RUSSIA

A HISTORY AND AN INTERPRETATION

IN TWO VOLUMES

VOLUME II

By MICHAEL T. FLORINSKY

——————————————————————

TOWARDS AN UNDERSTANDING OF THE U.S.S.R.

FASCISM AND NATIONAL SOCIALISM

THE SAAR STRUGGLE

WORLD REVOLUTION AND THE U.S.S.R.

RUSSIA: A HISTORY AND AN INTERPRETATION

RUSSIA

A HISTORY
AND
AN INTERPRETATION

IN TWO VOLUMES

BY

MICHAEL T. FLORINSKY

VOLUME II

THE MACMILLAN COMPANY

NEW YORK · 1955

Copyright, 1947, 1953, by The Macmillan Company

All rights reserved—no part of this book may be reproduced in any form without permission in writing from the publisher, except by a reviewer who wishes to quote brief passages in connection with a review written for inclusion in magazine or newspaper.

PRINTED IN THE UNITED STATES OF AMERICA

Second Printing

CONTENTS

VOLUME II

PART III. THE ST. PETERSBURG PERIOD (Cont'd.)

Chapter XXV. ALEXANDER I: THE MAN AND THE RULER   629
The Enigmatic Tsar, 629. The Liberal and the Man of Action, 633. Mysticism and Orthodoxy, 638. Arakcheev, 646. Fedor Kuzmich, 650.

Chapter XXVI. ALEXANDER I: NAPOLEONIC WARS AND THE HOLY ALLIANCE   651
The First Steps, 651. The Third Coalition, 1805–1807, 653. The Franco-Russian Alliance, 1807–1810, 661. The War of 1812, 671. "The War of Liberation," 1813–1815, 679. The European Alliance, 1815–1825, 685. An Appraisal, 692.

Chapter XXVII. ALEXANDER I: GOVERNMENT, FINANCE, TRADE, INDUSTRY, AND SOCIAL CONDITIONS   693
Unfulfilled Promises, 693. Speransky and the Reaction, 696. Finland, 702. The Kingdom of Poland, 705. Public Finance, 708. Foreign Trade, 709. Industry, 712. Social Conditions, 715.

Chapter XXVIII. CULTURAL DEVELOPMENTS AND POLITICAL MOVEMENTS, 1800–1825   722
Schools, 722. Censorship, 727. Literature, Art, and the Theater, 728. Secret Societies, 735. The Dynastic Riddle, 745. The Insurrection of December 14, 1825, 748.

Chapter XXIX. NICHOLAS I: THE APOGEE OF ABSOLUTISM   753
Emperor Nicholas, 753. The Polish Insurrection, 1830–1831, 757. The Police Regime, 765.

Chapter XXX. NICHOLAS I: SOCIAL AND ECONOMIC CONDITIONS   774
The Nobility, the Peasants, and the Burghers, 774. Finance, Railways, Commerce, and Industry, 786.

v

Chapter XXXI. NICHOLAS I: SCHOOLS, INTELLECTUAL MOVEMENTS, LITERATURE, AND ART 797
"Official Nationalism" and the Schools, 797. Intellectual Movements, 807. Censorship, 812. Literature and the Theater, 815. Art, 820. The Cleavage, 824.

Chapter XXXII. THE EASTERN QUESTION, 1825–1855 826
Nature of the Conflict, 826. The years 1825–1830, 827. The July Revolution and the Crisis of 1833, 834. The Threat to India, 841. *Rapprochement* with England, 844. The Revolution of 1848, 850. The Gathering of the Storm, 1850–1853, 858. The Crimean War, 1854–1856, 869.

Chapter XXXIII. ALEXANDER II: THE REFORMS 879
The Tsar-Liberator, 879. The Emancipation of the Serfs, 882. Local Self-Government, 896. The Judiciary, 902. The Army, 906. The Polish Insurrection, 1863, 909. Finland and Autocracy, 919.

Chapter XXXIV. ALEXANDER II: SOCIAL AND ECONOMIC DEVELOPMENTS 921
The Peasants, 921. The Nobility, 928. Industry, 929. Communications, 934. Trade, 937. Finance, 941. Russian Capitalism, 945.

Chapter XXXV. ALEXANDER II: EUROPE, AMERICA, AND ASIA 947
The Treaty of Paris, 947. *Rapprochement* with France, 951. Europe and the Polish Insurrection, 956. Intervention in Greece and Rumania, 958. Russia and the Unification of Germany, 961. Revision of the Treaty of Paris, 967. Alliance of the Three Emperors, 1873, 970. Sale of Alaska, 973. Expansion in the Far East, 977. Expansion in Central Asia, 979.

Chapter XXXVI. ALEXANDER II: PANSLAVISM AND THE EASTERN QUESTION, 1875–1881 987
Panslavism, 987. Revolt in Herzegovina, 991. Russia and Serbia, 993. Panslavism and the Russian Government, 995. Agreement with Austria, 996. Russia's War Preparations, 998. The Conference of Constantinople, 1000. The Russo-Turkish War, 1877–1878, 1002. International Complications, 1005. The Armistice and British Counter-measures, 1007. The Treaty of San Stefano, 1010. On the Verge of a New War, 1014. The Congress of Berlin, 1017. Russia and the Treaty of Berlin, 1022. Revival of the Three Emperors' League, 1026. A Retrospect, 1856–1881, 1027.

Contents

Chapter XXXVII. ALEXANDER II: SCHOOLS, ART, LITERATURE, AND POLITICAL MOVEMENTS — 1030
Schools, 1030. Science, 1048. Music, 1050. Art, 1052. Literature, 1054. Political Movements, 1064.

Chapter XXXVIII. ALEXANDER III: THE LAST AUTOCRAT — 1086
Alexander III and His Advisers, 1086. Administrative Counterreforms, 1090. Social and Economic Policies, 1100. Censorship, Schools, Nationalism, and Political Movements, 1111. Foreign Relations, 1124. Alexander III's Legacy, 1139.

Chapter XXXIX. NICHOLAS II: TWILIGHT OF ABSOLUTISM, 1894–1905 — 1141
The Tsar and the Tsarina, 1141. Beginning of the Reign, 1147. The Bolsheviks and the Mensheviks, 1148. The Socialist Revolutionaries, 1152. The Liberals, 1155. Finland, 1157. The Village and the Factory, 1159. University Students, 1163. The Revolutionary Tide, 1166. The Revolution of 1905, 1171.

Chapter XL. NICHOLAS II: THE CONSTITUTIONAL MONARCHY, 1906–1914 — 1184
Witte and the Constitutional Framework of 1906, 1184. Political Parties and Elections to the First Duma, 1188. The First Duma, 1190. Stolypin's Administrative Methods, 1193. The Second Duma, 1197. The Third and Fourth Dumas, 1199. The Triumph of Reaction, 1200. Nationalism, 1202. Stolypin's Murder, Kokovtsov, and Goremykin, 1204.

Chapter XLI. NICHOLAS II: ECONOMIC AND CULTURAL DEVELOPMENTS, 1894–1914 — 1206
Public Finance, 1206. The Land Reform, 1211. Industry, Banking, Labor, and Foreign Trade, 1224. The Schools, 1232. The Press and Literature, 1238. Painting, Music, Drama, and the Ballet, 1245. *L'Ancien Régime:* An Appraisal, 1255.

Chapter XLII. NICHOLAS II: FOREIGN RELATIONS, 1894–1914 — 1258
Two Eventful Decades, 1258. Universal Peace and Disarmament, 1260. The Far East, 1894–1903, 1262. The Russo-Japanese War and After, 1904–1914, 1270. Relations with France, Austria, and Germany, 1894–1905, 1283. The Anglo-Russian Convention, 1907, 1286. The Bagdad Railway, 1289. The Bosnian Crisis, 1907–1909, 1291. The Balkan Wars, 1911–1913, 1299. Russia and Constantinople, 1911–1914, 1305. On the Eve of World War I, 1309.

Chapter XLIII. IMPERIAL RUSSIA AND THE FIRST WORLD WAR: I — 1312
The Vortex, 1312. Fortunes of War, 1319. Imperial Diplomacy: The Epilogue, 1335.

Chapter XLIV. **IMPERIAL RUSSIA AND THE FIRST WORLD WAR: II** 1353
The Economic Effects of the War, 1353. The Government in Wartime, 1361. Social Unrest, 1374.

Chapter XLV. **THE TWO REVOLUTIONS OF 1917: I** 1380
The Fall of the Monarchy, 1380. The Provisional Government, 1383. The Soviets, 1388. "Dual Power," 1392. Lenin and the Bolsheviks, 1400.

Chapter XLVI. **THE TWO REVOLUTIONS OF 1917: II** 1406
The Army, 1406. The Peasant Revolution, 1412. Labor and Economic Disintegration, 1417. Separatist Movements, 1421.

Chapter XLVII. **THE TWO REVOLUTIONS OF 1917: III** 1426
The First Coalition Government, 1426. The July Uprising, 1430. The Second Coalition Government, 1433. Substitutes for Parliament, 1434. The Kornilov "Mutiny," 1436. The Third Coalition Government, 1441. The Bolsheviks on the Eve of October, 1442. Overthrow of the Provisional Government, 1447.

Chapter XLVIII. **THE MORROW OF THE OCTOBER REVOLUTION** 1451
Peace, Land, and Soviet Power, 1451. Resistance to Bolshevism, 1454. Dissensions Within the Bolshevik Party, 1458. Early Legislation, 1459. The Constituent Assembly, 1461. National Self-Determination: Finland and Ukraine, 1464. Brest-Litovsk, 1467. The "Inevitability" of Bolshevism, 1474.

AUTHOR'S NOTE 1477

GLOSSARY OF SELECTED RUSSIAN AND OTHER UNFAMILIAR TERMS 1479

PRINCIPAL SOURCES 1482

INDEX xxv

MAPS

RUSSIA FROM 1800 TO 1914 1280–1281

RUSSIA AFTER THE TREATY OF BREST-LITOVSK, MARCH 3, 1918 1472

PART III. THE ST. PETERSBURG PERIOD (Cont'd.)

CHAPTER XXV

ALEXANDER I

The Man and the Ruler

THE ENIGMATIC TSAR

"It is not easy to form a just opinion of the character of the emperor," Count de La Ferronays, French ambassador at St. Petersburg, wrote in April, 1820. "It is composed of too many contrasts to be understood or grasped; some who appraised it several years ago surely would not recognize it today. Deep dissimulation is, perhaps, in his case less a pose (*étude*) and a fault than a necessary result and, so to speak, a consequence of the very inconsequences (*une conséquence des inconséquences même*) of his character. He talks of the rights of man, of those of peoples, of the duties of a monarch, as the disciple of a philosopher can and should talk, but at the same time he enforces his most arbitrary wishes with greater despotism and ruthlessness than Peter I would have. He espouses with enthusiasm any idea that he likes, he pursues it with ardor, he supports it with all the means of an authority which knows no limits and no restraint; and this idea itself may be superseded by another one to the execution of which everything will again have to be sacrificed, and this is what is so disturbing in the character of this prince." The judgment of posterity has confirmed in large measure that of the French diplomat, and Alexander I has gone down in history and literary tradition as the "sphinx" and the "enigmatic tsar." An authoritative appraisal of his views and policies has been rendered all the more difficult by the systematic and wanton destruction by his successor, Emperor Nicholas I, of many pertinent records, especially private papers.

The highly abnormal conditions under which Alexander spent his early years and the nature of his education may help, nevertheless, to explain some of the puzzling inconsistencies of his character. Born on December 12, 1777, the elder son of Paul was removed from the care of his parents and was brought up under the supervision of his grandmother, Empress Catherine II. His principal teacher was César La Harpe, an ardent Swiss revolutionary who, however, was not unwilling to compromise with autocracy when he deemed it expedient. An enthusiastic disciple of Gibbon, Mably, Locke, and Rousseau, La Harpe endeavored to introduce his pupil to the enchanted realm where the abstract notions of reason, justice, equality, and the common good assumed an appearance of reality and moved majestically amidst the romantic figures of heroes and social reformers drawn from ancient and modern history. Although much of the teaching of La Harpe was beyond the grasp of Alexander, an indolent boy still in his teens, his instruction by the Swiss tutor left a strong imprint on his mind and he developed for the philosophy of the Enlightenment a sincere emotional attachment which he retained in a strangely perverted form to the end of his days. Alexander spoke fluent English and excellent French, a language he almost invariably used in his correspondence, but he had an inadequate and hesitant command of the Russian tongue. As to the actual conditions in the vast empire over which he was soon to rule, he learned nothing from his mentor. After the marriage of Alexander in September, 1793, the time available for study was curtailed, and a year later La Harpe was dismissed and soon left Russia. The formal schooling of the future emperor was brought to an end when he was only seventeen.

While at the court of Catherine, Alexander was surrounded by an atmosphere of indolence and superficial liberalism, but at his father's residence in Gatchina, where he was a frequent visitor in the later years of his grandmother's reign, he was initiated into the manly art of warfare according to the Prussian model. The meticulous and ruthless discipline so dear to Emperor Paul had for the young grand duke an appeal at least as strong as that of the liberal teaching of La Harpe, and an influence even more lasting, for he remained throughout his life a devotee of that type of regimentation which finds its fullest expression in well ordered army barracks. It was at Gatchina that he formed a friendship with Arakcheev, eventually one of his closest collaborators. It will be remembered that relations between Catherine and Paul were openly hostile and that the empress had made up her mind to disinherit her son in favor of Alexander. A letter written by the latter to Catherine on September 24, 1796, leaves little doubt that he was aware of this plan and that it had his approval. The position of Alexander with his grandmother and her favorites, on the one hand, and with his father, on the other, was one of extreme delicacy, and the necessity of presenting a serene appearance in the two warring camps of the Winter Palace and of Gatchina probably contributed to his consummate mastery of the art of dissimulation, so often emphasized in contemporary reports. His uncanny ability, early acquired, of never allowing the pupil of La Harpe to be seen behind the drillmaster of Gatchina, and vice versa, made it possible for him to combine in later years the seemingly sincere belief in liberal principles with the most reactionary domestic and international policies. The palace revolution of March 11, 1801, which led to the murder of Paul, was carried out, as has already been stated, with the knowledge and connivance of Alexander. None of the participants in the conspiracy was tried or suffered official punishment; and while the career of some of the conspirators, for instance, Panin and Pahlen, was soon brought to an end, others—like Bennigsen—continued to occupy important positions and were recipients of marks of favor not only from Alexander but also from the dowager empress. There are indications, nevertheless, that Alexander never entirely freed himself from the haunting memories of the night of March 11. Arakcheev, who had an exceptional insight into the mysteries of Alexander's character, instituted an ostentatious and elaborate cult dedicated to the memory of Emperor Paul, and in his letters to Alexander he frequently emphasized his loyalty to his late master. Far from taking offense at these seemingly tactless demonstrations, the son of the murdered man accepted them as evidence of Arakcheev's devotion to himself and of his loyal friendship.

Alexander, fair, tall, and handsome, was slightly lame, having been thrown from his horse in 1794, and early in life he became affected with progressive deafness. The studied simplicity and courtesy he almost invariably displayed in his relations with people, irrespective of their station in life, won him a reputation for kindliness and charm. He had a real gift for proffering those thoughtful marks of personal attention to which no recipient is ever indifferent, especially when they come from the occupant of the throne. For instance, during his state visit to the imperial residence of Tsarskoe Selo in July, 1821, the French ambassador, Count de La Ferronays was surprised and delighted to discover that every member of the large retinue of servants assigned to his private apartments spoke faultless French. Women were particularly susceptible to the gallantry of a monarch who came to be known as "the angel" and *"le grand charmeur."* Married when he was less than sixteen to Elizabeth, formerly Princess Louise of Baden and one year his junior, Alexander was for a time very happy with his affectionate and pretty wife. The romantic and sentimental nature of his German bride found a ready response in the mind and heart of the grand duke, brought up in the tradition of Rousseau's *Émile*. In a much quoted profession of faith made to Prince Adam Czartoryski in 1796, the future emperor not only castigated despotism, class privileges, and the very institution of hereditary monarchy, but also voiced his determination to renounce his rights to the Crown and to live the life of a private citizen in the picturesque rural surroundings of Switzerland or the Rhineland.

The marital bliss of Alexander and Elizabeth proved as ephemeral as were their dreams of a rural idyll. Court gossips ascribed to Alexander numerous amorous adventures, and in 1804, or perhaps earlier, began his official liaison with the beautiful Pole Maria Naryshkin, *née* Princess Czetwertynski, wife of Dimitry Naryshkin, a wealthy nobleman, high court official, and the most indulgent of husbands. This relationship pursued its uneven course until 1819 and resulted in the birth of several children whom Alexander recognized as his own, although he was aware that Madame Naryshkin had other lovers. Time and the conversion of Alexander to mysticism, however, eventually wrought important changes in his outlook and private conduct. La Ferronays reports (dispatch of April 13, 1820), on the authority of Madame Naryshkin herself, the disappointment which awaited her on her return to St. Petersburg after a protracted stay abroad: the emperor "talked to her of nothing else except the cross and divine love (*il ne lui parle que de croix et d'amour divin*), a language rather novel to this lady, who, complaining that her lover had turned into a father confessor, had but one wish—to return at once to Paris." This wish was fulfilled, and the death in 1818 of Alexander's sister, the Grand Duchess Catherine (married, first, to Prince George of Oldenburg and, after his death, to the king of Württemberg) removed, almost simultaneously with the departure of Madame Naryshkin, another important feminine influence from the life of the emperor. The letters of Alexander to this sister, even after they had passed the rigorous censorship of their editor, the Grand Duke Nicholas Mikhailovich, and presumably that of Emperor Nicholas II, still contain indiscreet passages which indicate a passionate attachment of a kind unusual between brother and sister. Catherine, ambitious, scheming, and very active, took a lively interest in domestic and foreign affairs and constantly discussed them with her brother.

Empress Elizabeth bore her conjugal misfortunes with dignity and fortitude, made but brief appearances at court functions, and lived for years in voluntary semi-retirement, an attitude which did not entirely protect her reputation from malevolent gossip. The death in their infancy of her two daughters, born in 1799 and 1806, contributed to her morbid disposition and made her seek consolation in religion, although she never shared the mystical beliefs of her husband. Throughout the many disappointments of her married life she had retained her affection for the prince charming of her youth, and she welcomed the signs of Alexander's desire for a *rapprochement*, which became apparent after his breach with Madame Naryshkin. Five years later the reconciliation of the estranged couple seemed complete, and the journey to Taganrog, which they undertook on the advice of the empress's physicians in the autumn of 1825, brought them even closer together. The idyll in the sleepy seaside town was reminiscent in many ways of the romantic dreams Alexander and Elizabeth had cherished some thirty years earlier, but it lasted for only a few weeks and was rudely terminated by the emperor's sudden death on November 19, 1825. On that day Elizabeth wrote to her mother, "Our angel is in heaven."

THE LIBERAL AND THE MAN OF ACTION

The liberalism of Alexander, although more deeply rooted than that of Catherine II, was almost as sterile in its practical manifestations. The ideas of the Enlightenment that he had learned from La Harpe remained the elegant and, in the Russian environment, the exotic adornments of a superficially cultured mind, glittering generalities which were duly aired before foreigners and French-speaking Russians in St. Petersburg, in the political and literary salons of Vienna, Berlin, Paris, and London, and at international congresses; but they had little influence on practical policies and were at best reflected in projected reforms that were fated never to become law. As Professor Kizevetter has so well put it, Alexander had grown accustomed to appreciate merely the esthetic aspects of liberal thought, and he "admired them in a purely detached manner as a tourist admires the beauty of a landscape from the window of a railway carriage—admires and speeds by." The same author astutely suggests that both the rise and fall of Speransky, the liberal statesman of the era of Alexander, were due primarily to his ability in translating the elusive radicalism of his master in terms of close-knit governmental institutions, in giving an accurate and practical interpretation to the vague and shapeless ideals of the disciple of La Harpe. Alexander was at first delighted to have met a man who not only understood him but who was also capable of giving his exalted political conceptions an appearance of reality. The very precision of the projects of Speransky, however, dispelled the enchantment of the dream, lifted the veil of mystery, did away with emotional and sentimental verbiage, and thus dealt a severe blow to some of Alexander's most treasured notions. The emperor resented the too precise limitation of autocracy suggested by Speransky, although it was the inescapable and logical deduction from the premises he had himself enunciated, and he disliked especially the finality of the project, which called for immediate action. With Speransky's dramatic and sudden disgrace in March, 1812, Alexander returned to his "phantasmagoric world of shapeless dreams." He did not, of course, admit or even realize his failure. An autocrat in Russia, in the newly organized grand duchy of Finland and in the kingdom of Poland, he played the part of a constitutional monarch. In an address delivered before the Polish diet in March, 1818, Alexander paid a ringing tribute to "free institutions" as compatible with the maintenance of order and the advancement of economic welfare, and proclaimed his intention of extending the benefit of such institutions to the whole of the empire.

With the spread of the revolutionary movement in western Europe in the 1820's, Alexander lost much of his former admiration for the very principles of representative government. Commenting on the murder of the Duke de Berry, he remarked to the French ambassador: "What are the masses? Inert and passive they suffer and groan under the fury of the despotism of factions, but they invariably submit to the one that triumphs" (dispatch of La Ferronays, February 25, 1820). In a remarkable letter to Prince Golitsin and Koshelev (dated Laybach, February 8–15, 1821), Alexander interpreted the revolutionary movement in Spain, Portugal, and the kingdom of Naples as directed not only against monarchy but primarily against Christianity. "This is nothing else," he wrote, "but the practical application of the doctrines preached by Voltaire, Mirabeau, Condorcet, and all the so-called philosophers known as the Encyclopedists." A year later, in a conversation with the French ambassador, he condemned the practice of representative government (*jeu du gouvernement représentatif*) as "a terrible and dangerous procedure where the interests of the state are often sacrificed to the private interests of political parties" (dispatch of La Ferronays, January 14, 1822). Little wonder, therefore, that the project of a Russian constitution embodying the federal principle, and drafted, at the request of the tsar, by Novosiltsev in 1818–1819, never became law.

Contrary to the widely held theory, which tends to explain Alexander's failings by the weakness of his character and the pernicious influence of his advisers, he was not easily swayed from the course he had once made up his mind to follow. Men whose judgment he trusted, moreover, were few, but most of them retained his confidence over long periods of years. Like his two immediate predecessors, Alexander assumed the direction of Russia's foreign relations; the titular heads of the ministry of foreign affairs were relegated to a subordinate position and at times were not even informed of important international negotiations, which were conducted by the emperor through other channels. In 1811, for instance, vital conferences with Austria were entrusted by Alexander to Koshelev, who, although a former ambassador to Copenhagen, had no official connection with the world of diplomacy. Both Count Stackelberg, Russian ambassador to Vienna, and Count Saint-Julien, Austrian ambassador to St. Petersburg, were instructed by the emperor to communicate directly with Koshelev, to the exclusion of the Russian chancellor, Count Nicholas Rumiantsev. Saint-Julien noted with malicious satisfaction in a dispatch to Metternich (August 20, 1811) the "truly most piquant" and irreconcilable contradiction between the objects and methods of Russian foreign policy as expounded by Rumiantsev, on the one hand, and by the emperor and Koshelev, on the other. Alexander was in the habit of communicating with foreign courts and statesmen through his personal representatives, who were not responsible to the minister of foreign affairs and who for all practical purposes superseded the duly accredited Russian ambassadors. The latter were at times left in ignorance of the mission of the tsar's special emissaries. There was therefore no exaggeration in Alexander's statement that he was his own chancellor (dispatch of Saint-Julien, April 14, 1811).

Crucial decisions in questions of foreign policy affecting the fate of the empire and of Europe bear the indelible mark of the tsar's personal will. Throughout the vicissitudes of a quarter of a century he remained the untiring champion of Prussia, his loyalty to a most unworthy ally being not unconnected with his admiration for Queen Louise, the beautiful and brilliant consort of the unprepossessing Frederick William III. The alliance with France in 1807, Russian leadership in the anti-French coalition of 1813–1815, and above all the creation of the Holy Alliance were policies that met with much opposition in Russia and could have been imposed on a reluctant country only by Alexander's unflinching obstinacy. Although Metternich succeeded without too much difficulty in gaining the upper hand over Alexander in the intricate game of European diplomacy, it is hardly correct to say, as does the historian of Alexander, the Grand Duke Nicholas Mikhailovich, that at the Congress of Verona the emperor "handed over to Metternich the conduct of foreign policy." By one of those inexplicable aberrations of mind to which Alexander was subject, he had succeeded in persuading himself that the crafty Austrian chancellor was actually serving the aims he himself had so much at heart. No less apparent is Alexander's personal part in the uneven course of domestic affairs, in the sporadic encouragement of liberal reforms and in their abrupt abandonment. The creation of military colonies, a sinister experiment that absorbed much of Alexander's attention during the second half of his reign, was his personal policy in the success of which even its chief administrator, Arakcheev, did not believe, although to please his imperial master he ruthlessly enforced it.

Alexander, moreover, especially before he sank in the morass of mystical religiosity, displayed at times real statesmanship and readiness to follow enlightened advice at the cost of some of his cherished ambitions. His romantic conception of the duties of kingship included that of sharing the hazards of military campaigns, even though he did not lead his troops in battle. The bloody lessons of Austerlitz and Friedland, where he was a witness of the defeats of the Russian army, did not alter this belief, and on the eve of the Napoleonic invasion of 1812 he established his headquarters with the forces massed on the

Polish frontier. He, however, yielded to the urgent request of Arakcheev, Balashov, and Shishkov (memorandum of June 30, 1812) to leave the conduct of military operations in the hands of army commanders and to withdraw to the capital. The Grand Duchess Catherine reinforced the plea of the three high officials by arguing that the primary duty of the tsar was to head the government and that he should not be put in a position where the odium arising from military reverses caused by errors of judgment would do irreparable damage to his authority. Alexander remained in St. Petersburg throughout Napoleon's Russian campaign and did not rejoin the army until the invasion was over. The appointment as commander in chief in the War of 1812 of Kutuzov, for whom the emperor had a deep personal dislike, is another instance of Alexander's sound instinct and willingness to sacrifice his personal feelings to the pressure of public opinion. At times shy and even inarticulate—Saint-Julien in his dispatch of November 28, 1809, speaks of Alexander's "stuttering (*bredouillement*) which makes one painfully await the end of a sentence"—the tsar rose in great moments to the highest standards of leadership. After the occupation of Paris by the allies in March, 1814, Alexander exercised an authority that no other statesman approached. "For a few weeks . . ." writes Waliszewski, who cannot be suspected of excessive friendliness towards the tsar, "he became the real leader whom the masses instinctively accepted and enthusiastically acclaimed and in whom the distressed souls, from the Seine to the Vistula, put their hopes for a future of peace, justice, and liberty."

Perhaps the best example of Alexander's statesmanship and foresight was his clear and essentially accurate analysis of the difficulties Napoleon would encounter in the course of his invasion of Russia, and the ability of the tsar to draw from it the correct conclusions. "The emperor expects the war; he considers it inevitable and nothing less than remote," wrote Saint-Julien to Metternich on January 29, 1812. "The emperor has little confidence in the talents of his generals . . . he puts his trust in the courage of his troops, their discipline and their passive obedience, but even more so in the obstacles which, in his dominions, are offered by the terrain—wooded, swampy, unimproved (*inculte*) and sparsely populated. His Majesty greatly relies on the difficulty of supplies and the rigor of the climate. The emperor also depends (*se repose*) on public spirit, the sacrifices which are promised to him in the name of the nation, and the justice of his cause which he considers sacred (*attache une confiance religieuse*)." These lines, written several months before the invasion, corroborate the report of an even more emphatic statement attributed to Alexander by Caulaincourt. "If Emperor Napoleon starts a war," the tsar said to Caulaincourt in May, 1811, according to the latter's memoirs (which, however, were written long after the event and therefore must be used with caution), "it is possible and even probable that he will defeat us, but this will not bring him peace. . . . We shall not compromise our position, we have vast spaces to which to retreat, and we shall preserve a well organized army. Under these conditions we shall never be forced to make peace, whatever may be our military reverses. . . . We shall leave it to our climate, to our winter to wage our war. . . . I shall withdraw to Kamchatka rather than cede any of my provinces or sign in my capital, occupied by the enemy, a peace that would be merely an armistice." Although the determination of Alexander to resist the invaders to the bitter end was doubted in 1812 even by some of those who knew him best, for instance, by his sister Catherine, there is no evidence that he ever contemplated abandoning the policy he had outlined to Caulaincourt. Indeed, he firmly turned down offers of peace proffered at the darkest moment of the war, when Napoleon was in the Kremlin and when it was expected that St. Petersburg would soon fall to the enemy. In his analysis of Napoleon's forthcoming doom, moreover, Alexander showed sounder judgment than have many historians.

MYSTICISM AND ORTHODOXY

Brought up in the tradition of eighteenth century skepticism and rationalism, Alexander in his early years and during the first half of his reign showed little interest in religious questions. But a fundamental change in his attitude towards religion took place, presumably, in 1812, although the paucity of the sources makes it impossible to obtain a clear picture of his spiritual evolution. It is reasonably certain, nevertheless, that his conversion to morbid religiosity was prompted by the influence of Prince Alexander Golitsin and Rodion Koshelev. Golitsin (1773–1844), scion of one of Russia's most illustrious families and a lifelong friend of Alexander, had for years led a life of dissipation and pleasure and had displayed a marked indifference towards Christian morals, in spite of the fact that he had since 1803 held the office of chief procurator of the Holy Synod. In

1810 he was appointed a member of the newly created State Council and was simultaneously put in charge of a department administering the affairs of religious denominations other than the Russian Orthodox Church, an office he combined with that of chief procurator. In 1816 he became minister of education and a year later minister of religious affairs and education; he retained this position until May, 1824, when, victim of a cabal led by Arakcheev, he was relegated to the obscure post of postmaster general, although Alexander continued to treat him as a close personal friend. A staunch conservative in politics, Golitsin became interested in the Bible, recanted the errors of his early manhood, and espoused a mystical brand of Christianity, an odd mixture of Protestantism with the traditional beliefs of Greek Orthodoxy.[1] The religious life of Golitsin was influenced by his close association with Koshelev, whom he first met in 1811. Koshelev (1749–1827) served in the Horse Guards, was for a brief time Russian ambassador to Copenhagen under Emperor Paul, traveled extensively abroad, where he established personal relations with the leaders of western European mysticism (Louis de Saint-Martin, Lavater, Eckartshousen, and the disciples of Swedenborg), and took an active part in the promotion of Russian Freemasonry. In 1810 he was appointed member of the State Council and, later, master of the imperial court, but he resigned all his offices and charges in 1812. He continued, however, to occupy an apartment at the Winter Palace, and devoted his energy to the preaching of mystical doctrines in aristocratic salons of St. Petersburg. Both Golitsin and Koshelev were members of Alexander's intimate circle, and carried on with the tsar an assiduous correspondence of which only fragments have been preserved. The failing eyesight of Koshelev making it difficult for him to read and write, Alexander adopted the practice of communicating with him through the intermediary of Golitsin in messages intended for both his friends. Foreign diplomats were not impressed by the intellectual and moral stature of Alexander's spiritual advisers. Koshelev, according to Saint-Julien, was "much more a courtier than a statesman" (dispatch to Metternich, August 20, 1811), and Count de Gabriac described him (April, 1820) as "a visionary old man who claims to entertain direct and tangible relations with heaven (*prétend avoir avec le Ciel*

---

[1] Golitsin, according to his own statement, read the Gospel for the first time in 1803. This was not unusual because the study of the Bible is not a common practice among even the devout members of the Russian Church.

des communications directes et visibles); he has succeeded in winning the confidence of the emperor and making him share his delirium." La Ferronays, who had doubts about the sincerity of Golitsin's conversion, pictured him as a man "of amiable disposition, but humble intellectual gifts (*un homme d'esprit, aimable, mais peu éclairé*)," a statement which contained a large element of truth, although it was probably too generous.

According to Golitsin, it was at his urgent request that Alexander first read the Bible in the summer of 1812. The emperor had given Koshelev a large share of credit for his conversion. "I owe you much," he wrote to Koshelev on December 13, 1815. "You have powerfully contributed to make me adopt the course I am now following by conviction and which alone has brought me success in the most difficult task the Very High One has assigned me."[2] The persistency and the nature of the extraordinary influence Golitsin exerted is suggested by an exchange of letters between him and Alexander on the occasion of the death of Sophie Naryshkin, the emperor's favorite daughter by his mistress. "God has miraculously wrested you from sin (*vous a arraché miraculeusement au péché*)," Golitsin wrote to the bereaved father on June 19, 1824, that is, a few weeks after the former minister had been deprived of his high office. "Humanly you did not know how to bring about the rupture of a link (*lien*), even though an illicit one, which made the happiness of your existence. Now He has withdrawn the fruit of this union which, so to speak, should have never seen the light of day, according to the holy will of God and, by this decision, He has corrected the fault due to your own will." "Your letter went straight to my heart," replied Alexander the same evening to this quaintly phrased expression of sympathy.

The mystical creed of Alexander, like most phenomena of this order, defies precise analysis. The essence of his faith, in so far as it can be ascertained, consisted in seeking self-expression through absorption in the Deity. The doctrines of Böhme, Swedenborg, Eckartshousen, Saint-Martin, and Jung-Stilling, the mystical teaching of

[2] It would be a mistake to ascribe the mystical leanings of Alexander entirely to the influence of Golitsin and Koshelev. The growing preoccupation of the emperor with mysticism is disclosed in a curious memorandum sent by him to his sister, the Grand Duchess Catherine. This document, which contains an obscure and haphazard critical survey of mystical doctrines throughout the ages, was not dated, but a reference to Prince George of Oldenburg indicates that it was written before the death of Catherine's first husband in December, 1812.

Freemasonry, inspirations derived from the reading of the Bible, and the dogmas and practices of some of the Russian sects, all these and many other elements contributed to the shaping of his religious belief. The study of the Bible, however, appeared to Alexander most of the time as the only reliable guide of personal conduct and the only safe road to salvation. In December, 1812, there was formed in St. Petersburg the Russian Bible Society modeled on the British and Foreign Bible Society of London. Golitsin became its president, Koshelev one of the vice presidents, and the emperor hastened to enroll among its members (February 15, 1813). The governing body of the society, which, unlike its British prototype, was financed by the government, consisted of laymen and of ecclesiastical dignitaries of the Russian Orthodox, the Roman Catholic, and the Lutheran Churches. According to a contemporary report of the French diplomat De Gabriac, the ultimate object the emperor and Golitsin hoped to achieve through the Bible Society was "the establishment of one Christian faith which will unite all Christian denominations." [3] Rumors to this effect were current at the time and alarmed both the Holy See, which prohibited the Catholics from participating in the work of the Bible Society, and the more conservative elements among the orthodox clergy. Seraphim, metropolitan of St. Petersburg, Eugen, metropolitan of Kiev, and the fanatical and fiery Archimandrite Photius eventually assumed the leadership of the opposition within the Orthodox Church.

The religious affiliations of Alexander and Golitsin were of a nature to justify the worst apprehensions of Orthodox churchmen and clergy. Even a partial enumeration of the religious and pseudo-religious leaders who were eagerly listened to by the tsar and his minister will give the measure of the unhealthy state of exaltation which possessed their minds. The range of these associations was extraordinarily broad, from the high-minded Quakers William Allen and Étienne de Grellet du Mobillier, a Frenchman long resident in the United States, to vulgar impostors such as Madame Bouche and obscure Russian sec-

[3] "Your last letter . . . in which you give an account of the work of the Bible Society has interested and moved me more than I can say," Alexander wrote to Golitsin on Jan. 25, 1813. "May the Supreme Being bless this enterprise! I consider it of the highest importance and believe that you are fully justified in your contention that the Holy Scriptures will supersede the Prophets. In general, evidence from all sides that we are getting nearer to the true reign of Christ causes me real joy. Have the best architects work on the project of my Temple. . . . May this Temple be the true Temple of our Savior and may it serve to bring men to the true Cult."

tarians. Alexander met Allen and Grellet in 1814 in London, and on his invitation they visited Russia in 1819. The two Quakers, according to Grellet, initiated the emperor into the sublime joy of "silent prayer." At Bruchsal, on his way from England, Alexander had a long conversation with the German mystic and author, Jung-Stilling. A year later, in 1815, there took place at Heilbronn the celebrated midnight interview between the tsar and Baroness von Krüdener, leader of a mystical sect and widow of a Baltic diplomat long in the Russian service. A *grande dame* turned adventuress, to use the apt expression of a recent historian, the Livonian baroness claimed direct communication with divine Providence and the gift of prophetic vision. For a time her influence on Alexander was great, and he was, indeed, a daily visitor to her lodgings in Paris, where she had followed the tsar after the defeat of Napoleon at Waterloo. Haunted by creditors and often in trouble with the police, who objected to her unorthodox religious practices, Madame Krüdener gave her association with the tsar a resounding publicity which provided the foundation for the seemingly erroneous theory that she was the actual author of the Holy Alliance. Her verbose and voluminous letters to Alexander are an unpalatable mixture of theological galimatias and fulsome flattery, to which the tsar was uncommonly susceptible.[4] The spell these crude artifices cast over Alexander weakened after his departure from Paris, although his correspondence with the baroness continued for several years. The appearance of Madame Krüdener, a close friend of Golitsin and Koshelev, in St. Petersburg in 1821 created a sensation and brought her many converts, but it failed to revive Alexander's interest in the Livonian prophetess; and when she unwisely espoused the cause of the Greeks against Turkey, a policy of which the Russian government disapproved, she was summarily ordered to leave the capital. She died in the Crimea in 1824.

In St. Petersburg the career of Madame Krüdener was successfully emulated by another Baltic German, Catherine Tatarinov, *née* Bux-

[4] The following excerpt from a letter written by Madame Krüdener to Alexander on June 23, 1815, a few days after their first meeting, is a fair example of her theology and epistolary style: "Il s'agit de vous vider de toute la vie d'Adam pour vous remplir de la vie du Christ, afin que le corps de la Résurrection puisse se former en vous, et que le Christ puisse comme le Soleil se lever en vous et que par vous aussi il en éclaire, allume d'autres." In a letter dated "Leipzig, December 1817," the baroness writes to Alexander about the happiness he must experience to see "Russia blossom (*entièrement fleurir*) under the holy laws of Jesus Christ."

höwden. Madame Tatarinov, widow of an officer in the guards, devoted herself to charitable work among the poor and frequented revivals of Russian sectarians who practiced communal singing and dancing as a means of stimulating religious emotions. Similar gatherings held by Madame Tatarinov in the apartments she occupied in one of the imperial palaces were patronized by the élite of St. Petersburg society, including Golitsin and Koshelev. After her admission into the fold of the Russian Church in 1817, Madame Tatarinov proclaimed herself endowed with the gift of prophecy. Alexander, who knew her personally, took a keen interest in the activities of her group, which prospered until 1822, when it fell under the ban imposed on all "secret" societies.

The ranks of the apostles of the evangelical and mystical brand of Christianity sponsored by the Bible Society, by Madame Krüdener, and by Madame Tatarinov were reenforced in 1819 and 1820 by the arrival in St. Petersburg of two renegade Roman Catholic priests from Bavaria, Lindel and Gossner, who, under the high patronage of Golitsin, preached to the aristocratic congregations of the capital a reformed Catholicism which amounted to the denial of the dogmas and institutions of the Church of Rome.

The real significance of these religious movements, ephemeral and unimportant in themselves, lies in the influence they exercised upon the tsar and, through him, on the entire course of Russian policy. Daily communion with divine power had filled Alexander with the burning desire to rebuild this imperfect world according to the principles of Christian morality, and close association with visionaries such as Koshelev, Baroness Krüdener, and Madame Tatarinov led him to imagine that he was the chosen instrument of Providence for the achievement of this supreme aim. Count Lebzeltern, a usually keen and penetrating observer, was for once grievously wrong when he wrote to Metternich on March 30, 1813: "As to the views of the emperor about the future, the most beautiful projects in the world, believe me. . . . I am neither so presumptuous nor absurd as to give them for a moment, even for a single moment, a serious thought; I attribute them to the pure kindness and high indulgence (*pure bonté et haute indulgence*) of His Majesty." The Austrian ambassador, however, displayed his customary acumen when he added: "I would have given everything in the world in order that this prince and Your Excellency should come to know each other better; I can think of no two more compatible human beings (*qui se convienderaient davantage*)." The "beautiful projects" which Lebzeltern so casually dismissed were soon to become the pivots of Russian policy, pursued by the tsar with almost fanatical determination. To Alexander the Holy Alliance established in September, 1815, was primarily an act of faith. "My faith is sincere and ardent," he wrote to Koshelev on January 25, 1813. "It is getting stronger every day and gives me joys I had totally ignored. . . . The reading of the Scriptures which I had known but superficially has done me a good it is difficult to express in words." It was in this spirit of religious exaltation that Alexander interpreted the aims of the Holy Alliance.[5] Its object, as stated in the holograph letter he wrote on March 18, 1816, to the Russian ambassador in London, Count Liven, was "to apply more efficaciously to the civil and political relations between states the principles of peace, concord, and love which are the fruit of religion and Christian morality. . . . The sole and exclusive purpose of the alliance cannot be other than the maintenance of peace and the rallying of all the moral interests of peoples whom divine Providence has been pleased to unite under the banner of the cross." Alexander specifically denied that the alliance might be used for territorial expansion or that it was directed against non-Christian nations, especially Turkey; on the contrary, its object was "to favor the domestic prosperity of every state and the general good of all." These statements, which have a strangely familiar ring today, were coupled with denunciations of the less exalted interpretations of the alliance as the work of the "evil spirit (*génie du mal*) terrified by the superior action of a Providence who disposes at will of monarchs and peoples."

In a letter of some five thousand words to Golitsin and Koshelev, Alexander gave the full measure of his religious obsession and its political implications. "According to my conviction," he wrote from Laybach on February 8–15, 1821, "I am far from harboring the seeds of such virtues as prudence, sagacity, circumspection, etc., but I feel that I am the depository of a sacred, holy mission (*dépositaire d'une œuvre sacrée, sainte*). . . . It does not depend on me to act against my inner feeling; when it speaks, I must give in and submit, and there are no human considerations for which I could transgress what this inner feeling demands." And again: "Let us abandon ourselves with faith to His guidance and His direction and 'see thou hurt not

[5] See pp. 685 *et seq.*

the oil and the wine' (The Revelation of Saint John, Chapter VI, verse 6) by mixing it with our own work which would be only too sadly human. . . . My only resource is the Lord." The "sacred mission" referred to by Alexander was the Holy Alliance, which he imagined to be under the special protection of divine power. "God has blessed our intentions," he wrote of the decision taken by the Congress of Troppau, "because they were pure and because they were based on faith in Him alone." The alliance being an instrument of Providence, any opposition to its policies was interpreted by Alexander as directed not merely against the legitimate monarchs, but primarily against Christian religion itself. The situation in 1820–1821, as he saw it, was similar to that in 1812–1814, but he held that "the present evil is more dangerous than the destructive despotism of Napoleon because today's doctrines are more attractive to the multitudes than the military yoke under which he kept them." The actual and formidable enemies were "the revolutionary liberals, radical levelers and *carbonari* in every corner of the world. . . . There is a general conspiracy of all these societies." After they became convinced, the emperor argued, that Christian religion forms the very foundation of the policies of European Powers, "all these sects, which are anti-Christian and are based on the principles of the so-called philosophy of Voltaire and his like, vowed their desperate vengeance to all governments." Hence, according to Alexander, came the revolutionary attempts in France, England, and Prussia, and the successful revolutions in Spain, Naples, and Portugal. The only hope of the Christian world was the Holy Alliance, whose members, Alexander again insisted, had no designs for territorial aggrandizement. He maintained, indeed, that no further territorial changes in Europe were feasible, which was a far cry from his cool and common-sense evaluation of the chances of Napoleon's Russian venture in 1812. The pupil of La Harpe, now a divinely inspired leader of militant Christianity, was determined to fight to the last against the "reign of Satan," as he put it in a letter to Golitsin on March 10, 1821. This peculiar frame of mind persisted until Alexander's death. In the summer of 1825 the emperor argued, according to La Ferronays (dispatch of July 9, 1825), that the king of Spain should not recognize the independence of the South American colonies because "the recognition of the independence of North America had been the signal for the French Revolution."

The religious evolution of the emperor had a far-reaching influence upon the course of domestic affairs. It is likely, as suggested by the Grand Duke Nicholas Mikhailovich, that the unfortunate experiment with military colonies was inspired, in part, by Alexander's religious fervor. Military colonies appeared to the tsar as the very embodiment of his vague notion of equality and social justice, pleasingly combined with that martial regimentation for which he had so strong a predilection. Reactionary trends in foreign relations had a fitting counterpart in the policy pursued at home. Alexander, moreover, was losing interest in mysticism and in the evangelical Christianity represented by the Bible Society. The conservative elements within the Russian Church had long been outraged by these unorthodox practices and were impatiently awaiting a propitious moment to get rid of the distasteful "new cult." Archimandrite Photius, a protégé of Arakcheev, of the Metropolitan Seraphim, and of the eccentric Anne Orlov (daughter of Count Alexis Orlov), became the instrument of a complex intrigue directed against religious innovations, Golitsin, and the Bible Society. This half-educated, militant, and shrewd cleric of unimpeachable Orthodoxy conducted a crusade against mysticism in all its forms, cleverly linking it with the revolutionary movement. The ascetic appearance, fanatical zeal, and violent language of Photius produced a strong impression upon Alexander, to whom he was introduced in June, 1822. On August 1, 1822, came the decree prohibiting all secret societies, a measure that dealt a death blow to Russian Freemasonry. Baroness Krüdener and Madame Tatarinov faded out of the picture, but it was not until May, 1824, that Photius and his supporters obtained the dismissal of Golitsin. Alexander, moreover, although tending more and more towards strict religious orthodoxy, refused to dissolve the Bible Society and merely curtailed its activities,[6] just as he shrank from ordering the persecution of secret political societies, although he was aware that they were preparing a revolutionary uprising.

ARAKCHEEV

The innately domineering and suspicious disposition that Alexander concealed behind an affable and courteous manner made the tenure of high offices precarious, except for utterly insignificant men

---

[6] On May 17, 1824, two days after he ceased to be minister, Golitsin was replaced as president of the Bible Society by the Metropolitan Seraphim. The society was dissolved in 1826, that is, after Alexander's death.

such as the minister of foreign affairs Count Nesselrode, who was not a statesman but the tsar's zealous and self-effacing secretary. The distinction of being Alexander's lifelong friend Prince Alexander Golitsin shared with Prince Peter Volkonsky, an active participant in the conspiracy against Paul and, later, chief of the general staff and prominent court official. However, Volkonsky, a man of mediocre ability, played no political part. More important was the close and lasting association of Alexander with Alexis Arakcheev, whose administration of the country in the later years of the reign has gone down in history under the awe-inspiring name of *Arakcheevshchina*. Arakcheev (1769–1834) came from a family of the lesser nobility and modest means. He studied at the military academy of St. Petersburg, received a commission in 1787, and five years later joined the garrison of Gatchina, where he attracted the attention of the future Emperor Paul as a punctilious and exacting drill-master and artillery expert. After the accession of Paul, Arakcheev advanced rapidly and had a brilliant career; in 1796, at the age of twenty-seven, he was promoted to the rank of major-general and received the magnificent property of Gruzino, in the province of Novgorod; he was created a baron in 1797, a count in 1799, and he held various high offices. Alexander met Arakcheev at Gatchina, and their correspondence, which began in 1796 and was conducted in the Russian language, leaves no doubt as to his affection for his friend. In 1803 Arakcheev was recalled from temporary retirement and was appointed inspector-general of the artillery, and in January, 1808, he was named minister of war. A few months earlier (June 27, 1807) he had been given the unusual power of issuing decrees in the name of the emperor. The rise of Arakcheev took place in the face of the opposition of court and bureaucratic circles and, oddly, coincided with the short-lived ascendancy of the liberal-minded Speransky. Taking offense at not being consulted about the establishment of the State Council, which formed a part of Speransky's plan of constitutional reforms, Arakcheev resigned the office of minister of war (January 1, 1810) and refused to reconsider his decision in spite of the supplications of the tsar. He accepted, however, the chairmanship of the department of military affairs of the State Council. Alexander, who showered on him favors and honorary distinctions, was in July, 1810, for the first time his guest at Gruzino, which he visited on ten more occasions in the course of following years. There is little doubt that the revengeful favorite, seldom forgetting an offense, played a part in bringing about the fall of Speransky in March, 1812. During the Napoleonic wars Arakcheev was Alexander's inseparable companion and trusted adviser, and after the struggle was over his influence was further enhanced. Appointed *rapporteur* of the recently established committee of ministers, he became the only link between that body and the monarch; that is, the decisions of the committee and the reports of individual ministers were, with rare exceptions, submitted to the tsar by Arakcheev and not by the heads of the executive departments or by the president of the committee of ministers. Thus, without holding a portfolio, Arakcheev actually occupied a position akin to that of a prime minister. Moreover, he was put in charge of the military colonies in which Alexander was so inordinately interested. His hold over the administration of affairs of state was further strengthened by the emperor's frequent and protracted absences from the capital. Possessed by a seemingly insatiable restlessness, the tsar spent much of his time spanning at record speed the vast expanses of his empire or in traveling abroad, and it was the common belief of contemporary observers that in the later years of Alexander's reign Arakcheev was all-powerful.

The influence of Arakcheev, however, was by no means as comprehensive as is often imagined. It will be remembered that Golitsin and Koshelev, both of whom Arakcheev hated, were during the same period very close to Alexander and that Golitsin was not deprived of his ministerial office until May, 1824. A year earlier Peter Volkonsky, another enemy of Arakcheev, was forced to resign as chief of the general staff and went abroad "for reasons of health," but he retained his court charges and was soon readmitted to the tsar's intimate circle. Arakcheev also failed, in spite of the powerful support of his creature, Photius, to bring about the dissolution of the Bible Society. These facts strongly suggest that Alexander did not unreservedly hand over to Arakcheev the reins of the government.

Historians have been greatly puzzled by the seemingly inexplicable partnership of Alexander and Arakcheev. Historical tradition, encouraged until early in this century by censorship restrictions, has pictured the favorite as a consummate villain of the darkest hue and has held him responsible for the harsh and reactionary nature of the closing years of Alexander's rule. Many allegations against his personal character are well founded. He was dissolute, reactionary, ambitious, rude, vindictive, and perversely cruel to a degree verging on sadism.

The murder of his mistress, Anastasia Minkin, by the exasperated serfs of Gruzino in September, 1825, was followed by bloody repressions typical of the man to whom Alexander had entrusted the fate of thousands of helpless military colonists. However, other aspects of the character of Arakcheev, which have been brought forth in more recent studies, help to explain the association between the pupil of La Harpe and the universally hated master of Gruzino. Strange as this may appear at first sight, the two men had many interests in common. They were both devotees of formal external order and took particular delight in the precise maneuvering of army units and in the thorough discipline obtained by incessant drilling. Regimentation on the Prussian model, so dear to Alexander, was enforced by Arakcheev not only in the army and in military colonies but even at Gruzino, where peasant cottages of the same pattern were neatly placed at regular intervals. Symmetry, order, cleanliness, and precision were in evidence everywhere. Pigs, which traditionally enjoy the free run of Russian villages, were rigorously excluded from the streets of Gruzino. Religiosity was undoubtedly another important link between the emperor and his minister. Like Alexander, Arakcheev was deeply religious, although he never shared the mystical leanings of the tsar and patiently worked for the elimination of the unorthodox influence of Golitsin, Krüdener, and the Bible Society.

For all his distasteful peculiarities, Arakcheev was an administrator of no mean ability. His reform of the artillery is held by military experts to have been successful and to have added to the fighting power of the army. His annotations on state papers disclose, according to Kizevetter, a keen practical mind, a desire to safeguard the public purse from spoliation and unnecessary expenditure, to champion the interests of the poor and especially to protect the serfs against excessive exactions of their lords, as well as to prevent abuses in the administration of justice. The executioner of Gruzino and the iron-handed administrator of military colonies pleaded at times for clemency and the mitigation of unduly severe sentences. These traits could not fail to appeal to the better side of Alexander's nature, even though it is probable that some of the more humane recommendations of Arakcheev were inspired by considerations of a not very high order.

Arakcheev, moreover, succeeded in firmly convincing the emperor of his unwavering devotion. He incessantly impressed upon his imperial master that he had no other interest and desire in life than to serve him and to carry out his wishes. By no means oblivious of his personal interests, Arakcheev strove to create the impression of unselfish disinterestedness. In 1809 he returned the insignia of the coveted order of St. Andrew, which Alexander wished to confer upon him on the occasion of peace with Sweden, and in 1814 he refused the baton of field marshal. Although he did not believe in the military colonies, he devoted himself to their administration and represented them to the tsar as a great success. A confirmed serfowner, he prepared in 1818, at the request of Alexander, a practical and businesslike project for the emancipation of the serfs which foreshadowed some of the important features of the reform of 1861. It would seem, therefore, that the term *Arakcheevshchina* attributes, by implication, to the favorite much greater influence than he actually enjoyed. He was the tsar's close and trusted, but not his sole, adviser and an important cog in the administrative machine of which Alexander, however, retained the control.

FEDOR KUZMICH

The air of mystery that shrouded Alexander in his lifetime persisted after his death. There came into existence a legend that the tsar did not die at Taganrog on November 19, 1825; he is said to have disappeared and after long peregrinations to have ended his days in Siberia in 1864 in the guise of a holy hermit, Fedor Kuzmich. Based on conjectures and guesses, this tale was revived by Prince Vladimir Bariatinsky in a study published first in Russian, and in 1929 in French. Maurice Paléologue, in a volume which appeared in New York in 1938, advances the even more fanciful theory that Alexander did not die in 1825 but made his way to Palestine in a yacht owned by an English peer. All available evidence, however, indicates beyond reasonable doubt that the tsar ended his terrestrial existence at Taganrog, unless one is prepared to accept the theory of a conspiracy involving a large number of people, including Empress Elizabeth. It is more than probable that such a conspiracy would never have succeeded even had it been attempted.

CHAPTER XXVI

ALEXANDER I

Napoleonic Wars and the Holy Alliance

THE FIRST STEPS

Napoleon's expansionist policies and their aftermath dominated the broad currents of European affairs in the first quarter of the nineteenth century. In the unfolding of the Napoleonic epic Russia played a prominent part and, after experiencing bitter humiliations and bloody defeats, she achieved for a brief time a position of international supremacy never attained before in her history nor duplicated since.

Like his predecessors, Catherine II and Paul I, Alexander began his reign by proclaiming his devotion to the ideals of international peace. "If I ever raise arms," he wrote on June 4, 1801, in a circular note to Russian diplomatic representatives abroad, "it will be exclusively in defense against aggression, for the protection of my peoples or of the victims of ambitions that endanger the peace of Europe. . . . I shall never participate in the internal dissensions of foreign states." The emperor announced his intention to honor "as far as possible" the international obligations he had inherited from his father, although "many of them were incompatible with national interest and some were out of keeping with the geographical position and mutual advantages of the contracting parties." The peace of Europe, according to Alexander, could be best safeguarded by an alliance of the great Powers, and in pursuance of this aim his government intended to seek a simultaneous *rapprochement* with London, Paris, and Vienna.

England was the first country to benefit by Russia's new political regime. Immediately after his accession Alexander ordered the recall of the Cossacks sent by Paul to conquer India. Count Simon Vorontsov, the former Russian envoy to London who had remained in England in a private capacity after the breach of diplomatic relations with that country, was reappointed ambassador to the Court of St. James's. The conciliatory attitude of the tsar prevented the outbreak of a naval war between Russia and Great Britain. On April 2, 1801, N.S., an English fleet, nominally under the orders of Sir Hyde Parker but actually commanded by Nelson, won a brilliant victory over the Danes at Copenhagen. No further operations in the Baltic against the members of the Second Armed Neutrality League, however, took place.[1] The war of embargoes between England and the Baltic states was called off, and on June 17, 1801, N.S., Lord St. Helens and Panin signed at St. Petersburg a convention that amounted to an abandonment by Russia of Armed Neutrality, although some minor concessions were made to the Russian point of view. With much reluctance Denmark (October, 1801) and Sweden (March, 1802) adhered to the Convention of St. Petersburg.

The murder of Paul and the resulting closer relations between St. Petersburg and London came as a shock to Bonaparte. In 1801 France was at war with Great Britain, and the first consul had made elaborate preparations for the sending of a French corps under Masséna to join Orlov's Indian expedition. With the recall of Orlov these plans and the hopes of a speedy conquest of India were shelved. The friendliness and courtesy displayed by Alexander towards General Duroc, Bonaparte's new envoy to St. Petersburg, could not disguise the fact —made clear by the Anglo-Russian convention of June 17—that Russia had chosen, at least temporarily, to cooperate with England rather than with France. Inconsistent and contradictory as Alexander's pronouncements and diplomatic moves during this period often were, it would seem that on the whole he distrusted Bonaparte, resented the unceremonious manner in which the first consul dealt with the crowned heads of the German and Italian states, and, perhaps, already nursed the ambition of succeeding the "usurper" as the arbiter of the destinies of Europe. There was, however, no indication of the imminence of a breach between France and Russia. The Franco-Austrian Treaty of Lunéville (February 9, 1801, N.S.) extended the dominion of France over Belgium, Luxemburg, a large portion of Italy, and the left bank of the Rhine, and granted to Paris the right to determine the indemnity due to the dispossessed princes. Alexander manifested lively interest in the fate of these rulers, and the nature of the indemnities to which they were entitled loomed large in

---

[1] See pp. 620–621.

the prolonged negotiations between Paris and St. Petersburg. In spite of the divergencies in the views held in the two capitals, a Franco-Russian treaty of friendship was signed on October 11, 1801, N.S. Although this treaty left many questions unsolved, and although Alexander failed to obtain an "adequate" compensation for the king of Sardinia, whose cause he championed with a zeal that one finds difficult to understand, the contracting parties undertook to act in close cooperation in all matters of common interest and to use their best endeavors for the maintenance of peace.

The *détente* in Anglo-Russian and Franco-Russian relations reflected the general trend of European affairs. A strong desire for peace manifested itself in both France and England. The retirement of Pitt (February, 1801) and the formation of a ministry under Addington led to the reopening of negotiations between Paris and London. The preliminaries of the Anglo-French peace were signed in London on October 1, 1801, N.S. and were followed by the Treaty of Amiens (March 27, 1802, N.S.). Treaties concluded in the course of 1802 between France, on the one hand, and Prussia, Bavaria, and Turkey, on the other, removed some of the more controversial issues and seemed to usher in an era of peaceful collaboration. In fact, however, Europe was spared the scourge of war for only a few months.

In the meantime Russia drew closer to Prussia. In June, 1802, Alexander, without consulting Count Kochubey, the titular head of the department of foreign affairs, visited at Memel King Frederick William III and Queen Louise of Prussia. According to the official version, the interview had no political significance; nevertheless, it established the foundation of a personal friendship between the two monarchs that survived the test of adversity throughout the years.

THE THIRD COALITION, 1805–1807

The Peace of Amiens was much more advantageous to France than to England and was subject to sharp criticism in the British parliament and press. The refusal of Bonaparte to mitigate the restrictions imposed on English commerce caused widespread disappointment in London business circles, which had sponsored a *rapprochement* with France. Napoleon, moreover, assumed a threatening attitude towards Great Britain and proceeded to mass troops and ships in the channel ports preparatory to an invasion of the island kingdom. London, on the other hand, refused to evacuate Malta, which under the Treaty of Amiens was to be restored to the Order of St. John of Jerusalem. Anglo-French relations reached an impasse, and on May 18, 1803, N.S., Great Britain declared war on France. A year later Pitt succeeded Addington as prime minister and became the chief architect of a new anti-French coalition.

The Franco-Russian treaty of October, 1801, like the Peace of Amiens, failed to bring a lasting improvement in the relations between the two countries. Bonaparte, who in August, 1802, became first consul for life, showed impatience with the support and encouragement given by the Russian court to French royalist *émigrés* and their agents. The manifestly pro-English attitude and royalist sympathies of Count Morkov, Russian ambassador to Paris, led to much friction, and in November, 1803, he was recalled at the request of the French government. A royalist conspiracy, financed and sponsored by England, for the overthrow of the consular regime was discovered by the French police early in 1804. The Duke d'Enghien, son of the Duke de Bourbon, was arrested by the emissaries of Bonaparte at Ettenheim, in Baden (March 14, N.S.), and although available evidence indicated that he was in no way involved in the plot he was tried by a military commission and shot at the castle of Vincennes, near Paris, in the early hours of March 21, 1804, N.S. The Russian court was put into mourning, and sharply worded protests were dispatched to the German imperial diet at Ratisbon (the arrest of D'Enghien was a violation of the territory of Baden) and to Paris. Bonaparte replied to the Russian note in an insulting rejoinder which drew an insidious comparison between the interest taken by St. Petersburg in the case of the Duke d'Enghien and its failure to prosecute the murderers of Emperor Paul. The French ambassador to Russia, Count d'Hédouville, was recalled, and after some further negotiations Peter Oubril, Russian chargé d'affaires in Paris, demanded and received his passports (August, 1804). In the meantime Bonaparte was proclaimed emperor of the French (May 18, 1804, N.S.).

There were, however, other and more general reasons for the intransigent attitude of Russia than indignation over the fate of a Bourbon prince. Reverting to the tradition of Catherine II and Emperor Paul, Alexander was swayed by a vast international scheme in which Russia's territorial aggrandizement and the expansion of her dominion were pleasantly blended with vague proposals for the maintenance of perpetual peace. In reply to a request of Bonaparte for Russian mediation of the Anglo-French conflict, Alexander outlined in the early summer of 1803 a plan of international settlement which provided, among other things, for the occupation of Malta by Russian troops. At the beginning of 1804 Prince Adam Czartoryski, a close friend of Alexander, became Russian minister of foreign affairs. Scion of a great Polish family and an ardent Polish patriot, Prince Adam was the untiring champion of the restoration of a unified, autonomous Poland under the Russian scepter. In November, 1804, Novosiltsev, then assistant minister of justice and, like Czartoryski, a member of Alexander's intimate circle, was sent to London on a highly secret mission. He was to present an elaborate proposal for the formation of an Anglo-Russian league, with the object of destroying the hegemony of Napoleonic France and establishing a new European order. The plan, as outlined in an instruction to Novosiltsev of September 11, 1804, specifically stated that Russia and England were fighting the French government, and not the French people, and provided that the states liberated from the yoke of Napoleon, including France herself, should not have forced upon them again inequitable governments, but should be granted the benefit of free institutions of their own choice. The future peace treaty, it was held, should declare the basic principles of the law of nations and should impose upon the states the obligation to submit their disputes to mediation before declaring war. The political boundaries of the new Europe were to follow "natural frontiers" determined by geographical and economic factors and the racial complexion of the populations. The statement of these broad principles, which will appear strangely familiar to the student of international affairs since 1917, was accompanied by practical proposals of far-reaching scope. According to the Russian plan, as unfolded in the course of the negotiations and in supplementary secret instructions to Novosiltsev, the recurrence of French aggression was to be prevented by the creation of federations of Italian and German states; the latter, moreover, were to be protected against domination by Austria and Prussia. Novosiltsev was directed to secure the extension of Russia's sovereignty over the whole of Poland (compensation to Austria and Prussia was to be provided for elsewhere) and, if opportunity presented itself, over Moldavia, Cattaro, Corfu, Constantinople, and the Dardanelles; in case of the partition of the Ottoman empire the tsar was to exercise "a decisive influence" in settling the fate of its Christian population and was to assume the title "Protector of the Eastern Slavs." [2] Russia also demanded Malta, substantial subsidies, and the amendment of the English maritime code.

Pitt was far more interested in securing Russian cooperation against Bonaparte than in building a new European order. He professed admiration for Alexander's lofty international ideals and agreed to some of the Russian proposals for European territorial settlement. He avoided, however, direct commitments concerning the future of Turkey (these proposals were not pressed by Novosiltsev) and refused to surrender Malta or to make changes in the maritime code, although he was willing to submit the latter question to the future peace conference. An Anglo-Russian treaty was finally signed on April 11, 1805, N.S. The two governments agreed to form a European league for the liberation from French domination of North Germany, Holland, Switzerland, and Italy. England undertook to pay an annual subsidy of £1,250,000 for every 100,000 men contributed by the continental Powers to the struggle against France, provided the total number was not less than 400,000. Napoleon indirectly assisted the successful conclusion of the delicate negotiations by proclaiming himself king of Italy (March 17, 1805, N.S.).

Both England and Russia made diplomatic preparations for the impending war. Sweden signed a secret convention with England in December, 1804, and a treaty of alliance with Russia in January, 1805. Austria, in spite of her suspicion of St. Petersburg and her military unpreparedness, yielded to the pressure brought to bear by the tsar. In November, 1804, she entered with Russia into a defensive agreement against France, and on August 9, 1805, N.S., joined the Anglo-Russian

[2] The instruction of September 11 made no definite territorial demands, and merely spoke of "certain advantages" to which Russia and England would be entitled at the end of a successful war. Russian territorial claims were listed in a secret memorandum dated "1804" and written, presumably, by Czartoryski (both documents are published in *Mémoires du Prince Adam Czartoryski et sa correspondance avec l'Empereur Alexandre I-er* [Paris, 1887], II, 27–45, 62–66). Prof. J. Holland Rose expresses doubts whether the Czartoryski memorandum was authorized by the tsar (*The Cambridge History of British Foreign Policy, 1783–1919* [Cambridge, 1922], I, 335). It is unlikely, however, that Czartoryski would have followed a personal policy in a matter of such importance, especially because Novosiltsev was Alexander's close friend and personal envoy. The program of 1804 was in agreement with the views expressed by Alexander in later years, at Tilsit, at the Congress of Vienna, and elsewhere. On the other hand, Novosiltsev, who imagined that his mission was a great success, failed to carry out instructions in full: according to Czartoryski (*Mémoires*, I, 376), Novosiltsev in his London conversations made no reference to Russian designs on Poland.

coalition. Prussia took no part in the hostilities in 1805 and clung to an uneasy neutrality in spite of the bribes, diplomatic pressure, and threats of war used freely by Paris, St. Petersburg, and London.

At the end of August, 1805, Napoleon, abandoning his plans for an invasion of England, marched his troops from the channel coast to the valley of the Danube. Hostilities began in September, Bavaria and other south-German states siding with France. The campaign proved short and disastrous to Russia and her allies. On October 19, N.S., the Austrian General Mack and some 25,000 men capitulated at Ulm, and on November 13, N.S., Napoleon was in Vienna. Kutuzov, commander in chief of the Russian army, endeavored to avoid an open encounter with the enemy and limited himself to delaying rear-guard action. His cautious strategy was severely criticized and was finally over-ruled by Alexander and Emperor Francis of Austria, who after the fall of Vienna had established their joint headquarters at Olmütz. The ill advised decision of the two emperors precipitated the catastrophe. An Austro-Russian army of some 90,000 men commanded by Kutuzov was routed at Austerlitz (December 2, 1805, N.S.) and retreated in disorder, leaving behind some 26,000 men and its entire artillery. Emperor Francis abandoned the struggle and on December 26, N.S., signed at Pressburg an onerous treaty of peace with France, while the shattered remnants of Kutuzov's army withdrew across the Russian border. The death of Pitt in January, 1806, dealt another severe blow to the moribund coalition. Prussia hastened to make a bargain with the victor. At the end of October, 1805, Alexander was the guest of Frederick William at Potsdam, and the two monarchs exchanged promises of eternal friendship. A Russo-Prussian convention (November 3, 1805, N.S.) bound the government of Berlin to present to Napoleon conditions of peace which were substantially those laid down in the Anglo-Russian treaty; in case of his refusal to accept them Berlin was committed to entering the war on the side of the allies. The military reverses of Austria and Russia made Frederick William change his mind; not only did the Prussian army fail to take the field, but Frederick William, in the middle of December, 1805, signed a treaty of alliance with France. This was soon superseded by the Treaty of Paris (February 15, 1806, N.S.). By virtue of this agreement Prussia annexed Hanover and closed her ports to British commerce. The contracting parties guaranteed each other's territories, as well as the integrity of the Ottoman empire and that of

Naples and of the German states. Frederick William ratified the treaty (February 24, N.S.), but assured Alexander that he was acting under duress and that he had no intention of fulfilling the obligations he had been forced to assume.

Double-crossing and the simultaneous assumption of mutually incompatible obligations, seldom absent from international relations, were a common practice in Napoleonic Europe. Alexander, who is said to have wept bitterly during the retreat from Austerlitz, soon regained his composure. The collapse of Austria, the annexation of the Dalmatian coast by France, and the Franco-Prussian alliance offered, for the first time, a real threat not only of a Poland restored and unified under the aegis of France but also of a French-dominated Turkey. A council held at St. Petersburg early in 1806 decided that the policy of Russia should be based on the British alliance and on the maintenance of friendly relations with both the Porte and the Christian population under the Turkish rule; and that every means, including promises of military assistance, should be used to win Prussia to the side of the allies. But there were also in St. Petersburg powerful influences favoring peace with France, among them Czartoryski and the dowager empress. A similar tendency manifested itself in England, where Fox, the successor of Pitt, hastened to reopen peace negotiations with Napoleon. These attempts, led by Lord Yarmouth, dragged throughout the summer and collapsed soon after the death of Fox (September 13, 1806, N.S.). Early in July Oubril, a Russian envoy, reached Paris, and within a fortnight (July 20, 1806, N.S.) signed a treaty of peace. Its provisions guaranteed the integrity and independence of the Ottoman empire, bound the contracting parties to bring about peace between Prussia and Sweden, settled the conflicting French and Russian claims in Italy and in the Adriatic, and imposed on France the obligation to withdraw her troops from Germany. The Russian government, however, refused to ratify the treaty on the questionable ground that Oubril had exceeded his instructions. In fact, St. Petersburg had undergone another change of heart. In the middle of June, after Oubril had left on his errand, Czartoryski resigned, and although Baron Budberg, his successor as minister of foreign affairs, did not close the door on further peace negotiations with Paris the prospects of a Franco-Russian *rapprochement* were dimmed.

The attitude of Prussia proved a decisive factor at this turn of European affairs. It was not long before Frederick William was led to regret his alliance with France. His adherence to the Continental System provided by the treaty of alliance led to the blockade of the Prussian ports by the English fleet, the seizure of hundreds of Prussian ships then in British harbors, and the declaration of war against Prussia by England and Sweden. In the meantime Napoleon proceeded to redraw the map of Germany and Italy and to carve out principalities for his relatives and marshals, without any regard for the historic rights and interests of his Prussian ally. In July, 1806, there was formed, under his protection, a Confederation of the Rhine from which Austria and Prussia were excluded. In August the Holy German Empire was declared dissolved, and its emperor, Francis II, renounced his title and became Francis I, emperor of Austria. The Anglo-Swedish blockade proved effective, and by driving Prussian commerce off the high seas struck a heavy blow at the very foundation of Prussia's economic life. Queen Louise became the leader of influential circles, condemning the French alliance both on political and on economic grounds. Suspicion and indignation were further aroused by the peace negotiations carried on in great secrecy between Napoleon, Lord Yarmouth, and Oubril. At the end of July Napoleon had offered the restitution of Hanover to King George III, subject to the compensation of Prussia elsewhere, and there were persistent rumors of French plans to transfer Prussia's Polish provinces to Russia, and Pomerania to Sweden. In dismay Frederick William turned to Alexander, who, like the Prussian king, was playing a double game. In July, 1806, Russia and Prussia concluded a secret treaty amounting to a military alliance, and on September 26, N.S., Frederick William, convinced that war with France could no longer be avoided, sent Napoleon an ultimatum demanding, among other things, the immediate withdrawal of French troops to a position behind the Rhine. His note reached Napoleon at Bamberg on October 7, N.S., and the next day the French troops that had been concentrated on the river Main were on the march. On October 14, N.S., Napoleon and Davout inflicted on the Prussians a double defeat at Jena and Auerstädt. Eleven days later (October 25, N.S.) the victorious French army entered Berlin. It was from the Prussian capital that Napoleon issued his celebrated decree proclaiming the blockade of the British Isles (November 21, 1806).

Alexander unhesitatingly acknowledged his obligation to the Prussian alliance, but Russia's aggressive designs against Turkey and the machinations of General Sebastiani, the French envoy at Constantinople, had borne their evil fruit, and in the middle of October, 1806, the tsar became involved in a war with Turkey which was to last for six years. The collapse of Prussia within a fortnight after the outbreak of hostilities had not been foreseen. It was not until November 25, N.S., that a slow-moving Russian corps under Bennigsen had its first encounter with the French, thirty miles west of Warsaw. Three days later Murat occupied the city. The Russian army of some 100,000 men was at first commanded by the aged Field Marshal Kamensky, but his cautious tactics met with so much criticism that early in January, 1807, he was replaced by Bennigsen. In the meantime the Prussian army had dwindled to merely 15,000. In the exceptionally bloody and inconclusive battle of Preussisch Eylau (February 8, 1807, N.S.), both the French and the Russians suffered heavy losses. Bennigsen, nevertheless, chose to regard it as a great victory, and although he deemed it prudent to fall back on Königsberg the valor of the Russian troops under most trying conditions cheered the allies and encouraged them to continue the struggle. Peace negotiations between France and Prussia began immediately after the Prussian debacle but met with insurmountable obstacles in the severe terms offered by Napoleon, in spite of his desire to end a winter campaign that had imposed terrible hardships on his troops. Alexander used every means at his disposal to keep his ally in the war. Early in April, 1807, he met Frederick William at Memel, where the Prussian court had sought refuge, and on April 26, N.S., the two monarchs signed the so-called Convention of Bartenstein. This treaty confirmed the Russo-Prussian alliance, invited the adherence of Austria, Great Britain, Sweden, and Denmark, and dealt with the various problems of future European settlement—including the restoration of Prussia—as if victory had already been won.

Unlike Russia, Great Britain kept aloof from the coalition until it was too late. The repeal, at the outbreak of war with France, of all restrictions imposed by Prussia on English commerce led to the resumption of Prussian diplomatic relations with London, but the vexed question of Hanover proved a stumbling block to effective cooperation. The formation of a Tory government with George Canning in the foreign office (March 25, 1807, N.S.) and the more conciliatory attitude of Berlin eased the Anglo-Prussian tension. Peace between Prussia and Great Britain was formally restored at the end of April, an agreement was reached regarding British subsidies and the sending of a British expeditionary force, and on June 27, N.S., Great Britain acceded to the Convention of Bartenstein. This, however, was a belated and empty gesture. On June 14, N.S., the anniversary of Marengo, the armies of Bennigsen were decisively defeated by Napoleon at Friedland, and a Franco-Russian armistice was signed on June 21, N.S. "An alliance of France with Russia has always been the object of my desires," Alexander wrote to Napoleon three days later, "and I am convinced that it alone can guarantee the happiness and peace of the world." The next day the two emperors met on a gaily decorated raft in the middle of the Nieman, near Tilsit.

THE FRANCO-RUSSIAN ALLIANCE, 1807–1810

Alexander's demand for an armistice and the subsequent peace negotiations were not entirely unexpected. The Russian army's power of resistance survived the defeat of Friedland, and the retreat of the Russians into the unconquerable vastness of their native plains might, from the purely military point of view, have prolonged the war indefinitely. There were, however, other factors that militated against the continuation of hostilities. The troops of Bennigsen, poorly equipped and suffering from shortage of supplies, were demoralized. Russian generals had demonstrated their incompetence and were seemingly more interested in petty intrigues and personal quarrels than in fighting Napoleon. The financial resources of the empire were at a low ebb; the English government had at first turned down pressing requests for subsidies, and when it finally made up its mind to provide financial assistance the sums offered were deemed inadequate at St. Petersburg. Even before Friedland some of the tsar's advisers believed the situation to be so serious that they urged him to leave the army and to return to St. Petersburg in order to safeguard his prestige from the damaging repercussions of probable military reverses, and also, perhaps, to eliminate his interference with the orders of the commanding officers. The disavowal of the Oubril treaty, moreover, did not discourage the supporters of immediate peace with France. At the tsar's army headquarters the Grand Duke Constantine, Czartoryski, Novosiltsev, and Paul Stroganov agitated in favor of peace. Alexander himself was disgusted with the lack of cooperation on the part of Austria and Great Britain. But if under these conditions the opening of peace negotiations with Napoleon had become something of a necessity, this cannot be said of the offer of a full-fledged alliance, so suddenly proffered by Alexander.

Although the actual reasons for the tsar's dramatic change of heart were never disclosed, there is little doubt that the courtesy and friendliness with which Napoleon received the emissaries of his defeated enemy after Friedland paved the way to reconciliation. The ultimate object of Napoleon, as Vandal puts it, was to establish European peace by the defeat of Great Britain. For the achievement of this aim he needed an alliance with Russia. No witness was present at the first meeting of the two emperors on the Nieman raft (June 25, N.S.), and no record of their conversation has been preserved. The following day Alexander, this time accompanied by Frederick William, again met Napoleon on the raft. Negotiations were later continued at Tilsit, where both the tsar and the king of Prussia established their headquarters. Queen Louise, too, came to Tilsit in the vain hope that her beauty and charm might soften the heart of the conquerer and win better terms for Prussia. The Russian plenipotentiaries were Prince Alexander Kurakin and Prince Dimitry Lobanov-Rostovsky, but all major issues were decided by Alexander himself. Baron Budberg, the Russian minister of foreign affairs, took no part in the negotiations; dismissed soon after these meetings, he was succeeded by Count Nicholas Rumiantsev. The Tilsit conversations covered a wide range and dealt in an often vague and dilatory fashion with the partition of Europe and the world into French and Russian spheres of influence. France was to enjoy a hegemony in western Europe, while Russia was to have a free hand in the east. Napoleon originally contemplated the dismemberment of Prussia, and he offered Alexander all territories east of the Vistula and of the Nieman. The tsar, however, faithful to his Hohenzollern ally, declined the offer, although he agreed to annex the district of Belostok, formerly held by Prussia. Article 4 of the Franco-Russian treaty signed at Tilsit on July 7, N.S. (ratified July 9, N.S.), stated specifically that the restitution to Frederick William of even a portion of his domain was made out of regard (*"par égard"*) for the Emperor of All the Russias. The Franco-Russian agreement was embodied in a public treaty of peace supplemented by "secret and reserved articles," and in a secret treaty alliance. These documents contained detailed provisions concerning the allocation of territories severed from Prussia. The most important change, from the Russian point of view, was the formation, under the aegis of the king of Saxony, of a duchy of Warsaw which was to comprise all Polish provinces formerly held by Prussia, except the Belostok district. Alexander officially recognized these changes, as well as other territorial arrangements previously made or contemplated by Napoleon, and yielded to France the Ionian Islands and Cattaro.[3] Alexander was to mediate between Great Britain and France while Napoleon was to mediate between Russia and Turkey. Great Britain was to be offered Hanover in exchange for the recognition of the equality of all flags on the seas and for the restoration of the French, Spanish, and Dutch colonies she had seized after 1805. If peace with England was not concluded by November 1 or if its terms were not fulfilled by December 1, 1807, N.S., Russia was to declare war on Great Britain. In that case the countries which had maintained a friendly neutrality towards Great Britain or were her allies—Austria, Sweden, Denmark, and Portugal— were to be compelled to take part in the anti-British coalition, and if Sweden refused (as seemed likely) Denmark was to be forced to join in a war against her. Arrangements concerning Turkey were less clear-cut and less stringent. Napoleon was to mediate an armistice between Russia and the Porte on condition that the armies of both countries were withdrawn from the Danubian principalities. If the sultan refused to accept French mediation or if the latter failed to produce satisfactory results within three months, France was to make common cause with Russia against Turkey, and the contracting parties were to reach an agreement concerning the liberation of the European provinces under the Ottoman rule, except for Constantinople and Rumelia. The term Rumelia, according to Vandal, was used because it was singularly vague and elastic. The secret treaty of alliance, which contained the more important of the above provisions, bound France and Russia to fight side by side in any European war, to the limit of their resources.

The Franco-Prussian treaty (signed July 9, 1807, N.S., and ratified three days later) deprived Prussia of about one-half of her territory and population and aligned her with France and Russia against England. The supplementary Convention of Königsberg (July 12, N.S.) provided for the evacuation of the French troops from Prussia, but

---

[3] The Dalmatian port of Cattaro was ceded to Napoleon by Austria in 1805 under the Treaty of Pressburg. It was occupied by Russian troops from Corfu in 1806.

made the withdrawal conditional on the payment of an indemnity of an unspecified amount. This crude device permitted Napoleon to retain the army of occupation in Prussia as long as he pleased.

Neither Alexander nor his inexperienced diplomatic advisers would seem to have grasped the momentous implications of the formidable documents they had helped to frame. The air of Tilsit, saturated with exuberant friendliness and loose promises of collaboration in distant lands, was not conducive to clear thinking. "God has saved us," the tsar wrote to his sister Catherine at an early stage of the negotiations; "instead of sacrifices we emerge from the struggle with a kind of luster." And he parted with his new ally on most affectionate terms.

Speransky held in 1811 that the Tilsit settlement contained practically all the elements of a future war between Russia and France. It forced Russia into an onerous and, from the national point of view, purposeless conflict with Great Britain; facilitated the consolidation of the French dominion over the Continent and the expansion of the Continental System; failed to free Prussia from French occupation; prepared the invasion of Russia by creating on her border the French-controlled duchy of Warsaw; alienated whatever pro-Russian feeling might still have existed in Poland; and proved ineffective in prompting Alexander's plans of aggrandizement at the expense of Turkey. It took time, however, before the true implications of the alliance were fully realized. General René Savary, first French ambassador to Russia after Tilsit, and his successor (December, 1807), Marquis de Caulaincourt (afterwards Duke de Vicence) were treated by Alexander with particular courtesy but were given a frigid reception in the salons of the Russian capital. Both Savary and Caulaincourt were involved in the unhappy affair of the Duke d'Enghien; feelings on this score were running so high among Russian aristocracy that Caulaincourt deemed it expedient to seek personal rehabilitation by a disingenuous *démarche* (April, 1808) designed to prove that he had no connection with the murder of the Bourbon prince.

Alexander in the meantime proceeded to carry out the obligations imposed on him by the alliance. His offer of mediation between France and England received a courteous but elusive reply from Canning, who was anxious to avoid, or at least to postpone, an open conflict with Russia. The Russian government, however, protested vigorously against the British attack on Copenhagen and the capture of the Danish fleet (September, 1807), and the final breach was precipitated by the indiscretions of the British representative in St. Petersburg, Sir Robert Wilson. Wilson was ordered expelled on the charge of circulating an anti-Tilsit pamphlet that contained unflattering allegations regarding the person of the tsar. On November 7, 1807, N.S., Russia severed relations with Great Britain.

War with Sweden was the next result of the Tilsit agreement. Gustavus IV Adolphus of Sweden, an uncompromising enemy of Bonaparte, stuck to his alliance with Great Britain in spite of the menacing attitude of Russia and France. The proximity of St. Petersburg to the Swedish border had long caused uneasiness in the Russian capital. Napoleon, directly (his letter to the tsar of February 2, 1808, N.S.) and through Caulaincourt, did everything in his power to encourage Russia's latent ambition to annex Finland. He promised Alexander full support in this venture, and went so far as to offer him Stockholm. Early in February, 1808, the Russian troops crossed the Swedish border, overcame without difficulty the small Swedish garrisons, and occupied Finland. On March 16, 1808, the incorporation of this province in the Russian empire was announced to foreign courts and four days later was proclaimed by an imperial manifesto. The Finnish population, however, refused to submit, and through the summer of 1808 conducted successful guerilla warfare against the invaders. The poor showing of the Swedish troops, political unrest in Stockholm, and Alexander's promises to safeguard the ancient rights and privileges of the Finns turned the scale once more in favor of Russia. In March, 1809, a Russian corps under Barclay de Tolly crossed the ice of the Gulf of Bothnia, occupied the Aland Islands, and reached the shores of Sweden. On March 28, N.S., a Finnish diet was convoked at Borgö by Alexander's orders, and the next day in Stockholm the erratic King Gustavus Adolphus was forced to abdicate the Swedish throne. He was eventually succeeded (June 5, 1809, N.S.) by his uncle, the Duke of Sudermania, who took the name of Charles XIII. A peace congress assembled at Frederikshamn in July, and by the treaty of September 17, 1809, N.S., Sweden ceded to Russia the Aland Islands and Finland; the new frontier was traced along the Torneo river. The outcome of the war was highly satisfactory to Alexander and his nationalistically-minded advisers, but it also emphasized the frailties of the Franco-Russian alliance, for Napoleon's promises of military assistance were not fulfilled, although he reaped some of the benefits of the defeat of Sweden. War between that country and Denmark was terminated in December, 1809, and in January, 1810, Charles XIII signed with France a treaty by which, in return for the recovery of Pomerania and the island of Rügen, he agreed to adhere to the Continental System and to impose embargoes on British commerce and ships.

Soon after the Tilsit settlement it became apparent that Russian and French policies in Turkey, Prussia, and Poland were hopelessly at variance. In violation of the agreement, Alexander showed no intention to withdraw his troops from the Danubian principalities, while Napoleon indefinitely postponed the evacuation of Prussia. Count Peter Tolstoy, Russian ambassador to Paris, warned his government in October and November, 1807, that Napoleon was planning the final dismemberment of that country; according to these reports Silesia was to be attached to the duchy of Warsaw. Nothing could have alarmed St. Petersburg more than the strengthening of Poland and the further weakening and possible destruction of Prussia. Napoleon hastened to divert the tsar's attention to Sweden and the east. In his letter to Alexander of February 2, 1808, N.S., he unfolded a grandiose plan for the joint action of the allies in Scandinavia, Turkey, and Asia. Within a few weeks after the beginning of the proposed campaign, Napoleon maintained, the Russian troops would be in Stockholm and an allied army on the Bosphorus on its way to India. This, according to Bonaparte, was the most effective way to bring Great Britain to her knees. The final arrangements for the great venture, he suggested, should be reached in a personal interview between the two monarchs. Napoleon's plan, which was developed in the instructions to Caulaincourt, envisaged the partition of Turkey, although no definite reference to this matter was made in the letter of February 2. Alexander accepted the proposal with all the outward signs of enthusiasm, and it was agreed that the two emperors should meet at Erfurt. The sincerity and earnestness of both Napoleon's offer and Alexander's acceptance have been questioned. Peter Tolstoy, whom Napoleon accused of "prejudice against and suspicion of France" and whose recall he demanded, wrote to his government (February 6, 1808, N.S.) that "Napoleon does not think about the partition of Turkey and merely seeks to gain time." Yet the extensive French preparations for the Indian expedition and the elaborate negotiations between Paris and St. Petersburg suggest that the two emperors were in earnest. Moreover, the powerful flight of imagination which inspired Napoleon's proposal is characteristic of his general approach to European and world problems, and it had a strong appeal to Alexander.

The discussion of the proposed campaign brought out the divergency of the views held by the two governments. France was willing to agree to Russian expansion in Turkey but would not concede the annexation of Constantinople and of the Dardanelles, and she refused to evacuate Prussia. Events in the Iberian Peninsula, however, basically changed the international situation and gave a new turn to the Franco-Russian negotiations. The bogus election of Joseph Bonaparte to the throne of Spain (March 10, 1808, N.S.) was followed by a revolutionary movement in that country and by war with France, which for a time claimed all the attention of Napoleon. In July he was reluctantly compelled to admit that plans for the invasion of Egypt and India would have to be indefinitely postponed; and orders were given for the recall from Prussia of some of the French troops urgently needed in Spain. Napoleon took care to give this decision the appearance of a special concession to Alexander for recognizing Joseph as king of Spain. The French government, moreover, was alarmed by the policy of rearmament inaugurated by Austria in the summer of 1808.

It was in an international situation vastly different from that of February, 1808, when the conference was first suggested, that Napoleon and Alexander met six months later at Erfurt (from September 27 to October 14, N.S.). The ancient Thuringian city provided a fitting setting for the somewhat theatrical display of might and splendor of which Napoleon was the unsurpassed master. On this occasion Bonaparte surrounded himself with an imposing and decorative array of German kings and princes who, kept at a respectful distance, emphasized by their submissive demeanor his seemingly unchallengeable power. The practical results of the Erfurt deliberations were hardly in keeping with these elaborate arrangements. After much wrangling behind the scenes the two emperors signed (October 12, N.S.) a convention which was to remain secret for two years. It confirmed the alliance and provided for an offer of peace to Great Britain on the basis of *uti possidetis*; that is, Great Britain was to recognize "the new order established by France in Spain," and the annexation by Russia of Finland, Moldavia, and Wallachia. France thus acquiesced in Russia's acquisition of the two Danubian principalities but assumed no obligation to assist Russia in a war with the Porte in case of the latter's refusal to agree to the annexation (unless Austria or another Power took the side of Turkey). On the other hand, if France was attacked by Austria, Russia was to declare war on the Hapsburg Monarchy.

Of greater significance than this half-hearted official agreement were the private negotiations between the princes and statesmen assembled at Erfurt. Talleyrand, although no longer Napoleon's minister of foreign affairs, played an important part in these unofficial activities. He had become convinced that the expansionist policies of Bonaparte and his violent methods spelled the ruin of France, and he secretly urged Alexander and Rumiantsev to make common cause with Austria in opposing Napoleon and in restoring the European balance of power. His advice fell on fertile soil, and Emperor Francis's representative at Erfurt, Baron Vincent, was surprised and pleased to discover that the attitude of the tsar towards Austria was as conciliatory and friendly as that of Napoleon was provocative and harsh. The ground for the future anti-French coalition was prepared at Erfurt, where the spell of Tilsit was definitely broken. "Bonaparte imagines that I am nothing but a simpleton *(un sot)*," Alexander wrote to his sister Catherine in September, 1808; "*rira le mieux qui rira le dernier.*" [4]

Peace negotiations with Great Britain were perfunctory and came to naught in December, 1808. In the meantime the success of the Spanish resistance spurred Austria to take up arms in a desperate attempt to throw off the domination of Napoleon. Metternich, the Austrian ambassador to Paris, acting on the advice of, and in secret agreement with, Talleyrand, urged the Vienna government to declare war on France. During the negotiations preceding the outbreak of hostilities, Alexander played an ambiguous part. He feared that war between France and Austria might lead to the strengthening of the duchy of Warsaw and the reopening of the Polish question. Yet by courting simultaneously Napoleon and Emperor Francis he actually precipitated the conflict that it was in his interest to prevent. On the

---

[4] The letter quoted has been the source of some confusion. In the volume of correspondence between Alexander and Catherine edited by the Grand Duke Nicholas Mikhailovich (*Perepiska Imperatora Aleksandra I s Sestroi Velikoi Kniaginei Ekaterinoi Pavlovnoi* [Correspondence of Emperor Alexander I with His Sister the Grand Duchess Catherine Pavlona], p. 17), it is erroneously dated "Weimar, May 26, 1807." The error was corrected in a later publication by the same historian (*Imperator Aleksandr I*, I, 55, 97), where the date is given as September, 1808. Alexander was not at Weimar in 1807, but he visited that city in September and October, 1808.

one hand, the tsar assured Caulaincourt of his attachment to the French alliance and his determination to fulfill its obligations; and, on the other, he intimated to the Austrian envoy, Prince Schwarzenberg, that Russia had no desire to fight Austria and that Emperor Francis had nothing to fear from him. Great Britain, although at war with France, did not effectively cooperate with Austria and, as in 1807, remained aloof until it was too late.[5] There was no formal declaration of war between Austria and France, but military operations began in April, 1809, and after an exceptionally bloody campaign the Austrian army was routed at Wagram on July 6, N.S. Fighting was terminated by the armistice of July 12.

The assistance given by Alexander to his ally was half-hearted. The Russian troops massed on the border of Galicia were marking time; they did not cross the frontier until early in June and took no part in the fighting, although they occupied Cracow on July 14, N.S., two days after the armistice. In striking contrast with their hostile attitude towards the army of the duchy of Warsaw, which had fought gallantly on the side of France, Russian officers and men treated the Austrians with utmost friendliness. Alexander was not represented at the peace congress which after difficult and protracted deliberations framed the Treaty of Schönbrunn (October 14, 1809, N.S.). The harsh provisions of this treaty deprived Austria of much of her territory, reduced her to the position of a second-rate Power, and aligned her with France against Great Britain. Western Galicia was annexed to the duchy of Warsaw, whereas Russia received a slice of eastern Galicia, a much smaller territory than the one allotted to the Polish state.

The Treaty of Schönbrunn produced in St. Petersburg an even more painful impression than Alexander's lack of enthusiasm for the Austrian war had created in Paris. The transfer of western Galicia to the duchy of Warsaw was regarded by the Russian government as a step towards the eventual reconstruction of a unified Poland and as a menace to Russia's Polish provinces. Napoleon, for all his irritation with the equivocal and dilatory policies of Alexander during the Austrian war, was still anxious to maintain the Russian alliance. Polish independence meant nothing to him. "His Majesty approves the idea

---

[5] The British expeditionary force did not sail until July 28, N.S., sixteen days after the Franco-Austrian armistice. It landed on the island of Walcheren, but accomplished nothing, and after suffering heavy losses was ignominiously withdrawn in December.

that the words Poland and Poles should disappear for ever not only from all political transactions, but even from history," the French minister of external relations, De Champagny (afterwards Duke de Cadore) wrote to Rumiantsev six days after the conclusion of the Treaty of Schönbrunn. This declaration was welcomed in St. Petersburg, but Alexander felt that the policy it represented should be made more definite and should take the form of precise treaty obligations. Napoleon in the meantime became engrossed in a new scheme which, he imagined, would assure the future of his dynasty and would cement his alliance with Russia. When question of his marriage with a Russian princess was raised in very general terms at Erfurt, he had gained the impression that the tsar would be willing to give his consent. In the autumn of 1809 Napoleon decided to divorce Josephine and to seek the hand of the Grand Duchess Anne, Alexander's fifteen-year-old sister. The very day (November 22, N.S.) when a French courier was to be sent to St. Petersburg with secret instructions concerning the offer of marriage, the draft of a Russian convention dealing with Poland was received in Paris. Article 1 provided that "the kingdom of Poland shall never be restored." In his anxiety to allay Russian suspicions and to create an atmosphere favorable to the acceptance of his matrimonial proposal, Napoleon directed Caulaincourt to sign the convention on Russian terms. The divorce from Josephine was pronounced in the middle of December, but the eagerly awaited reply of Alexander was slow in coming. Napoleon, having become convinced that the tsar's procrastination would be followed by a rejection of his proposal, announced with dramatic suddenness his betrothal to Archduchess Marie Louise of Austria (February 6, 1810, N.S.). The Russian court was informed of the decision in two separate messages: an antedated note withdrew Napoleon's marriage demand while a postdated one brought the news of his engagement to the daughter of Francis I. These communications crossed a letter from the tsar which, as Napoleon had anticipated, was a refusal courteously disguised as a deferment for two years because of the youth of the prospective bride.

These rather shoddy matrimonial negotiations had direct repercussions on the fate of the Polish convention. The Russia text was signed at St. Petersburg by Caulaincourt and Rumiantsev and was ratified by Alexander on January 4, N.S., but on February 10, N.S., four days after his betrothal to Marie Louise, Napoleon repudiated the signature of his ambassador and made counter-proposals. Futile parleys were resumed, but no agreement was reached and the matter was dropped in July. For a while Napoleon clung to the illusion that the "system of Tilsit" had been maintained intact. It was felt in St. Petersburg, however, that his policy in Poland was incompatible with the preservation of the territorial integrity of the Russian empire. The external shell of the alliance was preserved, but confidence, good faith, and belief in the community of interests—never too conspicuous in Franco-Russian relations—had vanished.

THE WAR OF 1812

The French alliance was never popular in Russia. Before Tilsit the government itself had vigorously promoted anti-French propaganda. An imperial manifesto read in November, 1806, from the pulpit of every church in the land stigmatized Bonaparte as the disturber of the peace of the world, the perpetrator of abhorrent iniquities, and the enemy of Christian faith. Seven months later he became the tsar's ally and friend. To the majority of the Russian nobility Napoleon was the son of the French Revolution, and there were persistent rumors that a French invasion of Russia would spell the doom of serfdom. Hostility to France found expression in a whole literature of pamphlets, novels, and plays; Rostopchin, the future governor of Moscow, particularly distinguished himself by the caustic vehemence of his invective. After Tilsit, in spite of Alexander's efforts, strong opposition to Napoleonic France persisted, and counted among its leaders the dowager empress, the Grand Duchess Catherine, and the Anglophile friends of the tsar, Novosiltsev and Stroganov, who in 1807 had favored peace with Napoleon but were not reconciled to the alliance. The economic consequences of the alignment of Russia with France proved disastrous. It will be remembered that at the turn of the eighteenth century Russian foreign trade was almost exclusively in British hands. Alexander's adherence to the Continental System, therefore, dealt a severe blow to firms engaged in foreign commerce and to the landed proprietors, who provided the chief articles of Russian export. The adverse balance of trade and the immoderate use of the printing press to meet war expenditures led to the catastrophic depreciation of the ruble, whereas prices, especially those of imported commodities, including colonial products such as sugar, increased manyfold. In spite of the annexation of Finland, war with Sweden was by no means universally popular, and there was much criticism of the inconclusive and protracted war with Turkey. The incorporation of western Galicia in the duchy of Warsaw in 1809 alarmed even such staunch supporters of the French alliance as Rumiantsev and Kurakin.

In 1810 and 1811 the state of Franco-Russian relations rapidly deteriorated. Napoleon, relentlessly pursuing his plans for the enforcement of the Continental System, proceeded to extend his direct dominion over the littoral of the Northern and the Baltic Seas and to make the blockade more stringent. The annexation of Holland by the French empire (July 9, 1810, N.S.) was followed by the so-called Trianon Tariff (August 5, N.S.), which imposed heavy duties on colonial products imported under the cover of a neutral flag. Napoleon requested Alexander (September and October, 1810) to adopt the rates of the Trianon Tariff, as the German states had done, and to close Russian ports to neutral shipping on the ground that neutrals (especially the United States of America) were merely agents of Great Britain and that goods of British origin found their way through Russia to European markets. The tsar not only eluded the acceptance of Napoleon's new demands but on December 19 (December 31, N.S.) issued a tariff which imposed heavy duties on articles imported over the land frontier, especially on certain luxuries, chiefly of French origin, whereas a much more liberal treatment was accorded to sea-borne imports, provided they were carried under the flag of a nation with which Russia was not at war. This legislation was considered in Paris as a direct violation of the Tilsit treaty. The French themselves, however, showed little respect for that agreement. On December 13, N.S., Napoleon annexed the northwestern coast of Germany, including the Hanseatic cities of Hamburg, Bremen, and Lübeck, and by a decree of January 22, 1811, N.S., took over the duchy of Oldenburg. The ruling house of that principality was closely related to the Romanov. George of Oldenburg, heir apparent to the duchy, was the husband of Alexander's sister Catherine, and the integrity of his domain was specifically guaranteed by the Treaty of Tilsit. Russia made a formal protest which the French government refused to consider.

Throughout 1811 and the early part of 1812 the fiction of the alliance was maintained, but ominous diplomatic incidents multiplied, the possibility of a Franco-Russian war was freely discussed, and both countries hurriedly prepared for it. Napoleon poured troops into Prussia and sent large consignments of arms to the duchy of Warsaw; Alexander hastened to complete the reorganization of the Russian military force and massed his armies on the western border. There was much open and surreptitious diplomatic activity, Austria and Prussia pursuing, as in the past, a devious course. Early in 1812 Napoleon concluded military alliances with Prussia (February 24, N.S.) and Austria (March 14, N.S.), but both Frederick and Metternich gave Alexander secret assurances that the participation of their countries in a war against Russia, if war was to come, would be purely nominal. At the end of 1811 the tsar sought the cooperation of his former minister of foreign affairs, Prince Adam Czartoryski, in winning over to the Russian side the duchy of Warsaw. He suggested the restoration of the kingdom of Poland under the scepter of the Russian emperor, who was to assume the title of king of Poland. Prince Adam, however, realized that this vague offer would not commend itself to his countrymen, whose mistrust of Russia was deep-rooted and only too well justified by past experience. Ignorant of Napoleon's profound indifference towards the independence of their country, the Poles had come to look upon him as their liberator. Czartoryski, therefore, gave Alexander no encouragement, and declined to participate in the execution of his project. Russia was more successful in her negotiations with Sweden. A treaty concluded with that country in April, 1812, removed the danger of a Swedish attack on Finland and St. Petersburg, in exchange for Alexander's promise to support the Swedish claim to Norway as a compensation for the territory ceded to Russia in 1809.

Of great practical importance was the timely termination of the war in which Russia and Turkey had been involved since 1806. Political and economic confusion in the Porte, military victories won by Russian armies after Kutuzov's appointment as supreme commander on the Turkish front (1811), and the abandonment of Alexander's claim to Moldavia and Wallachia permitted the conclusion of peace, in spite of Napoleon's anti-Russian agitation at Constantinople. By the Treaty of Bucharest (May 28, 1812, N.S.) the Porte ceded Bessarabia to Russia; the *status quo ante bellum* was restored on the Caucasian frontier of Turkey, Russian troops withdrawing from the Black Sea port of Anapa, which they had previously occupied.[6] In

---

[6] Russian expansion in the Caucasus led to a war with Persia. The annexation

July, 1812, after the outbreak of war with France, Russia entered into military agreements with Great Britain and with Spain, whose relentless resistance to Napoleon was a major factor in his eventual downfall.

In May, 1812, Napoleon, accompanied by Marie Louise and a brilliant suite, left Paris for Dresden, where he conferred with Emperor Francis, Frederick William of Prussia, and a galaxy of German kings and princes. He then took leave of Marie Louise and proceeded to the Russian border. On June 24, N.S., the French army, without a formal declaration of war, crossed the Nieman and entered Russian territory. When the news of the invasion reached Alexander the same evening at Vilna, he immediately sent to the French headquarters his minister of police, Alexander Balashev, with an eleventh-hour appeal for the preservation of peace. Napoleon, however, had reached the irrevocable decision to fight Russia, even though it would seem that he had neither a clear conception of the ultimate object nor a strategic campaign plan. The Grand Army participating in the invasion has been estimated at 575,000 men; of this number 420,000 crossed the Nieman in June and 155,000 came later as reinforcements. Only about one-third of this huge force were Frenchmen, the others being soldiers drawn from Germany, Italy, Portugal, Poland, Holland, Switzerland, and other countries. The total effectives of the three Russian armies opposing the invaders, and commanded, respectively, by Barclay de Tolly, Prince Peter Bagration, and General Alexander Tormasov, were officially estimated at 220,000, but the actual number was even smaller, and probably did not exceed 180,000 men.

The numerical inferiority of the Russian forces determined the character of the campaign: Alexander's generals had no choice but to retreat. It will be remembered that as far back as 1811 the tsar had envisaged the possibility of a withdrawal and had expressed the belief that the absence of roads, the rigors of the climate, and the vastness

---

of Georgia by Emperor Paul (Jan. 18, 1801) was confirmed by Alexander (Sept. 12, 1801) and was followed by sporadic fighting between Russian troops and local chieftains. War with Persia began in 1804 and lasted until 1813. By the Treaty of Gulistan (Oct. 12, 1813), negotiated with the aid of Great Britain, Russia was granted the right to maintain a fleet in the Caspian Sea and also obtained the recognition of her sovereignty over a vast stretch of mountainous country extending from the Black Sea to the Caspian Sea. This territory comprises the bulk of the oil wealth of the Caucasus. The involvement of Russia in the struggle against Napoleon was an important factor in bringing about the termination of the Turkish and the Persian wars.

of Russia were her best defense.[7] Retreat, however, is an onerous and unpopular policy. Nevertheless Alexander and Barclay wisely discarded a plan devised by the tsar's mentor, the Prussian General Phull, to make a definite stand at Drissa, on the Dvina River.[8] Under the steady pressure of the enemy the Russian troops were withdrawn to the east, avoiding contact with the main body of the French army. Although Barclay, then minister of war and senior commanding officer at the front, resorted to the strategy of retreat merely as a matter of expediency, his conduct of the campaign was bitterly attacked on the ground that he lacked courage, determination, and vision. On June 28, N.S., Napoleon entered Vilna amid the jubilation of the Polish population. The two Russian armies of Barclay and Bagration effected a junction at Smolensk (August 3, N.S.); but, contrary to general expectations, Barclay decided to surrender the city, which the French occupied on August 18, N.S., after a bloody battle with a small rearguard force of General Nicholas Raevsky. This was a great shock to Russian public opinion, and the position of Barclay became intolerable; among his most violent critics were Bagration and the Grand Duke Constantine, who accused him of treason and of "leading the enemy to Moscow." Alexander had left the army in July and after a brief visit to Moscow had returned to St. Petersburg. Two days after the fall of Smolensk he appointed the aged and venerable Field Marshal Prince Michael Golenishchev-Kutuzov (1745–1813) to the

[7] See p. 637. The views of the tsar were shared by some of the more enlightened contemporary observers. Professor Tarle quotes, for instance, the following letter, written on June 5, 1812, N.S., by Count Simon Vorontsev, Russian ambassador to London: "The whole world anxiously watches the events about to take place on the Dvina, Dnieper, and Vistula. I am afraid only of political and diplomatic repercussions, for the military situation inspires in me no fear. Even if at the start we should suffer military reverses, we might win nevertheless by persisting in a defensive war and by fighting while we retreat. If the enemy pursues us, he is lost because the further he is from his stores of foodstuffs and arms and the deeper he advances into a country which has no roads and no supplies . . . the sooner he will be reduced to a pitiful state, and he will end by being annihilated by our winter, which has always been our most trusted ally." Rostopchin voiced a similar opinion. "I am not afraid of military reverses," he wrote to Alexander; "your empire has two powerful defenders in its vastness and its climate. The emperor of Russia will always be formidable in Moscow, terrible in Kazan, and invincible in Tobolsk."

[8] Phull has been severely criticized by military writers, and is usually held as a shining example of ineptitude and pedantry. Alexander, however, in a letter dated Dec. 12, 1813, paid him a warm tribute. "It is you," he wrote, "who have conceived the plan which, with the help of Providence, had as its consequence the salvation of Russia and Europe."

supreme command.[9] Kutuzov, however, found himself compelled to follow the unpopular strategy of his predecessor, and when he finally decided to meet the enemy in open battle at Borodino it was probably, as Clausewitz has suggested, because he was forced to do so by the clamor of "the court, the army, and the whole of Russia." It did not seem possible to surrender Moscow without a struggle. The battle of Borodino, described later by Napoleon as the most terrible of all the battles he ever waged, took place on September 7, N.S. The fighting was exceptionally severe and the outcome inconclusive, although both sides claimed victory. The Russian losses in killed and wounded were 58,000 men out of 112,000 combatants; those of the French, 50,000 out of 130,000, with forty-seven generals among the casualties. Bagration, mortally wounded, died a few days later. Kutuzov believed that Moscow could not be defended, and on September 13, N.S., in the village of Fili, he ordered the army to evacuate the capital and to withdraw in the direction of Riazan. The next day Napoleon entered Moscow, but he found there a situation very different from the one he had anticipated: the majority of the population had fled, and a fire that broke out the same evening destroyed three-fourths of the city before it was brought under control on September 18, N.S. The actual cause of the conflagration was never established, but Napoleon ascribed it to arson perpetrated by the Russians themselves.

The invasion had been received by the nation with mixed emotions. There was undoubtedly a genuine outburst of patriotism, especially during the tsar's visit to Moscow in July. Nobles and merchants subscribed large sums for the defense of the realm; wealthy landowners raised and equipped at their own expense whole regiments; people of all classes flocked to the banners and filled the ranks of the militia (*opolchenie*) and organized themselves into bands of "partisans" or guerrillas. There was, however, another side to the picture. The retreat, the inaction of the army, and finally the fall and destruction of Moscow inevitably produced a widespread feeling of discouragement and resentment. It was feared that St. Petersburg would be the next objective of the invaders, and there were many in Alexander's entourage, including his brother Constantine, who after the fall of Smolensk considered the war already lost and demanded immediate peace. "The capture of Moscow has caused extreme exasperation," the Grand Duchess Catherine wrote to Alexander on September 18,

[9] See p. 637.

N.S.; "discontent has reached its highest point and you are no longer spared. . . . You are openly accused of having caused the misfortune of your empire, general destruction and the ruin of private individuals, and, finally, of having lost the honor of the country and your own. It is not one class but all of them that unite in condemning you."

Napoleon had harbored the illusion that the occupation of Moscow would force Russia to seek peace. During the thirty-three days he spent in the Russian capital, he made three peace overtures; but the tsar ignored them all, and severely reprimanded Kutuzov for granting an interview to General Lauriston, an emissary of Napoleon. In the meantime the position of the invaders, in the middle of a hostile country, hundreds of miles away from their bases and depots of supplies, had become precarious. The approach of the Russian winter threatened even greater hardships, and disturbing news was reaching the conqueror both from Paris and from Spain. Somewhat suddenly Napoleon decided to abandon his costly conquest. On October 19, N.S., began the retreat of the Grand Army, accompanied on its long trek to the Polish border by a huge train of vehicles loaded with booty, with the sick, the wounded, and with French and allied civilians and their families who had stayed in Moscow and now fled Russian vengeance. The retreating French blew up parts of the Kremlin and other public buildings. Kutuzov, faithful to his cautious strategy, followed the withdrawing enemy but avoided open battle or even contact with the French rearguard. These tactics brought upon him the trenchant criticism not only of those who had long disliked him—Alexander, Bennigsen, and the British representative Sir Robert Wilson—but even of some of his admirers and friends. Kutuzov's deliberate refusal to engage the body of the French army at Maloiaroslavets (October 24, N.S.) appeared to many as akin to treason. His plan of campaign facilitated Napoleon's escape, and thus indirectly prepared the way for Russia's participation in the "War of Liberation" of 1813–1815, to which Kutuzov had been so relentlessly opposed. His chief and only object was to free the Russian soil from the invaders at the least possible cost; the tsar and some of his advisers, however, were intent on the total destruction of Napoleon. The clash of these conflicting points of view bore its evil fruit at Berezina. On November 8, N.S., Napoleon had reached Smolensk, and on November 27 and 28, N.S., he crossed the Berezina River. According to a plan prepared at St. Petersburg, the army of Kutuzov was to execute jointly with those of Admiral Paul Chichagov and of Prince Peter Wittgenstein a maneuver designed to prevent Napoleon from crossing the river. If successfully carried out, the operation would have resulted in the encirclement of the enemy and in the capture of the French emperor. Napoleon's army, which numbered about 110,000 men when he left Moscow, had dwindled by the end of November to 80,000; it was scattered along Russia's impassable roads and had lost much of its discipline and cohesion. Kutuzov's army, too, had been reduced by illness, death, and desertions from 97,000 to a mere 27,000. But Wittgenstein had 34,000 and Chichagov 24,000 men who had seen little fighting because Prince Schwarzenberg's Austrian corps, which opposed them, had remained notoriously inactive. The ineptness of the Russian generals, aggravated by their petty quarrels and mutual distrust, gave Napoleon his great opportunity. Military writers are in agreement that the crossing of the Berezina presents a striking example of his military genius. It postponed his downfall for nearly two years and plunged Europe into new and bloody wars. Hunger and an exceptionally severe winter, however, completed the task begun by Russian troops and guerrillas. Some 30,000 men, demoralized and in rags, were all that was left of the once proud Grand Army when its last detachments recrossed the Nieman on December 14, N.S. A few days earlier (December 6, N.S.) Napoleon appointed Murat supreme commander and left for Paris, where he arrived a fortnight later. The invasion was over. On December 23, N.S., Alexander triumphantly entered Vilna.

It will be noted that during his Russian campaign Napoleon failed to make use of a weapon that some of the Russian landowners particularly dreaded: he did not attempt to proclaim the emancipation of the serfs and to enlist in the service of his cause the latent forces of social discontent. He explained to the French senators (December 20, 1812, N.S.) that he had considered this plan but had abandoned it because its execution, in view of the brutality *(abrutissement)* of the Russian peasantry, would have meant death to a large number of innocent families. This statement seems disingenuous. Social reforms, moreover, are hardly compatible with foreign invasion and a regime of military occupation. It is unlikely, therefore, that a proclamation of the emancipation of the serfs by Napoleon would have had any substantial effect upon the course and the ultimate issue of his Russian campaign.

"THE WAR OF LIBERATION," 1813-1815

It was fervently hoped in Russia that the retreat of the Grand Army would bring the war to an end. The condition of the country and of the army was pitiful, and the inadvisability of carrying the war into foreign territory was urged upon the tsar by men as far apart in their views and sympathies as the Grand Duke Constantine, Kutuzov, Rumiantsev, Arakcheev, and Rostopchin. Alexander, however, flushed with what appeared to him as an almost miraculous victory, thought differently. He had revived the project of reestablishing a unified Poland under the Russian aegis, and as early as October, 1812, had resumed negotiations to this end with Czartoryski and other Polish leaders. He was, moreover, possessed with a newly acquired messianic zeal, heavily tinged with religious ardor and a desire to play the part of the savior of Europe and the founder of a new international order. For personal and patriotic reasons these aspirations were fostered by influential foreign members of the tsar's entourage: Sir Robert Wilson, always mindful of British interests; the Prussian statesman Freiherr Henry von Stein, a refugee from Napoleonic persecution; Count John Capo d'Istria, a native of Corfu and since 1809 in the Russian diplomatic service; the future Russian ambassador to Paris Count Charles Pozzo di Borgo, a Corsican like Napoleon and one of his inveterate enemies; and several aristocratic Poles headed by Prince Adam Czartoryski. After joining the army in December, 1812, Alexander expressed his resolve not to leave it again until the campaign about to begin was over. He was critical of his generals and distressed by the shabby appearance of the troops and by their "loss of discipline." Rigorous drilling was resumed at once and was continued from Vilna to Paris.

On January 13, 1813, N.S., a Russian army of some 110,000 men crossed the Nieman. Although secret negotiations between Russia, Austria, and Prussia had been in progress for some time, the first defection among Napoleon's allies occurred on December 30, 1812, N.S., when the Prussian general von York, acting ostensibly on his own authority, declared his corps neutral and practically invited the invasion of the Prussian territory by the Russians. A secret understanding with Austria (January, 1813) opened to the tsar's armies the gates of Warsaw; Prince Schwarzenberg's Austrian corps which had occupied that city, the government of the duchy, and the Polish troops under Prince Joseph Poniatowski, who had remained loyal to Napoleon, withdrew to Galicia. On February 28, N.S., Russia and Prussia concluded a military alliance (Treaty of Kalish) and on March 13, N.S., Frederick William declared war on France. The allied troops under the supreme command of, first, Kutuzov and, after his death (April, 1813), of the Russian Field Marshal Count Wittgenstein were confronted with a new and powerful French army. Their defeat at Lützen (May 2, N.S.) and the bloody but indecisive battle of Bautzen (May 20, N.S.) were followed from June to August by an armistice brought about by a French proposal of peace. This move was probably a fatal mistake on the part of Napoleon. Not only did it afford the allies an opportunity to strengthen and reorganize their battered forces but it also permitted them to enlarge the scope of the coalition. The allies were joined by Sweden and were assured of the indispensable financial assistance of Great Britain (Treaty of Reichenbach, June 14, N.S.). On June 27, N.S., by the secret Treaty of Reichenbach, Austria concluded a military alliance with Russia and Prussia and undertook to declare war on France should the terms of the allies be rejected by Napoleon. Peace negotiations having broken down, Emperor Francis duly entered the war against his son-in-law (August 12, N.S.).

According to authoritative estimates, the allied armies under the supreme command of the Austrian Field Marshal, Prince Schwarzenberg, numbered well over 500,000 men, including 185,000 Russians, while there were more effectives at the disposal of Napoleon, perhaps as many as 700,000. The battle of Dresden (August 26 and 27, N.S.), the first major encounter between the French and the new coalition, was a great victory for Napoleon, but the allies defeated the French at Kulm (August 30, N.S.) and dealt them a shattering blow in the gigantic battle of Leipzig (October 16 to 19, N.S.), where 120,000 men are said to have been killed or wounded. The French army was forced to retreat behind the Rhine, the Confederation of the Rhine collapsed, and the German kings and princes hastened to desert Napoleon and to join the ranks of the allies. In spite of these costly successes the ultimate victory of the coalition remained uncertain. "At the end of 1813," writes C. K. Webster, "the alliance appeared to be dissolving into fragments. It had neither military nor diplomatic unity." There were futile peace negotiations with France, while the uncoordinated moves of allied commanders permitted Napoleon to win a number of local victories during the final phase of the campaign, which was fought on French soil. Some appearance of diplomatic unity was restored after the arrival on the Continent, early in 1814, of Viscount Castlereagh, the British minister of foreign affairs. The Treaty of Chaumont (dated March 1 but actually signed on March 9, 1814, N.S.), which established the Quadruple Alliance, bound Great Britain, Russia, Prussia, and Austria not to conclude a separate peace with Napoleon. The provisions concerning postwar territorial settlements did not include Poland.

General war-weariness in France was probably the decisive factor in Napoleon's impending doom. Alexander, informed of France's desperate plight by Talleyrand, with whom he carried on a secret correspondence, and learning of it from other sources, succeeded in overcoming the reluctance of Schwarzenberg to press an immediate advance on Paris. The progress of the allied armies was favored by the defection of French commanders; Paris capitulated, and on March 31, N.S., Alexander, accompanied by Frederick William, made a triumphal entry into the French capital. Emperor Francis and Castlereagh choosing, for reasons of their own, to remain in the background, Alexander assumed the leading role not only in framing the Treaty of Fontainebleau (April 11, 1814, N.S.), by which Napoleon abdicated the throne of France and became the sovereign of Elba, but also in establishing the first Peace of Paris (May 30, 1814, N.S.), which terminated war with France. The relatively generous and liberal character of these treaties was a tribute to Alexander's determination and singleness of purpose, for his program was opposed by the Prussians and received only half-hearted support from Castlereagh. The tsar, however, made a major concession to the wishes of his allies when he reluctantly agreed to the restoration of the Bourbons. He had other candidates for the French throne, and had even gone so far as to consider establishing a republic in France. The acceptance by the other Powers of the provision that Louis XVIII should return to Paris as a constitutional and not as an absolute monarch made Alexander's capitulation somewhat more palatable for him. The influence of Talleyrand, in whose house in rue Saint-Florentin Alexander resided during his stay in Paris, was instrumental in the tsar's unwilling conversion to legitimism and in determining his general pro-French attitude.

The stupendous task of rebuilding a new European order out of the fragments of the Napoleonic empire devolved upon the Congress of

Vienna (September, 1814, to June, 1815). The original object of the allies in summoning the congress was to obtain its sanction for the territorial and political arrangements previously agreed upon by the principal Powers. It happened, however, that no such agreement on a number of the major issues was reached either in Paris or in London, which was visited by the allied potentates and statesmen in the spring and summer of 1814. During their stay in England, moreover, both Alexander and his sister Catherine, by a tactless display of liberalism, demonstrative association with the Whigs, contempt for conventions, and discourtesy towards the prince regent (later King George IV) greatly shocked the court, the Tory government, and conservative circles. The resulting animosity of official London towards the tsar embittered Anglo-Russian relations and contributed to the feeling of distrust Russian policies inspired in every European capital. Although the Congress of Vienna was attended by a host of crowned heads and by delegates of every European state, its actual business was transacted, chiefly in informal conversations, by the representatives of only five Powers—Great Britain, Russia, Austria, Prussia, and France. C. K. Webster observes that "the congress of the whole body of plenipotentiaries never came into existence" and that "no appreciable difference would have been made in the final settlement at Vienna if the large majority of the plenipotentiaries had never appeared there at all. They merely acted as a picturesque and expensive background to the real Congress of Vienna."

The real stumbling block in the path of the Congress of Vienna was the Polish question. The eastern Powers had previously reached definite, albeit seemingly contradictory, arrangements concerning the future of Poland. By the Treaty of Kalish (February 28, 1813, N.S.) Frederick William had abandoned to Russia a large part of his Polish claims in return for compensation in Germany which would restore Prussia to the position she had occupied in 1806. By the Treaty of Reichenbach (June 27, 1813, N.S.), however, Russia, Austria, and Prussia agreed to partition the duchy of Warsaw among themselves, and provisions for an amicable settlement of the Polish question were inserted in the Treaty of Teplitz (September 9, 1813, N.S.), which confirmed the alliance of the three Powers. In spite of these commitments Alexander demanded at Vienna that the entire duchy of Warsaw should be put under Russian sovereignty and that Prussia should be compensated by the annexation of Saxony. The future of Poland thus became inextricably tied up with that of Saxony, and on the latter, again, depended the solution of the riddle of the territorial boundaries of practically every German state. The bargaining position of Russia and Prussia was strengthened by the fact that, like other great Powers, they were in possession of the coveted territories: Poland was entirely under Russian occupation, and on November 8, 1814, N.S., the Russian general Prince Nicholas Repnin, whose troops were stationed in Saxony, transferred the supreme command of that country to Prussia, a move against which the German states and the French vigorously protested.

Russian designs on Poland met with the opposition of other Powers, especially Great Britain and Austria. Castlereagh felt (to quote Webster again) that it was necessary "to unite Europe against Russia." Metternich held that Austria would rather perish than tolerate the establishment of a Russian Poland. Talleyrand, then minister of foreign affairs of Louis XVIII, sided with Castlereagh and Metternich and was particularly active in championing the case of Saxony. The Prussian minister of foreign affairs, Prince Charles Hardenberg, was inclined in the early stage of the negotiations to seek a compromise with the Anglo-Austrian point of view, but he was overridden by Frederick William. In the heat of the conflict diplomatic niceties were forgotten, and in December the tsar refused to have any further personal dealings with Metternich. This was an ominous decision, because Alexander in person conducted all negotiations, although he received advice from Czartoryski, Stein, Capo d'Istria, Pozzo di Borgo, and La Harpe (officially a member of the Swiss delegation). Count Charles Nesselrode, who in August, 1814, had succeeded Rumiantsev as Russian minister of foreign affairs, an office he held for forty-two years (until 1856), played a subordinate part and was seldom consulted on major issues. By the end of 1814, the discussion of the Polish and Saxon problems having reached an impasse, the two opposing groups of Powers made preparations for war. On January 3, 1815, N.S., Castlereagh, Metternich, and Talleyrand signed a secret treaty of military alliance directed against Russia and Prussia; Hanover, Bavaria, Holland, and other states were invited to join the new coalition. It is a moot question whether the existence of this treaty became known to the tsar and prompted him to enter the road of compromise, as is claimed by the apologists of Castlereagh, or whether Alexander's change of heart was due to other causes.[10] Whatever may have been the real reason, the diplomatic crisis of early January was followed by a *détente*, and after laborious negotiations, rendered easier by Castlereagh's determination to create a strong Prussia (contrary to the wishes of Metternich), a settlement of the troublesome question of Poland and Saxony was agreed upon by the Great Powers in February, that is, before Napoleon left Elba and landed at Cannes (March 8, 1815, N.S.). By the Final Act of the Congress of Vienna (June, 1815), Prussia received the Polish territories known as the grand duchy of Posen, and Austria recovered Galicia, including eastern Galicia ceded to Russia in 1809. Cracow became a free city under the protection of Austria, Russia, and Prussia. The greater part of the former duchy of Warsaw was transferred to Russia and was given the status of a constitutional kingdom, with the Russian emperor as king. The other territorial changes made by the Congress of Vienna need not be discussed here, although Alexander took a prominent part in deciding the fate of some of these distant lands.

The position of Alexander in the council of the allies was undermined by the wrangle over Poland and by the escape of Napoleon from Elba, which was regarded at Vienna as a consequence of the tsar's unwarranted leniency in 1814. No Russian troops were available in western Europe in the spring of 1815, and Wellington curtly rejected Alexander's request for his own nomination as supreme commander of the allied army. The Russians took no part in the battle of Waterloo (June 18, N.S.), and it was the British and the Prussians who occupied Paris on July 7, N.S. In 1815 Wellington assumed the leading role Alexander had played a year earlier. The tsar did not reach Paris until July 10, N.S., two days after Louis XVIII, whose restoration he opposed, was installed by Wellington at the Tuileries. The rapacious vindictiveness of the Prussian generals and the stern realism of the British dominated the political scene. The second Peace of Paris (November 20, 1815, N.S.) reduced France to her frontiers of 1790 (instead of the frontiers of 1792 stipulated by the first Peace of Paris), imposed a heavy indemnity, and provided for an allied army of occupation of 150,000 men which was to remain in France for no longer than five years. Of this number 30,000 were Russians. Napoleon

---

[10] The text of the treaty was communicated to Alexander in April, 1815, by Napoleon, who found it in Paris during the Hundred Days.

in his final desperate plight had sought asylum in England, but he was treated as a prisoner of war and was banished to the inaccessible island of St. Helena, from which there was no escape. There he died in 1821.

THE EUROPEAN ALLIANCE, 1815–1825

The war of 1813–1815 and the Congress of Vienna revealed once more the inherent weakness of international coalitions. Divided by ancient hatreds, deep-rooted suspicions, conflicting policies, and irreconcilable ambitions, the allied Powers were most of the time more concerned with plotting against one another than with fighting the common enemy. Absorbed in squabbles over the division of the spoils, the monarchs and statesmen assembled at Vienna gave but cursory and passing attention to proposals for the establishment of a new European order, in the possibility of which few of them believed. Alexander, however, was not prepared to relinquish his recently acquired and already threatened position as the "new Agamemnon." Consumed by messianic fervor and spurred by personal ambition, he persuaded Frederick William and Emperor Francis to sign the Treaty of the Holy Alliance, which he dramatically announced to the world on September 26, 1815, N.S. This document, unique in the history of diplomacy, bound the signatories to be guided in their relations among themselves and with their peoples by the principles of Christian morality. What this actually meant no one knew at the time, nor has anyone since been able to ascertain, but as it did not seem advisable to antagonize the tsar all the European rulers—with the exception of the pope, the sultan, and the prince regent of Great Britain—adhered to the Holy Alliance. The future King George IV shielded himself behind constitutional technicalities and merely gave his personal endorsement to the treaty of September 26, avoiding any commitments that might have involved the British government. The United States, repeatedly approached by Russia in 1816–1820 with invitations to join the Holy Alliance, avoided direct refusal; but on July 5, 1820, N.S., John Quincy Adams, then secretary of state, notified the American minister at St. Petersburg, John Middleton, of "the president's absolute and irrevocable determination" not to participate in any European league.[11]

[11] J. C. Hildt, *Early Diplomatic Negotiations of the United States with Russia* (Baltimore, 1906), pp. 101, 148.

The Holy Alliance created no binding obligations. Alexander regarded it primarily as an act of faith,[12] and it was wildly acclaimed by those who believed in the magic power of exalted formulas. Goethe is said to have welcomed it as "the greatest and the most beneficial thing ever conceived in the interest of humanity." To Castlereagh, however, the Holy Alliance was "a piece of sublime mysticism and nonsense," and to Metternich "a loud-sounding nothing." Abbé de Pradt wittily described it as "the Book of Revelation of diplomacy." The treaty of September, 1815, according to W. Alison Phillips, "was of immediate practical importance only in so far as it tended to complicate the diplomatic relations of the allies . . . owing to the Russian claim, persistently repeated, that it committed the Powers to Alexander's ideal of a 'universal union,' which they in fact repudiated."[13] In literary and historical tradition the Holy Alliance has become the symbol of extreme reaction in both foreign and domestic policy.

The real basis of the ill fated attempt at international cooperation in the 1820's was not the Holy Alliance but the treaty of the Quadruple Alliance of November 20, 1815, N.S. As has already been stated, an alliance of Great Britain, Russia, Austria, and Prussia was formed at Chaumont in March, 1814. Although designed to last for twenty years, it was shattered by the Treaty of January 3, 1815, N.S., which aligned Great Britain, Austria, and France against Russia and Prussia. The reappearance of Napoleon made the allies for a time forget their differences, and on March 25, 1815, N.S., the Quadruple Alliance, renewed by the Treaty of Vienna, received its final formulation in the Treaty of November 20, 1815, N.S. The idea of putting the Quadruple Alliance on a permanent basis originated with Castlereagh and was enthusiastically approved by the tsar. Article 6 of the treaty of November 20 provided that "in order to consolidate the connections which at the present moment so closely unite the four sovereigns for the happiness of the world, the high contracting parties have agreed to renew their meetings at fixed periods, either under the direct auspices of the sovereigns themselves or by their respective ministers, for the purpose of consulting upon their common interests, and for the consideration of the measures which at each of these periods shall be considered as the most salutary for the repose and prosperity of nations

---

[12] See p. 644.
[13] *The Cambridge Modern History* (Cambridge, 1902–1911), X, 10.

and for the maintenance of the peace of Europe." This provision inaugurated what is sometimes called the "congressional era" of European politics. Directed originally against France and the revolutionary spirit she represented to contemporary statesmen, the European or Grand Alliance (as the Quadruple Alliance is usually called, especially since 1818, when France joined it) endeavored to carry out in practice the principle which had been gradually evolved during the Congress of Vienna; namely, that the "great" Powers had special rights and obligations in assuring the international order and domestic stability of Europe and of the world. The international conferences of the 1820's, even though Alexander played a leading part in them, have little bearing on the history of Russia and will be noted here only in barest outline.

In 1815–1818 the European Alliance functioned chiefly through ambassadorial conferences held in Paris, London, and Frankfort. The first full-fledged congress of the alliance met in October and November, 1818, at Aix-la-Chapelle and was attended by the monarchs of Russia, Austria, and Prussia, by a score of statesmen and diplomats, including Wellington, Castlereagh, Metternich, Nesselrode, Capo d'Istria, and—somewhat illogically, since the alliance was directed against France—by the Duke de Richelieu, minister of foreign affairs of Louis XVIII. The congress disposed of the troublesome question of French reparations and ordered the withdrawal of the army of occupation. France was invited to join the European concert; but on the same day (November 15, N.S.) the four allied Powers secretly agreed to continue to watch over France and to protect her against the danger of revolution. The Russian proposal to convert the alliance of the great Powers into a "universal union" which would guarantee the territorial *status quo* and political order (based on "wise" constitutions to be granted by the sovereigns to their peoples) of every state was successfully resisted by Great Britain. Castlereagh refused to assume further international commitments, especially those involving intervention in the internal affairs of countries other than France. Alexander's attempt "to give the soul of the Holy Alliance a body" thus came to naught. Castlereagh also defeated the proposal that congresses of the European Alliance should meet at regular intervals, but he promised that Great Britain would participate in such gatherings when called in emergencies.

Russia and Great Britain drifted further apart as a result of five revolutions which broke out in Europe in 1820–1821: in Spain, Naples, Portugal, Piedmont, and Greece. Alexander, supported by Prussia, insisted on joint allied action for the suppression of revolutionary movements and on the restoration of "legitimate" governments, while Castlereagh upheld the British position of non-intervention in the domestic affairs of foreign states. The policy of Austria and France was less clear-cut but was finally swayed in favor of intervention. The Congress of Troppau (October to December, 1820) and the Congress of Laybach (January to May, 1821) were attended by Alexander, Metternich, and the crown prince of Prussia, but Great Britain and France were represented merely by observers. In the decisions of these congresses the principle of intervention received its official formulation and its practical application. Alexander, now in full agreement with Metternich, went so far as to put at the disposal of the allies his armed forces and to issue orders for the organization of an expeditionary corps of 100,000 men to be used against the Italian "rebels." The speedy defeat by Austria of the revolutionaries in Naples and Piedmont, however, rendered superfluous the proposed intervention of Russian troops, which none of the other allies wanted.

The suicide of Castlereagh (August, 1822) precipitated the dissolution of the European concert. His successor, George Canning, was opposed to entangling alliances and, even more than Castlereagh, hated the reactionary policies of the great continental Powers. Nevertheless he sent the Duke of Wellington to represent Great Britain at the Congress of Verona (October to December, 1822), the last important meeting of the sovereigns and statesmen of the European Alliance. The decision of the congress to intervene in Spain was followed by the invasion of that country by a French army (April, 1823) and by the restoration at the point of French bayonets of the absolutist rule of Ferdinand VII. It took all the eloquence of Metternich, Wellington, and the French plenipotentiary, Duke de Montmorency, to dissuade the tsar from sending a Russian army of 150,000 men to fight the Spaniards. With intervention in Spain Canning would have nothing to do, and after the Congress of Verona Great Britain practically withdrew from the European Alliance. "Things are getting back to a wholesome state again," Canning wrote Sir Charles Bagot, British ambassador at St. Petersburg, on January 3, 1823, N.S.[14] "Every nation for itself, and God for us all. The time for Areopagus and the like of that, is gone by." The European Alliance, nevertheless, was not

[14] *The Cambridge Modern History*, X, 37.

officially dissolved, although it became dormant; it was invoked against France in 1830 and again in 1848. The principle of intervention continued to be upheld by Russia, Austria, and Prussia. It was asserted for the last time by Emperor Nicholas I in 1849, in his crusade against the revolution in Hungary.

The Turkish or "eastern" question, which came to play an increasingly important part in European affairs in the nineteenth century, was brought to the fore by the outbreak of the Greek revolt in March, 1821. Alexander found himself on the horns of a dilemma: on the one hand, the Greek insurrection presented tempting possibilities of intervention on behalf of Russia's co-religionists, a policy that would have been consistent with the tradition of Catherine II and his own wishes and which commanded the support of an influential and vocal body of public opinion; on the other hand, the Greeks were rebels against their lawful sovereign and as such had nothing to expect from the founder of the Holy Alliance. Metternich and Castlereagh, temporarily brought together by their common fear of Russian expansion in Turkey, had no difficulty in persuading Alexander that it was the duty of Russia to keep hands off Turkey and Greece. An appeal for Russian help made by the leader of the insurgents, Prince Alexander Ypsilanti, an officer in the Russian service and aide-de-camp to the tsar, was rejected. Capo d'Istria, the zealous Greek patriot who since 1815 had shared with Nesselrode the office of Russian minister of foreign affairs, was dismissed in 1822, and retired to Geneva. The protracted character of the insurrection, Turkish atrocities, which received wider publicity than those perpetrated by the Greeks, and the rising tide of pro-Hellenic feeling in England, Russia, and other countries indicated that the policy of aloofness could not be maintained indefinitely. In March, 1823, Canning recognized the Greeks as belligerents, thus marking another breach between Great Britain and the eastern allies. Alexander, too, gradually departed from the attitude of rigid support of "legitimacy." In 1824–1825 he formulated compromise proposals for the settlement of the conflict, but they were rejected by both the Porte and the Greeks. Great Britain was not even represented at an abortive conference held at St. Petersburg in the spring of 1825. A semi-official exchange of views between the Russian and the British governments took place in the latter part of the year; the agreement it foreshadowed, however, was not reached until after Alexander's death in December.

It was only logical that the tsar's attachment to the principle of "legitimacy," which interfered with Russian intervention on behalf of the insurgent Greeks, should have made him a partner of Spain in her endeavor to recover her South American colonies. After the Napoleonic wars the question of Latin America loomed large in the preoccupations of European statesmen and was repeatedly discussed at the congresses and conferences of the European Alliance, especially at Aix-la-Chapelle and at Verona. The Russian diplomats Count Dimitry Tatishchev, in Madrid, and Pozzo di Borgo, in Paris, agitated in favor of action by the European Alliance to restore the rule of the Spanish king over his overseas domain. Alexander and his agents, however, could be of little practical assistance to Spain. The sale to that country of a squadron of Russian ships in which to transport Spanish troops across the Atlantic did not bring the expedition any nearer because the vessels delivered proved unseaworthy. Castlereagh and Canning were opposed to intervention in South America by the European Alliance, and the designs on that continent entertained by the European Powers were viewed with concern in the United States.

Alexander had professed warm admiration for Jefferson and the United States Constitution, and it was by his command that formal diplomatic relations with America were established in 1808, when Andrew Dashkov was appointed Russian "chargé d'affaires near the Congress of the United States." In 1809 John Quincy Adams arrived in St. Petersburg as the first duly accredited American minister.[15] In September, 1812, Alexander offered his mediation in the war that had just broken out between the United States and Great Britain. President Madison accepted the proposal with somewhat excessive haste and without ascertaining the attitude of London. The consequences proved disappointing. American plenipotentiaries, after spending considerable time in Europe, returned home empty-handed: Great Britain had declined the tsar's offer, and Alexander, in the midst of his French campaign, had seemingly lost all interest in the matter.

Of far greater consequence to the United States and to the world were the repercussions of Russia's territorial claims in North America and of her advocacy of intervention in the Spanish colonies. Following Bering's voyages of discovery between 1728 and 1741, Russian adventurers and hunters, attracted by the prospects of a lucrative fur

---

[15] The first American minister to Russia, Francis Dana, reached St. Petersburg in 1781 but returned home in 1783 without having been received at court. The first American consul at St. Petersburg was appointed by Washington in 1794.

trade, began to settle on the Aleutian Islands, in Alaska, and along the northwest coast of America. In 1799 an imperial decree established the Russian American Company, which was granted a trade monopoly, exclusive jurisdiction of the American coast north of the fifty-fifth degree north latitude, and the right to occupy further vacant territories in the name of the Russian Crown. The monopolistic privileges of the company led to much friction with American traders and to inconclusive negotiations between the two governments. The discussion entered an acute stage in 1821, when an imperial decree (September 16, N.S.) laid claim to the exclusive right of Russian subjects to "the pursuits of commerce, whaling, and fishing, and all other industry" north of the fifty-first degree, and prohibited foreign vessels from approaching Russian-held Pacific islands and coasts "within less than one hundred Italian miles." [16] John Quincy Adams, then secretary of state, rejected both Russian contentions as contrary to international law. The willingness of the Russian government to negotiate, however, prevented a breach. In the minds of American statesmen Russia's policy of expansion in North America was closely associated with the plans of European Powers for intervention in the Spanish colonies. Early in 1822 the United States had recognized the independence of the South American states; the principles of her policy in the western hemisphere—the Monroe Doctrine—were stated in the presidential message to Congress on December 2, 1823, N.S. This celebrated document declared (1) that "the American continents . . . are henceforth not to be considered as subjects for future colonization by any European Power" and (2) that the United States "should consider any attempt on their [European Powers'] part to extend their system to any portion of this hemisphere, as dangerous to our peace and safety." In the formulation of this doctrine, especially of its first principle, the policies of Alexander—which were the antithesis of those expounded by Monroe—played an important part. Oddly, the Russian government showed no annoyance with the Monroe Doctrine, parleys with the United States proceeded smoothly, and a treaty was signed on April 17, 1824, N.S. It reduced Russian territorial claims to the area north of the fifty-fourth degree forty minutes and restored freedom of navigation and fishing in the Pacific Ocean. Russia's readiness to compromise was presumably due to the relative unimportance of her interests on the wild coast of distant America. The Russian

[16] Hildt, *op. cit.*, p. 159.

American Company was dissatisfied with the treaty, and President Monroe held it as a victory for American diplomacy. The treaty, in fact, meant the abandonment by Russia of her policy of expansion in America.

AN APPRAISAL

The net balance of the diplomatic wizardry and the many wars of Alexander the Blessed, as the tsar was called after 1814, eludes precise evaluation. Finland, Bessarabia, and vast territories in Poland and in the Caucasus were added to the already boundless expanses of the sparsely populated empire. It cannot be repeated too often, however, that territorial aggrandizement is always costly and that it is not an unmixed blessing. Poland and Finland remained for over a century hostile elements in the body of Russian politics, and their subjugation by Russia proved but a stage in their long martyrdom, the end of which is not yet in sight. The War of 1812, known as the "patriotic war," has assumed in national and literary tradition a place grossly out of proportion to its true significance. It is too often overlooked (perhaps because Tolstoy's *War and Peace* is an admirable as well as a very long novel) that the Napoleonic invasion lasted less than six months and the retreat of the Grand Army barely seven weeks, and that it was preceded and followed by more protracted and devastating Russian invasions of a score of European countries. The Holy Alliance never reached the status of the "universal union" of Alexander's dreams, and its influence in world affairs was largely negative. Castlereagh remarked once that "the tsar is half a madman," and it is possible that Alexander was not absent from Jefferson's mind when he wrote, on June 11, 1823, N.S.: "I have ever deemed it fundamental for the United States never to take active part in the quarrels of Europe. Their political interests are entirely different from ours. Their mutual jealousies, their balance of power, their complicated alliances, their forms and principles of government, are foreign to us. They are nations of eternal war. All their energies are expanded in the destruction of labor, property, and lives of their people." No sovereign or statesman has ever wished for peace more ardently and sincerely than did Alexander, yet Jefferson's sad reflections fully apply to Russia under the rule of that monarch.

CHAPTER XXVII

ALEXANDER I

Government, Finance, Trade, Industry, and Social Conditions

UNFULFILLED PROMISES

The accession of Alexander was greeted with jubilation in court, military, and bureaucratic circles. To the vast majority of those who acclaimed the young emperor, the forcible removal of Paul meant liberation from an arbitrary and tyrannical regime and the restoration of their privileges. To a small group of educated Russians familiar with western Europe, however, the new reign brought the promise of far-reaching constitutional and social reforms. These expectations were based on Alexander's reputed liberalism and were fostered by the enlightened character of his early measures: repeal of the vexatious restrictions enacted by Paul, provision for a broad and comprehensive amnesty, liberalization of trade, removal of the prohibition on traveling abroad, permission to import foreign publications, and partial mitigation of the harshness of the penal procedure. Although the accession manifesto proclaimed Alexander's intention to govern "according to the laws and the spirit" of Catherine II, the emperor was critical of her rule. He confirmed the privileges of the *dvoriane*, as defined in the Charter of the Nobility (decrees of March 15 and May 5 and manifesto of April 2, 1801), and he restored the local government act of 1775. He, however, abolished the security police, that mainstay of Catherine's administrative order, declaring it incompatible with the principles she had professed. "In a well governed state," read the manifesto of April 2, 1801, "all crimes must be provided for, tried, and punished by the general laws."

The feverish administrative and legislative activities at the beginning of Alexander's reign included a partial remodeling of the institutions of central government. The council of the sovereign, since 1769 the Crown's chief advisory body,[1] was abolished on March 26, 1801, and four days later (March 30) twelve elder statesmen were appointed as a "permanent council" (*nepremennyi soviet*), which, like its predecessor, acted in an advisory capacity. Alexander professed, as had Catherine and Paul, detestation of arbitrariness, and he voiced the determination to establish his government on the immutable foundation of the law. A commission appointed on June 5, 1801, resumed the ungrateful task of codification so unsuccessfully tackled by eighteenth century committees. Preliminary steps were taken towards "restoring" the Senate to a position of administrative supremacy which, as a matter of fact, it had never actually enjoyed in the past.

Alexander, however, was harboring much more ambitious plans of reform. The formulation of these projects was entrusted to a "non-official committee" (*neglasnyi komitet*) consisting of the emperor's personal friends, Count Paul Stroganov, Nicholas Novosiltsev, Prince Adam Czartoryski, and Count Victor Kochubey, wealthy young aristocrats of pronounced liberal and even radical leanings. Stroganov had been brought up by a French tutor, the well known mathematician and revolutionary Gilbert Romme, in whose company he had frequented the Jacobin clubs of Paris. Kochubey was educated in England, a country where both Novosiltsev and Czartoryski had spent considerable time and whose constitution and social structure the emperor's "young friends" greatly admired. The chief object of the "non-official committee," according to Stroganov (memorandum of May 9, 1801), was "to become thoroughly acquainted with all existing constitutions, to digest them, and on the basis of their principles to prepare a constitution for Russia." The "non-official committee," which had no standing in law, functioned, at intervals, from June, 1801, to probably the end of 1803,[2] and for a brief time it took an important part in framing both domestic and foreign policy, but it failed to produce a constitutional charter. Its dilatory and confused deliberations, indeed, left hardly any imprint on the government and the social structure of the Russian state. This committee was respon-

---

[1] See pp. 550, 614.
[2] The work of the committee was shrouded in secrecy, and although its last meeting, the minutes of which have been preserved, was held on Nov. 19, 1803, it is not impossible that it continued to function after that date.

sible for only two administrative reforms: the substitution of ministries for the former administrative colleges and a legislative attempt at defining the powers and duties of the Senate. A law of September 8, 1802, abolished the colleges and divided executive functions among eight ministries: war, navy, foreign affairs, justice, interior, finance, commerce, and education. The reform, however, was more apparent than real, since the collegial principle had long been inoperative and was practically eliminated by Emperor Paul.[3] The law of September 8 merely changed the names of the former colleges and added a few central departments to those already in existence; otherwise it left things pretty much as they were before. In another law of the same date an effort was made to establish the Senate as the highest organ of judicial and administrative control. This object, however, was not achieved, and an imperial edict issued in 1803 specifically denied to the Senate power to challenge any decrees of the Crown promulgated in contravention of the law, a right which the majority of the senators believed was granted to them by the law of September 8.

The administrative reforms of the first years of Alexander's reign were thus both limited and disappointing. Liberal tendencies were more in evidence in the attitude of the government towards the promotion of schools and the liberalization of censorship, matters which will be discussed in the next chapter. Preparations for the war with Napoleon and Russia's participation in the Third Coalition (1805–1807) absorbed for a time all the attention of the tsar and his advisers, while the never too promising outlook for domestic reforms was further dimmed. There were, moreover, disturbing signs that Alexander was gradually abandoning his tepid liberalism and professed attachment to legality. In September, 1805, on the eve of his departure for the army, the emperor created a committee on which he conferred broad powers to deal with cases affecting public order and safety. Originally a provisional institution, the committee was reorganized on a permanent basis in 1807 and proved a worthy successor to the security police of Catherine II.[4]

[3] See pp. 378–379, 553–554, 615.
[4] The "committee of public safety of January 13, 1807," functioned until 1829. Senator Makarov, who had succeeded Sheshkovsky as head of Catherine II's security police, was one of the committee's three original members. The detection of subversive activities was prosecuted with even greater zeal by the so-called "special chancery" of the ministry of the interior; in 1826 this was superseded by "Section III" of His Majesty's Own Chancery.

SPERANSKY AND THE REACTION

Russia's military defeats in 1805–1807, the unpopular alliance with Napoleon, and the hardships and financial losses inflicted upon foreign trade and landed interests by the adherence to the Continental Blockade led to an alarming growth of discontent and disaffection which the government could not ignore. Alexander, moreover, influenced by the example of Napoleon's tireless administrative activities, after Tilsit turned once more to domestic reforms. This time he found an exceptionally able collaborator in Michael Speransky (1772–1839), a newcomer in high bureaucratic circles. Son of a village priest (a status which, in Holy Russia, imposed almost insurmountable social handicaps), Speransky was educated in a theological seminary and had taught for a while in an ecclesiastical institution. He was soon transferred to the civil service, and thanks to his intelligence, attractive personality, and rare capacity for work, as well as to the powerful patronage of the Princes Alexander and Alexis Kurakin and, later, of Count Victor Kochubey, he had a rapid rise and a brilliant career. It was at the request of Kochubey, then minister of the interior, that Speransky in 1803 prepared one of his first drafts of constitutional reform. He became personally known to the tsar, accompanied him to Erfurt, and in December, 1808, was appointed assistant minister of justice and in 1810 secretary of state. From 1809 to the beginning of 1812 Speransky's influence with Alexander was very great. "M. Speransky is the emperor's factotum (*faiseur*), a kind of minister of innovations," Caulaincourt wrote to Champagny on March 3, 1811, N.S. "He is not allied with anyone (*il n'est lié avec personne*). His influence extends to everything." Commissioned by the tsar at the end of 1808 to draft a plan of constitutional reform, Speransky completed this work by October, 1809. His project, which is little known outside Russia, although it has been much discussed by Russian historians and jurists, need not be examined here in detail because only fragments of this comprehensive and carefully thought-out scheme were enacted into law. In a truly remarkable preamble, perhaps the most striking part of the plan, Speransky submitted the then existing political, administrative, and social order to trenchant and unsparing criticism. His proposals for reform, while retaining the monarchical principle, endeavored to fit it into the framework of a state governed by law. This was to be achieved by a strict application of the doctrine of separation of powers—legislative, executive, and judicial—all of them emanating from the Crown. Distinct and parallel sets of institutions, outlined in some detail in the project, were to administer the three principal branches of government. Judged by the standards of our time, many of Speransky's proposals were unduly cautious and even reactionary. Franchise was limited by property qualifications; elections to the central legislative body, the State Duma, were indirect and were arranged in four stages; the powers of the legislative assembly were parsimoniously measured out. The project, moreover, contained no provision for the emancipation of the serfs and excluded the servile population from participation in government, although Speransky favored the eventual abolition of serfdom and, indeed, considered this measure and the broadening of the franchise as essential elements of his reform. He realized, however, the immensity of the obstacles to emancipation and was willing to proceed by slow stages. According to the eminent historian and constitutional lawyer Baron Boris Nolde, Speransky's plan was "at least a generation ahead of the French consular and imperial constitutions and of the constitutional charters of the European states within the French orbit."

Alexander studied the plan carefully and with seeming approval, but finally, for reasons that never have been fully disclosed, shrank from putting it into effect. Speransky succeeded in salvaging only two elements of his scheme. A manifesto of January 1, 1810, established the State Council (*Gosudarstvennyi Soviet*), and the manifestoes of July 25, 1810, and June 25, 1811, basically reorganized the executive departments (ministries). In Speransky's original plan the elective State Duma did not enjoy the right of legislative initiative, but provision was made for a State Council, a body consisting of ministers and other high officials to be appointed by the Crown, which was to draft legislative bills and advise the monarch on all other matters. When it became clear that Alexander would not agree to the creation of an elective legislative assembly, Speransky substituted for it the State Council but eliminated from the constitution of the latter all judicial and executive powers (provided by the original draft). The State Council thus became a purely legislative assembly, and one suffering from obvious limitations: it was an appointed and not an elective body; its decisions were not binding on the Crown; and it was denied the right of legislative initiative. It is held, nevertheless, that from the point of view of constitutional theory the establishment of the

State Council was an important departure: it introduced for the first time in Russian history a clear-cut formal distinction between a law, that is, a measure examined by the State Council and confirmed by the emperor, and an executive decree. Although the sphere assigned by Speransky to "laws" in the sense just indicated was broader and more comprehensive than that within the purview of most European legislatures, the practical consequences of the reform were slight. The members of the State Council, appointed by the tsar, did not enjoy permanency of tenure, and the emperor was free to approve either the majority or the minority decision, or to reject them both. It is self-evident, therefore, that the State Council imposed no effective limitation on the powers of the Crown. The subtle distinction between a law and an administrative decree, moreover, was often disregarded between 1810 and 1906, when Russia finally was granted an elective legislative assembly and when the constitution of the State Council was revised and amended. In this modified form the State Council survived until the revolution of 1917.

The legislation of 1810–1811 dealing with the ministries, unlike the law of 1802, brought about a fundamental reconstruction of the executive departments. The total number of ministries and central administrations (*glavnoe upravlenie*) enjoying similar status was increased to eleven by creating a ministry of police and central administrations of transportation, of financial control, and of religious denominations other than the Russian Orthodox Church, while the ministry of commerce was abolished. The gist of the reform was the personal responsibility imposed upon the ministers, the careful delimitation of the functions of the executive departments, the elimination of their interference with legislative and judicial matters, and the formulation of precise and comprehensive rules for their own administration. This legislation, which remained in force with but minor changes until the revolution of 1917, has been aptly described as the "organic charter" of Russian bureaucracy. Of Speransky's ambitious plan the State Council and the ministries were all that he succeeded in preserving. His proposal for a reform of the judiciary met with much criticism in the State Council and was shelved for half a century. The net result of the reform was the modernization of the bureaucratic machine, which continued to govern the country until the end of the empire. The autocratic powers of the Crown remained intact, and the great constitutional changes Alexander and his minister dreamed of were indefinitely postponed.

Speransky made another significant contribution to the strengthening of the framework of the bureaucratic state. A decree of April 3, 1809, provided that court appointments no longer entitled their holders to a "rank" under Peter I's Table of Ranks; that is, they became merely honorary distinctions which carried none of the prestige attached to rank, with the privileges and possibilities of promotion or transfer to the civil service. A decree of August 6, 1809, laid down the rule that appointment to positions above a specified rank was conditional on the passing of a stiff examination or the holding of a university degree. These measures greatly improved the educational levels of the civil service; but they created consternation in court and bureaucratic circles, especially among the older members, who had little hope of mastering the mysteries of geography, physics, statistics, economics, history, and law, on the knowledge of which the promotion of office-holders was made to depend.

Speransky's financial program was equally unpopular. In view of the desperate position of the treasury and the calamitous depreciation of the ruble he proposed the suspension of issues of paper currency, curtailment of expenditure, increases in direct and indirect taxation, and the floating of a domestic loan secured by state properties. A truly revolutionary innovation was the introduction in 1812, as an emergency measure, of a progressive tax on incomes derived from landed estates. Contrary to precedent, the tax was computed on the basis, not of the servile population on such estates, but of their revenue. The rate of the tax, 1 per cent on incomes of 500 to 2,000 rubles, was increased 1 per cent on each 2,000 rubles of income over 2,000, until it reached 10 per cent on incomes of 18,000 rubles, when the rate became stationary.[5] The hostility of the landed nobility towards the new impost was all the greater because Speransky's financial program, which was never made fully effective, failed to stop the depreciation of the ruble.

It is probable that these infringements of the privileges of the bureaucratic and landowning class, rather than any organized opposi-

[5] The law provided that declarations of income were to be based on "good faith and honor," no information concerning alleged concealment being accepted. The yield of the tax was 4.9 million paper rubles in 1813 and only 2.4 million in 1819. In 1820 the tax was repealed. The income tax was introduced in 1916.

tion to Speransky's constitutional ideas, precipitated his downfall. His plan of reform was unknown outside a small group of higher officials. It will be remembered that Arakcheev, Alexander's trusted friend, was not taken into the tsar's confidence concerning the proposed establishment of the State Council and that in protest he resigned the office of minister of war.[6] The air of mystery that surrounded Speransky's activities added to the alarm and apprehensions of the conservative elements. The breath-taking rise of an obscure employee to the summit of the bureaucratic hierarchy had created resentment and jealousies, and in spite of his affable demeanor he had wounded the susceptibilities of many and had made powerful personal enemies. In 1811 and 1812 aristocratic and bureaucratic St. Petersburg was militantly anti-French, whereas Speransky had the perhaps not entirely undeserved reputation of being Napoleon's admirer. A cabal headed by the Grand Duchess Catherine, Arakcheev, and the historian Karamzin spared no effort in proving to the tsar that his trusted adviser was a traitor who had brought the country to the rim of the abyss. The decisive factor in the disgrace of Speransky, however, was in all probability the basic incompatibility between his logical, forceful, and precise mind and the tsar's faltering emotional liberalism.[7] In the evening of March 17, 1812, the all-powerful minister was summoned to the palace, and after a two-hour audience with his imperial master, the nature of which has remained a closely guarded secret, he was exiled first to Nizhni-Novgorod and later (September, 1812) to Perm.[8]

[6] See p. 647. Information bearing on Speransky's plan was long withheld. A summary and lengthy excerpts from this document were published for the first time by N. I. Turgenev in his volume *La Russie et les russes* (Paris, 1847). Baron M. A. Korff, in a two-volume biography of Speransky (St. Petersburg, 1861), made but cursory and veiled references to the proposed reform. A. N. Pypin, in 1885, and V. I. Semevsky, in 1888 (the latter on the basis of archive materials), gave good factual and analytical accounts of Speransky's abortive constitutional charter, but its text and related documents were not published until 1905, one hundred years after they were written.

[7] See pp. 633–634.

[8] In the middle of 1814 Speransky was permitted to reside on one of his remote estates. His direct appeals to the tsar having remained unanswered, he bowed to the inevitable and, chastened and humbled by his experience, sought the patronage of his former enemy, Arakcheev. The intervention of the latter proved successful. In August, 1816, Speransky was appointed governor of Penza and in 1819 governor-general of Siberia. In 1821 he returned to St. Petersburg, where his reappearance created a short-lived sensation. He was given a large estate and was appointed a member of the State Council and of the commission on codification, but Alexander

With Speransky's eclipse all practical attempts at constitutional reform came to an end. Converted to morbid religiosity and engrossed in Napoleonic wars and, later, in the promotion of an illusory new international order and in the suppression of foreign revolutions, the tsar had little time for domestic reform. He clung, however, to the cherished dreams of his youth. As has been already stated, in 1818 Alexander announced his intention of extending to Russia the benefit of "free institutions," which had been granted to Poland, and he commissioned Novosiltsev to draft an imperial constitution embodying the federal principle. Although based on Speransky's plan, the Novosiltsev project was considerably less liberal and contained no reference to an even eventual emancipation of the serfs. It was never acted upon and remained just another "highly secret" state paper.

There was a striking contrast between Alexander's craving for the rule of law, on the one hand, and, on the other, the arbitrariness of Russia's administrative practice, especially in the second half of the reign of that monarch. "Living in this country one learns to be suspicious and distrustful," wrote La Ferronays on April 11, 1820, N.S. "The impregnable secrecy with which important questions are decided . . . is a worthy subject for meditation and anxiety. . . . In no other country, no doubt, is corruption so general; it is, in a sense, organized, and there is, perhaps, not a single government official who could not be bought at a price. . . . Really important matters, however, remain secret because they are decided by the emperor alone, who confides them at the utmost to two or three of his ministers. . . . The silence reigning around his throne, which can be reached by no petition, by no complaint except through the channel of the ministers interested in deceiving their master, makes the emperor ignore the cost at which his wishes are fulfilled. When he rapidly traverses his vast empire he finds everywhere his orders executed, he sees merely the governors of his military districts, and therefore receives nothing but flattering and encouraging reports. He mistakes the results of force and violence for those of wisdom and good administration. He imagines that he builds while he merely disorganizes, because there are

---

had lost interest in his former friend and mentor and did not receive him in 1824 or 1825. In the meantime Speransky's view underwent a radical change. In 1825 nineteenth century Russia's greatest liberal statesman wrote a pamphlet eulogizing military colonies, for which, at heart, he had nothing but contempt. His new-born conservatism and administrative abilities opened to him a field of fruitful activity in the reign of Nicholas I.

no institutions anywhere, because everything is forced, everything is exaggerated; he allows himself to be blinded by a brilliant scaffolding under which no foundation has been built."

FINLAND

Approximations to a constitutional regime, so sadly wanting in Russia, were tried in Finland and in Poland. The invasion of Finland by Russian troops in February, 1808, was preceded by the publication of an imperial proclamation (February 6) which promised the inhabitants of the territory still to be conquered "the preservation of their privileges, religious freedom, liberties, rights, and other advantages," and invited them to send deputies, elected in the customary manner, to a diet that was to meet in Abo. The object of this move was to enlist local support and to create an agency for the eventual ratification of the proposed annexation. The speedy collapse of Swedish armed resistance was followed by the announcement of the annexation of Finland embodied in a circular note to foreign courts on March 16 and in an imperial manifesto of March 20, 1808. In the meantime the proposal for the convocation of a Finnish diet was temporarily abandoned, Russian authorities having decided that the administration of the oath of allegiance would be a less cumbersome method of clothing the conquest with an appearance of legality. Beginning in May, 1808, a reluctant Finnish population (the majority, according to Russian claims) was induced to take the oath, and a manifesto of June 5, 1808, addressed to the new subjects of the Russian Crown, reiterated the finality of the annexation and the promise of safeguarding local institutions and privileges. The next step—the summons to St. Petersburg of Finnish deputies to deliberate on the future organization of Finland—disclosed a novel factor which was destined to play an important part in the relations between Russia and Finland: the sturdy determination of the Finns to resist any infringement of their laws, customs, and liberties. The Finns vigorously protested against the method of elections devised by Russian authorities; they held that it violated the law of the land, and although they complied with the stern orders of the Russian commanding officer, the delegates, on their arrival in St. Petersburg (November, 1808), presented to Alexander a memorial in which they stated that their election was invalid and that they were unable, therefore, to discuss any question within the jurisdiction of the diet. The demonstration was impressive, and Alexander, then still under the influence of the constitutional ideas of Speransky, complied with the wishes of his new subjects. The provisional statute on the government of Finland, promulgated without the participation of the Finnish delegation on November 19, 1808, provided for the convocation of a Finnish "general and constituent assembly." The delegates were dismissed, and on January 20, 1809, Alexander, in his new capacity of grand duke of Finland, issued letters patent summoning a Finnish diet to be elected in conformity with local laws and customs. An imperial manifesto of March 15 (March 27, N.S.), 1809, promulgated on the eve of convening of the diet at Borgö, "confirmed and certified the religion, fundamental laws, rights and privileges which each 'estate' in the duchy, in particular, and all subjects residing therein, from the lowest to the highest, had enjoyed in the past according to their constitutions." In his opening address to the diet Alexander repeated his promise to maintain "your constitution, your fundamental laws," and restated it in a manifesto of March 23, 1809, issued on the occasion of the administration to the members of the diet of the oath of allegiance.

These enactments and statements of official policy, as well as the Treaty of Frederikshamn (September 17, 1809, N.S.) by which Sweden ceded Finland to Russia, failed to make clear Finland's position in the framework of the Russian empire. The acrimonious and inconclusive legal controversy concerning the constitutional status of Finland was eventually taken up by politicians, and envenomed the relations between the two countries. The essence of the difficulty would seem to have been that the term "constitution" and "constitutions," so freely used by both Alexander and the Finns, was not quite applicable to the situation that existed in 1808–1809 and that its meaning was open to more than one interpretation. The part of Finland annexed in 1808–1809 (with which the Finnish provinces held by Russia since 1721 and 1743 were merged in 1808) had not previously constituted an autonomous state but merely a province of Sweden. Finland before 1809 had neither her own parliament nor her own executive. The central government institutions of the new grand duchy—the diet, the executive council of fourteen members appointed by the Crown (which became the Finnish Senate by virtue of a manifesto of February 9, 1816), the governor-general, and the secretary of state for Finland (an office created in 1826)—were not provided for by Swedish law. In certain cases, for instance, in the composition of the diet, the new Finnish institutions were based on analogy with Swedish law, but in many instances no such analogy existed.[9] The diet of Borgö, unlike its Swedish prototype, was an advisory and not a legislative body. "The diet is requested merely to express opinions and not to issue decrees," Speransky wrote to Barclay de Tolly on June 27, 1809, and the assembly kept its work within the prescribed narrow limits. The Finnish executive council and its successor, the Finnish Senate, were specifically enjoined to refrain from legislation (law of August 6, 1809). The diet, moreover, was soon dissolved, and was not reconvened until 1863, when it began to meet regularly, and in 1869 it was reorganized as a legislative assembly vested with comprehensive powers. Under Alexander I and Nicholas I the Crown alone legislated for Finland, as it did for the rest of the empire.

It does not follow from the above analysis that Alexander's promises of safeguarding ancient Finnish institutions and privileges were empty and meaningless. On the contrary, they allowed Finland to retain the Swedish civil and criminal codes and to enjoy the benefit of Swedish law in all matters pertaining to taxation, the budget, the judiciary, local government, the Church, the legal status of various social groups, and so on. Although the governors-general, with the exception of the first incumbent of that office, J. M. Sprengtporten, were Russians, the secretary of state for Finland was almost invariably a native of the grand duchy. Infringements of local laws and customs undoubtedly occurred, but on the whole Finland enjoyed a degree of autonomy unique among the territories of the empire, except for the kingdom of Poland in 1815–1830. It would seem, nevertheless, that contrary to the contention of Finnish constitutional lawyers endorsed by some eminent international authorities, Finland was not—until the reforms of Alexander II—an autonomous constitutional state under the suzerainty of her grand duke, who was also emperor of Russia, but rather an integral part of the empire governed largely, but not exclusively, by her own laws and institutions.

[9] Some Swedish laws were obviously inapplicable, for instance, those governing succession to the throne and the provision that the monarch must belong to the Lutheran Church. On the other hand, the Russian Orthodox and the Roman Catholic Churches, Russian schools, military and naval establishments, and land and water transportation in Finnish territory were governed by Russian laws.

THE KINGDOM OF POLAND

The constitutional position of Poland was less controversial. The agreement reached at the Congress of Vienna and incorporated in its final act provided that the Polish territories transferred to Russia should form a constitutional kingdom with the Russian emperor as king. "His Imperial Majesty," read the treaty, "reserves to himself the right to give to this state, enjoying a distinct administration, the interior improvements which he shall judge proper." Although the armies of the duchy of Warsaw had fought valiantly against the Russians in 1812 and, according to a recent Polish historian (General M. Kukiel), had lost 72,000 men out of 96,000, Alexander showed no resentment, and put a generous and liberal interpretation on the obligations imposed upon him, with his consent, by the Treaty of Vienna.[10] As early as May, 1815, in a proclamation drafted by Prince Adam Czartoryski, the tsar laid down the principles of the future organization of the Polish state. A constitution prepared by his Russian and Polish advisers and revised by Alexander was promulgated on November 15, 1815. According to its provisions, the kingdom of Poland was a hereditary monarchy under the scepter of its king, who was also the Russian emperor. Except for foreign relations, the conduct of which was reserved to the imperial government, the kingdom was granted a broad and comprehensive autonomy. It had its own army, only Polish citizens were eligible for public office, and the Polish language was used in the administration and in the courts. The Crown was represented in Poland by a viceroy acting with the assistance of an appointed state council. The diet consisted of the king and two houses: the Senate, whose members were appointed for life by the Crown, and the lower house, elected by the landed nobility and the burghers. Both franchise and eligibility for membership in the diet

[10] During the first half of his reign Alexander gave no encouragement to autonomous Polish institutions. A decree of Emperor Paul (Dec. 12, 1796) restored the autonomous elective judiciary in the Polish provinces then under the Russian rule and led to the revival (although with greatly restricted jurisdiction) of the "dietines," or local assemblies of the Polish nobility which had controlled the administrative machine before the partitions. The traditionally rebellious and unruly character of these assemblies caused much friction, and by virtue of legislation passed in 1802, 1805, and 1809 they were made subject to supervision by Crown officers. After 1809 the separate Polish judiciary functioned largely on the basis of Russian and not of Polish law, as intended by Emperor Paul. It was abolished by a decree of Jan. 1, 1831.

were restricted by property qualifications. The diet was to meet every two years, but the Crown had the power to postpone its convocation and actually only four sessions of the diet were held between 1815 and 1830. The diet was denied legislative initiative but was entitled to petition the Crown. There were five central executive departments or ministries whose heads, under the presidency of the viceroy, formed the executive council. The landed nobility and the well-to-do burghers were granted effective participation in local government, and they elected the judges of the lower courts. The constitution guaranteed protection of civil rights, freedom of worship, and freedom of the press, but it denied the poorer classes, the peasantry and the Jews, any part in government.

Judged by the standards of its time, the Polish constitution, which was largely based on that of the duchy of Warsaw and on Speransky's ill fated projects, was a liberal and enlightened document. Yet it brought to Poland nothing but disappointment and misery. A large share of blame for the disaster is usually attributed to the higher officials representing the tsar at Warsaw. Contrary to general expectations, the office of viceroy was filled, not by Prince Adam Czartoryski, but by General Joseph Zaionczek, who, having fought the Russians under Kosciuszko and Napoleon, had since become reconciled to the Russian rule. This gallant soldier was a mediocre administrator and proved subservient to the wishes of the Grand Duke Constantine, commander in chief of the Polish army. Constantine was not really hostile to Poland, but he was erratic, rude, and a ruthless disciplinarian. His avowed contempt for constitutional government and his capricious outbursts of ill temper did much to embitter the relations between Warsaw and St. Petersburg. Even more nefarious was the influence of Novosiltsev, the once-liberal-minded friend of Alexander, who became high commissioner of the imperial government in Poland, an office not provided by the constitution. Alexander reveled for a while in the part of a constitutional monarch. His address to the Polish diet in March, 1818, contained a warm eulogy of Poland's constitutional regime and announced his intention of extending the benefits of "free institutions" to the other parts of the empire. This declaration, which was inspired by Koshelev, was received with enthusiasm in Poland and in liberal circles in Russia and Europe. This honeymoon of constitutionalism, however, was brief. In the closing years of his reign Alexander, obsessed by the fear of revolution, was tending more and more towards reactionary policies, whereas Polish public opinion was not only jealously guarding the country's constitutional liberties but was demanding their extension.

Polish nationalism, a mighty factor which had held the nation together through more than a century of subjugation by foreign Powers, clamored for reunion with the kingdom of the Lithuanian provinces acquired by Russia in the eighteenth century, an aspiration that Alexander himself had indirectly encouraged. Secret societies with a strong nationalistic, political, and social tinge were common in those days in Poland, as they were in Russia and in other European countries. The spread of the Polish underground movement invited Russian repression, which in turn fostered surreptitious activities. In May, 1819, censorship of newspapers and periodicals was introduced by the viceroy acting on the order of the tsar, and in July this was extended to all publications. The session of the diet in 1820 proved stormy, two important bills introduced by the government were voted down, and there was much bitter criticism of the administration. The arrest in April, 1822, and the trial two years later, of the leaders of a secret "Patriotic Society," which had for its object the independence of Poland, greatly added to popular excitement. The diet was not reconvened until May, 1825. In February of the same year Alexander amended the constitution by providing that the deliberations of the diet must be conducted *in camera*. Stern police measures and the exclusion of the leaders of the opposition produced the immediate effect desired, and the session of 1825, the last one to be held in Alexander's lifetime, was completed without untoward incidents. But the frailty of the Polish constitutional regime had been convincingly demonstrated, and the ground was prepared for the great explosion which came five years later and led to the abrogation of the constitution of 1815.[11]

[11] A minor experiment in local autonomy was attempted in Bessarabia after its annexation by Russia in 1812. Under the Turkish rule this province, formerly a part of the principality of Moldavia, had enjoyed a degree of self-government. Legislation enacted in 1812, 1813, and 1818 granted Bessarabia the use of the local language in her courts and administrative institutions, confirmed the rule of local law within a wide sphere embracing taxation and all civil cases, and gave the elected representatives of the landed nobility an important part in the administration of public affairs. In 1824 and 1825, however, the curtailment of these privileges began, and in 1828 the statute of 1818, which had superseded earlier legislation and which was the cornerstone of Bessarabian autonomy, was repealed. The experiment thus came to an end, although some local features in the struc-

PUBLIC FINANCE

In comparison with Alexander's spectacular international activities and far-reaching, albeit unfulfilled, projects of constitutional reform, the economic advancement under his rule appears singularly dull and unimpressive. Public finance, that sensitive barometer of national health, showed disquieting signs of deterioration due in part to the financial disorder inherited from the previous reigns but chiefly to the exorbitant burden of war expenditure, economic backwardness, the devastation wrought by the Napoleonic invasion, and unsound methods of financing. The principal manifestations of the financial malaise were recurrent budget deficits, depreciation of paper currency, and the growth of the public debt. In spite of the establishment of a ministry of finance in 1802 and its reorganization in 1811, no unified budget or orderly budget procedure existed in Russia before 1863. Imperfect as were the estimates of revenue and expenditure during the earlier part of the century, they offer ample evidence of the dire plight of the treasury. Deficits of 20 to 25 per cent were common in the opening years of Alexander's reign, and in 1808, after the first round of Napoleonic wars, expenditure approached the impressive figure of 250 million rubles, while revenue was slightly over 111 million. To meet urgent demands for funds the government, following in the footsteps of Catherine and Paul, proceeded to issue paper money. The volume of inconvertible paper currency, or assignats, in circulation was 156 million rubles in 1796 and 213 million in 1800; this increased to 319 million in 1806, to 477 million in 1808, and reached the high mark of 836 million in 1817. In 1801 the value of the paper ruble had declined, in terms of silver, to 50 copecks; and, although it improved somewhat in 1803–1804 as a consequence of the revival of Russian exports under the more liberal commercial regime introduced by Alexander, the war of 1805 led to a new depreciation. By 1808 the paper ruble was worth 48 silver copecks and in 1810 it reached the low level of 20 copecks. In the same year the government, in a half-hearted attempt to carry out Speransky's financial program, prohibited further issues of paper currency and established the silver ruble of specified weight and fineness as the new monetary unit (manifesto of February 2, 1810). The experiment, however, was abandoned almost at once, and 46 million paper rubles were issued before the end

---

ture of governmental institutions in this province and a limited application of local law were retained.

of the year, a decree of April 9, 1812, making the paper ruble the only legal tender. Whereas the treasury determined the official parity of the paper ruble in terms of gold and silver coins, which circulated freely and were much in demand, in practice these rates varied within a wide range from place to place and from month to month, thus adding to the financial chaos. Count Dimitry Gurev, minister of finance in 1810–1823, fearing the further depreciation of the assignats if gold and silver were made legal tender, repeated on May 8, 1817, the order prohibiting the acceptance of precious metals by government agencies in payment of taxes and other obligations. Gurev's policy aimed at strengthening the paper ruble by reducing the volume of bank notes in circulation. The proceeds of four domestic loans floated in 1817, 1818, 1820, and 1822 were used to retire 240 million rubles of paper currency. The volume of assignats thus declined from 836 million rubles in 1817 to 596 million in 1823, but the value of the paper ruble in terms of silver was raised by merely 2.5 per cent. Count Egor Kankrin, who succeeded Gurev in 1823, made no further use of the printing press, and the volume of paper currency in circulation remained at the 1823 level until the monetary reform of 1839–1843.

In view of her budget and monetary situation it is not surprising that Russia found it difficult to borrow abroad. Her participation in the Napoleonic wars was financed by England, but through subsidies, not through loans. In 1817 the Russian public debt, including paper currency, was 1,202 million paper rubles, or approximately one billion rubles more than at the end of Catherine's reign. Of this huge sum only 107 million rubles represented foreign borrowing. By 1823 the public debt had increased to 1,345 million paper rubles. The first domestic interest-bearing loan was floated in 1809. The total interest-bearing public debt in 1823 was 213.6 million silver rubles requiring annual interest payments of 11.7 million silver rubles, or 41.1 million paper rubles. The service of this debt, including interest and amortization, amounted to 66.3 million paper rubles, or 15 per cent of the state revenue (440.2 million paper rubles in 1823).

FOREIGN TRADE

The first quarter of the nineteenth century brought no appreciable change in the volume, composition, and direction of Russian foreign trade. Under the impact of wars, shifting international alliances, and the vagaries of Russian and foreign tariff policies, the volume both of exports and of imports fluctuated within a wide range, but displayed a tendency to increase towards the end of the period:[12]

Russian Foreign Trade, 1801–1825

Years	Exports	Imports
	(Yearly average in thousand gold rubles)	
1801–1805	75,108	52,765
1806–1808	43,169	31,819
1812–1815	61,986	39,106
1816–1820	91,712	70,049
1821–1825	81,372	72,250

The chief articles of export at the beginning of the century were grain (18 per cent of the total value of exports), animal fats (15 per cent), raw hemp (15 per cent), raw flax (9 per cent), copper, iron, and steel (7.5 per cent), articles manufactured of flax and hemp (5.5 per cent), and furs (4 per cent). In the middle of the century the composition of exports was similar, except that exports of metal had sunk into insignificance and Russia had begun to send abroad a considerable amount of wool and timber.

The export of grain (that is, wheat, rye, barley, and oats) was affected, in addition to the factors mentioned above, by the frequent failure of crops, for instance, in 1820 and in 1821:

Value of Grain Exports, 1802–1825

Years	Yearly average in million paper rubles	Per cent of total exports
1802–1807	11.8	18.7
1812–1815	18.0	10.5
1816–1820	74.2	31.2
1821–1825	17.5	8.4

Volume of Grain Exports, 1801–1825

Years	Yearly average in thousand poods *
1801–1805	19,873
1806–1810	5,120
1811–1815	9,089
1816–1820	29,655
1821–1825	10,071

* One pood = 36 lbs. = 0.016 ton

[12] No official data for the period 1809–1811, when the Continental Blockade was in full force, are available.

According to Kulisher, the export of grain during this period was on the average only slightly over 1 per cent of the total yield. Wheat accounted for most of the grain exports.

At the beginning of the century the chief articles of import were cottons (16.5 per cent of the total value of imports), woolens (16.5 per cent), sugar (12.5 per cent), dyes (6.5 per cent), wine and spirits (6.5 per cent), tea (4 per cent), and salt (4 per cent), that is, commodities consumed largely by the well-to-do classes. This characteristic of the imports became even more pronounced during the subsequent decades.

Sea-borne commerce retained its predominant position, although there was some increase in the share of overland trade. The bulk both of exports and of imports continued to flow, as in the eighteenth century, through the ports of the Baltic Sea, and England remained Russia's chief customer and principal source of supply. Domestic shipping made hardly any progress, Russian imports and exports being carried, as in the past, in foreign bottoms. Although the number of ships of Russian registry entering Russian ports increased, their tonnage was insignificant and Russian ownership often fictitious.[13] Foreign interests exercised a quasi-monopoly of Russian foreign commerce, except for trade with China, from which they were excluded by Russian law.

The tariff and commercial policy of the imperial government did not favor the development of international trade. The brief era of relative commercial liberalism inaugurated after Alexander's accession gave place in 1808 to a regime of partial exclusion of foreign goods, in fulfillment of the obligations of the French alliance. The tariff act of 1810 was on the whole protective, and while it facilitated the entry of certain articles it prohibited the importation of many "luxuries." The tariff act of 1816 marked a further step in the same direction; it

[13] Number and Capacity of Ships Entering Russian Ports

Years	Total Number	Total Capacity in thousand lasts	Ships of Russian registry Number	Ships of Russian registry Capacity in thousand lasts
1802–1804	7,530	576	697	54
1814–1815	7,558	584	1,866	158
1820–1821	8,023	637	1,379	118
1824–1826	7,415	607	1,199	82
1848–1850	13,202	1,209	2,110	193
1851–1853	17,752	1,560	2,202	178

The increase in the number of ships of Russian registry in 1814–1815 was due to the taking over of a number of Finnish vessels engaged in coastal trade.

imposed stiff duties, and although it shortened somewhat the list of prohibited imports it still excluded many important commodities, among them a wide range of metal goods, cottons, woolens, linen, footwear, hats, tableware, and tea. An important revision of this restrictive regime was brought about by a convention concluded between Russia and Prussia in 1818. Whereas the convention dealt primarily with the trade relations of the kingdom of Poland, it also provided for the liberalization of Russian commercial practices and specifically did away with the prohibition on the importation of woolen, linen, and leather goods consigned by Prussian exporters. The Russian tariff act of 1819, which was a direct consequence of the convention of 1818, retained a fairly high level of duties but, much to the distress of Russian vested interests, removed all prohibitions on imports. Landed proprietors lamented the loss of foreign markets, the industrialists foresaw the necessity of closing down their establishments, and all united in predicting the inevitability of an adverse balance of trade, flight of precious metal, and the collapse of the ruble. The government soon gave in and, without awaiting a reply to the representations it had made in Berlin for the revision of the convention, issued in 1822 a tariff act which restored the high protective rates and the prohibitions of the act of 1816. This obstructive and unenlightened regime was maintained with but minor modifications for three decades.

INDUSTRY

The presentation of a picture of Russian industrial development in the first half of the nineteenth century presents the difficulties already noted in dealing with the earlier period: the inadequacy and unreliability of available data and the neglect of this aspect of economic history in Russian literature.[14] The nature of the sources and the difference in the legal status and in the conditions of manufacture (*obrabatyvaiushchaia promyshlennost*), on the one hand, and of mining and metallurgy (*gornozavodskaia promyshlennost*), on the other, necessitate separate examination of these two industrial fields.[15] Ac-

[14] This regrettable state of affairs was emphasized by Prof. M. I. Tugan-Baranovsky in his volume on the Russian factory (first published in 1898) and by A. G. Rashin in a recent well documented study of the rise of the Russian proletariat (Moscow, 1940).

[15] Metallurgy, in Russian terminology, is used to denote the extraction of metals from their ores; enterprises engaged in the fabrication of metal articles are classified as manufactures.

cording to official data, the number of manufacturing enterprises increased from 2,339 in 1804 to 5,261 in 1825, and the number of workers employed from 95,200 to 210,600. These figures, however, must be used with caution. Some enterprises, for instance, distilleries and armament and powder factories, were not included in the official computations; others escaped registration because their owners, in order to evade taxation, failed to report them. A major source of uncertainty is the already noted indiscriminate use of the terms *fabrika* and *zavod* (factory or industrial enterprise), which as late as the 1880's were applied to small and large enterprises alike. For instance, Russia's seven tobacco "factories" in 1804 were manned by a labor force of only nineteen men. Moreover, the use of machines was practically unknown and some of the large establishments were not manufactories in the modern meaning of the term: productive processes were carried on, not on the premises owned by the entrepreneur, but in the workers' own cottages or in small workshops. In 1814, of the 3,573 manufacturing enterprises (employing 170,700 workers) on which information is available, 70 per cent had less than 15 men each and accounted for merely 7 per cent of the total number of workers, whereas establishments employing more than 100 workers each represented 9 per cent of the total number of enterprises and 75 per cent of the total number of workers (Rashin). The average labor force per establishment was 35 in 1804, 39 in 1819, and 48 in 1830, but in view of the marked difference in the size of the enterprises these average figures mean little. The larger and most important enterprises during this period were in the cotton, woolen, and linen industries. The greatest progress was registered by the cotton manufactories; their number increased from 199 in 1804 to 484 in 1825, and the number of workers employed from 8,200 to 47,000. A modest start was made in sugar refining: in 1804 Russia had ten sugar refineries employing 108 workers; in 1825 the respective figures were 47 and 1,374. In 1825 the chief manufacturing regions were the provinces of Moscow (45,000 workers out of 210,600), Vladimir (35,000), and Kaluga (13,500); the province of St. Petersburg, with 5,600 industrial workers, trailed far behind.

Manufacturers continued to depend, as in the eighteenth century, partly on servile and partly on hired labor, with the latter gradually displacing the former. According to official data, of the 45,500 workers employed in manufacturing establishments in 1767, 17,800, or 39 per cent, were hired; in 1804 the number of hired workers was 45,600, or 48 per cent, and in 1825 it increased to 114,500, or 54 per cent. The sources of hired labor were the same as in the eighteenth century: state peasants, the urban population, and serfs paying their masters a fixed annual tribute (*obrok*).[16] Hired labor was unevenly distributed among the branches of industry; in 1825 the highest percentage was to be found in cotton textiles (95 per cent), with leather (93 per cent), and ropemaking (92 per cent). In other industries, however, the trend was towards increasing employment of serfs. In woolen manufactories, for instance, the number of serfs employed rose from 10,800, or 38 per cent, in 1804 to 38,600, or 61 per cent, in 1825, and in the glass and crystal industry the figures were, respectively, 1,300, or 34 per cent, and 3,700, or 64 per cent. The higher percentage of employed serfs worked in industrial enterprises owned by the nobles, who enjoyed a monopoly of this source of labor.[17] Other manufacturers ran their establishments largely by hired labor, although not infrequently they hired workers en bloc from a noble landowner instead of engaging them individually. By this arrangement the serfs had, of course, nothing to gain, and the practice, although prohibited by a law of June 16, 1825, was common in the reign of Nicholas I and led to abuses and exploitation of the workers. A significant development was the appearance of an increasingly important group of manufacturers who were themselves bondsmen. Among the pioneers of the cotton textile industry were many serfs of Count Sheremetev, and the village Ivanovo, owned by that nobleman, in the province of Vladimir, became a great textile center. The initial success of the cotton industry was due to the exclusion of British textiles during Russia's participation in the Continental Blockade and, later, to tariff protection and

[16] The urban population, according to Miliukov, was 1.3 million (4.1 per cent) in 1796; 1.7 million (4.4 per cent) in 1812; and 3.0 million (5.8 per cent) in 1835. Rashin considers these figures too low. According to his computations, the urban population was 2.3 million in 1794; 2.9 million in 1811; 3.5 million in 1825; and 4.9 million in 1840.

[17] The only exception was the so-called possessionary works (see p. 390), which might be owned by non-*dvoriane* and were endowed with a permanent servile labor force. In manufacturing industries, however, labor of this group was losing its relative importance. The number of possessionary workers in manufactories in 1804 was 30,200, or 32 per cent of the total number of workers employed, and declined to 29,400, or 14 per cent, in 1825. Serfs, who must be distinguished from possessionary workers, remained an important source of industrial labor. The number of serfs employed in industrial enterprises owned by their masters (*votchinnaia fabrika*) increased from 19,000, or 20 per cent, in 1804, to 67,000, or 32 per cent, in 1825.

the expanding domestic market. Some of the serfs who had built up one of Russia's great industries did not succeed in throwing off the yoke of bondage until the emancipation of 1861, although they had accumulated vast fortunes and enjoyed freedom in the management of their enterprises.

The position of mining and metallurgy was different from that of the manufacturing industry. Enterprises of this group belong to the class of possessionary works which were created by Peter I in 1721 but received their chief development in the middle of the eighteenth century, especially in the decade 1753–1763. They were manned exclusively by servile workers and were subject to minute and oppressive government control in all matters pertaining to volume, methods, labor relations, and the technique of production. Early in the nineteenth century mining and metallurgical enterprises numbered about 200 and were owned either by the state or by a small group of wealthy entrepreneurs. In these industries, located chiefly in the Ural Mountains, where 70 per cent of their total labor force was concentrated, were employed some 100,000 regular workers, and 354,000 peasants were permanently attached in a subsidiary capacity to such enterprises (1802–1806). The average number of regular workers per enterprise was over 400, but in some as many as 1,000 or 2,000 were employed. The frequent uprisings of the servile workers and the stifling effects of government regulations (even though they were often not enforced, especially those bearing on wages and conditions of work) were largely responsible for the stagnation of these industries. The contrast offered by the plight of mining and metallurgy, on the one hand, and, on the other, the rapid progress of the cotton industry, which employed almost exclusively hired labor, was an indication that serfdom was incompatible with the exigencies of the nascent Russian capitalism.

SOCIAL CONDITIONS

Wholesome signs of a partial awakening of public opinion to the evils of serfdom may be discerned in the activities of the St. Petersburg Free Economic Society. In 1812 this influential organization, which counted among its members many of the intellectual élite of the day, offered prizes for the best discussion of the relative merits of free and servile labor. The opinions of the fourteen authors who submitted manuscripts were equally divided, with the supporters and the opponents of serfdom equal in number (seven and seven), while the sympathies of the society may be gathered from the fact that the first and second prizes went to the partisans of free labor; the third prize was awarded to a monograph expounding the view that the position of Russian bondsmen was more favorable and their work more productive than that of the landless laborers in western Europe. The question of the emancipation of the serfs, or at least of the curtailment of the serfowners' powers, occupied much of the time of the "non-official committee" and was repeatedly discussed by the State Council. In addition to Speransky's projects and the proceedings of the Free Economic Society there have been preserved some twenty-five memoranda dealing with the "peasant question." Of this number, according to Semevsky, more than half came to the attention of the tsar, and some, for instance, Arakcheev's project (1818), were written at his request. There is no doubt that Alexander hated serfdom and until 1820 cherished the hope that it might soon be abolished. A mutiny in October, 1820, of the Semenovsky regiment, of which the tsar was the honorary colonel, would seem to have convinced him that all such plans were premature. Although the outbreak was traceable to the cruel discipline enforced by a newly appointed commanding officer, the proclamation issued by the rebellious soldiers contained a bitter indictment of the political and social system, and Alexander, who received the news of the Semenovsky affair at the Congress of Troppau, persisted in the belief (fostered by Arakcheev) that it was inspired and directed by international revolutionaries. The regiment was disbanded, and all projects for the improvement of the serfs' position were put aside. In 1820 Alexander vetoed the proposal of a group of wealthy aristocratic landowners to form a society for the betterment of the status of the serfs and for their gradual liberation.

Next to nothing was accomplished during Alexander's reign to alleviate the position of the servile population, and in some respects it was, indeed, worsened. A decree of May 28, 1801, prohibited advertising in the press of sales of serfs without the land; this mild restriction was easily circumvented by substituting "hire" for "sale," the true meaning of the subterfuge being generally understood. Alexander discontinued the practice of making gifts of populated estates, so freely indulged in by Catherine II and Paul, but such estates continued to be distributed as hereditary leases (*nasledstvennaia arenda*). In 1810 some 350,000 male serfs lived on estates so granted, and their position is said to have been appalling. A decree of December 12, 1801, extended to the merchants, burghers, and state peasants the right to own agricultural land. The initiative of Count S. P. Rumiantsev, a wealthy nobleman educated in Germany, led to the promulgation on February 20, 1803, of a law creating a new rural class, the "free farmers" (*svobodnye khlebopashtsy*). This status, conferred exclusively on freemen owning land, was intended specifically for the benefit of serfs who had obtained freedom by voluntary agreement with their masters, in accordance with the rules laid down by the law of February 20. The application of this legislation led to some confusion, and a decree of December 14, 1807, prohibited the emancipation of *whole villages* of serfs without land, although the liberation of *individual* serfs without land was permitted. The law of February 20, 1803, appeared to many liberal-minded Russians as the dawn of a new era, but its practical results were disappointing. The total number of male serfs emancipated by virtue of this act in Alexander's reign was under 37,000 and in that of Nicholas I 67,000, a mere fraction of the servile population. The price paid by the bondsmen for their freedom varied within a wide range, from 139 rubles to 5,000 rubles per male person. Failure on the part of the liberated serfs to live up to the provisions of their emancipation agreements was punishable by restoration to their former status. Two instances of such reversion to serfdom are known to have occurred, in 1826 and in 1828.

In 1810 wealthy merchants were permitted to own populated agricultural estates, provided they were purchased from the Crown and not from private individuals. This measure, which constituted an infringement of one of the nobility's treasured prerogatives, was enacted in connection with Speransky's unsuccessful attempt to raise funds by the sale of state properties. "Personal nobles" [18] were prohibited in 1814 from acquiring serfs, although they were allowed to retain until their death those already in their possession. A decree of July 14, 1808, made it illegal to sell serfs "like cattle" at markets and fairs; in spite of heavy penalties (confiscation of the serfs sold and fines) the practice continued without interference until the emancipation of 1861. In 1809 Alexander repealed the decree of 1765 which allowed the owners to sentence serfs to penal servitude, but the right to deport them to Siberia was confirmed in 1822, although the deportees were no longer credited towards the owner's quota of army recruits. As has already been stated, the hiring out of serfs by owners

[18] See p. 571.

to manufacturers was prohibited in 1825, but this law was never enforced.

Nothing was done to regulate the economic relationship between masters and serfs, and so far as can be ascertained, from avowedly incomplete information, the financial burden of the servile population tended to rise. The average annual payment (*obrok*) exacted by the owners was raised from five rubles per male serf at the end of the eighteenth century to eight rubles in 1819. There were, of course, important deviations from these approximate average figures, but the general trend towards higher payments was unmistakable. The serfs of Count Sheremetev, for instance, paid thirteen rubles per male person in 1815, and twenty-two rubles in 1824. In some cases the *obrok* was forty rubles or more. The depreciation of the ruble makes it difficult to determine the real meaning of the figures quoted, but it may be well to remember that the price of bread in Moscow in 1811–1825 was almost three times as high as it was at the beginning of the century.

It is a curious coincidence that the emancipation of serfs in Russia should first have been tried in the Baltic provinces, where the nobility was solidly German and the servile population Estonian and Lithuanian, just as constitutional government was introduced in Finland and in the kingdom of Poland almost a century before Russians were given even a taste of a parliamentary regime. The exploitation of the peasantry by the Baltic landowners and the resulting peasant uprisings forced the intervention of the St. Petersburg government, which in the early years of Alexander's reign was keenly concerned with the peasant question. A law of February 20, 1804, based on a project approved under pressure by the reluctant *Landtag* (organ of corporate self-government of the Baltic nobility) of Livonia, relieved the serfs of personal dependence on the landowner, attached them permanently to their allotments, recognized their property rights, and defined both their obligations towards the owner of the estate and the powers of the latter. By a law of August 27, 1804, this regime, somewhat modified in a way unfavorable to the peasantry, was extended to the province of Estonia, but it was not applied in the province of Courland. In spite of its seemingly enlightened character the reform, by "freezing" the existing land relationships and by making difficult the introduction of more progressive methods of cultivation, provoked much hostility both among the noble landowners and among the peasants, led to new peasant uprisings, and contributed to the agrarian depression the Baltic provinces experienced in 1807–1816. The whole question was reopened almost at once, and after lengthy deliberations the law of May 23, 1816, conferred personal freedom upon the peasants of Estonia but deprived them of their allotments, which then became the unencumbered property of the noble landowners; thus there came into existence a class of tenant farmers who enjoyed property rights and whose relations with their former masters were regulated by voluntary agreements. The law, however, imposed restrictions on the peasants' freedom of movement and of settlement, curtailed the traditional rights of village self-government, and vested the noble landowners with comprehensive police powers. This legislation was extended to Courland (law of August 25, 1817) and to Livonia (law of March 26, 1819), and in the three Baltic provinces it altered the economic and legal status of some 416,000 male serfs. There is general agreement among historians that the emancipation of the Baltic peasants without land dealt a severe blow to small farming; its enforcement was accompanied by a fresh wave of agrarian disturbances. The advantages this type of emancipation presented, from the point of view of the serfowners, did not escape the *dvoriane*, and several projects submitted on their behalf proposed a similar solution for the Russian provinces. No action, however, was taken.

The perennial shortage of funds and the desire to maintain Russia's military might at a high level led Alexander to experiment with a novel type of army organization, the military colonies. The idea of military colonies was probably inspired by the practice of old Muscovy, where the holding of land allotments was conditional on the performance of military service; by the somewhat similar organization of the Cossacks; by the example of the Austrian military agricultural settlements in Transylvania; and by the plan for the organization of frontier forces advocated by the French general Servan de Gerbey, with which Alexander was familiar. Military colonies were first tried in Russia in 1810, when the entire population of a commune in the province of Mogilev was removed to make place for the soldiers of one of the regiments. The negative results of this experiment did not discourage Alexander, and in 1816, at the end of the Napoleonic wars, he launched a more ambitious program of military colonies. Under this plan the population of the districts designated as military colonies was no longer removed but was incorporated in the regiments assigned to these districts. The soldier farmers were to live in model agricultural settlements built according to a uniform plan and were to provide for the maintenance of their military units as well as to perfect themselves in the art of warfare. Alexander took a passionate interest in this curious venture, in which he saw the possibility not only of relieving the treasury of the burden of military expenditure but also of improving the lot of the common soldier, who was to enjoy the advantages of family life and agricultural pursuits combined with the benefits of army discipline, so dear to the tsar. Entrusted to Arakcheev's energetic administration, military colonies rapidly expanded, and by the end of the reign comprised 375,000 soldiers. Some foreign observers, misled by the appearance of order and prosperity maintained in the colonies by Arakcheev, imagined they discerned in them the instruments of Russia's future irresistible military might. In fact, however, the experiment was a dismal failure. In spite of Arakcheev's financial wizardry the colonies were costly and, far from bettering the lot of the common soldiers, subjected them to a fantastic regime which combined the worst features of both serfdom and army barracks. A personal tour of inspection of the colonies by Nicholas I in 1826 led him to the conclusion that "after eight years of sustained efforts and incalculable expenditure, the colonies present a most distressing picture." They survived, nevertheless, although on a greatly reduced scale, until 1857.

The position of the peasants being what it was, sporadic uprisings among them were frequent. Recurrent rumors of imminent liberation reached a high pitch during the Napoleonic invasion of 1812. A small minority of the serfs put their hopes in the magnanimity of the French emperor, whereas the majority came to believe that emancipation would be granted by the tsar as a reward for fighting the invaders. Such, for instance, was the belief of the militiamen who rebelled in Penza in December, 1812. The government, needless to say, did not share this view.

No significant change took place in the position of other social groups. The growth of the urban population continued at a slow rate and, although there was some expansion in the volume of domestic commerce, the merchants, as in the past, had no voice in public affairs.[19] The nobility retained its privileges and prerogatives but dis-

---

[19] "The burghers, a respected and influential class in all other states, are with us contemptible, poor, tax-ridden, and deprived of means of existence," wrote a keen contemporary observer, A. A. Bestuzhev. "In other nations they populate the cities, but our cities exist merely on maps."

played signs of increasing apprehension and restlessness. Count de Noailles was right when he wrote on September 28, 1816: "The emperor does not like the nobility and is not liked by it." The conservative majority of the *dvoriane* disapproved of the casual manifestations of Alexander's liberalism and dreaded any thought of emancipation, while the small progressive minority was losing faith in promises of reform that never were fulfilled. For the first time, perhaps, the conflict between the Crown and the nobility emerged from the familiar sphere of purely selfish interests and palace revolutions and entered the broad arena of political and social issues.

Kliuchevsky acutely remarked that a foreign observer familiar with Russia's political and social order at the end of the eighteenth century would have noticed no change had he returned to that country in 1825: on the surface everything was much as it had been before. The shock of the Napoleonic invasion, like the great upheaval Muscovy experienced in the first decade of the seventeenth century, left no imprint on her political and social structure. Behind the imposing façade of the empire, however, there was a growing realization of its inherent and fatal weakness. In the preamble to his plan of constitutional reform Speransky wrote that he found in Russia "only two classes: the slaves of the autocrat and the slaves of the landowners. The former is free merely by comparison with the latter; in actual fact there are no free men in Russia except beggars and philosophers. The relationship between these two classes of slaves totally destroys the energy of the Russian people." The more enlightened representatives of the nobility—the only articulate group during this period—came to realize, as did Speransky, that autocracy offered no way out of the tragic impasse.

CHAPTER XXVIII

CULTURAL DEVELOPMENTS AND POLITICAL MOVEMENTS, 1800–1825

―――――※―――――

SCHOOLS

Kliuchevsky's pessimistic appraisal of conditions in Russia during the first quarter of the nineteenth century does not apply to her intellectual history. Reaction in politics, social inequities, and economic stagnation not only failed to check liberal thought or to discourage literary endeavor but, on the contrary, would seem to have spurred them to unprecedented activity. Closer contact with western Europe and western civilization, as well as, perhaps, Alexander's own shifting attitude towards liberalism, acted as a powerful stimulant in awakening Russia from her century-long slumber. The genius of the nation, so long dormant, asserted itself with a brilliancy and vigor that entitle this period to a distinct place in the cultural history of the empire.

The government's direct contribution to this development was negligible. Alexander and the members of the "non-official committee" were in agreement that rebuilding from the ground the practically non-existent school system was a matter of utmost urgency. The creation in 1802 of a ministry of education was a useful preliminary step in the right direction. Oddly, Russia's first minister of education was Count Peter Zavadovsky, an elderly courtier whom Alexander described (in a letter to La Harpe dated July 7, 1803) as "a nonentity" ("*il est nul*"). According to the tsar, however, school reform was safely in the hands of a board which had among its members some of his trusted advisers—Novosiltsev, Czartoryski, Michael Muravev. The foundation of the new school system was laid in the "provisional statute of schools" of January 26, 1803, which divided Russia into six school regions each headed by a curator who resided in St. Petersburg and was an ex officio member of the central school board. There were to be four types of schools: universities, provincial schools or gymnasiums, county schools, and parish schools. The plan provided for a university in each region; a provincial school in the capital city of each province (*guberniia*); a county school in the chief town of each county (*uezd*); and at least one parish school for every two parishes (*prikhod*). Russia had at the time three universities: a Russian university in Moscow, a Polish university in Vilna, and a German university established in Dorpat by Emperor Paul at the request of the Baltic nobility. There were practically no state-sponsored secondary schools (except military academies) and no elementary schools. The plan required the opening of three universities, 42 provincial schools, 405 county schools, and a large but undetermined number of parish schools. The government assumed charge of financing the universities and the provincial schools, but the county and parish schools were to be provided for by local authorities. The school system was closely integrated, in both administration and academic curriculums. The governing body of the university, which was to act as chief representative of the ministry of education in each region, had the specific duty of supervising the provincial schools; the director of a provincial school was also superintendent of the county schools of his province; and the director of a county school exercised similar control over the parish schools within his county. The course of instruction was one year in parish schools, two years in county schools, and four years in provincial schools. The curriculums were so arranged as to facilitate promotion from the lower to the higher schools and to eliminate duplication as far as possible. In parish schools were taught reading, writing, and the rudiments of religion and arithmetic; in county schools there were somewhat more advanced courses in religion and arithmetic, as well as in geometry, grammar, geography, history, elementary physics, natural history, and technology. Provincial schools provided no instruction in religion or Russian, but they offered an ambitious program which included logic, psychology, ethics, aesthetics, natural and public law, political economy, mathematics, physics, commerce, and technology. The graduates of provincial schools were expected to continue their studies at the universities.

The execution of this program met with difficulties similar to those that had confronted Russian school reformers in the eighteenth century: lack of funds; the deep-rooted distrust of the community towards government-controlled schools; and the absence of teachers. The school reform imposed a substantial burden on the treasury; and the outbreak of the Napoleonic wars, followed by the rapid deterioration in the state of public finance and the depreciation of the ruble, put an effective check on educational activities. Enrollment in secondary schools and universities was encouraged (although, as will appear later, not very successfully) by the decree of August 6, 1809, which made promotion in the hierarchy of civil servants conditional on the passing of an examination or the holding of a university degree. The primary task of the authorities, however, was to provide the schools with teachers. Russia's only teachers' college, founded in St. Petersburg in 1786, had closed its doors in 1801. It was revived in 1803 and after several transformations became in 1819 the University of St. Petersburg. Two new universities were established at Kazan and at Kharkov; although they received their charters as early as November 5, 1804, they bore for a number of years little resemblance to institutions of higher learning. The primary object of a university, as defined in 1804, was to train government employees, whereas the advancement of science, which was stipulated among the duties of the professors, was relegated to a subordinate place. Each university comprised four departments (or faculties): moral and political science, physics and mathematics, medicine, languages and literature. In their internal organization the universities enjoyed, in theory, complete autonomy. Academic corporations were independent of the authorities, elected their own officers, and had their own courts, which enjoyed comprehensive jurisdiction. In practice, however, autonomy, which had been borrowed from the statutes of German universities, remained a dead letter. The curators and other administrative officials paid little attention to the provisions of the charters and treated the members of the academic corporations as their subordinates. The conflict between the faculty members and the government entered an acute stage after 1816, when Golitsin was appointed minister of education. The tide of extreme reaction sweeping over Europe, which found its expression in the policies of the Holy Alliance, moved Alexander and his lieutenants to start a crusade against the allegedly liberal, ungodly, and revolutionary tendencies in Russian higher schools. University teaching was to be brought in line with the principles of Christianity as interpreted by the tsar, Golitsin, and their mystically inclined friends of the Bible Society. Michael Magnitsky, Speransky's former collaborator who had since recanted his liberal creed and become converted to militant conservatism and religiosity, directed a purge in 1819 of the University of Kazan. Shortly thereafter appointed curator of the Kazan region, he instituted at the local university a crude parody of a monastic order. The University of St. Petersburg was the victim of a similar campaign waged by Dimitry Runich, the curator of that region. Runich, among other things, brought proceedings against four well known professors on the charge that they taught philosophy and history "in a spirit inimical to Christianity." Under this extravagant regime little was left of university autonomy and academic freedom.

Another cause of the inability of the universities to fulfill their function was the composition of the teaching staff. Since few Russians were qualified to teach in higher or even in secondary schools, the government, reverting to the eighteenth century tradition, secured the services of foreign, especially German, professors. Some of them were scholars of distinction, but they found it difficult to adapt themselves to Russian conditions and to reconcile the enlightened provisions of university charters and the promises given to them on their appointment with the unpalatable realities of their new academic surroundings. There was much jealousy and mutual recrimination between Russian and foreign faculty members, and many of the latter were dismissed, especially during the second half of Alexander's reign. Not knowing Russian, foreign professors could not use it in their teaching, and lectured chiefly in Latin, a language with which their students were not familiar. The resulting grotesque situation led the government to abandon the policy of recruiting foreign scholars and to adopt the more sensible procedure of sending for training in foreign universities the more promising Russian students. Another method of solving the language difficulty was the introduction in secondary schools, or gymnasiums, of intensive courses in Latin. Proposed by the curator of the St. Petersburg region, Count S. S. Uvarov, this change in curriculums was first tried in 1811 in St. Petersburg; in 1817 it was adopted in all secondary schools. Whereas its original object was primarily utilitarian—to enable the graduates of those schools to follow university courses given in Latin—it became the basis of classicism, which was retained in secondary schools long after Latin ceased to be the language of university classrooms.

The practical consequences of the school reform, which were not vastly different from those of Alexander's other high-sounding projects, may be gathered from the following figures. The university student body (excluding the Finnish University of Helsingfors and the Polish University of Vilna) increased from 450 in 1809 to 1,700 in 1825. Of this number the University of Moscow had the lion's share. In 1824, for instance, Moscow had 820 university students; Kharkov 337; Kazan 118; and St. Petersburg only 51. Enrollment in secondary schools rose from 5,600 in 1809 to 7,700 in 1825.[1] No comprehensive data for the lower schools are available, but information for separate regions indicates that attendance remained consistently small (4,043 in 1810 and 4,465 in 1824 in the vast St. Petersburg region). The predilection of the nobility for private schools, which put great emphasis on French, dancing, and other "useful" accomplishments, may be gathered from the fact that in 1824 these schools in the St. Petersburg region had over 2,000 students, whereas the government-sponsored secondary school had 450 and the university, as has already been stated, 51 students. The few parish schools established in villages, presumably under official pressure, were soon closed for lack of funds and of local support. To the 69 parish schools in existence in 1801, 349 were added by 1825, practically all of them, according to Miliukov, located in urban areas. The villages continued to be denied school facilities; education remained the privilege of a tiny minority.

A noteworthy feature of the school policy was the novel attitude towards the Jews expounded in a law of December 9, 1804. Jewish children and youths were to be admitted to Russian schools without restriction and were to be eligible for university degrees, while Jewish communities were allowed to maintain, at their own expense, confessional schools.[2] This seemingly liberal legislation was received by

[1] The above figures quoted by Miliukov do not include students enrolled in military academies and other specialized institutions. Facilities for the education of boys of the upper class were augmented by the founding of a *lycée* at Tsarskoe Selo (1811), a *lycée* at Yaroslavl, and a college at Nezhin. The two latter schools were privately endowed.

[2] The other provisions were less liberal. The law of Dec. 9, 1804, retained the Jewish pale (see p. 605) and extended it to include the Caucasus and the province of Astrakhan. Within the pale the Jews were to enjoy "the protection of the law on the same basis as the other subjects of the Crown"; they were divided into four legal categories: farmers, manufacturers and artisans, merchants, and burghers. The Jews, however, were debarred from leasing agricultural land, from keeping inns and distilling or selling intoxicating beverages, that is, the very trades in which many of them were engaged. The consequence of the law, therefore, was the mass eviction of Jews residing in rural districts but not engaged in farming. A plan for

Orthodox Jewry, that is, by practically the entire Russian Jewish population, at first with indifference—Russian schools were too few to be a cause for alarm—and later with growing hostility. Still fanatically attached to an ancient tradition of racial and religious exclusiveness, the Jewish communities interpreted the law as an attempt at destroying the very basis of the national and religious organization that had safeguarded the identity of the nation through centuries of dispersion and persecution.

CENSORSHIP

The printed word is, like the schools, an essential medium of progress, and its efficacy is obviously determined by the circle of readers it reaches and by the degree of freedom allowed to the press. In eighteenth century Russia the powers of censorship were not defined by law, and all matters relating to the publication of books and periodicals were left to the discretion of administrative officials. By an irony of fate Radishchev, who later became an outstanding victim of this vicious system,[3] held as early as 1790 that "censorship of printed works belongs to the public: it bestows a crown upon the author or uses the sheets of his book for wrapping paper." In the early years of Alexander's reign the tsar and his advisers were keenly concerned with the protection of authors and publishers from administrative arbitrariness. The government's true attitude towards freedom of the press, however, may be gathered from the significant deletion, in the official Russian edition of Jeremy Bentham's treatise on civil and penal law, of a passage containing a vigorous indictment of censorship.[4]

The Russian censorship law of July 9, 1804, was modeled on that of Denmark and required preliminary examination by officials of the ministry of education of all manuscripts submitted for publication.

---

the organization of Jewish agricultural colonies in the south of Russia, inaugurated in 1806, brought no appreciable results. In 1825, as a measure against smuggling, an order was issued for the removal of all Jews residing outside the cities within fifty versts (thirty-three miles) of the frontier.

[3] See p. 599.

[4] The three-volume Russian translation of Bentham's *Traités de législation civile et pénale*, edited by P. E. L. Dumont, was published by imperial command in 1805–1811 and was dedicated to the tsar. Bentham, whose brother Samuel was in the Russian service, visited that country in 1786–1787. His works had attracted much attention in Russia, he corresponded with Alexander and several high-placed Russians, and was eager for a time to devote himself to the proposed reform of Russian law. The incompatibility of Bentham's liberal views with the policies of the Holy Alliance led him to abandon this project.

So long as the ministry was controlled by men of fairly liberal views this regime was not too oppressive. Foreign books (but not periodicals), moreover, if consigned to private individuals, were exempt from censorship, and there were loopholes which permitted booksellers to distribute foreign publications banned by the authorities. This era of relative tolerance lasted for only a few years. With the revival in 1807 of the security police as a permanent institution, that agency began to interfere with censorship, and the ministry of the police established in 1811 was given broad, albeit ill defined, powers to deal with domestic and foreign publications. There were numerous instances of confiscation by the police department of books and articles passed by the ministry of education. The conflict between these two agencies continued even after the reactionary Golitsin became minister of education (1816), although his stern handling both of the press and of the publishers left little to which the police could take exception. Golitsin prohibited (February 10, 1817) the discussion in print of government activities without preliminary authorization by the minister concerned. It was further officially explained (May 14, 1818) that "all questions pertaining to government policies may be discussed only in accordance with the wishes of the authorities, who know better what information should be given to the public; private persons must not write on political topics, either for or against." The ban applied specifically to the discussion of constitutional reform and emancipation of the serfs. In 1825 Arakcheev communicated to the minister of education an imperial order prohibiting the publication of magazine articles on military colonies, except those supplied by himself. But even strict compliance with these Draconian rules offered no real protection to authors and publishers. The popular journal *Dukh Zhurnalov* (Review of Reviews), which had many clashes with the censors, printed in 1820 articles on the constitution of the United States of America and on representative government. It was suspended in 1821. Censorship of purely literary works was equally capricious, unpredictable, and stringent. It was against these overwhelming odds that the nascent Russian literature and journalism had to struggle for a place in the sun.

LITERATURE, ART, AND THE THEATER

At the beginning of the nineteenth century western influence dominated Russian literature. The form and content of Russian literary works, even the emphasis on national themes that became the fashion under Catherine II, were of a distinctly foreign origin. Literature, and particularly versification, moreover, became the handmaiden of politics, subservience to government wishes being particularly marked in the writings of Russia's two most talented eighteenth century poets, Lomonosov and Derzhavin. The brutal persecution of Radishchev for overstepping the narrow boundaries of officially tolerated criticism effectively silenced any expression of independent thought. Stale pseudo-classicism and affected sentimentalism were the prevalent literary tendencies; it was only gradually that they were superseded by romanticism and, later, by realism.

Since literary opinion was then still in a state of flux, one would hardly be justified in speaking of definite "literary schools." It may be said, nevertheless, that individual authors, as well as the numerous and often ephemeral coteries of literati, supported at various times one of the following three literary movements: (1) Alexander Shishkov's [5] and Derzhavin's ultra-reactionary group, which extolled the imaginary glories of Russian eighteenth century literature and particularly insisted on the necessity of safeguarding the Russian language against pernicious foreign influences (Old Slavonic, they argued, was the fountainhead of the Russian tongue, and should be drawn upon to bring the Russian vocabulary in line with modern requirements): (2) Karamzin's group, which combined rigid political conservatism with a spirited defense of a simplified and "westernized" literary language; and (3) the informal organization of the younger men whose views tended towards liberal romanticism and political radicalism. It was not uncommon for the authors to shift their allegiance from one movement to another.

The outstanding literary figure at the turn of the century was Nicholas Karamzin (1766-1828). His *Letters of a Russian Traveler*, first published in 1791-1792, and several stories which in the years immediately following appeared in the periodicals he edited, made his

---

[5] A. S. Shishkov (1754-1841), a man of mediocre ability, began his career in the navy. His patriotic *Discourse on Love for One's Country* won Alexander's whole-hearted approval and led to his appointment as secretary of state (1811). In 1824 Shishkov succeeded Golitsin as minister of education, an office he held until 1828. He was opposed to the Bible Society and was instrumental in its liquidation in 1826. From 1816 to 1841 Shishkov was president of the Russian Academy (see p. 597), which he used as a vehicle for the dissemination of his reactionary views. After his death the academy was closed and its functions were taken over by the newly established division of Russian language and literature of the Academy of Science.

literary reputation. In 1803 Karamzin was appointed Russia's official "historiographer," and in 1816 were issued the first eight volumes of his monumental *History of the Russian State*, followed by four more volumes, of which the last was published posthumously. His work had an immediate and resounding success and was heralded by contemporary opinion as ushering in a new era both in Russian letters and in historiography. Subsequent developments and scientific criticism have largely revised this too favorable verdict. Karamzin's chief claim to fame is his contribution to the evolution of the literary language. Believing that one should write as one talks, he carefully avoided the clumsy rhetorical adornments and artificial constructions affected by other eighteenth century authors. Karamzin, moreover, added to the flexibility and power of expression of the Russian tongue by adopting a number of words and grammatical constructions translated or borrowed from the French. These innovations, to which Shishkov and his friends took exception, have withstood the test of time and have gained general acceptance. Karamzin's own style, however, although once considered a model of elegance and simplicity, was soon to appear hopelessly dated and labored. His work, nevertheless, facilitated the evolution of the literary language achieved by his younger and more talented contemporaries, especially Zhukovsky and Pushkin.

His influence in directing Russian literature and history into new channels was less fruitful. He is rightly regarded as the founder of the short-lived Russian sentimentalism, which, as in other countries, was a reaction against pseudo-classicism and rationalism and was inspired by foreign authors (Rousseau, Bernardin de Saint-Pierre, Sterne, to mention only a few). In Karamzin's case, however, sentimentalism was a literary manner rather than the expression of a deep-felt conviction, of a consistent philosophy. His immensely popular stories, written in a sentimental vein, dealt with Russian themes but were just as remote from Russian realities as were the works of the pseudo-classicists. In Pypin's apt phrase, Karamzin's outlook was that of "sentimental optimism which eventually made him a staunch reactionary." The *History of the Russian State*, acclaimed by contemporary opinion as a work of unsurpassed erudition and literary charm, is seldom consulted today. Miliukov established (in 1897) that while Karamzin had used some hitherto unknown archive materials he had, on the whole, leaned much too heavily on the writings of earlier historians, especially those of Prince Shcherbatov. The philosophy of history expounded by Karamzin was summarized with particular clarity in his lengthy *Memorandum* (Zapiska) *on Ancient and Modern Russia*, submitted to Alexander in 1811 and directed against the reforms of Speransky. Fanatically opposed to constitutional and social changes, the celebrated historian urged the retention of serfdom and held that all that was needed was "good" provincial governors and "good" priests. "Autocracy," he wrote to Prince P. A. Viazemsky, on August 21, 1818, "is the soul, the life of Russia," an opinion undoubtedly shared by the vast majority of the *dvoriane*. Karamzin, however, at the same time claimed (as Catherine II had done) that he was "republican at heart." His aggressive emotional nationalism and reactionary views won him the lasting admiration of the ultra-conservative among his countrymen, but he had no disciples and founded no historical school. His literary influence was even briefer. Contrary to contemporary opinion, therefore, his work was not the beginning of a new era, and belonged to the tradition of the eighteenth rather than to that of the nineteenth century.

The progress of political and literary thought was fostered by the appearance of numerous translations. Some of them, for instance, Bentham's treatise, Delolme's study of the British constitution, and Raynal's philosophical study of European trade in the Indies, were published by imperial command. An increasing number of younger poets, more skillful than the older generation in the art of versification, showed interest in foreign authors. Nicholas Gnedich (1784–1833) translated Ducis, Schiller, Voltaire, Shakespeare, and the *Iliad* (translation published in 1829). Constantine Batiushkov (1787–1855), whose fruitful work was brought to an end in 1820 by a mental ailment, paraphrased and translated Latin classics, Voltaire, La Fontaine, Parny, and Torquato Tasso. Vasili Zhukovsky (1783–1852), the illegitimate son of a Russian nobleman and a captive Turkish woman, obtained his first great literary success with a Russian version of Gray's *Elegy in a Country Churchyard* (1802). His translations and adaptations covered an exceptionally wide range and comprised La Fontaine, Florian, Millevoye, Bürger, Schiller, Goethe, Oliver Goldsmith, Klopstock, Uhland, Geibel, Walter Scott, and many others. Towards the end of his life he published a translation of the *Odyssey* (1849). The work of these authors and of other less notable littérateurs familiarized educated Russians with western literary movements and at the same time contributed to the evolution of their own literary language. Pseudo-classicism receded to the background, and sentimentalism, which still held sway, acquired in the poems of Batiushkov and especially in those of Zhukovsky a sincerity and intimate quality that were lacking in Karamzin. Zhukovsky, whose verses reached a high degree of perfection, is regarded as the founder of Russian romanticism.

The emergence of a national Russian literature, of original contributions that could withstand the test of time, may be traced to the almost simultaneous appearance of three exceptionally talented authors: Krylov, Griboedov, and Pushkin. Ivan Krylov (1768–1844), a man of obscure antecedents, humble education, and questionable conduct, entered the world of letters when he was still under twenty, and for a number of years wrote indifferent plays and edited commonplace satirical journals. His genius was unexpectedly revealed in 1809 with the publication of a volume of fables which made him famous. From that time he continued to write nothing but fables, his productivity declining rapidly with the passing of the years. Krylov's fables, whether adaptations or original productions, are masterpieces of wit, homely wisdom, and imagery. He had a unique gift for drawing vivid, concise word pictures, and an unsurpassed mastery of the popular tongue. High-minded critics have condemned his work on the ground that his moralizing was not always of a very high order. His fables, nevertheless, have been for over a century an indispensable element in the education of every Russian child, and his apt and quaint dictums, continually quoted by Russians, have retained their persuasive power. Krylov is the only eminent representative in Russian literature of the genre in which he excelled.

Alexander Griboedov (1795–1829) received a careful education, was an accomplished linguist, a diplomat, and a man of the world. He took an early interest in the theater, translated and adapted several foreign plays, and collaborated in writing others with Prince Alexander Shakhovskoy. These early attempts, like those of Krylov, were entirely undistinguished. His only truly great work was the comedy in verse, *The Misfortune of Being Wise*, which he began probably in 1816 and completed in 1823, when it was circulated in manuscript copies and created a sensation in literary and aristocratic circles.[6] A

[6] Excerpts from *The Misfortune of Being Wise* were first published in 1825, and a carefully censored version in 1833, but the full text was not permitted to appear until the 1860's. The comedy was performed for the first time in 1831.

mordant satire on Moscow's contemporary upper class, *The Misfortune of Being Wise* was an unprecedented phenomenon from the point of view of its content, structure, and language. Without sacrificing the rich flavor of Russia's early nineteenth century, Griboedov's genius succeeded in unfolding a revealing picture of human relationships which, like all true works of art, transcends national boundaries and defies time. That is why, 130 years after this play was written, it has lost none of its appeal or social significance. According to authoritative opinion, no other play in Russian literature has ever reached the level of Griboedov's comedy. The richness, aptness, and wit of its language has been a source of delight to generations of Russians, who quote Griboedov as freely as they quote Krylov. The author did not live to see his work in print or on the stage: he was murdered in 1829, victim of a popular rebellion in distant Teheran, where he represented the imperial government.

Alexander Pushkin (1799–1837) came from an aristocratic though impoverished family, and had in his veins a strain of African blood. He received a superficial education in the newly founded *lycée* at Tsarskoe Selo, and on graduation in 1817 was attached to the ministry of foreign affairs. In 1820, his verses having brought upon him the wrath of the government, he was expelled from the capital, where he was not permitted to return until 1827. During his exile Pushkin lived chiefly in Kishenev and Odessa, visited the Caucasus, and spent the last two years of his banishment in almost complete seclusion on his estate in the province of Pskov. By extensive reading he succeeded in nearly filling the gaps in his education. When he entered the *lycée* in 1811, Pushkin, later the greatest master of the Russian language, had difficulty in writing his native tongue, and even in his later years he admitted that he was more at ease in French. His interest in Byron led him in the 1820's to acquire a fluent knowledge of English. Although Pushkin professed a deep admiration for Karamzin, the only Russian authors who left an imprint on his own work were Zhukovsky and Batiushkov. Like most of his contemporaries, he was influenced by the ancient classics (especially Anacreon), and also by Voltaire, Parny, Byron, Shakespeare, and Walter Scott. These influences, however, were not allowed to overshadow Pushkin's powerful individuality. He began to write when he was a mere child. In 1814 his verses appeared for the first time in print, and by the end of 1825 he was the author of several major poems (*Ruslan and Liudmila*, 1820; *The Cau-*

casian Prisoner, 1821; *The Bakhchisarai Fountain,* 1822; *The Gypsies,* 1823-1824; *Count Nulin,* 1825), the historic drama *Boris Godunov* (1825), the first two chapters of his great novel in verse, *Eugene Onegin,* and a number of shorter works. The distinguishing characteristic of Pushkin's genius was its universality, that is, unlike Krylov and Griboedov, he excelled in every form of literary endeavor. He had a remarkable command of every shade of the Russian language, from the solemn recitations of biblical texts to the vernacular of the common people. His lyrics, whether light or sentimental, his historical poems and dramas on Russian and foreign themes, his popular tales, his stories and other prose works have remained a hundred years after his death the best examples of their kind Russian literature has to offer. Pushkin's works powerfully contributed to the defeat of pseudo-classicism, sentimentalism, and romanticism, although he had himself experienced the influence of these movements, and they cleared the path for the triumphant progress of realism which was to bring so rich a harvest in the latter part of the century. The radiance of his genius won for Russian literature, and especially for poetry, freed at last from subservience to the court and purged of low selfish motives, a recognition and a position of dignity it had never known before. It is with good reason, therefore, that Pushkin is regarded as the real founder of a national Russian literature.

This statement, however, needs qualification. Madame de Staël rightly observed that in Russia "a few noblemen occupy themselves with literature," and the pertinent question has been raised whether a literature, irrespective of its intrinsic merits, has a claim to be called "national" so long as it is accessible to merely a tiny minority of the people. In Pushkin's day both the contents and language of Russian literature were beyond the grasp of the illiterate masses. If the above theory is accepted, the conclusion is inescapable that Russian literature did not acquire a "national" character in the sense just indicated until many years later.[7]

The theater, which became popular in the first decades of the nineteenth century, did not fare so well as belles-lettres. Pseudo-classicism

[7] It is noteworthy that the events of 1812 were neglected in contemporary writings and produced no literary works of real merit. The authors that dealt with the Napoleonic wars limited their treatment to somewhat standardized expressions of patriotic joy over the defeat of the enemy and to often hyperbolical descriptions of feats of arms, but they passed over in silence the deeper social aspects of the upheaval.

and sentimentalism were still supreme on the stage, and the comedies and tragedies of even the most successful dramatists—Vladislav Ozerov (1770–1816), Prince Alexander Shakhovskoy (1777–1846), and Michael Zagoskin (1789–1852)—were no great improvement on those of the earlier playwrights. Acting was in the "grand manner," pompous and conventional. The spell of the old tradition was not broken until the second quarter of the century, when the works of Griboedov, Gogol, and Ostrovsky ushered in the era of realism. A development of some importance was the founding of the Moscow state theater (1806), which in 1823 became known as the Small (*Malyi*) Theater. In the same year M. S. Shchepkin (1788–1863), a serf until he was thirty-three, joined its company and eventually became one of Russia's greatest actors.

Under the watchful supervision of the Academy of Arts, architecture, painting, and sculpture continued to move slowly along the familiar path of academic classicism. Foreign talents were still greatly appreciated in St. Petersburg, and Russian artists were invariably trained abroad or under foreign masters. The more important Russian architects were Andrew Voronikhin (1760–1814), Adrian Zakharov (1761–1811), and Vasili Stasov (1769–1848). Voronikhin, a former serf of Count Stroganov, was the architect of the Kazan Cathedral in St. Petersburg, a monument severely criticized at the time as a poor imitation of St. Peter's in Rome, but viewed more favorably by some recent authorities (for instance, Grabar). Zakharov was responsible for the striking admiralty building (1806–1815), and the Frenchman Thomas de Thomon (1754–1813) for that of the St. Petersburg stock exchange (1805–1816). These works were not without merit, but they were in no way representative of national Russian architecture. Levitsky and Borovikov, already mentioned in an earlier chapter, remained the leading painters, and I. P. Martos (1750–1835) and Count Fedor Tolstoy (1783–1873) may be added to the list of sculptors. Unlike belles-lettres, the other arts had not yet freed themselves from the academic tradition, but a revolt against its stifling influence was soon to break out.

SECRET SOCIETIES

"Russians are generally concerned with and seek in everything the superfluous without having even the necessary," wrote Count de Noailles on July 23, 1817. "They have an army, an administration where corruption is pushed to the extreme degree; they bend under a yoke softened merely by the generous character of their master or by the right they arrogate to dispose of him if they dislike him; and in a state of society so remote from perfection and resembling in many ways oriental governments, a young Russian officer, armed with his knout, subject of an absolute sovereign, surrounded by his own slaves, talks to you of the rights of peoples, of liberty, like a citizen of the United States!" The radicalism of a section of Russia's upper class noted by the French ambassador to St. Petersburg had its roots in western liberal and revolutionary ideas, which had become increasingly popular since the days of Catherine II. It was not until the second decade of the nineteenth century, however, that there emerged a semblance of organized political opposition; this took the form of secret societies which attempted the abortive *coup d'état* of December 14, 1825. This opposition was manifested exclusively by members of the upper class, particularly young officers in the guards, and bore an imprint of its social origin.

There were many reasons why young guardsmen risked sacrificing the advantages of an easy and promising career for the uncertainties and dangers that beset the path of political and social reformers. Alexander himself had indirectly encouraged the transformation of eighteenth century Russia's vague theoretical liberalism into a movement demanding fundamental reforms and, in the last resort, revolutionary action. His personal preference for constitutional government and his abhorrence of serfdom were well known in aristocratic and military circles. He had given proof of his attachment to these ideals in the constitutions granted to Finland and Poland, in his advocacy of a constitutional regime in France after the fall of Napoleon, in his disapproval of Ferdinand VII for abrogating—on his restoration—the Spanish constitution. Hopes of a Russian constitutional reform were kept alive by Alexander's pronouncements (for instance, his address before the Polish diet in March, 1818) and by officially sponsored constitutional projects, of which the last, it will be remembered, was prepared by Novosiltsev in 1818–1819. Liberal-minded Russians, therefore, were justified in believing that their aspirations were basically in agreement with the monarch's own wishes. Constitutionalism in Finland and Poland, moreover, appeared to many as a national insult. Patriotic feelings were outraged by the bestowal of representative government on "defeated" Finland and Poland, whereas it was denied to the tsar's Russian subjects, who regarded themselves as the saviors of Europe. They were alarmed by the persistent and not unwarranted rumors that Alexander was considering the incorporation of the Lithuanian provinces with the kingdom of Poland. The emperor, moreover, had the unfortunate habit of expressing his contempt for the land of his birth; he blamed the maladministration of public affairs on the absence of able and honest men, and he had among his confidential advisers an uncommonly large number of foreigners (Czartoryski, La Harpe, Stein, Capo d'Istria, Pozzo di Borgo).[8] Just as unpopular were his frequent and protracted journeys abroad and his boundless confidence in the universally hated Arakcheev.

The desire for reform was spurred by the distressing state of internal affairs. The courts were notoriously corrupt, and the low salaries paid to government officials made graft and spoliation a practical necessity. In overcrowded prisons starving convicts were treated with inhuman cruelty. Economic stagnation and the crushing burden of taxation brought about the impoverishment of every social group, including the nobility. The position of the clergy, according to the future Decembrist (that is, participant in the movement which led to the rebellion of December 14, 1825) Paul Pestel, was "bitter and pitiful: priests barely earn their daily bread and in their old age have no shelter." According to another Decembrist, Alexander Iakubovich, "the clergy is ignorant and not always virtuous"; the Russians, therefore, "have little respect for their pastors, who have no influence with the people."[9] The plight of the peasantry was a matter of particular concern to liberal-minded Russians, and the emancipation of the serfs was regarded as an essential reform, although there was no agreement concerning the manner in which it was to be achieved. In dealing with this problem considerations of humanity and equity were reinforced by those of enlightened self-interest. The Decembrist Prince Serge Trubetskoy, for instance, believed that nothing short of the abolition of serfdom would prevent a social upheaval.

As most of the members of the secret societies were army officers,

[8] Of Alexander's forty-five aides-de-camp general (*general-adiutant*) who formed his immediate circle, thirteen were foreigners (including the Baltic Germans).

[9] The subservience of the higher clergy was such that even Alexander, fond as he was of flattery, found it unbearable. "I am so disgusted (*excédé*) with the flat panegyrics delivered to me in every town where there is a bishop," he wrote to Prince Alexander Golitsin on Sept. 28, 1817, "that I have decided to prohibit the practice by a ukase to the Synod."

the condition of the armed forces was the source of much discontent.[10] The normal term of service for privates was twenty-five years, and this could be extended indefinitely in case of delinquency. The granting, as a measure of economy, of protracted leaves of absence, which became customary after 1815, sometimes worked to the disadvantage of enlisted men who, having lost all contact with their native villages, had nowhere to go. The pay of infantry privates was 9 rubles 50 copecks a year, and of privates in the guards from 16 to 25 rubles. After 1815 soldiers were permitted to supplement their meager pay by outside earnings; for this purpose they were granted annual furloughs for periods of six to eight weeks. The commissariat department was a notorious hotbed of corruption; discipline was harsh and often ruthless. None of these evils was new, but the resentment they naturally provoked became more apparent and more vocal when, at the end of the Napoleonic wars, the army returned to its peacetime quarters. The movement of disaffection was particularly pronounced among the guards who were the immediate victims of incessant drilling, which was a real obsession with Alexander and his three brothers: Constantine, Nicholas, and Michael. For instance, the number of steps infantry was to make per minute was regulated by imperial orders, and any failure to keep the prescribed pace brought upon the delinquent unit severe penalties. The size of the army, moreover, was raised from 394,000 in 1800 to an average of 950,000 in the closing years of Alexander's reign; this meant, of course, that a larger percentage of young men were drafted for military service. There were numerous desertions, much discontent, and occasional mutinies, of which the most notable was that of the Semenovsky regiment of the guards in October, 1820. In May, 1821, the guards were moved to Vilna preparatory to the campaign to put down the Piedmont revolution. In fact, however, the government used the proposed Italian expedition as a convenient pretext for clearing the capital of regiments regarded as unreliable. The guards did not return to St. Petersburg until the middle of 1822.

Russia's participation in European campaigns, especially in the War of 1813–1815 and in the following three-year occupation of France,

---

[10] Peacetime service was still regulated by the antiquated army regulations of 1716, which remained in force, with but minor modifications, until 1839, although new regulations governing the status of the army in wartime were issued in 1812.

was probably the most potent single factor in promoting the desire for constitutional and social change. Direct intimate contact with western Europe, shattered as it was by decades of war and revolution, brought to thousands of young Russians a clear realization that countries enjoying some degree of constitutional government offered their citizens advantages and opportunities that were not to be found in their own homeland. These seeds of liberalism fell on fertile ground: progressive ideas were expounded in the teaching of the more enlightened professors not only in the universities and in the *lycée* of Tsarskoe Selo but also, strange as this may seem, in the government-sponsored military academies where many officers received their training. There was an unprecedented demand for political literature, and the epigrams and verses of Pushkin (and also those of the less well known poets) ridiculing abuses and extolling the virtues of freedom were circulated in thousands of handwritten copies. Alexander complained that "Pushkin has flooded Russia with revolutionary poems: all young people know them by heart." However, since Russian history was still inadequately studied, liberalism often acquired a nationalistic tinge and strove to discover elements of popular government in the ancient institutions of the *veche* and *zemskii sobor*, or to glorify the attempt at imposing limitations on autocracy in 1730, when Anne of Courland mounted the Russian throne.

The policies of the imperial government after 1815 moved in a direction the very opposite of the one so ardently desired by the small minority of the educated class. Obscurantism, personified in the two irreconcilable enemies Golitsin and Arakcheev, found its expression in the ever expanding activities of the security police,[11] the extravagance of censorship, the promotion of military colonies, the campaign against the universities, the triumph of mysticism and, later, of militant religious orthodoxy. The course of European events had a twofold effect upon the growth of Russian revolutionary ideas. On the one hand, the policies of the Holy Alliance, interpreted as a betrayal of the principles of liberty and national independence so often extolled by Alexander, cast discredit upon the government: intervention in Spain and Italy was as unpopular as was the abandonment of Greek

---

[11] The army being suspected of disaffection, a special branch of the security police in the armed forces was inaugurated in 1821, first in the brigade of the guards and later in the Second Army quartered in the south of Russia. Its agents spied on officers and men both on and off duty.

insurgents to the mercy of the Turks. On the other hand, revolutionary outbursts in western Europe inflamed the imagination of the more ardent Russian radicals. The German student Karl Sand, who in March, 1819, murdered the well known German dramatist, reactionary, and agent of the Russian government, Augustus von Kotzebue, became a hero and a martyr not only in his native land but also in Russia. His bloody exploit was celebrated by Pushkin in a poem (*The Dagger*) which many officers knew by heart. The revolutions in Spain, Naples, Piedmont, Portugal, Greece, and Central and South America were followed with sympathy and close interest in Russian progressive circles as object lessons worth emulating.

The origin of Russian secret political societies is linked with the Masonic movement. The persecution of Novikov by Catherine II dealt the never too vigorous Russian Freemasonry a blow from which it only partially recovered. In the first two decades of the nineteenth century the lodges were tolerated, but under the close supervision of the police they remained, to quote Semevsky, "numerically weak, financially insecure, and hopelessly timid." With rare exceptions they shunned political and social issues, displayed marked indifference towards the emancipation of the serfs, and were concerned chiefly with the performance of seemingly meaningless rituals. Many of the future Decembrists were affiliated with the lodges, and the influence of the Masonic tradition is traceable in the structure and aims of the secret political societies. The first organization of this type—the Union of Salvation (*Soiuz Spaseniia*), otherwise known as the Union of the True and Faithful Sons of Russia (*otechestva*)—was founded in St. Petersburg in 1816 by a small group of officers of the guards and of the general staff. Among its members were Prince Serge Trubetskoy, the brothers Serge and Mathew Muravev-Apostol, the brothers Alexander and Michael Muravev, their second cousin Nikita Muravev, and Paul Pestel.

The aims of the society, which never had more than twenty members, were not clearly defined, but its general object, so far as it can be ascertained, was the establishment of a representative government, preferably a constitutional monarchy.[12] The Union of Salvation

[12] Information on the aims and organization of political societies is regrettably incomplete. The two chief sources are the depositions made by the members before the commission of inquiry appointed after the rebellion of Dec. 14, 1825, and the memoirs written in later years by some of the participants. Depositions

achieved little, except that it led to the formation of a new secret society, the Union of the Public Good (*Soiuz Blagodenstviia*), which was organized in 1818 when the Union of Salvation was dissolved. The Union of the Public Good was modeled on the German *Tugenbund*, the importance of which its Russian admirers grossly exaggerated.[13] The declared objects of the union were social work (supervision of hospitals, orphanages, and prisons, the promotion of a more humane attitude towards the serfs), advancement of education, social justice (including the prevention of abuses in the courts and by administrative officials), and the promotion of economic welfare by encouraging agriculture, industry, and commerce. The political objects, which were not stated in the written statute (the so-called *Green Book*), were the establishment of a representative government, the abolition of serfdom, and propaganda for the achievement of these aims. The union, which consisted of semi-autonomous local organizations subordinated to a central executive board (*korennaia duma*), was only slightly more successful than its predecessor. Its total membership probably never exceeded two hundred and, according to Trubetskoy, was at times as low as fifty-six, whereas its cultural activities were limited to the opening of a few army schools and a certain mitigation of discipline in the units commanded by officers, members of the union. Of greater significance was the decision of the central executive board, which, under the influence of Pestel, declared itself in 1820 in favor of a republic. This decision, however, was not accepted as binding by some of the members, and it precipitated a conflict between the radical group, led by Pestel, and the more conservative elements, who refused to be drawn into a political conspiracy. At a conference held in Moscow in January, 1821, the union was declared dissolved. It is a moot question whether this decision was the actual expression of the views held by the leaders or, as is believed by some historians, a

---

submitted by defendants fighting for their lives tend in many cases to give a one-sided and even a distorted picture. Memoirs written many years after the event and without access to documents are also open to serious criticism as a source of information. Few contemporary documents bearing on the secret societies have been preserved. The membership of these societies, moreover, like that of the Masonic lodges, was composed of degrees, the actual aims being revealed only to the members belonging to the higher degrees. This may account, according to Shchegolev, for discrepancies in the statements of aims given by individual members.

[13] The *Tugenbund*, an association "for the revival of morality, religion, good taste, and public spirit," was founded in Königsberg in April, 1808, and received official recognition in June. It was officially dissolved in December, 1809.

maneuver to get rid of lukewarm and unreliable members, but the former hypothesis seems more plausible. Pestel, then colonel of a regiment stationed in the south of Russia, was not present at the Moscow conference, and refused to submit to its decision. There thus came into being the secret Southern Society, with Pestel as its leader and a modest initial membership of nine. In St. Petersburg and Moscow, however, the work of the secret society was discontinued and was not resumed until the end of 1822, after the guards had returned to the capital.

The less zealous members of the secret organization had good reasons for feeling uneasy and hesitant. The mutiny of the Semenovsky regiment and the revolutionary outbreaks in western Europe had made the government increasingly suspicious and watchful. In 1821 General Alexander Benckendorff, chief of staff of the guards, submitted to the tsar a detailed and fairly accurate report describing the activities of the subversive organizations and listing the officers involved. Major Vladimir Raevsky, son of a hero of the War of 1812 and one of the most active members of the Union of the Public Good and of the Southern Society, was arrested in February, 1822. A decree of August 1 in that year prohibited all secret societies, including Masonic lodges, and directed army officers and civil servants to make written statements concerning their affiliations with such organizations and to pledge themselves to discontinue them at once. In spite of these unmistakable warnings the Union of the Public Good was revived in St. Petersburg at the end of 1822 and took the name of the Northern Society. Its leaders were Nikita Muravev, Prince Serge Trubetskoy, Prince Eugene Obolensky, Nicholas Turgenev, and the poet Konrad Ryleev. According to Trubetskoy, the total number of members was thirteen.

Cooperation between the Northern Society and the Southern Society, which both considered essential, was made difficult by the relative conservatism of the former and the radicalism of the latter. The members of the secret societies, united as they were in their desire to establish a representative government and to emancipate the serfs, were hopelessly at odds concerning all practical aspects of the proposed reform and the methods by which it was to be achieved. There were some, like Nicholas Turgenev and General Michael Orlov, an admirer of Joseph de Maistre, who favored the creation of a Russian peerage. The unfinished project of a constitution, on which Nikita Muravev had been working since 1821, provided for the establishment of a federated Russian state under a constitutional monarch. It guaranteed the equality of all citizens before the law and freedom of the press and religion, but restricted by high property qualifications the right to vote and the right to be elected to parliament or public office. The project, while safeguarding the interests of the landed aristocracy, called for the emancipation of the serfs: the former serfs were to receive small land allotments and were to form a class of tenant farmers.

Pestel, in his *Russkaia Pravda* (Russian Truth) expounded a very different program.[14] The Russia he visualized was a unified, centralized, egalitarian, and democratic republic where there would be no room for privileges arising from birth, rank, or wealth. Serfdom was to be abolished, and every citizen was to be entitled to enough land to support himself and his family. By a rather intricate division of land into publicly and privately owned, Pestel hoped to achieve general security without undermining property rights. His political, social, and economic radicalism went hand in hand with the most aggressive nationalism. He demanded the ruthless Russification of all territories comprised in the Russian empire, the abolition of Finnish autonomy, the exclusive use of the Russian language throughout Russia, the annexation of Moldavia, of the still unconquered parts of the Caucasus, and of the lands inhabited by the Kirghiz and other Mongolian tribes. The only exception to his program of assimilation was Poland, which Pestel proposed to establish as an independent state and even to expand eastward, provided Poland adopted a political and social system similar to that of the new Russian republic and entered with it into a political alliance.[15] The main points of this proposal were endorsed by the secret Society of the United Slavs, founded in 1823 by

[14] Named after the collection of laws ascribed to the Kievan prince Yaroslav, *Russian Truth*, a draft instruction for the use of the future provisional government, was to consist of ten chapters, of which only five were actually written. In 1822 the draft was submitted to the executive board of the Southern Society, which approved it, with some revisions, a year later.

[15] Pestel was critical of the Jews, especially of their exclusiveness, which was incompatible with his conception of a unified state. He favored strong measures for the breaking down of the power of the rabbis and for the assimilation of the Jews, but he considered even more desirable their wholesale eviction and the formation of a Jewish state in Asia Minor.

Lieutenant Peter Borisov with the object of bringing about a federation of Slavic peoples. In 1825 this organization was merged with the Southern Society.

The striking contrast between the views advocated by the leaders of the Southern and Northern societies may be explained not only by the personal preferences of Muravev and Pestel but also by the social complexion of their respective organizations. The aristocratic and wealthy guardsmen in St. Petersburg tended towards a constitutional monarchy and the preservation of proprietary rights, whereas the lesser nobility, which served in the regiments of the line and formed the bulk of Pestel's following, were not averse to the more radical solution, although there were dissenting voices in both camps. Friction between the two societies increased in 1823-1825, when attempts were made to reach a practical understanding for joint action. Both parties agreed on the necessity of creating a provisional government after the successful *coup d'état*. Pestel, however, insisted that this government should remain in power for a protracted period, perhaps for eight or ten years, and that it should carry out on its own authority the proposed reforms. Prince Serge Trubetskoy, who at the end of 1823 had succeeded Nikita Muravev as leader of the Northern Society, held that the rule of the provisional government should be brief and that no fundamental changes should be made without the approval of a constituent assembly, which was to be summoned at once. His great concern was to preserve intact the administrative apparatus and to maintain, as far as possible, the traditional authority of the government. Trubetskoy, indeed, would seem to have nursed the illusion that determined pressure might be sufficient to wrest from the emperor the desired reforms, thus avoiding the necessity of overthrowing the dynasty. Pestel, on the other hand, clamored for a revolutionary dictatorship. A visit he paid to St. Petersburg in the spring of 1824 accentuated the difference separating the two factions. The proposed establishment of an independent Poland and the agreement concluded in January, 1824, between the Southern Society and the Polish revolutionaries appeared to some of the St. Petersburg members as akin to treason. The land program of the *Russian Truth* was branded as utopian by Nicholas Turgenev, whose views on economic matters carried great weight. An element of personal rivalry embittered the dispute, and Pestel left the capital without bringing any nearer the cooperation between the Southern and the Northern societies which had been the object of his journey. His faith in the success of the revolution and his eloquent advocacy of the necessity of regicide and of the physical destruction of the imperial family, however, produced a strong impression upon some of the members of the Northern Society, especially Ryleev and Obolensky. At the end of 1824 Trubetskoy went south, and returned to St. Petersburg early in November, 1825, with the conviction (which events soon proved to be unfounded) that the southern army was ready for an uprising. Ryleev, who in Trubetskoy's absence had administered the affairs of the Northern Society, was forced to admit that the St. Petersburg garrison was hopelessly unprepared for revolutionary action; but, carried away by his revolutionary enthusiasm, he put his faith in the support of of the people. The date for the uprising was provisionally set for the spring of 1826. The death of Alexander on November 19, 1825, caught the conspirators unprepared and precipitated the tragic *dénouement*.

THE DYNASTIC RIDDLE

Alexander having died childless, his brother Constantine was under the law of 1797 next in line of succession to the throne. Officially known as the "tsesarevich," a title associated with the position of heir apparent but conferred upon him by Emperor Paul as far back as 1799, Constantine had shown an early disinclination to shoulder the burden of kingship. It was a combination of factors of a private nature, however, that led him to renounce his hereditary right. In 1801 his first wife, a princess of Saxe-Coburg, went to live with her parents and refused to return. Constantine's repeated requests for a divorce and permission to marry a commoner (he had several romances with women of non-royal blood) were not granted by Alexander and the dowager empress until March, 1820. A few weeks later (May 12) he married morganatically the Polish Countess Jeanette Grudzinska, a Roman Catholic, who received the title of Princess Lowicz. On April 17, 1818, the tsar's second brother, the Grand Duke Nicholas, became father of a son, the future Emperor Alexander II. The continuation of the dynasty was thus assured, and this was probably the reason why Alexander had intimated to Nicholas in the summer of 1819 that some day he would be called upon to wear the Crown. The renouncement by Constantine of his right to the throne in favor of Nicholas was a condition attached to his divorce and the permission to marry Countess Grudzinska.[16] In a letter to Alexander dated January 14, 1822, Constantine confirmed his decision to transfer his title to the throne to "the next heir," an arrangement sanctioned in the tsar's reply of February 2. Thus a question of paramount importance to the empire was dealt with as a purely family matter in private negotiations between the two brothers. A manifesto written by Philaret, archbishop of Moscow, and signed by Alexander on August 16, 1823, appointed Nicholas heir apparent. This action was not, however, made public. A sealed envelope containing the original text of the manifesto and the two letters mentioned above was deposited in the Moscow Uspensky Cathedral with the direction that the package should be returned to the tsar if he so desired and that, in case of his death, it should be opened "before any other action" was taken. Three copies of each document were made by Prince Alexander Golitsin and, for safe custody, were handed in sealed envelopes and with similar instructions to the State Council, the Senate, and the Synod. Nicholas knew that he was destined to succeed Alexander, but neither he nor Constantine was aware of the legal form that had been given to the unusual transaction. Constantine remained the official heir apparent and was thus referred to in state documents and Church services. It is impossible to suggest a rational explanation for these mysterious and quaint arrangements which precipitated a dynastic crisis.

At the time of Alexander's death in Taganrog (November 19), Nicholas was in St. Petersburg and Constantine in Warsaw. The news was not received in the capital until November 27. The factor that determined the conduct of Nicholas during the following three weeks was the attitude of the guards. The future emperor, a ruthless and exacting disciplinarian, was in daily contact with the troops of the St. Petersburg garrison and was extremely unpopular with both officers and men. Constantine, although as severe and cruel a drill-master as his brother, had the advantage of having been away from the capital for over a decade. His personal frailties were largely forgotten, but it was known that the Polish army he commanded was better equipped and received higher pay than the Russian army and that in Poland the term of service for privates was eight years instead of the twenty-five prescribed by the Russian law. These facts, together with the per-

[16] In 1814 Constantine had visited his wife in Germany and offered her a reconciliation for dynastic reasons, but his plea was rejected.

sistent, though unfounded, belief that Constantine favored the abolition of serfdom, made him a formidable potential adversary of Nicholas.[17] Consulted by Nicholas on November 25, when news from Taganrog became alarming, Count Nicholas Miloradovich, military governor-general of St. Petersburg, took the position, shared by many high officials, that an act of the former monarch not promulgated in his lifetime had no binding power and that since an interregnum must be avoided at any cost there was no choice (in case of the emperor's death) but to administer the oath of allegiance to Constantine without delay. The guards, it was believed, would not countenance the accession of Nicholas unless Constantine had freely and publicly renounced his right to the throne. Conscious of the vulnerability of his legal title and fearful of a mutiny of the guards, Nicholas, on receipt of the news of Alexander's death, immediately took the oath of allegiance to Constantine and ordered that it should be administered throughout the empire. The State Council, after having acquainted itself with the documents enclosed in the mysterious package, decided, not without misgivings, to follow his example. The Senate, that custodian of legality, and Philaret and the Moscow authorities deemed it wise to ignore the orders of the late emperor, and took the oath to Constantine without opening the envelopes entrusted to them by Alexander. Except in Warsaw, the army, government officials, and the populace followed suit. The reign of Constantine had begun.

This strange comedy went on for nearly three weeks. Constantine, contrary to the expectations entertained by some in St. Petersburg, remained faithful to his decision to refuse the Crown; but, blaming Nicholas and his advisers for a truly grotesque situation, he declined either to come to the capital or to issue an official statement that would remove all doubts concerning his real attitude, as his brother and the dowager empress implored him to do.[18] His final curt refusal was received in St. Petersburg on December 12 simultaneously with a report by Baron Ivan Dibich, from Taganrog, disclosing the existence of a conspiracy among the officers of the southern army and the guards. This information was confirmed the same day in a personal report

[17] The legend of Constantine's magnanimity persisted in later years, and delegations of the servile population flocked to Warsaw seeking redress of their grievances. With characteristic dry humor the grand duke referred the petitioners to Benckendorff, the head of the security police.

[18] Constantine took the oath of allegiance to Nicholas and administered it to the Warsaw garrison on December 21, after the new emperor's formal accession.

made to Nicholas by Jacob Rostovtsev, a young officer whom Prince Eugene Obolensky had vainly sought to enroll in the Northern Society. There was no time to lose and no help to expect from Warsaw. Nicholas ordered the preparation of a manifesto announcing his accession [19] and directed that the new oath should be administered on December 14. He took no steps, however, to arrest the officers listed in Dibich's report. There were persistent rumors that Constantine and his younger brother, Michael, who was known to be close to him and who during these eventful weeks served as a liaison officer between St. Petersburg and Warsaw, were under arrest. Nicholas feared that the apprehension of popular officers at this time would add to the excitement of the troops and might unleash the mutiny it was his hope to avoid.

THE INSURRECTION OF DECEMBER 14, 1825

While the state of confusion created by Alexander's death offered the secret societies their golden opportunity, it also made clear their inherent weakness. Their membership was pitifully small, and it consisted, moreover, almost exclusively of junior officers. This was important, because the *coup d'état* envisaged was a military revolution that would depend for its success on the willingness and ability of the officers to sway their men to the side of the insurgents, and obviously appeals by junior officers were less effective than the formal orders of their superiors. One of the conspirators, Captain Alexander Iakubovich, did preach popular rebellion with mass murders and arson as the best method of seizing power, but his declamations were discounted by most of his colleagues as mere rhetoric: in the events of December 14 the part of the "fiery Caucasian," as Iakubovich was called by his friends, proved to be singularly unheroic. Trubetskoy, who resumed his place as the central figure of the conspiracy, believed that armed forces, controlled by their officers, should be the tool, but merely the tool, of the proposed *coup d'état*. The guards, he argued, had decided the fate of the throne in the eighteenth century; they would now give Russia a constitutional government. He was particularly anxious to avoid "the dangerous participation of the populace," and he stated later that since the mutiny of the St. Petersburg garrison appeared inevitable the secret society had the duty of directing the

---

[19] To this act were attached the letters exchanged by Alexander and Constantine in 1822, the manifesto of August 16, 1825, and Constantine's letters to Nicholas and the dowager empress confirming his decision to decline the Crown.

Cultural Developments and Political Movements, 1800–1825

forces of discontent into orderly channels. The more radically minded Ryleev was inclined to believe that the seizure of the Winter Palace and the arrest of the imperial family were essential to the success of the insurrection.

The practical activities of the Northern Society during these decisive weeks were limited to propaganda among the officers and to attempts at winning the support of the rank and file by circulating the legend that Nicholas had suppressed a "testament" in which Alexander had decreed the shortening of the army service term. The conspirators based their hopes of success on the anticipated refusal of a portion of the St. Petersburg garrison to take the "new" oath and on the simultaneous uprising of the southern army. The plan, in so far as this term is applicable to the results of confused and shapeless deliberations, was to prevent the State Council and the Senate from taking the oath to Nicholas and to force the latter body to issue a manifesto summoning a constituent assembly and appointing a provisional government of two or three prominent statesmen, among them Speransky. Thus the fiction of "legality" was to be preserved, and Trubetskoy hoped that Nicholas might be induced to capitulate and to accept the decisions of the future constituent assembly. The execution of this plan for what Pokrovsky aptly called a "non-revolutionary revolution" demanded the occupation of the Senate Square by the insurgent troops at the time when the senators were assembled to take the oath to Nicholas.

Most of the conspirators had little faith in the success of their enterprise. Trubetskoy, realizing the insignificance of his following, was particularly despondent, and Ryleev, who proclaimed in a burst of enthusiasm that "the tactics of revolution are summed up in one word —daring!" admitted in his more lucid moments that "it is possible that our dreams will come true, but it is probable, indeed much more than probable, that we shall all perish." He consoled himself with the thought that their sacrifice would redound to the good of future generations. The conspiracy, however, had gone too far to be abandoned or postponed. Rostovtsev had sent to Obolensky a copy of the report he had submitted to Nicholas on December 12 informing him of the plot. In case of the new emperor's uneventful accession, reckoning was certain to follow swiftly.

The insurrection of December 14 proved a ghastly failure. In the morning of that day the majority of the St. Petersburg garrison took the oath to Nicholas in an orderly and decorous fashion, although in some cases with a conspicuous lack of enthusiasm. The case of Nicholas was helped by the arrival in the capital at 8 A.M. of the Grand Duke Michael, whose personal appearance in the barracks of the less reliable regiments put to rest the tale that both he and Constantine were under arrest. Some seven hundred men of the Moscow regiment, however, led by Captain Michael Bestuzhev and Captain Prince Dimitry Shchepin-Rostovsky (who was not a member of the secret society and did not even know of its existence), refused to take the oath. Shouting that they wanted Constantine, they marched to the Senate Square, where they were joined by rebellious soldiers from other regiments, the total number of insurgents rising to three thousand men and thirty officers. This demonstration, however, was pointless. The State Council had taken the oath to the new emperor on the night of December 13, and the Senate at 7 A.M. on December 14, that is, before the arrival of the rebellious troops. The appointed leaders of the insurgents—the "dictator" Trubetskoy and his designated assistants Colonel Alexander Bulatov and Captain Iakubovich—made but a brief appearance in the Senate Square. Ryleev, too, wandered away from the square in search of reinforcements and was not seen there again. Prince Eugene Obolensky assumed command of the insurgent forces, but neither he nor his followers knew what to do, and remained inactive while government troops under the personal direction of Nicholas poured into the square and the adjoining streets. There were some victims of desultory shooting, among them Count Miloradovich, who was fatally wounded by Lieutenant Peter Kakhovsky. Cold, hungry, and leaderless, the insurgents nevertheless refused repeated suggestions that they surrender; they were encouraged to resist by crowds of civilians who mixed freely with the soldiery and sporadically attacked government troops with stones and logs. As the short winter day drew to an end and darkness set in, it became probable that unless the situation was handled with firmness other troops might join the insurgents and that the military mutiny might assume the character of a popular rebellion. Cavalry charges having failed, the four field pieces constituting the government artillery were brought into action. After the third volley the formation of insurgents broke down and they fled in disorder pursued by the loyal troops. In a few minutes the Senate Square was cleared, except for seventy or eighty dead, among them some civilians. The insurrection was over.

"*Voilà un joli commencement de règne,*" Nicholas remarked to one of his generals.

The southern army had no part in the events of December 14. General Dibich, having found among the late emperor's papers at Taganrog a report on the proposed mutiny, on December 13 arrested Pestel and the other leaders of the Southern Society. Lieutenant Colonel Serge Muravev-Apostol, who was among the arrested officers, succeeded in regaining his freedom and at the end of December raised the banner of rebellion in the Chernigov regiment. His hopes for the support of the other units of the southern command were not realized, and in the first encounter with government troops, on January 3, 1826, his followers suffered a defeat. The military insurrection in the south proved no more successful than it had been in the capital.

The liquidation of the uprising was conducted by a commission of inquiry under Nicholas's direct supervision. Most of the Decembrists had hastened to surrender to the authorities, and in the overwhelming majority of cases (Pestel was one of the few exceptions) the evidence they gave was imbued with a spirit of almost insufferable humility and burning repentance. The defendants, indeed, seem to have vied in their zeal to tell everything and even to implicate people who had no connection with the conspiracy or with the secret societies. Nearly six hundred persons were investigated by the commission, among them Griboedov, who was especially brought to St. Petersburg from the Caucasus. Of this number 121 were finally put on trial by a specially constituted high criminal court consisting of members of the State Council, the Senate, the Synod, and high officials. Speransky was the most active member of the tribunal, which conducted the trial in such a manner that some of the defendants did not realize that they had had a hearing before a court. The final verdict, after the emperor had exercised his prerogative of clemency, provided five death sentences by hanging (among them Pestel, Ryleev, and Serge Muravev-Apostol), and penal servitude and deportation to Siberia for more than one hundred of the accused. Some of the Decembrists were accompanied to Siberia by their wives and families, and displayed in exile a fortitude and dignity of which there had been little evidence during the investigation and trial. Partial commutation of their sentence was granted from time to time (penal servitude for life, for instance, was terminated in 1839), but it was not until the coronation of Alexander II in 1856 that the twenty-nine Decembrists still in Siberia were restored to their former legal status and were permitted to reside wherever they pleased in Russia, except St. Petersburg and Moscow.

It should not be concluded from the above account that the dark forebodings of Trubetskoy and Ryleev were entirely justified and that the failure of the insurrection was a "historical inevitability." It is significant that some of the insurgent leaders, for instance Shchepin-Rostovsky, were not members of the secret societies and that of the many officers who knew of the conspiracy only one, Jacob Rostovtsev, reported it to the authorities. The possibilities offered by the dynastic crisis and Nicholas's personal unpopularity should not be underestimated. The sympathies of a section of the populace were clearly with the insurgents, and had the movement shown any signs of success the hesitant allegiance of the "loyal" troops might have easily been swayed to the rebels' side. There is an unconfirmed story that Speransky, when asked whether he would take part in the proposed provisional government, replied: "You must win first, then everyone will be with you." Had the leaders of the insurgents displayed greater vision, courage, and a sense of reality, the issue of the fateful day of December 14—and also, perhaps, the subsequent history of Russia—might have been very different.

The Decembrist insurrection had far-reaching repercussions. It increased the watchfulness of the government, although it has been unjustly blamed for the severity of the police regime instituted under Nicholas: Russia's eighteenth century tradition and Alexander's rule could hardly have been improved upon in this respect. The crushing of the rebellion dealt Russian liberalism a shattering blow. The deterrent effects of trials, executions, and deportations were great, and many of the former liberals zealously devoted themselves to erasing the compromising memories of their earlier associations: not a few of those who were affiliated with the secret societies but had escaped Siberia had a brilliant military and administrative career under Nicholas. On the other hand, those whose personal convictions precluded surrender were driven deeper into underground revolutionary work. For later generations the Decembrists became the symbol of self-sacrificing struggle against autocracy and serfdom and the founders of the nineteenth century revolutionary tradition. Ryleev was not altogether wrong when he spoke of the value of seemingly aimless sacrifices for a great cause. The secret societies were wiped out on December 14, but the ideals they stood for could not be destroyed.

CHAPTER XXIX

NICHOLAS I

The Apogee of Absolutism

EMPEROR NICHOLAS

The character of Nicholas I, under whose rule (1825–1855) Russian nineteenth century absolutism reached its fullest development, presents none of the complexities that have baffled Alexander's biographers. Born in 1796, Nicholas received a good education, spoke Russian, French, German and English, studied Latin and Greek, and was initiated by distinguished scholars (Professors Storch, Balugiansky, and Kukolnik) into such disciplines as political economy, government, constitutional law, jurisprudence, and public finance. In these subjects, however, the young grand duke took little interest, and his learned mentors succeeded merely in inspiring their pupil with a profound aversion for what he contemptuously called "abstractions." The notion of legality, as Presniakov rightly observes, remained foreign to Nicholas's mind. "Sound morals are the best theory of law," he once remarked; "they must be present in the heart of every man, irrespective of any abstraction, and must be based on religion." For the science of warfare, especially for military engineering, however, Nicholas showed great aptitude and, like his three brothers, remained throughout his life an expert, enthusiastic, and exacting drill-master. He was fond of drawing, played the flute, and assiduously patronized the opera, the ballet, the drama, and fancy-dress balls. Nicholas's scholastic career came to an end in the middle of 1813. In 1814 he joined the Russian army abroad and in later years traveled extensively both in Russia and in foreign countries. On July 1, 1817, he married Princess Charlotte of Prussia, daughter of King Frederick William III and sister of the future King Frederick William IV. By his wife (who on her admission to the Russian Orthodox Church assumed the name of Alexandra Fedorovna) he had four sons and three daughters. Although destined to succeed Alexander, Nicholas in his brother's lifetime had no part in the administration of public affairs; he merely commanded a brigade of the guards and was inspector-general of army engineers.

Close family ties with the House of Hohenzollern greatly influenced the future tsar's outlook and policies. He was an admirer of Frederick William III, and patriarchal monarchical rule on the Prussian model appeared to him the ideal form of government. A firm believer in autocracy, Nicholas held that a monarch "by the grace of God" (and he recognized no other source of monarchical power) should be both the fountain of law and the actual head of the administration. This theory, of course, was by no means novel, but Nicholas gave it a peculiar twist by emphasizing the importance of the dynastic and religious factors, by stressing the element of duty and discipline, and by insisting on conformity with national tradition. He visualized a state organized and functioning like a well drilled army unit, that is, a polity embodying the principles of hierarchical subordination, close delimitation of the duties of each member, and the unchallengeable authority of the anointed leader. Nicholas held that "the entire life of a man must be regarded merely as service, for everyone has to serve." This clear-cut and simple philosophy, cleverly summed up by Nicholas's minister of education, S. S. Uvarov, in the celebrated formula "Orthodoxy, autocracy, and nationality," was, needless to say, at variance with the practice of the Russian government.

The uprising of December 14 left an indelible imprint on the emperor's mind. The shock was all the greater because the rebellion involved the army, especially the guards, whom Nicholas regarded as the mainstay of the throne. He not only supervised in person the investigation of the conspiracy, meted out to its leaders crushing penalties, and to the end of his life continued to manifest keen interest in the doings of the Decembrists lingering in Siberia, but he also made a careful study of their grievances. A. D. Borovkov, secretary of the commission of investigation, prepared by imperial command a comprehensive summary of the evidence submitted by the accused men. His report, which contained a bitter indictment of Russia's maladministration and social inequities, ended with the sweeping recommendation that steps be taken "to correct innumerable disorders and abuses." Nicholas is said to have kept this document on his desk and to have consulted it frequently.[1] He was aware of Russia's predicament and

[1] A revealing instance of the interest taken by Nicholas in the views held by

realized the necessity of reform. In agreement with his philosophy the program of his reign was formulated in the manifesto of July 13, 1826, stigmatizing the Decembrists as "a handful of monsters *(izvergi)*" inspired by outlandish ideas "incompatible with the ways and character of the Russian people," and proclaiming that improvement was to be brought about "not by insolent and always destructive dreams but by the gradual betterment, from above, of national institutions." This promise was not fulfilled, and in spite of numerous "secret committees" and a flood of proposals and reports no important reform was enacted. The general attitude of Nicholas and his government is well illustrated by the tsar's remarks on the emancipation of the serfs, the most urgent domestic question of the day. "There is no doubt that serfdom, in its present form, is a flagrant evil which everyone realizes," he declared in the State Council on March 20, 1842; "yet to attempt to remedy it now would be, of course, an evil even more disastrous." Nicholas's rigid conservatism, fear of the masses, and desire to safeguard absolutism and to protect the interests of the landed nobility proved an insurmountable bar to reform. The result was that his supposedly benevolent and paternal rule degenerated into a dictatorship, an arbitrary, stifling, and despotic police regime that sought to regulate the lives of individuals in minute details.

The tsar's reactionary views determined Russian foreign policy, over which he exercised personal control. Attachment to the outworn fiction of the Holy Alliance and to legitimacy, and persistent opposition (with some exceptions to be noted later) to the principle of national self-determination which swept nineteenth century Europe, brought him in conflict with every democratic and liberal movement in England and on the Continent. An inconsistent, aggressive, and arrogant policy in Asia and the Near East antagonized European Powers and

---

the Decembrists is offered by the case of one of them, Alexander Kornilovich, a young historian and social scientist of some promise. Recalled to St. Petersburg in February, 1828, from Siberia, where he was serving an eight-year sentence of penal servitude, Kornilovich, though he was incarcerated in the fortress of Peter and Paul, was treated with consideration and kindness, was supplied with newspapers and books, and was ordered by the tsar to submit his views on "whatever subject he might choose." Twenty-two of Kornilovich's memoranda, which have been preserved, deal with topics such as Russian trade with Asia, relations with Persia, administration of the Caucasus, the Polish question, school reform, and so on. Although these reports were favorably commented upon by the tsar and by Benckendorff, chief of the police, they failed to win the prisoner complete forgiveness. In 1832 Kornilovich was released from the fortress and was sent as a private to a regiment stationed in the Caucasus, where he died two years later.

generated suspicion. The wanton destruction of Polish autonomy added to the dislike with which Russia was regarded in many European capitals. Nicholas, moreover, in the apt phrase of his German historian, Theodor Schiemann, dwelt in the imaginary world of "dynastic mythology" where international questions were settled in direct dealings between crowned heads, and private letters and personal views of monarchs and statesmen assumed the character of binding international obligations. This peculiar personal diplomacy played a part in bringing about the disaster of 1853–1856. A reign that began with some notable military and diplomatic successes ended in the catastrophe of the Crimean War, which exposed the frailties of imperial diplomacy and exploded the fiction of Russia's military might. Michael Bakunin, the well known revolutionary, was not far from truth when he wrote in 1847: "Our internal situation is deplorable. It is complete anarchy under the label of order. The veil of bureaucratic formalism conceals terrible wounds; our administration, our courts, our finances —all are sham: sham to deceive foreign opinion, sham to lull the conscience of the tsar, who pretends to believe it all the more willingly because he is afraid to face realities." Nicholas, however, was not unaware of the tragic failure of his rule, and whatever illusions he might have retained were dispelled by the Crimean War.

In his private life, too, Nicholas was unable to live up to the ideals of duty he professed. While scrupulously preserving the appearance of a devoted husband, and often extolled as such, he for years had a liaison with Barbara Nelidov, a lady-in-waiting to the empress.[2] Frustration and failing health made Nicholas, whose manner was often curt, increasingly irritable, and towards the end of his life he became subject to spells of melancholy which were partly responsible for the persistent rumor that his death (February 18, 1855) was not caused by illness but was due to suicide by poisoning. Although available evidence does not warrant this conclusion, careful and reputable his-

---

[2] According to Presniakov, children born of this union were adopted by P. A. Kleinmichel, who in the closing years of the reign occupied at the court a position akin to that of Arakcheev under Alexander I. A contemporary observer, Baroness M. P. Fredericks, states in her memoirs that Madame Nelidov showed great tact, and never exploited her influence with the tsar for selfish or political ends. After Nicholas's death Madame Nelidov, at the request of Emperor Alexander II and the dowager empress, continued to reside at the imperial palace, and remained a member of Alexandra Fedorovna's intimate circle. She died in 1897.

torians (N. S. Stackelberg, Presniakov) believe that it cannot be entirely dismissed.

THE POLISH INSURRECTION, 1830–1831

Events in Poland, like the Decembrist rebellion, exercised a profound influence on Russia's destiny. The infringements of the Polish constitution by Alexander and the arrest in 1822 of the members of the secret Patriotic Society stimulated political unrest. In a manifesto published on his accession, Nicholas promised to uphold the Polish constitution; but it was generally known that he had little liking either for the Poles or for representative government, and was unalterably opposed to the reunion with the kingdom of the Lithuanian provinces which Polish nationalists regarded as a part of their lawful heritage. The investigation of the Decembrist rebellion disclosed the existence of a link between the reconstituted Polish Patriotic Society and the Russian Southern Society, and although the Polish underground movement was not involved in the events of December 14, 1825, a number of prominent Poles were arrested, among them Colonel Severin Krzyzanowski, the leader of the Patriotic Society. After a protracted investigation and much legalistic bickering, Nicholas agreed to have the accused men tried (in accordance with Article 152 of the Polish constitution) by a special court of Polish senators, a procedure advocated by the Grand Duke Constantine, who unexpectedly rallied to the defense of the Polish constitutional charter. The verdict rendered in June, 1828, was mild: Krzyzanowski was sentenced to three years in prison, other defendants received even lighter sentences, and some were acquitted. Although Nicholas believed that the accused were guilty of high treason and deserved the death penalty, he was prevailed upon to confirm the verdict (March, 1829), not, however, without severely reprimanding the Polish Senate for its leniency.[3] This incident added to the bitterness of Russo-Polish relations.

In May, 1828, Nicholas, accompanied by the empress and the heir apparent, paid a state visit to Warsaw; on May 12 he was crowned king of Poland and took the oath to support the constitution. He re-

---

[3] This constitutional procedure was used in the case of only eight of the accused Poles, all of them citizens of the kingdom. Twenty-four Polish defendants, subjects of Russia, were tried by the Russian Senate and received much more severe sentences.

turned to Warsaw a year later (May and June, 1830) for the meeting of the Polish diet. The legislative program submitted to the diet was strictly limited, and although a divorce bill sponsored by the government was voted down and sharp criticism of the administration developed in the commissions, the session was permitted to run its course and closed in June in a decorous fashion. There were numerous signs of restlessness and discontent, but little to indicate the imminence of an explosion.

Polish nationalistic and revolutionary agitation centered in underground clubs and associations of which the most important was the secret society organized in 1828 by Peter Wysocki, a young lieutenant in the guards and an instructor in the Polish Military Academy. The membership of the society was small, and consisted of cadets, army officers, university undergraduates, and intellectuals, among them the popular historian Joachim Lelewel, a former professor in the University of Vilna. These ardent nationalists were particularly alarmed by the unmistakable process of the integration of the Lithuanian provinces in the administrative framework of the empire, a policy which made rapid progress under the rule of Nicholas and indicated his determination to prevent the reunion of these territories with the kingdom. The more extreme elements in the society craved revolutionary action. Plans were made for insurrection and the seizure of the imperial family during the coronation and, again, during the session of the diet in May and June, 1830, but they were not carried out.

The French revolution of July, 1830, followed by the Belgian revolution in September, gave new strength to the Polish national movement and precipitated the conflict between Russia and Poland. Nicholas made feverish preparations for military intervention in western Europe and proposed to use the Polish army as a part of the Russian expeditionary force. No policy could have been more unpopular with the Poles, and insurrection appeared to their radical leaders as the only way to prevent Nicholas from forcing Poland to fight France and Belgium under the banners of legitimacy and reaction. Moreover, the police were on the track of the conspirators, and further delays might well have proved their undoing. In the evening of November 29, 1830, N.S., a small band of cadets and students invaded the Warsaw Belvedere Palace, residence of the Grand Duke Constantine, while a larger group led by Wysocki attacked the Russian cavalry barracks. Although the insurgents failed to capture Constantine or to dislodge the Russian troops, they succeeded in occupying a part of the city with the help of an excited populace to whom they distributed arms. A number of high Polish officials and generals were murdered. It is widely believed that Constantine, by a timely display of energy, might easily have suppressed the uprising in this early stage. He chose instead to withdraw from Warsaw with the loyal troops, among them some Polish regiments. The insurgents having no definite plan of action, the leadership of the revolutionary movement passed temporarily into the hands of the conservative Polish elements. Prince Ksavery Lubecki, Polish minister of finance since 1821, and *persona grata* with the Russian court, summoned the executive council, which was reinforced by Prince Adam Czartoryski and several other prominent Poles. On November 30, N.S., the executive council issued, in the name of Nicholas, an appeal condemning the events of November 29 and calling the population to maintain order. The object of the conservative Polish circles was to prevent a social revolution, to uphold the constitution of 1815, and to avoid war with Russia. General Joseph Chlopicki, a veteran of the Napoleonic wars, who was appointed commander in chief of the Polish army (December 3, N.S.) and two days later became military "dictator," did not believe in the possibility of a Polish victory. The radical elements did not support the modest program sponsored by Lubecki and his associates, and organized themselves into a Patriotic Society of which Lelewel was the president (December 1, N.S.). The struggle between the conservative and the radical factions continued unchecked until the defeat of the revolution, and largely determined its course.

The insurgent movement rapidly spread throughout the country. On December 1, N.S., the executive council was forced to drop some of its more unpopular members and to substitute for them men acceptable to liberal opinion. Two days later, however, Lubecki was compelled to resign, the executive council faded away, and was replaced by a provisional government of seven members headed by Czartoryski. In the provisional government the members of the Patriotic Society held the majority of seats. In the meantime Polish authorities negotiated with Constantine. The grand duke undertook not to attack Warsaw without direct orders and without giving forty-eight hours' notice; not to call the Lithuanian army corps which was under his command; and to recommend amnesty for the insurgents. He declined, however, to endorse the Polish demand for incorporation in the kingdom of the Lithuanian provinces. Constantine displayed on the whole a surprising magnanimity: he authorized the Polish regiments, which had accompanied him, to return to Warsaw, and on December 12, N.S., withdrew with the Russian troops behind the frontiers of the kingdom. Nicholas showed none of this kindly disposition towards the Poles. He refused to deal officially with the emissaries of the Polish government, among them Lubecki, who were sent to St. Petersburg, receiving them merely as private individuals. Mobilization orders were issued at once, and an imperial manifesto promised amnesty on the condition of immediate surrender (December 24, N.S.).

The extraordinary Polish diet which met in Warsaw on December 18, N.S., took a similarly uncompromising attitude. It proclaimed the insurrection a national movement, and voiced the determination of the Polish people to fight until they had achieved independence and the liberation of the Lithuanian provinces. Reconvened in January, 1831, the diet voted the dethronement of Nicholas and the deposition of the Romanov (January 25, N.S.). Chlopicki having in the meantime resigned his ephemeral "dictatorship," the diet formed a national government of five members under Czartoryski, the radical faction being represented by Lelewel. All hopes for a peaceful solution of the crisis having vanished, the issue was to be determined by force of arms. For the momentous struggle against Russia's military might Poland was singularly ill prepared. Torn by inner dissensions, the national government strove in vain to reconcile the aspirations of the landed aristocracy with the demands of the radical and liberal groups. The inescapable fact that the whole-hearted support of the peasantry was essential to the victory of the national cause led the diet to discuss in April, 1831, measures for the improvement of the status of the serfs, but the stubborn opposition of the landed interests forced the assembly to postpone decision until the end of the struggle. Nicholas showed better judgment, and in May, 1831, issued a decree lightening the burden of the peasants in the Polish provinces occupied by Russian troops. This measure was not without effect. The response of the Polish peasants to the insurgents' call to arms was lukewarm, and lends support to Friedrich Engels's description of the Polish insurrection as "a conservative revolution" (his speech of February 22, 1848, N.S.). Lack of national unity inevitably hampered the action of the Polish government and led to frequent changes in leadership. European Powers, especially France and England, approached by the insurgents, were prolific in expressions of sympathy for Poland but did nothing to help her. Austria and Prussia, fearing the repercussions of the insurrection in their own Polish provinces, were even more reserved. At the moment of supreme trial Poland had to face Russia alone.

Early in February, 1831, Field Marshal Dibich crossed the Polish border at the head of a Russian army some 120,000 strong. Although at the beginning of the campaign the insurgent forces were only half that number, Poland's military situation was not desperate. In March, according to the Polish historian S. Askenazy, the Poles had under arms 100,000 men. Moreover, the Russian Lithuanian corps (38,000) in the expeditionary force had a large proportion of Polish officers and privates whose loyalty to the Russian Crown was not above suspicion. The Poles, however, were handicapped by lack of artillery, arms, munitions, and experienced officers. The first encounter (battle of Stoczek, February 14, N.S.) was a victory for Poland, but it was followed by the crushing defeat of the insurgents at Grochow, near Warsaw (February 25, N.S.). Dibich, however, did not press his costly success (his losses were estimated at 10,000 men), and the fall of the Polish capital, which at the time was considered imminent, was delayed for six months. Fighting continued with intermittent success, the insurgents lending military support to anti-Russian uprisings in the provinces of Podolia, Volynia, Minsk, and Vitebsk, where Poland had many adherents among the nobility and the well-to-do classes. The peasantry remaining largely aloof, these uprisings were soon suppressed by Russian troops. Dibich's relative inaction, which brought upon him the displeasure of the emperor, had some justification in the heavy losses suffered by his army not only at the hands of the enemy, who fought with great courage, but also from epidemics. The Russian commander in chief himself died of cholera on June 10, N.S., and was replaced by Paskevich, recently recalled from the Caucasus. In the middle of July a Russian army 60,000 strong crossed the Vistula near the Prussian border and converged on Warsaw. In the meantime the Polish campaign in Lithuania had ended in a fiasco, and the position of the insurgents had become desperate. An uprising of radical elements in Warsaw (August 15, N.S.) led to the resignation of Czartoryski and the national government. Power passed to the hands of General John Krukoviecki and, three weeks later, to General Casimir Malachowski (September 7, N.S.). At that time the struggle was practically over. By the middle of August, Paskevich was at the gates of Warsaw, and when negotiations for the surrender of the city failed he took it by assault on September 8, N.S. Sporadic fighting continued for a few more weeks, the bulk of the Polish troops being forced into Austria and Prussia, where they were disarmed, while the remnants of the insurgent army were rounded up by the Russians. Early in October the insurrection was finally suppressed.

The retribution was gradual but thorough. An imperial manifesto of October 20, 1831, granted an amnesty to the insurgents, with the exception of the instigators of the uprising of November, the members of the revolutionary government and diet, and the army officers who emigrated after the fall of Warsaw. This act of clemency, however, received a restrictive interpretation: not a few of the Polish soldiers who returned to their homeland were assigned to distant garrisons, chiefly on Russia's Asiatic frontier. The amnesty did not apply to residents of the Lithuanian and Ukrainian provinces, which were not a part of the kingdom of Poland. A special court tried the cases of the principal participants in the insurrection. Most of the defendants having fled abroad, Nicholas in 1834 commuted 258 death sentences (among them those of Czartoryski and Lelewel) to perpetual banishment. The government decreed wholesale confiscation of the estates held by insurgent Polish noblemen. According to Z. Lensky, at least one-tenth of the land owned by the Polish nobility was confiscated in 1832. The bulk of these properties passed into Russian hands, chiefly through the distribution of entailed estates to Russian generals and high officials.

The Polish constitution of 1815 was superseded by the Organic Statute of February 14 (February 26, N.S.), 1832, which proclaimed the kingdom of Poland "an indivisible part" of the Russian empire; the Russian emperor therefore was no longer required to be crowned king of Poland.[4] Poland retained her civil liberties (freedom of worship and of the press, inviolability of person and property), her civil and criminal code, institutions of local government, the use of the Polish language in the courts, in the administration, and in the schools.

[4] The constitution of 1815 was not formally abrogated. The Polish statesman Marquis Wielopolski held in 1860 that the constitution had been merely modified by the Organic Statute but was not entirely put aside. A similar view was advanced in 1907 by Dmowski, a Polish deputy to the second Duma.

These promises, however, remained a dead letter. The Organic Statute provided for a Polish administration distinct from that of the rest of the empire. The government was to comprise two sets of institutions: one established by appointment of the Russian Crown, and the other by the vote of the local population. The chief administrative organ was an appointed executive council headed by the viceroy and consisting of higher officials. It was assisted by an appointed Polish state council which dealt, among other things, with the drafting of legislative measures and the preparation of the budget, but this in an advisory capacity, its decisions being subject to the approval of the Russian State Council. The law did not require that the members of the executive council and of the state council should be natives of the kingdom of Poland, and a number of Russians were actually appointed to both bodies. The lower administration consisted of a hierarchy of appointed boards and officials. The second and rather elaborate set of institutions provided by the Organic Statute—those elected by the people—need not be described here: it was not called into being until 1861–1862, and was almost immediately suppressed as a consequence of the Polish insurrection of 1863.

The failure of the imperial government to make effective the more liberal provisions of the Organic Statute was in harmony with the views held by Paskevich, Russian viceroy and practically dictator of Poland from 1832 to his death in 1856. Created prince of Warsaw in September, 1831, Paskevich, in whom Nicholas had unbounded confidence, was an outspoken opponent not only of Polish autonomy but even of the modest institutions provided by the act of 1832. "The best thing to do would be to merge the kingdom of Poland with the empire and to put it under the Russian administration," Paskevich wrote in 1847, and although he was not blind to the danger of excessive centralization it was in this spirit that he carried out his mandate. In 1837 the provincial government of Poland was reorganized on the Russian model. In 1841 the Polish state council was abolished and the functions of the Polish supreme court were taken over by the Russian Senate. The Polish Criminal Code introduced in 1846 was an almost verbatim translation of the Russian Code of 1845. In 1850 the customs barrier between Russia and Poland was removed and the Russian customs regime was applied to the kingdom. The imperial government took over the administration of Polish roads and means of transportation in 1846 and of the post office in 1851. Russian and French, but not Polish, were the languages used in the higher administrative agencies.

The program of Russification was applied to Polish schools, intellectual pursuits, and to the Church. The University of Vilna was closed in 1832, and its medical school in 1842. A similar fate befell the *lycée* of Kremenchug and the University of Warsaw. In 1839 was established the school region of Warsaw, subordinated directly to the Russian ministry of education. Secondary school instruction was conducted in the Russian language. The University of Kiev, founded in 1834 as a substitute for the disbanded higher school of Poland, ran into serious difficulties in 1837–1838 when it was suspected of carrying on subversive Polish propaganda. Closed for several months, it was permitted to reopen its doors only after a drastic purge which deprived it of half its faculty and almost its entire student body. Censorship was vigilant, imaginative, and brutal, and prohibited even the mention of such respected Polish authors as Adam Mickiewicz, Sygmunt Krasinski, and Lelewel. The Church, too, felt the heavy hand of the oppressors. A Russian Orthodox diocese of Warsaw was created in 1838. In 1841–1843 the estates of the Catholic Church were secularized and the Catholic clergy given fixed salaries. In 1842 the Vilna Catholic theological seminary was transferred to St. Petersburg. Government supervision of the activities of Catholic clerics became particularly stringent, but the chief effort of militant Orthodoxy was directed to the reunion of the Uniats with the Russian Church. Under the unscrupulous and energetic leadership of Joseph Semashko, bishop of Lithuania, this movement made rapid progress. A number of Uniat monasteries, among them the revered sanctuary of Pochaev, were taken over by the Orthodox Church, while other Uniat monasteries were closed. In 1839 Semashko, with the assistance of the Russian government and the Holy Synod, achieved his object, and the Uniats officially returned to the fold of the Russian Church.[5] In his report of May 24, 1851 (which contained no reference to the Organic Statute), Paskevich accurately summarized the results of his stewardship when he wrote that "after the insurrection the administration of the kingdom of

[5] The resulting frictions with the Holy See did not prevent the conclusion in 1847 of a concordat which regulated the position of Catholic institutions in Russian Poland.

Poland has been properly revised and brought in line, as far as possible, with the administrative order of the empire as a whole."

The broader consequences of the Polish insurrection were the strengthening of administrative centralization and of reactionary trends in Nicholas's domestic and foreign policies. The relentless anti-Russian agitation conducted by large and influential groups of Polish *émigrés* abroad, especially in Paris, was not without effect on the attitude of the European cabinets towards Russia, and the tsar's detestation of the Poles and his fear of a new Polish uprising had a part in charting the course of Russian foreign relations.

THE POLICE REGIME

Fear of revolution and distrust of any independent manifestation of public opinion, on the one hand, and the realization of the necessity of reforms, on the other, were the main, if conflicting, forces behind Nicholas's domestic policy. The emperor, as has already been stated, was aware of the inequities of Russia's political and social structure, but he believed that reforms should come exclusively from the Crown, without any participation of the community; changes, moreover, were to be introduced by imperceptible steps, under the guise of maintaining the existing order. Hence the extraordinary development of the agencies of the tsar's quasi-personal rule and the plethora of "secret committees" whose objects and activities were, or were supposed to be, unknown even to ministers, so as to prevent "disturbing rumors" and "unwarranted expectations." Attempt at reforms while retaining things as they are is akin to the squaring of the circle and, needless to say, Nicholas and his advisers failed to solve the problem. In his reign, in spite of the steady stream of legislative proposals, the social structure underwent no significant change and the governmental machine continued to function as it had before, except for marked tendencies towards centralization, bureaucratism, and oppressive police control, hardly novel departures in Russian administrative practice.

The legislative program and methods of the reign were influenced by the proceedings and recommendations of the so-called "committee of December 6, 1826," first in the long line of secret committees instituted by Nicholas. Count Victor Kochubey, former collaborator of Alexander I, was appointed chairman of the body, which consisted of five high officials, among them Speransky and Dibich. The committee was to study the legislative projects found among the papers of the late emperor and to draft proposals for the amelioration of practically every part of the machinery of government. To the latter task the committee devoted most of its time. It took cognizance of the grievances of the Decembrists summarized in Borovkov's report,[6] acknowledged that they contained "much truth" although the scope of the evils had been exaggerated, but suggested no adequate remedies. Speransky, long since cured of his reformatory zeal and radicalism, concurred in the statement that the committee's aim "was not the complete revision of the existing administrative order, but its improvement by certain partial changes and amendments." Not only did the committee remain faithful to this uninspiring program but, by using spurious logic and legalistic niceties, it developed amazing virtuosity in drafting proposals which, under the faint pretense of reform, left the situation unaltered. As appears from the tsar's annotations on the minutes of the committee, even Nicholas, for all his conservatism and dislike of change, was at times puzzled by the verbal trickery indulged in by his high-placed advisers. Professor Kizevetter shrewdly observes that the work of the committee followed a definite pattern: warm endorsement of some general principles (for instance, that of the permanency of tenure of the judiciary, or of separation of legislative, judicial, and executive functions, which at the time were exercised simultaneously and in a haphazard fashion by the State Council, the Senate and the committee of ministers [7]); more or less ingenious explanation of why the application of these principles was not feasible under Russian conditions; and proposed amendments of no practical consequence or value to existing legislation. Although bureaucracy was the very mainstay of the regime, Nicholas, unlike the representatives of enlightened absolutism, had little confidence in its miracle-working powers. When the committee of December 6 suggested the creation of supervisory boards in provinces and counties, the tsar mournfully argued that the required five hundred reliable officials could not be found in the empire. Since participation of the

---

[6] See p. 754.

[7] The committee of ministers, created by the law of Sept. 8, 1802, which substituted ministries for the former administrative colleges, was reorganized in 1811 (see p. 697). Its functions, however, were ill defined, and its position among the other institutions of central government was uncertain.

community in government was to be kept within narrow limits, and bureaucracy was not to be trusted, any attempt at reforms inevitably moved in a vicious circle.

The committee of December 6 completed its main work early in 1830. In addition to projects of purely technical reforms, it submitted proposals for the reorganization of the State Council, the Senate, the institutions of provincial government, and a bill defining the rights, duties, and privileges of the social groups or "estates" (*sostoiane* or *soslove*). None of these measures, however, were enacted into law, and only the bill on the "estates" was discussed in the State Council, where it met with much criticism. The July revolution in France and the Polish insurrection were soon to strengthen reactionary influences opposed in principle to any change, however innocuous. Nevertheless some of the proposals made by the committee of December 6 were taken up by subsequent committees, and the general trend of its deliberations set a pattern which was closely followed by legislation in the latter part of the reign.

Under the rule of Nicholas the formal structure of central government underwent no appreciable modifications. The new statute (*polozhenie*) of the State Council of April 15, 1842, followed closely the lines of its predecessor of 1810. The State Council retained its limited legislative powers, that is, each law was to be examined by that body although its decisions were not binding on the Crown. Yet in practice the authority of the State Council, which was never great, suffered further diminution. Although usurpations of the council's legislative functions by the committee of ministers, frequent under Alexander I, became less common, the actual drafting of legislative measures passed largely into the hands of secret committees. Moreover, the statute of the ministry of war issued in 1836 provided that enactments dealing with military matters were outside the jurisdiction of the State Council. Nicholas and some of his more forcible ministers (for instance, Kankrin) inclined to regard as an insult to autocracy the very discussion by the State Council of bills sponsored by the Crown. The tsar at times forwarded to the State Council proposed laws with the annotation that there should be no "superfluous debates," or with the curt order that he wished the measure approved. Under these conditions the State Council had little real influence on legislation, and acted merely as a rubber stamp. The Senate, for which Nicholas displayed marked contempt, fared no better. Without any change in its legal status, it ceased almost completely to exercise the function of administrative control which, according to the law, was one of its important duties. The committee of ministers, too, was relegated to a subordinate position. The numerous and detailed annotations made by the tsar on the minutes of the committee prove, according to the historian of that institution, Professor Seredonin, that "every question was decided by the tsar himself and that he rigorously insisted that the ministers should be merely the strict executors of his will, of his wishes. . . . One may say that Emperor Nicholas killed the committee of ministers, reduced it to the status of almost his private chancery." Changes in the structure of the ministries were perfunctory and need not be discussed here.

The most notable development in the field of central government was the mushroom growth of His Majesty's Own Chancery, which expanded its jurisdiction over an ever increasing range of activities formerly exercised by executive departments. Section I of the chancery dealt with questions requiring the tsar's personal attention and with the execution of imperial commands; in 1846 it was assigned the additional duty of control over the civil service. In 1826 Section II on codification and the notorious Section III in charge of state police were organized. In 1828 there was formed Section IV for the administration of the charitable and educational institutions bearing the name of the Dowager Empress Maria Fedorovna, who had died in October of that year. In 1836, in connection with a reform affecting the status of the state peasants, there was established Section V, which two years later was reorganized as the ministry of state domains. Section VI for the administration of Transcaucasia was added in 1843. The expansion of the sphere of activity of His Majesty's Own Chancery was rather a symptom of the tsar's attitude towards the organs of central government than the inauguration of novel administrative methods. Distrusting bureaucracy as much as he distrusted public opinion, Nicholas sought to solve problems that did not automatically fall within the purview of existing institutions by putting them in the hands of specially created agencies under his quasi-personal control. In fact, however, this control remained nominal, the vast sections of the chancery being essentially similar to the other organs of central government. In either case the will of the monarch was supreme, but it was actually felt only in deciding major issues or in matters such as the police, in which he took particular interest.

It was the same distrust of the government over which he presided that made Nicholas seek advice, not of the State Council, the official consultative legislative assembly, but of secret committees appointed *ad hoc*. Desire for secrecy led at times to grotesque situations. For instance, a secret committee created in 1839 to draft proposals for the improvement of the position of the peasantry was officially labeled "a committee for the equalization of local-government dues and charges in the western provinces." The object of this curious device was "to prevent suspicions and conjectures." The public was not only excluded from participation in legislation but was to remain ignorant of the fact that reforms were under discussion, until the tsar and his intimate advisers had reached a decision.

The framework of provincial administration, like that of central government, was retained with only minor changes, although the local government reforms of Catherine II had proved a failure, and in the first half of the nineteenth century provincial Russia was at the mercy of notoriously corrupt petty bureaucrats. Gogol, in *The Inspector-General, Dead Souls*, and other works, has traced a vivid and telling picture of this unhappy state of affairs. The abolition of the office of governor-general (except in specially designated areas) and the partial reorganization of agencies of local government (laws of 1837 and 1845) contributed to administrative centralization by enhancing the position of the governor of the province. While centralization and bureaucratism were the distinctive features of local administration during this period, there gradually came into being institutions dealing with economic needs, where representatives of the community took part side by side with appointed officials. Such were the provincial road commissions (1833), the provincial commissions on provisioning (1834), and committees on local dues and charges (1851). Although these agencies played a subordinate role and participation in their work by local representatives was largely perfunctory, they are often regarded as precursors of the local self-government act of 1864 (Kizevetter, Polievktov).

The slow growth of cities and towns and the decay of a system of municipal government that was ostensibly based on the act of 1785 but actually run by the police called for legislative action, especially under a regime that firmly believed in the salutary effect of administrative fiat. Various departments and special committees had for years busied themselves with plans for the betterment of city government. The meager outcome of their labor was the statute of the municipal government of the city of St. Petersburg (February 13, 1846). According to Kizevetter, this complex and characteristic enactment "was in certain respects a step backwards in comparison with the municipal act of 1785. . . . The system of autonomous municipal institutions it erected proved in practice nothing but a fiction" and merely emphasized "the triumph of bureaucratic tutelage, that cornerstone of the policy of this reign. . . . The municipal reform of 1846 was a purely paper reform."

Codification was the only field of government to which the regime of Nicholas made a constructive and lasting contribution. For almost two centuries innumerable commissions had wrestled with the task of revising and amending the Code (*Ulozhenie*) of 1649 but had failed to make any progress. In 1826 the commission on legislation established by Alexander I was reorganized as Section II of His Majesty's Own Chancery, and under the able guidance of Speransky its work was brought to fruition in 1833 with the publication of (1) the *Complete Collection of Laws of the Russian Empire*, which contained 35,993 enactments, from those embodied in the Code of 1649 to those issued previous to January 1, 1830 (fifty-one volumes), and (2) *The Code* (Svod) *of Laws of the Russian Empire*, a systematic collection, in fifteen volumes, of laws still in operation. Provisions were also made for the periodical amendment and revision of these collections, which are of inestimable value to courts, administrators, and historians even though the methods of the codifiers were not always above criticism. The *Complete Collection*, for instance, did not reproduce the enactments (to mention only a few) bearing on the constitutional limitations imposed on Empress Anne on her accession, or on the new order of succession to the throne established by her in October, 1740, as well as the manifesto issued by Catherine II after the murder of Peter III.[8] The Code, although modeled on the *Corpus Juris* of Justinian, suffered from lack of consistency and integration, omissions, and inclusion of documents other than legislative enactments. Speransky's original plan provided for the preparation of an entirely new Code, that is, a systematic collection of laws in force, with necessary revisions and amendments, but this proposal was vetoed by Nicholas on the ground that it was too theoretical and abstract. Nevertheless partial revisions of the Code along the lines advocated by Speransky were authorized, and

[8] See pp. 441–442, 448, 502.

resulted in the publication of a new Criminal Code (1845) and of several collections of a more specialized nature (army and navy regulations, certain types of taxation). The Lithuanian Statute (1588), formerly in force in the western territories, was abrogated in 1840 in the provinces of Kiev, Podolia, Volynia, Minsk, Vilna, and Grodno and in the Belostok district, and in 1843 in the provinces of Chernigov and Poltava. The operation of the Russian Code was thus extended to the western and southwestern provinces, marking another stage in the policy of unification and Russification characteristic of this period.

The state and security police, thoroughly reorganized and endowed with vast powers, formed the core of Nicholas's regime. In January, 1826, General Benckendorff, who five years earlier had warned Alexander of the activities of the secret societies, submitted to Nicholas a memorandum in which he argued that the Decembrist rebellion had convincingly proved the ineptness of the Russian police, and he urged the creation of a powerful centralized gendarmery under a special minister.[9] This plan appealed to the emperor, but instead of the proposed ministry there was organized Section III of His Majesty's Own Chancery (June 25, 1826, the tsar's birthday). Its official functions were those of the "higher police," or, more specifically, collection of information on counterfeiting, religious sects and dissenters, and "all happenings without exception"; control of foreigners and persons under police supervision; administration of places of detention for state prisoners; and deportation of "suspicious or undesirable (*vrednye*)" persons. Actually, the jurisdiction of Section III was far more comprehensive than is suggested by this list. A contemporary observer, N. M. Kolmakov, relates in his memoirs that Section III "very often assumed judicial functions and determined the guilt of persons in matters which had nothing to do with public safety." M. Lemke, author of an admirable and well documented study on Section III, holds that "there was no aspect of Russian life that would escape its control." The creators of this all-powerful police regime imagined that it would not only ensure public safety but would eradicate corruption and maladministration and bring reward and happiness to the

[9] According to the Decembrist Prince Volkonsky, the idea of a Russian gendarmery was suggested to Benckendorff by the example of France, where he spent some time at the Russian embassy; he is said to have made proposals to this effect in the closing years of Alexander's reign. The term "gendarme" was first introduced in Russia in 1792 by Emperor Paul, but the troops whose members were so designated played no important part until the accession of Nicholas.

law-abiding subjects of the tsar. The chief aim, however, was to avoid the repetition of the events of December 14, 1825, and, by nipping in the bud subversive activities, to prevent well meaning people from being led astray. To achieve this object, according to the conservative historian Shilder, the government "had to know what was going on among the people, what were their thoughts, what they talked about, what occupied them; . . . it became necessary to penetrate into men's hearts and most secret thoughts." This melancholy task had been pursued in the past by the *oprichnina* of Ivan IV and by a long line of police agencies since the days of Peter I. It need not be emphasized that they merely bred arbitrariness, exploitation, and the worst abuses.

Section III operated through two sets of agents: the gendarmery and secret informers. The gendarmery was a uniformed military force under the orders of the director of Section III, who was also in charge of the emperor's military establishment. The whole of Russia was divided into five (later eight) gendarmery districts commanded by their own officers. The government endeavored, not without success, to enhance the prestige of this branch of the police by enrolling among its officers men of good education and representatives of some of Russia's most distinguished families. The network of secret agents was presumably large, and included not only men and women drawn from every stratum of society but even school children. The real source of the power enjoyed by Section III was the exceptional position of its director. Benckendorff (created a count in 1832) held that office from 1826 to his death in 1844; he was succeeded by Count (later Prince) A. F. Orlov. Both were Nicholas's intimate friends on whom he showered marks of his affection. The director of Section III was a member of the committee of ministers but, according to Butenev, was "actually a kind of prime minister," and the institution over which he presided, to quote Herzen, was "outside and above the law." [10] This agency was the principal channel through which Nicholas exercised his personal rule. He scrutinized diligently police reports; although these often failed to disclose what was in the hearts and thoughts of his unhappy subjects, they invited arbitrary interfer-

[10] Section III retained the control of the police for over half a century. In 1880 it was reorganized as the department of the police (*departament politsii*) which survived until 1917.

ence with sometimes purely private matters and brought about Draconian verdicts against which there was no appeal.

Nicholas, steeped in the military tradition, liked to refer to his vast empire as his "command." Members of his military establishment, his aides-de-camp, and the generals who had distinguished themselves on the parade ground and whom he knew personally appeared to him eminently fitted for the highest offices of state. He put them in charge of the Holy Synod, the post office, the ministries of the interior, finance, and communications. A cavalry general, Prince Menshikov, for years controlled the navy. The same small circle of army officers with court connections was freely drawn upon to supersede the civilian authorities as special emissaries of the Crown. Disregard for the methods of government provided by law, the omnipotence of the police, its close identification with the emperor, and predominance of soldiers in the administration gave the era of Nicholas its peculiar character of a quasi-personal and quasi-military dictatorship of the tsar.

CHAPTER XXX

NICHOLAS I

Social and Economic Conditions

THE NOBILITY, THE PEASANTS, AND THE BURGHERS

The pusillanimity so conspicuous in all attempts of Nicholas's government at constitutional and administrative reforms was again in evidence in its approach to the urgent question of rejuvenating Russia's antiquated social structure. Relations between the tsar and the nobility were far from harmonious, the Decembrist rebellion having produced an estrangement. Nicholas was suspicious, sulky, and vindictive, an attitude that was reciprocated by the more liberal groups among the *dvoriane*. Yet, by the compelling force of circumstances the two dominating elements of the Russian state—the Crown and the landed nobility—were irresistibly drawn together. In moments of emergency the tsar spoke of the *dvorianstvo* as "the mainstay of the throne" and proclaimed himself the unwavering defender of its interests; indeed, he occasionally described himself as "first among the noblemen" and "one of St. Petersburg's landed proprietors." The majority of the noble landowners, confronted with an acute economic crisis, blindly sought salvation in a return to "the good old days," and, while stubbornly opposing any innovation that might be interpreted as inimical to its narrow class interests, looked to the emperor for the preservation and expansion of its "ancient" privileges. In spite of mutual animosity and suspicion, the Crown and the landed nobility were forced into an uneasy partnership by the common fear of the masses and of a repetition, perhaps on an even larger scale, of the Peasant War of 1773–1774.

The Charter of the Nobility (1785) notwithstanding, Nicholas held, like Emperor Paul, that the primary duty of the *dvorianstvo* was to serve the state as army officers or civil servants. The nobility was to retain its privileges but was not, as a group, to play any independent political part. The policy of the government, although never clearly formulated, tended to achieve a double object: (1) the further integration of the organs of the corporate self-government of the nobility with administrative services; and (2) the raising of the social status of the nobility and the impartment to its corporate organs of a more exclusive character. The chief measure for the advancement of these aims was the statute (*polozhenie*) of December 6, 1831, on the corporations of the nobility. The immediate reason for the publication of this enactment was the vagueness of many provisions of the 1785 Charter and the lack of interest on the part of noble landowners in the activities of their corporate institutions. The statute of 1831 redefined, with a greater degree of precision, the functions of the provincial and district assemblies of the nobility and the procedure for the election of various officials. The number of such officials was increased, and they were given the same status (promotion in the bureaucratic hierarchy, decorations, and so on) as the members of the civil service. At the same time the control of the provincial governor over the corporate institutions, as well as over the officials they elected, was strengthened, and both were brought under the supervision of the ministry of the interior. However, the right of the nobility to present petitions was expanded to include all matters affecting local interests, even if those of the *dvoriane* were not directly involved.

The statute of 1831 raised the property qualifications entitling the noble landowners to participate in corporate activities. The right of direct vote was made conditional on the ownership of not less than one hundred male serfs or 3,000 dessiatines [1] of land. The 1785 Charter provision making the attainment of Rank Fourteenth in the civil service (or a corresponding rank in the army) a prerequisite for voting was retained. In the case of noblemen who had reached Rank Five in the bureaucratic hierarchy (or the rank of colonel in the army), the property qualifications were lowered, by a law of 1836, to five male serfs or 150 dessiatines of land. Other *dvoriane* owning not less than five male serfs or 150 dessiatines voted through representatives, being entitled collectively to one vote per each hundred serfs or 3,000 dessiatines of their aggregate holdings. Their less fortunate brethren who failed to satisfy the above property requirements were disfran-

---

[1] One dessiatine = 2.7 acres.

chised. This legislation, the object of which was to enhance the prestige of the corporations by excluding the impoverished *dvoriane*, did not succeed in injecting new life into moribund corporate institutions. In spite of fines (25 to 250 rubles) for non-participation, without good reason, in the assemblies, absenteeism, according to Kizevetter, was prevalent in the reign of Nicholas, and the corporations remained a mere parody of self-government.

The more aristocratically minded landowners had long agitated for the repeal of the provision of the Table of Ranks (1722) conferring the title of nobility on civil servants and army officers who had reached a specified rank. The committee of December 6, 1826, endorsed this demand and recommended that *anoblissement* should be not a matter of routine but a distinct mark of imperial favor. The government, however, rejected this view and chose the road of mild compromise. By virtue of a manifesto of June 11, 1845, hereditary nobility was to be conferred thenceforth on civil servants who had reached Rank Five in the bureaucratic hierarchy, instead of Rank Eight as provided by the Table of Ranks, while advancement to Rank Nine brought merely the title of "personal" nobility.[2] Government service thus remained the chief source of *anoblissement*, although opportunities for achieving the coveted status were somewhat restricted. Another old wish of those *dvoriane* who were alarmed by the breaking up of large estates and the resulting impoverishment of noble families was partly gratified by a law of 1845 prescribing rules for the creation of entails (*zapovednyia imeniia*). Since no estate could be entailed unless it comprised at least 400 peasant households and 10,000 dessiatines of improved (*udobnoi*) land and brought an annual revenue of not less than 12,000 silver rubles, the application of this measure was limited. The *dvoriane* won some other minor concessions. By a law of 1829 they were given special facilities for promotion from non-commissioned to commissioned ranks in the army. The school policy, as will appear later, was designed to perpetuate the class principle by providing education for the children of each "estate" according to what was deemed to be their social status. Finally, impoverished nobles were settled, with government assistance, on Crown lands east of the Volga and in Siberia.

These concessions to the nobility were accompanied by outright infringements of the privileges granted by the Charter of 1785. In

[2] See p. 571. Army ranks entitling their holders to either hereditary or "personal" nobility were correspondingly raised.

1831 the government forbade the sending abroad of men under eighteen to study in foreign schools. In 1834 the length of foreign residence permitted to the *dvoriane* was limited to five years, and in 1851 the term was reduced to three years. (The term of lawful residence abroad for the non-*dvoriane* was, respectively, three and two years.) A law of 1837, repeated in 1840, barred the young nobles from service in central institutions unless they had completed a specified term in provincial administrations. Children of hopelessly impoverished noble families were sent to the schools for commoners, and young *dvoriane* unable to support themselves and untrained for government service were drafted into the army and deprived of their title of nobility.

The real issue between the Crown and the nobility, however, was serfdom. Count Uvarov, the ablest ideologist of the regime, expressed the views of the conservative elements when he held that "serfdom is closely tied up with autocracy and even with the preservation of imperial unity (*edinoderzhavie*): they are two parallel forces which have grown together; both spring from the same historical source and follow the same law of development." Uvarov described serfdom as "a tree which has taken deep root—it protects (*oseniaet*) the Church and the throne and cannot be uprooted." "Political religion has its dogmas, immutable like those of Christianity," Uvarov argued in 1832. "With us they are autocracy and serfdom; why touch them when, fortunately for Russia, they have been preserved by a powerful hand?" Nicholas, although he placed Uvarov and other inveterate enemies of emancipation (for instance, Prince Alexander Menshikov) at the top of the bureaucratic hierarchy. did not fully share this view. As has already been stated, he believed that serfdom was a "flagrant evil" but that the time was not ripe for emancipation and that premature action would lead to the worst disasters. Little wonder, therefore, that while the discussion of the "peasant question" was kept alive in both bureaucratic and liberal circles, the tangible results achieved were practically nil. The general tone of official deliberations was set by the committee of December 6, 1826, which ruled out emancipation and limited itself to proposals for the betterment of the position of the serfs. These proposals were not immediately acted upon, but some of them were taken up later as a basis for discussion by specially appointed bodies. In the following two decades nine successive secret committees wrestled hopelessly with measures designed to benefit the serfs without infringing on the prerogatives of the serfowners. Any proposal tinged however lightly with liberalism invariably met with stubborn opposition and was either shelved or emasculated to a degree that made it meaningless. Among the outspoken opponents of change were the emperor's brothers, Constantine and Michael, and his son, the future tsar-liberator.

The seemingly most potent measure of the reign was the law of April 2, 1842, on the "obligated" peasants (the Russian term *obiazannye krestiane* is as awkward as its English equivalent), which was inspired by, and bore a close resemblance to, the law of February 20, 1803, on the "free farmers."[3] The law of 1842 was sponsored by P. D. Kiselev (created count in 1839), one of Nicholas's few collaborators who believed not only in the necessity of emancipation but also in the grant to the peasants of adequate land allotments. A memorandum submitted by Kiselev and a draft based on it were discussed for two and a half years by a secret committee appointed in 1839 and by the State Council. The law of 1842 permitted noble landowners to enter with their serfs into voluntary agreements transferring to the use of the bondsmen land allotments in return for suitable compensation. The law provided that the landowners were to retain title to the land so transferred, but left the determination of the size of the allotments and of the obligations of the peasants (money payments, deliveries in kind, and services) to the agreement of the parties. Kiselev's original draft contained provisions defining the size of the allotments and the compensation to which the owners were entitled, but these proposals were severely criticized and were dropped in the course of the discussion. Although the law could not have been more innocuous from the serfowners' point of view, it created much uneasiness among the landed nobility as a possible forerunner of emancipation, while the government took extraordinary precautions to prevent anticipated peasant disturbances. Both apprehensions proved equally unfounded. The country remained calm and the law practically a dead letter. It was rarely applied, and by the end of Nicholas's reign the number of male serfs transferred into the class of "obligated" peasants was only 24,708.

Other legislation dealing with the serfs was equally paltry. Sales of serfs without land by public auction in settlement of private debts, and all sales involving the breaking up of peasant families were prohibited by a law of May 2, 1833. In 1841 noblemen who did not own

[3] See p. 717.

populated estates were barred from purchasing serfs without land. A law of June 12, 1844, allowed landowners to emancipate their household serfs (*dvorovye*) [4] without land by entering with them into private agreements the contents of which, however, were not regulated. The power of the landowners to inflict punishments on their servile population was redefined in 1845 and 1846 without losing anything in severity. A decree of November 8, 1847, granted the serfs the privilege of buying their freedom if the estate on which they lived was sold at public auction; two years later, under the pressure of ultra-conservative opinion, the exercise of this right was made subject to the approval of the bankrupt owner. By virtue of a law of March 3, 1848, serfs were allowed to acquire landed properties, but only with the approval of their lord; they were, moreover, denied the right to take action for the recovery of such properties purchased previous to the passing of the law. With the outbreak of the revolution of 1848 in Europe, even these meager efforts to improve the position of the servile population petered out.

The reluctance of Nicholas and his advisers to intervene in the relations between landowners and serfs was put aside in the case of the western provinces annexed from Poland, where the landed nobility was largely Polish and the peasantry Russian. The weakening of the power of the landowners, in this case, was a part of the general policy of Russification followed by St. Petersburg after the insurrection of 1830–1831. There was, however, no question of emancipation, and the method chosen was that of "inventories" or regulations determining the mutual rights and obligations of owners and serfs. The introduction of inventories in Russia proper was often suggested, but it was invariably vetoed on the ground that it would constitute an intolerable interference with the prerogative of the landed nobility, whom Nicholas, in his more mellow moments, flatteringly described as "my police" (speech of March 21, 1848). To the former Polish provinces these considerations did not apply. Sponsored by D. G. Bibikov, an ardent Russian nationalist who was appointed governor-general of the southwestern provinces in 1838, and by Kiselev, the introduction of the inventories proved to be an extremely difficult matter. The methods adopted were at first different in the southwestern provinces (Kiev, Volynia, and Podolia), on the one hand, and in the northwestern provinces (Vilna, Grodno, Kovno, and Minsk) and the White Rus-

[4] See p. 572.

sian provinces (Vitebsk and Mogilev), on the other. An order of April 15, 1844, provided for the establishment in the provinces just mentioned of committees of appointed officials and elected representatives of the landed nobility for the preparation of inventories for each estate. In June, 1846, however, Bibikov informed the government that the inventories submitted by the committees of his governorship-general were so heterogeneous and unreliable as to be worthless. Comprehensive rules for the preparation of the inventories were then issued by the government on May 26, 1847—they were revised and amended on December 29, 1848—and were put into effect in the southwestern provinces. In the other Polish provinces, however, the inventories prepared by local committees were not challenged, and were gradually put into operation in 1845, 1846, and 1847. In August, 1852, Bibikov became minister of the interior, and in December he endeavored to extend the application of the inventory rules of 1847-1848 to all western provinces. The protest of the northwestern and White Russian landowners, supported by the heir to the throne, led to the reopening of the question, and the revision of the inventories in this area was ordered in April, 1854. New regulations for White Russia were issued in May, 1855; but the revision of the inventory rules for the northwest was never completed, and these provinces retained, until the emancipation, the less stringent inventory regime established by local committees in 1845-1847.

The introduction of the inventories created great agitation both among landowners and among serfs, although it is a moot question whether it eased the lot of the bondsmen. Yuri Samarin, an exceptionally keen and well qualified contemporary observer, maintained that while both the methods used by Bibikov and the inventory rules of 1847-1848 for which he was largely responsible were objectionable and crude, the reform as a whole was favorable to the serfs. A. I. Koshelev, another authoritative contemporary observer, took a more pessimistic view. In a report submitted to Emperor Alexander II in 1858, Koshelev wrote that the inventories unfortunately "did not justify expectations; the landowners retained practically unimpaired their powers over the serfs, the peasants made little use of the safeguards offered to them, and only the police are kept busy and collect no mean profits."

The general picture of agriculture in the decades preceding the emancipation is by no means clear, but most authorities agree that

Nicholas I

farming was passing through a severe crisis, although they differ widely as to causes. The expansion of the domestic and foreign market is said to have undermined an economy based on serfdom. Agricultural production was, no doubt, stimulated by increasing exports of farm produce, especially grain; yet the importance of this factor has often been exaggerated.

Volume of Grain Exports, 1826–1860

Years	Yearly average in thousands of poods *
1826–1830	23,950
1831–1835	18,469
1836–1840	28,831
1841–1845	27,205
1846–1850	51,211
1851–1855	45,396
1856–1860	69,254

* One pood = 36 lbs. = 0.016 ton.

As in the earlier period, the sharp fluctuation in the volume of grain exports was due to wars, poor harvests, and changes in the tariff policy of Russia and the importing countries. Russian export dues on grain were not substantially reduced until the 1850's, and they were finally abolished in 1865. England being the chief importing country, English Corn Laws were a factor of paramount importance, and it was only after their repeal in 1846 that the Russian grain exports increased briskly from 27 million poods in 1841–1845 to 51 million in 1846–1850, that is, by almost 90 per cent. The principal grain exported was wheat, and the bulk of this trade went through the ports of the Black Sea and the Sea of Azov, especially Odessa. Although the volume of grain export increased threefold from 1826–1830 to 1856–1860, it was still only a small fraction of domestic production: 0.6 per cent to 2.5 per cent in the 1830's, 2.7 per cent in 1851–1855, and 5.1 per cent in 1856–1860.[5]

The domestic market for agricultural produce, like that for exports, expanded but slowly. The social and legal structure of Russia, with

[5] M. N. Pokrovsky, dean of Soviet historians until his death in 1932, has grossly overemphasized the importance of grain exports and grain prices as factors in the breakdown of serfdom. His views are properly repudiated by recent Soviet historiography.

the forcible attachment of the vast majority of the population—serfs and state peasants—to rural districts, was inimical to the development of urban life. In 1851, according to Miliukov's widely quoted figures, urban population did not exceed 3.5 million, or 7.8 per cent.[6] In a report for the same year the ministry of state domains estimated that only one-fourth of the total yield of grain reached the market, one-eighth of this amount representing exports. Grain producers, moreover, were handicapped by the absence of roads and by the instability of grain prices, which from year to year varied within a surprisingly wide range, and also according to the remoteness of producing areas from centers of consumption and their accessibility to southern ports. Nevertheless there developed gradually a fairly steady demand for agricultural produce in the less fertile and more industrialized northern and central provinces that drew their supplies from the southern black-soil regions. This process, however, was slow, and it is believed that supply exceeded demand and was largely responsible for the stagnation of agriculture and the financial difficulties of the landowners.[7]

A small minority of the progressive *dvoriane* sought a way out in the improvement of agricultural technique. The Moscow Agricultural Society, its journal, and similar organizations in the provinces displayed marked interest in up-to-date methods of cultivation. On a few estates the three-field system, prevalent in Russia in its most primitive form, was replaced by more diversified rotations of crops. Attempts were made to use better seeds, to combine production with processing, to introduce agricultural machinery of foreign or domestic make. Among the more important developments was the rapid growth of the sugar industry and the spreading of sheep breeding in the southwest and the south. With the exception of sugar refineries, however, ventures into rationalization were notably unsuccessful and almost invariably ended in heavy losses for those who put their faith in technical progress.

[6] Kornilov holds that the above percentage is incorrect and should read 5 per cent. It will be remembered, on the other hand, that Miliukov's figures were challenged as unduly low by Rashin, a Soviet economist. Rashin estimates the urban population in 1856 at 5.7 million.

[7] The above explanation, although widely accepted, is not universally held. The distinguished historian and economist P. B. Struve, for instance, argued in his study *Krepostnoe khoziaisvo* (Economics of Serfdom) (Moscow, 1913) that farming experienced great prosperity in the 1850's and that emancipation therefore was not an economic necessity.

Rationalization demanded investments, but the only capital at the disposal of the majority of landowners was that represented by their serfs, who on a rationally organized farm were a liability rather than an asset. Moreover, the instability of agricultural prices and the restricted capacity of the domestic and foreign market offered little guarantee that the heavy outlays involved would bring financial reward. The more clear-sighted landowners were gradually driven to the conclusion that serfdom was incompatible with economic progress and with their own interests. In isolated instances estates were cultivated by hired labor, but these were rare exceptions.

The alternative to emancipation and improved agricultural technique was the more thorough and ruthless exploitation of servile labor, a solution that commended itself to the vast majority of the landowners. There was a pronounced tendency, especially in the black-soil provinces, to expand the area directly farmed by the owner, either by bringing under cultivation meadows and waste land, or by encroaching on the allotments of the serfs, much to the latter's detriment. The proportion of landless household serfs increased between 1835 and 1859 from 4.1 per cent to 6.8 per cent of the total servile population. There also developed the practice of removing serfs from their allotments and converting them into landless laborers (*mesiachniki*, or "monthly workers"). Not only were the allotments of the serfs reduced but the burden of their payments became greater. The once clear division of serfs into those paying annual tributes (*obrok*) and those performing services (*barshchina*) lost its former sharpness. In the 1850's about one-sixth of the serfs were subject to a mixed regime, that is, they were required both to make money payments and to perform services. It is believed (Semevsky, Ignatovich, Picheta), although information on this and other aspects of serfdom is unreliable and fragmentary, and precise computation is precluded by the uncertain value of the ruble, that between the 1820's and the 1850's the average amount of the *obrok* increased considerably, perhaps by as much as 50 per cent. The law of 1797 which required that serfs under *barshchina* should not work for their masters more than three days a week was generally disregarded. The expansion of the grain trade added to the serfs' tribulations. In the 1840's, according to the contemporary observer Zablotsky (quoted by Kulisher), some 800,000 serfs in the summer and as many as 3,000,000 in the winter were employed in transporting grain by road. There is ample evidence of growing exploitation and increasing impoverishment of the peasantry. As in earlier decades it led to agrarian disturbances. The ministry of the interior reported 556 uprisings in rural districts between 1826 and 1854, but this figure comprises merely the more serious outbreaks and fails to give a true picture.[8]

It is not surprising that the landed nobility, as a group, derived little economic advantage from the misery of the peasantry, its unwilling partner in the common enterprise. Superficially the position of the nobility was one of great power. In 1859, on the eve of the emancipation, 102,870 nobles owned 30.6 per cent of the territory of Russia. Yet the vast majority of the landowners were men of modest means and humble social status, and practically all of them suffered from financial stringency. Estates of less than one hundred male serfs represented 76.2 per cent of the total, and those of over five hundred male serfs, 3.6 per cent. The mortgage debt accumulated rapidly and foreclosures were common. It was the small proprietors who experienced the greatest difficulties. Between 1835 and 1859 the proportion of estates of twenty or fewer male serfs declined from 53.5 per cent to 41.0 per cent, that is, over 12 per cent of the noble landowners were presumably forced to dispose of their land. The number of male serfs, too, declined from 10.9 million in 1835 to 10.7 million in 1859.

The slight decline in the number of serfs was more than offset by the increase in that of the state peasants, which rose from 10.6 million in 1835 to 12.8 million in 1859.[9] Euphemistically described by the Code of 1833 as a "free rural 'estate'" (*svobodnoe selskoe sostoianie*), the state peasants were for all practical purposes in bondage to the state, and the defenseless prey of petty officials. Emperor Paul's measures for the introduction of self-government among the state peasants (law of August 7, 1797) and for the promotion of their welfare failed to achieve their object, and in the 1830's the legal and economic status of this large and growing group of the people was as unhappy as it was

---

[8] In 1842, for instance, the ministry of the interior registered one peasant uprising in the province of Saratov, while according to local data the number of disturbances was thirty-seven.

[9] See p. 576. The total population, both male and female, was estimated at 60 million in 1835 and at 74 million in 1859. These figures, as well as those given in the text, are at best crude approximations. The divergency in the statistics quoted by the authorities is distressing. S. A. Kniazkov, for instance, in the authoritative publication *Velikaia reforma* (The Great Reform), II, 209, gives the number of male state peasants in 1833 as 7.6 million. Figures in the text are taken from G. T. Robinson, *Rural Russia Under the Old Regime* (New York, 1932), p. 63.

chaotic. The accumulation of large arrears in payments due from the state peasants was among the reasons that made Nicholas turn his attention to their plight. Moreover, here was an opportunity to tackle the peasant question without infringing on the privileges of the nobility. In 1834 General Kiselev, freshly returned from Moldavia and Wallachia, where he had established a *de facto* Russian protectorate, submitted to the tsar a comprehensive plan of reform dealing with the state peasants. After some fruitless discussion by a secret committee, the execution of his proposal and the administration of the state peasants were entrusted to the newly formed Section V of His Majesty's Own Chancery (April, 1836), a department which was soon reorganized as the ministry of state domains (December, 1837). Kiselev was appointed head of the new ministry, an office he held for eighteen years. An enemy of serfdom, he aimed at the creation of a class of rural freemen, organized into self-governing, economically prosperous communities, a class with which the emancipated serfs would eventually merge. But Kiselev was also a bureaucrat to the core, and although he had keen sympathy with the peasantry and had acquired good first-hand knowledge of its needs, the regime he instituted was hardly less tyrannical than the one that preceded it. The original regulations for the administration of state peasants (April 30, 1838) and related documents comprised over four thousand articles and invited both evasion and abuse of power. The organs of village self-government they created were subordinated to appointed officials, especially the police. Some of the measures inaugurated by Kiselev, however, benefited the peasantry. A cadastral survey completed in 1855 permitted the reassessment of the tax and recruitment obligations on a more equitable basis. The attempt at improving the economic status of the state peasants by equalizing the size of their allotments (this involved colonization and resettlement) was only partly successful, and at the time of the emancipation the inequality in the size of the holdings was still considerable. The welfare program—erection of fireproof buildings, medical assistance, promotion of temperance and education—brought no striking results. Yet it was claimed by the ministry of state domains that in the eighteen years of Kiselev's administration the number of schools under its jurisdiction increased from sixty to 2,551 and the number of students from 1,800 to 111,000, including 18,000 girls. This was certainly a commendable achievement even though the number of students remained insignificant as a percentage of the number of state peasants. The peasantry showed little appreciation of the reform, and discontent found its expression in agrarian disturbances followed by customary punitive expeditions. A characteristic instance is found in the "potato riots" provoked by the forcible introduction of a crop the benefits of which the peasants at the time were unable to perceive.

Little need be said about the burghers. The only measure deserving notice was the Law of February 10, 1832, which instituted the "estate," or social class, of "honorary citizens" (*pochetnye grazhdane*), a quaint group designed to occupy an intermediate position between the common herd and the nobility. The law of 1832 was the adaptation, with substantial modifications, of a proposal made by the committee on December 6, 1826, recommending the abolition of government service as a source of *anoblissement*. The latter recommendation, it will be remembered, was not enacted into law, and honorary citizenship, as established in 1832, was primarily intended to enhance the prestige of the merchants. Honorary citizenship was either hereditary or personal, and brought with it exemption from recruitment, from the poll tax, and from corporal punishment. It was conferred, under conditions specified in the law, on merchants, scientists, artists, university graduates, government employees who did not reach a rank entitling them to nobility, and on children of "personal" nobles and of the clergy. The law of 1832 served no useful purpose and merely added to the complexities of Russia's cumbersome social structure.

FINANCE, RAILWAYS, COMMERCE, AND INDUSTRY

Russian financial and economic policies in the second quarter of the nineteenth century were strongly influenced by the views and proclivities of Count Kankrin, minister of finance from 1823 to 1844. It was only during the administration of his successors, F. P. Vronchenko and P. F. Brok (appointed, respectively, in May, 1844, and in April, 1852), that the St. Petersburg government, under the impact of the Crimean War and of the liberal ideas that were gaining ground in western Europe, especially in England, gradually departed from Kankrin's cautious and ultra-conservative program. The principal financial measure of the reign was the attempt to stabilize the ruble and to eliminate depreciated paper currency, that plague of Russian finance since the days of Catherine II. The reform was facilitated by the general financial policies pursued by Kankrin with great tenacity. While he did nothing to improve the budget situation, which remained chaotic until 1863. Kankrin was a firm believer in the homely and unpopular virtue of economy and had a wholesome dislike for the piling up of national debt, especially foreign debt; and although he was compelled by the force of events (the Persian and the Turkish wars, the Polish insurrection, famines, and, later, the building of railways) to conclude several foreign loans, foreign borrowing played during his administration a relatively minor part. Kankrin, moreover, resisted all pressure to use the printing press to meet extraordinary expenditure, and he maintained the volume of paper currency (assignats) in circulation at its 1823 level, that is, 596 million rubles. Simultaneously he took measures to encourage the flow of precious metals to the treasury. Reversing earlier regulations, silver (1827–1830) and gold (1833) were made legal tender for all payments due the government. In spite of the fact that the ratio of the assignats to silver and gold was officially determined, it was subject in practice to wide fluctuations which made financial transactions uncertain, and hampered domestic and foreign trade. The reform of 1839–1843 had for its object the remedy of this situation. The silver ruble, under the terms of a manifesto of July 1, 1839, became the basic monetary unit; the assignats were retained as legal tender but they could be accepted only at the official parity of 3.50 assignat rubles to one silver ruble. In 1841 there was issued a new paper currency, the treasury notes (*kreditnye bilety*), redeemable on call. A manifesto of June 1, 1843, decreed the compulsory exchange of the assignats for treasury notes (renamed *gosudarstvennye bilety*) which were backed not only by "all the resources of the state" but also by a special reserve fund of precious metals for not less than one-sixth of the notes in circulation, a ratio deemed adequate to ensure their convertibility. The retirement of the assignats reduced the volume of paper currency from 596 million rubles to 170 million. The later part of the reform, especially the compulsory retirement of the assignats, was the emperor's own idea, and was enacted over the opposition of Kankrin, who was soon forced to resign. The legislation of 1839–1843, by failing to establish an independent bank of issue and by leaving the management of the new paper currency in the hands of the treasury, invited disaster. The temptation to use the reserve fund for purposes other than those for which it was intended proved irresistible, and the printing press was soon as busy as ever. By 1848 the volume of treasury notes increased to

310 million rubles, by 1855 to 356 million, and by 1858 to 733 million. Convertibility was restricted in 1854 and was soon abandoned altogether. In 1855 treasury notes were quoted below official parity. Russia had returned to the regime of inconvertible paper money, which was maintained until the adoption of the gold standard in 1897.

Almost as unrewarding was the attempt to bring some order into the administration of the revenue from spirits. The farming out of the tax on spirits, prevalent in the eighteenth century, had the advantage of simplifying the task of the tax-collecting agencies, which under this system had to deal with a relatively small number of tax farmers (*otkupshchiki*). The financial and social effects of this method, however, proved most unsatisfactory. It created for the tax farmers a quasi-monopolistic position which they grossly abused, to the detriment both of the consumers and of the treasury. In 1817 the sale of spirits was made a state monopoly, but the change merely led to widespread corruption and to the eventual decline of revenue. Kankrin, although aware of the pitfalls of tax farming, urged its reintroduction on the curious ground that the excessive and often illicit gains of the tax farmers were likely to benefit industry, while spoliation and embezzlement by government officials, characteristic of the state monopoly, were a net loss. This argument did not fail to appeal to Nicholas, and in 1827 the state monopoly was discarded in favor of the farming-out method. The reform brought an increase in revenue, but its pernicious effects soon became so apparent that the question was reopened in 1841. Certain technical changes introduced in 1846 failed to improve the situation, and after further deliberations it was decided in 1854 to abandon the farming-out system and to substitute for it free distillation and sale of spirits, subject to the payment of excise. This measure, however, was not made effective until 1863.

It is unnecessary to deal at length with public debt. In spite of Kankrin's aversion to borrowing, the national debt continued to grow; but the bulk of the indebtedness was incurred after his resignation— largely as a consequence of Russia's intervention in European affairs, the Hungarian campaign, and especially the Crimean War. In 1843 the national debt was 586 million silver rubles (2,049 million assignat rubles); by 1858 it reached 1,759 million rubles. The foreign debt in 1855 was 278 million rubles. In the budget for 1857, of the total revenue of 258 million rubles, 100 million rubles were earmarked for the service of the loans. A peculiar and unhealthy method of financing was the "borrowing" from state-owned banks; the amount thus raised reached 507 million rubles in 1855 and eventually precipitated the banking crisis of 1857-1859.

Financial considerations played a part in determining the policy of the imperial government in the building of roads, especially railways. The deplorable state of the highways and the emperor's interest in engineering caused the authorities to devote particular attention to the development and improvement of internal communications. Some 8,000 versts [10] of hard-surface roads, many of them of strategic importance, were built between 1825 and 1855. Unfortunately, the department of internal communications, headed since 1842 by the tsar's favorite, Count Kleinmichel, fully earned its reputation for corruption and inefficiency, and the poor condition of the roads greatly handicapped the movement and supply of troops during the Crimean War. A proposal made in 1835 by a Viennese professor, von Gerstner, to build a comprehensive network of railways met with a hostile reception. Kankrin was opposed to the plan on the ground that it was unnecessary, too costly and, moreover, a danger to "public morals." Railways, he argued, "encourage frequent purposeless travel, thus fostering the restless spirit of our age." Nevertheless the line between St. Petersburg and the imperial residence of Tsarskoe Selo (25 versts), the first Russian railway, was opened to the public in 1837. In 1839 there was begun the construction of the Warsaw-Vienna line, and in 1842 of the Moscow to St. Petersburg line, which was completed in 1851. By the end of the reign Russia had 980 versts of railways; that is, her network was about one-fifth of that of France and one-sixth of that of Germany. Some progress was made with river shipping, steamship service being maintained on the Volga, Dnieper, Neva, and other principal waterways.

Foreign trade continued its upward trend without, however, undergoing any drastic change.

RUSSIAN FOREIGN TRADE, 1826-1860

Years	Exports	Imports
	(Yearly average in thousand gold rubles)	
1826-1830	85,715	79,687
1831-1835	94,319	80,999
1836-1840	118,435	101,096

[10] One verst = 0.66 mile.

RUSSIAN FOREIGN TRADE, 1826–1860

Years	Exports	Imports
(Yearly average in thousand gold rubles)		
1841–1845	132,323	119,864
1846–1850	151,757	131,522
1851–1855	133,173	129,962
1856–1860	225,594	205,866

In spite of the increase in the value both of exports and of imports, Russia's share of world trade remained practically stationary: according to the computations of Gulishambarov it was approximately 3.7 per cent at the beginning of the century, and 3.6 per cent fifty years later. Sea-borne trade still accounted for the bulk of Russian foreign commerce, although in 1850 the share of overland trade rose to 17 per cent of exports and 37 per cent of imports. In the middle of the century over 80 per cent of the sea-borne imports came through the ports of the Baltic Sea, but with the growth of grain exports about one-third of all exports left from the ports of the Black Sea and the Sea of Azov. There was little change in the range of commodities sold to, and bought from, foreign countries, except for a somewhat higher percentage of grain and other agricultural produce among Russian exports.[11] As in the eighteenth century, England remained Russia's chief customer and main source of supply. According to V. I. Pokrovsky, England in 1846–1848 took 37 per cent of Russian exports and provided 29 per cent of her imports, while the respective figures for Germany were 8 per cent and 16 per cent, and for France 10 per cent and 9 per cent.

The well established predominance of foreign firms in Russian foreign trade was fully maintained. G. P. Nebolsin, author of a useful survey of Russian foreign commerce published in 1850, held that in 1847, when Russian exports reached 134 million rubles, the share of purely Russian firms was merely 3 million rubles, or less than 2 per cent. According to the same author, the export trade of the southern ports was almost exclusively in the hands of Greeks and Italians. Russian merchants were active only in commerce with China, from which foreigners were excluded by law, but Russia's eastern trade in the middle of the nineteenth century did not exceed one-tenth of her total foreign trade. Nebolsin ascribed to their lack of proper education the

[11] See pp. 710–711, 781.

failure of Russian merchants to assert themselves; the real reason, however, would seem to have been the status of social inferiority traditionally attached to the merchant class, a deep-rooted prejudice which led many of the better educated and enterprising members of the merchant families to seek other occupations—especially government service—that would gain them admission into the ranks of the nobility. The Russian mercantile marine made little progress, import and export goods being carried predominantly in foreign bottoms.[12]

There was little change in Russian tariff and commercial policy. The tariff act of 1822, with its exorbitant duties and prohibitions of many imports, was prepared with the participation of Kankrin, and remained the basic charter of Russian commerce until nearly the end of Nicholas's reign. Although Kankrin opposed in principle prohibitions on the ground that they retarded industrial progress, deprived the treasury of revenue, and encouraged contraband, he did next to nothing to liberalize tariff legislation. A number of prohibitions were dropped in 1836, 1838, and especially in the tariff revision of 1841, but these changes affected articles of secondary importance, while a comprehensive range of vital commodities (woolen and cotton goods, iron, pig iron, metal articles, sugar, mirrors, tableware, and many others) remained on the black list. Moreover, protective duties substituted by Kankrin for prohibitions were often so high as to be prohibitive; for instance, duties on certain linens were 600 per cent ad valorem and those on ink twenty times its price. The trend towards freer trade in western Europe led to the gradual abandonment of the more objectionable forms of Russian protectionism. The tariff act of 1850 was the first modest step towards the removal of prohibitions and the lowering of tariff rates, especially those on raw materials; the tariff act of 1857 went a great deal further, with the result that almost all prohibitions on imports disappeared and the tariff rates, while still high and distinctly protective, were at least not entirely prohibitive. In contemporary Russian economic literature the opponents of protection have advanced, among others, the argument that restrictions on imports, by forcing foreign ships to call in ballast at Russian ports, added to freights and thus hindered exports.

Under the regime of high tariff protection, although not because of it, industry continued to expand. The number of enterprises engaged in manufacturing increased from 5,261 in 1825 to 10,943 in

[12] See p. 711, n. 13.

1855, and to 15,338 in 1860. It will be remembered, however, that many of these establishments were small and employed only a few workers. The leading industries in 1825–1860 were textiles, sugar, and the fabrication of metal goods. In 1825 Russia had 484 cotton manufactories employing 47,000 workers; in 1860 the number of enterprises increased to 1,200 and that of the workers to 152,000. Woolens came next, the number of enterprises having risen from 324 in 1825 to 706 in 1860, and the number of workers employed from 64,000 to 120,000. The progress of sugar refining was particularly striking. In 1825 there were 47 sugar refineries with a labor force of less than 1,400; in 1860 the respective figures were 467 and 65,000. The fabrication of metal articles showed a substantial, although less spectacular, advance from 274 enterprises with 24,000 workers in 1825, to 854 enterprises with 63,000 workers in 1860. On the other hand, the ancient linen industry lost ground because of the competition of cheap cotton goods and the shrinkage, with the advent of steamships, of the English market for sail cloth.

The number of workers engaged in manufacturing industries increased from 210,000 in 1825 to 483,000 in 1855, and to 565,000 in 1860. The average size of the enterprises changed but slightly, from 48 workers in 1830 to 53 workers in 1860. From these general averages those of individual industries differed widely. In 1860, for instance, the average number of workers per enterprise in the cotton industry was 170; in sugar 139; in woolens 127; in tobacco 18; in hides and leather 6. The province of Moscow retained its place as the leading industrial center, with 107,000 industrial workers in 1860; next came Vladimir (87,000) and St. Petersburg (33,000). The province of Kiev, which had only 3,000 industrial workers in 1825, held fourth place in 1860 with 32,000 workers, the expansion being due to the rapid growth of sugar refining. The industrialization of other provinces was even less advanced, Tambov occupying fifth place with less than 17,000 workers. Although there is no official information on the relative position of servile and hired labor during the period 1825–1860, there is much evidence to support the widely accepted view that the former was gradually crowded out by the latter. In 1860, according to the tentative computations of Rashin, of the 565,000 workers employed in manufactures 17,000 were possessionary workers, 117,000 to 118,000 were serfs compulsorily attached to industrial establishments owned by their masters, and 430,000, or the bulk of the labor force, were hired workers. No comprehensive data on the employment of women and children are available, but it is known to have been high. Some of the enterprises of the cotton and woolen industries employed more women than men, as well as many children. In 1858–1859 in the sugar refineries, according to Professor Vobly, 25.6 per cent of the workers were women and 10.8 per cent were children.

The evolution of mining and metallurgy proceeded along somewhat different lines. It will be remembered that most of the enterprises of this group were located in remote provinces, chiefly in the Urals, and were manned almost exclusively by servile labor. Most of these were possessionary works which paid for the privilege of a permanently attached labor force by being compelled to submit to rigid government regulations. Throughout the eighteenth century and the early part of the nineteenth, industrialists who did not belong to the nobility had demanded and at times enjoyed the right of acquiring serfs for employment in industrial enterprises, a privilege finally revoked by Alexander I in 1816. In the second quarter of the nineteenth century, however, the situation was reversed, and the owners of possessionary works frequently petitioned the government for the removal of the special status attached to their enterprises. One of the reasons for these requests, as stated in a memorandum presented in 1837 by the Moscow industrialists, was the notable ineptitude of the servile workers and their inability or unwillingness to adapt themselves to improved industrial technique. Compulsory industrial labor, moreover, had proved particularly unmanageable, and the history of possessionary works is a distressing story of recurrent violent disturbances. Even more reprehensible from the owners' point of view was the stifling bureaucratic control which regulated even minute details of the organization of possessionary works and specifically determined the volume and character of production; these rules, combined with the obligation of providing employment for all the workers attached to the enterprise, effectively prevented industrial progress. With the rapid improvement in the methods of production and the spread of technical knowledge, the position of possessionary works became unbearable and their unsatisfactory performance a matter of much concern. That government regulations, rather than servile labor, were chiefly responsible for the plight of possessionary works is suggested by the fact that sugar refining, one of the most progressive and successful industries of this period, depended on servile workers to an extent estimated at one-half (Vobly) or even two-thirds (Pazhitnov) of its total labor force.

The government gradually yielded to the plea of the hard-pressed owners of possessionary works. In 1835 they were granted authority to issue passports to their servile workers entitling the latter to seek outside employment, on the condition, however, that the volume of production should not be reduced and that the *obrok* paid by the dismissed workers should go to a communal fund and not to the owners. A law of June 18, 1840, went further and gave the owners the power to emancipate their possessionary workers. The owners were entitled to an indemnity of 36 silver rubles per male worker if the workers emancipated were acquired for a consideration; if, however, as was often the case, the acquisition had been through a public grant, no indemnity was forthcoming. The emancipated workers were given the option of joining either the burghers (*meshchane*) or the state peasants. In the latter case the owners were to make an allowance of 50 assignat rubles per each male and 20 assignat rubles per each female, plus 20 assignat rubles per each person, irrespective of sex, to cover the cost of transportation to the new place of settlement. It thus appears that in the case of workers who were not acquired for a consideration and who chose to join the state peasants, the emancipation authorized by the act of 1840 imposed a financial burden on the owners. The law of 1840 was never promulgated and does not appear in the official collection, probably because the government feared that it might lead to disturbances among the possessionary workers. Nevertheless, according to Tugan-Baranovsky, the owners of at least twenty-six possessionary works availed themselves of this law, and petitions of many others were filed but were not acted upon until the emancipation of 1861.

Rashin estimates the total number of workers employed in mining and metallurgy in 1860 at 245,000, and the proportion of hired labor among them at 30 per cent (hired workers were common in privately owned gold mines and salt pits). This brings the total of workers engaged in 1860 in all industrial pursuits (manufacturing, mining, and metallurgy) to approximately 800,000, or slightly more than 1 per cent of the population, four times their number at the beginning of the century, with servile labor accounting for 33 per cent or 34 per cent of the 1860 total. Rashin emphasizes that his computations have no claim to exactness but are rather indicative of general trends.

The inadequacy of statistical data, the amazing variety in the rates paid for the same kind of work, and the fluctuations of the ruble present seemingly insurmountable obstacles to the determination of the level of industrial wages. Nevertheless Professor Tugan-Baranovsky has reached the conclusion that in the reign of Nicholas the trend of wages was favorable to the workers, that is, wages both nominal and real were rising. He explains this by the rapid pace of industrial development, the relative shortage of labor due to serfdom, and the preference of the peasants for cottage industry, which in the decades preceding emancipation successfully competed with large industrial establishments. So long as machines were little used, the relatively simple processes involved in manufacturing could be performed as successfully by small artisans as by large establishments. It was only with the introduction of machines that cottage industry lost some, although by no means all, of its importance. The mechanization of Russian industry became a vital factor in the late 1840's, especially after the removal in 1842 of the prohibition on the export of machines from England. Although there was some progress in Russian domestic production of machines, it remained both insignificant in volume and inferior in quality.

IMPORT OF MACHINES AND TOOLS

Year	Machines	Tools
(Yearly average in thousand rubles)		
1841–1845	668	373
1846–1850	1,681	505
1851–1855	2,103	412
1856–1860	7,503	859

The effects of mechanization were first felt in the textile industry, particularly in cotton spinning and weaving.

Russia's first venture in factory legislation was a law of May 24, 1835, on "the relations between the owners of industrial enterprises and the workers they hire." It prohibited the workers from leaving their jobs or asking for higher wages until the expiration of their contracts. The owners, however, were permitted to dismiss workers at any time for inefficiency or bad behavior. The law required that each enterprise should keep a pay roll and that workshop rules should be prominently posted, a rather fine point since the vast majority of the workers were illiterate. No penalty was provided for the infringement of these regulations. Of greater potential significance was a law of

August 7, 1845, prohibiting night work for children under twelve years of age. This enactment, like the law of June 18, 1840, was not promulgated, did not appear in official collections, and was never enforced. Beyond these futile gestures the factory legislation of this period did not go.

CHAPTER XXXI

NICHOLAS I

Schools, Intellectual Movements, Literature, and Art

"OFFICIAL NATIONALISM" AND THE SCHOOLS

It is one of the paradoxes of history that the oppressive regime of Nicholas, barren as it was of political and social progress, coincided with a period of remarkable intellectual activity which produced some of the greatest masterpieces of Russian literature and contained the germs of practically every later cultural movement. These developments were all the more striking because they took place in spite of the government's effort to regiment intellectual life with a degree of thoroughness that probably was never exceeded until the appearance of the modern totalitarian states. The ideological and educational program of the reign was expounded by Count S. S. Uvarov, a man of culture, knowledge, and immense ambition, who forsook the liberal views of his early years for a brilliant bureaucratic career. Uvarov's appointment as minister of education, an office he held from 1833 to 1849, was preceded by his report to the tsar (December 4, 1832) in which he expounded the theory that the only way to counteract the influence of subversive western European ideas was a system of education based on "the truly-Russian conservative principles of Orthodoxy, autocracy, and nationality, our last anchor of salvation and the best guarantees of Russia's strength and greatness." Uvarov argued that "in view of existing conditions and the prevalent state of mind one must multiply, as far as possible, the number of 'intellectual dams.' Not all of them, perhaps, will prove equally solid, equally effective in the struggle against destructive principles; but each may have its relative merit, may serve its immediate purpose." The tripartite formula—Orthodoxy, autocracy, and nationality—became the slogan of the reign, and was extolled in official pronouncements and in the patriotic press.

What was meant by autocracy is too obvious to need elaboration. Orthodoxy, to quote Presniakov, was understood as "one of the pillars of secular power; it was not the 'inner truth' of an autonomous and authoritative Russian Church the slavophiles dreamt about, but a concrete system of Church control over the spiritual life of its members. The Church, moreover, was autocracy's political tool, obedient to lay authorities and administered by the chief procurator of the Holy Synod." [1] The concept of nationality, unlike that of Orthodoxy

[1] The appointment of the members of the Holy Synod (a purely ecclesiastical body), under the terms of a decree of 1803, for only brief terms increased the dependence of that institution on the chief procurator. That official was not entitled to vote in the Synod, which in theory was the supreme organ of the Church, yet the members of the assembly were well described by Bishop Nicodimus of Enissei (in a memorandum written in 1873) as "birds without wings." The autocratic powers of the chief procurator were due to the fact that he had complete control over the business activities of the Synod, dealt in its name with lay and ecclesiastical authorities, and was the sole intermediary between the Synod and the Crown. From 1836 to 1855 the office of chief procurator was filled by N. A. Protasov, a colonel in the hussars of the guards and an adherent of Uvarov's ultra-conservative doctrines. He treated ecclesiastical dignitaries as if they were cavalry subalterns and used his position to make the Church an instrument for the unifying and nationalistic policies of the state. The persecution of the old-believers and other dissenters, resumed in the closing years of Alexander I's reign, was carried on with new vigor under Nicholas, and assumed a distinctly political character. The object of the government this time was not merely to prevent the spread of religious sects but to exterminate them altogether. Although a decree of May 21, 1841, containing a number of restrictive measures, proclaimed that their purpose was to "safeguard the Orthodox faith of our forefathers," the political character of the anti-sectarian legislation was disclosed by the fact that in the classification of dissenters undertaken in 1837 the group of "the most pernicious sects" comprised, among others, not only the *skoptsy* (castrates) and the *khlysty* (flagellants) but also the *molokhane* and the *dukhobory*, whose moral doctrines and personal behavior were entirely unobjectionable. What mattered, however, was the attitude of the dissenters towards the state to which the two last-named sects were inimical. The measures taken against the dissenters included curtailment of civil rights (in 1850, for instance, they were debarred from attending secondary schools and universities); closing of their monasteries, places of worship, hospitals, and charitable institutions; liquidation of the settlements of some of the sects, their members being forcibly enrolled in the Caucasian army or deported to Siberia. The government struck with particular viciousness at the *bezpopovtsy* (the priestless), a sect which refused to pray for the tsar and denied Church hierarchy and the sacrament of marriage. By a law of 1838 children of the members of this group were declared to be illegitimate and were forcibly converted to Orthodoxy. The anti-sectarian legislation could not be fully enforced. A check of the dissenters disclosed that their actual number greatly exceeded the official figure, which in 1826–1855 was under one million; the real figure, according to General N. N. Oberuchev (quoted by Kornilov) was over 8

and autocracy, conveyed no clear meaning. The Russian term *narodnost* used by Uvarov has no definite connotation and, although much has been written on the subject, the scope and implications of the militant nationalism for which it stood have never been fully elucidated. The assumption by Uvarov of the mantle of prophet of Russian nationalism was somewhat ironical because, as Solovev has pointed out, he "had never read a Russian book and continuously used French and German in his own writings." It was widely believed, according to Pypin, that in the original version of Uvarov's formula the precise term "serfdom" was used instead of the vague one "nationality." The nearest English equivalent of what was meant by nationality is perhaps "official patriotism" or "official nationalism," the qualification "official" being almost invariably attached in Russian literature to Uvarov's brand of glorification of Russia's past and present. A succinct definition of the doctrine was given by Benckendorff in an admonition to Chaadaev: "Russia's past is admirable; her present more than magnificent; as to her future, it is beyond the grasp of the most daring imagination; this is the point of view . . . from which Russian history must be conceived and written." This statement of the Baltic-German nobleman was appropriately delivered in French.

M. P. Pogodin, professor of history in the University of Moscow, vied in enthusiasm with the director of the police. "Providence," Pogodin wrote, "guides the history of every nation, but this is particularly true of Russia. How great, indeed, are its merits. . . . No other history contains so many marvels." And again: "How great is Russia! How large is her population! How many nationalities it comprises! How immense are her national resources! Finally, is there anything the Russian state could not do? A word—and a whole empire ceases to exist, a word—and another disappears from the face of the earth!" This was the normal tone of the officially inspired press, although Uvarov expressed himself at times with greater moderation. "The term 'nationality,'" he wrote in a report to the tsar covering the first ten years of his administration (1833–1843), "has provoked the animosity of ill-wishers by its courageous affirmation of the ministry's

---

million. Evasion and its concomitant—wholesale bribery of officials—were prevalent, and in spite of the zeal of home missionaries the number of dissenters, it is believed, continued to increase. The net result of persecution was much bitterness and suffering among people whose only crime, in a large number of cases, was that they did not admire the Russian brand of autocracy and that they worshiped God in a manner of which the government did not approve.

contention that Russia has reached maturity and is entitled to advance not *behind* but at least *side by side* with other European nations." The practical manifestations of "official patriotism" were stagnation at home and arrogance in foreign relations, a factor in more than one international crisis.

The application of the principles of Orthodoxy, autocracy, and nationality to education called for a policy that would assist in preserving the existing social order and in eliminating liberal, and therefore outlandish and subversive, influences. To achieve these objects it was considered essential (1) to discourage students from pursuing studies above the station to which they were entitled by their social origin; and (2), in the words of Uvarov's report just quoted, "to collect and consolidate in the hands of the government the control of all intellectual resources, theretofore scattered, of all means of general and private education that had failed to gain recognition and had partly escaped supervision." Neither of these objects was fully attained.

It will be remembered that the school reform of 1803 embodied the principle of integration, that is, the curriculums of schools of various grades were so arranged as to encourage, at least in theory, the advancement of students from parish schools through county and provincial schools to the universities. The unity of the school system was further emphasized in the supervision by the executive officers of the higher schools over the lower schools.[2] The school legislation adopted under Nicholas, in the framing of which Uvarov had a prominent part even before he became minister, sprang from the very opposite theory: each type of school was to aim primarily at providing a complete education designed to meet the practical needs of the social group from which it drew its student body. Admiral Shishkov, minister of education in 1824-1828, argued that since no more than one out of a hundred graduates of county schools reached the universities, the function of these schools as a preparatory stage to higher education was mere fiction. He proposed that parish schools should cater chiefly to children of peasants, burghers, and artisans; county schools to those of merchants, minor officials, and lesser nobility; and provincial schools (gymnasiums) to the offspring of the nobility, although he added that "children of other social classes should not be excluded."

The law of December 8, 1828, on provincial, county, and parish

[2] See p. 723.

schools was an important step towards putting this program into effect. It introduced no change in the curriculum of parish schools and their relationship with county schools. The course of instruction in county schools, however, was extended from two to three years, and their curriculums were made to correspond to those of the junior years of the gymnasium. The central government assumed charge of the county schools which had been supported from local taxes. The course of instruction in the gymnasium was lengthened to seven years. The purpose of these schools was to provide their students with "solid rather than comprehensive education" and to prepare them for the practical tasks they would have to face on graduation. The broad humanitarian subjects, formerly a feature of the gymnasium program, were gradually dropped. The long-standing controversy between the supporters and the opponents of classicism received a compromise solution. Beginning with the fourth year, these schools were to offer two parallel sets of courses: one included classical languages and was intended for the students who wished to continue their studies at a university; the other omitted classical languages, emphasized natural history, mathematics, and law (the German *Realschule*), and was to be taken by those students who did not intend to go to a higher school. The result of the experiment was not a happy one. According to an authoritative statement in the Russian *Journal of the Ministry of Education* in 1864 "the gymnasium broke with classical tradition but failed to become a *Realschule*. . . . It proved incapable of providing either broad cultural background or specialized instruction. On the one hand, the young men whose education ended with the gymnasium were possessed of merely haphazard and largely useless information; on the other, the graduates of these schools were poorly prepared for university work with the result that, according to many professors, the standards of higher education declined."

The traditional dislike of the nobility for government-sponsored secondary schools (except military academies) was partly overcome by the establishment of boarding schools "for boys of noble descent" (*blagorodnye pansiony*). There were 47 such boarding schools in 1849 and 61 in 1863. It was originally intended that boys at the boarding schools should attend classes in the local gymnasium but should receive additional instruction in "arts befitting the upper class," such as French, music, dancing, fencing, and riding. Many of the boarding schools, however, were converted at the request of local nobility into regular boarding schools offering instruction in accordance with a somewhat abridged program of the gymnasium. This new type of school was an unforeseen and unwanted by-product of the reform. The encouragement of the *dvoriane* to send their children to the gymnasium went hand in hand with measures designed to prevent the enrollment of children of the non-privileged groups. Admission of the latter was made subject to certain burdensome formalities (presentation of "certificates of leave" from village and urban communities to which the boys officially belonged). The increase in 1845 in tuition fees (first introduced in 1817 for fiscal reasons) had the same object, and was officially motivated by "the excessive influx into higher and secondary schools of young men born in the lower strata of society for whom higher education is useless, indeed, an unnecessary luxury which tends to drive them away from their natural surroundings without benefit to themselves or to the state." In spite of these measures the proportion of gymnasium students belonging to the nobility declined from 78 per cent in 1833 to 70 per cent in 1864. The program of segregating children, according to their social origin, in schools of various grades met with limited success. In 1853, of the 424 students enrolled in the University of St. Petersburg 125 belonged to the non-privileged groups, while of the 7,613 students of the parish schools in the St. Petersburg region 883 were children of noble parents. Private schools, which it was the original intention to close and which Uvarov discouraged by various restrictive measures, held their ground well. In 1853 in the St. Petersburg school region, private schools accounted for more than 6,000 students, while the gymnasiums had fewer than 3,000 and county schools fewer than 5,000 students. The Uvarov experiment merely proved, as Miliukov observes, that while it was feasible to reserve certain schools, such as the boarding schools and a few others, exclusively for the education of children of noble parents, it was impossible to carry the class principle throughout the entire school structure.[3]

[3] Some of Uvarov's contemporaries understood the impracticability of his program. Miliukov quotes the following statement by Prince K. A. Liven, minister of education in 1828–1833: "In the Russian state where there is no middle class . . . ; where an artisan is in a position essentially similar to that of a farmer . . . ; where a well-to-do peasant may at any time become a merchant and is often both; where the nobility is so heterogeneous as to extend all the way from the steps of the throne to almost the peasantry; where every year many burghers and peasants join the ranks of the nobility through promotion in the army or in the civil service; in

The law on the school regions of June 22, 1835, and the charter of the universities of July 26, 1835, did away with the hierarchical administrative subordination of the schools, which was a feature of the reform of 1804. Under the new legislation the curator was to reside in the university city of his region and to supervise provincial, county, and parish schools, directly or through special agencies. The university ceased to be the principal organ of the ministry of education in the school region and was itself brought under the control of the curator. The charter of 1835 did not abrogate university autonomy (which existed only on paper) but greatly reduced its scope. The rector, deans, and professors were still elected by the corporation; the minister, however, was given discretionary powers to fill professorial chairs with men in good standing and possessed of appropriate degrees. The university executive board, which dealt with administration and financial matters, was subordinated to the curator. University courts were abolished; an inspectorate under the orders of the curator was to look after the behavior, manners, and even the appearance of the students who were put in uniform. Uvarov's tripartite formula was reflected in the revised curriculums. Theology, Church history, and Church law were made compulsory for all students. The department (faculty) of law offered courses in contemporary Russian law designed to train government employees rather than learned jurists. There were established new chairs of Russian and Slavic history. The first holder of the chair of Russian history in the University of Moscow was Pogodin, a sample of whose views has already been quoted. The corresponding chair in the University of St. Petersburg was held by N. G. Ustrialov. His doctor's dissertation *A Pragmatic System of Russian History*, published in 1836, was an elaboration of Uvarov's nationalistic doctrines and pictured the reign of Nicholas as the full expression of Russia's national genius, both socially and politically. Ustrialov later acquired considerable notoriety as the leading exponent of the view that Russia was the chief factor in the history of Lithuania and that the Lithuanian provinces were historically Russian and not Polish. Regarded with profound distaste by contemporary Russian liberal opinion, these theories were welcome in official circles and lent a semblance of historical justification to the policy of Russification of the western borderland.

---

the Russian state [so constituted] such an organization of schools [on the class principle] presents great difficulties."

The legislation of 1835 was soon followed by new restrictions. Uvarov was disturbed by the trickle of students from lower classes who were finding their way into the universities. As in secondary schools, the admission of such students was hindered by legalistic formalities and an increase in tuition fees (1845). The French revolution of February, 1848, had grave repercussions on the position of Russian higher schools. In March of that year officers of the ministry of education, including members of the teaching profession, were forbidden to travel abroad, and in April the number of students not in receipt of government stipends was limited to three hundred per university (exclusive of the faculty of medicine). With unconscious irony the same order suggested that young noblemen, as descendants of "ancient knights" (*drevnee rytsarstvo*), should prefer to a civilian career the army, which did not require university training. By this time the personal position of Uvarov was greatly shaken. Persistent rumors of the impending closure of the universities led him to cause the publication of a mild article in their defense. To this article the censorship authorities took exception, and in September, 1849, Uvarov was forced to resign. His successor, the ultra-reactionary Prince P. A. Shirinsky-Shikhmatov, rapidly disposed of the remnants of university autonomy and academic freedom. An amendment to the university charter (October 11, 1849) provided that the rector should be appointed, not elected, and should not hold a chair; the minister was empowered to remove elected deans and to substitute for them men of his own choice. In 1850 the deans were directed to exercise the strictest supervision over the contents of lectures delivered by the members of the faculty. The teaching of philosophy and of the constitutional law of European states was discontinued, and logic and psychological instruction was entrusted to professors of theology to make it conform with the doctrines of the Orthodox Church. Nicholas, indeed, was fighting revolution not only on the plains of Hungary but also in the lecture room.

There was, however, a brighter side to the picture. In the early years of Nicholas's reign the government, faced with an acute shortage of university teachers, sent a number of the more promising Russian students to the University of Dorpat and then to Germany and France to prepare for an academic career. The venture proved rewarding and produced a nucleus of university professors who, in spite of the limitations of Russian academic surroundings, maintained high standards in their teaching and scientific work. Around some of them gathered small but enthusiastic groups of students keenly interested in scientific, social, and political problems. From the collaboration of these two elements—the teachers and the student body—the cultural tradition of Russian universities was born. Among the more outstanding professors, whose contributions to knowledge were significant and lasting, were T. N. Granovsky (1813–1855), historian; N. I. Lobachevsky (1793–1856), mathematician; V. J. Struve (1793–1864), astronomer and founder of the Pulkovo observatory near St. Petersburg (1839); N. N. Zinin (1812–1880), chemist; N. I. Pirogov (1810–1881), surgeon and educator. Special mention must be made of S. M. Solovev (1820–1879), professor of history in the University of Moscow, who has been so often quoted in these pages. The first of the twenty-nine volumes of his monumental *History of Russia from Ancient Times* was published in 1851, subsequent volumes appearing regularly each year until his death. His industry was immense and, although many of his interpretations are no longer acceptable, his *History* is indispensable to every earnest student of Russia's past, and remains a mine of information. It may be no exaggeration to say that Russian historiography as a science—if it is a science—began with Solovev.[4]

The appearance of the first Russian scholars capable of original scientific work and the enthusiastic response of selected audiences to gifted teachers, such as Granovsky, should not obscure the fact that education was still the possession of the chosen few. The number of university students increased from 1,700 in 1825 to 4,600 in 1848 and declined to 3,600 in 1854. The University of Moscow retained its leading position with an enrollment of 1,061 students in 1854; that of St. Petersburg held the lowest rank with 379 students. The student body of the gymnasiums increased from 7,700 in 1825 to 18,900 in 1848, and declined to 17,800 in 1854.[5] The decrease in the number

---

[4] The study of Russian history was assisted by the activities of the committee on public records (*arkheograficheskaiia komissiia*) established in 1834, and by the organization of provincial archive committees in 1850 and of central archives in Kiev, Vitebsk, and Vilna in 1852. Useful work was performed by the Imperial Odessa Society of History and Antiquities, founded in 1839, which in 1849 became the Imperial Archaeological Society, and by the Archaeological and Numismatic Society, founded in 1846. In the 1840's a number of valuable historical documents for the first time appeared in print.

[5] These figures refer merely to schools under the ministry of education. Several government-sponsored military academies, technical schools, and boarding schools for girls were established during this period. The St. Petersburg teachers' college

of students between 1848 and 1854 was due, in both cases, to the restrictive legislation described above. According to official statistics, in 1857 the ministry of education maintained 463 county schools with 32,400 students and 2,214 schools of lower grades, with 105,500 students. Practically all these schools were located in urban areas. The needs of the rural community were cared for by other government departments. The reports of the Holy Synod disclose that the number of primary Church schools increased from 100 in 1837 to 4,820 in 1853, when they provided instruction for 98,300 students, including 10,600 girls. The ministry of state domains, as has already been stated, in 1854 maintained 2,551 schools with 111,000 students, including 18,000 girls. In 1853 the ministry of appanages reported 204 schools with 7,500 students. The two latter types of schools were supported from the proceeds of local taxes. These figures, humble as they are in relation to a population estimated at well over 70 millions, probably give too optimistic a picture. Official statistics dealing with primary schools, especially those of the Holy Synod, are recognized as notoriously inflated. The standard of instruction in all these schools —when they existed not merely on paper—was almost incredibly low; the schools of the ministry of state domains were often cited in later years as shining examples of heartless formalism and crass stupidity. Whatever smattering of literacy the peasant children succeeded in gaining was obtained largely from informal classes where the rudiments of reading and writing were taught by unqualified teachers, often retired soldiers. No wonder that on the eve of the emancipation a literate peasant was a rare exception.[6]

(*pedagogicheskii institut*) was revived in 1828. In 1835 was founded in St. Petersburg a law school (*uchilishche pravovedeniia*) for the legal training of boys of noble descent.

[6] Although the school legislation of this period contained no discrimination against Jews, the number of Jewish students in Russian schools remained small. Of some 15,000 students enrolled in 58 gymnasiums of 1853, only 155 were Jews. Nicholas was no friend of the Jews, whom he described in his diary in 1816 as "regular leeches." The policy of his reign was to bring about the assimilation of the Jews through the elimination of their "religious fanaticism and racial exclusiveness." Translated into concrete terms, this meant the breaking up of Jewish autonomous communal organizations, the bringing of Jewish schools under the control of Russian authorities and, as a final aim, the destruction of Judaism through conversion of Jews to Greek Orthodoxy. The German-born and German-educated liberal Jewish leader Dr. Marx Lilienthal, who agreed in 1841 to cooperate with Uvarov in a campaign for the "enlightenment" of orthodox Jewry, left Russia in 1845 for the United States, deeply disappointed and with the conviction that the

INTELLECTUAL MOVEMENTS

Alexander Herzen was not far from the truth when he wrote in 1860 that "thirty years ago the Russia *of the future* existed exclusively among a few boys just emerging from childhood; they were the legatees of universal science and of the true popular Russian tradition." Yet the period 1825–1855 proved highly significant in the history of Russian social and political thought. The repressions that followed the Decembrist uprising could not stop all independent intellectual activities. In St. Petersburg, in Moscow, and in the provinces there came into existence informal groups interested in philosophical, scientific, social, and political questions, and united, to quote Herzen, "by a profound feeling of alienation from official Russia." The influence of these groups, which included practically everyone who counted in Russia's intellectual life, was out of proportion to their size. Although there was no coordinated program and the members of these coteries changed their allegiance freely and at times took opposite sides in the passionate war of ideas, a fairly clear pattern of intellectual evolution emerges in retrospect from the confused clash of opinions. As an escape from the unpalatable realities of the police regime and as a protest against the rationalism and empiricism of French eighteenth century philosophers, Russian intellectuals of the 1820's and 1830's endeavored to lose themselves in the glittering generalities of Schelling's idealistic and romantic philosophy. Schelling was first introduced to the Russian reading public early in the nineteenth century, but it

---

only way for the Russian Jews to make peace with the government was "by bowing down before the Greek cross." The first step along the path of assimilation was the decree of Aug. 26, 1827, which abolished the exemption tax and made Jews liable to compulsory military service. The term of service being twenty-five years, this measure was received with consternation by the Jewish communities. The Statute on the Jews of 1835 redefined the area of the Jewish pale and codified the disabilities to which the Jews were subject, such as a prohibition against employing gentiles. By a law of June 22, 1842, all Jewish schools were brought under the supervision of the ministry of education, and a law of November 13, 1844, provided for the establishment of Jewish parish and district schools on the Russian model, under a mixed body of gentile and Jewish teachers. A secret rescript of the same date declared the emperor's intention of getting rid gradually of Jewish confessional schools. The dissolution of the kahals, or Jewish autonomous communities, was ordered by a decree of Dec. 19, 1844. The wearing of the traditional Jewish dress was prohibited in 1850, and the following year Jewish women were forbidden to shave their heads upon entering marriage, as required by religious custom. Compulsory assimilation failed in the case of the Jews as it did in that of the old-believers. Evasion was general, and police and other officials throve on the misery of the Jews.

was not until a quarter of a century later that he won there a number of ardent followers. From Schelling the seekers after truth turned to Kant, then to Fichte, and finally to Hegel, whose influence proved powerful and lasting, partly because the interpretations or misinterpretations of his views lent themselves equally well to the support of either radical or conservative doctrines. Seriously as Russian intellectuals took German metaphysics—divergencies in the interpretation of some obscure term of Hegelian philosophy are known to have broken life-long friendships—some of them became disillusioned with philosophical systems that centered on the eternal and insoluble problems confronting man, with little attention to current social issues. The inequities of Russian conditions were too flagrant to be indefinitely ignored; they inevitably fostered a craving for social justice and led the more restless minds to seek guidance either in the study of Russia's past or in the doctrines of French socialists—Saint-Simon, Fourier, Proudhon, Leroux, Cabet, and Louis Blanc. The novelist and publicist Alexander Herzen (1812–1870), who in the 1830's was under the influence of Saint-Simon, continued in a different guise the revolutionary tradition of the Decembrists. The beginnings of Russian socialism are traced to his early activities, although Lenin, while paying a warm tribute to Herzen as a revolutionary leader and to his mastery of Hegelian dialectics, which he called "the algebra of revolution," emphasized that Herzen never became a convert to "scientific" or Marxian socialism.

In the early 1840's the divergent currents of Russian thought were merged in two opposing schools, the westerners and the slavophiles. Both terms were misnomers. The westerners were primarily Russian humanitarians. "Their aim," writes Professor Guerie, "was not the substitution of western for national institutions, but the education of Russian society in the ideas of an European universal culture in order to lift Russian national development to a super-national level where it would acquire world significance." [7] The westerners were not bound by any definite set of principles, and drew their following from a heterogeneous group of people who believed in European science, favored constitutional government, freedom of thought and of the press, and

[7] The term "westerners" therefore seems more appropriate than "westernizers" used by B. H. Sumner in *Russia and the Balkans, 1870–1880* (The Clarendon Press, Oxford, 1937). "Westernizers" has a derogatory connotation suggestive of the criticism of the westerners by the slavophiles, which most of them did not deserve.

deplored, often platonically, serfdom and the gulf separating the educated few from the illiterate masses. Of the three outstanding leaders of the westerners—Granovsky, Herzen, and the literary critic Vissarion Belinsky—the first was a man of moderate liberal views and an opponent of socialism, while Herzen and, after 1842, Belinsky leaned towards socialism and political radicalism.

Slavophilism was not, as is suggested by its name, identical with panslavism. The term "slavophile" was first applied to Shishkov and his friends, who advocated the purification of Russian literary language by substituting words derived from Old Slavonic for those of foreign origin.[8] The slavophile doctrine of the 1840's as expounded in the writings of its founders (the brothers Ivan and Peter Kireevsky, Ivan and Constantine Aksakov, Alexis Khomiakov) was a highly romantic nationalism which extolled the imaginary virtues of the truly Russian national ways as superior to those of the decadent west and saw in the Orthodox Church the source of Russia's strength in the past and her chief hope for the future. The harmonious course of Russian history, according to this view, was interrupted by the reforms of Peter I; constitutional government was foreign to the spirit of the Russian people and would only lead, as it did in western Europe, to social discord and class struggle which, Constantine Aksakov imagined, were alien to Russian national tradition. His celebrated formula demanded for the government "unlimited power of state action," and for the people "unrestricted moral freedom, freedom of life and spirit"; the government should have "the right of action and therefore of lawmaking; the people—the right of opinion and therefore of expression." The voice of the people should be heard through a free press and a consultative popular assembly organized on the lines of the seventeenth century *zemskii sobor*. The slavophiles were enthusiastic about the village commune (*obshchina* or *mir*), and their insistence on its merits is regarded by some historians as the cornerstone of their teaching. In later years the village commune was upheld by Herzen and the radical wing of the westerners, not, however, as a "sacred national institution," to quote the slavophile A. I. Koshelev, but because they discerned in it the elements of the future socialist society.

The slavophile doctrine had many points in common with "official patriotism," but there were also essential differences. The slavophiles were as unsparing as the westerners in their criticism of the existing

[8] See p. 729.

order, and they particularly deplored the subjugation of the Church by the state. Some of their leaders (Yuri Samarin, Prince Vladimir Cherkassky) took a prominent part in the emancipation of the serfs. The movement's religious exclusiveness determined its attitude towards panslavism. Accepting the supremacy of Greek Orthodoxy as its principal dogma, slavophilism regarded as traitors to the cause of Slavdom Slavic nations that had embraced a different creed. The slavophiles were particularly hostile to Catholic Poland, and Samarin and Cherkassky were among the most ruthless and uncompromising agents of the Russification of Poland after the Polish uprising of 1863. But even in their attitude towards the Slavic nations professing Greek Orthodoxy the slavophiles tended to uphold the supremacy of Great Russia (*Velikorossiia*), and were, for instance, hostile to Ukrainian nationalism, which they branded as separatism. Until the Crimean War they showed but casual interest in the fate of the Balkan Slavs. In later years, soft-pedaling its criticism of the government, slavophilism became identified with many official reactionary policies. Its following was limited, and came chiefly from the landed nobility. Ivan Aksakov admitted in 1856 that while the name of Belinsky was revered by every thoughtful young man in provincial Russia, the slavophiles were practically unknown.[9]

Slavophilism was frowned upon by the government. The Slavic question, according to Uvarov's circular of May 30, 1847, "may be used by ill intentioned persons for the excitement of minds and the spreading of dangerous propaganda, criminal and obnoxious"; when Russia suffered and needed assistance, the circular argued, she was not helped by other Slavic nations who "now stretch out to us their arms and beg for protection, not so much from motives of brotherly love as from considerations of petty and not always disinterested [*sic*] selfishness." The first issue of the slavophile publication *Moskowskii Sbornik* (1852) was allowed to appear, but the second issue was prohibited, publication was suspended, and the editor suffered a penalty. The journals of the westerners fared no better.

With the approach of the stormy year 1848, Russian intellectuals found it increasingly difficult to dwell in the ivory tower of philosophi-

[9] Alexis Veselovsky, a distinguished literary critic, notes that slavophilism, as a romantic and sentimental national literary movement with a strong mystical and messianic tinge, is a universal phenomenon. Similar movements are found in Germany, Poland, Denmark, Sweden, Norway, and among the Czechs, as well as in other countries.

cal speculations or to engage in sterile discussions about the relative merits of western and national culture. In 1847 Herzen left Russia never to return; in 1855 he founded in London a Russian printing press and in 1857 began the publication of the newspaper *The Bell* (*Kolokol*), which for years exercised exceptional influence. Those who remained in Russia were less fortunate. Among the first notable victims of the rising tide of reaction was the Kiev Brotherhood of Cyril and Methodius, a secret society which grew out of an informal group organized by N. I. Kostomarov, professor of history in the University of Kiev, for the study of Saint-Simon and Fourier. The program of the brotherhood, which was founded in January, 1846, called for emancipation of the serfs and advancement of Ukrainian nationalism through the creation of a federated Slavic republic based on broad national autonomy. Some of the leaders of the brotherhood, for instance, Kostomarov and the historian P. A. Kulish, relied on peaceful methods of propaganda, but others, including the Ukrainian poet and artist Shevchenko, favored revolutionary action. In April, 1847, the members of the brotherhood were arrested. Kostomarov and Kulish escaped with light sentences, but Shevchenko had to spend ten years as a private in a remote garrison under strict supervision, being specifically forbidden to write or to draw.[10]

The case of the so-called Petrashevsky group was even more tragic. M. V. Butashevich-Petrashevsky (1821–1866), a graduate of the aristocratic *lycée* of Tsarskoe Selo and a minor official in the ministry of foreign affairs, was a man of versatile interests and a warm admirer of Fourier. He was co-author of a *Pocket Dictionary of Foreign Words* (published by N. Kirillov in 1845–1846) in which the ideas of pre-Marxian socialists were conscientiously but cautiously expounded. The dictionary, indeed, was dedicated to one of the grand dukes. Petrashevsky's Friday literary receptions were popular with the intellectual élite and aroused the suspicion of the police. After the revolution of 1848, Petrashevsky and his more intimate friends discussed the desirability of forming a secret society for revolutionary propaganda,

[10] Taras Shevchenko (1812–1861), born a serf, was sent to St. Petersburg to study drawing. His talent as poet and painter won him the friendship of men influential in the world of art and letters (the poet Zhukovsky, the actor Shchepkin, the painters Brüllov and Venetsianov), and through their efforts a fund was raised to purchase Shevchenko's freedom (1858). The poetry of Shevchenko is imbued with intense Ukrainian patriotism and a deep feeling for the suffering of the peasantry. His lyrics and poems written in Ukrainian still enjoy wide popularity.

but no such organization was established. They, however, held a dinner in memory of Fourier (April 7, 1849) at which the idyllic world of this least violent of social thinkers was extolled in terms befitting the occasion. Enthusiastic references to Fourier's *phalanstères* and the impending doom of the cities was later interpreted by imaginative police officials as a plot for the destruction of the Russian capital. On April 22, 1849, thirty-nine members of the group were arrested. Although nothing could be proved against them except a "conspiracy of ideas," an offense unknown to the criminal code, a specially constituted military court sentenced fifteen of the accused to death and six to forced labor or deportation to Siberia. At the last moment, after the convicted men were brought to the place of execution, death sentences were dramatically commuted to imprisonment. Among the victims of the Petrashevsky affair was the poet A. N. Pleshcheev and Fedor Dostoevsky, whose first works had only recently appeared in print. Dostoevsky was sentenced to four years of hard labor to be followed by six years of army service in a Siberian garrison.

CENSORSHIP

The rigor and absurdity of censorship under Nicholas are proverbial. The censorship law of June 10, 1826, a voluminous enactment in 230 articles, made it the duty of the censors to watch over science and education, to ensure good behavior of the citizens and internal safety, and to direct public opinion according to "the existing conditions and the views of the government." Under this law the powers of the censors were practically unlimited and opportunities for arbitrary action boundless. After the resignation of Shishkov and the appointment of Prince Liven as minister of education, the act of 1826 was superseded by the more liberal censorship law of April 22, 1828, which directed the censors merely to prevent the appearance of "harmful" publications and relieved them of the duty of directing public opinion and correcting "mistakes" of fact or even the style of the authors. The law of 1828 remained in force throughout the reign of Nicholas, but it was amended and interpreted in a manner which for all practical purposes was a return to the principles of the act of 1826. Censorship restrictions began to pile up after the French revolution of 1830, and especially following the appointment of Uvarov as minister of education in 1833. The most distressing feature of the censorship regime was, perhaps, the multiplicity of agencies vested with ill defined powers over what might or might not be printed. Such authority was exercised by practically every government department, even the post office, the committee for the building of the Cathedral of St. Isaac, the committee on archaeology, and the department of horse breeding. According to one of the censors, A. V. Nikitenko, "if one were to count all officials in charge of censorship their number would greatly exceed the number of books published annually." The emperor himself acted occasionally as censor, for instance, in the case of Pushkin, but this mark of imperial attention, over which the poet at first unwisely rejoiced, did not exempt his work from censorship by other agencies. Section III of His Majesty's Own Chancery was particularly active, and it was customary for editors and authors to receive orders from Benckendorff and his lieutenants as to how they should handle literary matters. No journal might be published without special authorization, which was often refused, and the suspension of periodicals, accompanied by deportations of editors and authors, was a common occurrence. Literary and other works circulated in manuscript were, like printed books, subject to censorship. Pushkin was severely reprimanded by Benckendorff for reading in the Moscow salons his *Boris Godunov* before it was submitted to the tsar. Yuri Samarin, in spite of his court connections, was imprisoned in the fortress of Peter and Paul for circulating the manuscript of a study in which he criticized official policies in the Baltic provinces. With the appointment on April 2, 1848, immediately after the outbreak of the revolution in France, of a secret committee on censorship under Count D. P. Buturlin, there began what is usually known as the "era of censorship terror," which lasted until the dissolution of the committee on December 6, 1855. The censors, spurred by threat of penalties for laxity and lack of zeal, used the red pencil with utmost freedom, deleting even such innocuous terms as "forces of nature" in textbooks on physics. Uvarov himself, as has already been stated, fell victim of this vicious system which owed him so much. There was probably no editor or author, however cautious and subservient to the wishes of the government, who did entirely succeed in escaping the wrath of the censors.

One of the most notable demonstrations of the official attitude towards dissenting opinions was the case of Peter Chaadaev (1793–1856). A brilliant officer in the guards' hussars, a dandy, a man of the world, and a favorite in the aristocratic salons of St. Petersburg and Moscow, Chaadaev was also a religious philosopher of deep convictions and literary ability. His mystical philosophy, which bore the imprint of Roman Catholicism, saw in the unification of the Christian churches the only road to establishment of the "Kingdom of God." He expounded his views in "philosophical letters" freely circulated in the aristocratic circles of Moscow, where Chaadaev lived after his retirement from the army in 1821. Several attempts to have the "letters" published were unsuccessful, but finally one of them appeared in the Moscow journal, the *Telescope*, in September, 1836. This celebrated profession of faith compared Russia with western Europe and drew the most unflattering conclusions. Russia, Chaadaev argued, did not belong to either east or west and was lacking in the cultural tradition of both. "Cast a glance over all the centuries we have lived, over all the territory we occupy," he wrote, "and you will find not a single memory that would arrest you, not a single monument that would bring out the past vividly, powerfully, concretely. We live in a state of indifference towards everything, with a narrow horizon, with no past or future." And again: "Hermits in the world, we gave it nothing and have received nothing from it; we contributed not a single thought to the sum total of the ideas of mankind; we have not assisted in perfecting human understanding and we have distorted whatever we have borrowed from it. During our entire existence as a society we have done nothing for the common good of man; not one useful thought has been born on our arid soil." The reason for Russia's alleged failings was her isolation from western Europe because of the polluted source of eastern Christianity. "Led by a malevolent fate," wrote Chaadaev, "we have borrowed the first seeds of our moral and spiritual enlightenment from decadent, generally despised Byzantium."

This avowedly inadequate summary of Chaadaev's not always very clear and consistent theories (he referred, for instance, to Russia's mission "to teach the world a great lesson" in some undetermined future) must suffice to convey the tenor of his argument. The "letter" created a sensation, supporters of "official patriotism" were outraged, and retribution came swiftly. The *Telescope* was suspended, its editor exiled, the censor who passed the article dismissed, and Chaadaev was declared insane. He was not, however, confined to an asylum, but had merely to endure for a year the daily visits of a doctor, and his freedom of movement was somewhat restricted. It is noteworthy that in spite of the vexations, rather than severe punishment, devised for Chaadaev by the emperor himself, his social position was enhanced by the persecution. The fact that he remained until his death one of Moscow's most popular and revered figures would seem to indicate that patriotism of the Uvarov brand had little support outside official circles.

LITERATURE AND THE THEATER

In spite of the obstacles besetting its path, the development of Russian literature in 1825–1855 was exceptionally fruitful; this period, indeed, has been called the golden age of Russian letters. Of the authors whose work does not extend beyond the chronological limits of Nicholas's reign, the most important were Pushkin, Lermontov, Koltsov, and Gogol. The literary output of Pushkin in the brief span between 1825 and January, 1837, when he died, was as rich as it was many-sided. He completed his great novel in verse, *Eugene Onegin* (1830), and wrote numerous lyrics, several major poems (including *Poltava*, 1828; *The Bronze Horseman*, 1833; and the delightful popular tales: *The Story of Tsar Saltan*, 1831; *The Mermaid*, 1832; *Le Coq d'Or*, 1834) and many prose works. It was not until 1827 that Pushkin turned to the latter medium of literary expression. His stories and a novel (*The Captain's Daughter*, completed in 1833 but revised later)—humane, humorous, and admirably written—were on as high a level as his poems. Pushkin, however, aspired to be a historian. Some of his fictional works show familiarity with Russian and European history, and he worked assiduously in archives, which were thrown open to him by order of the emperor. The outcome of this labor was *The History of the Pugachev Rebellion* (two volumes, 1834), the original title *History of Pugachev* being changed by Nicholas on the ground that a criminal could have no "history." Pushkin's ambition was to write a history of Peter I, for which he collected materials; but, as appears from his notes, the more he learned about his hero, the better he realized the brutality of Peter's methods and the terrible price Russia had to pay for conquests and reforms. Having long admired and extolled Peter, Pushkin found himself on the horns of a dilemma. He knew, moreover, that nothing but a panegyric of the tsar-reformer would be passed by the censorship. Whatever the reason, the history of Peter remained unwritten, as did many other projected literary works (among them a novel of contemporary life), notes for which were found in Pushkin's papers after his death.

The volume and scope of Pushkin's literary activity are all the more astonishing because the years 1825–1837 were a disturbed and unhappy period in his life. Pushkin was close to many Decembrists, and after the uprising of December 14, 1825, expecting arrest, he burned his papers. In 1826, however, he had an audience with Nicholas, and not only made his peace with autocracy but accepted the personal patronage of the emperor. A love marriage (1831) with a pretty woman, fond of society, did not bring him happiness. He lived beyond his means and found himself under the necessity of appealing to the tsar for financial assistance and of accepting money gifts, a sinecure at the ministry of foreign affairs, and the court office of *kammer-junker* (a position usually held by men younger than Pushkin was at the time, and therefore an "honor" he bitterly resented). The resulting dependence on the munificence of Nicholas and on the good graces of Benckendorff, intermediary in his relations with the tsar, preyed heavily on Pushkin's mind. He found himself in an ambiguous and awkward position, incompatible with his sincere and often expressed belief that a poet should be free from outside, especially official, influences. He made several half-hearted and futile attempts to break his chains and escape the stifling atmosphere of St. Petersburg. Scandalous gossip involving his wife added to his torment and led to a duel in which he was killed.

Michael Lermontov (1814–1841), a descendant, according to tradition, of a Scotch bard, was a wealthy aristocrat and an officer in the guards' hussars. Passionate, uncontrollable, and restless, he filled his brief life with violent incidents that culminated in his death in a duel. A master, like Pushkin, of both verse and prose, Lermontov relished depicting unhappy and powerful characters, contemptuous of mankind, proud of their solitude, and marked by fate for some mysterious destiny. The kinship of his work with that of Byron has often been emphasized by critics. The philosopher Vladimir Solovev saw in the foreboding figures drawn by Lermontov the forerunners of Nietzsche's superman. Lermontov's most representative poem was *The Demon*, first written in 1829 and revised several times in later years but not published in his lifetime because of censorship. His admirable novel *The Hero of Our Time* presented a vivid and realistic picture of contemporary society, even though its central character, Pechorin, was not free from romantic traits, and he wrote many lyrics expressing the feelings of the ordinary man. The purity of Lermontov's language, the perfection of his verse, the versatility of his genius, the simplicity and sincerity of many of his poems and the depth of feeling they reveal entitle him, in the opinion of Russia's most authoritative literary critics, to a place "among the giants not only of Russian but of European literature."

Unlike Pushkin and Lermontov, Alexis Koltsov (1808–1842) was a true son of the people. Born into the family of a small merchant in a forlorn provincial town, he had one year of schooling. Associated with his father in business, he spent his life among illiterate or semi-literate tradesmen, although in later years he paid several visits to Moscow and St. Petersburg. He learned to write poetry from books of verse and a manual on versification he chanced to pick up in shops and at country fairs. His genius and perseverance, however, triumphed over all obstacles. His poems began to appear in journals in the early 1830's, and the first small volume of his verse was published in 1835. Koltsov's first-hand knowledge of peasant life, not as an outsider looking on from the aloofness of the manor house, but as one of the common people; his appreciation of the homely beauty of the countryside, which he visited frequently on business trips; his genuine understanding of the joys and sorrows of those who, like himself, had little to expect from life; and his mastery of the popular tongue, gave his work its unique quality. He was at his best in popular songs, which received immediate recognition and remain unsurpassed in Russian literature. By presenting for the first time an unadorned yet poetical and moving picture of the life of the underdog, Koltsov introduced into Russian literature an important new theme which was successfully developed by later writers—the poet N. A. Nekrasov, I. S. Turgenev (in his *Sportsman's Sketches*), and Maxim Gorky.

Nicholas Gogol (1809–1852), born in Ukraine of a family of lesser nobility and modest means, received a meager education in the *lycée* of Nezhin. In 1828 he went to St. Petersburg, did some tutoring, and held for a short time a chair of history in the University of St. Petersburg, an episode that added nothing to his reputation. In 1836 he went abroad and, paying but brief visits to Russia, lived for many years in Rome, which he regarded as his second home. Gogol's literary career began in 1830 with the publication of stories and short novels dealing with Ukrainian life, legends, and history. These early works, vivid, picturesque, and humorous, were in the romantic vein and contained many poetical exaggerations and historical and ethnographic inaccuracies. They were followed by the so-called "St. Petersburg stories" and plays on subjects drawn from the everyday life of the lower middle class, which revealed Gogol as the leading author of the realistic school. In 1836 there was published his celebrated comedy *The Inspector General*, and in 1842 his great masterpiece *Dead Souls*. This extraordinary novel without a plot (Gogol called it a poem) unfolded with a force and insight of which there are few examples in world literature, a broad canvas of provincial and rural Russia. It was a telling human document and, by implication, an indictment of the existing social order, tempered, however, by a profound understanding of human frailties and by that peculiar and gentle humor which is one of the characteristics of Gogol's genius. Written in a sometimes ungrammatical, yet inimitably picturesque and irresistible style of which Gogol had the secret, it was probably the most truly national major literary work ever to appear in Russia. Its essentially national character and the difficulties of interpreting Gogol in foreign languages without losing the flavor of the original is presumably responsible for the fact that *Dead Souls* is less generally known abroad than are some of the other great and near-great Russian works.

Dead Souls won the acclaim of liberal opinion but was denounced by the conservative press as a vile caricature. The author came to resent applause more than he did detractions. The founder of Russian realism was a moralist and a religious mystic. He conceived his mission to be that of a divinely inspired teacher of mankind, but he was not interested in political or social reforms; moral betterment, he believed, was the source from which was to spring the glorious world of the future. This peculiar frame of mind, revealed in a few isolated passages in *Dead Souls*, became more pronounced with the passing of years, when, under the influence of Roman Catholicism, Gogol drifted into morbid religiosity and extreme political conservatism. In 1847 he published his *Correspondence with Friends*, a eulogy of Russian autocracy and serfdom; he went to the extreme of maintaining that the police and administrative institutions of Russia, so sublimely ridiculed in his own writings, were of divine origin: "God had invisibly guided the hands of the tsars." Repudiating his earlier work, Gogol proceeded to write volume two of *Dead Souls*, which was to present the positive side of Russian life not to be found in volume one. It is believed that he contemplated the writing of a vast trilogy modeled after Dante's *Divine Comedy:* volume one of *Dead Souls* was to be the *Inferno*. Gogol, however, too sensitive and sincere an artist to do violence to truth, failed miserably in his new undertaking. Dissatisfied with his draft of volume two, he burned it in 1843, rewrote it, and burned it again in 1845. Whatever was preserved of the text was published posthumously, only to prove that Gogol used good judgment in destroying the manuscript. It was not in his power, however, to undo his own work. Pushkin and Lermontov had contributed to the defeat of sentimentalism and romanticism, but Gogol is regarded as the true founder of realism. His influence, combined with that of foreign authors—George Sand, Stendhal, Balzac, Dickens, Thackeray (the two latter were translated into Russian by I. Vvedensky in the 1840's) —paved the way for the great novels of Turgenev, Dostoevsky, and Leo Tolstoy.

The tradition of the newborn school of realism, or naturalism as it was called in Russia, was carried on by an unusually large group of distinguished authors whose literary work began previous to the accession of Alexander II, although their major contributions were made in the second half of the nineteenth century. Among them were the novelists Turgenev, Goncharov, Dostoevsky, and Leo Tolstoy, and the poets Nekrasov, Tiutchev, Fet, Maikov, and Polonsky. It is characteristic of Russian conditions that some of these men of letters (Goncharov, Tiutchev, Polonsky) were also censors.

The theater was less prone than literature to respond to new literary tendencies because, perhaps, it was under the particularly strict control of the government. The stage was dominated by sentimental melodramas steeped in "official patriotism." The more popular playwrights of this uninspiring school were N. A. Polevoy (1796–1846) and N. V. Kukolnik (1809–1868). Translations of Kotzebue's hair-raising melodramas and adaptations of light French comedies were the normal fare of Russian theatergoers. Relief from this distressing mediocrity was offered by the production of a few plays of Molière, Shakespeare, and Schiller. Russian realism, however, began to assert itself on the stage in the 1830's with Griboedov's *The Misfortune of Being Wise* and the comedies of Gogol, scored further victories in the 1840's with the plays of Turgenev, and won final recognition in the work of Alexander Ostrovsky (1823–1886). Ostrovsky, a minor employee in a Moscow commercial court, had an intimate knowledge of lower middle-class life which he used effectively as the milieu of some fifty plays. The first of them was produced in 1853 and proved a resounding success. With the plays of Griboedov, Gogol, Turgenev, and Ostrovsky the spell of sentimental melodrama was broken.

The ascendancy of realism was greatly helped by literary criticism, which played an important part in educating the public and in developing appreciation of new authors. Vissarion Belinsky (1810–1848) was the first and, according to historians of Russian letters, the greatest professional literary critic in Russian history. He was not a mere commentator on current books, but a student of literature and art and a social philosopher of uncommon insight and power. To a modern reader his literary criticisms, penetrating as they are, may appear to be overloaded with German metaphysics (he never completely freed himself from the influence of Hegel, although he formally repudiated him in 1840) and lacking in restraint and a judicial approach. Understatement was not a characteristic of the writings of Belinsky, whom his friends nicknamed "Vissariono furioso." He enjoyed a position of influence that no other critic has ever attained, and his enthusiastic endorsement of Pushkin, Griboedov, Lermontov, Koltsov, and Gogol, to mention only a few, was a real service to Russian literature. Belinsky's *Letter to Gogol*, a passionate rejoinder to *Correspondence with Friends*, was a literary event, and it is said to have been committed to memory by practically every liberal-minded Russian youth, although its full text did not appear in print until 1905.[11] It is believed that only death saved Belinsky from arrest. Apollon Grigorev (1822–1864) was another distinguished literary critic, but his influence was not nearly so great as Belinsky's.

ART

Startling as was the progress of Russian literature during this period, it was in some degree the result of previous developments. The situation with music was different. Until the late 1830's Russia had no national operatic or concert music worthy of the name. Folk songs

[11] Belinsky had advocated in 1837–1840 views similar to those expressed by Gogol in his unfortunate *Correspondence*. Belinsky was at the time under the strong influence of the Hegelian formula: "What is rational exists, and what exists is rational." This led him to "reconciliation with reality" (a literal translation of *Die Versöhnung mit der Wirklichkeit*, which occurs in Hegel's *Philosophie des Rechts*), and, as a consequence, to an apologia for the existing social and political order. It took him two years to realize the incongruity of his position, and in October, 1840, he repudiated with his customary passion "my disgraceful desire for reconciliation with a disgraceful reality."

were transmitted orally from generation to generation, and the few transcriptions available were so inadequate as to impair, rather than preserve, this priceless heritage. The Orthodox Church had jealously protected its chants from lay influence; moreover, since no instrumental music is used in Orthodox services, the Russian Church could not have contributed to its development, as did, for instance, Roman Catholicism. No music schools existed in St. Petersburg or Moscow, and the teaching of music was in the hands of private instructors, chiefly foreigners. The few "Russian composers" of the eighteenth and early nineteenth century were either foreign expatriates, technically competent but alien to the spirit and melodies of their adopted country, or native Russians ignorant of the art they professed. An outstanding example of the former was the Italian Caterino Cavos (1776–1840), a resident of St. Petersburg since 1798 and *Kapellmeister* of the imperial opera house. He wrote over fifty operas, ballets, and other pieces, but even when his scenarios were Russian (for instance, the super-patriotic opera *Ivan Susanin*) his treatment and music—not of a high order—remained Italian. His successful Russian contemporary Alexis Verstovsky (1799–1862), author of six operas (among them the popular *Tomb of Askold*), had no knowledge of harmony, orchestration, or counterpoint. What passed in Russia for operas were not operas in the accepted meaning of the term, nor was there any symphonic music. The most popular compositions were romances, some of them melodious and pleasing, but technically deplorably low.

It is this humble background that gives the full measure of Glinka's achievement. Michael Glinka (1804–1857), the first great Russian composer, studied for several years in Italy and Germany, and later in France, and assimilated the musical culture of western Europe. His genius led him to apply European technique to national musical themes with which he had been familiar from his childhood. The resulting compositions were original and at the same time on a level with those of European masters. Glinka wrote two operas: *A Life for the Tsar* (1836)—the name has been changed in the Soviet Union to *Ivan Susanin*—and *Ruslan and Liudmila* (1842). Good music, however, needs a public capable of appreciating it. *A Life for the Tsar*, although criticized at first by aristocratic audiences as *musique de cochers*, at once won a permanent place in opera repertory because of its patriotic subject. *Ruslan and Liudmila*, which is regarded by music critics as superior to *A Life for the Tsar*, was favorably received but was withdrawn after one year and was not produced again in Glinka's lifetime. Deeply discouraged, the composer could not force himself to write another opera. Glinka's influence on Russian music was great and may be traced in the work of practically every nineteenth century Russian composer. Tchaikovsky held that, although Glinka wrote no symphonies, the entire Russian symphonic school is contained in his *Kamarinskaia* (Russian dance) "as an oak in an acorn." Glinka's numerous romances are among the best in Russian musical literature.

Alexander Dargomyzhsky (1813–1869), author of several operas, among them one of Russia's favorites, *The Mermaid*, was not so eminent a composer as Glinka, by whom he was strongly influenced, but his work has distinct merit, originality, and sound workmanship. Alexander Serov (1820–1871), although he wrote three operas, is best remembered as Russia's first competent music critic.

The evolution of painting, while slower and less spectacular than that of literature and music, showed a similar tendency. The Academy of Arts, mainstay of the pseudo-classical tradition, was still the supreme arbiter whose theories few painters dared to challenge. Portraits and biblical, mythological, allegorical, and historical subjects were the only ones considered worthy of the attention of an artist, landscapes and interiors being tolerated if they depicted elegant parks and the residences of the wealthy, or scenes of sunny Italy. Russian scenery and Russian life, except for romanticized historical episodes, were not deemed suitable subjects for pictures. Most of the painters were trained abroad, especially in Italy, where they were taught to copy slavishly the works of the masters of the Renaissance. Any departure from convention was discouraged by the Academy. The Society for the Encouragement of Artists, founded in 1820 with the object of sending Russian painters abroad, instructed its fellows to adhere strictly to the academic program. Under these conditions there was little opportunity for originality, and Russian painting (with the exception of the work of a few portrait painters, for instance, O. A. Kiprensky, 1783–1836) was hardly more than a feeble reflection of western European art. The most outstanding representatives of the academic school were K. P. Brüllov (1799–1852) and F. A. Bruni (1800–1875). Brüllov's *Last Days of Pompeii* (1836), a vast, ambitious composition with striking light effects, created a furor. Brüllov, however, did not remain entirely faithful to the academic manner; he defended the right of the artist "to come closer to nature," and the best of his portraits, in the opinion of art critics, offer the first examples of realism in Russian painting. He was, moreover, broad-minded and tolerant, and extended his powerful patronage to younger men, for instance, to Paul Fedotov, who had partly broken away from the academic tradition.

Genre painting, that is, portrayal of scenes from ordinary life, was introduced in Russia by A. G. Venetsianov (1780–1847), although he had a few obscure predecessors. Venetsianov believed that one should paint, "not in the manner of Rubens or Rembrandt," but, as he quaintly put it, "*à la* nature," as the artist sees life around him. His first picture dealing with peasant life was exhibited in 1824 and was followed by several others on similar themes. Venetsianov's realism, however, was limited to his subjects; his treatment of rural scenes remained academic and divorced from Russian realities, some of his peasant women looking distressingly like Italian Madonnas. The work of Paul Fedotov (1815–1852) marked a step away from conventionality; his pictures portraying the life of the lower middle class, humorous but never sardonic, were highly successful, and won him the reputation of founder of realism in Russian painting. Fedotov enjoyed Nicholas's special favor and, although genre painting was frowned upon by the Academy, he was elected a member of the august body. The place of Alexander Ivanov (1806–1858) among Russian artists is more difficult to determine. A painter of great talent, he detested academic tradition and dreamed of revolutionizing Russian art. Yet he was made a member of the Academy in 1836 and, in spite of the merit of his work and his heroic efforts to throw off the shackles of tradition, he did not succeed in freeing himself from the conventional approach or in creating a manner of his own. Ivanov spent most of his life in Italy working on a vast canvas, *Appearance of Christ to the People*, which was well received in Italy but proved a failure in Russia, where it was finally exhibited in 1858. It is believed, nevertheless, that Ivanov did exercise a profound influence on Russian art. The almost ascetic restraint of his composition, coloring, and use of light was in striking contrast with the flamboyant effects and labored artificiality of Bruni's and Brüllov's historical and biblical paintings.[12]

---

[12] A Soviet publication issued under the auspices of the Academy of Science describes Ivanov as "one of the world's greatest painters" (*Istoriia S.S.S.R.*, ed. M. V. Nechkina [Moscow, 1940], II, 377). This is surely a gross exaggeration.

Improvement in public taste was evidenced by the remarkable progress in the subtle art of engraving, illustrating, and bookmaking. The 1830's and 1840's are said to have produced some of the finest books ever printed in Russia.

Sculptors found it more difficult than did painters to free themselves from academic conventions; here technical progress still followed traditional lines. In the compositions of Count Fedor Tolstoy, already mentioned in an earlier chapter, mythological and classical subjects acquired new vigor and freshness. The modest beginnings of realism in sculpture are found in the work of Baron P. K. Clodt (1805–1867), especially in his bas reliefs on Krylov's monument portraying the quaint animal world of Russian fables.

Architecture was the least fortunate of the arts. Plans for churches, public buildings, and in some cases private dwellings were required to be submitted for government approval. Nicholas took a personal interest in architecture, and his belief in the infallibility of his taste had dire consequences. The "Russian *empire*" of the eighteenth and early nineteenth centuries, which was not without grace and charm, gave place to a deplorable eclecticism, a haphazard mixture of styles borrowed from western Europe. Eclecticism was superseded by a quasi-Russian national style, an unfortunate invention of Professor K. A. Ton (1794–1881), who endeavored to combine in his plans and drawings what he believed to be the elements of Byzantine and ancient Russian architecture. In 1841 Ton's "Russo-Byzantine" style—a fitting counterpart of "official patriotism"—was sanctioned by the emperor and was made obligatory for the designers of churches, public buildings, and even cottages in military settlements. The most notable examples of Ton's work were the Grand Palais in the Kremlin and the Church of Christ the Savior in Moscow, which was demolished to make place for the Palace of the Soviets.

THE CLEAVAGE

The intensification of intellectual activity and the emergence of a vocal public opinion critical of official policies and demanding reforms were perhaps the most significant and portentous traits of Russia's social history in the second quarter of the nineteenth century. The opposition was still unorganized and numerically insignificant, but it was no longer a tiny group of disaffected noblemen, such as the Decembrists. It drew its leadership and following not only from the nobility but also from the middle and lower middle class (Belinsky, Koltsov) and even the former serfs (Shevchenko). The severity of censorship notwithstanding, the press, literature, and the theater reflected to some extent the growing feeling of uneasiness and dissatisfaction. Although the masses of the people remained outside the current of protest against serfdom and autocracy, they had among the intellectual élite ardent champions, precursors of the liberal and revolutionary movement which seventy years later was to make a clean sweep of the monarchy. To all demands for reform the government opposed the blind wall of bureaucratic complacency and the determination to suppress liberal thought by every means at the disposal of a quasi-omnipotent police regime. Hence the deep cleavage between "official Russia," on the one hand, and nascent liberal opinion, on the other. The Crimean War temporarily strengthened the position of the government by silencing dissenting voices and by increasing the popularity of the crude doctrines of "official patriotism." But this was merely an ebbing of the tide which ended with the debacle of Sevastopol.

CHAPTER XXXII

THE EASTERN QUESTION, 1825–1855

The early Victorian era was an age of optimism where history counted for little and abstract theory for much.
—HAROLD TEMPERLEY, *England and the Near East: The Crimea* (London, 1936), p. 246.

NATURE OF THE CONFLICT

In the second quarter of the nineteenth century the "eastern question"—that is, the control of Constantinople and the Straits (the Bosphorus and the Dardanelles), the fate of the Christian population in Turkey and, in the last analysis, the survival or dissolution of the Ottoman empire—became the central question of Russian foreign policy. Economic rivalries, although an important factor in the struggle for the domination of the Near East, do not alone explain the tortuous course of European diplomacy which led to the Crimean War. Modern historiography inclines to the view that the clash between Russia and the European coalition was not inevitable, and should be traced to factors other than the interplay of immutable economic forces. The personal element, so contemptuously dismissed as trivial by the believers in economic determinism, played probably a decisive part in shaping the course of events. Nicholas, in agreement with his minister of foreign affairs, Nesselrode, espoused the theory that the maintenance of the *status quo* in Turkey was in Russia's best interest. The soothing effect of this conciliatory attitude, which was expressed in several international agreements, was unfortunately destroyed by the tsar's belief, disclosed in his utterances, that the demise of the "sick man" on the Bosphorus was inevitable, and by his insistence on making arrangements for this problematic contingency in the imminence of which Nesselrode, among many others, did not believe.[1] In view of the emperor's dual attitude and Russia's past record in dealing with Turkey, it is not surprising that official Russian pronouncements were readily discounted in European capitals, while sinister interpretations of every move of the imperial government received wide credence. Nicholas's attachment to the principle of legitimacy made him a lukewarm supporter of the national aspirations of the Greeks and the Balkan Slavs, in spite of the pressure brought to bear upon him by the numerically small but vocal Russian Orthodox and panslav circles. Since his disinterestedness in the fate of his coreligionists under Turkish rule (in whom he was inclined to see rebels against their legitimate monarch) was at variance with Russia's encroachments on Turkish sovereignty in Moldavia and Wallachia, it was plausibly interpreted abroad as mere deceit and hypocrisy. The tsar's detestation of revolution and liberalism determined his hostile attitude towards France and precluded the *rapprochement* with England which Nicholas repeatedly sought, while his inability to grasp the nature of the British constitutional government and the limitations it imposed upon the queen and her ministers led him into serious errors of judgment. Perhaps as crucial were the consequences of the personal failings of the other leading figures of this period: Napoleon's impatience with the snubs administered to him by the Russian court and his longing for quick victories and military laurels; Lord Aberdeen's indecisions and hesitant leadership; and, above all, the militant hatred of Russia by Lord Palmerston and Sir Stratford Canning (later, Viscount Stratford de Redcliffe), British ambassador, but actually proconsul at Constantinople. "The anti-Russian feeling of these two men," writes Temperley, "was one profound cause of the war." The mutual distrust of leaders tended to inflame public opinion, and throve on the loose wording of international agreements.

1825–1830

In accordance with tradition Nicholas began his reign by proclaiming his adherence to the foreign policy of his predecessor. His first important diplomatic move, however, resulted in the weakening of the

[1] In his conversations with Sir George Hamilton Seymour, the British ambassador, in January–February, 1853, and on many other occasions, Nicholas actually used the expression "sick" and "dying bear." The substitution of "man" for "bear" in the Blue Book was made "from a mistaken sense of decorum." Harold Temperley, *England and the Near East: The Crimea* (Longmans, Green and Company, Ltd., London, 1936), p. 272.

Holy Alliance, through abandonment of Russia's former attitude of non-intervention in the Greek war of independence. The poor showing of the Turkish troops against the Greeks forced Sultan Mahmud II reluctantly to appeal for military help to his powerful vassal Mehemet Ali, pasha of Egypt, and the landing in Morea (February, 1825) of a well disciplined Egyptian army under Ibrahim Pasha, Mehemet Ali's son, threatened not only the collapse of the Greek insurrection but also the extermination of the Greek population. An Anglo-Russian agreement on the Greek question was foreshadowed by informal negotiations between the two governments in the closing months of Alexander I's reign.[2] The Duke of Wellington, a staunch Tory, was therefore assured of a cordial reception when he arrived in St. Petersburg to offer his government's felicitations on the accession of the new tsar. Wellington's political mission, however, was only partly successful. On April 4, 1826, N.S., there was signed in St. Petersburg an Anglo-Russian protocol which provided for British mediation in establishing an autonomous Greek state under the suzerainty of the sultan; Russia promised to assist Great Britain, "as and when required," in carrying out this plan; mediation failing, Great Britain and Russia undertook to pursue a common policy towards Greece with the object of achieving her independence. This reversal in the policy of George Canning, then secretary of state for foreign affairs, was motivated primarily by his desire to prevent Russia's independent action in Turkey. The tsar, however, who had little real sympathy for the insurgent Greeks, was not prepared to entrust to Great Britain the mediation of other issues pending between Russia and the Porte, as suggested by Canning and Wellington. Without consulting Wellington, Nicholas sent to Constantinople in March, 1826, a virtual ultimatum demanding the withdrawal of Turkish troops from the Danubian principalities, the restoration in these provinces of the autonomous institutions abolished by Mahmud in 1821, the immediate release of Serbian deputies imprisoned by the Turks, the granting to the Serbs of privileges stipulated by the Treaty of Bucharest (1812), and the convocation of a Russo-Turkish conference. The internal difficulties experienced by the Porte and the endorsement, although by no means uniformly enthusiastic, of Russian demands by the representatives of the great Powers in Constantinople, made the sultan accept these conditions. Russian and Turkish delegates met at Akkerman and on October 7, 1826, N.S.,

[2] See p. 689.

signed a convention which settled the question of the Danubian principalities and Serbia according to Russia's wishes,[3] recognized Russian sovereignty over certain disputed areas on the Caucasian littoral, and granted Russian merchantmen free passage through the Straits and the right of navigation in Turkish waters.

If London was shocked by the Russian ultimatum to Turkey, Vienna and Berlin were even more distressed by the St. Petersburg protocol. Metternich was horrified at the very thought of "mediation" on behalf of the "Greek rebels," and saw in the Anglo-Russian agreement the death blow to the Holy Alliance. Neither Great Britain nor Russia, however, showed any haste in fulfilling the obligations they had assumed towards Greece. Canning, while dreading Russia's isolated action, was reluctant to go to war with Turkey over Greece; Nicholas hesitated to jeopardize the advantages so recently secured at Akkerman. Futile negotiations dragged on for months, and it was not until April, 1827, that the offer of mediation embodied in the St. Petersburg protocol was submitted to the sultan and met with court rejection. It became clear that coercive measures against Turkey could no longer be postponed if Greece was to be saved from destruction. Canning believed, however, that the safest method of preventing the war from spreading would be a concerted action by at least some of the great Powers. On July 6, 1827, N.S., the St. Petersburg protocol was converted into the Treaty of London, signed by Great Britain, Russia, and France. This document recapitulated the determination of the signatory Powers to establish Greece as an autonomous state, a tributary of the sultan. A secret article provided that, by using "means which circumstances may suggest to their prudence" but "without . . . taking part in the hostilities," the three governments should bind themselves to induce Turkey and Greece to accept an armistice within a month. Both Austria and Prussia having refused to sign the Treaty of London, Nicholas voiced his regret at having to enter into an international agreement which did not include his two partners in the Holy Alliance. While Metternich endeavored to persuade Turkey and Greece to accept his mediation, the control of events slipped from the hands of diplomats and passed into those of naval commanders.

[3] The privileges granted to Serbia were as follows: freedom of worship; local autonomy; restoration of districts severed from Serbia; tax reform; the right to carry on commercial pursuits in Turkey; the right to maintain schools, hospitals, and printing presses; the denial to Muslims, except members of the armed forces garrisoned in Serbia, of the right to reside in that province.

An allied fleet consisting of British, French, and Russian squadrons assembled in the Aegean Sea in order to force Turkey, by preventing supplies from reaching Ibrahim in Morea, to accept an armistice. In the Bay of Navarino, without any declaration of war and, it would seem by accident, the allied naval forces under the British admiral Sir Edward Codrington became involved in a major battle with the Turkish fleet, which was destroyed (October 20, 1827, N.S.). The Porte, incensed by what she regarded, not unnaturally, as an unwarranted and treacherous attack, demanded compensation and an apology; these being refused, the allied representatives left Constantinople and the sultan issued a manifesto denouncing the Christian Powers, especially Russia, annulling the Akkerman convention, and calling the faithful to a holy war (December 20, N.S.). Nicholas's proposal for strong military and naval action met with some support in France but none in England. George Canning, prime minister since the spring of 1827, had died in August and was succeeded by Viscount Goderich and, in January, 1828, by Wellington. The Iron Duke disapproved of Canning's Greek policy, and his mistrust of Russia was not allayed by an agreement of the three Powers (December 12, 1827, N.S.) not to seek exclusive benefits in case of a war with Turkey. The king's speech at the opening of parliament (January 29, 1828, N.S.) "deeply lamented" the Navarino battle as an "untoward event" (although Codrington was decorated for his part in the affair and was cleared of all blame by a court of inquiry), and the next day Wellington, speaking in the House of Lords, referred to Turkey as an "ancient ally" whose "existence as an independent and powerful state" was "necessary to the well-being" of England. Reversing Canning's policy of cooperation with Russia, Wellington, by refusing "to become party to the war," permitted the tsar and the sultan to fight out the issue between themselves. In view of the Turkish manifesto and the bellicose spirit displayed by Nicholas, war between the two empires could not be long deferred.

Russia, however, did not declare war on Turkey until April, 1828, partly because she was already engaged in a war with Persia. The annexation of the bulk of the Caucasus by the Treaty of Gulistan (1813) [4] strengthened the position of Russia's commerce in the Caspian Sea and enhanced her prestige in Teheran. Both these developments were resented not only by the Persians but also by the British,

---

[4] See p. 673, n. 6.

who saw in the Russian expansion in the Near East a menace to their trade and a potential threat to India. The fear of Russian designs on India became, indeed, an obsession with a long line of British statesmen from Wellington and Palmerston to Lord Curzon. The government of the shah, not without the instigation of English agents, denounced the Treaty of Gulistan, and in June, 1826, Persian troops crossed the Russian border. After some initial success, however, they met with reverses at the hands of a Russian corps commanded first by Ermolov and later by Paskevich, and in 1827 hostilities were transferred to Persian soil. The taking by assault of Erivan (October 1, 1827) was followed by an advance of Russian troops towards Teheran and by the capitulation of the Persians. By the Treaty of Turkmanchay (February 22, 1828, N.S.) Russia acquired the provinces of Nakhichevan and Erivan and obtained the right to maintain a navy in the Caspian Sea. The tsar was now free to deal with Turkey.

The Turkish campaign proved very different from the "military excursion" imagined by Nicholas and his generals. Though Russian troops occupied Moldavia and Wallachia without resistance, after crossing the Danube early in June, 1828, they encountered stubborn Turkish opposition. Varna, an important stronghold on the Black Sea, was taken towards the end of the year. The Russians, however, failed in their attempt at subduing the fortresses of Shumla and Silistria, and were forced to retreat behind the Danube, where they established winter quarters. The 1828 campaign in the Caucasus, although conducted by a much smaller force than that on the Danube, was far more successful. The Russians gained possession of the Black Sea littoral with the ports of Anapa, Sukhum-Kale, and Poti, while a corps under Paskevich freshly arrived from Persia took by storm the reputedly impregnable fortress of Kars (June 23) and by autumn had reached the upper basin of the Euphrates. With the appointment early in 1829 of Field Marshal Dibich as commander in chief of the Russian Danubian army, the campaign in that theater entered into a new and decisive phase. The Turks suffered a major defeat at Kulchava (May 30), Silistria capitulated (June 18), and a daring march over the Balkans brought Dibich to Adrianople, which surrendered without offering any resistance (August 8). By the end of August the Russian troops were within a few miles of Constantinople. Meanwhile Paskevich took Erzerum and was preparing to advance on Trebizond and Batum. Although the position of Dibich was precarious, with large undefeated Turkish armies in his rear and with his own force depleted by epidemics, Sultan Mahmud—distrustful of his commanders and troops, fearful of a revolutionary uprising, and pressed for concessions by the representatives of the great Powers, who were alarmed by the prospect of a Russian occupation of Constantinople—hastened to end the war by signing, on Russian terms, the Treaty of Adrianople (September 14, 1829, N.S.).

Russia had fought the Turkish war alone. From the beginning of the crisis, Metternich assumed a militantly anti-Russian attitude, endeavored to rally the European Powers to the defense of Turkey, and was suspected in St. Petersburg, although without sufficient ground, of warlike intentions. Wellington, too, was critical of Russian policy, but remained faithful to his determination to keep England out of the war. Curiously, the alliance of Great Britain, Russia, and France for the settlement of the Greek problem was maintained throughout the Russo-Turkish War. Desperately clinging to the fiction that the Greek question was unrelated to the war between Russia and Turkey, the three Powers continued to negotiate with the Porte for the establishment of an autonomous Greek state, in accordance with the London treaty of July 1827.[5] A protocol signed by the three Powers in London on July 19, 1828, N.S., authorized the sending of a French expeditionary force to Greece, but by the time the French troops reached their destination Sir Edward Codrington had arranged with Mehemet Ali for the withdrawal from Morea of Ibrahim and his Egyptian soldiers. Laborious negotiations resulted in the signature by Great Britain, Russia, and France of the London protocol of March 22, 1829, N.S., which, amending earlier agreements, provided for the establishment and defined the frontiers of an autonomous Greek state, tributary of the sultan, under a prince chosen by the signatory Powers. Wellington's manifest unwillingness to support the Greek cause was due, in part, to the election by the Greek national assembly (March, 1827) of Count Capo d'Istria, a former close associate of Emperor Alexander and a well known partisan of Russia, to the office of chief executive. Nevertheless British and French envoys were dispatched to Constantinople to negotiate with Turkey on the basis of the pro-

[5] In order to facilitate this quaint diplomatic game, Russia, in June, 1828, renounced her status as a belligerent in the Mediterranean, but resumed it in October of the same year by proclaiming the blockade of the Dardanelles, a move resented in England.

tocol of March 22. The Treaty of Adrianople made this *démarche* superfluous.

By the Treaty of Adrianople Russia annexed the mouth of the Danube and territories in the Caucasus, including a stretch of the Black Sea littoral, with Anapa and Poti. The Porte recognized Russia's recent territorial acquisitions from Persia and guaranteed freedom of Russian trade in Turkey, free passage of Russian merchantmen through the Bosphorus, and freedom of trade and navigation in the Black Sea. Moldavia and Wallachia, although remaining nominally under Turkish suzerainty, were to receive an "independent national government" and were placed under Russian protection. Serbia was granted the benefits conferred upon her by the convention of Akkerman. Turkey agreed to demilitarize the right bank of the Danube, to dismantle her military establishments in Moldavia and Wallachia, and to withdraw her troops from these provinces. Article X of the treaty provided for the settlement of the Greek question in accordance with the protocol of March 22. The Porte was to pay a large indemnity, the gradual withdrawal of Russian troops from the occupied territories being contingent on the performance of this obligation.

Although the terms of the Treaty of Adrianople could not have been influenced by the decisions of the conference on the future of Turkey held in St. Petersburg in September, 1829 (it met two days after the treaty was signed), they were in harmony with the conference's principal conclusions; namely, that from the point of view of Russia's interests "the advantages of preserving the Ottoman empire exceed its disadvantages." But if Russia favored the maintenance of the *status quo* in European Turkey, she was nevertheless determined to reap the fruits of her victory. In a letter to the Grand Duke Constantine, dated February 12, 1830, Nesselrode described the Ottoman empire as a country which "could now exist only under the protection of Russia and must comply with her wishes." This seemingly inescapable implication of the Treaty of Adrianople was realized abroad, especially in London and in Vienna. "I am not quite certain," Wellington wrote on October 4, 1829, N.S., "that what will exist will not be worse than the immediate annihilation of the Turkish Power." In an attempt to restore the British position in the Near East, Wellington and the Earl of Aberdeen, who in the middle of 1828 became secretary of state for foreign affairs, proposed that both Greece and Turkey should be placed under the guarantee of the Treaty of Vienna. This proposal being rejected by Russia, the British government endorsed Metternich's plan to make Greece an independent state, less likely—it was argued privately—to fall under Russian influence than if she was forced to remain a vassal of the sultan. Nicholas accepted this proposal, and the status of Greece as an independent hereditary kingdom under Prince Leopold of Coburg, uncle of the future Queen Victoria, was sanctioned by a protocol of the three Powers on February 3, 1830, N.S. The execution of this plan, however, was delayed by the July revolution, which played havoc with diplomatic alliances.

In the meantime the already precarious situation of Greece rapidly deteriorated. Leopold withdrew his acceptance of the proffered Greek throne (May, 1830). Capo d'Istria, who had made himself unpopular with liberal Greek circles, was murdered in October, 1831, a blow from which Russian influence in Greece never recovered. Finally the Greek Crown was bestowed by the three Powers upon the seventeen-year-old Prince Otto, second son of King Louis of Bavaria, and in January, 1833, the youthful monarch, accompanied by a retinue of Bavarian officials and some 3,500 Bavarian troops, landed on the ancient shores of his turbulent kingdom. It soon became apparent that the new government resented Russia's unceremonious interference in Greek affairs. In spite of her religious ties with Russia, Greece leaned towards the western Powers and remained outside Russia's political orbit.

THE JULY REVOLUTION AND THE CRISIS OF 1833

By the end of 1829 relations between Russia and Austria had greatly deteriorated. The French revolution of July, 1830, followed by the Belgian revolution (September), the Polish insurrection (November), and a wave of political and social unrest in Italy and Germany revived, however, the specter of the Holy Alliance which Metternich had only recently declared to be dead (his report to Emperor Francis I, October 9, 1829, N.S.). A week after Louis Philippe had become king of France, Metternich and Nesselrode signed the so-called *"chiffon de Carlsbad"* (August 6, 1830, N.S.), which voiced the intention of the two governments to protect the existing international order and "the internal peace of European states" against subversive French influence. Prussia adhered to the Carlsbad agreement, but the formal renewal of the alliance did not take place until 1833. It was in vain that Nicholas advocated in Berlin and in Vienna a crusade for the restoration of the Bourbons in France and the forcible return of Belgium to rule by the king of Holland. The Polish insurrection put an end to his plan for armed intervention in western Europe, and Nicholas was forced to grant recognition to Louis Philippe, "the king of the barricades." In the meantime, following the defeat of the Tory government in London, Lord Grey in November, 1830, formed a Whig ministry. Palmerston was appointed secretary of state for foreign affairs, a position he held with but one short interruption until the autumn of 1841. At the foreign office, in the opposition, at the home office, and as prime minister he remained until his death (1865) a dominating influence in British politics.

In spite of the stormy developments in western Europe and Poland, the eastern question continued to claim the attention of St. Petersburg. The Treaty of Adrianople established a virtual Russian protectorate over Moldavia and Wallachia. A commission of local notables, working in accordance with an instruction received from St. Petersburg and guided by the Russian viceroy, General P. D. Kiselev, drafted the "organic statute" (constitution) of the two Danubian principalities. Under the provisions of this charter each principality was to have an autonomous government headed by a hospodar, who was to be elected for life by a small group of ecclesiastical dignitaries, nobles, and landed proprietors. It is surprising, in view of Nicholas's unbounded admiration for autocracy, that the statute embodied some of the principles of constitutional government (separation of powers, representative elected assemblies, although on the basis of a limited franchise), as well as provisions for the development of the school system and the regulation of the relationship between the landowners and their peasant farmers. The statute was approved by a specially appointed committee in St. Petersburg and by assemblies of Moldavian and Wallachian notables. The Porte had merely the dubious privilege of formally sanctioning the charter and putting it into effect. For a time the immediate future of the principalities remained uncertain. Kiselev favored their outright annexation by Russia, but Nesselrode doubted the economic gains to be derived from this move and dreaded its international repercussions. Nicholas sided with his vice chancellor, and after the Porte had enacted the statute into law early in 1834 Russian troops were withdrawn. This decision was influenced by the change that had taken place in Russo-Turkish relations, and by the tsar's desire to allay the suspicions of Austria, the alliance with which had been renewed in 1833.

In 1832 the eastern question entered an acute phase. In November, 1831, Mehemet Ali, pasha of Egypt, rebelled against Sultan Mahmud II, and by the middle of the following year Ibrahim Pasha, commander of the insurgent army, conquered Syria and threatened Constantinople. The sultan appealed for help to the western Powers but met with indifferent success. Metternich merely went through his usual intricate diplomatic motions. The attitude of France was even more ambiguous. Mehemet Ali was her protégé, and his rebellion was not altogether unwelcome in Paris because it tended to facilitate French designs on Africa, which later led to the conquest of Algeria. England, whose friendship for the Porte Wellington had so recently and so solemnly proclaimed, proved hardly more responsive than had Austria and France. Palmerston turned a deaf ear to Stratford Canning's ardent plea for the immediate dispatch of a naval force to the Levant and the conclusion of a formal alliance with Turkey. He would not commit himself beyond promises of diplomatic intervention, and he did not agree to send a naval squadron to the Archipelago until May, 1833, that is, after Mahmud had come to terms with Mehemet Ali.

Unlike the western Powers, Russia was eager to give Turkey military assistance. The Turko-Egyptian War offered a golden opportunity for the consolidation of Russia's hold over the "sick man" on the Bosphorus. Nicholas, moreover, saw in Mehemet Ali a rebel against his suzerain and a tool in the hands of revolutionary France. Both the tsar and Nesselrode professed, and probably believed, that the establishment of the pasha at Constantinople would have made the Turkish capital a center of subversive agitation and a meeting place of the revolutionary "rabble" (including Polish *émigrés*), an eventuality they were determined to prevent at any cost. In the middle of November General N. N. Muravev was sent to Constantinople and Alexandria on a double mission: to assure the sultan of Nicholas's unfaltering friendship and to persuade Mehemet Ali to make peace with Mahmud. A supplementary instruction dated December 6, 1832, N.S., directed Muravev and A. P. Butenev, Russian ambassador to the Porte, to place at the disposal of the sultan for the defense of his capital a Russian squadron of five sails of the line and four frigates. Although Muravev reached Constantinople on December 21, N.S., the very day of Turkey's crushing defeat at Konieh, the Ottoman government showed no haste in accepting the Russian offer. It was not until February 2, 1833, N.S., when the position of Turkey became truly desperate, that Mahmud requested not only Russia's proffered naval aid but also her military aid. In the apt and much-quoted phrase of a high Ottoman official, "A drowning man clings to a serpent."

The news of the impending arrival of the Russians alarmed British and French representatives in the Turkish capital. The new French ambassador, Admiral Roussin, reached Constantinople on February 17, N.S., and at once assumed the part of mediator between Mahmud and Mehemet Ali. On the same day Butenev was requested by the Porte to countermand, at least temporarily, the dispatch of Russian troops. The Russian squadron, however, had already sailed from Sevastopol, nor was the tsar in a mood to yield entirely to French and British pressure. He canceled his earlier orders for the advance towards Constantinople of the Russian Danubian army of some 25,000 to 30,000 men, but nine Russian men-of-war entered the Bosphorus on February 20, N.S., and came to anchor opposite the Russian embassy at Buyukdere. Flattery, intrigues, and threats used by Turks and foreign diplomats to bring about a speedy withdrawal of the Russians were of no avail. Convoys carrying Russian troops entered the Bosphorus on April 4, and April 22, N.S., and landed some 10,000 men on the Asiatic shore. As often happens, the ultimate result of Russia's impetuous move was, at least in some respects, the very opposite of the one intended. Although the sultan reviewed in person the Russian expeditionary force, he could not but feel apprehensive about the consequences of his momentous decision, which he made, it would seem, against the advice of his ministers. France, Great Britain, and even Austria and Prussia exerted themselves to terminate a situation they regarded as intolerable. To both the Porte and the western Powers almost any solution appeared preferable to the entrenchment of the Muscovites on the Bosphorus. Peace between Mahmud and Mehemet Ali was restored by the convention of Kiutayeh, negotiated under the auspices of the western Powers in April and early in May, 1833. This agreement, to which Butenev vainly objected, amounted to the capitulation of the sultan. More favorable terms might have been arranged had the Russians kept away from the Straits. But even after the conclusion of peace the situation remained highly explosive because of the uncertainty concerning Russia's ultimate designs. The belated appearance in the vicinity of the Dardanelles of British and French naval squadrons was fraught with possibilities of war between those countries and Russia. It was, however, once more that the unexpected happened.

On July 9, N.S., after Count A. F. Orlov, the tsar's special envoy to Constantinople, received the news of Ibrahim's withdrawal behind the Taurus Mountains, the Russians boarded their ships and the next day sailed from the Bosphorus to the Black Sea. It was surely no mere coincidence that the embarkation order was issued the day after Orlov had appended his signature to the Treaty of Unkiar Skelessi.

General Orlov, the tsar's aide-de-camp and personal friend, arrived in Constantinople early in May. An ardent nationalist, he had advocated the advance of the Russian Danubian army towards the Turkish capital, irrespective of the Porte's wishes. Orlov, however, was a courtier and a man of the world. He ingratiated himself with Mahmud and showered presents and honorary distinctions on Ottoman officials, but the Russian squadron and expeditionary force formed the necessary background for the delicate negotiations of the Russo-Turkish alliance in which he was engaged. "I follow with the Turks the method of caressing them with one hand, and squeezing them in my fist with the other," Orlov wrote to Kiselev on July 9, 1833, N.S. It is a moot question whether the idea of the alliance embodied in the Treaty of Unkiar Skelessi (July 8, 1833, N.S.) originated with Nicholas or with Mahmud.[6] The treaty provided for "eternal" peace, friendship, and alliance between the two empires, although its term was only eight years. It confirmed the earlier treaties concluded between the two countries and bound them to defend each other's dominions against aggression. The tsar promised to maintain the independence of Turkey in case the latter should again ask for Russian naval or military assistance. A secret article provided that Turkey "shall limit her action in favor of Russia to closing the Straits of the Dardanelles, that is, to not allowing any foreign vessel of war to enter them under any pretext whatever." In spite of the secrecy with which the treaty was negotiated, its contents became known to Lord Ponsonby, British ambassador to Constantinople, four days after the signature, and a version of it was published in the English press in August, 1833. The disclosure created a sensation, chiefly because it was believed that the secret article just quoted guaranteed to Russia free passage for her warships through the Straits while it closed the entrance of the Black Sea to every other Power. The article contained no direct statement to this effect and, according to the Russian view, merely restated

[6] For an illuminating discussion of this point, see Temperley, *op. cit.*, pp. 69–70, 412–413.

the "ancient rule" sanctioned by the Anglo-Turkish treaty of 1809 which prohibited all war vessels from entering the Straits. Nesselrode insisted in vain that the treaty "does not impose on the Porte any burdensome condition and does not cause it to contract any new engagement" (August 17, 1833, N.S.). The sincerity of this opinion, which was generally disbelieved, would seem to be proved by Nesselrode's confidential report to the tsar of January 16, 1838. The chancellor argued that the existing treaties imposed on Turkey the obligation *"to close* the entrance of the Dardanelles to any foreign war flag, but they by no means oblige her *to open* it to us. The Treaty of Adrianople, confirmed by that of Constantinople [Unkiar Skelessi], stipulates explicitly in our favor only free passage for *merchant* ships; but no stipulation authorizes us to request (*exiger*) the admission to the Bosphorus of our warships." [7]

The real significance of the Treaty of Unkiar Skelessi, from the Russian point of view, was the provision by which the two monarchs "promise to come to agreement without reserve (*sans réserve*) on all matters concerning their respective tranquility and safety and, for this purpose, mutually to lend each other material aid and most effective assistance." Nesselrode felt justified in claiming that "our intervention in the affairs of Turkey has acquired a basis of legality" (letter to Prince Liven, July 24, 1833). "Russia's real aim in making the treaty of 1833," writes Mosely, "was therefore to secure recognition from the Porte of her paramount interest in Turkey and of her previous right of intervention, to the exclusion of the alliance and intervention of other Powers." And although intervention was permissible only "under the guise of friendly assistance to the Porte," Nesselrode was convinced (and Orlov shared this view) that the tsar would be called "in a year or two" to send a new expeditionary force to the Bosphorus under conditions which, perhaps, would allow it to stay.

It thus appears that if European statesmen and public opinion misconstrued the secret article, their interpretation of Russia's ultimate

[7] Not only was the erroneous interpretation of the Treaty of Unkiar Skelessi prevalent among contemporary statesmen but it has gained acceptance among the historians. See Philip E. Mosely, *Russian Diplomacy and the Opening of the Eastern Question in 1838 and 1839* (Cambridge, 1934), pp. 9-24. The text of Nesselrode's report was first published by Mosely, pp. 141-147. Temperley (*op. cit.*, p. 413) agrees that the documents quoted by Mosely seem "to prove that Russia meant to close the Dardanelles to all warships at Unkiar Skelessi." Herbert C. F. Bell, *Lord Palmerston* (Longmans, Green and Company, Ltd., London, 1936), I, 183, follows the traditional but, it would seem, no longer defensible interpretation.

purpose was not wholly unwarranted. The Porte, according to Guizot, became Russia's "official client" and the Black Sea a "Russian lake," and Palmerston believed that Russia would "exercise a kind of protectorate over Turkey." France and England sent to St. Petersburg a vigorous joint protest declaring that they reserved the right to act as if the Treaty of Unkiar Skelessi did not exist, a declaration which was, of course, rejected by Nesselrode. There followed a period of political tension, French and British squadrons in the Mediterranean were reinforced, and there was much loose talk of the imminence of war. But the storm blew over and Russia celebrated a great diplomatic victory. Her triumph, however, had an unfortunate aftermath. "Unkiar Skelessi is a true turning point in the attitude of English statesmen towards Russia," writes Temperley. "It bred in Palmerston a fatal hostility to Russia and converted even Whigs to the Tory policy of bolstering up Turkey."

Russia's ascendancy in Turkey appeared all the more ominous because it took place simultaneously with a *rapprochement* of the three eastern Powers. In September, 1833, the emperors of Russia and Austria and the crown prince of Prussia met for ten days at Münchengrätz, in Bohemia. This gathering (which, according to Nesselrode, had for its sole object an *épanchement de cœur*) led to the formal renewal of the Holy Alliance as a three-Power league for the preservation of the European order established by international treaties, especially those of 1815 (convention of Berlin, October 15, 1833, N.S.). The Turkish question was dealt with in an Austro-Russian convention signed at Münchengrätz on September 18, N.S. The two emperors declared that "their close alliance during the recent events in Egypt has powerfully contributed to the preservation of the Ottoman empire," and they promised "to accept this principle of unity as the basic rule of their policy in the Levant." They agreed "to maintain the existence of the Ottoman empire under its present dynasty," and to oppose any change in the form of Turkish government. In two secret articles Russia and Austria undertook (1) to prevent Mehemet Ali from acquiring any direct or indirect influence in any part of European Turkey, and (2) to maintain their unity and to act in concert in case the dissolution of the Ottoman empire should become inevitable. Russia's chief object in concluding this convention, which restricted her freedom of action in the Near East, was to secure the cooperation of Austria should a new crisis arise on the Bosphorus. Although the convention was clearly designed to preserve the Ottoman empire, Palmerston was convinced that its object was the partition of Turkey. Metternich unsuccessfully pleaded with the tsar for permission to reveal the secret articles, a step which would have eased international tension. Palmerston's anxiety to restore the balance of power, threatened by the Holy Alliance, was among the reasons which led to the conclusion of the Quadruple Alliance of Great Britain, France, Portugal, and Spain (April, 1834).

THE THREAT TO INDIA

"Palmerston, like all men of his generation, was impressed by general principles," writes Temperley. "He believed that Europe was convulsed by a struggle between despotic and constitutional principles, and that this war of opinion was the great fact of the moment. The opposed forces were the despotic military monarchies, Russia, Prussia, Austria, Turkey; and the constitutional states, England and France." [8] But since what Palmerston understood to be British interests demanded the preservation of Turkey, he had little difficulty in persuading himself, as did Stratford Canning, that under enlightened British guidance the Porte could be transformed into a modern constitutional state. He held no such hope for Russia, however, and with the appearance of the bogey of Russia's threat to India the area of potential conflict between Muscovy and Great Britain was expanded so as to include not only Europe and the Bosphorus but also the Caucasus, Persia, Asia Minor, and central Asia. British policies and public opinion were influenced by the views of men who held responsible positions in the Near East. The British ambassadors to Constantinople, Lord Ponsonby (1832–1841) and Stratford Canning (1841–1858), were militant Russophobes.[9] Dr. John McNeill, author of the inflammatory volume *Progress and Present Position of Russia in the East*, became in 1836 British minister to Teheran. An anti-Russian campaign of extraordinary violence was in progress in England. The writings of David Urquhart, a pronounced radical, fanatical hater of Russia, and for a brief time (1835–1836) secretary of the British embassy at Constantinople, were particularly notable for the vehemence of their invectives. In his blind fury Urquhart turned eventually

[8] Temperley, *op. cit.*, p. 60.
[9] In 1833 Stratford Canning was appointed ambassador to St. Petersburg; but Nicholas refused to receive him.

against his former patron Palmerston and demanded his impeachment as an agent of the tsar. There were, of course, dissenting voices and attempts to pour oil on the stormy waters of journalistic and public passion. Lord Melbourne in 1837 deprecated Ponsonby's "ridiculous Russophobia." Richard Cobden in his pamphlet *Russia* (1836) and throughout his long career argued that Great Britain was not called upon to interfere between Russia and Turkey. He expounded the plausible theory that even the establishment of the Muscovites on the Bosphorus would not injure British commerce because backward Russia was not in a position to compete with England. But these cooler counsels met with little public support and their very moderation and soundness tended to increase the violence of the anti-Russian attacks.

Russia's alleged threat to India, which became an article of faith with British statesmen of the Palmerstonian school, made London watch with growing anxiety the activities of the tsarist government in the regions deemed suitable as the starting point of the expected invasion. It was imagined, with scant regard for formidable geographical and physical obstacles, that Russia might strike at India either indirectly through Persia or directly through the passage between the Caspian and the Aral seas and the valley of the Oxus, occupied by the principalities of Khiva and Bokhara. Russian expansion in the Near East offered a semblance of justification for the apprehensions entertained by the imaginative statesmen, publicists, and historians. The treaties of Turkmanchay (1828) and Adrianople (1829) had consolidated and extended Russia's hold over the Caucasus and had pushed the southern frontier of the empire to the upper valley of the Euphrates, one of the potential routes for the invasion of India. The formal annexation of the Caucasus, however, was followed by a protracted struggle for the subjugation of the rebellious and freedom-loving mountaineers. The principal insurgent movement broke out in 1830 and assumed the character of a holy war of Islam. In 1834 Shamil was elected leader of the insurgents, and he successfully resisted the conquerors until 1859. There were numerous other less stubborn yet determined and bloody uprisings, and the pacification of the Caucasus was not officially completed until 1864. British statesmen, especially Ponsonby and Palmerston, who doubted the legality of Russia's claim to the Caucasus, followed the progress of the struggle with keen interest and offered the insurgents moral encouragement and material assistance. Late in 1836 a small British vessel, the *Vixen*, carrying salt, according to London, and arms, according to St. Petersburg, was captured by the Russian navy off the Caucasian shore. The *Vixen* voyage was engineered by Urquhart, but it would seem that Palmerston, who knew of the plan, did not approve of it, as claimed by Urquhart. The incident created an uproar in both countries and strained their relations almost to the breaking point.

Anglo-Russian rivalries in Persia centered on the domination of Afghanistan, not yet a united state, and especially on the control of the commercially and strategically important cities of Herat and Kabul. Mohammad, who became shah of Persia in 1834, was a partisan of Russia, and at the instigation of the Russian minister to Teheran, Count Simonich, he embarked in the autumn of 1837 on a campaign for the conquest of Herat. At the same time the Russians succeeded in strengthening their diplomatic influence in Kabul: the British emissary Captain Alexander Burnes was withdrawn from that city, leaving the field to his Russian colleague and antagonist, Captain Vitkevich. Viewed from London and Calcutta, these were serious setbacks; the probable annexation of Herat by Persia and the entrenchment of Russian influence at Kabul were regarded as a menace to British commerce in the Near East and as important landmarks on Russia's road to India. Russian successes, however, were short-lived. Palmerston, as an English historian puts it (G. P. Moriarty), addressed himself to the problem "in a spirit of confidence and ardor." A British expeditionary force organized by Lord Auckland, governor-general of India, landed on the shores of the Persian Gulf in the spring of 1838; the siege of Herat was raised in September; Simonich, whose recall Palmerston had long demanded, was finally withdrawn; and in August, 1839, a ruler acceptable to London was installed in Kabul by a victorious British army.

Even more lamentable was the outcome of a Russian expedition for the conquest of Khiva. St. Petersburg had long complained that the khan of Khiva had plundered Russian caravans, and in 1839 the tsar announced his intention of asserting in that part of Asia the influence which "rightly belonged to Russia." Palmerston perceived in the Khivan venture a new threat to India, and spoke to the Russian ambassador of retaliatory measures that might lead to war. His apprehensions were again ill founded. A small Russian expeditionary force of some 5,000 men with two field guns, accompanied by a huge train of 10,000 camels carrying supplies and munitions, started on its long trek through a mountainous desert country in November, 1839. The rigors of the climate and the absence of roads took a frightful toll both of men and of animals, and ten weeks later General V. A. Perovsky, who commanded the expedition, was forced to turn back without having even sighted the enemy. The outcome of Russia's Persian intrigues and of the Khivan expedition strongly suggests that danger to India was not so real as Palmerston believed.

RAPPROCHEMENT WITH ENGLAND

Constantinople, however, remained the focal point of the potential European conflict. The Peace of Kiutayeh (1833) did not end the feud between Mahmud and Mehemet Ali. The sultan was not reconciled to the humiliation and loss of territory and revenue inflicted on him by his rebellious vassal, while the pasha of Egypt was harboring plans for complete independence. A Turkish attack on Egypt was prevented in 1834 by St. Petersburg's firm statement that since the Treaty of Unkiar Skelessi was defensive, Russia would not countenance an unprovoked aggression by the Porte. The long-expected crisis did not break out until 1839.

In the meantime the ground was prepared for a new alignment of Powers and for their concerted intervention in the eastern question. Palmerston was resolved to prevent Mehemet Ali from acquiring control of Syria, partly because he foresaw a possible reconciliation between Russia and Egypt and pictured the junction of the armies of the two countries in Iraq and their advance down the Euphrates to threaten the British flank in India. Alliance with France remained one of the pillars of British policy and an essential element in the balance of power; but there were disturbing signs that the French government and public opinion favored Mehemet Ali and might, therefore, fail England at the very time when action would be needed. Palmerston did not believe in Russia's disinterestedness and her professed intention to preserve the Ottoman empire. He was anxious, however, to weaken Russia's hold over Turkey by merging the Treaty of Unkiar Skelessi "in some general compact of the same nature" (letter to Ponsonby, September 13, 1838, N.S.).

Russia had her own reasons for seeking an understanding with England. The Holy Alliance had proved lifeless and offered little guarantee of common action in the Near East. Prussia was specifically exempted from the obligation to intervene in the Levant (letter of Nicholas to

Frederick William III of October 5, 1833, N.S.), and the attitude of Metternich gave no assurance that he would live up to the somewhat indefinite obligations assumed at Münchengrätz. Contrary to expectations, the Treaty of Unkiar Skelessi did not make Turkey a Russian dependency; the influence of Ponsonby at Constantinople was, indeed, much greater than that of Butenev. This treaty, moreover, was to expire in 1841, and Nesselrode argued in a confidential report to the tsar (August, 1839) that, its renewal by the Porte being unlikely, a comprehensive international agreement for the closure of the Straits to warships was highly desirable. There were other considerations of a more general nature which drew St. Petersburg closer to London. An understanding with England offered the tempting possibility of isolating France and of reviving the Quadruple Alliance of Chaumont (1814) which had defeated Napoleon. To Nicholas, France was the very embodiment of the subversive revolutionary spirit; but, much as he hated representative government, he admired England and would welcome her as a member of the Holy Alliance. There was, moreover, a significant shift in the attitude of the leading St. Petersburg diplomats towards the objects and methods of Russian policy. Baron Ernest Brunnow, senior diplomatic adviser to Nesselrode, prepared a remarkable survey in 1838 of Russia's foreign relations for the use of the heir to the throne, the future Emperor Alexander II. Brunnow argued against Catherine II's policy of territorial aggrandizement as containing the seeds of future complications. He was critical of the partition of Poland and especially of the Treaty of Kuchuk Kainardzhi (1774), which, by giving the imperial government ill defined powers in the administration of the Danubian principalities, had invited arbitrary Russian intervention in the internal affairs of Turkey and had led to costly and purposeless conflicts. Although, according to Brunnow, this policy had been basically revised by Nicholas, its ill effects continued to poison relations between Russia and foreign countries, especially England.[10] It is noteworthy that the author of this

[10] "The policy of the Russian court in the reign of Catherine unfortunately justifies only too well the suspicion which today is being disseminated concerning the intentions of our government," wrote Brunnow. "The English always remember that the countries which were once under the protection of Russia have all ended by losing their independence; that Russia has extended her protection to Poland in order to bring about her partition; that she has freed the Georgian tribes from the Ottoman dominion and has subjugated them; that she has recognized the independence of the Crimea to annex it to her empire. Examples of the past, therefore, hamper the present, and the noble motives of our policy today are denied

indictment was sent to London on two special missions in 1839 and represented Russia at the Court of St. James's until 1854. The above changes in the attitude of the Powers must be kept in mind in order to understand the "diplomatic revolution" of 1840.

War between Turkey and Egypt began at the end of April, 1839, when the Ottoman army crossed the Euphrates and invaded Syria. This conflict was brief and disastrous for the Porte. On June 24, N.S., the Turks were overwhelmingly defeated at Nezib and the entire Ottoman fleet went over to Mehemet Ali. The sultan died on June 29 and was succeeded by his son Abdul Mejid, a boy of sixteen. In the apt words of Guizot, "In three weeks Turkey had lost her sultan, her army, and her navy." Ibrahim, who commanded the Egyptian forces, had won his greatest and also his last victory. Hostilities were suspended, and Abdul Mejid hastened to make peace overtures to his formidable opponent.

There followed a period of extraordinary diplomatic activity. The Maritime Powers dreaded Russian intervention under the Treaty of Unkiar Skelessi and took precautions accordingly. They were divided among themselves, however, in that France favored the retention by Mehemet Ali of some of the fruits of his victory, while England wanted to prevent any substantial weakening of Turkey. Metternich, forgetting the obligations assumed at Münchengrätz, agitated in favor of collective action by the great Powers. The attitude of the Russian government was at first ambiguous. It was unwilling either to lend military assistance to Turkey or to give up Russia's special position at Constantinople. Nicholas curtly refused to be represented at an international conference in Vienna sponsored by Metternich and Palmerston. Such a conference, it was argued in St. Petersburg, would be necessarily directed against Russia. Yet on July 27, 1839, N.S., the ambassadors of Great Britain, France, Russia, Austria, and Prussia presented to the Porte a joint note informing the Ottoman government that "an agreement on the eastern question has been reached by the five great Powers" and urging Turkey "to suspend all definite decisions without their concurrence, pending the effect of their interest in the Porte's welfare." This was the first indication that, abandoning

---

because memories of distant events are still alive in the minds of foreign governments who are alarmed by and envious of our might." Quoted in S. S. Tatishchev, *Vneshniaia politika imperatora Nikolaia pervago* (Foreign Policy of Emperor Nicholas I) (St. Petersburg, 1887), pp. 465–466, 480.

her previous position, Russia was prepared to support collective action. In September Brunnow came to London with the offer to allow the Treaty of Unkiar Skelessi to lapse, provided a satisfactory agreement on the eastern question was reached by the great Powers. Palmerston was informed of Russia's readiness to participate in a coalition of all states, although the tsar favored the exclusion of France. This proposal was well received, and negotiations were resumed when Brunnow returned to London in December. Prussia and Austria supported the Russian plan, but the rift between England and France over the treatment to be accorded to Mehemet Ali widened, especially after Marshal Soult's government was defeated (February 29, 1840, N.S.) and Thiers assumed the direction of French policies. Palmerston then decided to break with his old ally. On July 15, 1840, N.S., the representatives of Great Britain, Russia, Austria, and Prussia, on the one hand, and Turkey, on the other, signed in London a convention which laid down the terms of settlement between Mehemet Ali and the Porte and provided for military and naval measures to enforce them. Article IV confirmed the "ancient rule" of closing the Straits to war vessels. The convention was not communicated to Guizot, the French ambassador, until July 17, two days after signature. Indignation in Paris was great, the Anglo-French alliance appeared to be dissolved, and war between France and the rest of Europe seemed imminent.

The crisis, however, was solved before Paris made up its mind to intervene. Mehemet Ali refused to accept the terms laid down in the convention of July 15, but the speedy and remarkably successful action of British, Austrian, and Turkish squadrons under Admiral Sir Charles Napier, and the revolt of Syria against Ibrahim made a clean sweep of the pasha's ambitious dreams of empire. The hostilities which began in September were over by the end of November, and Mehemet Ali accepted the terms negotiated for him by the great Powers.

The final liquidation of the long-drawn-out Turko-Egyptian struggle came a few months later when France resumed her place in the European concert by signing the Straits convention (July 13, 1841, N.S.). This agreement pledged the signatory Powers (Great Britain, Russia, France, Austria, and Prussia) to observe the rule that the sultan, "so long as he is at peace," will admit no foreign warships in the Straits, except light vessels in the service of legations of friendly

Powers. Under the convention of 1841 Russia retained the rights secured by the treaties of Kuchuk Kainardzhi, Akkerman, and Adrianople, but she relinquished her special position under the Treaty of Unkiar Skelessi. The latter, indeed, was permitted to lapse. The integrity of Turkey became a matter of concern to the five Powers, and the regime of the Straits could not be altered without a conference of the European concert. Both Palmerston and Nesselrode claimed the convention of 1841 as a triumph for their respective policies. "The treaty of Unkiar Skelessi, though annulled to all appearances, has been really perpetuated under another form," Nesselrode wrote ten years later. "The new act which has replaced it and been recognized by all the Powers, forbids foreign warships to enter the Dardanelles, and assures us henceforth against all naval attack." British and French statesmen, however, took a different view and, as Temperley makes clear, were devising plans to have the Dardanelles open to their fleets in an emergency. Even Aberdeen, the most scrupulous of British ministers, argued (September 22, 1853, N.S.) that "urgency is sufficient to dispense with all obligations." In spite of the appearance of a political *rapprochement*, a "wide cleavage arose in practice" between Russia and England. "Europe had imposed peace for a moment, but imposed a peace full of danger," writes Temperley. "A peace which stimulated Russia to increase her fleet inside the Black Sea and England and Turkey to increase their fleets outside it was unlikely to last long. For such a peace had in it the seeds of war. It is remarkable that the peace, which signalized cooperation between England and Russia, ultimately drove the two Powers to make war upon one another." [11]

The unhappy consequences of the 1841 convention, however, did not become apparent until a decade later. Meanwhile Nicholas worked assiduously for the isolation of France and the inclusion of England in the Holy Alliance. In December, 1840, he made overtures to this effect to Marquis Clanricarde, British ambassador at St. Petersburg, and since a formal treaty did not seem feasible he expressed his readiness to be satisfied with a mere promise of the London government. Palmerston declined the offer on the ground that it was contrary to British policy to enter into commitments concerning situations which had not yet arisen (Nicholas pleaded for British assistance against France "in a war of revolutions this year or later"), and he stated that an informal promise of a British ministry would be "scarcely consistent

---

[11] Temperley, *op. cit.*, p. 150.

with the spirit of the British constitution" and would not be binding on future cabinets. Nicholas, however, was not discouraged, and endeavored to achieve his object through personal negotiations with the British government. In 1839 his son, the future Emperor Alexander II, had visited London, where he was cordially received. In the summer of 1844 the tsar himself went to England and spent some time at Windsor as the fêted and admired guest of Queen Victoria.[12] Aberdeen, who after the defeat of the Whigs in August, 1841, succeeded Palmerston at the foreign office in the government of Sir Robert Peel, was the recipient of Nicholas's overtures. A memorandum summarizing the London conversations was drafted by Nesselrode and was submitted to Aberdeen.[13] Both Russia and England, the memorandum argued, were vitally interested in the maintenance of the independence and territorial integrity of Turkey. The fate of the Christian population under the Ottoman rule depended largely on the concerted action of the great Powers whose duty it was "to use all their influence to maintain the Christian subjects of the Porte in a state of submission to their sovereign authority." The Turkish empire, however, contained many "elements of dissolution," and the Russians held that the adverse effects of this unwanted event would be minimized if St. Petersburg and London would agree on a common course to be followed in case of the breakdown of the Ottoman empire. During the tsar's visit to England, according to the memorandum, Nicholas and the British government had agreed (1) to maintain as long as possible the *status quo* in Turkey, and (2) in case of the dissolution of the Porte to reach a preliminary understanding concerning the establishment of a new order. It was argued that in the latter eventuality Austria was bound by the convention of Münchengrätz to act in concert with Russia and that France would have no choice but to acquiesce in the decision of the three Powers. Aberdeen, after some delay, admitted "the accuracy of the statement," but he would not commit himself any further. Nicholas, Nesselrode, and Brunnow, on

---

[12] Relations between Russia and France further deteriorated in 1842, when the Russian ambassador to Paris and the French ambassador to St. Petersburg were recalled. Until the revolution of 1848 the two countries were represented in each other's capital by a chargé d'affaires.

[13] The text of the memorandum, which was written in French, is published in A. M. Zaionchkovsky, V*ostochnaia voina 1853–1856 gg. v sviazi s sovremennoi ei politicheskoi obstanovkoi* (The Eastern War of 1853–1856 and Its Contemporary Political Background) (St. Petersburg, 1908), Vol. II, Pt. II, pp. 132–134.

the other hand, imagined that the 1844 conversations had produced a new political system. "The English cabinet has entered a new road," Brunnow wrote to Nesselrode on December 3, 1844, N.S. "It has taken it as a rule to have an understanding with Russia before concerting with the other courts of Europe. This system . . . only dates from the month of June of this year." If Brunnow had some misgivings as to how the agreement would work in practice, it was to Aberdeen merely one "of mutual expression of opinion" in no way binding on his successors. Palmerston, who returned to the foreign office in 1846, would seem to have held a similar view, as did the subsequent British ministers of foreign affairs. For this curious misunderstanding Aberdeen and his colleagues share the responsibility with Nicholas and Nesselrode.

The severance of the Anglo-French *entente cordiale,* as a consequence of the quaint incident of the "Spanish marriages" (1846) and Palmerston's anger with Louis Philippe, favored the *rapprochement* between England and the eastern Powers. Palmerston had protested with utmost vigor in 1836, when the tiny republic of Cracow, which was regarded by the Holy Alliance as a center of subversive Polish agitation, was occupied by the allied troops. Ten years later Metternich, with the connivance of Russia and in violation of the Treaty of Vienna, annexed Cracow, but the formal protest of London was, in Palmerston's own words, "as civil and moderate" as it could be made. Nesselrode was justified in saying that the ease with which the annexation of Cracow was accomplished "surpasses my expectations." On the eve of the revolution of 1848 the isolation of France, one of the chief objects of Nicholas's policy, was largely achieved.

THE REVOLUTION OF 1848

The French revolution of February, 1848, which terminated the reign of Louis Philippe, spread like wildfire over the continent of Europe, led to the establishment of constitutional regimes in Austria and Prussia, and gave a strong stimulus to the movements for national liberation among the Italians, Hungarians, Poles, Czechs, Rumanians, and the Irish. Unlike its numerous predecessors, the revolution of 1848 had a distinct proletarian and socialist character: early in that year Marx and Engels published the *Communist Manifesto,* which seventy years later was to exercise so profound an influence on the destinies of Russia.

Nicholas, having little liking for Louis Philippe, derived from the fall of the Orléans dynasty a personal satisfaction which was shared by Palmerston, still smarting under the defeat of his policy in the vexed question of the "Spanish marriages." Constitutional governments and national movements, however, appeared to the tsar as direct assaults on the very foundations on which rested his own rule. There were, indeed, indications that revolutionary disturbance might spread to Russia. In spite of the rigors of censorship, Russian liberal and radical circles showed keen interest in European developments. Nicholas's first reaction to the news from Paris was to break diplomatic relations with France and to mass some 400,000 troops along Russia's western border, preparatory to a march to the Rhine. The rapid progress of the revolution and the capitulation of the Austrian and the Prussian governments before the onslaught of radical forces put an end to these bellicose plans. A manifesto of March 14, 1848, written by the tsar himself, dolefully admitted that "rebellion and lawlessness" have engulfed Austria and Prussia and are threatening "our holy Russia." Nicholas called his subjects to rally to the ancient slogan "for faith, tsar, and country," and somewhat unexpectedly closed the manifesto with the ominous but not very clear statement: "God is with us! Understand, ye people, and submit: for God is with us!" This solemn proclamation further embittered relations between St. Petersburg and Paris, but it had no other direct consequences. Although Nicholas was forced to abandon his plans for military intervention in France, he exercised considerable influence upon the course of events. The policy of the St. Petersburg government was primarily directed to the maintenance of Russia's position in Turkey, the suppression of the Polish national movement, the bolstering of Austria, and the preservation in Germany of the *status quo* established by the treaties of 1815.

The revolution of 1848 infused new strength in the Rumanian national movement. Uprisings directed against both Turkey and Russia broke out in Moldavia and Wallachia, and there was much unrest in Bessarabia. Russia's appointee, Prince Dimitry Bibesco, forced to abdicate, fled to Austria, and revolutionary governments were set up in the Danubian principalities. A Turkish army crossed the Danube and took possession of Bucharest; in July, 1848, Russian troops occupied Moldavia and Wallachia, the administration of the turbulent provinces passing into the hands of Russian military authorities. Rumanian nationalists, encouraged by Stratford Canning, counted on the support of England and France. Palmerston, however, accepting Nesselrode's assurance that Russia had no intention of annexing the Danubian principalities, refused to intervene. By the agreement of Balta-Liman (May 1, 1849, N.S.) Russia and Turkey sanctioned the drastic amendment of the constitutions of Moldavia and Wallachia proposed by St. Petersburg. The hospodars, formerly elected for life, were now appointed by the sultan for a term of seven years; consultative bodies nominated *ad hoc* were substituted for the elective legislative assemblies provided by the earlier constitution. New hospodars were appointed by agreement between Russia and the Porte, and commissioners representing the two Powers exercised joint supervision over the administration of the principalities. Nicholas, however, kept the promise he had given to Palmerston: early in 1851 Russian (and also Turkish) troops were withdrawn from Moldavia and Wallachia.

The easy success of the revolutionary movement in Vienna dealt a rude blow to Nicholas's confidence in his Austrian ally. Replying to a letter in which Metternich, on the eve of his flight to England, announced his resignation, Nicholas wrote on March 23, 1848, "In my opinion with you disappears a whole system of mutual relationships, ideas, interests, and common action." He was particularly alarmed by the failure during the early stage of the revolution of the Austrian authorities to suppress the Polish national movement, which threatened to spread from Galicia to Russian Poland. But, as Nesselrode put it, Russia "cannot allow the downfall of the Austrian monarchy, this is a vital question to us." Nicholas therefore lent to Emperor Ferdinand I financial and diplomatic support in his struggle with the insurgent Italian provinces and was gratified by the decisive defeat inflicted by the Austrian field marshal Count Joseph Radetzky on Charles Albert, king of Sardinia, who headed the Italian forces (battle of Custozza, July 25, 1848, N.S.). Austria's control of Lombardy was secured, and she was soon to restore her dominion over the entire north of Italy. Just as pleasing to St. Petersburg was the suppression of the Czech revolution after the bombardment of Prague by Field Marshal Prince Alfred Windischgrätz (June, 1848). Reaction was, indeed, making rapid progress in the Hapsburg Monarchy. On October 31, N.S., Windischgrätz recaptured Vienna, which had been held for three weeks by the revolutionaries, a conservative government, headed by Prince Felix Schwarzenberg took office, the feeble-minded Emperor

Ferdinand I abdicated (December, 1848), and was succeeded by his eighteen-year-old nephew, Francis Joseph. The complexion of the new government and Nicholas's professed paternal affection for the young Austrian emperor helped to strengthen the fragile link uniting the courts of St. Petersburg and Vienna. By the end of 1848 the stage was set for Russian intervention in Hungary.

The Hungarian revolution broke out in March, 1848, simultaneously with that in Austria. Under the leadership of Louis Kossuth, it assumed the character of a struggle for national independence, complicated by the century-old feud between the Magyars, on the one hand, and the Croatians, Slovaks, and Rumanians, on the other. These tendencies precipitated a conflict between Budapest and Vienna, with the result that on October 3, 1848, N.S., the Austrian government declared war on Kossuth and his supporters. Ably assisted by a large number of Polish *émigrés*, among them General Joseph Bem, who had fought against the Russians under Napoleon and in the Polish insurrection of 1830–1831, the Hungarians in spite of numerous reverses held their ground well. Austria, weakened by a year of revolutionary disturbances and involved in an onerous war in Italy, sought to restore her control over Hungary with the assistance of foreign troops. In March, 1849, Schwarzenberg, on the advice of Windischgrätz, appealed to Russia for military help. Nicholas accepted at once, not only because of his devotion to legitimacy and his belief that the success of the Hungarian national movement was a threat to the Hapsburg Monarchy but also because he perceived in the establishment of an independent Hungary an immediate danger to Russia's Polish provinces and a menace to Russian influence in the Balkans. Moreover, early in 1849 a detachment of Russian troops had entered Transylvania at the request of a local Austrian commander and had suffered a humiliating defeat at the hands of Bem. There were the usual delays in setting the Russian military machine in motion. The main body of the Russian army under Paskevich crossed the Carpathians in June and invaded Hungary, while additional troops came from Wallachia and Bukovina. The total Russian effectives were estimated at 170,000 men with 576 field guns; the Austrian army in Hungary was approximately equal in numbers to that sent by Nicholas. Although the forces at the disposal of Kossuth were considerably smaller, the campaign proved arduous and costly. The Hungarians put up courageous resistance, and epidemics, due to the inadequate organization of supplies, wrought heavy losses among the invaders. Paskevich's strategy was severely criticized in Russia, where the Magyar cause, moreover, had many warm supporters. But temporary setbacks could not alter the issue of the uneven contest, which was a foregone conclusion. After several defeats of the Magyars Kossuth abdicated his powers as governor-president and fled to Turkey. Two days later (August 13, 1849, N.S.) the Hungarian army laid down its arms and threw itself on the mercy of Nicholas. The struggle was over. By the middle of September the Russian troops were withdrawn except for one division which remained somewhat longer in Transylvania. The Hungarian officers and men who had surrendered to Paskevich were handed over to the Austrian government. Thirteen generals were executed and 386 officers received prison sentences, a decision that shocked even Nicholas and was condemned by him as "purposeless cruelty." Hungary's gallant struggle against the forces of reaction was followed with deep sympathy in France and England, but neither country came to her rescue. Louis Napoleon was too absorbed in consolidating his rule and too anxious to retain a free hand in dealing with Italy to intervene. Palmerston was even more reluctant to take action because, like Nicholas, although for different reasons, he considered a strong Austria an essential element in the balance of power.

The aftermath of the gruesome Hungarian affair brought Russia and the western Powers to the brink of war. Some 3,600 Hungarian and 800 Polish refugees (among them Bem and General Henry Dembinski, another irreconcilable enemy of Russia) had fled to Turkey. Nicholas and Francis Joseph peremptorily demanded their surrender; but, although the request was justified by the existing treaties, the Porte, at the instigation of England and France, refused to comply (August 30, 1849, N.S.). Diplomatic relations between the two imperial courts and Turkey were then suspended. Concern over the fate of the refugees so suddenly manifested by Louis Napoleon, and especially by Palmerston, who had looked complacently upon the destruction of the Hungarian national movement, was primarily due to the fact that they interpreted the Austro-Russian demand as an infringement of Turkish sovereignty and a step towards the subjugation of the Porte by the eastern Powers. On October 7, N.S., Palmerston directed Stratford Canning to assure Turkey of "the moral and, if necessary, the material support" of Great Britain and France. British public opinion, stirred to a high pitch by accounts of atrocities perpetrated on the Hungarians, was solidly behind the government.[14] A British squadron under Admiral Sir William Parker reached Besika Bay, outside the Dardanelles, on October 27, N.S., and on November 1 entered the Straits and anchored between the inner castles and Point Nagar. Twelve days later it was withdrawn. Whether the appearance of British warships inside the Straits was or was not a violation of the convention of 1841 is a controversial and somewhat academic question. Russia and Austria believed that it did constitute a violation, and Palmerston, in replying to their protest, admitted that Parker was in error and promised not to repeat the offense. The refugee question, however, was disposed of by direct negotiations between Turkey and Russia. Fuad Pasha, a special emissary of the sultan, arrived in St. Petersburg and was received by the tsar on October 16, N.S. Three days later it was officially announced that the imperial government had dropped its demand for the surrender of the Polish refugees. It is possible that Nicholas's decision was influenced by the firm attitude of England and France, but it could not have been due to the movement of the British squadron, which did not reach Besika Bay until October 27, N.S. Diplomatic relations between Russia and Turkey were resumed by the end of 1849. Austria proved more recalcitrant, but the question of refugees was finally settled by the repatriation of some 3,000 Hungarians who had accepted an amnesty. Kossuth and other Hungarian leaders remained behind and early in 1851 sailed for the United States, while General Bem and several other Poles became Mohammedans and entered the Turkish service.

The desire to prevent the unification of Germany under the leadership of Prussia was one of the underlying reasons for the support lent to Vienna by St. Petersburg. After the Napoleonic wars, especially in the second quarter of the nineteenth century, the German national movement had made rapid progress and, indeed, was one of the powerful factors behind the revolution of 1848. The maintenance of the loose German confederation created by the treaties of 1815 and the retention by the heterogeneous Austrian empire of its preponderant position among the German states was regarded as a check on the growth of extreme German nationalism, although the full conse-

[14] A notable exception was Queen Victoria. "What business have we to interfere with Polish and Hungarian refugees in Turkey?" she asked Lord John Russell on Sept. 12 (Bell, *op. cit.*, II, 20). Temperley, however, maintains that on the question of refugees "the queen . . . for once saw eye to eye with her foreign minister" (Temperley, *op. cit.*, p. 263).

quences of the latter could not, of course, be foreseen at the time. German nationalism, moreover, was closely associated with political liberalism, so deeply hated by Nicholas; nor was the tsar unmindful of the fact that the Frankfort *Vorparlament* had proclaimed its sacred duty to cooperate in the restoration of an independent Poland (March, 1848). Nicholas had reasons to be dissatisfied with his brother-in-law, Frederick William IV of Prussia, who had succeeded his father in 1840. The policies of the new king were often puzzling and contradictory, and his outlook was heavily colored with extravagant romanticism and pietism, early symptoms, perhaps, of a mental ailment which in 1857 necessitated his withdrawal from public life and the establishment of a regency. Frederick William fully shared the Russian emperor's devotion to legitimacy and his aversion for constitutional government. He would not agree to the abolition of the formula "by the grace of God" as the preamble to his title, nor would he accept the imperial Crown offered to him by the Frankfort constituent assembly (March 1849) because a Crown proffered by an elective body was to him "a Crown of shame" (*Schandkrone*) and the constitutional limitations attached to it "a necklet of slavery." He shared, however, the national aspirations of the liberal groups and, unlike Francis Joseph, having once granted his subjects a constitution he despised, he refused to repeal it.

Russia's animosity towards Prussia and German nationalism was revealed by the attitude of St. Petersburg in the thorny question of Schleswig and Holstein which was raised by the inopportune death of King Christian VIII of Denmark (January 20, 1848, N.S.). Stripped of its baffling dynastic and legal complexities, the issue may be reduced to a contest between the German confederation and Denmark for the possession of the duchies.[15] In March, 1848, Schleswig and Holstein rebelled against the Danish Crown and applied for admission to the German confederation. The Frankfort assembly enthusiastically responded to this appeal, and at the end of April the Prussian army, acting on behalf of the confederation, invaded the duchies, which had been previously occupied by the Danes. Russia, England, and France took the side of Denmark. A Russian squadron was sent into Danish waters, and Nicholas curtly informed Frederick William that he would

---

[15] "The former history of Denmark and the duchies seems to be so confused and so full of irregular transactions, that some events may be quoted in support of almost any pretension," Palmerston wrote to Queen Victoria on Oct. 23, 1850.

declare war on Prussia unless hostilities in Schleswig and Holstein were brought to a speedy end. The tsar was motivated in his ultimatum by his determination to maintain the political structure erected by the Congress of Vienna. There followed protracted negotiations; hostilities between Prussia and Denmark were twice suspended and resumed, but a peace treaty on the basis of *status quo ante bellum* was finally signed by the two Powers (July 2, 1850, N.S.). It was a complete victory for the Danes.

Even more humiliating was the outcome of Frederick William's attempt to bring about the unification of Germany under Prussian leadership. Although attachment to legitimacy long prevented him from openly challenging Austria's traditional supremacy in the Germanic world, he sponsored in May, 1849, a constitution which provided for a closer "union" among the purely German states headed by Prussia, and a "perpetual" alliance between this "union" and Austria. The "union" made a good start and won the adhesion of a number of German states, but it soon ran into serious difficulties caused by the defection of some of its most important members and by the stubborn opposition of Austria and Russia. The Austria-dominated old German confederation, which had ceased to function, was revived in September, 1850, and Nicholas hastened to show his approval by appointing an ambassador to the reconstructed Frankfort diet (November, 1850). The uneasy coexistence of the two rival associations of Germanic states was terminated as a consequence of a conflict between the elector of Hesse-Cassel and his local diet (September, 1850), a conflict that nearly led to war between Austria and Prussia. Both these countries, claiming the dubious privilege of restoring order in the electorate, moved their troops into Hesse-Cassel. St. Petersburg displayed keen interest in the dispute. At an interview held in Warsaw in October, Nicholas told Schwarzenberg and Count William Brandenburg, prime minister of Prussia, that he upheld Austria's right to intervene, and early in November he intimated to Berlin that a refusal to comply with Austria's demand for the withdrawal of Prussian troops would be regarded by Russia as a *casus belli*. Palmerston having turned down Prussia's plea for British assistance, Frederick William found himself forced to abandon the struggle. The capitulation of Prussia was sanctioned by an agreement negotiated at Olmütz by Schwarzenberg and the new head of the Prussian government, Count Hans Manteuffel (Brandenburg had died on November 6), under the watchful eye of the Russian ambassador to Vienna, Baron P. K. Meyendorf. By the Olmütz "punctation" (November 29, 1850, N.S.) Prussia not only accepted all Austrian demands concerning Hesse-Cassel and Holstein, but renounced her plans for a German "union" and adhered to the old confederation established in 1815. The Olmütz agreement came as a shock to Prussia, but the wrath of the public was directed against Russia rather than against Austria. A few months later, indeed, Frederick William and Francis Joseph concluded a secret military alliance (May 16, 1851, N.S.). On the surface, the relations of the three eastern Powers remained cordial, and a visit paid by Nicholas to Berlin and Vienna in the spring of 1852 was a personal triumph for the tsar. To many contemporary observers he appeared to be on the pinnacle of power. Yet the Holy Alliance, on which he continued to rely, existed merely in name. Prussia did not forget Nicholas's part in frustrating her cherished national ambitions, while the Hapsburg Monarchy resented the country's increasing dependence on an impetuous ally and dreaded the growth of Russian influence in the Balkans.

THE GATHERING OF THE STORM, 1850–1853

The course of the French revolution, which in its initial stage Nicholas had planned to destroy by armed force, led to a gradual improvement in the relations between the two countries. The suppression by General Louis Cavaignac of a radical uprising in Paris (June, 1848) was rightly interpreted in St. Petersburg as the turning point ushering in the triumph of reaction. The strong-handed domestic policies of Louis Napoleon, who became president of France in December, 1848, commended themselves to Nicholas, and although the prince-president's military intervention in the dispute between Pope Pius IX and his rebellious subjects raised a number of thorny international questions, these were of greater immediate concern to Austria and England than to Russia. The capture of Rome, after a siege, by the French troops (June 30, 1849, N.S.) and the unconditional restoration of pontifical authority was another defeat for the revolution and a victory for the legitimacy that Nicholas so ardently championed. The issue of legitimacy, however, was soon to interfere with the harmonious relations between Paris and St. Petersburg. When it appeared that Louis Napoleon contemplated the revival of the empire, the tsar instructed his chargé d'affaires in Paris, Nicholas Kiselev, "tactfully" to dissuade the prince-president from taking a step regarded in conservative circles as a violation of the 1815 treaties. Meanwhile Russia, Austria, and Prussia had reached a preliminary agreement to indicate their displeasure at the French *coup d'état*—and also to mark the difference in the status of a monarch "by the grace of God" and one deriving his powers from popular election—by officially addressing the head of the French state as "Emperor Louis Napoleon" and "good friend," instead of "Napoleon III" and "brother." But when the empire was actually proclaimed (December 2, 1852, N.S.) Nicholas alone adhered to the terms of this agreement, Austria and Prussia choosing at the last moment to use (as did England and the other states) the formula requested by France. The incident could not have been more trivial, yet it was only after a delay and against the advice of his ministers that Napoleon resigned himself to overlooking Russia's discourtesy which, to quote Nesselrode (his report to the tsar for 1852), caused the French emperor "profound bitterness and irritation." Nesselrode held the submission of France to be a diplomatic victory for Russia, and he triumphantly opposed the "firmness" of his policy to the "timidity" of England, which raised no objection to Napoleon's title, although the conservative government of Lord Derby did not approve of it. Events were soon to prove that the tsar and his chancellor had grossly misjudged the situation.

With the peaceful solution of the 1849 crisis over Polish and Hungarian refugees, relations between Russia and England improved. The forced resignation (December, 1851) of Palmerston, whom Brunnow described as "not a revolutionary" but one who "profits by revolutions" and promotes them, caused vivid satisfaction in St. Petersburg. The brief administration of Lord John Russell and that of his successor, Lord Derby, were not unfriendly to Russia. In December, 1852, the Derby government was defeated and a new ministry was formed under Aberdeen, who since the tsar's visit to England in 1844 was *persona gratissima* with the Russian court. Lord John Russell came to the foreign office, and although Palmerston was a member of the cabinet he was relegated to the relatively obscure and seemingly innocuous post of home secretary. The dispute about the Holy Places (to be discussed presently) having embittered Franco-Russian relations and reopened the eastern question, Nicholas, disregarding Nesselrode's objections, once more attempted to reach an understanding with England by personal negotiations. His aim was to prevent a *rapprochement* between Great Britain and France and to arrive at an agreement concerning the future of Turkey. In January and February, 1853, Nicholas had four interviews with Sir Hamilton Seymour, British ambassador to St. Petersburg. The tsar reiterated the familiar argument that the Turkish "bear" was dying, and insisted on the necessity of an understanding between Russia and England as to the future of Turkish territories. He made it clear that he would not tolerate the establishment of England in Constantinople, and, while disclaiming any intention of annexing that city, he admitted that it might temporarily be occupied by the Russians. He proposed the creation of an independent Moldavia, Wallachia, and Serbia under Russian protection, and of an independent Bulgaria. Egypt and Crete were magnanimously assigned to England, and the Turkish coasts of the Adriatic and the Archipelago to Austria.[16] In making this proposal Nicholas not only unwisely assumed that it would command the support of Austria but also underestimated the military might of France and misjudged the probable reaction of the British cabinet. In Seymour's opinion the Russian offer was inspired by a desire to reduce Turkey to a state of vassalage, and Russell hastened to reject the plan (even before it had been fully developed by the tsar to the British ambassador) on the ground that the dissolution of the Porte was a mere conjecture, that any partition of Turkey would require consultation with France and Austria, and that even a temporary occupation of Constantinople by the Russians would be fraught with "numberless hazards" and might lead to annexation (February 9, 1853, N.S.). In spite of this rebuke Nicholas persisted in his belief that his overtures to Seymour had contributed to a better understanding between St. Petersburg and London. In a letter to Queen Victoria, written at the height of the crisis (November 1, 1853, N.S.), the tsar referred to the definite obligation of the two governments to consult one another whenever the fate of Turkey was at stake, and he quoted his conversations with Seymour as evidence of his good faith.[17] British opinion did not share this view; and when

[16] An undated contemporary memorandum written in French in Nicholas's own hand provided for a somewhat different distribution of Turkish territories. This tentative plan envisaged the establishment of Constantinople as a free city, with Russian and Austrian troops in control, respectively, of the Bosphorus and the Dardanelles. Text in Zaionchkovsky, *op. cit.*, Vol. I, Pt. II, pp. 357–358.

[17] "*C'est fort amical, mais cela ne conclut rien,*" Nicholas wrote peevishly on Victoria's non-committal reply to his letter. He still clung to the belief that his London conversations (1844) had produced a "new system" which it was in the power of the queen to enforce.

the official report of the Seymour conversations was published in 1854, together with the text of Nesselrode's memorandum of 1844, these documents were held as convincing proof of "the dark ambitions of a foreign despot." Modern historiography inclines to be more lenient towards Nicholas's ill advised plan. "Though not a crime . . . it was nevertheless a blunder," writes Temperley. "And penalty for blunder is exacted in this world."

The Franco-Russian dispute about the Holy Places was the immediate cause of the Crimean War. The status of the European Powers with regard to the right of protection of Christians and Christian churches in Turkey was confused. The French claim was based on a long line of treaties going back to 1528, and especially on the capitulations of 1740. Austria, too, had treaty rights to intervene on behalf of Roman Catholics, and somewhat similar rights were conceded at different times to Great Britain, the Netherlands, and the republic of Venice. The Russian case rested on usage, sultan's decrees and, in the later phase of the dispute, on the Treaty of Kuchuk Kainardzhi (1774). In 1839, as part of a comprehensive program of westernization of Turkish institutions, the Porte proclaimed complete equality of all Ottoman subjects, Moslems and Christians (the *Gulhané* or "Chamber of Roses" decree); but this legislation was never made effective. In the second half of the eighteenth century and in the first four decades of the nineteenth, the French government showed little interest in the Holy Land. The number of Catholic pilgrims to Palestine was insignificant and the custody of the sanctuaries passed largely into the hands of the Orthodox Church, whose members flocked to Jerusalem in ever increasing numbers. The first indication of the revival of French interest in the Holy Land came in 1842, when, as a consequence of the Near East crisis of 1840-1841, Paris turned its attention to Palestine and made an unsuccessful claim for the privilege of repairing the Church of the Holy Sepulchre. In 1847 Pope Pius IX transferred to Jerusalem the Latin patriarchate of that city, formerly an honorary office whose incumbents had for centuries resided in Rome. Catholicism was making a bid to assert its influence in the Holy Land. It found an ardent champion in Louis Napoleon, who in his struggle for power relied on the support of militant clerical groups.

In the middle of 1850 the prince-president sent to the Porte a formal request for the restoration to the Catholics of the position to which they were entitled by the capitulations of 1740. The French claimed the possession of the key to the great door of the Church of Bethlehem and the right to replace a Latin silver star marking the birthplace of Christ, an emblem sacrilegiously stolen by the Greeks in 1847. There followed a diplomatic controversy that lasted for two and a half years. Louis Napoleon, backed by Austria and by Catholic opinion, pressed his demands; Nicholas sternly warned the Porte that he would not tolerate a change in the *status quo*. In case of non-compliance France threatened to use her fleet against Tunis and Tripoli; Russia, which had occupied Moldavia and Wallachia until early in 1851, threatened to reinvade the principalities. In its predicament the Ottoman government sought salvation in the familiar method of procrastination: special commissions busied themselves with nice questions of archaeology and diplomacy, such as the validity of the "*traité du Khalif Omar*" of the year 636. An ingenious temporary solution was found in February, 1852, when the Porte sent a note to France granting her demands, while a *firman* (sultan's decree) confirmed the privileges traditionally enjoyed by the Greeks. The Russian court was simultaneously given secret assurances that in spite of the "French note" the *status quo* would be maintained. It was not long, however, before the duplicity of the quaint diplomatic subterfuge was discovered in both Paris and St. Petersburg. In the early summer of 1852 France exacted from the sultan permission to send to Constantinople a warship, the *Charlemagne*. Russia, Austria, and England protested against this violation of the convention of 1841, but the appearance in Turkish waters of the screw-propelled and heavily armed French man-of-war made a strong impression in Constantinople, as did the arrival of a French squadron in the Bay of Tripoli (July, 1852) to enforce the surrender by Turkish authorities of two French deserters. The show of determination and force by the prince-president was an important factor in tipping the scale of Turkish indecision in favor of France. Early in December, 1852, the dispute about the Holy Places was settled in accordance with the wishes of Paris: the coveted keys were handed over to the Catholics, and soon thereafter the Latin patriarch with much solemnity deposited a new silver star in the Church of the Nativity (December 22, N.S.).

The announcement of the French diplomatic victory at Constantinople came almost simultaneously with the assumption by Napoleon of the imperial title. Nicholas retaliated by mobilizing two army corps in the south of Russia. He, too, was determined to make a show of force. Having supported Austria in a conflict with Turkey over Montenegro then in progress, the tsar was confident of the friendly attitude of the Hapsburg Monarchy, while his optimism concerning an amiable understanding with Aberdeen was evidenced by his overtures to Seymour. War with Turkey, however, was regarded in St. Petersburg as a remote possibility, and it was believed that a timely display of firmness would force the sultan to capitulate. At the end of February, 1853, Prince Alexander Menshikov, special envoy of the tsar, arrived in Constantinople. The ostensible object of the mission of the forcible Russian ambassador, whose refusal to negotiate with the Turkish foreign minister Fuad Pasha had led to the latter's resignation, was to bring about the restoration of Greek rights over the Holy Places. It transpired, however, in the course of the negotiations, which lasted almost three months, that Russia had other far-reaching objects in view. Menshikov, in accordance with his instructions, demanded a treaty of secret alliance with Turkey and the guarantee by the Porte of the privileges not only of the Orthodox Church, its possessions, and dignitaries, but also of Orthodox laymen, that is, some twelve million Ottoman subjects. The latter demand, according to the Russian view, was a mere emendation of the Russian rights enjoyed by virtue of Article VII of the Treaty of Kuchuk Kainardzhi,[18] but it was regarded by the Porte and the European Powers as incompatible with Turkish sovereignty and as a definite step towards establishing a Russian protectorate over the Orthodox Christians in the Ottoman empire. Lord Stratford de Redcliffe, reappointed for the third time in succession ambassador to Constantinople, returned to his post early in April and used his influence with the Porte to bring about the speedy settlement of the dispute about the Holy Places. "The problems of keys, stars, doorkeepers, gardens, domes, and outbuildings," to quote F. J. C. Hearnshaw,[19] were decided to the satisfaction of the Orthodox by a

[18] The Treaty of Kuchuk Kainardzhi was first introduced in the dispute by M. Ozerov, Russian chargé d'affaires at Constantinople, in December, 1852, that is, when the controversy had lasted for over two years. "It can be proved that neither Nicholas nor Nesselrode nor Brunnow knew much about the treaty or the claims it put forward," writes Temperley (*op. cit.*, p. 304). Seymour quotes "on most certain authority" Nicholas's statement that "his conduct would have been different [in 1853] but for the error into which he had been led" as to the rights secured to him by the Treaty of Kuchuk Kainardzhi (Temperley, *op. cit.*, p. 469).

[19] *The Cambridge History of British Foreign Relations* (Cambridge University Press, Cambridge, 1923), II, 348.

firman of May 5, N.S. Stratford, however, opposed the granting by Turkey of Russia's other demands, because he believed that they "would eventually prove fatal to the Porte's independence." The English influence prevailed, and on May 21, N.S., Menshikov, after several postponements, finally left Constantinople without achieving his object. Nesselrode informed the Porte (May 31, N.S.) that unless Menshikov's demands were accepted within eight days Russian troops would occupy the Danubian principalities, "not to make war on the sultan . . . but to obtain material guarantees" which were to be retained until the Ottoman government complied with Russian requests.

Contrary to the textbook version, the religious issue was not an essential factor in the Franco-Russian dispute. Edouard Drouyn de Lhuys, French minister of foreign affairs, admitted that the question of the Holy Places was in itself unimportant and merely provided an opportunity for breaking down the continental alliance which for nearly half a century had paralyzed France. Nicholas, it will be remembered, disliked the panslav movement. In 1826 he told Wellington that the Russian people cared nothing about those who shared their religious faith. In May, 1853, Menshikov intimated to the Turkish government that the dispute about the Holy Places was "a secondary matter and could be easily abandoned." It is significant that the granting by the Porte, under Stratford's influence, of important concessions to its Orthodox subjects (June 7, 1853, N.S.) failed to improve the situation. The real issue was one of broad "national interests" as interpreted by monarchs and statesmen. In England and France the government was influenced by public sentiment, which responded to the intense anti-Russian campaign conducted by patriotic and liberal organizations, and perhaps by financial and trading groups. It is more difficult to detect such influence in Russia because under the regime of rigorous censorship the outcry of militant Orthodox circles, which are often said to have forced the hand of the tsar, could not have been heard except with government permission. Russia had no important economic interests in the southern sea routes. Although the export of wheat, which went chiefly through the ports of the Black Sea and the Sea of Azov, had increased from 1825 to 1850, it still remained relatively insignificant, and there is nothing to indicate that grain exporters had any part in determining the government's near-eastern policy.

Until the real object of Menshikov's mission became known in May, 1853, the British government had kept aloof from the "churchwarden's quarrel." Early in that year the attitude of the London cabinet towards St. Petersburg was conciliatory, and Russell went so far as to admit that the Russian claim to protect Orthodox Christians was "prescribed by duty and sanctioned by treaty" (February 9, 1853, N.S.). Aberdeen entertained none of Palmerston's and Stratford's illusions about the perfectibility of Turkey, disliked Napoleon, and shared the curious fear of many of his countrymen that England was in grave danger of French invasion. Although the Seymour conversation had alarmed London, as late as the end of April not only Aberdeen and Lord Clarendon (who in February had succeeded Russell at the foreign office) but even Palmerston refused to suspect the tsar's good faith. Referring to the near-eastern situation, Aberdeen wrote on March 21, N.S., to Russell, then leader of the House of Commons, that "we must take special care to avoid entering into any agreement with France"; and the British cabinet, overruling the British chargé d'affaires at Constantinople (H. H. Rose), declined to join the French in an anti-Russian naval demonstration in the Aegean. The impression produced in England by the Menshikov mission strengthened the anti-Russian faction in the cabinet and forced Aberdeen to yield reluctantly to his colleagues. At the end of May, simultaneously with Nesselrode's ultimatum to Turkey, the British government approved the rejection of Russian demands by the Porte and ordered the Mediterranean fleet to Besika Bay, where it was joined by a French squadron. On June 13-14, N.S., an imposing Anglo-French naval force was anchored at the entrance of the Dardanelles. Turkey having refused to comply with the Russian ultimatum (June 16, N.S.), the Russian legation left Constantinople; and on July 1, N.S. a Russian army under Prince Michael Gorchakov crossed the Pruth and invaded the Danubian principalities. The Porte offered no resistance and there was no declaration of war.

This abnormal situation obviously could not last long. England, France, and, to the tsar's sorrow, Austria and Prussia protested against the occupation of the principalities, but the chief effort of diplomacy was directed to the peaceful solution of the crisis, and not less than eleven projects of pacification were produced in the second half of 1853. The only important proposal, however, was the "Vienna note" which was submitted to Russia and Turkey on behalf of England,

France, Austria, and Prussia (July 28, N.S.). The final text of this document, drafted by Napoleon, after reciting the pertinent articles of the treaties of Kuchuk Kainardzhi and Adrianople, provided that "the Sublime Porte . . . promises that the existing state of things shall in no wise be modified without previous understanding with France and Russia." Nicholas, who was officially but secretly informed of the contents of the note and, it is believed, had influenced its tenor and wording, accepted at once (August 5, N.S.), but Turkey demurred and suggested amendments to which Russia was not likely to agree and which therefore amounted to a rejection (August 20, N.S.). There were various reasons for the intransigence of the Porte. Russian arrogance and the occupation of the principalities had fanned nationalistic feelings and religious fanaticism to a point where there was a widespread popular demand for a holy war. The military position of the Ottoman government was strengthened by the arrival at Constantinople of the Egyptian army and fleet and by the presence in Besika Bay of the Anglo-French squadrons, which were practically committed to assist Turkey in case of a Russian attack. Stratford, whose own plan for the settlement of the dispute had been discarded in favor of the "Vienna note," made no secret of his disapproval of the latter, although officially he urged its acceptance.

Temporarily Russia appeared in a stronger diplomatic position than Turkey: she had accepted the offer of the four Powers which the Porte had rejected. In the middle of September, however, it became known that St. Petersburg had read into the "Vienna note" a much wider right of intervention in Turkish affairs than was intended by its authors. This "violent interpretation," as Clarendon called it, was held in England and France to be conclusive evidence of the tsar's duplicity. Alarmed by the turn of events, Nicholas endeavored to reassert his influence with his Austrian and Prussian allies and to placate the Maritime Powers. On September 26, N.S., he visited Francis Joseph at Olmütz, and a week later the two emperors and the king of Prussia met at Warsaw. The tenor of the Olmütz conversations was conciliatory. The tsar expressed solicitude about the British fleet in Besika Bay and suggested that it might enter the Dardanelles during the autumn storms; he spoke of evacuating the Danubian principalities as soon as Turkey accepted his conditions; and he dropped the "violent interpretation" of the "Vienna note." The Olmütz meeting produced a new proposal, transmitted to England and France by Count Karl

Buol-Schauenstein, Austrian minister of foreign affairs. The "Buol project" was based on the "Vienna note," which was modified by the Russian pledge to refrain from direct intervention in Turkey and merely to exercise the right "of watching that the engagement contracted by the Ottoman empire in the Treaty of Kuchuk Kainardzhi is strictly observed." Napoleon was, for once, favorably impressed by Nicholas's unexpected moderation; but the British cabinet, more than ever distrustful of the tsar, turned down the "Buol project" (October 8, N.S.), overruling Aberdeen, who to the end of his life believed that its acceptance might have prevented the war.

Diplomatic activities, however, were rapidly overshadowed by military events. On September 14, N.S., four armed steamers, two French and two British, entered the Straits at the request of the Turkish government. In the opinion of Stratford, who was upheld by eminent English historians, this constituted an "evasion" and not a "violation" of the convention of 1841, a subtle and not very convincing distinction. On September 27, N.S. Aberdeen and Clarendon, under pressure from France and without consulting the cabinet, ordered the British fleet to Constantinople. On October 4, N.S., Turkey declared war on Russia and demanded the withdrawal of Russian troops from the principalities within fifteen days. Hostilities began on October 23, the day after the Anglo-French squadrons, which had been intentionally delayed by Stratford, passed through the Dardanelles and came to anchor at the entrance of the Bosphorus. The imperial manifesto of October 20 (November 2, N.S.) announced that Russia had been forced to take up arms against Turkey in order to protect "the sacred rights of the Orthodox Church." The last chance of localizing the conflict vanished when in the battle of Sinope, in the Black Sea, a portion of the Turkish fleet was annihilated by a Russian squadron under Admiral P. S. Nakhimov (November 30, N.S.). While the Russians noisily celebrated their victory, a wave of righteous indignation swept over France and, especially, over England. Although, unlike Navarino, the Sinope affair was, to quote Temperley, "a perfectly legitimate operation of war" and "is now generally accepted as such," it was denounced in western Europe as a hideous crime. The *Times* wrote that peace "was no longer compatible with the honour of the country," and the *Globe* that Russia was not "accessible to the ordinary motives of the rest of the human family." [20] The popular press

[20] Temperley, *op. cit.*, pp. 371–374.

was, if possible, even more virulent. Aberdeen still argued privately that Russia "had done nothing we had any right to complain of," but Palmerston's resignation from the cabinet (December 14, N.S.), although actually due to a disagreement over the reform bill, was widely interpreted as a protest against the government's eastern policy.

Palmerston had consistently argued that the occupation of the Danubian principalities should be regarded as a *casus belli* and had urged the sending of the British fleet to the Bosphorus and the Black Sea. His influence in parliament and on public opinion was great, and daily increasing. Probably no other Englishman had done more to foster what H. C. F. Bell aptly calls "the curious eagerness for war" which took possession of England. In the emotional atmosphere created by the "Sinope massacre" the bellicose statesman became "indispensable," and on December 24, N.S., to the regret of the queen and Aberdeen, he withdrew his resignation and resumed his place in the cabinet. Napoleon, whose prestige was involved in the dispute about the Holy Places and who strove to revive the glories of the first empire, had insisted throughout 1853 on forcible and dramatic action. He became even more militant when, in spite of Aberdeen's anti-French feelings, England committed herself to cooperation with France. At the end of December the irrevocable decision was taken: the British and the French fleet received orders to take over the control of the Black Sea and to protect not only Turkish shores but the Turkish flag; "all Russian vessels, other than merchantmen, met in the Black Sea" were required to return to Sevastopol. Early in January, 1854, the Anglo-French squadron sailed through the Bosphorus on its new mission. The die was cast, and although desultory diplomatic moves for the preservation of peace continued, they were due rather to force of habit than to any real hope of success. At the beginning of February diplomatic relations between St. Petersburg, on the one hand, and Paris and London, on the other, were severed. France, England, and Turkey concluded a treaty of alliance on March 12, N.S., and France and England a treaty of defensive and offensive alliance on April 10, N.S. An Anglo-French ultimatum (February 27, N.S.) demanded the withdrawal of the Russian troops from the Danubian principalities by a specified date in April and stated that failure to comply would be considered equivalent to a declaration of war.[21] This communication

[21] The ultimatum took the form of two separate letters from Clarendon and Drouyn de Lhuys. The date for the evacuation of the principalities was set as April

remained unanswered and, instead of evacuating the principalities, the Russian troops in March crossed the Danube. A contingency Nicholas had so long refused to admit became an accomplished fact: war with Turkey was merged into a war with a European coalition.[22]

THE CRIMEAN WAR, 1854–1856

Austria and Prussia, like England, adopted an attitude that Nicholas had not foreseen. The Anglo-French treaty of alliance (Article V) invited all European states to join the anti-Russian coalition, and Clarendon, to quote W. F. Reddaway, "was not wholly proof against the normal British illusion that foreign nations may well be proud to fight for a cause which had been sanctified by British adhesion." Fortunately for Russia this illusion was not universally shared. Spain and Denmark, in spite of considerable pressure, refused to be drawn into "the battle of civilization against barbarism" in which their interests were in no way involved. Sweden, whose geographical position was of great importance in a naval campaign against Russia, ignored the discreet bait of reconquering Finland and maintained her neutrality which, however, tended to favor the allies. Of all the European states the kingdom of Sardinia alone, eager to secure the patronage of France and England in the impending struggle with Austria over Lombardy and Venice, became a full-fledged member of the coalition on January 26, 1855, N.S., and in May sent 15,000 Piedmontese soldiers to the Crimea. The allies were particularly anxious to win over Austria and Prussia, whose attitude might well have proved decisive. The monarchs of the three eastern Powers, however, were united by the bonds of the Holy Alliance, devotion to legitimacy, and detestation of revolu-

---

15, N.S. in the French and April 30, N.S. in the English communication. The time allowed for a reply was not mentioned by Drouyn de Lhuys, but was stated as six days by Clarendon.

[22] The part of Lord Stratford de Redcliffe in the events that led to the war cannot be discussed here. It is one of the disputed points of British diplomatic history, and his detractors are as numerous as his apologists. It may be noted, however, that Stratford, as W. F. Reddaway puts it, "in many ways resembled an independent potentate rather than an ordinary public servant" (*The Cambridge History of British Foreign Relations* [Cambridge, 1923], II, 365). His policies were often not only independent from, but even opposed to, those of the cabinet, and Aberdeen repeatedly accused him of "dishonesty." The motives, objects, and consequences of Stratford's separate moves are open to more than one interpretation, but there is little doubt that his passionate Russophobia was important among the factors working against the preservation of peace.

tion. Nicholas had suppressed the Hungarian insurrection and as recently as 1852–1853 had supported Francis Joseph in the conflict with Turkey over Montenegro. Frederick William IV was the tsar's brother-in-law and warm admirer. Yet throughout the Crimean War Prussia remained neutral and played a subordinate and ambiguous part, while Austria, although not a belligerent, pursued a definitely anti-Russian policy which brought her twice to the verge of war and facilitated the victory of the coalition.

In January, 1854, Count A. F. Orlov, of Unkiar Skelessi fame, arrived in Vienna on a secret mission. In return for Austria's declaration of friendly "armed neutrality" he offered the guarantee of her territory and, in case of Russian victory, a joint protectorate with Russia over Serbia and the Danubian principalities. The proposed pact, which was to include Prussia, provided for the close diplomatic collaboration of the three courts. Francis Joseph, however, rejected this offer and ominously moved to Transylvania an Austrian army corps. On April 9, N.S., Austria and Prussia joined England and France in proclaiming the integrity of the Ottoman empire and in demanding the evacuation of the Danubian principalities. A few days later (April 20, N.S.) Berlin and Vienna signed an offensive and defensive alliance which, by removing the danger of war between the two countries, allowed Francis Joseph to follow a more active policy in the Danubian region. Frederick William tearfully pleaded with the tsar that, since Prussia was determined not to fight Russia, the alliance was really in the latter country's interest because it would prevent Austria from falling entirely under the influence of the western Powers. These hopes were only partly realized. An Austro-Turkish convention (June 14, 1854, N.S.) bound Vienna to secure the evacuation of Moldavia and Wallachia, if necessary by force of arms. The Austrian government peremptorily demanded the withdrawal of the Russians, a *démarche* in which Prussia concurred. The tsar at first refused, but the concentration of Austrian troops in Transylvania and the reverses suffered by Gorchakov forced him to yield. In September the Russians retreated behind the Pruth and, by agreement with Turkey, the Danubian principalities were occupied by the Austrians. Nevertheless the hostile attitude of Vienna compelled Russia to maintain on the Austrian border a sizable army that might have been profitably used in the main theaters of war.

At the Vienna conference Austria, France, and England formulated (August 8, 1854, N.S.) the following four-point program, which became the basis of peace negotiations: (1) substitution of a European guarantee for the Russian protectorate over Moldavia, Wallachia, and Serbia; (2) freedom of navigation of the Danube; (3) revision of the Straits convention of 1841; (4) abandonment of the Russian claim to protect Orthodox Christians in Turkey and the substitution for it, by the five Powers, of a collective guarantee of Christians, irrespective of denomination. These proposals were at once communicated by Buol to St. Petersburg, but it was not until November that military reverses and the deterioration of the domestic situation forced Nicholas to accept them as a basis for negotiations. Meanwhile Austria had concluded with the western Powers a treaty of alliance (December 2, 1854, N.S.) which, however, did not impose upon her the obligation to participate in offensive operations against Russia. The hope of a speedy termination of the war, which had been raised by the death of Nicholas (February, 1855), came to naught when the Russian representative in Vienna, Prince Alexander Gorchakov, would not consent to the naval limitation on which the allies insisted. The war dragged on for another ten months, the Russians refusing, even after the fall of Sevastopol in September, to accept the allied terms. It was Austria who broke the deadlock and dealt Russia the final blow. In December, 1855, Vienna presented to St. Petersburg an ultimatum demanding immediate peace negotiations on the basis of the original four points, supplemented by two new conditions: the rectification of the Bessarabian frontier in favor of Moldavia, and the right of the allies to submit to the future peace congress further demands the nature of which was not disclosed. In case of refusal, Austria threatened to proceed at once with warlike measures. Russia was in no position to face a new war, and Frederick William urged Nicholas's successor, Emperor Alexander II, to yield. On January 16, 1856, N.S., the St. Petersburg government signified its acceptance, and a peace congress met in Paris at the end of February.

Nicholas's foreign policy thus ended in a ghastly fiasco. Had the tsar lived to see the end of the war, he might have found some solace in the fact that his arch-enemy Palmerston was bitterly disappointed with the outcome. Palmerston, prime minister since February, 1855, was an advocate of peace with victory. Victory, however, meant to him something different from what it meant to his allies. He wrote to Russell on May 26, 1854, N.S., that to expel Russia from the Danubian principalities "would be only like turning a burglar out of your house, to break in again at a more fitting opportunity. The best and most effectual security for the peace of Europe would be the severance from Russia of some of the frontier territories acquired by her in later times, Georgia, Circassia, the Crimea, Bessarabia, Poland, and Finland . . . she will still remain an enormous Power, but far less well posted for aggression on her neighbours." [23] Napoleon and Francis Joseph, however, showed little enthusiasm for this program, and Palmerston had to accept their decision.

The military campaign, like the diplomatic situation, did not develop according to plan. Nicholas, who, as appears from a memorandum he wrote early in November 1853 and from other documents, attached great importance to the anticipated uprising of the Christian subjects of the Porte, outlined a comprehensive program of measures designed to encourage the national aspirations of the Slavs and the Greeks. Although the memorandum of 1853 indicated that these proposals were inspired by fear of Great Britain's assuming leadership in "the emancipation of Christians in Europe" rather than by any real sympathy for the subjugated populations, Nesselrode did not fail to perceive the contradiction between the measures advocated by the tsar and Russia's traditional policy. In a remarkable report (November 8, 1853) the chancellor argued that the emancipation of Slavs and Greeks necessarily meant the dissolution of the Ottoman empire which Russia had invariably held it to be her interest to preserve; that, having consistently opposed the national movement in Poland, Hungary, and Italy, the imperial government could not very well promote it among Slavs and Greeks; that so flagrant a departure from traditional policy would open Russia to charges of duplicity and would invite intervention by Turkey and her allies on behalf of the Mohammedans under Russian rule; and that the sacrifice of the principle of legitimacy and the encouragement of national aspirations among the Balkan peoples was likely to alienate the sympathies of Austria and Prussia. Nesselrode held that the situation would be basically changed and the program proposed by the tsar justified in case of a spontaneous uprising of the Christian populations, but that Russia should do nothing to promote it.[24] Nicholas did not entirely agree with his chancellor's too logical and surprisingly outspoken criticism, but the

[23] Bell, *op. cit.*, II, 105.
[24] The text of the tsar's memorandum and Nesselrode's report, both written in French, are published in Zaionchkovsky, *op. cit.*, Vol. II, Part II, pp. 321–326.

failure of the Danubian campaign, the occupation of the Piraeus by the allies in May, 1854, and the measures taken by Austria effectively prevented any large-scale insurrection of Christians in support of Russia. Nicholas's predecessors had experienced similar disappointments in their wars with Turkey.

Disappointments were, however, not all on Russia's side in a war in which the allied navies were called upon to play a prominent part. Odessa was bombarded in April, 1854; in July a British squadron occupied the Aland Islands off the shores of Finland; and the British fleet attacked points as far apart as the ancient Solovtsky Monastery on the White Sea (July) and Petropavlovsk in Kamchatka (August). These naval demonstrations alarmed St. Petersburg, but it soon became clear that the British Baltic squadron, commanded by Sir Charles Napier, had failed to live up to the sanguine expectations of London and that the issue of the struggle was to be decided in the Black Sea region. The military advantages derived by Russia from the fact that the war was waged on her territory, or in areas adjoining it, were largely illusory. Russian railways were few, and there were none south of Moscow. Because of the poor state of the roads, the transport of troops, munitions, and supplies to the Danubian principalities, to the Crimea, and the Caucasus—the three main theaters of war—presented in the case of Russia obstacles at least as formidable as those encountered by the allies, who controlled the sea and had at their disposal a large fleet of steamships. The technical equipment (rifles, field and heavy guns, and munitions) of the French and British armies were vastly superior to the obsolete models still used by the Muscovites. With the appearance in the Black Sea of allied screw-propelled and heavily armed ships, the Russian navy, which consisted largely of sailing vessels, was reduced to inaction, while many units of the Russian Baltic fleet were so antiquated as to be practically unseaworthy. In spite of the technical advantages enjoyed by the allies, the war proved longer, more difficult and costly than had been expected in London and Paris.

The Danubian campaign, which Nicholas had hoped might lead to the invasion of the Balkans, was short and disastrous. It will be remembered that in July, 1853, the Russian army of Prince Michael Gorchakov had "peacefully" occupied Moldavia and Wallachia and in March, 1854, had crossed the Danube. Gorchakov's attempts to subdue the Turkish fortress of Silistria, first by siege and later by assault, were equally unsuccessful. The threatening attitude of Austria, the concentration of a large allied expeditionary force in the Black Sea port of Varna, military reverses, and epidemics among the troops compelled the Russians to retreat. In July Gorchakov recrossed the Danube, in August the Ottoman commander in chief Omar Pasha entered Bucharest, and in September the Russians evacuated the principalities and withdrew east of the Pruth. Thus did the Danubian campaign come to an inglorious end.

The idea of sending an expeditionary force to the Crimea, which had become the chief battlefield of the war, would seem to have originated with Palmerston.[25] After elaborate preparations an allied armada of some three hundred transports, escorted by ninety men-of-war and carrying 62,000 troops (28,000 French, 27,000 English, and 7,000 Turkish), powerful artillery and ample war supplies, sailed from Varna (September 7, 1854, N.S.) and a week later landed in Eupatoria, in the Crimea, without meeting any resistance. The naval base of Sevastopol, regarded in London and Paris as the pillar of Russian influence in the Black Sea, was the object of the invasion. On the river Alma, in the first encounter with the French and the British, the Russians, hopelessly outnumbered, but fighting stubbornly, were defeated, not, however, without inflicting heavy losses on the enemy (September 20, N.S.). The allies having failed to press home their victory, Prince Alexander Menshikov, commander of the Russian forces in the Crimea (the aged Field Marshal Paskevich was the Russian commander in chief), succeeded in disengaging his battered divisions and retreated to Sevastopol. To avoid encirclement and prevent the severance of his lines of communication, Menshikov decided to leave the city, and he withdrew with the bulk of his troops to Bakhchisarai (September 24, N.S.). Simultaneously a portion of the Russian fleet was sunk at the entrance of the harbor which runs along Sevastopol's north side. This heroic measure prevented the allies from attacking the fortress from that direction in an amphibious operation of their fleet and land forces. They then decided to invest Sevastopol and to assault it from the south, where it was known to be practically unfortified. The encircling movement was completed by the end of September; but further operations were suspended until the arrival of heavy artillery, and the actual bombardment did not begin until October 17, N.S. This delay afforded the defenders a much-needed respite. In

[25] Bell, *op. cit.*, II, 105.

the early stage of the siege the garrison did not exceed 18,000 men, chiefly sailors of the Black Sea fleet. They were commanded with great skill, courage, and devotion to duty by naval officers Admiral V. K. Kornilov, Admiral P. S. Nakhimov, and Admiral V. I. Istomin. General E. I. Totleben, a military engineer of outstanding ability and indomitable energy, succeeded in record time in throwing around the fortress a line of fortifications which for eleven months withstood the onslaught of the enemy. Russian resistance came as a shock to the allies. The British government had approved the plan of the expedition on the theory that Sevastopol could not be defended by land; therefore no preparations had been made for a winter campaign. For this facile optimism allied soldiers paid a price as terrible as the ordeal they inflicted on the Russians.

While the garrison and population of Sevastopol repulsed repeated attacks and endured with admirable fortitude incessant bombardments, both sides received substantial reinforcements. Hopes that the siege might be lifted, however, were not fulfilled. Menshikov's attempt to dislodge the British from their encampment at Balaklava ended in the rout of his troops (October 25, N.S.), and at Inkerman (November 5, N.S.) some 35,000 Russians suffered another crushing defeat, although their opponents numbered merely 16,000. These reverses were in part responsible for Nicholas's belated acceptance of the offer of the western Powers to negotiate on the basis of the "four points." Meanwhile hostilities continued, and in February, 1855, General Khrulev led an unsuccessful assault on Eupatoria, the allies' principal port in the Crimea. Soon after, Menshikov was recalled, and Prince Michael Gorchakov was appointed his successor. In spite of the spectacular victories of Balaklava and Inkerman, the indecisive character of the campaign, the high mortality among the allied troops, especially from cholera, the breakdown of the medical service, and widely publicized tales of laxity, corruption, and sheer stupidity on the part of allied high command and responsible officials at home provoked a storm of indignation in both England and France. In January, 1855, the Aberdeen government met with ignominious defeat. Napoleon considered going himself to the Crimea, and there were important shifts in the allied high command. A great diplomatic and military effort was made to bring the war to a speedy end. Beginning in February, with Palmerston in control of the British government, attacks on Sevastopol increased in ferocity, taking a heavy toll both of assailants and of defenders. Kornilov was killed at the beginning of the siege; Istomin in March, 1855; Nakhimov, Kornilov's successor and chief organizer of the defense, in July, 1855; and in the same month Totleben was grievously wounded. Gorchakov's last desperate attempt to relieve the besieged fortress by engaging the allies on the river Chernoi (August 16, N.S.) ended in failure, the Russians losing some 8,000 men. Further resistance became impossible. On September 9, N.S. the assailants finally broke through the fortifications and took possession of the smoldering shambles of Russia's once-great naval base.

In addition to the region around Sevastopol the allies occupied Kerch and Enikale, gateway to the Sea of Azov; Anapa on the Caucasian littoral; and Kinburn in the delta of the Dnieper. On the Caucasian front, where the Russians had to deal with Turkish troops and local insurgent movements, the course of the campaign was much more satisfactory from the Russian point of view than it was in the Crimea. The most important Russian victory was won towards the end of the war, when, after a protracted siege, the fortress of Kars capitulated to N. N. Muravev (November 28, 1855, N.S.). Although this belated success could not affect the outcome of the struggle, it bolstered Russian morale and provided a useful bargaining point at the Paris peace congress.

Like all wars, the Crimean campaign produced many instances of selfless courage and abnegation which are the theme of nationalistic textbooks and historiography. The stock example, on the side of the allies, is the celebrated but futile charge of the British light cavalry brigade, at Balaklava, of which the French said, "c'est magnifique, mais ce n'est pas la guerre." The defense of Sevastopol is ranked among Russia's great national epics. An unforgettable record of the indomitable spirit and the sufferings of its defenders has been preserved in *The Tales of Sevastopol* by Leo Tolstoy, who fought in the ranks of the besieged. Heroism, however, is always costly. According to Russian estimates, in the siege of Sevastopol alone the Russian army lost in killed and wounded 102,000 men, and Sir Spencer Walpole puts the total loss of lives, including men who died from disease, at 600,000.

The war of 1854–1856 was a severe personal blow to Nicholas. He lived to witness not only the collapse of his diplomatic system but also the defeat of his army, in which he had taken particular pride.

Nationalistically minded Russian historians have interpreted the war as a conspiracy of the western Powers, jealous of Russia's might and greatness, to prevent the fulfillment of her "historic destinies" in the Balkans and on the Bosphorus. British historians have often extolled the wisdom of Palmerston and Stratford in safeguarding the "vital" routes of British commerce and saving Europe and Asia from Russian domination by blocking her progress in the Balkans, the Near East, and on the road to India.[26] There is more truth in the official Soviet interpretation (1940) of the Crimean War as a conflict of bourgeois and liberal Europe with the forces of reaction personified by Nicholas. The tsar's ultra-conservatism was largely responsible for the formation of the anti-Russian coalition and, although there are no conclusive proofs that he actually intended to destroy Turkey, there are reputable Russian historians who believed, as did Palmerston, that this was Nicholas's ultimate object. Professor S. M. Seredonin, for instance, wrote (in 1911) that in the 1840's Nicholas "had set as the aims of his policy the suppression of revolution and the elimination of Turkey" and, in the final analysis, the establishment of "Russian hegemony over Europe." On the other hand, John Bright spoke of "the 50,000 Englishmen who died in the Crimean war to make Lord Palmerston prime minister." Although the prejudices, theories, and personal ambitions of the chief actors in the great drama—Nicholas, Napoleon, Palmerston, Stratford—contributed to the making of the war, it is nevertheless more likely that the course of events was determined rather by spontaneous decisions, the consequences of which were not fully realized, than by any preconceived plan. Referring to the two momentous British moves—the sending of the fleet to Constantinople in September and to the Black Sea in December, 1853—Temperley judiciously remarks that neither "was taken from clear motives or on the basis of an agreed policy. Both were influenced by misconceptions of the moment."[27] This observation applies to practically every phase of the conflict and goes a long way to make intelligible how (if not why) the British, the French, and the Italians came to fight the Russians in the Crimea.

From the Russian point of view the war had one redeeming feature:

[26] Even the usually sound and clear-sighted W. F. Reddaway maintains, for instance, that the decision to send an expeditionary force to the Crimea "was in many respects unimpeachable," certainly a most questionable statement. *The Cambridge History of British Foreign Policy*, II, 383.

[27] Temperley, *op. cit.*, p. 511.

by forcibly exposing the administrative, economic, and social ineptness of autocracy it convinced even conservative elements (for instance, the historian Solovev) that far-reaching reforms could be no longer postponed.

CHAPTER XXXIII

ALEXANDER II
The Reforms

THE TSAR-LIBERATOR

The reign of Alexander II (1855–1881) is known in Russian historiography as "the era of great reforms" and the emperor whose name it bears as the tsar-liberator. Although Alexander is formally entitled to this appellation, he was singularly ill qualified by education, convictions, and temperament for the part of reformer he was fated to play. The eldest son of Emperor Nicholas I, Alexander was born in Moscow on April 17, 1818. His principal tutor, the poet and courtier Vasili Zhukovsky, devised for the education of his pupil a vaguely humanitarian program which did more credit to its author's imagination and zeal than to his pedagogical abilities. This program, moreover, although approved by Emperor Nicholas, was never fully carried out, and court festivities and military parades, whose effects on the character of the grand duke Zhukovsky particularly dreaded, absorbed much of the boy's time. An indifferent and indolent student, Alexander nevertheless acquired a good knowledge of Russian, French, German, English, and Polish, and in 1838 he attended brief courses on military arts, finance, and diplomacy given respectively by General Baron Jomini (formerly chief of staff of Marshal Ney), Kankrin, and Brunnow. From an early age Alexander traveled extensively in Russia and abroad; his progress from place to place, however, was usually so rapid as to offer little opportunity for anything except official receptions, inspections of troops, and worship at local shrines. In 1837, for instance, he visited in seven months thirty Russian provinces, including Siberia, where no other member of the imperial family had ever been. Two years later, during the grand duke's European tour, Zhukovsky complained to the empress that because of the pressure of official engagements the time left for visits of an educational character was so short as to render them tiresome and useless. Unlike his father, Alexander was called before his accession to take an active part in government. He held various military commands, was a member of the State Council (from 1840) and of the committee of ministers (from 1842), and during Nicholas's absences he acted as his deputy.

The nebulous, sentimental humanitarianism of Zhukovsky left little imprint on his pupil's character, except perhaps in fostering public display of his emotions, accompanied at times by copious tears. During the War of 1877–1878 Alexander wished to relieve the sufferings of the wounded by attending them as a male nurse (*brat miloserdiia*). Though these manifestations of imperial tender-heartedness greatly impressed his official biographers, they did not prevent the tsar from maintaining a police regime of extreme severity and from sending thousands of people into exile without even the formality of a trial. Unwillingness to face obstacles and a tendency to follow the line of least resistance, noted by his devoted governor Captain Charles Merder as early as 1831, were perhaps Alexander's outstanding traits. He seldom showed leadership (his initiative in pressing the cause of emancipation in 1856 was one of the rare exceptions), and he exercised his influence over the destinies of Russia chiefly through the selection of his advisers; the uncertainty as to his personal views is made all the greater by his practice of maintaining in responsible offices, simultaneously and for years, men whose opinions and policies were irreconcilably opposed (for instance, the liberal Dimitry Miliutin and the reactionary Count Dimitry Tolstoy). Although Alexander's political philosophy, to quote Presniakov, eludes precise definition, there is much evidence to show that he was an admirer of the quasi-dictatorial regime instituted by Nicholas, and shared the latter's predilection for autocratic and bureaucratic methods. The nobility and other groups were consulted on some aspects of the reform, but decisions were invariably made by bureaucratic agencies and tended to perpetuate administrative tutelage. There is no justification, moreover, for the traditional division of Alexander's reign into two parts: the era of liberal reforms ending in 1866, when the first attempt against his life was made, and that of reaction following this date; both liberal and reactionary tendencies manifested themselves in varying degrees throughout the entire period.

Until his accession Alexander showed no sympathy for the cause of emancipation and, as has already been noted, lent his support to the reactionary elements. His change of heart, it is believed, was due to the revelation of Russia's ineptitude and weakness in the Crimean War and to his conviction that emancipation was the only way of preventing a peasant revolution. All subsequent reforms were largely the consequence of the abolition of serfdom. Alexander, however, proceeded reluctantly and slowly; he rejected the demands of liberal opinion for the limitation of autocracy and the introduction of a representative government. In a manifesto (February 19, 1855) issued the day after his accession, he paid tribute to the guards for "saving Russia" in December, 1825. Yet at times he gave indirect encouragement to the constitutional aspirations of Russian liberals. In 1863, in an address to the Finnish diet reconvened for the first time since 1809, Alexander held that "in the hands of a wise nation . . . liberal institutions not only are not dangerous, but are a guarantee of order and well-being," and fifteen years later he was instrumental in establishing a constitutional regime in liberated Bulgaria. He would not agree, however, to any curtailment of the powers of the Russian Crown. The lack of a definite legislative program and the reactionary attitude of many of Alexander's closest collaborators impaired the usefulness of the reforms, which, moreover, fell short of the expectations of even moderately liberal circles. "The great reforms," important as they are in Russian history, were not therefore a charter of liberties granted to the nation by high-minded statesmen conscious of the needs of the time and led by the tsar-liberator, but half-hearted concessions on the part of those who (with some exceptions) hated to see the disappearance of the old order and tried to save as much of it as circumstances would allow.

The half-heartedness and indecision characteristic of Alexander were well illustrated by his role in the War of 1877–1878. He did not assume the command of the troops, but established his headquarters with the army and by his interference with the course of military operations added to the confusion and hazards of the campaign.

In foreign relations, as in domestic affairs, Alexander clung to the tradition of Nicholas I. In spite of the bitter lessons of the Crimean War, he retained an emotional attachment to the Holy Alliance, although the course of international events prevented him from following consistently the policy of close cooperation with Berlin and especially with Vienna. Ties with Germany were strengthened by Alexander's marriage (1841) with Princess Wilhelmina Maria of Hesse-Darmstadt, known in Russia as Maria Aleksandrovna. A love match which led to the birth of six sons and two daughters, the union with the German princess nevertheless did not withstand the test of time. After several brief liaisons Alexander (about 1864) came under the spell of Princess Catherine Dolgoruky, then a girl of seventeen. He had by her four children, and after the death of the empress (May, 1880) married morganatically Princess Dolgoruky (July, 1880) and conferred upon her the title of Princess Yurevsky. Following Alexander's assassination, Princess Yurevsky lived chiefly in France, and died in Nice in 1922. Contrary to the contention of Maurice Paléologue, there is no reason to believe that she "is entitled to an important place in Russian history."

THE EMANCIPATION OF THE SERFS

The death of Nicholas and the accession of Alexander II were received with a feeling of genuine relief by all those—and their number had greatly increased during and after the Crimean War—who believed in the necessity of reform. The young emperor's conservative views were little known outside court circles, and he was generally regarded as the champion of emancipation which was to usher in a new era in Russian history. Rumors, freely circulated, about the impending abolition of serfdom alarmed the conservative majority of the serfowners and gained wide credence among the peasants who, for instance, imagined that service in the militia established during the Crimean War (decree of April 3, 1854, and the manifesto of January 29, 1855) was to free the militiamen and their families from bondage. Hence the enthusiastic response of the serfs to the call to arms, refusal to obey authorities, and a wave of agrarian disturbances which swept over many provinces. There was little, however, in Alexander's early measures to justify the expectations of the liberals and of the peasantry. The hopes of the militiamen were dampened by flogging and by punitive military expeditions. Most of the ministers of the former reign remained in office, the few newcomers belonging to the old bureaucratic school. Bibikov, minister of the interior, was dismissed in August, 1855, because Alexander disapproved of his policy of "inventories" as unduly harsh on the landowners.[1] His successor, the elderly

[1] See p. 780.

S. S. Lanskoï (created a count in 1861), eventually a partisan of emancipation, announced on taking office that the tsar had entrusted to him the duty "to safeguard unwaveringly (*nerushimo*) the rights conferred upon the nobility" by former monarchs. This statement was no mere figure of speech. Although the emancipation forced by the government upon the reluctant majority of the *dvoriane* destroyed their most valuable privilege, Alexander regarded the landed aristocracy, in his own words, as "the mainstay of the throne." When the abolition of serfdom was decided in principle, he endeavored to persuade the serf-owners to accept the inevitable, to cooperate with the government, and to assume a share both of responsibility and of credit for the reform. He was eager to protect the economic interests of the noblemen, although he would make no concessions to their political aspirations. Emancipation "cannot be accomplished without sacrifices," Alexander told the representatives of the *dvoriane* on September 4, 1859, "but I wish that these sacrifices should be as light as possible. I shall exert myself to help you." On January 28, 1861, he reiterated this assurance, and with scant respect for truth enunciated the doctrine that initiative in freeing the serfs came from the nobles. His concern with the interests of the *dvoriane*, as K. K. Arsenev has noted, explains much in the course and character of the reform.

The manifesto of March 19, 1856, announcing the termination of the Crimean War, contained the first indications that important changes might be in the offing. Veiled references to the benefits Russia was to derive from the new era of peace were meant to render more palatable the humiliating terms of the Treaty of Paris. The phraseology of the manifesto, however, was so guarded and vague as to mean almost anything, and the cynics were inclined to think that it meant nothing. For once they proved to be wrong. A few days later (March 30) Alexander, addressing an assembly of the Moscow nobility, referred to rumors concerning his plans for the emancipation of the serfs. "I consider it necessary to inform you that I have no intention to do this now," the emperor said. "But, of course, you understand yourselves that the existing order of serfdom cannot remain unchanged. It is better to begin to abolish bondage from above than to wait for the time when it will begin to abolish itself spontaneously from below. I request, gentlemen, that you think over how this could be accomplished. Convey my words to the *dvoriane* for their consideration." This statement, which took by surprise even Alexander's closest collaborators, for instance, Lanskoï, failed to bring a response. Inveterate serfowners did not wish to encourage the tsar in a course of which they disapproved, and they sought solace in his assertion that he did not intend to abolish serfdom *now*. Noblemen, partisans of the reform, welcomed the emperor's unexpected initiative but, as one of them (Yuri Samarin) put it, "dreaded equally popular wrath and the sudden, unprepared action by the government." Whatever the reason, the corporations of the nobility manifested no inclination to follow Alexander's lead.

Confronted with the inertia of the *dvoriane*, the government fell back on the trusted method of bureaucratic agencies. A secret committee composed of higher officials, most of them large landowners and opponents of emancipation, was appointed at the end of 1856, and faithfully conformed to the familiar pattern established by its numerous predecessors. It decided that serfdom was an evil but should be remedied "gradually and with due caution." Caution was pushed to such extremes that the committee, even after the Grand Duke Constantine, the tsar's brother and a proven friend of emancipation, was appointed as its chairman (August, 1857), preferred to use in its deliberations the circumlocution "betterment in the condition of the serfs" rather than the distasteful terms "emancipation" and "abolition of serfdom." After much procrastination the committee produced a report (August 18, 1857) which outlined three stages in its future work: (1) secret collection of information by the minister of the interior, no time limit being set for this task "in order not to embarrass" that official; (2) preparation on the basis of information so assembled of proposals dealing with the "period of transition," which was to be not less than ten years; and (3) final liquidation of serfdom. The committee's composition, procedure, and the nature of its report, which was confirmed by the tsar, justified the fondest hopes of the serfowners: in the hands of an expert bureaucratic body inimical to the reform, collection of information and drafting of proposals might well have gone on until the object in view had been lost in the flood of official verbiage.

At this juncture, however, once more the unexpected happened. At the end of October, 1857, V. I. Nazimov, governor-general of Vilna, Grodno, and Kovno, arrived in St. Petersburg as bearer of a petition in which the nobles of that area requested of the tsar permission to free their serfs *without land*. This seemingly magnanimous offer was wangled from the nobility by Nazimov's threats of reimposing "inventories" (which were then in the process of revision) of a type far less favorable to landed interests than was the reform they proposed. The secret committee to which was referred this sole and belated response to the emperor's speech of March 30, 1856, spent three weeks in desultory debate without being able to reach a decision. In the meantime Alexander had shifted to the side of those who favored speedy emancipation. He had read some of the numerous memoranda stressing the urgency of emancipation, for instance, those of Yuri Samarin and K. D. Kavelin (such memoranda were circulated in manuscript, no discussion of the emancipation being permitted in the press until the end of 1857). Pressure was brought to bear upon the tsar by the partisans of the reform: the Grand Duke Constantine, the Grand Duchess Helen (formerly Princess of Württemberg, widow of Alexander's uncle the Grand Duke Michael), and by some of the bureaucrats, among them Lanskoï. The petition presented by Nazimov offered an opportunity for action. An imperial rescript to Nazimov (November 20, 1857) approved the "initiative taken by the nobles of the Lithuanian provinces," and directed them to establish provincial committees of landowners to draft within six months detailed proposals "for the future organization of the serfs and the betterment of their condition." These proposals, however, were to embody the following arrangements, which differed widely from the emancipation without land requested by the petitioners: (1) noble landowners were to retain legal title to the whole of their land, but peasants were to be entitled to the possession of their homesteads, which they were to acquire within a specified time by purchase; they were also to be entitled to allotments of farm land, adequate in size to provide for their needs, including taxes and payments to the landowner; for the use of this land the peasants were either to pay an annual tribute (*obrok*) or to perform services; (2) peasants were to be organized into village communes (*obshchina*), noble landowners retaining police powers; and (3) provisions were to be made to ensure the collection of taxes and other obligations due from the peasants. The rescript of November 20 and Lanskoï's accompanying instruction, which spoke of "the abolition of serfdom," proved an important turning point on the road towards emancipation. On November 24 these documents were circulated to all provincial governors and provincial marshals of the nobility "for their information and guidance" in case the nobility in their provinces "expressed the wish" to follow the example of the landowners of Lithuania. On December 5 a rescript drawn in terms similar to those of the rescript of November 20 was given to the governor-general of St. Petersburg, ostensibly in reply to a request for the introduction of "inventories" made by the landowners of that province early in 1857. Both rescripts were published in the newspapers on December 17. The government had at last announced its intention to proceed with the reform, although the rescripts left many questions unanswered and even though their wording was lacking in clarity and in part was contradictory. But the veil of secrecy was finally lifted, and the press was permitted to discuss emancipation. Jubilation in liberal circles was boundless; Herzen in his London publication paid a warm tribute to Emperor Alexander.

The nobility had no choice but to comply with the wishes of the government and to petition the tsar for permission to establish the committee provided by the rescript of November 20, which was modified by subsequent instructions. The corporation of the nobility, slow in toeing the line, received pointed reminders from the minister of the interior. Between January, 1858, and April, 1859, committees were set up in every province. Each committee consisted of the provincial marshal of the nobility (the chairman), two members from each county (*uezd*) elected by the county assemblies of the nobility, and two members appointed by the provincial governor from among local noble landowners. The appointed members were supposed to speak for the peasants, who were not otherwise represented. According to Lanskoï, of the approximately 1,400 members (in all committees) hardly one-tenth took active part in the work, the vast majority meekly following the leaders. Professor Kornilov, author of a detailed study of the provincial committees, does not agree with this verdict. In his opinion the members interpreted accurately the attitude of the landed aristocracy, which as a body opposed the reform. Since serfdom, however, was doomed, the landowners were determined to sell the liberation of the serfs at the highest possible price. The explanation of the great variety in the recommendations made by the provincial committees lies in the diversity of economic conditions throughout Russia rather than in the "conservative" or "liberal" views held by the delegates. Quality of the soil, prevalent forms of farming and estate management (*barshchina* or *obrok*), and density of population were among the chief factors determining the attitude of the landowners.

In the predominantly agricultural provinces, especially in the fertile black-soil belt, where land constituted the chief value of the estate, the owners were prepared to waive all claims to indemnification for the liberation of the serfs, provided no great sacrifice of land was involved. In the more industrialized and less fertile central and northern provinces, where absentee ownership was common and the landowners derived their chief revenue from the *obrok* (annual money tribute) paid by the serfs, there was willingness to grant generous land allotments in return for high indemnities. The provincial committees displayed a larger degree of agreement in recommending the retention by the landed nobility of comprehensive administrative and police powers over the peasant population, although on this question, too, there were dissenting opinions. Given the composition of the committees, their recommendations inevitably reflected the interests and aspirations of the landed nobility.

The task of the provincial committees was completed by the end of 1859. Their reports were forwarded to the central committee, as the former secret committee was renamed on January 8, 1858. The actual drafting of the emancipation statutes (*polozheniia*) was done by two editorial commissions established on February 17, 1859; although they sat as a body the plural in the title of this institution was never dropped. General J. I. Rostovtsev, who as a young officer had informed Emperor Nicholas of the proposed Decembrist uprising,[2] was made chairman of the editorial commissions, which consisted of high officials and appointed "experts" selected among aristocratic landed proprietors. Some of the members of the editorial commissions were opponents of the emancipation (Prince F. I. Paskevich, Count P. A. Shuvalov); others believed in the necessity of the reform (Rostovtsev, Yuri Samarin, Prince V. A. Cherkassky, Nicholas Miliutin). Rostovtsev, a conscientious bureaucrat, was uneasy about the fact that all the members of his commissions belonged to the class of wealthy landowners; he proposed that there should be attached to the editorial commissions an advisory body consisting of landed proprietors of modest means and practical experience, as well as managers of agricultural estates and even village elders. Though this proposal was formally approved, it was never made effective: Rostovtsev died in February, 1860, and was succeeded as chairman of the commissions by Count V. N. Panin, minister of justice and a well known opponent

[2] See above, pp. 747–748.

of the reform. Moreover, although the representatives of the provincial committees were summoned to St. Petersburg, they were not permitted, in violation of a promise given to the nobility by Alexander, to take an active part in the framing of the statutes, a decision against which the delegates protested with unusual vigor. A predominantly bureaucratic agency, the editorial commissions went about their work in a businesslike fashion and completed the drafting of the statutes by October 10, 1860, when the proposed legislation was submitted to the central committee. The drafts differed in many essentials from the recommendations of the provincial committees, and Rostovtsev and Miliutin (a high official of the ministry of the interior) are deservedly given credit for making them in some (although not in all) respects less objectionable than they would have been if these recommendations had been more closely followed. The drafts were revised several times in a sense unfavorable to the peasants: first, by the editorial commissions themselves under the pressure of the provincial committees; then by the central committee; and finally, by the State Council, which was given by the tsar a mere fortnight for its deliberations. The statutes were promulgated on February 19, 1861, the end of serfdom being solemnly proclaimed in an insincere and pretentious manifesto written by the Metropolitan Philaret, another enemy of emancipation.

The statutes of February 19 comprised twenty-two enactments, and were originally published in a bulky volume of 360 pages; they were repeatedly amended in later years. The conflict of opinions within the agencies responsible for the framing of the emancipation acts, lack of legislative experience on the part of the members, and the great pressure under which they worked account for the numerous obscurities and inconsistencies in the official texts. History has proved that the statutes of February 19 failed to provide an adequate solution for the admittedly immense difficulties raised by the reform. The social, economic, and administrative regime created in 1861 was one of baffling complexity. The liquidation of serfdom was to extend over an undetermined but protracted period and was to be achieved in three stages. During the first, or introductory, stage there were established, before the end of 1861, agencies which took over the administrative and judicial functions formerly exercised by the noble landowners. The personal dependence of the serfs on their masters was brought to an end. They were free to marry, acquire property, engage in trades, and bring actions in courts. Each estate owner was to prepare within one year after the promulgation of the statutes an inventory (*ustavnaia gramota*) determining the area of land actually in possession of the peasants, specifying whether this area met with the requirements laid down by the law (to be discussed presently), and defining the *obrok* (annual payment) or *barshchina* (services) due from the liberated serfs. The inventories were then submitted for confirmation to the arbitrator (*mirovoi posrednik*), an official appointed by the provincial governor from among local noble landowners. The arbitrator, jointly with the representatives of the peasantry of the estate, examined each inventory, settled disputed points, made revisions and amendments if the original text did not conform with the law, and finally put the inventory into operation by reading it at the village assembly. In case of failure of estate owners to prepare inventories within the prescribed time (one year), the performance of this task devolved upon the arbitrator. The introduction of inventories was to be completed within two years, by February 19, 1863, when the process of emancipation was to enter its second phase. During this period relations between landowners and their "temporary-obligated" (*vremenno-obiazannye*) peasants, to use the inelegant official term, were determined by the inventories; this relationship continued until it was superseded (either by voluntary agreement of the parties or at the request of the landowner) by the regime of redemption payments through which the former serfs eventually became owners of their allotments. The statutes of 1861 established no time limit for the period of "temporary obligation." They merely provided that the charges prescribed by the "inventories" were to be revised after twenty years, that is, in 1881. By the law of December 28, 1881, however, the redemption of allotments was made compulsory as from January 1, 1883. The redemption debt, the amortization of which constituted the chief feature of the third stage of the emancipation, was computed by capitalizing at 6 per cent the annual charges assessed on peasant allotments. The government advanced to the landowners interest-bearing securities to the amount of 75 or 80 per cent of the total indemnification to which they were entitled, the peasants usually providing the balance (and sometimes additional payments), except when the redemption operation was imposed by the landowner without the peasants' consent. According to the law, advances made by the government to the owners were to be repaid by the peasants by annual installments extending over forty-nine years and equal in amount to the share of the advance assessed on each allotment, plus interest. It was only after the fulfillment of this obligation that the process of emancipation was terminated and the former serf acquired a clear title to his allotment. Redemption payments being far in excess of the value of the allotments the plan inevitably broke down. Arrears accumulated, were written off, accumulated again, and necessitated the reassessment of the outstanding portion of the redemption debt over a long stretch of years, well into the 1950's (law of May 13, 1896). The impoverishment of the peasant farmers and the revolutionary disturbances of 1905 forced the government to abandon this preposterous scheme: by a manifesto of November 3, 1905, all redemption payments were finally canceled.

The bewildering complexity of the general emancipation procedure was fully matched by the provisions bearing on the basic questions on which depended the future of rural Russia: size of the allotments; charges imposed on the peasants; land tenure and village self-government; and the legal status of the liberated bondsmen. Realizing that emancipation without a grant to the peasants of any land was a practical impossibility, the framers of the legislation of 1861 upheld the view that the former serfs should be provided with homesteads and "adequate" allotments of farm land. What constituted an "adequate" allotment, however, was necessarily a matter of opinion. For reasons of expediency rather than on theoretical grounds, the legislators accepted the principle that pre-reform allotments should be regarded as "adequate," a questionable assumption, since under serfdom the peasants were expected to spend at least half of their time working for their master. In practice, however, even this modest safeguard was sacrificed to the interests of the landowners. The statutes of February 19 emphasized voluntary agreements as the best method of settling the post-emancipation relationship between the peasants and their former lords. The disparity in the size of the pre-reform allotments, however, was known to be great, and the law made a weak attempt to remove some of the most striking inequalities. To achieve this object the whole of Russia was divided into a number of territorial zones, maximum and minimum norms for allotments per male serf being established for each zone. The maximum norms varied from 12 to 2.75 dessiatines; [3] the minimum norm was one-third of the

---

[3] One dessiatine = 2.7 acres.

maximum. As a rule (although there were important exceptions) the allotments actually received by the peasants were within the limits of the maximum and the minimum norms. If pre-reform allotments exceeded the maximum norm, the landowner was entitled to cut them down to that level; if they fell below the minimum norm, he was obliged to increase them to that standard. In most agricultural provinces, however, the landowners had the right to retain one-third (and in some provinces one-half) of their non-waste land, irrespective of the effect that this might have on the size of the allotments. There were also the "gratuitous" or "beggarly" allotments introduced in the statutes at the last moment by the State Council. A "gratuitous" allotment was equal to one-fourth of the maximum norm, and could be granted only with the consent of the peasants, the owner waiving all claims to indemnification. The inequity and economic unsoundness of these involved arrangements is disclosed by the fact that in numerous instances the maximum norms, although they exceeded by as much as 100 to 300 per cent the allotments proposed by many provincial committees, were substantially smaller than the pre-reform peasant holdings.

Acceptance by the peasants of the land assigned to them was compulsory for the first nine years, that is, until 1870, and could be rescinded after that date only by complying with cumbersome conditions. These restrictive measures were inspired by the well founded apprehension that in view of the heavy obligations attached to the possession of allotments the former serfs might choose to give them up altogether. The charges imposed on the peasants took the form of either payments or services. According to the statutes of 1861, however, the former method was the normal one: commutation of payments into services was not permitted without the peasants' consent; on the other hand, the peasants could obtain the substitution of payments for services, irrespective of the wishes of the owner. In determining the amount of the charges the law ostensibly departed from the principle that landowners were entitled to indemnification only for the land ceded; the government repeatedly proclaimed that it would not tolerate even the discussion of compensation for loss of servile labor. Adherence to this program would have inflicted considerable sacrifices on many landowners, especially those in the less fertile regions, where labor, not land, constituted the real value of an estate. Always mindful of the interests of the landed nobility, the acts of 1861 introduced an elaborate gradation of charges clearly designed to provide for the landowners the ransom that was officially denied to them. For the provinces of Great Russia (Velikorossiia), for instance, the law established a scale of charges corresponding roughly to the division of that area into zones according to the size of the allotments. There were four maximum annual charges of 12, 10, 9, and 8 rubles which were imposed on the holders of maximum allotments in the respective zones. These charges, however, did not reflect the market value or the productivity of the land, nor were they reduced in proportion to the decline in the size of the allotments. In the industrial non-black-soil zone half of the total charge fell on the first dessiatine of the allotment; one-fourth, on the second dessiatine; and the balance was equally assessed among the subsequent dessiatines. For example, if the maximum annual charge was 12 rubles and the maximum allotment 4 dessiatines, the apportionment of the burden was as follows: the first dessiatine was assessed at 6 rubles; the second at 3 rubles; the third and fourth at 1.50 rubles each.[4] That is, the smaller the allotment, the larger the average charge per dessiatine. In other words, the gradation of charges was based on a principle which is the converse of that of the modern income tax, an arrangement probably unique, according to Professor Vorms, in the history of emancipations. The conclusion is inescapable that the greater charge on the smaller holdings comprised indemnification for the liberation of the person of the serf. To realize the full implications of these arrangements one must keep in mind that the burden of the redemption debt was determined, as has already been stated, by capitalizing the charges imposed by the statutes of 1861. The result was that redemption payments were often in excess of the rental value of the allotments. Moreover, no payments made before the redemption operation was put into effect were credited towards the final settlement.

The statutes of February 19 established several new agencies of village government but did not alter the prevailing forms of peasant land tenure, nor did they make the former bondsmen free in the accepted meaning of the term. After 1861, as under serfdom, the peas-

[4] In the agricultural black-soil zone the apportionment of charges was somewhat different. The first dessiatine of the allotment was uniformly assessed at 4 rubles, the balance being apportioned among the remaining dessiatines. Thus, if the annual maximum charge was 10 rubles and the maximum allotment 4 dessiatines, the first dessiatine was assessed at 4 rubles, and each of the subsequent three dessiatines at 2 rubles.

ants were organized into communal groups described in the emancipation acts by the term "village commune" (*selskoe obshchestvo*).[5] Village communes were of two types: those with hereditary household tenure (*podvornoe vladenie*) and those with repartitional tenure, or land communes (*obshchinnoe vladenie*). In either case land was allotted to the commune, not to individual households. In the communes of the first type, which were to be found almost exclusively in the western and southwestern provinces, homesteads as well as strips of arable land were assigned by the commune to households in heredity and were not subject to repartition. In communes with repartitional tenure, homesteads alone were assigned to households in hereditary tenure, arable land being subject to periodical repartitions by a two-thirds' vote of the assembly of the householders. Under both systems arable land was usually divided into a number of intermingled strips assigned to the households, an arrangement which necessitated a common rotation of crops. Moreover, even in communes with hereditary tenure, some of the land, for instance, pastures, remained in communal use. The members of the commune were thus linked together by a multitude of economic interests, and the pre-reform legislation and administrative practice invariably treated a village commune, for fiscal and police purposes, as an entity.

The legislation of 1861 retained the village commune as the basic unit of peasant organization but superimposed on it a new territorial-administrative subdivision, the township (*volost*).[6] A township com-

[5] Robinson, *op. cit.*, pp. 66–71, gives an illuminating account of the ambiguities in the use of the term "village commune" and of the resulting confusion. Prof. Robinson's book is the best study available in English of rural Russia before 1917.

[6] The relative merits of communal and individual tenure have been the subject of a heated controversy which goes back to the 1850's. In 1856 there began in the columns of Russian periodicals the debate between B. N. Chicherin and N. D. Beliaev on the origins of the land commune (*obshchina*). Chicherin held that the land commune was the product of the administrative practice of the Russian state, while Beliaev expounded the theory that it had grown from the patriarchal organization inherent in the immemorial customs of the Russian people. The land commune had its partisans among both slavophiles and westerners. Some of the slavophiles (Constantine Aksakov, Khomiakov) upheld it primarily on moral and religious grounds, as a product of Russian national genius and the embodiment of the ideals of "love" and Christianity. The socialist-minded westerners (Herzen, Chernyshevsky) argued that communal tenure was intrinsically more favorable to the technical improvement of agriculture than was individual farming. Other westerners (I. V. Vernadsky) opposed this view and described communal tenure as the chief obstacle to the development of private initiative, which to them was the real source of progress. Some of the slavophiles (Koshelev, Yuri Samarin) favored the

prised one or several village communes with a total male population of from 300 to 2,000 and dealt exclusively with the affairs of the peasantry. In theory both the commune and the township enjoyed some degree of self-government. The assembly of the householders of a village commune elected a village elder and the assembly of the householders of a township—a township elder, an executive board (*volostnoe pravlenie*), and a court which tried minor civil and criminal cases involving only peasants. The powers of the assemblies and of the executive board being strictly limited and their members usually illiterate and unfamiliar with the art of government, much of peasant self-government proved a fiction. According to competent authorities (for instance, Kornilov), the actual administration of peasant affairs was carried on by the village and the township elders or, not infrequently, by the appointed secretary of the township executive board (*volostnoi pisar*). The township and the village elders, moreover, were subordinated to appointed administrative and police officials vested with comprehensive disciplinary powers. To these imperfect organs of peasant self-government were transferred the administrative, judicial, and police functions formerly exercised by the estate owners.

The village commune was jointly responsible, as before the emancipation, for taxes and other obligations imposed on its members. Assessment of these charges among the householders, collection of payments due, and maintenance of public order were the chief functions of peasant officials whose salaries were paid by the commune and who wielded disciplinary powers over their fellow villagers. For infringements of police regulations the elder could impose fines, arrest the delinquent member, or assign him to compulsory work. If taxes and other payments of a household were in arrears, the village assembly could sentence the householder or any member of his family to compulsory labor, corporal punishment, army service, confiscation of most

---

land commune chiefly for practical reasons: it was, they maintained, a form of tenure that had sprung up and developed on Russian soil and could not be abolished, at least for the time being, without disrupting the existing economic, social, and perhaps even the political order. This was the point of view that prevailed in the editorial commissions and was reflected in the legislation of 1861. Rostovtsev, answering the advocates of individual farming, gave two reasons for the preservation of communal organization: (1) "the people still need a strong authority to take the place of that of the landowners;" and (2) "without the commune the landowners will never obtain the payments and services due to them, and the government will not collect taxes."

of his property, and, under certain conditions, to banishment. Membership in a village commune was compulsory for every peasant. The emancipation acts, moreover, retained the traditional organization of peasants into households (*dvor*), or family groups, which the law regarded as a unit. The household elder (head of the household) exercised an ill defined authority over the property of the household and over the person of its members. No peasant could absent himself lawfully from the village without obtaining a passport, which was issued only with the permission of the household elder (if the applicant was a junior member of a household) and of the village authorities. Withdrawal from a commune was hedged with conditions so burdensome and complicated as to make it, in most cases, an impossibility.

It thus appears that although the liberated serfs were described by the emancipation acts as "free village dwellers" (*svobodnye selskie obyvateli*), they were actually in bondage to the commune controlled by government officials. In conformity with Russian historical tradition the peasants constituted a segregated social group which had few rights but many duties and disabilities. The emancipation, as has already been stated, terminated the personal dependence of the former serfs on the landowner. Peasants could marry freely, own property, engage in trades, enter into legally binding obligations, sue and be sued in courts. But the village commune was given quasi-dictatorial powers over its members. The property relationships of the peasant family (for instance, the right of inheritance), as well as the rights of householders to land held in communal tenure, were governed not by law but by obscure unwritten local customs. Peasants were subject to corporal punishment (abolished for other social groups in 1863), they paid the poll tax, provided recruits for the army, and performed various other obligations (billeting, repair of roads) from which the privileged "estates" were exempt. It was only gradually that these burdens and disabilities were removed: recruitment in 1874; the poll tax in 1885; joint responsibility of the village commune in 1903; corporal punishment in 1904; passport restrictions in 1906; and finally, between 1906 and 1911 the attempt was made to free rural Russia from the deadening grip of communal organization. Some of the limitations attached to the status of a peasant, however, remained in force until the revolution of 1917.

The provisions of the emancipation acts dealing with land tenure and peasant government were applied, with but minor modifications, to all peasants throughout the empire. There was greater variety in arrangements bearing on the size of the allotments and the charges attached to them. The household serfs (*dvorovye*), as a rule, received no land, and many of them drifted to the cities in search of a living. In the western provinces, where the peasantry was predominantly Russian and the landed nobility Polish, the size of the allotments was determined by the inventories of 1845–1848;[7] consequently, peasant holdings suffered no diminution at the time of the emancipation. After the Polish uprising of 1863 allotments in these provinces were increased and redemption charges scaled down for political reasons. Peasants living on the estates of the imperial family (appanages)[8] and state peasants[9] received, by virtue of special legislation passed in 1863 and 1866, land settlements on terms more generous than those granted to the former serfs: their allotments were larger and their charges less onerous.

LOCAL SELF-GOVERNMENT

The long-overdue reform of local government was a corollary of the emancipation. It will be remembered that the provincial administration created by Catherine II fell short of self-government; although numerous local offices were filled by election, provincial Russia in the first half of the nineteenth century was actually governed by appointed officials. The deliberations and reports of the provincial committees of 1858–1859 made it clear that the landed nobility expected to be compensated for its loss of dominion over the serfs by the extension of its participation in government, especially in local administration. The provisions of the emancipation acts which excluded the noble landowners from the control of the affairs of townships and village communes and subordinated these institutions to Crown officials were particularly resented by the *dvoriane*, both conservative and liberal. In their criticism of this aspect of the reform many noblemen were motivated by selfish class interests; but there were others who sincerely believed that social and economic progress was incompatible with bureaucratic regimentation. A. M. Unkovsky, provincial marshal of the nobility of Tver, expressed the views of the liberal minority when he wrote in 1859: "The entire life of the people

[7] See pp. 779–780.
[8] See pp. 575, 578, 615, 623.
[9] See pp. 575–577, 784–786.

is under governmental tutelage. No question, however trifling, can be dealt with by the people themselves; . . . they dare not [without official sanction] to repair a miserable bridge or to hire an elementary-school teacher. . . . The whole of our administration is a vast system of malfeasance raised to the dignity of state government." Unkovsky urged "the emancipation not only of the peasants but of the people as a whole."

The first official steps towards the reform of local government were taken early in 1858. A year later, in March, 1859, the drafting of appropriate legislation was entrusted to a bureaucratic committee under the chairmanship of Nicholas Miliutin, then assistant minister of the interior, but in April, 1861, both Miliutin and his chief and patron Lanskoï were dismissed as unduly liberal—a criticism they hardly deserved—and the chairmanship of the committee went to the new minister of the interior, P. A. Valuev (created a count in 1880). Valuev favored the predominance of the nobility in the proposed zemstvos (institutions of local self-government), which, however, he wished to keep under close administrative supervision to prevent them from becoming "a state within the state." The draft prepared by the Valuev committee was revised in the light of criticisms submitted by Nicholas Miliutin and Count M. A. Korf and of views expressed during the discussion of the bill in the State Council. The government, anxious to win over liberal opinion, agreed to eliminate some of the most inequitable and reactionary provisions of the Valuev draft. It was this draft, nevertheless, that determined the general character of the statute (*polozhenie*) on provincial and district zemstvos promulgated on January 1, 1864.

Each provincial and county zemstvo consisted of an assembly and an executive board (*uprava*). The members of the county assembly were chosen by the population of the county voting in three separate electoral colleges: (1) individual landed proprietors, irrespective of whether they belonged to the nobility or to other social groups ("estates"); (2) urban population; and (3) village communes. The right to participate in the first and second electoral colleges was conditional on the possession of property qualifications, that is, ownership of a specified area of land or, chiefly in the cities, of property of equivalent value. The third electoral college (village communes) consisted of delegates chosen by township assemblies. The number of representatives sent by each college to the county assembly was determined by the aggregate area of land (or by the value of the property) owned by its members.[10] The county zemstvo assemblies chose the members of the provincial zemstvo assemblies, which, like the county assemblies, were elected for three years and met once a year. The provincial and the county marshals of the nobility were, respectively, chairmen of the provincial and the county zemstvo assemblies. The membership of these assemblies, both county and provincial, varied from 10 to 100; they elected their executive boards which carried on the business of local government when the assemblies were not in session. The chairmen of the county executive board were confirmed in office by provincial governors, and the chairmen of the provincial executive boards by the minister of the interior. It was originally intended to install zemstvo institutions without delay in 33 provinces; actually however, they were established in 19 provinces in 1865; in 9 provinces in 1866; and in 6 provinces in 1867–1875.[11]

The functions and powers of the zemstvos were carefully defined and kept within narrow limits. The zemstvos were to concern themselves primarily with "local economic needs": upkeep of roads and bridges, providing of means of conveyance for police and other officials; maintenance of prisons, hospitals, and lunatic asylums; promotion of industry, commerce, and agriculture; prevention of famine; advancement of public health and education; relief of the poor. In the exercise of these functions the zemstvos were autonomous, at

[10] The property qualifications entitling to a vote varied from county to county. The right of direct vote was granted to landed proprietors owning, approximately, the equivalent of 100 maximum allotments as established for their county by the emancipation acts (see p. 890). The owners of holdings smaller than the property qualification prescribed by the statute of 1864 (but not less than one-twentieth of that norm) voted through representatives they elected; the number of these representatives was arrived at by dividing the aggregate area of such holdings by the statutory norm qualifying for direct vote. Each electoral college was entitled to one delegate per, approximately, each 3,000 maximum allotments (or their property equivalent) owned by its members, but no college could have more delegates than the two others taken together. The above provisions of the statute were less inequitable than the corresponding sections of the Valuev draft which provided that the property qualification of the *dvoriane* should be one-half of that required from other social groups (50 and 100 maximum allotments, respectively) and their representation twice as large as that of the peasants (one representative per 3,000 maximum allotments for individual landed proprietors, that is, chiefly the nobility, and one representative per 6,000 maximum allotments for the village communes).

[11] The zemstvos established in the territory of the Don Cossacks in 1876 were abolished in 1882. In 1911 zemstvo institutions were introduced in 6 provinces and in 1913 in 3 provinces. On the eve of the War of 1914 zemstvo institutions functioned in 43 of the 70 provinces into which Russia was subdivided.

least in theory, but they had no executive powers and depended for the carrying out of their decisions on the cooperation of police and other Crown officials over whom they had no control. Their work was further handicapped by lack of funds. The revenue of the zemstvos was derived from local rates on agricultural land, urban real estate, commerce and industry, that is, sources already heavily drawn upon by the central government. Although the power of the zemstvos to levy taxes was limited by law, their aggregate revenue increased from 5.6 million rubles in 1865 to 24.2 million in 1870 and to 33.1 million in 1880; nevertheless it remained considerably below the legitimate demands on their treasury. Moreover, zemstvo budgets were burdened with expenditures which had no direct bearing on local needs (for instance, maintenance of the justices of the peace; transportation and lodgings for certain judicial officials; outlays connected with army drafts; relief of families of men killed while serving with the colors). These and other "obligatory" expenditures absorbed 50.8 per cent of zemstvo revenue in 1870 and 45.3 per cent in 1880. It was only towards the very end of the century that this burden was substantially lightened.[12] In spite of these handicaps the zemstvos strove to expand their cultural activities. Expenditure on public health increased from 1.3 million rubles in 1868 to 3.9 million in 1875 and to 9.4 million in 1885; and that on schools from .7 million rubles in 1868 to 3.3 million in 1875 and to 6.8 million in 1885. These figures are unimpressive, especially for a country as vast as Russia, but they were a straw in the wind and marked the starting point of a novel departure which was to bring results in the future. To give a striking example, in 1877 the zemstvos employed one agronomist; in 1912 the number of zemstvo agronomists was nearly 5,000.

Denial of adequate revenue was one manifestation of the hostility with which the ruling bureaucracy regarded the institutions of local self-government. The statute of 1864 achieved its object of bringing the zemstvos under the control of the nobility; in 1865–1867 42 per cent of the members of the district and 74 per cent of the members of the provincial zemstvo assemblies were noblemen or government officials. Yet the very existence of autonomous local institutions was a

[12] "Obligatory" expenditure reached its high mark in 1890, when it stood at 18.5 million rubles, or 42.0 per cent of the revenue; it was reduced to 6.8 million rubles, or 7.7 per cent, in 1900, and to 4.5 million, or 2.1 per cent in 1912, when the aggregate revenue of the zemstvos was 220.1 million rubles.

thorn in the flesh of those who cherished the tradition of the omnipotent police state. "The term 'zemstvo,'" the liberal-minded Grand Duchess Helen wrote to Nicholas Miliutin in January, 1862, "inspires fears in high circles." The zemstvos, according to their historian A. A. Avinov, were treated in Russian administrative practice, not as an organic part of local government, but "as an accidental appendix, tolerated but often unwanted, without which local government could exist and function." S. Witte, in his memorandum on *Autocracy and the Zemstvo*, held that the statute of 1864, "a compromise between two hostile views," produced institutions which "failed to meet the requirements of self-government" and yet could not be integrated in the bureaucratic order. Hence the conflict between the bureaucracy and the supporters of autonomous local institutions, a conflict in which the central government invariably had the upper hand. "The zemstvos," to quote Lenin's somewhat mixed metaphor, "were doomed from the very beginning to play the part of the fifth wheel on the coach of Russian state administration, a wheel tolerated by the bureaucracy only so long as its own powers were not at stake." The autonomy of the zemstvos, even within the narrow sphere assigned to it by the law, was not maintained. From 1866 on, restrictive legislation inexorably expanded administrative controls over all zemstvo activities.

In view of the nature of the 1864 statute and of the subsequent administrative practice it is hardly surprising that the enthusiasm with which the beginnings of local self-government were greeted by liberal and radical opinion soon gave place to disappointment and decline of interest in zemstvo institutions, as evidenced by the extraordinarily low percentage of voters who participated in the elections and the mass absenteeism of members of zemstvo assemblies. Until the 1880's the struggle of the zemstvos against the central government centered on the defense of their rights from infringement by the bureaucracy. It was only after the War of 1877–1878 that the liberal zemstvo leaders began to take a more active part in the movement for constitutional reforms. The liberalism of some of the zemstvos is partly explained by the fact that they had in their midst a large number of *dvoriane* of modest means, traditionally affiliated with progressive movements. Another important factor in shaping the political orientation of the zemstvos was their growing army of hired employees—doctors, nurses, teachers, agronomists, veterinarians, engineers, statisticians—drawn chiefly from the ranks of the radical intellectuals. The formation of this group goes back to the 1870's, but it was not until a quarter of a century later that it developed into a sizable progressive and revolutionary force. The actual influence in the zemstvo councils of the "third estate," as hired employees were usually known, was much greater than is suggested by the humble status of its members.

The condition of city government on the eve of the emancipation was, if possible, even more chaotic than that of the provincial administration. The municipal institutions heralded by the 1785 Charter simply did not exist, and the conduct of city affairs was in the hands of makeshift agencies unknown to the law. Preparations for the municipal reform began in 1862, when, in fulfillment of an imperial order, the minister of the interior decreed the establishment in cities and towns of representative committees to make proposals for the reorganization of city government. The reports of the 509 committees actually formed disclosed a surprisingly democratic spirit and unanimity in demanding autonomy for the city administration, although the committees were not always clear how this object was to be achieved. In 1864 the ministry of the interior completed the draft of a bill on the reorganization of the municipalities; this bill, repeatedly revised and amended by various bureaucratic agencies and by the State Council, was finally promulgated on June 16, 1870. Under this legislation city government was to consist of a municipal council (duma), an executive board (*uprava*), and a mayor (*golova*). The municipal council was elected for four years by local residents who paid city taxes of a specified amount. Following the Prussian model (elections to the *Landtag* under the constitution of 1850), the electorate was divided into three groups on the basis of tax assessments. The composition of each group was determined from a list (prepared in each city) in which taxpayers were arranged in the order of their decreasing contributions to the city treasury. The large taxpayers, whose names appeared at the top of the list and who together provided one-third of the municipal tax roll, formed the first group; taxpayers next on the list, who provided another third of the tax roll, formed the second group; and small taxpayers at the bottom of the list formed the third group. Each group voted separately and elected one-third of the members of the municipal council. Under this system the representation of the larger taxpayers was, of course, out of proportion to their number. In Moscow, for instance, the first and second group, which elected two-thirds of the municipal council, comprised 13 per cent of the electorate, and in Saratov merely 8 per cent. The municipal council elected the municipal executive board and the mayor. The mayors of the larger cities were confirmed in office by the minister of the interior, and those of the smaller cities and towns by the provincial governor. In the 1870's the new municipal institutions were introduced throughout the empire, except in Poland and Finland, which retained their original city government.

The functions and powers of the municipal institutions were similar to those of the zemstvos. They were to deal primarily with local economic needs, had no executive power to enforce their decision, were limited in the right to levy taxes, were burdened with heavy "obligatory" expenditure unrelated to municipal affairs, and were subject to oppressive controls by Crown officials.

With all their glaring inequities and shortcomings the zemstvos and the new city government were from the point of view of both theory and practice a marked improvement on their predecessors. In place of the medieval principle of representation by social class ("estate") they introduced that of property qualification, generally accepted in nineteenth century Europe. Moreover, the new system proved workable; and, in spite of their many disabilities, the new municipalities, and especially the zemstvos, eventually succeeded in building up public services on a scale Russia had never known.

THE JUDICIARY

"The statutes of the judiciary (*sudebnye ustavy*) of November 20, 1864, would never have been enacted if it were not for the emancipation of 1861," wrote S. I. Zarudny, one of the authors of the reform. "No real need for equitable courts existed under serfdom. The only true judges then were the noble landowners over whom ruled a supreme and arbitrary authority. They had to accept its decision; but in their hands was concentrated the power over the immense majority of the people! Lynch law was the method used by the peasants in settling their grievances against their masters. After February 19 even our higher bureaucrats perceived the necessity of speedy and equitable administration of justice." Russian courts before the reform of 1864 were notoriously inequitable and corrupt. Their chief characteristics were the inhuman severity of punishments; multiplicity of judicial agencies; complexity of the procedure which allowed cases to drag on for decades; secrecy and arbitrariness equal to that of the Star

Chamber; heartless formalism; centering of preliminary investigations —often a determining factor in the issue of the case—in the "unskilled and unclean hands" of the police (to quote the eminent jurist A. F. Koni); hopeless confusion of judicial and executive powers; subservience of judges not only to the bureaucracy but also to wealth and birth; low moral and educational standards of even high judicial officials (in the middle of the nineteenth century, according to M. P. Chubinsky, most of the judges of the lower courts were illiterate or half literate, and some of the members of the highest court, the Senate, could barely sign their names). Casuistry, procrastination, and bribery were so prevalent as to make a lawsuit synonymous with disaster. Thousands of innocent people suffered ruinous and degrading punishments and lingered in prisons and in Siberia while notable, well born and wealthy lawbreakers escaped retribution.

The unspeakable disorder of the courts was a matter of common knowledge. In the reign of Nicholas I the reform of the judiciary was repeatedly discussed in official circles, but it was not until 1850 that there was appointed a committee under the distinguished jurist Count D. N. Bludov to draft pertinent legislation. The work of this committee, although wanting in many respects, paved the way for the reform of 1864. At the end of 1861 the committee was enlarged to include several competent jurists, the aged Bludov faded from the picture, and leadership in the movement for new law courts passed into the hands of S. I. Zarudny and D. N. Zamiatin, who in the autumn of 1862 succeeded the reactionary Count Panin as minister of justice. On September 29, 1862, the "basic principles" of the reform of the judiciary received imperial sanction and were given wide publicity. Universities, the courts, and private jurists were invited to offer criticism and suggestions; 446 such comments, published later in six bulky volumes, were actually submitted and were examined by the committees which completed the drafting of the statutes in December, 1863. The bills were then discussed and amended by the State Council and became law on November 20, 1864.

The statutes of the judiciary embodied, with a varying degree of thoroughness, the accepted principles of western European jurisprudence: equality of all before the law; access to an impartial tribunal and the right to be heard; acceptance of the maxim *nullum crimen, nulla poena sine lege*, that is, no action is punishable unless adjudicated, after a fair trial, as a violation of the law; uniformity and relative simplicity of judicial procedure; separation of the judicial from the legislative and the executive power; irremovability of the judges, except for misconduct in office; publicity of proceedings; representation of the parties in civil cases and of defendants in criminal cases by qualified members of the bar; trial by jury; election of judges of the lower courts; preliminary investigation of criminal offenses by examining magistrates (*sudebnyi sledovatel*, the French *juge d'instruction*) instead of by the police.

The new system of law courts was one of great simplicity. Minor civil and criminal cases were tried by justices of the peace elected by county zemstvo assemblies or, in St. Petersburg and Moscow, by municipal councils. Appeals from the decisions of these courts were taken to the county session (*mirovoi sezd*) of the justices of the peace. In provinces that had no zemstvos the justices of the peace were appointed by the Crown. The more important cases were tried, with or without jury, by district courts (*okruzhnoi sud*), and might be appealed to the local higher courts (*sudebnaia palata*). The judges of these two sets of courts were appointed by the Crown from lists of candidates submitted by the judiciary. The reorganized Senate was retained as the supreme court.

Contrary to the original plans, the new law courts, like the zemstvos, were not introduced at once. They were inaugurated in 1866 in the ten provinces forming the judicial districts (*okrug*) of St. Petersburg and Moscow, but their establishment in the other parts of the empire was extended over decades and was, in some instances, accompanied by substantial modifications of the 1864 statutes. Trial by jury, for example, did not apply in Poland, the western provinces, or in the Caucasus. The official explanation of the delay was lack of funds and shortage of trained jurists, but the hesitations of the government were also due to other causes. The ideas of the supremacy of the law, independence of the courts, and equality of all at the bar of justice were irreconcilable with those of autocracy and bureaucratic omnipotence and were in conflict with Russia's medieval social structure and traditional administrative practice. That is why liberal opinion both in Russia and abroad acclaimed the reform as the forerunner of far-reaching constitutional and social changes. These changes reactionary forces entrenched in palace and bureaucratic circles were resolved to prevent. Their opposition left its imprint on the statutes of 1864, and determined the subsequent evolution of judicial institutions. In the spring of 1868 Zamiatin was dismissed. Count C. I. Pahlen, an enemy of the reform, became minister of justice, an office he was to hold for ten years.

The principles proclaimed by the statutes of 1864 were not consistently applied in practice. Military courts, ecclesiastical courts, and township courts dealing with petty cases involving only peasants were retained. Their functions were by no means unimportant. Ecclesiastical courts, for instance, tried divorce cases, while the jurisdiction of military courts was soon extended to crimes against public safety. Offenses committed by government officials in the performance of their duties were tried in accordance with special rules, proceedings against alleged offenders being initiated only with the permission of their superiors. The unfortunate and ambiguous provision of the 1864 statutes that "executive power may take measures provided by the law to prevent crimes (*prestupleniia*) and illegal activities (*prostupki*)" received a broad and unwarranted interpretation. It was used as an excuse for the perpetuation of a comprehensive extra-judicial penal system administered outside the courts. As was the case before the reform, men and women considered undesirable by the bureaucracy were, without a trial, deprived of their livelihood, assigned to compulsory places of residence, deported to remote parts of the country, and sometimes imprisoned. The Crown exercised not only the prerogative of pardon but also that of increasing the severity of sentences. Disturbances of public peace were suppressed by police measures, participants being meted out summary punishments, usually flogging, by virtue of the extra-judicial powers vested in administrative officers. The independence of the judges was impaired by the fact that they were government officials and that their advancement, or transfer to less desirable posts, depended on their superiors. In contravention of the law judicial vacancies were often filled by men who were not endorsed by the bench. Count Pahlen, moreover, devised the vicious subterfuge of appointing examining magistrates pro tem; he claimed that the holders of such temporary appointments were not entitled to judicial immunity. The acceptance of this theory gave the government powerful means of influencing the selection of future judges, who usually began their career as examining magistrates. Trial by jury suffered a partial eclipse. An ever increasing category of cases was withdrawn from the competence of the district courts, that is, defendants in such cases were denied trial by jury. A law of December 12, 1866, transferred cases involving the public press to the jurisdiction of local higher courts (*sudebnaia palata*); crimes against the state, by virtue of a law of June 7, 1872, were tried by a special court of the Senate; a law of August 9, 1878, gave governors-general and military governors discretionary powers to direct the trial by military courts of cases involving resistance to lawful authorities or attempts against the life of officials. A law of May 19, 1871, entrusted to the security police (gendarmery) the preliminary investigation of crimes against the state and empowered the Crown to decide such cases without a trial. A law of April 17, 1863, abolishing the worst forms of corporal punishment, revolutionized the penal system, but it did not entirely do away with flogging. Flogging was retained among the penalties inflicted upon the peasants by the township courts, in disciplinary battalions of the armed forces, and as a punishment for deportees and prisoners, including women, in Siberia. It remained the accepted method used by the police in exacting arrears from the peasants and in quelling public disturbances. Among the defenders of corporal punishment, whose efforts were partly responsible for the retention of flogging, was Count Panin, for twenty years minister of justice, and the Metropolitan Philaret, author of the flowery emancipation manifesto.

In spite of these violations of both the spirit and the letter of the 1864 statutes, the post-reform courts were immeasurably superior to their predecessors. The personnel of the tribunals established under the regime of Zamiatin comprised men of learning, integrity, and devotion to duty. They succeeded in building a tradition that subsequent government pressure was never able completely to destroy. Within the sphere of their jurisdiction the courts proved reasonably efficient, businesslike, and honest. If the reform failed to make the Russian's home his castle, it was because real guarantees of individual rights against administrative arbitrariness are incompatible with the very nature of the autocratic authoritarian state. The reform had to its credit the establishment of a bar which attracted progressive and well educated lawyers and in later years produced many leaders of the liberal movement.

THE ARMY

The state of the Russian army in the 1850's was as lamentable as that of local government and the courts. The Crimean War had proved that sheer weight of man power and perfection of drilling, so impressive on parade grounds, was no substitute for modernized equipment, organization, and training. Of some 2,200,000 men called to the colors by 1856, a mere fraction took an active part in fighting. The ruinous cost of maintaining this huge force and its failure to prevent the disastrous outcome of the war pointed to the necessity of fundamental army reforms. Moreover, it became increasingly clear, especially after the emancipation, that a system of recruitment resting exclusively on the shoulders of the lower classes, and conditions of service akin to penal servitude, could not be indefinitely maintained. The reorganization of the army was the work of General Dimitry Miliutin (created a count in 1878), assistant minister of war from 1858 and minister of war from 1861 to 1881. General Miliutin, like his brother Nicholas, was a man of vision and progressive views. He had the tsar's confidence, and his long tenure of office gave his reforms a degree of consistency and continuity not to be found in other fields.

Miliutin's program was comprehensive and thorough. Important technical improvements were introduced in the organization of the ministry of war, the general staff, the territorial distribution of the troops, the commissariat, medical service, army engineers, military courts. The obsolete weapons of the Crimean period were gradually replaced by up-to-date arms and equipment. Military schools, formerly under a separate central department, were brought in 1863 within the purview of the ministry of war and were reorganized in accordance with a liberal program which compared favorably with that of corresponding schools under the ministry of education. Miliutin's greatest achievement, however, was the humanization of discipline, the betterment of conditions of service, and the introduction of conscription borne equally by all social groups.

In the pre-reform period the normal term of service in the ranks was twenty-five years. Contingents of men required by the armed forces (usually in the age group 20 to 34) were raised through a system of recruitment which applied exclusively to "estates" liable to the poll tax, that is, to peasants, artisans, and burghers (*meshchane*). The nobility was exempt from military service, as were merchants, who paid instead a special tax. Army service was, in a sense, a collective rather than a personal obligation; quotas of recruits were apportioned to village and urban communities which, through their authorities, designated the recruits. The latter, however, could escape the draft by providing "voluntary" substitutes (*okhotnik*) whose services, of course, were purchased at a price. Discipline in the forces was harsh, corporal punishments numerous and cruel. The army, therefore, was properly regarded by the community and by the law as a penal institution: terms of service with the colors were among the penalties imposed by the courts. After the Crimean War these intolerable conditions were gradually removed. The term of service was shortened to fifteen years; the worst forms of corporal punishment were abolished, flogging being officially retained only in disciplinary battalions; troops were provided with better living quarters and more adequate maintenance. The sharp and final break with the past, however, was the conscription law of January 1, 1874, which followed the lines of similar legislation adopted by most European countries in the nineteenth century. It was based on the idea of substituting for a large and costly standing army a much smaller force supported by trained reserves that could be called in wartime.

Under the new law army service became the personal obligation of every able-bodied male on reaching the age of twenty, irrespective of his social status. The normal term of active service was six years, followed by nine years in the reserve and five more years in the militia (*opolchenie*). The reserve and the militia, however, were mobilized only in emergencies. Not all men of twenty were actually drafted. They were classified into several categories according to their family status. Breadwinners and only sons, for instance, formed Category 1, which could be called only by special imperial order. The category not entitled to preferential treatment was called first, then came the next category, and so on. The order of drafting within each category was determined by lot, men being inducted in the order of the numbers they drew, until the prescribed quota was filled. Special privileges were granted to holders of academic diplomas. The term of service for the graduates of elementary schools was shortened to four years; for those of secondary schools to three years or to eighteen months, according to the class of the institution; and for those of higher schools to six months. Graduates of secondary and higher schools, moreover, were entitled to enlist as "volunteers," that is, without drawing lots; in this case their terms of service were halved, university graduates, for instance, being required to serve merely three months.

The importance of these reforms cannot be exaggerated. They removed some of the worst survivals of Russian medievalism. Miliutin, moreover, inaugurated in 1875 a program of training which provided for the schooling of privates not only in the art of warfare but also in the rudiments of reading and writing, an innovation all the more welcome because elementary schools were still practically non-existent. The new method of conscription was a step towards social equality, even though shorter terms of service for holders of diplomas favored proprietary groups. The softening of discipline and emphasis on educational activities gave the army an opportunity for contributing to the enlightenment of the masses. Much of the old brutality in the treatment of the men by their officers no doubt remained and, indeed, lingered until the end of the empire. But the pre-reform army, as a penal institution, was gone. Men with criminal records were excluded from the forces. Strange as this may seem, it was in the army, that stronghold of tradition and conservatism, that Russian democracy scored one of its first modest, yet real, successes.

THE POLISH INSURRECTION, 1863

Except for Poland and Finland, the reforms of the 1860's had little effect upon the constitutional framework of the empire. With the accession of Alexander II relations with Poland entered upon a new and turbulent phase. The ruthless regime maintained in Warsaw by Nicholas I failed to stamp out Poland's longing for national statehood. The tradition of Polish independence was kept alive by large *émigré* groups, divided though they were among themselves on other issues. The conservative and aristocratic wing accepted the leadership of Hôtel Lambert, the Paris residence of Prince Adam Czartoryski; this faction, known as the "Whites," favored the return to the Polish constitution of 1791, and put its faith chiefly in the diplomatic intervention of France and England. The more radical elements gave their allegiance to the Polish Democratic Society which was founded in France in 1832 but later transferred its headquarters to London. The Democratic Society (or the "Reds") sought the salvation of Poland "not only in a military uprising against the foreign yoke but also in a radical democratic revolution." It sponsored and directed several minor unsuccessful uprisings in Poland. General Ludwik Mieroslawski, one of the leaders of the Democratic Society who had fought on the side of the revolution in Germany in 1849 and later in Sicily, established in Italy (September, 1861) a Polish military school to train officers for the future army of liberation. The national cause was extolled in the popular writings of distinguished Polish authors, Adam

Mickiewicz, Julius Slowacki, and Zygmunt Krasinski. Both Whites and Reds had adherents in the homeland, and they spared no effort to fan the flame of Polish nationalism.

The death of Nicholas I, followed closely by that of Paskevich (February, 1856), seemed to usher in a new era in Russo-Polish relations, even though Alexander II's address to Polish notables in Warsaw (May, 1856), conciliatory as it was in part, contained statements that could not but give offense to Polish susceptibilities. The emperor voiced his intention of maintaining in Poland the order established by his father. "The happiness of Poland," Alexander held, "depends on her complete union with the peoples of my empire," and he admonished the Roman Catholic bishops to impress on their parishioners the necessity of "union with Holy Russia." Ominously and with much emphasis the emperor repeated twice: "Point de rêveries!" These harsh and tactless words, however, were accompanied by conciliatory moves. Unlike his predecessor, the new viceroy, the venerable Prince Michael Gorchakov, believed in concessions to Polish opinion. An amnesty for Polish *émigrés* and deportees to Siberia was granted in May, 1856. In the summer of 1857 there was established in Warsaw a medical school which, it was hoped, would eventually grow into a Polish university. In November of the same year was founded the Agricultural Society, an organization of landed proprietors, that is, the nobility; under the leadership of Count Andrew Zamoyski it soon acquired great political influence.

These modest concessions not only failed to reconcile Poland to the Russian rule but probably contributed to political unrest. The repatriated *émigrés* and exiles provided the Polish national movement with leaders craving for action. They found enthusiastic disciples among the undergraduate body of the medical school, and the Polish students scattered through the Russian universities. Polish nationalists, their imagination inflamed by the success of the Italian Risorgimento, overrated the strength of Russian liberals and revolutionaries and their sympathy with Polish national aspirations. Hatred of Russia was the only real link between Polish conservatives and radicals. The Whites, represented by the Agricultural Society, dreaded the military uprising advocated by the Reds.

The state of nationalistic exaltation that had taken possession of many Poles found its expression in political and religious manifestations. The first of these demonstrations took place in Warsaw in

June, 1860, when some 20,000 mourners marched behind the coffin of the widow of a Polish general killed in the insurrection of 1831. It became customary for women in deep mourning and men in Polish attire to foregather in churches on anniversaries of national events and to give vent to their feelings by singing patriotic songs. Two huge demonstrations held in Warsaw in February, 1861, were dispersed by Russian troops; five participants in the second demonstration (February 27, N.S.) were killed, and many were wounded. Tension in the Polish capital having reached a high pitch, Gorchakov deemed it wise to allow a self-appointed "delegation" of left-wing elements to assume responsibility for the maintenance of public order. For forty days the "delegation" practically ruled Warsaw with the assistance of a newly formed municipal guard of some 2,000 men. The events of February forced the Agricultural Society to depart from its cautious non-political attitude. An exceptionally well attended congress of the society then in session in Warsaw framed proposals for a drastic land reform (commutation of compulsory services for money due, and eventual transfer of land to the peasants) and petitioned the tsar, in terms which, however, were lacking in precision, for the restoration of Polish autonomy.

After a brief delay the imperial government decided to grant some of the Polish demands. The policy of reconciliation was urged by the viceroy and had influential supporters in St. Petersburg (the Grand Duke Constantine, Prince Alexander Gorchakov, Valuev). Marquis Alexander Wielopolski, author of proposals for a limited autonomy embodied in the Russian official program, was called to take the leading part in the new Polish administration. Wielopolski, a wealthy Polish landowner, was the London representative of the Polish national government in 1831, but he had changed his mind since and had become an advocate of close cooperation with Russia. His ultimate object was the restoration of the constitution of 1815; he was willing, however, to proceed gradually and to be satisfied at first with less. The government of Poland announced in an imperial decree of March 14 (March 26, N.S.), 1861, and established by legislation passed in 1861 and 1862, was largely a return to the regime of the Organic Statute of 1832. The Polish state council was revived, and there was created a committee on religion and education, as well as institutions of local self-government (elective provincial, district, and municipal councils) endowed with comprehensive powers. From April to October, 1861, and from June, 1862, to June, 1863, Wielopolski held important offices in the reorganized Polish government. His actual influence, however, depended on the political situation and on relations with the viceroys, who followed one another in rapid succession. He succeeded, nevertheless, in carrying out the major part of his program: the new administrative institutions were duly organized; a Polish university (officially styled "higher school") was established; the Polish language was reintroduced in schools and in the administration; the legal disabilities of the Jews were removed; and a land law did away with the compulsory services of the peasants.

Although at least some of these reforms, which were introduced gradually, should have been welcomed by Polish opinion, Wielopolski was extremely unpopular. Polish nationalists could not forgive him his cooperation with Russia, and most of his countrymen resented the ruthlessness of his methods. Wielopolski would have nothing to do with the opposition. His early measures included the abolition of the "delegation," the disbandment of the municipal guard, and the dissolution of the Agricultural Society. Several hundred people were killed or wounded when the troops fired on a demonstration of protest against the closing of the society. The vacillations and inconsistencies of St. Petersburg, reflected in the choice of viceroys, contributed to the turmoil. Michael Gorchakov died in May, 1861, and was succeeded as viceroy pro tem by the minister of war, General N. O. Sukhozanet, an administrator in the worst tradition of Nicholas I. Wielopolski tendered his resignation but was prevailed upon to withdraw it when Count Charles Lambert, a Roman Catholic and a supporter of reconciliation, was appointed viceroy (August, 1861). In the meantime a new wave of unrest had swept over Poland. On order from St. Petersburg a "state of emergency" was proclaimed in October. Patriotic manifestations and memorial services held on the anniversary of Kosciuszko's death (October 15, N.S.) were broken up by troops that invaded the churches and made over 1,600 arrests. The Roman Catholic clergy retaliated by ordering the closure of the churches. After a stormy interview with the viceroy, General A. D. Hershtenzveig, governor-general of Warsaw, committed suicide. Wielopolski and Lambert resigned. General Count A. N. Liders, a disciplinarian of the Paskevich school, succeeded Lambert. Wielopolski's eventful career, however, was not yet closed. He was called to St. Petersburg, where the supporters of conciliation once more had the upper hand. At the end of May, 1862, the Grand Duke Constantine was appointed viceroy, and

Wielopolski preceded him to Warsaw as head of the civilian administration. What Polish revolutionaries thought of the change may be gathered from the fact that within a few days they attempted to murder Liders, the grand duke, and Wielopolski. A significant development was an address presented by the Polish nobility to its unofficial leader, Count Zamoyski. An indirect reply to Constantine's appeal for cooperation, the address declared that Poles would support only a Polish government, and claimed for their country "the territory designated for her by God and sanctioned by history," that is, the frontiers of 1772. Zamoyski was deported abroad, but the address of the nobility indicated that the government could not count on the collaboration of conservative groups. In an eleventh-hour attempt to stem the revolutionary tide by removing the most restless elements, Wielopolski decreed a levy for the army. In violation of a law of 1859, which provided that the order of drafting was to be determined by lot, the decree was so phrased as to apply to men active in the national movement. It was put into effect on January 15, 1863, N.S., and became the signal for the insurrection.

For the struggle against Russia, Poland in 1863 was far less prepared than in 1830. The insurgent movement was directed by the Central National Committee, an agency of the Reds established in 1862 and led by Stefan Bobrowski and Zygmunt Padlewski. The rival organization of the Whites ("Citizens' Directorate") was at odds with the National Committee on practically every issue except the demand for the restoration of Poland within the frontiers of 1772. The superficial reconciliation of the two factions in the spring of 1863 did not eliminate deep-rooted animosities and suspicions, and the lack of unity inevitably impaired the efficacy of the insurgents' effort. On January 22, 1863, N.S., the National Committee declared "a state of insurrection" and issued a manifesto proclaiming the equality of "all sons of Poland irrespective of religion, origin, and social status." The manifesto, which was read from the pulpit of every church in Poland, promised the peasants the ownership of the land they farmed; the large landowners were to be indemnified by the state. After some hesitation the Whites endorsed this program. In March the National Committee was reorganized to include representatives of the Whites, and in May it assumed the name of National Government. The insurgents were short of funds, troops, military supplies, and officers. With the adherence of the Whites the financial stringency was somewhat relieved by contributions from proprietary groups, but the other handicaps remained. Polish leaders put their hopes in popular enthusiasm, foreign intervention, and the support of the Russian revolutionary movement. The latter illusion was widely shared abroad. "The Poles are doing well," Engels wrote to Marx on February 17, 1863, N.S. "If they keep up until March 15 the whole of Russia will be in a state of insurrection." Conscious of their weakness and faithful to Poland's romantic tradition, the National Committee and, later, the National Government established military "dictatorships" which, however, proved ephemeral. Mieroslawski, a Red hastily summoned from Paris, was the first "dictator." He was followed by General Marian Langiewicz, a White who had fought under the banners of Garibaldi. Towards the end of the insurrection, in October, 1863, arose the "dictatorship" of Romuald Traugutt, a former officer of the Russian army and a veteran of the Crimean campaign. It is noteworthy that organs of the Polish revolutionary government functioned not only in areas held by the insurgents but throughout Poland, including Warsaw, which remained under Russian control. In spite of the wide and real sympathy for the Poles in western Europe, the intervention of the Powers, as in 1831, did not go beyond diplomatic representations.[13] The only practical result was the imperial manifesto of March 31, 1863, promising amnesty to those insurgents who laid down arms by May 1, an offer rejected by Polish leaders.

From the purely military point of view the position of Poland was hopeless. The insurgents had under arms 10,000 men inadequately trained and poorly armed; the Russians, over 80,000 regular troops. The striking discrepancy in the size of the armed forces determined the character of the campaign, which, unlike most nineteenth century revolutions, was fought not on the barricades of the large cities but in forests and marshes. The partisan character of the warfare conducted by small detachments of the insurgents explains why, in spite of Russia's overwhelming superiority, Polish resistance lasted for eighteen months. Most of the time military operations were confined to the territory of the kingdom of Poland, especially its southern part. In the spring of 1863, however, the movement spread to Lithuania, White Russia, and Ukraine, but this was a mere flare-up which was suppressed within a few weeks.

The bulk of the insurgent forces was recruited from the middle and

---

[13] See pp. 956–958.

the lower middle class: the lesser nobility, government officials, university undergraduates, artisans, the Roman Catholic clergy. The Polish peasants, in spite of promises of equality and land, were slow and hesitant in answering the call to arms. Their attitude, however, according to Lensky, was one of "passive approval" rather than hostility. Lenin regarded the insurrection as a truly national revolutionary movement. In the Ukrainian and Lithuanian provinces, where relations between large landowners and peasants were embittered by racial and religious issues, the Russian peasants often sided with the authorities against the insurgents led by Polish noblemen and Catholic priests.

The reaction of Russian radical and liberal circles did not justify the sanguine expectations of Polish leaders. The revolutionaries—Herzen, Michael Bakunin, and the organization Zemlia i Volia (Land and Freedom) [14]—rallied whole-heartedly to the support of the Polish cause, but the uprising in Russia on which the insurgents had counted was not forthcoming. The appeals addressed to the troops by Herzen and Land and Freedom not to fight against the Poles brought no response, except that a few officers went over to the rebels. The attitude of Russian liberals was even more disappointing from the Polish point of view. Few of them resisted the sway of nationalistic emotions (Herzen called them "nationalistic syphilis") raised by the attack on Russian sovereignty (especially Poland's claim to the Lithuanian and Ukrainian provinces) and by the diplomatic intervention of the western Powers. Corporations of the nobility, municipal councils, universities, religious bodies, and peasant communes deluged St. Petersburg with patriotic addresses. The Russian westerners took the questionable position that since the emancipation of 1861 Russia had been the true standard-bearer of western civilization in eastern Europe. The erstwhile liberal journalist Michael Katkov argued in the influential *Moskovskiia Vedomosti* (Moscow News) that the insurgents represented the Polish nobility and the Catholic clergy, not the Polish people; that they were fighting for the further subjugation of the masses, not for national independence. The slavophile point of view was expanded in *Den* (The Day) by Yuri Samarin. He interpreted the insurrection as the latest stage in the secular struggle between Orthodox Slavdom, on the one hand, and Latinism represented by Poland, on the other. He demanded suppression of the uprising by methods of military dictatorship and by improving the lot of the

[14] See p. 1074.

peasantry; eradication of Polish influence in Lithuania and Ukraine, thus assuring the predominance in these provinces of Russian and Orthodox elements; and abolition of the last vestiges of Polish autonomy and the incorporation of the kingdom in the administrative framework of the empire.[15] The bulk of Russian liberal opinion endorsed this program, which the imperial government made its own and to which it remained faithful for half a century.

This policy was first applied in the northwestern provinces. By a decree of March 1, 1863, the state of "temporary obligation" [16] in this area was terminated and peasants were transferred to the regime of redemption payments. At the same time General Michael Muravev (created a count in 1865) was appointed governor-general of Vilna and was given dictatorial powers. A brother of the Decembrist Alexander Muravev, and himself once a member of the secret societies, Michael Muravev was a stern administrator and of sinister reputation. An opponent of emancipation in Russia, he became the champion of the peasants in the Lithuanian provinces. With slight regard for the law, Muravev ordered the revision of existing arrangements between the landowners and their former serfs, with the result that (according to Ianson) the size of peasant allotments was increased by 25 to 70 per cent and redemption charges were reduced by 2 to 16 per cent. Polish landowners were subjected to a reign of terror. Muravev instituted a military dictatorship, organized a peasant militia which preyed on the landowners and Catholic clergy, arrested and deported recalcitrant noblemen and priests, burned manor houses, and in the two years of his tenure of office (March, 1863, to April, 1865) carried out 240 public executions. Polish nobles, at the mercy of the dictator, were induced to petition the tsar for pardon and clemency. Russification proceeded

---

[15] Samarin was particularly bitter in his attacks on the Catholic Church. "From the thickness of the woods . . . a band of insurgents is making its way to the village," he wrote in *Den* of May 11, 1863. "At the head of the column rides a Catholic priest. Merely an hour ago he might have celebrated the holy mass. In one hand he still holds the cross, in the other . . . what would you think? Perhaps the sword of Peter, that symbol of secular power? No, this sword which had once threatened the universe had long dropped from the senile hand. It had been relegated to the arsenal and in its stead the servant of the Roman Church holds a six-barrel gun. Where words are powerless a bullet will do the job and will crush the skull of those, whether men or women, who resist exhortations. Before the tribunal of the Church all, of course, are equal."

[16] See p. 889.

at a rapid pace. Polish officials were dismissed, schools were reorganized so as to eliminate both Polish and Catholic influence. Teaching in primary schools was conducted in the Russian language, except that religious instruction of non-Orthodox children was permitted in their native "dialect" (decree of March 23, 1863). The tradition of Muravev was carried on by his successor, General C. P. Kaufman, and by the governor-general of the southwestern provinces, A. P. Bezak. In December, 1865, persons of Polish descent were prohibited from acquiring agricultural estates in the nine western provinces, and Polish landowners, deported because of their participation in the insurrection, were ordered to sell their landed properties within two years; such estates could be bought only by Orthodox Russians. Great pressure was exercised to encourage conversion to Orthodoxy. Addressing in Vilna a group of peasants who had joined the Russian Church, Alexander II declared: "I feel sure that you have embraced the ancient faith of this region sincerely and by conviction; you must know that I shall never tolerate converts to Orthodoxy returning to Catholicism" (June 13, 1866).

The repercussions of the insurrection were even more severe in the kingdom of Poland. In the summer of 1863 Wielopolski and Constantine were dismissed. The new viceroy, Count Theodore Berg, was an admirer of Paskevich and Muravev, whose methods he successfully emulated. The ultimate fate of Russian Poland, however, was entrusted to a commission presided over by Nicholas Miliutin. The commission, in which the slavophiles Prince V. A. Cherkassky and (for a time) Yuri Samarin played the leading part, dealt first with the peasant question. By a decree of February 19, 1864, Polish peasants were given land allotments substantially larger than those received by their Russian brethren. No redemption charges were attached to the possession of allotments, indemnities paid to the landowners being recovered through a land tax on all landed proprietors. The 1864 decree, moreover, retained a complicated system of easements which entitled Polish peasants to use extensively the woods and pastures of their former masters. The *gmina*, the new Polish administrative rural subdivision, unlike its Russian counterpart (township or *volost*), included not only the peasants but all local landed proprietors. In the *gmina* the noble landowners were outnumbered by peasant farmers and were brought into uncomfortably close contact with the Russian police, which dominated the *gmina* even more completely than it did the Russian township. These measures were obviously designed to court the peasants at the expense of the landed nobility.

The reorganization of the Polish government was thorough but less swift. Between 1867 and 1869 all institutions established by the Organic Statute of 1832 and the Wielopolski reforms were abolished, and Russian Poland, a kingdom only in name, was brought under an administrative regime identical with that of the other parts of the empire. Administrative assimilation was made all the more unpalatable by aggressive Russification. Polish officials were replaced by native Russians, who received a privileged status in the civil service (law of June 30, 1867). The Russian language was introduced in the administration and in the courts. With the appointment of Count Dimitry Tolstoy as minister of education (1866), Russification was extended to schools. Polish schools were gradually but inexorably crowded out by Russian schools. A drive for the elimination of the Polish language in secondary schools was inaugurated in 1869, and in primary schools in 1871. By a law of 1885 all instruction in Polish primary schools was to be given in Russian, except for classes in the Polish language, and in religion for Roman Catholics, which might be conducted in Polish. In 1869 the University of Warsaw was reorganized as a Russian university; its faculty was appointed by Russian authorities. The Catholic Church was made to pay a heavy price for the part taken by the clergy in the insurrection. A number of Catholic and Uniat monasteries and convents were closed in 1864. Two years later Uniats were debarred from espousing Catholicism. Bribery, intimidation, and outright coercion were successfully used to force the Uniats to repudiate their allegiance to Rome: in 1875 the Uniat diocese of Kholm was readmitted to the fold of Greek Orthodoxy.

The one redeeming feature of the ill advised and ill fated insurrection of 1863 was the land reform of 1864. According to the distinguished Polish authority Roman Dmowski, the reform, by creating a large and economically sound class of peasant owners, contributed to the prosperity and social stability of Poland. It is arguable, however, that since the necessity of the economic emancipation of the peasantry was recognized by Polish opinion, a liberal land reform would have been enacted, irrespective of the St. Petersburg government. Russian political objectives in Poland were not achieved. Generous treatment did not reconcile Polish peasants to Muscovite domination, and Poland's national aspirations survived repressions, administrative assimilation, and Russification. The insurrection of 1863 and its aftermath merely added to the heavy heritage of bitterness and mutual suspicion which explains much in the course of subsequent Russo-Polish relations.

FINLAND AND AUTOCRACY

The progress of Finland towards constitutional government stands in sharp contrast with the vicissitudes experienced by Poland. Throughout the reign of Nicholas I relations between Russia and Finland remained uneventful and harmonious. Hard-working, orderly, and prosperous Finland lived her own life, and St. Petersburg did not interfere with the autonomous institutions established in the grand duchy in 1809. Nicholas I, indeed, would seem to have accepted the view that Finnish laws could not be altered without consulting the diet. The diet, however, had not been convened since 1809, and after the accession of Alexander II Finnish opinion, under the influence of the rising tide of nationalism, showed restlessness and an unmistakable desire for a more active part in government. St. Petersburg endeavored to meet the Finns halfway. An imperial manifesto of April 10, 1861, summoned a commission of representatives of the four Finnish "estates" constituting the diet (nobility, clergy, burghers, and peasants) to discuss urgent legislation; the decisions of the commission, pending the convocation of the diet at some undetermined date, were to receive the force of law. Finland's vigorous protest against this unconstitutional procedure forced the imperial government to abandon its plan and to announce (August 11, 1861) that the commission would act in a purely advisory capacity. After further hesitations and delays Alexander, in June, 1863, ordered the convocation of the diet, which met in September. The emperor's opening address, prepared in collaboration with his Finnish advisers, contained the already quoted reference to "liberal institutions" as "a guarantee of order and well-being," and indicated that the diet was to function as a legislative assembly. After 1863 the diet met at regular intervals. Its functions and constitution (based on the old Swedish law of representation by "estates") were defined by a statute passed by the diet in 1867 and confirmed by the tsar on April 15, 1869, N.S. This statute laid down the rule that the "fundamental laws" of Finland could not be altered without the consent of the diet. Thus the powers of the Crown in

Finland were limited, and the Russian emperor, as grand duke of Finland, became a constitutional monarch. No serious attempt at infringement of the legislative prerogatives of the diet was made by the Russian government until the very end of the nineteenth century.

No corresponding constitutional reform took place in Russia. The only modification in the machinery of the Russian central government was the creation of the council of ministers. Established in 1857 and reorganized in 1861, the council had ill defined duties, and functioned hardly at all. It met seldom after 1862, and slipped into oblivion in 1883. In the reign of Alexander II, in spite of incessant agitation, proposals for representative government never passed the discussion stage. The "great reforms" had no direct effect on absolutism, and until 1905 the Crown retained all its autocratic powers.

CHAPTER XXXIV

ALEXANDER II

Social and Economic Developments

❋

THE PEASANTS

The emancipation, for all its imperfections, was a factor of paramount importance in Russian history; yet in the first two or three decades following the reform its social and economic consequences were surprisingly slight. The statutes of February 19, 1861, bore the imprint of rigid conservatism and avoidance of clear-cut decisions which Alexander II and his advisers had inherited from the previous reign. The transition of the peasants from bondage to a status of political and economic equality with other social groups could hardly have been more gradual. The reaction of the serfs to the emancipation edicts was one of bewilderment and disappointment. The intricacies and legal niceties of the emancipation procedure have for decades puzzled historians and economists, and have defied the efforts of the Senate (supreme court) to interpret them intelligibly and consistently. Although they were beyond the grasp of the peasantry, the shrewd common sense of the muzhik told him that the "land and freedom" granted to him under the conditions I have described was not what he had hoped for and what he vaguely believed to be his due. To the popular mind some of the stipulations of the emancipation acts seemed a mockery. According to Koshelev, the provision that the redemption operation was to extend over forty-nine years—"two generations"—was greeted by the peasants of his estate with derisive laughter. There came into being the widely accepted legend that the acts of February 19 were not the "real emancipation," that the tsar's ukase had been falsified by landowners and officials, and that "true emancipation" would follow when the treachery had been exposed or, more precisely, on the expiration of the introductory two-year period provided by the statutes of 1861. The Crown was forced to take cognizance of these persistent rumors. "Reports have reached me that you are expecting a new emancipation," Alexander sternly told a delegation of Tula peasants in August, 1861. "There will be no emancipation except the one I have granted you. Obey the law and the statutes! Work and toil! Be obedient to the authorities and to noble landowners!" This not very inspiring admonition was not heeded at once. There was much passive and open resistance to the execution of the reform. A common manifestation of the former was the refusal of the peasants to approve the "inventories" (*ustavnaia gramota*),[1] the application of which constituted the introductory stage of the emancipation. Sporadic peasant revolts flared up in many localities, and reached particular force in the provinces of Penza and Kazan, where thousands of former serfs refused to work for the landowners and attacked manor houses. The movement, however, was short-lived. In 1861 acts of insubordination were reported in 1,176 estates; in 1862 in 400; in 1863 in 386. The government was prepared for the emergency, and troops were effectively used to quell the disturbances. A particularly bloody incident, involving the death of some 50 and the wounding of over 350 insurgents, occurred in the village of Bezdna, in the province of Kazan. Courts-martial, executions, deportations to Siberia, and flogging once more crushed popular revolt. In 1864 outbreaks were reported in only 75 estates. Peace and order were restored by methods that augured ill for the success of the reform.

The statutes of February 19 were instrumental in perpetuating the economic dependence of the liberated serfs on their former masters. It will be remembered that the law set no time limit for the duration of the period of "temporary obligation,"[2] which in its economic aspects differed but little from serfdom. According to the computation of Prince D. I. Shakhovskoy, the regime of redemption payments superseded that of "temporary obligation" on about one-half of all peasant allotments in 1862–1866 and on two-thirds of the allotments in the first decade following the emancipation (1862–1871). The inducement of substantial subsidies granted by the government to the landowners on the conclusion of redemption agreements was largely

[1] See p. 889.
[2] See p. 889.

responsible for the initial success of the redemption operation. Yet in the early 1880's, when redemption of allotments was finally made compulsory (law of December 28, 1881), some 14 per cent of the former serfs were still living under the regime of "temporary obligation."

There were, however, other and more permanent factors that worked against the economic rehabilitation of the peasantry. As has already been stated, the charges imposed on the liberated serfs were grossly in excess both of the yield of their land and of its market value, while the average size of the allotments (except in the western provinces) fell considerably below that of their pre-reform holdings. The decline was particularly marked in the fertile southern and southeastern provinces; in the province of Samara, for instance, it was as high as 42 per cent. The consequences of the contraction of the area of peasant tenure were all the graver because, to repeat, pre-reform allotments were intended to provide employment for only half of the serfs' time, the other half to be spent in work for their master. The statutes of February 19, moreover, deprived the former serfs of their customary right to timber and firewood from manorial forests, and denied them the use of meadows and pastures, which the landowners often retained in their own possession.

The total area of allotment land transferred to the peasants in 1861–1870 was 111.6 million dessiatines.[3] In 1877 the distribution of land in European Russia was as follows: state and public bodies (appanages, the Church, municipalities), 166.3 million dessiatines, or 44.1 per cent; peasant allotments, 116.7 dessiatines, or 31 per cent; private owners, 94.0 million dessiatines, or 24.9 per cent. Much of the vast state domain consisted of forest and unimproved land, unsuitable for cultivation. The landholdings of the Church were relatively small (2.1 million dessiatines in 1877). Of the 94.0 million dessiatines owned privately, 73.2 million belonged to the nobility and 5.0 million to individual peasants and peasant communes; the land owned privately by the peasants was not subject to the legal restrictions attached to the allotments. The average size of allotments *per male person* varied according to the class of peasants to which their owners belonged before the emancipation. The average allotment per serf was 3.2 dessiatines; per appanage peasant 4.9 dessiatines; and per state peasant

[3] The above figure is for European Russia, exclusive of Poland, Finland, and the Caucasus. One dessiatine = 2.7 acres.

6.7 dessiatines. The average allotment *per household* (*dvor*) in European Russia in 1877 was 13.2 dessiatines, or more than 35 acres.[4] In view of the pronounced inequality in the size of peasant holdings, these average figures are of little value. Nevertheless Professor Robinson is right when he writes that, judged by western European standards, the Russian peasant "was not badly off, in so far as the mere extent of his acres was concerned." Yet historians and economists are in general agreement that, given the existing methods of cultivation, allotments failed to provide for the needs of a peasant family (to say nothing of taxes and other charges) or to offer full employment for its labor. Clearly the size of allotments and financial burdens, including a disproportionately large share of indirect taxes, do not alone explain the plight of the farmers in the post-reform period.

The economic backwardness of Russia, the stifling influence of the village commune, and the short-sighted policy of the government were the chief obstacles to the progress of peasant farming. The introduction of intensive methods of cultivation was effectively precluded by lack of technical knowledge and expert guidance, by insufficiency of capital and credit, and by a communal organization under which the land assigned to peasant households was subdivided into narrow intermingled strips necessitating a uniform rotation of crops. The three-field system was prevalent not only in the 1860's and 1870's but for decades thereafter; this meant that one-third of plowland was annually left fallow. The use of improved machinery and fertilizers was practically unknown, and the possibility of repartition of land (even though the rule of periodical repartitions was often not enforced) tended to discourage the farmers from taking good care of their fields. The yield of grain was low and remained nearly stationary, increasing from an average of 29 poods per dessiatine in 1861–1870 to but 31 poods in 1871–1880,[5] that is, it failed to keep pace with the rapid growth of the rural population. Idle man power, however, was firmly bound to the hungry village. The statutes of 1861 made no provision for internal migration. The resettlement of state peasants in the eastern provinces of European Russia, in the Caucasus, and in Siberia,

---

[4] A. N. Antysferov and others, *Russian Agriculture During the War* (New Haven, 1930), pp. 20, 306; Robinson, *op. cit.*, p. 97. The figures quoted are at best approximations. Russian land statistics are notoriously incomplete, unreliable, contradictory, and misleading. For a good discussion of this point see Robinson, *op. cit.*, especially notes on pp. 288–290.

[5] In 50 provinces of European Russia. One pood = 36 lbs. = 0.016 ton.

inaugurated by Kiselev in the 1830's, was conducted on a modest scale (the number of such settlers from 1831 to 1866 was slightly over 300,000 males), and was discontinued in 1866, when the emancipation acts were extended, with some modifications, to the state peasants. No comprehensive data on the number of settlers are available for the 1860's, 1870's, and early 1880's, but whatever migration took place was illicit and in contravention of official regulations. Migration without a permit from the authorities was specifically prohibited in 1881. In that year only 36,000 male settlers went to Siberia, and in 1883 the figure was still as low as 46,000. Obstacles to internal migration were relaxed in the late 1880's and were finally abolished in 1906. The earlier policy of obstruction was inspired by the desire to assure big landowners an ample supply of cheap labor. The same preoccupation was in part responsible for the legal restrictions which made it practically impossible for the peasants to withdraw from the village commune and made it difficult for them to seek even temporary employment in industry, trades and professions. It will be remembered that a member of a village commune could not lawfully absent himself without securing a passport, the issuance of which could be refused by communal authorities and, if the applicant was a junior member of the household, by the household elder. The slow development of industry, moreover, offered little opportunity for employment in factories. In 1861–1870 8.7 million passports were issued, and in 1871–1880 18.9 million. The annual average number of passports per 1,000 of the peasant population (male and female) was 13.9 in 1861–1870 and 26.8 in 1871–1880.[6] In spite of this increase the outflow of man power from the village was too small to provide any real measure of relief.

The extension of peasant acreage was achieved through the purchase and lease of land. The use of the former method, however, was restricted by lack of capital and credit facilities. The first peasant bank was not established until 1883. Nevertheless, of the 50 million dessiatines that changed hands from 1863 to 1882 about 3 million were bought by individual peasant farmers and 2.5 million by village communes and peasant associations. Leasing of land proceeded on a much

[6] These data are for fifty provinces of European Russia. There were important deviations from these average figures. The largest number of passports per 1,000 was issued in the central industrial provinces, where it stood at 39.4 in 1861–1870 and at 71.9 in 1871–1880; the respective ratios for the eastern provinces, which occupy the opposite end of the scale, were 2.6 and 7.5.

greater scale but its extent and economic implications defy precise analysis. Estimates of the area of peasant renting vary within an extraordinarily wide range, from 10 million dessiatines to 50 million. The economic character of these transactions is highly controversial. Russian economists have long upheld the theory that peasant leasing was an absolute necessity, that is, peasant farmers were forced to extend the area of their tenure, irrespective of rents charged, in order to provide the bare minimum of existence for themselves and their families. This theory of "subsistence" or "hunger" leases has been challenged by more recent students, especially by Professor S. N. Prokopovich (in 1924). In his opinion peasant leasing was governed not by the fear of starvation but by a desire to obtain the most advantageous combination of the essential factors of agricultural production: labor, capital (machinery, implements, domestic animals), and land; in other words, Russian land leases did not differ from those in any other country. Whatever the right explanation, the fact is indisputable that peasants took on lease vast areas of land and that the rents they paid were high and constituted a heavy burden on their meager budgets.

Poverty, backwardness, administrative tutelage, restrictions on freedom of movement, and the inherent conservatism of the rural community all combined to perpetuate the survival of serfdom. Peasant land leasing, especially when born of necessity, as it was in many instances, bore close resemblance to the pre-emancipation *obrok* (annual money due). *Barshchina* (*corvée*), too, survived in a slightly modified form in arrangements under which peasants paid for the right to farm a portion of a neighboring estate by cultivating, for the benefit of the owner, another portion with their own horses and implements. Sometimes estates were farmed on a crop-sharing basis, the landowner providing the land, and the peasants labor, horses, and implements. According to the computations of Lenin, who carefully scrutinized statistical returns for every evidence of nascent Russian capitalism, the farming of estates by pre-emancipation methods was prevalent in the late 1880's in 55.8 per cent of the 43 provinces of European Russia for which information was available. The element of legal compulsion, characteristic of serfdom, had disappeared, but economic necessity stepped in in its place and the economic relations between landowners and their former serfs were in many cases not very different from what they were prior to 1861. "Twelve years have passed since the emancipation," wrote A. N. Engelgardt, a keen contemporary observer and owner of an estate in the province of Smolensk, "but the methods of farming on most of our estates are the same as of yore." From the peasants' point of view the change was even less perceptible; although their personal dependence on the landowner was terminated they found themselves at the mercy of communal and township authorities, whom the representative of the local nobility—first the arbitrator (*mirovoi posrednik*) and, after 1874, the permanent member of the county peasant board (*nepremennyi chlen uezdnago po krestianskim delam prisutstviia*)—ruled with an iron hand.[7] There was, indeed, old wine in the new bottles.

The emancipation thus failed to establish peasant farming on a sound economic basis or even to eliminate many of the abuses of serfdom. A few energetic and aggressive householders succeeded, no doubt, in overcoming the equalitarian tendencies of the village commune and in improving their status through leases and purchases of land, as is evidenced by the acquisition of 3 million dessiatines by private peasant owners. But the majority of the villagers continued to live in abject poverty, with little chance of bettering their position. Their predicament has often been described in Russian economic literature as "shortage of land" or "rural overpopulation." "Overpopulation," of course, was not used in the accepted meaning of the term, since Russia was less densely populated than any other European country; it implied the inability of a large portion of the farmers, under then existing conditions, to make a living from their acres and to employ on them fully the labor of their families. The appropriation by the peasants of all land owned by the state and the nobility, although at best a palliative, came to be regarded by the masses as the only possible remedy for the "shortage of land," and as an act of justice long overdue. In spite of Alexander II's warning to the Tula delegates, the belief in the inevitability of a "second emancipation" persisted, gaining momentum. This "latent socialism without a doctrine," to use

[7] "The arbitrator is everything," Engelgardt wrote in the 1870's. "Opening of schools, closing of taverns, collection of donations—all stem from the arbitrator. If the arbitrator so wishes, the peasants will proclaim their desire to have in every township not only a school, but a university. If the arbitrator so wishes, a resolution will be adopted that the peasants of a certain township, recognizing the advantage of gardening, have resolved to contribute so many copecks per head to some society in Haarlem for the cultivation of hyacinth bulbs. If the arbitrator so wishes, the peasants of any village will drink vodka in one tavern and close another."

Baron Boris Nolde's felicitous phrase, formed the background of Russian history for a half-century, and proved a decisive factor in the revolution of 1917.

THE NOBILITY

The landed nobility, whose interests the statutes of 1861 strove so diligently to protect, derived, like the peasants, little economic benefit from the emancipation. The process of decay of large-scale farming noted in the earlier part of the nineteenth century continued unabated after the reform. The ill effects of technical backwardness, lack of capital, inertia, inefficiency, and attachment to traditional methods of husbandry were in evidence on big estates almost as much as they were on peasant holdings. The nobility received substantial subsidies in indemnification for land transferred to the former serfs, but the financial relief thus obtained proved largely nominal. Of the nearly 600 million rubles to which the landowners were entitled for acreage ceded during the first ten years after the emancipation, almost half reverted to the treasury in settlement of outstanding mortgage loans. Only a small portion of the balance was invested in agricultural improvements, machinery, and livestock. In the meantime borrowing continued, and in the early 1880's the mortgage debt of the nobility had risen to 400 million rubles, that is, it exceeded the pre-emancipation level. In the pre-reform period estates were cultivated by servile labor, horses and implements being provided by the serfs. Transition to capitalist forms of management—employment of hired labor working with horses and agricultural machinery supplied by the owners—proved a slow and difficult business. Most of the noble landowners were unwilling or unable to make the necessary outlays and, as has already been stated, they either rented their land to the peasants or cultivated their estates by methods substantially similar to those of the pre-emancipation era. The yield per acre on estates was in 1860–1870 some 14 per cent higher than on peasant farms, but the difference was due not so much to improved methods of cultivation as to the fact that the big owners had retained the best arable land as well as most of the meadows and pastures. The average yield per acre on privately owned land (that is, chiefly estates of the nobility) in Russia was much lower than in other European countries.

The stagnation of Russian agriculture (and its concomitant, recurrent famine) was all the more striking because of the rapid growth of

Russian grain exports, which were greatly stimulated by the building of railways connecting the hinterland with the southern ports. The annual average export of wheat, rye, barley, and oats increased from 69 million poods in 1856–1860 to 120 million in 1866–1870, and to 257 million in 1876–1880. Grain for export, however, was obtained, not by higher yield per acre, but by extension of the tilled area, especially in the southern provinces. The grain trade was poorly organized and was largely in the hands of middlemen, chiefly merchants, who reaped most of the profits.

The decline of the nobility was evidenced by the relentless shrinkage of its landholdings. According to Professor Oganovsky, the area owned by the nobility in 47 provinces of European Russia declined from 87.2 million dessiatines in 1862 to 80.7 million in 1872, and to 71.2 million in 1882; in 1911 it was reduced to 43.2 million dessiatines. The acres over which the *dvoriane* once lorded were passing, at an ever increasing pace, into the hands of merchants, burghers, and peasants.[8]

INDUSTRY

Russian industry maintained in the second half of the nineteenth century a fairly steady, if somewhat uneven, rate of progress, interrupted by recessions of a cyclical character. The business expansion of the middle of the 1850's was followed by a depression which lasted from about 1858–1859 to the late 1860's. New depressions developed in 1873–1876, in 1882–1887, and in the early 1890's. The closing years of the nineteenth century were a period of intensive business activity. According to Professor Tugan-Baranovsky, Russia's foremost authority on business cycles, cyclical fluctuations in Russia conformed closely to similar trends in western Europe and in the United States, although they were, of course, affected by local conditions. The recovery of the 1870's for instance, is traceable to the government-sponsored program of railway construction. The emancipation of the serfs was a contributing factor in the depression of the 1860's, but its effects should not be overemphasized. It will be remembered that employment of hired

[8] Much of the land sold by the nobility in the decades immediately following the emancipation was acquired by merchants and burghers. In 47 provinces of European Russia individual peasants, peasant associations, and village communes owned privately 5.7 million dessiatines in 1862; 7.3 million in 1872; 10.7 million in 1882; and 30.4 million in 1911. These figures do not, of course, comprise allotment land.

labor was prevalent in industry long before 1861; in the case of most industrial establishments, therefore, the recruitment of labor was not appreciably affected by the reform. Those branches of production, however, which had previously depended on servile workers went through a painful process of readjustment. Peasants attached to possessionary works [9] hastened to throw off the hated yoke, sold or even abandoned their homesteads, and moved away from the localities where their forefathers had slaved for generations. Between 1861 and 1865 the possessionary mines and metallurgical works of the Urals lost some 30,000 workers, or about one-fourth of their labor force. The output of pig iron in that region declined from 14.5 million poods in 1860 to 10.5 million in 1862, and increased but slowly to 12.4 million in 1867. The woolen and other industries, in which previous to the emancipation the percentage of servile labor was high, were similarly affected, the control of such establishments tending to pass from the nobility to the merchants, a process that had been manifest long before 1861. The depression of the 1860's was strongly felt by the cotton industry although it employed chiefly hired labor. The drastic contraction of production and employment in this industry, however, was due to an external cause: the shortage of cotton experienced by European markets as a consequence of the Civil War in the United States.

The chaotic state of Russian statistics precludes a precise analysis of industrial development. A major source of confusion (already mentioned with reference to the earlier period) is the indiscriminate use of the term "factory" (*fabrika* and *zavod*) to denote large and small enterprises alike. Lenin, limiting the term "factory" to enterprises which employed at least 16 workers, computed that Russia had approximately 2,500 to 3,000 factories in 1866; 4,500 in 1879; 6,000 in 1890; and 9,000 in 1903. The number of workers engaged in the manufacturing, mining, and metallurgical industries in fifty provinces of European Russia increased from an annual average of 798,000 in 1861–1870 to 946,000 in 1871–1880, to 1,160,000 in 1881–1890, and to 1,638,000 in 1891–1900.[10] The province of Moscow retained its position as the chief industrial area, with 135,000 industrial workers

[9] See pp. 389–390, 793–794.
[10] According to Rashin, from whose study these figures are borrowed, the data he quotes, although derived from official sources, are neither comprehensive nor accurate, but are merely indicative of general trends.

in 1861–1870 and 163,000 in 1871–1880. The rich mining regions of southern Russia were still practically untouched by industrialization: the province of Ekaterinoslav had merely 5,200 industrial workers in 1861–1870 and 8,700 in 1871–1880; the respective figures for the Don region were 1,500 and 8,700. The manufacturing of cotton textiles, after recovery from the depression of the 1860's, remained Russia's leading industry. Although the number of cotton mills and manufactories in European Russia declined from 724 in 1865 to 575 in 1880, the number of workers they employed increased, during the same period, from 76,000 to 167,000. A reverse process took place in the woolen industry: from 1865 to 1880 the number of enterprises increased from 683 to 766, but that of the workers fell from 109,000 to 97,000. Progress was registered in machine building. In 1865 European Russia had 126 machine-building plants employing 18,000 workers; in 1880 the number of plants had risen to 202 and the number of workers to 44,000.

The concentration of production due to mechanization is illustrated by the following table based on data collected by Lenin:

Distribution of Industrial Enterprises According to Size, 1866–1879 (European Russia)

Number of workers per enterprise	Number of enterprises 1866	Number of enterprises 1879	Number of workers In thousands 1866	Number of workers In thousands 1879	Per cent of total 1866	Per cent of total 1879
100 to 499	512	641	109.1	141.7	47	36
500 to 999	90	130	59.9	91.9	26	24
1,000 and over	42	81	62.8	156.8	27	40
Total	644	852	231.8	390.4	100	100

The rapid growth of very large enterprises employing 1,000 and more workers each is particularly notable; in 1866 they accounted for 27 per cent of the workers, in 1879 for 40 per cent. In 1879, according to Lenin, enterprises employing 100 and more workers each represented 4.4 per cent of all industrial establishments (large and small) and provided employment for 66.8 per cent of all industrial workers.

The advent of large-scale capitalist enterprise was accompanied by abuses which ushered in the machine age in every country: long hours, harsh and unsanitary conditions of work, increased employment of women and children, low wages. None of these evils was novel in the post-emancipation Russia; they merely perpetuated, and sometimes made worse, the situation that existed under serfdom. The working day was seldom shorter than twelve hours, and often rose to fourteen, fifteen, sixteen, and even eighteen hours. In the manufacturing of rush mats the twenty-one-hour day appeared to be prevalent, although it is difficult to see how this could have been enforced for any length of time. Night work was common for men, women, and children. With rare exceptions, workshops and living quarters were crowded and, according to the standards of a more enlightened age, unfit for occupancy. Workers, irrespective of sex and age, were herded into filthy barracks, where they slept on the floor or on bare bunks arranged in tiers. In 1887 (no earlier data are available) of the 789,300 wage earners reported by the department of commerce and manufactures, 192,500, or 24.4 per cent, were women. In some industries the ratio of female labor was higher; in the textile mills of St. Petersburg in 1881, for instance, it was 42.6 per cent. Juvenile labor was extensively used. According to a study made by E. Andreev (quoted in Rashin), of the 548,000 workers employed in 1882–1883 in 3,316 enterprises 49,500, or 9.2 per cent, were under fifteen. The majority of the juvenile wage earners (41,700) were in the age group twelve to fifteen; 960 were children under ten. The largest number of workers under fifteen was employed in textile mills (30,200), in mining and metallurgy (7,700), and in the food industry (6,500). A common abuse was the long delay in paying wages. It was customary to pay workers three or four times a year, or even only twice (on Easter and Christmas), an arrangement under which the determination of earnings was necessarily left to the discretion of the factory administration. Another inequitable practice was that of imposing fines. Fines as high as three months' wages were not unusual in the John Hughes ironworks in southern Russia. Strikes were prohibited by the penal code of 1845 (Section 1792) and were punishable by arrest for a term not exceeding three months; "willful disobedience to factory owners or managers," however, if expressed in collective action, was deemed "rebellion against lawful authorities," and might bring a sentence of penal servitude (Section 1791). Strikes, nevertheless, took place, and their pressure, combined with that of a public opinion increasingly conscious of the evils of the Russian sweating system, led the government to give thought to the betterment of factory conditions. Beginning with the late 1850's, official committees busied themselves with drafting proposals for the improvement of the lot of the workers, but no action was taken until 1882.

The determination of the trend of industrial wages is difficult for reasons already given in an earlier chapter: incompleteness and unreliability of statistical records, lack of uniformity in the wage rates throughout the country, vagaries of the price level, and the uncertain purchasing power of the paper ruble. Nevertheless Russian economists are in general agreement with Tugan-Baranovsky that while *money* wages in most industries rose between the 1860's and the 1890's, *real* wages declined by perhaps as much as 20 or 30 per cent. The displacement of the produce of many cottage industries by cheap machine-made articles swelled the army of men and women seeking employment in factories. The growth of industry, however, was too slow to absorb available man power. With the supply of labor exceeding demand, the standards of wages, low as they were, deteriorated still further, except for a few occupations where skill was at a premium. It was not until the rapid industrial expansion of the closing years of the century that real wages, as well as money wages, showed a tendency to rise. The majority of industrial workers, moreover, were peasants who had not entirely severed the link with their native villages. Most of them retained an interest in the remote homestead where their families often continued to live. This permitted Russian workers to accept lower wages than would have been necessary if they had had to maintain a family establishment near their place of employment. Conversely, higher wages were an essential prerequisite before the "link with land" could be definitely broken. The wage problem in Russia would, indeed, seem to have moved in a vicious circle.

The importance of the "link with land," however, should not be overstressed. Sample investigation of the permanency of industrial employment discloses a high degree of stability. For instance, of the 12,000 wage earners employed in the Moscow textile mills in 1881 only 22.8 per cent were connected with that industry for less than three years, while 20.1 per cent had worked in textile mills from fifteen to twenty-five years, and 18.3 per cent for over twenty-five years. The examination of a smaller sample (4,391 workers) shows, according to the same author (P. A. Peskov, quoted in Rashin), that 42.8 per cent of the Moscow textile workers in 1881 were sons (or daughters) of factory workers. An analysis of the record of 18,600 male workers engaged in various industries in 1884–1885 brings this ratio to 55.5 per cent (E. M. Dementev, quoted in Rashin). These and other partial investigations do not warrant broad generalization, especially since samples are usually weighted in favor of old established industries (textile and metallurgy). They suggest, nevertheless, that a class of "hereditary proletarians," to use Rashin's phrase, was in a process of formation. The appearance of an industrial proletariat, on the one hand, and of entrepreneurs closely connected with financial and banking circles, on the other, was perhaps among the most significant developments of the post-emancipation era.

COMMUNICATIONS

The construction of railways was the chief single factor in fostering Russia's economic progress. The difficulties in supplying the army during the Crimean War had abundantly demonstrated the military importance of modern methods of communication. Their economic value, moreover, was no longer questioned. In the 1860's few would argue, as Kankrin did a generation earlier, that railways were a harmful luxury. In 1855 Russia had less than 1,000 versts [11] of railways, to which some 500 versts were added by 1860, when the pace of construction was greatly accelerated. Two thousand versts were open to traffic in 1861–1865; 6,400 in 1866–1870; 7,500 in 1871–1875; and 3,500 in 1876–1880. In 1881 railway mileage reached 21,000 versts and in 1895 33,000 versts. This was a notable achievement even though Russia had fewer miles of railway lines per unit of territory or population than any other major European country.

The financial aspects of railway construction were less satisfactory. Some of the higher bureaucrats, for instance, the ministers of communications General P. L. Melnikov (1863–1869) and Count A. P. Bobrinsky (1872–1874) believed that railways should be built exclusively, or at least chiefly, by the state, and they deprecated the granting of concessions to private interests on the ground that it led to graft, abuses, inefficiency and, finally, to heavy treasury losses. Bobrinsky held that no concession should be given to private companies unless they were subject to thorough government supervision. The opposite view had its protagonist in Count Michael Reutern, minister of

[11] One verst = 0.66 mile.

finance from 1862 to 1878. Reutern was concerned primarily with the stabilization of the paper ruble and the improvement of Russia's balance of payments through the strengthening of her export position. Railway construction was an essential element in his program for the development of Russian national resources, which he regarded as necessary to assure the country some degree of prosperity. In Reutern's opinion, however, the treasury was unable to finance the building of railways. The only practical solution, according to this view, was to enlist the services of private, especially foreign, capital. It was also argued that the government's record in railway building was not encouraging: it took the state nine years (1842–1851) to complete the St. Petersburg-Moscow line, and the cost per mile was exorbitant. Financial stringency, pressure of powerful interests affiliated with the higher bureaucracy, and Reutern's influence with the emperor determined the character of Russian railway policy.

Its basic principles were laid down in an imperial decree of January 26, 1857, which established the General Company of Russian Railways nominally headed by the Russian banker Baron Alexander Stiglitz (son of a German expatriate who made one of the largest fortunes in Russia and eventually became banker to the imperial court) but actually controlled by a syndicate of Dutch, English, and French banking houses. The company undertook to build within ten years 4,000 miles of railway lines; it was given the privilege of operating them for ninety-five years, the government guaranteeing 5 per cent interest on the capital invested. In spite of the highly advantageous terms of the concession, the General Society soon ran into financial difficulties and proved unable to meet its commitments. In 1861 its charter was amended; the company received substantial subsidies and was relieved of the obligation of building some of the lines stipulated in the original agreement; its headquarters, however, were transferred from Paris to St. Petersburg, and four of the fourteen members of the managing board were appointed by the Russian government. In spite of this inauspicious start the government persevered in a policy of concessions accompanied by official guarantees. Until 1865 it was the practice to grant railway concessions only to foreign companies. Russian financial disorders and the spread of the revolutionary movement in the early 1860's, however, dealt a severe blow to Russian credit abroad, and attempts at organizing new foreign companies, in spite of the exceptionally favorable terms offered by the government, ended in lamentable failure. Encouragement was then given to Russian financiers, and in the middle of the 1860's there began a real orgy of railway promoting and speculation in railway securities. Confidence in Russia having in the meantime been restored, railway issues found eager purchasers abroad, especially in Germany and England. The scandalous involvement of higher bureaucrats in railway promoting forced the government to prohibit responsible officials from participating in private railway companies (1868); this rule, however, was never fully enforced. There was much irregularity in securing concessions and in railway financing and management. "The existence of many of our railway companies is fictitious," wrote the minister of communications, Count A. P. Bobrinsky, in his report to the tsar in 1873; "their firms are a mere front; their managing boards are irregular; their shareholders are straw men; their shares were never actually subscribed." Bobrinsky complained that when the management of companies remained formally within the law, the ministry of communications was reduced to the role of a helpless observer of activities "contrary to the interests of the government, the company, and the fisc"; but even when the law was clearly violated the government was compelled, at a heavy cost to the treasury, to condone illegal actions in order to protect Russian credit. By January 1, 1880, the total indebtedness of private railway companies to the government amounted to 1,091 million rubles. "The financial disorders of our railways have reached the limit," A. A. Abaza, minister of finance in 1880–1881, declared in the committee of ministers in February, 1881. "No more than five or six of our railway companies are in a position to pay their shareholders dividends in excess of the returns guaranteed by the government; the majority, however, burden the treasury with requests for payments of almost the full amount of the official guarantee, and a great many cannot even meet their operating expenses. . . . The bulk of private railway companies operate exclusively with government funds and present a highly abnormal phenomenon: on the one hand, expenditure of public money without adequate control; on the other, private management without the stimulus of private interest." Abaza's criticisms and his proposal that in the future construction of railways should be undertaken by the government were endorsed by the committee of ministers. Such was the stern yet fully justified appraisal of Russia's first major venture in capitalist enterprise.

The Russians, never having excelled in navigation and shipbuilding, were only partly successful in their efforts for the promotion of a mercantile marine. Typical of the shipping concerns of the post-reform period was the Russian Steamship Company for the advancement of commerce in the Black Sea and the Sea of Azov; the company, founded in 1856, was under the patronage of the emperor and was the recipient of generous subventions and other bounties. In 1860 11,000 seagoing ships with an aggregate tonnage of 2.1 million called at Russian ports; in 1880 15,400 ships with a tonnage of 5.4 million; in 1900 the number of ships declined to 10,600, but their tonnage increased to 8.7 million. Russia's share in her sea-borne trade, however, shrank. In 1850 vessels of Russian registry accounted for 15.1 per cent of the tonnage of ships calling at Russian ports; in 1900 this ratio had fallen to 11.8 per cent. On the high seas and internal waterways sailing vessels were gradually replaced by steamships. The number of river steamers rose from 400 in 1860 to 2,500 in 1895.

Postal and telegraph services were operated by the government and were administered, at different times, either by the ministry of the interior or by a special department. Postage stamps for domestic mail were introduced in 1857 and for foreign mail in 1864; ten years later Russia was among the founders of the Universal Postal Union. The number of letters sent through the mail had risen from 33.9 million in 1854 to 198.8 million in 1878, hardly an impressive figure for a population of some 80 or 90 million. Between 1855 and 1880 the length of the telegraph network increased from 2,000 to 75,000 versts. In 1866 the importation of telegraph equipment was discontinued, all necessary materials and apparatus being then manufactured in Russia. Shipbuilding, on the other hand, in spite of government subsidies, made little progress. As late as 1914, 85.4 per cent of the tonnage of Russian steamships was built abroad, chiefly in England.

TRADE

The second half of the nineteenth century was a period of rapid expansion of international markets. Population growth, rising standards of living, technical inventions, and revolutionary changes in methods of transportation (steamships and railways) were all important elements in this process, which had a profound effect upon the volume and character of Russian foreign trade. Its progress is indicated in the following table:

Russian Foreign Trade, 1860–1900

Years	Exports	Imports
	Yearly average in million gold rubles	
1861–1865	225.9	206.7
1866–1870	317.3	317.8
1871–1875	470.6	565.8
1876–1880	527.3	517.8
1881–1885	549.9	494.3
1886–1890	630.9	392.4
1891–1895	621.4	463.5
1896–1900	698.2	607.3

It will be noted that the rate of expansion was particularly rapid in 1861–1875; it was slowed down later by tariff restrictions and by the competition in the grain market offered by the United States and other overseas countries. Russia's share of world trade was 3.8 per cent in 1880 and 3.4 per cent in 1899; that is, practically the same as in the earlier part of the nineteenth century.[12] With the advent of railways overland trade increased in importance, and in 1896–1898 it accounted for 27 per cent of exports and 46 per cent of imports. England lost her former position of predominance in the Russian market. In 1896–1898 Germany took 32 per cent of Russian exports and supplied 28 per cent of her imports; the respective figures for England were 19 and 20 per cent; and for France 4 and 7 per cent. The United States began to show a real, if somewhat one-sided, interest in the trade possibilities of the distant empire. United States exports to Russia increased from an annual average of 6.3 million rubles, or 4.9 per cent of total Russian imports, in 1846–1848 to 54.6 million rubles, or 9.3 per cent, in 1896–1898; on the other hand, Russian exports to the United States declined from the low annual average of 2.6 million rubles, or 1.6 per cent of total Russian exports, in 1846–1848 to 2.4 million rubles, or 0.3 per cent, in 1896–1898. The principal article of United States exports to Russia was cotton; Russia shipped to the United States wool and raw hides.

The most striking development in the structure of Russian trade was the steady growth of grain exports.

[12] See p. 790.

VOLUME OF GRAIN EXPORTS, 1856–1897 *

Years	Yearly average in million poods †
1856–1860	69.3
1861–1865	74.9
1866–1870	120.0
1871–1875	181.3
1876–1880	257.1
1881–1885	269.1
1886–1890	367.9
1891–1895 ‡	377.5
1896–1897	433.9

* Wheat, rye, barley, and oats.
† One pood = 36 lbs. = 0.016 ton.
‡ Grain exports in 1892 were exceptionally low because of a severe famine. The average yearly exports for the four years 1891, 1893, 1894, and 1895 were 432.3 million poods.

Grain represented 15 per cent of the total value of Russian exports in 1836–1840, 31 per cent in 1846–1850, and about 50 per cent from 1871 to the end of the century. Russia's international credit position and her ability to meet her large commitments abroad came to depend on the sale of her grain, irrespective of the price level and of the state of domestic supplies. In 1851–1855 2.7 per cent of the grain produced was shipped to foreign lands, in 1861–1865 4.6 per cent, in 1871–1875 9.1 per cent. From 1875 to 1897 the ratio (average for five-year periods) of grain exports to production fluctuated within the narrow margin of 14 to 16 per cent. There were, of course, deviations from these averages. The highest point was reached in 1888, when 17.6 per cent of the grain produced was exported; the lowest, in the famine year 1892, when it fell to 8 per cent. The grain trade was carried on chiefly through the southern ports. The consignment from the Baltic ports (St. Petersburg and Libau) and over the European land frontier of more than half of the grain exported in the 1870's and the early 1880's was a temporary diversion due to the uncertainties of the Near East situation and the Turkish war. In 1865–1870 66 per cent, and in 1886–1890 64 per cent, of grain exports were shipped from the ports of the Black Sea and the Sea of Azov; in 1891–1895 77 per cent was shipped from these ports. Odessa, Nikolaev, Rostov, Taganrog, and Novorossisk were the chief centers of the grain trade.

Among the principal changes in Russian imports was the increase in purchases of cotton yarn, steel, iron, and metal goods. In 1855–1860 Russia bought 7.5 million rubles worth of machines per year; in 1876–1880 she bought 51.0 million.

The tariff policy of the imperial government in the 1850's and the 1860's was inspired by liberal principles, a welcome change from the oppressive protectionism of the Kankrin era. The tariff act of 1857 removed a number of import prohibitions and substantially lowered the rates of duty, especially those on machines, industrial raw materials, and semi-manufactured goods. Even after the two 10 per cent rises decreed in 1859 and 1861 tariff rates did not exceed 16 per cent ad valorem. Almost all export prohibitions were removed in 1864, and the tariff act of 1868 reduced the duty rates to a very moderate level. The immediate object of this liberal policy was fiscal. It was hoped that encouragement to imports would yield a substantial increase in customs revenue and relieve the pressure on the ruble. This object, however, was not achieved. The adverse balance of trade in the early 1870's contributed to the depreciation of the ruble in terms of foreign currencies, and made it difficult for Russia to meet her financial obligations abroad. Industrialists, of course, were clamoring for protection. The government, moreover, was anxious to replenish its gold reserve in view of the approaching war with Turkey. In 1877 custom duties were made payable in gold instead of in paper rubles, a measure equivalent to an increase of the tariff by 30 to 50 per cent. In June, 1880, iron and pig iron were removed from the free list; at the same time rates on metal articles were raised. A flat 10 per cent upward revision of rates on all dutiable articles was ordered in December, 1880. Russia thus gradually reverted to a policy of protection which was to become more ruthless under Alexander II's successors.

Little factual information is available on the Russian domestic trade of this period. Its turnover, however, is believed to have been several times that of foreign trade, and was tentatively estimated by V. I. Pokrovsky at 4,442 million rubles in 1898. Of this amount 923 million rubles were spent on manufactures and textiles; 880 million on grain and flour; 612 million on tea, coffee, sugar, and groceries; 188 million on coal, firewood (used for fuel in every Russian household), and building materials; 186 million on vodka, wine, and beer; 180 million on cattle, meat, game, eggs, and vegetables. Approximately 492,000 persons were engaged in domestic commerce in 1867 and 832,000 in 1899.

Some 400,000 commercial enterprises with an aggregate capital of 20.3 million rubles were operating in 1898. There were 14,000 licensed itinerant merchants in 1867 and 33,000 in 1898-1899, but the number of persons actually engaged in this kind of commerce was probably considerably larger. Consumers' cooperative societies made their appearance in 1865; in 1897, however, there were only 307 cooperative stores, including 56 in rural localities. Improvement in communications, especially the development of a network of railways, tended to deprive some 2,700 fairs of their former significance; trade, once quasi-monopolized by the fairs, was gradually diverted to less picturesque but more regular channels. Fairs, of course, did not disappear, and some of them, for instance the great Nizhni-Novgorod fair, continued to play an important part in the machinery of distribution until the end of the empire.

FINANCE

The government of Alexander II, like its predecessors, struggled in vain to bring some order out of the chaos of Russian finance. Poverty and economic backwardness were obstacles formidable enough to tax the ingenuity of statesmanship and expert knowledge, neither of which was to be found among the St. Petersburg bureaucracy. The task of financial rehabilitation was rendered hopeless by the mounting cost of military adventures: the Crimean War, the Polish insurrection, expansion in central Asia, and the Turkish war of 1877-1878. The taxpayers of the 1950's need not be reminded that war is an expensive business. Russia could certainly ill afford the wars waged under Alexander II.

Some of the financial reforms—establishment of the State Bank, unification of the budget, legislation dealing with private banks—were both beneficial and long overdue. The immediate reason for the founding of the State Bank was the crisis experienced in 1857-1859 by the state-owned banks. The government had borrowed from these institutions, especially during the Crimean War, large amounts (in 1857 indebtedness under this heading exceeded, according to Khodsky, 500 million rubles) which were used to defray current expenditures or were reloaned to the nobles on the security of their estates. In July, 1857, as a measure of economy, the rate of interest on deposits was lowered from 4 to 3 per cent. The depositors retaliated by mass withdrawals of funds; the banks, being short of liquid assets, found themselves on the verge of bankruptcy. The crisis was overcome through a series of intricate credit transactions, but it led to the liquidation of the state-owned banks. In their place was established in May, 1860, the State Bank, which took over the assets and liabilities of the defunct institutions. Its statutory object was the promotion of commerce and the stabilization of the ruble, although its capital was merely 15 million rubles and it had no control over the issue of paper currency. The State Bank nevertheless became, especially after the amendment of its charter in 1897, the central financial institution of the empire.

In January, 1862, Reutern was appointed minister of finance, an office he held for sixteen years. His program of economic reconstruction comprised, in addition to the building of railways, the revision of budget procedure and of the tax system, the creation of private banks and, above all, the stabilization of the ruble by linking it to precious metals. The reform of the budget enacted on May 22, 1862, and put into effect on January 1, 1863, was prepared by a committee under V. A. Tatarinov, who had made a study of financial administration in western Europe. Previous to 1862 Russia had no budget in the accepted meaning of the term; important sources of revenue were administered independently by various departments over which the ministry of finance had no control. The annual confidential summaries of revenue and expenditure compiled by the minister of finance were grievously incomplete and often misleading. The legislation of 1862 achieved the important object of creating a single treasury and of centralizing the accounts of all departments in the ministry of finance. The methods of audit, although purely bureaucratic, were vastly improved. The budget, from 1863, and the reports of the state controller, from 1866, were made available to the public. These were real technical improvements, but they could not, of course, check the arbitrariness in spending public money inherent in an autocratic regime. The budgets and reports of the minister of finance, moreover, had a strong tendency towards over-optimism, and at times contained questionable figures that failed to give a true picture of the financial situation. S. A. Greig, Reutern's successor at the ministry of finance, mournfully admitted in his report to the tsar in 1878 that "our government and our financial administration are among the most costly in the world."

The tax system, in spite of the incessant labors of various committees, underwent few modifications. The only changes worth mentioning were the substitution in 1863 of excise for the farming-out of the tax on spirits (a measure decided upon as far back as 1854) and the abolition in 1880 of the salt tax. The treasury leaned heavily on indirect taxation, which in 1880 represented 69 per cent of the total revenue. Excise on spirits accounted for 31.5 per cent (138 million rubles) of revenue from all sources in 1869, and for 34.5 per cent (228 million rubles) in 1879. The poll tax held first place among direct taxes. In 1869, when the revenue from direct taxes was 83 million rubles, the poll tax yielded 38.5 million, or 46 per cent, and in 1879 52 million rubles out of 117 million. The main burden of the land tax was borne by the peasantry. The average rate of the land tax paid by the peasants exceeded that of "private landowners" by approximately 20 per cent; the difference between the two rates was much greater in some localities, especially if redemption payments are taken into account. In the early 1890's, for instance, in certain counties of the province of Novgorod the assessment per dessiatine of land "owned privately" was 8 copecks, and that of the peasants 90 copecks (including redemption payments). Needless to say, the poorer classes paid a disproportionately large share of the indirect taxes. Expenditures provided for by the state budget increased from 432 million rubles in 1863 to 563 million in 1870, and to 793 million in 1880, but in only five years during the period 1855-1881 were the accounts closed, at least nominally, without a deficit. War and other "extraordinary" expenditures were not included in the budget. The cost of military and naval establishments consumed much of Russia's meager financial resources. In 1860 appropriations for the armed forces were 129 million rubles, or 36 per cent of total expenditures. The budget of 1881 provided 226 million rubles for the ministry of war and 17 million for the ministry of education. Little wonder that the soldiers who fought in Europe and Asia for the cause of Russia's imperial greatness were mostly illiterate.

Reutern was keenly interested in the promotion of private banking, which was practically non-existent in Russia prior to the 1860's. By 1879-1880 Russia had 126 savings banks with deposits of 7 million rubles, 278 municipal banks with deposits of 188 million rubles, 33 joint-stock commercial banks with a capital of 93 million rubles, 92 societies for mutual credit whose discount and loan operations in 1879 reached 114 million rubles. In 1865, in a village in the province of Kostroma, was founded the first loan and savings association; in 1882 there were 727 such associations with a membership of 202,700 and a capital of 14.5 million rubles. Mortgage loans being discontinued by the government with the closing of state-owned banks in 1859, some 20 joint-stock banks and associations for mortgage credit were established in the 1860's and the 1870's. The growth in the volume of banking transactions may be gauged from the following figures for 1855 and 1879: discount of bills, 93 million and 417 million rubles; short-term loans on securities and movable property, 10 million and 271 million rubles; long-term mortgage loans, 650 million and 853 million rubles. Private banks were active in promoting industrial enterprises. In 1879, according to V. I. Pokrovsky, Russia had 566 joint-stock companies with a capital, chiefly of Russian origin, of 757 million rubles. The great flow of foreign investments in Russian industrial enterprises did not begin until the closing decade of the nineteenth century.

The cost of the Crimean War was estimated at 800 million rubles and that of the Turkish war at 1,000 million. Vast sums were spent on the construction of railways. The budget was seldom balanced, and then merely on paper. Taxation could not provide the large amounts urgently needed by the treasury. There was no alternative except borrowing and the use of the printing press. Under these conditions the stabilization of currency had little chance of success. The Crimean War, it will be remembered, was instrumental in defeating the earlier attempt at stabilization. In 1855 the volume of paper rubles in circulation rose to 356 million and in 1858 to 733 million, while the reserve fund [13] declined from 152 million to 142 million. Convertibility was suspended, and in 1862 the paper ruble was quoted at 87 metal copecks. Reutern, a firm believer in stable money, addressed himself to the problem with more zeal than wisdom. The proceeds of a loan of £15 million, successfully floated in England early in 1862, were applied to the redemption of paper currency. Convertibility at rates fixed in advance by the treasury was restored on May 1, 1862, but the operation was so unskillfully planned that it had to be discontinued in August, 1863, after most of the proceeds of the loan had passed into the hands of currency speculators. In 1864 the volume of paper money declined to 637 million rubles, but the reserve fund sank to 68 million, the lowest point in twenty years. Reutern, however, blaming (it would seem without sufficient justification) the Polish insurrection for the failure of his financial maneuver, was not discouraged, and proceeded patiently to build up the reserve fund. In 1874–1876 the volume of

[13] See pp. 787–788.

paper money, which had been steadily mounting, was kept stable at 797 million rubles, while the reserve fund rose in 1875-1876 to 231 million, a level never attained before. In the meantime the paper ruble continued to fluctuate from the low point of 76 metal copecks in 1867 to 87 copecks in 1875. The Turkish war of 1877-1878 brought the inevitable setback. Reutern vainly argued in his report to the emperor in October, 1876, that financially Russia was unprepared for the conflict and that a declaration of war would create almost insurmountable obstacles to the payment of interest on her large foreign loans, would wipe out the achievements of the last twenty years, and would retard her economic development for at least two generations. His laments fell on deaf ears. In the summer of 1878 Reutern resigned without having achieved his major object, the stabilization of currency. By 1880 the volume of paper rubles in circulation rose to 1,162 million, the reserve fund declined to 173 million, and the paper ruble was quoted at 63 metal copecks. The regime of paper currency was to continue for another seventeen years.

Borrowing was used even more extensively than the printing press. The total national debt, according to Professor P. P. Migulin, increased from 2,180 million gold rubles in the late 1850's to 6,046 million in 1881.[14] Of the latter amount 812 million rubles were railway loans guaranteed by the government. According to another estimate, the total foreign debt of Russia in 1880 was 1.169 million rubles. The rate of interest on loans was from 4 to 5 per cent but, since the price of issue was substantially below par (in some cases as low as 67 for 100), the actual cost to the treasury was considerably higher, and varied from 5.5 to 7 per cent. Commissions charged by foreign bankers, moreover, were exorbitant, reaching 10 per cent on some of the railway loans. The country had to shoulder the burden. Appropriations for the service of the public debt kept pace with the growth of the budget and in 1860-1880 represented, roughly, from one-fourth to one-third of total expenditure.

RUSSIAN CAPITALISM

The Russia of Alexander II was, both socially and economically, in the stage of transition from *ancien régime* to capitalist society. Many

[14] Loans being issued in paper and metal rubles and in foreign currencies, their reduction to a common denominator presents great technical difficulties. The margin for error is considerable, and figures given in the text are mere approximations.

features of the old order appeared almost unchanged, yet under the pressure of economic and social forces they were gradually superseded by relationships of a novel type, a process which was to gain momentum in the decades to come. Reflecting in the late 1890's on the slow rate of progress of Russian capitalism, Professor Tugan-Baranovsky, an eminent and thoughtful historian, ascribed it to *nekulturnost* (a term of which Russians are fond, meaning literally "lack of culture," but better translated, perhaps, as "crudeness" or "lack of cultural tradition and civilized habits"). The capitalist evolution of the tsarist empire was still too little advanced to warrant broad generalization, nor should it be forgotten that the birth of modern society has been, in every country, difficult and painful. Tugan-Baranovsky's observation, nevertheless, is suggestive and fruitful, and it helps to explain not only the period he wrote about but other phases of Russian history as well.

CHAPTER XXXV

ALEXANDER II

Europe, America, and Asia

THE TREATY OF PARIS

A quarter of a century of Russian foreign policy is epitomized by the Congress of Paris (1856) and the Congress of Berlin (1878), the two great international events at the beginning and at the end of Alexander II's reign. Although both congresses, and the treaties they framed, dealt primarily with the perennial eastern question, their deliberations and decisions reflected with considerable accuracy the alignment of Powers and the broad trends of European politics. The liquidation of the Crimean War was the most urgent task inherited by Alexander II from his predecessor. As has already been stated, the fall of Sevastopol in September, 1855, did not terminate hostilities, the *coup de grâce* being administered to Russia three months later by Austria, her partner in the Holy Alliance.[1] The two imperial councils, which under the chairmanship of Alexander discussed the Austrian ultimatum, agreed with but one dissenting voice that Russia could not continue the war with any chance of success. It was rightly believed that the rejection of the Austrian demands would merely prolong the agony and bring even more exacting terms from the allies. Kiselev, arguing in favor of immediate peace negotiations, stressed the state of unrest in Russian borderlands: pro-Swedish sympathies in Finland; profound discontent in the southwestern provinces annexed from Poland; and the eagerness of the Poles to rise as one man against the Russian rule the moment an opportunity presented itself. Prospects of a tolerable peace were enhanced by dissensions among the allies. As is usually the case, the members of the coalition, after having

[1] See p. 871.

achieved their main purpose, drifted apart. Crimean victories, in the opinion of Napoleon III, offered France full vindication for the defeats of 1812–1815, and both the emperor and French opinion showed coolness towards Palmerston's plans for the further humiliation of Russia and the ruin of her position in the Near East. The British government, on the other hand, would have nothing to do with Napoleon's proposal for the restoration of an independent Poland. In the autumn of 1855 Paris made overtures to St. Petersburg through indirect channels. It was intimated that the interests of France and Russia were basically identical and that Napoleon was only too anxious to secure for the defeated enemy "peace with honor." Alexander nursed for a while the naive illusion that the failure of crops in France would lead to a revolution in that country ("Former revolutions have always begun in this manner," he wrote to Michael Gorchakov in October, 1855, a quaint rule that presumably did not apply to Russia), but French advances were too tempting to be ignored, even though Nesselrode put little faith in Napoleon's profession of friendship and offer of good services. It soon appeared that his suspicions were unfounded.

The Congress of Paris met on February 25, 1856, N.S. It was attended by the representatives of France, Britain, Sardinia, Turkey, Austria, and Russia. Prussia, whose pro-Russian sympathies Palmerston resented, was invited to participate in only the closing sessions of the congress, when the Straits convention of 1841, of which Prussia was a signatory, came up for revision. The Russian delegation was headed by Prince A. F. Orlov and Brunnow, the French by Count Alexander Walewski, who presided; the English by Lord Clarendon, the Austrian by Buol, the Sardinian by Count Camillo di Cavour. Both Napoleon and Palmerston were actively engaged in pulling the strings behind the scene. The broad lines of the peace settlement were determined in advance by the four-point program formulated by the allies in Vienna and by the supplementary conditions laid down in the Austrian ultimatum.[2] These terms having been accepted by Russia in January, the task of Orlov and Brunnow was somewhat limited: they endeavored to give the allied program the most lenient interpretation and to prevent its modification to the detriment of Russian interests. Whatever success they achieved was due largely to the friendly support of Napoleon and Walewski, who sustained Russian objections to the more

[2] See pp. 870–871.

extreme demands made by Clarendon and Buol. Anti-Russian feeling in England was still running high; the prevailing British attitude was well expressed by Lord Ripon when he referred to Russia (in 1854) as "that great, grim, shadowy power which sits brooding over Europe and Asia, and of which no man knows really whether it be strong or weak." Palmerston, however, would take no chances, and vigorously pressed every point detrimental to the tsarist empire. For instance, he urged the congress to investigate the validity of the Russian title to the territories on the eastern shore of the Black Sea, with the ultimate object of proclaiming the independence of the Caucasian peoples, a proposal which Orlov and Walewski succeeded in defeating. Yet the support lent to Russia by France was delicately molded so as not to give undue offense to London or to impair the Anglo-French alliance. The final settlement embodied in the Treaty of Paris (March 30, 1856, N.S.), while less harsh than it might have been in view of Russia's inability to resume the war, was unpalatable enough, especially to the nationalistic-minded Russians.

By virtue of this treaty all occupied territories were restored, Sevastopol being "exchanged" for Kars, but Russia was forced to cede to Moldavia a strip of southern Bessarabia bordering on the Danube "to safeguard the freedom of navigation" on that river, which was open to all nations. The Sublime Porte was "admitted to participate in the advantages of the public law and system of Europe." The signatory Powers undertook "to respect the independence and territorial integrity of the Ottoman empire," to consider any violation of this obligation "as a question of general interest," and in case of any "misunderstanding" between one of them and Turkey to resort to mediation before having recourse to the use of force. The treaty paid a high tribute to the sultan's recent *firman* (decree) providing religious and legal equality for all Turkish subjects, and renounced on behalf of the signatory Powers the right to interfere, collectively or severally, in the domestic affairs of the Porte. Although the *firman* was euphemistically described in the treaty as "emanating spontaneously" from the sultan's "sovereign will," it was actually exacted from the padishah by Stratford de Redcliffe four days before the opening of the Congress of Paris, and was never made effective. The "ancient rule" concerning the closure of the Straits to warships was retained; the Black Sea was neutralized, its ports and waters being thrown open to merchantmen of all nations but prohibited "in perpetuity" to men-of-war. Russia and Turkey were thus deprived of the right to maintain navies in the Black Sea or arsenals on its shores. Moldavia and Wallachia remained under Turkish suzerainty, their privileges and immunities being jointly guaranteed by the signatory Powers. Serbia was given a similar status but, unlike the Danubian principalities, continued to be garrisoned by Turkish troops. A special convention attached to the treaty bound Russia to maintain no military or naval establishments on the Aland Islands. The congress concluded its work with the celebrated Declaration of Paris dealing with maritime law.

The Russian delegation claimed as a great success the fact that the Polish question, although raised several times by Napoleon and Clarendon in private conversations with Orlov, was never brought before the congress. Prospects of a Franco-Russian *rapprochement*, however, were dampened by the disclosure that Britain, France, and Austria signed on April 15, 1856, N.S., a secret convention binding them to treat as a *casus belli* any infringement of the Treaty of Paris. The convention was unmistakably directed against Russia, and the unfortunate impression it created in St. Petersburg was but partly offset by the fact that its contents were confidentially disclosed to Orlov by Walewski and that Napoleon was profuse in the expression of his reluctance to enter into a commitment which he represented as the mere fulfillment of a pledge given in 1854.

The end of the war was universally welcomed in Russia, even though the treaty offered little gratification to Russian *amour propre*. The abandonment of the Christian population of the Ottoman empire to the tender mercy of the Turks was deplored by the slavophiles, but their lamentations met with no response in official circles. Orlov wrote from Paris (February 19) that the interests of the Danubian principalities were "a question of purely secondary importance," and Nesselrode held (March 3) that "Moldavia and Wallachia have given so many proofs of their ingratitude for the benefactions obtained for them at the price of Russian blood that no more Russian blood should be shed on their behalf." The cession of a slice of Bessarabia and the neutralization of the Black Sea, however, were thorns in the flesh of Russian officialdom and of nationalistic groups. The Russian manifesto announcing the signature of peace dwelt on the imaginary benefits secured for the Turkish Christians and contained veiled references to forthcoming domestic reforms. The Treaty of Paris, curiously, was almost equally unpopular in England, where it was decried by statesmen and hissed by the London populace.[3]

RAPPROCHEMENT WITH FRANCE

Several major themes are discernible in Russian European policy during the quarter-century following the Congress of Paris. Two of them were born of the 1856 treaty: the determination to throw off the shackles of the Black Sea neutralization and to recover the ceded portions of Bessarabia. Friction with France and England over Poland, repercussions of Russian territorial expansion in the Far East and in central Asia, and the intensification of Russia's interest in the Balkans were other important factors in determining her place in the alignment of Powers and her part in European affairs. Moreover, Alexander II and his advisers never succeeded, in spite of many bitter lessons, in entirely freeing themselves from the tradition of the Holy Alliance. Addressing the diplomatic corps in February 20, 1855, two days after his accession, Alexander II proclaimed his allegiance to the principles of the foreign policy followed by Alexander I and Nicholas I. "These principles," he said, "are those of the Holy Alliance. If this alliance no longer exists, the responsibility is certainly not my father's." The predatory Austrian moves in the closing months of the Crimean War would seem to have dispelled the last illusions of the St. Petersburg court. The tripartite alliance, according to a confidential Russian memorandum of April 5, 1856, "was no more; the influence it enjoyed in Europe has been destroyed by Austria's conduct." Yet the conservative tradition linking the governments of St. Petersburg, Berlin,

[3] "The condition of England's happiness in the nineteenth century, and the cause of that peculiar belief in 'progress' as a law of history which cheered the Victorian mind, was the fact that we were not engaged in any great war for a hundred years after Waterloo," writes G. M. Trevelyan. "The Crimean War (1854-56) was no exception. It was merely a foolish expedition to the Black Sea, made for no sufficient reason, because the English people were bored with peace, in spite of the flood of pacific talk in which they had indulged three years before at the time of the Great Exhibition at Hyde Park. The bourgeois democracy, played upon by its favorite newspapers, was worked up to a crusading ardor on behalf of the Turkish rule over the Balkan Christians, which, in the following generation the same forces, when led by Gladstone, precisely reversed. We fought the Crimean War on the principle of limited liability and broke it off when the desire for foreign adventure had been satisfied. It is a fact in our social history that foreign policy was becoming less of a mystery of statesmen and more of an interest of the people at large. Whether statesmen or people have been most foolish is perhaps difficult to say."— *English Social History* (Longmans, Green and Company, Ltd., London, 1942; copyright, 1942), p. 548.

and Vienna refused to die. It was formally revived in the "three emperors' league" of 1873 and again in 1881, after the stormy interlude of 1877–1878.

Throughout the reign of Alexander II the conduct of Russian foreign affairs was officially in the hands of Prince Alexander Gorchakov. Born in 1798, Gorchakov spent his life in the diplomatic service, conducted preliminary peace negotiations in Vienna in 1854–1855, succeeded Nesselrode as minister of foreign affairs in April, 1856, was made vice chancellor in 1862 and chancellor in 1867. A man of uncertain abilities, ambitious and vain, Gorchakov owed much of his international reputation to his long tenure of office and to his unsurpassed mastery of diplomatic French, which he skillfully used to clothe his most trivial pronouncements with a semblance of importance and dignity. Some of his epigrams and dictums are classic examples of the subtle art of appearing to say much when really saying nothing—for instance, his celebrated statement in a circular note of August 21, 1856: "La Russie boude, dit-on. La Russie ne boude pas. La Russie se recueille." It would be idle to seek a definite political program or deep convictions behind the easy flow of Gorchakov's elegant and often witty, if somewhat pompous, verbiage. "What one often mistook in Europe for his policy," writes Baron Boris Nolde, "was in reality but a series of improvisations which manifested themselves in phrases rather than in actions. Granville described him once as the 'immense talker.' This characterization should be retained by the historian." Final decisions concerning Russian foreign affairs, moreover, rested with the tsar, not with the chancellor, and although Gorchakov enjoyed the confidence of Alexander there were other influences at the Russian court which at times proved stronger than that of the titular head of the ministry of foreign affairs.

The Crimean War and the Treaty of Paris generated in Russian official circles a profound hatred for England and Austria. Palmerston, prime minister of Great Britain until his death in October, 1865 (except for the brief interval February, 1858, to June, 1859), fully reciprocated Russian feelings. The execution of the Treaty of Paris proved an arduous task, Palmerston maintaining throughout this trying period, as he had during the Congress of Paris, a militantly anti-Russian attitude. When the Russians attempted, in tracing the new frontier of Bessarabia, to interpret the loose wording of the treaty in a sense favorable to themselves, the British fleet was peremptorily dispatched to the

Black Sea, a move that alarmed Constantinople as much as it did St. Petersburg.[4] Hostility towards England and Austria drew Russia closer to Prussia and France. The proceedings at the Congress of Paris paved the way for a Franco-Russian *rapprochement*, which was favored by Gorchakov and by Kiselev, Russian ambassador to France. Alexander, however, inclined to closer cooperation with Prussia, distrusted Napoleon, and disliked the latter's "revolutionary" methods. The tsar's uncle, Prince William of Prussia (prince regent since 1857), who became King William I in January, 1861, was active in fostering anti-French sentiment at the Russian court. In the 1850's, 1860's, and 1870's obstacles to the proposed Franco-Russian alliance proved insurmountable. Napoleon was eager to win Russian support in his intricate game of international politics, but his overtures to the tsar were subordinated to the exigencies of the Anglo-French alliance, which followed an eventful course. The French emperor was prepared to endorse Russian claims for the abrogation of the obnoxious provisions of the 1856 treaty; he demanded in exchange, however, the revision of the treaty of 1815 and considerable latitude in redrafting the map of Europe, policies that fitted ill with Alexander's legitimism and conservatism. The insoluble Polish question, moreover, was a constant threat to the entente between Paris and St. Petersburg. Nevertheless there was in 1856–1859 an ostentatious display of Franco-Russian friendship. The respective ambassadors of the two countries in St. Petersburg and in Paris were recipients of flattering attention. In September, 1857, Alexander and Napoleon conferred for three days at Stuttgart. The meeting, however, was held under a cloud: the Russian empress had refused to meet Empress Eugénie, a discourtesy which, according to Kiselev, grieved the consort of Napoleon III. The French emperor, moreover, unwisely pleaded with the tsar the case of Poland, a *démarche* interpreted by Alexander as a personal insult. Although the practical consequences of the Stuttgart conversations

[4] According to Palmerston, the Turkish request for the withdrawal of the British fleet was "an act of impertinent folly" and "the basest treachery." He was even less complimentary, if possible, about the Russians. "How mean, how unworthy, how disgraceful it is for a Power whose territory stretches from the White Sea to the Black, from Behring's Straits to the Baltic, to be throwing away its reputation (if it ever had it) for good faith and for a sense of honour and self-respect by haggling and bargaining for a few thousand souls (bodies they ought rather to call them, though the tyranny of the government is such that the poor people cannot as the saying runs, call their souls their own) and a few square miles of useless land." Bell, *op. cit.*, II, 164, 166.

were slight, Gorchakov described them to Bismarck as exceeding all expectations and as a "historical event." The French hopes for a closer understanding with Russia were further dampened by the fact that from Stuttgart Alexander went to Weimar, where he met Emperor Francis Joseph of Austria.

In spite of these setbacks the efforts of the advocates of Franco-Russian cooperation (Napoleon, Walewski, Gorchakov, Kiselev) were not entirely sterile. In enforcing the Treaty of Paris Napoleon, as Queen Victoria put it, left it to Great Britain "to act the part of the executioner, while he acted that of the generous victor." France and Russia concerted their policies in the Danubian principalities. The union of Moldavia and Wallachia was opposed by Palmerston, Austria, and the Porte on the ground that a new unified Danubian state would be likely to fall under Russian domination. Vienna, moreover, apprehended the effects of the union upon the large group of Rumanians within the Austro-Hungarian borders. Napoleon, realizing the importance to France (in the impending struggle with Austria) of a friendly Danubian state, espoused the cause of the union (which Russia favored chiefly because it was opposed by England and Austria), and took the leading part in the establishment of the principality of Rumania (1858–1866).[5] He also supported Russian policies in Serbia, where the pro-Austrian Prince Alexander Karageorgevich was deposed by a local assembly (December, 1858) and was succeeded by the pro-Russian Milosh Obrenovich. French and Russian intervention on behalf of the Montenegrins, who rose against the Turks and inflicted upon them a severe defeat at Grahovo (May, 1858), not only saved the insurgents from the probable effects of their dangerous victory but even led to the revision of the Montenegrin boundaries in a sense favorable to the Black Mountain. Napoleon's immediate objective, in which he partly succeeded, was to win Russian support for his Italian policy. By a secret treaty of March, 1859, the St. Petersburg government bound itself to maintain friendly neutrality towards Paris in case of a Franco-Austrian war. The war fought by France in alliance with Sardinia actually broke out in April, and the massing of Russian troops on the Austrian frontier facilitated the rapid French victory,

---

[5] For the spurious arguments and derisive tactics used by Palmerston and, especially, by Stratford de Redcliffe in opposing the union of the principalities, see R. W. Seton-Watson, *A History of the Roumanians* (Cambridge, 1934), pp. 248–258.

although Alexander refused to carry out a similar military demonstration against Prussia. Gratifying as the defeat of Austria was to the tsar, he was alarmed by its consequences, particularly by the overthrow of the ruling houses of Tuscany, Parma, Modena, and Naples, developments incompatible with the maintenance of the principle of legitimism and the 1815 treaties. Napoleon's political maneuvers, inconsistent as they often were, were on the whole too heavily tinged with sympathy for national and liberal movements to inspire confidence in St. Petersburg, where Prussian influence was strengthened with the arrival of Bismarck, Prussian ambassador to Russia from 1859 to 1862. In October, 1859, at a Warsaw conference attended by the tsar and the Russian ambassadors to London, Paris, Berlin, and Vienna, Kiselev vainly pleaded for a formal Franco-Russian alliance. Nevertheless a new *rapprochement* between St. Petersburg and Paris took place in the spring of 1860, when the French government supported Gorchakov's proposal for the concerted action of the Powers to enforce the fulfillment by the Porte of the obligations it had assumed, under the Treaty of Paris, towards its Christian subjects. A conference on the eastern question held in the French capital in the summer of 1860, however, concerned itself chiefly with the situation in Syria, where massacres of Christians had occurred, and the conference sanctioned the occupation of that country by the French. A Russian proposal for a collective *démarche* of the Powers on behalf of all Christian populations under Turkish rule was rejected; Russia, this time, was not supported by France and was opposed by Great Britain.

Secret negotiations concerning a common policy in the Near East were still pursued by Kiselev in Paris, but they came to naught. Alarmed by the events in Italy, the Russian government was unsparing in its criticism of Victor Emmanuel and Garibaldi, and blamed Napoleon for fostering Italian liberal and national aspirations. When in September, 1860, Sardinian troops, without a declaration of war, occupied the Papal States, the Russian mission was withdrawn from Turin and diplomatic relations with the unified kingdom of Italy were not established until August, 1862. Fear of revolutionary and national uprisings in Hungary, Galicia, Russian Poland, and the Balkans and the belief that these movements were instigated by England and France drew St. Petersburg, Berlin, and Vienna closer together. The Warsaw meeting between Alexander, Francis Joseph, and the prince regent of Prussia in October, 1860, was properly regarded in Paris, in spite of

Gorchakov's protestations, as a grave setback to the Franco-Russian *entente*. With the rising tide of discontent in Poland, the pro-Polish attitude of Napoleon and of French public opinion added to the tension. In the middle of 1862 the Francophile Kiselev was recalled and was succeeded at the Russian embassy in Paris by Baron Andrew Budberg, a diplomat of the Nesselrode school and an adherent of the tradition of the Holy Alliance. At the request of the new ambassador the French consul-general in Warsaw, Ségur, was ordered home for alleged secret dealings with subversive Polish groups. On the eve of the Polish insurrection in January, 1863, Franco-Russian relations had greatly deteriorated.

EUROPE AND THE POLISH INSURRECTION

The reaction of the western world to the Polish insurrection was one of deep sympathy for the Poles. Bismarck, prime minister of Prussia since September, 1862, however, hastened to offer St. Petersburg his country's assistance in the struggle with the rebels. A Russo-Prussian convention of February 8, 1863, N.S., authorized Russian troops in pursuit of the insurgents to cross into Prussian territory. It was believed in European chanceries that the convention was a prelude to a full-fledged military alliance. Napoleon at once offered to join Great Britain in a protest to Berlin, but Palmerston and the British foreign secretary, Earl Russell (formerly Lord John Russell), countered with the proposal for a joint representation to *"le grand coupable,"* that is, Russia, a step Napoleon at first hesitated to take. In spite of Queen Victoria's passionate opposition to British intervention in Polish affairs, Russell dispatched to St. Petersburg on March 2, N.S., a sharply worded note in which he branded the Russian action as a violation of the treaties of Vienna and urged the tsar to grant full amnesty to the insurgents and to restore in Poland the political regime instituted by Alexander I. This peremptory request, as was to be expected, was rejected by St. Petersburg, except that a partial and conditional amnesty was offered to the insurgents in the imperial manifesto of March 31. After a hasty exchange of views between London, Paris, and Vienna, the three governments presented to St. Petersburg on April 17, N.S., simultaneous but not identic notes. The British note elaborated the argument advanced in Russell's previous communication; the French made no reference to the 1815 treaties but lamented the effects of Polish disorders on the peace of Europe; the Austrians emphasized the probable repercussions of the uprising in Galicia. The three governments, however, were unanimous in urging the termination of bloodshed in Poland. In his lengthy replies Gorchakov refuted all charges of Russian responsibility for the outbreak and expounded the view that the insurrection was the work of international revolutionaries whom it was in the interest of all Powers to suppress. In the meantime Napoleon and Palmerston invited other European governments and the United States to intercede with Russia on Poland's behalf. The invitation was declined by the United States, who would have nothing to do with the disputes of the Old World, by Prussia, and by other German courts; Switzerland and Belgium also replied in the negative because of their special status as neutral states. Spain, Sweden, Italy, the Netherlands, Denmark, Portugal, and Turkey, however, complied with the Anglo-French request and made appropriate representations to St. Petersburg. Pope Pius IX, grieved by the fate of Catholic Poland, sent a personal letter to the tsar. This meek demonstration of quasi-European solidarity had no effect upon the policies of St. Petersburg. On June 17, N.S., Great Britain, France, and Austria sent to Russia separate notes outlining a six-point program for the solution of the Polish problem.[6] By that time, with the insurrection well under control, Gorchakov curtly refused to admit any interference by the Powers in the relations between Russia and Poland; he proposed, however, the consultation of states directly interested, that is, Russia, Prussia, and Austria. Napoleon's final move for the convocation of a European congress found no support, even in London.

Napoleon and Palmerston had persevered in their well intentioned but unwise course, in spite of repeated warnings from the French and the British ambassador to St. Petersburg that the Anglo-French policy was irresponsible and courted disaster. "The revolt is spreading on the hope of foreign intervention," the British ambassador Lord Napier wrote on May 17, N.S. "If the English government do not mean to fight, let them say so, and stop the loss of life and suffering attendant on a rising which, unaided, cannot succeed." The truth of the matter is that neither Napoleon, hopelessly involved in his Mexican expedition, nor Palmerston was prepared to go to war; and when it became

[6] The Powers demanded general amnesty; a national government in accordance with the constitution of 1815; access of Poles to public offices; freedom of conscience and removal of restrictions imposed on the Catholic Church; exclusive use of the Polish language in the administration, the courts, and the schools; army recruitment regulated by law.

clear that Russia would not yield to diplomatic pressure they abandoned Poland, as on so many previous occasions, to her unhappy fate.

The principal consequence of this inglorious diplomatic episode was the further estrangement of Russia from France and England and the paving of the way for the Russo-Prussian alliance which was to dominate the European scene for thirty years. Of lesser moment, but nevertheless important, was the severance of diplomatic relations between Russia and the Holy See. Incensed by the Holy Father's denunciations of the persecution of Catholics in Poland, St. Petersburg, in the late spring of 1864, recalled its ambassador to Rome. An exceptionally violent altercation of the Russian chargé d'affaires, Baron F. K. Meyendorff, with Pope Pius (December, 1865) led to the break in diplomatic relations and was followed by the abrogation of the concordat (imperial decree of November 27, 1866).

INTERVENTION IN GREECE AND RUMANIA

In spite of the tension produced by the Anglo-French diplomatic intervention of 1863, Russia, Great Britain, and France succeeded in coordinating their action in Greece, which since its establishment as an independent state was under the joint "protection" of the three Powers. Agreement on a common policy in Greece was at times difficult to achieve. King Otto feared the expansion of Russian influence in the Balkans; his consort, the former Princess Amalia of Oldenburg, however, took pride in her connection with the reigning family of Russia and became eventually the guiding spirit of the Orthodox party, which desired to put on the Greek throne an Orthodox sovereign, a proposal that commended itself to St. Petersburg. The Crimean War was regarded in Athens as an opportunity for the aggrandizement of the Hellenic kingdom, and even as a chance for the ejection of the Turks from Europe and for the restoration of the Byzantine empire. Greek attempts at organizing uprisings of Christian populations under the Turkish rule, however, were nipped in the bud by the occupation, in May, 1854, of the Piraeus by the French and English troops, which were not withdrawn until February, 1857. In the meantime the government of King Otto, heavily in debt to the Protecting Powers and incapable of cooperating with liberal opinion, which became particularly restless with the success of the liberation movement in Italy, was drifting towards its doom. In October, 1862, a revolution forced the king and the queen to flee from Greece on board a British warship.

Although the fall of Otto was not unexpected, the choice of his successor raised a number of thorny questions. According to engagements entered into by the Protecting Powers in 1827–1832, the members of their reigning families were excluded from the Greek throne. Moreover, a treaty of 1852 between the Protecting Powers and Greece embodied the provision of the Greek constitution of 1844 which required that the successors to the Crown must profess the Orthodox religion. In spite of these commitments the Russians, suspecting that London coveted the Greek Crown for Prince Alfred, the second son of Queen Victoria, supported the candidature of the Duke of Leuchtenberg who was related to the Russian dynasty. An understanding, however, was soon reached, and the Protecting Powers informed the Greek provisional government (December 13, 1862, N.S.) that the members of their royal houses were not eligible to the vacant throne. This declaration notwithstanding, the Greek national assembly elected Prince Alfred (December 6–15, N.S.), ratifying the election in February, 1863. In accordance with the policy agreed upon by Russia, England, and France, Alfred refused the proffered Crown, and after several other candidates (King Ferdinand of Portugal, Duke Ernest II of Saxe-Coburg-Gotha, the Duke d'Aumale, Archduke Ferdinand Maximilian Joseph of Austria) declined or were found wanting, the choice of the Protecting Powers fell on Prince William of Denmark. William signified his acceptance, was unanimously elected by the Greek national assembly (March 30, 1863, N.S.), and assumed the name of George I.[7] The new king was a Lutheran, but it was stipulated simultaneously with his election that his successors should profess the faith of the eastern Orthodox Church, a condition on which Russia particularly insisted. Russia, England, and France took official cognizance of the deposition of the Bavarian dynasty in Greece (protocol of May 27, 1863, N.S.) and by the Treaty of London (July 13, 1863, N.S.) the Protecting Powers and Denmark recognized the succession of George I and the union with Greece of the Ionian Islands, which had been conquered by Great Britain in 1809–1814 and had manifested a

---

[7] William was the second son of Prince Christian of Schleswig-Holstein-Glücksburg, who in November, 1863, became King Christian IX of Denmark. In March, 1863, Christian's daughter, the future Queen Alexandra of England, was married to the Prince of Wales; in October, 1866, his other daughter, Princess Dagmar (known in Russia as Maria Fedorovna) became the consort of the future Emperor Alexander III. In September, 1867, King George I of Greece married the Grand Duchess Olga, a niece of Emperor Alexander II.

desire to take their place among the territories of the Hellenic kingdom. The whole involved international transaction was wound up by the Treaty of London of March 29, 1864, N.S., concluded between the Protecting Powers and Greece. Recapitulating a number of previous agreements, the treaty officially established the Hellenic kingdom as a constitutional monarchy under King George I and under the guarantee of Great Britain, France, and Russia. The Greek imbroglio was thus peacefully solved by negotiations and mutual concessions, probably because the conflict of interests of the great Powers in this part of Europe was more imaginary than real.

It proved more difficult to arrive at a satisfactory compromise in 1867–1869, when the Greek question again threatened the peace of Europe. The outbreak of a revolt in Crete, an island under the rule of the sultan, was used by Russian agents in Turkey to foster discontent among the Christian populations. Gorchakov, in concert with France, the German confederation, and Italy, urged the Porte to transfer Crete to Greece (April, 1867) while the Russian Mediterranean fleet was busy maintaining the liaison between the rebellious islanders and the Hellenic kingdom, which supported the insurrection. England, however, having taken a stand against any weakening of the Ottoman empire (although London recognized the necessity of improving the position of the Christian population in Crete), the Russian proposal was rejected by Constantinople. Meanwhile the uprising was suppressed with great ruthlessness, and in December, 1868, the Porte sent Greece an ultimatum demanding the cessation of assistance to the insurgents. Athens refused and the Greek coast was threatened with blockade by a Turkish fleet commanded by a retired British officer, Hobart Pasha. A conference of great Powers hastily summoned in Paris in January, 1869, advised King George to comply with the Turkish terms. Gorchakov concurred in this decision and pressed upon the king of Greece the necessity of accepting Turkish demands. George had to follow the unpalatable course prescribed by the great Powers. Peace was preserved, Crete received some degree of self-government, but the vagaries of Russian policy proved costly to the Cretans and did not add to Russia's prestige in Athens.

In the Danubian principalities, as in Greece, international rivalries were entangled with the dynastic questions. In February, 1866, Prince Alexander Cuza, ruler of both Moldavia and Wallachia since 1859, was forced to abdicate. A local national assembly elected Prince

Charles of Hohenzollern-Sigmaringen, son of a former prime minister of Prussia, to succeed Cuza. The election was of questionable validity because the choice of the assembly was restricted, by a convention of August, 1858, to a native of the principalities. Nevertheless Russia's demand for severe measures against Rumania (as the Danubian principalities became officially known after their union in July, 1866) was not supported by England, France, and Prussia. The Porte recognized the rights of Charles and his descendants to the Rumanian throne in October, 1866, but Russia withheld recognition for two years.

RUSSIA AND THE UNIFICATION OF GERMANY

In the 1860's, however, the focal point of diplomatic activity was not the Balkans, but southwestern and central Europe, where the growth of the national movement led to the unification of Italy and of Germany. Alexander and Gorchakov took advantage of these developments to achieve some of their own purposes. It was a fixed principle of Bismarck's policy, even before he became prime minister, to prevent a Franco-Russian alliance unless it was enlarged to include Prussia as a third member. Gorchakov had favored such a tripartite alliance, but the resentment created in St. Petersburg by the French diplomatic intervention of 1863 forced the abandonment of this plan. Mindful of Berlin's friendly attitude during the Polish crisis, the Russian government drifted towards an ever closer collaboration with Prussia in spite of the fact that the personal relations between Gorchakov and Bismarck, once so cordial, threatened to become almost openly hostile.

It is known that the series of bold strokes which resulted in the formation of the German empire was, in its initial stage, the personal policy of Bismarck carried out with persistency and determination in spite of the opposition of King William I, Crown Prince Frederick (afterwards Emperor Frederick III), the Prussian house of representatives, liberals, and many conservatives. The struggle for the possession of Schleswig and Holstein was the first major move towards the attainment of Bismarck's aim. Lord Russell, referring to the Schleswig-Holstein question, wrote that "nothing is more embarrassing and more intricate than it, if examined in detail" (December 28, 1863, N.S.). In 1848 Emperor Nicholas I, in concert with England and France, prevented the separation of the duchies from Denmark.[8] The integrity

[8] See pp. 856–857.

of the Danish monarchy was thus preserved; but in the course of subsequent negotiations with the great Powers King Frederick VII of Denmark undertook to safeguard the autonomous political institutions of the duchies, to secure equal treatment of their German and Danish inhabitants, and to abstain from any step towards the administrative incorporation of Schleswig. The question of King Frederick's successor proved particularly troublesome. After much diplomatic bickering and erudite, if inconclusive, probing of the historic titles to Schleswig-Holstein claimed by various reigning houses, the five great Powers (Russia, England, France, Austria, and Prussia) and Sweden concluded with Denmark the Treaty of London (May 8, 1852, N.S.) which settled the entire succession to the Danish Crown (including the two duchies together with Lauenburg, which had shared their fate since the Congress of Vienna) upon Prince Christian of Glücksburg, his consort, and their male issue. It was, however, only under strong diplomatic pressure that Austria, and especially Prussia, acceded to the Treaty of London in the framing of which the Russian representative Brunnow took a prominent part.

The Treaty of London, "in some of its consequences beyond all doubt one of the most unfortunate achievements of European diplomacy" (according to Sir A. W. Ward), became the source of interminable complications and failed in its ultimate object, the preservation of the integrity of the Danish monarchy. Denmark, Schleswig-Holstein, the German confederation, Austria, and Prussia, were all dissatisfied, although for different reasons, with the regime established in 1852. The representative assemblies ("estates") of Holstein complained that Denmark infringed upon their constitutional prerogatives; the German confederation watched the situation closely and from 1858 on threatened Denmark with "federal execution," that is, the occupation of Holstein by federal troops until Denmark had agreed to make the administrative changes deemed equitable by the confederation. The Danes meanwhile pursued an increasingly intransigent policy. A Danish royal charter (March 30, 1863, N.S.), precursor of the new constitution, incorporated Schleswig, reducing it to the status of a Danish province; the same charter imposed heavy financial burdens on Holstein, which, however, was allowed to retain its administrative autonomy. A wave of indignation swept over the Germanic world, and although neither Prussia nor Austria favored the emancipation of the duchies the two great German Powers, competing for the favors of the minor German states, bowed to public opinion and somewhat reluctantly assumed the leadership of the movement for drastic action against Denmark. On July 9, 1863, N.S., the federal diet sent to Denmark an ultimatum demanding, under threat of "federal execution," the withdrawal of the March charter. Denmark refused, and the diet decided to proceed with punitive measures (October 1, N.S.). The death of King Frederick VII of Denmark (November 15, N.S.) and the accession, in accordance with the Treaty of London (1852), of Christian of Glücksburg under the name of Christian IX complicated the situation. Christian at once put into force the constitution announced by the March charter; the federal diet retaliated by sending Hanoverian and Saxon troops into Holstein, which they occupied without meeting any resistance (December, 1863).

At this juncture a sharp cleavage in the attitude of the German states towards the Schleswig-Holstein question became apparent. Prussia and Austria, both of them signatories of the London treaty, recognized Christian as the duke of Schleswig-Holstein and ostensibly insisted on merely the fulfillment by Denmark of the 1852 agreements, while the smaller German states clamored for the establishment of the duchies as a sovereign state under Prince Frederick of Augustenburg, whose father in 1852 had renounced, although in somewhat ambiguous terms, his title to Schleswig-Holstein. The Austro-Prussian policy being unpopular in Germany, the federal diet refused to continue "federal execution" in support of the 1852 regime (January, 1864). Prussia and Austria then took the matter in their own hands, sent Denmark an ultimatum demanding the repeal of the November constitution and, when this was refused, declared war on Denmark. Schleswig and Holstein were overrun by the Austro-Prussian troops within a few weeks. Foreign assistance, which had saved Denmark in 1848, was not forthcoming this time. A conference of the Powers, signatories of the 1852 agreements, met in London but broke up without results. By the Peace of Vienna (October 27, 1864, N.S.) Schleswig, Holstein, and Lauenburg were ceded by Denmark to Prussia and Austria. Their ultimate fate was still to be decided and was finally settled within the framework of the broader issue, the struggle between Prussia and Austria for supremacy in the Germanic world. The Austro-Prussian convention of Gastein (August 14, 1865, N.S.), by which Prussia was to administer Schleswig and Austria was to administer Holstein, proved a mere stopgap. Bismarck used the breathing space thus provided to improve Prussia's international position before striking the final blow. He reached an understanding with Napoleon, concluded an alliance with Italy, and in June, 1866, proceeded to occupy Holstein on the pretext that Austria had violated the Gastein convention. There followed a brief war between Prussia and Austria, the former fighting in alliance with Italy, the latter with several German states. In spite of the poor showing of the Italian troops, Prussia won a rapid and decisive victory; an armistice was concluded on July 22, N.S., preliminaries of peace were signed at Nikolsburg four days later, and by the Peace of Prague (August 24, 1866, N.S.) Prussia acquired Schleswig-Holstein and certain other German territories, while Venice was awarded to Italy. The most significant consequence of the war was the exclusion of Austria from the German confederation and the formation of a new north German confederation whose armed forces and foreign relations were placed under the control of Prussia.

In these momentous events, which altered the balance of power and transformed the political map of central Europe, Russian diplomacy had an indirect but important part. It will be remembered that the various Prussian moves outlined above were largely the personal policy of Bismarck, carried out in the face of strong opposition both at home and abroad. The attitude of the western Powers was, to a certain extent, conditioned by that of St. Petersburg, and a timely display of leadership and firmness by Alexander and Gorchakov might have frustrated Bismarck's ambitions by aligning France and perhaps England against Prussia. Russian diplomacy, however, showing little consistency, vision, or courage, unwittingly facilitated the unification of Germany under Prussia, which it was probably in the Russian interest to prevent. London, Paris, and Vienna vied with St. Petersburg in ineptness, shortsightedness, and facile optimism. Russia was one of the principal sponsors of the regime established in Schleswig-Holstein in 1852 and was therefore committed to the maintenance of the integrity of the Danish monarchy. Gorchakov, although suspicious of Bismarck, was at first unaware of his ultimate object—the annexation of the duchies. In November, 1863, the Russian foreign minister defended "federal execution"; in January, 1864, he approved the invasion of Schleswig and Holstein by Austria and Prussia and intimated his intention to concentrate Russian troops in Finland if Sweden came to Denmark's assistance. Yet Gorchakov still believed that the separation of the duchies from Denmark should be resisted, fearing that their independence might lead to the formation of a unified Scandinavian state inimical to Russia. At the abortive London conference (April–June, 1864) the Russian representative Brunnow pleaded for the fulfillment of the 1852 agreements and, when it became clear that Prussia and Austria were resolved to terminate the allegiance of the duchies to the Danish Crown, Brunnow pressed the claims to Schleswig-Holstein of the Duke of Oldenburg, to whom Emperor Alexander II, as the titular head of the house of Holstein-Gottrop, had transferred his hereditary rights. In Berlin, in June, 1864, the tsar told Bismarck that he was opposed to the annexation of Schleswig and Holstein by Prussia; nevertheless no protest was raised in St. Petersburg when four months later Denmark ceded these provinces to Prussia and Austria.

As relations between the two great German Powers deteriorated, the Russian government manifested pro-Prussian sympathies, even though Gorchakov criticized Bismarck's proposal for the revision of the German federal constitution by the Frankfort diet; in the opinion of the Russian foreign minister the constitution of the German confederation established by the Congress of Vienna could not be altered without the consent of all great Powers. During the brief Austro-Prussian War Russia remained neutral, but her government showed uneasiness when the nature of the peace terms Bismarck intended to impose upon Austria became known. At the very time when the preliminaries of peace were signed at Nikolsburg, St. Petersburg, reviving a proposal made by France and England before the outbreak of the Austro-Prussian War and accepted at the time by Prussia, urged the convocation of an international conference. Bismarck, however, demurred and he had little difficulty in persuading the Russians to drop their proposal. Gorchakov feared the strengthening of Prussia and the unification of Germany; Alexander was particularly distressed by the deposition of several German dynasties necessitated by the Prussian annexation of Hanover, Hesse-Cassel, and Nassau, and by the curtailment of the sovereign rights of the other German states under the new federal constitution. The unilateral action of Prussia, the tsar believed, was a violation of the principle of legitimism and of the 1815 treaties. General Schweinitz, the Prussian military attaché in St. Petersburg, told Alexander that King William could not, without provoking a revolution, renounce the fruits of his victory or permit the intervention of foreign Powers in German affairs; he added that if the Powers persisted in their demand for a conference Bismarck would seek an alliance with the militant German nationalistic groups and with the forces of discontent in the neighboring countries, that is, in Hungary and Poland. General Manteuffel, Prussia's special emissary to St. Petersburg, and King William, in his letters to the tsar, argued that Prussia was the last stronghold of the monarchical principle in Europe, which was undermined by the mere existence of petty and weak dynasties. A strong Germany under Prussia, it was held, was the best safeguard against the spreading of revolutionary agitation. The tsar was not entirely convinced, yet he assured William that under no condition "would Russia join the enemies of Germany" (letter of July 31, 1866). There was another aspect of the negotiations that influenced the attitude of the Russian government. Gorchakov told Manteuffel that while he did not demand at that time the abrogation of the obnoxious provisions of the Treaty of Paris, he would expect Prussian support whenever a favorable opportunity for their repeal presented itself. Alexander made a similar statement to Manteuffel which he charged him to transmit to King William.

The Franco-Prussian War provided the opportunity Gorchakov so anxiously awaited. Between 1866 and 1870 the *rapprochement* between St. Petersburg and Berlin made further progress. Austria, excluded from the German confederation, showed increased interest in her Hungarian and Slavic provinces and in the Balkans. In 1867 the Hapsburg state became the dual Austro-Hungarian empire. Its chancellor, Baron (afterwards Count) Frederick Beust, a personal enemy of Bismarck, endeavored to reach an understanding with Napoleon, thus indirectly contributing to the closer cooperation between Russia and Prussia. Ostentatious manifestations of Russo-Prussian friendship were not lacking. In June, 1870, William and Alexander, accompanied by Bismarck and Gorchakov, conferred at Ems. Assurance that Russia would not side with the enemies of Prussia and would neutralize any Austrian move to assist France encouraged Bismarck to pursue a daring and provocative policy which was made possible by Napoleon's blind obstinacy and arrogance. On July 19, 1870, N.S., France declared war on Prussia. Less than six weeks later Napoleon, after suffering several major defeats, was captured at Sedan, the third empire was overthrown by a revolution, and a provisional government of national defense was formed in Paris (September 4, N.S.). The war nevertheless continued until the middle of February, 1871. It was terminated by the Treaty of Frankfort (May 10, 1871, N.S.), which transferred Alsace and Lorraine to Germany, and imposed on France a heavy indemnity. In the meantime the unification of Germany had been completed, King William of Prussia being proclaimed emperor of Germany in the Gallery of Mirrors of the Versailles Palace (January 18, 1871, N.S.).

REVISION OF THE TREATY OF PARIS

Immediately after the outbreak of the Franco-Prussian War the Russian government announced its decision to maintain neutrality, provided Austria-Hungary would do the same. The French minister of foreign affairs, Duke de Gramont, was informed that if Austria should attack Prussia, Russia would attack Austria. In August, 1870, Gorchakov, on the invitation of the British secretary of state for foreign affairs, Lord Granville, signed with Great Britain, Italy, and Austria a pact which bound the four Powers not to abandon neutrality without serving notice on the other cosignatories. Under this arrangement Austria and Italy could not intervene on behalf of France without previously informing Russia. Close understanding with Prussia, the success of the German armies, and the state of confusion prevailing in Europe created a situation that was judged opportune by Gorchakov for exploding the diplomatic bombshell he had carefully prepared. On October 31, 1870, N.S., three days after Marshal Bazaine's capitulation at Metz, the Russian chancellor sent to the Powers, signatories of the Treaty of Paris (1856), a note repudiating the Black Sea provisions of that treaty. Gorchakov argued that the Russian action was justified on two grounds: (1) *de jure*, because the treaty had been violated in several of its essential clauses (specific reference was made to the unification of Rumania and to admission of warships in the Black Sea); and (2) *de facto*, because it was inadmissible that "the security of Russia should depend on a fiction which had not stood the test of time." The Russian announcement provoked a diplomatic crisis of the first magnitude, although a change in the status of the Black Sea had long been anticipated. Palmerston had told General Ignatev and Brunnow that the restrictive provisions would not last more than ten years.[9] Gladstone, prime minister in 1868–1874, had consistently opposed the neutralization of the Black Sea as an indefensible affront to Russia. Beust, who held that the Black Sea clauses placed Russia "in a situation unworthy of a great Power," had proposed in 1867 the convocation of a conference to remove the disability. King William of

[9] *The Cambridge History of British Foreign Policy*, III, 45.

Prussia in 1866 and Bismarck as recently as September, 1870, had assured Alexander of their full cooperation in bringing about the amendment of the Treaty of Paris according to Russia's wishes.[10] It was the attitude of Prussia, coupled with the success of the German army, that decided the Russian government to issue the declaration of October 31, N.S., even though Bismarck, informed of the contents of the note when it was still on its way to European capitals, considered the time inopportune and vainly pleaded for a deferment.[11]

The real reason for the hostility abroad to the Russian move was not any opposition to the abrogation of the Black Sea clauses, which were regarded as inequitable and, in the long run, unenforceable, but objection to the procedure adopted by Gorchakov. The unilateral repudiation of an international agreement was incompatible with Russia's traditional defense of legitimism and sanctity of international treaties; moreover, the position taken by the Russian chancellor was palpably inconsistent: he repudiated certain clauses of the Treaty of Paris, on the ground that the treaty had been previously violated, but at the same time proclaimed his adherence to the other clauses. The Powers concerned, especially England, protested vigorously and refused to accept the *fait accompli* which, it was held, not without exaggeration, threatened the very foundation of the international order. A breach of diplomatic relations between Russia and England appeared imminent for a time, and Brunnow, Russian ambassador to London, urged the withdrawal of Russian deposits from English banks. Granville's stern note of protest to Gorchakov, however, ended with the conciliatory statement that the British government "would not have refused to examine the question in concert with the co-signatories to the treaty." There followed an outburst of diplomatic activity. Lord Odo Russell was sent by Granville to Versailles, where he conferred with Bismarck. The German chancellor made no secret of the fact that he did not object to the abrogation of the Black Sea clauses, although he disapproved of the timing of the Russian move and of the procedure chosen by St. Petersburg. He would do nothing, however, to antagonize Alexander and Gorchakov, who continued to render Prussia valuable services by declining Granville's proposal to participate in the formulation of peace terms acceptable to neutrals, or to bring pressure on Berlin to refrain from the annexation of Alsace and Lor-

[10] S. Goriainow, *Le Bosphore et les Dardanelles* (Paris, 1910), pp. 154, 162.
[11] *Ibid.*, p. 167.

raine. Bismarck, nevertheless, suggested an international conference, and after some further bickering this face-saving device was accepted by all the governments concerned. Gorchakov, probably under the influence of Brunnow, who took a pessimistic view of the situation, adopted a conciliatory tone without, however, abandoning the Russian demands. He assured Granville that all that Russia really wanted was "the abrogation of a theoretical principle without immediate application." To make things more palatable to England and the other Powers, the invitation to the conference was sent "on the express understanding that it should be in no way prejudiced by any previous assumption as to the result of its deliberations."

The seven-Powers conference (Russia, Germany, Austria-Hungary, France, Great Britain, Italy, and Turkey) met in London in January, 1871. The German plenipotentiary, Count Albrecht Bernstorff, a personal friend of the Russian delegate Brunnow, was instructed by Bismarck to work in close cooperation with his Russian colleague. The conference began its labors by issuing a pusillanimous declaration to the effect that international engagements could not be modified "unless with the consent of the contracting Powers by means of an amicable agreement." Brunnow signed the declaration only after referring it to Gorchakov and on condition that it would not operate retroactively. This bit of diplomatic *chinoiserie* safely out of the way, the conference settled down to its real business, the ratification of Russia's unilateral repudiation of the Black Sea clauses. By the treaty of March 13, 1871, N.S., the pertinent articles of the Treaty of Paris were abrogated; the principle of the closing of the Bosphorus and the Dardanelles was maintained but the sultan was given authority to open them in time of peace to warships of friendly and allied Powers "in case the Sublime Porte should judge it necessary in order to secure the execution of the stipulations of the treaty of Paris"; the other provisions of the 1856 treaty were "renewed and confirmed." Both Russia and Turkey were thenceforth free to maintain navies in the Black Sea and fortifications and arsenals on its shores. Russian *amour propre* was gratified, and Gorchakov was rewarded with the title of Highness. The other consequences of Russian diplomatic victory were less pleasing. The improvement in Russo-Turkish relations which Gorchakov had professed to anticipate failed to materialize. Gladstone and Granville were bitterly attacked in the British parliament and press for a shameful surrender to Russian threats. Anti-Russian feeling in England, which had subsided after the Crimean War, again ran high. Russia, moreover, did not avail herself at once of her newly recovered freedom to rearm in the Black Sea. Hardly any warships were launched in these waters in the next few years, and during the Russo-Turkish War of 1877–1878 naval operations played an insignificant part.

ALLIANCE OF THE THREE EMPERORS, 1873

The events of 1870–1871 marked an important stage on the road of Russo-Prussian cooperation. "Prussia will never forget that she owes it to you that the war has not assumed extreme dimensions," William telegraphed to Alexander announcing the signature of the preliminaries of peace with France. "I am happy that I was in a position to prove to you my sympathy as a devoted friend," the tsar replied. "Let the friendship uniting us assure the happiness and glory of our two countries." On the day when the German troops made their triumphal entry into Paris, Alexander was appointed honorary colonel of the Prussian grenadiers of the guards; simultaneously William and his generals were recipients of high Russian military honors. In spite of the friendly trend of Russo-Prussian relations, Bismarck was still haunted by the fear of a possible alignment of Russia and Austria-Hungary with France. The surest method to foil the dreaded combination was to bring both empires definitely within the German political orbit. Gorchakov, too, was suspicious of Bismarck, and felt uneasy about the rapid reconciliation between Berlin and Vienna and the rumors of an impending Austro-German alliance. Changes in the Viennese government favored the *rapprochement* of the three imperial courts. Beust, heartily disliked in both St. Petersburg and Berlin, was dismissed in the autumn of 1871; Count Julius Andrássy, a Magyar and a former opponent of Russia who had been reconciled to the necessity of collaboration with that country, became minister of foreign affairs. Bismarck assured Vienna that he had no designs on the German provinces of the Hapsburg Monarchy and encouraged her to seek compensation in the east for recent territorial losses. Andrássy, on the other hand, persuaded Gorchakov that Austria-Hungary was vitally interested in the preservation of the Ottoman empire and did not wish, as it was rumored, to annex Bosnia and Herzegovina. The sincerity of these statements was doubted in influential Russian circles led by Ignatev, Russian ambassador to Constantinople, but Gorchakov accepted them on their face value. In his report to the tsar for 1873 the

Russian chancellor, after paying a personal tribute to Andrássy, voiced his conviction that for the time being "the political situation and the interests of Austria-Hungary" offer a guarantee of her desire to maintain the *status quo*. Gorchakov admitted at the same time that the dual monarchy, as a great Power bordering on Turkey and comprising a large Slav population, had legitimate interests in the welfare of the Christian subjects of the sultan. This admission was an important departure from Russia's traditional attitude as the sole protector of the Slavs under Turkish rule. The willingness to conciliate the rival Russian and Austrian claims in the Balkans made possible the alliance of the three emperors which Bismarck was striving to achieve.

The *rapprochement* of the three imperial courts was brought about gradually. In August, 1871, the emperors of Germany and Austria-Hungary conferred at Ischl. In June, 1872, a group of Austro-Hungarian officers headed by the Archduke William attended Russian army maneuvers near St. Petersburg, where they were given a warm reception. In September the tsar, at his own request, was invited to visit Berlin at the same time as Francis Joseph. In April–May, 1873, William was Alexander's guest at St. Petersburg, and in June the tsar paid a state visit to Vienna, his first appearance in the Austrian capital since the Crimean War. In February, 1874, Francis Joseph returned the Russian emperor's visit. On each occasion the monarchs were accompanied by their ministers of foreign affairs.

The revival of the Holy Alliance in the guise of the alliance of the three emperors is usually identified with their meeting at Berlin. Although the Berlin conversations, in the words of Gorchakov (letter to Brunnow of September 11, 1872, N.S.) produced "no positive engagements that would modify our freedom of action, . . . nothing for the diplomatic archives," their "moral result was immense." William's visit to St. Petersburg led to the conclusion of the secret Russo-German convention (May 6, 1873, N.S.) which stipulated mutual military assistance in case Russia or Germany were attacked by another European Power. A month later (June 6, N.S.), during the stay of the tsar in Vienna, Alexander and Francis Joseph affixed their signatures to the quaintly worded secret convention of Schönbrunn which professed to ensure the unity of action of the two emperors, irrespective of changes that might occur in the composition of their governments. The monarchs bound themselves not to allow any divergency of interests in "special questions" that may arise to prevent them from adhering to, and if necessary enforcing, "the principles of a higher order (*les considérations d'un ordre plus élevé*) which they regard as essential to the protection of the peace of Europe from any subversive attempts (*bouleversements*)." In case of aggression by a third Power, the contracting parties agreed to seek common understanding, not to conclude outside alliances, and if necessary to make arrangements for joint military action. On October 22 N.S., Emperor William acceded to the Schönbrunn convention. Both conventions (May and June) could be denounced on serving a two-year's notice.

The realignment of the Powers evidenced by the cordiality in the relations of the three emperors was a political factor of paramount importance; it was interpreted as a return to the principles of the Holy Alliance of the pre-Crimean era, and as an attempt to maintain the *status quo* through the concerted action of the three conservative courts. The most notable feature of the new European situation was the reconciliation of Germany and Russia with Austria-Hungary. Relations between Russia and Germany were not appreciably affected by the developments of 1872–1873.

If the international significance of the *entente cordiale* of the three emperors is clear, the practical usefulness of the two conventions of 1873 is open to serious doubt. The Russo-German convention of May 6, N.S., was the handiwork of the military, not of the diplomats. Bismarck, fearing its repercussions on the relations between Germany and Austria-Hungary, refused to countersign it. "What precise meaning and how much significance should be attached to this convention it is impossible to estimate without more evidence than is at present available . . . ," writes Sumner. "The Russian foreign office seems to have left the convention pigeon-holed . . . and the tsar, who was always vague about engagements, seems to have forgotten it. At any rate it played no part in the succeeding years, during which no reference appears to have been made to it." It was specifically abrogated, however, by the treaty of June 18, 1881 N.S.[12] The Schönbrunn convention, the only written basis for the "three emperors' league," is properly characterized by Sumner as "jejune and vague"; according to the same author, "Russian and Austrian archives have not yet revealed any specific reference to action being taken under the convention in the following years." [13]

[12] Sumner, *op. cit.*, pp. 91–92.
[13] *Ibid.*, p. 90.

Alexander II 973

The frailty of an alliance based on commitments so ill defined and broad as those of the Schönbrunn convention was demonstrated in the spring of 1875, when the diplomatic world was disturbed by persistent, albeit unwarranted, reports of Germany's intention to launch a "preventive" war against France. Throughout the crisis Andrássy maintained an attitude of utmost reserve, while Gorchakov uncautiously assumed the part of the champion of France and of European peace and, characteristically, did not resist the temptation to claim credit for averting the imaginary conflagration. This diplomatic incident brought to a head the latent hostility between Gorchakov and Bismarck, and subjected the "three emperors' league" to a severe strain.

SALE OF ALASKA

In the nineteenth century St. Petersburg was gradually awakening to the fact that Russia was not only a European but also an Asiatic Power. European affairs remained the chief preoccupation of Russian diplomacy, yet the potential significance of the Pacific area and of the Asiatic continent could no longer be ignored. The problems of these distant and little known regions, however, were envisaged primarily from the standpoint of European politics. In the reign of Alexander II the two principal developments of Russian eastern policy were the liquidation of Russian colonies in North America and the acquisition of vast territories along the Amur River and in central Asia.

Russian expansion in North America brought the tsarist empire into close geographical proximity with the United States. The two countries, however, had no economic or political interests in common, except for their traditional antagonism towards England. Edward Stoeckl, Russian minister to Washington, expressed the view of his government when he held that "the United States in rivalry with Great Britain 'was the best guarantee against the ambitious projects and political egotism of the Anglo-Saxon race.' " [14] The American Civil War and the Polish uprising of 1863 brought a temporary and superficial *rapprochement* between Russia and the United States, a *rapprochement* based in part on misunderstandings. During the Civil War England being suspected, not without reason, of favoring the Confederate States, Gorchakov hastened to assure the federal government of his sympathy with the North and with the cause of American unity. "The

[14] Foster Rhea Dulles, *The Road to Teheran* (Princeton, 1944), p. 54.

disintegration of the United States, as a Power, is, from our point of view, most undesirable," Stoeckl wrote to Gorchakov in February, 1862. "The American confederation is a counterpoise to English might and, in that sense, its existence is an element in the world balance of power." Gorchakov expressed his agreement with Stoeckl's argument, and in 1862 rejected English and French proposals for European mediation between the North and the South. A year later, as has already been stated, the United States reciprocated by refusing to participate in the collective *démarche* on behalf of Poland. In the autumn of 1863 the unheralded appearance of the Russian fleet in New York and San Francisco was acclaimed by American opinion as a tangible evidence of Russia's readiness to lend her support to the federal government in case of foreign intervention in the Civil War. This interpretation was unwarranted: Russia, fearing a war with the European Powers over Poland, was endeavoring to remove her weak fleet from the reach of the potential enemy, and sent it to America because, to quote Dulles, "there was in fact nowhere else the Russian vessels could go." American exuberance and ignorance of Russian conditions was responsible for another somewhat awkward demonstration of Russian-American solidarity. In April, 1866, a Russian revolutionary, Dimitry Karakozov, made an unsuccessful attempt to murder the tsar. In July a delegation of the United States Congress, headed by the assistant secretary of the navy, Gustavus V. Fox, arrived in St. Petersburg to congratulate Alexander on his "miraculous escape." Unfortunately the congressional address to the tsar represented Karakozov as a member of the Russian nobility seeking vengeance for the emancipation of the serfs. The Russian press took considerable pains to explain that the error was understandable and that it was the American gesture of good will, not the motives behind it, that really mattered. Imaginative Russian writers seized this occasion to picture the United States as a new "European Power" anxious to obtain Mediterranean bases to protect the Black Sea from English and French fleets and to share, in concert with Russia, in the impending partition of the Ottoman empire.

These fantastic, albeit no doubt officially inspired, speculations helped to reconcile the nationalistic-minded Russians to the unpalatable fact that the Russian flag was about to be hauled down in Alaska. The decision to dispose of the Russian possessions in America was due to economic and political considerations. Since the checking of Russian expansion on the American continent by the Monroe Doctrine and the treaty of 1824,[15] the affairs of the Russian American Company, never too prosperous, had gone from bad to worse. In spite of its monopolistic position, and perhaps because of it, the company experienced extreme financial difficulties and was hopelessly in debt to the government. In the late 1840's, with the opening of Chinese ports to foreign commerce, the company's fur trade with China, on which it largely depended, dwindled at an appalling rate, while the inferior grade of the pelts produced by the Russian colonies made it difficult for them to compete successfully with foreign furs in the more exacting western European markets. There was much inefficiency and mismanagement. Russian colonies in America, according to the report of an interdepartmental committee (May, 1863) "present a picture of complete stagnation in all matters of colonization, industry, commerce, and citizenship; in general, the Company has not justified the confidence placed in it by the government."

Political considerations in favor of the sale of Alaska were no less weighty. It was realized in St. Petersburg that the colonies could not be defended and that sooner or later they would be annexed either by the United States or by Great Britain. At the beginning of the Crimean War the belief in the inevitability of a British attack on Alaska led to the fictitious transfer, for a period of three years (May 1, 1854, to May 1, 1857), of the properties of the Russian American Company to an American company, thus putting them under the protection of the American flag. This subterfuge proved unnecessary. A convention of neutrality negotiated by the Russian American Company and the neighboring British Hudson's Bay Company was ratified by the British and the Russian governments; under this arrangement the territories held by the two companies were excluded from the sphere of military operations. "This act of magnanimity seemingly incompatible with British selfishness had a secret motive," Stoeckl wrote to Gorchakov five years later (December 23, 1859). "It was rumored at the time that we intended to sell the colonies to the United States, and it was in order to prevent this transaction that the British government ratified the convention." From 1854 on, the sale of Alaska to the United States was informally discussed by St. Petersburg and Wash-

---

[15] See pp. 690–692. A good account of the history of the Russian American Company and of Russo-American relations up to 1867, based on Russian archives, will be found in S. Okun, *Rossiisko-Amerkanskaia Kompaniia* (The Russian American Company) (Moscow-Leningrad, 1939).

ington, but action was deferred, the Russian ministry of foreign affairs insisting that, in order not to antagonize Great Britain, the matter should be postponed until the expiration of the charter of the Russian American Company on January 1, 1862.

The rumored and then actual (1862) discovery of gold in Alaska increased the apprehensions of those in St. Petersburg who, like the Grand Duke Constantine, realized that the retention of the American colonies would only lead to international complications and to Russia's eventual defeat. Considerations of a broader political nature were not overlooked. Reutern, the Russian minister of finance, argued in 1866 that by acquiring Alaska the United States "will have a common border with the British colony not only in the south but also in the northwest." This, in his opinion, "must lead to the strengthening of our friendly relations with the United States and is bound to increase the opportunities for disagreement between the United States and England." In December, 1866, the Russo-American negotiations, interrupted by the Civil War, were resumed and were conducted in great secrecy by William Henry Seward, secretary of state, and Stoeckl. By the treaty of March 29, 1867, N.S., all the properties of the Russian American Company were transferred to the United States for a payment of $7,200,000, that is, $2,200,000 more than the minimum price of $5,000,000 Stoeckl was authorized to accept. In spite of the unpopularity of the transaction in the United States, the treaty was ratified by the Senate on April 9 N.S., by a majority of 27 to 12. Studies by American historians, especially the works of Dulles, have established that the support of the Washington politicians was obtained at a price. Information from American sources shows that Stoeckl's figure of $200,000 used on "secret expenses" was probably near the mark. There was a loud outcry in the American press. Although funds to meet the purchase price were not voted by the House of Representatives until July, 1868, the United States officially took possession of Alaska on October 18, 1867, N.S.: in an elaborate ceremony at Sitka the Russian flag was hauled down and the stars and stripes hoisted in its place. Russia had withdrawn from the American continent.

There was some criticism of the cession of Alaska in the closely controlled Russian press. "Today we hear rumors of the sale of the Nikolaevsky [Moscow to St. Petersburg state-owned] railway line; tomorrow, of the Russian colonies in America," wrote *Golos*. "Who would vouch that the day after tomorrow we shall not get rumors of the sale of the Crimea, Transcaucasia, the Baltic provinces?" Censorship at once silenced the recalcitrant journal, although stringent measures were hardly necessary. To the vast majority of even educated Russians Alaska was but an empty sound and its fate a matter of indifference.

EXPANSION IN THE FAR EAST

The abandonment by Russia of her strategically indefensible and economically burdensome American colonies went hand in hand with the acquisition of important territories on the Asiatic littoral of the north Pacific. In the middle of the nineteenth century these regions were under Chinese sovereignty, but the Celestial Empire exercised little effective control over its distant, sparsely populated, and economically unimportant borderlands. Russian penetration along the Pacific shore and in the valley of the Amur was due largely to the energy and the adventurous spirit of Nicholas Muravev, governor-general of eastern Siberia from 1847 to 1861. Vested with practically unlimited powers, cut off from St. Petersburg by immense distances and lack of rapid communications, and meeting with no armed resistance on the part of the Chinese, Muravev carried out his gigantic enterprise with remarkable ease. Russian inroads into Chinese territory were at first made in the guise of trading activities by the Russian American Company, supported by a surprisingly small number of troops, in some cases less than a dozen men. In 1850 the post of Nikolaevsk was established on the Amur, a few miles from the estuary; in 1852–1853 the Russians crossed to Sakhalin Island, and then gradually extended southward their occupation of the littoral of the mainland. In 1854 a force led by Muravev sailed up the Amur and founded the city of Khabarovsk, named after a Russian seventeenth century explorer and soldier of fortune. Traders and soldiers were followed by settlers; there was ample evidence that the Russians had come to stay.

Russian encroachments on Chinese territory coincided with the outbreak of keen rivalry among the Powers for the markets of the Far East, and with the forced abandonment by China of her traditional policy of seclusion and non-intercourse with the western world. The Anglo-Chinese Treaty of Nanking (1842), which terminated the infamous Opium War, opened five Chinese ports to foreign commerce and laid the foundation of the system of extraterritoriality that was to govern the relations between China and the western Powers for decades to come. The new international regime did not work smoothly, and it was responsible for the war of 1857–1858 fought by China against England and France. The Russians took advantage of China's predicament to exact the formal cession of the territories over which they exercised a *de facto* control. In May, 1858, a local Chinese commander, yielding to Muravev's persuasions and threats, signed the Treaty of Aigun (a city on the Amur), which recognized Russian sovereignty over the left bank of the Amur from the Aigun River to the sea; put the Ussuri region (from the junction of the Ussuri River to the shore) under a joint Russo-Chinese administration; and granted Russian and Chinese nationals the exclusive right of navigation on the Amur, the Ussuri, and the Sungari. Almost simultaneously, by the Treaty of Tientsin (June, 1858), the Russian emissary to China, Admiral Count E. V. Putiatin, obtained for Russia all the privileges secured previously by England, France, and the United States. Peking, however, would not ratify the Aigun treaty, and did not concede Russian territorial claims until driven to extremes by the so-called Taiping Rebellion, the occupation of the Chinese capital by the Anglo-French troops, and the looting of the Forbidden City (1860). The Russians in the meantime continued their penetration along the Pacific littoral, where they founded, in the vicinity of the Korean border, the city of Vladivostok (July, 1860). The Treaty of Peking (November 14, 1860, N.S.), tracing the new Russo-Chinese frontier, recognized Russian sovereignty not only over the territories ceded by the Aigun treaty but also over the vast region between the Ussuri and the Gulf of Tartary, and granted Russia trading privileges in Mongolia and in Chinese Turkestan. The next year Russia, England, and France established permanent legations in Peking.

A further infringement of China's territorial integrity occurred a decade later, in connection with the Russian expansion in central Asia. A revolt against Peking in the districts of Kashgar and Yarkand, in Chinese Turkestan, brought about the occupation by the Russians of the province of Kuldja (1871). Although the occupation was ostensibly a provisional measure and the rebellion was suppressed by 1877, the Russian troops were not withdrawn. There followed complicated negotiations. By the Treaty of Livadia (1879) China ceded to Russia a large portion of Kuldja, including the Tian Shan mountain passes, but the Chinese government disavowed its envoy and refused to ratify the treaty. For a time an armed conflict between the two countries appeared likely; the matter, however, was settled by the Treaty of St. Petersburg (August, 1881) by virtue of which Russia retained a smaller slice of Kuldja than she had secured in 1879, received an indemnity of 9 million rubles, and was granted new trade privileges in China, Mongolia, and Chinese Turkestan.

Expansion in the north Pacific brought Russia for the first time in conflict with Japan. Unable to prevent Russian encroachments in Sakhalin, the Japanese were forced to agree, by a treaty of 1855, to the joint administration of the island. This arrangement, however, proved unworkable, the Russians gradually extending their settlements and crowding out the Japanese. By the Treaty of St. Petersburg (1875) Japan ceded Sakhalin to Russia in exchange for the recognition of Japanese sovereignty over the Kurile Islands, which since the end of the eighteenth century St. Petersburg had claimed as Russian territory. From the Japanese point of view the exchange was a poor bargain exacted under duress.

The expansion in the Amur and the Pacific regions was effected, especially in its early stage, against the wishes of the Russian ministry of foreign affairs. In the delicate international situation of the period before and after the Crimean War, Nesselrode, and later Gorchakov, feared the repercussions of the imperialistic schemes launched, with little regard for diplomatic niceties, by Muravev and his subordinates. Yet territorial aggrandizement in the Far East had a strong appeal to the tsar and the nationalistically-minded bureaucrats and generals. It offered the solace Russian *amour propre* craved after the defeat suffered in the Crimean War. In 1858, on the occasion of the signature of the Aigun treaty, Muravev was rewarded with the title of "Count Muravev-Amursky," although some of his lieutenants had only recently been threatened with court-martial for the unauthorized seizure of the very territories in the possession of which the imperial government now gloried. The ambition of Russian imperialism was suggested by the name of the newly founded Vladivostok, which means in Russian "Rule over the East."

EXPANSION IN CENTRAL ASIA

Russian expansion in central Asia was on a larger scale than in the Far East; the military and financial effort involved was vastly greater, and the relentless southward movement of the Russian frontier, until it reached the Afghan border, had a profound effect on Russian relations with England and therefore on the international situation.

In the middle of the nineteenth century no definite borderline existed between Siberia and the steppes and deserts of central Asia where roamed the Kirghiz (Kazakh), Turkoman, Kalmyk, and other nomad tribes. Effective Russian control extended, roughly, west and north of a curve drawn up the Ural River and along latitude 51° to the Altai Mountains. Russian penetration south of this curve began in the 1820's. In the 1830's Russian military outposts and settlers appeared in the Orenburg steppes; by 1846 they reached the Aral Sea and the mouth of the Syr-Darya (Jaxartes) River. In 1853 a column commanded by V. A. Perovsky, governor-general of Orenburg, made its way up the Syr-Darya and established the fort of Perovsk some 350 miles southeast of the Aral Sea. Simultaneously the Russians were converging on central Asia from the northeast; in 1850–1854 they occupied the Ili basin (Semirechensk) and founded on the Alma-Ata River the fort of Verny (today the city of Alma-Ata). These inroads into the Asiatic steppes brought the tsarist forces to the threshold of the settled Moslem khanates of Kokand, Khiva, and Bokhara. In the meantime the long-drawn-out resistance of the Caucasian mountaineers was overcome with the capture of Shamil (1859) and the defeat of the Circassians (1864), giving Russia complete control of the western shore of the Caspian Sea north of the Persian border.

Kokand, Bokhara, and Khiva were loosely organized, semi-feudal states engaged in endless internal feuds and wars with one another and with the turbulent nomads of the steppes. Kokand, the largest of three khanates, bordered in the east on China, in the west on Bokhara, and in the north on the territories claimed by Russia. The principal city of Kokand was Tashkent, an important trading center with a population of some 100,000 in the middle of the nineteenth century. The territory of Bokhara lay to the southwest of Kokand and comprised the ancient commercial cities of Samarkand and Bokhara, with a population of from 60,000 to 70,000 each. The khanate of Khiva occupied the lower basin of the Amu-Darya (Oxus), north of the Bokhara border. The khans of Kokand and Khiva were hereditary lay rulers, while the ameer of Bokhara was both the hereditary head of the khanate and the spiritual leader of the Moslems of central Asia.

A new chapter in the history of Russian conquest in central Asia was opened in 1864 when Colonel (afterwards General) M. G. Cherniaev was sent on the modest mission of establishing a line of forts from Perovsk to Verny. The immediate object of the expedition was attained within a few weeks with the Russian occupation of the cities of Turkestan and Chimkent. Events, however, took a turn St. Petersburg had not foreseen. In October Cherniaev stormed Tashkent but met with determined resistance and was forced to retreat. The offensive was resumed in 1865, and Tashkent fell in June; but the ameer of Bokhara having declared a holy war, the Russians proceeded to occupy a part of that khanate. In 1866 the territories seized by Russia after 1847 were annexed and became the governorship-general of Turkestan; General C. P. von Kaufman, a stern and ruthless administrator, was appointed governor-general. Meanwhile warlike operations on Bokhara continued, the city of Bokhara being captured by the Russians in May, 1868. The defeat of the two khanates terminated the hostilities, at least for a time. By a treaty of January, 1868, Kudair, the Russian-sponsored khan of Kokand, ceded to Russia the territories she occupied and accepted for the khanate the status of a Russian protectorate; a similar treaty was imposed on Bokhara in June, 1868. The turn of Khiva came five years later. In the spring of 1873 that country was overrun by Russian troops and, in spite of the courageous resistance of the Turkoman warriors, capitulated on Russian terms. Khiva ceded to the victors the right bank of the Amu-Darya, conferred exclusive privileges on Russian commerce and shipping, paid an indemnity, and became a Russian protectorate. The latter status was retained by Bokhara and Khiva until the end of the empire. Kokand fared even less well. A revolt against Kudair Khan in 1875 became a holy war against Russia and brought upon the unhappy natives punitive expeditions led by Kaufman and, later, by General M. D. Skobelev. In February, 1876, the khanate of Kokand disappeared from the map, its territory being annexed by Russia under the name of the Ferghana region.

In the 1870's St. Petersburg turned its attention to the still unconquered area extending from the eastern shore of the Caspian Sea to the frontiers of Persia, Afghanistan, Bokhara, and Khiva, a region occupied by the warlike Tekke Turkoman tribes. Krasnovodsk, a port established by the Russians on the eastern littoral of the Caspian in 1869, provided a convenient base for military operations in this arid and largely unexplored land. The Russian campaign of 1879 having ended in disaster, it was not until 1881 that Skobelev succeeded in taking by assault the stronghold of Gheok Teppe, a victory which permitted the speedy subjugation and annexation of the Turkoman country. Russian dominion was extended further south in 1884, when the tsar graciously granted the petition (exacted by appropriate pressure) of the city and region of Merv to be annexed to Russia. With these acquisitions the territorial expansion of imperial Russia was virtually closed.[16]

What were the causes of Russia's advance in central Asia and of its acceleration in the 1860's and the 1870's? The official explanation formulated by Gorchakov in the lengthy circular dispatch of November 21, 1864, may be summarized as the doctrine of historical necessity. According to this view, considerations of security and the interests of trade compel any state situated in close geographical proximity with territories occupied by warlike tribesmen to bring them under its dominion. "The United States in America, France in Africa, Holland in her colonies, England in India," Gorchakov wrote, "were all forced to take the road of expansion dictated by necessity rather than by ambition, a road on which the chief difficulty is to know where to stop." The truth of the latter statement was abundantly demonstrated by the history of Russian conquests. Gorchakov, however, conveniently forgetting his basically sound premise that one annexation was likely to lead to another, assured foreign governments (in his November dispatch) that Russia would not advance beyond Chimkent. He was unaware at the time that several weeks earlier Cherniaev had made his first and unsuccessful attempt at capturing Tashkent, a city far beyond the line approved by St. Petersburg as the limit of Russian penetration. The officially inspired theme—defense of frontiers and trade routes—was enthusiastically taken up by the nationalistic press. There were, of course, the inevitable references to Russia's "civilizing mission," although the methods employed by Kaufman, and especially by Skobelev, while not unparalleled in the colonial history of other Powers, were notable for utter disregard of the elementary rules of humanity and decency. Slavery, it is true was abolished, at least on paper, by the treaties with Bokhara and Khiva, but the newly acquired provinces remained for years notable examples of corruption and maladministration.

The popular Marxist theory, endorsed by Lenin, that Russia's ad-

[16] Russia secured in 1895 a minor rectification in her favor of the frontier in the Pamir region, and in 1898 wrung from China a lease on the Liaotung peninsula with Port Arthur, which, however, she was forced to cede to Japan in 1905.

vance in central Asia was the "inevitable" by-product of capitalist development, with its demand for colonial markets, is not in accordance with available facts. Economic considerations, while a part of the background of conquest, were not the determining factor. Russian trade with Asia increased from the 1830's to the 1860's; it remained small, however, and did not justify the cost of military expeditions and administration. The ministry of finance opposed the policy of expansion. A few enterprising merchants and industrialists were sanguine about the opportunities for lucrative concessions and high profits, but their expectations were seldom realized. "Actually the commercial and economic perspectives were widely exaggerated," writes Sumner; "most of the early Russian ventures failed; in the seventies there was much dispute as to the growth of trade with Russia, disputes much aided by the lack of accurate figures." [17] It was not until two or three decades later, with the pacification of the Asiatic possessions and the building of railways, that the economic outlook became brighter.

It is the inner logic (or what may be called the mechanics) of conquest in a primitive and distant country that offers the key to the understanding of Russian expansion in central Asia. Remoteness from the capital and the absence of rapid communications necessitated, as in the Far East, the delegation of broad powers to local administrators and made it impossible for St. Petersburg to control effectively military commanders. Empire building appeals to professional soldiers, and offers opportunities for promotion and reward. The pace of the Russian advance was intensified by the rivalry of high local administrative officials, especially Kaufman, governor-general of Turkestan (1867–1883), and the tsar's brother, the Grand Duke Michael, viceroy of the Caucasus (1863–1881); both enjoyed practically autocratic powers within the areas under their respective jurisdictions, Kaufman (like Muravev in the Far East) being granted the right to make treaties with native rulers. Less highly placed, yet influential, administrators and soldiers (for instance, Cherniaev and Skobelev) vied in zealous efforts to hoist the Russian flag over the once great Asiatic cities and to extend Russian dominion to the wilderness of steppes and mountains. The policy of the imperial government was hesitant and self-contradictory. Some of the higher bureaucrats favored expansion, others opposed it. There was, on the one hand, much satisfaction with

[17] Sumner, *op. cit.*, p. 46. Prof. Sumner gives an admirable summary of the nature of Russian expansion in central Asia (pp. 35–56).

the victories over the tribesmen which permitted the assertion of Russian supremacy in Asia; on the other hand, the danger of unduly offending English susceptibilities was realized. Gorchakov's attempts at restraining the military failed, and his efforts to placate London were only moderately successful. The tsar, subject to conflicting influences, swayed uneasily from drastic measures against his impetuous proconsuls to whole-hearted approval of annexations carried out, at times, in contravention of his own orders.

As often as not local commanders forced the hand of the imperial government by confronting it with a *fait accompli*. Tashkent was captured by Cherniaev, contrary to the instructions given him, and was annexed without reference to St. Petersburg. Gorchakov proved unable to prevent the occupation of Kuldja. In January, 1873, Russia's special envoy to London, Count Peter Shuvalov, assured Lord Granville that "the emperor not only does not wish to take possession of Khiva, but has given definite orders that such an eventuality should be prevented," and that the instructions sent to Kaufman directed him to impose on the khan terms which would make a lasting occupation of Khiva impossible. In August, however, Khiva became for all purposes a Russian dependency. Two years later Kokand was annexed, according to Sumner, against the tsar's will. Under these conditions Gorchakov's repeated assurances that each advance was the last carried little weight. It was clear that either Russian professions were disingenuous, or the imperial government was incapable of controlling its agents in Asia. The practical consequences in either case were the same.

Russian inroads in Asia were followed in England with keen interest and anxiety. A powerful group of British statesmen, publicists, and civil servants took a grave view of the situation, and suspected Russia of the most sinister intentions. Shrill voices were again raised, sounding the half-forgotten Palmerstonian battle cry of Russia's "threat to India." Sir Henry Rawlinson, influential with government circles and the general public, pleaded in his articles (reprinted in 1875 in a volume entitled *England and Russia in the East*) the necessity of stopping the Muscovites before they had entrenched themselves in Merv and had at their mercy Herat, "the pivot to the whole eastern question" and the "key to India." Although the armed invasion of India by way of Afghanistan and Persia was a mere flight of fancy, the danger of an Anglo-Russian conflict in Asia was real and, indeed, inherent in the facts of the case. Great Britain was expanding her Asiatic dominion from the south, Russia was doing the same from the north. The vast distance once separating the territories the two Powers controlled was rapidly shrinking, until in the 1870's the British lion and the Russian two-headed eagle were glowering angrily at one another across the uncertain frontiers of Afghanistan. This was a situation pregnant with dangerous possibilities. In 1865 Lord Russell attempted to negotiate an agreement delimiting the respective spheres of influence; all he obtained were vague assurances of Russia's peaceful intentions. Lord Clarendon proposed in 1869 the recognition of Afghanistan as the neutral zone between British and Russian possessions. Gorchakov accepted in principle, but the negotiations dragged on for several years because the two parties could not agree what territories should be comprised in Afghanistan. The agreement finally reached in January, 1873, was almost immediately invalidated by the subjugation of Khiva, in violation of Russian promises. Internal changes in England contributed to the tension. In February, 1874, the Gladstone administration resigned and was succeeded by the cabinet of Disraeli, with Lord Derby at the foreign office and Lord Salisbury at the India office. The change was a victory for an aggressive British foreign policy and a triumph for the so-called "forward" policy which, according to W. H. Dawson, "wished to anticipate a development of events already assumed to be inevitable and at once bind all the frontier rulers and chiefs to the British government by means of alliances, missions, and, where necessary, subsidies in the form of money and material of war." [18] The most spectacular, although by no means the most important, manifestation of "forward" policy was the proclamation of Queen Victoria as "Empress of India" (1877). The rise of Disraeli accentuated the Anglo-Russian differences in Afghanistan and strengthened the hand of those in England who regarded Russia as a menace to the vital interests of the British empire. Anti-Russian feelings reached a high pitch reminiscent of the eve of the Crimean War.

"It will always be a point of dispute how far the suspicion of Russian designs, which was diligently fostered by a powerful party in England through the 'seventies, accentuated the very danger against which it was directed," writes Dawson, and he adds that while "Russia had, of course, just the same right to approach Afghanistan from

[18] *The Cambridge History of British Foreign Policy*, III, 72.

the one side as Great Britain had from the other . . . Russian diplomacy was not as straightforward as it might have been."[19] The pessimistic predictions and vituperations of Rawlinson and his political friends were, indeed, not without effect on Russian opinion and even, perhaps, on the course of Russian expansion in Asia. In the light of English alarmist pronouncements, to which Russian nationalists tended to attach excessive importance, the annexation of the deserts and crumbling cities of Asia acquired a new and greater significance. The long drawn-out contest between the two empires, it was imagined in some Russian circles, might well be settled on the plains of Asia. "In the event of a war produced by European complications," wistfully wrote the Russian publicist M. A. Terentev, in the early 1870's, "we shall clearly be obliged in our own interest to take advantage of our proximity to India, which is afforded by our present position in central Asia." Skobelev, one of the architects of Russia's Asiatic expansion, prepared in 1876–1877, when he was military governor of the Ferghana region, detailed plans for the invasion of India. Success, in his opinion, was assured to an expeditionary corps 50,000 strong. He believed, moreover, that India was seething with discontent and that the mere appearance of even a small Russian force on her frontier "would probably lead to a general uprising in India and to the ruin of the British empire." The overthrow of the British power in India, Skobelev maintained, might well provoke "a social revolution" in the metropolis, and "will be the beginning of the fall of England." Four years later, after experiencing the hardships of the trans-Caspian campaigns, Skobelev revised his views as to the feasibility of the Indian expedition, which he no longer held practicable.

Subsequent events have proved that all speculations concerning the "threat to India" were unfounded. Rawlinson's prophecies of the invasion did not come true even though Russia annexed Merv in 1884. Friedrich Engels's dogmatic assertion (1858) that the Russian advance in Asia "will soon relegate England to a secondary place on that continent" was not borne out by history. Intrigues and serious friction in Persia and Afghanistan continued, but the long-heralded "inevitable" Anglo-Russian war in Asia is still to come.

[19] *Ibid.*, p. 75.

CHAPTER XXXVI

ALEXANDER II

Panslavism and the Eastern Question, 1875–1881

PANSLAVISM

The eastern question came to the fore in 1875 with the outbreak of an anti-Turkish revolt in Herzegovina. The far-reaching repercussions of this event, not in itself unusual in the annals of the Balkans, can be explained only in terms of the general European situation outlined above. An important new factor in shaping Russian policies was the rise of the panslav movement.

The shock of the Crimean defeat was probably one cause of the transformation of the nugatory and romantic slavophilism of the earlier period into what is known as Russian panslavism. A term covering a multitude of loosely coordinated theories and opinions, Russian panslavism is aptly characterized by Sumner as "the connecting link between slavophilism and panrussianism"; eventually the movement crystallized into "a very pronounced form of Great Russian nationalism" operating through "crude appeals to national mass emotions."[1] The panslavs were in general agreement that it was the historic mission of Russia to liberate the Slavs from a foreign religious and political yoke; they differed widely, however, as to the source of her claim to leadership and in the practical conclusions they drew from it. Ivan Aksakov, faithful to the tradition of the slavophiles, extolled Greek Orthodoxy as the only true form of Christianity and the fountainhead of the alleged supremacy of Slavic, and especially Russian, civilization. The alleged conflict between the Slavs and western

---

[1] Sumner, *op. cit.*, p. 57. This chapter owes much to Sumner's detailed and thorough study. I differ, however, from Prof. Sumner in many of my interpretations.

Europe, in his opinion, was primarily one between Orthodoxy and Catholicism, Protestantism being regarded as a relatively minor evil. Unity of faith, according to Aksakov, was the cornerstone of Slavdom's glorious future, and its advancement, the moral right and duty of Orthodox Russia. This doctrine had the political disadvantage of excluding from the fold of Slavdom not only the Poles (whom all Russian panslavs detested) but also the Czechs, the Croats, and the Slovaks unless they recanted their Catholic "heresy" and became reunited with the Russian Church, a most unlikely contingency.[2] The panslavs of the Aksakov brand, moreover, stressed Russian cultural supremacy and assumed towards the western Slavic nations a patronizing attitude which the latter, better acquainted with their own history and cultural tradition than their Russian mentors, found it difficult to accept.

The less mystically inclined Russian panslavs soft-pedaled, or even discarded altogether, the slavophile claim to Russia's religious and cultural dominance, and emphasized instead the "historic" struggle between the Slavs and western (especially German-Magyar) Europe, a struggle in which Russia, the only great Slavic Power, was called upon to play the leading part. The best known propagandists of this group were R. A. Fadeev and N. Ya. Danilevsky. Fadeev, an army officer who had seen service in the Caucasus, in Egypt (where he was in charge of the khedive's army), and later in the Balkans, formulated at length the panslav doctrine in the provocative articles *Opinion on the Eastern Question*, published in 1869 and widely read in Russia and abroad. According to his interpretation, an armed conflict between Slavdom and the West was inevitable if Russia was to fulfill her historic destiny. Russia, Fadeev argued, could not maintain her position in Europe unless she achieved the emancipation of the Slavic lands; this task could be accomplished only through the destruction of both the Ottoman empire and Austria-Hungary, and would of necessity lead to a war with Germany, committed as she was to defend German predominance in the Danubian valley. Russian victory was assured by the whole-hearted cooperation of the Balkan peoples, and

---

[2] The total Slavic population of the world at the end of 1906 was estimated in round figures as 150 million. Of this number 70 per cent were members of the Greek Orthodox Church, 23 per cent Roman Catholics, 2.7 per cent Uniats, 2.3 per cent Russian sectarians, 1 per cent Protestants, and 1 per cent Moslems. T. D. Florinsky, *Slavianskoe plemia* (The Slavs) (Kiev, 1907), p. 13.

would result in their emancipation and in the formation of a Slavic federation under Russian leadership. Similar views were expounded by Danilevsky in the celebrated study *Russia and Europe* (1869), except that the federation he proposed was to comprise, in addition to the Slavs, also the Greeks, the Rumanians, and the Magyars, and was to have its capital in Constantinople, which, under Fadeev's plan, was to be a free city. The broad lines of the panslav political program at times found support among Russian ultra-conservatives, for instance, the influential reactionary publicist M. N. Katkov, who cared little for the ideological and historical trappings of panslavism.

The significance of panslavism lies, not in its half-baked pseudo-historical schemes,[3] but in the unfortunate impression they produced abroad and in the fact that the movement became the rallying point of aggressive panrussian agitation. Virulent diatribes against the decadent West and prophecies of an impending armed struggle were not conducive to harmonious foreign relations. With the accession of

[3] A. N. Pypin, in an admirable study *Panslavism v proshlom i nastoiaschem* (Panslavism, Its Past and Present), which retains its significance although it first appeared in 1878 (reprinted in 1913), offers a keen and devastating analysis of the fallacies of the panslav doctrine. Pypin makes it clear that the basic concept of Russian panslavism—the existence of Slavdom as a coherent cultural entity inexorably moving towards close political union—corresponds to no historical reality. Unlike the Germans and the Italians, whose unification contributed to the awakening of nationalism in the Balkans, the Slavic peoples had lived for centuries knowing next to nothing of one another; they were subject to different political and cultural influences, had no common religion, no common language, no common cultural tradition. Panslavism, according to Pypin, owed its beginnings to the "archaeological discovery" of the common ethnographic and linguistic origins of the Slavs, but it ignored subsequent developments. The political and cultural tradition of the Poles, Czechs, Croats, and Slovaks was derived from western Europe, not from Muscovy. "Slavic civilization . . . ," writes Pypin, "is in no sense integrated, exceptional, peculiarly Slavic. It cannot be spoken of as we speak of the German, the French, or the Italian civilization." This being the case, the opposition of Slavdom to the "decadent" West was meaningless. Prior to the Crimean War Russian interest in "Slavic brethren" was sporadic and of little practical consequence. In the second half of the nineteenth century the Balkan Slavs, in their quest for national statehood, turned with hope to Russia, but few of them (there were exceptions) were willing to exchange the rule of the Austrians, the Magyars, or even the Turks for that of Russian autocracy. The experience of the Poles was not encouraging. Russia, Pypin held, if she was to play an effective part in the advancement of unity among the Slavic peoples, should renounce all claims to cultural and political domination and accept the principles of political freedom, religious tolerance, and linguistic and national equality. Needless to say, this was not the program of the Russian panslavs.

Alexander II, moreover, the slavophiles or panslavs (the two terms were still interchangeable) gained a measure of official recognition, partly because of the relaxation of the police regime and partly because of their more friendly attitude towards the government, especially their support of the emancipation. In 1858 was founded the Moscow Slavonic Benevolent Committee; in 1868–1870 similar committees were organized in St. Petersburg, Kiev, and Odessa. The object of the committees was to provide facilities for Slavic students in Russian theological seminaries and universities, to supply books to Slavic lands, and to disseminate panslav ideas through the preparation and publication of appropriate studies. The membership of the committees was small, and consisted of university professors, ecclesiastical dignitaries, and others interested in educational and charitable endeavor. The political orientation of the committees may be gathered from the fact that Professor Pogodin, a sample of whose nationalistic pronouncements has already been quoted,[4] was among the founders and presidents of the Moscow committee. An ethnographic map of Slavdom issued by the St. Petersburg committee failed to list Ukrainian among the Slavic languages, an omission characterized by Pypin as "odd and indecent." At the Slavic ethnographic exhibition and congress held in Moscow in 1867, the Poles were not represented, and when the Czech delegate Rieger referred in guarded terms to this regrettable gap in the ranks of the "fraternal union" he was sternly reprimanded by Prince Cherkassky. In spite of the unexceptionable Russian nationalism of the Slavonic Benevolent Committees, panslavism was but grudgingly tolerated by the government and was heartily disliked by Alexander and Gorchakov: too many of its doctrines ran contrary to official policies. The panslavs, nevertheless, made a number of converts in court and bureaucratic circles, especially in the entourage of the heir to the throne. The most influential adherent of political panslavism (which in his case was but another name for Russian ultra-nationalism) was General N. P. Ignatev, Russian minister and later ambassador to Constantinople (1864–1877). Prior to 1876 the Slavonic Benevolent Committees had hardly any following in Russia; they maintained, however, fairly close relations with the Slavic countries especially Bulgaria and Serbia, where, with the powerful assistance of Ignatev and his agents, they kindled the flame of nationalist agitation.

[4] See p. 799.

REVOLT IN HERZEGOVINA

The revolt that broke out in Herzegovina at the end of June, 1875, cannot be traced to the activities of the Russian panslavs; it was the natural consequence of the general situation in that part of the Balkans and of the inequity and harshness of the Turkish rule. Herzegovina and Bosnia, which soon became involved in the insurrection, were two Turkish provinces bordering, roughly, in the west and north on the Austrian territories of Dalmatia, Croatia, and Slavonia, and in the east and south on Serbia and Montenegro, self-governing principalities under the suzerainty of the sultan. The bulk of the population of Bosnia and Herzegovina was Slav by race, Serbian by language, and Orthodox in religion; there was, however, a strong Catholic minority, while the upper landowning classes were Moslems. The secular antagonism between peasant farmers and their lords, who wielded semi-feudal powers, was thus embittered by the religious issue. The administrative, economic, and social structure of Bosnia and Herzegovina was such as to keep their population in a state of continuous ferment fostered by the restless Montenegrins across Herzegovina's southern border. The immediate cause of the outbreak of 1875 was probably the visit paid by Emperor Francis Joseph to Dalmatia in the spring of that year. It created great excitement among the Slavs on both sides of the Austro-Turkish frontier and was accompanied by impressive demonstrations of pro-Austrian sympathy. In the early stage of the revolt the Catholic element played a prominent part.

The rapid spread of the disturbance and the threat of a general uprising of Christians in Turkey called for the intervention of the European Powers. The initiative came from Vienna acting in concert with St. Petersburg and Berlin, and reflected the attitude of the three governments. Andrássy did not wish to precipitate the violent dissolution of the Ottoman empire; if, however, this was to take place, he was determined that Bosnia and Herzegovina should be brought under Austrian control. His chief concern was to prevent the formation of a strong Slavic state that would exercise a powerful attraction for its sister provinces in the dual monarchy. The tsar and Gorchakov, like Andrássy, desired to localize the conflict. "The sick man . . . is agonizing, but I do not want his corpse; we would not know what to do with it," Alexander wrote to Emperor William on October 11, 1875, N.S. "The agony must be prolonged." Since Germany had no immediate interests in the Balkans, Bismarck's main preoccupation was the preservation of good relations between Russia and Austria, which he regarded as essential to German security. The three eastern Powers therefore endeavored to restore peace and order by mediation. The two attempts made in that direction in 1875—the appointment of a consular commission of the great Powers in August and the comprehensive plan of reforms in Bosnia and Herzegovina to be carried out under the supervision of a mixed commission of Christians and Moslems (the "Andrássy note" of December 30, N.S.)—proved equally futile. Both proposals were made jointly by Austria, Russia, and Germany and were accepted by France, Italy and, with great reluctance, by Great Britain. Disraeli and his foreign secretary Lord Derby, suspicious of Russia, did not believe that foreign mediation was warranted or expedient. A "hands off" policy was urged upon London by Sir Henry Elliot, British ambassador to Constantinople (1867-1877), an ardent Turkophile and Russophobe in the tradition of Stratford de Redcliffe. Disraeli's grudging approval of the Andrássy note was due partly to the fear that, in the case of refusal, the Powers would act without Great Britain. The British government, however, rejected the next proposal for a collective *démarche* known as the Berlin memorandum (May 13, 1876, N.S.). The memorandum was drafted by a conference in the German capital which was attended by the tsar, Gorchakov, and Andrássy; it restated the demands of the Andrássy note (which was accepted but not acted upon by the Porte) and reinforced them by the threat of "effectual measures that may appear necessary in the interest of general peace." Disraeli's rejection of the Berlin memorandum (previously approved by France and Italy) and the simultaneous dispatch of the British fleet to Besika Bay confirmed Constantinople in the belief that England, as in 1854, would stand by Turkey in the hour of need.[5]

[5] "If the effect of the British government's action at this point was to encourage Turkey in obstinacy, another was to throw her still more upon Great Britain's hands and support," writes Dawson. "It is not too much to say that, from that time forward until the eve of the settlement of the eastern question, the main lines of the Turkish policy were determined in London. The political and moral responsibility which fell upon the British government and nation in consequence were incalculable. Henceforth, it was impossible to shake the sultan's faith that Great Britain stood behind him, ready to protect him to the last extreme against the designs of his enemies; and this faith encouraged the Porte again and again in opposing the collective pressure of the Powers." *The Cambridge History of British Foreign Policy*, III, 98.

In the meantime the internal situation in Turkey deteriorated. Sultan Abd ul-Aziz was forced to abdicate (May 20, 1876, N.S.), and shortly afterwards was murdered or committed suicide; three months later a similar fate befell his nephew and successor, Murad V. It was under these inauspicious conditions that Abd ul-Hamid, Murad's brother, began what was to be a long and eventful reign (September 1, N.S.). In the summer of 1876 Constantinople was in the throes of anarchy; Moslem fanaticism ran high, officials were murdered, while the flame of the anti-Turkish revolt was spreading to new territories. In May an insurrection broke out among the Slav and Orthodox population of Bulgaria, a non-self-governing province which, however, in 1870 was granted an autonomous church administration (exarchate), independent of the Greek patriarch of Constantinople. The ferocity with which the Turks suppressed the Bulgarian rebellion created a stir in the Balkans and throughout the world. In June Prince Nicholas of Montenegro and Prince Milan of Serbia concluded an alliance and early in July opened hostilities against the Porte.

RUSSIA AND SERBIA

It was generally believed, especially in England, that the action of Serbia and Montenegro was instigated by Russia. This statement, although it contains a large element of truth, needs qualification. To begin with, the Slavic populations of Turkey, divided as they were on many issues, had behind them a long tradition of opposing Moslem oppressors, a tradition cemented by ties of racial and religious solidarity. There were in Montenegro and elsewhere warlike elements to whom fighting the Turks was a normal and honorable pursuit. As weeks and months of the revolt went by and rumors and evidence of atrocities piled up, Slav and Christian fanaticism, like its Turkish and Moslem counterpart, mounted. To discount unduly the intensity of this feeling tends to distort the picture. Alexander and Gorchakov, moreover, had no sympathy for Slav nationalists, and in 1875 and in the first half of 1876 worked diligently for the localization of the conflict. In August, 1875, Milan inquired whether he could count on Russian and Austrian support if Serbia declared war on Turkey, but met with a curt rebuttal. He was told in October that Russia would do nothing to prevent a Turkish occupation of Serbia unless the latter refrained from any aggressive measures against the Porte. Russia and Austria administered an even sterner rebuff to Milan and Nicholas in March,

1876, when the terms of the proposed Serbo-Montenegrin alliance became known in St. Petersburg and Vienna. As late as June, 1876, the tsar directed A. N. Kartsov, Russian consul general in Belgrade, not to permit Serbia to enter the war.

The failure of these admonitions to impress the Serbs and Montenegrins, like the failure of official professions of good faith to allay the suspicions of the European Powers, was due to an unprecedented outburst of activity on the part of Russian panslav organizations and their highly placed supporters. The Herzegovina revolt vitalized the hitherto academic and lifeless panslav movement. The Slavonic Benevolent Committees busied themselves with the collection of funds for relief and Red Cross work among the insurgents. There was a great outpouring of panslav propaganda, which for the first time reached a wide public. Newspapers and journals, irrespective of political allegiance, vied in denunciations of Turkish savagery, misrule, and wickedness, and in extravagant eulogies of Slavic virtues. Morbid curiosity was treated to lurid and grisly pictures of Turkish atrocities. Ecclesiastical dignitaries, with but a few exceptions, became willing tools of panslav propaganda. Inflammatory sermons were delivered from pulpits, money for the Slav cause was collected in churches, and special services were held in honor of the victims and heroes of the new crusade. In May, 1876, the Russian General Cherniaev, conqueror of Tashkent and a militant panslav, arrived in Belgrade and assumed command of the Serbian army. Former escapades and acts of insubordination had brought upon him the wrath of the minister of war, Miliutin, and had forced his retirement from active service. Although acclaimed by the nationalist press, Cherniaev's appearance in Serbia was a defiance of the tsar and the Russian government. After Serbia's declaration of war in July, the Slavonic Committees proceeded to recruit volunteers for the Serbian army. Some 4,000 or 5,000 men, including 800 officers, were enrolled and departed for the Balkans amidst scenes of wild enthusiasm. The bulk of the volunteers were adventurers and soldiers of fortune in search of excitement, promotions, and booty; others went to Serbia because they believed in the panslav ideals or imagined that the war, by undermining autocracy, would expedite constitutional reforms or even lead to the social revolution which was favored by some of the Balkan secret societies.

The enthusiasm and brotherly feelings so much in evidence at Moscow's tumultuous farewells withered away, however, under the impact of the grim realities of the Serbian struggle. It was not long before the Serbs and the Russian volunteers discovered that, both literally and figuratively, they did not speak the same language. In spite of the chaotic conditions prevailing in Constantinople, Cherniaev's campaign was brief and inglorious. At the end of August Milan and Nicholas sued for peace. Cherniaev was defeated and his headquarters at Deligrad captured on September 1, N.S. The Guaranteeing Powers intervened diplomatically; hostilities, suspended and again resumed, were terminated, after a new crushing defeat of the Serbs, by an armistice which the tsar exacted from the Turks under threat of a severance of diplomatic relations (October 30, 1876, N.S.). Peace between Turkey and Serbia was restored four months later on the basis of *status quo ante bellum* (February 28, 1877, N.S.). After the October debacle Cherniaev returned to Russia followed by many of the disgruntled volunteers. There was disillusionment and much mutual recrimination between Serbs and Russians. Even the most ardent panslavs had to admit that Serbia had not justified their expectations, although her defection, of course, could not compromise the cause itself. Bulgaria, Aksakov wrote in December, 1876, "is much more important for us and for the future of Slavdom than Serbia."

PANSLAVISM AND THE RUSSIAN GOVERNMENT

The ascendancy of panslavism in 1875–1876 is puzzling. It is certain that much of its doctrine and policies was repugnant to Alexander II and was incompatible with Gorchakov's "diplomatic system" revolving around the "three emperors' league." Yet the tsar and his chancellor were finally forced into the position of champions of the panslav cause. The familiar argument that even an autocracy has to bow to the pressure of public opinion is not entirely convincing. Panslavism, for all its short-lived effervescence, was never a broad popular movement. The masses in Russia, as well as in other Slavic countries, cared nothing for the cause of Slavdom. Sumner rightly notes that "very few of the volunteers seem to have been from the peasantry." But even among the tiny minority of educated Russians, who constituted what may be called public opinion, by no means all were swept off their feet by the tempest of panslav and nationalist propaganda. A keen contemporary observer, Prince P. A. Viazemsky, in a letter to a relative, characterized the Russian policy of this period as a "nightmare," and begged his correspondent to preserve for posterity his bitter indictment as an evidence that "in drunken Russia sober voices could still be heard." Pypin, writing in 1878, held that interest in panslavism was probably a fad and that "a great many" of its supporters during the war years were people "who merely felt the urge to do something in order to escape insufferable apathy and boredom." These were hardly the elements of an irresistible popular movement. The imperial government, moreover, was not in the habit of yielding to public opinion, however articulate. Propaganda, collection of funds, and recruiting of volunteers were impossible without the knowledge and connivance of high officials. Why should the government give the greatest leeway to, and finally capitulate before, a handful of panslav visionaries?

It is easier to raise this question than to answer it conclusively. One reason for official tolerance was that panslavism, especially in its later manifestations, was not inimical to autocracy and was closely associated with the Church, on which the Crown traditionally leaned. The panslavs, moreover, enjoyed the patronage of the tsarevich, commanded the support of such pillars of ultra-conservatism as Katkov and K. P. Pobedonostsev, and, as has already been stated, had many adherents among the higher bureaucracy and at the court. The empress, as head of the Red Cross, took a personal interest in relief work in the Balkans and was known to be favorable to the panslavs. Another, and perhaps decisive, factor was that peculiar half-heartedness, so characteristic of Alexander II, which made him keep at the key embassy in Constantinople Ignatev, whose views were sharply at variance with those of the chancellor. The anti-Austrian and pro-Slav activities of Ignatev and his carefully selected agents counted more in Serbia and Bulgaria than did Gorchakov's ingenious diplomatic schemes and polished rhetoric. Little wonder that in foreign capitals the pronouncements of the chancellor were discounted as window dressing, while Aksakov, Katkov, Ignatev, and their peers were listened to as the true spokesmen of official Russia. There gradually developed a situation where the abandonment of the panslav cause would be interpreted both at home and abroad as the betrayal of a policy to which the government appeared to be definitely committed.

AGREEMENT WITH AUSTRIA

In the summer of 1876, with Bulgaria, Serbia, and Montenegro in the fray and the Moscow campaign for the recruitment of volunteers in full swing, panslav and nationalist agitation reached a high pitch. During the next nine months, until Russia's declaration of war on Turkey, the imperial government pursued two distinct yet inter-related, although somewhat contradictory, policies: (1) preparation, both diplomatic and military, for war; and (2) endeavor to settle the conflict through the collective intervention of the Powers. The uneasy sway from the one course to the other was determined by the events in the Balkans, the international situation, the ebb and flow of panslav agitation, and the degree of influence enjoyed with the tsar at any particular time by either the partisans of war or its opponents. Of great practical consequence were the personal struggle between Gorchakov and Ignatev, and the ascendancy of the latter.

From the Russian point of view the attitude of Austria was a matter of paramount importance. A few days after Serbia's declaration of war, Alexander and Francis Joseph, accompanied by their foreign ministers, met at Reichstadt and reached an agreement concerning a common policy in the Balkans (July 8, 1876, N.S.). The agreement provided for two contingencies: if Turkey won the war, Russia and Austria were to concert their action to protect the Christian populations and to enforce a minimum of administrative reforms; if Turkey lost the war, the two Powers bound themselves to work together for the establishment of a new political order in accordance with an agreed program. There was to be no large Slav state. Russia was to acquire the districts of Bessarabia, severed in 1856, and unidentified territories in Asia Minor; Austria was to annex Bosnia and, according to Andrássy (but not to Gorchakov), Herzegovina.[6] Other Turkish territories in Europe were to be partitioned among Bulgaria, Serbia, Rumania, Montenegro, Greece, and Albania. Constantinople was to become a free city.

The Reichstadt agreement left Alexander and Gorchakov unconvinced that Austria would not side with the enemies of Russia if the latter went to war with Turkey. The "three emperors' league" was still too recent and untried an alliance to put to rest the memories of the hostility that had characterized the relations between St. Petersburg and Vienna since Austria's defection during the Crimean War. In September, 1876, after the defeat of Serbia, the tsar bluntly inquired in Berlin whether Germany would be prepared, in case of an Austro-

---

[6] There was no joint official text of the Reichstadt conversations, the Austrian and the Russian version differing in some essentials.

Russian war, to fight Austria as Russia had promised to do in 1870. Bismarck's reply to this indiscreet question was not forthcoming until the first day of November, and was couched in guarded and non-committal terms. The reserve shown by Berlin was a blow to Gorchakov and especially to Alexander, who, like his father, thought of international relations in terms of personal loyalties and close monarchical and family ties with the House of Prussia. Bismarck, moreover, disclosed the Russian move to Andrássy, thus adding to the difficulties of the laborious Austro-Russian negotiations then in progress. These negotiations dragged on throughout the winter and led to the conclusion of two secret conventions, one military and the other political, both dated January 15, 1877, N.S., although the political convention was not actually signed until the middle of March. The military convention provided that, if Russia went to war with Turkey, Austria-Hungary was to maintain a benevolent neutrality and was not to participate in any action under the treaty of April 15, 1856, N.S.[7] Russia was permitted to occupy Bulgaria; Austria was to occupy Bosnia and Herzegovina if and when she deemed this desirable. Serbia, Montenegro, and the portion of Herzegovina comprised between the two principalities were to constitute a neutral zone prohibited to Russian and Austrian troops. The second convention dealt with the political and territorial changes resulting from the war or from the dissolution of the Ottoman empire. It restated briefly the arrangements agreed upon at Reichstadt, sanctioned the annexation by Austria of Bosnia and Herzegovina, and the annexation by Russia of the Bessarabian districts ceded in 1856, but did not mention any Russian acquisitions in Asiatic Turkey. The two Powers promised mutual support if the proposed territorial changes were brought before an international conference. Although the negotiations proceeded in an atmosphere of distrust bordering on hostility, which augured ill for the future, the conventions offered Russia some guarantee of Austrian neutrality in the forthcoming war.

RUSSIA'S WAR PREPARATIONS

The Serbian defeat came as a shock to Russian nationalists and panslavs, the more so because the Serbian army was commanded by a Russian general and comprised Russian volunteers. There was a loud outcry in the press and a demand for vigorous action. The most

[7] See p. 950.

urgent need was for an armistice to save the insurgents from annihilation. Early in August Gorchakov had vainly sought to induce Andrássy and Bismarck to initiate armistice negotiations, to be followed by a conference of the great Powers. When, after the Serbian debacle, the European cabinets took up the matter with the Porte, progress proved difficult and slow. Flushed by their victories and confident of the support of Great Britain, the Turks were intransigent and stubborn, marking time while the position of the insurgents grew increasingly critical. The Russian government, despairing of the effectiveness of representations made by the European concert, was hesitantly and reluctantly driven to the conclusion that it would have to act alone. The scene of important decisions which made war likely, if not yet inevitable, was Livadia, in the Crimea, where the tsar, the tsarevich, the court, and many high officials were spending the autumn. The already bellicose atmosphere of court circles was intensified by the arrival of Ignatev, who relentlessly preached the urgency of energetic action and decried any concessions to, or arrangements with, Austria. He interpreted the success of Gladstone's celebrated campaign against Turkish atrocities in Bulgaria as conclusive evidence that the days of Anglo-Turkish friendship were over. The time for Russia to strike had arrived. Ignatev's eloquence was not without effect, although he complained later in his memoirs that his warnings went unheeded.

In mid-October Alexander conferred at Livadia with high officials on the question of war and peace. Some of his advisers—notably Miliutin, the minister of war, and Totleben, the hero of Sevastopol—were lukewarm to nationalist and panslav plans; Reutern, the minister of finance, objected violently, arguing in a secret memorandum that war would spell the ruin of Russian finance.[8] In spite of this opposition far-reaching measures were adopted: partial mobilization was decided upon; a plan of the Balkan campaign drawn by General N. N. Obruchev was approved; the Grand Dukes Nicholas and Michael, the tsar's brothers, were appointed commanders in chief, respectively, of the Danubian and the Caucasian armies. On October 30, N.S., as has already been stated, Alexander sent Turkey an ultimatum demanding an immediate armistice with Serbia on pain of severance of diplomatic relations. Addressing the nobility and the burghers of Moscow in the Kremlin on November 11, N.S., the tsar paid a warm tribute to the Montenegrins but referred disparagingly to the Serbs. "I know," he

[8] See p. 945.

said, "that all Russia joins me in taking the deepest interest in the sufferings of our brothers by faith and origin." Alexander expressed the hope that the conference of the great Powers which was to meet shortly at Constantinople would make unnecessary the shedding of Russian blood, but declared that he was determined, if necessary, to act independently in order "to fulfil our sacred mission." This was a momentous pronouncement and seemingly an unqualified endorsement of the panslav creed. Aksakov, Katkov, and their friends were properly jubilant. Words were followed by deeds. Partial mobilization was ordered on November 13, N.S., although the actual concentration of troops would seem to have started in October. At the end of November Prince Cherkassky, who had earned a sinister reputation as the "Russificator" of Poland after 1863, was appointed civil governor of Bulgaria, a province of Turkey with which Russia was still at peace. Early in 1877 the Grand Duke Nicholas established his headquarters in Kishinev, Bessarabia, at the head of an army of some 190,000 men.

THE CONFERENCE OF CONSTANTINOPLE

These were moves of the utmost gravity, yet the tsar, Gorchakov, and the peace-minded bureaucrats (for instance, the ministers Reutern, A. E. Timashev, and P. A. Valuev) had not abandoned hope of avoiding war. There was still the possibility that the conference, to which Alexander referred in his Moscow speech, and Russia's display of firmness might prevent the conflagration. The formal invitation to the conference was issued by Lord Derby on November 5, N.S., two days after the British ambassador, Lord Augustus Loftus, had a long audience with the tsar at Livadia. Alexander informed the ambassador that in view of Turkish procrastination and bad faith he might be forced to take independent action. If this was to come, a temporary occupation of Bulgaria by Russian troops was likely. He repudiated, however, any designs on Constantinople; its annexation would be a misfortune to Russia, although the possibility of its provisional occupation was not excluded. The British fears for India, Alexander scornfully remarked, were sheer nonsense, and the much-discussed Russian campaign against India an impossibility. He urged Anglo-Russian cooperation and the convocation of an international conference.

Although Beaconsfield [9] was not impressed by the tsar's statement, he agreed to sponsor a conference of six Powers (Great Britain, Russia,

---

[9] Disraeli was created Earl of Beaconsfield in August, 1876.

Germany, Austria-Hungary, France, and Italy), which met in Constantinople in the middle of December, 1876. Russia was represented by Ignatev, England by Lord Salisbury, then secretary of state for India, and Elliot. The delegates of the great Powers agreed on a program of reforms which comprised the creation of a western and an eastern Bulgaria, autonomous states under the suzerainty of the sultan. The Turks were then admitted to the conference, but they rejected its proposals in spite of the substantial softening of the original demands in the course of subsequent negotiations. The conference thus ended in a deadlock (January 20, 1877, N.S.), and as a sign of protest the delegates of the six Powers, including ambassadors to the Porte, left Constantinople. One reason for the conference's failure was the discord within the British delegation. Salisbury despised the Turks, and spoke of the Crimean War as a "deplorable folly" that should never be repeated; Elliot was an ardent Turkophile and Russophobe. The Porte, however, was convinced that Elliot, not Salisbury, represented the true views of London, and it acted accordingly.[10]

In spite of the Constantinople fiasco, the search for a peaceful solution continued. After involved negotiations, in which Russia took a prominent part, the six Powers signed in London a protocol (March 31, N.S.) embodying an emasculated version of the Constantinople demands. The protocol was presented to the Porte together with a Russian declaration which provided for the simultaneous demobilization of the two armies, on the condition that Turkey gave proof of good faith and concluded an armistice with Montenegro. It was unfortunate that the adherence to the protocol by the British government synchronized with the appointment to the Constantinople embassy, as successor to Elliot, of Sir Henry Layard, another notorious Turkophile and antagonist of Russia. On April 9, N.S., the Porte curtly rejected the protocol and the Russian declaration. Ten days later Alexander left St. Petersburg for Kishinev, where on April 24, N.S., he signed a manifesto declaring war on Turkey.

[10] The Ottoman government opposed any interference by the European Powers as incompatible with Turkish sovereignty, and shielded itself behind the pleasing fiction of recent administrative reforms (December, 1875) and of the new liberal constitution of December, 1876. All these reforms, like their many predecessors and those enacted in February, 1877, remained a dead letter.

THE RUSSO-TURKISH WAR, 1877–1878

Rumania was destined by geography to play the unenviable part of furnishing the base of Russian military operations against European Turkey, and St. Petersburg hastened to make necessary arrangements with Bucharest. Negotiations between the two governments had been carried on in a dilatory fashion since November, 1876. The chief stumbling block was Alexander's well known desire to recover the portions of Bessarabia lost after the Crimean War. Rumania's public opinion was opposed to the cession of these provinces, and many of her leaders preferred neutrality or an anti-Russian alliance with Vienna, London, or even Constantinople, to collaboration with the Muscovites. The imminence of the Russo-Turkish War and of the invasion of Rumania by the Russians put an end to these hesitations. On April 16, 1877, N.S., Russia and Rumania signed two conventions, one military and the other political. The military convention regulated the passage of Russian troops through Rumanian territory, the use of railways, and kindred matters. The political convention bound Russia "to maintain and respect the political rights of the Rumanian state ... as well as to maintain and defend the actual integrity (*intégrité actuelle*) of Rumania." The Porte retaliated by declaring war, and on May 21, N.S., Rumania proclaimed her independence. At first, however, St. Petersburg discouraged Prince Charles from joining in the fighting. "Russia," Gorchakov tartly informed Bucharest in May, "does not need the assistance of the Rumanian army." It was not until the severe reversals of midsummer that, at the urgent request of the Grand Duke Nicholas, the Rumanian troops took the field.

The war was fought simultaneously in the Danube-Balkan area and in Transcaucasia; of the two fronts the European was by far the more important. At the outbreak of hostilities Grand Duke Nicholas, commander in chief of the Danubian army, had under his command some 190,000 men, including 145,000 combatant troops, and approximately 500 guns; the trained or partly trained reserves comprised another 150,000 men and 200 guns. The Russian army in the Caucasus under Grand Duke Michael numbered some 60,000 troops with an approximately equal number in reserve battalions. Another 70,000 men and 200 guns were assigned to the defense of the Black Sea coast. The strength of the Turkish army in Europe was estimated at 300,000;

of this number 160,000 to 180,000 were concentrated in Bulgaria. The Ottoman effectives facing the Grand Duke Michael were probably between 70,000 and 100,000. The Russian army, although numerically not inferior to the Turkish, was handicapped in many respects. The conscription reform of 1874 had not yet been completed, and there was a shortage of reserve officers and trained cadres. The technical equipment of the Russian troops left much to be desired, the bulk of the infantry being armed with old-fashioned rifles and the artillery with antiquated field pieces, while up-to-date weapons were used by the majority of the Turkish units. Russian medical and supply services were as inefficient and inadequate as they had been during previous wars with Turkey; their failure was scandalous and became the source of attacks on the government and army leaders. The difficulty of the campaign was aggravated by the inadequacy of the railways and highways and by the length of the lines of communication, which increased as the Russian troops pushed forward. Not less grievous was the lack of competent leadership and unity of command. Neither Nicholas nor Michael had any aptitude for the art of warfare, and both were devoid of the ability to rise above petty quarrels and trivial interests of the guards' mess room and court circles. Few of their generals, excepting perhaps Totleben, measured up to the responsibilities thrust upon them, although some of them, especially Skobelev, have gone down in history as intrepid and dashing heroes. Moreover, the continuous presence of the tsar at the European front, from June to December, destroyed the unity of command, in spite of his studious adherence to the fiction that military leadership rested solely with his brother. In actual fact, however, important strategic decisions were referred to imperial headquarters. The confusion on what is called today the "upper levels" was worse confounded by the fact that various commands were held by the tsarevich, Prince Charles of Rumania, and a plethora of Russian grand dukes. These royal personages and their retinues of civil and military dignitaries, greedy for sinecures, promotions, and decorations, engaged among themselves in private wars of intrigue which had little to do with the liberation of the "Slavic brethren" or with the national struggle. It was fortunate for Russia that an even greater state of disorder prevailed in the Turkish army.

The early course of the campaign would seem to have justified the most sanguine expectations of the Russian high command. On

April 24, N.S., the day when war was declared, Russian troops poured simultaneously into Rumania and Asia Minor. The Caucasian army took by storm Bayazid (end of April) and Ardahan (middle of May) and besieged Kars. In the meantime the forces of the Grand Duke Nicholas virtually occupied Rumania; the Danube was crossed on June 27, N.S., Nicopolis capitulated (July 16, N.S.), and while the main body of the Russian army was advancing in Bulgaria a flying column (variously estimated at 10,000 to 16,000 men) under General J. V. Gurko seized the Balkan pass of Shipka (July 19, N.S.), overran the valley of the Tundzhi, captured Kazanlik, and headed towards Adrianople.

These initial successes, however, were followed by reverses. On July 20, N.S., the Russian assault on the important road junction of Plevna was repulsed by Osman Pasha with heavy losses to the attackers. The second assault on Plevna (July 30, N.S.) proved an even more disastrous failure. On the same day Gurko's advance was checked by the superior force of Suleiman Pasha, and the Russian column was forced to retreat hastily over the Balkans. The Shipka pass, however, defended with courage by General F. F. Radetsky, remained in Russian hands. News from Transcaucasia was equally alarming: the Russians, compelled to relinquish their conquests and to lift the siege of Kars, had by the beginning of August withdrawn behind their frontier. These reverses, especially the second defeat of Plevna, exposed the vulnerability of the Russian position, created a dismay at imperial headquarters, and brought a public clamor for extraordinary measures. The guards, who were not called for combatant service during the Crimean War, were hastily summoned to the Balkans. The Rumanian army, some 50,000 strong, only recently snubbed by Gorchakov, was pressed into service on Prince Charles's own terms. These measures, however, proved unequal to the emergency. The third assault on Plevna (September 11–12, N.S.) was an even worst disaster than its two predecessors: all Russo-Rumanian attacks were repulsed with the loss of some 15,000 men. The Grand Duke Nicholas, despairing of the situation, urged immediate withdrawal behind the Danube, but he was overruled both on military and on political grounds, and the conduct of operations against Plevna was entrusted to the level-headed Totleben, who was recalled from semi-retirement and reached army headquarters by the end of September. Totleben vetoed any further assaults on Plevna and proceeded instead with the painstaking investment of the Turkish stronghold. This cautious strategy brought its fruit. The Turkish garrison, having exhausted its supplies, made an unsuccessful eleventh-hour attempt to break through and was forced to surrender (December 10, N.S.).

The capitulation of Plevna ushered in the final phase of the war. Heartened by this victory and by the improvement of the situation in Asia Minor, where Kars had fallen to the Russians (November 16, N.S.) the Grand Duke Nicholas won, over the objections of Totleben, the approval of his plan for the energetic pursuance of the campaign. In subzero weather and blinding snowstorms the tide of Russian invasion swept over the Balkans. Demoralized and tottering, the Turkish army offered only sporadic resistance and surrendered en masse. Early in January Gurko entered Sofia, Adrianople was captured on January 20, N.S., and advanced Russian units were racing towards Constantinople. Its back to the wall, the Porte sued for peace. Hostilities were terminated by the armistice of January 31, 1878, N.S.

INTERNATIONAL COMPLICATIONS

The Russo-Turkish War reopened the eastern question and revealed the insecurity of Russia's international position. The looseness of the "three emperors' league" was suggested by the appointment in April, 1877, of a German and an Austrian ambassador to the Porte, to replace those demonstratively withdrawn as a protest after the failure of the Constantinople conference. Gorchakov protested against these appointments with unusual vehemence and somberly reflected that the tsar "must rely solely on God and his sword" (report of April 22, 1877, N.S.), an opinion in which Alexander concurred. The chief opposition to Russia's still ill defined aspirations in the Balkans, and in the Near East, however, came from London. The militant Russophobia of Queen Victoria,[11] Beaconsfield, and the majority of the cabinet thrived on Loftus's and Layard's alarmist reports. Stirred by Gladstone's campaign against "Bulgarian atrocities," English opinion in 1876 showed hostility towards Turkey. In 1877 and 1878 these recriminations were forgotten, and Russia again became the chief ob-

[11] According to Algernon Cecil, the interference of Queen Victoria with foreign relations, countenanced by Beaconsfield, was particularly marked during Derby's tenure of the foreign office (1874 to March, 1878). "It may probably be no exaggeration to say," writes Cecil, "that at no time during the nineteenth century was the conduct of foreign affairs regulated on lines so monarchical." *The Cambridge History of British Foreign Policy*, III, 602.

ject of invective and denunciation. The intensity of anti-Russian agitation, which rose with the victories of the Russian armies and receded when they met with reverses, reached its zenith after the Turkish collapse in January, 1878.

The Russian press, not to be outdone by the British, expounded the view that, but for English intrigues, war could have been prevented; and it gave prominence to the fact that the Turkish fleet was commanded by a British admiral, while several British officers held positions in the Ottoman army.

There was a close correlation between the trends of British opinion and the foreign policy of the British government, the former being influenced by the latter. London, indeed, lost no time in voicing its disapproval of Russia's declaration of war. Replying to a circular note in which Gorchakov endeavored to justify the outbreak of hostilities, Derby rejected the contention that war was forced upon Russia by Turkish intransigence and was "in accordance with the sentiments and interests of Europe." On the contrary, he argued, Russia was guilty of a breach of the Treaty of Paris. In a note of May 6, 1877, N.S., handed to Count Peter Shuvalov, Russian ambassador to London, Derby warned that Great Britain would be unable to remain neutral if her vital interests were threatened; he referred specifically to the Suez Canal, Egypt, Constantinople, the Straits, and the Persian Gulf. The Russian reply gave London the desired assurances concerning the Suez, Egypt, the Persian Gulf, and India; Gorchakov, moreover, recognized that the fate of Constantinople and the Straits, should this question arise, was a matter of European interest to be decided by general accord (*entente générale*) and that Constantinople, if it was to change hands, was not to belong to any of the great Powers (note of May 30, N.S.). Shuvalov, however, simultaneously informed Derby that a temporary occupation of Constantinople was not excluded, a reservation which aroused the worst suspicions of the British government. On June 30, N.S., three days after the Russians crossed the Danube, the British fleet was ordered to Besika Bay. As the armies of the tsar advanced deeper into Turkey, the British government decided (July 21, N.S.) that a declaration of war might become necessary in case of a Russian occupation of Constantinople, and Shuvalov was notified (July 28, N.S.) that the British fleet might be ordered to enter the Straits. Meanwhile (May to August) Beaconsfield was engaged in secret negotiations with Andrássy with the object of a joint Anglo-Austrian naval and military action against Russia, but he failed to obtain definite commitments. Tension between St. Petersburg and London was somewhat eased during the period of Russian military reverses; it increased, however, after the fall of Plevna (December 10, N.S.). Three days later, Beaconsfield informed Gorchakov that Great Britain would not remain indifferent if Constantinople were occupied, even temporarily; and he unsuccessfully pressed the chancellor to accept mediation. In view of Beaconsfield's attitude and Vienna's keen interest in the proposed Balkan settlement, the nature of Russian peace demands became a matter of primary importance not only from the point of view of Turkey and the Balkan nations but also that of maintaining peace among the great Powers.

THE ARMISTICE AND BRITISH COUNTER-MEASURES

During the war St. Petersburg had no fixed peace program, officially sponsored proposals being amended and revised as the military and international situation developed, and also to meet the predilections of those whose influence with the tsar was uppermost at the time. The importance of the latter factor must not be underestimated. Broadly speaking, Gorchakov and the senior members of the diplomatic service, especially Shuvalov and E. P. Novikov, ambassador to Vienna, were opposed to panslavism and worked for a settlement acceptable to England and Austria. The principal spokesman in official circles of nationalist and panslav views was the formidable Ignatev, seconded by many, although by no means all, commanding officers. As Sumner makes clear, the tsar's presence at the front from June to the end of 1877 tended to weaken the influence of the ministry of foreign affairs. Although Gorchakov followed Alexander to the Danubian area, he lived in Bucharest, paying but casual visits to imperial headquarters, to which Ignatev was attached. The Grand Duke Nicholas had his own diplomatic chancellery headed by A. I. Nelidov, an antagonist of Gorchakov. The foreign office in distant St. Petersburg was in charge of N. K. Giers, assistant minister of foreign affairs, who like his chief was inimical to the panslavs. The Grand Duke Nicholas, Gorchakov, and Ignatev were on the worst possible terms, the commander in chief, moreover, making no secret of his contempt for the diplomatic service. The lack of unified direction of foreign policy and the personal animosity and jealousy among those in a position to influence it led to much uncertainty and confusion, especially since the chancellor was occasionally left in ignorance of important decisions made at army headquarters. This situation was at least in part responsible for the reputation of duplicity and half-heartedness which Russian diplomacy of that period earned abroad. The dramatic change in the fortunes of war which, within a few weeks, destroyed Turkish resistance and brought the victorious Russian armies to the gates of Constantinople was not conducive to moderation.

Under the Russian peace plan as finally evolved (December, 1876 to January, 1877), the liquidation of the war was to comprise three stages: armistice; preliminary peace between Russia and Turkey; and the final settlement by the European Powers of all questions of "general interest," presumably at an international conference. The granting of the armistice, however, was conditional on the acceptance by Turkey of a formidable list of demands which were eventually embodied, with some modifications, in the Treaty of San Stefano (to be discussed presently). Turkish plenipotentiaries were summoned to Adrianople, where the Grand Duke Nicholas had moved his headquarters, and were coerced into signing the armistice and the attached bases of peace (January 31, 1878, N.S.). Austria and Great Britain protested even before the armistice was signed. Andrássy, apprised of the Russian demands, informed Gorchakov that he would not recognize as valid any peace terms incompatible with Austrian interests, or any changes in the regime established by the treaties of 1856 and 1871, unless they were confirmed by all signatories. The British government made a similar declaration (January 15, N.S.), and when the information reached London that the question of the Straits was to be settled by Russia and Turkey alone, the British fleet was ordered to Constantinople (January 23, N.S.). This order, however, was countermanded the next day, and on January 26, N.S., Gorchakov announced that his government regarded the regime of the Straits as a matter of "general concern."

The armistice, far from relieving the tension, precipitated a new crisis. More than ever distrustful of Russia, the British government was convinced that armistice negotiations were a mere sham to facilitate the seizure of Constantinople and the Straits. As far back as May, 1877, Loftus had urged Beaconsfield to occupy Constantinople the moment the Russians crossed the Danube. On February 5, 1878, N.S., Layard, acting on official albeit erroneous Turkish information, telegraphed to his government that in spite of the armistice, which provided for a neutral zone between the two armies, the Russians continued to advance. Official London was aroused. Queen Victoria, threatening to lay down her "thorny crown," demanded an immediate declaration of war. The cabinet, however, demurred from so drastic a step but instead ordered the British fleet to proceed from Besika Bay to Constantinople "for the protection of British life and property" (February 8, N.S.). Disregarding the protests of the sultan, who feared that the British move would precipitate the occupation of his capital by the Russians, British warships entered the Dardanelles (February 13, N.S.); as a concession to Abd ul-Hamid's plea, however, they cast anchor off the island of Prinkipo, some distance from Constantinople. A large credit was voted by the House of Commons in the middle of February, and war preparations were energetically pushed forward.

The appearance of British men-of-war in the Straits threw the Russian government and press into a frenzy of patriotic indignation. The hoisting of the cross on Saint Sophia was the dream and the battle cry of the Russian panslavs. General Obruchev advocated in December, 1877, the seizure of Constantinople and the Straits as the prerequisite to the granting of an armistice. National aspirations and expert opinion, it was argued, were brushed aside in deference to British susceptibilities; and now *la perfide Albion*, on the flimsiest pretext and in violation of international conventions, had sent her fleet to Constantinople to deprive Russia of the legitimate fruits of a hard-won victory. Many Russians who had formerly opposed the occupation of Constantinople, for instance, Shuvalov, considered it now inevitable. Alexander became convinced that this was the only course to follow. From February 10, N.S., to April, when the Grand Duke Nicholas was relieved of his command, the tsar bombarded his brother with telegrams, orders, and instructions, not always clear and in part contradictory, but all directed to one object—the seizure of Constantinople and of both shores of the Bosphorus. The grand duke was in a predicament. At the end of January he himself had favored the occupation of the Turkish capital. Three weeks later, however, the situation had changed, not to Russia's advantage, and the difficulties facing the high command were daily more apparent. The number of combat troops was small; they were worn out by an arduous campaign; there was no fleet, and the army was suffering from an acute shortage of munitions, supplies, and heavy artillery; the length and chaotic state of the lines of communication made the arrival of reinforcements problematic. The Turks, on the other hand, held strong positions in the hills dominating Constantinople, had massed in its vicinity a large number of troops, and could presumably count, in case of a Russian attack, on the support of the British fleet. Negotiation for entry into the Turkish capital by agreement with the sultan having failed, the grand duke was increasingly uneasy about the hazards of any attempt to take it by force. Yet the tsar was pressing for an immediate advance. A temporary solution was found in the occupation of San Stefano, a town on the Sea of Marmora six miles from the outskirts of Constantinople. This extension of Russian occupation was carried out on February 24, N.S., with the sultan's consent exacted by threat of force.

THE TREATY OF SAN STEFANO

The Russians in the meantime were pressing for a speedy conclusion of the preliminary peace. Ignatev, who was in charge of the negotiations, was given broad powers in interpreting the peace terms already accepted by the Turks. Leaving St. Petersburg at the end of January, he reached Adrianople on February 8, N.S.; negotiations began four days later at the grand ducal headquarters, and the treaty was signed at San Stefano on March 3, 1878, N.S., after the resistance of the Turkish delegation had been broken down by threat of the immediate occupation of Constantinople. The Treaty of San Stefano was to transform the political map of the Balkans. Bulgaria was to become an autonomous principality under the nominal suzerainty of the sultan, to whom she was to pay an unspecified tribute. Her frontiers were to comprise, broadly, the territory lying between the Danube, the Black Sea, and the Aegean, including Rumelia and Macedonia, but excluding Adrianople and Salonika.[12] The new principality was to have an elected prince, elective assembly, and national militia. Turkish garrisons were to be withdrawn, and the installation of the new regime was to be supervised, for two years, by a Russian commis-

[12] The territory of Bulgaria provided by the Treaty of San Stefano was essentially similar to (although not identical with) that proposed by Ignatev at the Constantinople conference. His proposal was accepted by the conference with the important modification, insisted upon by Salisbury and the Austrians, that there was to be not one, but two Bulgarias, the western and the eastern. The reason for the partition was that eastern Bulgaria, which was to comprise the approaches to Constantinople, the Black Sea coast, and the Balkan passes, would be controlled by Turks and Greeks, not by Slavs, thus escaping Russian domination.

sary supported by a Russian army of occupation of not more than 50,000. All Turkish fortresses on the Danube were to be razed. The Porte recognized the independence of Montenegro, Serbia, and Rumania. The territory of Montenegro was to be trebled at the expense of Herzegovina, the sanjak of Novibazar, and Albania, and was to include the Adriatic ports of Spizza, Antivari, and Dulcigno. Serbia was to make less impressive territorial gains in Novibazar and in Old Serbia, south of her former frontier. The Dobrudja and the delta of the Danube were to be ceded to Russia, who reserved the right to transfer them to Rumania in exchange for the Bessarabian districts lost in 1856. The Porte promised to introduce in Bosnia and Herzegovina the administrative reforms proposed by the Constantinople conference, subject to such modification as might be agreed upon by the Porte, Russia, and Austria-Hungary. The political institutions granted to Crete in 1868 were to be extended to Epirus, Thessaly, and "other parts of European Turkey for which no special organization is provided in this treaty." Armenians living in the districts of Asia Minor to be evacuated by Russian troops were promised "suitable" administrative reforms and protection against Kurds and Circassians. The Porte undertook to pay Russia an indemnity of 1,410,000,000 rubles. Of this amount 1,100,000,000 were credited to Turkey for the cession of Dobrudja and, in Asia Minor, of the districts of Ardahan, Kars, Batum, Bayazid, and parts of Armenia to the Saganluk range. Russian troops were to be withdrawn, except from Bulgaria, within three months after the conclusion of the final peace. Significantly, the treaty made no reference to the Straits, except that they were to remain open, both in peace and war, to neutral merchantmen bound for or from Russian ports. Gorchakov, it will be remembered, had announced (January 26, N.S.) that the question of the Straits was reserved for European settlement; nevertheless the armistice concluded five days after the chancellor's statement contained a provision for a separate agreement with Turkey concerning the Straits. Ignatev attached the greatest importance to a direct Russo-Turkish understanding on this question, and relentlessly pressed this condition upon the Turkish delegation, in spite of Gorchakov's repeated admonitions. Unsupported by his foreign office and meeting with the obstinate resistance of the Porte, he finally abandoned this part of his plan.

Taken as a whole, the Treaty of San Stefano was a great personal triumph for Ignatev and a victory not only over the Porte but also over Gorchakov and the foreign office. The chancellor had favored a preliminary peace agreement couched in rather general terms and embodied in a protocol; he felt that the conclusion of a treaty in the "preliminary" stage of the negotiations would expose Russia to charges of violating the treaties of 1856 and 1871 and would make difficult the final settlement in concert with other Powers. Ignatev, on the contrary, was determined that preliminary peace should be as definite and binding as he could make it. He hurried the Porte through the necessary formalities, and on March 17, N.S. ratifications were exchanged in St. Petersburg. The preliminary Treaty of San Stefano thus acquired an ominous air of finality, although it was subject to review by the members of the European concert.

The Russian nationalist press acclaimed the treaty as a monument of statesmanship and moderation. This interpretation, however, was not shared abroad. Even the Balkan countries, with the exception of Bulgaria and Montenegro, showed disillusionment, bitterness, and resentment. Serbia, fallen from grace after her ignominious defeat in 1876, did not re-enter the war until after the capitulation of Plevna, partly because she was discouraged by the Russians themselves, but chiefly because her army was disorganized and her treasury empty, the much-needed Russian subsidies being parsimoniously measured out and delayed. Her alleged lack of military prowess and the brevity of her belligerency (six weeks) were unceremoniously rubbed in by Ignatev. Serbian territorial claims, moreover, were blocked by the fact that Bosnia and Herzegovina, under the Reichstadt agreement, were an Austrian preserve (even though the Treaty of San Stefano appeared to ignore it), while Macedonia was assigned to Bulgaria. In spite of independence and territorial gains bestowed upon them at San Stefano, the Serbs, remembering the heyday of Cherniaev and of the Russian volunteers, felt betrayed and despoiled. Greece, divided between the desire to establish her claim to territorial compensation and mistrust of Russia and the fear of rumored British designs on Crete, had maintained an uneasy neutrality until it was too late; she finally entered the war on February 1, 1878, N.S., the day after the signature of the armistice of Adrianople, but she was at once peremptorily ordered by the Powers to withdraw her troops, which had crossed the frontiers. The inclusion of Macedonia and the Aegean littoral in Bulgaria dealt to Greek national aspirations a blow which was not mitigated by the paltry promises of reforms in Epirus and Thessaly, the

Turkish record in matters of reform being what it was. Rumania, Russia's unwilling yet loyal and indispensable partner in the war, had more serious grudges. The tsar's unalterable decision to annex the Bessarabian districts was officially communicated to Bucharest at the end of January, 1878. The Russians remained unmoved by the protests of Prince Charles and by the resolution of the Rumanian parliament not to accept any change of frontier. In reply to the argument that the Russian decision was a violation of the convention of April, 1877,[13] Gorchakov propounded the theory that the obligation "to defend the actual integrity of Rumania" could be invoked only against Turkey. The Rumanians remaining unconvinced, measures of exemplary severity were applied against the recalcitrant country. When the Rumanian government, having had no part in drafting the armistice and the Treaty of San Stefano, announced that it could not accept that treaty (March 28, N.S.), Gorchakov countered by threats of occupation and demand for the disarmament of the Rumanian army. There were ominous movements of troops on both sides of the frontier, Bucharest pinning its hopes on Austrian and British intervention. Yet discreet negotiations for a suitable compensation were not abandoned, and as more sober counsel prevailed in St. Petersburg the situation was sufficiently improved to allow the conclusion of a convention regulating the position of Russian troops in Rumania.

The two principal beneficiaries of San Stefano were Russia's old protégé Montenegro, a belligerent throughout the war, and peasant Bulgaria so recently discovered by the Russian panslavs.[14] Surely the imperial government could not be sufficiently interested in their fate to challenge European opinion and risk a major war. A study of the Treaty of San Stefano suggests that Ignatev was not primarily concerned with the emancipation of the Slavic populations or the ad-

[13] See p. 1002.
[14] There was little love lost between Russians and Bulgars, and their relationship was not improved by close contact. ". . . First hand acquaintance with the Bulgars had cured the Russian troops of any enthusiasm for shedding their blood to emancipate Bulgaria," writes Sumner. ". . . In sober fact they found themselves in a foreign land among a close-fisted peasantry who, in most cases, seemed to show little spontaneous joy at their 'liberation.' . . . Few occupying armies commend themselves to the occupied: none when the period of occupation is likely to prove fluctuating. If the Russians disliked the Bulgars, the Bulgars equally disliked the Russians. Yet . . . the Bulgars knew that in the last resort only through the Russians could their freedom be won; Alexander to them was the Tsar Liberator: and there were bonds of a kind between the two peoples which in the years to come were never fully effaced. . . ." *Op. cit.*, pp. 337–338.

vancement of the cause of Orthodoxy, these leitmotivs of the panslav press. The real meaning of San Stefano must be sought elsewhere. The creation of a large Bulgaria surrounded by hostile countries and dominated by St. Petersburg would have put Russia in an exceptionally strong position in the Balkans and would have made possible the extension of her influence in southeastern Europe and the eventual annexation of Constantinople and the Straits. This is what no one in Europe wanted and what Vienna and London were resolved to prevent.

ON THE VERGE OF A NEW WAR

Although the text of the Treaty of San Stefano was not officially communicated to the European capitals until after its ratification, the tenor of Russian peace terms was known in Vienna, Berlin, and London before that date. An outline of the proposed settlement was sent by Alexander to the emperors of Germany and Austria-Hungary on December 9, 1877, N.S. Francis Joseph's reply, which was not forthcoming until January 8, 1878, N.S., was a sharp criticism of Russian terms on the ground that they violated the Reichstadt agreement and the convention of January, 1877. The Austrian emperor emphatically opposed the preliminary peace concluded without consulting Vienna, the creation of a big Bulgaria and her occupation by Russian troops; he claimed the right to annex Bosnia and Herzegovina and refused to recognize the validity of any changes in the Treaty of Paris unless they were confirmed by all signatories. Alexander conceded at once (January 16, N.S.) the Austrian claim to the occupation or even the annexation of Bosnia and Herzegovina and, in principle, agreed to the convocation of a European conference, but he rejected the other demands. In spite of this divergency of views between the two courts, Gorchakov, oblivious of his recent condemnation of the "three emperors' league," [15] maintained that the close cooperation of the three imperial governments was the only hope of neutralizing the hostility of England and of preventing a European war. Berlin, however, proved nearly as disappointing as Vienna. The letters of Emperor William to the tsar could not have been more affectionate; they invariably harped on the memories of 1870 and his undying loyalty, but Bismarck would not bring any pressure on Austria, which was what Gorchakov wanted him to do. Relations between St. Petersburg and Vienna continued

[15] See p. 1005.

to deteriorate. The armistice terms were regarded by Andrássy as far more objectionable than the preliminary peace program of December. Nevertheless, early in February he issued a formal proposal for the convocation of a conference of the signatories of the Treaty of Paris. Gorchakov accepted on the condition that it should be a full-fledged congress attended by leading European statesmen. By the end of February Bismarck reluctantly agreed to sponsor a congress in Berlin, but no decision was reached as to its exact date and terms of reference. The Treaty of San Stefano precipitated a new crisis. Meanwhile Austro-Russian negotiations, including a visit by Ignatev to Vienna at the end of March, dragged on until early in May without producing an agreement. Bismarck, faithful to the doctrine expounded in his "honest broker" speech (February 19, N.S.), would not intervene between St. Petersburg and Vienna, even though he was anxious that they should reach an understanding. The aloofness of Germany, the intractability of Austria-Hungary, and the hostility of Rumania were important factors in forcing St. Petersburg eventually to assume a more conciliatory attitude towards London.

The reaction of the British government to Russian peace terms, as evidenced by the dispatch of the fleet to Constantinople, left no doubt that Beaconsfield was not prepared to bow to a *fait accompli*. London refused to participate in the proposed congress unless every item of the Russo-Turkish settlement was brought within its purview (March 16, N.S.), a condition that Russians declared unacceptable. The Treaty of San Stefano was greeted in Great Britain with an almost hysterical outburst of Russophobia. On March 27, N.S., the cabinet decided to call up reserves, to bring Indian troops to Malta and Asia Minor, and to occupy portions of Turkish territory, presumably Cyprus and Alexandretta, in order to restore the balance of power in the Mediterranean. The latter decision led to the resignation of Derby, foreign secretary only in name, the prime minister having assumed the actual conduct of foreign relations. Derby's successor, Salisbury, began his tenure of office by issuing an indictment of the Treaty of San Stefano (circular note of April 1, N.S.). Russia, Salisbury argued, in violation of international agreements, and with complete disregard for the interests of the non-Slav populations of the Ottoman empire, aimed at establishing herself as the dominating Power in the Balkans and in the Near East. Turkey was to be reduced to the *de facto* status of a Russian vassal, and since the Porte controlled the Straits and territories in Asia Minor vital to British and European commerce, the British government could not accept her subjugation by Muscovy. Salisbury conceded that reforms in the Christian provinces of Turkey were needed; such reforms, however, could be brought about only by an international congress free to reach decisions in accordance with the interests of all its members and those of the populations immediately concerned. Gorchakov, while contesting every assertion of Salisbury, challenged the British government to say not only what it did not want but also what it wanted (April 9, N.S.), thus leaving the door open for future negotiations. There was no immediate response to this hint, and, indeed, in March and April war between Russia and England, in alliance perhaps with Austria-Hungary and Rumania, appeared almost inevitable. In the middle of February Beaconsfield resumed secret but inconclusive negotiations with Andrássy, who, however, showed no eagerness to plunge into a war for which he knew Austria was not ready.

Ignatev, back in St. Petersburg in the middle of March, was at the height of his power. Russian military and naval preparations, including plans for a diversion in central Asia and the fitting of privateers in the United States, were feverishly pushed. The Grand Duke Nicholas was snowed under by an avalanche of pressing orders to occupy, if necessary by force, the shore of the Bosphorus (and sometimes also Constantinople and Gallipoli) so as to forestall a British landing and to prevent the entry of British warships in the Black Sea. The Porte, however, would not yield to diplomatic pressure, and the grand duke hesitated to take the irrevocable step that would precipitate a new war. In the middle of April, on the pretext of ill health, he was relieved of his command. His successor, Totleben, after a survey of the situation reached the conclusion that the mining of the Bosphorus insisted on by the St. Petersburg strategists was not feasible and that the British fleet could not be kept out of the Black Sea; the occupation of the shores of the Bosphorus, therefore, would serve no useful purpose. The storming of Constantinople, Totleben believed, would be risky and onerous; even if successful, it would bring merely temporary advantages and would involve Russia in a protracted war for which the epidemic-ridden army, poorly supplied and dependent on long and insecure lines of communication, was ill prepared. The failure of the attack would have had even direr consequences. These disheartening findings were submitted to the tsar in a report of May 9,

N.S., accompanied by the unheroic recommendation that the army should withdraw to Adrianople, provided the Turks evacuated the fortresses of Shumla and Varna. The military argument was reinforced, from other quarters, by equally weighty economic and political considerations: financially Russia was not in a position to fight another war, and the spreading of disaffection and revolutionary activities (discussed in the next chapter) was a warning not to be ignored. There were sobering thoughts. By the end of April war fever in St. Petersburg had subsided, although panslav agitation in the press continued. Totleben's report received imperial sanction. In the second half of May, Ignatev, much to the relief of Gorchakov and the foreign office, withdrew to his estate. His career, as a diplomatist, was closed. It befell his old enemy, Shuvalov, to lead Russia out of the impasse of San Stefano.

THE CONGRESS OF BERLIN

The alternative to war was an international congress, which, however, had no chance to succeed without a preliminary agreement among the leading Powers. Negotiations with Andrássy being barren of results, an understanding with England became imperative. Shuvalov in London had worked patiently and assiduously to stave off a break with Great Britain. Parleys initiated by Bismarck early in April for the simultaneous withdrawal of Russian troops from San Stefano to Adrianople and of the British fleet outside the Dardanelles suggested that the mediation of Berlin might be extended to include other and more basic issues. When the German effort at mediation failed (April 27, N.S.), Shuvalov was authorized to offer Salisbury direct negotiations (April 29, N.S.), a method recommended also by Bismarck. Beaconsfield and Salisbury accepted, and the road towards a *rapprochement* was at least cleared. The Shuvalov-Salisbury conversations were carried on in great secrecy, Bismarck alone among foreign statesmen being informed of their progress. Preliminary British proposals were taken by Shuvalov to St. Petersburg, and on his return to London a secret agreement was signed after its final text had been telegraphed to the tsar and had received his approval. The agreement was in the form of three memoranda, two dated May 30, N.S., and one May 31, N.S. It represented (as will appear from the discussion of the Treaty of Berlin which incorporated its provisions) a drastic revision of the Treaty of San Stefano and, in spite of substantial concessions made to Russia, was a signal success for British diplomacy. A number of explosive questions were left unsettled, but the progress achieved justified, even before the formal signature of the agreement, the convocation of an international congress. The invitation issued by Bismarck (May 14, N.S.) stated specifically that the president of the congress "confirms the free discussion" (*confirme la libre discussion*) of the Treaty of San Stefano, another victory for the British point of view.

The British, however, were not content to rest on their laurels, and proceeded to secure further strategic and diplomatic advantages. On May 24, N.S., Beaconsfield demanded that the sultan conclude an alliance with England, pledging Great Britain to defend Turkish domains in Asia against Russian attacks. In return the Porte was to "assign the island of Cyprus to be occupied and administered by England" in order to enable her "to make necessary provision for the execution of her engagement." British control over this "key to western Asia" was to counterbalance Russian acquisitions in Asia Minor. The sultan, threatened in case of refusal with "capture of Constantinople and the partition of the empire," had to comply with the ungenerous demand of his old friend and protector. A convention to that effect was signed on June 4, N.S., but was not announced until July 8, N.S., the day after the British occupied Cyprus. No less significant was an agreement between Salisbury and Andrássy (June 6, N.S.) which bound Great Britain to support Austrian demands in the Balkans and thus assured the cooperation of the two governments at the forthcoming congress. The diplomatic outlook for Russia was not too promising; it was not improved by the appointment of Gorchakov as first Russian plenipotentiary. Shuvalov was the original choice, but the tsar could not resist the plea of his eighty-year-old chancellor, who was consumed by ambition to shine at a great international gathering. Bismarck was hostile to Gorchakov, and the latter's appointment led to the German chancellor's refusal to preside at the congress, a position which he reversed only at the express request of the tsar. Bismarck, however, was on excellent terms with Shuvalov, the second Russian delegate, and lent him loyal support. The burden of defending Russia's cause was shouldered by Shuvalov, the ailing and senile Gorchakov taking but a minor part in the proceedings.

The Congress of Berlin held its first session on June 13, 1878, N.S. The leading personalities at the congress, in addition to Bismarck,

Gorchakov, and Shuvalov, were Beaconsfield, Salisbury, and Andrássy. The French and the Italian plenipotentiaries, W. H. Waddington and Count Luigi Corti, remained in the background, while the Turks hardly counted at all and were treated by Bismarck in the most cavalier fashion. The Balkan states, except Bulgaria (still officially a province of Turkey), sent delegations but did not participate in the work of the congress, although Greece and Rumania were given the opportunity to be heard, a formality which had no effect upon the decisions. The proceedings resolved themselves into a duel between Shuvalov, on the one hand, and Beaconsfield, seconded by Salisbury and Andrássy, on the other, with Bismarck in the part of an umpire, impartial yet lending a discreet—but on several occasions decisive—support to the Russians. In spite of the preliminary agreements the discussion was often stormy, Beaconsfield threatening to leave Berlin if his demands were not accepted. Shuvalov's unfailing tact and conciliatory spirit and Bismarck's firm and skillful handling of awkward situations triumphed over all obstacles: on July 13, N.S., the Treaty of Berlin was signed. It was in more than one way a revealing document. In the clash of imperial ambitions of the great Powers the fate of the Balkan Slavs and the Christian populations in Turkey, ostensibly the cause of the war, was largely forgotten. Bismarck professed supreme indifference for the Balkan peoples, whom he regarded as outside the pale of European civilization and of no consequence in themselves. Beaconsfield was intent on limiting Russian influence and on prodding Turkey (from whom he had just wangled Cyprus), an attitude fatal to the national aspirations of the Greeks. Both Gorchakov and Shuvalov knew little and cared less about the Bulgars, Serbians, and Montenegrins, whom the Magyar Andrássy was only too willing to sacrifice to the aggrandizement and security of Austria-Hungary. The lack of sympathy on the part of the statesmen assembled in Berlin for the peoples whose destinies they were molding profoundly affected the new order in the Balkans.

By the Treaty of Berlin Russia acquired the coveted districts of Bessarabia and, in Asia Minor, Kars, Ardahan, and Batum (still held by the Turks), which became a free port "essentially commercial," but she renounced Bayazid and the valley of the Alashkert ceded to her at San Stefano. The city and district of Khotur were transferred by Turkey to Persia. Bulgaria, shorn of the littoral of the Aegean, lost more than half of the territory assigned to her by the Treaty of San

Stefano and was split into two parts: (1) north of the Balkan range was formed the politically autonomous principality of Bulgaria tributary to the sultan and governed by representative institutions and an elected prince "confirmed by the Sublime Porte with the consent of the Powers"; (2) the Bulgarian districts south of the Balkans constituted the administratively autonomous province of Eastern Rumelia, which remained "under the direct political and military authority" of the sultan. Turkish fortresses in the principality of Bulgaria were razed, and Ottoman troops were withdrawn. The Porte was allowed to maintain fortifications and military and naval establishments on the frontiers of Eastern Rumelia, including the Balkan range which formed the boundary between Bulgaria and Rumelia; but Turkish armed forces could be brought into the other parts of Eastern Rumelia only at the request of its Christian governor and after notification to the Powers. Police functions in Eastern Rumelia were entrusted to a native gendarmery assisted by local militia. The use of irregular troops, bashi-bazouk and Circassians, was prohibited. Bosnia and Herzegovina were occupied and administered by Austria-Hungary, who also secured the right to maintain garrisons and "military and commercial routes" in the sanjak of Novibazar, which otherwise remained under Turkish administration. The independence of Montenegro, Serbia, and Rumania received official recognition. The San Stefano frontiers of Montenegro were revised to its detriment, although less drastically than those of Bulgaria. Montenegro was deprived of substantial regions in Novibazar, Herzegovina, and Albania. The Adriatic port of Spizza became a part of Dalmatia, and that of Dulcigno was restored to Turkey. On the Adriatic littoral Montenegro had to be satisfied with a precarious foothold at Antivari, which, moreover, was demilitarized, closed to warships of all nations, and made subject to the control of Austrian naval and sanitary police. Serbia, the stepchild of San Stefano, lost some territory in Novibazar but was partly compensated by accretions on her southeastern frontier at the expense of former large Bulgaria. Rumania's protest against the re-cession of the Bessarabian districts and the plea of her delegation that Russian troops should not be evacuated through her territory went unheeded. As a compensation for her territorial losses Rumania was given the delta of the Danube, the isle of the Serpents, and the Dobrudja, whose borders were pushed further west than under the San Stefano treaty. Bulgaria, Montenegro, and Serbia were made responsible for a portion of the Ottoman public debt. Greece gained nothing except the nugatory promise of frontier rectification and the reassertion of the San Stefano provision that the 1868 regime in Crete would be scrupulously observed and extended to the European province of Turkey not otherwise provided for by the treaty. The Armenians were handed over to the mercy of the Turks with the jejune and studiously vague assurance of reforms and protection, a restatement of the benevolent platitudes of San Stefano. The congress, however, took good care to eradicate Russian influence in the administration of the Balkan and Asiatic settlements by substituting a maze of European commissions for the Russian agencies provided at San Stefano. The term of the Russian occupation of Bulgaria was cut down from two years to nine months from the day of the ratification of the treaty; Rumania was to be evacuated within three months after the Russians had withdrawn from Bulgaria. The Russian commissary in Bulgaria was retained, but he was to function jointly with a Turkish commissary and with delegates of the other Powers. In case of disagreement, decision rested with the conference of the representatives of the Powers at Constantinople.

The treaty of Berlin reaffirmed the internationalization of the Danube and disposed of the question of the Straits by providing that the treaties of Paris (1856) and London (1871) were to be maintained in so far as they were not abrogated by the present treaty. This provision was unanimously accepted by the congress on July 6, N.S. On July 11, however, Salisbury startled the delegates by reading to them a declaration which stated that "the obligations of Her Britannic Majesty relating to the closing of the Straits do not go further than an engagement with the sultan to respect in this matter His Majesty's independent determination in conformity with the spirit of the existing treaties." The Russians rejoined (July 12, N.S.) that the closing of the Straits was a European principle binding on all the Powers, not only as regards the sultan but also the other signatories of the treaties of 1841, 1856, and 1871. Salisbury made no reply, and the text of the Treaty of Berlin was not amended. The ambiguous and unexpected British declaration, nevertheless, created bewilderment and apprehension in St. Petersburg and had important political repercussions.[16]

---

[16] Russian plenipotentiaries, according to their declaration, were "unable to comprehend the exact meaning" of Salisbury's statement. Their puzzlement is shared by many international lawyers who hold that the British contention was

RUSSIA AND THE TREATY OF BERLIN

The execution of the Treaty of Berlin was a formidable task not made easier by the lack of confidence among the signatory Powers. There developed considerable difficulties in enforcing the territorial and administrative changes ordained with little knowledge of, or consideration for, local conditions. The Berlin plenipotentiaries were vague not only about the geography and ethnography of the Balkans and Asia Minor but even about the very names of some of the peoples whose fate they decided.[17] Transfer of territories is always a painful process; those arbitrarily decreed at Berlin met in some instances with stubborn resistance. The Albanians fought spiritedly and successfully against the annexation of a portion of their homeland by Montenegro, with the result that the Berlin boundary was revised, Montenegro being compensated by the acquisition of Dulcigno. The desperate resistance of Bosnia and Herzegovina to Austrian occupation was broken down only after three years of bloody struggle. Macedonia and other Turkish provinces were seething with discontent, and appeared on the verge of a revolt.

From the European point of view, however, the crucial question was whether Russia would withdraw her army from Turkey, Bulgaria, and Eastern Rumelia. Although there were many, especially in London, who believed that evacuation was likely to be indefinitely postponed, this was not the intention of the Russian government. At the end of September, after the Turks had surrendered Shumla, Varna, and Batum, Totleben transferred his headquarters from San Stefano to Adrianople, and some of the Russian troops were sent home. Otherwise the situation remained unchanged. The necessary prerequisite for evacuation, according to the Russian view, was the conclusion of a final peace with the Porte which would supersede that of San Stefano and would settle a number of questions (for instance, indemnities) not dealt with at Berlin. The tsar pressed for a speedy termination of the negotiations, but the sultan, as procrastinating as ever, demurred, partly because of the disturbed political situation in Constantinople and frequent changes in government, and partly because

---

irreconcilable with treaty obligations. See C. Phillipson and N. Buxton, *The Question of the Bosphorus and Dardanelles* (London, 1917), pp. 156–162; Baron Boris Nolde, *L'Alliance franco-russe* (Paris, 1936), p. 243 *et seq.*; Goriainow, *op. cit.*, p. 381 *et seq.*

[17] See, for instance, Sumner, *op. cit.*, p. 506 n.

of Layard's tireless anti-Russian intrigues. Such, at least, was the explanation conveyed to Alexander by Prince A. B. Lobanov-Rostovsky, the new Russian ambassador to the Porte. Nevertheless the final Russo-Turkish peace treaty was signed on February 8, 1879, N.S., and the withdrawal of Russian troops from European and Asiatic Turkey began at once. The last Russian detachment left Adrianople in the middle of March, and a few days later Totleben departed from Varna for Odessa. Simultaneously the British fleet repassed the Dardanelles.

There still remained, under the Treaty of Berlin, the Russian army of occupation in Eastern Rumelia and in Bulgaria. By the end of March, 1879, the administrative statute of Eastern Rumelia, prepared by a European commission, was confirmed by the sultan, and the new governor, Aleko Pasha, a Christian Greco-Bulgar and a partisan of Russia, was installed in Philippopolis. In Bulgaria, under the energetic leadership of the Russian commissary, Prince A. M. Dondukov-Korsakov, things moved equally fast but not entirely in accordance with the wishes of the Russian government. In February, 1879, the draft of a fairly liberal organic statute of the principality, prepared in Bulgaria under the direction of Dondukov-Korsakov but revised in St. Petersburg and confirmed by the tsar, was submitted to an assembly of Bulgarian notables. After six weeks of deliberation the draft was returned to Dondukov-Korsakov in the guise of the Bulgarian constitution, with important amendments (universal suffrage, limitations of the powers of the Crown, freedom of the press, assembly, and association) that were sadly at variance with the tradition of Russian autocracy. The tsar nevertheless directed Dondukov-Korsakov to confirm the constitution. The elections of the prince took place at the end of April under the new constitutional charter. Prince Alexander of Battenberg, a nephew of the Russian empress and a relative of Queen Victoria, was unanimously elected. Although Prince Alexander was a nominee of Russia and had served with the Russian army during the war, his brief reign (he abdicated in 1886) was filled with clashes with the Russian government and his numerous Russian advisers. Russian officers in the service of the new principality were concerned chiefly with the building up of the Bulgarian army (and the surreptitious distribution of arms in Eastern Rumelia), preparatory to the unification of Bulgaria and Rumelia, which was regarded in Russian military circles as imminent. Ostensibly, however, the stipulations of the Treaty of Berlin were observed; the evacuation of the Russian troops of occupation began early in May, 1879, and was completed in September.

The Congress of Berlin, conscious perhaps of the evanescence of its work, shrank from providing a collective guarantee for the enforcement of its decisions. Beaconsfield's claim that he had brought back from Berlin "peace with honor" did not commend itself to the opposition or even to many of his followers. It was rightly felt in England that Turkey had been shabbily treated. For different reasons the treaty was almost uniformly unpopular in Russia. Taken by itself, that is, irrespective of San Stefano, the Berlin pact was a victory for Russian imperialism. The "humiliation" of 1856 was wiped out; sizable territories were annexed in Asia Minor; Turkey was dealt a shattering blow; the Slav and Christian peoples of the Ottoman empire had achieved (or were promised) independence or autonomy. That the treaty was by no means unsatisfactory was the view taken by some of the higher officials of the ministry of foreign affairs, for instance, Giers and Lobanov-Rostovsky,[18] but this opinion was timidly and imperfectly reflected in the press. In both content and form the Treaty of Berlin was the undoing of that of San Stefano, and the comparison of the two made a substantial victory appear a crushing defeat. The wrath, dismay, and sorrow of the panslavs and the nationalists were voiced by Aksakov in a celebrated speech delivered on July 4, N.S., a few days before the signature of the treaty. To him the work of the congress, especially the partition of Bulgaria and the Austrian occupation of Bosnia and Herzegovina, was a shameful betrayal of the "sacred cause" for which Russian soldiers had shed their blood. "We are burying today," Aksakov exclaimed, ". . . the principles and traditions of our forebears, our own wishes; we are burying Russian glory, Russian honor, Russian conscience. . . ." and he demanded the continuation of the war, if necessary against England and Austria-Hungary, on the optimistic assumption that "the Russian tsar cannot be defeated if he carries high the banner of Slavdom and eastern Christianity." The author of this philippic was chastized by expulsion from Moscow; nevertheless the feeling of disillusionment to which he gave vent was shared, in a varying degree, by the majority of the reading public and the bureaucracy.

The attitude of Alexander towards the treaty was, as usual, ambigu-

[18] Letter of Giers of July 5, 1878, N.S., and letter of Lobanov-Rostovsky of July 1, 1878, N.S., quoted in Nolde, *op. cit.*, pp. 208–209.

ous and shifting. "What will Russia and our gallant army say if you fail to take Constantinople," the tsar wrote to the Grand Duke Nicholas in a moment of nationalist exaltation (April 1, 1878, N.S.). Yet he approved the Shuvalov-Salisbury agreement, and no important decision in Berlin was made without his sanction. According to Giers, he was at first satisfied with the results obtained at Berlin.[19] Soon, however, he changed his mind. Shuvalov, only recently mentioned as the most likely candidate for the chancellorship, was given on his arrival at St. Petersburg from Berlin a frigid reception. In May, 1879, he left the London embassy on a long leave of absence, and his diplomatic career was virtually over. More significant was the tsar's resentment against Germany, especially against Bismarck, whom he pictured as the instigator, and chief agent at the Berlin congress, of a European conspiracy to humiliate and despoil Russia.

This aberration, which lasted for only a few months, may be ascribed partly to the panslav and nationalist influences in his entourage (the tsarevich, Pobedonostsev, Katkov) and partly to the intrigues of Gorchakov, an inveterate enemy of Shuvalov and Bismarck. The aged chancellor was disappointed with Berlin on personal rather than on political grounds. The congress proved distressingly unlike the Areopagus of his dreams, where his polished discourses had enthralled respectful throngs of admiring statesmen. Gorchakov, moreover, shrewdly endeavored to escape his share of responsibility for the work of the Russian delegation by shifting in advance (as he did in his letters to the tsar) on Shuvalov and Bismarck the blame for the inevitable but unpopular decisions. His recriminations against Bismarck were a great deal more than manifestations of a personal feud between two elderly statesmen. They meant, if persisted in, the abandonment of the German alliance which Gorchakov had championed, with but minor defections, since the 1860's. This was, indeed, the course he was now determined to pursue. "In our opinion," he wrote to Novikov on February 14, 1879, N.S., repeating almost verbatim what he had said in 1856 and in April, 1877, "the agreement of the three emperors is terminated by the actual conduct of our two allies. Today our chief task is to wind up the liquidation of the past and to rely entirely on ourselves." The Russian press, instigated by the foreign office, launched a violent attack on Austria-Hungary, Germany, and Bismarck personally. The high tariff bill then pending before the

[19] Letter of July 5, 1878, N.S., quoted in Nolde, *op. cit.*, p. 208.

Reichstag and the imposition of a German embargo on certain articles of Russian export, because of an outbreak of the plague in the province of Astrakhan, provided additional fuel for the Russian press campaign. Bismarck was no friend of Gorchakov's, and retaliated in kind. In the spring of 1879 the bloodless "war of the two chancellors" was raging in newspaper columns.

REVIVAL OF THE THREE EMPERORS' LEAGUE

These seemingly trivial happenings threatened to have grave political repercussions. On August 15, 1879, N.S., Alexander, without consulting his ministers, sent his uncle, Emperor William, a recriminatory letter in which he denounced the alleged anti-Russian activities of German diplomatic agents on the various commissions established under the Treaty of Berlin, pointedly recalled the "unforgettable" services rendered by Russia to Germany in 1870, and closed with a vague but ominous reference to the gravity of the situation, pregnant with disastrous possibilities for both countries. The eighty-two-year-old German emperor was greatly perturbed. After a hasty exchange of messages Alexander and William met at the frontier station of Alexandrovo (September 3–4, N.S.). The tsar fell at once under the spell of his venerable uncle, confessed that his letter was written on the spur of the moment, and retracted his charges against Bismarck. The two emperors parted on most friendly terms.

The tsar's unconditional abandonment of his anti-German attitude cannot be entirely explained by his affection for William coupled with dynastic loyalties, strong as these motives were. For several months Alexander was subject to the pressure of a group of advisers convinced of the necessity of an alliance with Germany. In the spring of 1879 Gorchakov went abroad for reasons of health and thenceforth made but rare appearances in the Russian capital. Giers, acting minister of foreign affairs, Miliutin, Lobanov-Rostovsky, and P. A. Saburov (appointed ambassador to Berlin in December, 1879) were all partisans of the German alliance. It not only appealed to the conservative tradition of the elder statesmen and of the foreign office but, it was argued, was dictated by the logic of the international situation. The events of 1877–1878 again demonstrated that Russia's chief enemy was England. Evidence of the impending conflict with Great Britain was not lacking: the Anglo-Turkish convention of July 4, 1878, N.S.; Salisbury's declaration on the Straits at the Congress of Berlin; the anti-Russian intrigues of the British agents in the Balkans and in the Near East; clashes with the British in central Asia. Reliance on one's own strength so glibly advocated by Gorchakov was obviously the counsel of despair. Alliance with Germany, Giers and his friends held, was from the Russian standpoint a necessity. After the meeting of Alexandrovo the tsar was won over to this program, and in the middle of September, 1879, Saburov, armed with an appropriate instruction, was dispatched to Berlin.

In the meantime Bismarck, distrustful of St. Petersburg, exasperated by the personal attacks of the Russian press, and fearing the isolation of Germany, took advantage of Alexander's uncautious letter to William to negotiate with Vienna a secret defensive alliance against Russia. The treaty of alliance was signed on October 7, 1879, N.S., the emperor of Germany being forced to ratify it (although he considered the alliance a base treachery to Russia) under threat of the resignation of Bismarck and the cabinet. Bismarck, without disclosing the exact nature of the Austro-German treaty, explained to Saburov that he had definite obligations towards Austria, and countered the proposal for a German-Russian alliance with the offer of reviving the "three emperors' league." The tsar signified his acceptance "in principle" (November, 1879), and negotiations followed which led to the conclusion, after Alexander II's murder, of the secret alliance of Russia, Austria, and Germany (June 18, 1881, N.S.). The salient feature of this treaty, which will be discussed in a later chapter, was the promise by Russia to respect the *status quo* in the Balkans (as revised by the agreement of the three emperors) in return for the guarantee of the existing regime of the Straits and Constantinople. In other words, the panslav dreams were sacrificed on the altar of what was deemed to be Russia's security.

A RETROSPECT, 1856–1881

The historian casting a glance over the quarter-century of Russian foreign policy from 1856 to 1881 may well hesitate to formulate a clear-cut verdict. Measured by the conventional standards of prestige and empire building, the achievements of Alexander II's reign were, indeed, impressive. Under his rule Russia firmly established herself on the shores of the Pacific, acquired vast territories in central Asia and in the Near East, threw off the vexatious restrictions of the Treaty of Paris, reduced to impotence her old enemy Turkey, and powerfully contributed to the liberation and national awakening of the Balkan Slavs. Seen at close quarters, however, the onward march of the empire loses much of its majesty, and appears in its true light as a haphazard and confused process set in motion by small men driven by petty ambitions. A country already oversized and underpopulated, hopelessly backward industrially and culturally, squandered her scant resources of men and treasure in conquests of the arid wastes of Asia and in unrewarding adventures in the Balkans. The expansion of the imperial frontier traced on the map in blood and iron flattered, no doubt, national *amour propre*; this superficial and unreasoned satisfaction, however, was purchased at the exorbitant cost of retarding Russia's political, social, and economic progress. An aggressive foreign policy, even if successful, contains the seeds of future conflicts. British Russophobia was unwarranted and foolish. Yet for antagonizing England in central Asia Russia paid dearly during the Turkish war and at Berlin.

By a cruel irony of fate victory over Turkey brought to many Russians disappointment as poignant as had the defeat of the Crimean War. No economic motives can be assigned to the War of 1877–1878. Neither before nor after the war had Russia any business interests in the peasant poverty-stricken Balkan lands. The few Russian firms which attempted to do business with Bulgaria and the Danubian area soon gave up after taking heavy losses. Poliakov and Günzberg, the two Russian-Jewish financiers active in promoting Bulgarian railways, were representative of international high finance, and had closer relations with Paris than with St. Petersburg or Moscow. Interpreted in strictly economic terms, Katkov was right when he wrote in 1883 that "Russia has no selfish interests in the [Near] East. This, on the one hand, is her strength, but, on the other, explains her clumsiness and lack of steadfastness in pursuing her aims. . . . Russia . . . has no excess population . . . excess labor or excess capital; . . . Russian labor and Russian capital . . . are barely adequate to develop her own untouched natural resources." It would be hardly correct, however, to interpret the War of 1877–1878 as "a crusade." [20] Aksakov's exalted messianic creed was never shared by the tsar or the foreign office. The panslav doctrine of the Ignatev brand, translated in terms of the San Stefano treaty, deliberately sacrificed Orthodoxy and Slavdom to aggressive Russian nationalism. The lamentable collapse of

---

[20] Nolde, *op. cit.*, pp. 173–174.

panslavism after 1878, not only as an official policy but also as a literary movement, is, perhaps, the most striking aspect of this remarkable episode. The renewal of the alliance of the three emperors amounted to the renunciation by Russia of further adventures in the Balkans. The timeliness of this alliance may well be questioned, since Beaconsfield's defeat in April, 1880, marked the termination of the era of "flamboyant" British imperialism and the relaxation of the Anglo-Russian tension in the Black Sea region. Although the "three emperors' league" proved of considerable service to Russia during the Anglo-Russian crisis over Afghanistan in 1885, the revival of the alliance was a sad comment on the unimaginative methods and stale ways of the Russian foreign office. It foundered in the Balkan crisis of 1886–1887.

When all this is said, and when full allowance is made for the vagaries and disingenuousness of Russian policy in the Balkans, the fact remains that the War of 1877–1878 is preserved in Russian and Balkan tradition as the "war of liberation" and that it introduced in the European situation a novel factor the effects of which are still strongly felt today.

CHAPTER XXXVII

ALEXANDER II

Schools, Art, Literature, and Political Movements

SCHOOLS

Craving for knowledge and the urge for self-expression through the medium of the written word and of the arts are potent social and cultural forces which the autocracies of the pre-totalitarian era never succeeded in fully controlling. Stern as was the police regime through most of Alexander II's reign it did not involve the physical destruction of all opposition or the silencing of every organ of public opinion that was not a mouthpiece of the government. Moreover, the unintelligent and obstinate refusal to make concessions to liberal opinion, coupled with the inconsistencies of official policies, defeated its own purpose by fostering political radicalism. Some of Alexander's advisers, as has already been stated, were men of enlightened views, and there were periods when the tsar himself appeared to favor liberal measures. The progress of science, arts, music, and literature noted in the earlier part of the nineteenth century was maintained and, indeed, won for Russia a foremost place among the European nations. Of even greater significance was the emergence for the first time in Russian history of an organized revolutionary movement aiming at the overthrow not only of the autocracy but of the social and economic structure of the empire as well.

The reconstruction of the school system, from the universities to the practically non-existent primary schools, was regarded in progressive circles and by the more enlightened bureaucrats as a necessity. The dismissal in 1854 of Shirinsky-Shikhmatov suggested that even Nicholas I had come to doubt the benefits of the obscurantist regime that ruled the universities. Shirinsky-Shikhmatov's immediate successors—A. S. Norov (1854–1858) and E. P. Kovalevsky (1858–1861) —although they would hardly qualify as liberals, were less hostile towards the higher schools than were the ministers who preceded them. Between 1855 and 1861 the most oppressive restrictions besetting the universities were removed. The school regions of Kharkov and Kiev, which in 1847–1848 were subordinated to the governors-general, returned to the jurisdiction of the curators; limitations on the size of the student body were lifted; Russian scholars were permitted to travel and study abroad; the conduct of students outside university grounds was no longer subject to the supervision of the inspectors; uniforms for undergraduates were abolished; chairs of philosophy and of European constitutional law were revived; lectures open to the general public were allowed; rectors were elected by academic corporations instead of being appointed; the 1850 instruction directing academic authorities to censor the views of faculty members was amended and made less stringent.

In spite of these welcome changes, universities became the scene of recurrent disturbances which, indeed, were to remain a permanent feature of Russian academic life until the end of the empire. Unrest among undergraduates was not unknown in the earlier part of the nineteenth century, but it was not until after the Crimean War that it assumed the character of a mass movement. At first the causes of the outbreaks were trivial and of no political consequence; students protested against vexatious regulations, unsatisfactory living conditions, petty tyranny and high-handed methods of academic authorities and the police. With the rising tide of discontent and disaffection, however, student demonstrations acquired a political tinge. One of the first manifestations of this nature was the church service and meeting in memory of the victims of the peasant revolt in the village of Bezna held by the undergraduates of the university and the theological academy of Kazan (April, 1861). Retribution followed swiftly: Professor A. P. Shchapov, who addressed the gathering, was deprived of his chair and nine students were expelled, but unrest among the students was not checked and caused concern to the government. Kovalevsky's program for restoring order being judged too mild, he was forced to resign in June, 1861. His successor Admiral Putiatin, of Far Eastern fame, was faced in the autumn of 1861 with severe outbreaks of student disorders which led to the temporary closure of the University of St. Petersburg and spread to Moscow, Kiev, Kharkov, and Kazan;

the University of Dorpat, immured in its Germanic tradition, alone remained peaceful and unaffected by the stormy currents of Russian academic life. Putiatin advocated forceful policies, but his proposals were disavowed by the tsar and he was dismissed in December, 1861. A. V. Golovnin, a man of liberal views, became minister of education.

Golovnin realized that repression was not enough and that the situation called for basic reforms. Opportunity for action was provided by the report of an official committee which since 1858 had been working, in collaboration with the faculty of the University of St. Petersburg, on revision of the charter of that institution. In December, 1861, the report, together with the observations of other Russian universities which were consulted, was examined by a committee of government officials and university professors. The outcome of their labor was the draft charter intended for the use of all Russian universities; it was translated into English, French, and German and was circulated to Russian and foreign institutions of learning, to educators, and to lay and ecclesiastical officials. Meanwhile the distinguished jurist Professor K. D. Kavelin was dispatched abroad to make a first-hand study of the organization of German, French, and Swiss higher schools. In the light of the information collected and of the comments received which were published in two bulky volumes, the draft was revised several times (partly by a committee of high officials under the chairmanship of the reactionary Count S. G. Stroganov), was approved by the State Council, and was promulgated on June 18, 1863.

The charter of 1863 restored university autonomy and did away with most of the restrictions imposed in and after 1835. University councils consisting of members of the faculty, and the officers they elected, were given wide control over academic and administrative matters. Curators of the school regions, however, retained the function of general supervision, while government-appointed inspectors were shorn of most of their powers. There were created elective university courts which, unlike those of 1804, had jurisdiction only over disciplinary offenses committed by the students. "Outsiders," that is, persons who did not qualify as students in good standing, were authorized to attend lectures, but the doors of the universities remained closed to women, although their admission was urged by the universities of St. Petersburg, Kiev, Kharkov, and Kazan. The University of Moscow, on the other hand, expressed itself against the admission of women on the curious ground that their presence was likely to have "a pernicious effect upon the studies of young men." Golovnin and many of the authorities consulted favored the legalization of student organizations and corporate activities, but no provision to this effect was included in the charter. This denial of opportunity for legitimate collective action invited disturbances and led to conflicts that eventually proved the undoing of university autonomy.

The virtues of the charter of 1863 have been often overstated, yet in spite of its limitations and of the fact that some of its provisions (for instance, those dealing with university courts) proved still-born, it was a step in the right direction. It was unfortunate, therefore, that the introduction of the charter was followed by assumption of control over Russian schools by Count D. A. Tolstoy, an implacable enemy of autonomy and academic freedom. On April 4, 1866, D. V. Karakozov, a youth of twenty-five, made an unsuccessful attempt to murder Alexander II. The shot he fired at the tsar reverberated throughout Russia and brought to the fore the forces of reaction. The would-be regicide was a former student in the universities of Kazan and Moscow, and the small circle of his youthful associates consisted of men with university connections. This offered the pretext for a violent attack on the ministry of education, long the *bête noire* of the ultra-conservatives. Golovnin was summarily dismissed and was succeeded (April 14) by Tolstoy, a sinister figure notorious for his savage persecution of Roman Catholics and his vicious opposition to the emancipation of the serfs. Chief procurator of the Holy Synod since 1864, Tolstoy retained that office after he became minister of education, and for fourteen years ruled with an iron hand both Church and schools. His administration left on educational institutions a lasting trace that was not entirely erased until the overthrow of the monarchy.

Obstinate, intolerant, and bigoted, Tolstoy was determined to eradicate by police methods the liberal and revolutionary spirit of the universities. An order of May 26, 1867, decreed close cooperation between academic authorities and the police in exchanging information concerning the political views of the undergraduates and their conduct in and outside the university, and prohibited all student activities, including concerts and theatricals for the benefit of student relief. Tolstoy's regime failed, of course, to restore academic peace, the years 1869, 1874, and 1878 being particularly stormy. In 1872 the minister requested the university councils to formulate proposals for the amendment of the charter of 1863 but met with scant response. A committee appointed in 1874 to investigate student disturbances recommended drastic curtailment of university autonomy, stricter government control over the character of teaching, and limitation of the size of the student body. In 1875 the drafting of a new charter embodying the above program was entrusted to a committee under the chairmanship of I. D. Delianov, later minister of education under Alexander III. There were sharp clashes between Tolstoy and the upholders of academic freedom, the venerable historian Solovev being forced to resign the rectorship of the University of Moscow. The draft charter was finally introduced in the State Council in February, 1880, but in April Tolstoy was dismissed and his successor, A. A. Saburov, hastened to withdraw the unpopular bill. It was revived in the reign of Alexander III and became law in 1884.

There was less delay in carrying out the reform of secondary schools, around which raged a heated controversy. The issue, the old one of classicism versus science, was not entirely academic because the teaching of the humanities was used by reactionary elements as a method for preventing boys of modest means and humble social status (deemed therefore particularly susceptible to revolutionary propaganda) from gaining access to higher schools, although this object was not openly proclaimed until 1887. Reform of secondary education had already been sponsored by Norov. The program outlined in his report to the tsar in 1856, while favoring classical studies, emphasized that real improvement in the scholastic and moral standards of the students should be brought about by better teaching of "the holy truths of the Orthodox faith," which, the minister imagined, would "warm up the hearts of the young." Golovnin's approach was different. A bill on secondary schools for boys, prepared by a committee of the ministry of education, like the university charter, was translated into foreign languages and was circulated to educational institutions and qualified persons at home and abroad. The 377 comments received, including 42 from abroad, filled six volumes; the bill was repeatedly revised, was amended and finally approved by the State Council, and was confirmed by the tsar on November 18, 1864.

In spite of this elaborate procedure the law of 1864 contained no striking innovation but was rather a return to the principles of the law of 1828. It provided for schools of two categories: gymnasiums with a seven-year course and progymnasiums with an abridged course comprising the four junior years of the gymnasiums. The gymnasium was either classical or of the *Realschule* type. The principal difference between the two was that Latin and Greek were taught only in classical gymnasiums. Gymnasiums of the *Realschule* type offered instead of classical languages more comprehensive instruction in mathematics, natural history, and courses in chemistry, physics, cosmography, modern languages, drawing, and drafting. Religion, Russian, literature, history, and geography were included in the curriculums of all gymnasiums. The aim of classical gymnasiums was to prepare students for the universities, which admitted holders of classical diplomas without entrance examinations; the aim of the gymnasium of the *Realschule* type was to provide adequate general education; universities were closed to its graduates but the latter might qualify for admission to higher technical schools. As a provisional measure, until the law of 1864 was made fully effective, half of the then existing gymnasiums were to teach Latin, one-quarter both Latin and Greek, and one-quarter had no classical languages. This compromise arrangement, which was due in part to the shortage of teachers of Greek, was claimed as a victory both by the supporters and by the opponents of classicism. Secondary schools were open to all boys "irrespective of faith or social status." Instruction was not free; the determination of the amount of tuition was left to the board of each school, and fees varied within a wide range, in 1881, for instance, from 5 to 100 rubles per annum.

Tolstoy's appointment ushered in a new phase in the history of secondary schools. Alexander, shortly after Karakozov's attempt on his life, decreed that education "must be conducted in the spirit of true religion, respect for the right of property, and preservation of the foundations of public order," and that "no school shall tolerate the propaganda, openly or secretly, of destructive notions equally inimical to the advancement of the moral and the economic well-being of the people" (rescript to the president of the council of ministers, Prince P. P. Gagarin, May 13, 1866). To the elimination of these "destructive notions" Tolstoy applied himself with great resourcefulness and tireless zeal. His policies were influenced by the views expounded in the columns of the ultra-reactionary *Moskovskiia Vedomosti* by his political friends Katkov and P. M. Leontev, who were very critical of Golovnin, especially of his "too liberal" school law of 1864. The only safe method of protecting the schools from the infiltration of revolutionary doctrines, according to Katkov, was to concentrate on the teaching of subjects that did not lend themselves to subversive interpretations; namely, classical languages and mathematics. Reviving theories prevalent under Nicholas I, Katkov argued (in an article published in 1871) that every social group should receive an education befitting its station. Elementary schooling ending at the ages of twelve and thirteen met the needs of the "lower trading classes"; more advanced education of the *Realschule* type should be provided for boys of the "better-off trading classes" who could afford to remain at school until the age of fifteen to seventeen; finally, higher education up to the age of twenty-one to twenty-five should be reserved for "the upper class which decides the fate of the nation and charts its future." This program Tolstoy endeavored to carry out even though he denied its class character.

Preparations for the revision of the law of 1864 began in the summer of 1866. Tolstoy, unlike his predecessor, did not consult the academic profession, and the bill was drafted by purely bureaucratic methods. Public criticism of the reform was silenced by an imperial order (reenacted two years later as the law of June 16, 1873) which was interpreted as giving the authorities the power to prohibit, in the public interest, discussion in the press of measures contemplated by the government. The interdict applied only to adverse criticism, laudatory comments being strongly encouraged. In spite of this precaution the bill met with stubborn opposition. Tolstoy's classicism *à outrance* had implacable enemies among the higher bureaucracy, including members of the State Council. It was in vain that the imaginative minister pleaded before that assembly that the ability of the students to read in the original the Gospel, the works of Church fathers, and "other religious chants [sic] . . . will not leave indifferent our common people . . . and will eventually endear to it the higher schools." Unmoved, twenty-nine members of the Council, among them the tsar's favorite, Dimitry Miliutin, voted against the bill, and only nineteen, including Tolstoy, voted for it. Alexander confirmed the minority decision, which thus became law on June 30, 1871.

The new law instituted in secondary schools a regime aptly described as "Greco-Roman bondage." Both classical languages were made compulsory in all gymnasiums, Latin beginning with the first year, Greek with the third; the number of hours per week assigned to each language varied from six to eight throughout the entire course, which in 1877 was extended to eight years. The number of hours allotted to mathematics and religion were also increased at the expense of other subjects, especially Russian, literature, history, and geography. It was officially explained that the "excessive" time formerly given to Russian and literature encouraged teachers "to indulge in generalizations not only useless but at times distinctly harmful." To discourage such practices Church Slavonic was included among the topics taught under the heading of "Russian."

Many educators shared and still share, although for different reasons, Tolstoy's predilection for the humanities. The framers of the law of 1871 claimed, indeed, that they were following in the footsteps of German, French, and English schools. Unfortunately Tolstoy's brand of classicism was perfunctory and shallow and his methods highly objectionable: study of ancient civilization was excluded from the classroom, the time and energy of students being devoted to mastering vocabulary and grammar, especially syntax. A high degree of proficiency was required from the young scholars: Russian texts dictated by the teacher were to be translated into Latin and Greek on the wing, so to speak, that is, without being first taken down in Russian. History and geography were taught with special reference to ancient Greece and Rome. Teachers were given minute instructions as to how to handle their subjects and what they should or should not say in class. For instance, only cursory reference was permitted to forms of government in foreign lands; in discussing the struggle between patricians and plebeians it was to be "strongly emphasized" that both parties "displayed at all time moderation and self-control"; the "positive" aspects of Russian history, including victorious wars, were to be dealt with at length, while the "negative" ones were to receive summary treatment. All textbooks were to be approved by the ministry.

The curriculums of classical gymnasiums were designed to provide formal training and to shield students from contact with problems that might have social or political implications. This austere intellectual fare was matched by an administrative regime that stressed discipline and obedience. In 1867 comprehensive annual examinations, abolished under Golovnin, were restored. The life of students, both in and out of school, was subject to close regimentation. Conduct in the classroom, the manner in which the boys were to address teachers and answer questions, church attendance, homework—all were carefully regulated. Enforcement of the rules was entrusted to a staff of inspectors whose duty it was to visit students in their lodgings and to be at all times informed of their whereabouts. There was a carefully graded list of penalties, from reprimand to expulsion, but no corporal punishment. To facilitate the task of supervision the students were put in uniform, which they had to wear even during summer vacations. The hard-earned classical diploma was the prerequisite for admission to universities without entrance examinations.

The reform of 1871 affected the composition of the teaching body. Russia had few men qualified to teach Latin and Greek, and the number of graduates of the St. Petersburg Historico-Philological Institute founded in 1867 to train teachers of classical languages was too small to make good the deficiency. A special seminar for Russian students of Greek and Latin was organized in Leipzig in 1873 and functioned until 1888. The immediate and pressing need, however, was met by the importation of classicists of Czech and other Slavic extraction, chiefly graduates of Austrian universities. These foreign teachers were often competent classical scholars; but they knew little about their adopted country, and some of them, at least, expressed themselves in what may be termed "basic" Russian. It was Tolstoy's policy to give preference to classicists, including the imported pedagogues, in making appointments to the more lucrative and responsible administrative positions in the schools, such as directors and inspectors. Students, thus, were not the only ones to bear the yoke of "Greco-Roman bondage." Moreover, bureaucratic regimentation was extended to the teaching body. The modest degree of self-government enjoyed under the law of 1864 by the school boards, which consisted of members of the teaching staff, practically vanished and gave place to the autocratic rule of the appointed director laboring under the watchful control of the ministry.

"The future historian . . . will dwell with particular gratitude on the school reform of 1871," wrote Katkov; "before this decade has run its course the beneficial effect of the reform will be widely felt and even the present generation will bless for it the reign of Alexander II." The verdict of posterity belied these sanguine expectations. Peter I had failed in his endeavor to turn Russians into sailors; Tolstoy and Alexander II were no more successful in their attempt to make classical scholars out of Russian schoolboys. From 1872 to 1890 only 4 to 9 per cent of the boys enrolled in gymnasiums completed the course within eight years; another 21 to 37 per cent managed to squeeze through after spending one or more extra years in the same grade;

the balance, that is, the vast majority, were either dropped or withdrew. There is a remarkable unanimity among competent observers that even the successful graduates were far from constituting that "aristocracy of intelligence, aristocracy of knowledge, aristocracy of labor" Tolstoy liked to talked about. Professor V. Modestov, writing in 1879, held that the reform dealt "the death blow" to classicism itself; the schools it created "dull intellectual faculties, lead to intellectual and moral mediocrity." The conservative publicist V. V. Rozanov characterized (1899) classical gymnasiums as "moral and intellectual prisons" in which no gifted child could survive long without suffering irreparable damage. The reform of 1871, according to Count P. Kapnist, curator of the Moscow school region from 1880 to 1895, "was based on principles hostile to the advancement of knowledge"; by methods "almost criminal" it produced instead of secondary education a kind of "antiseptic for the destruction of free thought, a bacteriological station for the inoculation of schoolboys with officially approved doctrines." But even the latter object was not achieved. The armor of classicism proved ineffectual against the dreaded "destructive notions." Ministerial circulars bear witness that revolutionary propaganda was rife among teachers and students and that counter-measures were often rendered useless by the fact that subversive ideas were encouraged by some of the parents.

The law of 1871 having abolished gymnasiums of the *Realschule* type, new *Realschulen* were established by the law of March 15, 1872.[1] The majority of the State Council voted against the bill when it was introduced by Tolstoy, but the tsar again confirmed the minority report. The new *Realschulen* offered a six-year course which, however, might be extended to seven years. The curriculums of the four junior years corresponded, broadly, to those of the gymnasiums, except that classical languages were not taught; the programs laid stress, especially during the two (or three) senior years, on physics, chemistry, engineering, and rural economy. A large number of hours throughout the entire course was given to drawing and drafting. *Realschulen* were intended for boys of the lower middle class, sons of merchants and burghers, and were aimed at providing technical or professional training rather than general education; their graduates were denied access to universities and were eligible for admission to the higher technical schools

[1] The Russian *realnoe uchilishche* is the literal translation of *Realschule*; I use the German term because no satisfactory equivalent appears to exist in English.

only on complying with specified requirements and on passing entrance examinations. According to the views of the ministry of education, the object of *Realschulen* was to prepare young men, not for advanced studies, but for employment in trades, commerce, industry, agriculture, and other business pursuits.

It is noteworthy that at the very time when the secondary schools of the ministry of education were submitted to a regime of either insufferable classical pedantry or narrow professionalism, an educational experiment along entirely different lines was carried on by the ministry of war. Desire for economy and for better educational standards among army officers led to the reorganization of the then existing military academies (*kadetskii korpus*) as higher military schools (*vysshee voennoe uchilishche*) and military gymnasiums (law of May 14, 1863). Specialized military training was provided by the higher military schools and lasted for two years; military gymnasiums offered a preliminary six-year course of a general educational character. The subjects taught were roughly the same as in the secondary schools of the ministry of education, except that military gymnasiums omitted classical languages and were free from the aggressive professionalism of the *Realschulen*. Strange as this may seem, military gymnasiums, judged by contemporary Russian standards, were liberal schools: there were no comprehensive examinations, no foolish and vexatious regimentation of teachers and students such as was practiced by Tolstoy. This enlightened regime was due to the common sense, vision, and determination of Dimitry Miliutin, minister of war from 1861 to 1881; it did not survive his resignation. The new minister of war, General P. S. Vannovsky, hastened to undo the work of his predecessor: in 1882 military gymnasiums (they numbered twenty-three in 1880) reverted to their former status of military academies.

While the boys' schools went through a period of painful experimentation, education of women registered substantial progress. In the first half of the nineteenth century secondary schools for girls, except for a few private institutions, were managed by the Administration of Empress Marie (*Mariinskoe Vedomstvo*, functioning since 1828 as Section IV of His Majesty's Own Chancery), which in 1855 maintained forty-six schools with an aggregate student body of seven thousand. Most of these schools were boarding schools (*institut*) intended primarily for daughters of noblemen and government officials. The educational levels were low, girls being trained chiefly in "useful accomplishments"—religion, French, handiwork, domestic arts, music, singing, and dancing; they were carefully protected from contact with the realities of everyday life and were reared, especially in the more exclusive schools, in an atmosphere of rarefied gentility. Towards the end of Nicholas I's reign the rules governing admission to the boarding schools were somewhat relaxed, partly under the pressure of financial considerations: day students and girls belonging to the less privileged groups were accepted by some of the schools. In 1865 all but seven of the boarding schools opened their doors to girls of every social group (except those subject to the poll tax), and the school of Kerch was authorized to admit daughters of Jewish merchants. The prohibitive cost of boarding schools, however, suggested that the solution of the problem of female education must be sought elsewhere.

A proposal for the establishment by the ministry of education of day schools for girls was made as early as 1846 but was abandoned for lack of funds. It was revived by Norov in 1856 and was acted upon by Kovalevsky. A law of 1858, amended in 1860, authorized girls' day schools with a six- and a three-year course to be financed by corporations of the nobility, municipalities, and private contributions. By a law of May 24, 1870, these schools received a new organization which they retained, but with minor changes, until the revolution of 1917. The law of 1870 provided for the establishment of girls' gymnasiums with a seven-year course (the eighth year was added for the students who wished to be trained as teachers) and progymnasiums with a three-year course. The state treasury appropriated a small subsidy towards the maintenance of these schools, but the bulk of their expenditure was defrayed, as under the law of 1864, from local sources. The control of the ministry of education over administrative and academic matters affecting the schools was extended in 1870, much to the detriment of the limited autonomy previously enjoyed by the school boards. The curriculums of girls' gymnasiums differed somewhat from those of the boys' schools, Tolstoy insisting on programs deemed suitable for preparing young women for their duties as future wives and mothers. Nevertheless Latin and Greek were introduced in 1874 as optional subjects in girls' gymnasiums. Beginning in 1858, the Administration of Empress Marie proceeded to establish girls' gymnasiums (day schools) which, unlike those of the ministry of education, were financed by the state treasury. Gymnasiums were open to all girls irrespective of their social status, but the fees charged made it difficult for impecunious parents to avail themselves of the opportunity.[2]

The spreading of secondary education for women led to the demand for their admission to the higher schools. The charter of 1863 having barred them from the universities, the alternative was the organization of higher schools for their exclusive use. Universities for women (*vysshye zhenkie kursy*), authorized by the government but established by private initiative and dependent on private support, were opened in Moscow in 1869 and 1871, in St. Petersburg in 1877, and in Kiev and Kazan in the 1870's. The faculties of these institutions were drawn from the teaching staff of local male universities and comprised some of Russia's most distinguished professors. The first medical school for women, affiliated with the Military Medical Academy, was founded in 1872. The immediate success of these institutions showed conclusively that they met a real need.

In the 1860's and 1870's a modest yet real beginning was made in the advancement of elementary education. It will be remembered that on the eve of the emancipation Russia had few primary schools and that those in rural areas were administered by departments other than the ministry of education.[3] An early manifestation of public interest in the spread of literacy was the movement for the establishment of Sunday schools, which, unlike their namesakes in this country, were concerned not so much with the teaching of the Gospel as with the rudiments of reading and writing. The first Sunday schools were founded in Kiev and St. Petersburg in 1859; in 1862 there were over 300 such schools with an attendance of some 20,000 scattered in 178 towns. The government, however, was suspicious of a spontaneous mass educational endeavor. In May, 1862, St. Petersburg was swept by recurrent devastating fires; the outbreaks were attributed to arson allegedly instigated by radical groups active in Sunday schools. The schools were closed; and although in 1864 they were permitted to resume operation they recovered but slowly, and never regained their former vitality.

In the meantime the ministry of education was busy with plans for school reforms. The necessity of a concerted effort for the promotion of village schools was urged upon the government from many

[2] In 1879 the annual fees in gymnasiums of the Administration of Empress Marie varied from 40 rubles in the provinces to 75 rubles in St. Petersburg and Moscow.
[3] See p. 806.

quarters, especially by the commissions drafting the emancipation acts. Two reports on primary schools were prepared in 1860, one by a committee of the ministry of education and the other by an interdepartmental committee; they were translated into foreign languages and were circulated (like those on universities and secondary schools) to competent institutions and persons at home and abroad. After much discussion, amending, and redrafting, the primary-schools bill was passed by the State Council and was confirmed by the tsar on July 14, 1864. The purpose of primary schools, according to the law, was to promote "true religious and moral principles" and to impart "useful elementary knowledge." The subjects taught were religion, reading (Russian and Church Slavonic), writing, arithmetic and, "wherever feasible," religious singing. Schools were to be established by the "free cooperation of the government, the clergy, village communes, and private persons," but required a license from the county school board. The ministry of education was to supply textbooks and to watch, with the assistance of the clergy, over the moral and political views of the teachers. The administration of schools was entrusted to provincial (*guberniia*) and county (*uezd*) school boards which consisted of officers of the ministry of education, the clergy, representatives of the zemstvos, and administrative officials. Chairmen of county boards were elected by their members and confirmed by provincial boards; local bishops were ex officio chairmen of provincial boards. The schools were to be supported by village and urban communities, participation of the state treasury being limited to small subsidies deemed adequate to encourage local endeavor. Tuition fees were permitted on the theory that the peasantry was suspicious of free schools. Instruction was conducted exclusively in Russian, although Golovnin had advocated the use of local languages.

The law of 1864, a compromise between the views of those who believed that primary education should be left in the hands of the clergy and those who favored lay zemstvo schools, was followed by measures for the unification of school administration in the ministry of education. In 1865 that department took over the schools of the ministry of appanages, in 1867 those of the ministry of state domains, and in 1874 the schools operating among nomadic tribes (Kirghiz, Bashkir, Tartar). Church schools, however, remained under the control of the Holy Synod, and as the number of zemstvo schools increased, the conflict between the supporters of lay or Church schools became acute. The question of compulsory primary education loomed large in the discussion of 1860–1864, as it did in later years. The interdepartmental committee of 1860 recommended compulsory school attendance, but this proposal was rejected, partly for financial reasons and partly because it was opposed by many liberals who dreaded the stifling effect of government intervention and naïvely put their trust in popular enthusiasm for education and in the miracle-working power of free initiative.

In the administration of Tolstoy primary schools, like all others, were brought under close government control. In 1868 rigid supervision was extended to private schools, even tutoring being permitted only to persons whose religious, moral, and political views were approved by the ministry. In 1869 the censorship of textbooks, especially those intended for primary schools, was tightened. In the same year was created the office of inspector of primary schools, one for each province; these officials were appointed by the ministry of education and were endowed with comprehensive powers seemingly incompatible with those vested in the school boards by the law of 1864. The resulting ambiguous situation was regularized by a law of May 24, 1874, which remodeled the administrative setup. Provincial and county marshals of the nobility became ex officio chairmen, respectively, of the provincial and the county school boards. The powers of the boards were restricted to financial and administrative matters, academic questions being dealt with exclusively by the officers of the ministry of education: the newly appointed directors of primary schools and the inspectors, whose number was increased. Appointments of teachers required approval by the inspector and confirmation by the county school board. In other words, the zemstvos, municipalities, and village communes financed the schools, but the ministry of education chose the teachers and dictated academic policies.

The process of overhauling extended to county schools.[4] By a law of May 31, 1872, they were reorganized as municipal schools (*gorodskoe uchilishche*) with courses that varied, according to the class of the school, from one to six years. Students who successfully completed a four-year course were eligible for admission to gymnasiums. In 1881, however, of the total number of 262 municipal schools only 33 offered courses of four or more years; in the vast majority of these schools the

[4] See pp. 723, 806.

length of study was three and two years (117 and 109 schools, respectively).

The real obstacle to the progress of elementary education was not so much the vagaries of official policies, unreasonable and obnoxious though they were, as lack of teachers, poverty, and reluctance of the communities to assume the burden of supporting a school. In the 1860's Russia had only two institutions for the training of primary-school teachers. There was, moreover, a persistent belief, shared by even some of the outstanding educators, that practically anyone—especially the lower clergy—was qualified to teach. It took time before the fallacy of this assumption was understood. The first government-sponsored schools for teachers (institutes and seminaries) were opened in 1871 and 1872; in spite of the rapid increase in number it remained inadequate. The question of school finance was even more difficult to solve. The law of 1864 left the founding of schools to local initiative, of which there was little evidence, especially in the villages, where merely a small group of the more well-to-do peasants showed any interest in literacy. It was slowly and gradually that the zemstvos emerged as the chief agency for the advancement of elementary education. Inexperienced, harassed by petty bureaucratic persecution and handicapped by lack of funds, they did little at first except to foster local initiative by granting subsidies, contributing to teachers' salaries, and making arrangements for the training of teachers. Their outlay on education, as I have stated elsewhere,[5] rose steadily, but the well equipped and properly organized zemstvo schools, of which Russian liberals were proud, did not materialize until the end of the century. From the very beginning most of the zemstvo schools were free.

Municipalities followed a school policy similar to that of the zemstvos, although with less skill, enthusiasm, and perseverance. In 1881 Russia was still overwhelmingly illiterate, yet the flame of elementary education had been kindled and darkness was no longer opaque. Referring to the school situation, Baron N. A. Korf wrote in 1876 that the pioneers of Russian self-government "inherited a desert; they leave to their successors a desert dotted with many oases the creation of which had cost immense labor and they have blazed trails that will be explored in the future."

Some idea of the state of education at the end of Alexander II's

[5] See p. 899.

reign may be gathered from the following figures. In 1881 Russia had eight universities [6] with a teaching staff of 600 and a student body of 9,860,[7] mostly gymnasium graduates (7,700). The largest universities were in Moscow and in St. Petersburg, with, respectively, 2,400 and 2,000 students; the University of Odessa held the lowest place with less than 400 students. Nearly half of the students (4,250) worked for degrees in medicine. There were several thousand students in the universities for women; over 900, for instance, were enrolled in 1881 in the women's university of St. Petersburg, and 400 in that of Kiev. In the same year there were 133 boys' gymnasiums and 82 progymnasiums, with 65,750 students, and 79 *Realschulen*, with 17,500 students. In 1881 the ministry of education maintained 97 girls' gymnasiums and 178 progymnasiums, with 51,400 students. Some 18,300 girls were studying in 1880 in the 61 secondary schools (including 30 boarding schools) of the Administration of Empress Marie. Finally, in 1881 there were 157 institutes and seminaries for the training of primary-school teachers, with 9,000 students.[8]

Statistics of elementary schools are even less impressive. In 1881 the ministry of education reported 229 county schools with 17,300 students; 262 municipal schools with 28,100 students; and 22,800 primary schools with 1,207,000 students, including 235,000 girls. Of the 10,285,000 rubles spent in that year on primary schools, 12 per cent was provided by the state treasury, 36 per cent by the zemstvos, 40 per cent by municipalities and village communes; the balance came from other sources. The majority of primary schools (19,900) were located in rural areas. Assuming a population of 92,000,000, the minis-

[6] The University of Odessa was founded in 1865 and that of Warsaw was reopened as a Russian university in 1869. The University of Tomsk, in Siberia, was officially founded in 1878 but did not begin to function until 1888. The University of Helsingfors, a Finnish institution, is not included in the figures given above.

[7] Of this number 1,360 were Roman Catholics and 1,260 were Protestants; there were 700 Roman Catholic students in the University of Warsaw and 950 Protestant students in the University of Dorpat, or, respectively, 71 per cent and 81 per cent of the student body of each of those universities.

[8] The above statement does not include the higher and secondary schools under the ministry of war and the Holy Synod (in 1880 the 4 theological academies and the 47 theological seminaries had 14,800 students). Also omitted are several specialized institutions (the Alexander *lycée* in Tsarskoe Selo, the Nicholas *lycée* in Moscow, the Demidov *lycée* in Yaroslavl, and a few others), as well as various technical and veterinary schools. The number of such institutions was small and the number of their students relatively insignificant. The omission does not distort the general picture.

try of education computed that in the empire as a whole (exclusive of Finland and the Caucasus) there was one primary school per 4,000 inhabitants, in the school region of Moscow one per 3,100 inhabitants, in eastern Siberia one per 7,600 inhabitants, in Turkestan one per 70,600 inhabitants. Less than 9 per cent of the children of school age (7 to 14), or one boy out of 6 and one girl out of 32, went to school. The level of instruction, moreover, was admittedly very low, and over 20 per cent of the students withdrew before completing the course. The school statistics of the Holy Synod are so erratic, inconsistent, and notoriously inflated as to be largely useless. Whether the 6,000 Church primary schools with 172,000 students—very humble figures indeed—actually existed in 1878, as officially reported, or were the product of the zeal and fancy of ecclesiastical statisticians is anybody's guess, but the latter assumption would seem more plausible.

A comparison of the above data with the school statistics for the 1850's quoted in an earlier chapter [9] will indicate a marked increase in the number both of schools and of students. The percentages of increase might be heartening, but the actual figures remained shockingly low when viewed in relation to the size of the population. The encouraging factor in an otherwise dreary situation was the growing realization by liberal opinion of the necessity of an aggressive school policy and the gradual recognition by the institutions of local government, especially the zemstvos, that the responsibility was theirs.[10]

[9] See pp. 805–806.
[10] The school legislation of the 1860's and the 1870's, like that of the earlier part of the nineteenth century, contained no discrimination against the Jews. The policy of the government was still one of "assimilation," but it was pursued by methods less objectionable than those used in the previous reign. The program of reorganizing Jewish schools on the Russian model (see p. 806, n. 6.) was canceled in 1873, and the decree of May 3, 1855, which virtually prescribed the liquidation of Jewish confessional schools by 1875, was not enforced and was repealed in 1879. Under this more liberal regime the popularity of Russian schools with the Jews increased. In the 1850's a Jew in a university or secondary school was a rare exception. In 1881 there were 848 Jewish students in universities, 8,200 (12 per cent) in gymnasiums and progymnasiums, and 1,400 (8 per cent) in *Realschulen*. In the Jewish pale the ratio of Jewish students was considerably higher; it was, for instance, 35 per cent in the gymnasiums and progymnasiums of Odessa and 27 per cent in those of Vilna. The influx of Jewish students was due partly to official policies and partly to the revolt of the Jews themselves against what S. M. Dubnow calls "the fierce superstition . . . and impenetrable fanaticism which was throttling the noblest strivings of the Jewish mind." Some of the legal disabilities weighing on the Jews were lifted or eased. The conscription law was amended to meet the wishes of the Jewish communities (1856). The privilege of residence outside the pale was extended to wealthy Jewish merchants, members

SCIENCE

Unlike most countries, Russia built her temple of knowledge from the top, not from the bottom, and was encumbered with an Academy of Science and a university long before she had any secondary or elementary schools. This anomaly affected the standards of the institution of higher learning, whose record until the second quarter of the nineteenth century was undistinguished. The improvement in the quality of teaching in the reign of Nicholas I ushered in a new era in which Russian science for the first time asserted itself and made significant contributions to knowledge. The basic anomaly, however, persisted. Science in Russia, like art (and in a smaller degree music), stemmed from a foreign tradition and was somewhat akin to a luxuri-

---

of the first guild (1859); to holders of higher academic degrees (1861), to skilled artisans and craftsmen (1865), and finally to all university graduates (1879). Of great practical importance was the provision of the conscription law of 1874 shortening the term of service for holders of academic diplomas. The combined effect of these measures, as well as the social prestige attached to secondary and higher education, created a strong inducement for Jewish parents to send their children to Russian schools. This attitude was in agreement with official policies directed towards assimilation and the eradication of Jewish exclusiveness. It found many supporters among the upper classes of the Jewry, beneficiaries of the above measures, and among Jewish intellectuals anxious to throw off the shackles of traditionalism and scholasticism of Jewish Orthodoxy and to exchange the narrow confines of the pale for a broader arena, the road to which led through gymnasiums and universities.

Assimilation, however, had its dangers not only from the point of view of supporters of the traditional institutions of the Jews and their way of life. The rapid ascendancy of Jewish businessmen in finance, industry, and commerce raised the familiar cry of their "exploiting" the easygoing gentiles; the equally rapid ascendancy of Jewish intellectuals in liberal professions—medicine, journalism, law (there was no restriction on their admission to the bar)—and their affiliation with liberal and revolutionary movements led to the no less familiar accusation that Jewry was fomenting disaffection and social revolution. The State Council and various committees wrangled for years over the Jewish question without being able to reach a clear-cut decision. A few bureaucrats favored the complete emancipation of the Jews, but the majority leaned towards a policy of restriction. The settlement of Jews in the agricultural areas of southern Russia, inaugurated under Nicholas I, was stopped in 1866. By the municipal government act of 1870 the ratio of Jewish members in municipal councils was limited to one-third, and a Jew could not be elected mayor. In 1871 Odessa was swept by a pogrom (instigated, it would seem, by the Greeks who competed with the Jews in the lucrative grain trade), while the police and troops complacently looked on. In 1878 the assassination of a girl in Kutais, in the Caucasus, led to a "ritual murder" trial which, however, ended in the acquittal of all defendants. Ugly anti-Semitism, encouraged by the future Emperor Alexander III, was becoming increasingly vocal. Russian Jewry was approaching an era of new severe trials.

ant exotic flower blossoming on the surface of a stagnant pool of ignorance and illiteracy. This analogy should not be pushed too far, because the discoveries of Russian scientists and the influence they exercised over the young generation became essential elements in the cultural and technological progress.

The young Russian intellectuals of the 1860's and 1870's were passionately interested in science—chemistry, physics, mineralogy, geology, zoology, botany, biology, and allied disciplines, including mathematics. This interest is explained by the brilliant discoveries of the nineteenth century and by the adoption by western European universities of the laboratory method of teaching, which brought the instructor and his students closer together in the common effort of solving scientific problems. Interest in science was, in a sense, a revolt against the scholasticism and metaphysics of many conventional beliefs and an expression of the desire to comprehend and explain the universe by using the seemingly more reliable tools of laboratory analysis. Moreover, natural sciences, being removed from politics, were less likely than social disciplines to bring the students into conflict with a stern government. The chief centers for the study of natural science were the universities of Kazan and St. Petersburg, but all future Russian scientists of note received at least a part of their training in the great schools of western Europe, especially in Germany; most of them had worked under the eminent German chemist Liebig. They returned home armed with modern scientific methods, often full of enthusiasm for their subject, and not a few of them succeeded in transmitting both to their own students. The equipment of Russian laboratories was improved; zoological, biological and other experimental stations were organized in Russia and abroad.

Interest in natural sciences found expression in the founding of learned societies, the organization of learned congresses, and the publication of scientific journals. The popularity of science was not limited to academic circles. An enterprising St. Petersburg firm in 1858 built a hall where public lectures on such abstruse subjects as "galvanism and its applications" were delivered before capacity audiences. Much of the work done in Russian laboratories was of high caliber and constitutes an integral part of the scientific heritage of mankind. It will suffice to mention the chemist D. I. Mendeleev (1843–1907), the biologist I. I. Mechnikov (1845–1916), and the physiologist I. P. Pavlov (1849–1936), whose names may be familiar even to the lay reader.

It is an indictment of Russian conditions, and a grievous loss to that country, although not to the world, that in 1882 Mechnikov was forced to resign his chair in the University of Odessa. In 1890 he joined the Institut Pasteur in Paris. Other scientists found it difficult to make a place for themselves in Russia. The brilliant woman mathematician Sophie Korvin-Krukovsky (Mrs. V. O. Kovalesky [1850–1891]) received no recognition in her native land but held with distinction a chair of mathematics in the University of Stockholm.

The progress of the natural sciences was duplicated, although on a less striking scale, in other fields, including history. It would be idle to attempt an even cursory survey of these achievements, nor would it serve any useful purpose to clutter these pages with names that would necessarily mean little except to the few initiated. I cannot refrain, however, from mentioning the historian V. O. Kliuchevsky (1841–1911), who began his academic career in 1871 and in 1879 joined the faculty of the University of Moscow. Practically every Russian authority quoted in this study went through the universities in the second half of the nineteenth century. The official list of publications by university professors in the years 1879, 1880, and 1881 fills 120 closely printed pages. These books and articles, written in many languages, deal with innumerable subjects and bear witness to the breadth of interest, scholarship, and industry of the academic profession. Russian science had come of age even though the country at large had still to learn how to read and write.

MUSIC

Music, like science, came with a degree of suddenness to the fore and assured Russia of the place she holds today in the affection of music lovers. It is no exaggeration to say that under the leadership of the Russian Music Society, founded in 1859, Russian standards were revolutionized, within a surprisingly short time, from the standpoint of both the teaching and the appreciation of music. The society established branches in Moscow and in some thirty provincial cities. Under its auspices were organized the conservatoires of St. Petersburg (1862) and Moscow (1866), as well as music schools in Kiev, Kharkov, Saratov, Tiflis, Odessa, and other centers. The society maintained symphony orchestras and sponsored concerts and recitals by Russian and foreign artists. The leading spirit behind this vast and remarkably successful venture was Anton Rubinstein (1829–1894), son of a Jewish manufacturer converted to Christianity. A boy-prodigy and later a world-famous pianist, Rubinstein was a prolific composer: he wrote nineteen operas, six symphonies, five concertos for piano, reams of chamber music, and nearly two hundred romances. His compositions, uneven in quality and conservative in manner, showed the strong influence of the German classical and romantic school. Much of his work, once so popular, is now forgotten, yet at least one of his operas, *The Demon* (1874), occupies a permanent place in Russian (if not in European or American) repertoire. Anton's brother, Nicholas Rubinstein (1835–1881), an accomplished pianist, was organizer of the Moscow branch of the Russian Music Society and director of the Moscow conservatoire.

Of paramount importance to the world of music was the appearance in the early 1860's of "The Five" (*Kuchka*), a group of exceptionally gifted composers—Balakirev, Cui, Mussorgsky, Borodin, and Rimsky-Korsakov—who rose in arms against the conservative tradition represented by the Rubinsteins and the conservatoire. Usually described as founders of the "neo-Russian school," The Five revered Glinka and Daragomyzhsky, strove for "realism" in music (they particularly admired Berlioz's and Liszt's "program" music), and held that a composer must in his work draw on national melodies and popular songs. The Five's spirited, if not always judicious, attacks on the classical school and on the partisans of Wagner and of Italian operas led to lively polemics in which Cui was very active. As a counter-poise to the conservatoire, the supporters of the neo-Russian movement established in St. Petersburg the Free School of Music (1862), which through its teaching and concerts exercised considerable influence. The cause of the neo-Russians was championed by the distinguished music and art critic V. V. Stasov (1824–1906).

Of The Five, M. A. Balakirev (1837–1910) alone, the leader of the group, was a trained professional musician, a pianist and conductor as well as a composer. C. A. Cui (1835–1918) was a general of army engineers, M. P. Mussorgsky (1839–1881) an officer in the guards and later a civil servant, A. P. Borodin (1834–1887) a noted professor of chemistry, and Rimsky-Korsakov (1844–1908) a naval officer and after 1871 a professor in the St. Petersburg conservatoire, although his connection with the navy was not severed until 1884. The Five differed too widely among themselves in their genius, background, and temperament to allow lasting close association. Indeed, they soon drifted apart, each pursuing an independent course not necessarily consistent with the views advocated in the 1860's. Cui, for instance, made little use in his compositions of popular melodies. Four of The Five were, strictly speaking, amateurs, handicapped at times by lack of technical training (which Rimsky-Korsakov overcame later by assiduous work); yet they made great contributions to their art and exercised, and still exercise, profound influence on the development of music at home and abroad. Borodin and Balakirev are regarded as the creators of the Russian symphonic school. Mussorgsky's *Boris Godunov*, Borodin's *Prince Igor*, and Rimsky-Korsakov's *Le Coq d'or*—to mention only a few of their operas—have been enjoyed by innumerable audiences in many lands. The luminous genius of Tchaikovsky marked another stage in the ascendancy of Russian music. A graduate of the aristocratic law school of St. Petersburg, P. I. Tchaikovsky (1840–1893) studied at the conservatoire of that city in 1862–1865 and then taught at the conservatoire of Moscow until 1877. His versatile talent embraced every form of composition from romances and chamber music to ballets, operas, and symphonies. Of his eight operas *Eugene Onegin* (1877) and *La Dame de Pique* (1890) are immensely popular in Russia, although they are less frequently produced abroad. On the other hand, Tchaikovsky's symphonies, particularly the celebrated Sixth (*Pathétique*), are favorites of the international concert platform and stand among the world's masterpieces. The great tradition established by these masters has been carried on by a distinguished company of talented, if perhaps less outstanding, composers and has added far more to the prestige and luster of the Russian name than have costly and uncertain victories on distant battlefields.

ART

On the morrow of the Crimean War, Russian intellectuals being in a recalcitrant mood, young painters, like young musicians, rebelled against convention and academic routine. The long-brooding revolt against the pseudo-classical tradition of the Academy of Arts came to the fore in 1863 when the entire graduating class refused to participate in the contest on the subject "Feast in Valhalla." This somewhat childish gesture proved less futile than might have been expected. The disgruntled art students organized themselves into an Association of Free Artists; although the association soon dissolved amidst the recriminations of its members, it led to the founding in 1870 of the

Society of Circulating Exhibitions, which maintained its activities until the end of the empire. The annual shows of the society toured the principal cities, were well attended, and became a factor in the cultural life of the country. Most of Russia's progressive artists were affiliated with the society. Unfortunately, the rebels against routine and tradition declared war not only on the academy and its preposterous rules but also on old masters. Art, according to this view, was to be brought within the reach of the toiling masses (which, of course, never attended exhibitions); composition, design, and color were said to be of minor importance; what mattered was the social content of the picture. The most worthy subjects, inspired by a deeply felt protest against social injustice, however, do not necessarily make works of art. The tragedy of the Russian painters was that their draftsmanship, sense of color, and knowledge of the principles of composition left much to be desired. The praiseworthy efforts of the pillars of the society, I. N. Kramskoy (1837–1887) and V. G. Perov (1834–1882), convincingly prove that these artists were mediocre painters, even though their hearts were in the right place. The once much-admired historical canvases by V. I. Surikov (1848–1916) and the huge battle pictures by V. V. Vereshchagin (1842–1904) are hopelessly dated and do not rise above a very humble level. The prolific, renowned, and unquestionably the most talented painter of this period, I. E. Repin (1844–1930), has no claim to any real contribution to art.[11]

These pessimistic observations should not be taken as evidence that the revolt of the 1860's and 1870's was entirely sterile. The repudiation of academic routine was a wholesome move, and contained possibilities of which the painters of later generations availed themselves. Viewed in retrospect "revolutions" in art often appear stale; this is particularly apt to be the case in a country like Russia, which in the nineteenth century still remained outside the artistic currents of western Europe. The backwardness of Russia, which hedged off progressive influences by the narrow traditionalism of the Church and the Academy of Arts, might help to an understanding of the situation but it does not alter it. If Russian composers won immediate recognition abroad while Russian painters (including those who, like

[11] Every evaluation of art necessarily comprises an element of subjective judgment. The official Soviet publication quoted in an earlier chapter (see p. 823 n. 12.) refers to Kramskoy, Perov, Surikov, Vereshchagin, and Repin in terms of unqualified admiration and praise. Russian pre-revolutionary art critics (V. M. Frich, A Benois) showed greater restraint and, I think, a better sense of values.

Vereshchagin, exhibited in western Europe and in the United States) were practically ignored, the reason is that the former had, and the latter had not, something of value to offer.

The trend towards realism was reflected in sculpture. Its two outstanding representatives, Antokolsky and Trubetskoy, belonged to the opposite poles of the social scale. M. M. Antokolsky (1843–1902), born in the slums of the Vilna ghetto, achieved local fame but is relatively little known outside Russia. Prince Paolo Trubetskoy (1866–1938), son of a Russian nobleman and an American mother, was born on Lago Maggiore, studied in Italy, and exhibited for the first time in Venice in 1883. His work is represented in many leading European and American collections, and the monuments he molded are scattered throughout the world, from St. Petersburg to Los Angeles.

The record of Russian architecture was even less distinguished than that of painting, although it is well to remember that the second half of the nineteenth century was responsible for some of the worst (and, unfortunately, time-resistant) specimens of bad taste to be found in the monuments and buildings of continental Europe, England, and the United States. Russia, with her lack of architectural tradition and low technical standards, was no exception to the general trend; in her case, however, its consequences were particularly dreary because this was a time of rapid growth of Russian cities and of the substitution of brick and stone for wood as the principal building materials. The two prevalent tendencies in Russian architecture were eclecticism, the more or less successful adaptation of western European styles or a mixture thereof, on the one hand, and abortive attempts at creating a national (but actually a pseudo-national) style, on the other. Among the architects of this period the names of K. K. Rachau (1830–1880), V. I. Hartmann (1834–1873), A. I. Resanov (1817–1887), D. I. Grimm (1823–1898), and I. P. Ropet-Petroff (1845–1908) may be mentioned at random, but it would be idle to claim that they have any title to the gratitude of posterity.

LITERATURE

Literature was a field of creative endeavor in which Russia's achievements in the 1860's and 1870's were particularly striking, in spite of the difficulties put in its way by a restless and suspicious government. In the closing years of Nicholas I's reign the regime of censorship was as oppressive as it was grotesque; it will suffice to remember that the very name of Gogol was not allowed to appear in print. The accession of Alexander II brought some relief and promise of a brighter future. In December, 1855, the Buturlin committee on censorship, of sinister memory, came to an unlamented end.[12] Some leeway was given to the periodical press. From 1845 to 1854 six newspapers and 19 magazines (exclusive of those issued by official agencies and learned societies) obtained publication licenses; in 1855–1864 the number of the former increased to 66 and of the latter to 156. Under Nicholas I periodicals were to be non-political, only four newspapers being permitted to comment on foreign and domestic affairs; in 1855 this restriction was removed. This was a good start, forerunner (some imagined) of a real liberalization of censorship, if not of its abolition. An extensive revision of pertinent legislation began in 1857 but was not completed until 1865. In the meantime the position of the press remained precarious, lack of a coordinated policy and the multiplicity of agencies in charge of censorship leading sometimes to the suspension of journals for the publication of articles duly passed by the censor.

The censorship law of April 6, 1865, was disappointing in more than one respect. It was not, as was originally intended, a comprehensive enactment superseding and consolidating earlier legislation, but a collection of "provisional rules" superimposed upon a maze of measures that were repealed only in part. This "provisional" law, which was to remain in force for forty years, introduced two seemingly important innovations: (1) partial abolition of preliminary censorship, and (2) partial substitution of judicial procedure for administrative methods in dealing with the offenses committed by publishers and editors. Books of over a specified number of pages and periodicals published in St. Petersburg and in Moscow were exempt from preliminary censorship. Licenses, which continued to be required for the publication of periodicals, were issued by the minister of the interior, who was also authorized to extend the privilege of exemption from preliminary censorship to the organs of the provincial press. If a book exempt from preliminary censorship was deemed to violate the law, action against the publisher was brought in the courts; censorship authorities, however, could seize at once the offending volume and withhold it from circulation until the case was decided, that is, for a period of several months to several years. Publishers and editors

[12] See p. 813.

of periodicals exempt from preliminary censorship were subject to two kinds of penal action: proceedings before the courts for violating the law or summary extra-judicial penalties; the minister of the interior was vested with the power to issue warnings and then suspend publication temporarily or to prohibit it altogether. The vital question was whether the judicial or the extra-judicial procedure would be the rule and whether the power to seize books would be used indiscriminately or only in exceptional instances, as the law would seem to provide. Faithful to the tradition of the police state, the government chose the latter course. According to a distinguished authority (K. K. Arsenev), literary matters practically never came before the courts, except for cases of libel, while administrative penalties, imposed at times clearly in violation of the law, were impartially and generously meted out to journals of every political persuasion, although it would seem that publications of slavophile leanings got somewhat more than their legitimate share. The law, however, did not succeed in unifying the control of the press in the ministry of the interior; there continued to exist quasi-independent agencies which exercised the functions of ecclesiastical and theatrical censorship and censorship of foreign publications. It thus appears that no appreciable relief was given to editors and publishers and that next to nothing was accomplished in curbing the arbitrary rule of administrative officials.

The history of Russian literature bears out the familiar generalization that censorship (at least in the pre-totalitarian era), pernicious and indefensible as it unquestionably was, was not an insurmountable bar to the creation of literary masterpieces. The second half of the nineteenth century, especially its opening decades, has been aptly called the age of the Russian novel. Turgenev, Tolstoy, and Dostoevsky— the three towering literary figures of this period and lineal descendants of Pushkin, Lermontov, and Gogol—gave the term "realism" a theretofore unsuspected depth and broad significance and opened new vistas in fiction writing which to this day hold the attention of the reading public and are a source of inspiration.

Turgenev, Tolstoy, and Dostoevsky entered the literary arena almost simultaneously. Ivan Turgenev (1818–1883), son of an impoverished squire and a wealthy heiress, was a man of good education and European outlook. He studied at the universities of Moscow, St. Petersburg, and Berlin, and spent much of his life abroad, in Germany and France, partly because of his attachment to the singer Madame Viardot

(Pauline Garcia), to whom he remained devoted for nearly forty years. Turgenev's early verses appeared in print in 1838; between 1843 and 1852 he wrote several plays, and in 1847 there began the publication in a magazine of his celebrated short stories from peasant life, issued in book form in 1852 under the title *A Sportsman's Sketches*. In the same year he was arrested for writing what was regarded by the authorities as a too eulogistic obituary of Gogol and was banished to his estate, where he spent eighteen months. *Rudin*, Turgenev's first novel dealing with contemporary Russian life, was published in 1855 and was followed by others: A *Nest of Gentlefolk*, 1858; *On the Eve*, 1860; *Fathers and Sons*, 1861; *Smoke*, 1867; and *Virgin Soil*, 1876. These novels and Turgenev's numerous short stories, which form a valuable part of his literary contribution, were immediately successful and brought their author fame and financial reward, even though he was attacked by left-wing critics for allegedly drawing in Bazarov, the hero of *Fathers and Sons*, a caricature rather than a true portrait of Russia's revolutionary youth. Turgenev was the first among his contemporaries to win recognition abroad, perhaps not only because of his mastery but also because of his general approach, which was akin to that of the western world. In spite of the Russian setting and the national atmosphere of his novels and stories, which were greeted as a revelation by his European admirers, he was far less aggressively "Russian" than Tolstoy, Gogol, or Dostoevsky. Tastes change, however, and Turgenev is regarded today in some literary circles as somewhat Victorian and dated. Yet he was a great novelist and a great story-teller, and his contribution to the treasure-house of world letters is precious and lasting.

Count Leo Tolstoy (1828–1910), member of an ancient aristocratic family, was brought up in a large well-to-do household and studied at the University of Kazan (1844–1847), which he left without taking a degree. From 1851 to 1855 he served in the army, first in the Caucasus and during the Crimean War in Wallachia and Sevastopol. Most of his life was spent on the estate of Yasnaia Poliana, where he was born and from which he dramatically escaped—with the intention never to return—shortly before he died. In 1857 and in 1860–1861 Tolstoy traveled abroad, but, unlike Turgenev, he found nothing to admire in western Europe. His first story, *Childhood*, was published in 1852; *The Tales of Sevastopol*, which began to appear in a magazine while the siege of the Black Sea stronghold was still on, established Tolstoy as one of Russia's leading authors. After the Crimean War he devoted himself exclusively to literary work, his stories, plays, and novels following one another in rapid succession. *War and Peace*, the monumental epic of the Napoleonic invasion, was published in 1869, and *Anna Karenina*, perhaps his greatest novel, in 1877. During this period Tolstoy was still a conservative; he was too much of an aristocrat to feel at ease in bohemian literary circles whose radical aspirations, moreover, he did not share. It is significant that both *War and Peace* and *Anna Karenina* were first published in a periodical edited by the reactionary Katkov. Yet the elements of revolt against conventional beliefs and the existing social order, which were soon to lead to Tolstoy's "conversion," were discernible in some of his earlier stories (*The Cossacks*, 1852–1853; *The Two Hussars*, 1856) and particularly in *War and Peace*. Tolstoy had a profound dislike for western civilization, for the artificiality of the accepted ways of life, and especially for the state and everything it stood for. Hence his predilection for simple, "unspoiled" characters (the Cossacks, Natasha, Nicholas Rostov, Platon Karataev in *War and Peace*) whose inherent goodness he brought out in sharp relief against the background of the unworthiness of his heroes, contaminated by the vices of civilization (Olenin in *The Cossacks*; Prince Andrew in *War and Peace*). In the later 1870's Tolstoy experienced an acute moral crisis which brought about his "conversion" and found its striking literary expression in *A Confession*, written in 1879–1882. He revealed himself as the prophet of a rationalized form of Christianity stripped of mysticism, dogmas, and rituals and built around the doctrine of non-resistance to evil. His political teaching was essentially anarchism: he condemned the state as an instrument of oppression, the Church that sanctioned the state, and private property, particularly ownership of land. He repudiated his own literary work as sinful and artistically wrong, and although he used the narrative form in his later writings they were to serve thenceforth the didactic purpose of spreading the Gospel of his brand of Christianity. Tolstoy's novels and stories are characterized by rare psychological insight and consummate artistry of which there are few examples in literature. Whatever one may think of his philosophical and religious views, his fictional works have assured him the place he rightfully holds today in the world of letters.

The evolution of Dostoevsky's tormented genius was both similar to and different from that of Tolstoy's. Fedor Dostoevsky (1821–1881), son of a well-to-do doctor, studied in a school for military engineers (1837–1841), was commissioned in the army, but resigned in 1844 and devoted himself to literary work. His first novel, *Poor Folk*, was published in 1846 and won him immediate recognition. His promising career, however, was interrupted by his arrest in 1849 as a member of Butashevich-Petrashevsky's ill fated circle: Dostoevsky was among the fifteen convicted men whose death sentence was commuted at the last moment to imprisonment.[13] He did four years of hard labor in Siberia and then served in a distant garrison, first as a private and later as an officer, until 1859, when he was amnestied and returned to St. Petersburg. He plunged at once into literary work and made for himself a leading place as a journalist, editor, and novelist. An exceptionally prolific author, Dostoevsky wrote innumerable articles, stories, and several major novels: *Humiliated and Insulted*, 1861; *Memoirs from a House of Death*, 1861–1862; *Memoirs from Underground*, 1864; *Crime and Punishment*, 1866; *The Idiot*, 1869; *The Devils*, 1871; and *The Brothers Karamazov*, 1880. He denied the statement frequently made that he was primarily a psychological novelist. "I am called a psychologist," he wrote in his diary; "this is not true, I am merely a realist in the higher meaning of the term, that is, I depict all the depth of the human soul." His insight into the dark mysteries of human consciousness and his genius in translating these intimate inner experiences in terms of fictional characters gave his work its universal quality and made him a precursor of Marcel Proust and James Joyce. There was, however, another side to Dostoevsky's work. During his incarceration in the House of Death in Siberia he experienced, like Tolstoy in the late 1870's, a religious and moral crisis; he repudiated the progressive ideas of his youth, especially socialism, and espoused Greek Orthodoxy and a brand of militant messianic nationalism tinged with slavophilism and mystical populism. Like Tolstoy, he despised western civilization, his contempt for Europe being strengthened by observations during his several protracted stays abroad. The essence of his political creed was the belief that Orthodox Russia was destined to triumph over the decadent and impious western world. The ultimate expression of Dostoevsky's political faith was formulated in his address on Pushkin (1880) in which he called Russian intellectuals to reconcile their western ideas with "popular truth" and "popular principles" (terms that elude translation or precise definition) which were to be learned from the common people, and

[13] See pp. 811–812.

he voiced his conviction that "our poverty-stricken land will, perhaps, finally bring a new message to the world."

Dostoevsky the penetrating analyst of human behavior and the creator of unforgettable fictional characters is far more significant than Dostoevsky the chronicler of Russian life and the mystical philosopher of a messianic nationalism. It is important to emphasize this point because his writings have been so often invoked in recent years to explain Russian events. "It would . . . be a mistake to regard his novels as *representations* of Russian life under Alexander II," writes the acute literary critic and historian D. S. Mirsky. ". . . Dostoevsky is in substance less true to life than any other writer. . . . He dealt in spiritual essences, in emanations of his own infinitely fertile spiritual experience. He only gave them the external realistic garbs of current life and attached them to current facts of Russian life." [14] Dostoevsky's personal record, like his literary genius, was out of the ordinary: he was an epileptic, a former convict who had lived through the harrowing experience of a death sentence and a long term in a penal institution, an inveterate gambler struggling through most of his life with crushing financial burdens, and the unhappy lover of a sinister and evil woman (Apollinaria Suslova) whom he himself described as "infernal." The world of his fictional characters is as sordid, unhealthy, and terrifying as it is fascinating. To quote Mirsky again, "It is food that is easily assimilated only by a profoundly diseased spiritual organism." Dostoevsky's novels and stories are a revealing and disturbing commentary on the human animal and his motives, but they are not, nor were they intended to be, a picture of Russian character or Russian conditions. To generalize from them about Russia is about as sound as to assume, on the basis of Proust's immortal novel, that homosexuality is one of the main preoccupations of the French.

Several authors, contemporaries of Turgenev, Tolstoy, and Dostoevsky, stand among Russian classics even though their work is less generally known abroad. The eldest member of this group is Serge Aksakov (1791–1859), a country squire who turned to literature late in life. His two most important books, A *Family Chronicle* (1856) and *Years of Childhood of Bagrov-Grandson* (1858), are models of unadorned, straightforward narrative and give a memorable picture of the more pleasing aspects of country life under serfdom. The great

---

[14] Prince D. S. Mirsky, A *History of Russian Literature* (New York, 1927), pp. 355–356.

literary reputation of Alexander Goncharov (1812-1891), author of several books, rests almost exclusively on his novel *Oblomov* (1858); its hero has become the symbol of dreamy inefficiency and paralysis of will characteristic of a section of the landed nobility. *Oblomov* is a strange and weird story which to this day has lost none of its significance and interest. Alexis Pisemsky (1820-1881), a novelist and a playwright, was a pessimist according to even Russian standards; appropriately, his first play was called *The Hypochondriac*. Pisemsky's skepticism, bordering on cynicism, and his disbelief in reforms brought upon him the wrath of the social-minded critics, including those who recognized his mastery in portraying human baseness and futility. His most important work is the novel *A Thousand Souls*, published in 1858. Michael Saltykov-Shchedrin (1826-1889), at one time vice governor of a province, enjoyed immense popularity as editor of a radical review and author of numerous stories satirizing the inequities and petty tyranny of officialdom. His novel *The Golovlev Family* (1872-1876), the foreboding chronicle of a clan of country squires, was written with a restraint and economy of means which reveal the hand of a master. Pavel Melnikov (1819-1883), an authority on religious dissenters, produced under the pseudonym Andrew Pechersky two voluminous novels, *In the Woods* and *On the Hills*, which have for their setting the communities of old-believers in the wilderness of the middle Volga. In spite of their somewhat artificial and labored style these epic narratives, packed with illuminating facts and apt characterizations, make fascinating reading and still retain their popularity. There were, of course, many other novelists of lesser distinction whose works were widely read at one time but are largely forgotten today.

The ascendancy of the novel was accompanied by the decline of poetry, although the tradition of Pushkin and Lermontov was carried on by several authors of the older generation. The poems of Fedor Tiutchev (1803-1873), a diplomat and a man of the world, began to appear in print in 1836, and the first volume of his verse was published in 1852. A typical representative of the upper class of the early nineteenth century, Tiutchev was a reactionary in politics and invariably used French in conversation, correspondence, and prose writing. Yet he ranks among the most accomplished Russian poets, coming next to Pushkin and Lermontov. Athanasius Fet (1820-1892), a cavalry officer and a chamberlain of the imperial court, and the two littérateurs from the well-to-do nobility, Apollon Maikov (1821–1897) and Jacob Polonsky (1819–1898), were competent poets of the "art for art's sake" school, while Alexis Pleshcheev (1825–1893), one of the victims of the Petrashevsky affair, made not very successful attempts at injecting civic motives in his verses. Greater originality was displayed by Alexis Tolstoy and Nekrasov. Count Alexis Tolstoy (1817–1875), a wealthy aristocrat and a lifelong friend of Emperor Alexander II, wrote lyrics, epic poems, and ballads, a historical novel (*Prince Serebrianyi*), and a dramatic trilogy in verse: *The Death of Ivan the Dread, Tsar Fedor,* and *Tsar Boris* (1866–1870). Some of his work has real merit, especially his lyrics and humorous poems. Under the pseudonym Kosma Prutkov, supposedly a clerk in the treasury, Tolstoy and his cousins the brothers Zhemchuzhnikov published witty satirical rhymes from which grew a whole school of nonsense poetry. Nicholas Nekrasov (1821–1877), born of the unhappy union of an impoverished Russian nobleman with an aristocratic Polish girl, received no formal education. By hard work and perseverance, aided by the use of somewhat unscrupulous methods, he became one of Russia's outstanding editors; many of the masterpieces written during this period appeared in the journals which he published. In his own writings Nekrasov was the bard of the underdog and was the first to use poetry as the vehicle for social protest and political satire in the grand manner. This attitude eventually endeared him to radical literary critics, although his first book of poems (1840) was roundly condemned as worthless by Belinsky, and his subservient attitude towards the authorities (inspired by base business considerations) was not easily reconcilable with the noble feelings expressed in his poems. From the purely literary point of view the merit of Nekrasov's work is debatable. Much of what he wrote was rhymed journalism of low order, but some of his poems in the folk-song manner and a few lyrics are on a very high level and show real inspiration and genius. His influence with the reading public was great. On the whole the achievements of these poets, none of whom were young, did not compare favorably with those of their predecessors.

The decline of poetry may be explained to some extent by the influence of a school of radical writers and literary critics who held that art, including literature, must serve primarily a social purpose. The leading members of this group, which drew its inspiration from Belinsky, were Chernyshevsky, Dobroliubov, Pisarev, Lavrov, and Mikhailovsky. Nicholas Chernyshevsky (1828–1889), son of a priest, began his literary career in 1855 with the publication of a treatise on the utilitarian nature of art. His remarkably popular articles in the review *Sovremennik* (The Contemporary), however, dealt chiefly with economic questions and expounded, within the boundaries imposed by censorship, the ideas of revolutionary socialism. After the emancipation of 1861, which he regarded as inadequate, Chernyshevsky became involved in revolutionary activities, was arrested in 1862, confined for two years in the fortress of Peter and Paul in St. Petersburg, and then deported to Siberia, where he remained until 1883. During his detention in the fortress Chernyshevsky wrote his celebrated novel *What to Do?* a tendentious revolutionary saga devoid of literary merit. It was received, nevertheless, as a revelation by the radical youth and established a fashion for political novels, at which many younger authors tried their hand.

Nicholas Dobroliubov (1836–1861), like Chernyshevsky, the son of a priest, was the literary critic of *Sovremennik*. Although he died at the early age of twenty-five, he had a profound influence on the development of the revolutionary movement. His criticisms were not concerned with the literary quality of the books about which he wrote; the latter were merely texts for the exposition of his own social and political views. This type of literary criticism, which is but a form of political journalism, took firm root in the Russian tradition, was preserved until the end of the empire, and in a perverted form survives under the Soviet regime. Dimitry Pisarev (1840–1868), a country squire by birth and education, rivaled Chernyshevsky and Dobroliubov as the idol of radical youth. His philosophy, expounded with great brilliancy in his essays, was that of nihilism (or, as it was quaintly called, "thinking realism"), that is, rejection of the past and assertion of individuality, guided exclusively by reason and science, as both the supreme aim of self-expression and the sole true instrument of social progress. Pisarev's crusade against traditional values extended to art and literature, to which he denied all virtue unless they served social and revolutionary purposes. Hence his attack on Pushkin. The career of Pisarev was brief. In 1862 he was arrested for spreading revolutionary propaganda, spent four years behind bars (most of his writing was done during his incarceration), and was accidentally drowned two years after his release. Peter Lavrov (1823–1900), army colonel and professor of mathematics in the Artillery Academy in St. Petersburg, made his literary *début* by writing some mediocre verse and philosophical essays which were met at first with hostility by the radical press. In 1862 he joined the revolutionary society Land and Freedom; in 1866 he was tried by a military court on the charge of spreading subversive doctrines and was exiled to a forlorn town in northern Russia. In 1868–1869 a St. Petersburg journal published Lavrov's *Historical Letters*, which presented the thesis that the educated classes have a definite "obligation towards the people" whose toil makes possible the advancement of civilization and that the obligation must be repaid by establishing a social order based on truth and justice. The remodeling of the social and political structure, according to Lavrov, could be accomplished only through the efforts of a small group of individuals capable of independent critical thinking; they are the moving force of history. For reasons difficult to comprehend today Lavrov's somewhat abstruse philosophical treatise created a sensation (much to the surprise of the author and of the editors of the journal) and became the Bible of revolutionary Russia. Belatedly vetoed by censorship, *Historical Letters* was surreptitiously circulated in foreign editions and was not reissued legally in Russia until 1905. In the meantime Lavrov escaped abroad (1870), came increasingly under the influence of Marxian socialism, joined the First International, and until his death carried on from Paris active revolutionary propaganda. Nicholas Mikhailovsky (1842–1904), a nobleman and a brilliant journalist and sociologist, expounded in the columns of a widely read St. Petersburg journal (*Otechestvennyia Zapisky*) ideas similar to those of Lavrov, emphasizing the theme of "obligation towards the people" and the duty of the nobility to do penance for the sins of its forefathers. His provocative literary criticisms, written in the manner of Dobroliubov, have a permanent place in the history of Russian literature. Mikhailovsky took little direct part in underground revolutionary activities, but his sympathies with the revolutionary movement were well known and his influence can hardly be overstated.

POLITICAL MOVEMENTS

The trend towards realism and political radicalism in literature, journalism, and art, while traceable to earlier developments, reflected the social unrest and disillusionment characteristic of the 1860's and the 1870's. It will be remembered that the accession of Alexander II was regarded by many as the beginning of an era of far-reaching social and constitutional reforms. There were, indeed, signs, that the bureaucracy was willing to let bygones be bygones. In the late 1850's the surviving Decembrists and the participants in the Petrashevsky affair were permitted to return from Siberia. The announcement of the government's determination to proceed with the emancipation of the serfs was greeted with unqualified approval not only by the slavophiles and the liberal westerners but also by the radicals—Herzen and Chernyshevsky. The era of reconciliation and sanguine expectations, however, was brief. The tenor of the emancipation acts, the bloody suppression of peasant revolts (especially, the massacre of Bezna), the Polish insurrection and its aftermath, and the general ultra-reactionary trend of official policies had a profound effect on public opinion. The conservative and nationalist groups rallied round the throne; but the liberals were estranged, and the radicals, who felt the full brunt of reaction, were driven underground and espoused the cause of political and social revolution.

The acknowledged leader of conservatism and militant nationalism was M. N. Katkov (1818–1887). A talented journalist, inspirer of many fateful decisions, he began his career as a humanitarian liberal and an admirer of constitutional government on the English model. A man of integrity, Katkov revised his views under the impact of the events of 1861–1866: the rise of nihilism and the Polish insurrection. His detestation of nihilism drove Katkov into conservatism of the darkest hue (although he favored the introduction of the zemstvos and the reform of the judiciary), while the Polish insurrection aroused his nationalism and made him a proponent of administrative centralization and of the Russification of all borderlands. According to his biographer, S. Nevedensky, "Nationalism became to Katkov an object of cult which he approached with passionate, almost religious fervor. He regarded Russian national policy as an article of faith and any departure from it as heresy." Katkov attacked Herzen, the liberals, and—a proof of real courage—some of the members of the government allegedly tinged with excessive liberalism, particularly the minister of the interior Valuev and the minister of education Golovnin. Valuev retaliated by showering penalties on Katkov's journal *Moskovskiia Vedomosti* and for a time forced him to curtail his activities. After Karakozov's attempt at regicide (April, 1866), however, the tide turned in favor of the Moscow publicist: Golovnin was dismissed; Alexander II, on his own initiative, granted Katkov an audience, expressed admiration for his articles, and pledged support in case of difficulties with the ministry of the interior. In 1867 Valuev was forced to resign, ostensibly because of a famine of which he appeared blissfully unaware. From his struggle with the bureaucracy Katkov emerged all-powerful. The oracle of a large section of the landed nobility, he exercised in official circles a degree of influence that no other Russian journalist ever attained, before or since.

The liberals, a small unorganized group of noble landowners and intellectuals, favored representative government, elimination of administrative arbitrariness, freedom of the press, and—although there was less agreement on this point—equality of all before the law, that is, the abrogation of the privileges of the nobility. These views were expounded in several influential periodicals to which Valuev gave leeway, not because he approved of the liberal program but because of these journals' hostility to his arch-enemy Katkov. With Valuev's dismissal the liberal press was practically reduced to silence. Sporadic echoes of liberal wishes came from a few corporations of the nobility and, later, from the zemstvos. Vigorous criticism of the bureaucratic methods employed in drafting the emancipation acts was voiced by some of the corporations of the nobility. The outspoken protest of the nobles of Tver led to the summary removal from office and deportation to Viatka of their provincial marshal A. M. Unkovsky (1859). In January, 1860, the nobility of Vladimir petitioned the government to adopt a comprehensive plan of reforms embodying broad self-government, the rule of law, the abolition of special privileges. The nobility of Tver went further. In a sharply worded address to the Crown (February, 1862), it argued that the emancipation acts violated the principles of justice and were economically unsound; in view of the patent bankruptcy of the bureaucratic government necessary reforms, including the abrogation of the privileges of the nobility, could be accomplished only through the summoning of a representative assembly. Similar, although less bluntly phrased, opinions were submitted by a small number of corporations of the nobility in 1862–1863. In January, 1865, the nobility of Moscow requested the Crown to convoke the representatives of the people; but, unlike the nobility of other provinces, they stressed the part of the landed aristocracy as the mainstay of the throne. This proposal, interpreted as an attempt at establishing an oligarchical rule, was not well received. The tsar refused to accept the address, and announced in a rescript to Valuev that initiative in constitutional matters was a prerogative of the Crown and that no social group has the right to speak for the nation. The Moscow address was the last attempt of the nobility to bring pressure for constitutional changes. The zemstvos and other reforms met halfway the wishes of the liberal element. Moreover, the tsar's displeasure with outside interference was made clear, and the fear inspired by the rise of the revolutionary movement had a part in forcing the nobility to preserve its traditional attitude of inertia and submissiveness to the wishes of the autocracy.

The zemstvos, which did not begin to function until the second half of the 1860's, at first kept aloof from broader political issues. Nevertheless, they experienced difficulties with the administration. Valuev, disapproving of the tenor of debates in the St. Petersburg zemstvo assembly and of its refusal to comply with restrictive tax legislation (law of November 21, 1866, which limited the power of the zemstvos to tax commercial and industrial enterprises), ordered the dissolution of that body and the deportation of its chairman, N. F. Krause, to Orenburg (January, 1867). Two laws promulgated on June 13, 1867, gave the presiding officers of zemstvo assemblies discretionary powers to determine the scope of the debates and prohibited the publication of the proceedings without the authorization of administrative officials. These rules applied likewise to the assemblies of the nobility and other public bodies. A. E. Timashev, Valuev's successor, being hostile to the zemstvos, they had to keep their activities within narrow limits, and public interest in the institutions of local government declined in the 1870's. With the spread of social unrest after the War of 1877-1878, the zemstvos manifested some interest in the revived movement for constitutional reforms. In the meantime the more progressive zemstvo leaders established an informal zemstvo union for the elaboration of common policies. In August, 1878, the government, alarmed by mounting revolutionary terror, appealed to all classes of the community to rally to the defense of public safety against the revolutionaries. In response to this appeal the zemstvo of Chernigov, led by I. P. Petrunkevich, drafted an address in which it stated that the absence of free press, free schools, free science, and independent public opinion precluded effective resistance to the forces of disruption and that nothing could be done until these conditions were removed. Petrunkevich was arrested and deported to Kostroma, and the police prevented the adoption of the address; nevertheless, its text was circulated to the other zemstvos. Few of them chose to follow the example of Chernigov. The zemstvos of Tver and Kharkov, however, expressed the hope that the constitutional liberties granted by the tsar to Bulgaria would be extended to his own subjects as the essential prerequisite for the restoration of peace and order. Beyond the formulation of these pious wishes liberal opinion did not go.

The slavophiles, whose doctrine has been discussed in earlier chapters, occupied an intermediate position between the conservatives and the liberals. Their nationalism and adherence to autocracy classed them among the conservatives, but their demands for the freedom of the press and the convocation of a consultative representative assembly, as well as their hostility towards bureaucracy and regimentation, made them allies of the liberals and brought upon them the wrath of censorship. The slavophiles, moreover, gave widely divergent interpretations to their own creed. Ivan Aksakov advocated in 1862 the extension of the privileges of the nobility to all other social groups and urged the nobles to petition the Crown for the permission "solemnly to abolish themselves as an 'estate.'" Yuri Samarin argued that constitutional government in Russia was premature. "We are not yet ready for a people's constitution," he wrote in 1862, "and a constitution that is not truly popular, that is, the rule of a minority acting without the consent of the majority, is but a lie and deceit." This statement was poles apart from the traditional slavophile view of autocracy as an immutable national institution.

While the liberals and the slavophiles moved within the orbit of conventional ideas and relied on desultory tactics such as sporadic appeals to the Crown, the radicals broke new ground and trod the thorny path of political and social revolution. In the 1850's Russia had no organized revolutionary movement. The only center of Russian subversive agitation was London, where Herzen, in collaboration with N. P. Ogarev, established a Russian printing press and in 1857 began the publication of the monthly, and early in 1858 the fortnightly, journal *Kolokol* (The Bell). Herzen, unsparing as he was in his criticisms of the bureaucratic government, was concerned chiefly with social and economic reforms, especially the abolition of serfdom; political and constitutional issues were to him matters of secondary importance. He believed that the changes he so ardently desired might come from the Crown, although after 1861 he did not shrink from advocating revolutionary action; some of his best known pronouncements took the form (much to Lenin's disgust) of "open letters" to the tsar. Until the middle of 1861 the program of *The Bell* was on the whole moderate: emancipation of the serfs on generous terms, freedom of the press, abolition of corporal punishments. A certain intransigence, however, was revealed in the demand that troops should not allow themselves to be used for the suppression of peasant uprisings. In spite of these occasional lapses into sedition, *The Bell* was read by everyone who mattered in Russia, and by many who did not. Herzen's critic, Professor B. N. Chicherin, expressed a widely held opinion when he wrote to him at the end of 1858, "You are a power in the Russian state." Highly placed sympathizers supplied the editor of *The Bell* with spicy bits of confidential information. His London retreat became the Mecca not only for radical *émigrés* but for distinguished men of letters, prominent officials, society matrons, and aides-de-camp to the tsar. Some of these visitors, according to Herzen, "looked wistfully at *The Bell* as if it was truffled." This adulation, however, did not last long. On the announcement of the emancipation (February, 1861) Herzen greeted Alexander as the tsar-liberator, but a study of the emancipation acts and the bloody suppression of peasant revolts made him reverse his judgment. On July 1, 1861, *The Bell* published an editorial entitled "What Do the People Need?" The "simple" answer was given in the celebrated sentence which became one of Russia's revolutionary battle cries: "The people need land and freedom (*zemlia i volia*)." Branding the emancipation of February as fraud, the editorial outlined what has been termed the first practical program of reforms set forth in a language within the grasp of the masses: generous land allotments for the liberated serfs to be farmed by the traditional methods of communal tenure (*obshchina*); no increase in the peasants' tax burden, the noble landowners to be compensated from other sources; drastic reduction of military and other government expenditure; "emancipation from officialdom," that is, broad local self-government; convocation of an elected popular assembly. This challenge to St. Petersburg was followed by others. Herzen advocated the establishment of underground printing presses and secret societies for agitation among the peasantry and in the army. In November, 1861, commenting on the closure of the universities, he urged the expelled students to go "to the people," thus coining another slogan that was to have a profound influence upon the course of the revolutionary movement.

The arrival in London at the end of 1861 of the impetuous anarchist Michael Bakunin, a champion of Polish independence, led Herzen to embrace the cause of Poland. The columns of *The Bell* were thrown open to Polish nationalists; Herzen appealed to Russian officers not to lead their men against the insurgents who were fighting the common enemy—the ruthless centralized Russian state. This courageous stand cost him the support of his nationalistically-minded Russian admirers and won him few followers. Radicals of the younger generation flocking to London, Paris, Zurich, and Geneva soon found Herzen too rhetorical, romantic, genteel, and tame for their taste. In spite of his association with Bakunin, Herzen abhorred anarchism and political terror; and, the acridity of his philippics notwithstanding, he was basically a humanitarian and a social reformer rather than a ruthless revolutionary such as Bakunin, Tkachev, Trotsky, or Lenin. His London headquarters, once so popular, were deserted. In 1865 Herzen transferred his printing press and editorial offices to Geneva, the new center of Russian political emigration, but daily contact with new arrivals from Russia merely emphasized his estrangement. The circulation of *The Bell*, which never exceeded 3,000 copies, declined substantially after 1863; publication was suspended in 1867 and attempts at reviving the journal in the French language came to naught. Profoundly disgusted with the ideas and mores of the younger *émigré* circles (so well described in Turgenev's *Smoke*), Herzen left Geneva a disillusioned and embittered man. He died in Paris in January, 1870, and was buried in Nice. His articles and his memoirs (*Byloe i dumy*), "one of the great biographies of the nineteenth century" according to V. S. Pritchett, reveal wide culture, literary skill, devotion to the ideals of the common good and social justice, and a large measure of naïveté. Leaders of a different metal were taking over the control of the nascent Russian revolutionary movement which Herzen had so greatly helped to build.

The three outstanding figures among the men of action who came to dominate Russian radical thought and revolutionary tactics were Bakunin, Nechaev, and Tkachev. Born in 1818, Michael Bakunin, son of a wealthy nobleman, was from the age of twenty-five the stormy petrel of every European revolution. "The great wanderer, the great homeless," according to Herzen, he was the natural center towards whom gravitated the malcontents "of every age and in every country." Endowed with a gift for making both friends and enemies, Bakunin was among the founders of Marx's International Workingmen's Association (or First International, 1864) but soon broke finally with Marx (there had been sharp disagreements between them on numerous previous occasions) and was expelled from the organization in 1872. Four years later he died in Berne on the morrow of his last futile attempt to raise the banner of social revolution in Italy. In his earlier career Bakunin was the proponent of a federation of Slavic nations and at times exhibited slavophile tendencies. He lives in history, however, as the father of revolutionary anarchism based on Proudhon's negation of the state which Bakunin pushed to its extreme logical conclusion and which he combined with the Marxian idea of collective ownership. His teaching, for all its oversimplification, inconsistencies, and obscurities, attracted a devout following, while the commanding figure of the great rebel inflamed the imagination of those who were not satisfied with mere theories but craved action.

Among these restless minds was the low-born schoolteacher and student in the University of St. Petersburg Serge Nechaev (1847–1883), a disciple and for a time a friend of Bakunin, whom he met in Switzerland. Nechaev was the first Russian revolutionary to outline a detailed matter-of-fact program for the organization of the revolutionary party and to formulate the principle of political terror (1869); attached to this program was a set of forbidding, austere rules of personal conduct which every member of the party was requested to follow.[15] Fanatically devoted to the cause, Nechaev believed that the end justifies the means. To build himself up as a leader he used the crudest artifices, such as spreading of news concerning his sham arrests, escapes, and even death, and when he came to doubt the blind obedience of his associate and fellow student Ivan Ivanov, he decreed and carried out his murder (November, 1869). This gruesome affair, portrayed in Dostoevsky's novel *The Devils*, led to Nechaev's extradition by Switzerland, where he had taken refuge, and to his trial. In court Nechaev behaved with unconcern and arrogance. The remaining years of his life were spent in the fortress of Peter and Paul; from his cell, however, he established regular contacts with his associates, directed terroristic activities, and devised fanciful schemes for popular uprisings which were to be provoked by specious imperial manifestoes.

[15] There is some uncertainty whether this document was written by Bakunin or Nechaev, but there is no question that Nechaev subscribed to the views it expressed.

The Ivanov affair and other revelations resulted in the repudiation of Nechaev by many revolutionary leaders, including Marx and Bakunin, but he lost none of his prestige with the more ruthless section of the revolutionary movement. Indeed, Zheliabov, organizer of the murder of Alexander II, hesitated for a time between regicide and the liberation of Nechaev; it was at Nechaev's own request that the murder of the tsar was given precedence.

Peter Tkachev, born in 1844, was first arrested for revolutionary activities at the age of seventeen. In the 1860's he made a name for himself as a radical journalist, was close to Nechaev and his group, and was arrested again in 1869, but four years later escaped abroad and from 1875 to 1877 published in Geneva the journal *Nabat* (The Tocsin); he died in Paris in 1886. Tkachev argued that the success of a revolution depends on determined leadership by a closely knit and well organized party. Strongly influenced by Auguste Blanqui, he held that the primary duty of the party was not to propagandize the masses but to overthrow the government and to seize power, a theory which won him the reputation of a Jacobin. Russia, in his opinion, was ripe for a socialist revolution, and delays due to excessive emphasis on propaganda would merely strengthen the bourgeois elements and jeopardize the chances of success. Although not a Marxist— Tkachev thought in terms of the peasantry, not of the industrial proletariat—he is properly regarded as a precursor of Lenin.[16]

From the confused clash of opinions voiced by Russian radical political theorists there gradually emerged a fairly coherent doctrine known as "populism" (*narodnichestvo*). Originating in Herzen's writings of the late 1840's and early 1850's, it was expanded a decade or two later by Chernyshevsky, Dobroliubov, Lavrov, Mikhailovsky, Bakunin, Tkachev, and Nechaev, to mention only a few. The essence of populism, with due allowance for the divergencies of views and emphasis in the presentation of various authors, may be reduced to four propositions: (1) the existing order was doomed and must be overthrown by a socialist revolution; (2) the historical development of Russia differed from that of other European countries and allowed direct transition to socialism, omitting the intermediate stage of capitalism; (3) the latter theory was based on the assumption that the

---

[16] The similarities of Lenin's and Tkachev's revolutionary tactics were emphasized by the Soviet historian M. N. Pokrovsky but are repudiated by later Soviet writers.

allegedly specifically Russian institutions—communal land tenure (*obshchina*) and associations of workingmen and craftsmen (*artel*) —were compatible with socialist principles; hence, according to this view, the introduction of capitalism in Russia would be a step backward, not forward; and (4) the peasants, "communists by instinct and tradition," were the real force behind the revolution. The populists, moreover, stressed the importance of "heroes" or leaders in the historical process. The doctrines of populism, which Lenin aptly called "peasant socialism," were unfounded, far-fetched, unduly optimistic, and impracticable, but they hardly deserve the contemptuous description "petty bourgeois" and "reactionary" applied to them by Soviet writers, even though Lenin used these terms in the heat of party squabbles.

There was little agreement among the populists concerning the methods by which their objectives could be achieved. Lavrov and his disciples held that Russia must be rebuilt "not only for the people but by the people," that "a revolution could not be artificially provoked" but was the product of an organic historical process. Revolutionary action, therefore, was to be limited to patient propaganda and agitation among the peasantry; premature uprisings would weaken the movement and postpone the establishment of a socialist commonwealth. The faction led by Bakunin took issue with Lavrov, and argued that the country was ready for an uprising; what was needed was not painstaking long-range propaganda but a resolute call to arms and assistance in coordinating the efforts of the insurgent groups—the more rebellions, the better. Tkachev and his friends agreed with Bakunin that a revolutionary situation existed in Russia but, as has already been stated, relied on the *coup d'état* by a small revolutionary party. The seizure of power appeared to them feasible and relatively easy because they believed that the government "hung in the air" and was not supported by any social class. Moreover Tkachev, like Nechaev, favored terrorism.

Populist doctrines survived in the teaching of the Socialist Revolutionary Party with which we shall meet later. Although a Russian section of the First International was formed in Geneva in 1870 and Volume I of Marx's *Capital,* first published in 1867, appeared in Russian in 1872, prior to its translation into any other foreign language, Marxism made little progress in Russia until the closing decade of the nineteenth century. In the 1870's populism—that quaint mixture of socialism and nationalism, idealism and brutality—was the creed of Russian radicals. Its practical repercussions were graver than might have been expected in view of the nebulous and fanciful character of its program.

Radical circles in Russia reacted to the emancipation in a manner similar to that of Herzen and *The Bell*. They gave vent to their disillusionment through the legitimate press and, to avoid the shackles of censorship, through underground channels. In the summer and autumn of 1861 appeared the first revolutionary proclamations printed in Russia, forerunners of a long line of underground publications. The police at once took action. The novelist and poet M. I. Mikhailov, arrested in September, 1861, for circulating subversive leaflets, was sentenced to penal servitude in Siberia; this was the first political trial in the reign of Alexander II. Many of the appeals issued by Herzen and other radical leaders were addressed to university youth. That they were not without effect was indicated by the outbreak in the autumn of 1861 of student disturbances; the movement had a political character and spread from St. Petersburg to Moscow and other university cities. Large recurrent fires of uncertain origin, but ascribed to subversive elements, swept St. Petersburg in the spring of 1862, adding to the state of public unrest. The government decreed stern reprisals: Pisarev and Chernyshevsky were arrested in July, radical journals were suspended, and many of their sympathizers were emprisoned or deported.

In spite of these measures centers of revolutionary activity began to appear on Russian soil. Early in 1862 Land and Freedom, the first secret society of some importance, was founded in St. Petersburg by a group of intellectuals, including several army officers. Chernyshevsky, although not a member, was in close touch with the organization, which established sections in Moscow and in many provincial cities and published two issues of the underground journal *Svoboda* (Liberty). Land and Freedom denounced autocracy, supported Polish insurgents, and carried on some propaganda among the students, peasants, and troops; but it met with indifferent success, and ceased to function in 1864. The Polish rebellion and its concomitant—chauvinistic nationalism—strengthened for a time the hand of the government. Radical leaders, from Herzen down, had to bear the odium of their advocacy of the cause of Poland. Mass arrests and deportations, moreover, had a sobering effect, while administrative reforms and the more humane regime instituted in the universities by Golovnin helped to bring about a degree of reconciliation. Though the revolutionary tide was at low ebb, it was merely the calm before a storm. The absurdity and crudity of Russian policies in Poland during the aftermath of the rebellion cured many liberal-minded Russians of their nationalistic inhibitions; the zemstvo reform was hardly less disappointing than the emancipation of the serfs; and although the voices of Chernyshevsky and Pisarev were no longer heard, their writings, as well as those of other Russian and European radical thinkers, were avidly read and discussed at informal gatherings that became the custom among university students.

Not all of these debating circles were academic and politically unobjectionable. The so-called Nicholas Ishutin group, which had met in Moscow since 1863, was impregnated with extreme radicalism, held that "all reforms" were futile, and devised daring, though childish, schemes for social revolution and the overthrow of the government. A member of this group, Dimitry Karakozov, against the advice of his friends, made an attempt on the life of Alexander II. On April 4, 1866, he fired point-blank at the tsar but missed him by accident. Though the redoubtable Count Michael Muravev, who was entrusted with the investigation of the abortive regicide, failed to discover any trace of the rumored wide-flung conspiracy, he pointedly remarked in his report that the overthrow of the monarchy had adherents in every social group, even among the members of the government. Karakozov was hanged, and thirty-four of his associates suffered lesser penalties. The consequences of his foolish gesture were mass arrests of innocent people, the strengthening of reaction, and the substitution of Dimitry Tolstoy for Golovnin as minister of education. The atmosphere of foreboding and reaction became even more oppressive after the Polish *émigré* Berezowski attempted to murder Alexander in Paris in May, 1867. In 1869 a new wave of student disturbances swept the universities, partly because of the vexatious regime introduced by Tolstoy and partly because of the general state of unrest accentuated by revolutionary propaganda. Tolstoy endeavored to restore order by decreeing a complex system of penalties which comprised expulsions accompanied by prohibitions to enroll in higher schools for periods of from one to three years or even altogether, except by permission of the central authorities. The director of the police (and later minister of the interior) V. K. von Plehve rightly held in 1882 that these vicious regulations, by making social outcasts of young men on the threshold of life, created a vast body of malcontents who were all but forced into the ranks of the revolutionary movement. Von Plehve's statement was supported by statistical evidence from police records.

The barring of women from the universities by the charter of 1863 proved another boon to the revolutionaries. Denied the right to higher education in their own country, Russian girls flocked abroad, especially to Zurich, that center of Russian revolution and emigration, where they were exposed to the teaching and personal influence of the inveterate enemies of autocracy and the existing order. Belatedly realizing its mistake, the imperial government issued in 1873 a statement informing Russian female students abroad that higher schools for women were about to be opened in Russia and directing them to return home by the end of the year under the threat of exclusion from Russian schools and government employ. The edict was generally complied with but for somewhat different reasons: the revolutionary groups were preparing a mass propaganda campaign among the peasantry. Unwittingly, the government facilitated these designs by helping to build up the cadres of the revolutionary army.

The revolutionary slogan of the late 1860's and early 1870's was Herzen's battle cry "To the people!" assiduously disseminated by *émigré* organizations through their publications, which were smuggled into Russia, and by informal populist groups at home. Yet the immediate objectives and methods of the proposed campaign remained vague and uncertain. The movement was colored with exuberant idealism, boundless faith in the inherent wisdom and goodness of the people, and ignorance of the conditions in the countryside. Of the many populist groups in Russia, the two better known were those led by N. V. Chaikovsky (Tchaikovsky) and A. Dolgushin. The Chaikovsky group, formed in 1869, concentrated at first on propaganda in the higher schools and factories, chiefly through the distribution of appropriate literature and the organization of discussion groups and evening classes. Its headquarters in St. Petersburg maintained a liaison with *émigré* circles and with numerous sympathizers throughout the country, and had agents in some thirty provinces. The group consisted of young intellectuals of the upper and middle class, university students, and army officers. Among its members was Sophie Perovsky (born in 1853), daughter of a former governor-general of St. Petersburg, and Prince Peter Kropotkin (1842–1921), scion of one of Russia's ancient families and a graduate of the aristocratic Corps des Pages, who had joined the First International and who eventually became a pillar of revolutionary anarchism. To dispel the distrust of workingmen towards upper-class propagandists, this group proceeded to organize workshops where its members were trained in manual tasks before they enrolled in factories in the manly effort to merge with the rank and file of the proletariat. The scant response of industrial workers to populist propaganda led to a change in tactics; beginning with 1873 the chief stress of the group's activities was shifted from the sullen factories to the hitherto unexplored and boundless expanses of rural Russia. The new orientation involved no sacrifice of principle. Chaikovsky and his friends opposed dictatorship and revolution by decree, believing that the overthrow of the existing order must be accomplished through the spontaneous action of the people; their aim was to arouse the revolutionary instinct of the masses. The Dolgushin group, inspired by Bakunin, deprecated this program and emphasized immediate rebellion as the real object of the movement "to the people." Organized in St. Petersburg in 1872, the group was soon transferred to Moscow, where it met with disaster: Dolgushin and the other leaders were arrested, tried, and convicted in the autumn of 1873; many of their followers, however, escaped the police and gave themselves with renewed zeal to revolutionary agitation.

The movement "to the people" began in 1873 and assumed the character of a mass phenomenon in the "crazy" summer of 1874. Worked up to a high pitch of excitement, and relying on optimistic reports that rural Russia was on the verge of rebellion, thousands of young men and women donned peasant garb and invaded the countryside; some endeavored to establish permanent centers of agitation, others moved from place to place preaching the revolutionary gospel. The immediate results of this unique crusade were nil. The villagers listened sometimes with approval but more often with bewilderment and suspicion, listened and went about their business. The police, moreover, were on the track of the revolutionaries. Their St. Petersburg organization was wiped out in the winter of 1873–1874, some 800 propagandists were seized by the end of the summer, and after a protracted investigation 193 were tried (October, 1877 to January, 1878). Of this number 153 were acquitted, and many of those found guilty received light sentences. The tsar, however, revised the sentences upwards, while a large number of the acquitted defendants were deported by the police to the northern provinces and to Siberia.

The revolutionary movement had suffered a severe blow; yet it would be an error to write off the 1874 adventure as a total failure. In his report on the case Count Pahlen, minister of justice, after noting that many people of wealth and good social standing approved of their sons' and daughters' part in the revolutionary campaign, observed that in view of the scope of the movement some of the underground organizations would inevitably elude detection and "continue their criminal activities." His apprehensions were justified. The revolutionaries, moreover, were learning from their mistakes and were partly cured of their illusions about the peasants. At the end of 1874 a group of former expatriates from Zurich, including several women, formed in Moscow a secret revolutionary society more closely knit than any of its predecessors. Its propaganda work in the Bakunin manner (incitement to rebellion) was carried on chiefly among industrial workers but was soon discovered by the authorities. Arrests of the leaders were followed by the "Trial of Fifty" (February and March, 1877). Several other conspiracies along similar lines suffered a like fate. Whatever its potential ultimate results, propaganda among the masses did not seem to weaken autocracy but depleted the ranks of its opponents. "The propagandist of the early 1870's," wrote S. M. Stepniak-Kravchinsky, one of the participants in the 1874 crusade, "belonged to a type common among the leaders of religious rather than revolutionary movements. Socialism was his creed, the people—his god. . . . He was too much of an idealist to withstand the forthcoming arduous and cruel struggle. He had either to change or to disappear. A new type of revolutionary—the terrorist—was getting ready to step into his place." The more gentle souls shrank from the alternative. Chaikovsky and some of his friends became converted to an obscure brand of mystical Christianity and sailed for the promised land of the United States, where they founded agricultural communes ostensibly based on principles of brotherly love. They soon hopelessly quarreled, the communes disintegrated, and the disgruntled brethren drifted back to their native shores.

After the debacle of 1874 the nature of populism underwent a change. The doctrine that revolution should be made by the people themselves and that the part of radical intellectuals should be limited to arousing the popular conscience was relegated to the background;

under the new interpretation the intellectuals were to fight autocracy in the name of socialism and the toiling masses. In other words, as one commentator put it, the populists "had lost faith in the people." The change of orientation came about gradually. In October, 1876, the populists reassembled in St. Petersburg founded a secret society, or party, which in 1878 assumed the revered name of Land and Freedom. The program still upheld traditional beliefs and provided for propaganda among university students, industrial workers, and peasants. A specially constituted "disorganizing section," however, was assigned the duty of rescuing arrested comrades, fighting the arbitrariness of the police and prison authorities, and protecting the party against the disloyalty of its members; betrayal of confidence was made treason, punishable by death. These were important concessions to the terroristic ideas of Tkachev and Nechaev. Propaganda tactics were revised: the practice of sending itinerant agitators into rural areas was declared unsound; instead there was to be established a carefully planned network of permanent propaganda centers directed by resident agents whose duty it was to win the respect and confidence of the peasants. To achieve the latter object the propagandists went to the villages in the guise, not of common laborers, but of personages of some importance—storekeepers, skilled workmen, teachers, and so on. A new movement "to the people" according to the revised program was attempted in 1877–1878 but was no more successful than its predecessor. The basic unsoundness of the whole scheme, the vigilance of the police, and the incurable indifference of the villagers were the reasons for its failure. Patient indoctrination of illiterate peasants in the bleak isolation of forlorn hamlets, moreover, did not appeal to the imagination of young intellectuals dreaming of quick results and heroic spectacular deeds. By 1879 the second crusade "to the people" petered out. A more promising attempt to arouse the countryside was made in the county of Chigirin, province of Kiev, where a handful of resourceful revolutionaries induced some 3,000 peasants to join an underground organization which ostensibly had for its object the defense of autocracy. The instigators of the movement owed their success to a spurious manifesto declaring in the name of Alexander II that the emancipation acts of 1861 were forgeries and that all land belonged to the peasants; the tsar's loyal subjects were urged to organize secretly and to get ready to liberate him from the usurpers—the nobility and the officials. This quaint plot in the tradition of Pugachev was uncovered in 1877 and led to the arrest of over one thousand men, including all the leaders. With the unprincipled Chigirin adventure Land and Freedom would have nothing to do.

Land and Freedom achieved some success in establishing connections with revolutionary groups in the provinces and in fostering unrest among university students and industrial workers. The years 1879–1880 were particularly stormy in the higher schools and in the St. Petersburg textile mills, where populist propaganda was rife. The party's principal activities, however, were of the "disorganizing" type, an indication that the influence of Tkachev and Nechaev was winning over that of Lavrov. The trend towards terrorism was intensified by the remarkable case of Vera Zasulich. In December, 1876, Land and Freedom staged in the Kazan Square in St. Petersburg what was intended as an impressive mass demonstration but turned out to be a miserable affair: the few dozen participants were roughly handled by the police and the crowd; their leaders were arrested, tried, and sentenced to long terms of penal servitude. For a minor breach of the prison routine one of the convicted men, Alexis Bogoliubov, a revolutionary of long standing and a member of Land and Freedom, was flogged by orders of the military governor of St. Petersburg, General F. F. Trepov. This occurrence provoked a near riot among the prisoners and created great excitement, especially in revolutionary circles. Clamoring for vengeance, several revolutionary groups made preparations for the murder of Trepov. Forestalling their plans, Vera Zasulich (1849–1919), acting independently, fired at and grievously wounded Trepov (January, 1878). Zasulich came from the lesser nobility, and in 1869–1871 had served a two-year sentence for revolutionary activities. She was not acquainted with either Bogoliubov or Trepov, nor did she make an attempt to escape. The crime having no personal motive, the trial of Zasulich assumed the character of an indictment of the regime. The verdict of "not guilty" rendered by the jury after a brief deliberation was received with wild enthusiasm by the packed courtroom and the huge crowds outside; according to eyewitnesses, some of the higher bureaucrats in the audience joined in the applause. Consternation in official circles was great. The order for the rearrest of Zasulich, issued the same evening (March 31, 1878), and the subsequent setting aside of the verdict by the Senate were of no avail: Zasulich was spirited abroad by her friends and returned legally to Russia after the amnesty of October, 1905.

The Zasulich case gave a powerful impetus to political terror; the verdict, interpreted as public endorsement of terroristic methods, swayed many populists who had formerly opposed political murders. Attempts on the lives of high officials and police officers became increasingly frequent. The most notable victims were General N. V. Mezentsov, a hero of Sevastopol and head of the security police (August, 1878); Prince Kropotkin, governor-general of Kharkov (February, 1879); General A. R. Drenteln, head of the security police, who, however, escaped unharmed (March, 1879). Arrests, trials, executions, and deportations brought retaliation by the terrorists. The underground leaflet "Land and Freedom," which reflected the views of the more extreme wing of the party, said early in 1879: "Political murder is primarily an act of vengeance. . . . Under existing conditions political murder is the only means of self-defense and one of the most effective methods of propaganda. By striking at the very center of the government it shatters with terrible force the entire system." The inescapable and logical conclusion drawn from this theory was regicide, which, indeed, was soon to absorb the energies of the revolutionaries. Land and Freedom, however, was still divided on this much-discussed issue. On April 2, 1879, one of its members, Alexander Solovev, fired five shots at the tsar, who once more escaped injury; Solovev used a gun provided by the party but he acted without its sanction. His attempt brought to a head the long-standing ideological conflict within the inner circle of Land and Freedom. Moreover, the influx of new members, some of them not personally acquainted with the older leaders, undermined the feeling of solidarity and paved the way for disintegration.

A preliminary secret conference of Land and Freedom attended by fourteen delegates from St. Petersburg and the provinces met at the resort town of Lipetsk in June, 1879. The conference approved the principle of political terror, set up a centralized governing body (executive committee) shrouded in secrecy, and unanimously endorsed the murder of Alexander II as one of the organization's immediate objectives. The Lipetsk decisions were referred to a larger conference, held a few days later in the woods near Voronezh. With the lone exception of George Plekhanov (later one of the leading Russian Marxists), who took an uncompromising stand and withdrew, the some twenty-five delegates present approved the proposals. The revised program voted by the conference recapitulated the familiar principles of propaganda among the peasants but emphasized that the weapon of terror must be used against higher officials, on whom depended Russia's policies, as well as against their subordinates. Declaring, oddly, that the question of regicide "remains open in principle," the conference decided to proceed with practical measures for the murder of Alexander II. This compromise program satisfied no one, some of the members of the St. Petersburg group refused to abide by it, and in October, 1879, Land and Freedom split into two independent organizations: *Narodnaia volia* (People's Will) and *Chernyi peredel* (Total Land Reapportionment).[17] The latter, led by Plekhanov, upheld the traditional populist ideology, accomplished nothing, and by 1881 faded away. The program of People's Will spoke in general terms of socialism, faith in the people, overthrow of autocracy, and the convocation of a freely elected constituent assembly. Under the fanatical leadership of Andrew Zheliabov and Sophie Perovsky, however, the group concentrated on a single object: the murder of the emperor. Between the autumn of 1879 and March 1, 1881, when the tsar was finally killed, People's Will is known to have organized seven attempts against his life, although the actual number was probably greater. These sinister enterprises required careful long-range planning and laborious preparations. Firearms, held too unreliable, were discarded in favor of high explosives, which were zealously manufactured by the terrorists. The attempt at blowing up the imperial train near Moscow in November, 1879, necessitated the purchase of a building adjoining the railway track, the digging of an underground gallery, and the laying of a mine. A similar technique was used in the final assault of March 1, when, the tsar having changed his itinerary, the mine was not exploded and he was killed by a bomb thrown by one of the conspirators. Even more daring was the attempt of February 5, 1880, when a carefully planned explosion shattered the banquet hall of the Winter Palace shortly before a scheduled gala dinner.

The mounting tide of terrorism and the ease with which the conspirators gained access to the imperial residence and carried out their designs called for extraordinary measures. At a conference of high officials, held under the presidency of the tsar three days after the Win-

[17] *Peredel* is the term for redistribution or reapportionment of land under communal arrangements (*obshchina*); *chernyi* literally means "black" but in the above phrase implies "total" or "all-inclusive" transfer of land to the peasants. My translation does not convey the fighting ring of the original; the real meaning would be better rendered by some such phrase as "All land to the peasants."

ter Palace explosion, the heir to the throne argued that the only effective way to fight the revolutionaries was coordination of all governmental activities, that is, the establishment of a dictatorship. A diluted version of this proposal was embodied in a decree of February 12 creating the Supreme Executive Commission. Its president, Count M. T. Loris-Melikov, formerly governor-general of Kharkov, was vested with comprehensive police powers, although similar powers conferred upon the governors-general by a decree of April 5, 1879, were not revoked. Loris-Melikov believed that police measures alone were not enough and that the government must seek reconciliation with moderate opinion. Stern and ruthless with the revolutionaries, he made some concessions to the liberals: Dimitry Tolstoy was dismissed; the noose of censorship was slightly loosened; the infamous Section III of His Majesty's Own Chancery was dissolved without, however, any relaxation in police supervision; and the functions of Section III were taken over by the newly created department of the police under the ministry of the interior. The "dictatorship of the heart," as the Loris-Melikov regime was called, met with the approval of the liberals but was attacked by the revolutionaries and by the conservatives, especially Katkov. An unsuccessful attempt to murder Loris-Melikov was made on February 20, 1880, by I. Molodetsky, a member of People's Will. Yet during the following months revolutionary terror appeared to subside, and the Supreme Executive Commission was dissolved in August, Loris-Melikov continuing in office as minister of the interior. In pursuance of his policy of reconciliation Loris-Melikov advocated a minor change in legislative procedure: the establishment of a commission to which the zemstvos and the municipalities of the larger cities were to send representatives and which was to examine, in a purely advisory capacity, legislative bills before they were submitted to the State Council.[18] This innocuous scheme, euphemistically described sometimes as the Loris-Melikov "constitution," received Alexander's approval on the fateful morning of March 1, 1881, a few hours before the tsar met his death at the hands of the conspirators. It was shelved by his successor.

[18] It will be remembered that the State Council was a consultative and not a legislative assembly, that is, its decisions were not binding on the Crown. The Loris-Melikov "constitution" was but a jejune version of a proposal made by Valuev in 1863, when reconciliation with the liberals was deemed desirable because of the Polish rebellion. Valuev revived his proposal in January, 1880, but it was defeated by the opposition of the future Alexander III.

Alexander II fell the victim of the fanatical perseverance of a small group of revolutionaries: only four men and two women were tried and sentenced to be publicly hanged for the bloody deed of March 1. One of them, Jessie Helfman, an expectant mother, escaped the gallows: her execution was deferred and she died in prison after giving birth to a child. All six were young, their ages ranging from thirty to nineteen. The two leaders of the plot, Zheliabov and Sophie Perovsky, began their revolutionary career as peaceful propagandists in the classical populist tradition; both ended as terrorists, Perovsky being involved in every one of the seven known attempts on Alexander II's life organized by People's Will. Zheliabov was arrested the day before the murder, but volunteered a confession when he learned that the only regicide in the hands of the authorities was Nicholas Rysakov, a boy of nineteen. Sophie Perovsky escaped arrest until March 10, and might easily have fled abroad; she chose to stay and share the fate of her lover Zheliabov, although she had no illusions as to what this meant. These details are not insignificant; like the case of Zasulich, they throw much light on the nature of the revolutionary movement in the 1860's and 1870's. Although some of the populist leaders (for instance, Zheliabov) came from the peasantry, most of rural Russia and of the industrial workers remained aloof from the revolutionary movement, which drew its following from among the intellectuals of the upper and the middle class. The indifference of the masses was the basic reason why the idealistic propaganda of the Chaikovsky type degenerated into bloody terror. The actual membership of secret societies was not large; but revolutionary ideas, and even terroristic activities, commanded wide support not only among university students, members of liberal professions, and zemstvo employees, but also in the army, the bureaucracy, and even the security police. Revolutionary organizations, moreover, had at their disposal considerable funds, some of the well-to-do converts (Peter Kropotkin, Sophie Perovsky, Dimitry Lizogub) having contributed their entire fortunes to the cause. These factors, coupled with the amazing laxity of the police, help to explain the extraordinary number of successful escapes from Siberia and from reputedly impregnable prisons, or the almost unbelievable Nechaev correspondence with his associates from his cell in the fortress of Peter and Paul, and the rather nonchalant peregrinations of Zheliabov and Perovsky (both of them police suspects) through Russia with trunks full of dynamite.

The emergence of the revolutionary movement may well be regarded as the most portentous development of the era of "great reforms." It is eminently fitting that Vladimir Ulianov, the future Lenin, and Joseph Dzhugashvili, the future Stalin, should have been born, respectively, in 1870 and 1879, within the brief span of a revolutionary decade.

CHAPTER XXXVIII

ALEXANDER III

The Last Autocrat

ALEXANDER III AND HIS ADVISERS

In the brief reign of Alexander III (1881–1894), Russian monarchical absolutism, like a late summer blossom whose evanescent glories are soon to be swept away by the autumn storms, asserted itself for the last time. Born on February 26, 1845, the future Emperor Alexander III was the second son of Alexander II, and became heir apparent after his elder brother Nicholas died of consumption in 1865. Although Alexander's early education had been somewhat neglected, as was evidenced by his inability to master Russian spelling, the eminent historian S. M. Solovev in 1865–1866 taught the future tsar a course on Russian history, which may account in part for his ardently nationalistic views. On October 28, 1866, Alexander married Princess Sophie Frederica Dagmar of Denmark (a sister of the future Queen Alexandra of England), known in Russia as Maria Fedorovna. Although the Danish princess had formerly been betrothed to Alexander's elder brother and her marriage with the new heir apparent had all the earmarks of a *mariage de convenance,* their union proved serenely happy; Alexander was a devoted husband and the father of five children born between 1868 and 1882. His private life was free from the irregularities so common among his predecessors, and his disapproval of Alexander II's liaison and subsequent morganatic marriage with Princess Yurevsky (who, moreover, according to Count Witte, used her influence to promote the interests of unscrupulous concession seekers) was one reason for the disfavor with which he looked upon the policies of the preceding reign. Powerfully built and awkward in manner, Alexander shunned the pomp and circumstance of the St.

Alexander III

Petersburg court; and as the years went by he sought more frequently the seclusion of the country residence of Gatchina, where in a small circle of intimate friends he gave free vent to his rough-and-ready joviality. He was fond of the theater and music, especially of the lighter kind, and at the Gatchina soirees occasionally played the trombone in a quartet. The private life of Alexander was uneventful except for an abortive attempt upon his life in 1887 and the escape of the imperial family in a serious train wreck a year later. He died of nephritis on October 20, 1894.

As heir apparent Alexander took the customary, albeit inconspicuous, part in the administration of the affairs of state; during the War of 1877–1878 he held without distinction a military command wherein he showed little aptitude for the art of warfare. After his accession, Alexander, a conscientious ruler, performed diligently the duties of his high office. His copious annotations on state papers, as well as his public and private pronouncements, disclose a dull and unimaginative mind; its outstanding characteristics, perhaps, were a straightforwardness of approach and a singleness of purpose seldom encountered among the occupants of the Russian throne. The emperor's political creed may be reduced to the tripartite formula devised some fifty years earlier by Uvarov: Orthodoxy, autocracy, and nationality (*narodnost*), with special emphasis on autocracy.[1] This was not a closely reasoned, consistent philosophy—Alexander III was incapable of abstract thinking—but rather an instinctive elemental attachment to the idea of the unfettered supremacy of the Crown, interpreted as the mainstay of the empire and the very essence of Russia's historical tradition.

The practical repercussions of these doctrines were far-reaching. The emphasis on autocracy tended to perpetuate bureaucratic tutelage by denying popular representation any part in the central government and by obstructing the institutions of local self-government in the exercise of their legitimate functions. Orthodoxy was to Alexander both a matter of personal faith (a devout churchman, he recorded for years in his diary his attendance at divine services, neatly adding the total at the end of the year) and an element of his militant, if somewhat shapeless, nationalism. In the 1870's the future tsar, as has already been noted, was under the spell of the panslavs, especially Aksakov. He retained to the end the panslav hostility towards Austria-Hungary and Great Britain, but he soon lost interest in the positive aspects of

---
[1] See above pp. 797 *et seq.*

the panslav program. Some of these were incompatible with his most cherished beliefs. The inclination of the Balkan Slavs towards democratic government of the western type, as evidenced by the Bulgarian constitution, was at variance with the glorification of autocracy, while the sizable, closely knit non-Orthodox groups among the Slavs were a challenge to the supremacy of the Orthodox Church. In the Russian policies of the 1880's and 1890's panslavism was not an objective in itself but a means for the achievement of Russian national aims. "I understand only one policy," Alexander commented on Saburov's dispatch of April 25, 1881: "To exact from every situation all that is needed by and is useful to Russia, to disregard all other considerations, and to act in a straightforward and resolute manner. We can have no policy except one that is purely Russian and national; this is the only policy we can and must follow." The application of the principles of Orthodoxy and nationality to domestic affairs manifested itself in the intensification of administrative centralization and in the persecution of ethnic and religious minorities.

The opinions of Alexander—unswaying, stubborn, and at times curt and irritable as he was—were profoundly influenced by the subtle, incessant pressure of Pobedonostsev and by the writings of Katkov. Constantine Pobedonostsev (1827–1907), a distinguished jurist and co-author of the reform of the law courts, was the tutor both of Alexander III and of his son and heir, the future Emperor Nicholas II; from 1880 to 1905 he held the office of chief procurator of the Holy Synod. Generally and rightly regarded as the most powerful man in Russia, Pobedonostsev owed his influence to his intimate understanding of his imperial master's character and mind, which he himself had largely molded. His voluminous correspondence with Alexander III, published by the Soviet government, reveals that the emperor followed closely Pobedonostsev's advice in deciding political issues and in making appointments to higher offices. The most momentous pronouncements of the reign, as will appear later, were written by the chief procurator. Pobedonostsev's letters—unctuous, imbued with boundless devotion to the tsar and his family, and replete with invocations of divine Providence and references to minute happenings of the imperial household—followed a definite pattern. Their author invariably posed, on the one hand, as the relentless enemy of the self-seeking, corrupt, and inefficient bureaucracy and of the equally self-seeking proponents of constitutional reforms, and, on the other, as the staunch champion of the common people and the spokesman of their unfaltering faith in the Crown. The impression was thus created that it was the lower classes—hard-working, uncontaminated by outlandish ideas, and deeply religious—who, through the crafty chief procurator, urged the tsar to lead Russia along the traditional path of autocracy to which she owed her happiness and greatness, and who rejoiced at every reactionary measure inspired by Pobedonostsev. "The moral union of the people and the government" was, according to Pobedonostsev, the very foundation of the Russian state (letter of May 16, 1877); by government, however, he meant autocracy. "The whole secret of Russia's order and progress is above, in the person of the monarch . . ." he wrote to Alexander on October 12, 1876. "The day may come when flatterers . . . will try to persuade you that it would suffice to grant Russia a so-called constitution on the western model, and all difficulties would disappear and the government could live in peace. This is a lie, and God forbid that a true Russian shall see the day when this lie will become an accomplished fact." Pobedonostsev upheld this theory with remarkable persistency. "I meet many people of different stations and rank," he wrote on December 14, 1879. "What I hear here [in St. Petersburg] from highly placed and learned men makes me sick, as if I were in the company of half-wits or perverted apes. I hear everywhere the trite, deceitful, and accursed word—constitution. This word, I fear, has made its way into high circles and is taking roots. But I also meet and talk with sane Russian people who are full of apprehension. . . . They fear primarily that basic evil, a constitution. The idea is everywhere taking shape among the people: a Russian revolution, an ugly upheaval, is preferable to a constitution. The former could be suppressed and order restored throughout the land; the latter is poison to the entire organism, destructive by its inherent deceit to which Russia's soul could never be reconciled." Towards the end of his career, in a letter of March 21, 1901, to Nicholas II, Pobedonostsev wrote of "the insane longing for a constitution, that is, the ruin of Russia." These theories, combined with religious bigotry and nationalistic intolerance, colored the reign of Alexander III and overlapped that of his successor.

The influence of Katkov, whom Pobedonostsev admired and sponsored, was exercised through his articles in *Moskovskiia Vedomosti* (Moscow News), which Alexander read regularly. Although Katkov occasionally went too far, and his indiscretions and attacks on the Russo-German alliance brought upon him in 1887 the displeasure of the emperor, his ultra-conservative and chauvinistic paper was properly looked upon as the inspirer and the mouthpiece of official policies.

ADMINISTRATIVE COUNTER-REFORMS

Bismarck, in a conversation with Saburov in the spring of 1881, complained that the Russians he met in Berlin appeared to be obsessed with the desire for representative government. Disparaging democratic institutions, the German chancellor argued that parliamentary regimes put innumerable obstacles in the path of constructive legislation, and expressed the wish that "Russia will preserve as long as possible the magic wand of absolutism (*pouvoir absolu*), if only to accomplish the reforms she needs" (Saburov to Giers, April 25, 1881). "All this is true and just," Alexander wrote on the dispatch. "May God will that every Russian, particularly our ministers, shall understand our situation as clearly as does Prince Bismarck and shall not strive to achieve unattainable fantasies and lousy (*parshyvyi*) liberalism." The tsar had profited by Pobedonostsev's lessons. This being the case, the fate of Loris-Melikov's innocuous and over-rated proposal for the modification of legislative procedure, approved by Alexander II a few hours before he was murdered, was a foregone conclusion. At a conference of high officials held on March 8, 1881, the Loris-Melikov project was defended by its author, by the ministers of war and finance Miliutin and Abaza, and by the tsar's uncle the Grand Duke Constantine (head of the navy and president of the State Council). Pobedonostsev, leader of the opposing faction, presented in an emotional speech an indictment of the reforms of Alexander II and, paraphrasing Poland's tragic warning "*Finis Poloniae*," prophesied that the adoption of the proposal would mean "*Finis Russiae*." Alexander sided with the chief procurator and, although no formal decision was taken, the bill was shelved.

Whatever expectation of constitutional reforms might have lingered in liberal circles was put to rest by the imperial manifesto of April 29, 1881. Engineered and written by Pobedonostsev, the manifesto was communicated to the other ministers—as final and not subject to revision—on the eve of its publication. It proclaimed that the tsar had assumed his duties "with complete faith in the strength (*sila*) and truth (*istina*) of absolute power," which he was "called upon to maintain and defend, for the good of the people, against all assaults." Loris-Melikov and Abaza resigned at once and were shortly followed into retirement by Miliutin and the Grand Duke Constantine, Pobedonostsev's particular *bête noire*. The vacant offices were filled by men chosen by the chief procurator. Count Ignatev, architect of the ill fated San Stefano treaty, succeeded Loris-Melikov at the ministry of the interior. The representation of his brief administration as relatively liberal (Kornilov, Miakotin) is hardly in accordance with the facts. His treatment of the press was anything but magnanimous. He was, moreover, responsible for the statute of August 14, 1881, which empowered the government to proclaim a "state of emergency" in any part of the realm; administrative officials in the areas under the "emergency" regime were vested with broad extra-judicial and executive powers (arrest, imposition of fines, and sequestration of property without a trial; transfer of whole blocks of cases from the jurisdiction of criminal courts to that of military tribunals; closing of schools; suspension of periodicals; removal of officials). Enacted as a "provisional" measure for three years, this widely used law was repeatedly renewed, and continued in force until the revolution of 1917. Ignatev, however, in spite of his Balkan disappointments, had maintained his affiliation with the panslav movement. It will be remembered that one of the basic tenets of slavophilism was the union of the Crown and the people represented through an elective advisory assembly. Ignatev endeavored to apply this idea in practice. He began cautiously by summoning in June and September, 1881, two commissions consisting, respectively, of fifteen and thirty-five "men of experience" (*sveduiushchie liudi*) to advise the government on the then pending measures for the betterment of the position of the peasantry. Although the members of the commissions were appointed by the minister, included in their number were several zemstvo leaders, and they were given some latitude in criticizing and amending official proposals. Encouraged by the friendly reception given in many quarters to the work of the commissions, Ignatev planned his next and more ambitious step. In great secrecy he prepared a draft manifesto announcing the convocation of a *zemskii sobor*, a huge consultative assembly of some three thousand representatives elected by various social groups, including the peasants. The opening session of the *zemskii sobor*, an antiquated institution borrowed from the uncertainties of Russian sixteenth and seventeenth century history, was to be synchronized with

Alexander III's coronation in Moscow in 1883. Pobedonostsev, to whom the draft manifesto was referred by the tsar, ridiculed the archaic and labored style of this odd document in which he detected the hand of Aksakov; he branded the proposal as "criminal folly," and warned Alexander that the convocation of any representative assembly would inexorably lead to "revolution, the ruin of the government, and the ruin of Russia" (letter of May 4, 1882). Ignatev was dismissed and was succeeded, on Pobedonostsev's recommendation, by Count Dimitry Tolstoy, whose reactionary views and policies as Alexander II's minister of education have been described in a previous chapter. Somewhat earlier (January, 1882) the well meaning but colorless Baron Alexander Nikolai was replaced as head of the ministry of education by Ivan Delianov, another appointee of Pobedonostsev and formerly Tolstoy's henchman at the ministry of education. With these appointments the course of the reign was set towards extreme reaction.

The reorganization of local government was among the pressing issues of the day. Loris-Melikov, while still in power, had ordered senatorial investigations of conditions—including those of local government—in eight provinces, and had directed the zemstvos (circular of December 22, 1880) to submit proposals for the reform of township (*volost*) and village administration. Senatorial reports and zemstvo proposals, which in a number of cases went beyond the terms of reference and dealt with local government as a whole, were not forthcoming until after Loris-Melikov's dismissal. In September, 1881, these documents were turned over to a committee presided over by M. S. Kakhanov, assistant minister of the interior, and consisting of higher officials and senators in charge of the investigations. The information furnished the committee unfolded a grim picture of mismanagement, inefficiency, corruption, and bureaucratic arbitrariness and procrastination. As was to be expected in view of the composition of the committee, its preliminary report, which was not available until the autumn of 1884, was in no sense revolutionary. The object of the committee, indeed, was to devise measures for the "integration" of institutions of local self-government with those of the Crown administration in order "to secure the maintenance of internal peace and to promote public welfare, these best shields against anarchic tendencies." Written by enlightened bureaucrats, the report, for all its limitations, suggested important technical improvements, and tended to strengthen in certain respects the element of self-government and to remove at least some of the abuses. In 1884, however, Tolstoy was already firmly in the saddle. A group of fifteen "local leaders," handpicked by the minister and led by A. D. Pazukhin, a county marshal of the nobility, subjected the recommendations of the committee to unsparing criticism as unduly liberal and even subversive. The report was amended to meet these objections, but it still failed to win the approval of the authorities. In April, 1885, the Kakhanov committee was dissolved; its archives were transferred to the ministry of the interior, and Tolstoy, with Pazukhin, who had been appointed director of the chancery of the minister of the interior, assumed full control of revising legislation on local government.

Both were avowed opponents of Alexander II's administrative reforms. The zemstvo act of 1864, according to their interpretation, went too far in the direction of social equality; by impairing the leading position of the landed nobility the zemstvos, it was argued, had undermined the historic "class" or "estate" (*soslove*) structure of Russia and had endangered her very existence as a national state. Just as pernicious and incompatible with Russian tradition, in the opinion of Tolstoy, were institutions of local self-government enjoying real autonomy (a situation that certainly did not prevail in Russia in the 1880's). Pazukhin formulated tersely the program of the reign when he wrote in an article published in 1885 that "our objective today should be to restore what was destroyed" by the administrative reforms of Alexander II. This desire to set back the clock of history, which inspired many official policies, justifies the appellation of "the era of counter-reforms" often applied to the rule of Alexander III. The reactionary program was championed by Katkov and endorsed by a section of the landed nobility. The centenary (in 1885) of Catherine II's Charter of the Nobility, held as a suitable opportunity for some recognition of the services allegedly rendered to the Crown by the *dvorianstvo*, brought forth a plethora of projects and rumors.

The principal and most characteristic legislation dealing with administrative matters in the spirit of counter-reform was the statute on land captains of 1889, the zemstvo act of 1890, and the municipal government act of 1892. Although all three became law after Tolstoy's death (April, 1889), they bore the imprint of his evil genius. His successor, Ivan Durnovo, assistant minister of the interior since 1882 and minister from 1889 to 1895, shared the views of his former chief, and retained Pazukhin as director of his chancery.

The Kakhanov committee, recognizing that the institutions of peasant self-government were ineffectual, recommended that the township *(volost)* should be reorganized on a non-class basis, that is, that it should comprise not only the peasants (as provided by the statutes of 1861) [2] but all residents of rural areas irrespective of their legal and social status. This proposal had the merit of acknowledging the community of interests of rural inhabitants and of doing away with insidious class distinctions. Fearing, however, that in township assemblies the numerically weak group of noble landowners would be submerged in the mass of peasant farmers, the committee recommended that the administration of townships should be entrusted to officials elected by zemstvo assemblies and possessed of educational and other qualifications. Tolstoy rejected the first proposal and twisted the second so as to make it serve his political aims. The law of July 12, 1889, retained the township as a purely peasant institution but made it subject to the control of a new official, the land captain *(zemskii nachalnik)*. The land captain was appointed by the minister of the interior from a list of candidates selected, in accordance with complex rules, by the provincial governor and the provincial and county marshals of the nobility. The law required that the land captain should belong, whenever possible, to the local hereditary landed nobility; if, however, no suitable candidates of that group were available, the minister of the interior was empowered to fill the vacancy by appointing some other person eligible for civil service. In practice, except in the provinces which had no landed nobility, the majority of land captains were local landowners and hereditary noblemen. Unlike his predecessors,[3] the land captain exercised both judicial and administrative functions. The law of July 12, 1889, abolished the justices of the peace, except in the larger cities; in rural areas most of the cases formerly tried by the justices of the peace were transferred to the jurisdiction of land captains, thus violating the principle of separation of powers which the 1864 statutes strove to establish. Land captains were subordinated to the county session of land captains, the provincial board, the governor of the province, and the minister of the interior. The county session *(uezdnyi sezd)* consisted of the county marshal of the nobility, the land captains of the county, and several other officials. The provincial board *(gubernskoe prisutstvie)* was a

[2] See pp. 893–894.
[3] See pp. 889, 927.

bureaucratic body with a sprinkling of representatives from the zemstvo and local nobility; it invariably complied with the wishes of its chairman, the provincial governor appointed by the Crown. Unlike the arbitrators (*mirovoi posrednik*) of 1861 who were confirmed by the Senate, land captains, as has already been stated, were appointed by the minister of the interior; that dignitary was empowered to take against them disciplinary action and to remove them from office.

The administrative powers of the land captain were similar to, albeit more stringent than, those of the former arbitrator. Township assemblies no longer elected their elders but merely two candidates from whom the land captain made the final choice. A similar procedure was applied to the appointment of members of the township courts. Land captains could suspend or remove elective peasant officials; arrest and impose fines on peasant officials and the rank and file of the peasantry without the formality of a trial; veto decisions of township and village assemblies as contrary to the law or to the interests of the community or of its members, even if the parties concerned declared themselves satisfied; and prepare the agenda of township and village assemblies. Indeed, nothing pertaining to the financial, economic, social, and cultural welfare of the rural community escaped the jurisdiction of land captains. Some of their decisions were final and not subject to review; others could be appealed to higher authorities—the county session and the provincial board.

To claim that the law of 1889 destroyed peasant self-government would be idle for the reason that, as related elsewhere, the peasant institutions created in 1861 were still-born. Nevertheless the new legislation, typical of Tolstoy's and Pazukhin's methods, was a step backwards. A sham self-government was preserved, yet peasant Russia was actually ruled by petty officials drawn from the midst of the landed nobility and controlled by the minister of the interior.

Similar principles prompted the zemstvo reform of June 12, 1890. "The chief cause of the unsatisfactory state of the zemstvos," Pazukhin and Tolstoy wrote in an explanatory memorandum accompanying the bill, "is the lack of integration of zemstvo and Crown institutions. The estrangement between the two is the natural consequence of the acceptance by our legislation in 1864 of the theory that the zemstvos and their interests are something apart from the state and its needs, a doctrine which led in practice to the granting to the zemstvos, acting through their elective executive organs, of autonomy in matters pertaining to local economy and welfare. Hence the lack of unity and concord in the work of state and zemstvo institutions, and not infrequently avowed hostility between them." The remedy, according to the memorandum, must be sought, "in changing the very approach to local self-government, in recognizing that zemstvo functions are state functions." The logical conclusion from these premises would seem to be the frank admission of the usefulness of local self-government and the elimination of bureaucratic interference with its lawful activities. Tolstoy and Pazukhin, by a perverted process of reasoning based on fallacious historical assumptions, reached the opposite conclusion: in their opinion, the acceptance of the view that the zemstvo functions were "state functions" made it mandatory for the central authority to limit still further their independence. This was to be achieved by strengthening the representation of the landed nobility and by increasing the severity of bureaucratic controls.

The act of 1890 retained the 1864 framework of zemstvo institutions [4] but introduced important modifications in their organization. Under the revised law the electors who chose the members of the county (*uezd*) zemstvo assemblies were segregated, on a strictly class ("estate") basis, in three electoral colleges: (1) nobles, both hereditary and "personal"; (2) all other electors, except peasants; and (3) peasants. Ownership of a specified area of land, or of real estate (buildings) of a specified value, was a prerequisite for participation in the first and second electoral colleges.[5] Peasants were entitled to vote irrespective of property qualifications but participated in elections indirectly: each township meeting chose one candidate; from the list thus obtained the provincial governor appointed the number of peasant members prescribed by the law. Only those entitled to vote in an electoral college could be elected by that college. Women were denied a direct vote but could exercise their electoral rights through male representatives. Jews were disfranchised, a provision written into the law by Pobedonostsev. The law specified the number of members in each county (and provincial) assembly and the distribution of seats among the three electoral colleges: 57.1 per cent (in thirty provinces)

[4] See pp. 897 *et seq.*
[5] Electors who satisfied the statutory property qualification had the right of direct votes; those whose property holdings were below the prescribed norm, but not less than one-tenth thereof, voted through representatives elected at preliminary meetings; the number of representatives was determined by dividing the aggregate property holdings of the group of electors by the statutory norm.

were assigned to the nobility, 29.6 per cent to the peasants, and 13.3 per cent to others. Since county assemblies, as under the law of 1864, elected from their midst provincial zemstvo assemblies, and marshals of the nobility were ex officio chairmen of county and provincial assemblies (except, in the latter case, when a special chairman was appointed by the Crown), the preponderance of the landed nobility throughout the entire zemstvo structure was assured.

Other provisions of the act of 1890 revealed, however, that its framers put little trust in the nobility whom they had ostensibly entrenched as master of the zemstvos. The minister of the interior, provincial governors, and bureaucratic provincial offices on zemstvo and municipal affairs (*gubernskoe po zemskim i gorodskim delam prisutstvie*) wielded broad discretionary powers over the entire field of zemstvo activities. Elections and appointments of zemstvo officials (the number of appointed officials—doctors, teachers, agronomists, statisticians—increased rapidly with the expansion of economic and social services) required confirmation by provincial governors. Chairmen and members of zemstvo executive boards (*uprava*) elected by zemstvo assemblies were subject to the disciplinary authority of the minister of the interior, including that of removal from office. Decisions of zemstvo assemblies dealing with specified subjects required confirmation by the governor or by the minister of the interior. All other decisions did not become effective until two weeks after they were adopted; during this period the governor could suspend them on the ground that they violated the law or were contrary to public policy or local interests. In the latter case the offending decision could be amended and promulgated by Crown officials without the approval of the zemstvo concerned, a procedure incompatible with the basic principles of self-government but seldom, if ever, used in practice. The loose wording of the act, moreover, offered provincial governors unlimited opportunities for meddling with zemstvo finance. Such, in brief, was the regime designed to justify the nobility's claim to leadership, and to promote harmonious relations between zemstvo and state organs.

The municipal government act of June 11, 1892, like the zemstvo act of 1890, preserved the framework of existing institutions [6] but altered the basis of franchise and tightened bureaucratic controls. The cumbersome franchise of 1870 gave place to a less complex but far

[6] See p. 901.

more restrictive one based on property qualifications. Under the act of 1892 the right to vote in municipal elections was limited to owners of real estate of a specified value and to the proprietors of the more important commercial and industrial enterprises (those holding "guild" certificates first class in St. Petersburg and Moscow, and "guild" certificates first and second class in other cities). Property qualifications being relatively high the bulk of the urban population was disfranchised. The electoral roll in St. Petersburg shrank from the modest figure of 21,000 to 8,000, in Moscow from 20,000 to 7,000, in Kharkov from 6,900 to 2,300, in Rostov-on-Don from 5,400 to 800. Jews were disfranchised, but in the cities and towns within the Jewish pale Jewish municipal councilors were appointed by the provincial office on zemstvo and municipal affairs; their number was not to exceed one-tenth of the council's membership. Elaborate controls over the appointment of municipal officials and the activities of municipal government duplicated, with minor changes, the provisions of the zemstvo act of 1890.

The administrative counter-reforms, impregnated as they were with shameless bias towards the landed nobility and proprietary groups, might well appear as standard examples of class legislation. This interpretation, although it contains an element of truth, needs qualification. The history of the acts of 1889, 1890, and 1892 reveals that they reflected the views and prejudices of a small group of statesmen and journalists—Pobedonostsev, Tolstoy, Pazukhin, Durnovo, Katkov— rather than those of the landed nobility as a whole or of the nascent Russian bourgeoisie. As has already been stated, the Kakhanov committee, although consisting of high officials and members of the landed nobility, sponsored a program far more liberal than that embodied in the acts of 1889–1892. The State Council, another aristocratic and bureaucratic body, rejected or toned down a number of the more reactionary proposals devised by the minister of the interior and his friends. Had Alexander III chosen to listen to more enlightened advisers than Pobedonostsev and his kind, he would have found many supporters among the nobility and the bureaucracy. The failure of administrative reforms, moreover, indicates how profoundly the tsar and his councilors misread the signs of the time or even the mind of the upper class. Government efforts notwithstanding, the decline of the nobility continued unabated, while hostility between organs of central and local government increased. The zemstvos, in spite of the predominance of the landed nobility in their midst, became the centers of liberal and radical opposition. Municipal councils showed greater readiness to toe the line. City fathers only too frequently displayed indifference to the promotion of social welfare. At the turn of the twentieth century there were large cities that had not a single municipal primary school (Vitebsk) or city hospital (Simferopol). Some of the municipal councils (Odessa) were notorious hot-beds of militant reaction and aggressive nationalism; others, however, courageously raised their voice in defense of political and social progress, and refused to bow to bureaucratic dictation. Interference by Crown officials hampered the work of zemstvos and municipalities, but it did not succeed in stamping out that longing for real autonomy which is the essence of self-government.

Independence of the judiciary being difficult to reconcile with the authoritarian methods prevalent under Alexander III, it was inevitable that the assault on the reformed courts, which had developed in the 1870's, should be resumed with great energy. Ironically, Pobedonostsev and Katkov, once proponents of the 1864 statutes, were now in the forefront of the reactionary clique clamoring for the curbing of judges and juries. The law of 1881, which extended (in areas where a "state of emergency" was proclaimed) the jurisdiction of military tribunals and clothed administrative officials with extra-judicial powers, was a blow to the orderly administration of justice. Emergency powers, however, even if widely used, were not regarded as adequate safeguards against the recalcitrant spirit of the courts. Irremovability of the judges, publicity of the proceedings, and trial by jury were singled out for attack as incompatible with public interest. This agitation, coming as it did from influential quarters, bore fruit even though it fell short of the wishes of its instigators. The disciplinary powers of the minister of justice over judges and other law officers were strengthened (law of May 20, 1885); the minister of justice, as well as the court, was authorized to order the hearing of a case *in camera* on such ill defined grounds as "protection of the dignity of the state power" (law of February 12, 1887); various offenses, including murders of, and assaults on, officials and the more serious breaches of duty by office-holders were to be tried by specially constituted courts without a jury (law of July 7, 1889). In 1889, as has already been stated, the justices of the peace were abolished and their duties were transferred, in rural districts, to land captains, and in urban areas to town judges (*gorodskoi sudia*) appointed by the minister of justice. The bar, like the bench, went under a cloud, but repressive measures were ordered only against the Jews. An imperial decree of November, 1889, directed that admission to the bar of persons of "non-Christian persuasion" shall be exclusively with the permission of the minister of justice. During the following decade, of the numerous Jewish applicants only one was successful.

The above measures, which violated the spirit and the letter of the 1864 reform, were enacted in spite of severe criticism by the State Council and quasi-unanimous condemnation by the legal profession. Had it not been for this opposition, the government might have gone further—for instance, so far as to grant Katkov's demand for the abolition of trial by jury. Yet the consequences of manifest official displeasure with the judiciary were greater than is indicated by a mere enumeration of restrictive legislative enactments. Autocracy made it clear that it would not tolerate independent law courts as it would not countenance autonomous self-government. The principle of judicial independence, moreover, was impaired by the power of appointment, transfer, reward, and advancement vested in the minister of justice by the statutes of 1864. The unscrupulous use of these powers furnished the government with effective means of molding the bench in its own image, and led to deterioration of the standards of the judiciary. Leo Tolstoy has given in *Resurrection* an unflattering account of Russian judicial mores; denounced by some as a vile parody and a libel, the picture he traced was acknowledged by others to be accurate and true to life.

SOCIAL AND ECONOMIC POLICIES

The deterioration of peasant farming in the decade following the emancipation reminded the government and the educated classes that the reform of 1861 had failed to create conditions that would allow rural Russia a reasonable opportunity for economic progress. Moreover, in spite of the lack of response on the part of the peasants to revolutionary propaganda and of the collapse of the movement "to the people," it was realized that the hungry village was a grave potential menace to social and political stability. Public interest in the predicament of the farmers was aroused by the publication in 1877 of Professor Ianson's widely read statistical study, which presented massive evidence to prove that the impoverishment of the peasants was due primarily to the inadequacy of their holdings and to the burden of taxes and redemption payments. According to Ianson, in the vast majority of cases (except for the western provinces where, for political reasons, the liberated serfs were given a favorable settlement at the expense of Polish landowners) allotments were too small to provide even bare maintenance for the tiller of the soil and his family, and produced no surplus for meeting his obligations towards the state. Mounting arrears on account of taxes and redemption payments lent color to these pessimistic computations. The government finally decided to take action. By a law of December 28, 1881, the period of "temporary obligation" [7] was terminated and the redemption of allotments was made compulsory for all former serfs; simultaneously redemption payments were scaled down. Measures were taken to promote the expansion of the area of peasant tenure: the leasing by village communes of state-owned land was facilitated by a law of May 22, 1881, and a year later the State Peasant Bank was founded with the object of assisting peasants in purchasing land. The operations of the bank, however, were conducted on a modest scale; from 1883 to 1895 the peasants acquired through the bank some 2.4 million dessiatines, while their land purchases independently of the bank were almost three times as large. The poll tax, source of many legal disabilities attached to the status of a peasant, was partly removed in 1883 and 1884, and was abolished as of January 1, 1887 (law of May 28, 1885). The State Council, in a resolution of May 14, 1885, argued that the continuation of the poll tax was incompatible with the rights granted to the peasantry by the emancipation acts; the tax, it was held, was responsible for the vicious system of joint responsibility and its concomitant, passport restrictions, which imposed severe limitations on the freedom of movement of the peasant population. With the impending abrogation of the poll tax, the State Council recommended that joint responsibility should be abolished and the passport rules revised, the reasons for both having disappeared. The government, however, was slow in following the counsel of logic and common sense: joint responsibility was not done away with until 1903, and under the passport law of June 3, 1894, a peasant could still not obtain a passport—that is, the right to seek employment outside his native village—without the consent of the village assembly and, if he was a junior member of a household, of the household elder. In the latter case the discretionary decision of the household elder could be set aside by the equally

---

[7] See p. 889.

discretionary authority of the land captain. Moreover, to compensate the treasury for the loss of revenue from the poll tax (some 55 million rubles) the excise on spirits was raised and the regime of redemption payments was extended to the former state peasants. By a law of June 12, 1886, the annual charges paid by this group of the peasantry under a law of 1866 were increased by approximately 45 per cent and were to continue for forty-four years.

The reasons for the devious course of peasant legislation are not far to seek: the attitude of the more enlightened bureaucrats, who had lost faith in Russia's medieval class structure and favored the removal of the legal disabilities borne by the peasants, was in conflict with that of the supporters of counter-reforms led by Pobedonostsev and Tolstoy. While the liberal westerners wished the peasants to take their legitimate place among the freemen of post-emancipation Russia, the conservatives strove to perpetuate their segregation; the slavophiles and the populists, for reasons of their own, opposed any drastic modification of peasant institutions. The law of March 18, 1886, on the breaking-up (or dissolution) of peasant households was a victory for the conservative point of view. It will be remembered that the emancipation acts retained the traditional organization of the peasants into family units or households (*dvor*) over which the household elder wielded discretionary powers. In a memorandum submitted to the State Council in January, 1884, Tolstoy argued that "the multiplication of dissolutions of households was one of the causes of the impoverishment of the peasantry" because small families "were deprived of the advantages of the division of labor." Although the State Council contested this view, the minister finally won all his major points: under the law of March 18 the breaking-up of a household was not recognized as valid unless it was approved by a two-thirds majority of the village assembly, each case being considered on its merits. This was, indeed, a triumph for the principle of "tutelage by the village commune" over its members, to which, according to Tolstoy, the government attached the greatest importance.[8] It would seem, however, that the law of

---

[8] Replying to the criticisms of his proposals by the members of the State Council, Tolstoy admitted in a memorandum of Oct. 23, 1885, that the dissolution of households was frequently caused by discords and the inability of the members of the family group to live together. He maintained, however, that "disagreements and quarrels were, in the majority of cases, the manifestations of the general decline of discipline among the peasants due to the absence of restraint, which fostered the spirit of insubordination and moral laxity." According to the minister's optimistic

March 18 failed to achieve its purpose, for the number of dissolutions remained large. Even more inimical to the interests of the peasantry was a law of June 12, 1886, which made a breach of contract by an agricultural laborer a criminal offense. Like the law on the dissolution of households, however, it was seldom enforced.

Of greater practical significance was legislation bearing on the nature of peasant land ownership. The emancipation acts were based on the theory that in due course of time the liberated serfs would become full-fledged owners of their allotments. "Gradually and almost imperceptibly," according to I. M. Strakhovsky, the concept of unrestricted peasant ownership as the ultimate object of the reform was superseded by one of allotment land as a distinct and restricted form of tenure. As early as 1884 the ministry of the interior sponsored a bill prohibiting the peasants from selling their allotments, but the proposal met with strong opposition and was withdrawn. Four years later the report of an interdepartmental committee, established under the auspices of the ministry of the interior, took the position that the principles of private ownership were not applicable to allotment land, which should be regarded as inalienable because the purpose of the allotments was to provide for the needs of the emancipated serfs and to ensure the fulfillment of their obligations towards the state. Peasant allotments, it was held, were passing rapidly into the hands of speculators, thus threatening to render landless a large number of farmers. In the course of a debate in the State Council, it transpired that these apprehensions were ill founded: from 1861 to 1889 the area of allotment land (96 million dessiatines) declined by merely 200,000 dessiatines, or 0.2 per cent; included in the latter figure was land taken over for railways, highways, cemeteries, and for other public purposes. Nevertheless a law of December 14, 1893, forbade the sale of communal land by village communes without the consent of administrative officials (the ministers of the interior and finance, if the amount involved exceeded 500 rubles), prohibited the mortgage of allotment land, and provided that it could be sold only to peasant purchasers. The law, moreover, repealed the provision of the emancipation acts which entitled a member of a village commune who had paid his share of the redemption debt to withdraw from the commune and

theory, "The realization by the members of peasant families of the impossibility of withdrawing arbitrarily from the family group will inevitably lead to a decline in the number of discords and quarrels."

acquire a clear title to his allotment. All withdrawals, under the law of December 14, were subject to the approval of the village assembly. A law of June 8, 1893, endeavored to regulate the activities of the village communes and made it the duty of the land captain to supervise the commune's most important function—the repartition of land among its members. The cumulative effect of these measures was to nullify the promise implied in the abolition of the poll tax as a step towards the removal of the legal, social, and economic disabilities besetting the peasants; in the last decade of the nineteenth century peasant Russia was still a closed world waiting for a true emancipation.

Some of the restrictions on internal colonization, however, were lifted, chiefly in connection with the building of the Trans-Siberian railway. Beginning with a law of July 13, 1889, the government endeavored to bring some order into the movement to Siberia of settlers, although this enactment and those immediately following dealt primarily with the suppression of illicit migration. A more liberal policy was inaugurated with the formation in 1893 of the Siberia Railway Committee modeled after the boards of American railroad companies. S. J. Witte, minister of finance since August, 1892, and a leading member of the committee, favored energetic action in organizing the colonization of Siberia, but he had to overcome the opposition of powerful ultraconservative landed interests. Their spokesman on the committee, Durnovo, the minister of the interior, professed to see in the large-scale eastward movement of settlers the danger of political unrest. According to Witte, however, Durnovo was actually concerned with the probable repercussions of the proposed policy on the economic position of estate owners: depletion of reserves of cheap labor and depreciation of land values. The adoption of Witte's program brought at first but meager results; the average annual number of settlers increased from 41,000 in 1882–1892 to 81,000 in 1893–1895, an unimpressive figure. On the other hand, in spite of administrative restrictions, the number of passports issued to peasants rose substantially: 24.6 million passports, or an annual average of 30.2 per 1,000 of the population (male and female), were issued in 1881–1890, and 50.4 million, or an annual average of 53.1 per 1,000, in 1891–1900.[9]

[9] As in the earlier period (see p. 925), the annual average ratio of passports per 1,000 varied widely from region to region. The central industrial provinces had the highest ratio, the eastern provinces the lowest: 75.5 and 7.4 respectively, in 1881–1890; and 113.1 and 15.8 in 1891–1900.

A beginning, not entirely negligible, was made in the field of factory legislation. A law of June 1, 1882, the outcome of long-drawn-out discussion initiated by official agencies as far back as 1859, prohibited the employment of children under twelve years of age and limited to eight hours the working day of those aged twelve to fifteen; juvenile wage-earners were not permitted to work on holidays or Sundays, and their employment schedules were to be so arranged as to allow school attendance. The enforcement of these regulations was entrusted to a newly created body of factory inspectors. A law of June 3, 1885, forbade night work in textile mills for women and young persons under seventeen; the prohibition was later extended to several other industries. Labor disturbances, which were officially ascribed to the evils of the Russian factory system,[10] forced the government to intervene in the relations between employers and workers. A law of June 3, 1886, sponsored by the minister of the interior Dimitry Tolstoy, laid down detailed rules for the conclusion and the termination of labor contracts, directed that wages should be paid at least once a month, prohibited payments in kind and the charging of interest on advances made to the workers, and introduced several other technical improvements. On the other hand, it increased penalties for strikes and instigation to strike, and made refusal to work an offense punishable by arrest. There were created in the principal industrial centers new supervisory agencies, the factory boards (*fabrichnoe prisutstvie*), which consisted of Crown officials, factory inspectors, and representatives of the judiciary, the zemstvos, and the municipalities. The powers of factory inspectors were broadened so as to include not only enforcement of factory legislation but also actual supervision of the administration of industrial enterprises and prevention of conflicts between employers and workers. Although the number of factory inspectors remained inadequate and compliance with the law was not uniformly secured, the act of June 3 was an important landmark in the history of Russian industrial relations: the freedom of employers to deal with their workers as they pleased gave place to a degree of government control. As in the case of the peasantry, however, labor policies were inconsistent and self-contradictory. Some of the measures for the protection of women and minors were, in part, repealed by a law of April 24, 1890, which empowered factory inspectors and other officials to lift the prohibition on night work for women and wage-earners under

[10] See pp. 931–933.

seventeen, and to allow the employment of children as young as ten years of age. Legislation for the protection of women and minors had the support of liberal circles and of many industrialists, especially in the St. Petersburg region, where the level of wages was higher than in the densely populated area around Moscow. The St. Petersburg manufacturers, therefore, had good reason to believe that the unrestricted employment of women and children worked to the advantage of their Moscow competitors, who, as a group, opposed all labor legislation. The partial removal of restrictions on night work and child labor was, thus, a victory for the more ruthless employers.

The shifts in peasant and labor policies may be explained, to some extent, by the predilections of the successive ministers of finance, even though the most progressive factory law of this period (the law of June 3, 1886) was framed by the ultra-reactionary Tolstoy. N. C. Bunge, minister of finance in 1881–1886, was a man of relatively liberal views; his successor, I. A. Vyshnegradsky (1887–1892), a successful businessman and, like Bunge, a former university professor, was an aggressive and unrepentant conservative. Since neither was a statesman of uncommon ability or influence, the course of financial policies was only too often determined by the immediate exigencies of the treasury, the sway of conventional economic and political doctrines, and the inertia of the bureaucratic tradition.

The wars of Alexander II and the unskillful and onerous methods of financing railway construction aggravated, as has been related elsewhere, the familiar disorders of Russian public finance: depreciated currency, unbalanced budget, large public debt, and the crushing burden of taxation borne almost exclusively by the lower classes. Both Bunge and Vyshnegradsky, like their predecessor Reutern, strove to prevent the depreciation of the paper ruble and to link it eventually to precious metal by building up the gold reserve. The printing press was used but sparingly. The volume of paper currency in circulation decreased from 1,133 million rubles in 1881 to 1,046 million in 1886, and remained at that level through 1891; it rose, however, to 1,196 million in 1893 and 1894. The outflow of gold which began during the Turkish war was checked, and from 1881 to 1887 the gold reserve was maintained at 171 million rubles; it rose to 211 million in 1888 and to 361 million in 1894. The paper ruble, nevertheless, continued to fluctuate: it was quoted at 66 metal copecks in 1882, at 56 metal copecks in 1887, at 73 metal copecks in 1890, and at 67 metal copecks in 1894. The stabilization of the ruble and the introduction of the gold standard did not take place until 1897.

In spite of the abolition of the poll tax, important as this measure was from the administrative and social point of view, the tax system underwent no substantial modification, the bulk of the revenue continuing to be paid by the low-income groups. An inheritance and gift tax (law of June 15, 1882) and a tax on income from "capital," that is, securities and interest-bearing deposits (law of May 20, 1885), enacted in Bunge's administration somewhat broadened the basis of taxation, but the rates of these taxes were low and their yield relatively insignificant. Proposals for the introduction of the income tax, which had been under discussion since 1861, were revived in 1882 and 1892 only to be indefinitely shelved. Rapidly mounting public expenditure was met primarily by indirect taxation which in 1892 accounted for 72 per cent of the total revenue. Excise on spirits was the most productive indirect tax. Yet the excise method was no longer regarded as adequate; and by a law of June 8, 1893, the state monopoly of spirits was tentatively introduced in four provinces of European Russia, and was gradually extended to the entire territory of the empire.

The public debt, including railway loans guaranteed by the Russian government and inconvertible paper currency, rose from 6,046 million rubles in 1881 to 6,488 million in 1886, and to 7,070 million in 1892. In 1889–1892 Vyshnegradsky carried out a series of loan conversions which resulted in the reduction of the rate of interest to the uniform level of 4 per cent. These operations were officially represented at the time as a great achievement, but they have since been criticized on technical grounds by financial experts. Conversions, nevertheless, relieved somewhat the immediate pressure on the treasury and, by lessening the dependence of St. Petersburg on the Berlin money market, contributed to the Franco-Russian *rapprochement*. In 1892 the service of the loans represented approximately 28 per cent of the total expenditure.

There was an important revision of railway policies. The building of railways by private companies had proved burdensome for the treasury, and called for a remedy. In 1878 a committee was appointed to investigate the railway situation; its findings, which were not available until three years later, supplied voluminous information on the abuses and inefficiency of the existing system and had considerable influence on the attitude of the government. Beginning with 1880, the state took an active part in the building and administration of railways. The non-interference with the affairs of private companies practiced during the previous decades gave place to an advanced degree of government control; a number of lines were built by the state, while others were purchased by the treasury and were operated under state management. Between 1881 and 1894 the government took over twenty-four lines with an aggregate mileage of 12,000 versts, or about one-third of the total network. This policy was adhered to until the end of the empire: in 1912, of the total mileage of 63,500 versts only 20,500 versts, or 32 per cent, were owned by private companies. The beneficial effects of state ownership, however, were slow in showing themselves: purchases of railways were almost invariably made on terms onerous to the treasury; construction of new lines proved costly; and until about 1910 state management resulted in heavy financial losses. The most important state-built line was the Trans-Siberian railway, which was started in 1891 but was not completed until the eve of the Russo-Japanese War. While the cost of construction was high, indeed greatly in excess of the estimates, the completion of the gigantic venture opened to colonization the virgin vastness of Siberia and gave a powerful stimulus to Russia's ambitions in the Far East, of which the Russo-Japanese War was merely one of the earliest and most unfortunate manifestations.

The tendency towards state intervention in business activities may be detected in the accentuation of protectionism already noted in the late 1870's. Partial upward revisions of the tariff in 1882, 1884, 1885, 1887, and 1890 were capped by the tariff act of June 11, 1891, in which protection reached a new high mark. Protective legislation, common as it was in continental Europe after 1870, had in Russia a distinct local flavor, even though fiscal considerations had everywhere a part in building up tariff walls. "An examination of archive documents and contemporary economic literature," according to Professor M. N. Sobolev, author of a monumental treatise on the Russian tariff in the second half of the nineteenth century, "discloses that the influence of social groups in framing tariff policies was relatively slight; thus, for instance, the zemstvos, the nobility, agricultural societies, and other bodies almost never advocated free trade. The domineering influence was exercised by the state, which, as a self-contained (*samodavleiushchee*) institution, endeavored to exact the maximum customs revenue." When the lowering of the tariff in the 1860's failed to bring about the anticipated higher yields, the government, realizing that the impoverishment of the country offered little hope of a substantial increase in the volume of imports, sought to achieve its fiscal aims by raising the rates of duties. The ministry of finance pursued simultaneously two somewhat contradictory objectives: higher customs revenue to cover chronic budget deficits, and improvement in the balance of payments by curtailing imports. These two themes—need for revenue and the desire to strengthen the international position of the ruble—dominated both the arguments advanced by official spokesmen in favor of protection and the debates on tariff measures in the State Council. Considerations of a more lofty nature were at times adduced in support of an unworthy cause. Bunge, for instance, professed to believe in 1882 that the inequities of the tax system would be mitigated by higher customs duties because imported articles were consumed chiefly by the higher-income groups. This contention would seem to have been disingenuous: the major increases he proposed were on articles of general consumption, such as herrings, tea, rice, iron, coal, raw cotton, and cotton yarn. Protection of domestic industries, of course, was not entirely overlooked. Russian industrialists clamored for protection on the ground that they were handicapped, in competing with foreign producers, by lack of transport facilities, the lower productivity of labor, and the higher cost of credit, raw materials, and industrial equipment. Since the industrialists insisted on prohibitive duties, while the government wished to increase customs revenue, the former seldom received full satisfaction. Yet the cumulative effect of successive tariff revisions was great: the tariff act of 1891 was far more protective than its predecessor of 1868. Of the total number of 620 tariff items, 114 (18 per cent) were transferred from the free to the dutiable list and 432 (70 per cent) were revised upward. The increase in nearly one-quarter of the rates was more than 100 per cent over those of 1868, in 35 instances more than 500 per cent, and in 16 instances more than 1,000 per cent.

The outbreak in 1893 of a tariff war between Russia and Germany led to the revision of the act of 1891. Friction over commercial policies was only one link in the chain of events that led to the Russo-German estrangement and the conclusion of the Franco-Russian alliance. In the 1870's and the 1880's the old established profitable trade relations between Russia and Germany were disturbed by the growth of protectionist tendencies, which manifested themselves simultaneously in both countries. From 1865 to 1879 grain, Russia's principal export, entered Germany free; it was made subject to moderate duties in 1879 and to much stiffer ones in 1885 and 1887. At the end of 1891 Germany concluded several commercial treaties (with Austria-Hungary, Italy, Switzerland, and Belgium) which reduced the rates on grain and other agricultural produce by as much as 30 per cent; the new rates were extended, by virtue of most-favored-nation treaties, to the chief European trading countries but were not applied to imports from Russia, ostensibly because the negotiations for a most-favored-nation treaty initiated by St. Petersburg early in the same year had come to naught. Russian exports to Germany were thus put in a position of distinct disadvantage. Witte, Russia's new minister of finance, with some reason considered the German action as unfriendly and discriminatory: the lower rates of the German tariff were applied to overseas countries, for instance, the United States, with whom Germany had no most-favored-nation treaty. In spite of the opposition of the Russian ministry of foreign affairs (especially Giers and Shuvalov), Witte obtained the approval of the tsar for strong counter-measures. On June 1, 1893, the rates of the Russian tariff were raised 15 to 30 per cent, but the new schedule was to apply only to countries which denied Russia the most-favored-nation treatment; imports from all other countries continued to pay the 1891 rates. Berlin retaliated by a 50 per cent increase of duties on imports from Russia; St. Petersburg immediately ordered a similar increase on goods shipped from Germany. The resulting state of economic warfare, which threatened the extinction of trade between the two countries, was terminated by the Russo-German commercial treaty of March 7, 1894. The treaty embodied the most-favored-nation principle, prohibited discrimination in matters of tariff and railway rates, prescribed the treatment of commercial firms and navigation, and provided for tariff concessions by both parties. Concluded for ten years, the treaty was renewed in 1904 after an extensive upward revision of the 1894 rates. The terms of both agreements, especially that of 1904, which was negotiated in the midst of the Russo-Japanese War, are regarded by competent authorities as far more advantageous to Germany than to Russia.

Although the reasons for high-tariff policies were primarily fiscal, protection fostered certain branches of industry and favored certain private interests. Vyshnegradsky and Witte were close to business circles, and industrialists, financiers, and promoters were often in a position to influence official decisions in matters such as tariff and railway rates, the geographical distribution of railway lines, taxation, loans, and so on. The ministry of finance, moreover, encouraged the flow of foreign capital seeking profitable investment. According to an authoritative Soviet source, foreign capital invested in Russian industrial enterprises increased from 98 million rubles in 1880 to 215 million in 1890; but these figures are at best crude estimates. There is little doubt, however, that foreign capital played an important part in the development of the rich coal and iron Don region in southern Russia. The helping hand of the government was extended to the hard-pressed landed nobility, which had been unfavorably affected by some of the tariff measures, for instance, the high duties on agricultural machines and iron. The State Nobility Bank, founded in 1885, provided mortgage credit for the noble landowners on terms more favorable than those offered by the Peasants' Bank. The Nobility Bank operated on a large scale, drew freely on funds supplied by the State Bank, but failed to achieve its statutory purpose—to check the liquidation of large estates and their passing into the hands of merchants, burghers, and peasants.

From the ensemble of the economic and social measures sketched above—none of them striking or original—there emerged a policy pattern aimed at increased intervention of the state in the economic affairs of the nation. Witte, in his report to the tsar for 1893, held that for historic reasons Russian financial administration must overstep the conventional boundaries of public finance. The Russian people, in his opinion, believed that the initiative of every measure affecting public welfare should emanate from the Crown. This statement describes well the philosophy of government held by Alexander III and his advisers. In theory it was the paternal rule of a benevolent and wise autocrat; in practice it became the regimentation of public and private initiative and the quasi-omnipotence of the bureaucracy.

CENSORSHIP, SCHOOLS, NATIONALISM, AND POLITICAL MOVEMENTS

The muzzling of the press remained an immutable policy of the regime. Commenting on Loris-Melikov's proposal for the revision of the censorship law, Pobedonostsev wrote to the future emperor Alexander III (October 31, 1880): "I believe that the government should not allow the control of the press to slip from its hands, that it should not relieve itself of this responsibility. To entrust it to the courts would give the press unbridled license; this would cause great injury to the state and the people." He frequently returned to this theme in later years. With the appointment of Ignatev as minister of the interior, the regime of censorship, somewhat relaxed during Loris-Melikov's administration, became increasingly oppressive. It was made even more burdensome by the "provisional" rules of August 27, 1882, which remained in force for over twenty years and strengthened the already powerful hold of the executive over the press. Devised by Tolstoy and enacted without consultation with the State Council, the rules of August 27 imposed preliminary censorship on newspapers and journals which had previously received three official warnings: forthcoming issues of such periodicals were to be submitted to the censors not later than 11:00 P.M. on the eve of the day of publication, a requirement with which most of the daily papers affected found it impossible to comply. Moreover, a committee consisting of the chief procurator of the Holy Synod and the ministers of the interior, education, and justice was given the power to suspend any periodical *sine die* or permanently and to debar its editors and publishers from being editors or publishers of other publications. This and other laws for the curbing of the press were extensively used, and the decline in the number of penalties imposed in the late 1880's and in the 1890's must not be ascribed to any softening of the censorship regime. The apparent leniency of the authorities, according to the historian of Russian censorship Arsenev, was due to the disappearance of many periodicals. While indirect but relentless pressure was brought to bear on those that survived, not all newspapers and journals were reduced to the status of mouthpieces of the government; but those that retained some independence paid for the privilege of continuing publication by exercising extreme caution and by refraining from comments likely to give offense to the authorities.[11]

[11] Katkov, anticipating theories which were to become popular some fifty or sixty years later, argued in *Moskovskiia Vedomosti* at the end of 1886 that "the press in Russia, and perhaps in Russia alone, is placed in a position approaching complete independence. We know of no organ of the foreign press that could be called independent in the true meaning of the term." In the "so-called constitutional states," according to Katkov, the press was not "an expression of public conscience" but a tool of party interests. Russia had no political parties, hence the Russian press was basically independent. The state supervision of the press in that country was not essentially different from any other measure for the protection of public

The school policy initiated by Dimitry Tolstoy under Alexander II was carried on by Count Delianov, minister of education from 1882 to 1897. Delianov was responsible for the drafting of the university charter that was submitted by Tolstoy to the State Council early in 1880 but was withdrawn after his forced resignation.[12] Following Delianov's appointment, the charter was reintroduced in the State Council, became the center of a heated controversy, and was finally voted down. The tsar, however, approved the minority report endorsing the Tolstoy-Delianov version, which was thus enacted into law (August 13, 1884). The new charter did away with university autonomy. Under its provisions the rector, deans, and professors were appointed by the minister of education instead of being elected by the university council, as under the charter of 1863. The powers of the curators of the school regions in dealing with university matters were extended. Maintenance of order in the higher schools was entrusted to inspectors subordinated to the curators. The granting of degrees was made conditional on the passing of state examinations held under the auspices of the ministry of education. The student body was denied all corporate rights, its members being regarded as "individual visitors," while the cost of higher education was increased by the imposition, in addition to tuition fees, of charges for the benefit of the professors (the so-called honorarium). Simultaneously measures were taken to limit opportunities for the higher education of women. The St. Petersburg medical school for women was closed in 1882, and admission to universities for women was either restricted or suspended altogether. Although these unenlightened policies were resented by the majority of the academic profession and the student body, they provoked no concerted movement of opposition; they did lead, however, to the resignation or dismissal of several professors, and contributed to the feeling of discontent and disaffection which produced a new wave of student disturbances in the 1890's.

The abolition of university autonomy went hand in hand with the revival of the educational theories of the 1830's; namely, that children should receive an education appropriate to their social status and that

order and safety. "What is not contrary to the law and institutions of the country," wrote Katkov, "what does not offend public morality, what is not deceit and incitement to violence—can be and is expressed in the press with utter independence."

[12] See pp. 1033–1034.

boys of the lower classes should be discouraged from entering gymnasiums and universities. Originating with Shishkov and Uvarov,[13] these theories were later endorsed by Katkov [14] and Pobedonostsev. "It is imperative to pay attention to the organization of secondary schools in which boys of the lower classes would be given an unpretentious (*nekhitroe*) but solid education, one that would prepare them for the realities of life and not for the advancement of science to which most of them cannot devote themselves," Pobedonostsev wrote to Alexander on March 22, 1881. "Unfortunately all our gymnasiums aim at leading the students further and further, to the universities; hence the fallacious trend towards higher education; and those half-educated students who fail [to get a degree] are doomed, having lost contact with the social environment to which they belong." The reactionary elements were particularly distressed by the provision of the secondary-schools act of 1864, retained in the act of 1871, that gymnasiums were to be open to all boys "irrespective of faith and social status." Four ministers, including Pobedonostsev, Delianov, and Vyshnegradsky, proposed an amendment that would bar from gymnasiums children of parents whose legal status was inferior to that of merchants of the second guild, or more precisely, children of small traders, burghers, and peasants. Although this proposal was vetoed by Alexander as "untimely and inopportune," the government endeavored to achieve the same object in a roundabout way. Delianov, in a notorious circular of June 18, 1887, directed school authorities to scrutinize applications for admission to gymnasiums from the point of view of the social and financial standing of the prospective students' families. If the latter were found wanting, admission was to be refused and the applicants were to be advised to send their children to schools offering instruction "more in keeping with their social status." Gymnasium students who allegedly exercised, because of their "unsuitable domestic environment," a pernicious influence on their fellow students were to be expelled. Simultaneously gymnasium and progymnasium tuition fees were raised to a minimum of 40 rubles per annum. "The strict enforcement of this instruction," the circular declared, "would free the gymnasium and progymnasium of children of coachmen, footmen, cooks, laundresses, small shopkeepers and other similar people whose children, with perhaps the exception of the most gifted ones, should

[13] See pp. 800–802.
[14] See p. 1036.

not be led to break away from the milieu to which they belong." Gymnasium education, according to the circular, had an undesirable effect upon youths of the lower classes: it bred "contempt for parents, dissatisfaction with their own station, and bitterness towards the existing and, in the nature of things, inevitable inequality in the financial position of various social groups." A gymnasium diploma being practically a prerequisite for admission to the universities, the circular of June 18 aimed at closing the doors of these schools to the lower classes. Another obstacle to the admission of impecunious students was the increase in university tuition fees from 10 to 50 rubles per annum (June 26, 1887). Professor Kizevetter relates in his memoirs that the circular of June 18, usually referred to as the circular on "cook's children," created indignation, but this, of course, did not prevent its enforcement.

The purge of the student body was not limited to "undesirable" Russian elements. The influx of Jewish students and their high scholastic attainments had caused irritation among influential anti-Semites and led the government to renounce its traditional policy of nondiscrimination against the Jews in matters of education. Two circulars issued by Delianov in July, 1887, introduced, for the first time in Russian history, quotas for Jewish students in higher and secondary schools. Within the Jewish pale the quota was set at 10 per cent of the student body, and outside the pale at 5 per cent, except in St. Petersburg and Moscow, where it was 3 per cent. Since the quotas were considerably below the actual number of Jewish students,[15] thousands of them were denied educational opportunities above the level of primary schools.

Bureaucratic centralization, emphasis on religious education, and aggressive nationalism were the outstanding features of official policies in elementary schools. Various types of schools that had theretofore escaped the control of the ministry of education (Evangelical, Protestant, Roman Catholic, and those maintained by the ministry of finance) were brought under the sway of that department. The supremacy of the ministry of education, however, was challenged by the supporters of the view that primary education should be entrusted to the Church. "The clergy must be given a predominant part in the administration of elementary schools," according to a unanimous resolution of the council of ministers, inspired, presumably, by Pobedo-

[15] See p. 1047 n. 10.

nostsev.[16] In 1887 and again in 1893 the question of transferring all elementary schools to the jurisdiction of the Holy Synod was studied by responsible officials, but the government shrank from so drastic a step. There was established instead an elaborate ecclesiastical primary-school administration paralleling that of the ministry of education, appropriations for church schools were increased, and the clergy was given important functions in connection with the working and supervision of the school system. In 1893 the zemstvos were peremptorily "invited" by the chief procurator to finance church schools, a suggestion which few of them deemed it possible to disregard. As a consequence of these measures the number of church schools (if the notoriously inflated statistics of the Holy Synod are to be trusted) rose from 5,000 or 6,000 in 1882 to 32,000 in 1894, but their educational standards remained, with rare exceptions, deplorably low.

One of the most vexatious and foolish expressions of belligerent nationalism characteristic of this period was the persecution of ethnic minorities and local languages. Under a law of 1885 instruction in the primary schools of the kingdom of Poland was conducted in Russian, except for classes in religion and in "the native tongue of the pupils." In 1887 a similar rule was applied to the Baltic provinces simultaneously with the introduction in that area of a primary-school administration on the Russian model. In the northwestern provinces, on which the government looked with particular suspicion, even classes in religion for students of Roman Catholic faith were given in Russian, severe penalties being provided for the teachers of secret Sunday schools using the Polish language (1892). In 1887 the ministry of education intended to make Russian the language of instruction in Moslem schools, but the proposal was abandoned because the ministry of the interior feared the resistance of the Mohammedan clergy. As a compromise, the teachers of these schools were ordered to learn Russian (1890). The fact that children in the borderlands did not under-

[16] "It is imperative for the welfare of the people that everywhere within its easy reach, namely, next to the parish church, there should be an elementary school, elevating every simple soul (*prostuiu dushu*) by the teaching of religion and of church singing," Pobedonostsev wrote to Alexander on March 28, 1883. "Orthodox Russians dream of the time when the whole of Russia will be covered with a network of such schools. . . . Today all sensible men realize that church schools, and no others, must be in Russia the principal and universal means of elementary education."

stand the Russian language mattered little: the government was eager to protect them from the allegedly subversive influence of local native traditions and especially from that of the Roman Catholic and Protestant clergy.

Bigotry and religious intolerance were but another manifestation of the rising tide of pan-Russian nationalism; indeed, it was at times difficult to know where the one ended and the other began. Pobedonostsev's letters to Alexander III were replete with invectives against Roman Catholics, Protestants, Jews, and Russian dissenters. Profession of a religious dogma other than that of the established Church, just like the use of local languages in the schools, came to be looked upon in conservative circles as akin to treason. After the Polish insurrections of 1830 and 1863 the traditional hostility of Orthodoxy towards Roman Catholicism became merged with the nationalistic drive for the assimilation of the western borderland, the Roman Church being penalized for the support of the insurgents by the Catholic clergy. Inroads on the liberties enjoyed by the Reformed Churches in the Baltic provinces offered a clearer case of religious intolerance: the Protestant population of this area was loyal, and the Baltic-German nobility had powerful court connections and ranked high among the servants of Russian autocracy. Yet, according to Pobedonostsev, in 1887 fifty-three of the 139 Lutheran ministers in the Baltic provinces were under indictment for alleged offenses against the Orthodox Church and Russian authorities. Local courts showed reluctance to try these cases, and the central government, in deference to the wishes of highly placed Baltic noblemen, hesitated to take administrative action against the accused clerics, thus encouraging, in the opinion of Pobedonostsev, resistance not only among the Protestant but also among the Catholic clergy (letter to Alexander III, December 21, 1887). Russian nationalistic ambitions in the Baltic provinces were symbolized by the imposing Orthodox cathedral built in the center of the medieval walled city in Reval (1893). This pretentious monument in a flamboyant pseudo-Russian style sorely out of keeping with its Germanic surroundings was a visual reminder to the Protestant population that Russian rule meant also the domination of Orthodoxy.

In view of the official attitude towards non-Orthodox denominations it was only natural that the persecution of the dissenters, which had reached its zenith in the reign of Nicholas I but had subsided in that of Alexander II, should be resumed under Alexander III. A law of May 3, 1883, dealing with the legal position of the dissenters was, nevertheless, less rigorous than the legislation still on the statute books but no longer enforced. The new law granted the dissenters, except for the *skoptsy* (castrates), a modicum of civil and religious rights: they were authorized to receive passports, engage in commercial and industrial enterprises, hold minor offices, and conduct religious meetings in their homes and houses of prayer. A number of disabilities, however, remained. Most important among them were the prohibitions against building new places of worship, wearing ecclesiastical garb outside houses of prayer, and carrying on religious propaganda. The minister of the interior, moreover, was given power to deal with each sect according to its merits, a broad dispensation which tended to nullify the modest degree of protection offered by the law of 1883. The work of the missionaries, aggressively promoted by Pobedonostsev, was aimed primarily at the dissenters. Proselytizing, under the law, was a prerogative of the Orthodox Church, conversion of an Orthodox to the faith of a dissenting group being punishable by imprisonment or exile to Siberia. The zealous apostles of Orthodoxy only too often relied in their missionary work on methods of coercion. "The Orthodox missionaries, without doubt, frequently overstep the boundaries established by the law of 1883, and resort to the civil authorities in cases where such cooperation is not justified by law," D. S. Sipiagin, minister of the interior, wrote in 1901 in his report to the tsar. "Local authorities, and especially the police, in the old way, sometimes entirely arbitrarily, interfere in the religious affairs of the schismatics [dissenters] and take measures which lead the latter to make justified complaints." [17]

The case of the Stundists and the Dukhobors offered the most notable example of religious persecution. The teaching of Stundism, which derived its name from German Evangelical eighteenth century communities (*Stunde*), had much in common with that of the Baptists. Its success after 1870, particularly in southern Russia, alarmed Orthodox missionaries and Pobedonostsev, who decried the movement as anti-Christian and anti-social. In 1894 Stundism was officially branded an "especially dangerous" sect and its group prayer meetings were prohibited. The Dukhobors, like the Stundists, stemmed from

[17] Quoted in John Shelton Curtiss, *Church and State in Russia* (Columbia University Press, New York, 1940), p. 144.

the Reformation, practiced a primitive communal form of Christianity, denied Church hierarchy and sacraments, and refused to bear arms. The army reform of 1874 which made military service a personal (instead of a group) obligation, by doing away with the hiring of recruits formerly practiced by the Dukhobors, brought the latter into conflict with the authorities. A number of prominent Dukhobors, including their leader, Peter Virigin, were incarcerated in monasteries or deported to Siberia, while the rank and file suffered cruel indignities at the hands of punitive expeditions. This intolerable situation was terminated by the exodus of the Dukhobors to Cyprus and in 1899 to Canada, the mass migration being arranged and financed by their friends in Russia and abroad.

Religious persecution, however, did not achieve its main object—the return of the dissenters to the fold of Orthodoxy. No reliable statistics on the number of dissenters are available, but it is believed that in 1897, when the first comprehensive Russian census was taken, there were 17.5 million dissenters of various denominations in a population of 117 million; [18] that is, the ratio of dissenters increased substantially after the middle of the nineteenth century. The government, nevertheless, clung to restrictive policies until the revolutionary year 1905, when the legal disabilities of the dissenters were finally removed.

Anti-Semitism thrives on nationalism and religious intolerance; in Russia, as in other countries, it had far-flung ramifications reaching at times into unexpected quarters. Dislike of the Jews was an integral part of Alexander III's simple faith. "We must not forget," he wrote in 1890 in the margin of a report depicting the plight of Russian Jewry, "that it was the Jews who crucified our Lord and spilled his precious blood." Pobedonostsev, Dimitry Tolstoy, and Plehve were inveterate Jew haters. The nationalist press, led by the influential conservative

---

[18] *Ibid.*, p. 139. A revealing explanation of the failure of Russian religious propaganda was given in 1905 by a conservative Orthodox churchman, Bishop Makary of Tomsk: "We must state the fact, sad as it is for an Orthodox person, that old-believers and sectarians . . . in literacy and knowledge of matters of faith stand far higher than the Orthodox. The old-believer knows how his denomination differs from others, the sectarian knows the Gospel and is everywhere prepared to read it and to explain it, and both know how to dispute according to their teachings with the Orthodox, who in the overwhelming majority are without reply and are even astonishingly ignorant" (*ibid.*, p. 166). This admission is all the more striking since the following of the dissenters was drawn largely (and in the case of the Stundists and the Dukhobors, exclusively) from the peasantry, while Orthodoxy had at its disposal all the resources of the established Church.

Novoe Vremia (New Times) and by *Grazhdanin* (The Citizen), a paper edited by Prince V. P. Meshchersky, who was close to the imperial court, indulged in persistent and insidious campaigns of Jew baiting. In the slavophile *Rus* (Russia) Aksakov passionately proclaimed that Judaism was incompatible with Christian civilization. Anti-Semitism, however, was not restricted to conservative and Orthodox circles. In the early 1880's the revolutionary organization People's Will used anti-Jewish slogans in its propaganda. The prominence of the Jews both in business and in the radical movement singled them out for attacks by revolutionaries and reactionaries alike.

The anti-Semitic elements made capital of the fact that a Jewish woman, Jessie Helfman, was involved in the murder of Alexander II. In the spring and summer of 1881 a wave of pogroms swept over southern Russia. These bloody anti-Jewish outbreaks, which occurred in more than one hundred localities, would probably have been impossible without the connivance and, in some cases, the instigation of the police. Public opinion at home and abroad was aroused, and although the situation was soon brought under control (according to Dubnow, only ten pogroms, none of them on a large scale, took place between 1882 and 1903) the government announced its decision to proceed with far-reaching reforms. The framing of the new legislation was ostensibly entrusted to a committee appointed in February, 1883, and presided over by the former minister of justice, Count Pahlen. In spite of the unimpeachable conservatism of the committee's members, its report, which was not available until 1888, proved a disappointment to the highly placed anti-Semites. A melancholy survey of some 650 anti-Jewish laws on Russian statute books, as well as considerations of a general nature, led the committee to the conclusion that discrimination brought nothing but disaster. "The very history of Russian legislation . . ." according to the report, "teaches us that there is only one way and one solution—the emancipation of the Jews and their assimilation with the rest of the population under the protection of the same laws." Instead of the new restrictions desired by Pobedonostsev, the committee recommended the gradual removal of the existing ones. These proposals were summarily dismissed; the policy of the government was inspired by the opposite principle—increasing discrimination against the Jews.

The "provisional" rules of May 3, 1882, which remained in force for more than a generation, forbade the Jews to settle anew in rural districts even within the pale, although the expulsion of those already residing in rural areas was not decreed. Five years later, to the detriment of the Jews, the boundaries of the pale were revised by excluding from its confines the cities of Rostov-on-Don and Taganrog. Then came the restrictive measures already described in this chapter: quotas for Jewish students in secondary and higher schools (1887), and the exclusion of the Jews from the legal profession (1889), the zemstvos (1890), and the municipalities (1892). The partial repeal in March, 1891, of a law of 1865 which permitted Jewish artisans to carry on their trades outside the pale led to the removal from Moscow of some 20,000 Jewish craftsmen. Finally, a law of 1893 made it a criminal offense for the Jews to use Christian given names, a common practice among the educated Russian Jews.

A mere listing of legal restrictions—and the above statement is not all-inclusive—does not convey the full measure of their tragic implications for the people of Israel. Discrimination invites evasion, for which the corruption of petty Russian officialdom offered ample opportunity. But the reprieve, purchased by bribes, from the enforcement of inequitable laws was necessarily precarious, and enclosed the unhappy victims and their venal protectors in a vicious circle of renewed exactions and lawbreaking. The other consequences of pogroms and discriminatory legislation were otherwise important: they were the starting point of the mass exodus of Russian Jewry to the United States and of the migration, on a much smaller scale, to Palestine; these early refugees from Russia to the Holy Land were the ideological forerunners of the Zionist movement which was to take shape in 1897. Moreover, the brutality of Russian anti-Semitism provoked a strong hostile reaction abroad, especially in the United States and in Great Britain; it deprived Russia of many useful citizens, and created for the monarchy a host of implacable and powerful enemies at home and abroad.

Political opposition bore the full brunt of the attack by the police regime, imbued as it was with narrow nationalism and religious and racial intolerance. Censorship and persecution, however, do not alone account for the ebbing of the liberal and the revolutionary movement. The regicide of March 1, 1881, was fraught with grave and unpredictable consequences. The loyal aristocratic elements, shocked by the murder of the tsar, went to the extreme of forming a secret counterrevolutionary organization, the Holy Host (*Sviashchennaia Dru-*

zhina), designed to fight the terrorists with their own weapons. Headed by Count I. I. Vorontsov-Dashkov, minister of the imperial household and later viceroy of the Caucasus, this militant group worked in cooperation with the police; but it seems to have achieved little, and was disbanded in 1882.[19] The liberals, no less dismayed than the conservatives, went through much heart searching. Many of them came to feel that in view of the rising tide of political terror the struggle for constitutional reforms should be relegated to the background and that the restoration of law and order, even if it required cooperation with a reactionary government, was the immediate and urgent task.

Paradoxically, it was among the revolutionaries themselves that the fulfillment of their cherished ambition—the murder of Alexander II—provoked the greatest crisis. As if exhausted by the effort involved in the organization of the regicide, the executive committee of People's Will appealed to Alexander III (March 10, 1881), and offered the cessation of revolutionary activities on two surprisingly mild conditions: political amnesty and the convocation of a representative assembly. The government, however, was in no mood for compromise. By 1883 all the members of the executive committee of People's Will who had not fled abroad were behind prison bars. The organization itself survived, more or less nominally, until the late 1890's, but gave few signs of its former vigorous vitality. Many populists drifted away from the old revolutionary slogans and sought an understanding with the liberals; small groups of irreconcilables, on the other hand, clung to the heroic tactics of political terror. Their most notable, albeit isolated, venture was the abortive plot to murder Alexander III (March 1, 1887). Five of the fifteen men indicted for this crime—all young university students—received the death penalty; among them was Alexander Ulianov, Lenin's older brother.

The crisis experienced by the revolutionary movement had deeper causes than the mere dispersal of leadership. The very course of events was a challenge to two basic tenets of populism as formulated in the program of People's Will: the efficacy of political terror, and the peasantry as the mainspring of the revolution. Regicide did not bring social revolution appreciably nearer; Alexander II was merely suc-

---

[19] Witte claims in his memoirs that the idea of the Holy Host originated with him. As a member of the society he went to Paris on an unsuccessful mission to organize the murder of a revolutionary who had taken refuge in the French capital. The whole episode would be quite incredible were it not given on the authority of Witte himself.

ceeded by Alexander III, and one reactionary government gave place to another, even more reactionary. The murder of the tsar, moreover, failed to arouse broad popular response; rural Russia remained sullen, still, and apparently unmoved. Indeed, the tragic fate of Alexander II was sometimes interpreted by the peasants as an act of vengeance on the part of disgruntled serf-owners. The conclusion was not unwarranted that the theory as well as the strategy of populism needed overhauling.

In search of a revolutionary doctrine less at variance with the facts than were their traditional beliefs, some of the disillusioned populists turned to Marxism. Outstanding among these converts to "scientific" socialism was George Plekhanov (1857–1918), who broke away from Land and Freedom in 1879, emigrated to Switzerland a year later, and in 1883 founded in Geneva the first Russian social-democratic organization, Liberation of Labor (*Osvobozhdenie Truda*). Its program, based on the Marxian analysis, may be briefly summarized as follows: The historical destinies of Russia were not different from those of other countries, that is, Russia had to pass through the stage of capitalism before reaching the higher stage of socialism; the traditional land organization of Russian peasantry (*obshchina*) contained no elements of the future socialist society; the industrial proletariat, not the peasantry, was the only class capable, by conscious effort, of accomplishing a social revolution; terrorism, although a useful subsidiary weapon, was not to divert the leaders from their main task—the creation of a disciplined, closely knit working-class party which was to lead Russia along the path of social revolution. This program being the negation of populism's most sacred principles, much of the time and energy of Russian Marxists was spent in polemics against the populists. Meanwhile the writings of Marx and Engels were translated into Russian, studied, and reinterpreted in the light of Russian conditions. Plekhanov, a man of culture and literary ability, was the author of several treatises which rank among the classics of socialist literature. Beginning with 1883–1884, small groups of Marxian socialists were formed in Russia, chiefly among intellectuals and university students. The existence of these groups, however, was precarious and their connection with the working class tenuous. The strikes which broke out in the 1880's and the early 1890's—including the huge strike (1885) at the Morozov textile mills in Orekhovo-Zuev employing some 11,000 workers—were traceable to economic grievances and were devoid of political significance; they were easily suppressed by the police and the troops. Russian Marxism was still in its infancy, a literary movement sponsored by a small coterie of radical intellectuals, rather than a fighting revolutionary organization. From these humble beginnings grew the Russian Social Democrat Party, its Bolshevik faction, and finally the Communist Party of the U.S.S.R.

FOREIGN RELATIONS

Alexander III lives in official Russian historiography as the tsar peacemaker; under his rule the empire remained at peace except for minor, albeit costly, military expeditions in central Asia. One factor working against war was the circumspect and cautious policy of Giers, *de facto* head of the foreign office in the closing years of Gorchakov's chancellorship and foreign minister from April, 1882, to 1895. Unlike his predecessor, Giers was not a spectacular international figure with a flair for glittering generalities and ambitious schemes. Contemporary observers and historians differ in their evaluation of the part actually played by Giers in directing Russian foreign policies. Witte in his memoirs speaks of Giers, whom he knew well, as "a very prudent man, a diplomat, a civil servant of average ability and limited vision but wide experience." According to the same source, Alexander III held that he was his own minister of foreign affairs, and treated Giers as a mere secretary, an attitude which, however, did not prevent the tsar from following at times the counsel of the compliant titular head of the foreign office. This view of Giers's role is accepted by many historians (for instance, Skazkin). On the other hand Nolde, author of an admirable study on the Franco-Russian alliance, maintains that Giers was a true statesman (*un véritable homme d'état*), that his reputed pliability was illusory, and that he pursued with determination and skill a policy of peace dictated by the international situation and Russia's best interests.[20] Even though this appraisal may well be regarded as unduly generous (especially in view of the vagaries and methods of Russian policy in Bulgaria), the fact remains that Giers successfully kept in check the aggressive nationalistic and expansionist influences to which Alexander was so susceptible, and repeatedly prevented the tsar from adopting a course that might have precipitated an international conflagration. The Russian minister, according to Bernhard von Bülow (letter to Bismarck of October 27, 1887, N.S.),

[20] Baron Boris Nolde, *L'Alliance franco-russe*, pp. 259, 278.

was convinced that a military defeat of Russia would unleash a revolution "which would make the Paris commune appear mere child's play." Giers, moreover, displayed a sense of reality and freedom from dogmatism; a proponent of close ties with Germany he led Russia, although not without hesitation and misgivings, along the road of the Franco-Russian *rapprochement* when the hostile attitude of Berlin forced St. Petersburg to seek new allies.

The principal developments in Russian foreign relations under Alexander III were the renewal of the "three emperors' league," the conflict with England in central Asia, the Bulgarian crisis, the termination of the Russo-German alliance, and the conclusion of the alliance with France. The revival of the alliance of Austria, Germany, and Russia (June 18, 1881, N.S.) [21] marked not only the end of Russia's political isolation resulting from the War of 1877–1878 but also the at least temporary renunciation by St. Petersburg of the nationalistic program which Ignatev had endeavored to impose upon Turkey and Europe at San Stefano. Under the terms of the secret treaty of June 18 the contracting parties bound themselves, in case one of them became involved in a war with a fourth great Power, to maintain towards their belligerent ally a policy of benevolent neutrality and to work for the localization of the conflict. The above provision was to apply to a war between one of the signatory Powers and Turkey, provided the three courts had agreed in advance "concerning the results of such a war" (Article I). St. Petersburg, Berlin, and Vienna undertook to coordinate their respective interests in the Balkans, Russia promising specifically to respect the new position created for Austria by the Treaty of Berlin. No modifications of the territorial *status quo* in the Ottoman empire were to be tolerated (*ne pourront s'accomplir*) except by agreement of the three imperial courts (Article II). The signatory Powers confirmed their adherence to the principle of the closure of the Bosphorus and the Dardanelles, as defined by the Russian representative at the Congress of Berlin on July 12,[22] and bound themselves to warn the Porte, when circumstances warranted such action, that an infraction of the above rule would be regarded as a *casus belli* by the injured party (*la partie lésée*) and would abrogate the guarantees of territorial integrity secured for the Ottoman empire by the Treaty of Berlin (Article III). A protocol attached to the treaty amplified the

[21] See p. 1027.
[22] See p. 1021.

vague stipulations of Article II by listing the eventual changes in the territorial *status quo* agreed upon by the three governments. Austria was conceded the right to annex Bosnia and Herzegovina "whenever she may deem the time opportune," as well as the sanjak of Novibazar, the latter provision being the confirmation of a secret understanding reached by Austria and Russia during the Congress of Berlin (July 18, 1878, N.S.). The three Powers were also agreed not to oppose the union of Bulgaria and Eastern Rumelia "if the issue was raised by the force of circumstances."

From the Russian point of view the virtue of the treaty of June 18 consisted in the guarantee of the closure of the Straits, which minimized the danger of the reappearance of the British fleet in the Black Sea. In exchange for the obligation to enforce the closure of the Straits, Russia promised Germany benevolent neutrality in case of a Franco-German war, sanctioned the consummation of Austrian ambitions in the Balkans, and undertook to respect the *status quo* (subject to the reservations mentioned above), that is, she renounced her freedom of action in the Balkan peninsula. The nationalistic and panslav program of the late 1870's was to be held in abeyance at least during the lifetime of the treaty, which was to run for three years. Thus under the guise of a return to the tradition of the Holy Alliance, an argument that appealed to the conservative instincts of Alexander III, an essentially new diplomatic situation was brought into being.

The renewal of the alliance was a personal triumph for Giers because the tsar, while well disposed towards Germany, had little liking for Austria, and adhered to the view that Constantinople should eventually belong to Russia. "We shall never get together with the Austrians, and no agreement with them is possible," Alexander wrote despondently in the margin of a memorandum, of May 9, 1881, from his foreign minister. Commenting on a statement by Saburov (April 25, 1881) that the proposed alliance with Austria and Germany might eventually lead to the Russian occupation of the Straits, Giers observed that the suggestion struck him as far-fetched. "This may be true today," Alexander wrote in the margin, "but in due course of time it [the occupation of the Straits] will be necessary." The tsar, therefore, was not unreservedly won over to the policy inaugurated by Giers, a policy which, moreover, was under attack from several influential quarters.

Although the treaty of alliance remained a closely guarded secret, the greater cordiality in the relations of the three governments aroused the suspicion and anger of Russian nationalist and panslav groups. Ivan Aksakov, in the columns of *Rus*, never tired of denouncing any understanding with the Germanic Powers as treason to the national cause. The popular General Skobelev, hero of the Turkish war and of Asiatic conquests, stirred nationalistic emotions by two resounding speeches delivered in January (St. Petersburg) and February (Paris), 1882, in which he voiced sympathy for the population of Bosnia, then in revolt against Austria, decried the pernicious influence of "the internal enemy" upon Russian diplomacy, and prophesied the inevitability of war between Slavs and Teutons. Nicholas Ignatev, the unrepentant author of the San Stefano treaty, was an even more formidable opponent of the policy of non-intervention in the Balkans and cooperation with Germany and Austria-Hungary. His influence with Alexander was for a time very great, and he was commonly regarded as Gorchakov's most likely successor. By a curious coincidence both Ignatev and Skobelev soon, and almost simultaneously, vanished from the scene: Ignatev's political career, as related earlier in this chapter, was terminated in May, 1882, and Skobelev died in July of that year.

The policy of Giers, however, was opposed by influential officials in his own department, although on grounds different from those adduced by Aksakov, Skobelev, and Ignatev. Saburov, Russian ambassador to Berlin, urged that the renewal of the alliance (due in 1884) should be seized as an opportunity for broadening its terms: Russia, according to this view, should be given a free hand in Constantinople and the Straits in return for suitable compensations to Germany and Austria. This proposal was supported by A. I. Nelidov, Russia's newly appointed ambassador to Constantinople. The Saburov amendment, if accepted, would have altered the character of the alliance: from an instrument for the maintenance of the *status quo*, and therefore of peace, it would have become an instrument for territorial expansion, and therefore of war. Giers successfully fought the influences inimical to his policy, Saburov was recalled from Berlin early in 1884, and on March 27, N.S., the treaty of alliance was renewed, with minor modifications, for another three years (until June 18, 1887, N.S.). A few months later it was put to the test during the Anglo-Russian crisis over central Asia.

With the defeat of Beaconsfield and the advent to power of Gladstone (April, 1880), the tension in Anglo-Russian relations subsided.

British statesmen and public opinion were, no doubt, disturbed by Russia's encroachments on the Turkman steppes: in 1881 Skobelev took Gheok Teppe, in February, 1884, the Russians annexed Merv, and early in 1885 they occupied the Penjdeh district; the Muscovites thus appeared to be moving towards Herat, which, it will be remembered, was regarded by many Englishmen as the "key" to India. Yet until 1885 the London government showed no particular anxiety. The occupation of Merv was mildly challenged by Lord Granville, the British foreign secretary, with the statement that the news of Russia's annexation "has not been received by us with indifference"; he took no action, however, except to send to St. Petersburg a recriminatory and somewhat academic note which listed Russia's many broken pledges in central Asia. In the opinion of the liberal government the solution of Anglo-Russian difficulties lay in the peaceful delimitation of the Afghan-Russian boundary rather than in provocative military demonstrations. This view was shared by the viceroys of India appointed by the Gladstone administration, the Marquis of Ripon and the Marquis of Dufferin and Ava. According to Dawson, Dufferin, a former ambassador to St. Petersburg, "gave the Russians credit for common sense and, within limits, good faith," and "regarded normal standards as applicable" to the tsarist empire.[23] This magnanimous attitude of high British officials paved the way for the resumption of negotiations on the Afghan frontier. An Anglo-Russian boundary commission was appointed in July, 1884, but ran into difficulties and made no progress. A source of complications was the explorations carried on in the previously little known Trans-Caspian region by a Russian, Paul Lesser. He discovered, among other things, that the chain of high mountains supposedly separating Herat from the Russian-occupied steppes did not exist. The Lesser discoveries led to the temporary suspension, at Russia's request, of the work of the boundary commission, to the drastic revision of Russian proposals for the frontier settlement (January, 1885), and to the occupation of the Penjdeh district (end of February, 1885). The latter development created a stir in England. Queen Victoria, as in 1875, made a personal appeal to Emperor Alexander, imploring him to prevent a clash between Russian and Afghan forces (March 4, N.S.), while orders were issued to have a British corps in readiness for the defense of Herat. Hasty negotiations resulted in the agreement of March 17, N.S., by

[23] *The Cambridge History of British Foreign Policy,* III, 188.

which the Russians promised not to advance further in Penjdeh pending the settlement of the boundary question. On March 30, N.S., however, there occurred a bloody battle near Ak-Teppe in which the Afghans were defeated. Although the Ak-Teppe affair took place in violation of instructions received from St. Petersburg, it was interpreted in London as evidence of Russia's bad faith. The two countries appeared on the verge of war. Giers requested Germany to fulfil her treaty obligations; Gladstone obtained from parliament large credits for the defense of India. The storm, however, blew over. The British prime minister, much to Giers's relief, refused to be swayed by pressure from nationalist quarters. Anglo-Russian negotiations for the settlement of the Afghan boundary (and also for the fixing of responsibility for the Ak-Teppe incident, which were eventually dropped) were resumed, and led to a preliminary agreement (May 22, N.S.), followed by the final delimitation of the Russo-Afghan frontier in the Penjdeh region (September 10, 1885, N.S.). Russia was awarded the Penjdeh district, but the Zulfkar pass, which she had claimed, was retained by Afghanistan. Negotiations for the tracing of the other sections of the disputed border were brought to a successful conclusion in 1886 and 1887.

A noteworthy feature of the 1885 crisis was the readiness with which Bismarck responded to the Russian appeal to bring pressure on Turkey. His instructions to the German ambassador at Constantinople, issued at the time when war appeared all but inevitable (April 9, N.S.), could not have been more forcible and unequivocal.[24] Russia owed it to his perseverance that strong representations to the Porte were made not only by Austria but also by France and Italy. The results of these efforts, from the Russian point of view, were gratifying: the sultan gave a formal promise that, in case of an Anglo-Russian war, the Straits would remain closed. It is more difficult to determine to what extent the closure of the Straits actually influenced the policy of the British government, though it is clear that the freedom of access to the Black Sea was uppermost in the minds of some leading Englishmen.[25] Be that as it may, Giers had reason to congratulate him-

---

[24] Full text in Nolde, *op. cit.*, p. 313.

[25] Lord Stratheden and Campbell, for instance, said in the House of Lords on May 7, 1885, N.S.: "The facility of operating in the Black Sea is most important to this country. It is the only area in which Russia has ever been successfully encountered by Powers wishing to restrain her. . . . If the Black Sea is closed for her advantage, Russia is entitled, by the history of the past, to deem herself invinci-

self on the effectiveness of the diplomatic instrument he had helped to forge. There was little at the time to indicate that the alliance of the three emperors was soon to founder under the impact of a political storm brewing in the Balkans.

The focal point of the disturbance was Bulgaria, where, in spite of the Treaty of Berlin, Russian influence in the early 1880's was paramount. Many factors seemed to presage a close if not necessarily harmonious cooperation between St. Petersburg and Sofia. Alexander of Battenberg, prince of Bulgaria, owed his Crown to Alexander II, and in the opening years of his rule relied chiefly on Russian advisers, who filled the more important offices in the Bulgarian government and in the army. With the withdrawal of Russian troops in 1879, a major cause of friction between Russians and Bulgarians was removed. The nascent Bulgarian nationalism was tinged with panslav doctrines, and the tradition of the "war of liberation" favored the spread of Russian influence. Moreover, the union of Bulgaria with Eastern Rumelia written by Ignatev into the Treaty of San Stefano and ardently desired by Bulgarian nationalists appeared eventually assured by the pertinent stipulation of the alliance of the three emperors. The provisions of the 1881 treaty were not known, but there was much evidence that Russia had worked for the unification of Bulgaria. In spite of these auspicious conditions, Russo-Bulgarian relations went from bad to worse, culminating in a break between the two countries at the very time when the union of the two Bulgarias became an accomplished fact.

Russia's inept policy in Bulgaria must be assigned prime responsibility for its failure. Although occasionally represented as astute and Machiavellian, it actually lacked a clear purpose, and invited disaster by attempting to achieve, often by indefensible methods, mutually incompatible objectives. On the one hand, the St. Petersburg bureaucrats were at a loss in dealing with an unfamiliar phenomenon such as Bulgarian nationalism, and they proved incapable of devising a policy that would reconcile Russian and Bulgarian aspirations; on the other hand, the tsarist diplomats had but an imperfect control of the situation, the majority of Russian officials in Bulgaria being army men who acted independently of the foreign office. While Giers thought

---

ble. . . . If he [the sultan] excludes Great Britain from the Black Sea, Russia may attempt Herat with absolute impunity." Quoted in C. Phillipson and N. Buxton, *The Question of the Bosphorus and Dardanelles* (London, 1917), p. 159.

in terms of the balance of power and the preservation of the *status quo*, Russian proconsuls in Sofia, as often as not, were bent on turning Bulgaria into Russia's military outpost if not into a Russian province; that is, diplomats and the military worked at cross purposes, occasionally taking malicious pleasure in each other's blunders and discomfiture. Moreover, the choice of Russian representatives, with few exceptions, was particularly unfortunate, and their unintelligent and tactless conduct antagonized many of Russia's best friends in Bulgaria.

Prince Alexander, a twenty-two-year-old dashing Prussian officer, disliked the democratic constitution unwillingly granted to the principality by Alexander II at the request of the Bulgarian national assembly in Tyrnowo,[26] and he repeatedly pleaded with the Russian government for its repeal. Alexander II and, later, Alexander III and Giers, while sympathizing with the prince's desire, warned him against rash constitutional changes that might lead to international complications. Nevertheless, on May 9, 1881, N.S., Prince Alexander executed a *coup d'état* which forced the resignation of the liberal government, set aside the constitution, and conferred upon him dictatorial powers for a term of seven years; these arrangements were eventually confirmed, under strong pressure, by a national assembly convoked *ad hoc* at Sistova (July, 1881). Meanwhile the Russian representative, General Ehrnroth, one of Prince Alexander's supporters, was appointed head of a provisional Bulgarian government. Alexander III approved the activities of Ehrnroth and, after the Sistova assembly, congratulated the Bulgarian ruler on the success of his enterprise, which of course could not have been carried out, or even attempted, without the connivance of Russian agents. Ehrnroth was soon recalled, but the newly formed conservative Bulgarian government included two Russian generals; and the princely dictatorship, resting on the cooperation of Bulgarian conservatives with Russian military officials, proved unworkable. Faced with an effective liberal and nationalist opposition, Prince Alexander found himself at odds with public opinion at home and with his Russian advisers. In July, 1882, in a desperate attempt to inject new blood into a moribund political combination, he formed a conservative government headed by the Russian general Sobolev, with another Russian, General Baron Alexander Kaulbars, in the war office. Sobolev applied in Bulgaria the administrative methods he had once used—successfully, so he imagined—in conquered Bokhara, with the

[26] See p. 1023.

result that the conservatives finally lost patience and in March, 1883, all Bulgarian ministers resigned. Disgusted with the "ingratitude" of its clients, the Russian government shifted its support from the conservatives to the liberals; the latter, however, were slow in showing their appreciation, reached an agreement with the conservatives, and in September of 1883, contrary to Russia's wishes, forced Prince Alexander to restore the Tyrnowo constitution. The Russian generals were ignominiously withdrawn, much to the detriment of Russian prestige in the Balkans.

The turmoil of 1881–1883 destroyed whatever influence Prince Alexander enjoyed in St. Petersburg. "I positively do not trust the word of the prince any more," Alexander III commented in September, 1883. Ionin, Russia's special envoy to Sofia, urged the disavowal and removal of the hapless Bulgarian ruler, but the tsar and Giers demurred. A new crisis broke out on September 18, 1886, N.S., when a group of Bulgarian nationalists arrested and conducted across the border the Turkish governor-general of Eastern Rumelia and proclaimed the union of the two Bulgarias under Prince Alexander. Alexander was forewarned of the impending *coup d'état*, and under the pressure of the nationalist leader, Stephen Stambulov, he accepted, although not without hesitation, the offer to head the movement for national unification. The Bulgarian army was mobilized on September 21, N.S., the prince made a ceremonial entry into Philippopolis (the capital of Eastern Rumelia), and the Bulgarian parliament approved the union.

The great Powers were called upon to define their stand on the new situation in the Balkans. Germany and Austria, having agreed in their treaty of alliance with Russia not to oppose the union, were prepared to accept the *fait accompli*. But a curious reversal took place in the attitude of Russia and England. Since San Stefano Russia had been the champion of the unification of Bulgaria, which England succeeded in defeating at the Congress of Berlin. In 1885, however, St. Petersburg protested against the union as a violation of treaty obligations, while Lord Salisbury, first British delegate at the Berlin congress and prime minister since August, 1885, rallied to its defense. The Russian government demanded the convocation of an international conference and ordered the withdrawal of Russian officers serving with the Bulgarian army. Stern anti-Bulgarian measures had the whole-hearted approval of the Russian nationalist press: Bulgaria and Prince Alexander, it was argued, had proved their "ingratitude" towards Russia; the union therefore was declared both inopportune and illegal. Aksakov, faithful to the panslav program, was the only one in the nationalist camp to raise a dissenting voice.

The events of September created great excitement in Serbia and in Greece, which clamored for appropriate territorial compensations. Milan of Serbia, who had assumed the royal status in 1882, started war on Bulgaria (November 14, 1885, N.S.), only to be decisively defeated within a fortnight. The occupation of Belgrade was avoided because of the intervention of Austria, with whom Serbia had a secret alliance. Peace was restored by the Treaty of Bucharest on the basis of *status quo ante bellum* (March 3, 1886, N.S.). A war between Greece and Bulgaria was prevented by a timely naval demonstration of the Powers. The constitutional position of Alexander was regularized by amicable arrangement with the Porte: the sultan appointed him governor-general of Eastern Rumelia and relinquished the right to maintain troops in that area. In legal theory Eastern Rumelia remained a Turkish province; in practice it was an integral part of united Bulgaria, represented in the Bulgarian parliament.

Prince Alexander had thus achieved notable political and military successes, but he had incurred the implacable hostility of Russia, which spelled his doom. During the night of August 20, 1886, N.S., a band of disaffected Bulgarian officers led by Radko Dmitriev, later commanding officer in the Russian army in the War of 1914–1918, invaded the palace. Alexander was arrested, forced to sign an act of abdication, and was transported into Russian territory. A provisional government of pro-Russian orientation was formed, but three days later it was overthrown by Stambulov and his nationalist followers. Alexander, on the invitation of the new government, returned to Bulgaria; when he crossed the border, however, he was informed by a Russian consular officer that an envoy of the tsar was on his way to Sofia to assume control of Bulgarian affairs. Prince Alexander telegraphed to Alexander III announcing his return and humbly imploring the tsar's approval. This being curtly refused, he made public his abdication (September 7, N.S.), appointed a board of regents, and left his stormy principality never to come back.

The disappearance of the despised Battenberg did not improve Russia's position in Bulgaria. The Russian emissary, General Baron Nicholas Kaulbars, brother of the former war minister, proved unable to stem the rising tide of anti-Russian sentiment. In spite of his objections a national assembly was held in November, and unanimously elected to the throne Prince Waldemar of Denmark, brother-in-law of Alexander III and of the future King Edward VII of England. The Russian government took retaliatory measures. Kaulbars and Russian consular representatives were withdrawn, and Waldemar was prevailed upon by the tsar to decline the proffered Crown. The search for a candidate was resumed. In December Prince Ferdinand of Saxe-Coburg-Gotha, proposed by the regents, tentatively accepted the vacant throne, subject to subsequent ratification by the national assembly. To prevent his election the Russian government made an attempt to persuade the Porte that the sultan, as suzerain of Bulgaria, had power to remove the regents and replace them by men more adaptable to Russia's wishes (thus blocking Ferdinand's election), an argument hardly compatible with Russia's traditional attitude as protector of the Balkan Slavs.[27] The Russo-Turkish negotiations having failed, Ferdinand was duly elected (July 7, 1887, N.S.); St. Petersburg protested, and withheld recognition until 1896. Meanwhile Russian policies in Bulgaria dwindled to the organization of disaffected *émigré* groups which carried on subversive activities in their homeland.[28] Such was the undignified and lamentable epilogue of the panslav crusade.

The events in Bulgaria caused a resurgence of patriotic fever in the Russian nationalist press. Katkov, in *Moskovskiia Vedomosti*, attacked Giers with unprecedented violence; he put the blame for the failure of Russia's Balkan policy on England and, particularly, on Austria and Germany and those Russian statesmen and diplomats who favored cooperation with the central Powers. Russia, in Katkov's opinion, should regain freedom of international action and enter into a defensive alliance with France. His crusade reached its high point in an article of March 8, 1887, which divulged the existence of the alliance of the three emperors. Alexander III, who read the articles of Katkov and was impressed by his views, was nevertheless aroused and angered by the indiscretion of the Moscow oracle. The intervention of Pobe-

[27] Nolde, *op. cit.*, pp. 454, 460–461.
[28] P. Pavlovich, ed., *Avantiury russkago tsarisma v Bolgarii* (Adventures of Russian Tsarism in Bulgaria) (Moscow, 1935), *passim*. This valuable collection of documents leaves no doubt that the activities of the *émigrés*, who had their center in Odessa and were financed by the imperial government, were violations of criminal law.

donostsev, however, saved Katkov from the consequences of his misdeeds. The public rebuttal decreed by the tsar was commuted to a discreet private warning, followed by an audience with the emperor. From this interview Katkov carried the impression that Alexander, while upholding official policies, was in sympathy with his own views. The Giers-Katkov feud, which might have led to the dismissal of the foreign minister, was terminated by Katkov's death in July, 1887. Three years later the policy he had advocated was espoused, under the pressure of events, by his arch-enemy Giers.

The vituperations of the Russian press, unjustified as they were by the policies of Germany and Austria during the Bulgarian crisis, appealed to Alexander's nationalistic emotions and were instrumental in sealing the fate of the alliance of the three emperors. Giers favored the renewal of the treaty of 1884, which was to expire in June, 1887, but he met with the resistance of the tsar. In January, 1887, Alexander startled his foreign minister by opposing, as incompatible with the feeling of the nation, an alliance with either Austria or Germany, and by declaring that Russia's only possible ally was Turkey. In so far as Germany and the Porte were concerned, this was merely a passing mood, and the tsar soon returned to sentiments more in keeping with his traditional policy. However, his inveterate dislike of Austria, strengthened by the resentment of the part she had taken in the Serbo-Bulgarian War in 1886, precluded the continuation of close political ties with Vienna. Giers, while hoping that the traditional alignment of Powers might eventually be revived, bowed to his master's will: an alliance with Germany was to replace the alliance of the three emperors. Bismarck, alarmed by the anti-German outbursts in the Russian press and haunted by the specter of a Franco-Russian alliance, welcomed the overtures of St. Petersburg. Negotiations were opened in Berlin in May and were conducted by the chancellor and the Russian ambassador Count Paul Shuvalov. The embarrassing situation created by the existence of the secret Austro-German alliance was cleared up in a frank and honorable manner: Bismarck read to Shuvalov the text of the 1879 treaty and explained that, although directed against Russia, it was strictly defensive. This awkward matter safely out of the way, negotiations proceeded swiftly; the secret Russo-German treaty was signed on June 18, 1887, N.S.[29]

[29] The text of the Austro-German treaty of alliance was published, by Bismarck's order, in February, 1888.

Under the terms of this agreement Russia and Germany promised, if either of them became involved in a war with a third great Power, to maintain a benevolent neutrality and to work for the localization of the conflict; this stipulation was not to apply to a war against France or Turkey resulting from a German or Russian attack (Article I). Germany recognized "the rights historically acquired" by Russia in the Balkans, "especially the legitimacy of her preponderant and decisive influence in Bulgaria and Eastern Rumelia"; no change in the Balkan territorial *status quo* was to take place without the consent of the contracting parties (Article II). The final article reiterated the provision of the alliance of the three emperors concerning the closure of the Straits. In an additional and highly secret protocol attached to the treaty, Germany undertook (1) to assist Russia "in reestablishing in Bulgaria a regular and legal government"; (2) not to countenance the restoration of Alexander of Battenberg; and (3) to accord Russia benevolent neutrality and moral and diplomatic support if the Russian emperor "should find himself under the necessity of assuming himself the task of defending the entrance to the Black Sea," that "key" to his empire. The "re-insurance" treaty, as the agreement of 1887 is usually known, was to remain in force for three years. From the standpoint of Russian imperialistic ambitions it was an advance over the treaties of 1881 and 1884. Bismarck had made important concessions to St. Petersburg in return for the promise of Russian neutrality in case of a Franco-Prussian war. No sacrifice of principles, however, was involved on his part. Throughout his long career Bismarck had consistently maintained that Germany had no direct interests in the Balkans and that the fate of Constantinople and the Straits was to her a matter of indifference.

In spite of the alliance, Russo-German relations deteriorated somewhat in 1887–1890, partly because of the increase in the German tariff on grain and partly because of the campaign against Russian funds indulged in by Berlin financiers, not without the connivance of Bismarck. Yet the two governments appeared to be satisfied with the treaty, and its renewal in 1890 was taken as a matter of course. Meanwhile the German situation had undergone important changes. The venerable Emperor William I died in March, 1888, his son and successor Frederick III followed him to the grave three months later, and in June, 1888, William II mounted the throne. The impression he made on Alexander III in the course of a state visit to Russia in July was unfavorable and was not improved by his subsequent political activities and pronouncements. Giers, indeed, had difficulty in persuading the tsar to return the visit as was required by custom; it was not until October, 1889, that Alexander finally went to Berlin. Nevertheless, so long as Bismarck remained in power, the continuation of the alliance appeared assured. Negotiations for its renewal, initiated in Berlin by Shuvalov in February, 1890, met with the unqualified approval of William and the chancellor. On March 17, N.S., however, Shuvalov, on his return to Berlin with final instructions, was confronted with the news that Bismarck had been forced to resign. Four days later (March 21, N.S.) William assured the Russian ambassador that the retirement of the aged chancellor would not affect German policy and that he was eager to renew the treaty of 1887. In the meantime pressure inimical to Russia was brought to bear on the emperor and the new chancellor, Count Leo Caprivi. High officials of the German foreign office argued that the Russian alliance was incompatible with the obligations assumed by Germany as a member of the Triple Alliance—Germany, Austria, and Italy—concluded in 1882 and extended for another five years in 1887. William and Caprivi were won over by this argument. On March 27, N.S., General Hans Schweinitz, German ambassador to St. Petersburg, was instructed to notify the Russian government that Germany, while desirous of maintaining close and friendly relations with Russia, had decided to abstain from the renewal of the 1887 treaty.

Alexander received the news of the termination of the alliance with equanimity bordering on indifference, and declared himself satisfied with the German professions of friendship. Giers, on the other hand, was genuinely distressed. The alliance was the pivot of his diplomatic system, and its disappearance left Russia, in the minister's opinion, isolated and helpless in the midst of an unsteady and hostile world. He made several attempts to revive the traditional bonds with Berlin —in May and, again, in August, 1890, during the visit of William and Caprivi to Russia, and even as late as April, 1893—but his overtures brought no response. Russia had no choice but to seek allies elsewhere, and since Vienna, London, and Rome were excluded, Paris was the alternative. The idea was not new: it was advocated by Katkov, had warm adherents in France among the supporters of *revanche* (for instance, General Georges Boulanger and the poet Paul Déroulède), and was endorsed, among others, by the historian Anatole Leroy-

Beaulieu. To Alexander, however, France was the breeding place of revolution and social discord. This opinion was shared by Giers. "How can these people, the French, be stupid enough to imagine that Emperor Alexander would march with the Clemenceau against his uncle," Giers told Bernhard von Bülow in December, 1886. "This alliance would be abhorrent to the emperor, who does not wish to pull the chestnuts out of the fire for the commune." Official distrust did not preclude a degree of cooperation. At the end of 1888 Russia placed in France a large order for army rifles. Beginning in 1888–1889, as a consequence of the anti-Russian maneuvers of the German bankers, Russian foreign loans were issued chiefly on the French money market. The success of these operations and the fact that French investors were holders of Russian securities favored the political *rapprochement* between the two countries.

The real stimulus, however, came from Berlin. Refusal to renew the Russian alliance was followed by other German moves that caused uneasiness in both St. Petersburg and Paris. The treaty with England (June 14, 1890, N.S.) by which Germany gave up claims to territories in Africa and acknowledged a British protectorate over Zanzibar in exchange for the cession of the island of Heligoland in the estuary of the Elbe was interpreted as a sign of closer relations between Berlin and London. Official references to the renewal for six years of the Triple Alliance (May, 1891), whose terms, however, were not disclosed, contributed to the state of political tension. Emperor William's visit to England in July, 1891, gave rise to persistent, albeit unwarranted, rumors that the Triple Alliance was to be joined by Great Britain.

The time was propitious for a formal Franco-Russian accord. A visit of the French fleet to Kronstadt, where it was given an enthusiastic reception, paved the way for the negotiations (July, 1891). The foundation of the future alliance was laid in an exchange of notes of August 27, 1891, N.S., in which the two governments agreed to come to an understanding on measures they were to adopt "immediately and simultaneously" in case of a threat to peace. This formula, accepted by the Russian ambassador to Paris, Baron Arthur Mohrenheim, went further in the direction of definite commitments than was intended by Giers. Because of his hesitation and procrastination the text of the supplementary military agreement was not signed until August 17, 1892, N.S. It provided that if France were attacked by Germany, or by Italy supported by Germany, or if Russia were attacked by Germany, or by Austria supported by Germany, the other contracting party would employ all her available forces to fight Germany. The mobilization of the armies of the Triple Alliance was to be countered by the immediate and simultaneous mobilization of France and Russia. The number of troops to be used against Germany was 1,300,000 for France and 700,000 to 800,000 for Russia. The general staffs of the two countries were to coordinate their plans, and Russia and France promised not to conclude a separate peace. The agreement was to have the same duration as the Triple Alliance. The momentous document of August 17 was signed by the French and Russian chiefs of staff, and its legal status therefore was somewhat uncertain. According to one authority (Nolde), it was "more than a project and less than a convention." Giers, disillusioned, aged, and ailing, resisted for months French pressure for the consummation of the alliance. German armaments, saber rattling in Berlin, and perhaps his own weariness finally triumphed over his scruples. By an exchange of letters between Giers and the French ambassador to St. Petersburg (dated, respectively, December 27, 1893, and January 4, 1894, N.S.), the convention of August 17 was ratified and became a binding obligation. Its contents were not disclosed until 1918.

ALEXANDER III'S LEGACY

A bird's-eye view of Russia under Alexander III may well suggest a country enjoying the blessings of social stability and peace. The police regime appeared to have achieved its object. No dissenting opinions were heard except those of men like Katkov and Aksakov, whose ultranationalism was shared by the tsar and by highly placed bureaucrats. The revolutionary movement was disorganized and helpless, its leaders in prison, in Siberia, or scattered abroad. The peasants, with characteristic submissiveness, carried their many burdens; even the great famine of 1891, in which they died by the thousands, failed to provoke a movement of revolt. On the threshold of the twentieth century Russian autocracy had surrendered none of its prerogatives; indeed, it had regained some of the ground lost in the reign of Alexander II. The international position of the empire offered no reason for alarm. If the Bulgarian venture was, admittedly, not a success, it was at least arguable that Russia had withdrawn from the Balkans without a war. Relations with England were vastly improved, and France had stepped in to take the place of Germany as Russia's ally.

Events were soon to show that both social stability and the strength of Russia's international position were illusory. The revolutionary forces, driven underground and kept in check by the police, were about to explode with unprecedented violence; and although international agreements are more honored in the breach than in the observance, and their importance should not be exaggerated, the fact remains that in the last analysis the Franco-Russian alliance proved as fatal to imperial Russia as it was to imperial Germany.

CHAPTER XXXIX

NICHOLAS II

Twilight of Absolutism, 1894–1905

THE TSAR AND THE TSARINA

Nicholas II, upon whose frail shoulders the heavy mantle of absolutism fell somewhat suddenly on October 20, 1894, was born on May 6, 1868. He studied under private tutors, was an accomplished linguist, and traveled extensively in Russia and abroad. In 1890–1891 he made a voyage around the world which took him to Egypt, India, and Japan. He held the customary commissions in the guards, rising, while still heir apparent, to the rank of colonel; in deference to the memory of Alexander III he refused to have his army status changed in later years. Prior to his father's death his participation in the affairs of state was limited to perfunctory attendance at meetings of the committee of ministers and the State Council. Alexander III did not deem it necessary to inform his heir of decisions affecting vital national issues; Nicholas, for instance, was initiated into the secret of the Franco-Russian alliance only after his accession.

Throughout his life Nicholas kept, with remarkable regularity, a diary which throws much light on his character and interests. The portions of this intimate chronicle published by the Soviet government disclose that hardly a day passed without a record of what its author regarded as the most noteworthy events. These entries, comprising merely a few lines each, noted official audiences and visits of innumerable relatives; dwelt with unfailing affection on the minute doings of his wife and children; and invariably mentioned the weather and out-of-door activities. Playing with dogs, gathering mushrooms, walking, tennis, skating, rowing, paddling, swimming, bicycling, riding, and—above all—shooting were among the emperor's usual pastimes. The bag of every shooting trip was carefully listed, special note being made of his own share, and when the pressure of business prevented him from indulging in his favorite sport he shot at crows in the parks of the imperial residence, recording the results in his diary. There were frequent enthusiastic references to maneuvers, military reviews, and visits to the headquarters of select regiments, but the major political events (the Japanese war, the revolution of 1905, the establishment of the State Duma), which one would expect to be uppermost in the emperor's mind, were almost completely ignored.

Witte relates in his memoirs that Alexander III hesitated at first to accept his suggestion that the heir apparent be appointed chairman of the Siberia Railway Committee established in 1893. "He is a mere boy," Alexander remarked; "his judgments are truly childish: how can he be chairman of a committee?" Witte was an unsparing critic of his young sovereign, and his evidence must be accepted with caution. Yet Nicholas's own diary would seem to corroborate the above statement. In 1893, for instance, he noted that "after partaking of refreshment" he and two of his friends "played hide-and-seek, just like small children." On September 27, 1894, less than a month before his accession, Nicholas reported with obvious relish that he and Prince George of Greece fought a battle with chestnuts: "We started in front of the house and ended on the roof." Two days later there was another encounter on the roof of the Livadia palace, fought this time with pine cones. These episodes are innocent and trivial enough; it may be significant, however, that Nicholas, a man of twenty-six, chose to mention them in the summary record of his daily activities.

The tsar's simple and straightforward political philosophy was singularly inappropriate for the part of constitutional monarch he was destined to play after 1905. Like his father and his former tutor and trusted adviser, Pobedonostsev, he believed in autocracy and in the sacred union between the Crown and the common people, and he rejected representative government, however limited, as both morally wrong and incompatible with the country's best interests. Although the revolutionary storm of 1905 compelled Nicholas to summon a representative assembly, the State Duma, and to limit the legislative powers of the Crown, he was never reconciled to the status of a constitutional monarch, and resented the surrender of absolute power as an indignity and a betrayal of his sacred trust. In 1913 he directed N. A. Maklakov, minister of the interior, to submit proposals for constitutional amendments that would reduce the legislative chambers to the position of mere consultative bodies. "The presentation to the sovereign for his choice and approval of both the majority and the minority opinions," wrote the tsar, "will be a welcome return to the former peaceful course of legislation which, moreover, is in accordance with the Russian tradition." Maklakov prevailed on the emperor to abandon a plan that was unconstitutional and impracticable. Nicholas yielded, but he never fully accepted the view that his will was not above the law. This attitude of the monarch explains much in the course of Russian events after 1905.

In his relations with courtiers and officials the tsar was considerate, courteous and kind, but his ministers could never be sure that the policies seemingly agreed upon would actually receive his assent, or that a gracious audience would not be followed by a curt dismissal from office. The cause of these sudden reversals may be traced to unofficial influences that flourished at the court. Notable was that of Prince V. P. Meshchersky, editor of the paper *Grazhdanin* (The Citizen). Meshchersky, whose private life was one of St. Petersburg's blatant scandals, nevertheless enjoyed the patronage of Alexander III and, until his death in the summer of 1914, exercised a peculiar sway over the mind of Nicholas. At times, indeed, Meshchersky's insidious press campaigns appeared to have been the factor determining official policies, especially appointments and dismissals of higher officials. Count V. N. Kokovtsov, who knew Nicholas well and was familiar with the mechanics of bureaucratic government, has given in his memoirs a telling picture of Meshchersky's methods. After 1905 the scheming journalist harped incessantly, in the columns of *Grazhdanin*, on the trite theme of the blessings of autocracy and the devotion of the Russian people to their anointed ruler; the Crown was extolled as the fountain of Russia's happiness, and the reign of Alexander III as a model of benevolent paternalistic government. This no longer popular political philosophy was subtly used either to discredit or to commend the incumbents of high offices. Meshchersky's actual motives were less lofty than he made them appear. His paper existed on subsidies paid from the public treasury by order of the tsar, and Meshchersky tirelessly besieged ministers for both funds and favors for his numerous shoddy clients. The ministers who complied with his requests were praised in *Grazhdanin*; those who demurred were denounced as traitors to the tsar and to Russia's tradition. This crude political blackmail was remarkably successful. Nicholas regularly read *Grazhdanin,* corresponded with its editor, received him occasionally, and only too often followed his counsel. Kokovtsov ascribes to Meshchersky a leading part in the intrigue that brought about Kokovtsov's dismissal as president of the council of ministers in January, 1914.

The dominating influence in Nicholas's life, however, was his wife, the former Princess Alice of Hesse-Darmstadt. Except for the well known ballerina Madame Kshesinsky, with whom he had a brief liaison in 1890, no other woman ever won his affection. His desire to marry Alix, as the future empress was called by her intimates, dated back to 1889, when she spent several weeks in St. Petersburg. What might well have been a passing infatuation grew into a deep and lasting attachment which eventually triumphed over the hesitations and objections of his parents. In April, 1894, Nicholas and Alix were betrothed; their marriage was celebrated on November 14 of the same year, shortly after the death of Alexander III. The tsar's diary, in which Alix, even before their marriage, was in the habit of making insertions, and their correspondence in later years bear witness that their union was an exceptionally happy one. Empress Alexandra Fedorovna, as Alix was known in Russia, fully returned her husband's passionate affection. Some of her letters written during the First World War breathe a warmth of feeling that suggests a young bride on a honeymoon rather than a middle-aged woman entering the third decade of married life. Nicholas remained to the end an exemplary husband and a devoted father.

This family bliss, marred only by the empress's failing health and the illness of the heir to the throne, had grave and unfortunate political consequences. Alix, a daughter of Princess Alice of England, was born in Germany but was brought up at Kensington Palace in London by her grandmother, Queen Victoria. English, often unidiomatic and misspelled, was the language she used in writing to her husband. Profoundly religious, she was at first reluctant to join the Orthodox Church, as required by Russian law. Having once overcome these scruples, however, she embraced her new faith with all the ardor of a high-strung emotional nature. In her exalted mind Orthodoxy and absolutism became merged (not perhaps without the influence of Nicholas and Pobedonostsev) in a belief in the mystical union of the Crown with "the people" and in an intense hatred of any restraint on autocracy. Her mysticism and religiosity were fostered by her self-imposed isolation and by the resurgence of terroristic activities which threatened the lives of the tsar and his family. Ailing, painfully shy and ill at ease at public functions, the empress made rare appearances in St. Petersburg society and saw few people outside a small group of mystically-minded friends. The successive births of four daughters impaired her health but failed to provide for the succession to the throne. Her longing for a son caused Alexandra to seek the guidance of charlatans and adventurers. A notable precursor of Rasputin was one M. Philippe, a Frenchman who would seem to have claimed the power to determine sex and was prosecuted in France for practicing medicine without a license. He was brought to St. Petersburg, where he enjoyed the confidence of the imperial couple and in 1902 persuaded the empress that she was again to become a mother. The impending happy event was given customary publicity, but in due course of time the unpalatable truth had to be faced: Alexandra was not pregnant. Philippe was soon forced to leave Russia. This embarrassing episode notwithstanding, the empress retained her faith in the French pseudo-prophet and in 1916 still referred to him as "one of the two friends sent to us by God." The second "friend" was Gregory Rasputin.

The ascendancy of Rasputin was the unhappy sequel of an intimate tragedy that befell the imperial family. The long-hoped-for heir to the throne, Alexis, was born on July 30, 1904. The joy of the proud parents, however, was soon to give place to grief and anguish: it was discovered, when the infant was ten weeks old, that he was afflicted with an incurable ailment—hemophilia—which manifested itself in severe bleedings. This rare disease was hereditary in the male line of the House of Hesse and was transmitted to the "little treasure," as Nicholas called his son, through his mother. Science has no remedy for hemophilia, and the empress in her distress turned to divine Providence, which alone could accomplish the miracle for which she prayed. The eagerly expected savior appeared in the uncomely guise of Gregory Rasputin, a half-literate peasant from the wilderness of Siberia. Rasputin belonged to the shiftless fraternity of pilgrims (*starets*), or unordained religious teachers, wandering from monastery to monastery and living by their wits and on donations from simple-minded believers. Erotic and mystical elements were inextricably bound up in Rasputin's shapeless doctrine. He appears to have preached that sexual indulgence is the true path to humility and, through humility, to eternal salvation. His powerful build, forceful personality, and obscure pronouncements won him a following among the sensation-hungry neurotic ladies of St. Petersburg society; he also enjoyed the patronage of several highly placed churchmen. Anastasia and Militsa, Montenegrin princesses married to Russian grand dukes, and Anna Vyrubov, lady-in-waiting and trusted friend of the tsarina, were among Rasputin's early disciples. The two Montenegrins, who had previously introduced Philippe to the tsarina, were now under the spell of the new prophet. "Today," Nicholas noted in his diary on November 1, 1905, "we made the acquaintance of the man of God Gregory, from the province of Tobolsk."

Rasputin immediately captured the imagination of Alexandra. He was presumably endowed with hypnotic power and, according to S. P. Beletsky, chief of the imperial police, had been trained by a professional medium. Credible witnesses agree that on several occasions Rasputin succeeded in stopping the bleedings of Alexis. His inexplicable success was the miracle in which the empress so firmly believed. Rasputin, moreover, fitted perfectly into her concept of Russia: an instrument of Providence, he was the living embodiment of the sacred union between the Crown and the peasantry, a son of "the people"—coarse, uneducated, uncouth—divinely sent to protect and save the heir to the throne. Reports concerning Rasputin's loose living and immorality were brushed aside as base slander. Blind faith in Rasputin led Alexandra to seek his counsel not only in matters pertaining to the imperial family but also on questions of state policy. It was only gradually that Rasputin became aware of the immense power so unexpectedly thrust upon him. Meanwhile his influence was exploited by unscrupulous ecclesiastics, bureaucrats, financiers, and adventurers. His activities attracted considerable attention in 1911 and 1912. There was an interpellation in the State Duma where Alexander Guchkov spoke bluntly of Rasputin's influence. This interference in what the tsarina regarded as a private and, indeed, a sacred matter confirmed her in her detestation of parliament and made her an implacable enemy of Guchkov.

Alexandra's increasing sway over her husband and the growing influence of Rasputin in public affairs cast their dark shadow over the monarchy on the eve of the Great War. "Show your mind and don't let others forget who you are," she had admonished her fiancé as far back as October, 1894. Ironically, the same theme was revived by her with remarkable persistency in the war years when, as will appear later, the tsarina—and through her Rasputin—all but superseded the emperor at the helm of the ship of state.

BEGINNING OF THE REIGN

The reign of Nicholas began inauspiciously with a disaster which marred the coronation celebrations. Because of the ineptitude of the authorities, the distribution of presents to the populace on the Khodynka field near Moscow led to a stampede resulting in the death of some 1,300 people, with many more injured (May 18, 1896). The imperial couple were much criticized for attending the same evening a ball given by the French ambassador.

Of worse augury and graver political consequence was the vigorous assertion by Nicholas of his militant conservatism. The death of Alexander III aroused the hope of progressively-minded Russians, especially zemstvo leaders, that the new monarch might be willing to follow the path of constitutional reform. The tsar availed himself of the earliest opportunity to put such speculations to rest. Addressing zemstvo delegates on January 17, 1895, he dismissed as "senseless dreams" rumors concerning the impending participation of zemstvo representatives in the administration of national affairs. "Let every one know," he declared, reading from a manuscript, "that . . . I shall safeguard the principles of autocracy as firmly and unwaveringly as did my . . . father." Whether this speech was written by Nicholas or, as has often been suggested, by Pobedonostsev, is of minor interest: there is no question that it expressed the tsar's conviction. Supporters of representative government were thus given a plain warning: they had nothing to hope for from the Crown.

The opening years of Nicholas's rule were uneventful. Most of the statesmen appointed by Alexander III, including Pobedonostsev and Witte, continued in office; as in the past, new ministers were drawn from the small group of seasoned bureaucrats. No fresh idea, no departure from sacrosanct administrative methods was permitted to disturb the immutable routine. On the surface the country, as under Alexander III, was docile, pliant, and firmly controlled by her masters.

Behind this serene façade, however, powerful forces were at work preparing the overthrow of autocracy and the destruction of existing social and economic institutions. Principal among these forces were the unyielding reactionary policies of the government; the progressive impoverishment of the peasantry; the emergence of an industrial proletariat, concomitant of rapid industrialization; and the formation of an organized opposition, that is, revolutionary and liberal parties and groups which carried on intensive anti-governmental propaganda. The shock of Russia's ignominious defeat in the Japanese war accelerated the pace of the reform and the revolutionary movements which had been gathering strength for over a decade, culminating in the violent outbreak known as the revolution of 1905.

The revival of the opposition movement may be traced to the great famine of 1891–1892 and the epidemic of cholera that followed it, grim evidence of the plight of the farmers. Confronted with an emergency with which it was unable to cope, the government was compelled to allow the zemstvos and other non-bureaucratic bodies to participate in relief work, thus grudgingly encouraging public initiative. Daily contact with the bleak misery of the villages stimulated anew the interest of populist-minded relief workers in the revolutionary potentialities of the peasantry. Intellectuals of Marxist leanings turned eagerly to the expanding army of industrial workers: the growth of industry, accompanied by the familiar abuses of nascent capitalism (low wages, long hours, intolerable living conditions), offered fertile ground for revolutionary propaganda. In the 1890's the two revolutionary groups—the Marxists and the populists—as well as the liberals gathered around the zemstvos, showed signs of increasing activity.

THE BOLSHEVIKS AND THE MENSHEVIKS

After the founding by Plekhanov in 1883 of the first Russian social democratic organization, Liberation of Labor, Marxian ideas made many converts among Russian intellectuals.[1] Until the middle of the 1890's, however, the scattered Marxist groups were engrossed in theoretical discussions and vehement polemics against the populists. No attempt was made to carry on propaganda in factories and workshops. A change in tactics occurred in 1895, when some twenty Marxist groups in the St. Petersburg region were merged, under the leadership of Lenin and Julius Martov (Zederbaum), into the Fighting Union (*Soiuz borby*) for the Liberation of the Working Class. Assuming that the emancipation of labor could be achieved only through the workers' own collective effort, the union put the brunt of its activity on agitation among the rank and file of the proletariat, using the economic grievances of the workers for the attainment of broad revolutionary

[1] See p. 1123.

aims. Similar unions were established in Moscow and in other industrial centers. The new tactics, it is claimed by Marxists, were successful: the country was swept by a wave of major strikes, those in the St. Petersburg textile mills in 1896–1897 being particularly notable. They led to the introduction of the eleven-and-a-half-hour day, restriction on overtime, and other improvements (law of June 2, 1897). Marxist groups operated several clandestine printing presses, issued publications abroad which were smuggled into Russia, and reached the public through legitimate channels. In 1897 they took over the St. Petersburg monthly *Novoe Slovo* (The New Word); in its columns cautiously worded articles by Lenin and Plekhanov appeared side by side with those of the eminent Marxian economists Peter Struve and Michael Tugan-Baranovsky, and the writings of Maxim Gorky.

A step towards the unification of the Marxist movement was the founding, at a congress held in Minsk on March 1 to 3, 1898, of the Russian Social Democratic Labor Party. Police vigilance, however, kept down attendance to nine delegates representing five local Russian organizations and the Bund, a social democratic association of Jewish workers established in 1897. Lenin was not present; arrested in December, 1895, he was in exile in Siberia, and did not return to St. Petersburg until 1900. The party made an unpromising beginning; its central committee and those of the organizations represented at the Minsk congress were soon arrested. Although many Marxist groups dropped their former names and called themselves "sections" of the Russian Social Democratic Party, the latter was still a thing of the future: it had no program, no charter, no executive agencies, indeed, nothing except a manifesto written by Peter Struve and regarded as unsatisfactory by many of the movement's supporters. The building of the party machine was to prove a difficult task. Marxism in Russia, like its counterpart in other countries, comprised all shades of opinion, from right-wing "revisionists" bordering on social reformers to uncompromising champions of the class struggle and the dictatorship of the proletariat. The history of Russian social democracy therefore is filled with factional strife accompanied by mutual excommunications and cleavages.

The founding of the newspaper *Iskra* (The Spark) marked a further attempt to evolve unity from the chaos of conflicting Marxist opinions. *Iskra*, which carried on its front page the proud device "From the spark—the conflagration," was edited jointly by Lenin and the leaders of Liberation of Labor (Plekhanov, P. B. Akselrod, Vera Zasulich). Its first issue appeared in Stuttgart in December, 1900. Factional dissensions persisted, however, and came to a head at the second party congress (June 17 to 30, 1903), which met in Brussels but was forced, by the intervention of the Belgian police, to transfer to London. The forty-three delegates representing twenty-six organizations, divided though they were on many vital issues, succeeded in agreeing on a program and charter. There were actually two programs, the maximum and the minimum. The former dealt with the party's ultimate objectives: socialist revolution, eradication of capitalism, and the establishment of the dictatorship of the proletariat. The minimum program outlined the party's immediate aims: the overthrow of autocracy, organization of a democratic republic, the eight-hour day, the removal of survivals of serfdom, and the restitution to the peasants of the land of which they were deprived by the emancipation of 1861. The latter provision was amended by the fourth party congress, held in Stockholm in April, 1906. The revised version demanded the confiscation of large estates and the "municipalization" of land, that is, its control by agencies of local government. The 1903 program, as amended in 1906, was retained until 1918. The party charter approved by the second congress defined the conditions of membership and the structure and inter-relationship of party agencies. The central organs were the central committee, the council (dropped by the third party congress in 1905), and the editorial board of *Iskra*, which became the party's official newspaper. The filling of agencies on these policy-making bodies precipitated a conflict. The majority, or Bolshevik, group led by Lenin having succeeded in electing its candidates to the editorial board, the minority, or Menshevik, group refused to participate in further elections, or to be represented in the central party agencies. In this inconspicuous manner Bolshevism, eventually a most portentous international movement, slipped almost unnoticed into a hostile world.

Disagreement over this minor administrative question was a symptom of deep-rooted ideological differences which brought about the parting of the ways. Its full import was not realized at the time even by the movement's leaders. Party opinion was still in a state of flux, and victories at congresses were inconclusive. By the summer of 1904 the Mensheviks had captured the central committee; Lenin resigned as co-editor of *Iskra*, and in January, 1905, proceeded to publish a Bolshevik-controlled newspaper *Vpered* (Forward). The cleavage was consummated in April, 1905, when the Bolshevik faction held in London the third party congress; simultaneously the Mensheviks met at a conference in Geneva. A perfunctory reconciliation of the two factions took place at the fourth party congress (Stockholm, April, 1906), but it failed to bridge the ideological gap. Six years later (January, 1912) a Bolshevik-sponsored conference in Prague expelled the Mensheviks from the Social Democratic Party. The Mensheviks convened in Vienna (August, 1912) at a conference organized by Leon Trotsky, who, however, disclaimed affiliation with either faction, and reasserted their allegiance to their own brand of social democracy.

The causes of the Bolshevik-Menshevik feud do not lend themselves to precise summary treatment. Their elusiveness is suggested by the fact that the leaders themselves shifted with remarkable ease from one camp to the other. Stripped of revolutionary verbiage and the personal element (although the latter cannot be entirely ignored), the controversy may be said to have revolved about two main points, one bearing on the philosophy of history and the attitude of the party towards bourgeois liberalism, and the other on the nature of party organization. The Mensheviks believed that the defeated monarchy must be superseded, for a protracted period, by a bourgeois democratic republic as a necessary stage in the establishment of socialism. They were willing, therefore, to ally themselves with the liberal bourgeois parties in their struggle against the monarchy, and to cooperate with them, after a successful revolution, in building up a democratic republic. Lenin and the Bolsheviks rejected this concept. According to their view the imperial government was to be succeeded, not by a democratic republic, but by the dictatorship of the proletariat. The bourgeoisie, like autocracy, was an implacable enemy: it might be used as a tool of the proletariat but should never be supported as an ally. In the matter of party administration the Mensheviks favored the "democratic" method, that is, the right of the rank and file to participate in the framing of policies, while Lenin advocated authoritarian centralism. Neither the Mensheviks nor the Bolsheviks, including Lenin, consistently upheld the above theories. The nature of the Bolshevik doctrine profoundly influenced the course of the revolution of 1917 and determined the character of the Soviet state.

THE SOCIALIST REVOLUTIONARIES

In the 1890's and, indeed, until the advent of the Soviets, Russian Marxism exercised none of that monopoly of revolutionary thought it has since achieved. Lenin, a young, astute, and forcible revolutionary was not yet the canonized, unerring prophet of Bolshevik legend, and disagreement with the Marxian gospel was not necessarily regarded as treason to the cause. Throughout this period the somewhat rejuvenated doctrines of populism and the heroic tradition of the People's Will had many supporters. At low ebb, like other opposition movements in the 1880's, populism was spurred to new activity by the famine of 1891–1892, and rode the tide of unrest that gained momentum towards the turn of the century. Populist groups in Russia and among the *émigrés* multiplied, and in the later 1890's assumed the name of socialist revolutionaries.

The formation of these groups was due to the initiative and influence of local leaders; their new name emphasized the uncertain line differentiating them from the old brand of populism, on the one hand, and from social democracy, on the other. Their ideologies and tactics varied within a wide range. After three attempts at unification (two in 1897 and one in 1898), which were frustrated by internal dissensions and the intervention of the police, representatives of several socialist revolutionary groups met in Kharkov in the summer of 1900 and founded the Socialist Revolutionary Party. Though its manifesto bore, as *Iskra* rightly noted, a striking resemblance to the program of social democracy and was much criticized in socialist revolutionary circles, by the end of 1901 the more important socialist revolutionary groups merged with the new party. This success may be explained by the fluidity of radical opinion and by the fact that the party was joined by several notable revolutionaries with a strong personal following: G. A. Gershuni, Michael Goetz, Catherine Breshko-Breshkovsky, and Victor Chernov, the party's theorist and future leader. A central committee was organized, and the party's newspaper, *Revoliutionnaia Rossiia* (Revolutionary Russia), formerly published in Russia, began to appear abroad under the joint editorship of Goetz and Chernov. The organization of the Socialist Revolutionary Party, however, was not completed until its first congress, held in Finland from December, 1905, to January, 1906, approved a program and a charter.

The socialist revolutionary doctrine expounded in its program and elsewhere retained a distinct populist flavor, but was akin in some respects to that of social democracy. Both had as their ultimate object the overthrow of the existing order and the establishment of a classless socialist society, and both advocated for the intervening stage far-reaching political, social, and economic reforms. There were, however, essential differences: (1) The socialist revolutionaries believed that since Russian capitalism was weak and ineffectual, the fall of the monarchy would lead, immediately and inevitably, to socialism; this assumption, incompatible with the tenets of Marxism, made them the advocates of cooperation with the liberal bourgeoisie in the struggle against autocracy. (2) The socialist revolutionaries assigned to the peasantry a greater and more independent part in the revolutionary process than did the social democrats. The party program, moreover, called for the "socialization" of land, a system of tenure which retained the basic features of the traditional village commune (*obshchina*).[2] (3) Centralization and bureaucratism, inherent in Marxian schemes, were deprecated by the socialist revolutionaries. Their program warned the working class against "state socialism" as a "deceitful system of half-measures and a peculiar form of state capitalism" designed "to bring industry and trade under the control of the bureaucracy which exploits them for selfish fiscal and political purposes." (4) The socialist revolutionary believed—and this was the distinctive feature of the movement—in the efficacy of political terror, a dogma that held together the loosely knit groups of party members. Unlike their precursor, People's Will, however, they admitted that terrorism alone was not enough but must be combined with propaganda. Social democracy looked upon individual terror as futile and even harmful (although the Marxists rejoiced at the bloody exploits of their revolutionary rivals), and relied upon the insight, wisdom, and strength of a disciplined working-class party supported by the masses of the toilers.

The Terroristic Organization (*Boevaia organizatsiia*) of the Socialist Revolutionary Party was founded in 1901. Shrouded in secrecy, and acting under the orders of the central committee, it devoted itself to the perpetration of political murders. Similar terroristic units were established by local socialist revolutionary groups. From 1902 until 1907, when the revolutionary tide ebbed and the police succeeded

[2] Although these proposals were ridiculed by the Bolsheviks, an attempt at putting them into effect was made by the Soviet government in 1917–1918. See pp. 1452–1453.

in rounding up most of the terrorists, the country was swept by waves of political assassinations carried out by socialist revolutionaries. As a side line the terroristic groups organized armed robberies euphemistically known as "expropriations." The party did not entirely approve of the latter type of activity, and endeavored, quite unsuccessfully, to restrict "expropriations" to seizures of government funds, involving no loss of life "except those of police officers."

The central Terroristic Organization was a small, carefully selected group of men and women fanatically devoted to the cause of the revolution. They came from every stratum of society, from penniless peasants and workers to successful professional men and wealthy aristocrats. Tatiana Leontev, daughter of the vice governor of Yakutsk, volunteered—and was authorized by the organization—to murder the tsar at a court ball, which, however, was opportunely canceled. The most notable leaders of the Terroristic Organization were Gershuni, Evno Azef, and Boris Savinkov. The latter, author of two successful novels published under the pseudonym of V. Ropshin, was a terrorist of immense daring, imagination, and resourcefulness. The barest account of his exploits makes a sensational "thriller" appear trite. Catherine Breshko-Breshkovsky, the revered "Granny of the Russian Revolution," extolled terrorism as a necessary political weapon and the magnificent manifestation of "revolutionary and civic valor." Unfortunately for this theory, Azef, one of the master minds of the Terroristic Organization, was simultaneously an agent of the security police. With rare astuteness and complete lack of scruple he served and betrayed his two masters, at times organizing and, by deceiving the authorities, facilitating the execution of terroristic acts, at other times denouncing his confederates to the police. Repeated accusations of treachery leveled against Azef were dismissed by his revolutionary associates as calumny and a "reflection on the honor of the party," until his duplicity was irrefutably established in 1908 by the *émigré* journalist and historian V. L. Burtsev. The disclosure created a major scandal and dealt political terrorism, already on the wane, a blow from which it never recovered.

It will appear from the above that there was little unity among the revolutionary groups, except for their ultimate aim of overthrowing the existing order. Highfalutin exhortations of iron discipline and "monolithic" organization notwithstanding, the revolutionaries were hopelessly divided, and squandered their energies and scant resources in factional strife. The membership of revolutionary parties was small. At the beginning of 1905 the Bolsheviks claimed a following of merely 8,000. Figures of underground group membership, however, are unreliable and deceptive. The strength of the revolutionary movement lay neither in the number of adherents on party rolls nor in the niceties of populist or Marxian theories, which were beyond the grasp of the masses, but in the deep-rooted discontent and disaffection prevailing throughout the country, which brought an eager response to revolutionary propaganda. In 1905 close-knit party organizations and carefully thought-out revolutionary tactics were still a thing of the future. Their import was not revealed until the fateful year 1917.

THE LIBERALS

The frail seedlings of Russian liberalism experienced to an even stronger degree than did Marxism and populism the invigorating effects of relief work during the famine years 1891–1892. Having tasted the satisfaction of participating in common endeavor, educated public-minded Russians were reluctant to return to the state of hibernation that was their lot in normal times. It is not altogether accurate to speak of liberalism while dealing with the somewhat shapeless aspirations of those who occupied the middle position between the revolutionaries and the supporters of autocracy. They differed from the former in their rejection of socialism and revolutionary methods, and from the latter in their detestation of bureaucratic arbitrariness and their longing for political, social, and economic reforms. The loose, untranslatable Russian terms *obshchestvo* and *obshchestvennost* used to describe this group connote a body of educated critical opinion opposed to the ruling bureaucracy, although most of the time not to the extent of contemplating forcible action.

In the 1890's the standard-bearers of liberalism in the sense indicated above were the zemstvos, which, in spite of the restrictive act of 1890,[3] showed an increasing spirit of independence and a desire for expanding the field of their activity. Emboldened by their experience in 1891–1892, the liberal zemstvos reverted, at first hesitantly and cautiously, to the tradition of their precursors of the 1860's and the late 1870's. Two elements of this tradition were the demands for some form of popular representation in central government, and for the creation of a central zemstvo organization. The eagerly awaited op-

[3] See pp. 1095–1097.

portunity, offered by the accession of Nicholas II, was greeted with an outburst of optimism: Empress Alexandra, for instance, was pictured as a staunch liberal because she once attended a German university and was the recipient of a doctor's degree. Some of the congratulatory zemstvo addresses to the tsar (notably that of Tver) contained carefully phrased references to the virtues of the rule of law and to the summoning of a representative assembly. The emperor's ungracious characterization of such proposals as "senseless dreams" was the official reply to these temperate and well meaning petitions. The attempt at establishing a national zemstvo organization fared no better. On the initiative of D. N. Shipov, chairman of the executive board of the Moscow zemstvo, the zemstvo leaders assembled in Moscow for the coronation (May, 1896) decided to hold regular conferences. With the approval of I. L. Goremykin, minister of the interior, the first of these conferences met in Nizhni-Novgorod in August, 1896; but the next meeting, scheduled for 1897, was prohibited by Goremykin on the ground that it was an innovation "incompatible with our constitutional order."

The zemstvos nevertheless were not unduly discouraged. Overstepping the narrow boundaries of their jurisdiction, they proceeded to pass resolutions dealing with national problems such as compulsory school attendance for all children and abolition of corporal punishment. In the middle of the 1890's the fast expanding body of hired zemstvo employees—teachers, doctors, nurses, veterinaries, statisticians, agronomists—began to show interest in the establishment of professional unions and, with the connivance of the zemstvos, they held conventions where political issues were discussed side by side with questions within the immediate purview of the members. It will be recalled that the "third element," as the hired zemstvo employees were known (the other two were Crown officials and the elected members of zemstvos), came chiefly from the ranks of radical intellectuals, many of them affiliated with revolutionary groups. The movement for the organization of professional unions was taken up by professional men other than zemstvo employees.

Viewing these developments with disfavor, the government endeavored to check them by customary police methods. Zemstvo petitions were ignored, elected zemstvo officials were refused confirmation in office, conventions of professional men were closely supervised or prohibited. In November, 1895, the St. Petersburg and the Moscow Committees for the Advancement of Literacy (*Komitety Gramotnosti*), privately supported agencies supplying schools and libraries with much-needed popular books, were taken over by the ministry of education, renamed Societies for the Advancement of Literacy (*Obshchestva Gramotnosti*), and were made subject, under their new charter of March 12, 1896, to vexatious and cumbersome official controls. The committees had enjoyed the patronage of men and women of unquestionable loyalty; the successful campaign against these organizations was provoked by Probedonostsev's gratuitous charges that they had engaged in subversive propaganda. In 1899 a like fate befell the highly respected Law Society, affiliated with the University of Moscow, because the eminent jurist Professor S. A. Muromtsev (later president of the first Duma) delivered before that body an address in which he gave the poetry of Pushkin an interpretation distasteful to the authorities. These and similar capricious and obnoxious policies estranged from the government those very groups on which it could have relied.

FINLAND

Just as unreasonable and, in their ultimate consequences, as fatal to the unity of the realm, were the encroachments upon the constitution of Finland. As long as St. Petersburg respected the constitutional arrangements sanctioned by Alexander I and Alexander II, the grand duchy remained peaceful and orderly, indeed, the best governed and the least troublesome part of the empire. Far-reaching plans for the Russification of Finland were prepared in the reign of Alexander III; pressure was brought to force Finnish institutions to use the Russian language, and a heated controversy developed over the Finnish penal code approved by the diet (1888) and confirmed by the emperor, but subsequently suspended and amended by Russian authorities. The dispute, however, was eventually settled (April, 1894) within the framework of the Finnish constitution. Most of the restrictive policies devised under Alexander III were not translated into law until after the accession of his successor. Alexander III, according to his admirer Witte, "had no great liking for the constitution of Finland." This observation (incidentally, one of the rare instances of understatement in Witte's memoirs) offers the only plausible explanation of the anti-

Finnish campaign. The hostility of Alexander III towards Finland was shared by Nicholas II and his entourage, particularly Pobedonostsev, Bunge, Goremykin, and General A. N. Kuropatkin, the future sorry hero of the Russo-Japanese War. The reactionary press dutifully filled its columns with officially inspired vituperation against Finland, and in 1898 A. I. Bobrikov, a proconsul notorious for his rabid nationalism, was appointed governor-general of the grand duchy.

The turning point in Russo-Finnish relations was the imperial manifesto of February 3 (February 15, N.S.), 1899, and the accompanying Fundamental Statutes, which provided that "general imperial legislation," that is, measures applying both in Finland and in the other parts of the realm, as well as legislation applying only in Finland but "affecting the common interests of the empire, or connected with the legislation of the empire," should fall within the jurisdiction of the Russian State Council. The Finnish diet was to participate in the elaboration of such laws in a purely advisory capacity. The decision as to what measures affecting Finland were to come before the State Council was reserved for the Crown. This momentous enactment, which might well have spelled the doom of Finnish autonomy, was followed by the absorption of the Finnish postal services by the imperial post office (August, 1899), the compulsory use of the Russian language in the records of the Finnish Senate and other agencies (June, 1900), and the disbandment of the Finnish army (June, 1901), which, under a law of 1878, consisted of natives of the grand duchy and was to be used exclusively for the defense of Finland. Thenceforth the Finns were liable to military service under the general provisions of the Russian conscription law.

Russification, especially the act of February, 1899, which violated the Finnish constitution (even though this was denied by Russian nationalists, including distinguished legal authorities), aroused the placid and unemotional Finns. Setting aside inner political and national dissensions (there was considerable antagonism between the Finnish and the Swedish element in the grand duchy) the country, with admirable discipline and singleness of purpose, resisted the assault on its liberties. The impressive demonstration of Finnish determination and unity was soon to force St. Petersburg to repeal the obnoxious legislation. Finland's confidence in Russia, nevertheless, had suffered irreparable damage, and mutual hostility born of this incident entered as a permanent and weighty factor in Russo-Finnish relations. The infringement of the constitution of Finland was criticized by Russian liberals and inspired in the Poles the darkest forebodings.

THE VILLAGE AND THE FACTORY

The scheming of revolutionary doctrinaires and liberal reformers, and the anti-Russian character of resurgent nationalism in tiny Finland, would not have constituted in themselves a menace to autocracy were they not part and parcel of the growing restlessness throughout the country. The famine of 1891–1892 was no mere accident due to the inclemency of the weather; disastrous failure of crops, albeit less severe than in 1891–1892, occurred in 1897, 1898, and 1901. By the end of the century the breakdown of the land arrangements decreed at the emancipation could no longer be ignored. Stagnation of agriculture and the impoverishment of the peasantry were traceable to crushing fiscal burdens and the deadening effects of communal tenure. Sporadic uprisings in rural areas emphasized the political and social implications of the dreary statistics of mounting arrears, low productivity of land, and shocking standards of living. In 1902 agrarian disturbances broke out in the provinces of Poltava and Kharkov; some ninety manor houses were plundered, but order was soon restored by punitive military expeditions. These outbreaks were due to economic causes, and gave no special ground for alarm. They were, however, symptoms of a fundamental maladjustment fraught with explosive potentialities and calling for drastic remedy.

The awakening of labor was another major factor in the making—to use the Marxian phrase—of the "revolutionary situation" of 1905. The strikes of the 1890's, although on a scale that in this age of organized labor may appear paltry, became a permanent disturbing feature of the Russian scene. According to official data, the number of strikers in the establishments under the jurisdiction of factory inspectors was 17,000 in 1894, 31,000 in 1895, 30,000 in 1896, 60,000 in 1897, 43,000 in 1898, 97,000 in 1899, 29,000 in 1900, 32,000 in 1901, 37,000 in 1902, and 87,000 in 1903. The accuracy of these figures has been questioned. L. Martov, for instance, maintains that they understate the actual number of strikers by at least 50 per cent. The average annual number of workers employed in the manufacturing, mining, and metallurgical industries in fifty provinces of European Russia in 1890–1900 was 1,638,000; in 1900, for the empire as a whole, it was nearly 2,200,000, a figure that changed but slightly in the course of the following three years. Compared with the statistics of total employment, the annual number of strikers even in the peak years 1899 and 1903 is not unduly high. Mass organized strikes, however, were still a novel phenomenon. The movement, which involved chiefly large establishments of the textile and metallurgical industries, originated in St. Petersburg and spread to Moscow and other industrial centers. In 1896–1897 some 260 establishments employing 90,000 workers (according to Martov, the actual number of strikers was at least 170,000) were affected by strikes, a development unprecedented in Russian history. The St. Petersburg strike, moreover, was directed by the social democratic Fighting Union for the Liberation of the Working Class. In spite of this revolutionary leadership the strikers' demands were non-political, reasonable, and moderate: shorter hours (the usual hours were 14 and 15 per day), higher rates so as to maintain the former level of earnings in spite of the proposed shorter hours, a half-day on Saturdays, regular payment of wages, and the elimination of other unfair practices.

The policy of the government swayed uneasily from conciliation to reprisals. Some of the strikers' demands were granted by the above-mentioned law of June 2, 1897, which introduced the eleven-and-a-half-hour day, restricted overtime to 120 hours per year, and made other concessions. Pressure was brought to bear on employers to raise wages and to remove the more flagrant abuses. Witte, a protagonist of industrial expansion, bluntly told the manufacturers (July 6, 1896) that since mismanagement was the chief cause of strikes, harsh and inefficient employers should not count on official support. Nevertheless, the law of 1897, an important labor victory in principle, was but loosely enforced. In the early 1900's, the length of the labor day in some industries was still maintained at the pre-1897 level, exceeding the statutory norm by as much as five or six hours. Evasion of the overtime provision was facilitated by subsequent amendments which practically explained it away. No penalty was prescribed for the violation of the law of 1897 except nominal fines of no more than 50 rubles. Other labor legislation was equally perfunctory. A law of June 2, 1903, established the financial responsibility of the employer in case of industrial accidents resulting in the disability or death of a worker,[4] and a law

[4] A totally disabled worker was entitled to a pension of two-thirds of his normal earnings, a widow to a pension of one-third of her husband's earnings. There were

of June 10, 1903, created a semblance of corporate labor organization in the guise of "factory elders" (*fabrichnyi starosta*). Under the terms of this act the workers elected, subject to the employers' consent, candidates from whose number the factory administration appointed the elders. These official spokesmen for labor could be removed from office, as politically undesirable, by the authorities. Thus constituted, the new institution was looked at askance by both employers and workers. By 1905 it functioned in merely thirty or forty enterprises, and had little effect upon industrial relations or the labor movement.

Viewed from the economic angle, the labor picture was cheerless. Tugan-Baranovsky's much-quoted assertion that both money and real wages rose somewhat in the 1890's has been contested by other students on the ground that the rise in money wages lagged behind that of the price of grain. The recession of 1899–1903, moreover, tended to depress wage levels, wiping out previous gains. Taken as a whole, the decade 1894–1903 failed to achieve any appreciable improvement in the condition of the working class. This being the case, the ultimate effect of official conciliatory moves was the opposite of the one intended: concessions such as the law of 1897 gave labor a taste of the efficacy of collective action but brought little tangible relief. Interpreted as disingenuous and a sign of weakness, they created hope followed by disappointment, and intensified the strike movement they were designed to prevent.

Another major facet of official labor policies was measures for the eradication of radical leadership. Professional agitators and strike leaders were expeditiously rounded up, and hundreds of their followers were dismissed and summarily sent back to their native villages. The minister of the interior directed local authorities (circular of August 12, 1897) to make use of their extra-judicial powers in dealing with the strikers. Such cases should not be referred to the courts "because in numerous instances it would be difficult to prove that the alleged offenses constituted breaches of the law."

A less trite method of combating subversive influences was the setting-up of police-controlled labor organizations. This curious experiment is associated with the name of S. V. Zubatov, a repentant revolutionary who became the chief of the Moscow security police

---

allowances for hospitalization, medical care, and funeral expenses. No claim for compensation arose if the accident was caused by the worker's "gross negligence." Compensation claims could be settled out of court by agreement of the parties.

(*okhrannoe otdelenie*). The influence of the revolutionaries with the working class, according to Zubatov, was due to the fact that they alone openly espoused the economic grievances of the workers and endeavored to promote labor organizations. Subversive elements must be fought with their own weapons, and the workers should be given an opportunity to express their legitimate demands through legally recognized and properly conducted labor associations. These theories were shared by many high police officials who showed readiness to sacrifice the interests of the employers on the altar of social peace, which they visualized as a police-sponsored *entente cordiale* between labor and the bureaucracy. The government hesitated, however, and the Zubatov plan was not tried on a large scale until the end of 1900. Meanwhile Zubatov carried out, with the assistance of an extensive network of spies and *agents provocateurs*, mass arrests among the revolutionaries, and for a time reduced their Moscow groups to inactivity.

The Zubatov labor organizations took the form of benevolent mutual-aid associations which catered to the spiritual as well as to the economic needs of their members and were controlled by agents of the security police. The associations' cultural program, inaugurated in May, 1901, included a series of talks by well known liberal professors of Moscow University. The unprecedented tolerance of the authorities towards the new movement aroused suspicion, and by the autumn of 1901 the liberal lecturers deemed it wise to withdraw. They were replaced by less eminent speakers recruited chiefly from the ranks of the clergy. At first non-political, although tinged with liberalism, the movement rapidly came under the influence of extreme reactionaries. On February 19, 1902, the anniversary of the emancipation, the associations staged in front of the monument to Alexander II a huge patriotic demonstration in which some fifty thousand workers took part. This success, however, contributed to their undoing. On the one hand, the very magnitude of the demonstration alarmed the government; on the other, the associations, intoxicated with their apparent strength and impunity, became unmanageable and turned from patriotic manifestations and discussions of such academic topics as British trade unionism to less abstruse and more vital issues: shorter hours, higher wages, better conditions of work. These demands they proceeded to enforce by the old method of strikes. Employers and their spokesman in the government, Witte, protested against industrial conflicts instigated by police-sponsored labor groups. In 1903 Zubatov was dismissed and exiled to Vladimir. Simultaneously police support was withdrawn from the Moscow associations and from most of their counterparts in St. Petersburg, Minsk, and other industrial centers. Deprived of official patronage, the movement collapsed, leaving the field free, and the ground well prepared, for the revolutionaries.

UNIVERSITY STUDENTS

In the closing decades of the empire, university students occupied in Russian political life a place grossly out of proportion to what may be regarded as their legitimate due. Youth has a natural craving for excitement and activity, at times boisterous and not necessarily wise. In countries of different political background and older *cultural* tradition than Russia (and this applies to relatively "new" countries such as the United States), the outlet for this enthusiasm and longing for action is provided by organized sports and extra-curricular activities which form an essential part of academic programs. Russia had no national pastime comparable to baseball, football, or cricket, and her higher schools did not initiate their students in the subtle art of "playing the game." Russian intellectuals looked down upon what is known today as athletics, and youthful highbrows, however undistinguished their academic record, derided sports as a shameful waste of time and a desecration of the temple.

The university charter of 1884, moreover, denied the student body the right of corporate organization, and outlawed even the most innocent non-political student associations and clubs. With such outlets for gregarious instincts blocked, energy and urge for public service were driven into underground channels. Radical and revolutionary doctrines command everywhere a following, especially among those who stand on the threshold of life. In Russia such doctrines thrived on the inequities of autocracy and, from the beginning of the revolutionary movement, had many adherents in the universities. The fatuous rules of 1884, however, unwittingly created for the revolutionary student organizations a position of quasi-monopoly. Membership in underground groups involves serious personal risks and calls for devotion and discipline. Although the latter was hardly a characteristic of the Russian revolutionary movement, revolutionary student organizations found themselves in a strong strategic position in the amorphous mass of undergraduates indifferent to, or vaguely in sympathy with, the not always clearly formulated objectives of a resolute minority. This strategic advantage the left-wing leaders jealously guarded: the collective energy of the student body was not to be dissipated on non-revolutionary enterprises. V. A. Maklakov relates in his memoirs the telling incident of the Moscow student orchestra and choir, the only student-sponsored activities enjoying official recognition. The non-political character of this highly popular venture was frowned upon by radically-minded undergraduates, among them Victor Chernov. By subtle maneuvers they took over in the early 1890's the administration of the orchestra and choir and used them as centers of propaganda, with the result that both were disbanded by the authorities. The same elements successfully opposed the movement for the legalization of fraternal mutual-aid associations (*zemliachestvo*, that is, fraternal societies open to students from the same locality) which existed without official sanction and had their central organ, the "central fund" (*tsentralnaia kassa*). In the early 1890's the leadership of the fraternities passed into the hands of radical students, supporters of legalization were reduced to silence or forced to withdraw, and the central organ, renamed "united council" (*soiuznyi soviet*), aligned the fraternities with the revolutionaries.

Radical tendencies in the universities benefited by the financial insecurity of a large portion of the student body, conclusive evidence that Dimitry Tolstoy's and Delianov's efforts to make higher education the preserve of the upper class had failed.[5] Crowded in dreary lodgings, living from hand to mouth on the proceeds of poorly paid tutoring and other white-collar odd jobs (occupations such as that of a waiter, so common in American colleges, were ruled out as involving a loss of caste), and rubbing shoulders with their carefree, well-to-do fellow students, the impecunious undergraduates were naturally attracted by political and social theories that promised a more equitable order. Liberal opinion, moreover, invariably took the side of the students against the authorities, and as the tide of social unrest neared its crest even eminent members of the academic profession (Struve, Miliukov)

---

[5] An investigation of the financial status of the student body of Moscow University in 1899–1900 disclosed that of the total number of slightly over 4,000, approximately half had no adequate means of support; nearly 2,000 were granted remission of fees, and about 900 received stipends, usually very small ones.

urged the undergraduates to put aside their textbooks and to throw themselves whole-heartedly into the struggle against autocracy.

Throughout the 1880's the universities were relatively quiet. In the 1890's, however, academic life entered upon a stormy phase; student disturbances, which became more frequent and violent, assumed an aggressively political character. In 1895 the Moscow united council, representing forty-five fraternities, was arrested. The reconstituted council announced (October, 1896) that the fraternities' chief object was "to fight against the lawlessness and arbitrariness of university administration" in order "to steel and prepare" the students for the struggle against the imperial regime. A demonstration (November, 1896) called by the council to commemorate the victims of the Khodynka disaster led to clashes with the police and to the arrest of over seven hundred students; of this number 660 were expelled, subject to subsequent reinstatement, while the others were meted out more stringent punishments. The next two years passed without major disturbances, but in 1899 disorders broke out with unprecedented force. Their immediate cause was trivial. Annoyed by an official warning that rowdyism, common during the annual fête of St. Petersburg University (February 8), would not be tolerated, the students of that institution rudely interrupted the customary celebration and, after being ejected from the university building, were dispersed by mounted police using whips, an act of unwarranted brutality. The same evening a mass meeting of students decreed the closure of St. Petersburg University; class attendance was to be prevented by what became known as "obstructions" (*obstruktsiia*), that is, the use of violence. Russia's first university strike proved remarkably successful: within ten days all higher schools in St. Petersburg and Moscow and all Russian universities throughout the land were forced to close their doors. The appointment of a committee, headed by the former minister of war General Vannovsky, to investigate the causes of the unrest did not relieve the tension. The strike spread to Riga and Warsaw, and by the end of March practically every higher school was officially closed until the autumn.

Meanwhile the government produced a program of pacification which leaned heavily towards reprisals. Steps were taken to improve the housing situation, and clubs under official guidance were encouraged, but any form of independent student activity remained prohibited; annual enrollment was limited, for each institution, "in order to prevent overcrowding"; and, last but not least, by virtue of the "temporary rules" of July 29, 1899, the students expelled and deprived of the right to resume studies for a specified length of time (one, two, or three years) were drafted into the army for the duration of the interdict, even if they were not otherwise liable to military service. Moreover, several St. Petersburg professors, allegedly in sympathy with the strikers, were deprived of their chairs. These measures, needless to say, did not remove the causes of the unrest, and the universities, although drastically purged, reopened in the autumn of 1899 in a turbulent mood. Serious disturbances occurred in Kiev in 1900. In February, 1901, P. Karpovich, a socialist revolutionary and a former student twice expelled, shot and fatally wounded N. P. Bogolepov, minister of education since 1898. This bloody deed was extolled by speakers at student demonstrations held in St. Petersburg, Moscow, and other university cities.

THE REVOLUTIONARY TIDE

Bogolepov's murder, the first political assassination in the reign of Nicholas II, ushered in an era of terror waged by the Socialist Revolutionary Party. In March, 1901, a zemstvo statistician, Lagovsky, fired four shots at Pobedonostsev but missed him. In April, 1902, a twenty-year-old student, S. V. Balmashev, wearing the uniform of an aide-de-camp to the tsar, gained admission to the building of the committee of ministers and mortally wounded the minister of the interior, D. S. Sipiagin. Simultaneously elaborate preparations were made for murderous attacks on Pobedonostsev and the St. Petersburg military governor, General Kleigels, but the would-be assassins (among them a young girl, Z. Iurkovsky, dressed for the occasion in the uniform of a male gymnasium student) faltered and failed to carry out their assignment. In July, 1902, a worker, F. Kachura, fired two unsuccessful shots at the governor of Kharkov, Prince Obolensky, and in May, 1903, a railway worker, E. Dulebov, shot and killed the governor of Ufa Bogdanovich. The latter crime led to the arrest of the leader of the Terroristic Organization, Gershuni, who was succeeded by Azef. The technique of the terrorists underwent a change: firearms were discarded for high explosives. The first victim to be blown up was the minister of the interior, V. K. Plehve; the assassination (July, 1904) was planned by Azef and Savinkov, but the bomb that killed the minister was hurled at his carriage by E. S. Sazonov, an expelled student and son of a wealthy conservative peasant merchant. In June, 1904, Bobrikov, governor-general of Finland, was murdered by Eugene Shauman, son of a Finnish senator. Although unconnected with the terror of the socialist revolutionaries, this act of political vengeance was probably inspired by it—violence is not a part of the Finnish tradition. After shooting Bobrikov, Shauman committed suicide.

These bloody exploits and threats that terror was merely beginning contributed to public unrest and caused dismay in official circles. The liberals, like the revolutionaries, became restless, vocal and, finally, daring. The zemstvos had good reasons of their own for alarm and disaffection. The government had under consideration a project for the taking over by the state of all schools, that is, the elimination of zemstvo schools—the liberals' most cherished creation. A proposal sponsored by Goremykin for the introduction of zemstvo institutions (or, more exactly, a hopelessly truncated version thereof) in the nine western and four other provinces was vetoed by the tsar (1899), presumably under the influence of Witte, who argued in a celebrated memorandum that local self-government, meritorious as it might be in a different political climate, was incompatible with autocracy. Goremykin, a dreary bureaucrat of unimpeachable conservatism, was dismissed (October, 1899), and was succeeded as minister of the interior by a flamboyant reactionary, Sipiagin. In June, 1900, the zemstvos were shorn of their statutory powers for the provisioning of the population, but the near famine of 1901 forced the government to revoke this ordinance for the duration of the emergency. In August, 1900, Sipiagin prohibited communications between zemstvos and municipalities having for their object joint or parallel representations to the government concerning matters outside their jurisdiction. A severe blow to zemstvo finances was a law of June 12, 1901, which limited rates to 3 per cent of the assessed value of real estate, unless special dispensation was granted by the authorities. These policies lent color to persistent rumors that Meshchersky's campaign for the abolition of local self-government was soon to bear fruit.

In the tense atmosphere of the early 1900's government hostility, far from intimidating zemstvo leaders, drove many of them to the conclusion that since autocracy is irreconcilable with social progress the former must give place to representative government under a constitutional monarchy. In spite of official prohibition, a "private" zemstvo conference convened in Moscow in February, 1901. Thereafter such conferences met at frequent intervals, becoming a quasi-permanent institution and the chief organ of liberal opinion. Meanwhile the basis of liberal opposition was broadened. In June, 1902, there appeared in Stuttgart the first issue of *Osvobozhdenie* (Liberation), a journal sponsored by zemstvo constitutionalists and edited, in cooperation with P. N. Miliukov, by P. B. Struve, author of the social democratic manifesto of 1898, who had drifted to the right wing of the socialist movement. The new journal, which was smuggled into Russia, advocated the overthrow of autocracy and the establishment of a constitutional regime. This program was endorsed by the Union of Liberation (Soiuz Osvobozhdeniia), an underground political organization founded at a zemstvo conference in Kharkov in September, 1903, and formally constituted in January, 1904. The union, directed by a council, built up an extensive network of local agencies and enlisted, in addition to zemstvo constitutionalists, many intellectuals and professional men. For the first time in Russian history liberalism was raised to the status of an organized political force.

The government retaliated with customary reprisals which became particularly oppressive after Plehve, a militant and ruthless reactionary, was appointed minister of the interior to succeed the murdered Sipiagin (April, 1902). One of his early measures was the discontinuance of an investigation of farming on the ground that zemstvo statisticians were allegedly politically unreliable. An imperial manifesto of February 26, 1903, acknowledging the state of public unrest, made it clear that no surrender of autocratic powers was contemplated, and outlined a program of social and economic reforms so vague and jejune as to satisfy no one. The zemstvos continued their agitation and, as has already been mentioned, took the leading part in organizing the Union of Liberation. Plehve's retaliatory move was the suspension of the provincial zemstvo of Tver, ostensibly because of the subversive activities of the Tver zemstvo employees, especially schoolteachers (January, 1904).

The outbreak of the Russo-Japanese War (January, 1904) somewhat eased the internal tension. Although the war, caused by a conflict of obscure ambitions in a distant and little-known country, was not popular, there were inevitable patriotic manifestations and a feeling among a large section of the liberal (but not of the revolutionary) opposition that this was not the time for domestic strife. The reconciliation between the government and the liberals, however, proved short-lived. Much to Plehve's chagrin the zemstvos were permitted to organize a union for the relief of wounded and sick soldiers and of the families of war dead. Plehve created innumerable obstacles to the work of the union, and denied confirmation to a score of zemstvo officials, including the very popular D. N. Shipov, who was reelected chairman of the Moscow zemstvo board. The latter decision was all the more capricious because Shipov, although a staunch champion of local self-government, opposed the program of the constitutionalists. The Shipov incident did much to estrange the liberals from the government.

The principal reason for the collapse of the short-lived *union sacrée*, however, was the unforeseen course of military events. At the beginning of the war few in Russia doubted final victory. Opinions differed merely as to whether it would be a short and relatively easy war, or a long and costly war. In actual fact the war proved to be an uninterrupted series of military and naval disasters for which the government was blamed. Many, indeed, came to feel that autocracy rather than Japan was the real enemy. In the heat of political passions the distant battlefields of Manchuria were all but forgotten. The inevitable explosion was precipitated by the assassination of Plehve and the appointment of Prince P. D. Sviatopolk-Mirsky as his successor (August, 1904).

For a high functionary of the ministry of the interior, Sviatopolk-Mirsky was a man of enlightened views. The "political spring," as his brief administration is known, was an attempt at tempering autocracy with the rule of law, and softening the harshness of bureaucratic government by cooperation with moderate liberal opinion. He repealed the more unpopular measures enacted by his predecessors, pardoned a number of political exiles, and announced that his policies would "conform to the spirit of true and broad progress," provided the latter "did not conflict with the existing order." By 1904, however, discontent and disaffection had reached too advanced a stage to be quelled by these well intentioned but paltry gestures, while the partial lifting of police restrictions, instead of promoting reconciliation, favored the onslaught of the opposition forces.

In September, 1904, a conference of Russia's radical and revolutionary groups was held in Paris on the initiative of the newly formed Finnish Party of Active Resistance. Shunned by the social democrats, both Bolsheviks and Mensheviks, but attended by representatives of the Union of Liberation (Struve, Miliukov), the socialist revolutionaries (Chernov, Azef), and by delegates of six organizations of national minorities (Finland, Poland,[6] Georgia, Armenia, and Latvia), the conference formalized the alliance against autocracy which had for some time been under discussion between the left-wing liberals and the revolutionaries. It bound the member organizations to work, by methods left to their discretion, for the overthrow of absolutism, the establishment of a representative government, and the safeguarding of the rights of national minorities.

The liberals, although lacking an agreed program, were in a fighting mood. In October, 1904, the Union of Liberation adopted a threefold plan of action: (1) to induce the zemstvos and their conferences to pass resolutions demanding constitutional government; (2) to carry on political agitation at banquets organized on the pretext of celebrating the fortieth anniversary of the reformed law courts; and (3) to promote professional unions which eventually were to constitute the Union of Unions. Early in November a conference of zemstvo leaders, unauthorized but tolerated by the authorities, met in St. Petersburg and adopted an eleven-point resolution which called for the granting of civil liberties, equality of all citizens before the law, democratization and expansion of local self-government, political amnesty, repeal of the "state of emergency" legislation, and—by a vote of 71 to 27—the summoning of a representative *legislative* assembly. The minority, led by Shipov, favored a *consultative* assembly, while the conference unanimously declared itself against a *constituent* assembly on the ground that the hoped-for constitution should emanate from the Crown.

The zemstvo resolution was the starting point of a nation-wide campaign. In November and December countless zemstvos, municipalities, corporations of the nobility, and other public and private organizations and groups passed resolutions clamoring for constitutional reforms. Some of them, especially the resolutions adopted at political banquets sponsored by the Union of Liberation, went further than the eleven-point program: they demanded not merely a *legislative* but a constituent assembly. The government's reply was the ukase of

---

[6] Poland was represented by two organizations, the Polish National Party and the Polish Socialist Party.

December 12, 1904, which added little to what had been promised by the manifesto of February 26, 1903. Sviatopolk-Mirsky's original draft provided for the broadening of the State Council by the inclusion of members elected by the zemstvos and other bodies. This provision, although approved by a conference of high officials under the chairmanship of the tsar, was struck out by Nicholas on the eve of publication.[7] An official announcement issued simultaneously with the ukase, moreover, blamed the opposition for the state of public unrest and branded its members as enemies of the country. The combined effect of the ukase and the announcement was to widen the gulf between the bureaucracy and unofficial Russia, especially after it became known that the innocuous "elected representatives" provision had been deleted by the tsar.

1905

On December 19, 1904, Port Arthur, Russia's Far Eastern stronghold, surrendered to the Japanese. The consternation created by this staggering defeat was immediately overshadowed by untoward domestic events. Early in January a strike broke out in St. Petersburg and within a few days spread to a number of factories employing tens of thousands of workers. The movement was directed by the Assembly (*Sobranie*) of Russian Workingmen, an association sponsored and financed by the police and headed by the priest George Gapon, who conceived the plan of a dramatic appeal to the tsar. On Sunday, January 9, 1905, columns of workers bearing a petition listing their grievances and wishes (they ranged from minor abuses to the convocation of a constituent assembly) converged from distant suburbs upon the palace square. The authorities were aware of the proposed demonstration. The marchers were peaceful and orderly, some of them, indeed, carried portraits of the tsar and sacred icons. They were stopped, nevertheless, by cordons of troops, and when they refused to

[7] Nicholas's characteristic reversal may be ascribed to the pressure of the empress and Pobedonostsev and to Witte's insidious arguments. Summoned to the palace on Dec. 11, Witte restated his favorite theory with which the tsar was already familiar; namely, that popular representation, however limited, was incompatible with autocracy and would inexorably lead to a full-fledged constitution. The choice, as Witte saw it, was between the abdication of absolute powers and the rejection of Sviatopolk-Mirsky's already approved proposal. The emperor decided on the latter course. Sviatopolk-Mirsky was not informed of the change until after the final decision was made. He tendered his resignation but it was not accepted.

disperse were fired upon. The actual number of victims was probably larger than the official estimate of 130 killed and several hundred wounded.[8]

The "Bloody Sunday" produced a tremendous impression both at home and abroad. Sviatopolk-Mirsky and the higher police officials resigned. To mitigate the sinister effects of the butchery, the tsar received a deputation of workers hand-picked by the newly appointed governor-general of St. Petersburg, D. F. Trepov (January 19). Labor, however, refused to be lured by this naive strategem, and some of the delegates were forced by the resentment of their fellow workers to give up their jobs. The zemstvos, municipalities, and other bodies resumed their agitation for constitutional reforms. Ridden by strikes and political demonstrations, the universities were closed until the autumn. On February 4 the Grand Duke Serge Aleksandrovich, commanding officer of the Moscow military region and the tsar's uncle and brother-in-law—he was married to a sister of the tsarina—was killed by a bomb hurled into his carriage by the socialist revolutionary I. P. Kaliaev, an expelled student and son of a police officer. The assassination was planned by Savinkov, and its perpetrators were shielded from the police by Azef.

Three ill assorted enactments appeared on February 18, 1905. A manifesto written without consultation of any of the ministers except Pobedonostsev inveighed anew against the opposition, and called upon all loyal Russians to rally round the throne. A rescript addressed to Sviatopolk-Mirsky's successor, A. G. Bulygin, announced the emperor's intention to summon "the elected representatives of the people" in order that they may participate "in the preliminary elaboration and discussion of legislative bills," that is, to convoke a consultative representative assembly. A ukase to the Senate upheld the right

---

[8] In spite of the large literature on Gapon, his actual motives remain unclear. His association with the security police went back to 1902, but although he consulted with police officials and received subsidies he was no ordinary *agent provocateur*. Documentary evidence suggests that his real object was to counteract revolutionary influences among the workingmen (even though some of the demands of the January petition were revolutionary) and to organize the loyal elements of labor into patriotic fraternal associations. The tearoom clubs he established were for a time remarkably successful. After Jan. 9 Gapon issued a denunciation of the tsar, the bureaucracy, and the army, was unfrocked (March, 1905), fled abroad and joined the Socialist Revolutionary Party, but soon resumed his relations with the security police and returned to Russia. He was hanged, by order of the central committee of the Socialist Revolutionary Party, in a lonely summer cottage in Finland in March, 1906. The assassination was planned by P. Rutenberg.

of every subject of the Crown "to be heard directly by the monarch" and ordered the council of ministers to examine proposals made by private persons and institutions, for the betterment of public welfare. The ukase appeared to invite and legalize the political agitation which the manifesto roundly condemned. Its practical effects, however, must not be exaggerated (Witte regarded the ukase as meaningless and an empty gesture), although it probably facilitated the propaganda campaign of the opposition, especially among the peasants. Of greater immediate importance was a decree of April 17 which proclaimed the principle of religious tolerance and abrogated the discriminatory laws affecting dissenters.

The pusillanimity and tardiness of official moves favored the more extreme elements of the opposition. By the time the government reluctantly conceded popular representation in an advisory assembly, the bulk of liberal opinion had rallied to the support of a constituent assembly to be elected in accordance with the quadripartite formula: universal suffrage and secret, direct, and equal vote. These slogans were propagated by the Union of Liberation and the fourteen newly founded professional unions [9] which in May, 1905, established a central organ, the Union of Unions (*Soiuz Soiuzov*), under the chairmanship of Miliukov. A similar program was advocated by the Peasants' Union organized by radical intellectuals in July. The zemstvo conferences held in February, April, and May moved, although more cautiously, in the same direction. The May conference elected a delegation which waited on the emperor (June 6), but the gracious audience failed to bring a reconciliation. In an intransigent mood, and regardless of police orders prohibiting the meeting, zemstvo leaders convened in Moscow in July. The conference approved the draft of a "fundamental law" (imperial constitution) which, like a similar proposal issued by the Union of Liberation in October, 1904, embodied the principles of western political democracy, and was widely circulated. An awkwardly phrased resolution proclaimed the intention of the conference "to enter into close contact with the broad masses of the people for the joint discussion of impending political reform" and "for the conquest of liberties necessary to make it effective." The loyal

[9] These were the unions of university professors, lawyers, agronomists and statisticians, doctors, veterinaries, railway employees, journalists and authors, members of zemstvo assemblies, engineers, bookkeeepers and accountants, teachers, pharmacists; also the union for the emancipation of women and the union for the emancipation of the Jews.

opposition was treading the slippery path that leads to revolutionary action.

Developments in Manchuria were not such as to strengthen the position of the government. In February Russia's army suffered a defeat at Mukden, and in the middle of May her fleet was annihilated in the straits of Tsushima. A few days later both belligerents accepted Theodore Roosevelt's offer to enter into peace negotiations. The domestic situation went from bad to worse. Agrarian disturbances broke out in many parts of the country, particularly in the Baltic and western provinces and in the Caucasus, and strikes, which had subsided in the spring, were again numerous and bitter. Early in June troops were used against the strikers in Lodz, and a general strike was declared in Odessa. The socialist revolutionary terroristic groups were again active, one of their more notable victims being the military governor of Moscow, Count P. P. Shuvalov (June 28). Disaffection spread to the armed forces. On June 14 the battleship *Potemkin* of the Black Sea fleet mutinied, raised the red flag, and wrote in the revolutionary annals a blood epic (ably, albeit romantically, portrayed in the well known Soviet film) which ended somewhat ingloriously eleven days later with the surrender of the mutineers to the Rumanian authorities at Constantsa.

The agitation of the opposition and the excesses of the revolutionaries invited retaliation on the part of the supporters of autocracy. The earliest organization of the extreme right was the Russian Assembly (*Russkoe Sobranie*) founded in 1901, an upper-class society for the dissemination of information concerning Russian achievements in art and science. To check mounting discontent, however, the assembly soon engaged in nationalistic and monarchical counter-propaganda, which may in part account for the appearance of ultra-conservative groups in the universities (the so-called academic unions) and throughout the country. Most of the latter were eventually absorbed in the Union of the Russian People (*Soiuz Russkogo Naroda*) established at the end of October, 1905, in St. Petersburg under the leadership of the notorious Dr. A. I. Dubrovin. The program of the union was an elaboration of Uvarov's formula—Orthodoxy, autocracy, and nationality—tinged, however, with hostility towards the bureaucracy as a barrier between the throne and the people. The movement's outstanding characteristic was its militant nationalism and intense hatred of Finns, Poles, and especially the Jews. As these sentiments were shared by Nicholas, who in December, 1905, accepted honorary badges of the union for himself and his son, and by many high officials (Pobedonostsev, Plehve, Goremykin), Dubrovin and his peers were assured of official patronage, of which they made extensive and unscrupulous use. The benevolent attitude of the authorities might explain the union's success in building up within a short time a network of some 3,000 local agencies. Most of its following came from the lower middle class, small tradesmen, minor government officials, and the clergy. The ultra-nationalistic leaders were, with rare exception, men of low intellectual and moral standards who did not hesitate to play up the baser instincts and prejudices of the masses.

The prominence of the Jews in the revolutionary movement made them an easy target of the reactionary clique. Although anti-Semitism flourished under Alexander III, few pogroms occurred from 1881 to 1903. The spell was broken on Easter Day (April 6) of the latter year, when a wholesale massacre of the Jews and looting of their property took place in Kishenev, Bessarabia. For two days a delirious mob had control of the city; over seven hundred dwelling houses and six hundred business establishments were ransacked, the number of victims killed and injured running into hundreds. The attack was planned and provoked by a group of anti-Semites led by P. A. Krushevan, editor of the Jew-baiting sheet *Bessarabets* (The Bessarabian), which used the apocryphal story of a ritual murder to incite the populace.[10] The police and the troops did not intervene until the end of the second day of rioting. While the pogrom was condemned by the government and by all shades of opinion, and the rioters were tried and suffered various punishments, there was much evidence to support the widely held view that the outbreak could have been prevented had the authorities so wished. The Kishenev pogrom was followed by one in Gomel (August, 1903) and by waves of pogroms in southern and western Russia in the autumn of 1904 and in the spring and summer of 1905. As in Kishenev, the riots were instigated by ultra-nationalistic groups and were made possible by the ineptitude and, sometimes, the con-

---

[10] Krushevan's brand of anti-Semitism was based on religious and not on racial grounds. He urged that the Jews should be given the option either to join the Russian Church or to be deported. Converted Jews were to be freed from all disabilities; even titles of nobility and decorations were to be distributed among the educated converts—by lot.

nivance of the authorities. These savage and despicable manifestations of racial intolerance added nothing to the stability and prestige of the monarchy which their perpetrators ostensibly had at heart.

The law of August 6, 1905, defining the procedure for elections to the State Duma, as the consultative assembly announced in February was to be known, was greeted with a chorus of abuse and derision. The franchise, based on the familiar theory that the peasants were devoted to the Crown, was so framed as to ensure, through an intricate system of indirect voting, a large representation of the peasantry, while high property qualifications disfranchised the bulk of the urban population, especially intellectuals and industrial workers. The conservatives disapproved both of the proposed assembly and of the method by which it was to be chosen. The opposition was of one mind that the Duma should be boycotted or should be used for propaganda purposes and the assembly "torpedoed from within." The government, moreover, had to bear the onus of the unpopular peace settlement agreed upon in the middle of August, although its terms were less severe than might have been expected in view of Russia's undistinguished war record.

A surprise law of August 27, 1905, granted antonomy to the universities. Irresistible outside pressure and the broad interpretation put on this loosely worded enactment by university authorities (now elected by academic corporations) turned the lecture halls into public forums where freedom of speech and of assembly blossomed immune from police intervention. Revolutionary oratory flowing from the rostrums deserted by the professors inflamed the imagination of eager audiences in which university students mingled with government officials, tradesmen, artisans, factory workers, soldiers, starry-eyed society matrons, housewives, and even children. The St. Petersburg Soviet of Workers' Deputies soon to be established, according to its president G. S. Khrustalev-Nosar, was a by-product of university autonomy.

Political tension having reached the breaking point, the long-expected mass action took the form of a general strike. In the second half of September the Moscow printers and bakers laid down their tools, while a sympathetic strike was declared in St. Petersburg, but by October 5 the movement seemed to subside. On October 7, however, a railway strike organized by the railway union, an association that functioned openly, although lacking official recognition, broke out in Moscow, and within a few days spread to the entire network, engulfed the telegraph and telephone services, and paralyzed practically all industry. The strikers' original demands—a constituent assembly, repeal of the "state of emergency" legislation,[11] civil liberties, and the eight-hour day—were soon supplemented by purely revolutionary ones: a democratic republic, political amnesty, disarming of the police and troops, and the arming of labor. This program was endorsed by the professional unions. Excited crowds carrying red banners and revolutionary posters roamed the streets. Banks, shops, schools, law courts, government, zemstvo, and municipal offices, even pharmacies and hospitals, closed their doors. There were no newspapers, no electricity, no gas, and in some localities no water. Barricades were erected on the streets of Kharkov, Ekaterinoslav, and Odessa. The economic and business life of the country came to a standstill.

On October 13 the St. Petersburg Soviet of Workers' Deputies convened for the first time, with thirty or forty delegates present; by the end of November their number had risen to 562. Theoretically there was one delegate per 500 workers, but actually, according to Leon Trotsky, one of the Soviet's leading figures, some of the deputies represented much smaller groups. The revolutionary parties had engineered the elections, and they dominated the Soviet and the executive committee it chose on October 17. The strongest influence was that of the Mensheviks. Lenin did not return to St. Petersburg from abroad until November, and he took little direct part in the work of the Soviet, although he was active behind the scenes. The Union of Unions and other left-wing groups acknowledged the leadership of the self-styled workers' parliament. On October 17 appeared the first number of *Izvestiia* (News), the Soviet's official organ.

On the same day the tsar signed a manifesto transforming Russia into a constitutional monarchy. In the enforced isolation of his country residence at Peterhof, which because of the strike was accessible only by sea, Nicholas since October 9 had been in touch with Witte. In August, 1903, Witte, a severe critic of Russia's Far Eastern policy, was dismissed from the office of minister of finance he had occupied since 1892 and was relegated to the honorary position of president of the committee of ministers. Recalled from semi-retirement in the summer of 1905 to head the Russian peace delegation, he returned to St. Petersburg in September, his reputation greatly enhanced by the

[11] See p. 1091.

Portsmouth Treaty, for which he was rewarded with the title of count, and by the attentions showered upon him in France and Germany, where he had powerful political and financial connections. In spite of his short temper and arrogant manner, Witte had many political friends both among conservatives and among liberals, and was, indeed, regarded as the only man capable of saving the dynasty. The advice he tendered Nicholas in the fateful days of October was to choose between a constitution and a military dictatorship. He was willing (and many said, eager) to head a unified government under a constitution; with a dictatorship, however, in the success of which he did not believe, he refused to be associated. The emperor leaned towards the latter solution, but after his uncle, the Grand Duke Nicholas Nikolaevich, the imperial family's "strong man," tearfully declined the proffered dictatorial powers, and after Witte had rejected a compromise proposal drafted by Goremykin, the tsar reluctantly accepted Witte's liberal program. The manifesto of October 17 written by Witte contained the following provisions: (1) guarantee of fundamental civil liberties—freedom from arrest, freedom of opinion, of the press, of assembly, and of association; (2) promise to amend the law of August 6 by enfranchising the groups excluded from participation in the elections to the State Duma, and to ensure the further extension of the franchise by the new legislative assembly; and (3) announcement of the "immutable rule" that no law should be promulgated without the approval of the State Duma, which was also to exercise effective control over officials appointed by the Crown. The above principles were elaborated in Witte's report, confirmed by the tsar, and issued simultaneously with the manifesto. The ministers were not consulted. According to the minister of finance, V. N. Kokovtsov, he knew nothing of the change until the manifesto was published.

The country, stirred by the October manifesto, responded with conflicting emotions. The conservatives were frankly dismayed. The liberals vacillated between wild enthusiasm and dark premonition that the government was not in earnest and that the manifesto was but an artifice. Miliukov, speaking on the evening of October 17, characterized the manifesto as a great victory but also as "a new stage of the struggle." The revolutionaries scornfully dismissed official promises even though they feared their repercussions on the unity of the revolutionary front. "Witte has come, but Trepov remains," Trotsky, one of the world's greatest pamphleteers, wrote in *Izvestiia*. ". . . The proletariat knows what it does and what it does not want. It wants neither the police thug Trepov, nor the liberal financial shark Witte; neither the wolf's snout, nor the fox's tail. It rejects the police whip wrapped in the parchment of the constitution."

The immediate reaction, however, was one of uncontrollable excitement. Intoxicated with their first taste of liberty, people of every station and age, from sedate gray-haired bureaucrats to factory hands and children, poured into the streets and joined in noisy demonstrations and counter-demonstrations. There were red banners, revolutionary songs, and inflammatory oratory. But there were also demonstrators who carried portraits of Nicholas and marched to the strains of the national anthem "God Save the Tsar." The two factions inevitably came to blows. The right-wing movement, although aided by the police, was not entirely synthetic. The general strike, by creating mass unemployment and disrupting the life of the community, provoked bitterness and resentment. Even before the publication of the manifesto the Moscow students, attacked by an angry mob, barricaded themselves in the university building. After October 17, however, patriotic fervor turned primarily against the familiar scapegoat, the Jews. Between October 18 and 25 hundreds of pogroms swept towns and hamlets in and outside the Jewish pale, the most notable being those of Kiev and Odessa. Organized by ultra-nationalistic groups, condoned and sometimes instigated by the police, the pogroms, with the opportunity for looting, attracted the criminal dregs of society. They inflicted cruel indignities and sufferings on thousands of innocent people, and shocked and antagonized the western world. This was one of the first consequences of the October manifesto which granted civil liberties to all the subjects of the Russian Crown.

The manifesto of October 17, by proclaiming civil liberties which the laws still in force denied or narrowly circumscribed, put the administration in an impossible position and led to temporary government atrophy. Police regulations were no longer enforced. Official censorship became dormant. A new and even more formidable censorship, however, was exercised by the printers' union, which refused to handle publications not to its liking, while scores of radical papers made their appearance and were freely circulated. The flames of revolt blazed throughout the borderlands. Finland, in the throes of a general strike, demanded the restoration of her constitutional liberties; mass demonstrations in Poland clamored for autonomy or independence.

The new government headed by Witte met the wishes of Finland. A manifesto of October 22 abrogated all legislation, beginning with the manifesto of February 3, 1899, to which the Finns objected. A very different treatment was reserved for Poland, where a "state of emergency" was proclaimed in the last days of October in order to combat activities "threatening the unity of the empire." Disaffection made further progress in the armed forces. Kronstadt and Vladivostok mutinied at the end of October, but both uprisings were swiftly suppressed.

The center of revolutionary agitation was the St. Petersburg Soviet, whose example was emulated by soviets organized in Moscow, Odessa, and other cities. It parried the October manifesto by decreeing that the general strike would continue. A strike, however, especially a political strike that brings no immediate economic benefits to the workers, is a double-edged weapon; unduly prolonged it tends to disorganize the ranks of labor, particularly in a country which, like Russia in 1905, has no trade unions. The soviet was forced by a spontaneous back-to-work movement to call off the strike (October 21), but it was made clear that the counter-order was a tactical retreat, not a surrender: the proletariat, it was announced, would "not lay down its arms" until the monarchy had been superseded by a democratic republic. The soviet, accordingly, proceeded to make plans not only for new strikes but also for an armed uprising. This uncompromising program notwithstanding, the soviet was not interfered with, partly because of the state of uncertainty and confusion prevailing in bureaucratic circles and partly, as Witte explains in his memoirs, because he deemed it wise to wait until the soviet had outlived its popularity with the masses of labor. In the meantime the soviet enjoyed a quasi-official status, met freely, issued orders, and negotiated with the head of the government. A partial amnesty granted on October 21 reinforced the ranks of the revolutionaries by permitting the return of many political exiles. It was not, however, regarded as adequate either by the soviet or by the liberal opposition, and accentuated the demand for a full amnesty.

From the teeming industrial cities the revolutionary movement overflowed into the boundless expanse of rural Russia. In the closing months of 1905 the countryside was ablaze with agrarian disturbances. The worst outbreaks occurred in the provinces of Samara, Saratov,

Chernigov, Kherson, and Tambov, and in the Baltic provinces, where the situation was complicated by the secular antagonism between the German landed nobility, on the one hand, and the Latvian and Estonian peasantry, on the other. Over two thousand manor houses were looted and burned, their owners were murdered or fled, and the damage caused in only ten of the most affected provinces was officially estimated at 29 million rubles. The basic causes of the conflagration were the rural arrangements described elsewhere in this book. The outbreak of 1905, however, must in part be attributed to the ukase of February 18 which invited private persons and institutions to make known their wishes for the betterment of public welfare. This dispensation was used for revolutionary propaganda among the peasantry by professional agitators and left-wing zemstvo employees. In August, 1905, the Peasants' Union, an underground organization directed by revolutionary intellectuals, held its first conference in Moscow. It reconvened openly in that city in November (6–12), and adopted a series of resolutions calling for the transfer of all land to the toilers of the soil, the summoning of a constituent assembly not later than February, and a political alliance with the industrial proletariat and organizations "defending the interests of the people." These demands were to be enforced by methods akin to a strike: refusal to comply with army drafts and to work for big landowners. The government, having somewhat recovered its bearings, met the challenge by proclaiming a "state of emergency" in the Baltic provinces and other affected areas, by dispatching punitive expeditions to suppress the riots, and by arresting the entire Moscow bureau of the Peasants' Union (November 14).

The soviet, meanwhile, was losing its hold over labor, if not its revolutionary ardor. A general strike ordered on November 1 met with scant response, and was called off on the 5th. The campaign for the forcible introduction of the eight-hour day by stoppage of work at the expiration of that period was abandoned after a few hectic days. The telephone and telegraph strike (November 16) sponsored by the soviet was no more successful. Witte judged the time opportune for the final showdown: on November 26 the president of the St. Petersburg Soviet, G. S. Krustalev-Nosar, a lawyer and a Menshevik, was arrested. The soviet immediately elected a presiding committee of three members, including Trotsky, and issued an appeal to the armed forces (November 27) together with a "financial manifesto" urging non-payment of taxes and withdrawals of gold (December 2).[12] The eight St. Petersburg papers which published the manifesto were seized by the police. On December 3 the building where the soviet met was surrounded by troops, and all the deputies present were arrested.[13] A substitute soviet was formed at once, but it enjoyed none of the ephemeral prestige of its predecessor. A strike called early in December proved a lamentable failure. Leadership for a while passed to Moscow, where a Soviet of Soldiers' Deputies was organized on December 4 and the supreme revolutionary weapon—armed uprising—was tried on the 10th. The population, however, did not support the insurgents, and a week later a loyal regiment of the guards, brought from St. Petersburg and supported by artillery, crushed the revolt. With the defeat of the Moscow uprising the overt resistance of the revolutionaries came to an end.

The government was still faced with the menace of sedition and disaffection in the armed forces. Serious instances of insubordination occurred among the troops of St. Petersburg, Moscow, Kiev, Reval, and other army and naval bases. In the middle of November a mutiny led by Lieutenant Schmidt flared up in Sevastopol. It was expeditiously suppressed, but not until the cruiser *Ochakov* had been set afire by shore batteries and some two thousand sailors and soldiers made prisoners. An alarming situation developed in the Far East, where hordes of rebellious soldiers of Russia's defeated armies impatiently awaited repatriation, which was delayed by railway strikes and by the low traffic capacity of the Trans-Siberian line. The commanding officers having lost control over their troops, the Trans-Siberian railway for nearly three months was in the hands of an unruly soldiery. Measures for speedy demobilization and the ruthlessness of hand-picked punitive expeditions sent to Siberia succeeded, however, in restoring order by the end of January, 1906.

[12] The manifesto was signed by the soviet and the executive committees of the Peasants' Union, the Social Democratic Party, the Socialist Revolutionary Party, and the Polish Socialist Party.

[13] Of the approximately 300 deputies in the hands of the government, only 52, charged with conspiracy to overthrow the existing order, were put on trial. The case was tried by a civil court, and lasted for two-and-a-half months (September to November, 1906). Fifteen of the defendants, including Trotsky, were sentenced to deportation to Siberia for life; two received brief prison sentences; all others were acquitted. Trotsky began the long trek to Siberia in January, 1907, but escaped before reaching his destination, and on March 2 was back in St. Petersburg. After spending a few weeks in Finland, he emigrated abroad.

The revolution of 1905 was over. Autocracy had foundered in the storm but the monarchy had survived, and the economic and social order emerged from the turmoil practically unscathed. The revolutionary forces were once more driven underground. Yet there was prophetic insight in Trotsky's dramatic summation of the 1905 defeat: *La révolution est morte, vive la révolution.*

CHAPTER XL

NICHOLAS II

The Constitutional Monarchy, 1906–1914

WITTE AND THE CONSTITUTIONAL FRAMEWORK OF 1906

It has often been said that while the representative form of government is the best, it is also the most difficult. The transformation of an ancient autocracy ruled by a huge bureaucratic machine into a democratic polity would be a formidable task under the most favorable conditions; in Russia in 1905–1914 the situation was such as to make the transition particularly difficult. The vast empire of many races was largely illiterate. It had but the scantiest experience of self-government, and no established political parties, which are indispensable to the functioning of democratic institutions. The liberals, although they counted among their leaders men of integrity and intellectual acumen, had still to learn the subtle art of compromise essential to the successful working of the complex mechanics of representative government. Moreover, the constitutional monarchy, born in the crisis of 1905, was heavily handicapped by the persistence of secular bureaucratic tradition and the heritage of rancor and dislocation the abortive revolution left in its wake.

The hastily written manifesto of October 17, its omissions and loose phraseology notwithstanding, supplied a foundation on which a constitutional regime might have been built, provided the principles proclaimed were applied in good faith and the framing of the new institutions was entrusted to men who believed in them and enjoyed the support of an enlightened public opinion aware of the fact that the remodeling of national institutions must, of necessity, be a slow and gradual process. These prerequisites did not exist in Russia. Constitutionalism was distasteful to Nicholas and Empress Alexandra; both developed for Witte, the father of the October manifesto, a dislike that became an aversion. Witte, in spite of the publication of his voluminous and highly indiscreet memoirs and of many of his state papers, remains an enigmatic political figure. He relished picturing himself as a staunch partisan of autocracy and an admirer of Alexander III, to whom he owed his dazzling, though brief, bureaucratic career. Nevertheless he took the leading part in persuading Nicholas to relinquish absolute power, and was looked upon by the tsar as a self-seeking candidate for the presidency of the Russian republic. The tribute Witte paid to Pobedonostsev in his memoirs did not prevent him from removing from office in October, 1905, that "wise elder statesman." The puzzling inconsistencies of Witte's views should not be entirely ascribed to the political maneuvers and the Byzantine atmosphere of the Russian court. His great abilities, rising at times to real statesmanship, were conceded by his severest critics. The essence of his political philosophy would seem to be the conviction that autocracy is incompatible with representative institutions. To Witte absolutism was the highest form of political organization, provided the monarch was endowed with wisdom, integrity, and clear-sightedness, qualities which he wrongly attributed to Alexander III but rightly denied to Nicholas II. In Witte's opinion the tragic impasse reached by autocracy in 1905 left the country no alternative but the introduction of a constitutional regime. Constitutionalism, therefore, was forced upon Witte by the personal failings of Nicholas and by the revolutionary situation, in spite of his predilection for absolutism. The resulting peculiar dualism colored his policies and public pronouncements. His already-quoted memorandum *Autocracy and the Zemstvo,* for instance, might be—and actually was—interpreted, according to the preference of the reader, either as a plea for the abolition of local self-government, or as an insidious argument for the introduction of representative institutions. Insatiable ambition, craving for activity, arrogance, and a most ungenerous attitude towards his political opponents, to whom he invariably imputed the lowest personal motives, were other traits of the founder of Russia's constitutional monarchy.

On his appointment as president of the council of ministers, Witte made a genuine effort to secure the support of liberal opposition. Several seats in the new cabinet were offered to the representatives of the zemstvos, but the negotiations were broken off because zemstvo leaders insisted on the convocation of a constituent assembly elected in accordance with the quadripartite formula. Attempts to win the active cooperation of other liberal groups proved equally fruitless: the persons consulted either declined to accept ministerial responsibilities, or made their participation in the cabinet subject to conditions which Witte regarded as inadmissible. The failure to reach an understanding with the opposition led to the formation of a purely bureaucratic government whose members ranged from the liberal-minded minister of agriculture, N. N. Kutler (who resigned in March, 1906, over the land question, joined the Constitutional Democratic Party, and was among the government's critics in the second and third Duma), to the vicious reactionary, P. N. Durnovo, in the all-important office of minister of the interior, an appointment Witte later regretted. The inability of opposition leaders to compose their differences with Witte and to join the cabinet injured the cause of democracy by depriving the liberals of any direct influence on the framing of new institutions and by strengthening Witte's reactionary proclivities.

Between November, 1905, and the end of April, 1906, when the State Duma met, the legal framework of the constitutional monarchy was hastily evolved in the seclusion of bureaucratic offices and committees. The legislation thus devised violated both the spirit and the letter of the October manifesto. Civil liberties were given a restrictive interpretation. Preliminary censorship of periodicals and books was abolished ("provisional rules" of, respectively, November 24, 1905, and April 26, 1906), but issues of journals containing matters allegedly in contravention of the law could be seized, subject to subsequent review by the courts, by order of administrative "committees on the affairs of the press." This procedure was inimical to the interests of periodical publications, particularly daily papers. Severe penalties, moreover, were provided for such ill defined offenses as the spreading of false information concerning state agencies and officials (decree of February 18, 1906), misrepresentation of the position of state-owned institutions of credit (decree of April 22, 1906), or favorable comments on criminal acts (decree of November 24, 1905). The right of assembly and of association (including trade unions), guaranteed by the "provisional rules" of March 4, 1906, was narrowly circumscribed and enmeshed in a maze of red tape offering wide scope for administrative arbitrariness.

Mistrust of democratic methods permeated the structure of the new legislature, which comprised two chambers, the State Duma and the State Council (manifesto of February 20, 1906). No law could be passed without the approval of both houses and the sanction of the emperor. Deputies to the State Duma, an elective assembly, were chosen under the law of August 6, 1905,[1] which was amended so as to provide a modicum of representation of urban population and industrial workers (law of December 11, 1905). Half of the members of the State Council were appointed by the Crown, the other half were elected by the clergy (six members), the zemstvos (56 members), the nobility (18 members), the Academy of Science and the universities (six members), commerce and industry (12 members), and the Finnish diet (two members). High property qualifications assured the representation of well-to-do classes. The upper chamber was singularly unrepresentative of the country at large: the vast majority both of appointed and of elected members belonged to the wealthy landed proprietors of the central provinces. The right of control over the public purse, parliament's most cherished prerogative, was kept within narrow limits. The budgetary rules of March 8, 1906, modeled on the Japanese constitution, excluded from legislative jurisdiction approximately one-third of national expenditure. The right of interpellation, designed to ensure the legislature's control over the executive, was even less effective. A vote of censure passed by a two-thirds majority was submitted to the emperor, but it did not involve the resignation of the cabinet or of the offending minister. Members of the government were responsible to the emperor alone. Moreover, the council of ministers, established by the decree of October 19, 1905, failed to achieve that unification of administrative policies which was its object. Its collective character remained a legal fiction, individual ministers continued to report to the tsar without consulting their colleagues, ministerial appointments were made by the emperor sometimes contrary to the wishes of the president of the council, and the dismissal of some ministers, including the president of the council, did not lead to the resignation of the cabinet.

On April 23, 1906, four days before the opening of the State Duma, the government issued the so-called Fundamental Laws, a codification of the principal enactments bearing on the constitutional structure of the empire. Witte notes with pride in his memoirs that he was instru-

[1] See p. 1176.

mental in revising the original draft in a sense favorable to imperial prerogatives. Unlike other statutes, the Fundamental Laws could not be amended except on the initiative of the Crown. In legal theory this safeguard was redundant, since the emperor had the right of veto over all legislation; in practice, however, it had the advantage of preventing the State Duma from taking legal steps for the revision of the constitutional arrangements, which is exactly what the opposition intended to do.

POLITICAL PARTIES AND ELECTIONS TO THE FIRST DUMA

The chances for the establishment of a constitutional regime were jeopardized not only by the obstructionism of the government but also by the intransigence of the more influential among the newly founded liberal political parties. Until October, 1905, no political parties, officially recognized and performing constitutional functions, existed in Russia. The Social Democratic and the Socialist Revolutionary parties were purely revolutionary underground organizations. In July, 1905, the zemstvo constitutionalists and the Union of Unions launched a drive for the founding of a liberal party which became known as the Constitutional Democratic, or "cadet" Party, and was led by Miliukov. Its inaugural congress, held in Moscow, coincided with the publication of the October manifesto. The program approved by the first and the second (January, 1906) party congress was a compromise between the views of the left- and the right-wing elements within its fold. The demands for a democratic republic and a constituent assembly elected by universal suffrage and direct vote were dropped. The party declared itself in favor of a parliamentary regime under a constitutional monarchy, demanded that the State Duma exercise full powers in framing the new constitution, and advocated comprehensive social and economic reforms, including the expropriation of large estates, whose owners, however, were to receive equitable indemnification.

The Constitutional Democratic Party represented the left wing of liberal opinion. The less radically-minded members of the opposition set up several political parties, of which the most important was the Union of October 17, or "Octobrists," founded in December, 1905, and led by A. I. Guchkov. The union, as suggested by its name, took its stand on the October manifesto; it criticized the more extreme political demands of the cadets and their social and economic program, especially the expropriation of land. Simultaneously the conservatives, as has already been stated, organized themselves into the Union of the Russian People. With the appearance of political parties and the convocation of the Duma, the zemstvos lost their former position as the chief organs of liberal opinion. A well attended zemstvo conference meeting in Moscow in November, 1905, and dominated by the cadets, demanded that the State Duma should function as a constituent assembly. This pronouncement was the zemstvos' political swan song. Their conferences were discontinued. The Union of Unions and its component elements, too, faded away. During the remaining years of the monarchy political battles were fought primarily on the floor of the new Russian parliament.

With the ebbing of the revolutionary tide and the publication of the statutes defining the constitution and functions of the legislature (February 20, 1906), political discussions centered on the elections to the State Duma announced for March. The limited powers of the lower chamber, with restricted franchise and indirect vote, fell short of the demands of the opposition. The socialist revolutionaries and the social democrats decided to boycott the election. Lenin, misjudging the situation, argued that the country was on the verge of an armed uprising and that participation in elections would merely tend "to disorganize and corrupt the proletariat," foster "constitutional illusions," and divert the forces of the revolution from their main task—the overthrow of the existing order. Party directives, however, were not universally obeyed, and the first Duma had a sprinkling of social democratic deputies, especially from the Caucasus, where the Mensheviks, whose attitude towards the Duma was less uncompromising than that of the Bolsheviks, had a strong following.

The liberal opposition, unlike the revolutionaries, entered wholeheartedly into the electoral campaign. The leading Russian intellectuals, including some of the country's best public speakers, flocked to the ranks of the Constitutional Democratic Party, which fought the election with enthusiasm and skill. The attractive, and to the Russians still novel, slogan coined by Professor Kizevetter—"Political freedom and social justice"—was the theme of eloquent orators throughout the land, and won for the cadets a resounding victory. Their jubilation, however, was dampened by the publication of the Fundamental Laws which greatly narrowed the jurisdiction of the Duma. Miliukov denounced the Fundamental Laws as a "conspiracy against the people" and a violation of the pledges of the October manifesto. Whatever may have been the validity of this contention, it was clear even before the Duma met that the government and the principal opposition party were poles apart and that a conflict between the two was imminent.

Meanwhile Witte, exasperated by the emperor's implacable hostility and by the merciless attacks of conservatives, liberals, and revolutionaries alike, tendered his resignation (April 14), which was accepted and made public on April 22, five days before the convocation of the Duma. His political career was over. His retirement was followed by the dismissal of all the members of the cabinet. Witte was succeeded as president of the council of ministers by the elderly Goremykin (1839–1917), a cynical bureaucrat and a believer in the comforting theory that except the will of the tsar nothing mattered in Russia and that representative institutions and public opinion were but "nonsense" and "idle talk." Such was the statesman chosen by Nicholas to preside over the installation of the constitutional regime. P. A. Stolypin, a newcomer to the St. Petersburg bureaucracy, was the new minister of the interior.

THE FIRST DUMA

The new legislature was inaugurated on April 27, 1906, with an imposing function at the Winter Palace. The tsar's brief address from the throne was dignified and conciliatory but contained no concrete legislative program and offered little to win over the lower chamber. The election law secured, as was its intention, a large representation of the peasantry but failed in its political objective—the creation in the Duma of a large body of conservative opinion. Of the total number of 524 deputies, 200 were peasants, who, however, contrary to the expectations of the conservatives, aligned themselves with the left-wing parties and voted solidly for the most radical solutions of the land question. Although not less than twenty-six parties and sixteen national groups were represented in the Duma, the assembly was dominated by the Constitutional Democratic Party (170 to 180 members) supported most of the time by the Labor Group (over 100 members).[2] The Labor Group (*Trudovaia gruppa* or *Trudoviki*) was formed by the merger of ten factions more radical than the cadets, especially

---

[2] The figures of party membership are somewhat uncertain because of frequent shifts in party allegiance and the arrival of new deputies from Asia, the Caucasus, and other outlying regions.

on the land question, but not committed to socialism or revolution. The national groups—Polish, Ukrainian, Latvian, Lettish, and others —commanded a combined membership of sixty to seventy; they favored national autonomy and tended towards political and economic radicalism. The eighteen social democratic members constituted a separate faction. The conservatives failed to elect a single deputy. The benches to the right of the cadets were occupied by thirty to forty representatives of the moderate wing of the liberal opposition, including a dozen Octobrists. Approximately 100 members, chiefly peasants, had no party affiliation, but voted usually with the radical groups. The cadets set the tone of the assembly. Its president, Muromtsev, and other officers elected by the Duma, belonged to the Constitutional Democratic Party.

In a petulant mood the Duma formulated its program in an "address to the throne" adopted unanimously, with eleven right-wing deputies abstaining. The principal demands were universal suffrage, direct vote, abolition of the upper chamber, parliamentary government, broad amnesty, and a land reform based on the expropriation of large estates. The tsar refused to receive the deputation which was to present the address. On May 13 Goremykin read in a low monotone to a hostile chamber a declaration rejecting all its demands and emphasizing that the proposed solution of the land problem was "totally inadmissible." The stormy session that followed ended with a vote of censure and a request (which, of course, was ignored) for the resignation of the government. The council of ministers, according to the minister of finance Kokovtsov, was of one mind that cooperation with the Duma was out of the question and that dissolution was inevitable. Nevertheless the Duma was permitted to function for another two months, while conflicts multiplied; these revolved chiefly around land reform, abolition of capital punishment, and misconduct of police officials in connection with the treatment of political prisoners and the Jewish pogrom at Bielostok (June 1). The appearance of ministers at the Taurida Palace (seat of the Duma, formerly the residence of Catherine II's favorite Potemkin) was invariably greeted with loud cries of "resign." The dissolution decree was finally promulgated on July 9; the new Duma was to convene on February 20, 1907.

The delay in administering the death blow to the first Duma may be explained by secret political maneuvers aimed at a reconciliation between the Crown and the opposition. In June, 1906, when the conflict with the lower chamber was at its height, the ultra-conservative D. F. Trepov, then governor of the imperial palaces and an intimate of the tsar, made overtures to Miliukov concerning the formation of a cadet ministry. Simultaneously A. P. Izvolsky, minister of foreign affairs, sponsored a somewhat different plan—a "coalition government" comprising both bureaucrats and representatives of the opposition. Nicholas approved, and Izvolsky and Stolypin were directed to open negotiations with the opposition leaders. On June 28 Shipov, a respected public figure and a man of liberal but moderate views, tentatively scheduled to head the coalition government, was summoned by the tsar. Having ascertained in the meantime that the cadets would not participate in the proposed political combination, Shipov urged the formation of a cadet ministry under Muromtsev. He argued that the Constitutional Democratic Party, once in office, would drop its more extreme demands and that the Duma would be willing to cooperate with a cadet government. Nicholas appeared favorably impressed and, indeed, on the verge of making a decision that might have altered the subsequent course of Russian history. His inborn conservatism, palace influences, and the admonitions of Kokovtsov and, presumably, Stolypin, however, defeated the liberals. Instead of the summons to the imperial palace confidently awaited by Muromtsev and Miliukov came the dissolution decree. On the same day Goremykin was dismissed and Stolypin was appointed his successor as president of the council of ministers.

Extraordinary precautions were taken to prevent public disturbances. Contrary to expectations, however, the dissolution provoked no violent reaction except among the members of the Duma. Barred by the troops from the Taurida Palace, some two hundred left-wing deputies, including 120 cadets, journeyed to near-by Viborg, in Finland, where they issued a call to "passive resistance": pending the convocation of the Duma the population was urged to refuse to pay taxes or comply with army drafts. The appeal, however, brought no popular response. Its only practical consequence was the indictment and trial (December, 1907) of the signatories, who were sentenced to three months in prison. This legal action involved disfranchisement and terminated the parliamentary career of the élite of the Constitutional Democratic Party.[3]

---

[3] Miliukov, not a member of the Duma because of his failure to meet the residence requirements of the election law, was the author of the Viborg appeal. The atmosphere at the Viborg gathering was tense, deliberations were cut short by the

STOLYPIN'S ADMINISTRATIVE METHODS

Peter Stolypin, born in 1862, was a country squire rather than a bureaucrat. A Kovno landowner, he was the appointed marshal of the nobility of that province from 1887 to 1902.[4] In 1903 he became governor of the adjoining province of Grodno, and a year later was transferred in the same capacity to Saratov, on the Volga. His ruthless efficiency in quelling the *Jacqueries* of the Saratov peasants won him a deserved reputation for determination and personal courage and led to his appointment as minister of the interior in the Goremykin cabinet in April, 1906. Stolypin's experiences, as landowner and agent of the Russian government, in the western borderland where the upper class was predominantly Catholic and Polish and the peasantry Orthodox and Russian, probably account for his militant pan-Russian nationalism, while his first-hand knowledge of the plight of the farmers convinced him of the necessity of a comprehensive land reform. Nationalism and the emancipation of the peasants from bondage to the land commune became the pillars of his political program. An implacable enemy of the revolution and a conservative, Stolypin in June, 1906, threw his influence against the formation of the proposed cadet ministry, not perhaps unmindful of the fact that the advent to power of Muromtsev or Miliukov would spell the end of his own political career. He was anxious, however, to secure the participation of prominent liberals in a government of which he was to be the head, and on his appointment as president of the council of ministers, an office he combined with that of minister of the interior, he resumed negotiations with the leaders of the liberal opposition. The negative outcome of these conversations was another victory for reaction. Stolypin's was the last attempt on the part of a head of the imperial government to reach an understanding with the opposition. Having failed in his endeavor, he had to be satisfied with presiding over a government consisting mainly of his former colleagues in the Goremykin cabinet.

Stolypin did not share the aversion of officialdom for the Duma. An

---

plea of the Finnish authorities, and many of the deputies signed the appeal against their better judgment, from a misguided sense of solidarity. The appeal was criticized in cadet circles and was disavowed, with some face-saving reservations, by the fourth congress of the Constitutional Democratic Party in September, 1906.

[4] After the Polish rebellion of 1863 elections of marshals of the nobility in the western provinces, including Kovno, were discontinued. Instead, marshals of the nobility were appointed by the central authority.

able and resourceful speaker, he intervened effectively in the debates, and some of his pronouncements made before the house (for instance, "We shall not be intimidated," or, "They want great cataclysms, we want a great Russia"), trite as they may sound today, were worshipfully acclaimed by a not too discriminating nationalistic opinion. Stolypin was sensitive to adulation and applause; the Duma was nevertheless to him a mere accessory to the executive. He leaned heavily on "emergency" legislation, interfered with the freedom of elections, and with blatant disregard for the constitution changed the election law in order to secure a chamber subservient to the wishes of the government.

Legislation under Article 87 of the Fundamental Laws was the principal method used by Stolypin to impose his will upon the legislature. The tsar was empowered by this article to promulgate emergency decrees "during the recess of the State Duma, if exceptional circumstances call for a measure that requires legislative action." Such measures, however, could not make changes in the Fundamental Laws, the statutes of the legislative chambers, or the election law, and they became inoperative unless introduced in the Duma within two months after its convocation and duly approved. This seemingly innocuous provision, which has its counterpart in many constitutions, was extensively used by Stolypin in order to confront the legislature with *faits accomplis*. Although the measures enacted under Article 87 were eventually submitted to the Duma, the fact that they had sometimes been in operation for a protracted period made their repeal extremely difficult. Some of the emergency decrees dealt with surprisingly trivial matters, such as the change in the title of an official from "military governor" to "governor"; others were of paramount importance, for instance, the decree of November 9, 1906, inaugurating revolutionary changes in peasant land tenure. The most flagrant case of abuse of Article 87 occurred in March, 1911, when the State Council rejected a government-sponsored bill providing for the introduction of zemstvos in six western provinces. The bill, sacrificing on the altar of nationalism the principles of the zemstvo act of 1890, favored the peasantry, which was Russian, at the expense of the Polish landowners. Approved by the Duma, it was voted down by the State Council on the ground that by alienating the landed nobility the bill undermined the zemstvos and imperiled Russian influence in an important frontier region. Stolypin, showing a cynical disregard for the intent and spirit of the statute, prorogued both chambers for three days and promulgated the disputed measure under Article 87.

Even greater ruthlessness permeated Stolypin's administrative policies. In 1906–1907 the government was confronted with a situation full of uncertainty and peril. After the defeat of the Moscow uprising the revolution was driven underground, but there was no assurance that it would not rise again. Belief in the imminence of an armed insurrection, which made Lenin scorn elections to the first Duma, was shared by many contemporaries; this was, indeed, the theory behind the Viborg appeal. The authorities had tangible reasons for watchfulness and anxiety. On July 17, eight days after the dissolution of the Duma, a mutiny broke out in the Russian garrison of Sveaborg, Finland; it spread to Kronstadt and to the battleship *Pamiati Azova* (Memory of Azov) of the Baltic fleet, but was suppressed by July 20. There was a powerful resurgence of political terror. In November, 1905, shortly after the October manifesto, the central committee of the Socialist Revolutionary Party decreed, over Savinkov's objection, the temporary suspension of terroristic activities. This directive, however, was not fully obeyed, and the first party congress (December, 1905 to January, 1906) set it aside and ordered the intensification of the terror. According to official data, nearly 1,600 persons (chiefly officials, ranging from generals to village policemen) were killed by the terrorists in 1906, and over 2,500 in 1907. On August 12, 1906, the "maximalists," a newly formed faction of the Socialist Revolutionary Party, blew up Stolypin's summer residence on the Aptekarsky Island. The explosion killed 32 people, including the perpetrators of the crime, and wounded 22, among them the minister's son and daughter, but Stolypin escaped unscathed.[5] The reign of terror would seem to justify strong measures against the revolutionaries. The methods adopted, however, were incompatible with the rule of law (*pravovoi poriadok*) which Stolypin claimed to be the corner-stone of his program.

[5] The central committee of the Socialist Revolutionary Party disavowed the outrage. In October, 1906, the "maximalists," using bombs and guns, carried a successful attack in Fonarny Street, in the center of St. Petersburg, on an official transporting government funds under military escort. The 400,000 rubles thus obtained were used to finance an independent Union of Socialist Revolutionary-Maximalists. The career of this terroristic organization was brief. Arrests forced the liquidation of its central organ in April, 1907, and practically all its local groups disappeared by the end of that year.

Most of the country was put under a "state of emergency" regime [6] reinforced by the formidable law of August 19, 1906. Under the provisions of that act, if the commission of a crime was established beyond reasonable doubt preliminary investigation could be waived at the discretion of the governor-general, or other officials vested with similar powers, and the case tried by a specially constituted military court without the participation of civil or military jurists. The court convened within twenty-four hours after the crime, its deliberations were limited to forty-eight hours, and the verdict—usually the death penalty —was carried out immediately. This summary procedure was extensively used until the spring of 1907, when the law of August 19, which was enacted under Article 87, was permitted to lapse.[7] A circular of September 15, 1906, directed provincial governors to maintain public peace and security "at any cost," and to enroll the services of "private persons in sympathy with the struggle against the revolution," especially those of "patriotic and monarchical organizations." The latter, however, had a well deserved reputation for lawlessness, and were known as the organizers of Jewish pogroms.

Nothing was more detrimental to the cause of decency and orderly government than the license enjoyed by the security police. The use of *agents provocateurs* enmeshed police officials—the supposed custodians of order and legality—in a web of lawbreaking. Stolypin condoned this vicious system, knew of Azef's activities, and appeared to have employed undercover agents to stage political frame-ups. *Agents provocateurs*, however, are a double-edged weapon. One of them, the "maximalist" Solomon Ryss, after being permitted to escape from prison, organized the explosion at Stolypin's summer residence and the Fonarny Street robbery. His treachery somewhat belatedly detected, he was arrested and hanged in 1908. The authorities, however, refused to learn their lesson, as evidenced by Stolypin's death. There were many less spectacular but equally illegal practices indulged in by the police. Civil liberties were flouted by searches, arrests, and deportations without court warrants. Men holding allegedly "undesirable" views were summarily expelled from government service. Private

[6] See p. 1091.
[7] The law was attacked by the opposition, and the appropriate bill was not introduced in the second Duma within the prescribed term (two months after convocation). In a surprise move the Duma passed (April 17) a bill abrogating the law of Aug. 19 three days before it was due to expire. The State Council, however, rejected the bill on technical grounds.

correspondence, including letters of the dowager empress, were tampered with. Witte wrote his memoirs abroad because he knew they were not safe in Russia.

Stolypin did not rely exclusively on suppression and force. In the interval between the first and the second Duma the government prepared a number of bills designed to implement a program of reforms announced in August. Measures regarded as urgent or particularly controversial were enacted under Article 87; others were submitted to the legislature for preliminary examination.

THE SECOND DUMA

The immediate concern of both the government and political parties, however, was the approaching elections (January to February 1907) to the second Duma. The first Duma having demonstrated its efficacy as a public forum, Lenin was among the first to realize that boycott was a mistake. Reversing their former stand, the social democrats and the socialist revolutionaries participated in the elections. The government, too, abandoned the hands-off attitude adhered to by Witte and threw its active support on the side of the Union of the Russian People and other reactionary groups. These organizations, their leaders and publications, were generously financed from secret funds of the ministry of the interior, an unholy partnership that continued until the end of the monarchy. The Constitutional Democratic Party, already weakened by the disfranchisement of the signatories of the Viborg appeal, bore the brunt of the onslaught from left and right. The revolutionaries, particularly Lenin, were unsparing in their denunciations of the cadets. Stolypin, in a secret circular of September 15, 1906, advised provincial governors that a political party may be prohibited "if its aims, although formally within the law, are not sufficiently clear," or if it "shows hostility towards the government." Civil servants were debarred from membership in such parties (circular of September 18). There was much discrimination against the cadets; their clubs were closed and their election meetings broken up by the police. The new situation in which the elections were held was reflected in the composition of the second Duma.

The party lines in the second Duma were more sharply drawn than in the first, and its complexion was more radical. The left wing comprised 65 social democrats, 34 socialist revolutionaries, 14 people's socialists (*narodnye sotsialisty*, formerly a right-wing faction of the Socialist Revolutionary Party), and 101 members of the Labor Group. The number of cadets shrank to 92. The Octobrists and other moderately conservative parties were represented by 32 deputies and the extreme right by 22, among them the fanatical and irrepressible V. M. Purishkevich and the organizer of the Kishenev pogrom, P. A. Krushevan. Some 160 deputies either had no party affiliation or belonged to national or local groups (Poles, 47; Moslems, 31; Cossacks, 17; and so on). The government could muster approximately 90 votes, a situation that augured ill for the future. The brief life span of the second Duma (February 20 to June 3, 1907) was filled with clashes between the right and the left factions, on the one hand, and with acrimonious conflicts between the government and the opposition, on the other. Of the many issues involved, the crucial one was the land question. Stolypin's reform of peasant tenure enacted under Article 87 was a challenge to the program of the cadets and the left-wing groups. The anticipated rejection of the government-sponsored land bill, which was duly introduced in the Duma, was the true, although not the official, cause of dissolution. A less unpopular pretext was to be found. At the end of March the government announced the discovery of a conspiracy to murder the tsar. On May 4 the police raided the rooms of the social democratic deputy I. P. Ozol, and claimed to have obtained evidence of plans for mutiny by the armed forces. The incriminating documents were supplied by an agent of the secret police, Catherine Shornikov. The alleged conspiracy had all the earmarks of a frame-up, although Kokovtsov denies in his memoirs that the government had any knowledge of Shornikov's connection with the police. On June 1 Stolypin requested the Duma to waive the parliamentary immunity of the social democratic deputies, but the chamber demurred and referred the matter to a commission. On June 3, before the commission completed its report, the Duma was dissolved. Simultaneously the government promulgated a new election law.[8]

Stolypin, while plotting the downfall of the Duma, appeared to have retained the belief that a working arrangement with the lower chamber was not beyond the bounds of possibility. He kept in touch with members of the liberal opposition, and as late as June 2 discussed with four cadet deputies, at a fruitless eleventh-hour conference, the ways and

[8] Most of the social democratic deputies were arrested, tried, and sentenced to hard labor or deportation to Siberia. They were liberated after the revolution of 1917.

means of averting dissolution. These political maneuvers notwithstanding, the government had made careful long-range preparations for what amounted to a *coup d'état*. The radicalism of the peasant deputies had shattered the faith of the bureaucracy and court circles in the conservatism of the peasantry. According to Kokovtsov, the revision of the electoral law was undertaken by the ministry of the interior, probably soon after the convocation of the first Duma. In the autumn of 1906 the election bill drafted by the assistant minister of the interior, S. E. Kryzhanovsky, was examined, in great secrecy, by the council of ministers. Its promulgation, without the approval of the legislature, on June 3, 1907, although lamely justified by references to the "historic powers" of the Crown and the tsar's responsibility to God for the welfare of the realm, was an arrant violation of the Fundamental Laws.

THE THIRD AND FOURTH DUMAS

The law of June 3 retained the framework of indirect voting provided by the law of August 6, 1905. Deputies were elected by provincial colleges consisting of delegates chosen separately by four groups: landowners other than peasants, urban population, peasants, and industrial workers.[9] The number of delegates allotted to each group was arbitrary. By the simple device of reducing the number of delegates chosen by peasants and industrial workers, and by increasing that of delegates chosen by landowners, the law of June 3 altered the composition of provincial colleges.[10] Under the act of June 3 the urban electorate was subdivided, on the basis of property qualifications, into two groups which voted separately for delegates to the provincial college, the wealthier but numerically smaller group being allotted the larger number of delegates. The minister of the interior, moreover, was given discretionary powers to split electoral districts into smaller units according to the property qualifications, residence, or nationality of the voters, a dispensation widely and effectively used in the elections

[9] Indirect elections were completed in two, three (industrial workers), or even four stages (peasants). Under the law of June 3 the direct ballot was used only in the cities of St. Petersburg, Moscow, Kiev, Odessa, and Riga. The three- and four-stage elections were unknown to the constitution of any other country.

[10] Under the 1905 law the peasants elected 2,529 delegates, landowners 1,963, and industrial workers 208. Under the 1907 law the respective figures were 1,168, 2,644, and 114. These data do not include the Caucasus, the kingdom of Poland, and Siberia.

to the third and fourth Duma. The 1907 law reduced the total number of deputies to 442, disfranchised the provinces of central Asia, and cut down the representation of national minorities by decreasing the number of deputies allotted to provinces with a substantial non-Russian population. The Duma, according to the manifesto of June 3, was to be "Russian in spirit."

The law of June 3, while violating every canon of democratic elections, served well Stolypin's immediate purpose. The third Duma, the only one to complete its full term (November, 1907 to June, 1912), was dominated by the conservatives. Parties of the right (right, moderate right, and the nationalists) and the Octobrists had approximately 150 members each, the cadets 53, the progressists, a faction akin to the cadets, 28; the social democrats and the Labor Group 14 each. The remaining deputies belonged to national groups (the Polish group was reduced to 11 members) or had no party affiliation. During the lifetime of the third Duma the nationalist faction sponsored by Stolypin increased its membership, at the expense of other right-wing parties, from about 20 to approximately 80. The fourth and last Duma (November, 1912 to February, 1917) was even more conservative than its predecessor. The parties of the right numbered 185 deputies, including 88 nationalists; the Octobrists 97, the cadets 58, the progressists 47, the social democrats 14, the Labor Group 10. The Socialist Revolutionary Party boycotted the elections and was not represented in the third or fourth Duma.[11]

THE TRIUMPH OF REACTION

Although an assembly elected under the law of June 3 was not representative of the true feelings of the country, the third and the fourth Dumas reflected to some extent the shift that had taken place in public opinion. Dispersion of the revolutionaries, weariness, disillusionment, cynicism, and longing for order and "normalcy" brought a swing to the right. The campaign of terror sponsored by the socialist revolutionaries, after having reached its zenith towards the middle of 1907, collapsed by the end of that year. Tracked by the police, the terroristic groups were rounded up and their instigators were arrested

[11] A by-product of electoral wizardry was the increase in the number of priests among the deputies and the shift in their party allegiance. The first Duma had six priests, of whom four belonged to the left. Of the 13 ecclesiastics in the second Duma, eight sat on opposition benches. The third Duma had 45 and the fourth 46 ecclesiastics, all of them members of right-wing parties.

or fled abroad. The central committee of the Socialist Revolutionary Party, which after the amnesty of October, 1905, had operated in Russia, emigrated at the end of 1907. The exposure in 1908 of Azef's treachery, moreover, while highly embarrassing to the government, very nearly wrecked the socialist revolutionary movement. Social democracy fared almost as badly. Torn by inner dissensions, its membership depleted by mass arrests, the Social Democratic Party broke into small uncoordinated groups whose sporadic attempts at propaganda met with scant response from the workers. Forced to admit that the "revolutionary situation" was over, Trotsky and, in December, 1907, Lenin took the road of exile, which was to last for ten years. Stalin, arrested in March, 1908, was deported to Vologda. By the spring of 1908 nearly all revolutionary leaders were in prison, in Siberia, or abroad.

Liberalism, like the revolutionary movement, was in full retreat. Many of the zemstvos, traditional strongholds of liberal opposition, passed under the control of the conservatives. Outstanding zemstvo liberals, such as Prince G. E. Lvov, failed to secure re-election. Reaction was triumphant all along the line. Under the high patronage of the tsar and the Grand Duke Nicholas Nikolaevich ultra-conservative organizations multiplied and became more vocal and daring. Prominent among them was the Council of the United Nobility (*Soiuz Obedinennago Dvorianstva*) founded in May, 1906, but the most active role was retained by the Union of the Russian People. Disagreement between Dubrovin and Purishkevich, respectively president and vice president of the Union of the Russian People, led to a split and the formation in 1908 of a rival Union of Michael the Archangel, led by Purishkevich. The influence enjoyed by the Union of the Russian People is all the more significant because its criminal activities, to say nothing of the pogroms, were a matter of public record. Dubrovin and his confederates, among them A. E. Kazantsev, a member of the security police, plotted and carried out the murders of two cadet deputies to the first Duma, M. I. Hertsenstein (June, 1906) and G. B. Iollos (March, 1907), as well as two unsuccessful attempts against Witte (January and May, 1907). These sinister exploits were permitted to go unpunished. Acknowledging an avalanche of telegrams from the local agencies of the Union of the Russian People clamoring for the dissolution of the second Duma, the emperor referred to the union as "the mainstay of the throne" and the standard-bearer of "legality and order."

NATIONALISM

Stolypin's land reform, an important landmark in Russian history, will be discussed in the next chapter. Nationalism, the second major element of his program, took the all too familiar form of persecution of national minorities. The representation of the borderlands in the Duma was drastically reduced by the law of June 3, 1907. The western-provinces zemstvo act of 1911 disfranchised the Jews and, by segregating voters into electoral colleges on the national principle, assured Russian predominance in zemstvo institutions. The act provided, moreover, that the majority of members of zemstvo boards and of zemstvo employees must be of Russian nationality, and encouraged the participation of the Orthodox clergy in zemstvo work. There were persistent attempts at forcing upon the minorities the use of the Russian language. Instruction in Ukrainian schools was given in Russian; and although periodicals, books, and plays in Ukrainian were permitted, the hostility of the government towards the Ukrainian national movement (suspected of separatist tendencies chiefly because of the autonomy enjoyed by the Ukrainians in the adjoining Austrian provinces) was unmistakable. This unintelligent, chauvinistic nationalism found its fullest expression in the Polish-provinces municipal government bill passed by the fourth Duma (that is, after Stolypin's death) but rejected by the State Council. The bill disfranchised the Jews, who formed a substantial portion of the urban population in Russian Poland, and it prescribed the exclusive use of the Russian language in municipal councils.

Incursions were made upon the liberties of Finland, whose constitution was modernized in July, 1906, by the introduction of universal suffrage instead of representation by "estates" (nobility, clergy, burghers, and peasants). That the revolution of 1905 and the stubbornness of the Finns had forced the abrogation of the unconstitutional manifesto of 1899 [12] was not forgotten by the Russian nationalists, who, with the St. Petersburg government once more firmly in the saddle, returned to the charge. A law of June 17, 1910, approved by the Duma and the State Council, provided that legislation affecting Finland should be enacted by the Russian legislature "if its effects are not limited to the internal affairs of that region." The Finnish diet was

[12] See pp. 1179–1180.

called upon to pass on such bills in an advisory capacity. The list of questions deemed to be of "imperial interest" included Finland's contribution to the Russian budget, taxation required to raise that revenue, army service, school curriculums, regulations bearing on the right of association and assembly, and so on. The law of June 17, in violation of the Finnish constitution, was promulgated without being submitted to the Finnish diet, which would have rejected it. This unwarranted curtailment of Finland's liberties embittered and antagonized the law-abiding and freedom-loving Finns.

The Jews, perennial victims of belligerent nationalism, derived no benefit from the illusory promises of the October manifesto, except that, by what seems almost like an oversight, they were entitled to participate in Duma elections and were eligible to serve in that body. In October, 1906, the council of ministers submitted to the tsar proposals for the liberalization of the anti-Jewish legislation. There was no question of emancipation, but merely of the removal of those discriminatory measures which experience had proved to be unenforceable and conducive to widespread corruption. The council of ministers argued that a conciliatory gesture towards the Jews would take off the edge of anti-Russian propaganda abroad and would weaken the opposition of powerful financial Jewish interests to Russian foreign loans. After a delay of several weeks the tsar rejected the proposals; the argument of the council of ministers, he wrote to Stolypin, was "entirely convincing," but "an inner voice" which "has never yet deceived me" prevented him from giving his consent. This being the case, Jewish disabilities were retained and, indeed, extended. To the discriminatory legislation already noted was added the otherwise commendable law of June 15, 1912, which restored the justices of the peace (abolished in 1889) but made the Jews ineligible for that office. Prior to 1912 there was nothing in Russian law to exclude Jews from the judiciary, although none were appointed to the bench in the reigns of Alexander III and Nicholas II. The crudest and truly medieval manifestation of anti-Semitism was the celebrated case of Mendel Beilis, who was accused of ritual murder. From March, 1911, when the body of the alleged victim of Jewish fanaticism was discovered, to October, 1913, when Beilis was tried and acquitted, and indeed long afterwards, the validity of ritual charges was heatedly discussed in the Russian press. I. G. Shcheglovitov, minister of justice from 1906 to 1915, was the master mind behind the prosecution. Nationalism, as understood by Stolypin and his disciples, far from strengthening the empire, worked for its dissolution.

STOLYPIN'S MURDER, KOKOVTSOV, AND GOREMYKIN

Viewed in terms of its immediate objectives, Stolypin's policy might appear as eminently successful. The revolution was defeated. The land reform, although not approved by the Duma until June, 1910, wrought profound changes in the economic and social structure of rural Russia. The third Duma was as cooperative and docile as its two predecessors were unmanageable and recalcitrant. The only serious conflict with the legislature—that over the western zemstvos—was with the upper chamber. The radical movement, indeed, became a negligible factor, and attacks on Stolypin came from the extreme right, which accused him of excessive liberalism. His boldness in handling the western zemstvos crisis in March, 1911, when by threat of resignation he exacted from the tsar the prorogation of the legislature and the suspension of two members of the State Council (V. F. Trepov and P. N. Durnovo) who led the opposition to the bill, did not, however, improve his relations with either the monarch or the chambers. The position of the emperor was particularly awkward because Trepov had informed him in advance—and without meeting with any objection—of his proposed stand on the zemstvo bill. Stolypin's high-handed action was condemned by the press of every shade of opinion; Nicholas was humiliated and resentful, and court influences inimical to Stolypin came to the fore. By the summer of 1911 his dismissal was a foregone conclusion, but fate willed otherwise. On September 1 he was shot and mortally wounded during a gala performance held in the imperial presence at the Kiev opera house. He died five days later. His assassin, Dimitry Bogrov, was a member of a revolutionary group and an agent of the security police.

Stolypin was succeeded as president of the council of the ministers by V. N. Kokovtsov, minister of finance from 1904 (except for the brief interval of Witte's administration), an office he retained after his appointment to the presidency of the council. A man of ability and culture, but a bureaucrat to the core, Kokovtsov dwells complacently in his memoirs on his harmonious relations with the third and fourth Dumas and on the success of his polished discourses delivered in the chamber. His real attitude towards representative government, however, was more accurately and tersely expressed in his celebrated repartee, "Thank God, we still have no parliament" (April 24, 1908). It was during his administration that R. V. Malinovsky, a member of the central committee of the Social Democratic Party and an agent of the security police, was elected to the fourth Duma with the connivance of the authorities. Malinovsky, a Bolshevik and chairman of the Duma social democratic faction, suddenly resigned and went abroad in May, 1914, when the police terminated his employment. The true reason for his seemingly inexplicable withdrawal from the Duma did not come to light until much later. In 1918 he was tried and executed by the Soviets. The Malinovsky episode gives the measure of the bureaucracy's contempt for representative institutions.

The years 1911–1914 brought two significant developments in the domestic situation: the ascendancy of Rasputin, as manifested in the appointments to higher offices, and the growing awareness of his influence by the public. In 1911 V. K. Sabler, a Rasputin appointee, became chief procurator of the Holy Synod. Scandals in Church administration involving Rasputin and an oddly assorted array of churchmen, from bishops to errant monks, received much publicity in spite of the emperor's efforts to keep them out of the newspapers. In March, 1912, the Octobrist leader Guchkov and the reactionary Purishkevich denounced Rasputin from the rostrum of the Duma. The attacks were renewed later in connection with the discussion of the budget of the Holy Synod. The depraved Siberian peasant had become a factor in Russian politics, and incidentally contributed to the revival of opposition sentiments among even the moderate groups in and outside the Duma.

At the end of January, 1914, Kokovtsov, created a count, was sent into retirement. The presidency of the council devolved again on Goremykin, then seventy-five years old, a senile and futile bureaucrat whose only qualifications for office were his blind devotion to the tsar and his intimacy with Rasputin. It was under his undistinguished leadership that Russia entered the great war.

CHAPTER XLI

NICHOLAS II

Economic and Cultural Developments, 1894–1914

✳

PUBLIC FINANCE

The establishment of the State Duma, its limitations notwithstanding, may well be regarded as an important step towards the modernization of the monarchy. In the two decades preceding World War I similar transformations were taking place in other spheres of national life.

No other reform, perhaps, was of greater economic import than the stabilization of the currency. The parsimonious policies of Bunge and Vyshnegradsky, who used the printing press sparingly and accumulated substantial reserves of precious metal, together with the fortunate fact that from 1878 to 1904 Russia was not engaged in any major war, permitted abandonment of the inconvertible paper currency in favor of linking the ruble to gold. The monetary reform, which extended over a period of six years, from the enactment of preliminary measures in 1893 to the codification of monetary legislation in 1899, comprised two main features: (1) the devaluation of the ruble to two-thirds of its former gold value; this was achieved by changing the denomination of gold coins (authorized by an imperial order of May 26, 1895, but not actually issued at the time) from 5 and 10 rubles to, respectively, 7.5 and 15 rubles while retaining their former weight and fineness (ukases of January 3 and November 14, 1897); and (2) convertibility of the paper ruble into gold *at par* and the establishment of a statutory ratio between the volume of paper currency in circulation and the size of the gold reserve. The latter was to represent not less than 50 per cent of the paper circulation up to a limit of 600 million rubles. Issue of paper currency in excess of 600 million rubles was to be covered in full, that is, ruble for ruble, by an increase in the gold reserve (ukase of August 26, 1897).

The reform was carried out with determination and skill by Witte, the new gold coins being, indeed, nicknamed "Wittekind" and "Mathilde d'or" after the minister of finance and his wife, Mathilde. Both devaluation and stabilization met with considerable opposition, especially on the part of the landed nobility whose estates were heavily mortgaged and who feared the adverse effects of the new currency on Russian grain exports. Devaluation, an unfamiliar device at the end of the nineteenth century, was criticized on the ground that it was a form of bankruptcy and therefore incompatible with national dignity and detrimental to Russia's credit. Many of the supporters of stabilization, moreover, favored the silver standard or bimetalism because, it was argued, a poor country such as Russia could ill afford the luxury of a currency based on gold. The opposition to Witte's proposals in the State Council was so strong that the minister of finance enacted most of the monetary measures by imperial decrees, without their preliminary examination by the council as required by law. The rate of devaluation was roughly equal to the then prevalent ratio of the paper ruble to the gold ruble (the former being quoted in 1894–1896 at 66 to 67 metal copecks), and permitted introduction of the new currency with a minimum disturbance of the price level, wage scales, and other financial arrangements; outside the small group of people interested in monetary questions the reform passed almost unnoticed.

The advantages of a stable currency based on gold need no elaboration. The Russian monetary reform, nevertheless, was open to criticisms on both technical grounds and those of economic policy. The management of the monetary system was entrusted to the State Bank, whose statute was amended but not thoroughly revised. The bank enjoyed none of that freedom from government interference which is an essential prerequisite for the proper functioning of a bank of issue. The international financial position of Russia, moreover, was such as to make the maintenance of the gold standard difficult and burdensome. In the closing years of the nineteenth century Russian annual payments abroad on account of interest on foreign loans amounted to some 150 million gold rubles, and another 75 million rubles were spent by Russians traveling abroad, while the domestic production of gold was approximately only 40 million rubles. To prevent a disastrous outflow of gold, which would have jeopardized the gold standard, the difference between the sums due abroad and domestic gold production had to be made good from other sources, chiefly foreign loans and the excess of exports over imports. The piling up of foreign indebtedness, not for productive purposes but for meeting past obligations, is obviously not a wholesome method of public finance or one that could be depended on indefinitely. The building up of a favorable balance of trade by reducing imports and by fostering exports became, therefore, the corner-stone of Russian international economic policy. It found expression in the intensification of an already aggressive protectionism and in the relentless drive for expanding the export of grain, the principal commodity shipped by Russia to foreign markets. The sinister dictum attributed to Vyshnegradsky, "We may go hungry but we must export grain," might well have been uttered by his successors Witte and Kokovtsov. The maintenance of Russian credit abroad and the preservation of the gold standard were, indeed, among Kokovtsov's chief preoccupations.

The Japanese war and the revolutionary upheaval of 1905 subjected the Russian monetary system to a severe strain. The circulation of paper currency, which stood at 578 million rubles on the eve of the war, increased to 924 million on the conclusion of peace, while the volume of gold coins in circulation declined from 775 million to 654 million rubles. Yet the State Bank did not formally exceed its statutory power of issue, although it used the questionable expedient of reckoning as a part of its metal reserve the gold held on its account by correspondents abroad, a practice permitted by the monetary legislation of some European countries but not sanctioned by the Russian law. At the end of 1905 the decline in revenue and the outflow of gold from the treasury made the position of the ruble so precarious that the government imposed a limit on individual withdrawals of gold and prepared a decree suspending convertibility. The ebbing of the revolutionary tide and a timely large foreign loan, however, restored the position of the treasury and made the suspension of convertibility unnecessary. The gold standard was maintained until the outbreak of the First World War.

Primarily because of large outlays on the building of railways and the cost of the Japanese war, the public debt (exclusive of railway loans guaranteed by the government and inconvertible paper currency) rose from 4,905 million rubles in 1892 to 6,679 million in 1903, and to 9,055 million in 1910. From 1908 to the end of 1913, however, few government loans were floated, and by January 1, 1914, the debt, owing to amortization, declined to 8,825 million rubles. In 1913 the service of the debt (424 million rubles) represented 13.7 per cent of the total expenditure. Students of Russian public finance have detected in the closing years of the empire a trend towards the lessening of dependence of the treasury on foreign money markets. While the bulk of the funds invested in Russian government securities prior to 1908 came from abroad, the situation would seem to have been reversed in later years. Although no comprehensive and reliable figures on the distribution of Russian government securities between domestic and foreign investors are available, it is believed that on the eve of the First World War more than 50 per cent of such securities were in Russian hands. It should be noted, however, that a Russian consolidated loan for the huge amount of 1,250 million rubles was issued in France in January, 1914, and was subscribed, with the approval of the French government, by a French banking syndicate.

The credit position of a country, according to the traditional view, depends on its ability to live within its means. A cursory examination of the Russian state budget prior to World War I suggests the pleasing picture of tidiness, mounting prosperity, and conservative financial administration. The total expenditure increased from 1,056 million rubles in 1890, to 1,889 million in 1900, 2,596 million in 1910, and 3,382 million in 1913.[1] Both Witte and Kokovtsov were firm believers in the homely virtue of balancing the budget, and through the entire period of their administration of Russian finance (1892–1913), with the exception of the war and revolutionary years 1904–1906, public accounts were invariably closed with a surplus. The rate of increase of public revenue was particularly notable in 1909–1913, when aggregate receipts, classified as "ordinary," rose by nearly 1,000 million rubles. The financial wounds inflicted by the Japanese war and the 1905 revolution were healed with speed and apparent ease. Practically the entire cost of the war (2,450 million rubles) was defrayed by borrowing, a mere 177 million rubles being met from the general revenue, that is, by curtailing expenditures and raising the tax rate. Moreover, in spite of the limited control exercised by the legislative chambers over the public purse, the budget was no longer a closely guarded prerogative of the bureaucracy. The budget speech of the minister of

[1] In 1905, during the Japanese war, budget expenditures rose to 3,204 million rubles, but declined sharply after the termination of hostilities.

finance was the occasion for a full-dress debate in both the State Duma and the State Council, and was widely and critically discussed in the press.

A closer study of Russian budget methods, however, tends to dim the heartening picture of financial bliss. Witte mournfully noted in his memoirs that while he achieved brilliant success in reorganizing public finance, he "could do very little to improve the economic well-being of the people," a failure for which, of course, he blamed others. Kokovtsov, also in his memoirs, showed less restraint and poorer judgment in claiming a major share of credit for Russia's economic progress. The balancing of the budget, desirable as it is, was achieved by methods not likely to commend themselves to students of public finance. At the end of Kokovtsov's administration, nearly four-fifths of the revenue was derived from indirect taxation, a much higher ratio than that prevailing in other major European countries. The budget leaned heavily on the yield of the state monopoly of spirits, which was introduced in four provinces in 1893 and by the turn of the century was extended to practically the entire territory of the empire. In 1913 the monopoly operated 328 wholesale and 25,733 retail stores which sold some 290 million gallons of alcoholic beverages (vodka). The earnings of the monopoly were steadily rising, and over the period 1904–1913 yielded the treasury an aggregate of 5,329 million rubles; in 1913 the receipts from that source reached the imposing figure of 899 million rubles, or 28 per cent of the total revenue (3,417 million rubles), the largest single item on the revenue side of the budget.

It was foolish to argue, as some did, that the state monopoly of spirits was the actual cause of the drunkenness prevalent in Russia. The average consumption of alcohol per head in that country was substantially lower than in France, Great Britain, Germany, or Belgium. The reasons for Russian intemperance were the drinking habits of the muzhiks, who, according to one authority, drank "irregularly and spasmodically," and the almost exclusive use of strong intoxicants —vodka—instead of the milder wine and beer. It was plausibly held by the supporters of the monopoly that the distribution of alcoholic beverages through the channels of private trade would deprive the government of a substantial revenue without conferring any corresponding benefit on the community and, indeed, was likely to lead to the worst abuses. Nevertheless a financial system that lent itself to the exploitation of the drinking proclivities of the population was open to objections on moral, social, and economic grounds. The problem of promoting temperance was brought to the fore by a bill which originated in the State Duma and came up for discussion in the State Council in November and December, 1913. Witte, the proud and unrepentant father of the monopoly, delivered a bitter attack on the administration of that institution by Kokovtsov, whom he accused of being concerned exclusively with the promotion of the sales of vodka, irrespective of their effect upon public health and morals. For once Witte's views were shared in high places. On January 29, 1914, Kokovtsov was dismissed. An imperial rescript addressed on the same day to P. L. Bark, the new minister of finance, spoke of the "distressing picture of impoverishment, desolation of homes, and economic decay, inevitable consequences of drunkenness," which the emperor had observed during his journey throughout Russia. The rescript called for "drastic reforms" and declared that "the welfare of the treasury should not be made dependent on undermining the moral and economic forces of a great number of our loyal subjects." This pronouncement was a blunt condemnation of the financial policy pursued from the beginning of the reign. The inspirer of the temperance crusade, according to Kokovtsov, was Rasputin. An inveterate drunkard, he could speak with authority on the ill effects of intemperance, and he sensed, of course, that the proposed policy would appeal to the tsar and the tsarina. Bark, a Rasputin appointee, inaugurated accordingly a perfunctory program of measures for the reduction of drunkenness, but he does not seem to have contemplated the abolition of the monopoly. With the mobilization of the Russian army in July, 1914, liquor stores were temporarily closed, and in August the sale of intoxicants was prohibited, thus eliminating the chief source of state revenue.

THE LAND REFORM

Great as were the evils of drunkenness and dismal as was the poverty of the peasant masses, the Rasputin-inspired picture of rural conditions outlined in the rescript to Bark would seem to have been unfair and unduly harsh. In the opening years of the twentieth century the government, in its approach to the land question, displayed unusual boldness and imagination, and carried out reforms which basically altered the economic and legal status of the peasantry. The familiar features of agriculture in the post-emancipation period—the low yield of the land, depressed living standards, accumulation of arrears by the peasantry because of taxes and redemption payments, impoverishment of the landed nobility and, above all, recurrent disastrous failure of crops and sporadic outbursts of agrarian unrest—clearly called for remedial action. Nevertheless, for nearly a decade after the accession of Nicholas II the preservation of the existing land arrangements and the bolstering of the village commune, one of the chief obstacles to agricultural progress, remained, as under Alexander III, the immutable foundation of official policies. In 1892 the aggregate arrears due to redemption payments alone reached the impressive figure of 72 per cent of the annual assessment,[2] the arrears of individual provinces varying from 10 per cent of the annual charge to as much as 562 per cent (province of Orenburg). By a law of February 7, 1894, issued in the reign of Alexander III, the repayment of arrears was permitted over a term of years after the expiration of the statutory amortization period (forty-nine years). The scope of this law was broadened under Nicholas II by allowing, at the request of the village communes, the reassessment of the entire outstanding redemption debt (that is, arrears and installments not yet due) over periods of fifty-six, forty-one, and twenty-eight years, extending the regime of redemption payments well into the 1950's (law of May 13, 1896).

Meanwhile several bureaucratic committees trod wearily the beaten path of their innumerable predecessors in the futile endeavor to find a solution of the agrarian problem within the framework of traditional policies. A committee on the needs of the landed nobility, established in 1897, met for nearly five years, but produced nothing except a stillborn law (1899) permitting noble landowners to entail their estates for the duration of two generations. Equally barren of results were the labors of a committee on the impoverishment of the central provinces of the black-soil belt (1899–1901) which reached the fatalistic conclusion that the regrettable shrinkage of the per capita size of peasant allotments, due to the growth of the population, "was inherent in the nature of things." The poor harvest of 1901 spurred the bureaucracy to new efforts: in November of that year a committee "for the study of the impoverishment of the central provinces in connec-

---

[2] The above figure is average for the whole of Russia except the western provinces, where, it will be remembered, the emancipated serfs were given more generous treatment (larger allotments and smaller redemption payments) than in the other parts of the empire.

tion with the development of the other parts of the empire" was created under the chairmanship of Kokovtsov. After spending two years in collecting statistical data, the committee held a plenary session in October, 1903, only to register sharp disagreement between the representatives of governmental departments and those of the zemstvos. The demands of the latter for political, social and economic reforms were ruled out by Kokovtsov as outside the committee's terms of reference, and the anodyne resolutions finally adopted dealt with such relatively non-controversial matters as financial assistance to the zemstvos, promotion of cottage industry, internal colonization, and the scaling down of redemption payments.

A greater sense of reality was shown by a special conference "on the needs of agricultural industry" proposed by Witte in 1898 but not convened until January, 1902. Under the energetic chairmanship of Witte the conference set up some six hundred local—provincial and county—committees to frame proposals for the reorganization of rural Russia. Although the special conference was a bureaucratic body and the local committees consisted of officials (including members of the zemstvo executive boards), an opportunity for the untrammeled expression of local opinion was provided by the widely used powers of the chairmen of the provincial and county committees (respectively, provincial governors and county marshals of the nobility) to consult "informed persons." The work of the local committees, begun in the summer of 1902, was completed early in 1903, and their reports were speedily published in fifty-eight volumes. This huge compilation threw considerable light on the state of public opinion concerning the agrarian problem. A cardinal point submitted for the discussion of the local committees was the issue of communal tenure versus private ownership. A substantial proportion of the committees declared itself in favor of the abolition of the village commune, although there was a wide divergency of views as to the manner in which transition from communal to individual tenure was to be effected. In the late 1890's Witte, once a supporter of the village commune, was in the forefront of its opponents. To the ultra-conservatives, however, the village commune was the essence of Russia's historical tradition and the mainspring of the police state. The conflicting influences brought to bear upon the tsar account for the inconsistencies of official pronouncements and policies. An imperial manifesto of February 26, 1903, spoke of the "immutability of communal tenure" as the basis of the land organization, while admitting that the members of village communes should be allowed to establish themselves as individual farmers if they wished. The Witte-sponsored law of March 12, 1903, however, terminated in most provinces the joint responsibility of the village commune for state obligations, thus substantially weakening the hold of the commune over its members.[3] Another Witte-sponsored law (August 11, 1904) removed corporal punishment from the list of penalties inflicted by the township (*volost*) courts. On March 30, 1905, the special conference was suddenly dissolved and its work was taken over by a committee presided over by Goremykin; the latter body accomplished nothing, and was abolished after Witte became head of the government in October, 1905.

The revolutionary storm of 1905–1906 broke at last the dam of secular prejudice and bureaucratic inertia. Although the imperial manifesto of November 3, 1905, merely pledged the government to relieve the distress of the peasantry "without doing injury to the other landowners," a ukase of the same date cut by half all redemption payments due in 1906 and abolished them as of January 1, 1907, except for the arrears on the 1906 installments. The total redemption debt written off exceeded 1,100 million rubles.

This long-overdue measure and the vague promises of the November manifesto fell short of the expectations of a restless public opinion and of the peasants themselves. By 1905, as related elsewhere in this volume, the expropriation of the property of large owners and the transfer of all, or most, of their land to the toilers of the soil had won the support not only of the revolutionaries but also of many liberals. Even some of the more clear-sighted conservatives among the landed nobility reluctantly came to believe that at least a partial expropriation of large estates was necessary to stem the revolutionary tide. Kutler, head of the department of agriculture in Witte's administration, prepared a bill for the expropriation, subject to indemnification, of the holdings of large landowners; but his proposals were rejected by the other ministers and by the tsar, and this led to Kutler's forced resignation. The conflict over the agrarian question persisted, however, and was among the main causes of the dissolution of the first and the second Dumas and of the revision of the franchise in 1907.

The land policy of the government in 1906–1914, while shunning expropriation, was nevertheless bold and even revolutionary in its

[3] Joint responsibility was finally abolished by a ukase of Oct. 5, 1906.

breach with an age-long tradition. Inaugurated by Stolypin soon after he became president of the council of ministers (July, 1906), the reform aimed at the abolition of communal tenure, enclosure of scattered strips in compact holdings, and the establishment of the peasants as individual farmers, owners of their allotments. As a preliminary measure a ukase of October 5, 1906, did away with a number of legal disabilities formerly attached to the status of the peasant. Peasants were brought within the purview of the general passport regulations, that is, thenceforth they could obtain passports allowing them to circulate freely throughout the empire, without reference to communal authorities or the household elder. By the same enactment the land captains were shorn of their disciplinary powers over the rank and file of the peasantry, although they retained these powers over the elected peasant officials.

The land reform was enacted by a ukase of November 9, 1906, issued without the approval of the legislative chambers as a "temporary" measure under Article 87 of the Fundamental Laws; after the lapse of nearly four years the third Duma confirmed and expanded the provisions of the November ukase by the law of June 14, 1910, and the land settlement act of May 29, 1911. The resulting legislation was of considerable complexity, especially since different rules were prescribed for the village communes holding land in repartitional tenure and in hereditary household tenure; [4] of necessity, it must be dealt with here in barest outline. The ukase of November 9 provided that every householder in a commune with repartitional tenure (in 1905 communes of that type comprised some 9 million households, or about three-quarters of the total number) was entitled to claim his share of arable land as his individual property, a claim the commune was bound to grant. The ukase dealt even more drastically with the communes with hereditary household tenure: such communes were declared to have passed to the regime of individual ownership, without even the formality of consulting the wishes of their members. The law of 1910 went further, and decreed that individual ownership had superseded communal tenure in all communes where no redistribution of land had taken place since the original allocation under the emancipation

---

[4] See p. 893. Good accounts of the Stolypin land reform are given by A. N. Antsiferov *et al.*, *Russian Agriculture During the War* (New Haven, 1930), pp. 318–343, and G. T. Robinson, *Rural Russia under the Old Regime* (New York, 1932), pp. 208–343.

acts, roughly one-third of the total number. The law of 1911 permitted the partition among the householders of pastures and grazing lands which, by the earlier legislation, were left under communal control.

The dissolution of communal tenure went hand in hand with a drive for the consolidation of scattered strips. The pertinent provisions of the consecutive land acts were so framed as to facilitate enclosures and encourage the peasants desirous of consolidating their holdings. The administration of this aspect of the reform was in the hands of a network of local committees operating under the direction of the central land settlement committee established in 1906. The number of surveyors employed by that organization increased from 200 in 1906 to nearly 7,000 on the eve of World War I. Enclosures were of various types, differing in the degree of completeness; but the object in view, as defined in an instruction to the local committees in June, 1911, was "the formation of independent farms" through the consolidation in one place of all the land (household plot, arable land, pastures) to which the owner was entitled.

The third major aspect of the reform was the abolition of the ancient institution of joint family ownership. The ukase of November 9 recognized the household elder as the sole owner of the allotment land of the household.[5] This drastic revision of the law helped to lift the fog of uncertainty that surrounded peasant ownership, even though the ukase remained silent on the disposition of the household's movable property. The sudden deprivation of the junior members of the peasant family of all title to the land, which they had traditionally regarded as their own, was made all the less palatable by the curious rule that they were still held liable for the taxes assessed on the household.

The reform was pressed with ruthlessness and determination. Although the state of land statistics precludes an accurate evaluation of the results attained, tentative estimates indicated that by the end of 1915 some 7.3 million households, or more than half of the 13 to 14 million households settled on allotment land in fifty provinces of European Russia, held land in hereditary tenure.[6] Included in this figure are the approximately 2.6 million households which voluntarily severed their ties with the commune under the provisions of the

---

[5] In the case of households that included members other than the lineal descendants of the household elder, the institution of joint family ownership was retained.

[6] Robinson, *op. cit.*, pp. 214–215.

ukase of November 9. Land organization, too, proceeded at a rapid pace. Between 1907 and 1913 almost 5 million farmers applied for the consolidation of their holdings, but the work was actually completed in only about 1.5 million cases (less than one-third of the applications received) and covered an area of 13 million dessiatines, or somewhat more than 10 per cent of the total area of allotment land.[7] By the end of 1915, when the work of land organization was slowed down by the war, some 2.4 million projects were completed. Of this number 1.2 million were enclosed farms of the two types favored by the government: *khutor* and *otrub*. The *khutor* was a farm of a type familiar in the United States and in England, with the farmhouse adjoining the fields. Under the *otrub* system the farmhouse remained in the village, the cultivable land being consolidated into one or two plots of arable land and pastures. The balance of the land-organization work consisted of partial enclosures of scattered strips so as to reduce their number, delimitation of boundaries, and the building of roads which, by making the scattered strips accessible, eliminated the necessity of a compulsory rotation of crops.

In addition to the legislation outlined above, Russian agrarian policy after 1905 comprised measures for internal colonization and for the increase of the area of peasant landholding. The chief agency for the sale of land to the peasants was the State Peasant Bank, founded in 1882, which at first conducted its operations on a modest scale. In 1895, however, the bank was permitted to purchase land on its own account (theretofore it merely financed purchases of land by the peasants), and in 1894, and again in 1898, the rate of interest on loans was reduced. By the laws of November 3, 1905, and November 15, 1906, the policies of the bank were liberalized to allow, among other things, loans to the full amount of the land bought instead of a part thereof, as was formerly the rule. The rate charged by the bank, including amortization over a period of fifty-five years, was reduced to 4.5 per cent, that is, it was below that charged by other credit institutions. The aggregate acreage sold to the peasants through the bank increased from 2.4 million dessiatines in 1883–1895 to 5.3 million in 1896–1905, and to 8.5 million in 1906–1913. Of the huge area sold by the bank to the peasants, or purchased by the bank for resale to the peasants, less than 1.5 million dessiatines had formerly been owned by the state and by the imperial family. Land was also bought by the peasants without

---

[7] Antsiferov *et al.*, *op. cit.*, p. 337. One dessiatine = 2.7 acres.

the assistance of the State Peasant Bank. Between 1905 and the end of 1914 the area of peasant landholding in forty-seven provinces for which information is available increased by 9.6 million dessiatines (from 160.9 million to 170.5 million). During the same period the nobility sold to the peasants and to other purchasers 10.2 million dessiatines. The acquisition by the peasants of a vast acreage inevitably led to the growth of the mortgage debt. In 1913 somewhat less than one-half of the non-allotment land held by the peasants in 47 provinces was mortgaged to the State Peasant Bank for 1,200 million rubles, and the accumulation of arrears on account of interest and amortization lent color to the contention that the land prices charged by the bank were excessive; the mortgage obligations incurred by the purchasers would seem to have exceeded their ability to pay.

The lending policies of the State Peasant Bank reflected the changing attitude of the government towards communal tenure. In 1883–1894 98.7 per cent of the loans made by the bank went to village communes and peasant associations, and were used for collective purchases of land, while only 1.3 per cent of bank loans went to individual householders; in 1906 the ratio of individual borrowers increased to 18.7 per cent, and in 1912 to 82.9 per cent. Much of the land purchased by individual peasants with the assistance of the bank was organized into enclosed holdings of the *khutor* and *otrub* type.

The expansion of peasant acreage through land purchases was a frontal attack on the perennial problem of "shortage of land." There was an endeavor, through internal colonization, to solve the same problem by relieving the population pressure in the congested areas. By the middle of the nineteenth century the once powerful flow of settlers to the southern and southeastern provinces of European Russia and to the Caucasus had dried up. Thenceforth the promised land of land-hungry plowmen lay behind the Urals, in the boundless expanses of Siberia and the Russian Far East. It will be remembered that the policy of obstruction to the movement of settlers maintained since the emancipation was revised in the early 1890's in connection with the building of the Trans-Siberian railway. The increase in the number of Siberia-bound colonists from 65,000 in 1894 to 190,000 in 1896, however, alarmed the government and brought forth new restrictive regulations. Migration was prohibited without a preliminary survey of the prospective areas of settlement by "scouting parties" (*khodoki*), and the paltry government allowance of some 100 to 150 rubles per family was cut to merely 30 rubles (circular of January 20, 1897). Nevertheless, after a drop to 86,000 in 1897, the annual number of colonists remained at a figure of over 200,000 in 1898–1900, and in the neighborhood of 120,000 in 1901–1903. The Far Eastern crisis of 1904–1905 caused a sharp reduction in the number of settlers, and in 1906 the official policy towards the colonization of Siberia was again dramatically revised. A law of March 10, 1906, proclaimed freedom of internal colonization, and extended to all settlers in Siberia government assistance and various privileges provided by a law of June 6, 1904. The peasants were not only permitted but urged to avail themselves of the opportunities offered by the vastness of Asiatic Russia. Pressure of economic necessity, official propaganda and, perhaps, the desire to take advantage of their newly acquired freedom of movement led many peasants to abandon their old homesteads and cross the Urals. In 1908 the number of colonists reached 759,000, an all-time high; it declined to 707,000 in 1909, and to 226,000 in 1911, but rose again to 328,000 in 1913. The sharp fluctuation in the movement of settlers indicated by these figures, and the large percentage of colonists who returned to European Russia (118,000 in 1908, 139,000 in 1909, 64,000 in 1911, and 23,000 in 1913) suggest that Siberia, with her rigorous climate, immense distances, shortage of water, absence of roads, and other formidable obstacles in the path of agricultural development, was not the land of milk and honey pictured by official propagandists. The inadequate organization of the colonization movement bore a heavy share of responsibility for the hardships and disillusionment experienced by many settlers, although the situation in this respect would seem to have gradually improved. Between 1896 and 1914 Siberia absorbed some 3.5 million colonists from European Russia. Significant and potentially important as was this movement, it did not substantially contribute to the solution of the problem of "shortage of land": the number of settlers remained small in comparison with the natural growth of the rural population, estimated, for the same period, at some 30 million.

The actual effects of the Stolypin land reform cannot be evaluated with any degree of accuracy. The task undertaken by the government —that of transforming the land organization, based on immemorial custom, of a primitive population of some 132 million—was a formidable one. The briefness of the time the agrarian legislation of 1906–

1911 remained in force and the chaotic and fragmentary nature of Russian land statistics make it impossible to arrive at precise and well founded conclusions as to the results achieved. Stolypin's statement in the third Duma that "the government has placed its wager not on the needy and the drunken, but on the strong—the sturdy individual proprietor," was interpreted by his critics as evidence of the determination to sacrifice the interests of the peasant masses to those of a well-to-do minority. It is arguable, however, that the elimination of communal tenure, which effectively barred agricultural progress, served, in the long run, the interests of all social groups, even though it had a political purpose and worked hardship in the case of the poorer section of the peasantry: prosperous farmers endowed with full property rights were regarded as a bulwark against the revolution. There is no adequate factual evidence, moreover, to substantiate the widely accepted view that the movement for severance from the commune and enclosures drew its main support from the very rich and the very poor peasants, the former because they wished to protect their holdings against possible encroachments by the commune, and the latter because they intended to sell their plots and start anew elsewhere or enter some pursuit other than farming. It would seem, however, that the process of differentiation within the peasantry, as an economic group, made some advance as a consequence of large sales of allotment land after 1905.

But even conceding that the abolition of communal tenure was desirable and, indeed, necessary, the method by which it was enforced was open to criticism. Paradoxically, the reform went both too far and not far enough. The legal arrangements and the administrative practice of the severance from the commune and enclosures were such as to enforce compliance with the demands of the supporters of official policies, irrespective of the wishes of the majority of the villagers. Whether less stringent methods would have succeeded in overcoming the inertia, ignorance, and traditionalism of an inarticulate and stubborn peasantry is necessarily a matter of opinion. The transition from communal to individual tenure, however, had little or no effect on the methods of farming unless the change was accompanied by the consolidation of scattered strips. The figures quoted above indicate that in 1906–1915 enclosures and other measures of land organization were carried out on less than one-third of the peasant holdings that had passed to the regime of individual ownership. The disproportion between the area of peasant acreage freed from communal tenure and the area actually reorganized into compact holdings of the *khutor* and *otrub* type (less than one-sixth of the former in 1906–1915) suggests a lack of coordination between the two essential elements of the reform which greatly detracted from its efficacy.

The removal of legal restrictions attached to the status of the peasants, far-reaching as it was, retained elements of traditional paternalism and fell short of establishing complete equality. The abolition of joint responsibility and of restrictive passport regulations did not free the peasants from the obligation of belonging to the "village commune" (*selskoe obshchestvo*),[8] although the revised status of membership no longer involved burdensome personal disabilities and duties. The ukase of October 5, 1906, granted to all subjects of the Russian Crown, except the Asiatic nomads and the Jews (graciously lumped together as *"inorodtsy"* or "non-Russians"), equal rights of entering government service, which, it will be remembered, was the normal road towards *anoblissement*. The provisions of the ukase were less significant than may at first appear, because government service, even before 1906, was open to all holders of a university diploma, irrespective of social origin. The local government of the lowest administrative subdivision, the township (*volost*), remained, however, a strictly peasant institution dominated by the land captain, although the latter was deprived of some of his former powers. Illogically, and in contradiction of the spirit of the agrarian legislation of 1906–1911, disabilities of some importance survived in the field of property rights. With relatively few exceptions, family ownership was abolished by giving the house elder a clear title to the allotment land, but peasant succession and the right of testamentary disposition were still regulated, not by the civil code, but by local customs which were often conflicting and uncertain, if not non-existent. Administrative practice, moreover, tended to nullify even the clear prescriptions of the law. For instance, in spite of the abolition of corporal punishment, flogging of peasants, either by virtue of emergency powers or in violation of the statutes, was extensively used by Stolypin in suppressing agrarian disturbances. Paternalism was particularly in evidence in the new regime of the allotment land, which, even after its transfer to the individual ownership of the householders, could not be mortgaged and could be sold only to bona fide peasants, with the number of allotments any indi-

[8] See pp. 893–895.

vidual was permitted to purchase limited to six. In spite of these survivals of the past, the peasant legislation of the last decade prior to World War I was a major step towards social equality. The old division of the population into privileged and non-privileged classes or "estates" (*soslove*) was retained, but for most practical purposes (except the organization of local government) it was hardly more than an empty shell.[9]

A notable development of an order different from those discussed above was the rapid growth of the cooperative movement after 1905. The first Russian cooperative societies appeared in the 1860's, but for four decades they made little headway. Between 1905 and 1914, however, the number of cooperative societies increased, roughly, from 5,000 to 32,000, and their aggregate membership from less than one million to over 10 million. In 1914 the most important branches of the movement were the credit cooperatives (13,000 societies with a membership of 8.3 million) and consumers' cooperatives (11,000 societies with a membership of 1.4 million). Agricultural and producers' associations were lagging behind (5,000 societies with 500,000 members). In comparison with the teeming millions of rural Russia, these figures are modest; nevertheless they suggest the possibilities of future fruitful developments. Some of the cooperative organizations, for instance, the Siberian creamery associations, were eminently successful.

The agrarian disturbances and the dislocation inherent in the transition from communal to individual tenure did not prevent some improvement in the methods of cultivation, reflected in higher yields. The average yearly yield of the main grain crops increased, on peasant land, from 39 poods per dessiatine in 1891–1900 to 43 poods in 1901–1910, and on non-peasant land from 47 to 54 poods. These average figures, however, which do not compare favorably with the corresponding data for the western European countries, are largely meaningless because of the wide variation in the yield of crops, especially on peasant land, from locality to locality and from year to year. There is no doubt that the standard of living of the peasants was very low. Sample investigations of peasant budgets between 1900 and 1915 indicate that the income of an average household, including supplies obtained from

[9] The democratization of the social structure was a departure from the earlier policy of the government of Nicholas II. In 1900 (ukases of May 28 and Aug. 2) a concession, although a minor one, was made to the aristocratic principle by revision, in a restrictive sense, of the regulations concerning acquisition of the status of a nobleman through government service.

the farm, varied from 200 rubles to slightly over 500 rubles a year, that is, from $100 to $250. S. N. Prokopovich's careful analysis of budget investigations reveals that the distribution of expenditure, irrespective of the size of the income, was remarkably uniform: 60 to 70 per cent was spent on food, and most of the residue on clothing and lodgings (construction and repairs). Next to nothing was left for church, medical assistance, tobacco, and so on. In the province of Viatka in 1900 the average outlay on schools, newspapers, and books was 14 copecks, or 7 cents, a year. The data on budget investigations inspire little confidence, and the conversion of Russian peasant incomes into dollars is not really helpful unless accompanied by a comparative table of Russian and American prices interpreted in the light of the entirely different standards prevalent in the two countries, a task that presents insurmountable difficulties. All that can be claimed for the above figures is that they confirm the impression obtained from other sources, that the standard of living of the peasants was shockingly low. "The dwelling of a Tula peasant is usually a cottage of 18 by 21 feet, and 7 feet high," according to the 1902 report of the Tula committee on the needs of agriculture. "Cottages having no chimneys are still very common, the smoke being let out through a hole in the roof. . . . Almost all cottages have thatched roofs which often leak, and in the winter the walls are generally covered with dung to keep the place warm. . . . Earth floors are the rule because in cold weather lambs, calves, pigs, and even cows are brought into the cottage. . . . In localities that have no forests the peasants use straw for fuel, and in the years of poor harvest even dung, thus depriving their fields of much-needed manure. . . . Bath-houses are practically non-existent. . . . The peasants almost never use soap. . . . Meat, meal, lard and vegetable oil appear on the family table only on rare occasions, perhaps two or three times a year. The normal fare consists of bread, kvass [a home-made drink], and often cabbage and onions. . . . In brief, the poverty of the peasant establishment is astounding." According to Professor A. A. Kaufman, the report of the Tula committee gave an accurate picture of the conditions of a large section, if not of the majority, of the peasantry in the fertile black-soil belt. There is no reason to believe that the situation was substantially improved between 1902 and 1914.

Of great political, social, and economic significance was the striking decline in the acreage held by the nobility. In spite of official efforts to bolster the landed aristocracy the area covered by the estates of that group shrank from 73.1 million dessiatines in 1877 to 49.8 million in 1905 and to 39.6 million in 1914.[10] The acceleration of this process of liquidation after 1905 suggests that the imperial government used poor judgment in resisting the demands of the first and the second Dumas for the expropriation of the big landowners. Assuming that Russian primitive collectivism (a term which does not accurately describe the village commune) was a major bar to economic progress, the Stolypin land reform, for all its shortcomings, was a move in the right direction. Coupled with a firm policy that would meet the unmistakable longing of the peasantry for more land, it might have had a profound effect upon the future course of Russian history, and might have saved the upper classes from the tragic fate that befell them in 1917.

INDUSTRY, BANKING, LABOR, AND FOREIGN TRADE

The quarter-century immediately preceding World War I was a period of boisterous growth of Russian industry. The pace of expansion was particularly rapid in 1893–1899; it slowed down in 1900–1909 but regained momentum in 1910–1913. The principal single cause of the intensification of business activities in the 1890's was the huge program of railway construction (some 15,000 miles of railway lines, including the Trans-Siberian, were built during that decade), while the political turmoil and social unrest of the opening years of the twentieth century retarded recovery from the business recession that had made itself felt in 1900. According to tentative estimates based on official returns (which, however, are neither comprehensive nor exact), the number of workers employed in manufacturing, mining, and metallurgy increased from 1.4 million in 1890 to 2.3 million in 1900, and to 3 million or 3.1 million in 1913. The value of the output of industrial establishments subject to the control of factory inspectors rose from 1,503 million rubles in 1890 to 5,738 million in 1913. The largest gains were made by the cotton, coal, iron, and steel industries. The number of workers employed in cotton mills increased from 214,000 in 1890 to 391,000 in 1901 and to 566,000 in 1914, and the number of spindles from 3.5 million in 1890 to 6.1 million in 1900

---

[10] The 1877 figure is for 50 provinces of European Russia, and the 1905 and 1914 figures are for 47 provinces. Although not strictly comparable, they indicate the general trend.

and to 9.1 million in 1913. The output of coal was 534 million poods in 1894 and 2,198 million in 1913; that of iron 92 million poods in 1890, 335 million in 1900, and 562 million in 1913; that of pig iron 59 million poods in 1890, 177 million in 1900, and 283 million in 1913; and that of manufactured iron and steel wares 42 million poods in 1890, 134 million in 1900, and 247 million in 1913.

In the south the Donets valley, rich in coal and iron deposits, was speedily transformed into Russia's leading center of mining and heavy metallurgy. The output of the Donets coalfields rose from 183 million poods in 1890 to 1,544 million in 1913. In 1890 the region produced 23 million poods of iron and 13 million poods of pig iron; in 1913 the respective figures were 420 million and 190 million. A less spectacular yet important advance was registered by the oil industry, which increased its output from 275 million poods in 1891 to 462 million in 1913. Most of the oil came from Baku, but other Caucasian oilfields, especially those of Grozny, were gradually brought under exploitation. Industrialization made hardly any inroads in Siberia, although the output of Siberian coal increased from less than 3 million poods in 1894 to 125 million in 1913.

Concentration of production, a characteristic feature of capitalist development already noted during the earlier period, made further progress in 1890–1914. In the latter year 56 per cent of the workers engaged in the manufacturing industries were employed in large enterprises with 500 or more workers each, such enterprises representing less than 8 per cent of the total number of industrial establishments. Enterprises employing 1,000 or more workers each provided employment for 32 per cent of the total number of workers in 1901 and 40 per cent in 1914.[11] Very large concerns were predominant in the textile and metal industries. The active participation of the banks in the promotion of industry favored mergers and the formation of trusts and cartels. A large and steadily growing portion of the coal, metal, textile, oil, tobacco, sugar, and other industries came under the control of industrial combinations, which in some cases (for instance, the Prodamet, a syndicate of metal-working firms) achieved a quasi-monopolistic position.

---

[11] The above computations are borrowed from Rashin. The total number of enterprises subject to the control of factory inspectors with which he deals was 11,729 in 1914 and the number of workers employed 2.2 million. Only enterprises employing 20 or more workers each were covered by the investigation.

The industrial expansion of 1890–1914 was due in no small degree to the generous flow of funds from abroad. Witte, a proponent of the view that foreign capital was indispensable to Russia's economic advancement, spared no effort to attract foreign investors. From 1856 to 1894, thirty-seven foreign companies with an aggregate capital of 134 million rubles were established in Russia. By 1914 the number of foreign companies increased to 327 and their aggregate capital to 1,343 million rubles, roughly representing one-third of the total capital investment of Russian industry.[12] It was this influx of foreign funds that made possible the rapid industrialization of the south. The reverse side of the medal was the pressure on the exchange position of the ruble resulting from the necessity of making large transfers abroad because of dividends and interest. The total foreign investment in Russian industrial, banking, and commercial enterprises in 1917 was estimated at 2,243 million rubles. Of this amount 834 million rubles were invested in mining, 392 million in metallurgy, 237 million in banking, and 192 million in textiles. The bulk of the investments came from France (33 per cent), England (23 per cent), Germany (20 per cent), and Belgium (14 per cent); the share of the United States was 5 per cent, and the balance was supplied by Holland, Switzerland, Sweden, Denmark, Austria, Italy, and Norway. France is said to have controlled nearly three-quarters of her ally's output of coal and pig iron.[13]

The development of banking kept in step with the expansion of industry with which financial circles were so intimately connected. In 1890 Russia had thirty joint-stock commercial banks with an aggregate capital of 174 million rubles and deposits and current accounts of 230 million; in 1915 there were fifty joint-stock commercial banks with an aggregate capital of 906 million rubles and deposits and current accounts of 2,873 million. In 1914 forty-seven commercial banks maintained 743 branch offices. The number of societies for mutual credit increased from 100 in 1899 to 1,108 in 1914, their membership from 71,000 to 634,000, and their aggregate deposits and current accounts from 160 million rubles to 595 million. In 1914 there were 319 municipal banks with an aggregate capital of 60 million rubles; their

---

[12] S. O. Zagorsky, *State Control of Industry in Russia During the War* (Yale University Press, 1928), p. 16.

[13] V. P. Ol, quoted in L. Pasvolsky and G. H. Moulton, *Russian Debts and Russian Reconstruction* (New York, 1924), pp. 182–183.

deposits amounted to 198 million rubles and their loans and discounts to 232 million. The number of state savings banks increased from 4,600 in 1903 to over 8,000 in 1912, and deposits in savings accounts from 860 million to 1,595 million rubles. A notable expansion took place in the network of small credit institutions in rural areas, the loan and savings association established in the 1860's, and the credit associations authorized by a law of 1895. Both types of associations were cooperative societies promoted by the zemstvos with the assistance of the State Bank. The credit associations were particularly successful, partly because their facilities were made available to nonmembers. In 1897 there were 619 loan and savings associations with a membership of 222,000, and in 1914 there were 3,479 with a membership of 2,045,000. The growth of the credit associations was even more rapid: from 121 with a mere handful of members in 1901 to 9,536 with 6,210,000 members in 1914. In 1897 the operating funds of the cooperative credit institutions were 25 million rubles; in 1914 the amalgamated financial statement of the associations showed a total of 614 million rubles. In 1904 the loan and savings associations and the credit associations won the right to organize themselves into credit unions, but progress along these lines was slow (partly because of the opposition of the bureaucracy, always suspicious of collective endeavor); nevertheless eighty-four unions comprising about one-fourth of all the associations were formed by 1916. Akin to credit cooperative societies were the zemstvo small-credit funds authorized by a law of 1904; their resources, however, were inadequate, and they played but a minor part in catering to the financial needs of the rural community. The structure of cooperative credit was topped by the Moscow People's (*Narodnyi*) Bank founded in 1912 with the object of "financing institutions of small credit and cooperative enterprises." The shares of the bank were held by the cooperative institutions and by small groups of proven friends of the cooperative movement. The share and reserve capital of the bank increased from one million rubles in 1912 to 10 million in 1917. The State Bank, which became the bank of issue by virtue of the monetary reform of 1897, occupied the central position in the banking system and performed primarily the functions of a bankers' bank. Its intervention and liberal loan policy during the depression of 1900 and again in 1904–1906 saved many commercial banks from disaster.

In spite of its numerical growth labor derived little benefit from the industrial expansion. Except for the establishment of sick benefit funds and the revision of the accident insurance law, the State Duma made no contribution to the meager labor legislation enacted prior to 1906. The "provisional rules" of March 4, 1906 (issued before the convocation of the Duma), legalized trade unions, as well as organizations of employers, but limited their functions to vaguely defined activities such as improvement in the conditions of labor, setting up of a machinery for the arbitration of industrial disputes, inquiry into wages, educational work, and management of labor exchanges. These provisions, if liberally interpreted, might have led to a fruitful development of the labor movement, even though each union was required to have a charter approved by administrative officials, and the amalgamation of unions was specifically forbidden. It would seem that unionism had made a promising start; and, according to somewhat controversial data, from 650 to 860 unions (authorities disagree as to the exact number), with an aggregate membership of perhaps 250,000, or about 10 per cent of the total number of workers, secured official recognition by 1907. Under the stern rule of Stolypin, however, they speedily disappeared, and the few smaller unions that managed to survive (for instance, the printers' and the woodworkers' unions) exercised hardly any influence. The anti-union policy was adhered to by Stolypin's successors. At a meeting of the council of ministers in August, 1915, Prince V. N. Shakhovskoy, minister of commerce and industry, admitted that "in many instances the liquidation of the trade unions has been carried out without sufficient justification by unduly active generals, or by too energetic provincial governors"; a similar opinion was voiced by Prince N. B. Shcherbatov, minister of the interior. "Abuses are frequent in dealing with the trade unions. . . ." he said. "The generals and governors prefer to close down the organizations they dislike rather than to look after them or be responsible for them." The only agencies of organized labor that gained a footing prior to the revolution of 1917 were the sick benefit funds established by a law of June 23, 1912. Some 2,800 funds, with an aggregate membership of over two million, were functioning in 1914. They were financed by contributions of workers and employers, and labor took an active part in their management. Their jurisdiction, however, was necessarily narrow, and they were in no sense a substitute for the trade unions. Another law of June 23, 1912, dealt with accident insurance, providing medical aid and relief during illness due to an industrial accident, pensions in case of disability, and pensions to the worker's family in case of his death.[14] The total cost of accident insurance was borne by the employer, a feature of the scheme that placed imperial Russia among the pioneers in at least one field of social legislation.

While the trade unions, although permitted by law, were virtually non-existent, strikes, which were forbidden as "disturbances of the social order," nevertheless occurred. The wave of strikes that swept the country in 1905–1906 receded but slowly, only to rise again with the revival of business activities. In 1907 there were 3,600 strikes involving 740,000 workers; in 1908 there were 900 strikes, with 176,000 participants. The lowest point in the strike movement prior to the outbreak of the First World War was reached in 1910, when the number of strikes declined to slightly over 200 and that of the strikers to 47,000, but in 1912 the respective figures were 2,000 and 725,000, and in January to July, 1914, 4,000 and 1,449,000. With the declaration of war the trend was dramatically reversed: in August to December, 1914, there were only 68 strikes, with less than 35,000 participants. Violent labor disturbances in St. Petersburg in July, 1914, which coincided—not entirely by accident—with Poincaré's visit to the Russian capital, were followed by mass arrests of the revolutionary leaders. Deprived of its leadership and swayed, perhaps, by patriotic emotion, labor appeared to be willing to make peace with the imperial government, or at least to postpone domestic strife until the end of the war.

It is believed that the trend of both monetary and real wages in the closing decade before the war of 1914 was favorable to labor. Even if one accepts this contention, which is based on flimsy evidence, the fact is inescapable that wages remained exceedingly low. In 1913 the average monthly wage in all industries was 22 rubles, ranging from 16 to 17 rubles in the textile industry to 33 to 34 rubles in the metal industry. Sample studies of workers' budgets indicate that practically their entire income was spent on the barest necessities—shelter, food, and clothing. Outlays on "recreation and cultural needs," which included such un-

[14] In case of total disability the pension amounted to the annual wage of the disabled person. If the accident resulted in the death of the worker, the pension of his widow was one-third, and that of his children and dependent brothers and sisters under 16, one sixth of his wage. The act of 1912 was an advance on that of 1903 (see p. 1160). It simplified the procedure for collecting disability benefits and closed a number of loopholes which, under the earlier law, permitted the employer to escape responsibility.

expected items as visits to public bath-houses, postage, and street cars, averaged half a ruble per month. The basic cause of low wages was the equally low productivity of labor. According to authoritative estimates, one thousand spindles in England were tended by three workers, in Russia by 16.6. Moreover, the "link with land," that is, the retention by industrial workers of an interest in the family farm, even though it tended to become less common with the sale of a large number of peasant holdings after 1906, was still a potent factor in keeping wages down.

Industrial expansion had a marked effect upon the flow of Russian foreign trade. Average annual exports increased from 698 million rubles in 1896–1900 to 941 million in 1901–1905, to 1,203 million in 1906–1910, and to 1,540 million in 1911–1913; average annual imports increased from 607 million rubles in 1896–1900 to 632 million in 1901–1905, to 910 million in 1906–1910, and to 1,239 million in 1911–1913. In 1913 Russian exports were valued at 1,520 million rubles and imports at 1,375 million. The bulk of the exports consisted of foodstuffs (55 per cent in 1911–1913) and raw materials and semi-manufactured goods (37 per cent), the share of manufactured goods (less than 6 per cent) and animal products (slightly more than 2 per cent) being relatively insignificant. In the first decade of the twentieth century wheat alone accounted for 48 per cent of the value of the export trade. The average yearly exports of grain rose from 442 million poods in 1891–1900 to 571 million in 1901–1905; these declined, because of agrarian disturbances, to 450 million poods in 1906–1908 but advanced to 672 million poods in 1911–1913. These average figures, however, tend to conceal the sharp fluctuation in the volume of grain exports from year to year. In 1904 Russia shipped to foreign markets 658 million poods of wheat, rye, barley, oats and maize; in 1907, 338 million; in 1910, 847 million; and in 1913, 647 million. In view of the dependence of Russia on grain exports to meet her international financial commitments, the ebb and flow of the grain trade was closely watched by the authorities. In April, 1914, Bark, the minister of finance, regretfully noted in the Duma that Russia's share in the grain imports of the principal consuming countries had declined from 25 per cent in 1908–1912 to 17 per cent in 1913. About 90 per cent of the grain trade went through the ports of the Black Sea and the Sea of Azov.

It will be noted that after 1905 imports increased more rapidly than exports. In 1913, 47 per cent of imports consisted of raw materials and semi-manufactured goods, 33 per cent of manufactured articles, and 18 per cent of foodstuffs. The principal items listed under the heading of raw materials and semi-manufactured goods were coal, cotton, oil, chemicals, dyestuffs, wool, silk, jute, iron, pig iron, steel, zinc, and lead. The import of commodities of which Russia had seemingly an unlimited potential supply is explained by the inability of the "primary" industries, such as mining and heavy metallurgy, to keep pace with the rapid expansion of the manufacturing industries. Another reason was the irrational geographical distribution of industry, due to some extent to historical causes, and the discovery of new sources of coal and ore. The important industrial region of St. Petersburg, for instance, found it more advantageous to use foreign sea-borne coal than the domestic supply transported by rail from the distant Donets valley, hence imports of coal, which in 1913 amounted to 8 million tons. A large portion of imports classified as manufactured goods consisted of machines, machine tools, railway equipment, and similar articles. The principal imported foodstuffs were tea, coffee, oranges, lemons, and tropical products.

In 1913 Germany took 32 per cent of Russian exports and supplied 47 per cent of Russian imports; England, 19 and 12 per cent. The shares of other countries were much smaller. In 1913 the exports of the United States to Russia amounted to 74 million rubles (5.8 per cent of Russian imports) but United States imports from that country were merely 14 million rubles.

The notable growth of Russian imports was achieved in spite of an aggressive and mounting protectionism. Witte would seem to have had some misgivings about the virtues of a high tariff policy; yet, as related in an earlier chapter, he was responsible for the upward revision (in connection with the tariff war against Germany in 1893–1894) of the already stiff rates of the 1891 tariff. A decree issued in July, 1900, ordered further increases ranging from 10 to 50 per cent of existing duties. This measure was motivated by the need of additional revenue because of the tense situation in the Far East. The revised rates were incorporated, with but few exceptions, in the tariff act of 1903, put into effect in February, 1906. Although somewhat mitigated by commercial treaties based on the most-favored-nation clause, Russian protectionism was among the highest in the world. Witte's successors in the ministry of finance, Kokovtsov and Bark, preoccupied as they were with the exchange position of the ruble, and therefore with a favorable balance of trade, made no change in a tariff system that imposed a heavy burden on consumers.

The brisk pace of industrialization, the concentration of production, and the expansion of the banking system and of foreign trade should not obscure the fact that on the eve of the First World War Russia remained a predominantly agricultural country. In 1913 the number of wage-earners engaged in industry, commerce, transportation, and other allied pursuits of a non-agricultural nature did not exceed 9 million, or approximately one-seventeenth of the total population.[15] Russian capitalism, so diligently fostered by Witte and nurtured by foreign investors, was still but a precocious infant.

THE SCHOOLS

The changes wrought in the two decades preceding World War I in the field of cultural endeavor were no less striking than those noted in the sphere of economics. The most important among them, perhaps, were the modernization and expansion of the school system, the creation of a vigorous and independent press, and the appearance of a host of new movements in literature and in the arts.

The universities, in spite of the autonomy granted to them more or less by accident in the midst of the revolutionary storm of 1905, made little progress towards real self-government. The "provisional rules" of August 27, 1905, restored the right of academic corporations to choose their executive officers and to fill professorial vacancies by election; but, while they relaxed the strict discipline formerly applied to the student body, they did not repeal the university charter of 1884.

[15] Zagorsky, *op. cit.*, p. 13. S. N. Prokopovich, in an essay published in 1918, advanced the opinion that in 1913 industry accounted for 25 per cent of Russia's national income. Investigations of national income are full of hazards, and Prokopovich's study was avowedly a pioneer effort. His estimate would seem to be far too high.

No reliable information is available on small artisans in urban areas and on peasants engaged in handicraft (cottage industry). Before World War I the number of the former was tentatively put at 1.2 million, while estimates of the number of the latter varied within a surprisingly wide range, from 750,000 to as much as 15 million. It is a moot question whether cottage industries (wood-working, furniture making, weaving, and the manufacturing of metal wares, sheepskin coats, felt boots, etc.) were as a rule subsidiary to farming or rather tended to become the craftsmen's principal occupation, as would seem more likely. The earnings of the peasant craftsmen were known to be low. An investigation of cottage industries in the province of Yaroslavl in 1904, regarded as representative of the conditions prevailing over a large section of the country, brought out that weekly earnings of 1.5 rubles were common, while 3 rubles per week was rated as "very good."

Autonomy, moreover, was flouted by the administrative practice of the ministers of education, A. N. Schwarts (1908–1910) and L. A. Kasso (1910–1914). In violation of the 1905 "rules," elected rectors, deans, and professors were arbitrarily dismissed, vacant chairs were filled by ministerial appointments, and the persecution of students for alleged political offenses went unabated. These unenlightened policies and the general feeling of restlessness manifested towards the end of Stolypin's administration led to the resurgence of student disturbances in the academic year 1910–1911. In January and February, 1911, strikes were in progress in practically every higher school. Kasso retaliated by mass expulsions, arrests, and deportation of students and by removals from office of "lax" or "undesirable" university officials. As a protest, a large group of members of the Moscow University faculty —among them the eminent historians Kliuchevsky, Paul Vinogradoff, and Kizevetter—resigned (February, 1911). Relations between the universities and the ministry of education remained highly strained until Kasso's death in November, 1914.

The stormy course of academic life did not prevent a substantial increase in the size of the student body. In the middle of the 1890's, according to the data quoted by the Soviet historian of education E. N. Medynsky, Russia had sixty-three higher schools, including ten universities, with an aggregate enrollment of 29,000, of which about 4 per cent were women. On January 1, 1914, according to the same source, there were sixty-seven higher schools with 90,000 students, including thirteen institutions for women with 21,000 students. Some 36,000 students were enrolled in the universities, 22,000 in engineering and other technical schools, and 10,000 in specialized institutions (agricultural colleges, archeological and philological institutes, and so on).[16]

Secondary schools fared, in a sense, better than the institutions of higher learning. In the late 1890's the Tolstoy brand of classicism provoked a strong movement of reaction even in official circles. Beginning

[16] The figures for the 1890's and 1914 are not strictly comparable. The former do, and the latter do not, include Finland. The 1914 data, moreover, do not include the higher commercial, military, theological, and art schools. Higher estimates are sometimes given. Professor Novgorotsov, for instance, states that "in 1914 there were in Russia considerably more than one hundred universities and higher technical schools with 150,000 students." The basis for this estimate and the method by which it is arrived at, however, are not given. D. M. Odinetz and P. J. Novgorotsov, *Russian Schools and Universities During the War* (Yale University Press, 1929), p. 146.

in 1899 the ministry of education was busy framing plans for the reform of secondary schools, and although most of the proposed legislation was never enacted the "Greco-Roman bondage" was speedily brought to an end. In 1902 the number of hours assigned to the classical languages was reduced, compulsory teaching of both Greek and Latin being retained in but a small number of gymnasiums. By 1914 Latin was, as a rule, the only classical language taught in these schools. Simultaneously the programs of the gymnasiums and the *Realschulen* were brought closer together, although the graduates of the latter were still denied admission to the universities. Ironically, the heaviest blows to Russian classicism were dealt during the brief administration of the ministry of education by G. E. Zenger (1902–1904), an enthusiastic classicist and author of a Latin version of Pushkin's long novel in verse *Eugene Onegin*. Some idea of the progress of secondary education may be gathered from the following figures. In the middle of the 1890's, according to Medynsky, there were 898 secondary schools of various types with 224,000 students; of this number 614 were boys' schools with 149,000 students and 284 girls' schools with 75,000 students. There was one secondary school student per 564 of the population. No comparable comprehensive data are available for the later period. In 1915, however, there were 441 boys' gymnasiums and 29 progymnasiums with 152,000 students, and 284 *Realschulen* with 81,000 students, and in 1914 there were 873 gymnasiums and 92 progymnasiums for girls with 384,000 students.[17] The larger number of schools for girls than for boys, as well as the larger enrollment of girl students, is explained by the fact that the above figures refer exclusively to schools under the jurisdiction of the ministry of education. An important proportion of the boys went to the schools over which the control of that ministry did not extend—commercial, technical, and trade schools, military academies, and theological seminaries. The gymnasiums, from which Dimitry Tolstoy and Delianov had endeavored to exclude the children of the lower classes, were becoming increasingly democratic. In the school region of Vilna, for instance, the proportion of gymnasium students coming from families of the nobility and government officials declined from 67 per cent in 1894 to 37 per

---

[17] Odinetz and Novgorotsov, *op. cit.* pp. 35–36. In 1895, according to Medynsky, Russia had 225 boys' gymnasiums and progymnasiums with 65,000 students, 107 *Realschulen* with 26,000 students, and 325 gymnasiums and progymnasiums for girls with 68,000 students.

cent in 1910, while that of students of peasant extraction increased from 6 to 18 per cent.

The most notable changes, however, took place in the field of primary education. The census of January, 1897, the only comprehensive census ever taken in imperial Russia, disclosed that merely 21 per cent of the population could read and write. The percentage of literacy was higher for men (29 per cent) than for women (13 per cent), and was considerably higher for the urban (45 per cent) than for the rural (17 per cent) population.[18] In the 1890's and the 1900's the benefits of literacy were no longer questioned except by a few ultra-reactionaries. Educational matters were widely discussed in the general press and in specialized periodicals such as *Russkaiia Shkola* (The Russian School) and *Vestnik Vospitaniia* (Messenger of Education), both founded in 1890, and *Tekhnicheskoe Obrazovanie* (Technical Education), which began to appear in 1892. Most of the zemstvos, some of the municipalities, and a host of private associations evinced keen interest in the promotion of primary education and in the improvement of scholastic standards. A passionate debate raged around two major issues: compulsory school attendance for all children and the question of school administration, that is, whether the schools should be managed by the state, by the Church, or by the institutions of local self-government. There was more agreement on the former than on the latter issue. A bill providing for the introduction of compulsory education was submitted by the government to the second Duma, but no action was taken because of the dissolution of that assembly. The third Duma, its conservative character notwithstanding, addressed itself with enthusiasm to the reform of primary schools. A law of May 3, 1908, based on the bill introduced by the government in the second Duma, provided for the gradual enforcement of compulsory school attendance for all children aged eight to eleven; instruction was free and lasted for four years. A far more ambitious plan of reform was embodied in a bill passed by the Duma in 1911 but voted down by the State Council. The organization and immediate supervision of primary schools, according to the Duma proposal, was to be entrusted to the zemstvos and the municipalities, the ministry of education retaining the function

---

[18] According to the 1897 census, the total population of Russia, exclusive of Finland, was 125.6 million. Of this number 16.8 million, or 13 per cent, lived in cities and towns. The census data were published in 1905, eight years after the census was taken.

of guidance and general control. Church schools were to be absorbed in the network of primary schools under the ministry of education. Scholastic programs were to be revised in a manner that would allow the graduates of primary schools to gain admittance to secondary schools. The use of local languages was to be permitted in localities with a predominantly non-Russian population. The administration of the schools was to be reorganized on a democratic basis, and teachers' salaries were to be raised. The State Council rejected every major provision of the bill, which never became law.

In spite of this setback some advancement was made towards the goal of compulsory education. Since the government was unwilling to broaden the taxing power of the zemstvos and of the municipalities as urged by the liberal groups, the funds needed for the expansion of the school system were to come (under the law of May 3, 1908, and subsequent legislation) largely from the state treasury, that is, appropriations were made to local government institutions that had agreed to participate in the scheme for the introduction of compulsory education. By 1914 arrangements of this nature were reached with 386 county zemstvos (out of 426) and with 257 municipalities.

The act of May, 1908, restricted primary-school attendance to children between eight and eleven years of age. Even within these artificial limits the task set by the law proved difficult of accomplishment. According to the estimates of the Duma, the number of children of school age in 1922, when the plan for compulsory education was to be in full operation, would reach 15.9 million and require 317,000 schools. Somewhat less than 100,000 schools existed in 1908. More than tripling the number of schools within the short span of fourteen years, the erection of school buildings and the training of an army of teachers required money and careful planning. The Duma estimate of the number of children in the age group eight to eleven, moreover, was probably too conservative. According to the ministry of education, there were 15.3 million children of that age in 1914. Both the zemstvos and the central government made sizable increases in their expenditure on primary schools. Zemstvo outlays under that heading rose from 5.3 million rubles in 1891 to 26.2 million in 1907 and to 42.4 million in 1910. Appropriations in the state budget for primary schools under the ministry of education were 3.1 million rubles in 1900, 8.3 million in 1906, 15.9 million in 1908, and 35.9 million in 1910.

In 1896 Russia had 65,000 primary schools, including 35,000 church schools, with an aggregate enrollment of perhaps 3.5 million. The school census of January, 1911, recorded 100,300 primary schools with 154,000 teachers and 6.2 million students. Included in these figures were 38,000 church schools with 46,000 teachers and 1.8 million students. In 1915 the number of primary schools increased to 122,000 and their student body to 8.1 million. Progress towards the goal of compulsory education, however, was slower than had been anticipated: according to the 1908 plan the number of primary schools was to reach 149,000 by 1914. It is unlikely, therefore, that even without the intervention of the war compulsory school attendance would have been fully enforced in 1922.

A significant development was the partial eclipse of the church schools. Fostered by Pobedonostsev and by state subsidies, which in the 1890's and the early 1900's more than doubled, the church schools had multiplied rapidly. In 1905 they numbered 43,000 and represented 46 per cent of the total number of primary schools (91,000). In 1911, as indicated by the figures quoted above, their relative position and even their actual number had declined. There was a real improvement in both the physical equipment and the educational standards of the schools, especially those maintained by the more progressive zemstvos. Yet on the eve of the First World War the promotion of literacy was still one of Russia's unsolved problems. In 1914, according to the estimates of the ministry of education, 49 per cent of the children 8 to 11 years old did not attend school. The picture would be even more cheerless if the school age were extended to include children aged 7 to 14. The proportion of children of this group who attended school in rural areas, according to the data quoted in the report on the census of 1911, was 9 per cent in 1880, 16 per cent in 1894, and 24 per cent in 1911.

The status of the primary schools of a more advanced type, those offering a six-year course, and of the so-called upper primary schools, which were reorganized by a law of June 28, 1912, and actually occupied an intermediate position between the primary and the secondary schools, was even less satisfactory than that of the schools of the lower grade. Until 1906 the six-year schools were under the jurisdiction of the Church. In 1906 the zemstvos were permitted to establish schools of that type, but owing to financial stringency few of them were actually opened. According to the 1911 census, many counties had no six-year primary schools. As to the upper primary schools, their development on the eve of the First World War was still in an embryonic stage. In 1912 there was one such school per 135,000 of the population and per 139 schools of the lower grade. In 1914 they numbered merely 1,300.

A seemingly more promising era in the history of Russian schools was ushered in with the appointment of Count P. N. Ignatev as minister of education (January, 1915). Filled with boundless enthusiasm and good will towards the zemstvos and the teaching profession, the new minister displayed feverish, if somewhat erratic, activity, and released a whole avalanche of legislative proposals which ranged from the establishment of numerous institutions of higher learning and the redrafting of the university charter on the basis of broad autonomy, to the far-reaching reorganization of secondary schools and the reform of primary education along the lines of the abortive Duma bill of 1911. Ignatev's dismissal in December, 1916, before any of the major bills he sponsored were enacted, and the revolution that broke out a few weeks later terminated this unexpected interlude in the history of Russian education.

THE PRESS AND LITERATURE

After 1905 the Russian press enjoyed a considerable degree of freedom in spite of the perils inherent in the censorship regime established by the "provisional rules" of November 24, 1905, and by subsequent legislation.[19] The penal code, moreover, provided heavy penalties not only for sedition, treason, and offenses against the Church but also for incitement to hostility between the various groups of the population, "especially between employers and workers" (Article 129), while the proclamation of a "state of emergency"—a common occurrence in 1906–1910—vested in administrative officials discretionary powers to suspend the publication of undesirable journals. Publishers, editors, and authors, however, were willing to take the risk and face criminal proceedings, administrative penalties, and financial losses resulting from the "temporary" seizure of allegedly offending issues of newspapers and magazines rather than to dodge burning issues or bow to official dictation. The 2,167 periodicals published in 1912 in 246 Russian cities and towns (Finland is not included) reflected practically every shade of opinion. The representative character of the

[19] See p. 1186.

press may be gauged from a brief enumeration of a few better known papers. On the extreme right were the totally disreputable *Zemshchina* and *Russkoe Znamia* (The Russian Flag), organ of the Union of the Russian People. The conservatives had their chief mouthpiece in the St. Petersburg *Novoe Vremia* (New Times), the liberals, in the Moscow *Russkiia Vedomosti* (Russian Chronicle) and the St. Petersburg *Rech* (The Speech), edited by I. V. Hessen and Miliukov. The principal organs of social democracy were the Menshevik daily *Luch* (The Ray) and monthly *Nasha Zaria* (Our Dawn); the Bolshevik daily *Pravda* (The Truth), which was founded in St. Petersburg in April, 1912, repeatedly ran into difficulties with the authorities, and was forced to suspend publication in July, 1914. Several political and literary monthlies—*Vestnik Evropy* (European Messenger), *Russkaia Mysl* (Russian Thought), and *Russkoe Bogatstvo* (Russian Wealth), to mention only a few—carried on with distinction a great literary tradition and compared not unfavorably with similar journals published in England, France, and Germany. Marxian writers encountered no insurmountable obstacles in presenting their views in print. An avowedly incomplete bibliography (prepared by the Communist Academy in 1924) of the social-democratic literature, both Bolshevik and Menshevik, published legally in St. Petersburg and Moscow in 1906–1914, lists nearly 3,300 items. In spite of the government's ill advised program of Russification, local languages were extensively used. The 2,167 periodicals issued in 1912 appeared in 33 languages: 1,585 in Russian, 234 in Polish, 69 in German, 47 in Lithuanian, 45 in Estonian, 31 in Hebrew and Yiddish, 21 in Armenian, 20 in Latvian, 13 in Georgian, 12 in Ukrainian, and so on, in order of diminishing importance. The status of the press in 1906–1914, even after allowance is made for the arbitrariness of the censorship regime, was the nearest approximation to one of freedom that Russia had ever experienced. In 1917, when freedom of the press was proclaimed by the Provisional Government, the publication of conservative papers was precluded by political considerations.

The intensification of political and economic activities towards the turn of the century, and the greater freedom of the press after 1905, had a vivifying effect upon literature and the arts. The brilliant tradition of realism established by the novelists of the 1860's and 1870's was maintained by a company of distinguished men of letters. The outstanding representatives of this school were Leo Tolstoy, Chekhov,

Gorky, and Bunin. Tolstoy, in spite of his "conversion" and repudiation of his earlier writings, remained Russia's leading literary figure. In the celebrated treatise *What Is Art?* he submitted to an unsparing criticism some of the acknowledged masterpieces of world literature, including the works of Shakespeare and Pushkin, and he attacked realism, as interpreted by his contemporaries and by earlier writers, on the ground that it was overburdened with superfluous details; to the "over-elaborations" of realism he opposed the austere simplicity of biblical tales. Extreme economy of means and avoidance of unnecessary "realistic" adornments became a characteristic feature of some of Tolstoy's work after 1880. In the thirty years between his conversion and his death Tolstoy wrote tracts expounding his religious doctrine and kindred subjects, numerous didactic popular short stories, longer stories of a psychological character, a novel, and several plays. Not all of this voluminous output was subject to the severe discipline enunciated in *What Is Art?* Some of Tolstoy's most successful works that appeared in his lifetime—the play *The Power of Darkness* (1887), the novel *Resurrection* (1899), and the longer stories—as well as those published posthumously, were written in his pre-1880 "realistic" manner. Although moral and religious preoccupations were ever present in his later writings, his literary genius seldom allowed them to assume undue prominence, while his artistry and the charm of his Russian style lent distinction even to treatises on such uninspiring and trite subjects as the evils of alcohol and tobacco.

Tolstoy's revolt against the established Church and his blasphemous attacks on its institutions led to his excommunication by the Synod (1901). His denunciation of the state and the Church and his rejection of the institution of private property played a part in fostering the revolutionary movement; but the following of his religious doctrine remained small, and his rationalized Christianity, after his neophyte exaltation had worn out, brought no real peace of mind to its founder. There was hostility between Tolstoy's family, on the one hand, and the small community of his religious followers led by the forcible and sinister V. G. Chertkov, on the other. A profound cleavage developed between Tolstoy and his wife, with whom he had been exceptionally happy but who shared none of his communist views. Increasingly conscious of the incompatibility of his doctrine with the life of ease and comfort he was leading on the family estate which he had made over to the countess, Tolstoy finally decided to cut the Gordian knot: at the age of eighty-two, accompanied by his daughter Alexandra and his doctor, he mysteriously vanished from Yasnaia Poliana. A few days later he was taken ill and died in the lodgings of the stationmaster of Astapovo, a railway junction in the province of Riazan (November, 1910).

Anton Chekhov (1860–1904) belongs, like Tolstoy, in the galaxy of world classics. Son of a former serf who became a prosperous merchant, Chekhov received a good education and in 1884 was awarded an M.D. degree by the University of Moscow, but he never practiced medicine. While still an undergraduate he contributed short humorous stories to cheap popular magazines. These early literary efforts, which were on a different level from his later writings, proved eminently successful with the indiscriminating public to whom they were addressed and brought their author popularity and financial reward. On leaving the university, Chekhov devoted himself exclusively to literary work. The first volume of his collected stories, published in 1886, attracted the attention of A. S. Suvorin, editor of *Novoe Vremia*. Behind the vulgarity and crude buffoonery that marred much of what Chekhov wrote during this period, Suvorin discerned his extraordinary genius and offered the young author a position with *Novoe Vremia* which freed him from dependence on the cheap magazines. Chekhov's association with Suvorin lasted until 1897, when it was broken off over the Dreyfus affair, Chekhov in the meantime having joined the ranks of the liberal opposition. In 1901 he married Olga Knipper, an actress of the Moscow Art Theater, where his plays scored some of their greatest triumphs. After 1897 ill health forced Chekhov to spend much of his time in the Crimea and at foreign resorts. He died of consumption at Badenweiler, Germany, at the early age of forty-four.

Chekhov's great literary reputation rests on his short stories, written after 1886, and on his plays. The main theme that runs through his work, to quote an acute literary critic (D. S. Mirsky), is "the mutual unsurpassable isolation of human beings and the impossibility of understanding each other." The Chekhovian world is not one of dramatic conflicts; what he deals with is despondency born of the triviality and drudgery of everyday life. This gloomy theme, developed with consummate mastery and relieved by touches of poetry and gentle humor, gives Chekhov's work its unique quality and its peculiar, if morbid, fascination. No other author has conveyed more convincingly the atmosphere of helplessness and distress which many foreign students have come to regard—perhaps without sufficient justification—as characteristic of the dark mysteries of the "Russian soul." The four principal plays of Chekhov—*The Seagull, Uncle Vania,* and especially *The Three Sisters* and *The Cherry Orchard*—are written in the same vein and rank among the masterpieces of the stage. Although the elusive character of his genius put his work in a class all its own, the influence of Chekhov on Russian and world literature has been great and enduring. It may be traced, among other things, in the predilection of the younger Russian authors for short stories rather than novels.

Maxim Gorky (1869–1936), whose real name was Alexis Peshkov, was, unlike Tolstoy and Chekhov, a self-made man. Born in a working-class family, at the age of five he lost his father and was soon forced to earn his living. He never attended school, and was taught to read and write by the cook of a Volga steamer where he was employed as a pantry boy. The formative years of his life were spent in wanderings along the Volga and in the south of Russia; he tried his hand at various jobs, had his full share of vexations, hunger, and unemployment, and acquired a profound insight into the psychology, and a familiarity with the ways, of tramps and "ex-men," who were his usual companions and whom he later portrayed in his books. Gorky's first story, *Makar Chudra*, was published in a Tiflis newspaper in 1892; three years later he was contributing to the influential St. Petersburg monthly *Russkoe Bogatstvo*, and in 1898 his collected stories were issued in two volumes and proved an immediate and immense success. In 1902 the Russian Academy of Science took the unprecedented step of electing the young author to membership in that august body; the annulment by the government, on political grounds, of his election merely added to the popularity of Gorky and brought about the withdrawal from the academy, as a protest, of two of its eminent members (Chekhov and V. G. Korolenko). The government's ill advised action was not without formal justification: Gorky was connected with the Social Democratic Party and most of the time supported its Bolshevik faction. He took a part in the revolutionary movement and was arrested in 1900 and again in 1905. In 1906 he came to the United States, but the triumphal reception accorded to him in New York was marred by the discovery —which created a sensation and brought protests and much unpleasantness—that he was not legally married to the woman who traveled with him as his wife. Gorky's disillusionment with America found its expression in a volume of stories published under the telling title of *The City of the Yellow Devil* (1907). The next few years were spent by Gorky chiefly in Capri, his time being divided between literary work and revolutionary propaganda. He returned to his native land shortly before the outbreak of World War I, was uncompromisingly opposed to Russia's war effort, and in spite of his occasional disagreements with the Bolsheviks emerged from the revolution of 1917 as the Soviet Union's leading proletarian author.

Realism and romanticism were inextricably mixed in Gorky's earlier works which laid the foundation of his literary reputation, with romanticism gradually fading away. The success of his writings was due not only to his great narrative power but also to the novelty of his theme—the underdog, the "ex-people"—and the picturesque and convincing manner in which it was developed. His celebrated play *The Lower Depths* (1902), an unconventional although somewhat romanticized story of "ex-people" gathered in the brutally realistic setting of a night refuge for the homeless, was a sensational success both in Russia and abroad. Realism seasoned with a rather large dose of social moralizing was the dominating characteristic of Gorky's work from 1899 to 1912. His massive novels *Foma Gordeev* (1899), *Three of Them* (1900–1901), *The Mother* (1907), *A Confession* (1908), *Okurov City* (1910), and *Matvei Kozhemiakin* (1911) unfolded a broad, dreary panorama of provincial Russia. These novels and a score of plays written by Gorky during this period were not well received (except for *The Lower Depths*) by the reading public and by Russian literary critics, who resented their tendentious moralizing which allegedly degraded belles-lettres to the level of political journalism. Gorky's creative power, however, reasserted itself in his autobiographical works *Childhood* (1913) and *Among Strangers* (1915), as well as in his later writings, and few would deny him today a place among the great contemporary authors.

Ivan Bunin, although he never achieved the international stature of Tolstoy, Chekhov, and Gorky, belongs in the forefront of the Russian realistic school. He was born in 1870 into a family of the landed nobility. His verse and prose writings began to appear in 1892. Outstanding among them are the remarkable stories *The Village* (1910), a masterful, unadorned picture of the Russian countryside, *The Dry Valley* (Sukhodol, 1912), a grim saga of the decline of the landed nobility, and *The Gentleman from San Francisco* (1916), a variation of rare effectiveness and restraint on the eternal and disquieting theme of the helplessness of man in the presence of death. These three stories alone would seem to assure Bunin a permanent place in world literature. A few other representatives of realism must be mentioned, however briefly: V. G. Korolenko (1853–1921), whose verse and stories, pathetic or humorous, were imbued with emotional radicalism and humanitarianism in the populist tradition; A. I. Kuprin (1870–1938), a former army officer and author of unflattering stories depicting conditions in the forces, and of a sensational novel about the life of prostitutes (*Yama*); M. P. Artsybashev (1878–1927), novelist, dramatist, and apostle of sexual freedom, whose novel *Sanin* (1907), preaching unbridled license, and whose plays built around the same theme created a tremendous, albeit short-lived, sensation. There were many other authors, representing various shades of realism, whose work, of necessity, cannot be mentioned here.

Meanwhile the virtues of realism, long the accepted creed of Russian men of letters, were challenged by writers of the younger generation. The closing decade of the nineteenth and the opening decade of the twentieth century witnessed, indeed, a strong movement of revolt against traditional theories and methods in every field of creative endeavor. While the opposition to accepted artistic values came from many quarters, it crystallized around a group of writers and painters known as *Mir Iskustva* (The Art World, after a review of that name published in 1898–1904) and led by Serge Diaghilev, of ballet fame, and the painter and art critic, Alexander Benois. According to contemporary Russian standards, the program of *Mir Iskustva* was revolutionary: "Art for art's sake," repudiation of realism, extreme individualism, and the study and acceptance of modern trends in western Europe and of the art of bygone centuries, both Russian and foreign, as guidance and a source of inspiration. The artists and authors who gathered under the banner of *Mir Iskustva* belonged to Russia's intellectual élite, and their campaign for the popularization of western ideas and a revival of interest in the past proved fruitful. The main literary movement stemming from *Mir Iskustva* was symbolism colored with mysticism. Derived from Baudelaire, Mallarmé, Verlaine, and Maeterlinck, Russian symbolism owed much to the proselytizing zeal and tireless activities of D. S. Merezhkovsky (1865–1941), a novelist, poet, essayist, and dramatist of ability and immense, although somewhat uncontrollable and even overwhelming, erudition. Merezhkovsky was a member of the *Mir Iskustva* group, and in 1903 he founded a review, *Novyi Put* (The New Way), which opened its columns to the young authors of the symbolist school but was forced to suspend publication after the defeat of the revolution of 1905, when Merezhkovsky, who had supported the revolutionary movement, deemed it wise to withdraw to Paris. The better known symbolist writers were Constantine Balmont (1867–1943), Valéry Briusov (1873–1924), Fedor Sologub (F. K. Terenikov, 1863–1927), Viacheslav Ivanov (born in 1866), Alexander Blok (1880–1921), Andrei Bely (B. N. Bugaev, 1880–1934), and Zinaida Hippius (wife of D. S. Merezhkovsky, born in 1867). Leonid Andreev (1871–1919), for a few years one of Russia's most discussed and successful authors, eludes precise qualification. Some of his writings (for instance, the well known story *The Seven That Were Hanged*, 1908) are in the realistic manner, while others, especially several of his plays (*The Life of Man*, 1907, and *He Who Gets Slapped*, 1914) are highly abstract and rhetorical, and might well have been the work of a full-fledged symbolist. A significant achievement of the symbolist school was the resurgence of poetry, so sadly neglected in the latter part of the nineteenth century, and a notable improvement in the level of prosody. The poems of Balmont, Briusov, Ivanov, Hippius, and Blok attained a high degree of technical perfection and revealed theretofore unsuspected possibilities of the Russian language as an instrument for conveying the intimate moods of the poet and for producing harmonious tonal effects. An offshoot of the symbolist movement was a futurism which, however, had no direct connection with its Italian namesake. Primarily a challenge to all literary conventions, Russian futurism made its appearance about 1910 and had its chief representative in Vladimir Maiakovsky (1894–1930).

Viewed as a whole, the Russian literary scene on the eve of the First World War was not lacking in diversity or vigor, whatever one may think of the merits of individual authors. Educated Russians, moreover, took literature seriously, and the publication of a new volume by a noted or promising author was something of an event.

PAINTING, MUSIC, DRAMA, AND THE BALLET

Symbolism in literature was but one manifestation of the aesthetic revolt of the 1890's. Dissatisfaction with the traditional schools of Russian painting, represented by the Academy of Arts and the Society of Circulating Exhibitions, was rampant among the younger painters, especially those who had studied in Paris. It was against the type of art sponsored by these two organizations that the thunder of *Mir Iskustva* was primarily directed. By the end of the century the old feud between the academy and the society was largely a thing of the past.[20] On the one hand, the academy relaxed its once intransigent classicism and even admitted to its midst several members of the society; on the other hand, some of the members of the society (for instance, Vladimir Makovsky, 1846–1920) adopted a manner of painting that conformed closely to the academic tradition. Repin, one of the pillars of the Society of Circulating Exhibitions, was simultaneously a member of the academy and for a time held the office of rector of that institution. The program of *Mir Iskustva*—"Art for art's sake," repudiation of both realism and the "social motive" so dear to the society, and the glorification of individualism—was a challenge to the accepted creed. A. N. Benois (born in 1870), an authority on art and a polemist of unusual power, and the other art critics associated with *Mir Iskustva*, launched effective attacks on the work of contemporary Russian masters, whom they criticized, among other things, for the staleness of their manner of painting and their inability to keep abreast of, or even to comprehend, modern trends in art. As if to confirm these accusations, Repin, in a letter of resignation from *Mir Iskustva*, which he had inadvertently joined, referred to the paintings of Millet, Dégas, and Puvis de Chavannes as "mediocre pastiches" (*posredstvennyia kartinki*).

The revolt against traditionalism succeeded beyond all expectation; indeed, it went further than the leaders of the "Art for art's sake" campaign had anticipated or desired. Spurred by polemics in the press, Russian painters flocked to Paris and, later, to Berlin and Munich, where they came under the influence of the most advanced art movements. Exhibitions of modern foreign masters, from the early French impressionists to Cézanne, Gauguin, and Picasso, were held in Russia and attracted a large, if occasionally bewildered, public. In 1898 there was inaugurated in St. Petersburg the Alexander III Museum of Russian Art, which included works by contemporary artists. The vast collection of Russian paintings assembled by the Moscow merchant P. M. Tretiakov was opened to the public in the 1880's and in 1892 transferred to the city of Moscow. The modern European school was exceptionally well represented in the private Moscow collections of

[20] See pp. 1052–1053.

Savva Morozov, S. J. and D. J. Shchukin, and S. M. Tretiakov; the latter collection was eventually incorporated in the P. M. Tretiakov gallery. There was a notable revival of interest in the art of past centuries, in icon painting and handicrafts, and a school of popular art was established in St. Petersburg in 1911.

Beginning in 1900 the progress and achievements of the "new" art were chronicled at the annual exhibitions of *Mir Iskustva*, which played a major part in the revolt against classicism, realism, and "social" painting. The leadership of *Mir Iskustva* as a progressive art organization, however, was soon challenged by more radical groups of artists such as *The Blue Rose* (1907) and the *Knave of Diamonds* (1910-1911). Freed from the shackles of tradition, Russian painters moved irresistibly towards limitless horizons. In 1900-1905 impressionism was the extreme left-wing movement; it was superseded by post-impressionism, expressionism and, around 1912, by futurism. To the follower of Picasso and Paul Klee the theories of *Mir Iskustva* were as stale and dated as classicism and realism were to Benois.

The rapid evolution of Russian art was not an unmixed blessing. It was responsible for much confusion of thought and scores of bad pictures. Nevertheless its accomplishments were substantial and real. The work of the more talented painters, who had experienced in varying degrees the influence of modern trends, was an advance from the mediocre level of their predecessors. The breach with the nineteenth century, as epitomized by the exhibitions of *Mir Iskustva*, manifested itself both in manner of painting and in subject matter. Academic restraint and conventional realism had given place to a much freer use of the brush and to more vivid, imaginative, and daring colors. Genre painting, especially that of topical character loaded with "social" content, was in the discard. The *Mir Iskustva* group produced several distinguished landscape painters: J. I. Levitan (1861-1900), perhaps Russia's first impressionist; K. A. Korovin (born in 1861), V. A. Serov (1865-1911), M. V. Nesterov (born in 1862), V. M. Kustodiev (1878-1927), and I. E. Grabar (born in 1872), also a writer on Russian art. Serov, moreover, ranks among Russia's best portraitists of the modern school. K. A. Somov (born in 1869) earned popularity by his exquisitely stylized evocations of the eighteenth century. M. V. Vrubel (1856-1910) was one of the founders of the Russian symbolist school. A prolific artist of impressionistic leanings was N. K. Roerikh (born in 1874), who has to his credit over three thousand canvases. Original work in illustrating Russian fairy tales and legends was done by A. Bilibin (born in 1876). The revival of religious painting, stimulated by interest in the old icons, proved disappointing. The most ambitious venture in this field, the murals by V. M. Vasnetsov (1848–1926) and Nesterov in the St. Vladimir Cathedral in Kiev, hardly justifies the extravagant praise bestowed upon them by contemporary art critics. Vasnetsov's labored and stylized Byzantinism singularly fails to provoke religious emotions. This artist, however, belonged to the older generation, and the Kiev murals were executed in 1886–1896. The greatest accomplishment of the *Mir Iskustva* group was in the field of decorative art. The stage settings by L. S. Bakst (1866–1924), Benois, Korovin, Kustodiev, Vrubel, Roerikh, and others constitute an important and exciting chapter in the history of the theater.

The evolution of Russian art brought to an end its isolation from the west. From 1900 on, Russian painters appeared regularly at international exhibitions. The Russian section organized by Diaghilev at the Paris Autumn Salon in 1906 was the object of favorable attention, but its success was rather a *succès de curiosité* than a tribute to the intrinsic merits of the pictures. The better known representatives of Russian cubism and futurism, M. Larionov and N. Goncharova (both born in 1881), received a degree of recognition abroad, especially in Germany.

Towards the end of the monarchy Russian painting had caught up with Europe, although in most fields it made no significant original contributions. Having telescoped within a decade developments that in other countries took a much longer time, modern Russian art bore the marks of its precocious growth: lack of tradition, a tendency towards extremes, slavish imitation of foreign masters, and the lingering survivals of realism and classicism; yet much of it had the virtues of youth—spontaneity, freshness, vigor, and daring. No national school of painting came into being; nevertheless it was not so much the achievements of Russian painters in assimilating and developing western trends, as the exotic element in their work, interpreted as national characteristics, that captured the fancy of the public at home and won applause abroad.

In the twentieth century, as in the nineteenth, music in Russia fared better than painting. The concerts sponsored by the Russian Music Society accomplished a great educational work in familiarizing the public with the works of Russian and foreign masters; the standards of teaching in the music schools, especially in the conservatoires of St. Petersburg and Moscow, were high; and last but not least, musicians of the younger generation proved worthy successors of their elders. The veteran composers Balakirev, Cui, and Rimsky-Korsakov continued their fruitful work well into the first decade of the twentieth century, and they were joined by talented younger men who, however, did not always see eye to eye with their teachers. The maturing of public taste and the better appreciation of music were evidenced by the rediscovery of Mussorgsky, whose scores violated the accepted canons and who was perhaps the most original and talented among The Five. The work of this great master of realism, with its apt characterizations and sardonic humor, proved far ahead of his time. Mussorgsky's genius found its full expression in his operas *Boris Godunov* and *Khovanshchina*. The former was produced at the St. Petersburg Imperial Opera House in 1874; but it was roughly handled by the critics and was soon dropped from the repertory, while the latter, unfinished at the time of his death (1881), did not see the footlights of the Imperial Opera House until many years later, although a complete score, reconstructed by Rimsky-Korsakov from the original material, was available as far back as 1883 and was produced by a private company in 1885. The other compositions of Mussorgsky were equally neglected in Russia; but they gradually won recognition abroad, were known to the young Debussy, and influenced the work of some of the modern European masters. Through Paris and Brussels the work of the long-ignored composer triumphingly returned to his native land. In 1904, after an interval of many years, *Boris Godunov*, edited and arranged by Rimsky-Korsakov (1896), was restored to the repertory of the St. Petersburg Imperial Opera House; the turn of *Khovanshchina* came in 1911, nearly thirty years after the opera was written. It is characteristic of the trend of musical opinion that the Rimsky-Korsakov version of *Boris Godunov*, which not only supplemented Mussorgsky's avowedly defective orchestration but also revised, or eliminated, some of the more iconoclastic passages, soon came under fire as a wanton distortion of a great masterpiece and that the original score has been used in the more recent editions.

The belated recognition of Mussorgsky roughly coincided with the opening of new inviting vistas by two young composers, Scriabin and Stravinsky. A. N. Scriabin (1871–1915), a mystic, a mediocre poet, and an accomplished pianist, was among the first to raise the banner of revolt against the tendencies prevalent in Russian music; he succeeded in creating works of real beauty expressed in a personal and unorthodox medium, but his influence outside Russia remained limited. The case of Igor Stravinsky (born in 1882) was different. His genius was most fully expressed in his celebrated ballets *The Firebird* (1910), *Petrushka* (1911), and *Le Sacre du printemps* (1913), works which shocked the conservatives but won the acclaim of influential critics and of vast audiences in Russia and abroad. In brilliance and originality of scoring and in aptness of characterization Stravinsky has few equals. The dominating principle that governed his art from *Petrushka* onward, according to one authority, "is the belief that music should make a purely physical appeal to the hearer and should be free from any literary or pictorial associations which address themselves to the intellect." Stravinsky's art has had a profound effect upon the development of music throughout the world.

Among the composers who shunned revolutionary innovations but carried on with distinction the classical tradition (even though their work showed occasionally the influence of the "neo-Russian" school), the leading place belongs to Serge Rakhmaninoff (1873–1943) and A. K. Glazunov (1865–1936), director of the St. Petersburg conservatoire in 1906–1917. A. S. Arensky (1861–1906) and A. T. Grechaninov (born in 1864) may be mentioned as other talented and competent composers of the more conservative school.

Of credit to Russian music was the brilliant array of Russian-trained interpretive artists whose names are internationally known. The roster of conductors included E. F. Napravnik, V. I. Safonov, Alexander Ziloti, Glazunov, Rakhmaninoff, and Serge Koussevitzky, conductor in 1910–1917 of his own admirable symphony orchestra, with headquarters in Moscow. Among the pianists and violinists were Josef Hofmann, Safonov, Scriabin, Rakhmaninoff, Ziloti, Nicholas Orloff, Vladimir Horowitz (whose professional career, however, did not begin until the early 1920's), Leopold Auer, Efrem Zimbalist, Mischa Elman, and the then boy-prodigy Jascha Heifetz. The list of opera and concert singers was headed by Fedor Chaliapin and Leonid Sobinov. In 1914 a new major star rose on the musical horizon: Serge Prokofiev (born in 1891) graduated from the St. Petersburg conservatoire with highest honors for piano playing. It may be claimed, indeed, that Russia was the Mecca of music lovers, particularly opera lovers. St. Petersburg had four opera houses, each offering a full season—the Imperial Mariinsky Theater, the Italian Opera, the People's Palace, where Chaliapin scored some of his brilliant successes, and the Musical Drama, which endeavored to do away with operatic conventions. Moscow, Warsaw, and the larger provincial cities (Kiev, Odessa, Tiflis) had their own opera houses with permanent companies and an eight- or nine-month season.

The Russian theater benefited greatly by modern trends in literature, painting, and music; the application of new ideas to the stage was facilitated by the removal of restrictions on private theatrical enterprise that had been in force until the 1880's. For nearly 150 years, from the establishment of the first state theater in 1756 to the end of the nineteenth century, state-owned theaters dominated the Russian stage. In 1826 the state or "imperial" theaters, as they were officially known, all of them situated in St. Petersburg and Moscow, were brought under the management of the ministry of the imperial court. Private theatrical enterprises existed, but their position was precarious and their record undistinguished. In 1856 Emperor Alexander II, alarmed by the spread of public unrest and fearing that the stage might be used for subversive propaganda, directed that "private theaters in the two capital cities shall not be permitted." Although this decision was merely embodied in a resolution penned by the tsar, on a report of the minister of the imperial court, and was not confirmed by law or decree, it established, according to a recent historian of the stage (S. S. Bogdanov), a monopoly of the imperial theaters in St. Petersburg and in Moscow. The fact that theatrical enterprises in the provinces were not affected was of little practical import. Provincial companies dated back to the end of the eighteenth century, and in 1875 numbered about seventy; their repertoires, however, were worthless, their artistic standards unbelievably low, and their casts recruited from the dregs of society. The monopoly of the imperial theaters, although not rigidly enforced, was among the causes that hindered the development of private theatrical enterprises.

The abrogation of the monopoly by a decree of March 22, 1882, followed by the aesthetic revolt of the 1890's opened to private initiative a fruitful field of activity. Of the privately owned theaters that came into being, the most notable was the Moscow Art Theater founded in 1897–1898 by the actor and producer K. S. Stanislavsky

(1863–1938) and by V. I. Nemirovich-Danchenko (1859–1943), a dramatist and novelist of some repute. The guiding principle of the new enterprise was the striving for harmonious ensembles, with the same meticulous attention paid to the details of the setting as to the acting of the leading performers. The "star" system was to be replaced by team-work of a high degree of perfection. "There are no minor parts but there are mediocre actors," was a contention of the Moscow Art Theater. Stanislavsky's enthusiasm and genius, an excellent cast, admirable stage settings designed by Russia's foremost artists, and a judiciously selected repertoire, which included plays by eminent Russian and foreign dramatists, combined to make the Moscow Art Theater an unqualified success. Its achievements have received world-wide recognition and have left an enduring imprint on dramatic art.

Modern trends—impressionism, expressionism, symbolism, cubism, and futurism—had their adherents among Russian producers and stage directors, and led to much exciting, if not uniformly successful, experimentation with the stage. Advanced theories were more readily tried by private entrepreneurs, for instance, by the talented actress and producer Vera Komissarzhevsky, and before long they invaded the imperial theaters whose honorable tradition was of necessity conservative. Several of the renowned stage designers of the modern school did their best work for the imperial theaters, and it was at the Imperial Aleksandrovsky Theater in St. Petersburg that V. E. Meyerhold, a resourceful and tireless innovator, staged some of his most striking productions. The example of St. Petersburg and Moscow was contagious: within a decade or two the levels of the provincial theater—from the point of view of repertoire, acting, and quality of production—was vastly improved. There was no lack of entertainment for those who found concerts, the opera, and the drama too heavy a fare. Light comedy, musical comedy, and vaudeville shows flourished on the Russian stage. Some of the companies specializing in lighter entertainment developed a genre of their own which, in later years, won considerable popularity abroad (for instance, Baliev's *Chauve Souris*).

The effervescence of the ballet was more sudden and perhaps more unexpected than the transformation of the other arts. First introduced in Russia in 1672, the ballet did not take firm root until a century later, when in 1779 Empress Catherine founded in St. Petersburg a ballet school modeled on that of Paris. The school, which exists to this day in the Soviet Union, subjected its students to a long and rigorous training and supplied the imperial ballet (and its successor) with a steady flow of highly skilled dancers. It is this institution, and not, as is sometimes imagined, any inborn aptitude of the Russians for dancing, that accounts for the technical perfection of the Russian ballet. Transplanted to the banks of the Neva from Paris, the ballet for over a century remained hermetically closed to Russian influences. Popular folk dances had no part in the formation of its tradition. Choreography, dance technique, and the methods of training were French, and foreign masters—French or Italian—ruled both the ballet and the ballet school. Charles Louis Didlo, a Frenchman, was the choreographer and leading dancer of the St. Petersburg ballet from 1802 to 1831. His countryman, and eventually his successor, Marius Petipas arrived in Russia in 1847, produced his first ballet in 1858, and until his death in 1910 remained the premier dancer and a dominating influence in the St. Petersburg ballet. In spite of his long residence in St. Petersburg he spoke a fantastic brand of Russian, and in his work he faithfully maintained the classical French tradition. At his best Petipas was a consummate artist, as evidenced by his masterpieces *Sleeping Beauty* (1890) and *Swan Lake* (1896) for scores by Tchaikovsky. Nevertheless his choreography, for all its technical perfection, was unimaginative and stale; some fifty ballets that he staged differed in costumes and décor but otherwise adhered closely to an immutable pattern. Moreover, the leading parts were usually assigned to French and, later, to Italian dancers, and it was not until the turn of the century that brilliant Russian ballerinas—Kshesinskaia, Preobrazhenskaia, Pavlova, Karsavina, Geltser—gained full recognition. The musical scores were, as a rule, as trite and conventional as the choreography. The earliest attempt at injecting into the ballet the "national" element was made in 1865 with the production of *Konek-Gorbunek*. Named after a mythical beast in a Russian fairy tale and staged by S. Leon, the new ballet differed from the others of the same period merely in its costumes and setting, which the French choreographer imagined to be inspired by Russian folklore. The personnel of the ballet was very large. In 1892–1893 the St. Petersburg establishment consisted of three choreographers, four stage directors, 153 ballerinas, 73 male dancers, and the students of the ballet school. Maintained at a considerable cost to the taxpayers and officially a national institution, the imperial ballet was actually an exotic growth alien to Russian tradition and aloof from the intellectual currents of Russian life.

The almost revolutionary transformation of the ballet in the opening years of the twentieth century was a result of mounting dissatisfaction with the French conservative tradition, an opposition that merged with, and became part and parcel of, the aesthetic revolt of the 1890's. Several factors combined to make possible the modernization of the ballet: the almost simultaneous appearance of a number of exceptionally gifted dancers and stage designers and, above all, the genius, vision, and perseverance of Michael Fokine, a young choreographer of the St. Petersburg ballet. The Fokine innovations, which horrified Petipas and against which the aging Frenchman waged a losing battle, affected both scores and choreography. Fokine chose the scores of his ballets exclusively from among the works of outstanding composers—Tchaikovsky, Balakirev, Rimsky-Korsakov, Glinka, Borodin, Glazunov, Stravinsky, Schumann, Wagner, Weber. As a choreographer he leaned towards the "neo-Grecian" school which stemmed from the "free dance" theory and technique of Isadora Duncan. His ballets were based on the principle of the "unity" of the performance, that is, the dancers were to interpret the meaning of the music, the two elements blending into one. In some of his ballets Fokine emphasized mass movements rather than solo dancing. The *corps de ballet* thus acquired a new importance instead of merely providing a background for the prima ballerina (for instance, in Borodin's *Polovetsky Dances*). Several of Fokine's best productions, however, were in the classical vein (*Les Sylphides, Le Spectre de la rose*). Costumes and settings of great originality and richness of color were designed by distinguished artists—Benois, Bakst, Sudeikin, Bilibin, and others. The "new" Russian ballet was dramatically revealed to the world by Diaghilev. In 1906 he brought to Paris Russian painting, in 1907 Russian music to be played at the Historical Concerts, and in the summer of 1909 he inaugurated at Le Châtelet his first celebrated season of the Russian ballet, which was followed by many others. The virtuosity and charm of accomplished dancers (Nijinsky, Pavlova, Karsavina), the beauty and originality of many scores, the magnificence of the décor, and the unrivaled synchronization of the performance took Paris and, later, the world by storm. Stretching the facts somewhat, it may well be said that while the classical French ballet was preserved and nurtured in St. Petersburg and Moscow (which had its own imperial ballet), the Russian ballet, as a distinct national achievement, was born in Paris. That at least two of its component elements—the all-important technique and many of the scores—were of non-Russian origin does not necessarily detract from an accomplishment that proved a landmark in the history of the ballet throughout the world.

L'ANCIEN RÉGIME: AN APPRAISAL

To those who had the good fortune to belong to the upper levels of the social structure, life in Russia on the eve of the First World War was not devoid of interest and charm, particularly if they happened to reside in St. Petersburg or Moscow and were reconciled to the rigors of the climate. There was intense intellectual activity, as indicated by the wide range of the political press and by diversity of currents in literature, painting, music, and the theater. The imperial court, contrary to what might have been expected, was not the center of social life. Court functions were rare, formal, and insufferably dull. Several of the grand duchesses and society matrons, however, kept salons which set the tone for the capital and the provinces. Outside the narrow circle of the tsar's and tsarina's personal friends, it was fashionable to be critical of the existing order, and the vast majority of educated Russians were probably, in some degree, in sympathy with the opposition. The State Duma was the rallying point of the politically-minded; parliamentary debates on the main issues were heatedly discussed in the press and elsewhere. Social conventions were less crystallized and less uniformly followed than in the Anglo-Saxon countries, leaving greater freedom of personal choice and introducing in social intercourse an element of the unexpected. For instance, the principal meal of the day, *obed*, or dinner, might be served at any time from noon to 10 P.M. Since it was customary both to make unannounced calls and to invite the visitor to partake of the family meal, a judicious arrangement of visits might have brought ample gustatory reward. Ties with western Europe were intimate and seemingly real. Children in Russian upper- and middle-class families were usually brought up by French, German, or, less frequently, English governesses; foreign books and journals were widely read; and European capitals and resorts were crowded with Russians. Familiarity with foreign languages and literature and visits abroad are not, however, conclusive evidence that the traditional estrangement of Muscovy from the west was over. In the process of transplantation to an alien soil, foreign ideas and practices inevitably suffer transformation and sometimes distortion. It may be symbolic that Miliukov, standard-bearer of western parliamentarism, appeared at the opening afternoon sessions of the Duma in a dinner (quaintly known as "smoking") jacket, an attire still novel in St. Petersburg. There was nothing wrong with Miliukov's sartorial innovation, except that it was worn at the wrong time of the day.

Moreover, western influences were restricted to the educated classes, and rapidly thinned out with the increase of the distance from the capital. St. Petersburg, with its baroque eighteenth and nineteenth century palaces built by French and Italian architects and its magnificent embankments—a dream metropolis in the eerie glow of the white nights—was both physically and spiritually the most westernized of the Russian cities. The court and the bureaucracy were susceptible to western ideas, and not indifferent to world opinion. Moscow, a maze of winding streets lined with sprawling houses and vast gardens and dominated by the somber medieval walls, towers, and domes of the Kremlin, was traditionally critical of the new capital, scornful of the bureaucracy, and hostile to foreign ideas. The imprint of the west was less noticeable in the small provincial towns than in the larger cities, and disappeared altogether in the remote urban settlements, which had no modern amenities and differed from villages only in name. Moreover, 87 per cent of the population (according to the census of 1897) lived in rural areas and were as untouched by any cultural influence as though they dwelt on another planet.

The gulf between the educated classes and the masses was the basic and fatal weakness of Russia's social structure. In appearance, customs, standards, and way of life the *barin* (a term applied by the lower stratum to social superiors) and the muzhik had nothing in common and, both literally and figuratively, spoke a different language. The Russian used by the educated groups differed sharply from the parlance of the peasants, nor had the two classes any common interests except, perhaps, the harvest and the weather, if the *barin* happened to be a landowner. The prevalence of illiteracy barred the great leveling influence of the popular press, even though by 1914 the ratio of those unable to read and write had probably declined from the 79 per cent of the 1897 census. According to official reports literacy among men drafted for the army increased from 38 per cent in 1894 to 56 per cent in 1904 and to 68 per cent in 1913. These figures, which still indicate a substantial percentage of illiteracy even in the selected group of younger men, must, however, be treated with caution. Experience shows that many of the soldiers reported as "literate" had attended school in their boyhood but had not since seen a book or a newspaper. They were actually unable to write a letter, and some had difficulty in signing their names. Russia had no organized sports (boxing, football, baseball, cricket) which have a universal appeal, create common interests, and obliterate, at least for a time, class distinctions. The Orthodox Church, with its long tradition of subservience to the state, low educational level of the clergy, and indifference to social activities, never exercised a unifying and cultural influence comparable to that of the Protestant or the Roman Catholic churches. The persecution of national and religious minorities—Finns, Poles, Jews, Ukrainians, and others—bred disaffection and separatist tendencies. Finally, the failure to produce a decent standard of living for the peasants and industrial workers weakened among these groups the stimulus to fight for the country against the external enemy and prepared a fertile ground for subversive propaganda. In 1914–1917, as in 1905, the strain and stress of the war brought to the fore the disruptive forces that had long been at work behind the imposing façade of the empire.

CHAPTER XLII

NICHOLAS II

Foreign Relations, 1894–1914

※

TWO EVENTFUL DECADES

The years 1894–1914 were a period of recurrent international crises and feverish diplomatic activity. The rapid industrialization of the more advanced countries in the second half of the nineteenth century, and the improvement in shipping and overland transportation, gave a powerful stimulus to overseas expansion in the form either of territorial annexations or of the establishment of spheres of influence. Conquest of distant lands, irrespective of their economic value, gained considerable public support through the uncritical acceptance of such ill defined notions as "the white man's burden" or *"la mission civilisatrice de la France."* The older colonial Powers—Great Britain, France, Holland—found themselves confronted in many parts of the world with the demands not only of their traditional rivals but also of impatient newcomers in the colonial field: Germany, Belgium, Japan, and the United States. Russia, although a backward agricultural country with vast undeveloped and underpopulated territories, had her empire builders bent on conquest. Overseas expansion, superimposed upon the secular antagonisms of the Old World, accentuated international rivalries and multiplied the causes of conflict. The growth of nationalism and the ceaseless quest for political alignments that would both gratify national ambitions and reconcile the supposedly "vital" interests of the great Powers produced a maze of diplomatic moves and counter-moves which culminated in the First World War. The inner link between these kaleidoscopic events is not obvious. Decisions affecting international issues of utmost gravity are made, even in democracies, by small groups of leaders whose tenure of office is often precarious. Subsequent ratification of such decisions by a representative assembly may obscure but cannot alter the fact that they reflect the personal views and prejudices of their framers. The familiar notion of the continuity of national policies, therefore, is in most cases unfounded, because it connotes a degree of cohesion and integration grossly at variance with the facts.

All these considerations apply to imperial Russia. Under the Fundamental Laws of 1906 the conduct of foreign relations remained, as before, a prerogative of the Crown. In actual fact, however, Nicholas exercised no unifying influence over foreign policy, and his sporadic interference with diplomacy invariably ended in embarrassment or disaster. Russian ministers of foreign affairs during this period were men of mediocre caliber. The aged Giers died early in 1895. He was succeeded, as head of the foreign office, by Prince A. B. Lobanov-Rostovsky (1895–1896), Count M. N. Muravev (1897–1900), Count V. N. Lamsdorf (1900–1906), A. P. Izvolsky (1906–1910), and S. D. Sazonov (1910–1916). Lobanov-Rostovsky and Muravev, former ambassadors in the grand manner, were courtiers rather than statesmen; both died in office. Lamsdorf, an industrious and unassuming bureaucrat who had never seen service abroad, considered it his duty faithfully to execute the policies decided upon by the tsar, even when he was in disagreement with them, as was the case in the Far East. Izvolsky, a diplomat of ability and experience, was an opportunist and the victim of an inveterate snobbishness and of a passion for social and diplomatic successes. To Izvolsky, according to Baron Taube, "the real interests of Russia were frequently lost in a vague mist characteristic of Russian thought, and political issues often interested him only in so far as they appeared to promise laurels to the minister of foreign affairs; hence the artificial character of many of the so-called 'great political questions' which actually had precious little to do with the real interests of the Russian state." [1]

Sazonov's rapid rise from the minor post of Russian representative at the Vatican to that of assistant minister (1908) and then minister of foreign affairs was due to his kinship with Stolypin (he was married to a sister of Madame Stolypin). Profoundly religious, retiring, timid, and pliable, Sazonov had but an inadequate grasp of the vast prob-

---

[1] Baron M. de Taube, *La Politique russe d'avant guerre et la fin de l'empire des tsars, 1904–1917* (Paris, 1928), p. 107. Taube, a distinguished international lawyer, was a high official of the Russian ministry of foreign affairs.

lems with which he had to deal. At his best he was a conscientious and well meaning functionary, but he had neither the vision nor the force of character needed to lead the nation in an emergency such as arose in 1914. From 1894 to 1903, and again in 1905–1906, Witte had a far greater influence on Russia's foreign relations than had Lobanov-Rostovsky, Muravev, or Lamsdorf. It was, indeed, his criticism of the Far Eastern policy that brought upon him imperial displeasure and dismissal from the office of minister of finance in 1903, when the tsar chose to follow the counsel of a clique of irresponsible adventurers. The ease with which Nicholas yielded to pressure from unofficial quarters introduced in Russian foreign relations a grave element of uncertainty. Moreover, in spite of the Franco-Russian alliance, the tradition of friendship with Germany had many adherents in St. Petersburg, while hostility towards England was intensified by London's pro-Japanese attitude during the Russo-Japanese War. In the entangled and confused diplomatic situation of the opening decade of the twentieth century the emergence of the Triple Entente, which in 1914 was to confront Germany, was by no means a certainty.

UNIVERSAL PEACE AND DISARMAMENT

Nicholas's dramatic appeal to the world for "the maintenance of universal peace and a possible reduction of the excessive armaments" stands outside the general current of Russian foreign policy. In a circular note of August 12, 1898, the imperial government lamented the financial, economic, and moral effects of the armaments race, and proposed the convocation of an international conference to deal with the issues involved. The real motives of this unexpected move remain obscure. Witte claimed that it originated with Muravev and himself, and was provoked by Austria's plan for the modernization of her artillery. Since St. Petersburg was unable for financial reasons to meet the Austrian challenge, limitation of armaments was suggested as a suitable method of preventing Vienna from gaining a military advantage. This explanation is not entirely convincing, and the possibility of more lofty considerations behind the Russian proposal should not be excluded.[2] If such motives actually existed, however, few contemporaries

[2] "I suppose Witte is the best man that Russia could have at the head of her affairs at present . . . ," Theodore Roosevelt wrote in Sept., 1905. "I cannot

believed in their sincerity; foreign statesmen and the press, while paying perfunctory homage to the nobility of the tsar's sentiments, made no secret of the fact that they regarded the Russian proposal as devoid of practical significance and designed to serve some sinister, selfish purpose. The time chosen for launching the disarmament move, moreover, was singularly inopportune. Muravev and Kuropatkin, the minister of war, sent abroad to canvass for the support of European governments, arrived in Paris in the midst of the Fashoda crisis which brought France and England to the brink of war. Russia's own devotion to the cause of peace was open to doubt. St. Petersburg had then only recently embarked on a policy of aggression in China. Kuropatkin argued in a report to the tsar (November 23, 1898) that general disarmament was not practicable until certain conditions had been fulfilled: partition of Austria-Hungary; Russian occupation of the Bosphorus; restoration of Alsace and Lorraine to France and, as compensation to Germany, the annexation by that country of Austria's German provinces. This program, it will readily be seen, was not conducive to universal peace. A Russian circular note of December 30, 1898, a watered-down version of that of August 12, while received with ill concealed hostility, nevertheless led to the convocation of the first peace conference held at The Hague in May and June, 1899, and attended by twenty European Powers, the United States, Mexico, Japan, China, Siam, and Persia. The amended Russian disarmament proposal—temporary "freezing" of armed forces and of appropriations for armaments—was defeated, but the conference agreed on rules of warfare and established a permanent court of arbitration. The second and last Hague conference, summoned on the initiative of the Russian government in 1907, dealt with kindred problems of international law which have little bearing on Russian history and need not be discussed here. A boon to international lawyers, the Russian 1898 proposal proved futile and sterile as a step towards peace and disarmament; similar efforts in the interval between the First World War and the second were equally barren of practical results.

say that I liked him, for I thought his bragging and bluster not only foolish but shockingly vulgar when compared with the gentlemanly restraint of the Japanese. Moreover, he struck me as a very selfish man, totally without high ideals." Quoted in Edward H. Zabriskie, *American-Russian Rivalry in the Far East, 1895–1914* (University of Pennsylvania Press, Philadelphia, 1946), p. 129.

THE FAR EAST, 1894–1903

In the 1890's and the early 1900's the political ambitions of St. Petersburg were focused on the Far East. In the opinion of Russia's leading statesmen the Trans-Siberian railway, which was slowly approaching completion, opened boundless vistas of Russian domination over China. In a report submitted to Emperor Alexander III (November 6, 1892), Witte, then newly appointed minister of finance, held that the Trans-Siberian line would eventually supersede the Suez Canal as the principal trade route to China and would flood Chinese markets with Russian goods. He advocated a Sino-Russian alliance as the best means of undermining the colonial supremacy of Great Britain, and pictured St. Petersburg in the part of arbiter between Asia and the western world. Reliable rapid communications linking Vladivostok with the metropolis would, in Witte's opinion, allow the strengthening of the Russian Pacific fleet and—in an international emergency—make the imperial navy master of "the entire commercial traffic of the Pacific." Eight years later (in 1900) Witte argued that the control of the Manchurian railway assured Russian predominance in the whole of China, including her rich southern provinces, and he consistently held that Russian objectives could be attained by "peaceful penetration." Exaggerated and, in part, illusory as were these schemes, they captured the imagination of nationalistic-minded Russians. Nebulous metaphysics was allied with faulty economics. Prince E. E. Ukhtomsky, an influential journalist and student of Buddhism and oriental art, as well as an administrator and a diplomat, extolled the spiritual kinship of Russia and Asia and wrote ecstatically about Russia's "Asiatic mission."

Nicholas was impressed by the arguments of Witte and by the rhetoric of Ukhtomsky, who had accompanied him on the voyage round the world. Emperor William of Germany encouraged Russian Far Eastern plans, partly because he wished to divert the attention of St. Petersburg from Europe and partly because he believed in the "yellow peril." Since Vladivostok was icebound several months a year, the execution of the Russian program required the acquisition of an ice-free port on the Pacific coast. "It is absolutely necessary that Russia should have a port open all year," the tsar wrote in April, 1895, in the margin of a report of the foreign minister. "This port must be on the littoral (southeastern Korea) and must be connected by a stretch of land with our . . . possessions." It was not fully realized in St. Petersburg that expansion in China would lead to conflicts not only with England but also with Japan and the United States.

The intervention of the western Powers in China, which was intensified in the 1840's, did not at first extend to Manchuria and Korea, the latter an autonomous kingdom under the suzerainty of the Manchu emperors of China. For geographical reasons these thinly populated territories, remote from the main trade routes, were of greater interest to Russia and, particularly, to Japan than they were to their western rivals. The contiguity of the Korean peninsula to the Japanese islands and its importance as the gateway to China and Manchuria invited Japanese penetration. Throughout the centuries Korea was repeatedly raided by its island neighbors; a particularly devastating invasion took place at the close of the sixteenth century, but the Japanese eventually withdrew and for over 150 years were satisfied with a small trading settlement at Fusan which they operated under highly restrictive conditions. In the early 1870's, when territorial aggrandizement became one of the principal objectives of Japanese foreign policy, the Korean problem came again to the fore, partly because attempts at southerly expansion had met with indifferent success. The Riukiu Islands were annexed by Tokyo in 1875, but a landing party sent to Formosa a year earlier accomplished nothing. In 1876 the Japanese exacted from Korea a treaty terminating her seclusion. The example of Tokyo was emulated by the western Powers, and treaties with Korea were concluded by the United States in 1882, by England and Germany in 1883, by Italy and Russia in 1884, and by France in 1886. The predominant influence in Korea, however, was Chinese and Japanese. The struggle between the two oriental empires for the control of Korea is a weird story of rebellions, massacres, and palace intrigues. Under the terms of the Sino-Japanese treaty of 1885, both Powers undertook to withdraw their troops from Korea with an agreement not to send them back without advance notice to the other signatory, an arrangement that recognized the right of Japan to intervene militarily in the affairs of Korea. The fear of Russian aggression loomed large in the Chinese policy of other nations. In April, 1885, Great Britain seized Port Hamilton off the Korean coast because of the alleged Russian intention to occupy Port Lazareff on the peninsula. St. Petersburg's protest and threats of retaliation, and the likelihood that Japan would use the seizure of Port Hamilton as a pretext for the establishment of naval bases in Korea, forced London to withdraw the expeditionary force (February, 1887).

The gathering storm burst in 1894 when an insurrection in Korea brought about the simultaneous intervention of China and Japan. Refusal to recall the Japanese troops after the suppression of the rebellion led to the Sino-Japanese War (July, 1894 to March, 1895) and the overwhelming defeat of China. The unexpected display of Japanese military might perturbed the European capitals and Washington. Proposals (autumn, 1894) sponsored by Great Britain and Russia for mediation by the western Powers were rejected by the United States and Germany. Confronted with Japan's mounting victories, St. Petersburg hesitated between two courses: determined resistance to Japanese expansion in continental China, or an arrangement with Tokyo for Russian acquisition, by way of compensation for Japanese gains, of an ice-free port in Korea and the cession to Russia of northern Manchuria, which would shorten the Chita-Vladivostok span of the Trans-Siberian railway by some six hundred miles. Russian nationalist opinion clamored for annexations, and Nicholas for a time favored the dismemberment of China. Witte, however, argued that the integrity of northern China must be maintained at all cost because Japanese penetration in southern Manchuria would lead to a Russo-Japanese war. The concessions desired by St. Petersburg could, in his opinion, be easily secured later from a Chinese government weakened by the struggle and grateful for Russian assistance. The policy advocated by Witte finally prevailed. Early in April, 1895, Russia was joined by France and Germany, but not by Great Britain, in a "friendly" representation to Tokyo to refrain from annexations on the Chinese mainland. The Sino-Japanese Treaty of Shimonoseki (April 17, 1895, N.S.), however, proclaimed the independence of Korea, imposed a heavy indemnity on China, and ceded to Japan the Liaotung peninsula as well as Formosa and the Pescadores Islands. The Liaotung cession was protested by Russia, France, and Germany (April 23, N.S.). Although Great Britain again remained aloof, Tokyo deemed it wise to heed the wishes of the three governments which had at their disposal sizable naval forces in Chinese waters. The Shimonoseki treaty was ratified but the Liaotung peninsula was restored to China, ostensibly in return for an increase in the indemnity.

The Russian government lost no time in reaping the fruits of its diplomatic victory. A Franco-Russian loan to China arranged by

Witte supplied the funds for the payment of the first installment of the indemnity. This skillfully planned operation defeated the proposal for an international loan to be secured by foreign controls over Chinese revenue. The Sino-Russian loan contract (July, 1895), moreover, provided for Russian participation in any international supervision of Chinese finance that might be established in the future. In December, 1895, there was founded, on Witte's initiative, the Russo-Chinese Bank, an institution operating in China and endowed with broad powers, including those of coinage, tax collection, and holding of concessions. The bank was under the patronage of the imperial government, but its capital was predominantly French. Russian overtures for railway concessions in Manchuria were at first resisted by the Chinese. An agreement, however, was reached in direct negotiations between Witte and the Chinese elder statesman Li Hung-chang, who came to Russia for the coronation of Nicholas II. Witte took good care that the Chinese envoy should not be exposed to undesirable European influences: Li Hung-chang was met at Suez by Prince Ukhtomsky and was transported on board a Russian steamer to Odessa and then by rail to St. Petersburg and Moscow. The secret Sino-Russian treaty of June 3, 1896, N.S., provided for a defensive alliance against Japan and granted the Russo-Chinese Bank a concession for the construction of the Chinese Eastern Railway across Manchuria.[3] In spite of the large bribe accepted by Li Hung-chang, he refused to give the concession to the Russian government, nor would he agree to Witte's demand for a branch line connecting the proposed railway with the Liaotung peninsula. The trans-Manchurian line, therefore, was built and managed by the Chinese Eastern Railway Company organized by the Russo-Chinese Bank. The company was nominally a private concern but was actually owned and operated by the Russian government. It enjoyed extensive privileges and exercised what amounted to sovereign powers (including that of maintaining an armed police force) within the territorial zone transferred to its jurisdiction. Like Manchuria, Korea was brought within the sphere of Russian influence. St. Petersburg and Tokyo agreed to respect the independence of that country and to cooperate in her administrative and financial rehabilitation, Russia assuming the status of the senior partner (protocol of June 9, 1896, N.S.). As a consequence of these

---

[3] The concession was for eighty years, but the railway might be repurchased by China after thirty-six years.

moves the Russian position in China was greatly enhanced. Other treaty Powers, among them the United States, which showed keen interest in Chinese markets and railway concessions, were disturbed by the Russian ascendancy. The policy of peaceful penetration, nevertheless, appeared to be eminently successful, and Witte had reason to be satisfied.

A new international crisis in China arose in November, 1897, with the seizure of Kiaochow by Germany. The official pretext was the murder of two German missionaries in Shantung, but the real reason was the desire of Emperor William and pan-German circles for a naval base in China. The question of the occupation of Kiaochow was raised by William during a visit to Russia in August, 1897, and he interpreted the tsar's somewhat evasive answer as consent. The seizure of Kiaochow was the signal for a scramble for Chinese territory on the part of the European Powers. To Germany's surprise and embarrassment Russia protested the occupation and threatened to send her fleet to Kiaochow Bay. The conflict, however, was speedily settled at the expense of China: in December, 1897, the Russian squadron came to anchor at Port Arthur, and demands for territorial concessions were presented to Peking. China had no choice except to comply with the requests of the great Powers. Germany secured a ninety-nine-year lease of Kiaochow and the adjacent territory as well as valuable concessions in Shantung (March 6, 1898, N.S.). Russia wangled a twenty-five-year lease of the Liaotung peninsula, including Port Arthur and Talienwan (Dalny), and the right to build a railway between Port Arthur and Harbin (March 27, 1898, N.S.). Great Britain and France clamored for and obtained their pound of flesh. Japanese resentment was temporarily allayed by a Russo-Japanese agreement which, revising the 1896 protocol, recognized Japan's special economic interests in Korea (April 28, 1898, N.S.).

From the beginning of the Kiaochow crisis the seizure of the Liaotung peninsula, advocated by Muravev, was opposed by Witte as an act of "unexampled treachery." Nevertheless, when it became clear that the St. Petersburg government was committed to a policy that Witte judged economically and politically unsound and incompatible with the spirit of the Chinese alliance, he used his influence and bribery to make Peking agree to Russian demands. Emperor William saluted the consummation of this sordid transaction by addressing

Nicholas as "master of Peking." Events were soon to prove him a false prophet.

The next major upset in the precarious balance in the Far East was precipitated by the Chinese themselves. The despicable treatment meted out by the great Christian Powers to China, a country of ancient and distinguished civilization, gave rise to a strong nationalist movement not untinged, perhaps, with fanaticism. Sporadic anti-foreign disturbances have long been a feature of the Chinese scene. In the closing years of the nineteenth century they became increasingly frequent, and were instigated and directed by the secret society of Boxers, which enjoyed the patronage of the Chinese court and counted many adherents among higher officials. The culminating point of anti-foreign agitation was the Boxer Rebellion, which broke out in May, 1900, swept over several provinces, led to the siege of the legations in Peking, and was finally suppressed by an international force under the command of the German field marshal Count Waldersee. Negotiations for a settlement were initiated in October, 1900, but were not concluded until September, 1901.

Russian Far Eastern policy during this period offers a nearly perfect example of shameless duplicity. On the one hand, St. Petersburg professed to uphold the territorial integrity of China and the principle of the Open Door; on the other hand, it worked for the dismemberment of the Chinese empire and the exclusion of non-Russian foreign influences from the territory north of the Great Wall. In December, 1899, Muravev endorsed, although with reservations and reluctance, the doctrine of the Open Door enunciated in September by John Hay, the American secretary of state. In July, 1900, Lamsdorf (Muravev had died in June) proclaimed Russia's determination to preserve "the true governmental structure of China" and to remove "everything that might lead" to her partition. Desirous of ingratiating itself with the Chinese government, St. Petersburg urged the early withdrawal of foreign troops from Peking and opposed the stiff and humiliating provisions written in by the other Powers in the peace settlement. These benevolent gestures did not prevent General Linevich, commander of the Russian expeditionary force, and other Russian officers, from participating in the looting of the imperial palaces after the seizure of Peking by the international corps.[4] Even less compatible with Rus-

---

[4] An unwelcome trophy was the original text of the Sino-Russian treaty of al-

sia's professed disinterestedness and friendship for China was a land concession in Tientsin exacted by the Russian military (November, 1900). Similar concessions were immediately demanded by Belgium, France, Italy, Austria, and Japan.

The touchstone of Russian policy, however, was Manchuria. Attacks by the insurgents on the Chinese Eastern Railway in July, 1900, brought Russian armed intervention and the occupation of the whole of Manchuria. Once in possession of the coveted territories, the Russians showed no desire to leave, official assurances to the contrary notwithstanding. There followed tortuous negotiations conducted, in part, by Russian military commanders. Disclosure that the arrangements contemplated amounted to the establishment of a *de facto* Russian protectorate over Manchuria and called for the exclusion of foreigners caused the United States, Japan, and Great Britain to enter vigorous protests. St. Petersburg appeared to yield: on April 8, 1902, N.S., Russia signed a convention recognizing Chinese sovereignty over Manchuria and promising to evacuate her troops within eighteen months; the withdrawal was to be accomplished in three stages, at six months' intervals, that is, the last Russian troops were to leave in October, 1903. The first stage of the evacuation was completed in accordance with the agreement, but then a deadlock arose: St. Petersburg made further withdrawals conditional on "guarantees" similar to those demanded during the earlier negotiations. Prodded by Washington, Tokyo, and London, the Peking government demurred, and the Russian troops remained in Manchuria.

The vagaries of Russian policy were the product not so much of Machiavellism as of divided counsel among the tsar's advisers. Disagreement was one of method, not of aim: Witte and Lamsdorf favored peaceful penetration, while their opponents urged a reckless aggressive policy both in Manchuria and in Korea. Prominent among the latter were the promoters of the so-called Yalu concession. This mysterious enterprise originated at the end of 1897 when two well connected retired guards officers, V. M. Vonliarliarsky and A. M. Bezobrazov, became interested in a vast timber concession on the Yalu and Tumen rivers on the northern border of Korea. Bezobrazov,

---

liance removed by the Russians from the bedchamber of the dowager empress of China, who had fled the capital. According to Witte, the embarrassing document was returned to the Chinese authorities as evidence that Russia remained faithful to the alliance.

leader of the group and a man of vivid and erratic imagination, by representing it as an outpost of Russian political, cultural, and military influence in the Far East, persuaded Emperor Nicholas to finance the Yalu venture (although most of the funds actually came from the state treasury). According to Bezobrazov, the concession, camouflaged as a private company, was to be the personal enterprise of the tsar and the instrument for the achievement of great national aims; that is, enrichment of the stockholders was not a primary object. The Yalu concession was held to be the antithesis of concessions to foreign capitalists favored by Witte, or of the Russo-Chinese Bank, which Bezobrazov castigated as a "Jewish-Polish" enterprise concerned exclusively with making profits. Witte, unsparingly critical of the Bezobrazov scheme, nevertheless provided the necessary funds when ordered to do so by the tsar.[5] Bezobrazov and Admiral A. M. Abaza, his cousin and principal lieutenant, reached the zenith of their influence in 1903, partly because of the support of their cause by Witte's implacable enemy Plehve, the minister of the interior. In May of that year Bezobrazov was appointed secretary of state (*stats-sekretar*), and was actually in charge of all matters pertaining to the Far East; in August Witte was dismissed from the office of minister of finance. These personal squabbles, trivial and petty as they were, explain much in the devious course of Russian policy.

The ascendancy of Bezobrazov dimmed further the none too bright prospects of an understanding with Japan. Russia's forcing Japan in 1895 to restore the Liaotung peninsula to China only to annex it two years later created a profound resentment in the island empire. The trend of Russian policy in China after the Boxer Rebellion intensified the anxieties and apprehensions of Tokyo, while the friendly attitude of Washington and London encouraged that section of Japanese opinion which, believing in the inevitability of war with Russia, demanded that action should not be delayed. After England's refusal to associate herself with St. Petersburg in insisting on the revision of the Shimono-

[5] The Yalu concession went through several legal transformations and had a small number of shareholders drawn chiefly from court circles. It remains uncertain whether they actually subscribed any funds or were straw men. The state treasury paid Bezobrazov and his associates well over two million rubles in loans and grants. In 1906, after the debacle of the Japanese war, the concession was sold to American interests. The details of this transaction and the purchase price were never revealed. The above account is based on an excellent study documented from Russian archive sources by B. A. Romanov, "Kontsessiia na Yalu" (The Yalu Concession), in *Russkoe Proshloe* (Russian Past), No. 1 (Petrograd-Moscow, 1923), pp. 87–108.

seki treaty, Tokyo and London were drawn closer together by their common hostility to, and fear of, Russia. At the end of 1901 Marquis Ito, an elder Japanese statesman and a proponent of an understanding with Russia, visited St. Petersburg, where his overtures, though well received, failed to produce a *rapprochement*. The Japanese government of Count Katsura decided instead in favor of an alliance with England, which was concluded, after protracted negotiations, on January 30, 1902, N.S. This was an ominous development, though hopes of a Russo-Japanese understanding were not abandoned. A final attempt at reconciliation was made by Tokyo at the end of July, 1903. Subject to the promise by both Powers to respect the territorial integrity of China and Korea and the principle of the Open Door, it was proposed that Russia should recognize Japan's "preponderant interests" in Korea, and that Japan should recognize Russia's "special interests in railway enterprises in Manchuria." The Japanese offer coincided with the announcement that the Russian provinces of Kwantung (with Port Arthur) and Amur had been reorganized as a viceroyalty. The viceroy, Admiral E. I. Alekseev, was an associate of Bezobrazov. The reorganization was significant in two respects. The provinces of Kwantung and Amur were separated by a vast stretch of Manchuria, and their administrative unification was interpreted as a notice of the impending annexation by Russia of the missing territorial link. The viceroy, moreover, was subordinated directly to the tsar, that is, he was exempt from the control of the foreign office and other ministries. Lamsdorf, Witte (who was still minister of finance), and their colleagues, except Plehve, learned of the change from the newspapers. With Bezobrazov in full control of Far Eastern policies, the Japanese proposal had little chance of success. The long-delayed Russian reply was rejected as unsatisfactory by Japan. On February 5, 1904, N.S., after further desultory negotiations, Tokyo broke off diplomatic relations with St. Petersburg and three days later, without a formal declaration of war, attacked the Russian fleet at Port Arthur and Chemulpo.

THE RUSSO-JAPANESE WAR AND AFTER, 1904–1914

Russia was ill prepared for a war she had done so much to provoke. The traffic capacity of the single-track Trans-Siberian railway was inadequate to meet the requirements of a huge modern army. Moreover, the line in the mountainous country round Lake Baikal was still under construction and, until its completion, reinforcements and supplies had to be transferred across the lake by steamers or, in wintertime, on sleds and over a light railway built on the ice. At the beginning of the hostilities the land forces of the belligerents were unevenly matched. Russian effectives in the Far East did not exceed 100,000 regular troops and 30,000 railway guards scattered over immense distances. The Japanese army numbered 180,000 men and had large trained reserves; the mobilization ordered in February more than doubled its peacetime strength. A large contingent of transports permitted the simultaneous embarkation of two fully equipped Japanese divisions, a force which could be landed in Korea less than twenty-four hours after leaving port. In the later stage of the war, with the improvement in the carrying capacity of the Trans-Siberian railway, the ratio of land forces swung in Russia's favor. The disparity in the navies available in Chinese waters at the outbreak of the war was less marked, the Russian battle fleet (according to Sir F. B. Maurice) being slightly superior to the Japanese. Russia, however, had only two naval bases some nine-hundred miles apart: Port Arthur, still under construction, and Vladivostok, icebound part of the year, while Japanese ships were within easy reach of numerous home ports. Diplomatically and internationally Japan was in a strong position because of her alliance with England and the quasi-unanimous support of British and American opinion. Influential British and American circles acted on the assumption that Japan was fighting in Manchuria not only her own battle but also that of Great Britain and the United States. Anglo-American help in financing the war was avowedly an essential element in Japanese victory. Theodore Roosevelt spoke for the majority of his countrymen when he wrote in May, 1906: "I have from the beginning favored Japan and have done all that I could . . . to advance her interests. I thoroughly admire and believe in the Japanese." Russia's international position was far less secure. The French alliance proved of limited usefulness in the Far East, and St. Petersburg had to rely chiefly on the none too dependable friendship of Germany.

Russian diplomatic and military agents abroad having repeatedly warned the home government that Japan was planning for war, the country's unpreparedness must be explained primarily by the belief—shared alike by the tsar, his advisers, and the general public—that victory was a foregone conclusion. The Japanese were contemptuously dismissed as the "little apes" (*makaki*) who, in the popular phrase, were to be snowed under by the caps of the Russian soldiers.

The levity and confusion characteristic of Russian prewar diplomacy persisted in the organization of the high command and in the conduct of military operations. General A. N. Kuropatkin, a veteran of the 1877–1878 campaign, and minister of war since 1898, was appointed commander in chief of the army in Manchuria. Although an advocate of expansion in the Far East, Kuropatkin was at odds with the Bezobrazov clique and owed his appointment to the support of nationalistic circles and the press. The viceroy, Admiral Alekseev, however, remained at his post and, as supreme commander and through his court connections, exercised considerable influence on the course of the campaign. The resulting situation was all the graver because the two men were not only personally incompatible but held irreconcilable strategic conceptions. Kuropatkin's plan provided for delaying action, gradual retreat, and avoidance of major engagements until the army had been built up to a strength that would assure it a reasonable chance of success. Alekseev deprecated this cautious and probably wise strategy, partly because he shared the popular misconception about Japanese weakness, and therefore regarded withdrawals as unwarranted, and partly because he attached great importance to naval warfare and urged the dispatch of a large fleet from Europe to the Far East. Port Arthur being Russia's only ice-free port, the maintenance of lines of communication between that naval base and the hinterland was deemed essential. The theories of Alekseev were shared by some of the tsar's counselors and by several of the commanding officers in Manchuria. Resistance on the part of the latter and contradictory orders from St. Petersburg made all the more difficult the execution of Kuropatkin's inherently unpopular plan. In October, 1904, Alekseev was recalled and a semblance of unified command was at last established, although interference from the capital continued. "I went through a painful inner struggle before I reached this decision," Nicholas noted in his diary, referring to the termination of the viceroy's inglorious and brief career.

The war in the Far East comprised three sets of distinct, although closely inter-related, operations: the siege of Port Arthur, the campaign in Manchuria, and naval warfare. During the opening weeks warlike activities were limited to the concentration of Russian forces in Manchuria, the landing of Japanese troops in Korea, and minor operations around Port Arthur. Japan's first major victory was won at the end of April, on the Yalu River, when General Zasulich, in contravention of Kuropatkin's orders, engaged a superior enemy force. Railway communications between Port Arthur and Harbin were severed a few days later. In the middle of May the Japanese captured the strongly fortified position of Nanshan on the narrow neck of the Kwantung peninsula, occupied the Russian commercial port of Talienwan (Dalny), and proceeded to invest Port Arthur. On December 19, 1904, after a siege lasting 148 days, the commander of Port Arthur, General A. M. Stessel, surrendered the fortress to the enemy. The besieged troops had fought gallantly and had inflicted heavy losses on the Japanese, but the capitulation does not seem to have been justified because the garrison still had some 25,000 able-bodied men and adequate supplies of food and munitions. According to some authorities, the prolongation of the resistance until the arrival of the Baltic fleet then on its way from Europe might have altered the outcome of the war. Stessel acted on his own responsibility, in disregard of the views of other senior officers of the Port Arthur command.

The Manchurian campaign put to a severe test the endurance of the contesting armies. The difficulties of the mountainous terrain, remoteness from supply bases, rigors of the climate, and the poor condition of the few available roads, which were often rendered impassable, even in the summer, by torrential rains, combined to add to the hardships of the troops. In that inhospitable country Kuropatkin pursued his plan of retreat and delaying tactics. Following Zasulich's defeat on the Yalu in April, 1904, the Russian armies steadily fell back, fighting rearguard actions and making occasional diversions to ease the pressure on Port Arthur. It was not until August that Kuropatkin decided, although not without misgivings, to meet the enemy in strength. At Liaoyang, a strongly fortified position sixty-five miles south of Mukden, 150,000 Russians engaged 135,000 Japanese. After a furious battle lasting for nine days, the Russians retreated to Mukden, establishing their advanced line along the Sha-ho River twenty miles south of that city. The withdrawal was executed in good order, but losses were very heavy on both sides. The inability of the Japanese to exploit their somewhat inconclusive victory, arrival of substantial Russian reinforcements, and pressure from St. Petersburg account for a dramatic change in Kuropatkin's strategy. On September 15 he issued a flamboyant order announcing that "the long-awaited moment to advance against the enemy" and "to force the Japanese to comply with our will" had at last arrived. The Russians attacked on a wide front along the Sha-ho River; but ten days of exceptionally heavy fighting failed to dent the Japanese lines, and the offensive petered out in spite of Kuropatkin's numerical superiority: 220,000 Russians against 160,000 Japanese. The Russians lost well over 30,000 killed, wounded, and prisoners, the Japanese about 20,000. The collapse of the offensive, notwithstanding the show of determination by Kuropatkin, silenced for a time his St. Petersburg and Manchurian critics and led to the recall of Alekseev. The long lull following the Sha-ho battle came to an end with the capitulation of Port Arthur, which set free 100,000 Japanese troops to join Marshal Oyama, the Japanese commander in chief in Manchuria. At the end of December 6,000 Cossacks under General A. V. Mishchenko carried out a daring raid on Japanese communications, penetrating as far as the naval base of Yingkow, one hundred miles within enemy territory, but they returned to their lines having accomplished little. In January, 1905, General O. K. Grippenberg, commander of the second Russian army, succeeded in turning the left flank of the Japanese and made some gains in the stubbornly defended area of Sandepu but was forced to retreat after Kuropatkin refused to send reinforcements. This operation cost Russia 10,000 killed and wounded. Grippenberg, proclaiming that victory under Kuropatkin was precluded, demanded to be relieved of his command. Branded by the commander in chief as a deserter, the rebellious general was recalled to St. Petersburg, where he found many admirers and was given a prominent position in palace councils.

In the meantime the Russian effectives massed round Mukden rose to 310,000 and those of the Japanese to about 300,000. The battle of Mukden, one of the greatest in history measured by the number of participants, began with the Japanese attack in the middle of February, 1905. A pincer movement, skillfully planned by Oyama and executed in subzero weather, threatened the encirclement of the entire Russian army and compelled Kuropatkin to withdraw north along the railway to Harbin. On February 25 Mukden was occupied by the Japanese, but the victors were too exhausted to pursue energetically the defeated enemy: the retreat did not become a rout. The Russian army lost nearly 90,000 men, including 25,000 prisoners, and an immense amount of stores and equipment; Japanese losses were over 70,000. Kuropatkin, at his own request, was transferred to a subordinate command and was succeeded as commander in chief by Linevich. A staggering defeat for Russia, Mukden nevertheless was not a Waterloo or a Sedan. The Russian army retained its cohesion and remained a formidable enemy. The new front was stabilized north of Mukden, and remained practically unchanged until the end of the war. The final blow which led to the peace negotiations was dealt to Russia on the high seas.

The story of Russian naval warfare in 1904–1905 is an almost unrelieved record of futility and disaster. At the outbreak of the war the Russian squadron in the Far East consisted of seven battleships, seventeen cruisers (nine first class, two second class, and six third class), twenty-five destroyers, and a large number of auxiliary craft. The majority of the ships, including all battleships, were at Port Arthur; four cruisers were at Vladivostok, and one at Chemulpo. Japan's predatory attack on Port Arthur in February, 1904, caught the Russian navy unprepared, and inflicted serious injuries on seven ships. This initial reverse and the blocking by the Japanese of the narrow entrance to the inner harbor immobilized for a time the Port Arthur squadron. The cruisers based on Vladivostok raided the northern shore of Japan and interfered sporadically with enemy transports but otherwise took little part in the fighting. The arrival at Port Arthur at the end of February of Admiral S. O. Makarov, commander of the squadron and a gallant and able officer, terminated the period of inaction. On April 13, N.S., however, Makarov went down with the battleship *Petropavlovsk*, which was sunk by a mine; on the same day another battleship, the *Pobeda*, was severely damaged. The Port Arthur squadron did not reappear on the high seas until June. Meanwhile the narrowing ring of the siege brought the inner harbor within the range of enemy artillery. On August 10, N.S., the fleet steamed out of Port Arthur in an attempt to break through to Vladivostok. It was intercepted by a Japanese force under Admiral Togo, the Russian commanding officer, Admiral V. K. Vitheft, was killed, and the entire squadron annihilated. Some of the ships succeeded in making foreign ports and were disarmed. Five battleships, one cruiser, and three destroyers—all severely injured—returned to Port Arthur but never put out to sea again.

The continuation of naval warfare depended on Russia's ability to reconstitute her Far Eastern squadron. Nationalistic opinion, abysmally ignorant of nautical matters, clamored for a spectacular naval expedition against Japan, a demand unsuccessfully opposed by the more level-headed bureaucrats and naval officers but endorsed by the tsar. In October, 1904, the hastily refitted Baltic fleet under Admiral Z. P. Rozhdestvensky sailed for the Pacific. Coaling service, for which Russia had no facilities, was assured by an agreement with the Hamburg-America Line. In the night of October 21, N.S., while crossing the Dogger Bank in the North Sea, the Russian ships opened fire on two of their own number, having mistaken them for Japanese torpedo boats. Several English fishing smacks from Hull were the innocent victims of this grotesque incident: one smack was sunk, two fishermen were killed and eighteen wounded. British opinion was incensed, anti-Russian feeling ran high, and for a few days the two countries appeared to be on the brink of war. The willingness of St. Petersburg to make amends, and the moderation and common sense of the British government, prevented a serious crisis: the Dogger Bank incident was referred for arbitration to an international commission of admirals which met in Paris in January, 1905. Under the commission's award Russia paid damages but otherwise was permitted to escape with as little loss of face as her unfortunate predicament would allow.[6]

After this inauspicious beginning Rozhdestvensky, whose squadron the British had threatened to detain at the Spanish port of Vigo, continued eastward, and in December reached Madagascar, where he remained until March, the fall of Port Arthur calling for a reconsideration of Russian plans. Various proposals for the strengthening of the expeditionary force were explored. There were mysterious abortive negotiations for the purchase of battleships from Chile or Argentina. The possibility of making use, in contravention of the Straits convention, of the Black Sea fleet was examined and abandoned. Finally the few antiquated vessels remaining in Baltic naval establishments were hastily reconditioned, and in February, 1905, sailed for the Far East under the command of Admiral N. I. Nebogatov; a reinforcement of most questionable value, they eventually joined the main force. On May 27, N.S., Rozhdestvensky, heading for Vladivostok, entered the Straits of Tsushima. His squadron consisted of eight battleships, four armored and eight protected cruisers, nine destroyers, and a number

---

[6] According to Witte, Rozhdestvensky was obsessed with the notion that European waters were infested with Japanese warcraft. A factual account of the Dogger Bank incident, based on Russian documents, is given in Taube, *op. cit.*, Chap. I, especially pp. 30 *et seq.* Taube was the legal adviser of the Russian delegation to the international commission of admirals. Rozhdestvensky's version of the incident, which was upheld by the St. Petersburg government and the Russian delegation, was, as Taube makes clear, an invention.

of auxiliary craft. About half of the ships were slow and obsolete. Attacked by Admiral Togo's superior and far more efficient force, the Russian squadron was within a few hours wiped out of existence. Only one cruiser and two destroyers reached Vladivostok. Four battleships, seven cruisers, and five destroyers were sunk; four battleships and one destroyer were captured; the other ships escaped to foreign ports and were disarmed. Rozhdestvensky, severely wounded, was made prisoner. The Japanese lost merely a few destroyers.

The Tsushima debacle produced a tremendous impression throughout the world, and by shattering Russia's naval illusions paved the way for peace. The war was never popular with the Russians except for the Bezobrazov lunatic fringe and a few reactionaries, like Plehve, who held that a "short victorious war" would restore the prestige of autocracy. A long disastrous war was a very different matter, as was evidenced by the rise of the revolutionary movement. After Mukden the chances of peace were freely discussed in the Russian press of every shade of opinion. The unbroken record of Japanese victories, moreover, alarmed not only the friends of Russia in France and Germany but also some of Japan's staunch supporters. Roosevelt came to feel that "the destruction [of Russia] as an eastern Asiatic Power would . . . be unfortunate." [7] Shortly after Tsushima Tokyo proposed that Roosevelt "on his own motion and initiative" invite the belligerents to enter into peace negotiations (May 31, N.S.). Emperor William, fearing for the future of the Russian monarchy, urged the tsar to avail himself of the good offices of the President of the United States (June 3, N.S.). After a brief exchange of views between Washington and St. Petersburg, the two belligerents accepted the invitation to a peace conference formally issued by Roosevelt on June 8, N.S. There was no armistice, but little fighting took place during the summer. The Japanese drove the Russians from northeastern Korea, made threatening moves towards Vladivostok, occupied the practically undefended Sakhalin Island, and landed a small expeditionary force at the mouth of the Amur. The Manchurian front remained quiescent.

The peace conference opened at Portsmouth, New Hampshire, on August 10, 1905, N.S. and was concluded in twelve sessions. Witte and

[7] Zabriskie, *op. cit.*, p. 114. "I wish I were certain," Roosevelt wrote in December, 1904, "that the Japanese at bottom did not lump Russians, English, Americans, Germans, all of us, simply as white devils inferior to themselves . . . to be treated politely only so long as would enable the Japanese to take advantage of our various national jealousies, and beat us in turn." *Ibid.*, p. 111.

Baron Komura, minister of foreign affairs, were the first delegates of, respectively, Russia and Japan. Witte's instructions barring indemnities and cessions of territory were incompatible with the original Japanese demands, and the apparent stubbornness displayed by both sides appeared for a time to endanger the success of the conference. The difficulties, however, were overcome with remarkable ease, not so much, perhaps, because of the frenzied diplomatic activities of Roosevelt and Emperor William or of Witte's alleged astuteness, but because of the realization by responsible leaders that neither country, although for different reasons, was in a position to continue the war. By the Treaty of Portsmouth (September 5, 1905, N.S.) Russia acknowledged Japan's "paramount political, military, and economic interests" in Korea, and ceded to Japan the southern portion of Sakhalin, the lease of the Liaotung peninsula, including Port Arthur and Talienwan (Dalny), and a section of the Southern Manchurian Railway from Port Arthur to Changchun, a locality some 150 miles south of Harbin. Both Powers undertook to evacuate Manchuria and to restore in that province exclusive administration by China. The Russian government declared that "they have not in Manchuria any territorial advantages or preferential or exclusive concessions in impairment of Chinese sovereignty or inconsistent with the principle of equal opportunity." The much-publicized claim, from which the Russians took heart, that the treaty imposed no indemnity was only formally correct. The transfer to Japan without compensation of "all public works and properties" in the Liaotung peninsula and of "all rights, privileges, and properties appertaining" to the Southern Manchurian Railway (including "all coal mines . . . belonging to or worked for the benefit of the railway") was akin to reparations in kind.

The Treaty of Portsmouth, in spite of the gains it conferred upon Japan, had a better press with the vanquished than with the victors. Japanese opinion blamed Roosevelt for what it regarded as excessive generosity towards the defeated enemy, and especially for the failure of the treaty to provide a large indemnity. It was insufficiently realized that war burdens weighed much more heavily on small Japan than on Russia, a country of almost unlimited resources. The war costs of each nation amounted to about $1,000 million, and the losses in killed and wounded, distributed nearly evenly between the two belligerents, reached 450,000. In the summer of 1905 the economic and human resources of Japan were dangerously strained, while those of Russia were not seriously impaired. Russia's weakness, including difficulties in floating foreign loans, was due primarily to the rise of the revolutionary movement and a state of political chaos. From a purely military and economic standpoint Russia might have continued war in Manchuria for many more months. The Russians, nevertheless, welcomed peace because of the absence of any real interest in the Far East, her disheartening war record, and political turmoil at home. The loss of Port Arthur, half of Sakhalin, and the Southern Manchurian Railway —unfamiliar, outlandish places—was accepted with indifference and almost without a murmur.

The years 1905–1914 witnessed a remarkable change in Russo-Japanese relations. While some of the St. Petersburg bureaucrats, supported by a section of the nationalist press, planned for a *revanche*, others favored an alliance with Japan. A proposal for such an alliance, cautiously advanced by Witte at Portsmouth, was ignored by the Japanese and disavowed by Lamsdorf. Nevertheless, it eventually brought fruit. The Russo-Japanese *rapprochement* was unwittingly fostered by the insistence of the Washington government on the territorial integrity of China and the principle of the Open Door, and by the ambitious schemes for the economic domination of Manchuria which were launched by a powerful group of American financiers headed by E. H. Harriman, Jacob Schiff, and J. P. Morgan. Their chief agent in China was Willard Straight, United States consul general in Mukden from 1906 to 1908. The Harriman plan provided for the control by a banking syndicate of the northern Chinese railways as well as of the Trans-Siberian line. Large investments of American capital in Manchuria, establishment of American banks, and loans to the Chinese government were advocated as a method of opening up profitable markets for American exports by developing the natural resources of northern China. Theodore Roosevelt favored these policies; and they were later aggressively pushed by President Taft and his secretary of state Philander Knox, author of a proposal for the "neutralization" of Manchurian railways by transferring them to the control of an international consortium (November, 1909). The American plans were defeated by the concerted opposition of Russia and Japan, and were formally abandoned after the Chinese revolution of October, 1911.[8]

[8] Incidentally, the protest of the people of Szechwan against the Hukuang railways concession granted by the imperial Chinese government in May, 1911, to a

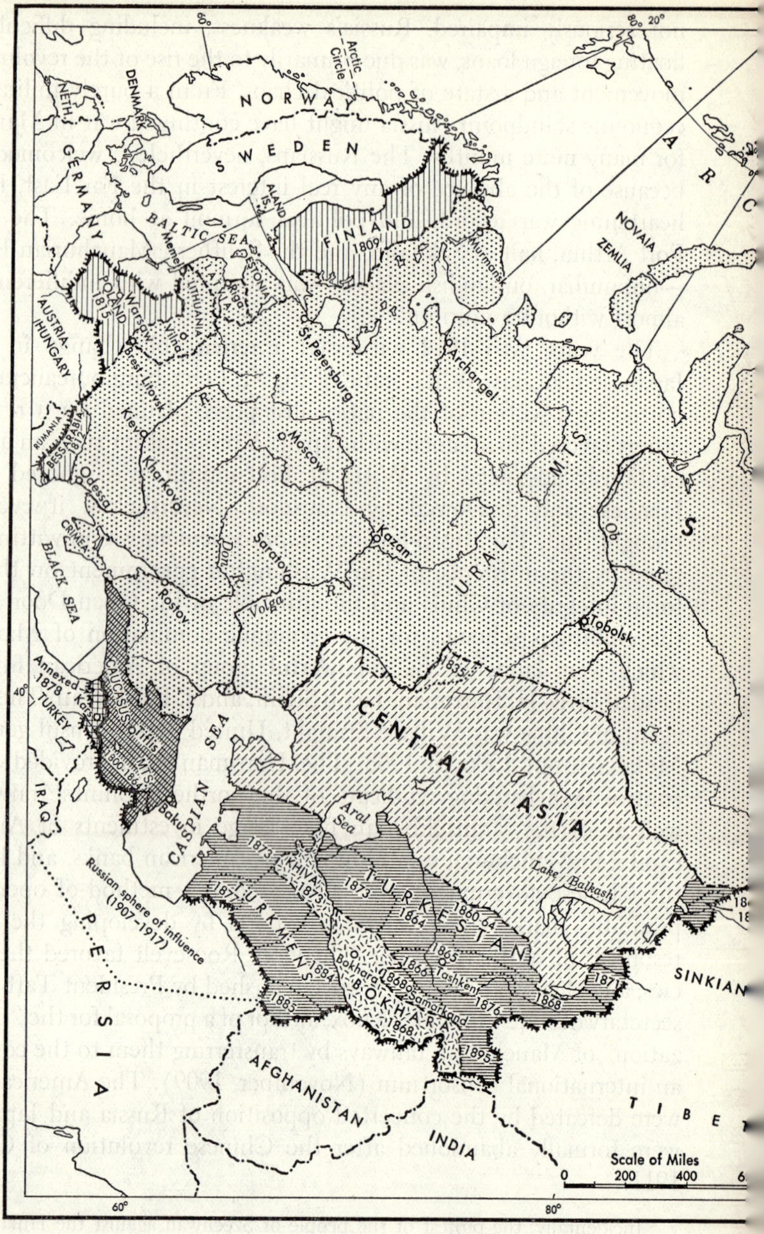

NORWAY
SWEDEN
DENMARK
NETH.
GERMANY
FINLAND
1809
ALAND IS.
BALTIC SEA
Memel
ESTONIA
LATVIA
Riga
LITHUANIA
Vilna
POLAND
1815
Warsaw
Brest-Litovsk
AUSTRIA-HUNGARY
RUMANIA
BESSARABIA
1812
Kiev
Odessa
CRIMEA
BLACK SEA
Kharkov
Moscow
St. Petersburg
Archangel
Murmansk
NOVAIA ZEMLIA
Arctic Circle
Don R.
Saratov
Volga R.
Kazan
Rostov
URAL MTS.
Ob R.
Tobolsk
1835
CENTRAL ASIA
CASPIAN SEA
CAUCASUS MTS.
Tiflis
Baku
Kars
Annexed 1878
TURKEY
1800-1864
IRAQ
Aral Sea
KHIVA
1873
TURKMENS
1877
1884
1885
TURKESTAN
1860-64
1864
1865
1866
1868
1871
1876
Tashkent
Samarkand
Bokhara
BOKHARA
1868
1895
Lake Balkash
SINKIANG
PERSIA
Russian sphere of influence (1907-1917)
AFGHANISTAN
INDIA
TIBET
Scale of Miles
0 200 400
60°
80°
40°
20°

RUSSIA
FROM 1800 TO 1914

- Russia at the end of the XVIIIth Century
- Caucasian conquest and annexations, 1800–1864
- Annexations in Asia, 1802–1856
- Annexations in Asia, 1857–1913
- Russian protectorates
- Annexations in Europe, 1809–1815 (Eastern Galicia, Russian 1809–1815, is not indicated on the map)
- Russian frontier in 1914
- 1871 Approximate boundaries with dates of conquests

ALASKA (Russian from middle of XVIIIth century to 1867)

SIBERIA

Yenisei · Lena · Yakutsk · Lake Baikal · Irkutsk · Chita · Okhotsk · Amur · AMUR DISTRICT 1858 · Khabarovsk 1860 · Vladivostok

KAMCHATKA · KOMANDORSKIE IS. · SEA OF OKHOTSK · KURILE ISLANDS (Russian, end of XVIIIth century to 1875) · SAKHALIN (Russia 1875) (Ceded to Japan, 1905)

OUTER MONGOLIA · MANCHURIA (Russian occupation 1900–1905) · KOREA · Port Arthur (Russian 1898–1905) · YELLOW SEA · SEA OF JAPAN · JAPAN · Tokyo

The threatened encroachment by American capital on Manchuria, traditionally regarded by St. Petersburg and Tokyo as their special preserve, and Russia's fear of the growing strength of Japan were the chief causes of the Russo-Japanese *rapprochement*. On July 30, 1907, N.S., two days after the conclusion of a Russo-Japanese treaty of navigation and commerce and of a fisheries agreement, the two Powers signed a convention in which they promised to respect each other's territorial integrity and to uphold in Manchuria the principle of the Open Door. The secret articles, however, gave Japan a free hand in Korea and recognized southern Manchuria and Inner Mongolia as the Japanese sphere of influence, and northern Manchuria and Outer Mongolia as the Russian sphere. These undertakings were made more definite in the Russo-Japanese treaty of July 4, 1910, N.S., which contained no reference to the integrity of China or the Open Door and, like the 1907 convention, included secret articles providing, among other things, for "common action . . . for the safeguarding and defense" of Russian and Japanese "special interests" in their respective spheres of influence. Six weeks later (August 29, N.S.) Japan annexed Korea. In December, 1911, Outer Mongolia, instigated by Russian agents, proclaimed its independence and became a *de facto* Russian protectorate.[9] The secret Russo-Japanese treaty of July 8, 1912, N.S., amplified and redefined the provisions of the 1907 and 1910 agreements bearing on the partition of Mongolia and Manchuria. These predatory arrangements were, of course, incompatible with the Manchurian section of the Treaty of Portsmouth. The Russo-Japanese *rapprochement* was countenanced by France and Great Britain, the two partners in the 1904 *entente cordiale* being linked to St. Petersburg and Tokyo by interlocking alliances and political agreements.

Economic factors, which are not to be confused with speculations concerning problematic future gains, played no part in Russian expansion in the Far East. Incursions into Chinese territory were not prompted by the pressure of financial or business interests (unless one chooses to regard the Yalu concession as a business enterprise), nor did they open up new channels of commerce. Russia's Chinese trade was negligible, and her railway ventures in China were unprofitable. In

---

financial four-Power group (the United States, Great Britain, France, and Germany) was the starting point of the organized movement that led to the revolution.

[9] The autonomy of Outer Mongolia was conceded by China, under strong Russian pressure, in the Kiahkta agreement of May 25 (June 7, N.S.), 1915.

1909 the minister of finance, Kokovtsov, favored the sale to American interests of the Chinese Eastern Railway, which owed the government 550 million rubles and was operated at a loss. A poor country, dependent on foreign capital for the development of her domestic resources, Russia had no funds to invest in the wilderness of Manchuria. The substantial sums frittered away in Far Eastern adventures, to say nothing of the cost of the Japanese war, had been a severe drain on the imperial treasury and might have been used more profitably elsewhere.

RELATIONS WITH FRANCE, AUSTRIA, AND GERMANY, 1894–1905

During the two decades preceding World War I, Russian policies in Europe and in the Near East pursued, as in the Far East, a devious course determined by the predilections of the statesmen in power and their interpretation of a highly fluid international situation. The Franco-Russian alliance, the Anglo-French *entente* of 1904, the intensification of the Anglo-German colonial and naval rivalries, the expansionist ambitions and provocative moves of Berlin, and the Bosnian crisis of 1908 were all instrumental in bringing about the *rapprochement* between Russia and England and a new alignment of Powers.

Franco-Russian ties were reasserted during Nicholas's stay in Paris in 1896, and the existence of the alliance was officially announced in August, 1897, when President Félix Faure paid a return visit to St. Petersburg. In the opinion of the Russian government, however, the Franco-Russian partnership was not incompatible with maintenance of close relations with Vienna and Berlin. Relations with Austria were put to a test by a new crisis in Turkey. The massacre of Armenians in Asia Minor and Constantinople (1894–1896) raised the question of the intervention of the great Powers. A council held in St. Petersburg in November, 1896, approved, over Witte's objection, the proposal of A. J. Nelidov, Russian ambassador to Constantinople, for the occupation—in some ill defined emergency—of the upper Bosphorus. Secret instructions to this effect were elaborated in considerable detail, and a Russian expeditionary force was held in readiness to sail from the Black Sea ports on the receipt of a code message from Nelidov. Although the situation in Turkey further deteriorated with the outbreak of war between that country and Greece in February, 1897, the plan for the Russian occupation of the Bosphorus, which had the whole-hearted support of the tsar, did not materialize. In May, 1897, St. Petersburg, reversing itself, concluded with Vienna an agreement which bound the two countries to maintain the *status quo* in the Balkans or, this failing, to consult in advance as to future territorial changes. Because of the "eminently European character" of the status of Constantinople and the Straits, the disposition of these areas remained outside the scope of the Austro-Russian conversations. No definite agreement concerning the allocation of other Balkan territories was reached. The Austrian note provided for the redrafting of the map of the Balkans and stipulated the right of Austria to annex Bosnia, Herzegovina, and a portion of the sanjak of Novibazar. Muravev in his reply, however, avoided committing Russia to the support of the Austrian program. The agreement of 1897 thus boiled down to a promise by the two countries to preserve the *status quo*; renewed during the meeting of Nicholas and Francis Joseph at Mürzsteg in October, 1903, it was of considerable value to Russia, especially in view of her involvements in the Far East.

Relations between St. Petersburg and Berlin, after the accession of Nicholas, retained their cordial character in spite of the unpopularity of Emperor William with both the tsar and the tsarina. Conflicts of policy produced at times a strain, for instance, during the Kiaochow crisis of 1897, but divergencies of view were invariably settled without creating lasting estrangement. William, it will be remembered, encouraged Nicholas's Far Eastern venture, German assistance made possible Rozhdestvensky's ill fated expedition to the Pacific, and the mediation of the German emperor helped to pave the way for the Russo-Japanese peace negotiations. The Dogger Bank incident somewhat suddenly brought to the fore proposals long entertained in St. Petersburg and Berlin for a Russo-German alliance which was to become the nucleus of a continental league directed against England. On October 27, 1904, N.S., Emperor William, who was passing through an acute phase of Anglophobia, wired to Nicholas that the English press was advocating stern measures to prevent the coaling of Russian warships by the Germans. "The result aimed at by such a threat of war would be the absolute immobility of your fleet and its inability to proceed for want of fuel," wrote William. "This new danger would have to be faced in common by Russia and Germany together, who would both have to remind your ally France of the obligations she took over in the treaty of dual alliance with you in the case of a *casus belli* arising." [10] "I have no words to express my indignation with England . . . ," Nicholas wired back (October 28, N.S.). "The only way [to make England more amenable] would be that Germany, Russia and France should at once unite upon agreements to abolish English and Japanese arrogance and insolence. Would you like to lay down and frame the outline of such a treaty?" William complied with the tsar's request and prepared, in collaboration with the Chancellor Prince von Bülow, a treaty of defensive Russo-German alliance which France was to be subsequently invited to join. The draft was at first approved by Nicholas with a few verbal changes. On second thought, however, it was realized in St. Petersburg that an alliance with Germany concluded without preliminary consultation with France, one which that country was merely invited to join after ratification, might well prove the undoing of the Franco-Russian alliance at the very time when Russia desperately needed the Paris money market for the floating of her war loans. Moreover, the conciliatory attitude of the British government in the Dogger Bank incident removed the immediate cause for alarm. Nicholas insisted that France should be taken into the confidence of the two imperial courts, while William regarded a preliminary notice to France as fatal to the proposed alliance. The draft treaty was finally dropped, Russia assuming instead the obligation to provide military assistance to Germany if the coaling of the Russian fleet should lead to a war between Germany and Great Britain (December, 1904). According to Izvolsky, the Russian foreign minister was not kept informed of these negotiations.[11]

The German emperor was disappointed but not discouraged. In the summer of 1905 he engineered a private meeting with the tsar, and in the seclusion of the imperial yachts, cruising in Finnish waters, secured the signature of Nicholas to a treaty of alliance similar to the one the Russian monarch had rejected eight months earlier (Treaty of Björkö, July 24, 1905, N.S.). The treaty, countersigned, under orders from the tsar, by the minister of the marine, Admiral A. A. Birilev, who was not permitted to read the text, was binding according to Russian law. "The morning of July 24, 1905 at Björkö became a turning point in the history of Europe, thanks to the Grace of God," William wrote (in English) to von Bülow. Nicholas was less sanguine.

[10] The two monarchs corresponded in English. Quotations in the text are given in the original version.
[11] *The Memoirs of Alexander Iswolsky* (London, 1920), p. 51.

It was not until September 12, N.S., that with considerable embarrassment he disclosed to Lamsdorf Russia's latest international commitment. The foreign minister was appalled and, for once abandoning his customary submissiveness, demanded the immediate annulment of a treaty which he considered incompatible with the obligations assumed by Russia towards France. Witte, informed of the Björkö agreement, took a similar view. He was a convinced supporter of an alliance of Russia, Germany, and France, but not of a Russo-German alliance concluded behind France's back and one to which the latter country was not likely to become a party. Nicholas had to admit that his venture in diplomacy was not a success. He pleaded with William for the revision of the Björkö treaty (which was to become operative on the ratification of the peace treaty with Japan) so as to bring it in line with the terms of the Franco-Russian alliance. The German emperor's impassioned retort concluded a bitter indictment of France with a characteristic statement: "We joined hands and signed before God who heard our vows! . . . What is signed is signed! and let God be our testator!" (October 12, 1905, N.S.). Witte and Lamsdorf, however, refused to be moved; and while the Björkö treaty was not formally abrogated, the German government was officially informed that the obligation of military assistance (in the event of either party being attacked by a European Power) did not apply in the case of a war with France and that the Franco-Russian alliance "remains fully in force until the three-Powers agreement has been reached" (November, 1905). The unfortunate Björkö incident was closed; it added little to the luster of imperial diplomacy (for the secret leaked out in spite of extraordinary precautions) and cast a dark shadow over Russo-German relations.

THE ANGLO-RUSSIAN CONVENTION, 1907

The traditional Anglo-Russian hostility, which was greatly accentuated by the developments in the Far East and reached its zenith during the Dogger Bank incident, subsided after the Russo-Japanese War. Izvolsky, the new Russian foreign minister and a former ambassador to Tokyo, had been opposed to the policy that brought about the conflict with Japan. A *rapprochement* with England, Japan's friend and ally, was an integral part of his program of reconciliation with Tokyo consummated in the Russo-Japanese agreement of July, 1907.[12]

[12] See p. 1282.

The fact that both Russia and England were linked to France—the former by the alliance of 1897 and the latter by the *entente cordiale* of 1904—worked for the establishment of friendly cooperation between St. Petersburg and London. There was still, no doubt, much anti-Russian feeling in England, and the excesses of the Russian revolution of 1905, the Jewish pogroms, and the treatment meted out to the State Duma, were repugnant to British leaders and to public opinion. London, however, was even more directly disturbed by the provocative gestures coming from Berlin, by Germany's apparent determination to win for herself a place in the colonial sun, and by her challenge to English naval supremacy. Ideological scruples are seldom permitted to stand in the way of what are deemed to be exigencies of *Realpolitik*. King Edward VII, Sir Edward Grey (afterwards Lord Grey of Fallodon), who became foreign secretary in December, 1905, Lord Morley, secretary of state for India, and Sir Charles Hardinge, former ambassador to St. Petersburg and since the autumn of 1905 permanent undersecretary at the foreign office, were advocates of an understanding with Russia. In April, 1906, British bankers participated, for the first time since the Crimean War, in the floating of a Russian international loan. In March, 1907, the Russian fleet visited Portsmouth and was the object of flattering marks of attention from both the general public and the British government.

The foundation of the future *entente* appeared to have been laid in Copenhagen in the course of an interview between King Edward and Izvolsky, Russian minister to Denmark from 1903 to 1905. Official conversations, conducted by Izvolsky and the British ambassador Sir Arthur Nicolson (afterwards Lord Carnock), began in June, 1906, and lasted for fifteen months. Izvolsky took the precaution of consulting von Bülow, and secured his assurance that Germany would not object to the proposed Anglo-Russian agreement, provided it did not affect her own interests. The convention signed by Izvolsky and Nicolson on August 31, 1907, N.S., defined the policies and delimited the spheres of influence of the signatory Powers in Persia, Tibet, and Afghanistan. The agreement on Persia amounted to a *de facto* partition of the country (which, of course, was not consulted), although the preamble contained the customary sanctimonious reference to the preservation of Persian integrity and independence. Ostensibly a purely Asiatic settlement, the Anglo-Russian convention nevertheless, by attempting to remove major causes of friction between Russia and

Great Britain, had an important bearing on the European situation. The support of London in revising the status of the Dardanelles was uppermost in Izvolsky's mind, while the British negotiators sought to prevent the formation of a continental coalition dominated by Germany and directed against England.

The Anglo-Russian convention, eventually one of the pillars of the Triple Entente, was not thought of in those terms in 1907 and, indeed, for several years thereafter. "The signature of the Anglo-Russian convention did not, by any means, imply the conclusion of an Anglo-Russian understanding," writes Harold Nicolson, Sir Arthur Nicolson's son and biographer. "The convention was regarded by M. Izvolsky as a purely negative insurance and one which should not be allowed to affect his relations with the central Powers. . . . Even as an Asiatic agreement the Anglo-Russian convention was a feeble and artificial growth. It was popular neither in England nor in Russia. It was cordially disliked by the government of India as well as by all the Russian and British officials on the spot. It proved unworkable and damaging in Persia, and was never recognized by the amir of Afghanistan. . . . Had the Anglo-Russian convention remained confined to Asia . . . it would unquestionably have led to a permanent estrangement between England and Russia. It was the violent attitude adopted by Austria and Germany in the Bosnian crisis which transformed what was a negative arrangement applicable only to Asia into a positive undertaking applicable mainly in Europe." [13] "If matters had been more tactfully handled by Germany and Austria," Lord Carnock wrote in the winter of 1916–1917, "I have little doubt that the general trend of Russian policy would have been most benevolent and intimate towards Berlin and Vienna and Russia would not gradually have drifted into a position which forced her to lean upon France and Great Britain and which eventually prevented any close intimate understanding between her and the Triple Alliance." [14] These evaluations of the real significance of the Anglo-Russian convention are judicious and eminently correct.

---

[13] Harold Nicolson, *Sir Arthur Nicolson, Bart., First Lord Carnock* (Constable and Company, Ltd., London, 1930), pp. 260–261. American edition, Harold Nicolson, *Portrait of a Diplomatist*, being the Life of Sir Arthur Nicolson first Lord Carnock, and a Study of the Origins of the Great War (Houghton Mifflin Company, Boston, 1930; Harcourt, Brace and Company, New York). References in the text are to the English edition.

[14] *Ibid.*, p. 260.

THE BAGDAD RAILWAY

Alarm over the growing power and imperial ambitions of Germany was the principal single factor working for the consolidation of the Triple Entente. This statement implies no element of moral judgment, foolish and unnecessarily provocative as many of the policies of Berlin unquestionably were: the record of the other great Powers in this respect is far from blameless. It was Germany's misfortune, however, that she succeeded in simultaneously antagonizing three of her most formidable potential opponents—France, Great Britain, and Russia—and thus brought into existence the coalition which eventually spelled her doom. The Franco-German conflict over North Africa (the Moroccan crisis of 1905 and the Agadir crisis of 1911) aroused the nationalist spirit in France, revived the desire for the recovery of Alsace and Lorraine, and contributed to the movement of national awakening led by that admirable, yet formidable, Frenchman, Raymond Poincaré. Germany's colonial demands were not liked in England, but they were not in themselves an insurmountable bar to a friendly understanding between the two countries. What made an Anglo-German *rapprochement* impossible was the program of naval rearmament launched by Berlin in 1898 and 1900 and intensified in 1908 when, after the conclusion of the Anglo-Russian convention and King Edward's visit to the tsar at Reval (June, 1908), "encirclement" became an obsession with Emperor William and German nationalist circles. The "big navy" policy was the pet child of Admiral von Tirpitz, secretary of the navy from 1897 to 1916, and had the enthusiastic support of William. To the London government, however, naval supremacy was a dogma admitting of no compromise. The dangerous implications of the von Tirpitz program were fully realized by responsible Germans. The resignation of von Bülow in June, 1909, was due to the opposition of William and von Tirpitz to a reasonable naval agreement with England.[15] Theobald von Bethmann Hollweg, chancellor from 1909 to 1917 and, like his predecessor, an advocate of naval concessions to Great Britain, twice offered his resignation in the vain attempt to check a policy that was leading Germany along the slippery path to war.[16] Count Metternich, German ambassador to London, and Albert Ballin, head of the Hamburg-America Line, favored the

[15] Sidney B. Fay, *The Origins of the World War* (New York, 1928), I, 259.
[16] *Ibid.*, p. 263.

revision of the German naval program so as to meet the wishes of England, but their arguments and efforts proved of no avail. Confronted with the German determination to challenge Great Britain's rule of the seas, London, much against its will, drifted into an ever closer partnership with France and Russia.

Russia, not a maritime or colonial Power, was not immediately concerned with Germany's naval program and schemes for overseas expansion; indeed, she was notably lukewarm in supporting her ally France during the Moroccan and Agadir crises. Nevertheless St. Petersburg viewed with disquiet the military ascendancy of Germany and resented German penetration in the Near East, particularly the ambitious plan for the Bagdad railway which was to link the Persian Gulf with Konia, the terminal point of the German-controlled Anatolian railway. The concession for the Bagdad line was secured by Germany from Turkey in 1902, and in spite of the opposition of Russia, England, and France the 200-kilometer stretch from Konia to Eregli was completed by the autumn of 1904. The construction work then came to a standstill. St. Petersburg and London objected to the Bagdad railway on political, strategic, and economic grounds, although the British had at first favored the German project. British, French, and Russian capital were discouraged from participation in the Bagdad railway, and the three Powers refused their consent (required by the existing treaties) to raise the Turkish tariff in order to provide the funds necessary to finance the railway company. When the increase in tariff rates was finally granted in September, 1906, the conditions attached made it practically impossible to use the proceeds of the levy to defray the cost of railway construction. Sporadic negotiations between Germany and the *entente* Powers went on, but they failed to produce an agreement. Approached by Emperor William at the end of 1907, Sir Edward Grey took the position that no settlement of the Bagdad railway question was feasible without consultation with, and the consent of, France and Russia. This attitude towards *entente* solidarity was not shared by the Russians. During a visit of the tsar and Sazonov to Potsdam in November, 1910, the Near East and the Bagdad railway were discussed as a part of a comprehensive attempt to wipe out the bitter memories of the Bosnian crisis (to be discussed presently). The Potsdam conversations led to the Russo-German agreement of August 19, 1911, N.S., by which Germany undertook to seek no economic concessions in northern Persia (that is, the Russian sphere of influence), while

Russia promised to withdraw all obstacles to the construction of the Bagdad railway. Although the Potsdam conversations were criticized in Paris and London as undermining the very foundation of the Triple Entente (according to Bethmann Hollweg, Russia and Germany reaffirmed in Potsdam their determination not to enter into hostile combinations against each other), the Russo-German agreement on the Near East appeared promising and fruitful. Following the example of Russia, Great Britain and the other Powers with interests in the Near East succeeded in composing their differences with Germany, and an agreement designed to ensure the completion of the Bagdad railway was initialed in mid-June, 1914. Its ratification was prevented by the outbreak of the First World War.

THE BOSNIAN CRISIS, 1907–1909

With the appointment of Izvolsky as foreign minister (1906), the emphasis of Russian diplomatic activity shifted from the Far East to Europe. The new minister endeavored to restore Russia's prestige—and to win the applause of his countrymen and of the world—by spectacular diplomatic action. He seized the opportunity offered by the international situation to reopen two venerable problems of *Grosse Politik*: the Aland Islands and the Straits of Constantinople. Both stemmed from the Treaty of Paris of 1856, imposed on Russia restrictions deemed incompatible with her status as a great Power, and unfolded tempting vistas of ingenious diplomatic combinations, highly secret negotiations, much-publicized conferences, and grandiloquent international treaties.

The gist of the Aland Islands issue was engagingly simple. By the Treaty of Paris Russia was forbidden to fortify this archipelago off the coast of Sweden. The dissolution in October, 1905, of the union between Sweden and Norway disturbed the *status quo* in the Baltic and raised a host of intricate questions of international law. Izvolsky judged the moment opportune for the abrogation of the restrictive Aland Islands clause, thus erasing the humiliation (of which most Russians were blissfully oblivious) inflicted upon Russia after the defeat of the Crimean War. Baron M. Taube, Izvolsky's chief legal adviser, argued in vain that in no conceivable contingency could the demilitarization provision work to the detriment of Russian interests.[17] Izvolsky refused to be swayed. He engaged in complex diplomatic maneuvers;

---

[17] Taube, *op. cit.*, p. 128.

secured, much to the annoyance of France and England, the approval of his proposal by Germany (secret agreement of October 29, 1907, N.S.), and was about to score his point when, following an appeal to the tsar by the king of Sweden, all direct references to the Aland Islands were dropped from the Baltic Declaration signed by Russia, Germany, Sweden, and Denmark (April, 1907). Izvolsky's first venture into the treacherous waters of *Grosse Politik* proved a dud.

While the Aland Islands issue was an artificial one of no practical consequence, the somewhat kindred problem of the Straits was loaded with explosive potentialities. According to the "ancient rule" recognized by the convention of 1841 and confirmed by the treaties of 1856, 1871, and 1878, the Straits of the Bosphorus and the Dardanelles were closed to war vessels. From the Russian point of view this regime had the advantage of making the Black Sea a *mare clausum* and of preventing, so long as treaty obligations were observed, the appearance of foreign warships in its waters. The obvious disadvantage was the limitation imposed by the above arrangement on Russia's freedom of action: warships for the Black Sea fleet could be built only in local shipyards and were denied the right of egress. In view of the weakness of the Black Sea naval establishments the latter restriction proved occasionally a blessing in disguise: legal obstacles to the dispatch of the Black Sea fleet to the Pacific during the Japanese war, resented as they were by the Russian government and nationalist opinion, actually saved men and ships from needless destruction. The closure of the Straits nevertheless was vexatious and, it was plausibly argued, incompatible with Russia's status as a great Power. The Austro-Russian agreements of 1897 and 1903 binding the two countries to uphold the *status quo* in the Balkans were indications that St. Petersburg had become reconciled, at least temporarily, to the existing situation, although plans for a drastic solution of the eastern problem—ranging from the opening of the Straits to the annexation of Constantinople—were sporadically discussed in court, bureaucratic, and army circles. Izvolsky, remembering perhaps that the abrogation (1870–1871) of the Black Sea neutralization clause of the Treaty of Paris won Gorchakov the title of Highness, was a proponent of the opening of the Straits to Russian men-of-war. He raised this issue in connection with the Anglo-Russian convention of 1907 but got nowhere; later Grey denied that the question had even been discussed.[18]

[18] Fay, *op. cit.*, I, 365–368, especially Note 20.

The opportunity Izvolsky sought was provided by Austria-Hungary. With the national awakening of the Balkan peoples, the government of Vienna became increasingly uneasy about the vast Slav population under its rule. It was believed that the growth of the national movement among the Balkan Slavs might well lead to the dismemberment of the Dual Monarchy. Since the Austro-Hungarian occupation of the predominantly Serbian provinces of Bosnia and Herzegovina (1878), the kingdom of Serbia had been watched with particular suspicion by the government of Vienna. Milan and his son Alexander, the two last Serbian kings of the Obrenovitch dynasty, maintained friendly relations with Austria. In June, 1903, however, King Alexander and Queen Draga were brutally murdered, the Obrenovich dynasty was deposed, and King Peter Karageorgevich mounted the Serbian throne. In spite of the inauspicious conditions surrounding his accession, Peter proved a popular and able ruler, and became the leader of the "Greater Serbia" movement which aspired to effecting the unification of all peoples of Serbian blood, that is, Serbs, Bosnians, Slovenes, Croats, and Dalmatians. He leaned heavily on Russian support, while Austro-Serbian relations rapidly deteriorated. The expiration in 1906 of the Austro-Serbian commercial treaty was followed by a tariff war disruptive of old established economic ties and conducive to much ill feeling in both countries. Baron (later count) von Aehrenthal, appointed Austrian foreign minister in October, 1906, had once advocated the revival of the alliance of the three emperors, but had changed his mind and had reached the conclusion that an active policy in the Balkans was imperative for the preservation of the integrity of the Dual Monarchy. Aehrenthal had spent some fifteen years in St. Petersburg, twice in minor diplomatic posts and finally as ambassador from 1902 to 1906. An eyewitness of the Russian revolution of 1905, he became convinced that Russia was not in a position to intervene effectively in the Balkans and that the moment was propitious for dealing with the Serbian menace.

In September, 1907, Izvolsky visited Vienna and confidentially informed Aehrenthal of his desire to have the Straits opened to Russian warships. The Austrian minister was non-committal but asked to be given advance notice of any action bearing on the status of the Straits; Austria was to follow a like course if and when she decided to annex Bosnia and Herzegovina. Professor Fay rightly notes that the Buchlau agreement of a year later "was foreshadowed" in Vienna in September,

1907.[19] Aehrenthal's next step, however, appeared to preclude further cooperation with Russia. In January, 1908, he announced the intention of Austria to build a railway through the sanjak of Novibazar, from Sarajevo to Mitrovitza; a connection of the proposed line (which was approved by the Porte a few days later) with the Macedonian railways would have established a link between the Austrian network and Salonika. This proposal was interpreted in St. Petersburg as a breach of the Austro-Russian agreements of 1897 and 1903. At a meeting of the council of ministers held on January 21 (February 3, N.S.), 1908, Izvolsky argued that Lamsdorf's policy of maintaining the *status quo* in the Balkans and collaborating with Austria was no longer in conformity with Russian interests. He favored, although with some reservations, strong action based on close military cooperation with England. Such a policy, according to Izvolsky, "would open tempting possibilities" and "was capable of achieving brilliant results and of contributing to the fulfillment of Russia's historic mission in the Near East." His plea, however, met with no response at the council. Minister after minister emphasized the country's unpreparedness for war. Summing up the discussion, Stolypin said that under the existing conditions "any policy other than a strictly defensive one would be the delirium of an insane government." In a few years Russia would recover her strength and reassert herself as a great Power. Meanwhile, "in case of serious complications in the Balkans," the government must rely on "the diplomatic skill of the minister of foreign affairs."

Military measures being thus ruled out, Izvolsky, somewhat chastened, turned once more to Austria and to the less ambitious portion of his program—the revision of the status of the Straits. In a discursive note to Aehrenthal he proposed that the opening of the Straits to Russian warships and the Austrian annexation of Bosnia and Herzegovina—although neither question could be settled without the consent of the other Powers, signatories of the Treaty of Berlin—should be examined by the two governments "in a spirit of friendly reciprocity" (July 2, 1908, N.S.). Aehrenthal agreed and promised, in return for Russia's "favorable and friendly attitude" towards the Austrian annexation of the Serbian provinces, to evacuate the sanjak of Novibazar and to enter into "a confidential and friendly exchange of views" concerning the Straits (August 27, N.S.). The outbreak in July, 1908, of the Young Turk revolution appeared to favor the Izvolsky-Aehren-

[19] Fay, *op. cit.*, I, 370.

thal plan. In August the Russian foreign minister went abroad on an exploratory tour of European capitals. In Carlsbad he met Count von Berchtold, then Austrian ambassador to St. Petersburg, and accepted his invitation to visit him at the castle of Buchlau in Moravia, where Aehrenthal was also to be a guest. The celebrated interview of the two ministers took place on September 15 and 16, N.S. It produced no written agreement, and the exact nature of some of the promises exchanged by Izvolsky and Aehrenthal became the center of a controversy. Both agreed not to oppose each other's demands—the opening of the Straits and the annexation of Bosnia and Herzegovina. Aehrenthal confirmed his earlier undertaking to withdraw Austrian troops from the sanjak of Novibazar and to abandon the Sarajevo-Mitrovitza railway project. A friendly understanding was reached on several other questions, among them the recognition of the impending independence of Bulgaria. But if the objectives in view were clearly defined, the methods by which they were to be achieved were lacking in precision. It would seem that Izvolsky left Buchlau under the impression that no date had been set for the annexation and that Vienna would postpone action until the attitude of the other Powers on this question, as well as on that of the opening of the Straits, had been ascertained. There is evidence, however, to show that Izvolsky knew more of Aehrenthal's plans and had made more far-reaching commitments at Buchlau than he would later care to admit. The Austrian minister acted expeditiously: the annexation of Bosnia and Herzegovina was announced on October 6, N.S., the day after Ferdinand of Bulgaria proclaimed the independence of that country and assumed the title of king. Izvolsky learned of the annexation from the French papers which published the news prior to the official announcement.

Aehrenthal's impetuous action created a stir in European chanceleries and in the press and provoked a movement of protest in Serbia, Turkey, and Russia. At first there seemed to be a consensus of opinion that the unilateral repudiation by Austria of a clause of the Berlin treaty should not be allowed to go unchallenged. The Serbian government clamored for the "autonomy" of the annexed provinces, demanded territorial compensations for Serbia, and made preparations for war. Turkey went through threatening military motions and attempted to boycott Austrian goods. Russian nationalist opinion was aroused, the loudly expressed feeling of indignation against Austria being shared by the tsar and the government. Izvolsky, whose incautious commitments at Buchlau had precipitated the crisis, did not sense at first the seriousness of his personal predicament. His policy after the annexation pursued the double objective already outlined in his negotiations with Aehrenthal: the opening of the Straits to Russian warships as a *quid pro quo* for the Austrian annexation, and the confirmation of the new status of the Straits and of Bosnia and Herzegovina by an international conference. After leaving Buchlau, but prior to the proclamation of the annexation, Izvolsky disclosed the nature of the Austro-Russian agreement to the German foreign minister Baron von Schön (at Berchtesgaden, September 26, N.S.) and to the Italian foreign minister Tittoni (at Desio, September 29, N.S.), meeting with no serious objections to the opening of the Straits. Pichon, the French foreign minister, consulted after the annexation took place, was sympathetic but non-committal. The shattering blow to Izvolsky's Straits proposal was dealt in London, where he arrived on October 9, N.S. Sir Edward Grey approved "in principle" the opening of the Straits to warships subject, however, to a condition—unacceptable to Izvolsky—that the new regime should be based on "reciprocity," that is, the Straits should be open to warships of all nations, both in peace and in war. The unyielding attitude of the British foreign secretary ended the negotiations for the revision of the status of the Straits. Izvolsky's disillusionment was all the greater because his plan had been predicated on the erroneous assumption that he could count on the support of London.[20]

Spurred by a personal resentment against Aehrenthal and by attacks in the press which accused him of having sold Serbia to her hereditary enemy, Izvolsky endeavored to undo the nefarious Buchlau bargain by bringing the issue of the annexation before a conference of the Powers signatory to the Treaty of Berlin. Nothing came of his efforts. It was felt in London, Paris, and Rome that the mere transformation of an occupation *sine die* into an outright annexation, even though in violation of international agreements and indicative of

[20] It was not until his return to St. Petersburg that Izvolsky learned of the secret Austro-Russian agreement of 1878 in which Russia promised to raise no objections to Austria's annexation of Bosnia and Herzegovina. About the same time the matter was brought to the attention of the tsar by Emperor Francis Joseph. "I never knew of the existence of such a secret paragraph," Nicholas wrote to his mother on Oct. 21, 1908, N.S., "and never heard about it either from Giers or Lobanov, in whose time all this happened."

Austria's aggressive designs in the Balkans, was not a sufficient reason to risk a European war. Aehrenthal carried out his program with determination and efficiency. He would not submit the annexation issue to an international conference unless a definite agreement was reached beforehand that the Powers would merely ratify the *fait accompli*. The recognition by Turkey of the new status of Bosnia and Herzegovina was purchased by a payment of 2.5 million Turkish pounds and the withdrawal of Austria from the sanjak of Novibazar (February 26, 1909, N.S.); and as Serbian agitation mounted—not without the instigation of Russia—portions of the Austro-Hungarian army were put on a war footing and troops were concentrated on the Serbian border. Tension was relieved by the intervention of Germany and by Izvolsky's final capitulation.

Berlin was not consulted on the annexation. Emperor William, taken by surprise, deprecated the Austrian move as an unjustifiable and inopportune attack on Turkey fraught with danger to European peace. Von Bülow, however, held that the very existence of the Triple Alliance was at stake and that Germany must support Austria irrespective of the merits of the case. This view having prevailed, Izvolsky was bluntly told in Berlin, where he stopped on his way home from London (October, 1908), that Aehrenthal had the unqualified backing of Germany. In the spring of 1909, when a war between Serbia and Austria appeared likely, Russia's Balkan policy was reviewed at a council held at the imperial residence of Tsarskoe Selo. The decision was similar to the one of February, 1908: both financially and militarily Russia was unprepared for a major war. On the same day (March 17, N.S.) Berlin confidentially proposed to St. Petersburg that the new status of Bosnia and Herzegovina should be recognized (and Article XXV of the Treaty of Berlin abrogated) by an exchange of notes in which the Powers would sanction the Austro-Turkish agreement; Russia was requested to signify her approval beforehand. Izvolsky's somewhat elusive reply was followed by a second German *démarche* (March 21, N.S.). Count Pourtalès, the German ambassador to St. Petersburg, was instructed "to make it quite clear" that Germany "expects a precise answer—Yes or No. Any evasive, complicated or ambiguous reply will be regarded as a refusal. . . . The responsibility for all that follows will rest exclusively on M. Izvolsky." This communication, which Izvolsky described to Sir Arthur Nicolson as "a 'diplomatic ultimatum' of the most violent character," although "not . . . an ultimatum since it did not actually threaten war," [21] produced the desired effect: the next day (March 22, N.S.) Izvolsky accepted unconditionally the German proposal. From his personal point of view the peaceful solution of the crisis had one important advantage: it removed the threat made by Aehrenthal to publish some of Izvolsky's indiscreet and incautious letters written in the summer of 1908.

Russia's forced lead in officially condoning the annexation was followed by the other great Powers. Serbia, too, yielded, but not until Austria had ordered a partial mobilization (March 29, N.S.). On March 31, N.S., the Belgrade government solemnly promised "to renounce the attitude of protest and opposition adopted since last autumn with regard to the annexation"; to live in the future "on good neighborly terms" with Austria-Hungary; and to demobilize the Serbian army and disband irregular forces on Serbian territory. The triumph of Aehrenthal—and the defeat and humiliation of Izvolsky —could not have been more complete.

The annexation crisis, trivial as were its immediate causes (the distinction between an occupation *sine die* and annexation being largely one of legal terminology) had profound repercussions on the European situation. It generated in Russia a deep animosity towards Vienna and Berlin. "I do not think that I exaggerate," wrote Count Pourtalès on May 6, 1909, N.S., "when I say that the present feeling against Germany is even more bitter than against Austria." The Serbian declaration of March, 1909, notwithstanding, and contrary to the expectations of Aehrenthal and the Austrian chief of staff Conrad von Hötzendorf, anti-Austrian agitation in Serbia continued with unabated force. Relations between the *entente* Powers became strained. "Our *entente*, I much fear, will languish and possibly die," Nicolson wrote to Grey two days after Russia's acceptance of the German ultimatum. His proposal for a formal Anglo-Russian alliance was not only unacceptable to Grey, but the Russophile ambassador was even enjoined by the London foreign office to refrain from using in official dispatches the expression "Triple Entente," on the ground that "if it appeared in a parliamentary blue book it would be assumed to have some special official meaning and might provoke inconvenient comment or inquiry" (May 6, 1909, N.S.).[22] In the summer of 1910

[21] Nicolson, *op. cit.*, p. 301.
[22] Ibid., pp. 305–308.

Nicolson was appointed permanent undersecretary at the foreign office, and was succeeded at the St. Petersburg embassy by Sir George Buchanan.

In spite of the imposing demonstration of Austro-German solidarity, the structure of the Triple Alliance, like that of the Triple Entente, was weakened by the annexation crisis. The Italian government disapproved of Aehrenthal's policy as inimical to Italian interests, and resented not having been kept abreast of events by Vienna and Berlin. In October, 1909, during a visit of the tsar to King Victor Emmanuel at the castle of Racconigi, Izvolsky and Tittoni signed a secret agreement which bound the two governments to pursue a common policy in the Balkans, a pact which contained a secret provision reminiscent of the Buchlau bargain: Russia promised "to view with benevolence" Italian interests in Tripoli and Cyrenaica, and Italy agreed to take a similar attitude towards Russian interests in the Straits. The Racconigi agreement and futile attempts at reconciling Serbian and Bulgarian jealousies in order to establish a Slav front against Austria in the Balkans closed Izvolsky's ministerial career. Since the Bosnian crisis he had been the target of a merciless press campaign, and his position in the government became untenable. It was not until September, 1910, however, that he left the St. Petersburg foreign office. In his new post of ambassador to Paris he worked relentlessly against any understanding with the central Powers.

THE BALKAN WARS, 1911–1913

The Austrian annexation and the proclamation of Bulgarian independence not only whetted the appetites of countries coveting Turkish territories but fostered the national aspirations of the Balkan peoples. A new round of wars for the partition of the Ottoman empire began. The Italian ultimatum to the Porte (September, 1911) led to the Italo-Turkish War and the annexation by Italy of Tripoli and Cyrenaica (Treaty of Lausanne, October, 1912). The Tripolitan war had an electrifying effect upon the Balkan states. Negotiations for the "amicable division" between Serbia and Bulgaria of spheres of influence in Macedonia were initiated by Belgrade in April, 1911; but it was not until the outbreak of the Tripolitan war that proposals for a military alliance, taken up in earnest, led to the conclusion of the Serbo-Bulgarian treaty of March 13, 1912, N.S.

In 1910–1913, as on numerous previous occasions, the Balkan policy of St. Petersburg was vacillating and contradictory. The Russian government had not abandoned its designs on Constantinople and the Straits; it was in sympathy with the aspirations of the Balkan Slavs, and it favored the formation of a Balkan League as a means of restraining Austria. Sazonov's slavophilism, however, was of a mild and nebulous variety. He did not wish to set Europe aflame in order to acquire the control of the Straits or to gratify the national ambitions, however legitimate, of Russia's Balkan clients; and while believing in the ultimate inevitability of an armed conflict in the Balkans, he strove for the maintenance of the *status quo* at least until Russia had completed her military preparations. He singularly failed to perceive that the support and encouragement given to Serbia, Bulgaria, Rumania, and Montenegro could not but precipitate the conflagration he desired to avoid. In July, 1911, moreover, Sazonov left St. Petersburg for reasons of health and did not resume his duties until the end of the year, his place being temporarily filled by A. A. Neratov. Sazonov thus exercised no control over Russian policy during the opening phase of the Balkan crisis, but even after his return to office he was often incapable of imposing his views on his subordinates. N. Hartwig and A. Nekliudov, Russian ministers in the key posts of Belgrade and Sofia, were protagonists of Russia's "historic mission" and the Slav cause, and were the true architects of the Balkan League. The continuation in office of diplomats who persistently disregarded the instructions of the St. Petersburg foreign office may be explained by the popularity of aggressive panslav policies in court and army circles and with a small but well organized and vocal body of public opinion. Temperamentally unfitted for drastic disciplinary action, Sazonov, because of the insecurity of his personal position after the assassination of his brother-in-law Stolypin (September, 1911), was all the more inclined to show excessive leniency towards those of his recalcitrant subordinates who enjoyed the patronage of highly placed persons and a degree of public support.

The Serbo-Bulgarian treaty of March, 1912, provided for the mutual guarantee of the territory and independence of the two contracting parties and promised military assistance in case of an attack on either of them, or of an attempt by a great Power to occupy, even temporarily, any Balkan territory under the Turkish rule, should such occupation be regarded by one of the signatories as inimical to its interests and as constituting a *casus belli*. These provisions, designed to protect Serbia and the sanjak of Novibazar against encroachments by Austria, fitted well into Sazonov's policy of preserving the *status quo*. A secret annex to the treaty, however, stipulated that if disorders in Turkey endangered the national interests of the contracting parties and the *status quo*, Serbia and Bulgaria should discuss joint military action. The ultimate decision as to whether armed intervention by the signatory Powers was necessary was reserved to Russia, who was also to mediate any disputes between them.[23] The annex also provided for the partition of the territories to be conquered from Turkey, the delimitation of the future boundaries in specified cases being left to the discretion of the Russian emperor. The secret annex was clearly an instrument for the destruction of the *status quo* which the body of the treaty professed to uphold. The pact of March 13 was supplemented by a Serbo-Bulgarian military convention (May 12, N.S.) which stated in detail the number of troops to be used in a war against Austria or Turkey, and by a Greco-Bulgarian treaty of military assistance directed against the Porte (May 29, 1912, N.S.). Russian diplomacy endeavored unsuccessfully to mitigate the aggressive character of the latter treaty. Sazonov was uneasy about the Serbo-Bulgarian accord, which was largely framed during his absence. He did not reveal its full text to Russia's French ally until Poincaré's visit to St. Petersburg in August, 1912. Shocked and alarmed, the head of the French government characterized the agreement as a "covenant for war" (*convention de guerre*).

The ingenious device of the Serbo-Bulgarian treaty granting Russia the veto power over the question of war and peace remained, as was to be expected, a dead letter. The gathering of war clouds in the Balkans in the summer of 1912 forced the great Powers to try preventive diplomatic action. At the end of September Sazonov, stopping in Paris on his way from London to St. Petersburg, agreed with Poincaré on a three-point program: (1) condemnation of any move on the part of the Balkan allies likely to lead to a breach of peace; (2) request that the Porte should introduce administrative reforms which, however, were not to impair the sovereign rights of the sultan or the unity of the Ottoman empire; and (3) non-recognition of any changes

---

[23] This curious arrangement was presumably inspired by a provision of the Russo-Montenegrin military convention of Dec. 15, 1910, N.S., which forbade King Nicholas any aggressive action without Russia's consent. Montenegro, however, received from Russia an annual subsidy of 600,000 rubles. The restrictive clause was a source of constant irritation to King Nicholas.

in the *status quo* if war should break out. Sazonov attached particular importance to the last point, not only because it fitted into his general policy but also because it safeguarded the interests of the Balkan allies in case of an unsuccessful war.[24] Duly consulted, London, Berlin, Vienna, and Rome concurred, and on October 7, N.S., Russia and Austria, acting on behalf of the European concert, dispatched a strongly worded admonition to the Balkan states. However, it proved totally ineffective. On October 8 Montenegro declared war on Turkey and within ten days was joined by Serbia, Bulgaria, and Greece.

The first Balkan war was brief and disastrous for the Porte. In less than a month the allies overran practically the whole of European Turkey. The Greeks took Salonika, the Serbians reached the Adriatic, and the Bulgarians were at the gates of Constantinople. Early in December Turkey asked for an armistice; peace negotiations began in London in the middle of that month but were interrupted in January, 1913. The resumption of warlike operations early in February completed the Turkish debacle; the Bulgarians occupied Adrianople, one of the few strongholds still in Turkish hands, and a new armistice was signed in the middle of April, Montenegro alone continuing the struggle until her troops took possession of Scutari (April 23, N.S.). By the Peace of London (May 30, 1913, N.S.) the Porte ceded to the victorious allies all her European territories west of the Enos-Midia line as well as the island of Crete. Unable to agree on the division of the spoil, the members of the anti-Turkish coalition came immediately to blows. The second Balkan war began with Bulgaria's predatory attack on Serbia, who fought in alliance with Rumania and Greece. Turkey joined the fray and recovered Adrianople. The defeat of Bulgaria was speedy and decisive. By the Treaty of Bucharest (August 10, 1913, N.S.) she was despoiled of most of her recent conquests from Turkey and lost to Rumania southern Dobrudja, which was a part of Bulgaria prior to the first Balkan war; while the Turko-Bulgarian Treaty of Constantinople restored Adrianople to the Porte (September 9, 1913, N.S.). There was profound disillusionment and bitterness in Sofia. The two Balkan wars, on the other hand, brought substantial territorial gains to Serbia, Rumania, and Greece, although they fell short of satisfying all the territorial and national ambitions of those states.

Sazonov, caught in the vortex of Balkan policies, uneasily rode the

---

[24] Serge Sazonov, *Fateful Years, 1909–1916* (London, 1928), pp. 68–69.

storm which Russian diplomacy had helped to release but which it was powerless to control. The ungrateful task of finding a way out of the Balkan imbroglio was undertaken by a conference of ambassadors of the great Powers which met in London under the chairmanship of Sir Edward Grey (December, 1912). The two principal antagonists were Russia and Austria, although on specific issues their governments advocated at times identical policies (for instance, in favoring the allocation of Kavala, a Macedonian port of the Aegean, to Bulgaria instead of to Greece). Sazonov, fearing Austrian expansion in the Balkans and the revision of the status of the Straits to the detriment of Russia, endeavored to save, if possible, some part of the *status quo* formula already rendered obsolete by the surprise victories of the allies in the first Balkan war. He wished Constantinople to remain in Turkish hands and to maintain the unity of the Balkan League, Russia's probable ally in a war with Austria. Simultaneously he supported Serbian demands, although not with the determination hoped for in Belgrade, and courted Bulgaria, Rumania, and Greece, where Russian influence was less firmly implanted than in Serbia and Montenegro.

The objectives of Austrian policy were definite and clear-cut. Count von Berchtold, who became foreign minister after Aehrenthal's death in February, 1912, believed that the strengthening of Serbia was a real menace to the Dual Monarchy and that it should be prevented, or at least circumscribed, at almost any cost. Like Sazonov, he tried to win the friendship of the other Balkan states, especially when their ambitions could be gratified at the expense of Serbia. The anti-Serbian tendency in Vienna was accentuated after the reappointment in December, 1912, of a relentless advocate of a "preventive" war against Serbia, Conrad von Hötzandorf, as chief of staff, a position from which he was removed in 1911. England, France, Germany, and Italy did not lend unwavering support to their partners in, respectively, the Triple Entente and the Triple Alliance but pursued independent policies of their own. The rivalries and ambitions of the great Powers were superimposed upon the secular jealousies and irreconcilable claims of the Balkan states. The inevitable result was a series of improvisations and compromises which satisfied no one and were instrumental in bringing about World War I.

Opposed to war on moral grounds [25] and mindful of Russia's un-

---

[25] "I was brought up in the conviction," Sazonov wrote in his memoirs, "that the only admissible type of nationalism is one that does not conflict with the funda-

preparedness, Sazonov preached moderation and conciliation to the Balkan allies while Hartwig and Nekliudov fanned the flames of Serbian and Bulgarian nationalism and excited pro-Slav crowds roamed the streets of St. Petersburg. The Russian minister gave tangible evidence of his desire to prevent a European war. His slavophile sympathies notwithstanding, he would not countenance the partition of Albania among Serbia, Greece, and Montenegro, but agreed instead to the demand of Austria and Italy for the creation of an independent Albania, that is, the exclusion of Serbia from the Adriatic. He dealt even more ruthlessly with Russia's traditional friend and client, Montenegro. The Montenegrin occupation of Scutari, which the Powers had vetoed in deference to the wishes of Austria, was terminated, on Sazonov's initiative, by the dispatch of an international squadron to Antivari. Russia, according to Sazonov, was not prepared to collaborate with Montenegro "in starting a world war in order that King Nicholas might cook an omelette." In October, 1913, when Berchtold sent an ultimatum to Serbia demanding the withdrawal of Serbian troops who had reoccupied portions of Albania, St. Petersburg decreed and obtained immediate unconditional compliance.

Russia, of course, was not the only Power to work for the localization of the Balkan war. Sir Edward Grey's patience and genius for compromise were invaluable to the London conference, even though some of the solutions adopted were never enforced and others proved highly nefarious. Berlin exercised at times a restraining influence in Vienna. When in July, 1913, shortly after the outbreak of the second Balkan war, Berchtold, fearing the defeat of Bulgaria, contemplated strong diplomatic pressure in Bucharest and Belgrade (to be followed, if necessary, by armed intervention), Bethmann Hollweg sternly discouraged his Austrian colleague from embarking on so dangerous a course.

Every European government had to reckon, although in a different degree, with the state of public opinion. The position of Sazonov in this respect was particularly difficult because of the instability of the tsar and the opposition of nationalist and panslav circles to a policy of conciliation and peace. Russian diplomacy was attacked in a section of the press for its alleged indifference to the Slav cause and Russia's

mental principles of Christian ethics" (Sazonov, *op. cit.*, p. 12). The translation of this high-sounding but elusive formula in terms of practical policies presents insurmountable obstacles.

"historic mission." The conservative *Novoe Vremia*, for instance, published articles on Russian Balkan policy under such vitriolic headlines as "Diplomatic Mukden" and "Diplomatic Tsushima." In March, 1913, at the very time when Sazonov counseled moderation to the Balkan allies, the president of the State Duma, M. V. Rodzianko, indulged in noisy manifestations at the Taurida Palace to celebrate Bulgarian victories. In a private audience he urged the tsar to accept Constantinople, which a delegation of Bulgarian generals begged "to lay . . . at His Majesty's feet." "We must take advantage of the popular enthusiasm," Rodzianko told Nicholas. "The Straits must become ours. A war will be joyfully welcomed, and will raise the government's prestige." The latter contention was inspired by pro-Slav and anti-Sazonov street demonstrations whose participants, according to Rodzianko, were "serious, well-conducted people—officers, society ladies, senators, government officials, etc.," that is, hardly a representative cross section of the population, and one, moreover, not likely to be called (except for the officers) to the armed forces in wartime.[26] It is much to Sazonov's credit that he refused to be unduly influenced by these manifestations of "popular enthusiasm."

RUSSIA AND CONSTANTINOPLE, 1911–1914

The Bosnian crisis and the Balkan wars awakened the long-dormant interest of St. Petersburg in the question of Constantinople. A renewed attempt at opening the Straits to Russian warships was made in October and November, 1911, and its immediate cause may be traced to Turkey's order for dreadnoughts (June, 1911) and her plans for building railways in eastern Anatolia.[27] In the opinion of the leading officials of the St. Petersburg foreign office, the challenge to Russia's supremacy in the Black Sea implied in the proposed strengthening of the Ottoman navy could be met by securing the free passage of Russian war vessels through the Straits: the Russian Black Sea fleet could then be reinforced by ships built in the Baltic shipyards or abroad. Although this theory was deprecated by Russian naval authorities who believed the seizure of the Bosphorus to be the only effective solution, the acting foreign minister, Neratov, decided to make over-

[26] M. V. Rodzianko, *The Reign of Rasputin: An Empire's Collapse* (London, 1927), pp. 78–86.

[27] An excellent, succinct account of this obscure and much-misrepresented incident is given by Philip E. Mosely, "Russian Policy in 1911–1912," *The Journal of Modern History*, XII, No. 1 (March, 1940), 71–74.

tures to the Porte. The Russian plan, framed with the participation of Izvolsky and presented to the Turkish government by the Russian ambassador to Constantinople, M. Charykov, comprised four distinct proposals: (1) removal of restrictions imposed by the Russo-Turkish agreement of 1900 on the building of railways in eastern Anatolia, such railways to be financed by French and Russian capital; (2) guarantee by Russia of the existing regime of the Bosphorus and the Dardanelles and of the adjoining territory in case of an attack on Turkey; (3) in order to facilitate the fulfillment of the latter obligation, consent by the Porte to the passage of Russian warships through the Straits, provided the proposed reinterpretation of the London convention of 1871 was approved by the other signatory Powers; and (4) transfer to Russia of the dreadnoughts ordered by the Porte. On Charykov's initiative the first overtures to Constantinople (October 14, N.S.) contained also the offer of Russia's good offices in improving the relations between Turkey and her Balkan neighbors. Neratov eventually disavowed this proposal, although he was favorably impressed at first and suggested to Hartwig and Nekliudov that provisions for the adherence of Turkey should be included in the Serbo-Bulgarian treaty of alliance then under negotiation. The Porte looked askance at the Russian plan and as usual played for time. Italy, bound to Russia by the Racconigi agreement (1909), raised no objection; France, Izvolsky's insistence notwithstanding, would not definitely commit herself; Germany was frankly hostile; and Sir Edward Grey merely reiterated his 1908 stand: if the status of the Straits was to be changed, the Bosphorus and the Dardanelles should be open to the warships of all nations. With the return of Sazonov to St. Petersburg early in December, the matter was dropped. In an interview with a correspondent of the London *Times*, Sazonov roundly denied that Russia was negotiating with Turkey. Charykov, having allegedly exceeded his instructions, was recalled in March, 1912, and was succeeded at the Constantinople embassy by M. N. Giers.

Throughout the Balkan wars Sazonov's policy was predicated on the assumption that no foreign Power other than Turkey should be permitted to control Constantinople. This preoccupation with the future of the Straits and with German penetration in the Near East accounts for his excessive nervousness in the Liman von Sanders affair (November, 1913 to January, 1914). The Young Turk government, as a part of the program for the modernization of its civilian administration and armed forces, secured the services of French, English, and German specialists. The British admirals Limpus and Sir Douglas Gamble were in charge of the reorganization of the navy, while General von der Goltz, assisted by a group of German officers, was engaged in infusing Prussian discipline in the Ottoman army. Von der Goltz withdrew, however, the failure of his efforts having been demonstrated by the lamentable showing of the Turkish troops in the wars of 1912–1913. In November, 1913, after protracted negotiations, he was succeeded by General Liman von Sanders, head of a mission of some forty German officers. Sazonov took the strongest exception to the von Sanders mission. Von Sanders, unlike von der Goltz, was appointed commander of a Turkish army corps stationed in Constantinople, an arrangement which put the ambassadors accredited to the Porte in a position of dependence on a German general. The question of the von Sanders appointment, moreover, was shrouded in secrecy. In May Emperor William discussed the matter with the tsar, who had come to Berlin to attend a family wedding, but the exact nature of von Sanders's duties was not revealed at the time. Bethmann Hollweg made no reference to the mission in a long conversation he had with Sazonov in Berlin in October, a reticence the latter resented. When the news finally broke out, Sazonov, supported by France, demanded strong concerted action by the *entente* Powers and contemplated coercive military measures (the occupation of Trebizond or Bayazid), but Sir Edward Grey demurred. The conciliatory attitude of Germany brought a speedy termination of the crisis. It was announced in the middle of January, 1914, that Liman von Sanders had been promoted to the rank of field marshal, which made him ineligible for the command of an army corps. He retained the office of inspector-general of the Turkish troops and director of the Military School, but was relieved of the command of the Constantinople garrison. Sazonov had won a modest diplomatic victory.

The Liman von Sanders incident instilled into Sazonov's mind a profound mistrust of Germany, and indirectly led to the re-examination of the position of Russia in the question of Constantinople and the Straits. In a lengthy report to the tsar (November 23, 1913) dealing with the Turkish naval program, Sazonov argued that while the regime of the Straits was on the whole satisfactory to Russia, the probability of the disintegration of the Ottoman empire required close study and advance preparation. Both on political and on economic grounds (Sazonov emphasized Russia's financial dependence on grain exports from her southern ports) the control of Constantinople by any foreign Power other than Turkey could not be tolerated. The breakdown of the Ottoman empire, if it was to come, was most likely to occur within the framework of a European war. The neutralization of Constantinople suggested in some quarters offered no guarantee against its subsequent seizure by an ambitious Power, for instance, Bulgaria. Russia, in spite of her heavy military expenditure, was unprepared for the landing of her troops on Turkish shores and was unable to meet the challenge of the Ottoman naval program. Sazonov therefore demanded the summoning of a special conference "to discuss the problems involved and to take appropriate decisions." The tsar approved, and a conference of high officials duly met on February 8 (February 21, N.S.), 1914. Meanwhile the issues raised by the Liman von Sanders mission were dealt with by Sazonov in several reports and memoranda and were examined, on December 31, 1913 (January 13, 1914, N.S.), by a small emergency conference under the chairmanship of Kokovtsov. Some of the proposals advanced, particularly those presented at the February conference, were not lacking in vigor and aggressive spirit, but the general trend of the discussion made it clear that in view of the international situation Russia was not in a position to carry them through. The recommendations of the February conference were, accordingly, perfunctory and tame: speeding-up of mobilization, improvement in the land and sea transportation in the Black Sea area, and the strengthening of the Black Sea fleet. It is dubious whether these paltry measures could have been seriously regarded as a step towards the conquest of Constantinople. The St. Petersburg gathering, often pictured as a sinister conclave of ruthless and crafty leaders bent on conquest, was actually a meeting of colorless bureaucrats going wearily through the routine motions of passing resolutions about a largely academic question. E. A. Adamov, a Soviet historian and editor of an important collection of documents on Constantinople and the Straits, has conveyed well the feeling of half-heartedness and futility that permeated the deliberations of the St. Petersburg officials. In 1914, as in 1911 and during the Balkan wars, the preservation of the *status quo*, and not preparation for a war of conquest, was uppermost in Sazonov's mind.[28]

[28] A very different interpretation of Sazonov's policy is given by an eminent American historian. The conference of Jan. 13, 1914, N.S., according to Professor

ON THE EVE OF WORLD WAR I

In the years immediately preceding the First World War, the Triple Entente, in spite of numerous setbacks and much friction among its members, was steadily gaining ground and expanding its influence. The intimate relations between St. Petersburg and Paris were not seriously disturbed by such factors as Russia's reserve during the Agadir crisis (1911) or the recall, at Sazonov's request, of the French ambassador to Russia, Georges Louis (February, 1913). A secret Franco-Russian naval convention was signed in July, 1912, and the visits of Poincaré to St. Petersburg in August, 1912, and in July, 1914, did much to cement the alliance.

Relations between Russia and England were less harmonious, and were at times subject to severe strain. The Russo-German agreement reached at Potsdam (1910) was regarded in London as "not in keeping with the understanding on which the other members of the Triple Entente had hitherto acted." [29] The Russian government viewed with suspicion any move on the part of the British for a *rapprochement* with Germany, for instance, Lord Haldane's mission to Berlin (1912), and it resented London's lukewarm support of Russian policy during the Balkan wars. The focal point of discord, however, was Persia, where

---

Fay, "reveals sharply the contrast between Kokovtsov's moderate, conciliatory, and restraining influence on the one hand, and, on the other, the dangerous policy of military pressure urged by Sazonov and the military and naval officials. . . . It was therefore an incalculable misfortune for Russia and the world that, a few days after this conference, M. Kokovtsov followed Count Witte into political retirement, and left the field free to M. Sazonov and the Russian Pan-Slavs and militarists" (Fay, *op. cit.*, I, 536). Count Kokovtsov has emphatically contradicted this theory. Writing in 1929, two years after Sazonov's death, he ascertained that "during the term of almost three years when I was the president of the council of ministers, no divergency of opinion on any question of importance arose between myself and . . . Sazonov. Under the laws of the Russian empire . . . the conduct of Russia's foreign policy was entirely in the hands of the minister of foreign affairs. . . . In spite of this, M. Sazonov never made the slightest attempt to prevent me from taking an active part in the direction of the most important and responsible problems of Russian foreign policy and on many occasions was the first to suggest our collaboration in the discussion of such problems. . . . It seems extremely doubtful that my resignation from the government was received by Sazonov with a feeling of relief, as a removal of a limitation on his freedom of action. . . . I have excellent proofs, on the contrary, that he looked upon my retirement with considerable regret." Michael T. Florinsky, "Russia and Constantinople: Count Kokovtsov's Evidence," *Foreign Affairs*, New York, VIII, No. 1 (October, 1929), 135–141.

[29] Sir George Buchanan, *My Mission to Russia, and Other Diplomatic Memories* (London, 1923), I, 93.

the Anglo-Russian agreement of 1907 had proved unworkable. Having assured the Persian government that "the agreement cannot fail to promote the prosperity, security and ulterior development of Persia in the most efficacious manner," the two signatory Powers, especially Russia, proceeded to interfere in Persia's domestic affairs. In Persia, as in the Far East and in the Balkans, the Russian foreign office proved incapable of restraining the nationalistic ardor of its agents. Torn between the desire for cooperation with England, on the one hand, and, on the other, the determination of Russian proconsuls in Persia to reduce that country to the status of a Russian protectorate, St. Petersburg became hopelessly bogged in the quagmire of Persian internal politics, drifted into military intervention, for a time occupied Teheran, and established a quasi-complete control of Azerbaidzan. Sir George Buchanan, shortly after his arrival in Russia at the end of 1910, informed Sazonov that "there was such strong feeling [in England] against the military measures undertaken by Russia in Persia" that in spite of Sir Edward Grey's "earnest desire to maintain the Anglo-Russian understanding intact" he "had almost despaired of being able to defend it." As late as June, 1914, the British ambassador told the tsar that he was afraid that "the trend of events in north Persia would end by creating a situation that might prove fatal to the Anglo-Russian understanding." [30] Nevertheless the common distrust of Germany, especially after the failure of the Haldane mission and the Liman von Sanders affair, drove the two countries closer together. In February, 1912, a representative British delegation went to St. Petersburg, and in June, 1914, a British squadron visited Kronstadt; both were accorded a cordial reception. Negotiations for an Anglo-Russian naval convention began in May, 1914, but were interrupted by the outbreak of the war.

Russian diplomacy registered gains in other directions. The notable improvement in Russo-Japanese relations all but erased the memories of the war of 1904–1905. Rumania, assiduously wooed by Sazonov, who supported her claims to Dobrudja after the second Balkan war and encouraged her ambitions in Transylvania, had gradually shifted from the orbit of the Triple Alliance into that of the Triple Entente. The Russo-Rumanian political *rapprochement* was about to be consummated by the establishment of dynastic ties: an exchange of royal visits (March and June, 1914) brought forth the semi-official announce-

[30] *Ibid.*, pp. 113, 115.

ment of the impending marriage between the tsar's eldest daughter and Prince Carol, son of the heir to the Rumanian throne.

Such, in broadest outline, was the international position of Russia in the summer of 1914 when the murder of the Austrian Archduke Francis Ferdinand opened a new chapter in the history of Europe and of the world.

CHAPTER XLIII

IMPERIAL RUSSIA AND THE FIRST WORLD WAR: I

THE VORTEX

In the summer of 1914 the heir apparent to the Austrian throne, Archduke Francis Ferdinand, was attending the maneuvers of troops stationed in Bosnia. On June 28, N.S., accompanied by his morganatic wife, the Duchess of Hohenberg, he paid a state visit to Sarajevo, capital of the recently annexed province. As the royal couple was driving to the town hall a bomb was hurled in their automobile, but both escaped unhurt, although a member of their suite and several bystanders were injured. The pre-arranged program, however, was not abandoned; at the town hall Francis Ferdinand listened, with understandable impatience, to the mayor's prepared address extolling the loyalty of the Bosnians to their new rulers. On the return journey from the town hall two shots fired point-blank mortally wounded the archduke and the duchess. The assassin, G. Princip, was a Bosnian student; he and his associates had only recently returned from Serbia, and were connected with Serbian nationalist and terrorist organizations. The Serbian government was not involved in the plot, although it had encouraged anti-Austrian agitation and had tolerated the participation of army officers and police officials in terroristic groups.

The Sarajevo assassination created a stir in the European capitals, but its broader implications were not at first grasped and it was not permitted to interfere with the summer plans of monarchs, ministers, and generals. The momentous consequences of the murder, a dramatic but not in itself politically important occurrence, may be traced to two sets of misconceptions held by European statesmen, one bearing on the "national interests" of their respective countries, and the other on the probable attitude of the other great Powers. The Viennese government, led by Berchtold and Conrad von Hötzendorf, espoused the familiar theory that the "greater Serbia" agitation was a deadly menace to the Dual Monarchy and should be eliminated once for all. It was felt in Vienna, however, that the nature of the action to be taken against Serbia depended on the degree of support Germany was prepared to give her Austrian ally. A letter from Emperor Francis Joseph to Emperor William (delivered on July 5, N.S.) did not mention military action against Serbia. The Austrian emperor (or, more precisely, Berchtold, who drafted the letter) argued, however, that the re-establishment of the influence of the Triple Alliance in southeastern Europe would "only be possible when Serbia, which at present forms the pivot of the panslav policy, is eliminated as a political factor in the Balkans." Berlin's response fulfilled the most sanguine expectations of Berchtold. William urged Francis Joseph to proceed immediately with the strongest possible measures against Serbia, while Bethmann Hollweg assured the Austrian ambassador that "whatever Austria's decision may turn out to be, Austria can count with certainty . . . that Germany will stand behind her as an ally and a friend." The *carte blanche* so incautiously given by Bethmann Hollweg to Berchtold was predicated on the assumption that the humiliation of Serbia would enhance the position of Austria-Hungary, Germany's principal ally. It was not expected either in Berlin or in Vienna that the chastisement of Serbia, however ruthless, would lead to a European war: "monarchical solidarity," according to this view, would prevent the tsar from taking up the defense of a country guilty of regicide; moreover, neither Russia nor France was ready for war. There was therefore no reason for alarm. On July 6, N.S., William left Potsdam for his customary cruise in the Baltic, and Berlin officials dispersed to their country estates and summer resorts. Meanwhile Berchtold, his determination to inflict an exemplary punishment on Serbia strengthened by Germany's unqualified endorsement, proceeded with the preparation of an ultimatum to Belgrade.

Germany was the only Power taken into Austria's confidence. Neither Italy, the third member of the Triple Alliance, nor London, Paris, or St. Petersburg, was informed. There was some uneasiness in the *entente* capitals as to Berchtold's seemingly inexplicable procrastination as well as to the nature of the demands Austria might make on Serbia, but there was no real premonition of the impending catastrophe. In the first half of July St. Petersburg, like Berlin, was deserted by many officials, among them Sazonov and several of the key men in the ministry of war. The higher Russian functionaries, however, reassembled in the capital towards the middle of July for the reception of the French president Poincaré, who sailed for Russia on July 15, N.S., to fulfill an engagement of long standing. The presidential visit (July 20 to 23, N.S.) and mass strikes of unusual violence somewhat overshadowed events in the Balkans. The Russian press and public opinion were on the whole anti-Austrian and pro-Serbian, but not too aggressively so. Sazonov did not anticipate the outbreak of war. Commenting on an interview with Count Szápáry, the Austrian ambassador, who assured him of the Viennese government's love for peace, Sazonov remarked, *"Il a été doux comme un agneau"* (July 18, N.S.). It was not until July 22, N.S., that the Russian minister betrayed signs of anxiety and instructed the Russian ambassador to Vienna "to point out the dangerous consequences of any action on the part of Austria of an unacceptable character with regard to the dignity of Serbia." The Austrian ultimatum dispelled whatever illusions the *entente* statesmen may have had.

The demands made by Berchtold on Serbia were deliberately framed so as to make them unacceptable. Count Stephen Tisza, the Hungarian minister-president, had opposed this provocative and intransigent attitude as a "fatal mistake," and it was not until July 14, N.S., that he agreed to support Berchtold's adventurous policy on the condition that war with Serbia would not lead to territorial acquisitions by the Dual Monarchy: annexation of Slav provinces, in the opinion of Tisza, was incompatible with Magyar interests. The text of the Austrian note was completed on July 19, N.S., but its delivery was delayed until the late afternoon of July 23, N.S., in order to make sure that the news would not reach St. Petersburg before Poincaré's departure. The note recited Serbia's alleged violations of the pledges given to Austria in March, 1909,[1] provided the text of an official condemnation of anti-Austrian activities to be issued by the Serbian government, and demanded the suppression of all anti-Austrian publications and organizations, the elimination of anti-Austrian tendencies in the schools, the removal of officials and army officers guilty of anti-Austrian propaganda, the prosecution of all persons connected directly or indirectly with the Sarajevo plot, and the supervision by the representatives of the Austro-Hungarian government in the execu-

[1] See p. 1298.

tion of the above program. An answer was requested within forty-eight hours; the Austrian minister to Belgrade, Baron Giesl, made it clear that unless the reply was satisfactory he and the members of his staff would leave at once.

The contents and tenor of the Austrian note, a chilly blast in the balmy warmth of a summer evening, aroused European statesmen to the seriousness of the situation. Sir Edward Grey called the ultimatum "the most formidable document he had ever seen addressed by one state to another, that is independent." "C'est la guerre européenne" was Sazonov's spontaneous reaction recorded by his collaborator and friend Baron Maurice Schilling. Sazonov, nevertheless, advised Belgrade to exercise "extreme moderation" in its reply to Austria, and suggested that in view of the helplessness of the Serbs "it would be better for them to offer no resistance but to address an appeal to the great Powers" (July 24, N.S.). He also sought, quite unsuccessfully, to obtain an extension of the time limit set in the Austrian ultimatum. The Serbian reply, delivered to Giesl by the prime minister N. Pashitch a few minutes before the expiration of the time limit, accepted all Austrian demands except the participation of Austro-Hungarian officials in the judicial inquiry, and offered, if Austria was not satisfied, to submit the dispute to the International Court at The Hague or to the great Powers. Abiding by the letter of his instructions, Giesl declared the reply unsatisfactory, announced the rupture of diplomatic relations, and half an hour later, accompanied by the staff of the legation, left Belgrade.

The dreaded specter of war evoked by the Austrian action spurred statesmen and diplomats to renewed activity. In the few days between the Austrian ultimatum and the outbreak of hostilities, a number of proposals were made for the peaceful solution of the crisis. Plans for settlement—reasonable, ingenious, overlapping, or contradictory, but all equally futile—came from London, St. Petersburg, Paris, Rome, and, finally, Berlin. The German government, which had at first stanchly and unconditionally supported its Austrian ally, shifted its attitude somewhat after the receipt of the Serbian reply. The latter convinced Emperor William, who had unexpectedly returned to Potsdam on July 27, N.S., that "on the whole the wishes of the Danubian Monarchy have been acceded to" and that "no more cause for war exists." Bethmann Hollweg's obstinate belief in the localization of the Austro-Serbian conflict was shaken by the information reaching him from St. Petersburg, Paris, and London. Reports of Russian military preparations (to be discussed presently) indicated that St. Petersburg would not remain indifferent to the fate of Serbia. Poincaré showed determination to stand by Russia. Most disturbing of all, Grey told the German ambassador Prince Lichnowsky that "Serbia had agreed to Austrian demands to an extent that he would never have believed possible," and the tenor of Grey's remarks led the ambassador to the conclusion that Germany "would no longer be able to count on British sympathy or British support" (July 27, N.S.). Beginning with July 27, N.S., Bethmann Hollweg made several *démarches* designed to induce Berchtold to accept some of the proposals for settlement advanced by Grey and Sazonov, and he offered a plan, originated by Emperor William, providing for the temporary occupation of Belgrade by the Austrians as a pledge for the fulfillment of Serbian promises. An exchange of telegrams between William and the tsar (July 29 to August 1, N.S.) marked the final stage of the abortive diplomatic negotiations to avert the catastrophe.

In a tense international situation such as that created by the Austrian ultimatum, the legitimate considerations of national defense were bound to find themselves in conflict with the equally legitimate desire to preserve peace, and as the situation developed the control of events tended to pass from statesmen and diplomats to the military. From the very beginning of the crisis Sazonov was faced with a dilemma: measures of military preparedness diminished the chances for a peaceful settlement, while abstention from warlike preparations involved the risk of dire consequences if the efforts to maintain peace failed. The experience of Sazonov, and his immediate predecessors in office, with Germany and Austria-Hungary had been unfortunate; and the policy of Vienna in July, 1914, and that of Berlin until July 28, N.S., would seem to justify the assumption that a European war could be avoided only at the price of sacrificing Serbia, a contingency which, rightly or wrongly, Russia was not prepared to countenance. The unwillingness or inability of Sir Edward Grey to side definitely with Russia and France—understandable and, perhaps, inevitable as it was in the light of British political tradition, lack of interest in Serbia, and the deep cleavage in the Asquith cabinet—deprived English diplomatic intervention of much of its effectiveness, encouraged the aggressive policies of Austria-Hungary and Germany, and indirectly strengthened the hand of those in Russia who demanded energetic measures of preparedness. There was also the insidious argument that a timely display of firmness might well have a sobering effect upon Austria. Moreover, Sazonov, like other European statesmen, was subject to the relentless pressure of an excited public opinion and of the military, whose business it is to see that the interests of national defense come first.

On receipt of the text of the Austrian ultimatum to Serbia, Sazonov decided to proceed with a partial mobilization directed against Austria. Although he had little hope that a European war could be prevented, partial mobilization appeared to offer the advantages of a middle course: it would secure a degree of preparedness, serve as a salutary warning to Austria, and give no undue offense to Germany. Sazonov discussed his plan with General N. N. Ianushkevich, chief of the general staff, and had it approved by two ministerial councils held on July 24 and July 25, N.S., the latter under the chairmanship of the emperor. Partial mobilization was decided upon only in principle: the issuance of the mobilization order was made dependent on the international situation, but measures preparatory to mobilization were put into effect at once. Although the proposal for partial mobilization met at first with no opposition from Ianushkevich and General Sukhomlinov, the war minister, it was held to be impracticable by their subordinates in the general staff. Partial mobilization is feasible only in a country that has a territorial system of completing the peace-time forces, which was not the case in Russia. No plan for partial mobilization was in existence, and the execution of the decision of the ministerial council would have thrown all mobilization arrangements into confusion. Nevertheless, a plan for partial mobilization was hastily drawn up, but Ianushkevich and, later, Sazonov, became convinced that it should not be made effective.

Meanwhile the international situation rapidly deteriorated. Partial mobilization of the Austrian army was ordered immediately after the rupture of diplomatic relations with Serbia (July 25, N.S.) and began on July 28, N.S.: on the same day Austria declared war on Serbia and Belgrade was bombarded on July 29, N.S. The Austrian declaration of war on Serbia prompted Sazonov to announce (July 28, N.S.) that the next day Russia would proceed with a partial mobilization which should not be interpreted as an aggressive move against Germany. In the morning of July 29, N.S., however, Ianushkevich secured the tsar's assent to general mobilization; but the order was rescinded the same evening (Nicholas having received in the meantime an encouraging telegram from William) and one for partial mobilization was substituted. The next day (July 30, N.S.) Ianushkevich and Sazonov prevailed upon Nicholas to revert to his earlier decision: the partial mobilization order was revoked and general mobilization was decreed instead.

The Russians were aware that the step they were taking was of the utmost gravity. On July 29, N.S., Sazonov was warned by the German ambassador that "further continuation of Russian mobilization measures would force us to mobilize." Sir Arthur Nicolson summed up well the situation when he observed, on the same day, that "the resources of diplomacy are, for the present, exhausted." Austria proclaimed general mobilization on July 31, N.S., and France and Germany on August 1, N.S. German ultimatums to Russia and France demanding the suspension of military preparations were rejected, and Germany declared war on Russia on August 1, N.S., and on France on August 3, N.S.; the Austrian declaration of war on Russia was delayed until August 6, N.S. The Italian government, after some abortive negotiations concerning the possibility of Austria's ceding the Trentino to Italy "by way of compensation," decided that the war was due to an "act of aggression" on the part of Vienna and that the *casus foederis* had not arisen; Italy therefore remained neutral. Sir Edward Grey had striven desperately to keep England out of the war. To the despair of Poincaré and Sazonov his non-committal attitude as to England's future course was maintained up to August 1, N.S. The German ultimatum to Belgium (August 2, N.S.) and a marked shift in British parliamentary and public opinion (even though Lord Morley and John Burns resigned from the cabinet on August 2, N.S., because of the decision to defend the French Atlantic coast against a German attack) triumphed over his hesitations. A British ultimatum to Berlin requesting that Belgian neutrality be respected was followed by a declaration of war (August 4, N.S.), a development William and Bethmann Hollweg had failed to foresee.

The financial, trade, and colonial rivalries of the great Powers had no immediate part in framing the fateful decisions of July and August, 1914, although they might have influenced the attitude of European statesmen. Big business, with its far-flung international connections, dreaded the disruptive and ruinous effects of war, and its efforts, especially in Germany and in Great Britain, were directed to the maintenance of peace. The political factors—national and nationalistic ambitions, naval and military rivalries, and the interplay of international alliances—were of course instrumental in determining national policies. It was, however, the inexorable logic of interlocking measures of military preparedness that actually precipitated the unwanted conflagration. Sir Eyre Crowe, permanent under-secretary at the British foreign office, saw the situation clearly when he wrote on July 27, N.S.: "I am afraid that the real difficulty to overcome will be found in the question of mobilization. Austria is already mobilizing. This . . . is a serious menace to Russia, who cannot be expected to delay her own mobilization, which, as it is, can only become effective in something like double the time required by Austria and Germany. If Russia mobilizes, we have been warned that Germany will do the same, and as German mobilization is directed almost entirely against France, the latter cannot possibly delay her own mobilization for even the fraction of a day. . . . It seems certain that Austria is going to war because that was from the beginning her intention. If that view is correct, it would be neither possible nor just and wise to make any move to restrain Russia from mobilizing." Nicholas and Sazonov hated war as much as did any other European statesman; nevertheless in July, 1914, they ordered measures that, imperative as they might have appeared at the time, practically ruled out the possibility of preserving peace.

"The lamps are going out all over Europe" Grey remarked on the eve of England's entry into the war. The new Europe that emerged from four years of darkness and fighting was an eloquent proof that the concepts of national interest held by the leaders of the three eastern empires were illusory and destructive of the cause they were supposed to serve.

FORTUNES OF WAR

The course of military events exercised a major and, in some instances, a decisive influence upon the destinies of the belligerent nations. With the exception of Belgium every Power engaged in the struggle had its share of victory and defeat, and the final outcome more than once hung in the balance. Even after full allowance is made for the importance of the geographical factor, the deadly effectiveness of the blockade, and the overwhelming superiority of the anti-German coalition in man power and economic resources (especially following the entry of the United States in the war), it would seem that the ability to withstand the shocks of adversity and the wear and tear of inaction during long periods of trench warfare provided the key to victory and the real test of the soundness of the political, social, and economic structure of the principal belligerents. That of Russia proved hopelessly inadequate to the task.

In spite of the boastful aggressiveness of the Russian nationalistic press and of some generals and bureaucrats, the irresistible "Russian steam roller," on which the allies pinned their hopes in the dark hours of the war, corresponded to no reality. Sukhomlinov's assurances to the contrary notwithstanding, Russia—both militarily and economically—was unprepared for the war. The Law on the Administration of the Army in the Field in Wartime, hastily enacted on July 16 (July 29, N.S.), 1914, that is, virtually on the eve of mobilization, conferred wide powers on the commander in chief and, in the "military zone" adjoining the front, superseded the civilian administration by the rule of the military, thus establishing a regime akin to a military dictatorship. With the retreat of the Russian armies in 1915, the "military zone" was extended to a substantial portion of European Russia, including the city of Petrograd (as the capital was renamed, in a flash of anti-German sentiment, shortly after the outbreak of the hostilities). The council of ministers was not mentioned in the law of July 16, and military authorities were under no obligation to communicate their decisions to the members of the government.

In view of the quasi-dictatorial powers vested in the commander in chief, who was responsible to the emperor alone, the character and qualifications of the occupant of that exalted office were a matter of paramount importance. The first incumbent was the uncle of the tsar, the Grand Duke Nicholas Nikolaevich. Although the grand duke was a professional soldier and had held a variety of high positions in the army, his appointment was unfortunate and came as a surprise to military circles. Nicholas Nikolaevich, according to one of the ablest Russian generals, A. A. Polivanov, minister of war in 1915–1916, "appeared entirely unequipped for the task and, to quote his own statement, on the receipt of the imperial order he spent much time crying because he did not know how to approach his new duties." The grand duke nevertheless enjoyed great popularity with the rank and file of the army, a popularity due, presumably, to his handsome military bearing and to the widely circulated tales of his rough-and-ready justice in dealing with high-ranking officers; these legends endeared him to the common soldier even though they were hardly conducive to the maintenance of military discipline. The demotion of Nicholas Nikolaevich in August, 1915, to the position of commander of the Caucasian front and viceroy of the Caucasus was received by informed opinion with consternation, not because of the confidence he inspired, but because his successor was the emperor himself. Nicholas II was even less versed in the art of warfare than his uncle, and his assumption of the high command was fraught (as will appear later) with the gravest consequences to the monarchy. Neither General Ianushkevich, chief of staff under the grand duke, nor General M. V. Alekseev, who was appointed to that position in August, 1915, was an outstanding military leader. The record of Ianushkevich, a courtier rather than a soldier, was undistinguished, while Alekseev—scholarly, conscientious, and unassuming—did not rise above the modest level of an average staff officer.

Incompetent leadership was a serious weakness of the Russian army. In the opinion of Sir Alfred Knox, shared by Colonel Engelhard, of the Russian general staff, "there were many excellent officers . . . up to the rank of company commander, but . . . the peace training of officers of a higher rank has been conducted on a false principle." [2] This statement is corroborated by the course of the campaign. In a report submitted to the emperor in August, 1915, the military and naval committee of the Duma complained that the filling of responsible commands, such as those of divisions and army corps, was governed by seniority, except when an officer happened to have strong personal backing in high places. Under this system "really able men, gifted military leaders . . . seldom have reached the higher commands." Although the committee held that "the present order of promotion is fatal to the cause of victory," the seniority rule was maintained. The officers corps, moreover, especially its lower levels, suffered heavy losses and with the rapid expansion of the army was diluted by the influx of half-trained civilians. As to the common soldiers—inherently pacific, largely illiterate, and ignorant of the objectives of the war—they fought well at times, but had little of the stamina and stubbornness needed to counteract the effects of poor leadership, inadequate supplies, disheartening defeats, and staggering losses.

[2] Major-General Sir Alfred Knox, *With the Russian Army, 1914–1917* (New York, 1921), p. 264. Knox, a keen British observer, was attached to Russian headquarters. Engelhard was a prominent member of the Duma.

The patriotic enthusiasm of the opening weeks of the war proved shortlived, and the never too aggressive spirit of the army was soon on the wane.

Russia's strategic plan called for defensive action against the Germans and a vigorous offensive against the Austrians; the object of the latter was to save Serbia from annihilation and to stave off the invasion from the south of Russian Poland, which protruded dangerously into enemy territory. Austria-Hungary, moreover, was rightly reckoned as a far less formidable enemy than Germany. The rapid German advance through Belgium into France and desperate French and British appeals for a diversion led the Russian high command to improvise the invasion of East Prussia, a plan which had its partisans among the directors of Russian strategy, for instance, the quartermaster general G. A. Danilov. The operation was planned as a pincer movement and was to be carried out by two armies: one commanded by General E. K. Rennenkampf, who had won high distinctions as a cavalry officer in the Japanese war, and the other by General A. V. Samsonov. Rennenkampf was to advance on Königsberg; Samsonov was to push forward south of Rennenkampf through the difficult region of the Masurian Lakes; then the two armies were to encircle the German troops sandwiched between them. The Russian offensive began on August 17, N.S., and met with some initial success. Von Hindenburg, called from retirement and ably supported by his chief of Staff Ludendorff, was in charge of the defense of East Prussia. The Russians were vastly superior in numbers, and although they had practically no air force and their artillery, especially heavy artillery, was no match for the German, Russian headquarters, according to General Danilov, "had every reason to view the East Prussian operation with complete confidence." In actual fact it proved to be the classic example of ineptness, unpreparedness, mismanagement, and lack of coordination. The Rennenkampf advance was disappointingly and almost inexplicably slow, while the Samsonov army—lacking in munitions and supplies and out of touch with Rennenkampf and Russian headquarters—moved forward blindly through a hostile and inhospitable country and was finally entrapped by the Germans in the wooded Tannenberg-Soldau region. Samsonov shot himself (August 30, N.S.), and two of his army corps surrendered to the enemy. By the middle of September, Hindenburg, reinforced by two corps transferred from the western front, drove across the border the totally demoralized Russians (Rennenkampf with his staff had fled to Kovno, losing all contact with his troops). Russian losses in East Prussia were estimated at 300,000 men and 650 guns. The shock of the defeat both at home and in allied countries was all the greater because of the high hopes raised by the Russian incursion in the stronghold of German militarism. Tannenberg, moreover, confirmed the Russian officers' corps and the rank and file of the army in the almost superstitious belief in the invincibility of the German military machine. The Russians reoccupied a fringe of East Prussia in October, 1914, but their attempts to resume the offensive in that direction (November, 1914, and February, 1915) were foiled and were finally abandoned with the great German eastward drive in 1915.

The Russian offensive in Galicia began simultaneously with that in East Prussia on August 18, N.S. In view of its ultimate outcome it is a moot question whether the Russian commanders in that theater—N. J. Ivanov, A. A. Brusilov, N. V. Ruzsky, Alekseev, and the fiery and picturesque Bulgarian Radko Dmitriev—actually deserve the praise bestowed upon them by many Russian and foreign historians.[3] The real causes of Russia's initial success in Galicia were perhaps the long-range planning of the offensive (even though the plans proved wanting in many essentials) and, above all, the inherent weakness of the Austro-Hungarian army, which had few of the solid military virtues of its German ally. Herein lies the principal difference between East Prussia and Galicia. Austrian staff work, the commissariat, and communication system, unlike those of Germany, were not substantially above the Russian level. The Austro-Hungarian army, moreover, contained a large Slav element (according to official estimates, the Germans and the Magyars accounted for only 48 per cent). Of course not all of the Austrian Slavs were pro-Russian. The Poles had good reason to prefer Vienna to Petrograd in spite of Russia's conciliatory gesture. In August, 1914, the Grand Duke Nicholas Nikolaevich issued a proclamation to the Polish nation which spoke of the "resurrection of the Polish people," "brotherly reconciliation" between Poland and Russia, the "obliteration of boundaries dividing the Poles," and "the reunion under the scepter of the tsar" of a

---

[3] For instance, C. R. M. F. Cruttwell, *A History of the Great War, 1914–1918* (Oxford, 1936), p. 51 and *passim*. General G. A. Danilov, in his book, is very critical of the Galician campaign, particularly of the part played in it by General N. J. Ivanov, commander of a group of armies known as the southwestern front.

Poland enjoying "freedom of religion, language, and self-government." The promises of the proclamation, which was written largely by Sazonov and Count S. I. Wielopolski, a wealthy Polish landowner and a member of the Russian State Council, were much too vague to overcome Poland's deeply rooted mistrust of Russia. A Polish legion organized by Pilsudski fought, indeed, with the Austrians against Russia. On the other hand, many of the Ukrainians, Slovaks, and Czechs serving with the Austro-Hungarian army surrendered en masse, either because they believed that Russia would favor their national aspirations or because they preferred captivity to the hazards of a war for the defense of the Dual Monarchy. The resulting disorganization and decline in morale favored Russian military plans, even though the Germans and the Magyars, as a rule, gave a good account of themselves and resisted the invaders with determination and courage.

The Russian offensive in Galicia on a front of three hundred miles checked the invasion of Russian territory planned by the Austrians and rapidly gained momentum. Lemberg (Lvov), the ancient capital of Galicia and an important railway junction, was captured on September 3, N.S. The Austrians retreated to the river San, and after the fall of the fortress of Yaroslav and the investment of the fortress of Przemysl, to and beyond the Wisloka, a tributary of the Vistula. In the southern sector the Russians took Czernovitz, the capital of Bukovina, and reached the southern slopes of the Carpathian Mountains and the passes leading to the plains of Hungary. Although the Russian advance stopped short of Cracow, one of the objectives of the offensive (partly because the troops needed for that operation were used, probably unwisely, in the long siege of Przemysl), it succeeded, within three weeks, in dealing Austria a staggering blow. Austrian losses of some 350,000 men exceeded those suffered by Russia in East Prussia and were far more grievously felt because of Austria's much smaller reserve of man power.

The Austrian high command, in dire straits aggravated by a reckless and disastrous attempt at crushing Serbia (August), turned for help to Germany. The Germans, intent on winning a speedy and decisive victory in the west, were unable to fulfill their prewar promise of an offensive in northwestern Poland to be launched immediately after the outbreak of hostilities. The great *élan* of the German armies, however, soon wore itself out against the impregnable barrier of allied resistance (battle of the Marne, September 6 to 11, N.S.). On the western front the days of large-scale maneuvers and sweeping advances were over, and the struggle gradually settled down to the weary routine of trench warfare, releasing troops for other theaters. Meanwhile Hindenburg, without awaiting the arrival of reinforcements, transferred the bulk of his army from East Prussia to Silesia, and on September 28, N.S., launched a powerful offensive in the southwestern provinces of Russian Poland, theretofore barely touched by the war. The Russian command met the challenge by moving twelve army corps from Galicia to Poland. These troops occupied positions behind the Vistula, especially in the region immediately north of Warsaw. The advancing Germans, therefore, met with relatively little opposition until they reached the area of Russian concentration. The Austrians, too, resumed the offensive, pushed the Russians back to the San, retook Yaroslav and relieved Przemysl, but within a few days they were forced to relinquish their gains and retreat to Cracow (October). The numerical superiority and stubborn resistance of the Russians, and the misadventures of the Austrians, compelled the Germans to withdraw in order to escape encirclement. On October 12, N.S., they were within six or seven miles of Warsaw; by the end of the month they had retreated well over one hundred miles and established their lines in the western sector of the Polish salient. The Russian pursuit was hindered by the methodical and thorough destruction of railway tracks, bridges, and highways.

This, however, was merely a strategic retreat. On November 1, N.S., Hindenburg was appointed a commander in chief of the German forces on the eastern front and was succeeded, as commander of the ninth German army operating in Poland, by General Mackensen, who had directed the October offensive against Warsaw. The second thrust against the Polish capital began on November 11, N.S., this time from the region of Thorn, on the northwestern border of the Polish salient. It was no more successful than the first in attaining the ultimate objective, and after much heavy fighting the front was stabilized in December along a line some thirty-five miles west of Warsaw. Particularly onerous to both sides was the long-drawn battle for the possession of the textile city of Lodz, which was finally captured by the Germans, with the help of freshly arrived troops, on December 6, N.S. The confusion and ineptitude of the Russian command made possible the escape of some 50,000 Germans entrapped in the Lodz-Lowitch region, a strategic blunder all the more vexatious because the success of the encircling movement and the capture of a vast number of prisoners were prematurely announced by the Russian authorities. A renewed Austrian drive in Galicia, which synchronized with the German offensive in Poland, accomplished nothing. With the arrival of winter the eastern front became quiescent.

The balance of the first four months of the war was not altogether unfavorable to Russia. Her armies had suffered a terrible defeat in East Prussia, but they had overrun and retained Galicia and had turned back the enemy from the gates of Warsaw. In view of the exposed geographical position of western Poland, the withdrawal from that area shortened the front and was justifiable on strategic grounds. The East Prussian, Polish, and Galician campaigns had relieved German pressure on the western front during the battle of the Marne and the first battle of Ypres (October and November), and the involvements of the Austrians in Galicia were instrumental in bringing about the dismal failure of their second assault on Serbia (November and December). There was, however, another and less heartening side to the picture. The first major encounters of the war disclosed the glaring imperfections of the Russian military machine: poor staff work; lack of coordination; shortage of planes, artillery, rifles, and munitions; helplessness of the commissariat in providing for the needs of the army; inadequacy of the communication and railway system and the deplorable state of the roads. The expenditure of munitions and rifles during the Galician and the Polish campaigns was far in excess of domestic production and deliveries from abroad and made dangerous inroads on the modest stores available. Losses of man power were very great. Last but not least, there were ominous signs of declining morale and lack of confidence in victory.

In the early spring of 1915 (March 22, N.S.) Przemysl capitulated after a siege of six months, netting the Russians nine generals, 2,500 officers, 120,000 men, and over 900 guns. With the fall of that center of resistance the control of Galicia appeared assured. From the very beginning the victors had treated the conquered province as a permanent acquisition. A swarm of Russian lay and ecclesiastical officials, headed by the governor-general Count G. A. Bobrinsky and the notorious Bishop Evlogius, a fanatical and unscrupulous crusader for Greek Orthodoxy, descended upon that unhappy country and proceeded to remodel it in the Russian image. The bulk of the Ukrainian population, which belonged to the Uniat Church, were at first not unfriendly to the Russians; but they were soon made to realize the price of "liberation" (a bitter lesson driven home to so many nations after the Second World War), and they became sulky and recalcitrant under a regime of crude Russification and ruthless implantation of Greek Orthodoxy. The Russian brand of panslavism that flared up in Galicia was inexorably opposed to the Ukrainian independence, or "separatist," movement, which had a sizable following, especially among the intellectuals, and had received some encouragement from Austria. The Russian administration, under the influence of zealous Orthodox missionaries, was even more implacable in its attitude towards the Uniat Church. "Separatist" newspapers, libraries, clubs, cultural societies, and schools were closed, and the more uncompromising leaders of the Ukrainian independence movement and of the Uniat Church were banished to Russia, where they were kept under police supervision. Among those deported were the well known historian Michael Hrushevsky and the metropolitan Count Andrew Szepticki, head of the Uniat Church.[4] Sazonov and the Russian high command were uneasy about the possible military and international repercussions of the policies followed by Russian proconsuls in Galicia. Early in 1915 N. A. Bazili, representative of the Petrograd foreign office at the headquarters of the Grand Duke Nicholas Nikolaevich, was sent on an exploratory mission to Galicia. His very unfavorable report, although approved by the grand duke, had but one practical consequence: its author was peremptorily ordered by General Ivanov to leave Galicia. At the end of April Emperor Nicholas visited the conquered province, including Przemysl. At a state function in Lemberg he spoke of an "indivisible Russia" reaching as far as the Carpathian Mountains. The time chosen for this utterance was singularly inopportune: the tsar had barely time to recross the frontier before the Germans and the Austrians launched their great offensive on the eastern front.

[4] The population of Galicia, including the region of Cracow, numbered 7.5 million; of this number 4 million were Poles, 3 million Ukrainians, and 500,000 Jews. In eastern Galicia Ukrainians equaled the Poles, but in the western districts the Poles predominated. "The drive against the Uniate Church . . ." writes Allen, "produced the strangely paradoxical situation that in western Galicia the Russian administration experienced fewer difficulties with the Poles and Catholics than in eastern Galicia, where the population was of Russian origin and 'half Orthodox.'" W. E. D. Allen, *The Ukraine: A History* (Cambridge, 1941), pp. 270, 272. It will be remembered that the Uniats followed the rites of the Orthodox Church but recognized the supremacy of the Holy See.

Until the spring of 1915 General von Falkenhayn, the German chief of staff, had denied Hindenburg's requests for large reinforcements, thus blocking all plans for a major thrust in the east. The inconclusive nature of the campaign in France, the patent military impotence of Turkey, which had entered the war at the end of October, 1914, the Dardanelles expedition that began in the middle of March, 1915, and, above all, the desperate plight of Austria forced von Falkenhayn reluctantly to yield to Hindenburg. Spurred by the fall of Przemysl, the Russians had resumed in March their offensive in the Carpathians. An invasion of the plains of Hungary, the granary of the central Powers, coinciding with the anticipated outbreak of war between Austria and Italy, might well have precipitated the military collapse of the Dual Monarchy. This eventuality had to be prevented at all cost. In the second half of April, at the very time Emperor Nicholas was making his triumphal tour of Galicia, eight German divisions were brought in great secrecy from France to the Cracow region. These troops, commanded by Mackensen and supported by the Austrians, launched on May 1, N.S., a formidable offensive on a fifty-mile front south of the Dunajec. A four-hour artillery bombardment on a scale the Russians had never experienced before (even though its intensity was less than that customary on the western front) and massive attacks, for the first time in the war, of the German air force paved the way for the break-through at Gorlice. The army of Radko Dmitriev, which held that sector, fell back in great confusion, whole units surrendering to the enemy. The Germans exploited their success skillfully. They pursued the Russians relentlessly in Galicia, and there was marked intensification of warlike activities along the entire nine hundred miles of the front, particularly on the Baltic littoral; the resulting uncertainty as to where the next blow would come worked against a rational distribution of Russian troops. The Franco-British offensive in Flanders and at Artois launched in the first half of May, partly in response to a plea by the Grand Duke Nicholas Nikolaevich, and Italy's declaration of war on Austria-Hungary (May 23, N.S.) brought no appreciable relief to the hard-pressed Russians. By the end of May their armies had withdrawn behind the San and the Dniester; Przemysl was evacuated on June 3, N.S., and Lemberg on June 22, N.S.

Having cleared practically the whole of Galicia of the enemy,

Hindenburg turned to Russian Poland and the Baltic provinces. Warsaw was taken on August 4, N.S.; the fortress of Novogeorgievsk, on the Vistula, held out for three weeks after it was invested, but the fortresses of Kovno and Brest-Litovsk offered hardly any resistance. Vilna fell on September 18, N.S. In the northern sector the Germans occupied Libau, Russia's only ice-free port on the Baltic, and advanced to the gates of Riga, which, however, remained in Russian hands. In the late summer the Austrians, who had played a subordinate part during the earlier campaign, resumed the offensive, but achieved little except the capture of the fortress of Lutsk. By the end of October, when fighting gradually died down, the front line ran through points immediately west of Riga and Dvinsk and from that city almost directly south to the Rumanian border. A narrow strip of Galicia east of the river Sereth, which the Russians retained until the final collapse of their army in the summer of 1917, was all that was left of their conquests of 1914 and early 1915.

The Austro-German armies massed in 1915 on the eastern front numbered approximately 1.3 million divided about equally between the two partners. Russian forces, measured in terms of battalions, were supposed to exceed those of their opponents by perhaps as much as 500,000 but were actually smaller than indicated by this figure. The strength of many Russian combat units was merely 25 per cent, or even less, of their nominal complement. The depletion was not due to any shortage of man power (by September, 1915, Russia had mobilized 9.7 million men, and her total losses by the end of that year amounted to 3.4 million, including over 300,000 dead and 1.5 million missing or prisoners of war) but to the lack of training facilities and the breakdown of the replacement service. The hordes of men inducted into the army remained idle for months. There was an acute shortage of officers, non-commissioned officers, guns, machine guns, rifles, munitions, uniforms, boots, and even of living quarters and food. At the height of the retreat the artillery in some sectors of the front was rationed to one or two shells a day per gun—and even these were not always forthcoming—and during an attack infantrymen in the second and subsequent rows advanced empty-handed on the optimistic theory that they would pick up the rifles of their fellow soldiers killed in front of them. Under these conditions the mass surrenders and desertions that actually took place would seem to have been legitimate and unavoidable. It is, indeed, surprising that the army—battered, emaciated, bleeding, and defeated—preserved a degree of cohesion and survived the ordeal.

The retreat of 1915 not only wiped out Russia's ephemeral conquests but brought the enemy well within her borders: the new front ran some two hundred miles east of Warsaw. If the loss of Galicia was damaging to Russian prestige and a blow to nationalistic opinion unduly exercised over the fate of "Carpathian Russia," the German occupation of the western provinces was a genuine setback from the political, military, and economic point of view. The social and economic dislocation inherent in any war, especially in an unsuccessful one, was made worse by the truly fantastic "scorched earth" policy inaugurated by the high command and patterned, it was believed, after the "retreat of 1812" which led Napoleon to Moscow and to his doom. It was strangely overlooked that in 1812 the French army had advanced along a few roads, while in 1915 the front stretched from the Baltic to the Rumanian frontier. From the early days of the war certain groups of civilians, chiefly the Jews, were forcibly removed from the military zone, allegedly for "security" reasons. During the retreat of 1915 this policy was extended to the entire civilian population: the advancing enemy was to encounter a desert. Farmers and townsmen were peremptorily ordered to leave their abodes while their stocks of grain and sometimes their homesteads were set aflame. Some of the evacuees were packed in freight cars and dispatched at a snail's pace by rail to an unknown destination; the majority departed by road. Highways leading east were jammed by a mass of bewildered and desperate humanity, with carts carrying a few belongings, and with domestic animals driven by their owners. At first no arrangements were made to deal with the emergency, and a large but undetermined number of *bezhintsy* (refugees), precursors of the displaced persons of the 1940's, died of hunger, exposure, and disease. The registered refugees numbered 2.7 million in December, 1915, and 3.3 million in May, 1916; a great many, no doubt, escaped registration. The council of ministers protested vainly against the folly of the high command. The position of the government was well stated by A. V. Krivoshein, minister of agriculture, at a meeting of the council of ministers on August 4, 1915. "Of all the grave consequences of the war," he said, "this is the most unexpected, the most threatening, the most irreparable. And what is worse—it is not due to a necessity or a spontaneous popular movement, but has been invented by the learned military experts as a deterrent to the enemy. . . . The great migration organized by headquarters leads Russia to the abyss, to revolution, to perdition."

Grave as was Russia's predicament at the end of 1915, the blow dealt by the Germans was not a knockout. The territory lost was small when compared with the boundless expanse of the empire; the army had not broken down; and despite the unfavorable developments in the other theaters of war the government and the bulk of public opinion were determined to go on with the struggle. On the western front the opposing armies were locked in the grip of a merciless and thankless war of attrition. In September, Bulgaria threw in her lot with the central Powers. Serbia and Russia's client Montenegro were conquered in October and November. The boldly conceived but shockingly mismanaged Dardanelles expedition went from bad to worse and ended pitiably with the withdrawal of allied troops from Gallipoli in December. All hopes for the establishment of a short reliable route between Russia and her allies had vanished. The outlook, indeed, was uncertain and bleak. It was realized, nevertheless, that the central Powers, too, were beset with formidable difficulties, that their plans for a short war had been foiled, and that time might well work to the advantage of the anti-German coalition.

From October, 1915, to March, 1916, all was quiet on the eastern front, except for an abortive Russian attempt at recapturing Czernovitz, in Bukovina. The lull was welcome and permitted Russia to recover her bearings. The shock of the 1915 defeat and the pressure of an aroused public opinion succeeded, up to a point, in overcoming bureaucratic inertia and complacence. The legislative chambers, the zemstvos, municipalities, business, and labor were invited to participate through newly established agencies (to be discussed later) in the work for the army. Their activities were fruitful and, together with substantial deliveries from abroad, brought a marked improvement in the supply of munitions, arms, and other war requirements. In June, 1915, the totally discredited minister of war Sukhomlinov was dismissed and was succeeded by the able and energetic General Polivanov.[5] The assumption of the supreme command by the tsar (Sep-

[5] A favorite of Nicholas II, Sukhomlinov, on his dismissal, was the recipient of a particularly gracious letter from the tsar. Public feeling against him, however, ran high. In March, 1915, Colonel S. N. Miasoedov, who was close to Sukhomlinov,

tember 5, 1915, N.S.) was, from the military viewpoint, a matter of minor importance, although Alekseev, the new chief of staff, was more competent than his predecessor Ianushkevich.

At an allied conference at Chantilly (December, 1915) Russia undertook to resume the offensive not later than June 15, 1916. Preparations were accordingly made for an assault in the region of Vilna, but in the middle of March an urgent Franco-British request for a diversion to relieve the pressure on Verdun made the Russian high command attack in the area of Lake Narotch, northeast of Vilna. This ill conceived operation, although supported by a much larger concentration of artillery than the Russians were able to command during the earlier campaigns, was repulsed with losses estimated at well over 100,000. Preparations for the Vilna offensive were resumed when, in the middle of May, there came another urgent plea for a diversion, this time from the Italians, whose entire front threatened to collapse as a consequence of an enveloping thrust by the Austrians in the Trentino. After the Lake Narotch experience the Russians were unwilling to advance the date (June 15) of the Vilna offensive; moreover, an attack on the Germans in Poland was not likely to affect immediately the Austro-Hungarian advance in Italy. The alternative plan for an offensive along the entire Austrian front was proposed by Brusilov and reluctantly accepted by Alekseev. The hastily prepared assault began on June 4, N.S., took the Austrians by surprise, and threw them into utter confusion which, without the speedy arrival of German reinforcements, might well have become a rout. Brusilov broke through the Austrian lines on the northern flank, in the direction of Lutsk, and in the extreme south, in Bukovina along the Rumanian border. The center, however, held firm, and although between June and September (when the offensive petered out) Brusilov had occupied some 10,000 square miles and had taken over 400,000 prisoners he achieved no significant strategic gains. The unexpected success

---

although he was long under suspicion and was publicly denounced by Guchkov in 1912, was tried by a court-martial, found guilty of treason, and hanged. After a protracted investigation charges of malfeasance, corruption, and treason were brought against Sukhomlinov. He was arrested in April, 1916, freed in October, and rearrested after the Revolution. Tried in the autumn of 1917 and sentenced to life imprisonment at hard labor, Sukhomlinov nevertheless is believed to have been innocent of the charges preferred against him, although he was obviously incautious, incompetent, frivolous, and unfit for the office he held. He escaped in 1918 and went to Germany, where he died in 1926 after writing his highly colored and untruthful memoirs.

of the offensive, especially in its earlier stage, led Alekseev to divert all available reserves to the southern front and to give up the proposed attack in Poland, except for an unsuccessful assault on the railway junction of Baranovichi, halfway between Vilna and Pinsk (July 2, N.S.).

The true significance of the Brusilov offensive lay in its effects upon the international military situation. Austria-Hungary was dealt a shattering blow that forced her to abandon her offensive in Italy and contributed to her disintegration. The Italian army was given the chance to extricate itself from a most unfortunate predicament. The transfer to the eastern front, between June and September, of eighteen German divisions from France and of three German and two Turkish divisions from the Balkans was of material aid to the western allies during the crucial battles of Verdun and the Somme, and at Salonika. Finally, the Brusilov offensive provided the ultimate argument in the protracted and tortuous negotiations with Rumania: on August 27, N.S., that country declared war on Austria. These were no mean achievements; nevertheless, from the narrow Russian point of view the heavy losses (over two million killed and wounded and 350,000 prisoners in 1916) were not justified by the results achieved. There was a loud outcry against the alleged failure of the high command to take full advantage of the break-through in Galicia. Criticism was widespread and there was a further decline in the morale of the troops.

The addition of Rumania to the roster of the allies in August, 1916, was not an unmixed blessing. Whatever might be the virtues of the Rumanian people, military prowess was not among them. No other country was less well prepared for the war and, it would seem, less willing to fight. By the end of 1916 three-fourths of Rumania, including Bucharest, were overrun by the enemy. It was not until the Rumanians had reached the fortified region of the Sereth, between the Danube and the border of Bukovina, and had secured large Russian reinforcements that they succeeded in stabilizing their lines. The net result of the 1916 Rumanian campaign was the lengthening of the eastern front by some 250 miles of which the Rumanian army held a mere fraction and the Russians the balance.

The Caucasian front, established after Turkey entered the war, occupied a subordinate place in Russian strategy, being part and parcel of the Near Eastern theater of war, where the leadership belonged to

Great Britain. Russo-Turkish hostilities started in the Black Sea. On August 10, 1914, N.S. two modern warships of the German Mediterranean squadron, the battle-cruiser *Göben* and the light cruiser *Breslau*, having escaped British vigilance, took refuge in the Dardanelles. After the fictitious sale of these vessels to the Ottoman government, they entered the Black Sea and on October 29 and 30 the Turkish fleet, without a declaration of war, bombarded Sevastopol, Odessa, Feodosia, and Novorossiisk. Russia, Great Britain, and France retaliated by declaring war on Turkey (November 2, 5, and 6, N.S., respectively). Meanwhile the Caucasian frontier had been denuded of much of its troops, which were sent to Poland and Galicia. A Turkish offensive in the Caucasus led by Enver Pasha met at first with some success and brought from the Grand Duke Nicholas Nikolaevich a request to Great Britain for a diversion (December, 1914); this plea was the starting point of the Dardanelles expedition. The Russians, however, were unduly alarmed. The ill equipped Turkish army was soon forced to retreat, and thousands of the assailants perished miserably in the icy wilderness of the snow-blocked mountain passes. The subsequent course of the war on the Caucasian front was as a whole favorable to Russia and led to the invasion of Armenia and the capture of Erzerum in February and of Trebizond in April, 1916.

In 1914 Russia's rather unimpressive navy, not yet recovered from the disaster of the Japanese war, consisted mainly of obsolete vessels. The inferiority of the Russian Baltic fleet to that of Germany, which controlled the exit from the Baltic, dictated extreme prudence in the use of Russian naval forces in these waters. The task of the Russian Baltic fleet was accordingly limited to the defense of the Gulf of Finland and to occasional support of the land forces operating on the littoral. The activities of the Black Sea fleet were conducted on an even more modest scale and were restricted to tasks of a local nature. Of the thrilling encounters upon the Seven Seas which fill the naval history of the maritime Powers Russian sailors knew nothing.

In January and February, 1917, an allied conference attended by the statesmen and military leaders of Great Britain, France, Italy, and Russia met in Petrograd. Plans were drawn for a joint offensive in which the Russian government pledged itself to participate as soon as the new divisions then in process of formation had been trained and equipped; simultaneously arrangements were made concerning credits and supplies which were to be made available to Russia. The imperial government was never called upon to fulfill the obligations of this agreement: less than three weeks after the adjournment of the conference (February 21, N.S.) the monarchy was swept away by the revolution.

IMPERIAL DIPLOMACY: THE EPILOGUE

On the outbreak of the war the Russian foreign office was confronted with novel problems which may be broadly subdivided into three groups: promotion of allied solidarity; negotiations with non-belligerents (Japan, Turkey, Italy, Bulgaria, Rumania, Greece), to ensure their friendly neutrality or eventual participation in the war on the side of the *entente*; and arrangements for a peace settlement that would provide at least a semblance of justification for the heavy sacrifices imposed by the struggle. Understanding and cooperation among the allies—a prerequisite for the coordination of their policies towards the neutrals and the achievement of their war aims—were made difficult by ancient rivalries, lack of confidence, and the clash of national ambitions and interests as interpreted by the leaders of the allied governments. The unpredictable course of military events and the progressive deterioration of the internal situation in Russia exercised a profound influence upon international negotiations.

The anti-German alliance was formalized by the treaty of September 5, 1914, N.S., which bound Russia, Great Britain, and France not to conclude a separate peace and to reach preliminary agreement concerning the future peace terms. Although these obligations were ostensibly adhered to, relations among the allies were at times subject to severe strain. The close personal bonds between Sazonov, on the one hand, and the French and British ambassadors to Petrograd, Maurice Paléologue and Sir George Buchanan on the other, were instrumental in preserving the appearance of allied solidarity. Count A. C. Benckendorff, Russian ambassador to the Court of St. James's from 1902 until his death in January, 1917, was *persona gratissima* with the British foreign office, and while Izvolsky at the Paris embassy was less popular in the French capital than Benckendorff was in London, the militancy of his anti-Austrian and anti-German feelings pleased Poincaré and the Quai d'Orsay. In July, 1916, however, Sazonov was dismissed. His successor, B. V. Sturmer, a contemptible product of Russian officialdom, inspired no confidence in either Buchanan or Paléologue and was believed by both ambassadors to be pro-German. At the end of November, 1916, Sturmer was dismissed and, after a brief interregnum, was replaced in December by imperial Russia's last foreign minister, N. N. Pokrovsky, a bureaucrat of integrity but as ignorant of international affairs as was his predecessor. The Russian foreign office, moreover, was subject to pressure from many quarters. The debacle of East Prussia and the retreat of 1915, impetuous requests by Russian headquarters for diversions on the western front and in the Near East, and the conflict of the policies pursued by the allies in the Balkans, did much to destroy the enthusiasm for Russia that swept France and England during the early weeks of the war. Russia, according to the draft of a letter written by Winston Churchill to Grey on March 6, 1915, N.S., "is a broken Power but for our aid, and has no resource open but to turn traitor —and this she cannot do." [6] "Excitement against Russia because of doubts concerning our willingness to participate in the military operations in the Balkans increases here daily in parliamentary, journalistic, and even governmental circles," Izvolsky telegraphed to Sazonov on October 12, 1915, N.S. It was held, according to the ambassador, that the delay of the Rumanian intervention, due allegedly to Russia's resistance to her demands, and the failure to send Russian troops to the Balkans had hopelessly compromised the policy and military plans of England and France.

Disillusionment with the allies, especially with Great Britain, was equally bitter in Russia. Trench warfare in France was regarded by many as a subterfuge to shift the full burden of the fighting to the eastern front. In the summer of 1916, for instance, a reactionary newspaper which Buchanan "had reasons to believe to be inspired" by the entourage of Sturmer (then president of the council of ministers and foreign minister), published "an outrageous attack on the British army, declaring, among other things, that it had only advanced two hundred yards in the course of two years." The ambassador endeavored in vain to obtain a retraction and an apology.[7] The Grand Duke Boris, according to Knox, indulged in malicious talk about the

[6] Winston Churchill, *The World Crisis, 1915* (London, 1923), p. 204. Churchill, then first lord of the admiralty, was incensed by Sazonov's objections to the participation of Greece in the Dardanelles expedition. The letter of March 6 was not sent because of Venizelos's dismissal from office.

[7] Sir George Buchanan, *My Mission to Russia, and Other Diplomatic Memories* (London, 1923), II, 20–21.

"bluff" of the Dardanelles expedition and Great Britain's keeping Russia out of Bagdad, and he prophesied that the next war would be between Russia and England.[8] Such allegations were, indeed, common, and can be summed up in the often-heard statement that the western allies were determined to fight the war "to the last drop of blood of the Russian soldier." The resulting atmosphere of irritation and mistrust was sadly at variance with official proclamations of unflinching allied solidarity and was not conducive to the smooth working of the complex mechanics of *entente* diplomacy.

Japan, Russia's recent antagonist, proved the most manageable among the Powers whose attitude towards the war was of immediate concern to the allies. Aware of the opportunity for expansion offered by the world conflagration, the Tokyo government responded to an appeal of its English ally by demanding the withdrawal of German warships from Japanese and Chinese waters and the surrender by Germany, "unconditionally and without compensation," of Kiaochow with a view to its "eventual restoration to China" (August 15, 1914, N.S.). No reply being received within the prescribed time limit of eight days, Japan declared war on Germany and seized Kiaochow and the German-owned Tsing-tau railway and Pacific Islands. After these exploits Japan took little direct part in the fighting, and her belligerency expressed itself chiefly in supplying Russia with much-needed arms and munitions. Japanese annexations were not to the liking of Great Britain, Australia, New Zealand, and the United States, and contained the seeds of future complications in the Far East. Japan's entry into the war, nevertheless, served the immediate objectives of the allies by helping to clear the Pacific of German warships and merchantmen and by removing the danger of a Japanese attack on Russia's Far Eastern possessions.

The complexities of the diplomatic situation were nowhere more in evidence than in the Near East and in the Balkans. At the outbreak of the hostilities the Young Turk government in Constantinople was hopelessly divided on the issue of war and peace. Both German and Anglo-French influences were entrenched in the Turkish capital, where it was realized that the Porte had little to gain by the victory of either belligerent group. Hostility towards Russia, however, was fairly general, and the German penetration in the Near East, for all its impetuosity, contained the possibilities of a fruitful development of Asia

[8] Knox, *op. cit.*, p. 429 *et seq.*

Minor by which Turkey might well have benefited. Germany, moreover, was a newcomer in the Near East, and therefore a relatively unknown factor, while in the light of the record the Ottoman government had little to hope for in case of a victory of the *entente* Powers. Whatever the reasons, the pro-German faction in the Turkish cabinet led by Enver and Talaat succeeded in concluding with Germany a secret treaty which bound the Porte to declare war if the intervention of Russia forced Germany to carry out her pledges to Austria-Hungary (August 1, 1914, N.S.). This obligation notwithstanding, the Ottoman government proclaimed its neutrality, and Enver Pasha, war minister and leader of the pro-German faction, made overtures to the Russian military attaché in Constantinople for the conclusion of a Russo-Turkish alliance and the participation of Turkey in the war on the side of the *entente*. Although this offer, which was presumably a maneuver to gain time, was not taken at its face value by the allied governments, who suspected and later obtained definite information about the Turko-German pact, it was deemed wise to explore every opportunity, however slight, to prevent the Porte from joining the central Powers. The allies were eager to keep the Straits open to mercantile shipping and to avoid the establishment of a Near Eastern front that would necessitate the dispersion of their war effort; London and Paris, moreover, feared the effects of a war against Turkey upon the large Moslem populations under their rule. Accordingly the protests of the *entente* governments against Turkey's fictitious purchase and subsequent admission into the Black Sea of the *Göben* and *Breslau* and the repeal of the capitulations announced by the Porte on September 9, N.S., were cautiously worded and moderate in tone.

Sazonov was willing to go further than his English and French colleagues along the road of concessions to Constantinople. He proposed a guarantee of Turkish territorial integrity and the transfer to Turkey of the Greek island of Lemnos (Greece was to be compensated in the Epirus), as well as of German railway and other concessions in Asia Minor. London and Paris, however, mindful of Greek susceptibilities, vetoed the cession of Lemnos. The attack by the Ottoman fleet on Russian Black Sea ports at the end of October terminated the negotiations. Turkish belligerency not only complicated the military and naval task of the allies by creating several new fronts but also severed the only reasonably short and dependable sea route between

Russia and her western partners. From the beginning of August the Porte had sporadically interfered with the movement of merchant vessels entering and leaving the Black Sea. On September 27, N.S., following the interception by the British of a Turkish destroyer which ventured into the Aegean Sea, the Dardanelles were closed to all merchantmen. Allied protests against this violation of international conventions while Turkey was still technically neutral were of no avail, and the Straits remained closed until the end of the war. Turkey's entry into the war, which Sazonov had so diligently tried to prevent, provided Russia with what was soon to become her major war aim and the dominant factor in her Balkan policy—the annexation of Constantinople and the Straits.

Negotiations with Italy were initiated after the proclamation of Italian neutrality and were conducted by Rome simultaneously with both belligerent groups in the spirit of what the Italian prime minister Salandra euphemistically called *"sacro egoismo."* Secret discussions of the terms on which Italy would agree to throw in her lot with the *entente* began in the Russian capital but were shifted, at the request of the Italian government, to London, a change of venue that ruffled Sazonov. Although the Italian demands were onerous, most of them were quickly conceded by the allies, who feared to be outbid by the central Powers. Sazonov, however, after having reluctantly accepted the main points of the Italian program, raised obstinate objections to other points which the British and the French regarded as relatively minor. There followed an acrimonious controversy over the apportionment of morsels of Albania and of the Dalmatian coast among Italy, Serbia, Greece, and Montenegro, and over the "neutralization" of patches of the eastern littoral of the Adriatic, Sazonov stanchly defending the right of Serbia to a free access to the sea and opposing the cession to Italy of territories inhabited by Slav populations. The intransigent attitude of Italy and the insistence of Grey and Delcassé, the French foreign minister, that the negotiations be brought to a speedy successful conclusion forced Sazonov to make further concessions. But even after the territorial questions were safely out of the way he nearly wrecked the agreement by demanding that Italy should enter the war by May 1, N.S., instead of at the end of that month, as proposed by Rome. It required much pressure from London and Paris, including a personal letter from Poincaré to the tsar, to overcome Sazonov's resistance. By virtue of the secret treaty signed by the four Powers in London on April 26, 1915, N.S., Italy was promised territorial annexations which included the southern Tyrol to the Brenner Pass, Goritza, Istria, and northern Dalmatia, as well as an unspecified share of Asiatic Turkey and the German colonies in Africa, if the latter were partitioned among the allies. A truncated Albania was to become what Sazonov termed an Italian protectorate. The Russian foreign minister was critical of the London treaty and of the manner in which it was negotiated. He believed that the importance of Italian belligerency was grossly overestimated by Grey and Delcassé and that the legitimate interests of the Balkan Slavs had been sacrificed to Italian ambitions. In a sharply worded letter to Benckendorff (April 21, 1915, N.S.) Sazonov characterised the proposed treaty as "a capitulation by the three Powers before the Italian demands." The pact, in his opinion, was "unfortunate from all points of view" and he had agreed to sign it only "under strong pressure from the allies." Grey, according to Sazonov, had made no real effort to scale down the Italian claims, however unreasonable, and the text of the treaty was drafted by the British foreign secretary and Paul Cambon, the French ambassador to London, without any participation by Russia; Sazonov's objections received only the most perfunctory attention. The experience of the London treaty, Sazonov argued, was of ill augury for the future of allied cooperation.

A tangled, indeed, a perplexing diplomatic situation confronted the *entente* Powers in Bulgaria, Rumania, and Greece. Both Sazonov and Grey believed that the surest method of reconciling the passionate nationalism of the small Balkan states, and of aligning them against Austria and Germany, would be the restoration of the 1912 Balkan League. Whatever may be the theoretical merits of this proposal, it met with insurmountable practical difficulties. While the principal territorial aspirations of Serbia (Bosnia, Herzegovina, the Dalmatian coast), Rumania (Transylvania, the Banat, Bukovina), and Greece (whose program of expansion was less clearly defined) could be realized only at the expense of Austria-Hungary and Turkey, Bulgaria was primarily concerned with the recovery of the territories she had lost to the Balkan allies by the Treaty of Bucharest (1913) which terminated the second Balkan war. Because of her location in the center of the peninsula and the size of her army Bulgaria was deemed to hold a key position in the Balkans. King Ferdinand of Bulgaria, a Coburg, and the prime minister, V. Radoslavov, graduate of Austrian and German schools, were pro-Austrian and militantly anti-Russian, even though in 1914 and 1915 they carried on negotiations with both belligerent groups (as did the other Balkan states and Italy) and were profuse in their assurances that under no conditions would Bulgaria take up arms against Russia, England, and France. The apple of discord was Macedonia, the recovery of which, according to A. A. Savinsky, Russian ambassador to Sofia, had become "a real obsession" with the Bulgars; they were less intent on the annexation of Thrace and were relatively indifferent to Dobrudja (dispatch to Sazonov of November 8, 1914, N.S.). Macedonia, however, was held by Serbia and Greece; the winning over of Bulgaria and the restoration of the Balkan League, therefore, depended on the ability of the *entente* to prevail upon these countries to relinquish, in exchange for suitable compensations, their share of Macedonia to Bulgaria, or to persuade Bulgaria, again by promises of compensations elsewhere, to modify her intransigent attitude towards the Macedonian question. In both these undertakings Sazonov, Grey, and Delcassé failed lamentably.

There was a basic difference between the international position of Serbia, on the one hand, and that of Bulgaria, Rumania, and Greece, on the other. From the very outbreak of hostilities Serbia was a belligerent irrevocably committed to the cause of the *entente*, while the other three Balkan states remained neutral for many months. Each was ruled by a German monarch, had a powerful body of pro-Austrian and pro-German opinion, and was assiduously courted by Berlin and Vienna. Serbia, however, in spite of her dependence on the allies, showed unwillingness to make the territorial concessions that alone might have prevented Bulgaria from siding with the central Powers. The Serbian ambassadors to Athens and Paris stated emphatically that their government would rather abandon the whole of Serbia to Austria than to cede a fraction of Macedonia to Bulgaria (November, 1914). Rumania and Greece demanded and obtained, as a part of the price of their friendly neutrality and eventual participation in the war on the *entente* side, guarantees of their territorial integrity; these guarantees were incompatible with the allied efforts to secure the cooperation of Bulgaria. On the horns of a dilemma, *entente* diplomacy in the Balkan capitals often worked at cross-purposes. Sazonov realized from the beginning that it was useless to count on Serbia's voluntary concessions to Bulgaria and that the territorial sacrifices regarded as essential by the allies could be only imposed upon Pashitch (dispatch to Benckendorff, August 29, 1914, N.S.). Grey, however, believed that the allied Powers should limit themselves to advice and counsel and should let the Balkan governments themselves work out an agreement, a proposal that never had a chance of success. It would seem that in the spring of 1915 the position of the British and the Russian government had been reversed: Grey, under the impact of the deterioration of the military situation, urged the bringing of strong pressure upon Serbia, but Emperor Nicholas demurred and would not go beyond an appeal by the heads of the allied states to Serbia's sense of duty and enlightened self-interest. It was argued that since the realization of Serbian national ambitions depended on an *entente* victory, which would be impaired by the hostility of Bulgaria, the sacrifice of Serbian Macedonia would be a legitimate and wise contribution to the common cause.

The Bulgarian issue was further complicated by Turkey's entry into the war and Russian designs on Constantinople. Believing that military occupation was an essential prerequisite of annexation, Sazonov demanded in December, 1914, that Bulgaria's declaration of war on Turkey (then regarded as likely) should be delayed until a Russian expeditionary force had landed in the Balkans. In February, 1915, however, he withdrew his objections, but continued to feel uneasy about the possibility of a victorious war in European Turkey in which Russia would have no direct part. Desultory negotiations with Bulgaria and Serbia dragged on for a year. Meanwhile the failure of the Dardanelles expedition and the retreat of the Russian armies in Galicia and Poland strengthened the hand of the pro-German party in Bulgaria and at the same time made the Serbs somewhat more amenable. The final allied offer to Bulgaria (September 14, 1915, N.S.), concurred in—although grudgingly and with reservations—by Serbia, proposed the immediate occupation by Bulgaria of Thrace up to the line Enos-Midia and the annexation, at the end of the war, of the "unconditional" zone of Macedonia as defined in the Serbo-Bulgarian treaty of 1912. The allies demanded in return that Bulgaria promise to declare war on Turkey "in the near future." This offer was a case of too little and too late. On September 3, N.S., Bulgaria had concluded an agreement with Turkey, and on September 6 she had signed a military convention with Germany obtaining the immediate occupation of a portion of Thrace and a free hand in Macedonia in return for the promise to declare war on Serbia. On October 5, N.S., allied representatives were recalled from Sofia, and a week later (October 12, N.S.) Bulgaria invaded Serbia.

Rumania, like Bulgaria, was a source of grave anxiety to allied headquarters and foreign offices. In spite of the *rapprochement* between Rumania and the entente Powers that prevailed in the years preceding the war, the ties between that country and the Triple Alliance were not severed, and pro-German and pro-Austrian sentiment was strong in Bucharest. In 1914 Rumania was a partner of Austria-Hungary, Germany, and Italy in a defensive alliance directed against Russia. The alliance, whose origins went back to 1883, was renewed as recently as the spring of 1913. Rumanian national aspirations, moreover, included not only Austro-Hungarian territories but also Bessarabia, which had been annexed by Russia in 1812. In the fateful days of August, 1914, King Charles, a Hohenzollern and ruler of Rumania since 1881, favored the immediate declaration of war on the side of the central Powers but was overruled by the Rumanian government headed by Ion Bratiano. Bratiano, ignoring Rumania's obligations towards Germany and Austria-Hungary (as a year later he was to ignore her obligation to come to the assistance of Serbia when the latter was attacked by Bulgaria), merely ordered measures "for the protection of national frontiers," assumed a waiting attitude, and proceeded to negotiate with both belligerent groups. Sazonov, who acted as chief spokesman for the allies, offered to Bratiano, in return for Rumania's benevolent neutrality, the guarantee of her territorial integrity and the eventual annexation of Austro-Hungarian territories inhabited by Rumanians. The offer was accepted (subject to the curious reservation that it should not be disclosed at the time to any one in Bucharest, including the king and the British and French ambassadors) and was embodied in the secret Russo-Rumanian agreement of October 3, 1914, N.S. Although the death of King Charles (October 14, 1914, N.S.) and the accession of Ferdinand removed a powerful pro-German influence from Rumanian politics, the agreement of October 3 proved to be but the starting point of a laborious and protracted process of diplomatic bargaining.

The Russian position was inconsistent. Sazonov, after having guaranteed the territorial integrity of Rumania, repeatedly urged Bratiano to make "voluntary" concessions to Bulgaria in Dobrudja (which, it will be remembered, Rumania had wangled from Bulgaria in 1913); he believed that this would be a salutary example to Serbia and Greece and would pave the way for the revival of the Balkan League. Bratiano, however, would not part with Dobrudja unless Rumania was compensated by the annexation of Bessarabia, a proposal Sazonov would not even discuss. Meanwhile Bucharest played for time, and as the fortunes of war turned against the *entente* the Rumanian demands became more exacting. The ethnographical principle which Sazonov proposed to make the basis of the allocation of Austro-Hungarian territories to Rumania was lost sight of in the process of discussion. The revised Rumanian claims comprised the districts of the Banat inhabited by Serbs and those of Bukovina inhabited by Ukrainians. There was a sharp divergence of opinion among the allies as to Rumania's part in the war. Sazonov advocated benevolent neutrality that would cut off the central Powers from Rumanian oil and wheat; Grey and Delcassé insisted on belligerency "at any cost," as the French foreign minister put it to Izvolsky in June, 1915. Russian military opinion on the desirability of Rumanian participation in the war was divided and shifting. In May, 1915, the Grand Duke Nicholas Nikolaevich held that in view of the intervention of Italy Rumanian belligerency was a matter of "secondary importance" and her demands "exorbitant and unacceptable." Six weeks later his chief of staff, Ianushkevich, wrote to Sazonov that, because of the unfavorable trend of military events, the declaration of war by Rumania was eminently desirable and her terms should be agreed to at once. In the summer of 1916 General Alekseev, a former opponent of Rumanian intervention, joined the allied military leaders in a peremptory request that Rumania declare war without further delay; in case of non-compliance the promises of compensation were to be null and void. It was this ultimatum, coupled with the success of the Brusilov offensive, that finally forced Bratiano to take the plunge. The convention signed by Rumania and the allied Powers on August 17, 1916, N.S., accepted practically in their entirety the Rumanian demands, including those Sazonov had long held to be inadmissible. Ten days later Rumania declared war. The decisive and speedy defeat of her armies and the seizure of most of her territory and natural resources by the enemy was a blow to allied hopes and, perhaps, a vindication of those who, like Sazonov, had opposed Rumanian intervention.

The international situation in Greece differed from the pattern observed in the other Balkan states. The so-called pro-German and pro-Austrian faction, which somewhat illogically was deemed to include all those who opposed intervention on the side of the allies, was headed by King Constantine, brother-in-law of Emperor William; the supporters of an active pro-*entente* policy were led by Venizelos, prime minister since 1910. Greece, a maritime Power, had traditionally adhered to a "western" orientation, with the result that Russian influence in Athens was much weaker than in Bucharest and the capitals of the Slav states. Russia, moreover, had taken no part in the Balkan campaigns, except for sending a small "token" force to Salonika. Allied negotiations with Greece, therefore, were largely in the hands of London and Paris, while Russian diplomatic intervention was sporadic and rather negative in character, that is, it aimed not at winning the good graces of Greece but at preventing policies which the Russians deemed to be contrary to their interests. The conflict between Petrograd and Athens arose in connection with the Dardanelles expedition and Russia's proposed annexation of Constantinople (about which more will be said presently). From the beginning of the war the forcing of the Dardanelles was a favorite project of Winston Churchill, then first lord of the admiralty, but it was not taken up in earnest by the British government until early in January, 1915, after the Grand Duke Nicholas Nikolaevich had made an urgent appeal to London for a diversion in the Near East. Churchill had envisaged the possibility that the navy alone might not be able to seize the Straits and that the landing of a large expeditionary force might become necessary. According to his view, the avowedly formidable difficulties of a combined sea and land attack on Constantinople would be mitigated if the allies could rely upon the cooperation of Bulgaria and Greece. The outlook in Bulgaria was uncertain, but Greece, even though she would not take up arms in defense of Serbia, appeared eager to participate in a war against Turkey. An offer to this effect was made to Great Britain by Venizelos in August, 1914, six weeks before Turkey declared war, but was rejected by Grey on the ground that its acceptance would have forced Bulgaria into the enemy camp. Five months later, with Turkey in the war and the Dardanelles expedition in the process of preparation, the situation had changed, and Grey offered Greece important territorial acquisitions in Asia Minor in return for military intervention (January 23, 1915, N.S.).

Sazonov, who in the meantime had made up his mind that Russia must annex Constantinople and the Straits, was negotiating to this effect with England and France, and viewed the Balkan situation from the narrow standpoint of the fulfillment of Russia's "historic mission." He was suspicious of Bulgaria [9] and Greece, both of which had their own "historic" claims on Constantinople, and he was determined to block any military move that might jeopardize the consummation of the Russian plan. At the end of January, 1915, he agreed to the occupation of Gallipoli by the Greeks proposed by Grey, on condition, however, that England and France would guarantee the non-interference by Greece with "Russian policies and Russian interests in Constantinople and the Straits." Grey and Delcassé hastened to give the required assurance; but on March 1, N.S., after the difficulties of a naval assault on the Straits had become apparent, Venizelos made a new proposal: the use of Greek troops in forcing the Dardanelles. Churchill and the British admiralty welcomed the offer, but Sazonov declared that "under no condition" would Russia tolerate "the participation of Greek troops in the entry of allied armies in Constantinople" (March 2, N.S.). Grey's argument that the use of the Greek army and navy would greatly shorten the operation against Constantinople and that the fact of military occupation had no bearing on the final disposition of the conquered territories (a principle applied, according to Grey, to the German possessions in the Pacific) left Sazonov unmoved. He reiterated that the acceptance of Venizelos's offer "would lead to endless complications and have the most serious consequences" and that the tsar would never agree to the participation of Greek land and naval forces in any operation in the region of the Straits (March 6, N.S.). King Constantine having disavowed the offer of March 1, Venizelos was forced to resign (March 6, N.S.). Negotiations with his successor led nowhere, and Greece had no part in the Dardanelles expedition. In view of the internal situation in Greece it is a moot question whether Venizelos would have succeeded in carrying out his plan even if Sazonov had not interposed a veto; it is also debatable whether Greek participation would have materially altered the course and outcome of the Dardanelles expedition. Churchill was among those who felt that Sazonov's obstinacy had compromised one of the most promising operations of the war. The subsequent untoward events in Greece—the allied landing in Salonika (October, 1915), the formation in that area of a rump

---

[9] Sazonov in his memoirs gives credence to the fantastic tale that King Ferdinand of Bulgaria had purchased from a theatrical company the regalia and robes of a Byzantine emperor and kept them on hand at his residence.

government headed by Venizelos (September, 1916), and, in the summer of 1917, the bombardment of Athens by an allied force, the deposition of Constantine, the return of Venizelos to Athens, and the declaration of war by Greece on the central Powers—were engineered by the western allies. Russia had the good fortune to play but a minor role in these developments.

Having stumbled into the war unprepared and more or less by accident, Russia was caught short not only of guns and munitions but also of that all-important requisite of modern warfare—war aims. Repetitious verbiage about brotherly love for Serbia and German arrogance and bestiality (in which the Russians who knew Germany well found it difficult to believe) was obviously not enough. Sazonov's first attempt at rationalizing the irrational—for war is always irrational—was singularly unimaginative and anemic. The program he outlined to Buchanan and Paléologue on September 14, 1914, N.S., provided for cession of Alsace, Lorraine, and parts of the Rhineland to France; the restoration of Belgium and the enlargement of her territory at the expense of Germany; the return of Schleswig and Holstein to Denmark; the restoration of the kingdom of Hanover; the reorganization of Austria-Hungary as a tripartite monarchy, with the Czechs as the third full-fledged partner; the transfer to Serbia of Bosnia, Herzegovina, Dalmatia, and northern Albania; compensation to Bulgaria in Serbian Macedonia and the annexation by Greece of southern Albania; the annexation of Valona by Italy; the partition of German colonies among England, France, and Japan; and a war indemnity. Russian territorial gains were limited to eastern Galicia and the region along the lower course of the Nieman as well as the inclusion of Posen, Silesia, and western Galicia in the future autonomous Poland, which was to be under Russian rule.

This dreary catalogue of "historic grievances" and "legitimate national aspirations" compiled from the dusty files of the foreign office was hardly of a nature to arouse enthusiasm in Russia. No claims of any kind were made on Turkey; it was not until September 26, N.S., that Sazonov, as an afterthought, amended his list by demanding the free passage of Russian warships through the Straits. The question of the partition of the Ottoman empire was first raised by the British. Sazonov agreed that if Turkey joined Germany "she must cease to exist," while he continued to exert himself to prevent this contingency.

If, as it is often alleged, Russia's desire to acquire Constantinople and the Straits was one of the chief causes of the war, no evidence of it transpired in the early confidential exchange of views between Sazonov and the western allies.

Turkey's entry into the war altered the situation and provided the opportunity to inject into Sazonov's academic program a dramatic element which, it was imagined, would have a wide popular appeal. The imperial manifesto issued on the occasion of the break of diplomatic relations with the Porte spoke of the approaching solution of "the historic task bequeathed to us by our forefathers on the shores of the Black Sea." The hint was taken up by the press and by the conservative and the liberal factions of the Duma. For instance, the popular liberal professor of the University of Moscow, Prince E. N. Trubetskoy, who had only recently held that expansion could do Russia nothing but harm, now expounded the theory that the "independence of Russia" was inextricably bound up with the possession of Constantinople. "With us," he wrote in 1915, "this is a question of our daily bread, of our whole political power, of our cultural mission, of the survival of the spiritual self of Russia," and he proclaimed that Russia's main task was the restoration of the cross on the basilica of St. Sophia (a venerable structure in Constantinople converted by the Turks into a mosque), which he extolled as "that pearl of the Gospel for which Russia should be willing to sacrifice everything she has." According to Miliukov, leader of the liberal opposition in the Duma, Russia "must acquire the Bosphorus and the Dardanelles, together with Constantinople and a portion of the littoral sufficient to ensure the defense of the Straits." The conservatives vied with the liberals in insisting on the fulfillment of Russia's "historic mission." Not all educated Russians shared these aberrations, but since dissenting opinions received no publicity it was easy to mistake the quasi-unanimous acclaim of the proposed annexation for the true expression of a genuine popular movement.[10]

[10] Among those who deprecated the conquest of Constantinople were high officials of the Russian foreign office. For example, Prince N. A. Kudashev, chief representative of the foreign office at the army headquarters in 1914–1916, and later ambassador to China, held that "neither spiritually nor physically are we ready for the annexation of the Straits. When I say 'spiritually' or morally this is what I mean: to establish ourselves in Constantinople, as crusaders proclaiming the triumph of the Orthodox Church, is out of the question because of our panslav sympathies and affiliations, our dislike of the Greeks, and the insufficient authority of our clergy with the Greek hierarchy. Of playing the part so brilliantly performed by England in Egypt we are utterly incapable. Then what will happen if by a decree of

Grey understood that resistance to the wishes of the Russian government might well wreck the alliance. He took the lead, and on November 9, 1914, N.S., told Benckendorff that in the event of the defeat of Germany the fate of the Straits and Constantinople must be decided in conformity with Russian interests. Subsequent negotiations between Petrograd, on the one hand, and London and Paris, on the other, gave concrete meaning to Grey's intentionally vague statement. The final Russian program, which was formulated in a memorandum of March 4, 1915, N.S., and was accepted by the British government on March 12, provided for the annexation by Russia of Constantinople, the western shore of the Bosphorus, the Sea of Marmara and the Dardanelles, southern Thrace up to the line Enos-Midia, the islands of Imbros and Tenedos, and a strip of the Asiatic littoral. The consummation of these promises was contingent on the successful termination of the war and the satisfaction of British and French claims in the Ottoman empire and elsewhere. Petrograd undertook to view annexations by the allies in a spirit of friendly reciprocity. These were far-reaching commitments. As early as November, 1914, a few days after Grey's statement to Benckendorff, Sazonov, consulted by London, approved "with particular pleasure" the proposed annexation of Egypt by Great Britain. The agreement about Constantinople became, indeed, the corner-stone of a complex, precariously balanced structure of secret treaties which led eventually to infinite international complications and, when disclosed, brought discredit to the cause of the allies. Viewed from the standpoint of Anglo-Russian relations, Grey's wartime policy in the question of Constantinople was a welcome sign that under the pressure of necessity the British foreign office had at last succeeded in freeing itself from the nefarious tradition of Palmerston and Stratford de Redcliffe.[11]

Providence we obtain possession of Constantinople, the Straits, and so on? Among other things we shall have against us the entire local population, antagonized by our backward administrative methods, particularly by our treatment of national minorities; also Bulgaria and Greece, who have quite definite views about the Straits, and especially about Constantinople; and then Rumania, whom we are trying to win over and who will hardly be pleased by the rumors concerning our desire to settle down on the Bosphorus, which would mean that she is bottled up in the Black Sea" (letter to Sazonov, Feb. 24, 1915, N.S.). Sazonov had shared these doubts and had at first opposed the acquisition of Constantinople; but, bowing to the will of the tsar and the pressure of what he believed to be public opinion, he became the leading advocate of annexation.

[11] In 1903 the British Committee of Imperial Defense, after a thorough study, had reached the conclusion that the exclusion of Russia from the region of the

The French government signified its adherence to the Anglo-Russian agreement on April 10, 1915, N.S., and the Italian government on December 2, 1916, N.S. The brief delay in the case of France was due to the reluctance of the Quai d'Orsay to discard its traditional policy towards Turkey, and to apprehensions concerning the future of large French investments in that country. The much longer delay in the case of Italy was caused by Sazonov's refusal to recognize her as a full-fledged ally until she had declared war on Germany, which Rome finally did in August, 1916. With the agreements duly signed and sealed, the acquisition of Constantinople by Russia—assuming the defeat of the central Powers—appeared assured, at least on paper. Sazonov, however, had little confidence in the validity of international agreements unless supported by force. He believed (as Kudashev put it to General Danilov in January, 1915) that "only that is firmly acquired which we have obtained ourselves, by our blood, by our endeavor." Hence his efforts to organize an independent Russian expedition against Constantinople to assure an adequate or at least a token participation of Russian forces in the Dardanelles expedition, to discourage that operation if the Russians could have no part in it, and to prevent the use in the region of the Straits of Bulgarian and Greek troops. The military, however, shattered the plans of the foreign minister. Sazonov was told by headquarters that neither men nor ships were available for an independent Russian campaign against Constantinople. The same argument obtained concerning the Dardanelles expedition, in the success of which the Grand Duke Nicholas Nikolaevich and Danilov did not believe but which they regarded as a useful diversion to relieve the pressure on the Caucasian front.[12]

Straits "was not for Great Britain a matter of primary naval or military interest." *History of the Great War Based on Official Documents, by Direction of the Historical Section of the Committee of Imperial Defence: Naval Operations*, by Sir J. S. Corbett (London, 1921), II, 204. This conclusion, which did not affect the policy of Grey in 1908 and 1911, was a restatement, although on different grounds, of the common-sense policy advocated by Richard Cobden some seventy years earlier (see p. 842).

[12] There was considerable confusion concerning the number of Russian troops available for landing in European Turkey. On Jan. 23, 1915, N.S., the British government was informed by the Grand Duke Nicholas Nikolaevich that he could not promise the participation of Russian land or naval forces in the Dardanelles expedition. This emphatic statement, however, was not regarded as final and, indeed, under the pressure of the tsar and Sazonov the high command appeared to be willing to revise its position. The size of the Russian expeditionary force was estimated by Churchill at 8,000 (Feb. 23, 1915, N.S.), by Kitchener at 47,000 (March 10,

The outlook became even dimmer with the deterioration of the military situation in 1915 and the change in the Russian high command. The Russian retreat, the failure of the Dardanelles expedition, and the declaration of war by Bulgaria drove the new chief of staff, General Alekseev, to the conclusion that peace with Turkey was the only way to prevent disaster (October, 1915). He returned to this subject in February, 1916, when the success of the Russians in Turkistan and the capture of Erzerum created a favorable situation for peace overtures to Turkey. Alekseev argued that it was idle to plan for conquest when the enemy held a large portion of the national territory. Nothing short of the concentration of all Russian resources on the Austro-German front would bring victory. Alekseev therefore tentatively suggested peace with Turkey on the basis of the *status quo ante bellum* even at the price of renouncing "some beautiful dreams." This proposal, however, had no sequel. The Petrograd foreign office, committed to the annexation of Constantinople, was not prepared to revise itself. On February 21, 1917, that is, virtually on the eve of the revolution, the new minister of foreign affairs, N. N. Pokrovsky, presented to the tsar a secret report in which he argued that the ultimate fate of Constantinople and the Straits would be decided, not by international agreements, but by the military situation at the end of the war, and that without a Russian occupation of these territories allied promises would prove "a mere scrap of paper." He therefore urged preparations for the landing of Russian troops on the shores of the Bosphorus. Army headquarters gave no encouragement to this proposal, which after the revolution was taken up by Miliukov, foreign minister in the Provisional Government.

Constantinople and the Straits were the major (but not the only) item of Russian postwar expansion endorsed by the allies. An Anglo-French agreement dealing with the partition of Asiatic Turkey was initialed on behalf of the two countries by Sir Mark Sykes and G. Picot on March 9, 1916, N.S. Amended in the light of Sazonov's criticisms, it was ratified by a Franco–Russian convention of April 26, 1916, N.S., and a few days later by England. Under the Sykes-Picot agree-

---

N.S.), and by Paléologue at 100,000 (statement to the Bulgarian ambassador to Petrograd, March 24, N.S.). The final (and only) concrete Russian offer of 4,500 men to be shipped from Vladivostok (May and June, 1915) was declined by Kitchener on the ground that the limited usefulness of this small force would not justify the technical difficulties and expenditure of transporting it from the Pacific.

ment Russia's share of the spoils included the districts of Trebizond, Erzerum, Bayazid, Vana, Bitlis, a slice of Kurdistan, and a strip of the Black Sea shore west of Trebizond. The question of annexations along Russia's western frontier was dealt with, in a more summary fashion, by an exchange of letters between the French and the Russian governments in February, 1917. Under the terms of this agreement, which was negotiated during the allied conference in Petrograd, Russia promised to support the French claims to Alsace, Lorraine, and the Saar, as well as the French plan for the establishment of an autonomous neutralized state on the left bank of the Rhine; in return the French government reaffirmed its adherence to the 1915 agreement about Constantinople and recognized Russia's freedom in determining her western frontier. The British were unaware of the Franco-Russian agreement, and when it came to their notice they protested vigorously.

Peace feelers through both official and unofficial channels met with no response from the imperial government. There were, of course, influential men in Petrograd (among them Witte) who believed that war against Germany was a fatal mistake and should be terminated at the earliest opportunity. These views received no encouragement in official circles; and at no time, not even during the brief months when the supposedly pro-German Sturmer headed the foreign office, did imperial Russia falter in its loyalty to the Allied cause.

Constantinople, however, was the chief trump card of Russian diplomacy. To bolster the declining morale of the nation and to stem the tide of anti-British propaganda that swept the country after the failure of the Dardanelles expedition, the agreements concerning Constantinople and the Straits, theretofore a closely guarded secret, were disclosed, with the consent of the allies, in the Duma on December 2, 1916, N.S. The announcement, coming as it did in the midst of an acute domestic crisis and alarming news of the defeat of the Rumanian army, "fell perfectly flat," to quote Buchanan. Not even the ultra-nationalist and conservative press and parliamentary groups seemed to care any longer about the fulfillment of Russia's "historic mission" or to believe in its possibility. The "Byzantine mirage," as Paléologue put it, had vanished in thin air.

CHAPTER XLIV

IMPERIAL RUSSIA AND THE FIRST WORLD WAR: II

THE ECONOMIC EFFECTS OF THE WAR

It cannot be repeated too often that while the political and diplomatic gains of war are tenuous and problematic, its costs are invariably high. Contrary to some expectations, Russia's backwardness proved no safeguard against the disastrous consequences of belligerency. Like the other countries engaged in the struggle, she experienced the full effects of the disorganization of agricultural and industrial production: shortage of man power, raw materials, foodstuffs, and consumers' goods; dislocation of transportation and foreign trade; and budgetary and monetary disorders with their familiar concomitants—rising prices, declining real incomes, and general impoverishment. The inevitable disruptive consequences of warfare were aggravated, in the case of Russia, by enemy occupation of her industrialized western provinces, by nearly complete isolation from her allies and the outside world, and by the ineptness of her government and its inability to organize the country for war.

Rational distribution of man power is a basic problem of war economy. The mobilization of 1914 and subsequent drafts made profound inroads on the labor force engaged in peacetime pursuits. The Russian peacetime army in 1914 was estimated at 1.4 million men; an additional 5.1 million were drafted in 1914, 5.2 million in 1915, 2.7 million in 1916, and 0.6 million in 1917, giving a total of over 15 million. These official figures, which are probably too low, indicate that in 1914 15 per cent of the male population of working age were serving with the colors, in 1915 25 per cent, in 1916 36 per cent, and in 1917 37 per cent. The resulting shrinkage of the labor supply was felt particularly in industry, which even in peacetime suffered from a shortage of skilled workers and which, moreover, depended largely on the seasonal labor of the peasant farmers that was no longer forthcoming. Nevertheless between 1914 and 1917 the total number of industrial workers increased, according to the tentative estimate of Rashin, by some 400,000. The new sources of labor included refugees, oriental labor (Persian and Chinese), and prisoners of war (some 376,000 prisoners of war were employed under the ministry of commerce and industry in 1917), as well as men of military age who before the war would not have sought industrial employment but were now eager to do so because of exemptions from army service provided for the workers in some of the war industries. There was also a marked increase in the employment of women and in juvenile labor. Before the war about one-third of industrial workers were women; by the end of 1916 they accounted for more than half of the total labor force. The large influx of new and inexperienced workers, combined with other wartime conditions, had an adverse effect upon the productivity of labor. For example, in spite of the lengthening of the working day and the increase in the number of overtime hours, the average monthly output per worker in the foundries declined from 181 poods in 1914 to 163 poods in 1915, to 143 poods in 1916, and to 119 poods in the first two months of 1917. Similar trends were observed in other industries.

The effects of mobilization upon agriculture were different in the case of peasant farming and in that of large estates. Excess of man power, it will be remembered, was one of the features of Russian "rural overpopulation"; the withdrawal of a large proportion of men of working age therefore actually meant a reduction in the number of idle hands rather than an impairment of the productivity of small farming. Under the stimulus of increased demand and high prices, the area under cereal crops sown by the peasants in European Russia (exclusive of the provinces occupied by the enemy) expanded by some 13 million dessiatines, from the annual average of 47 million in 1909–1913 to 60 million in 1916. The large estates, on the other hand, in spite of the fact that many refugees, oriental workers, and prisoners of war were employed in agriculture, did not succeed in replacing the some 300,000 to 400,000 workers they had lost through army drafts, with the result that in European Russia (exclusive, again, of the provinces occupied by the enemy) the area under cereals on the large estates declined by 15 million dessiatines, from the annual average of 21.3 million in 1909–1913 to 6.5 million in 1916. This shrinkage was of great national importance because the large estates produced primarily for the market, while a considerable proportion of the grain grown by the peasants was consumed by the farmers themselves. Moreover, the total area under crops (excluding Finland and Poland) declined, chiefly because of enemy occupation, from 99.5 million dessiatines in 1913 to 90.6 million in 1916. The shortage of foodstuffs experienced during the war, however, may be traced to three principal factors: the appearance of a huge new demand represented by the armed forces, the breakdown of the railways, and the unwillingness of the peasants (whose production accounted, on the average, for 88 per cent of the cereal crop and for 78 per cent of the grain actually marketed) to part with their grain.

The expansion of the armed forces not only reduced the economic war potential by absorbing a large percentage of the male population but also simultaneously created a new highly urgent and inelastic demand for the innumerable requisites of warfare (arms, munitions, uniforms, and so on), as well as a substantial increase in the demand for foodstuffs. The nutrition standards of the peasants were exceedingly low, and the army fare, which included meat, fish, butter, eggs, and a generous allowance of sugar, was greatly in excess of what the peasant soldier used to get at home. Moreover, while the peacetime pittance of the peasants was derived, with but a few minor exceptions (sugar, vodka), from their own farms, the mobilized men (and also the refugees) had to be provided for by the government; hence the increased demand for foodstuffs and the additional strain on the inadequate transportation system, perhaps the weakest spot in Russia's weak economic armor. The geographical distribution of the railway network was uneven, its density declining in the east; that is, most of the lines were located in the western provinces occupied by the enemy or in the vicinity of the front. The carrying capacity of the railways was low and the rolling stock insufficient. This unhappy state of affairs was due in some degree to the policies of S. V. Rukhlov, minister of transportation in 1909–1915. He succeeded in bringing some order to the finances of the state-owned railways, which controlled about two-thirds of the total mileage; but the elimination of perennial deficits was achieved at the price of drastic retrenchments of maintenance expenditures and curtailment of capital outlays, much to the detriment of the efficiency of the network. The movement of millions of troops and refugees and of a huge volume of army freight imposed upon the weak and under-developed railways system a burden that proved beyond its capacity. The number of railway engines in working order declined from 20,000 in 1914 to 17,000 in 1916, and to 9,000 in 1917; the number of railway cars declined from 540,000 in 1914 to 463,000 in 1916, and to 174,000 in 1917, while the production of rails fell from 43 million poods in 1914 to less than 12 million in 1917. The practical monopolization of the meagre and dwindling railway facilities by army services accounted, in part, for the severe shortages experienced by the civilian population.

The nature of war economics was not as well understood in 1914 as it is by generations enlightened by the experience of two world wars. What many Russian economists feared at the outbreak of hostilities was not shortages but overproduction due to the shrinkage of the markets. In August, 1914, for instance, Prince D. I. Shakhovskoy argued before the influential Moscow Agricultural Society that because of the suspension of exports "wheat, finding no buyers on the home market, may well lose all value"; he therefore urged government intervention in support of grain prices. Many manufacturers, laboring under a similar delusion, cut production by 25 or even 50 per cent. These apprehensions were soon belied by events. Army demand more than filled the gap created by the disruption of exports, and both industry and agriculture found themselves deluged with orders. Nevertheless the economic policy of the early months of the war adhered to the principle of "business as usual," and no government intervention was contemplated except in the areas immediately adjoining the front. It was not until the military reverses of the spring of 1915, accompanied by a calamitous shortage of war supplies, breakdown of the railways, and the rapid deterioration of the economic situation that the "business as usual" approach was superseded by that of "mobilization of industry" for the needs of the army. The new policy, carried out by specially created agencies (to be discussed later) in which both management and labor were represented, achieved a degree of success: by the end of 1916, because of increased domestic production and large shipments from allied countries, the supply of the army was vastly improved. This result, however, was attained at the price of diverting practically all industrial capacity to war purposes, with a corresponding reduction in the output of consumers' goods and articles needed by the farmers, such as fertilizers and agricultural machinery and implements. The resultant shortages led to an orgy of speculation, inflicted considerable hardships on the civilian population, and deprived the peasants of the incentive to sell their grain.

Government control over the distribution of foodstuffs was introduced gradually and in a haphazard fashion. The initial period of almost unrestricted economic freedom was followed by the institution of partial controls and the splitting of the market into two sections, of which one—catering to the civilian population—continued to enjoy a large measure of freedom, while the other—embracing army supplies—was brought under increasingly stringent state regulations. It was not until the autumn of 1916, when the failure of this dual method became apparent, that an attempt was made to extend state control, including fixed prices, to the entire field of food supply. Fixed prices, however, were maintained at too low a level, were subject to frequent revisions, invited evasion, and instead of stabilizing production and supply merely added to the confusion. Rationing of consumption (food cards) was first tried in the latter part of 1916, and became fairly general in 1917. The state monopoly of grain trade was finally proclaimed by the Provisional Government in March, 1917. At the end of 1916, and especially in 1917, however, disorganization had reached a stage where government orders were no longer enforced, and much of the economic legislation of the later period of the war remained a dead letter. By the end of the empire the prices of the principal foodstuffs were two, three, or four times above their prewar level; in 1917 the upward price movement was accelerated, and assumed catastrophic dimensions.

Isolation from the outside world was a factor in Russia's economic predicament. With the outbreak of the war the land frontier with Germany and Austria-Hungary was closed. The German blockade of the southern Baltic and the Danish straits, and the closure of the Dardanelles by the Turks, deprived Russia of her principal sea routes. The two direct routes open were those of the Pacific Ocean and of the White Sea. The Pacific route, however, involved a rail journey across Siberia and, as a means of communication with Europe, a voyage around the globe. Archangel, the only sizable port on the White Sea, is icebound part of the year, and is connected with the hinterland by a railway of doubtful efficiency. The building of a railway linking Petrograd with the ice-free port of Murmansk in the extreme north began in October, 1915, but it was not completed until November, 1916. There still remained the possibility of transit trade by way of Sweden, by far the shortest and safest route in wartime. Its practical usefulness, however, was impaired by the British blockade (using the term "blockade" in its non-technical meaning) of the Scandinavian countries. The Swedish government vigorously resisted British interference with its freedom of commerce and used Russian transit trade as a lever to wangle concessions from London, a policy of legitimate self-defense that did not, of course, facilitate Russian trade by way of Sweden.

The war wrought revolutionary changes in Russian foreign trade. Exports and imports dropped precipitously in the first year of the war; although both recovered subsequently, exports remained at a level below one-third of their 1913 value, while imports exceeded their pre-war value by 20 per cent in 1915–1916 and were nearly twice as high in 1916–1917. For the three years August, 1914, to July, 1917, the excess of imports over exports aggregated 2,531 million rubles. The mounting deficit in foreign trade accounts indicated the deterioration of Russia's international financial position and was in sharp contrast with the "favorable" balance of trade so carefully husbanded by Russian ministers of finance of the pre-war period. Figures of value expressed in rapidly depreciating rubles, however, do not tell the whole story, and may be misleading. In spite of the increase in the value of imports, their volume, measured by weight, was but two-fifths of the corresponding figure for the three years immediately preceding the war; the volume of exports, of course, suffered a much greater decline. No less striking were the changes in the direction and composition of foreign trade. Commerce with Germany, formerly Russia's principal customer and source of supply, and with other enemy countries, was discontinued, and the bulk of Russian exports went to Finland and Great Britain; the commodities exported were chiefly semi-manufactured goods such as hemp, lumber, and flax. With the closure of the Dardanelles and of the Baltic sea route, small amounts of grain were exported by way of Archangel (18 million poods in 1915 and 21 million in 1916); in 1917 they dwindled to less than 2 million poods, that is, grain exports became practically extinct. Russian wartime imports came chiefly from Great Britain, the United States, France, and Japan, and consisted of arms, munitions, and equipment necessary for the manufacturing of war supplies.

The course of Russian public finance during the war conformed closely to a dreary and familiar pattern. The one significant departure from the conventional approach was the decree of August 22, 1914, extending for the duration of the war the prohibition of the sale of liquor previously ordered for the period of the mobilization. This venture into compulsory temperance would seem to have been a personal decision of the tsar, inspired, presumably, by Rasputin. As recently as July 27, the Duma had approved a bill, introduced by the minister of finance Bark, for an increase in the price of vodka. The abolition of the monopoly of spirits eliminated the largest single source of state revenue, an action believed to be unprecedented in the history of any country confronted with a grave emergency. The social effects of prohibition were similar to those in the United States under the Eighteenth Amendment. Prohibition was but loosely enforced, bootlegging flourished, peasants turned to various forms of home brew, and drunkenness was as prevalent as ever. Much of the home-brewed liquor, moreover, was not fit for human consumption, and its use was detrimental to public health. An unforeseen by-product of prohibition was the substantial savings realized by the peasants which added to their purchasing power, reduced the stimulus to sell grain, and exercised an inflationary pressure on the market.

The elimination of the liquor revenue was but one—although a major one—of the losses suffered by the treasury. Receipts from taxes fell because of enemy occupation of a portion of the territory, curtailment of peacetime activities (foreign trade, non-military railway traffic), and for other reasons, while expenditure increased by leaps and bounds. In 1914–1917 some 5,000 million rubles were spent on allowances to the families of service men and over 700 million on refugees. No official estimates of Russian war costs are available; but according to the authoritative computations of M. Dementev they amounted to 1,655 million rubles in 1914, to 8,818 million in 1915, to 14,572 million in 1916, and to 13,603 million in the first eight months of 1917, giving a total of 38,650 million. The rise in tax rates and the new taxes introduced during the war (including the income tax and the war profit tax, both enacted in 1916) were barely sufficient to fill the gap created by the loss of revenue. War expenditure, therefore, was defrayed by borrowing and by the use of the printing press. Between the outbreak of the war and September 1, 1917, the public debt increased by 23,908 million rubles; of this amount 8,071 million were foreign loans secured in part by the transfer to England of a portion of the Russian gold reserve. Convertibility of paper rubles into gold was suspended on July 23, 1914, and the volume of paper currency in circulation rose from 1,633 million rubles on the eve of the war to 2,946 million at the end of 1914, to 5,617 million at the end of 1915, and to 9,097 million at the end of 1916; paper circulation nearly doubled in 1917, reaching 18,917 million in October, when the Bolsheviks overthrew the Provisional Government. Simultaneously the rate of exchange of the ruble declined from the pre-war parity of 9.46 to the pound sterling to an average of 11.40 rubles in 1915, to 15.55 rubles in 1916, and to 25.52 rubles in July and October, 1917. Economic backwardness, indeed, proved no defense against the disruptive consequences of belligerency.

The war of 1914 brought a notable reversal in Russia's traditional attitude towards enemy aliens. During the Napoleonic wars, in 1800 and in 1807, the St. Petersburg government embargoed English ships and commercial establishments and imposed certain restrictions on the use of enemy property of non-commercial character, but these precedents did not create a tradition and were not followed in the later part of the nineteenth century. During the Russo-Turkish War of 1877–1878 and the Russo-Japanese War of 1904–1905, enemy nationals were permitted "to continue their residence and carry on their peaceful occupations under the protection of the Russian law." In August, 1914, the imperial government reaffirmed the above policy by proclaiming that "the inviolability of private property of enemy nationals is a principle firmly recognized by international law." This magnanimous attitude, however, was almost immediately reversed; beginning with October, 1914, the government embarked on a program of measures carried out under the slogan of "liberation from the German yoke" and directed towards the liquidation of the property rights not only of enemy aliens but also of settlers of enemy extraction, subjects of the Russian Crown, whose families in a vast number of cases had resided in Russia for generations.[1] The concept of war as a struggle between armed forces—a concept which the Russians upheld in an age less ruthless or, at least, less thorough than our own—was superseded by one of totalitarian war that tends to obliterate distinctions between combatants and non-combatants. The totalitarian doctrine of warfare

---

[1] Baron Boris E. Nolde, *Russia in the Economic War* (New Haven, 1928), pp. 3–17 and *passim*. The area of agricultural land held by enemy (chiefly German) settlers and subject to expropriation was estimated in June, 1916, at nearly 8 million acres. *Ibid.*, p. 114

found its full acceptance and application in the Second World War in measures such as internment of enemy aliens and seizure of their property, impounding of funds owned by neutral states and nationals, wholesale blacklisting of neutral firms suspected of trading with the enemy, saturation bombing of open cities, and, finally, the use of the atomic bomb.

THE GOVERNMENT IN WARTIME

Viewed in its broader aspects, the imperial government on the eve of the war was a blend of medievalism and western democracy. The former was typified by the jealously guarded prerogatives of the Crown and by hostility towards any extension of the sphere of popular government, while the latter was represented, however imperfectly, by the State Duma and the institutions of local self-government. Curiously, the war strengthened both these antagonistic tendencies. Medievalism asserted itself in the resurgence of the personal rule of the tsar, the ascendancy of the empress and Rasputin, and the decay of the bureaucratic system; the advance of democracy was evidenced by the enhanced stature of the Duma, the wider field of activity open to the zemstvos and municipalities, and the broadening of the social basis of government through the creation of wartime agencies which included representatives of the legislative chambers, management, and labor. The strengthening of both the democratic and the anti-democratic strain accentuated the conflict between the two and contributed to the disintegration of the entire system.

Prior to 1914 Nicholas exercised little control over the day-by-day administration of public affairs except through the selection of his ministers, who, however, were largely drawn from the upper levels of the bureaucracy and usually possessed (at least in theory) the qualification of experience acquired by virtue of tenure of high offices. The ever present influence of the empress was not unduly felt, although the activities of Rasputin (who, it will be remembered, was introduced to the imperial couple in 1905) had caused much unfavorable comment and were the subject of an interpellation in the Duma in 1912. Sabler in 1911 and Goremykin and Bark in January, 1914, owed their ministerial appointments to Rasputin's support. Nevertheless before the war his interference with the affairs of state was sporadic and of no serious consequence, and it was not until the departure of the tsar for the army in 1915 that it assumed the character of a major national problem. A novel and untoward development was the fanatical determination of the empress to devote herself to the service of the dynasty and of the nation. Her blind acceptance of Rasputin's guidance and the total domination she exercised over her consort produced a situation that might well have appeared incredible had it not been established beyond a shadow of doubt by the correspondence between Nicholas and Alexandra Fedorovna.[2] The empress, writing in unidiomatic and ungrammatical English, incessantly urged her husband to be "more autocratic" and "to show his mind." It did not occur to her that these admonitions were incompatible with the tsar's meek compliance with her own wishes. Guided by Rasputin, she imagined herself to be an instrument of Providence.

In August, 1915, the tsar assumed the command of the army. This fateful decision was partly due to his romantic concept of the duties of kingship and partly to the pressure brought to bear upon him by Rasputin and the empress. Alexandra Fedorovna feared the popularity of the Grand Duke Nicholas Nikolaevich with the troops and quite unjustly suspected his loyalty. She greeted the assumption of the high command by the emperor as the opening of a "glorious page" in his reign and in Russian history, and she prophesied that his critics would soon be forced to realize the "great wisdom" of his decision. Meanwhile she was eager to fill the place left vacant by the emperor's absence from Petrograd. "I long to poke my nose into everything . . . to wake people up, to put order into all, and unite all forces," the tsarina wrote in September, 1915. Nicholas warmly encouraged her ambitions. "Truly, you ought to be my eyes and ears there in the capital, while I have to stay here," he wrote a year later. "It rests with you to keep peace and harmony among the ministers—thereby you do a great service to me and our country. . . . I am so glad . . . that you have found at last a worthy occupation."

The enthusiasm of the emperor for Alexandra Fedorovna's interference in the affairs of state was not shared by the majority of his ministers and by the leaders of the Duma and public opinion. In the late summer of 1915 the council of ministers had among its mem-

---

[2] *The Letters of the Tsaritsa to the Tsar, 1914–1916*, with an introduction by Sir Bernard Pares (London, 1923); *The Letters of the Tsar to the Tsaritsa*, with an introduction by C. H. Hagberg (London, 1929). Pertinent excerpts from this correspondence are quoted in M. T. Florinsky, *The End of the Russian Empire* (New Haven, 1931), Chap. III, and in Sir Bernard Pares' *The Fall of the Russian Monarchy* (New York, 1939), *passim*.

bers an unusually large number of men of integrity and—for a Russian imperial government—of liberal leanings who were willing to work with the Duma and the newly created wartime agencies.[3] After the outbreak of the war the position of the civilian government was an exceptionally difficult one. The law of July 16, 1914, on the administration of the army in the field virtually deprived the council of ministers of any real authority.[4] Prince Shcherbatov stated at the meeting of the cabinet on July 16, 1915, that he "was deluged" with telegrams from provincial governors "depicting the intolerable situation created by the military authorities. The slightest objections of civilian officials are met with severe rebukes and threats—sometimes of imprisonment. It is impossible to find out whose orders should be executed. They come from everywhere and are often contradictory. The result is complete confusion and disorganization." Four weeks later (August 11) Shcherbatov complained that "even in Petrograd . . . the minister of the interior is a mere man in the street who is permitted to act only in so far as this does not interfere with the fanciful orders of the military." It will be remembered that the retreat which led to the mass movement of refugees and which was patterned after that of 1812 was devised and carried out by army headquarters regardless of the protests of the council of ministers.

The emperor's decision to lead the army was reached without consulting the cabinet and was received by that body with dismay. It was believed that the assumption by the tsar of direct responsibility for the conduct of military operations, at a time when the troops were in full retreat and the possibility of the evacuation of Petrograd and even Moscow was not excluded, might well prove the undoing of the monarchy. Over the objections of Goremykin, who vainly pleaded that

[3] Important changes in the composition of the council of ministers took place in midsummer of 1915. The minister of war Sukhomlinov was succeeded by Polivanov, who enjoyed great popularity in Duma circles. The minister of justice Shcheglovitov, a notorious arch-reactionary, was replaced by A. A. Khvostov, a conservative of less flamboyant hue. Prince N. B. Shcherbatov, a nobleman of liberal views, became minister of the interior, an office formerly held by the reactionary N. A. Maklakov. Sabler, Rasputin's appointee, was relieved of the duties of chief procurator of the Holy Synod. His successor was Samarin, a highly respected Churchman. The appointments of Polivanov and Samarin were made during the emperor's visit to headquarters, and they greatly distressed the empress. The changes undergone by the council of ministers in the summer of 1915 indicate that prior to the assumption by the tsar of the high command the influence of Alexandra Fedorovna and Rasputin was not yet supreme.

[4] See p. 1320.

"the will of the tsar must be obeyed like the Gospel," ten (out of twelve) ministers took the unprecedented step of sending to the emperor a joint letter begging him to reconsider his decision; a blunt reference to the "inadmissible divergence of opinion" within the council of ministers was tantamount to a request by the signatories to be relieved of their duties.[5] "The ministers are rotten," was the empress's verdict; Goremykin was "shocked and horrified," and the appeal to the tsar went unheeded.

With the ministers at odds and practically on non-speaking terms with their president, the Duma and the country increasingly restless, and the empress clamoring for the heads of those members of the council who had the temerity to oppose her own and Rasputin's wishes, the reconstruction of the cabinet could not be long delayed. The manner in which it was accomplished, however, was such as to defeat its avowed objects—national unity and administrative efficiency. Goremykin's extreme unpopularity and the realization that his appearance in the Duma would lead to hostile demonstrations forced Alexandra Fedorovna to agree that he could no longer remain at the helm of the government. In January, 1916, he was succeeded by B. V. Sturmer, an even more contemptible specimen of the St. Petersburg bureaucracy than his predecessor. The new president of the council, according to N. N. Pokrovsky, one of his colleagues, "gave the impression of a man of extremely limited gifts, one suffering from acute sclerosis due to advanced age," and incapable of formulating the simplest thought without first putting it down in writing. Sturmer, moreover, was surrounded by a group of unscrupulous adventurers and was suspected, it would seem on good grounds, of questionable financial dealings. The empress nevertheless held that he was the "right man" because he "very much values Gregory, which is important," and "completely believes" in Rasputin's "wonderful, God-sent wisdom." While in office Sturmer made weekly reports to Alexandra Fedorovna and kept in close touch with her through her friend and confidante Madame Vyrubov. In November, 1916, he was forced into retirement by a bitter personal attack upon him and the empress, which was launched in the Duma by Miliukov. The next president of the council, A. F.

---

[5] The letter was signed by eight civilian ministers, but the ministers of war and of the navy (Polivanov and Admiral J. K. Grigorovich) informed the tsar of their solidarity with their colleagues. Goremykin and the minister of justice A. A. Khvostov took no part in the collective *démarche*.

Trepov, a conservative who would not make obeisance to Rasputin, was appointed by the tsar against the wishes of Alexandra Fedorovna, but his tenure of office lasted merely five weeks. At the end of December, that is, after Rasputin's murder, Trepov was succeeded by the elderly Prince N. D. Golitsin, a wealthy nobleman devoid of political ambitions and inexperienced in the art of government but personally known to the empress. His appointment was as much of a shock and surprise to Golitsin as it was to the country at large. He was imperial Russia's last president of the council of ministers.

The vicissitudes of the presidency of the council epitomized the decay of the bureaucratic government. Of the ten ministers who were signatories of the appeal to the tsar in August, 1915, three were dismissed in September and October of that year and four in 1916; of the remaining three still in office in February, 1917—Bark, the minister of commerce and industry Prince V. N. Shakhovskoy, and Grigorovich —the former two owed their good fortune (if good fortune it was) to their friendship with Rasputin. The correspondence of Nicholas and Alexandra Fedorovna leaves no doubt that these and other changes in the government were due to her influence. With few exceptions the new ministers had the endorsement of the empress and Rasputin. Some of them maintained themselves in office for a few months, others merely for a few weeks. Changes in the cabinet were extraordinarily frequent, and were aptly described by the ultra-conservative deputy Purishkevich as the "ministerial leapfrog." Even Nicholas came to realize the consequences of his misdeeds. "All these changes make my head go round," he wrote in September, 1916; "in my opinion they are too frequent. In any case they are not good for the internal situation of the country, as each new man brings with him alterations in the administration." The names of shadowy office-holders lured by the illusory glamour of power need not be recorded here. It was a grotesque and sinister procession of nonentities and adventurers, pebbles—not milestones—on the road that led the monarchy to ruin. An exception, however, must be made in the case of A. D. Protopopov, an outsider in the bureaucratic circles of the capital. Protopopov was long connected with the zemstvos, belonged to the left wing of the Octobrist Party, was a member of the third and fourth Duma and its vice president since 1914. He was among the founders of the Progressive Bloc (about which more will be said below), and in the summer of 1916 he headed the Russian parliamentary delegation to the allied countries. Protopopov thus ranked high in liberal circles. His acceptance in September, 1916, of the office of minister of the interior under Sturmer, followed by revelations of his association with Rasputin and Madame Vyrubov, led to a breach with his former associates. Public feeling against Protopopov ran so high that it virtually ruled out the possibility of his appearance before the Duma over which he had so recently presided. Bitter attacks upon him in the Duma and in the press, his tenacious determination to remain in office, and the insecurity of his position appear to have unbalanced his mind. The progressive deterioration of his mental condition was noted by his colleagues in the government and is corroborated by the voluminous evidence he submitted to the committee of inquiry appointed after the fall of the monarchy. The odd ways of the minister who "jumps from one idea to another and cannot make up his mind on anything" did not escape his imperial master. In November, 1916, Nicholas decided to dismiss Protopopov; but the empress took up his defense, and a man verging on insanity remained at the head of the ministry of the interior until the revolution. His case gives the measure of the decadence of the bureaucratic system.

A bureaucratic government is inherently inflexible and finds it difficult to adapt itself to the demands of an emergency. It was this inability of the central authorities to cope with the problems raised by the war that primarily accounts for the greater freedom of action conceded to the institutions of local self-government. In Russia, as in other countries, the war generated a movement for national unity and a desire to put aside internal dissensions, at least until the struggle was over. In the case of the liberals this conciliatory attitude was motivated not only by nationalistic emotions but also by the vague belief that a war waged in alliance with the French and British democracies might well prove the forerunner of an era of constitutional and social reforms at home. The zemstvos were among the first to offer their services to the government. On July 30, 1914, the representatives of thirty-four provincial zemstvos met in Moscow and founded the All-Russian Union of Zemstvos for the Relief of Sick and Wounded Soldiers. All zemstvos, with the exception of the notoriously reactionary zemstvo of Kursk, joined the union, which was modeled on a similar organization established during the Russo-Japanese War. Prince G. E. Lvov, head of the 1904–1905 intra-zemstvo organization, was elected president of the union. Received by the tsar, he was assured of the whole-hearted cooperation of the government, a promise that was not fulfilled. The municipalities followed the example of the zemstvos and established the Union of Towns; characteristically, the imperial sanction (August 16) limited the existence of the union to the duration of the war. At first the two unions concerned themselves exclusively with the relief of the sick and wounded; they maintained hospital trains and built an extensive network of hospitals, canteens, and medical stores. Beginning with the summer of 1915, when the retreat of the Russian armies disclosed the inadequacy of war supplies, the unions participated in the drive for the mobilization of industry. This work of the unions was carried on chiefly through a joint committee "for the supply of the army," known by the abbreviated name of Zemgor. It took the form of assistance to the government in placing war orders, establishment of factories and plants, evacuation of industrial enterprises from areas menaced by the enemy, and shipment of supplies needed by the army in the field. The bulk of the vast sums spent by the unions came from the public treasury, only a small fraction of the funds they handled being raised directly by the zemstvos and municipalities. Although the work of the unions both in providing relief for war sufferers and in helping to overcome the supply crisis of 1915 was on the whole successful, it was not free from serious shortcomings. There was, perhaps inevitably, much waste and duplication of effort by other relief and supply agencies, and the accounting methods of the unions were notoriously loose. The unions, moreover, were the haven of draft-dodgers—the so-called "zem-hussars"—whose gaudy uniforms, ultra-martial bearing, and assiduous attendance at night clubs attracted some public attention and aroused amusement not unmixed with irritation. The fact that the unions, in spite of these shortcomings, enjoyed great popularity and commanded the allegiance of thousands of employees closely linked with the army and with provincial and rural Russia assured them a prominent place in the conflict between the government and the liberal opposition that developed in 1915 and 1916.

War is inimical to representative institutions and, even in countries with a deeply rooted parliamentary tradition, tends to curtail the control of the legislative over the executive. With the outbreak of hostilities the constitutional functions of the Duma, limited as they were, suffered further diminution. Under the Russian law the "war budget," which comprised the bulk of expenditure in wartime, was exempt from legislative control. Moreover, legislation under Article 87, that is, by "temporary" decrees subject to subsequent ratification by the chambers, received wide application. In the premiership of Goremykin (January, 1914, to January, 1916) no less than 384 measures were enacted by virtue of Article 87, some of them of questionable constitutional validity (for instance, the imposition of taxes). The Duma was thus *de facto* shorn of much of its lawmaking power and largely lost whatever degree of control it had formerly exercised over the public purse. These developments, together with the fact that the Duma, elected as it was on the basis of a highly restricted and selective franchise, was not a truly representative assembly, might well have justified the expectation that it would sink into utter insignificance. Events, however, followed a different course.

The Duma, convened for a one-day session on July 26 (August 8, N.S.), 1914, rode the wave of emotional patriotism and proclaimed its whole-hearted support of the government in the prosecution of the war. The only signs of dissent were the abstention of the Labor Group and the social democrats from voting war credits, and the resolution, proposed jointly by the Bolshevik and the Menshevik factions of the Social Democratic Party, which condemned war and the political and economic order that allegedly brought it about. However, like the socialist parties in western and central Europe, the Mensheviks and the Labor Group led by Alexander Kerensky, while disclaiming any imperialistic ambitions, agreed to cooperate with the government in waging a defensive war. The Bolsheviks alone took the intransigent position that the proletariat in every country should strive to defeat, not the opposing armies, but the bourgeois and imperialistic regime at home. In November, 1914, the five deputies constituting the Bolshevik faction in the Duma were arrested. They were tried, together with a few accomplices, by a civilian court on charges of subversive activities, found guilty, and sentenced to deportation to eastern Siberia (February, 1915). Contrary to the expectations of the authorities, the arrest and trial provoked hardly any protest among the workers. With the removal of the turbulent Bolshevik faction, cooperation between the Duma and the government appeared assured.

During the recess that followed the adjournment of July 26, the Duma did not disperse, but continued to function informally as a provisional committee for the relief of war sufferers. M. V. Rodzianko, president of the Duma, was chairman of the committee, which included all the deputies who happened to be in the capital. The committee met regularly, kept in close touch with the deputies in the province or serving with the forces, as well as with the Unions of Zemstvos and Towns, and gradually became the center not only for the exchange of war information but also for the discussion of political issues and the formulation of common policies. The three-day session of the Duma held at the end of January, 1915, was preceded by the appearance of the leading ministers before a private meeting of the budget committee. The attitude of cynical contempt and indifference displayed by Goremykin, Sukhomlinov's facile optimism, and the deliberate rudeness of N. A. Maklakov, minister of the interior, produced a painful impression in Duma circles. At the public session the pledges "to safeguard the moral unity of the nation" were renewed, but the reiteration of stereotyped patriotic slogans could not conceal the profound uneasiness felt by many deputies. The session of January, 1915, proved, indeed, the beginning of the parting of the ways which was soon to develop into a wide cleavage between the Duma and liberal opinion, on the one hand, and the Crown and officialdom, on the other. The informal program of liberal opinion (using "liberal" in the broadest meaning of the term) crystallized around four main issues: convocation of the Duma and its effective participation in the conduct of public affairs; removal of the particularly odious ministers; participation of the non-bureaucratic agencies in supplying the army; and "a government enjoying the confidence of the nation," a formula involving no constitutional changes but merely calling for the appointment to ministerial offices of men acceptable to liberal opinion. After the departure of the tsar for army headquarters in August, 1915, these issues were gradually merged with, and superseded by, that of the ascendancy of the empress and Rasputin.

In the spring and summer of 1915 the government took several halfhearted steps to placate the opposition. Four of the more unpopular ministers—Sukhomlinov, Shcheglovitov, Maklakov, and Sabler—were dismissed, but Goremykin continued in office. The Duma was convened on July 19 for a protracted session, and the non-bureaucratic agencies were at least permitted to participate in the work of supplying the army. The implementation of the policy of "mobilization of industry" adopted in the summer of 1915 was largely in the hands of three newly created institutions: the special councils, the war industries committees, and the already mentioned joint committee of the Unions of Zemstvos and of Towns (Zemgor). Legislation initiated in the Duma and enacted in August, 1915, provided for the establishment of five special councils—for national defense, transportation, fuel, food supply, and refugees. The object of the councils, which were given comprehensive powers, was the coordination of policies within their respective fields. Each council consisted of representatives of government departments, the legislative chambers, the Unions of Zemstvos and of Towns, and the central war industries committee. The establishment of the war industries committees, whose purpose was the self-mobilization of industry for national defense, was due to the initiative of business circles. The committees enjoyed a considerable degree of autonomy, their work being carried on with the approval of the government but not by its orders or under its control. The central war industries committee, with headquarters in Petrograd, directed the activities of an extensive network of provincial and local committees. Each committee consisted of representatives of government departments, the Unions of Zemstvos and of Towns, management, and labor. A. I. Guchkov, a former president of the Duma and a prominent business and political leader, was chairman of the central war industries committee. The work of the special councils, war industries committees, and the Zemgor—hasty improvisations in the midst of a great war—was lacking in coordination and has been much and deservedly criticized. Nevertheless these agencies had an important part in overcoming army supply shortages and opened to public initiative a new and fruitful field of activity.

The inclusion of representatives of labor in the war industries committees, a revolutionary departure from Russia's traditional administrative practice, caused a sharp disagreement within the Social Democratic Party. The Mensheviks favored participation, while the Bolsheviks opposed it on the ground that the proletariat must not support a bourgeois government engaged in an imperialistic war. These conflicting views were reflected in the results of the election of labor delegates. In September, 1915, the Bolsheviks succeeded in blocking the election of labor representatives to the central war industries committee, but the new election held in November reversed the decision; by May, 1916, labor was represented on some 120 local committees.

The military reverses of 1915 produced a strong movement of alarm and discontent which the paltry concessions to public opinion outlined above proved unable to quell. The retention of Goremykin at the head of the council of ministers was conclusive evidence that no real change of policy could be expected. Basic changes of policy, however, came to be looked upon as a *sine qua non* of a successful prosecution of the war; this theme, indeed, dominated the debates in the Duma, which reassembled in July, 1915. The demands of the parliamentary majority were formulated in the program of the Progressive Bloc, a parliamentary combination which included the deputies of six of the leading parties in the Duma (ranging from the "progressive nationalists" led by V. V. Shulgin, on the right, to the Constitutional Democratic Party, on the left), and the members of three of the less reactionary groups in the State Council. The program announced at the end of August, 1915, dwelt, in a preamble, on the necessity of a "united government consisting of persons who enjoy the confidence of the country and are in agreement with the legislative chambers as to the execution . . . of a definite program." The program aimed at the elimination of the "distrust of public initiative" that had hitherto governed official policies, and proposed to achieve this object by the strict enforcement of the rule of law, curtailment of the interference of the military with the civilian authorities, a change in the personnel of local administration, and removal of the more odious measures inspired by racial, religious, and class discrimination. More concretely, the program demanded amnesty for persons convicted, or deported without trial, on religious and political grounds; the repeal of discriminatory measures against Poles, Jews, Ukrainians, and religious minorities; non-intervention in the domestic affairs of Finland; repeal of anti-trade union regulations; removal of the legal disabilities attached to the status of a peasant; amendment of the zemstvo act of 1890 and the municipal government act of 1892, and extension of the field of local self-government.

The majority of the ministers were in agreement with the program, or at least regarded it as offering a basis for negotiations. Goremykin, however, took the position that a parliamentary combination including members of the two chambers was unconstitutional and that "its scarcely disguised purpose was the limitation of the powers of the monarch." After an audience with the empress he went to headquarters and secured an imperial order proroguing the Duma (September 3). This action was regarded in parliamentary circles as a deliberate provocation and spelled the end of all pretense at maintaining the fiction of a *union sacrée*. According to Rodzianko, some of the deputies went so far as to advocate open defiance of the prorogation order and urged the Duma to proclaim itself a constituent assembly. Negotiations between several of the ministers and the leaders of the Progressive Bloc were broken off, but public agitation continued. Demands similar to those advanced by the Progressive Bloc were forthcoming from many quarters—the Red Cross, the war industries committees, the Unions of Zemstvos and of Towns, and individual zemstvos and municipalities. The resolutions passed by some of these bodies went further than the Progressive Bloc, and called for a government not merely "enjoying the confidence of the nation" but one responsible to the Duma. The Progressive Bloc, even though it remained faithful to its moderate program and had among its members outspoken opponents of parliamentarianism (for instance, Kokovtsov, leader of one of the groups in the State Council affiliated with the Bloc), had unwittingly fostered the more radical demands. The multiplicity of political parties and the absence of a stable majority in the Duma were regarded as a serious obstacle to parliamentary government. With the formation of the Progressive Bloc this objection lost some of its force.

In the second half of 1915 and in 1916 the political situation rapidly deteriorated. Frequent changes among the ministers produced cabinets sadly at variance with a government "enjoying the confidence of the nation" for which public opinion was clamoring. To Alexandra Fedorovna the leaders of the opposition were traitors and the members of the Duma "impertinent brutes"; she wished Rodzianko could be hanged, urged the tsar to send Lvov, Gutchkov, Miliukov, and Polivanov to Siberia, and plotted the dissolution of the Duma and the abolition of the war industries committees and of the Unions of Zemstvos and of Towns.

Meanwhile the activities of Rasputin had become a matter of grave public concern, and soon overshadowed all other issues. Sturmer, Goremykin's successor, endeavored to obtain the assurance that Rasputin's name would not be mentioned from the rostrum of the Duma. Although his request was not granted, the Duma was convened, after a considerable delay, on February 6, 1916. On the opening day of the session Nicholas paid his first and only visit to the lower chamber. This step was instigated by Rasputin on the theory that the tsar's personal charm—an accepted dogma in court circles—would win over the deputies, but the results proved disappointing: by the time the Duma was prorogued on June 20 the Crown and the legislature had drifted further apart. On November 1 the Duma reassembled in a turbulent and angry mood. Miliukov bitterly attacked the regime and denounced the "dark forces" behind the throne, mentioning by name Alexandra Fedorovna and Sturmer as the leaders of the pro-German clique. He ended each peroration with the question: "Is this stupidity or is this treason?" Miliukov subsequently explained that he favored the former interpretation, but public opinion inclined to accept the latter. The speech created a sensation and forced the dismissal of Sturmer (November 10), but otherwise the situation remained unchanged. A few days later the ultra-conservative deputy Purishkevich delivered in the Duma a passionate oration directed against Rasputin and his associates. He wound up with a dramatic appeal to the ministers "to throw themselves at the feet of the emperor, and beg him to believe in all the horror of Rasputin's influence." Although both speeches were suppressed by the censorship, they were circulated in thousands of mimeographed and typewritten copies and were widely read.

The November debate, of which the Miliukov and Purishkevich speeches were the high-lights, expressed accurately the fears and aspirations of the upper and the middle class, and added greatly to the moral stature of the Duma. Appeals to the tsar to put an end to irresponsible influences and to reach an understanding with the Duma came not only from institutions and personalities identified with the opposition but also from the British ambassador and such conservative groups as the members of the imperial family, the State Council, and the Council of the United Nobility. Nicholas refused to be moved. His obstinacy drove some of the conservative Russians to the conclusion that the elimination of Rasputin and, perhaps, of Alexandra Fedorovna and even of the emperor himself might well prove the only way to save the dynasty. There was much inconsequential talk about schemes for a palace revolution in the manner of the eighteenth century. Finally a conspiracy to murder Rasputin was organized by Purishkevich, the Grand Duke Dimitry Pavlovich (a nephew of the tsar), and Prince Felix Yusupov, who was related by marriage to the imperial family. Rasputin was induced to take poison, and when it failed to work he was shot dead in the palace of Prince Yusupov on December 17, 1916. His body was recovered from under the ice, where it was thrown by the conspirators, and was secretly buried in the grounds of the imperial residence in the presence of the emperor, the empress, and their children. No legal action was taken against the participants in the murder, although Yusupov was exiled to his estate and Dimitry Pavlovich was sent to the Persian front. The disappearance of Rasputin was greeted with a general feeling of relief, but it had no appreciable effect upon the course of domestic policies and brought no relaxation of the political tension.

SOCIAL UNREST

The Rasputin epic was an element in the making of the revolution of 1917. It did untold damage to the prestige of the monarchy, and alienated from the throne the very social groups upon which the Crown might otherwise have relied. Nevertheless, the importance of Rasputin as a factor in the revolution has been grossly exaggerated. The educated Russians who took an interest in politics, read newspapers, and understood what they read were a tiny minority in the midst of the amorphous, inarticulate millions of the illiterate and half-literate peasants. Moreover, many of the intellectuals favored social revolution and were out of sympathy with programs of moderate reforms such as those sponsored by the Progressive Bloc. Because of the restricted franchise and the manipulation of elections by the ministry of the interior, the State Duma and the institutions of local self-government were not representative of the true feeling of the country. The handful of left-wing deputies in the Duma commanded a much larger following than is indicated by their number. The influence of what I have called the liberal opposition, a vocal and fairly well organized political group, should not be underestimated; yet the fact remains that it was numerically weak and was hopelessly out of touch with the masses, which were incapable of even understanding the issues so passionately debated on the floor of the Duma. If Alexandra Fedorovna was disliked by the common people, it was not because of her association with Rasputin or her interference with the affairs of state but because she was German and therefore suspected—contrary to all available evidence—of favoring the enemy. The true causes of the revolution must be sought not in the aberrations of the empress and the Rasputin extravaganza, grave as were some of their consequences, but in the inequities of Russia's political, social, and economic structure and in the additional burden thrust upon the country by the exigencies of a great war. Rasputin was a symptom, not the cause, of a pathological condition that led the monarchy to its doom.

The breakdown of national morale came about gradually. The nationalistic and patriotic emotions that swayed the Duma at the session of July, 1914, were shared at the time, in some degree, by every social group. Large pro-Serbian and anti-Austrian and anti-German crowds gathered in the streets and, in St. Petersburg, looted the German embassy. Mobilization was carried out in an unexpectedly orderly manner, and cases of draft evasion were few. The strike movement, which in the summer of 1914 had reached the highest point since 1905–1906, collapsed. The country appeared to be solidly behind its leaders and determined to fight the war to a victorious end. This heartening picture of the nation united in a great common cause began almost immediately to fade away. The process of social disintegration that set in and gained momentum as months went by must be viewed against the background of discord, bitterness, and lack of national unity that had accumulated for generations. The immediate causes of the mounting discontent and disaffection were military reverses, the heavy losses suffered by the army, the plight of the refugees, economic disorders, administrative chaos, and general weariness with a war whose object was not understood and, perhaps, could not be satisfactorily explained. The Duma spoke with authority for the majority of the upper and the middle class; labor and the peasantry, however, took little interest in politics, and their increasing restlessness was due primarily to economic hardships and a longing for peace.

Causes for grumbling and legitimate complaints were not lacking. Spiralling prices, shortages, lines in front of food shops, and overcrowding imposed a severe strain upon the urban population, especially its poorer section. Although the monetary wages of industrial workers increased appreciably during the war, they lagged behind the rise in the cost of living, with the result that, with the exception of the higher-paid workers in war industries, real wages in 1915 and 1916 declined from the already low prewar level. The position of the families of workers drafted into the army was truly desperate because separation allowances paid by the government were calculated merely to provide nutrition, and made no provision for other expenditures (lodging, fuel, clothing, and so on). The changing mood of labor was evidenced by the resurgence of the strike movement. After the outbreak of the war Russia enjoyed a brief period of almost undisturbed industrial peace. The situation, however, underwent a change in the spring of 1915. Over 1,000 strikes involving 553,000 workers occurred in that year, and 1,400 strikes involving 1,086,000 workers in 1916; the strike movement was further intensified in January and February, 1917. This was a disturbing development, even though the number of both strikes and strikers was still considerably below the respective figures for January to July, 1914 (4,000 and 1,449,000), when the total number of workers was smaller by some 400,000 than in 1916. Moreover, prewar strikes were predominantly "political," that is, they had objectives other than the advancement of the economic welfare of the workers, while wartime strikes, according to M. G. Fleer, the Soviet historian of the labor movement, were spontaneous, free from trade-union leadership, and inspired chiefly by economic motives. The one exception was the strikes of the relatively highly-paid metalworkers, who had been traditionally in the front rank of class-conscious, politically-minded militant labor. The authorities dealt sternly with labor disturbances, especially in industries working for national defense. Strikers of military age were drafted into the army and either sent to the front or retained at their jobs, no longer as "free" workmen, but as soldiers subject to military discipline. The government might have derived some comfort from the fact that industrial workers participated, through duly elected representatives, in the war industries committees. The official attitude towards organized labor, however, was one of mistrust, dislike, and suspicion, as illustrated by the case of the labor group on the central war industries committee. With the connivance of the authorities, an agent of the security police, Abrosimov, was elected a labor representative to that body, and early in 1917 the entire labor delegation was arrested, it would seem without good reason, by the mentally unbalanced Protopopov.

Economically, the farmers would seem to have fared somewhat better than the industrial workers. As related elsewhere in this chapter, the area cultivated by the peasants was extended during the war. Savings due to prohibition, allowances to the families of service men, and receipts for requisitioned livestock and the like are said to have increased the average real income of a peasant family by some 18 per cent. It is also held that the peasant establishment being largely self-sufficient, the rural community was less severely affected by the rise of commodity prices than was the urban population. Even if these optimistic assertions are correct—and one cannot be overcautious in dealing with Russian income statistics—the peasants failed to realize their blessings and, moreover, had valid reasons for restlessness and discontent. Russia's total casualties in World War I were officially estimated at slightly over 7 million men; included in this figure were 644,000 dead, 2,589,000 wounded, and 3,638,000 prisoners of war and missing. The peasants, who bore the brunt of these huge losses, never understood the purpose of the war, and after the excitement of the opening weeks of the struggle was over showed disinclination to continue the sacrifices. In the summer of 1915 Prince Shcherbatov, the minister of the interior, informed the council of ministers that "the calling of new classes is becoming more and more difficult. The police are unable to deal with the large number of men who are trying to evade military service. Men are hiding in the woods and in the fields." The minister expressed the fear that if new classes of the reserve were called the government "would not get a single man" unless—and this was an unwarranted assumption characteristic of the upper-class approach—the draft were sanctioned by the Duma. Observers in close touch with the rural community, moreover, did not share the optimistic conclusions quoted above concerning the effects of the war upon the peasantry. According to a secret report by the state police department, a document of unusual astuteness and foresight that was prepared in October, 1916, and published subsequently by the Soviet government, "the high cost of living is felt in the villages as keenly as in the towns; and here it is accompanied by rumors even more extravagant than those circulated in the cities. . . . The attitude of rural Russia towards the war has been negative from the very beginning because, more than the cities and towns, it felt the departure of mobilized men. Now it has lost all faith in the successful issue of the war. . . . Everybody is impatiently waiting for the end of this 'damned war.' . . . There is a marked increase in hostile feelings among the peasants not only against the government but also against all other social groups." Even if some of the premises on which the authors of the report based their conclusions are questionable (for instance, the assertion that the rural community was more adversely affected by the war than were the cities), the general picture of the attitude of the peasants presented in the report is judicious and true to facts.

A modern conscript army is a cross section of the population. In Russia it was, of necessity, a peasant army connected by innumerable intimate ties with the rural community and sharing its sorrows, forebodings, and hopes. The peasant soldier had even more compelling reasons than the peasant farmer to look askance at the war. The low educational standards of the masses made the rank and file of the army singularly unresponsive to the idea of sacrifice for a common cause, and the general trend of events at the front and in the rear— the almost unrelieved record of defeats, staggering losses, poor leadership, and shortages of arms, munitions, and equipment—did nothing to improve the morale of the troops. This statement does not imply that Russian soldiers never fought well but rather that they were poorly equipped to withstand the strain of adversity which was their lot. Signs of demoralization became apparent during the early stage of the campaign. In December, 1914, the chief of staff, Ianushkevich, wrote privately to Sukhomlinov of "mass surrender to the enemy . . . sometime on the initiative of wartime officers." "A Tambov peasant is willing to defend the province of Tambov, but a war for Poland, in his opinion, is foreign and useless," Ianushkevich wrote in July, 1915, to Krivoshein, the minister of agriculture. "The soldiers therefore surrender en masse." The chief of staff proposed an announcement to the effect that soldiers who have suffered disablement or have given proof of exceptional courage would be rewarded with land grants, while the land of those who surrendered to the enemy would be confiscated. A few days later the minister of war, Polivanov, told the council of ministers that "the army is no longer retreating but simply fleeing. . . . The slightest rumor about the enemy, the appearance of an insignificant German detachment leads to panic and the flight of whole regiments." Polivanov put his faith "in immeasurable distances, impassable roads, and the mercy of St. Nicholas, patron of Holy Russia." The report of the state police department (October, 1916) referred to above quotes with approval the following statement of an official of the Union of Zemstvos: "Every one who has approached the army cannot but carry away the belief that complete demoralization is in progress. The soldiers began to demand peace a long time ago, but never was this done so openly and with such force as now. The officers not infrequently refuse to lead their units against the enemy because they are afraid of being killed by their own men." General V. J. Selivachev, commander of the seventh army, put the matter in a nutshell when he wrote in his diary on March 10, 1917, "I am firmly convinced that the common soldier today wants only one thing—food and peace, because he is tired of the war." The defeatist spirit of the country and of the army was fatal to the imperial government, engaged, as it was, in a major war. The obstinate refusal to acknowledge the real mood of the nation and to draw from it the inevitable conclusions proved equally fatal to the Provisional Government which succeeded the tsar in 1917.

The rising tide of discontent and disaffection was a spontaneous movement surprisingly free from leadership by the revolutionary parties. The police repressions that followed the strikes of June and July, 1914, all but wiped out the underground revolutionary organizations. It was not until the end of 1915 that the central committee of the Bolshevik faction of the Social Democratic Party began to function again in St. Petersburg, and then on a greatly reduced scale. Its activities were limited to the surreptitious printing of proclamations which were circulated in a small number of copies. The arrest and trial of the Bolshevik faction of the Duma failed to arouse the working class, nor did the Bolsheviks succeed in their attempt to prevent the election of labor representatives to the war industries committees. The future revolutionary leaders were far away from the Russian capital. Lenin was in Switzerland, Stalin in Siberia; Trotsky, after being expelled from several European countries, finally landed in New York and found a temporary haven in the congenial surroundings of the Bronx. Yet if the organized revolutionary movement was emasculated and practically dormant, thousands of its members and sympathizers were scattered throughout the army and the various wartime organizations, which offered them ample opportunity for revolutionary propaganda. If their efforts succeeded beyond all expectations, it was neither because of their astuteness and skill, nor because of a revolutionary master plan devised by Lenin, but because of the deterioration of the general situation which the imperial government was incapable of preventing and to which, indeed, it had greatly contributed.

CHAPTER XLV

THE TWO REVOLUTIONS OF 1917: I

THE FALL OF THE MONARCHY

For all the talk about the imminence of the revolution, its timing, scope, and the character it assumed took every one by surprise. In the opening weeks of 1917 the excitement created by the murder of Rasputin subsided. The interallied conference held in Petrograd completed plans for the 1917 military campaign and adjourned on February 8 (February 21, N.S.). The Duma was convoked on February 14, and on the 22 the emperor left Tsarskoe Selo for army headquarters in Mogilev. On the surface everything was peaceful and normal. On February 23, however, serious disturbances broke out in Petrograd. Originating, apparently, in lines of disgruntled householders waiting in front of food shops, they spread rapidly to the working suburbs and overflowed into, and then submerged, the central thoroughfares and squares of the capital. At first the police and the troops had the situation well in hand, and in the evening of February 25 the emperor, encouraged by optimistic reports, telegraphed to General S. S. Khabalov, commanding officer of the Petrograd garrison, that "disorders in the capital must be stopped tomorrow." This order could not be carried out. On the contrary, street demonstrations grew in violence, crowds were in an increasingly ugly mood, there were frequent encounters with the police, and police stations and other public buildings were set aflame. Isolated instances of defection among the troops occurred on the 26, and by the evening of the 27 the bulk of the garrison had gone over to the insurgents. The fate of the empire was sealed.

The Duma was prorogued in the evening of the 26 but, after some hesitation, decided to remain informally in session and on February 27 elected a provisional committee which consisted of the leaders of the Progressive Bloc with the addition of representatives of left-wing factions: A. F. Kerensky (Labor Group) and N. S. Chkheidze (social democrats). The committee was given the loosely worded mandate "to restore order and to deal with institutions and individuals." On the same day (February 27) there was organized in the Taurida Palace, seat of the Duma, the Petrograd Soviet (Council) of Workers' Deputies which on March 2 changed its name to that of Soviet of Workers' and Soldiers' Deputies. Thus even before the abolition of the empire the Taurida Palace, its stately halls overrun by disheveled and unruly mobs, became the center of the new revolutionary authority and the focal point upon which converged seemingly endless columns of excited soldiers and civilians. The imperial administration collapsed; by the evening of February 28 most of the ministers and many high officials of the fallen regime were under arrest in the Taurida Palace. In the great national emergency it was to the Duma that many Russians turned for the direction and leadership that would restore order out of chaos and perhaps usher in the new era of liberty and social justice. Unexpectedly and illogically, the conservative fourth Duma crested for a few days the tidal wave of the revolution.

As the crisis developed, the president of the Duma, Rodzianko, a wealthy landowning aristocrat and an official of the imperial court, begged the tsar, first, to grant a representative government and, later, to abdicate. Nicholas, however, bided his time and postponed decisions until his return to the capital. In the night of February 28 the imperial train left Mogilev for Petrograd but was prevented from reaching its destination and was re-routed to Pskov, headquarters of General N. V. Ruzsky, commander of the northern front. The chief of staff General Alekseev and the commanding officers of the various army groups, including the Grand Duke Nicholas Nikolaevich, joined Rodzianko in urging the emperor to abdicate in favor of his son, with the tsar's brother, the Grand Duke Michael Alexandrovich, as regent. The attempt of Rodzianko to meet the emperor at Pskov was frustrated by the opposition of the Soviet, but the provisional committee of the Duma succeeded in sending to headquarters two of its members, Guchkov and V. V. Shulgin. Both were supporters of the monarchy, although Guchkov, it will be remembered, was a severe critic of Nicholas and Alexandra Fedorovna. It was still believed in many quarters that the abdication of the tsar, which the emissaries of the Duma were to secure, might save the dynasty. In the afternoon of March 2 Nicholas decided to abdicate in favor of Alexis, and signed documents to this effect, but by the time Guchkov and Shulgin reached Pskov in the evening of the same day he had changed his mind and, pleading the inability to part with his son, abdicated in favor of Michael Alexandrovich. Throughout the ordeal Nicholas preserved almost inhuman composure and self-control. On March 3, on the train which bore him into captivity and to his eventual doom, he wrote in his diary: "I had a long and sound sleep. Woke up beyond Dvinsk. Sunshine and frost. . . . I read much of Julius Caesar."

Meanwhile the revolutionary situation in Petrograd moved towards a climax and called for a far more drastic solution than that envisaged in liberal, army, and court circles. The Soviet was clearly determined to play a major part in shaping the structure and policies of the new Russian state. On March 2, after laborious negotiations with the Executive Committee of the Soviet, the provisional committee of the Duma announced the formation of a Provisional Government. It became evident in the course of that day that the establishment of a constitutional monarchy was no longer feasible. Miliukov's reference, at a meeting in the Taurida Palace (March 2), to the impending accession of Alexis and the regency of Michael provoked a storm of protests, and Guchkov, on his return from Pskov in the morning of March 3, was detained for a time by railway men hostile to the retention of monarchical government. A few hours later the Grand Duke Michael, after consultation with the Provisional Government and the provisional committee of the Duma, declined the Crown unless it was proffered by the Constituent Assembly, and urged all citizens to rally round the Provisional Government pending the convocation of the Constituent Assembly which was to determine Russia's future political organization. This was an untoward development which the liberals had not foreseen or desired; their dream of a constitutional monarchy, with a boy emperor on the throne and an insignificant and effaced grand duke as regent, faded away. The continuity of the historical tradition was broken. The Provisional Government, a purely revolutionary institution, although begotten by a conservative Duma, was forced into the position of the supreme organ of state authority; it was, moreover, committed to the convocation of a Constituent Assembly, a hazardous venture in the midst of a great war and in a country whose population was largely illiterate and ignorant of democratic methods.

The overthrow, or rather collapse, of the monarchy was accomplished with remarkable ease, even though the number of victims (killed, wounded, and injured) in Petrograd was officially estimated at 1,500. According to General Denikin, only two generals offered to the tsar their services for the suppression of the revolution. The solitary attempt to use combat troops against the insurgents—the sending from Mogilev to Tsarskoe Selo of two battalions of the "Knights of St. George" (Russia's highest military decoration) under the command of General N. I. Ivanov, as spearhead of divisions to be taken from the front—came to naught. The *coup d'état* was carried out by soldiers and populace of the capital. The rest of the country and the army had no direct part in the revolution but accepted it without protest, some with enthusiasm and high hope, others with foreboding and fear, but all with the recognition of its inevitability.

THE PROVISIONAL GOVERNMENT

The Provisional Government of March 2 was the embodiment of that "government enjoying public confidence" which liberal opinion had so long demanded. With few exceptions—Kerensky, M. I. Tereshchenko, N. V. Nekrasov—the new ministers were the very men whose names appeared in the tentative lists of future liberal cabinets circulated in Duma and zemstvo circles prior to the fall of the monarchy. It was a bitter irony of the revolution that the members of the Provisional Government not only proved mediocre statesmen—they would probably have done better under conditions less chaotic—but that they also lacked public support outside the tiny group of the educated upper and middle classes. And it was Kerensky, Tereshchenko, and Nekrasov who remained longest in office, even though it was merely for a few months.

Prince G. E. Lvov, minister of the interior and president of the first Provisional Government, belonged to an ancient aristocratic family. He had worked hard in his youth to restore failing family fortunes, was a wealthy landowner, and a well known zemstvo leader. In 1906, after the dissolution of the first Duma, of which he was an inconspicuous member, he was consulted by Stolypin in the abortive attempt to form a liberal cabinet. Prince Lvov's popularity during the First World War was due to his leadership of the Union of Zemstvos and also, perhaps, to the simplicity and kindliness of his manner, which endeared him to those who worked under him or had the opportunity to deal with him (and their number was large during the war). A lukewarm member of the Constitutional Democratic Party,[1] Prince Lvov was a zealous social reformer; in England he would have been a right-wing Fabian, and in the United States of the 1930's a remorseless New Dealer. A Russian to the core, however, he had leanings towards slavophile doctrines and had an unshakable faith in the "Russian soul" (about which he talked far too much) and the goodness and wisdom of the Russian people. In the light of his 1917 record his pre-revolutionary reputation as an outstanding administrator may appear incomprehensible. According to his biographer and lifelong friend, T. I. Polner, however, Prince Lvov had a genius for administrative improvisations, coupled with aversion for formal administrative schemes. His imaginative approach is said to have served him and Russia well under the conditions of war emergency, but it was a handicap for a prime minister and minister of the interior called upon to restore a semblance of order in the midst of revolutionary chaos.

The philosophy of the head of the Provisional Government is well illustrated by his statement to the press early in March, 1917. "We must not shut our eyes to the difficulties and dangers of the situation," said Prince Lvov. "The newly born freedom will encounter great and, perhaps, exacting trials; but I face the future with confidence. I believe in the inherent strength and wisdom of our great people which has proved its greatness by the powerful thrust towards freedom that overthrew the old regime. It will prove it again by the determined wholehearted effort to implement the principles of liberty and to defend them against external and internal enemies. I believe in the great heart of the Russian people filled with love for fellow men; I believe in this fountain of truth, verity, and freedom. It will assert the full measure of its glory, and the rest will take care of itself." The grim realities of the revolution, however, at times shook even Lvov's optimism. On April 25 he told General A. N. Kuropatkin that the revolution had gone much further than had been expected and that the government had no control over the situation. "We are tossed about," he said, "like flotsam on a stormy sea." Yet two days later (April 27), in an address before a joint session of the four Dumas, Lvov was again in an optimistic and lyrical mood. "The great Russian revolution is truly marvelous in its majestic, undisturbed progress . . . ," he said. "What is

---

[1] After the dissolution of the first Duma, Lvov attended the gathering of liberal leaders in Viborg but was one of the few party members, if not the only one, present who refused to sign the appeal. See p. 1192.

marvelous about it . . . is the kernel of its leading idea. The freedom of the Russian revolution is impregnated with elements of universality, catholicism. . . . The soul of the Russian people has proved to be, by its very nature, the universal democratic soul. It is ready not only to merge with the democracy of the entire world, but to take its place ahead of it and to lead it along the path of human progress inspired by the great principles of freedom, equality, and brotherhood." And again in the same address: "We can consider ourselves the happiest of men; our generation is fated to live in the happiest period of Russian history. . . ." It would be probably an error to dismiss this and similar statements as mere official verbiage. They expressed Lvov's most sacred beliefs, and it was between the extremes of romantic exaltation and bleak despondency that the overworked, harassed, and physically exhausted head of the Provisional Government swung uneasily until, a broken and prematurely aged man, he terminated his public career by resigning in July, 1917.

Miliukov, the minister of foreign affairs, and Guchkov, the minister of war and navy, ranked high, like Prince Lvov, among the leaders of the liberal opposition, and were apparently exceptionally well qualified for their respective offices. Miliukov, head of the Constitutional Democratic Party since its inception in 1905, was a historian of international repute and the Duma's chief opposition spokesman on foreign affairs. Guchkov, founder and leader of the Octobrist Party and chairman of the central way industries committee, had won a national reputation as an authority on military matters, and was instrumental in the removal from office and indictment of the minister of war Sukhomlinov. Miliukov was dogmatic, logical, imperturbable, and stubborn; Guchkov was reputedly a man of action.[2] Both were relentless critics of Nicholas, Alexandra Fedorovna, and the Rasputin regime, and both were cordially detested at court; yet at the fateful meeting in

[2] Born in 1862 into a family of wealthy Moscow merchants, Guchkov was prominent in business as well as in municipal and national affairs. A supporter of Stolypin's national program, he was elected president of the third Duma in 1908 but resigned in March, 1911, as a protest against the prorogation order by Stolypin to allow the enactment of the western zemstvos legislation (see p. 1194). Guchkov was the stormy petrel of Russian politics. He went to Asia Minor during the Armenian massacres, fought against the British in the Boer War, had a hand in the Macedonian uprising of 1903, headed the Russian Red Cross in the Russo-Japanese War, and was made prisoner at Mukden. At home he was frequently involved in sharp conflicts with political opponents, once challenged Miliukov to a duel, and fought another duel for which he served a brief prison sentence.

the afternoon of March 3 Miliukov and Guchkov were the only ones to urge the Grand Duke Michael to accept the throne. They were also the first ministers to be dropped by the Provisional Government. The effervescence of their ministerial career—merely eight or nine weeks— was additional evidence of the inability of liberal opinion to interpret correctly the mood of the masses.

Most of the other ministers of the Provisional Government were also well known public figures, but they left no imprint on the course of events and their names need not be recorded here. Some of the ministerial appointments, however, were unexpected and, presumably, were due to accident. The provisional committee of the Duma which, jointly with the representatives of the Soviet, selected the ministers worked under terrific pressure; its members had no proper sleep or food for days and were mercilessly buffeted by the revolutionary throngs that had taken possession of the Taurida Palace. A government had to be formed, and time was pressing; a casual nomination which met with no determined opposition had a chance to slip through. This probably explains how M. T. Tereshchenko became minister of finance and N. V. Nekrasov minister of transport. Tereshchenko, reputedly one of the richest men in Russia, was young, well groomed, and good company; he was chairman of the Kiev war industries committee but had never been thought of as candidate for high public office. This statement holds true of Nekrasov, a little-known member of the Constitutional Democratic Party and for a brief time vice president of the fourth Duma. If Tereshchenko and Nekrasov remained in the government longer than their more illustrious colleagues, it was because they hooked their wagon to the rapidly rising star of Alexander Kerensky, another newcomer in the broad political arena whose name had never appeared in the pre-revolutionary lists of cabinets "enjoying public confidence." The inclusion of Kerensky in the Provisional Government, however, was no accident.

A lawyer looking surprisingly young for his middle thirties (he was born in 1881), Kerensky was a deputy to the fourth Duma, where he led the Labor Group, a small radical faction of non-Marxian persuasion. He had attracted some notice as a left-wing politician and defense counsel in political trials, but had largely remained in the margin both of the liberal and of the revolutionary movements and prior to February, 1917, was not regarded as a prominent political figure. Trotsky, an acute but unfriendly critic, speaks contemptuously

The Two Revolutions of 1917: I

of Kerensky as not a revolutionary but a "hanger-on of the revolution" lacking "theoretical training, political schooling, capacity to think in general terms, and political will." This characterization is unfair and does not explain Kerensky's meteoric ascendancy. If sublimation of the revolution, and that particular type of imagination which transforms mutinous soldiers and rebellious workmen into standard-bearers of the new order, are prerequisites of a revolutionary, Kerensky was a revolutionary par excellence. Unlike most of his colleagues, he was in his element in the midst of the milling throngs that swept through the Taurida Palace; seemingly dominating the events, he displayed determination and authority born of a fervent belief in the righteousness of the revolution and the glorious future it opened before the nation. His passionate oratory was not, perhaps, of a very high order and, as Trotsky rightly notes, appealed to emotions rather than to intelligence and will, but it reached his audiences and for a time proved extraordinarily effective.

Shulgin has traced in his memoirs a vivid picture of the contrast between the mood of despondency and despair of most of the Duma members (including Chkheidze, leader of the Social Democratic Party), on the one hand, and the theatrical, erratic, but relentless and triumphant activities of Kerensky, on the other. Kerensky welcomed regiments which came to swear allegiance to the Duma, addressed impromptu meetings, issued peremptory orders, arrested dignitaries of the imperial regime; "pallid and with an outstretched arm" he cut through the crowds "like the flaming torch of revolutionary justice" to wrest from the hands of an infuriated soldiery Protopopov and Sukhomlinov: deserved punishments would be meted out to the enemies of the people, but the revolution must not be desecrated by lynching. His burning faith in the greatness of the cause had a magnetic effect upon the masses. A Soviet chronicle of the events of 1917 (published in 1924) notes that when Kerensky "exclaimed with inimitable passion, 'I am sent by the revolution,' 'I am empowered by the revolution,' and so on, no one doubted the truth of his words." N. N. Sukhanov, a left-wing social democrat and a member of the Executive Committee of the Soviet, shrewdly observes that Kerensky "had the conviction of his special mission . . . and was highly irritated by those who failed to perceive its existence." Closely affiliated with the Socialist Revolutionary Party, which he joined after the revolution, Kerensky was influenced by the populist tradition and, not unlike Prince Lvov, never tired of extolling the virtues of the "Russian soul." The two messianic elements—personal and national—blended into a heartening, although somewhat shapeless, creed which was well within the grasp of the masses.[3] Whatever the reason, within a few days—indeed, a few hours—after the outbreak of the revolution Kerensky rose from relative obscurity to a position of undisputed leadership. A government without him was unthinkable. Moreover, as vice chairman of the Soviet, Kerensky was the only link between what came to be known as "revolutionary democracy" (that is, the Soviets) and the "bourgeois" Provisional Government in which he was minister of justice. Chkheidze, chairman of the Soviet, was offered the ministry of labor but declined. Kerensky, in a phrase which he seemed to like, was thus "the hostage of democracy" in the camp of the bourgeoisie. His nationalistic and patriotic exaltation and his opposition to Bolshevism notwithstanding, Kerensky—emotionally and by training—belonged to the left, an attitude that had a bearing on the course of events.

The fact that the Provisional Government was formed by the Duma, consisted predominantly of well known public figures, and included but one socialist, gave the revolution an appearance of moderation and respectability. It became almost immediately clear, however, that real authority rested, not with the Provisional Government, but with the Soviet of Workers' and Soldiers' Deputies.

THE SOVIETS

If the Provisional Government had no basis in constitutional law and was unrepresentative of the true feelings of the country, the origins and complexion of its formidable opponent, the Petrograd Soviet of Workers' and Soldiers' Deputies, were even less impressive from the standpoint of both theory and practice of democratic government. The initiative in summoning the Petrograd Soviet cannot be traced to any individual or organized group, but the idea of reviving the 1905 revolutionary assembly would seem to have occurred more or less simultaneously to a number of radical intellectuals and labor leaders. In the afternoon of February 27, when the mutiny of the

---

[3] Kerensky's book *The Catastrophe*, published ten years after the fall of the Provisional Government (London, 1927), and his subsequent pronouncements and activities as an *émigré* in Europe and the United States indicate that he has lost none of his faith and illusions.

Petrograd garrison was in full swing, left-wing members of the Duma, political prisoners just released from incarceration (among them some of the labor representatives on the central war industries committee only recently arrested by Protopopov), and a motley assortment of professional men (journalists, doctors, lawyers, zemstvo employees, and so on) foregathered in the Taurida Palace and set up the provisional Executive Committee of the still non-existent Petrograd Soviet. In the evening of the same day the first plenary session of the Soviet —a large, tumultuous assembly of uncertain provenance—was held at the Taurida Palace and confirmed the Executive Committee. None of the participants in this haphazard gathering, nor indeed any one else, realized at the time that the birth of the Petrograd Soviet was to prove a turning point in the history of Russia and of the world.

Information on the mechanics of elections to the early Soviets is scarce and fragmentary. It was clearly impossible to devise an orderly and uniform electoral procedure in the hectic days of February and March, but even later, after a scheme of representation in the Soviets was officially adopted, the situation remained chaotic. On March 3 the Petrograd Soviet had 1,300 members, a week later nearly 3,000; of that number 800 represented factory workers and the balance army units. The disproportion was all the more striking because in Petrograd workers by far outnumbered soldiers. Rules approved by the Petrograd Soviet on March 18 provided for one deputy for each 2,000 of either workers or soldiers, a measure designed to reduce the assembly to a manageable size and to restore the balance between the two elements represented in the Soviets, but these regulations were honored more in the breach than in the observance. Trotsky, the proud father of the 1905 Soviet, notes that in 1917 the Soviets in Petrograd and elsewhere comprised "numerous casual intruders, adventurers, impostors, and talkers used to the tribune," who represented "various problematic groups and, as often as not, but their own ambitions." The Taurida Palace was unable to accommodate the huge assembly, and the plenary sessions of the Soviet were transferred, first, to the Mikhailovsky Theater (formerly the home of the Italian Opera and of a French dramatic company) and, later, to the Naval Academy. The membership of the Soviet was highly fluid, its jurisdiction was undefined, it had no fixed rules of procedure, and the bulk of its members were possessed with an irresistible desire to talk; the usefulness of the Soviet as an effective organ of administration and control, therefore, was limited and its business was actually transacted by the Executive Committee, or, more precisely, by a group of leaders within that body.

The Executive Committee, formed on February 27, had fourteen members. Its chairman, Chkheidze, and one of the two vice chairmen, M. I. Skobelev, were Mensheviks; Kerensky was the other vice chairman. During March the membership of the committee rose to nearly forty by the addition of representatives of various socialist and revolutionary groups. The first conference of the Soviets (March 29 to April 2) reorganized the Executive Committee by adding to it delegates from provincial and army Soviets. The enlarged committee thus assumed the character of a national institution, but its membership of ninety proved unwieldy and led to the formation of a permanent bureau of twenty-four members, the actual managing board of the Soviet. The first congress of the Soviets, which was held in June, formally established a national executive agency by electing the All-Russian Central Executive Committee, an assembly of over 250 members which, however, was dominated by the leaders of the Petrograd Soviet.

The example of the capital was emulated throughout the country. Soviets of various types were rapidly set up, and by the end of August their number was officially estimated as 600, representing theoretically some 23 million voters. The complexion, jurisdiction, and methods of local Soviets were, if possible, even more casual and haphazard than those of the Petrograd Soviet, yet their authority was great, not perhaps because of the whole-hearted support of the masses but because of the disintegration of state authority. Local Soviets played an important part in dealing with local situations and as agencies for carrying out directives from the center, but they made no significant contribution to the shaping of national policies, which were determined by a small group of leaders at the head of, first, the Petrograd Executive Committee and, later, the All-Russian Central Executive Committee.

In the early weeks of the revolution the social democrats (both Menshevik and Bolshevik) and the socialist revolutionaries who controlled the Petrograd Executive Committee shared the belief that a degree of cooperation between socialist and liberal forces was essential to prevent the restoration of the old regime; and, as has already been stated, the Provisional Government, which was to include two representatives of the Soviet (Chkheidze and Kerensky), was formed by the provisional committee of the Duma after consultation with, and with the approval of, the Executive Committee. A plenary session of the Soviet held in the morning of March 2 repudiated the agreement, however, and the Executive Committee, reversing itself, passed a resolution prohibiting socialists from serving in a bourgeois cabinet. Chkheidze bowed to this decision, but Kerensky's passionate appeal to the plenary session of the Soviet resulted in the approval, by acclamation, of his participation in the Provisional Government. The interdict of the Executive Committee was not rescinded, yet Kerensky remained both minister of justice and vice chairman of the Executive Committee.

At the time of its inception and, indeed, for weeks to come the Soviet showed no intention of superseding the Provisional Government. The slogan "All power to the Soviets" was coined early in March by the garrison of the Kronstadt naval base. At first it met with little response in the capital, although the Bolshevik's *Pravda*, which resumed publication on March 5, denounced in its early issues the Provisional Government as a "government of capitalists and landowners" and called for a "democratic republic" to be established by the Constituent Assembly. With the return to Petrograd of a group of exiled Bolshevik leaders in the middle of March, these attacks became less virulent. The attitude of the Soviet towards the Provisional Government was formulated in an ambiguously worded resolution of March 3: The Soviet would support the policies of the Provisional Government "in so far as they correspond to the interests of the proletariat and of the broad democratic masses of the people." A contact committee [4] was appointed by the Executive Committee "to inform the Soviet of the intentions and activities of the Provisional Government, to inform the latter of the demands of the revolutionary people, to bring pressure upon the Provisional Government in order to ensure the satisfaction of these demands, and to exercise ceaseless control over the execution of appropriate measures" (resolution of March 8). The resulting situation was not cooperation, but what came to be known as the regime of "dual power" (*dvoevlastie*), the Soviet relentlessly encroaching upon the prerogatives and functions of the Provisional Government. During the period of their uneasy co-existence (March to October, 1917) both the Provisional Government and the Soviet evolved towards the left; but this trend was less pro-

[4] Later its duties were taken over by the bureau of the Executive Committee.

nounced in the case of the former than of the latter and, with the final breakdown of the army and the flood tide of social unrest and economic disorganization, inexorably led to the advent to power of the more extreme, resolute, and ruthless political faction—the Bolshevik Party led by Lenin.

"DUAL POWER"

The policies of the Provisional Government followed the lines of a program agreed upon by the provisional committee of the Duma and the Executive Committee of the Soviet and announced in a manifesto of March 6. Its principal provisions, in so far as they bore on the domestic situation, were the convocation of a Constituent Assembly, the immediate removal of restrictions on civic liberties and the granting of equal rights to all citizens, the democratization of local government, and a broad political amnesty. In view of Russia's historical tradition the implementation of this program, especially in the midst of war and revolution, presented baffling difficulties. The amnesty decree (March 6) actually sanctioned the release of political prisoners that had already taken place; simultaneously the government assumed the cost of repatriation of political exiles and *émigrés*, a logical and inescapable measure which, however, the Provisional Government was soon to have good reasons to regret. The death penalty was abolished on March 12, and disabilities resulting from the inequality of legal status, race, and religion were done away with on March 20. For the first time in Russian history Jews acquired full civic rights.

The ready acceptance of the revolution in the provinces did not signify easy transition from the old to the new administrative order. Provincial governors were abolished on March 6, and their functions were transferred to the chairmen of provincial zemstvo executive boards, who, however, were usually wealthy landed proprietors and inspired no confidence in the Soviets and committees which sprang up everywhere and rapidly crowded out the former administrative agencies. Prince Lvov refused to admit the threat of mounting administrative anarchy (which, perhaps, he was powerless to check), and held that local issues "should be dealt with not from the center but by the people themselves" and that the self-appointed revolutionary agencies formed "the very core of the future democratic self-government" (statements of March 7 and 19). A committee was set up to draw new municipal and zemstvo statutes along democratic lines; meanwhile the complexion of municipal councils and zemstvo assemblies and boards was changed beyond recognition by the forced resignation of many former members and the influx of representatives of revolutionary organizations, a spontaneous development sanctioned by the Provisional Government at the end of March. The new organs of provincial administration, however, paid little attention to the Provisional Government and looked for leadership to the Soviet. A central land committee and local land committee were established on April 21 to collect information and draft recommendations for a comprehensive land reform. Preliminary steps for the convocation of the Constituent Assembly were taken at the end of March, but the special council on elections to the Constituent Assembly did not meet until late in May and its work was not completed until the end of September.

The above measures were carried out by the Provisional Government under the pressure of, but without serious friction with, the Soviet. The first major conflicts inherent in the system of "dual power" arose over the issue of army organization and that of foreign policy. The agreement reached by the provisional committee of the Duma and the Executive Committee of the Soviet in the night of March 1 (published on March 3) contained two provisions dealing with military matters: army units participating in the revolution were not to be disarmed or removed from the capital, and soldiers were to be granted full civic rights compatible with the maintenance of army discipline. Both provisions were seemingly innocuous and capable of moderate and reasonable interpretation; in practice, however, they worked for the undoing of the Provisional Government. Immunity from service at the front fanned the revolutionary zeal of the Petrograd garrison, which became a kind of praetorian guard of the Soviet and had the Provisional Government at its mercy. The principles underlying the second provision found their fullest expression in Army Order No. 1, which was prepared by the army section of the Soviet on March 1 and was published the next day in *Izvestiia* under the signature of the Petrograd Soviet. "The only worthy document of the February revolution," according to Trotsky, Order No. 1 decreed the establishment of elective committees in every army unit; immediate election, by regiments which had not already done so, of deputies to the Soviet; subordination of all political activities in the army to the direction of the Soviet and army committees; compliance with the orders of the military committee of the Duma in so far as they did not conflict with those of the Soviet; control by battalion and company committees of all arms which "under no condition should be handed over to officers"; maintenance of discipline while on duty but otherwise the exercise of full civic rights; abolition of compulsory salute and introduction of simplified formulas in addressing officers. Rudeness on the part of officers and misunderstandings between officers and men were to be reported to company committees.

It will be remembered that the disorganization of the army was well advanced long before the revolution; mass arrests and murders of officers occurred in many parts of the country prior to the publication of Order No. 1, and were particularly ferocious at the naval bases of Kronstadt, Sveaborg, and Helsingfors. Nevertheless Order No. 1 struck at the very foundation of army discipline and contributed powerfully to the breakdown of the armed forces. The Executive Committee of the Soviet, which was not consulted by its army section,[5] issued on March 5 Order No. 2, emphasizing, among other things, that Order No. 1 did not sanction the election of officers by army committees. Two days later the Executive Committee published an additional statement explaining that Order No. 1 applied merely to the garrison of Petrograd. These belated attempts to mitigate the effects of Order No. 1 were of no avail. Committees were rapidly set up in army units at the front and in the rear. Guchkov, the minister of war, and the new commander in chief General Alekseev were under no illusion as to the effect upon the army of the committee system and of Soviet intervention in military matters, but they accepted the *fait accompli*. A commission for the revision of army regulations appointed by Guchkov (March 6) and presided over by General Polivanov meekly endorsed the proposals elaborated by the army section of the Soviet. By an order of April 16 Guchkov belatedly legalized army committees. The "Declaration of the Rights of Soldiers" approved by the Polivanov commission was but a restatement of a document issued by the Soviet on March 13. The declaration, which added nothing of importance to Order No. 1, was not promulgated, however, until May 11, that is, after Guchkov was succeeded at the war office by Kerensky.[6] In spite of Guchkov's surrender to the Soviet

[5] Kerensky claims that he read for the first time the text of Order No. 1 in London, in December, 1918. *Op. cit.*, p. 47.

[6] Kerensky subsequently criticized Guchkov and Polivanov for subservience to

he made no secret of his detestation of the new regime introduced in the armed forces nor did he conceal his forebodings about the future. He was cordially disliked in Soviet circles, and at the end of April *Izvestiia* launched an attack on the minister accusing him of reactionary and anti-Semitic tendencies. On April 30 Guchkov resigned. His resignation, however, was due not only to the conflict with the Soviet over army reforms but also to the acute crisis over foreign policy that split the Provisional Government.

The Provisional Government at first espoused the theory of its minister of foreign affairs that the revolution had no effect on Russia's foreign policy. "The minister of foreign affairs," Miliukov wrote in 1921, "conducted this policy in the spirit of traditional cooperation with the allies and he did not admit the thought that the revolution might have weakened the international position of Russia by a sharp change in orientation and a novel approach to agreements concluded and obligations assumed. In all his pronouncements he emphasized the pacific aims of the war of liberation but he invariably linked them with Russia's national objectives and interests." In the manifesto of March 6 the Provisional Government proclaimed its determination to bring the war to a "victorious end," "faithfully to observe the treaties of alliance binding us with other Powers," and "unswervingly to fulfill the agreements entered into with the allies." These assurances were, of course, welcome in the capitals of the allied Powers and in the United States. Washington recognized the Provisional Government on March 9, and London, Paris, and Rome two days later. At a reception in honor of allied ambassadors on March 11, Miliukov expounded the theory which became the corner-stone of his policy; namely, that the revolution was primarily a protest against the failure of the imperial government to organize the country for the war. Now that the obstacle had been removed, Russia "was determined to use her best endeavor and to make all sacrifices . . . to create conditions for a lasting peace through victory." This heartening theory was at variance with the realities of the Russian situation. The war, indeed, was an important factor in the overthrow of the monarchy, but the revolution was a protest against the war as such, and not against the

---

the wishes of the Soviet. He held that he had purged the "Declaration of the Rights of Soldiers" of some of its most obnoxious provisions, for instance, the power of army committees to pass on the appointment of officers. The Polivanov commission was abolished by Kerensky. *Op. cit.*, pp. 181, 187, 189.

alleged half-heartedness of the war effort under the imperial government. The obstinate refusal to face the facts and futile attempts to force the army, which was resolved to go home, to continue the struggle spelled the doom of Miliukov and, later, of the Provisional Government.

Foremost among the "national objectives and interests" championed by Miliukov was the annexation of Constantinople. It will be remembered that on the eve of the revolution Pokrovsky made plans for the seizure of the Straits.[7] Although this project was deprecated by General Alekseev on the ground that Russia could ill afford a diversion of her dwindling resources from the German front, Miliukov on taking office revived Pokrovsky's proposal. He was no more successful than his predecessor. N. A. Bazili, representative of the foreign office at headquarters, informed Miliukov (letter of March 23) that preparations for a descent in Turkey were countermanded by Guchkov and Alekseev (orders of March 19 and 21) and that the shortage of shipping made unlikely the landing of Russian troops on the Bosphorus "this year" or, indeed, at any future date. Miliukov, however, "the only man left in Russia who still thinks of Constantinople, St. Sophia, and the Golden Horn"—and this "because he is a historian," according to the French ambassador Paléologue,—was not in a mood to renounce Russia's rights to annexations secured by wartime agreements.

As long as the Soviet was dominated by the Mensheviks and the socialist revolutionaries it proved incapable of formulating a consistent policy on the issue of war and peace. With the outbreak of the war in 1914 some of the future Soviet leaders, like their socialist colleagues in western Europe, rallied to the support of the national government in the struggle against the foreign enemy; others, however, took an uncompromising attitude towards the "imperialistic war" which they believed the proletariat should unwaveringly oppose. It was not easy to reconcile these conflicting views when their proponents met in the Soviet. A temporary escape from the dilemma was found in the widely held belief that the Russian revolution would lead within the near future to revolutions in western countries. This naïve faith—shared by leaders as far apart as Plekhanov and Kerensky, on the one hand, and Lenin, on the other—inspired the "Manifesto to the Peoples of the World" issued by the Soviet on March 14. An emotional,

[7] See p. 1351.

verbose, and confused document, the manifesto invited the peoples of belligerent nations "to wage a decisive battle against the annexationist programs" of their governments. "Russian democracy, conscious of its revolutionary strength," said the manifesto, "declares that it will resist by all means the policy of annexations" of Russian ruling classes. However, "the Russian revolution shall not retreat before the bayonets of conquerors and shall not allow itself to be crushed by outside military force." The peoples of the world, especially the German proletariat, were urged "to refuse to be the weapons of annexations and violence in the hands of kings, landowners, and bankers." Revolutions in western Europe would lead to the end of the war, to the establishment of "international unity," and the "complete liberation of humanity."

The Russian socialist press greeted the manifesto as a momentous pronouncement inaugurating a new era in international relations. From the standpoint of Russia's "traditional policy," as understood by Miliukov, the manifesto had the advantage of committing the Soviet to the continuation of the war as long as no revolution had occurred in Germany. However, it also called for the revision of war aims and inaugurated a nation-wide campaign for peace "without annexations and indemnities," an ambiguous formula which lent itself to innumerable interpretations. *Izvestiia* (March 17) proposed that the slogan "War to victory" should be replaced by that of "War for freedom."

The immediate reaction to the manifesto appeared to be favorable to a defensive war. There were mass patriotic demonstrations of the Petrograd garrison and populace. The sudden attack by the Germans on the Stokhod River (March 21), which resulted in the heavy defeat and withdrawal of the Russians, was a timely reminder that the war was not yet over, and had a sobering effect upon some of those who put their faith in the efficacy of the peace manifesto. Although these developments tended to obscure the basic motives behind the appeal —fatigue with the war and passionate longing for peace—these motives immediately reasserted themselves. Socialist newspapers led by the Bolshevik *Pravda* harped incessantly on the theme that the war was caused by the greed and imperialistic ambitions of the ruling classes. The revolutionary government of Russia should take the lead in inviting the Allies to revise their war aims and to renounce all plans for territorial expansion. As the novelist Merezhkovsky put it in an article in the newspaper *Den*, "The new Russia must have a new foreign policy."

The foreign office, as we know, took the opposite view. On March 23, the day when the grandiose funeral of the victims of the revolution was held in Petrograd, Miliukov, commenting in a press interview on President Wilson's statement concerning the reasons for American participation in the war, outlined Russian war aims: liberation of the Slavic peoples of Austria-Hungary, "merging of the Ukrainian provinces of Austria-Hungary with Russia," and the annexation of Constantinople and the Straits. According to the minister, "No one could accuse Russia of territorial ambitions" because "the possession of Constantinople has always been regarded as an immemorial objective of Russian national policy."

The interview had the effect of a bombshell. An announcement authorized by Kerensky and published on March 24 stated that Miliukov expressed his personal opinions and not those of the Provisional Government. Newspaper agitation rose to a new high pitch, and innumerable committees passed resolutions demanding the clarification of the government's peace policy. *Pravda* argued that either Miliukov or Kerensky should go, but this proposal met with no immediate support. Changes in the Provisional Government were still deemed unthinkable, and both Miliukov and Kerensky "indispensable." After protracted negotiations with his colleagues and the contact committee of the Soviet, Miliukov, while refusing to send a note to the allies, agreed to issue a "Declaration on War Aims" addressed to the Russian people. The object of a free Russia, according to the declaration (March 27), was "not domination over other peoples . . . not the forcible annexation of their territory, but the establishment of durable peace on the basis of national self-determination." However, the Russian people "would never tolerate that Russia should emerge from the great struggle humiliated, undermined in her vital strength." The Provisional Government, therefore, was resolved "to protect national rights while strictly fulfilling the obligations assumed towards the allies." Miliukov, as he has subsequently explained (1921), was given the assurance that he would be allowed to interpret the intentionally vague phraseology of the declaration in accordance with the policy he had formerly pursued. The Soviet leaders deemed it opportune, although not without misgivings, to approve the declaration, which was accordingly acclaimed by the left-wing press as a great victory for Soviet democracy. The foreign minister, however, persisted in the belief that he had surrendered none of his principles or policies. The reconciliation resting on misunderstanding and deceit could not last long.

After the flurry of self-congratulation provoked by the declaration had subsided, the Soviet-controlled press returned to the charge: the Provisional Government was to take up the question of war aims with the allies. To this demand was soon added another one—the publication of secret agreements. The foreign office, however, refused to budge. *Rech*, Miliukov's mouthpiece, wrote on April 9 that the Provisional Government had done its part and that the next move was up to Germany, not to Russia and her allies. At a conference of the Constitutional Democratic Party in Moscow, Miliukov expounded the view that the declaration of March 27 contained nothing new but was a restatement of principles often proclaimed by the leaders of the western democracies. He was immediately accused of being the tool of the Allies. These allegations fell on fertile ground. Anti-allied sentiments were inflamed by the obstacles set up by England, France, and Canada to the return of Russian political *émigrés*, particularly the arrest of Trotsky and his companions in Halifax (April 3). Moreover, influential members of the Provisional Government—Kerensky, Tereshchenko, Nekrasov, and Prince Lvov—openly supported, or leaned towards, the formula of peace "without annexations and indemnities." Miliukov was finally prevailed upon to communicate officially to the allies the declaration of March 27. His covering note of April 18 denied any intention on the part of Russia to conclude separate peace, voiced "the will of the nation to pursue the war to decisive victory," and reiterated Russia's faithfulness to wartime agreements. The note, interpreted as a challenge to the Soviet, precipitated a crisis of unprecedented violence. There were mass demonstrations and counter-demonstrations in front of the Marinsky Palace, seat of the Provisional Government. Some of the throngs supported Miliukov, but the majority carried banners demanding peace without annexations and indemnities, end of the war, and the resignation of Miliukov. Although a semblance of order was restored and civil war was averted, the reconstruction of the government became imperative. The Executive Committee, after considerable hesitation, once more reversed itself and agreed to allow members of the parties affiliated with the Soviet to hold office in the Provisional Government (May 1). Guchkov resigned on April 30 and Miliukov two days later. He was asked by his colleagues to exchange the foreign office for the ministry of education, but this he refused to do. With two of the most unpopular ministers out of the way, the Provisional Government was reorganized on May 5 on a coalition basis, that is, with the participation of parties represented in the Soviet. In theory, at least, the regime of "dual power" came to an end.

LENIN AND THE BOLSHEVIKS

The formation of the coalition government was preceded by an event which, trivial in itself, nevertheless ushered in a new and decisive phase of the revolution: on April 3 Lenin returned to Petrograd. Since the end of 1907 Lenin had remained abroad; at the outbreak of the war he was arrested by Austrian authorities at Poronino, in Galicia, but was soon released, went to Switzerland, and lived in Berne and later in Zurich. During his stay in Switzerland Lenin's attitude towards the war, which was to play so crucial a part in Russian events in 1917, was formulated in numerous writings, especially in *Theses on the War* (August, 1914), a book on imperialism (1916), and various papers and pronouncements in connection with the Zimmerwald (September, 1915) and Kienthal (April, 1916) conferences called in an unsuccessful attempt to revive the Second International, an organization of socialist parties that ceased to function with the outbreak of hostilities. The gist of Lenin's argument was that imperialism and its concomitant, war, were inherent in a bourgeois society; struggle for peace, therefore, was a revolutionary struggle against capitalism; the imperialistic war must be transformed into a civil war; socialists had the duty to strive for the termination of the slaughter, and cooperation on their part with national bourgeois governments (voting for military credits, participation in war cabinets, as was the case in Belgium, France, and England) was treason to the cause of the working class. Although these preachments had little immediate effect, they are essential to an understanding of Lenin's subsequent activities.

Viewed in retrospect and against the background of the communist revolution, the figure of Lenin has acquired the elements of legendary greatness, and it is often taken for granted, not merely in Soviet historiography, that he was endowed with almost superhuman power of foresight and infallibility of judgement.[8] The Lenin legend, like any other legend, does not withstand close scrutiny. While his singleness of purpose is not open to doubt, his judgement was often at fault, and he had moments of discouragement and despondency when even his robust faith in the imminence of the revolution faltered. On the eve of the Russian revolution he was passing through an acute phase of pessimism. The Zimmerwald and Kienthal appeals brought but meager response both in allied and in enemy countries, and the war dragged on. In dire financial straits, cut off from Russia, enmeshed in interminable factional squabbles with his political associates, Lenin lost touch with Russian realities. On January 9, 1917, that is, seven weeks before the fall of the monarchy, an event that was foretold with great accuracy by the security police and was common gossip in the salons of the grand duchesses, Lenin told a Zurich audience that men of his generation were not likely "to live to see the decisive battles of the approaching revolution." The glad news of the overthrow of the tsar carried Lenin to the opposite extreme. His *Farewell Letter to Swiss Workers* closed with the bold assertion: "The transformation of the imperialistic war into a civil war *is becoming* a fact. Long live the socialist revolution which *is beginning* in Europe." It is in this frame of mind that Lenin left Switzerland on March 27. He and a group of Russian émigrés traveled to Sweden through Germany in a "sealed" railway carriage. Arrangements for the journey were made by Swiss socialist leaders. In the evening of April 3 Lenin reached Petrograd and was given a triumphal reception by the huge crowds that filled the square in front of the Finland Station. His speech to the assembled throngs ended with the vibrant call, "Long live the socialist revolution!" This, however, was not at the time the attitude of the Bolshevik Party.

The Bolsheviks had played no independent part in the overthrow of the monarchy. In February, 1917, their recently revived Petrograd organization consisted of merely three men of whom V. M. Molotov (Scriabin), then in his middle twenties, alone was to hold an important place in the future Soviet government. *Pravda*, as has been noted, took at first an aggressively hostile attitude towards the Pro-

[8] E. H. Carr (*The Bolshevik Revolution, 1917–1923*, Vol. I [New York, 1951]), for instance, speaks of Lenin's "astonishing achievements," "far-sightedness," "immense learning," "analytical skill," "outstanding intellectual power"; "everything was clear-cut, brilliant, decisive." Lenin, according to Carr, was "a great constructive statesman."

visional Government, but with the return from Siberia of Stalin and L. B. Kamenev (March 13) it adopted a more conciliatory tone and, like other socialist newspapers, supported the policy of defensive war. In March, 1917, the Petrograd Bolsheviks shared the Menshevik faith that the fall of the monarchy must be followed for a protracted period by a bourgeois democratic republic and that a socialist revolution at that stage would be premature and doomed to failure.

Lenin had eagerly watched from abroad the trend of Bolshevik opinion, and he lost no time in making his own views known. On April 4 he presented his celebrated *April Theses* to two meetings of delegates to the All-Russian Conference of the Soviets, held at the Taurida Palace. The first meeting was attended by Bolsheviks alone, the second by both Bolsheviks and Mensheviks. On April 7 the *Theses* were published in *Pravda*. The program outlined by Lenin comprised ten points. (1) In view of the bourgeois character of the Provisional Government the revolution had not altered the imperialistic nature of the war, and "revolutionary defensism" was inadmissible. A truly revolutionary war was impossible until three conditions were fulfilled: state power had passed into the hands of the proletariat and the poorest strata of the peasantry; annexations were definitely abandoned; and ties with capitalist interests were severed. Mass propaganda in the army must explain that no democratic peace was possible without the overthrow of capitalism, and soldiers should be encouraged to fraternize with the enemy.[9] (2) No less momentous was Lenin's second point. "The peculiarity of the present situation in Russia," he wrote, "consists in *the transition* from the first stage of the revolution, which gave power to the bourgeoisie because of the insufficient consciousness and organization of the proletariat, to *the second* stage, which must place power in the hands of the proletariat and the poorest strata of the peasantry." Revolutionary tactics must be revised to meet this new situation. (3) No support should be given to the Provisional Government. Its predatory nature must be mercilessly exposed; it was deceptive and inadmissible to make "demands," which merely foster illusions, that "*this* government of capitalists should *cease* to be imperialistic." (4) The Soviets of Workers' Deputies were "the only possible form of revolutionary government." How-

---

[9] "The German proletariat is the most trustworthy, the most reliable ally of the Russian and the world proletariat." Lenin, *Letter to Swiss Workers*, March 27, 1917.

ever, as long as the Bolsheviks were a minority in the Soviets their work should be limited to propaganda on behalf of the Soviet form of government, that is, Lenin did not advocate the immediate seizure of power by the Soviets. (5) Administration through Soviets at every level was the aim. The establishment of a parliamentary republic would be "a step backwards." The Soviet state would have no police, no army, and no bureaucracy—a theme to which Lenin returned frequently and which he developed at considerable length five months later in a celebrated little volume *The State and the Revolution*. (6) The agrarian program, which was to be administered by Soviets of Agricultural Laborers' (*batraki*) Deputies, called for the nationalization of all land, the expropriation of large estates, and the organization of large model farms financed from public funds. (7) All banks must be immediately merged into a single national bank controlled by the Soviets. (8) The *"immediate* goal" was not " 'the introduction' of socialism but *immediate* transition to *control* by Soviets of Workers' Deputies over social production and distribution." (9) The Bolshevik Party must convoke without delay a party congress, amend its program, and change its name from "social-democratic" to "communist." (10) The final point dealt with the rebuilding of the International.

The *April Theses*, especially the points dealing with the non-support of the Provisional Government, rejection of defensive war, and transition to the socialist stage of the revolution, ran contrary to the accepted dogmas of Russian social democracy and were received with stupefaction and consternation even by Lenin's closest associates. On April 4 his program was overwhelmingly rejected by the Petrograd committee of the Bolshevik Party (13 votes to 2, with 1 abstention), and on April 8 *Pravda* wrote editorially that Lenin's proposals were unacceptable in so far as they were based on an erroneous interpretation of the revolution (immediate transition to the socialist stage). The reaction outside Bolshevik circles was as contemptuous as it was hostile. A keen contemporary observer (V. B. Stankevich) noted that the opponents of Lenin were relieved: "A man who talks such nonsense is not dangerous." Plekhanov, Lenin's old mentor and erstwhile associate, but in 1917 leader of a right-wing socialist group, wrote scornfully *On the Theses of Lenin, Or Why Delirium Is Sometimes Interesting*. According to the most charitable view Lenin had lived too long abroad and did not understand the Russian situation; he would soon recant his errors. The consensus of Russian opinion being what it was, David F. Francis, United States ambassador to Petrograd, should not be judged too harshly for cabling to Washington on April 21, N.S.: "Extreme socialist or anarchist named Lenin making violent speeches and thereby strengthening government; designedly giving him leeway and will deport opportunely." [10]

Lenin seldom, if ever, doubted the correctness of his judgement, and he was not disturbed by the inimical reception given to his revelation. In the night of April 3 he was driven, atop an armored car, from the Finland Station to the palace of Madame Kshesinsky, the well known ballerina whose residence was seized by mutinous soldiers during the revolution and became the headquarters of the Bolshevik Party. From the balcony of the boudoir where the dancer had only recently entertained the flower of the Petrograd *jeunesse dorée,* Lenin tirelessly harangued a seemingly endless stream of men and women eager to listen to his revolutionary gospel. The niceties of the Marxian analysis underlying the *April Theses* were beyond the grasp of the masses, but the simple and clear-cut conclusions drawn from them by Lenin could not be more accessible. If the assumption on which rested his theoretical structure—the imminence and inevitability of socialist revolution in the western countries—was unsound and unwarranted, the slogans he coined reflected accurately the innermost aspirations of a war-tired and land-hungry nation. "End of the war" and "All land to the peasants," immediately and without waiting for the Constituent Assembly, were exactly what the peasant soldiers were thinking about. The two slogans constituted an irresistible program to which, moreover, there was no practical alternative. The success of Lenin's propaganda was instant, unmistakable, and overwhelming. Its revolutionary potentialities could not be ignored, and they triumphed over the doctrinaire scruples of all but the most inveterate pundits of Marxism in the Bolshevik fold. The Bolsheviks traditionally belonged to the left wing of the revolutionary movement, and Lenin's radicalism, how-

---

[10] "Francis was a charming old gentleman with no appreciation of what was going on in Russia and without any other particular qualification for his difficult post." Philip C. Jessup, *Elihu Root* (New York, 1938), II, 354. In this instance, however, Francis might have obtained his information from a seemingly unimpeachable source. On April 30, N.S., Miliukov told the British ambassador that "the troops were ready to arrest" Lenin and "the Government were but waiting for the psychological moment. . . ." Buchanan, *My Mission to Russia, and Other Diplomatic Memories,* II, 119.

ever unorthodox, appealed to them. Party opinion swung rapidly to his side, and the All-Russian conference of the Bolsheviks held on April 24 to 29 approved by a large majority the program which party leaders had rejected three weeks earlier. The slogan "All power to the Soviets" endorsed by the conference was not yet a call for the immediate overthrow of the Provisional Government but a program of long-range revolutionary action: the strengthening of the Soviet system and the bringing of the Soviets under Bolshevik control. Bolshevik leadership was still to experience reverses, but as long as the party retained the monopoly of the only policy (peace and land) that commanded the support of the masses freed from restraint, its ultimate victory was merely a matter of time. The Bolsheviks had an important part in the events of April which led to the resignation of Guchkov and Miliukov and the reconstruction of the Provisional Government. Kerensky and his fellow ministers in the coalition governments of May–October endeavored to check the agrarian revolution and the spontaneous demobilization of the army by upholding the fiction of Russia's will to fight the war to a victorious end and by promises of a land reform. These policies did not meet the wishes of the masses, and the government was powerless to enforce them. Therefore they were bound to fail.

CHAPTER XLVI

THE TWO REVOLUTIONS OF 1917: II

✳

THE ARMY

The onward march of Bolshevism was favored by political, social, and economic disintegration, which in turn was fostered by Bolshevik propaganda. In no other sphere except that of government were the consequences of war and revolution more immediate and momentous than in the army. A report of the quartermaster-general A. S. Lukomsky dated March 18 presented a graphic picture of the conditions in the armed forces on the morrow of the revolution. Food stocks were running short; production of arms and munitions declined sharply; no reinforcements were to be expected because of the demoralization of reserve battalions; and the breakdown of the railways precluded large-scale movements of men and supplies. The morale of the troops inspired the gravest apprehensions. "The army is sick," said the report. "It will take two or three months to improve relations between officers and men. Meanwhile the officers are dispirited, men are restless, and desertions have greatly increased. The fighting capacity of the army has been lowered, and it is difficult to expect that at the present the troops could be prevailed upon to advance." It would therefore be impossible, according to the report, to undertake offensive operations in the spring; the army must remain on the defensive, and the allies should be informed that Russia was not in a position to fulfill the obligation, assumed at the conferences of Chantilly and Petrograd, to participate in the proposed offensive. This was a sober and realistic appraisal of the immediate situation. The report, however, was over-optimistic in anticipating speedy reconciliation between officers and men, and shrank from drawing the inescapable conclusion: an army unwilling to advance is also unfit to wage a defensive war.[1]

[1] The views expressed by Lukomsky were contested by other army leaders. On

The army breakdown of 1917 must be viewed against the background of the low morale and war weariness inherited from the imperial regime. Yet the immediate and basic cause of the collapse was the committee system and the profound mistrust of officers fanned by revolutionary agencies which shattered the traditional notions of discipline and hierarchical subordination, that last frail barrier between the soldiers' elemental longing for peace and spontaneous demobilization. Mistrust of officers led, in its most extreme form, to mutiny, murder, assault, demotion, or ejection of unpopular commanders. There were many cases of army units electing their officers. Fantastic rumors were given credence, and misunderstandings over trifles grew into major conflicts. For instance, an officer of the commissariat was ejected by the men of his unit because of his refusal to lend them some pen points, an action allegedly designed to obstruct the elections to the Constituent Assembly. Every order, including combat orders, was subject to close scrutiny by committees and the men themselves, and led to interminable vexatious negotiations. Any pretext was good enough for a company, regiment, division, or army corps to refuse to take positions in the front line. The formula "Peace without annexations and indemnities," interpreted as a pledge to engage exclusively in defensive war, involved the peasant soldier in insoluble problems of semantics. For what is a defensive war? Is a reconnaissance, or the digging of trenches a few yards in front of those held, but for some reason made unusable, a defensive or an offensive operation? These and similarly weighty questions were debated *ad nauseam*, were decided according to the whims of committee leaders, and placed the commanding officers in a truly intolerable position. The artillery, where morale was higher than in other branches, was threatened by the infantry into silence lest the enemy return fire. No less ominous were the spreading of fraternization and the speedily mounting number of deserters.

Various means were tried to check the disintegration of the army. Civilian commissars, chosen chiefly among members of revolutionary

---

March 18, the very day when he wrote his report, five high commanding officers led by Brusilov wired to the war minister that, in their opinion, the army was fully capable of offensive operations and that Russia should fulfill her military obligations towards the allies, although, perhaps, on a somewhat reduced scale.

Most of the documents on which the present discussion is based are published in the official collection of documents, N. E. Kakurin, ed., *Razlozhenie armii v 1917 godu* (Breakdown of the Army in 1917) (Moscow-Leningrad, 1925).

parties, were attached to the larger units in an endeavor to bolster the morale of the troops, to fight defeatist influences, and to iron out the ever recurrent conflicts between officers and men. With the appointment of Kerensky to the war office more imaginative methods were tried. Salvation was sought in the creation of "shock" or "death" battalions of "revolutionary volunteers" who took a romantic oath and wore gaudy red-and-black insignia. General Alekseev saw no merit in the "shock" troops; on May 22, however, he was succeeded as commander in chief by Brusilov, a protagonist of the scheme. For a while the "shock" troops were the vogue, but in spite of the volunteers' solemn promise to execute all orders and to accept "death for the country and for Russia's freedom" as "happiness," the combat record of "shock" troops was undistinguished; the experiment gradually petered out and was abandoned in the middle of October. The formation of national troops—Polish, Ukrainian, Lettish, Latvian, Moslem, Georgian, Armenian—was regarded in some quarters as an effective way to counteract demoralization. Actually, however, the resulting reorganization was a disruptive factor and a source of confusion. The women's combat battalions formed in June under the leadership of the formidable Madame Bochkareva were mere oddities.[2] They were subsequently denounced as counter-revolutionary and, in part, disbanded by some of the Soviets.

Kerensky, however, relied chiefly on persuasion as a method for reviving the fighting spirit of the troops. Like Prince Lvov, he had his moments of despondency. On April 29, addressing in a somber mood a congress of army delegates, Kerensky exclaimed that he was no longer sure that "we have before us conscious citizens building a new order" and not "rebellious slaves." Nevertheless his faith in the revolution remained unshaken, and he was eager to infuse his passion into the soldiers.[3] Revolutions, like churches, have their dogmas, rituals, and divinely inspired leaders. Throughout the summer of 1917, the inroads of Bolshevism notwithstanding, Kerensky retained his extraordinary popularity. While the peasant soldier showed an unmistakable disinclination to fight, Soviets and committees passed sheaves of resolutions proclaiming his determination to die for the

[2] Another woman, Valentina Petrova, petitioned Kerensky to organize a women's battalion of "Black hussars of death," but no action was taken on her proposal.

[3] "We are told: the Provisional Government is powerless," Kerensky said in Moscow on May 26. "This is not true. Our strength resides in our confidence in the creative forces of the people, in our profound faith in its wisdom and conscience."

revolution, and the appearances of Kerensky at army meetings were, in spite of Bolshevik interruptions, notable personal triumphs. These manifestations of popular enthusiasm carried greater weight with the temperamental minister than the gloomy reports of former tsarist generals and timorous commissars, and he had no difficulty in persuading himself and the government that Russia should launch a major offensive, a decision which was endorsed, although not without opposition, by the Petrograd and other Soviets.[4] It was believed that even a moderate military success would check internal disintegration, relieve German pressure on the western front, and shorten the war. Allied governments urged Kerensky to resume active operations, although practically every Russian army leader, as well as some of the allied statesmen, realized that the offensive was bound to fail and that its likely consequences would be the final dissolution of the Russian front and the seizure of power by the extreme elements. To these counsels of caution Kerensky would not listen. He made an extensive tour of the front, addressing mass meetings of soldiers. The apparent spontaneity and ardor of the response to his emotional oratory convinced him that revolutionary Russia had awakened and was ready to follow the leader. The evanescence of popular adulation and the shallowness of support that expressed themselves in applause and ovations were soon to be convincingly demonstrated.

In spite of many technical shortcomings the offensive was prepared with great care. The main blow was to be dealt in the direction of Lemberg (Lvov), in Galicia, and was to be supported by thrusts at various points along the entire front. The Russians had an overwhelming superiority both in men and in guns. Indeed, the artillery fire which preceded the attack was on a scale unprecedented on the Russian front. On June 18 the offensive began, and met with some initial success; the advancing troops occupied a number of strategic points and took several thousand prisoners. However, enemy resistance did not crumble and there was no prospect of an immediate peace, as many soldiers had naïvely imagined. The question arose, and was debated by front-line committees, whether the continuation of the offensive was compatible with the principles of defensive war. The answer was inconclusive, but the *élan* of the troops was broken and by July 1 the advance in Galicia came to a standstill. On the other sectors of the front the offensive failed at an even earlier stage. In some cases the troops

---

[4] The Petrograd Soviet approved the offensive, 472 to 271, with 39 abstentions.

marched in parade formations through enemy positions flattened by artillery fire, only to return at once to their own lines. Other units, including whole divisions, refused to budge. On July 6 the Austro-Germans launched in Galicia a counter-offensive which met with hardly any resistance. In the section of the Sereth River, for instance, two Russian divisions fled before three enemy companies supported by a few machine guns. All semblance of discipline vanished and the retreat became a rout, the fleeing soldiers perpetrating unspeakable atrocities on the defenseless population. On July 11 the Russians evacuated Tarnopol, which had been thoroughly plundered, and on July 20 Czernovitz, the capital of Bukovina. If by the end of July the front line was stabilized somewhat east of the pre-war frontier with Galicia, it was because the enemy decided not to press its advance.

The news of the debacle, which was released on July 8, created consternation, especially because it was preceded by over-enthusiastic reports of earlier victories. An official statement of July 9 described the retreat as an "immeasurable calamity that threatens the ruin of revolutionary Russia." On July 7 General L. G. Kornilov (about whom more will be said below) was appointed commander of the southwestern front, which included Galicia. He demanded the immediate suspension of all offensive operations and the introduction of death penalty and military courts in the theater of war. These demands were endorsed by Brusilov, by influential commissars (Savinkov, M. Filonenko), and by a large section of public opinion. Without awaiting the reply of the government, Kornilov decreed the use of machine guns and artillery against bands of deserters and units refusing to obey orders. Kerensky, who became president of the Provisional Government on July 8, approved the measures taken by Kornilov and directed army committees not to interfere with combat orders and the appointment and removal of commanders. By a decree of July 12 the Provisional Government restored the death penalty in the army and established revolutionary military tribunals to deal with the major offenses against discipline and public order. Further measures for the restoration of the morale were to be studied by a commission which included Kerensky, Savinkov, and army leaders. Friction, however, arose immediately between Kerensky and the generals who made no secret that they blamed the Provisional Government, and particularly Kerensky, for the breakdown of the army. Nevertheless on July 18 Kornilov was appointed commander in chief.

It is unlikely that any measures taken in the summer and autumn of 1917 could have restored order and discipline in the army. Those enacted in July were clearly inadequate. A number of disaffected units were disbanded, but no one seemed to know what to do with their contingents. Surely, the reassignment of mutinous soldiers to other units was no solution. The make-up of the military revolutionary tribunals—three officers and three non-commissioned ranks—was ill-adapted to the existing situation. Contrary to the intent and letter of the decree of July 12, the tribunals dealt chiefly with petty cases, not with major breaches of discipline. Army committees were unwilling to accept any limitation of their powers, and many of them protested the restoration of the death penalty, which, moreover, was seldom, if ever, applied. Nor is it certain that Kerensky was reconciled to the stern measures which he had himself approved.[5] At the Democratic Conference in September he disclaimed any intention of signing death warrants. The situation at the front deteriorated still further after the Kornilov "mutiny" (end of August). Eastbound trains were packed with deserters whom no one even tried to stop. In October, according to an official report, the army was but "a huge crowd of tired, poorly clad, poorly fed, embittered men united by common longing for peace and general disillusionment." Its fighting capacity, to quote a later report (December), was "equal to zero."

The demoralization of the Russian army not only altered the strategic situation but had direct repercussions abroad. Following the revolution the Russian brigades in France and Macedonia rapidly disintegrated, mutinied, and were disbanded.[6] Their example was

[5] Kerensky, in an address before the Congress of the All-Russian Soviet of Peasants' Deputies on May 5, formulated as follows his notion of discipline: "I, a stranger in military circles, shall instil in the troops iron discipline, and it will be the discipline of honor and duty towards the country."

[6] The request for the sending of Russian troops to the western front was made by England in August, 1914. Sir Edward Grey offered to arrange for the transportation, within a week, of four army corps from Archangel, but the Russian government demurred. The request, this time for 300,000 troops, was revived by Paul Doumergue, the future president of France, who came to Petrograd on a special mission in December, 1915. General Alekseev disliked the proposal, and was particularly uneasy about "exchanging human beings for armaments." Nevertheless four Russian brigades were shipped to France: one from Dairen, on the Pacific, to Marseilles in January, and three from Archangel to Brest between July and November, 1916. Two brigades remained in France and the other two were transported from Marseilles to Salonika. The total Russian expeditionary force, not counting replacements, numbered 43,500 men and 745 officers. The experiment proved unrewarding, though the Russians did some creditable fighting for a few months both

probably not without influence upon the widespread mutinies that broke out among the French troops in the spring and summer of 1917, although the French disorders were primarily due to other causes and were successfully quelled by Pétain's display of firmness, moderation, and skill.[7]

THE PEASANT REVOLUTION

The army was linked to the peasantry by innumerable ties, and its breakdown may well be viewed as a phase of the peasant revolution, even though the tempo of events was slower in the village than it was in the barracks and in the trenches. The soldier—a "peasant in uniform" (to use a phrase which Lenin liked)—had a decisive part in the overthrow of the monarchy, but the peasantry, as a group, remained aloof from the March revolution. News of the events in the capital spread but slowly into the countryside and was at first received with bewilderment and suspicion; it was only gradually that the farmer came to realize that his secular dream was, at last, to come true. To the Russian peasant the "freedom" heralded by the new order had a

---

in France and in Macedonia. The first major instance of insubordination occurred in Marseilles, in August, 1916, when a mutinous Russian regiment murdered its colonel. The morale of the Russian troops in France declined rapidly after the revolution, and early in June, 1917, the Russian brigades were moved to camps in the rear, where they indulged in political meetings, factional quarrels, drunkenness, debauchery, and mutinies which were suppressed by armed force. The situation in Macedonia was analogous except that the process of disintegration was somewhat slower and the Russian troops remained in the trenches until January, 1918, although refusals to carry out combat orders occurred in October and fraternization was common in November and December.

In May, 1917, the French government stopped replacements from Russia. Frantic efforts to arrange for the repatriation of the Russian troops having failed because of the shortage of shipping, the French command proceeded in December with the "sorting out" (*triage*) of Russian contingents. Three possibilities were offered to the men: combat service with the French army; labor battalions; or internment in North Africa under conditions similar to those of prisoners of war. Of the 19,000 Russian soldiers then in France, 11,500 chose labor battalions, nearly 5,000 the African prison camps, and only a few hundred volunteered for combat service; 2,500 sick account for the balance. A similar procedure was applied to the Russian troops in Macedonia. The men who chose active service formed the Russian legion which in November, 1918, numbered 564 men—the last remnant of the Russian steam roller.

[7] "Pétain was the ideal restorer of order and confidence. His marble calm was never shaken. Of all the great chiefs of the war, he understood the common man best. His massive simplicity, so sincere, so completely unselfconscious, above all his justice, made him a true soldier's friend." C. R. M. F. Cruttwell, *A History of the Great War, 1914–1918*, p. 415.

definite and concrete meaning. It was not the right to vote, parliamentary government, the Constituent Assembly, or the removal of legal disabilities. In the popular mind "Land and freedom," Herzen's old battle cry, was tautology: for freedom *was* land, and land *was* freedom. "Land," moreover, meant, not any scheme of nationalization, socialization, or municipalization devised by the learned theorists, but the partition, among the villagers, of the large estates which they had so long and so passionately coveted. This was the one supreme gift the revolution could bestow upon them, and they were determined not to let the opportunity slip by. While Lvov, Miliukov, and Kerensky clung to the fiction that the revolution was an expression of the nation's eagerness to win the war, official reports agreed that in rural areas, as early as the spring of 1917, "war was often almost completely forgotten." What was true of the village was true of the army. The impending redistribution of land was uppermost to the peasant soldier when he turned a deaf ear on combat orders, threw away his rifle, and deserted by the thousand.

The Provisional Government was in sympathy with the aspirations of the peasants and was anxious to clear the way for a radical land reform, but it believed in legality and orderly methods of land transfer. "The land problem cannot be solved by force," said an official appeal of March 17. "Violence and pillage are the worst way of dealing with economic relationships. Only the enemies of the people would push the peasants along this road to ruin. . . . The land problem must be settled by a law approved by a popular representative assembly. The careful study and drafting of the land law are impossible without thorough preparatory work, collection of information, registration of the land reserve, classification of landed properties, examination of conditions and forms of land tenure, and so on. The Provisional Government considers it its pressing duty to complete within the shortest possible time the preliminary work bearing on the land question in order to submit all materials and information to the representatives of the people," that is, the Constituent Assembly. This program was, on the whole, adhered to by the Provisional Government until the very end, and its fatal weakness was that it could not be enforced in the midst of the agrarian revolution. Lenin, too, professed to believe in legality, but he gave the familiar notion a characteristic twist. "We advocate the immediate transfer of land to the peasants with the maximum of orderliness," he said on April 28 at the congress of the

Bolshevik Party. "We are absolutely opposed to anarchistic seizure." Earlier in the same speech, however, Lenin stated that "what matters to us is revolutionary initiative, and the [land] law must be its result. If you wait until the law is written and will not yourself generate revolutionary energy, you will get neither the law nor the land."

In spite of the multiplicity of peasant organizations that sprang up in 1917, the agrarian revolution was a spontaneous movement free from centralized leadership. Soviets of Peasants' Deputies began to appear soon after the revolution, and on March 19 a conference of peasant delegates who assembled in Moscow decided that the peasant Soviets should take their place side by side with the Soviets of Workers' and Soldiers' Deputies. The objectives of the peasant Soviets, as determined by the Moscow conference, were to study the land question, which, however, could be settled only by the Constituent Assembly; to exercise control over the organs of the state administration; and to represent the peasants in the various agencies, particularly in the Soviets of Workers' and Soldiers' Deputies. In April arrangements were made for the convocation of an All-Russian congress of the Soviets of Peasants' Deputies. It was provided—and this was important—that the deputies need not be peasants, although they must be elected by the peasants. The congress met in Petrograd from May 4 to 28. Its proceedings paralleled those of the Soviet of Workers' and Soldiers' Deputies and were dominated by intellectuals belonging to the Socialist Revolutionary Party. The Bolsheviks were a tiny minority. In the elections to the Executive Committee Kerensky and Chernov received over 800 votes each, while only 20 votes were cast for Lenin. The resolution on the land question approved by the congress on May 25 was radical. It embodied the principles of the socialist revolutionary doctrine and called for abolition, without compensation, of private ownership in land and the establishment of a system of equalitarian labor tenure involving no payment of rent. The final settlement of the land question, however, was reserved for the Constituent Assembly. Meanwhile all land relationships were to be controlled by local land committees. The other resolutions approved by the congress differed little from those of the Soviet of Workers' and Soldiers' Deputies during that period, that is, from the formation of the coalition government early in May to the capture of the Petrograd Soviet by the Bolsheviks at the end of August. They called for the support of the Provisional Government, the continuation of a defensive war, peace without annexations and indemnities, strengthening of army discipline, and the establishment of a republic. Chernov, minister of agriculture and a leading figure at the congress, deprecated the seizure of estates, and emphasized that the Provisional Government had no power to carry out a land reform.

The Executive Committee of the peasant Soviet set up by the congress included most of the leaders of the Socialist Revolutionary Party and, like its parent body, was largely concerned with problems of national policy. For instance, it enthusiastically endorsed the Kerensky offensive. With few exceptions, the composition and activities of local peasant Soviets conformed to those of the All-Russian congress and its Executive Committee; their policies, therefore, were singularly unrepresentative of the true aspirations of the peasantry. The same observation applies to the central, provincial, and county land committees established under the law of April 21 to gather information for the impending land reform, in spite of Chernov's efforts to broaden their functions and strengthen their influence. Township (*volost*) committees, including township land committees, were closer to the peasantry than committees and Soviets on higher levels; and although they included at first many radical intellectuals the latter were gradually crowded out by the peasants. Moreover, the Socialist Revolutionary Party, by far the most active party in rural areas, was hopelessly divided. The right-wing elements which controlled the Executive Committee of the peasant Soviet stood by Kerensky and the Provisional Government, while the left-wing faction leaned increasingly towards the Bolsheviks and often worked at cross purposes with the party leadership. The more extreme group had by far the better chance to survive in the township committees and to make its influence felt. The peasants, distrusting outsiders unless they told them what they wanted to hear, took the law into their own hands. The principal agencies of the agrarian revolution were the village assemblies, a traditional peasant institution, and the township committees.

The agrarian revolution went through several stages, although its objective—the partition of landed estates among the peasants—remained unaltered. There were instances of arson, pillage, and murder in the early days of the revolution, but their number was relatively small. The peasants, apprehensive about the future, and mindful perhaps of the repressions that followed the agrarian disturbances of 1905, proceeded at first cautiously and by quasi-legal methods: wages of agricultural laborers were raised to prohibitive levels; refugees and prisoners of war employed on large estates were withdrawn and distributed among the farms of mobilized men; owners were coerced into leasing out land at low rents or selling it at nominal prices; estate managers and supervisors were ejected; the use of agricultural machinery and the exploitation of forests were prohibited; there were much trespassing and wanton destruction of timber and woodlands. When these transgressions achieved their purpose and life on the estates came to a standstill, peasant committees took over arable land, meadows, forests, machines, and livestock on the ground that the owners were incapable of managing their properties. The agrarian movement, moreover, was directed not only against the landed nobility but also against the well-to-do peasant farmers, especially those who by virtue of the Stolypin legislation had severed their connection with the village commune (*obshchina*). At times the committees made use of patriotic motives—provisioning of the army and safeguarding of standards of agricultural production. Estate owners deluged the government with complaints and appeals for protection. Prince Lvov repeatedly condemned lawlessness, exhorted every one to be reasonable, to think of the common good, and to wait patiently for the decision of the Constituent Assembly, and he directed the frightened and hopelessly outnumbered militiamen to maintain law and order. The practical results of these admonitions were nil. In radical circles agrarian unrest was ascribed to the machinations of the landed proprietors who allegedly endeavored to defeat the agrarian revolution by breaking up their estates into small holdings: the future land law was not expected to affect farms below the specified acreage. Sales of land, often fictitious, were, according to this view, the basic cause of agrarian disturbances. A law of July 12, sponsored by the minister of agriculture Chernov, prohibited mortgages and sales of land except by permission of the provincial land committees and the minister of agriculture. This law was no more effective in stemming lawlessness than Prince Lvov's appeal to the wisdom and genius of the Russian people.

Statistics of the agrarian revolution are fragmentary and difficult to interpret. For example, the reduction of the number of outbreaks in a county was usually evidence, not of the ebbing of the movement, but rather of the fact that most of the estates in that county had been taken over by the peasants. Nevertheless official data analyzed by Soviet economists (for instance, A. V. Shestakov) shed some light on the course of the peasant revolution. They indicate that the movement did not reach its peak until July and became particularly violent in September and October. Of the 930 reported cases of seizure of estates, 686 occurred in July to October, and of the 350 cases of plunder of manor houses 271 took place in September and October. Punitive military expeditions which, beginning in August, were sent to the countryside failed to restore order. Indeed, not infrequently the troops went over to the side of the rebellious peasants. The pillage of estates and large peasant farms was ruthless, systematic, and thorough. Manor houses and farm buildings were razed to the ground, sometimes by the use of explosives. Trees were felled, and parks, gardens, and orchards plowed into fields. Everything imaginable was done to make sure that the owners would never come back. The violence of the summer and autumn outbreaks may be traced to the dynamics of the agrarian revolution, which gathered momentum and thrived on the impunity of earlier excesses and the patent impotence of the authorities; to the influx of deserters, some of them carrying arms; and to Bolshevik propaganda. It would be a mistake, however, to attach excessive importance to the last factor. The peasants had made up their minds about land long before they had heard of the Bolsheviks. Trotsky summed up the situation well when he wrote that "the peasants did not read Lenin" but "Lenin read clearly the thoughts of the peasants."

LABOR AND ECONOMIC DISINTEGRATION

From the first days of the revolution industrial labor, unlike the peasantry, was in the forefront of revolutionary forces. Its influence was exercised through the Soviets of Workers' and Soldiers' Deputies, the trade unions, and the factory committees. The Soviets, however, especially their central organs in Petrograd, functioned as a quasi-parliament rather than as an agency for the advancement of the professional interests of the working class, even though labor policies were not, of course, neglected. Trade unions and factory committees, irrespective of the political views held by their leaders, reflected more accurately than the Soviets the aspirations of the rank and file of the workers.

Although the trade unions were legalized in 1906 and made a promising start, few of them survived the reaction of 1907–1911, and by early 1917 they were ineffectual and numerically weak. The revolution gave a strong impetus to the trade-union movement. According to official data over 2,000 unions, including 130 in Petrograd and Moscow, were organized in March and April.[8] Most of them were very small, their membership being limited to the workers employed in one establishment.[9] There followed a brisk campaign for unionization and merger. Regional central councils and central bureaus of trade unions were set up in Moscow and Petrograd in March and somewhat later in the provinces. Fifty-one central bureaus and 976 unions with an aggregate membership of 1,475,000 participated in the third all-Russian conference of trade unions in June, but many of the small unions were not represented. The conference elected the All-Russian Central Council of Trade Unions and passed resolutions dealing with the eight-hour day, unemployment, female labor, arbitration of industrial disputes, factory inspection, professional press and cultural activities. Further encouragement was given to the amalgamation of small unions, a process that was not completed until after the October revolution. An investigation carried on by the first all-Russian congress of trade unions in January, 1918, covered 157 unions (one union failed to answer the questionnaire) with an aggregate membership of 2,253,000. The average membership for each union was 14,300, but more than half of the members (1,257,000) belonged to 16 unions with a membership of over 20,000 each; at the other extreme were 21 unions with less than 3,000 members each and an aggregate membership of 37,000. The textile industry (15 unions with 571,000 members) and the metal industry (35 unions with 526,000 members) were the strongholds of unionism. Practically all unions were organized on a local basis, that is, their membership was drawn from among the workers employed in the same locality and, not infrequently, in the same establishment.

Trade-unionism, like any mass movement, cannot be improvised on the spur of the moment. Born in the midst of a revolutionary upheaval,

[8] L. V. Meller and A. M. Pankratova, editors of a valuable collection of documents, *Rabochee dvizhenie v 1917 godu* (The Labor Movement in 1917) (Moscow-Leningrad, 1926), emphasize the incompleteness and unreliability of trade-union statistics for 1917 "and, indeed, for a long time to come."

[9] For instance, Baku reported 27 unions in May. Of this number only three unions had more than 1,000 members (seamen, 4,800; oil workers, 3,000; and bookkeepers, 2,000), while the membership of the majority of the unions varied from 700 to as little as 35. Some of the unions, however, were large, and their membership increased rapidly. The Petrograd union of metalworkers had 16,000 members in March, 70,000 in June, and 138,000 in August.

and lacking in tradition and organizing skill, Russian trade unions did not become in 1917 an effective instrument for the advancement of the professional interests of the working class. Their activities often duplicated, or were in conflict with, those of the Soviets, on the one hand, and those of the factory committees, on the other. The latter were by far the more important agency in the struggle of labor against the employers.

Factory committees (*fabrichno-zavodskie komitety*) were formed spontaneously in many industrial enterprises at the beginning of the revolution. On March 5 the Petrograd Soviet decreed the establishment of factory committees, and on March 10 the Petrograd Association of Manufacturers negotiated with the Soviet an agreement sanctioning the new committees, whose functions, however, were narrowly delimited. Moscow and the provinces followed suit. Under a law of April 23 which recapitulated the principal provisions of the agreement of March 10 factory committees were elected by direct secret ballot in any enterprise, or part thereof, at the request of not less than one-tenth of the workers concerned, or of the factory administration. The committees were empowered to represent the workers in negotiations with the management bearing on matters such as wages, hours, and conditions of work; to settle conflicts among workers; to represent workers in relations with the government and public agencies; and to promote the cultural and economic well-being of the workers. Committee members could not be dismissed from the enterprise without the approval of a court of arbitration or of the committee itself, which meant in practice that they could not be dismissed at all. On the invitation of a committee or its chairman, outsiders could participate in the work of the committee.

Factory committees did not consider themselves bound by the restrictive provisions of the law of April 23, and redress of professional grievances and cultural work were but one facet of their activity. They did press, jointly with the Soviets of the trade unions, for the eight-hour day and higher wages. The eight-hour day without reduction of pay was conceded by the Petrograd Association of Manufacturers in the agreement of March 10, but the scope of the agreement was limited to the capital, and even there it was not uniformly enforced. The eight-hour day was introduced by factory committees in many enterprises in spite of the opposition of the management, and it remained a popular battle cry of organized labor until the Bolshevik revolution.

Clamors for higher wages, sometimes unreasonable and indeed confiscatory, came from every side. Factory committees insisted on, and not infrequently secured, the adoption of the "closed shop," the right to supervise the hiring and dismissal of workers, the removal of technical and managerial personnel. There were many other oddly assorted demands that had no bearing on industrial relations: progressive profits tax, fixed prices, control by revolutionary agencies over production and distribution, dissolution of the State Duma and State Council, reduction of salaries and pensions of commanding officers and officials of the old regime, deportation of "agents of foreign imperialism," and the imprisonment (as the workers of the factory "Dynamo" put it) of the "vampire Romanov" (the former tsar) and of "the vampire's family." The main objective of the factory committees, as formulated by the first conference of factory committees, which was held in Petrograd (May 30 to June 5), was the establishment of "workers' control," that is, the effective supervision by workers' committees of the administration of business enterprises. A favorite idea of Lenin, workers' control became the law of the land in November, after the fall of the Provisional Government. Meanwhile there were sporadic seizures of factories and the systematic crowding out of owners, managers, and engineers. The Provisional Government admonished factory committees to keep within the provisions of the law, and threatened the application of penalties which everyone knew it was powerless to enforce.

Political and social anarchy superimposed upon the dislocation caused by the war precipitated an economic crisis of unexampled severity. The greatly overtaxed capacity of the railways declined sharply. State revenue fell, expenditure mounted, and the volume of currency in circulation practically doubled between January and October, 1917 (9,097 million rubles and 18,917 million, respectively). The general price level in 1917 was three and a half times that of 1916.[10] The position of the low-income groups was truly desperate, and industrial labor had a strong case for wage increase. When the textile workers argued in August that their children "died like flies" and that they were faced with "misery and starvation," their statement was no mere propaganda. Yet the economic demands of labor, to say nothing of its political demands, were as often as not exorbitant, and

[10] As computed by Strumilin, the general index of prices (1913 = 100) rose from 203 in 1916 to 673 in 1917.

spelled the ruin of industry. According to a memorandum submitted to the Provisional Government at the end of May by the Association of Industrialists of Southern Russia, the additional charges imposed upon the metallurgical industry by increased labor and other costs were 10 times higher than "gross profits" and 43 times higher than dividend payments in 1916. Both employers and workers agreed that industry was heading towards disaster, but the recognition of the impending catastrophe did not bring them any closer together. Driven into despair, many employers petitioned the government to take over their establishments or suspend production. The closing down of factories was of daily occurrence in the summer and autumn of 1917. Faced with unemployment, the workers interpreted these decisions as counter-revolutionary and sabotage. The solution advocated by the Bolsheviks and espoused by many labor organizations was the tightening of the screw of workers' control. Meanwhile the flow of industrial production thinned to a mere trickle.

The invasion by the factory committees of the fields traditionally regarded as a preserve of the trade unions, and the prominent part they played in the labor movement, created keen rivalry between the two branches of organized labor. Factory committees, moreover, were under strong Bolshevik influence, while throughout most of 1917 the Mensheviks and the socialist revolutionaries largely controlled the trade unions. There arose bitter disagreements on matters of principle and policy. Workers' control, for instance, was unpopular in trade-union circles. To the orthodox trade-unionists factory committees were usurpers and rabble; to the supporters of factory committees trade-unionism was the doctrinaire survival of the capitalist age, which in Russia was about to disappear. The resulting conflict threatened to split the labor movement; it was not resolved, at least formally, until February, 1918, when the factory committees were officially incorporated in the trade unions, which in the meantime had been taken over by the Bolsheviks.

SEPARATIST MOVEMENTS

Among the casualties of the revolution was the notion that "the Russian state is one and indivisible" which appeared in the Fundamental Laws of 1906. With the fall of the monarchy the policy of Russification and administrative centralization brought its fruit: the long pent-up aspirations of the national minorities came to the fore and found their expression in demands, first, for cultural and administrative autonomy and, later, in some cases, for independence.

Of the Russian border territories Poland and Finland had the strongest claim to independence. The case of Poland presented no serious difficulty because her right to secede was admitted in Russian radical and liberal circles. The principle of Polish independence was proclaimed by the Petrograd Soviet on March 14, and on March 16 (March 29, N.S.) the Provisional Government issued a manifesto calling upon the Poles to fight by the side of the Russians, "shoulder to shoulder, and hand in hand, for our and your freedom." The Poles were promised, subject to approval by the Constituent Assembly, "an independent Polish state comprising all territories inhabited predominantly by Poles" and "united with Russia by a free military alliance." Since the whole of Russian Poland was held by the enemy, the manifesto was of small practical significance, except that it encouraged the formation of national Polish troops. Small Polish units (Legion of Pulawy, the Polish Rifle Brigade) fought as a part of the Russian imperial army, but they did not enjoy an independent status. A strong movement for the creation of a national Polish army developed after the revolution and led to the organization of three Polish army corps which succeeded in maintaining discipline in the midst of Russian demoralization and, according to Polish sources, saved some of the Polish estates from Russian marauders during the debacle of the Kerensky offensive, but otherwise achieved little and were finally disarmed by the advancing Germans.

As Finland was not occupied by the enemy, the Finnish question called for immediate measures and a constructive policy. In a manifesto of March 7 the Provisional Government repealed all legislation incompatible with the Finnish constitution, amnestied the Finns imprisoned for political offenses, promised the extension of Finnish autonomy, and ordered the convocation of the diet. Finnish nationalism, however, was not satisfied with these concessions. National independence was much in the air in 1917, and the Finns had excellent reasons for throwing off any vestige of the Russian rule. The obscurities of Finland's constitutional position have long been a boon to international lawyers. In 1917 eminent legal authorities took the view that the abdication of the tsar had severed all links between Finland and Russia, an interpretation that naturally commended itself to Finnish nationalists. The Provisional Government, however, held fast to the theory that it was the successor to the powers formerly vested in the tsar, both as emperor of Russia and grand duke of Finland, and that this sacred trust must be handed over intact to the Constituent Assembly. Desire for independence was shared by every political group in Finland, but there were sharp differences as to timing and methods. Finnish social democrats, who held a small majority in the diet that met in the spring, showed little patience with the constitutional and legal technicalities on which the more conservative Finnish parties relied to some extent and which kept Russian and Finnish jurists busy. On July 5 (July 18, N.S.) the diet gave a first reading to a bill which virtually proclaimed the independence of Finland, although the Russian government was to retain the control of foreign affairs and of the army. The Provisional Government vetoed the bill as unconstitutional and with the concurrence of the Finnish Senate (by a 7 to 6 vote) dissolved the diet and ordered new elections. The Finnish social democrats, however, refused to submit. On September 15 (September 28, N.S.), practically on the eve of election day, eighty of the 200 deputies met in what they held to be a lawful session of the diet (the Russians regarded the assembly as illegal and tried unsuccessfully to prevent it) and passed, by giving it the required three readings, the controversial bill of July 5. Nevertheless elections were held, and gave a narrow majority to the non-socialist parties. The new non-socialist government headed by Svinhufud resumed half-hearted negotiations with Petrograd, and the diet was convened on November 1, N.S., less than a week before the overthrow of the Russian Provisional Government. With the advent of the Bolsheviks negotiations came to an end, and the independence of Finland was proclaimed on December 19, N.S.

Other national minorities, unlike Poland and Finland, were not endowed in modern times with national institutions of their own, and their claim to autonomy or independence rested on racial, linguistic, and religious grounds supported by historical arguments drawn from a distant and nebulous past. None of these claims was more persistent and vital to Russia than that of Ukraine. The resurgence of Ukrainian nationalism took the Russians by surprise because Ukraine, in spite of her name, was seldom thought of as borderland. Its fertile plains were the granary of the empire, and the Donets Valley was a major coal and metallurgical region. The Ukrainian language is easily understood by those who speak Russian and, rightly or wrongly, was generally considered a Russian dialect. To the man in the street the separation of Ukraine from Russia seemed absurd and unthinkable. Moreover, the Ukrainian national movement, at least in Russian Ukraine, was a weak and artificial growth; it was nurtured under Austrian auspices in Galicia and its influence was limited to a small group of intellectuals (the historian M. Hrushevsky, the novelist M. Vinnichenko, the journalist S. Petlyura) who, taking advantage of the Russian disorders, succeeded for a while in imparting to the frail Ukrainian nationalism a semblance of vitality.

The Ukrainian movement, like the other national movements, went through several successive stages: cultural autonomy, administrative autonomy, and independence either within or outside the Russian federation. In the middle of March a self-appointed Ukrainian delegation waited on the Provisional Government and requested the immediate introduction of the Ukrainian language in Ukrainian schools, courts, and administration and the creation in Petrograd of a central agency to deal with matters pertaining to Ukraine. Meanwhile the Ukrainian Central Rada (Council), an assembly of doubtful provenance, was set up in Kiev, gradually assumed the powers of a parliament, and endeavored to extend its authority throughout Ukraine, whose boundaries were still a matter of dispute between the Ukrainians and the Provisional Government. In June the Rada elected a general secretariat which was to function as a cabinet. The organization of a Ukrainian army proceeded rapidly, some of the regiments being taken over by the Ukrainians in contravention of the orders of the Russian command. In September the ships of the Black Sea fleet hoisted the Ukrainian flag. The official record of the Ukrainian movement was one of astonishing progress, and the new state appeared to be in the making. Yet these gains were largely illusory. The Soviets in Kiev and elsewhere in Ukraine paid little attention to the Rada, which was unrepresentative of the population and exercised no real authority (as the head of the general secretariat, Vinnichenko, admitted later).[11] Ukrainian soldiers paraded bravely in their picturesque uniforms, but their discipline, morale, and fighting spirit were no better than those of the Russians. For all the trappings of statehood the government of the Rada was but a stage setting behind which the true forces of the revolution were at work. The Rada and the general secretariat, nevertheless, engaged in long-drawn negotiations with the Provisional

[11] W. E. D. Allen, *The Ukraine: A History*, p. 280 *et seq.*

Government. The Russian ministers objected to what they regarded as excessive and unreasonable demands, protested, bargained, gave in, and at times withdrew the concessions granted. This tedious and inconclusive chapter of Russo-Ukrainian relations was closed by the October revolution. In the midst of the confusion and civil war that followed, the Rada proclaimed the independence of Ukraine, which, however, proved but a prelude to her reincorporation in the Russian (Soviet) state.

Developments in Ukraine were typical of what was taking place in the other borderlands, although in the Baltic provinces national movements rested on a firmer foundation and proved more viable. Latvia, Estonia, Lithuania, Belorussia (White Russia), Georgia, Armenia, Azerbaidzhan, the Crimean Moslems, and the peoples of Russian Asia and the far north were seized with a passion for autonomy and protection of national rights. With the approval of the Provisional Government a congress of national minorities, attended by about 100 delegates, met in Kiev in September. Nearly twenty national, ethnic, and religious groups (but not Poland and Finland) and twelve Cossack communities either sent representatives or pledged support. The congress outlined a program for the reorganization of Russia as a federation of independent states. The object in view was to be achieved through the cooperation of the central government with local constituent assemblies and administrative agencies. The aspirations of some of the minorities, however, went further and aimed at complete independence. Latvia, Estonia, and Lithuania achieved this status shortly after the Bolshevik revolution, and retained it until the outbreak of the Second World War.

CHAPTER XLVII

THE TWO REVOLUTIONS OF 1917: III

THE FIRST COALITION GOVERNMENT

The breakdown of the army, the agrarian revolution, labor unrest, seizure of factories, economic dislocation, and the loosening of the framework of the empire under the impact of surging local nationalism formed the somber setting for the desultory efforts of a tottering Provisional Government to maintain itself in power. There were six socialists and nine non-socialists in the coalition cabinet that took office on May 5; unlike their predecessors, the new ministers were delegated by the political parties and organizations to which they belonged and were deemed responsible to them. In the case of socialist ministers this meant responsibility to the Soviet. In the Provisional Government of May 5 Prince Lvov retained the office of president and minister of the interior, and Tereshchenko, formerly minister of finance, succeeded Miliukov at the foreign office. Kerensky became minister of war and navy. The most radical member of the government was Chernov, the minister of agriculture, a socialist revolutionary who had taken part in the Zimmerwald conference. As the coalition was formed with the sanction of the Soviet, the regime of "dual power" formally came to an end, but since no real reconciliation between the socialists and the non-socialists took place the conflict, as Trotsky noted at the time, was merely transferred to the cabinet. In other words, the coalition solved nothing, and the April-May crisis proved but the first of several reorganizations that deprived the Provisional Government of even a semblance of stability.

The program of the new cabinet (declaration of May 6) embodied the Soviet formula of "peace without annexations and indemnities" and a promise "to take preliminary steps" for a war-aim agreement with the allies, based on the Russian declaration of March 27,[1] but otherwise it merely restated the vague clichés of the earlier official pronouncements. Some of them were contradictory and mutually incompatible, for instance, the professed intention to strengthen both the fighting capacity of the army and the army committee system; nor was it feasible to revise the war aims "in agreement" with the allies. The interpretation of the program by Soviet leaders and nonsocialist ministers differed. According to *Izvestiia* (May 9) Russia henceforth would negotiate not only with allied governments but also "over the head of these governments, with the peoples themselves." Tereshchenko, who remained foreign minister until the October revolution, did not subscribe to this doctrine. There were surprisingly few changes in the higher personnel of the foreign office and no marked departure from the traditional methods of diplomacy. The exchange of views between Petrograd and allied capitals, including Washington, accomplished little except to make clear that, while allied governments would welcome the renunciation by Russia of her claims to Constantinople and other annexations, they saw no reason to revise their own war aims. Moreover, as Miliukov observed in his history of the revolution, Tereshchenko, in spite of his predilection for revolutionary phraseology, would seem to have remained faithful to the interpretation of Russia's "national interests" as expounded by his predecessor in office. Discussing at the Council of the Republic on October 16 the policies to be followed by the Russian delegation at the forthcoming allied conference in Paris, Tereshchenko stated that Russia must oppose territorial changes that would block her access to the Baltic and that "no Russian would agree to a peace that would humiliate Russia and infringe upon her national interests"; he demanded that "the territory of Russia should remain intact and that conditions safeguarding the economic development of her northern and southern regions should receive legal recognition." The latter statement was, presumably, a veiled reference to the Dardanelles and the Straits. The Soviet took a different view. As early as June 20 the all-Russian congress of the Soviets endorsed the principle of self-determination for national minorities, "including the right of secession," and the instruction drawn by the Central Executive Committee early in October for its delegate (Skobelev) to the proposed Paris conference spoke of "the full right of self-determination for Poland,

[1] See p. 1398.

Latvia, and Lithuania," and contained other provisions inacceptable to the Russian foreign office. To the very end the Provisional Government and the Soviet remained far apart on the issue of war aims.

The deep cleavage which developed within the coalition government had little to do with party lines. The leading group within the cabinet consisted of Kerensky, Nekrasov (constitutional democrat), and Tereshchenko (non-party but distinctly "bourgeois"), and was usually supported by Prince Lvov, while Kerensky and Chernov, both members of the Socialist Revolutionary Party, were at swords' points most of the time. The real menace to the Provisional Government and the less extreme socialist parties which controlled the Soviet, however, came from the Bolsheviks. The demonstration of April revealed the strength of the Bolshevik movement. Early in May the ranks of the extremists in Petrograd were reinforced by the arrival of Trotsky. Even before he joined the Bolshevik Party at the end of July, Trotsky was, next to Lenin, the most ardent, tireless, uncompromising, eloquent, and influential protagonist of the Bolshevik cause. The external progress of Bolshevism was not spectacular. In the Soviets, in various committees, and in the municipal councils elected under the democratic law of April 15 (proportional representation, universal suffrage, direct and secret ballot) the number of Bolsheviks remained small or even negligible. Of the 800 or 900 delegates attending the first all-Russian congress of the Soviets in June, slightly over 100 were Bolsheviks; together with the small supporting factions they controlled less than one-fifth of the votes. One should not, however, exaggerate the importance of these figures. In Russia, a country lacking in democratic tradition, party allegiance meant little. It is safe to say that few of the voters who cast their ballots for various socialist parties had a clear notion of the merits of their respective programs. Some of the meetings which elected unanimously Menshevik or socialist revolutionary delegates passed, also unanimously, resolutions endorsing Bolshevik slogans. Moreover, the non-Bolshevik socialist parties, by their participation in the coalition government, laid themselves open to the charge of having sold themselves to the "bourgeoisie." The reassuring evidence of the numerical weakness of Bolshevism notwithstanding, the swing of the masses towards the left was unmistakable. Few people had illusions as to what this meant. Indeed, in the months following the April demonstration the Provisional Government and those who did not believe in the benefit of an immediate socialist revolution lived in constant fear of a Bolshevik insurrection.

The Bolshevik demonstration which was planned in Petrograd for June 10 but was called off at the last moment caused considerable alarm. The congress of the Soviets denounced the proposed manifestation as a breach of the united revolutionary front, serving the interests of counter-revolution. This largely imaginary danger inspired the ill advised decision of Soviet leaders to hold on June 18 a peaceful demonstration of "the united revolutionary democracy" aligned behind the Provisional Government. The Bolsheviks eagerly seized the opportunity, turned out in force, and on June 18 banners bearing Bolshevik slogans ("End of the war," "Down with the capitalist ministers," and so on) by far outnumbered those calling for the support of the Provisional Government.

The authority of the government was flouted openly and with impunity. On March 17 the Kronstadt Soviet repudiated the Provisional Government and transferred its allegiance to the Petrograd Soviet. Although a perfunctory reconciliation was speedily arranged, the incident established a precedent and invited insubordination, while Kronstadt carried on, as before, a systematic nation-wide campaign against the government. Another somewhat fantastic storm center was the Durnovo summer estate (*dacha*) on the outskirts of the industrial Viborgsky suburb. Self-styled anarchists occupied the estate in the early days of the revolution and remained in possession unmolested until they created a minor sensation by a daring raid on a newspaper office (June 5). The Provisional Government ordered their eviction, but the Viborgsky workers went on strike and, supported by Kronstadt sailors, rallied to the defense of the anarchists. The Petrograd Soviet and the congress of the Soviets intervened and, while condemning the unauthorized action of the workers, set aside the eviction order. The anarchists, unexpectedly supported by the Soviets, won an easy victory over the government.

The Provisional Government was torn by profound dissensions. On June 18 the minister of commerce and industry, A. I. Konovalov, a wealthy Moscow industrialist and a liberal, resigned because of his disagreement with Skobelev, the socialist minister of labor. Concessions granted to Ukrainian nationalists by Kerensky, Tereshchenko, and Tsereteli (a Menshevik Soviet leader and minister of post and telegraph) led to the resignation on July 2 of four ministers, members of the Constitutional Democratic Party. It will be remembered that the offensive in Galicia began on June 18 and bogged down by the end of the month. It was at this critical juncture that a weakened and disunited Provisional Government was faced with a near insurrection.

THE JULY UPRISING

In the closing days of June the political atmosphere of the capital was charged with electricity. The Petrograd garrison was hostile to the offensive; and persistent rumors of the impending transfer of the "revolutionary" regiments to the front, as well as the refusal of the government to grant the customary summer furloughs to the older classes of the mobilized men, added to the restlessness of the troops. Closing of the factories, shortages of supplies, and the spiraling of the cost of living demoralized the workers and fomented discontent. It was believed that the calling off of the Bolshevik demonstration of June 10 was but a postponement, a belief strengthened by the massive display of Bolshevik slogans during the manifestation of June 18. Moreover, the patent helplessness of the Provisional Government invited revolt. The more extreme elements among the idle soldiers and workers craved action and grew impatient with the seemingly inexplicable timorousness and procrastination of the revolutionary leadership.

The initiative of the uprising which began in the late afternoon of July 3 came from the First Machine-Gun Regiment, a unit noted for its revolutionary zeal. Although friendly to the Bolsheviks, the machine gunners would seem, in this instance, to have acted contrary to the wishes not only of the Petrograd Soviet but also of Lenin and other Bolshevik leaders who opposed insurrection *at this time* and counseled patience. The call to armed rebellion met with ready response. Kronstadt sent a contingent of eager sailors; troops and workers poured into the streets; and huge crowds advanced menacingly towards the Taurida Palace. The insurgents clamored that the Central Executive Committee should immediately supersede the Provisional Government. This the committee refused to do and, indeed, branded the uprising as treasonable and "a stab in the back of our gallant army" (July 3). The Bolshevik Party, however, assumed the leadership of the movement, ostensibly to direct it into peaceful channels and to prevent counter-revolutionary outbreaks. Bolshevik headquarters at the

Kshesinsky palace became the general staff of the rebellion. In disregard of the prohibition of street demonstrations, columns numbering perhaps 500,000 formed on July 4 and converged upon the Taurida Palace. After long delays the delegates of the crowd were admitted in the palace; they demanded the adoption of the Bolshevik program and engaged in a long-drawn verbal wrangle with a sulky and frightened yet stubborn Central Executive Committee.

The demonstration was relatively orderly, although there were outbursts of violence and some desultory shooting; two or three scores of people were killed and over one hundred wounded. The real intentions of the Bolsheviks, however, were not known, and for a while the position of the Provisional Government, according to Miliukov, appeared desperate. Not all of the Petrograd troops were involved in the uprising; but as some of the regiments had declared their "neutrality" the effectives at the disposal of the government were exceedingly small. In the evening of July 3 Kerensky barely escaped arrest as his train left for the front shortly before the arrival of mutinous soldiers at the railway station. Chernov, the minister of agriculture, was roughly handled, and might have suffered a worse fate had it not been for the timely intervention of Trotsky. The other ministers, however, were not molested, and no steps were taken to occupy public buildings. The Bolshevik leaders did not seem to wish to push things to extremes. This being the case, the demonstration became pointless. The interminable discussions in the Taurida Palace damped enthusiasm, and the crowds, after waiting idly for hours in the adjoining streets and squares, drifted away. Even the Kronstadt sailors boarded their ships and went home. Meanwhile the minister of justice, P. N. Pereverzev, communicated to the "neutral" regiments of the guards documents which allegedly established that Lenin was a paid German agent. The disclosure produced a strong impression, and the guards, abandoning "neutrality," put themselves at the disposal of the government and the Central Executive Committee. The tide of the revolt was ebbing. In the early hours of July 5 the Central Executive Committee adopted a resolution of confidence in the Provisional Government. The editorial offices and printing plant of *Pravda* were raided and wrecked on July 5, and the next day the two strongholds of Bolshevism—the fortress of Peter and Paul and the Kshesinsky palace deserted by the Bolshevik leaders—were taken over without offering resistance; simultaneously the anarchists were ejected from their pleasant rural abode, while troops loyal to the government arrived from the front. In the morning of July 6 a Bolshevik leaflet announced that "the demonstration was over." To the Bolsheviks the July affair was a *ballon d'essai*. They were not yet sure of their ground and were not prepared for a real insurrection. Red guards, that is, armed detachments of workers, marched in the demonstration, but their number was small. The government could still count on loyal troops; the attitude of the workers and of the Petrograd garrison had not yet crystallized, and the revolt had few repercussions outside the capital. Lenin referred to the July rebellion as "something considerably more than a demonstration but less than a revolution." The immediate consequences to the party were dreary, but the experience taught the Bolsheviks a lesson by which they profited in October.

The documents incriminating Lenin and other Bolshevik leaders found their way into the newspapers in spite of the efforts of the government to stop publication. Kerensky held that the premature disclosure had prevented the apprehension of Lenin's accomplices and thus greatly weakened the case against him. Pereverzev was forced to resign. Other ministers, however, were unconvinced that the evidence was valid, and they questioned the reliability of the source from which it was obtained. The publication of the documents, nevertheless, created a sensation. In wartime, spy hunting is a popular sport, and the sinister activities of the German agents offered a facile explanation of Russia's disorders and the breakdown of the army. To the general public the fact that Lenin returned to Russia by way of Germany was conclusive evidence of his guilt.[2] The assumption that the participants in the July revolt were German agents or their dupes soothed the pangs of socialist conscience and simplified the task of retribution. On July 6 warrants were issued for the arrest of Lenin, Zinovev, and Kamenev. Lenin, however, went into hiding, first in Petrograd and later in Finland. Zinovev, too, eluded the police. Both protested their innocence but declared that they could not count on a fair trial. A special commission was appointed to investigate the ramifications of the revolt. There were numerous arrests, including those

[2] Miliukov and Kerensky (to mention only two) have maintained in their writings published in exile that Lenin and his friends were German agents financed from Berlin. This theory is implausible; and even if it could be proved—which, so far as I know, has never been done—that Lenin received funds from Germany this would not be conclusive evidence that such payments influenced his opinions and policies. His devotion to the cause of socialist revolution is not open to doubt.

of Trotsky and A. V. Lunacharsky (July 23). The government enacted emergency legislation dealing severely with incitement to crime and insubordination; if carried on in the armed forces such activities were deemed treasonable. Regiments participating in the uprising were disbanded and the men sent to the front; in some cases resistance was encountered and force had to be used. The circulation of Bolshevik papers at the front was prohibited, and several of these papers were closed.

The sudden display of energy and firmness on the part of the government was due not only to the revolt but also to the breakdown at the front. It will be remembered that the death penalty and military tribunals in the theater of war were instituted, at Kornilov's request, on July 12. This unexpected turn of events raised the hopes of the more conservative elements and brought forth a flood of approving resolutions from intrinsically weak yet conspicuous right-wing organizations, such as the Military League and the Officers' Union. The resurgence of their activities was watched with concern in Soviet circles and raised the dreaded specter of counter-revolution and military dictatorship. Some of the local Soviets, trade unions, and other "democratic" bodies passed resolutions exonerating the Bolsheviks and condemning official policies.

THE SECOND COALITION GOVERNMENT

Paradoxically, the Provisional Government which put up a brave show of authority was itself living through a crisis, with several ministerial posts vacant and portfolios changing hands. On July 8 the distraught, bewildered, and exhausted Prince Lvov resigned because of his disapproval of socialist trends among his colleagues, especially of Chernov's agrarian policy. He was succeeded as prime minister by Kerensky, whose rump cabinet a joint session of the two Central Executive Committees (Peasants' and Workers' and Soldiers' Deputies) proclaimed "the government of the salvation of the revolution," clothed with "plenary powers"; the same resolution, however, provided that the socialist ministers should report to the Central Executive Committees "at least twice a week" (July 9). The following fortnight was filled with tortuous negotiations, doctrinaire discussions, and obscure political maneuvers, including Kerensky's resignation on July 21. The outcome of complicated moves, counter-moves, and compromises was the formation on July 24 of the second coalition government. Kerensky was the prime minister as well as minister of war and navy, although his deputies, with the title of minister, were in charge of the two service departments. Tereshchenko retained the foreign office and Chernov the ministry of agriculture. Of the eighteen members of the cabinet eleven were socialists; nevertheless, as Miliukov rightly noted, the second coalition was less radical than that of May 5, in which the socialists were in a minority. This distinction, however, was tenuous: the tenure of ministerial offices was increasingly ephemeral, and the Provisional Government became identified, in practice, with the person of Kerensky. The members of the July cabinet were his personal appointees. Kerensky, Tereshchenko, and Nekrasov (vice premier and minister of finance) were the only survivals from the first Provisional Government. Contrary to precedent, the new government issued no joint declaration of policy but merely an appeal signed by the prime minister. Written in Kerensky's unmistakable flamboyant style, the appeal spoke of the necessity of "iron rule" (*zheleznaia vlast*) and asserted that "freedom welded by national unity and enthusiasm cannot be defeated. The Russian people will carry it out through blood and sufferings into a radiant future, will create for the good (*blago*) of mankind a new, free, and great Russia." It would have been difficult to draw a more misleading picture both of Russia's conditions at the time and of prospects for the future.

SUBSTITUTES FOR PARLIAMENT

The brief span between the formation of the second coalition and the October *coup d'état* was the twilight of the regime of which Kerensky was the head, the inspiration, and the symbol. As viewed from the Smolny, headquarters of the Soviet,[3] and from the Winter Palace, where Kerensky established his residence after the July uprising, Russia's liberties were threatened from two sides: the real and growing danger of Bolshevism, on the left, and the spurious and problematic menace of counter-revolution and military dictatorship, on the right. From the inception of the Provisional Government its claim to national leadership was vitiated by its inability to rely upon a representative popular assembly. The Soviets reflected the views of but a segment of socialist opinion and, even after the formation of the coali-

---

[3] The transfer of the Petrograd Soviet to the Smolny, a former convent and girls' school, was necessitated by the remodeling of the Taurida Palace for the meeting of the Constituent Assembly.

tion, tended to dictate their will to the Provisional Government rather than to support it, an attitude which undermined the very principle of partnership between the socialist and the non-socialist groups. Although the provisional committee of the Duma continued to function, it was heartily disliked in left-wing circles as a suspicious relic of the past. The abolition of the State Duma was, indeed, a perennial demand of the Soviets. The statute on the elections to the Constituent Assembly was promulgated, after several postponements, in September, and elections were set for the middle of November. Time, however, was pressing as the position of the government became increasingly insecure. Hence the attempts to provide a substitute for parliament that would express more completely than the Soviets the feeling of the nation.

The earliest experiment along these lines was the one-day session of the members of the four State Dumas held on April 27. In the midst of the July crisis Kerensky, on the initiative of a non-socialist minister (I. V. Godnev), decided to convene what became known as the State Conference, which met in Moscow on August 13 to 15. A huge gathering of nearly 2,500, the State Conference consisted of the deputies to the four State Dumas, and representatives of the Soviets, local governments, cooperative societies, trade unions, associations of manufacturers and landowners, universities, national minorities, the army, and liberal professions. The Bolsheviks were prevented from taking an active part in the proceedings but marked the opening of the conference by organizing a general strike in Moscow. The State Conference, contrary to the hopes of its sponsors, merely emphasized the deep cleavage of public opinion. The next move came from the Soviets. Aroused by the Kornilov affair (about which more will be said below) and by "counter-revolutionary opinions" expressed by a section of the State Conference, the Central Executive Committee organized in Petrograd the Democratic Conference (September 14 to 22). Its membership was even more haphazard than that of the State Conference and, broadly speaking, was drawn from the groups constituting the left wing of that assembly. Although the Provisional Government at first denied any official status to the Democratic Conference, a compromise was eventually reached and led to the appointment of the Provisional Council of the Republic (or pre-parliament), an advisory assembly with a membership of 550, including 150 non-socialists. It met on October 7, but the Bolsheviks withdrew at the opening session and took no part in its work. The Council of the Republic was still arguing about "strong authority" and "iron rule" when it was dispersed by the Bolsheviks on October 25, a few hours before the overthrow of the Provisional Government.

THE KORNILOV "MUTINY"

The quest for a "strong government" was at the root of the unhappy Kornilov affair, which threw Russia into a state of political turmoil. The July uprising and the disaster of the military offensive laid bare the weakness of the central authority and provoked much loose talk about the establishment of a "democratic" or military dictatorship. The revolution, however, produced few leaders of national stature, and in the summer of 1917 discussions of "iron rule" revolved around the names of Kerensky and Kornilov. In spite of the unrelieved record of disaster and futility, Kerensky was still held as "indispensable" even by many of those who disagreed with his policies (Prince Lvov, Miliukov, Savinkov, and—prior to August 27—even Kornilov).[4] His still great popularity and the fact that alone among the prominent revolutionary leaders he was definitely committed to cooperation with the non-socialist elements—a cooperation deemed necessary both by the liberals and by the non-Bolshevik socialists—made Kerensky the pivot of any ministerial combination based on the preservation of the existing balance of political forces. In July and August Bolshevism was seemingly in retreat and Kornilov appeared to many as the alternative to Kerensky, unless a way was found to bring the two leaders to

[4] The former emperor was among Kerensky's admirers. Welcoming his appointment as prime minister, Nicholas wrote in his diary on July 8 that Kerensky "was the right man in the right place. The more power he gets, the better." The events of June and July had a profound effect upon the destinies of the imperial family. On the morrow of the revolution Kerensky announced that Nicholas, Alexandra Fedorovna, and their children would be conveyed, under his supervision, to Murmansk and then would sail for England. This generous plan was never carried out. The British government, having at first agreed to provide asylum for the tsar, a first cousin of King George V, eventually withdrew its offer, nor were the Soviets prepared to let their victims escape. Since the early days of March the former emperor, empress, and their children had been under arrest at the palace of Tsarskoe Selo. In the summer the possibility of a German advance on Petrograd, as well as the threatening attitude of the extreme revolutionary groups, particularly the Kronstadt sailors, led to the removal of the prisoners. On Aug. 1, 1917, they left Tsarskoe Selo and were transported to Tobolsk, in Siberia, where they were confined in the residence of the governor. In the spring of 1918 they were moved to Ekaterinburg and on July 16 of that year were slaughtered in the cellar of the Ipatev house which served as their last place of detention.

work together in a Provisional Government reconstructed on a broader basis.

The rise of Kornilov was nearly as spectacular as that of his political rival. Born into a poor Cossack peasant family, General Kornilov was captured by the Austrians in 1915, made a spectacular escape, and became something of a national hero. He was in command of the Petrograd garrison in the early weeks of the revolution, a position he resigned after the April demonstration when the troops refused to obey orders unless they were counter-signed by the Soviet. The failure of the Galician offensive made Kerensky turn for assistance to the plain-speaking, forceful general who enjoyed a high reputation for integrity, firmness, and personal courage. Kornilov was appointed, first, commander of the southwestern front and, on July 18, commander in chief. His early measures for the restoration of discipline met with Kerensky's unreserved support. The fact that the enemy advance came to a stop and that headquarters and the government spoke at last the language of authority greatly enhanced Kornilov's reputation as a man of action, but this display of determination inevitably aroused the apprehensions of those who dreaded counter-revolution and the emergence of military dictatorship. Kerensky shared these fears.

Kornilov was not a statesman, had no understanding of the weird cross-current of Russian socialism, and in political matters depended on the counsel of an ill assorted group of adventurers clustered about the Mogilev headquarters. Like most professional soldiers, he hated the Soviets and army committees but was prepared to put up with them, at least temporarily, provided their activities were confined within narrow bounds, a pious hope in the conditions prevailing in the summer of 1917. Kornilov's program for the restoration of order at the front and in the rear was approved "in principle" by Kerensky as well as by Filonenko, commissar at headquarters, and Savinkov, acting minister of war, but its implementation met with insurmountable obstacles. Both temperamentally and in their political views Kerensky and Kornilov were poles apart, and neither trusted the other. Their mutual suspicions thrived on rumors, not all of them unfounded, which circulated in Petrograd, Moscow, and Mogilev. Kornilov knew that Kerensky was looking for a new commander in chief, and Kerensky knew that he was hated by the officers' corps and that his removal was common talk at Mogilev. Moreover, Kornilov, like Kerensky, enjoyed the external attributes of power. His communications to the Provisional Government had the metallic ring of combat orders, and on his public appearances he was invariably surrounded by an escort of picturesque, fierce-looking Caucasian horsemen. The estrangement between the prime minister and the commander in chief was demonstrated at the Moscow State Conference: Kornilov's address (August 14) brought delirious ovations from the right, while Kerensky was enthusiastically applauded by the left.

Military events precipitated the conflict. On August 18 the Germans launched an attack in the northern sector of the Russian front, crossed the Western Dvina River, and on August 21 (September 3, N.S.) occupied Riga. The road to Petrograd lay open and the evacuation of the capital appeared imminent. This tragic eventuality raised a thorny political issue: Petrograd was the heart and the brain of the revolution, and its proposed evacuation was resisted in Soviet circles as a counter-revolutionary move.[5] The military reversal called for strong remedial action, but the government could not make up its mind to adopt Kornilov's program, partly because of the Soviet opposition to the reinstatement of the death penalty in the rear. On August 24 Savinkov told Kornilov that a Bolshevik demonstration was expected in Petrograd on the 28 or the 29, and requested that a cavalry corps should be moved to the capital to protect the Provisional Government. This request was in agreement with a decision reached independently by Kornilov. The Moscow State Conference and the fall of Riga confirmed him in the belief that the salvation of Russia depended on the establishment of a "strong" government dominated by the commander in chief. The participation of Kerensky in the reconstructed cabinet was deemed desirable (although some of Kornilov's advisers strongly opposed it), and the execution of the plan was to be secured, if necessary, by the use of force. Hence the dispatch of a cavalry corps to Petrograd.

In this perilous and explosive situation the well meaning indiscretions of V. N. Lvov had the effect of the spark that starts the detonation. V. N. Lvov (who is not to be confused with Prince G. E. Lvov) was chief procurator of the Holy Synod in the Provisional Govern-

[5] Kornilov's reference in his address at the State Conference to the probable fall of Riga is used in recent Soviet historiography as conclusive evidence that the abandonment of that city was deliberately planned by the Russian high command. These strictures were rejected, on solid grounds, by earlier Soviet historians, for instance, Kakurin (*Razlozhenie armii v 1917 godu*, pp. 182–184).

ments of March to July. A politician of conservative affiliations, Lvov espoused, with more enthusiasm than wisdom, the cause of the Kerensky-Kornilov reconciliation. In a conspiratorial fashion he injected himself into the political picture (August 22 to 26) and unwittingly succeeded in creating the impression that he was Kornilov's spokesman at the Winter Palace and Kerensky's spokesman in Mogilev. The outcome of this truly fantastic misunderstanding was an "agreement" under the terms of which all power was to be transferred to the commander in chief and the Provisional Government was to resign. Kerensky was to put himself under the protection of Kornilov and to hold office in the reconstructed cabinet, although even Lvov, who was not noted for perspicacity, realized that Kerensky might be arrested or even murdered. Nevertheless on the face of it the "agreement" (August 26) paved the way for the "legal and peaceful" transfer of power to a government headed by Kornilov, of which Kerensky would be a member. But what was "agreement" to Lvov and Kornilov was "ultimatum" and "conspiracy" to Kerensky. As soon as Lvov's proposals, represented as Kornilov's demands, were authenticated by witnesses concealed in the prime minister's office and by cryptic teletype messages to and from the army headquarters, the hapless go-between was arrested by order of his "friend" Kerensky. Kornilov was relieved of his command but refused to submit; he branded as a "pack of lies" the official statement explaining his dismissal, and proclaimed that "the Provisional Government, under the pressure of the Bolshevik majority of the Soviets, acts in full agreement with the plans of the German general staff, kills the army, and destroys the country internally" (August 27).[6]

The peremptory dismissal of Kornilov did not entirely settle the issue of "mutiny." Kerensky's political friends (Tereshchenko, Filonenko, Savinkov) were of the opinion that the Lvov incident was a ghastly misunderstanding. Commanders of army groups expressed their confidence in Kornilov and urged that he should remain at his post. General Alekseev declined the offer to become his successor. It would seem that even Kerensky's faith in the "mutiny" theory,

[6] On Aug. 27 the Bolsheviks did not yet control the Soviets. Kornilov's proclamation gives the measure of his ignorance of the political situation, although in 1917 it was common practice in conservative circles, especially among army officers, to lump together Bolsheviks, Mensheviks, socialist revolutionaries, and the Soviets. To Kornilov "counter-revolution" meant the restoration of the monarchy, which was not a part of his plan.

of which he was the originator, faltered. In the early hours of August 28 he made a belated appeal to the newspapers to cancel the publication of the official indictment, but his request could not be complied with for technical reasons. With the publication on August 28 of charges and counter-charges the breach between Kornilov and the government was complete and the offer of mediation made the same evening by Sir George Buchanan on behalf of the diplomatic corps had no practical consequences. Kerensky issued stringent orders to check the advance of the cavalry corps which Savinkov had sought as a defense against the Bolsheviks. Exaggerated rumors of the progress of the troops created near panic among the supporters of the government. These fears were devoid of foundation. The movement of the echelons was obstructed by the railway workers and, what was far more important, the morale of the Cossacks and cavalrymen under Kornilov's orders was not different from that of the rest of the Russian army: the men did not wish to fight, least of all in a civil war. As Miliukov tersely put it, "The issue here, as at the front, was decided not by the leaders but by the common soldiers." Kornilov's reputation as a stern disciplinarian responsible for the restoration of the death penalty in the army was not an asset. Moreover, the commander in chief, suffering from a severe attack of fever, had remained at his headquarters in Mogilev. Leaderless, scattered along railway tracks with no facilities for feeding men or horses, subject to the relentless propaganda of the local Soviets, the idle and hungry soldiers of the "counter-revolutionary" army spent endless hours in debating the insoluble issue: Who was the real traitor—Kornilov or Kerensky? On August 30 General Krymov, commander of the cavalry corps, was arrested at Luga and sent to Petrograd, where, after an interview with the prime minister, he shot himself. On the same day (August 31) delegates of the Kornilov troops were received by Kerensky and pledged obedience to the Provisional Government. The "mutiny" was over.

Contrary to expectations Kornilov, reputedly entrenched in Mogilev with a strong body of loyal troops, surrendered without firing a shot (September 1) and, with several other army leaders, was imprisoned in Bykhov. On August 30 Kerensky became commander in chief, an office he combined with that of prime minister. Simultaneously General Alekseev took over the duties of chief of staff, but he resigned ten days later because the government insisted on trying the officers involved in the "mutiny." He was succeeded by General N. N. Dukhonin, the last chief of staff under the Provisional Government.

The Kornilov affair is often represented as the decisive turning point in the history of the revolution. Leaving aside the Lvov imbroglio, it is clear that Kornilov, on his own admission, was resolved to bring about the reorganization of the government, if necessary, by force. Technically this was mutiny, or came dangerously close to it. Yet many of his level-headed contemporaries saw the situation in a different light. "Kornilov did not seek power for himself," General Alekseev wrote to Miliukov on September 12, 1917. "His aim was the creation of a strong, dependable government consisting of men capable of leading Russia to her salvation. But this is the wish and ambition of all honest people who love their country." The personal issue between Kerensky and Kornilov is of minor interest. The real significance of the Kornilov episode—for it was no more than an episode—was to expose the groundlessness of hope for, and fear of, a counter-revolution. In August, 1917, a "strong" government resting on principles such as professed by Kornilov, Alekseev, Miliukov, and also Kerensky—continuation of the war, restoration of discipline, respect for the right of property—was beyond the realm of possibility. Unlike the revolutions of February and October, the Kornilov "counter-revolution" introduced no new factors in the situation but merely accentuated the existing trends. It probably shortened the life span of the Provisional Government, but it did not cause, nor could it have prevented, its downfall.

THE THIRD COALITION GOVERNMENT

Whatever the historic significance of the Kornilov "mutiny," its immediate consequences were grave. On August 26 all the ministers placed their resignations in the hands of Kerensky but, at his request, continued in office on a day-to-day basis. Kerensky thus became a quasi-dictator, his position being enhanced by his assumption of the office of commander in chief. On September 1 there was formed the "directory," an inner cabinet of five members headed by Kerensky and vested, in theory, with plenary powers. A score of ministers, among them Chernov and Savinkov, were dismissed, and new men were appointed by Kerensky to the vacant offices. Kerensky wished to reconstruct the government on a coalition basis but met at first with the opposition of the Central Executive Committee, which took the view that the involvement of the Constitutional Democratic Party and other "bourgeois" groups in the "mutiny" disqualified their members from holding office. Nevertheless, after protracted negotiations which had a Talmudic flavor the third coalition government was formed on September 25. Headed by Kerensky, it consisted of ten socialist and six non-socialist ministers and remained in power until the Bolshevik *coup d'état*. Meanwhile Kerensky, to placate his left-wing supporters, enacted several measures demanded by the Soviets. On September 1 Russia was proclaimed a republic, a step to which the non-socialists foolishly took strong exception on the ground that it was a usurpation of the powers of the Constituent Assembly. The Kornilov program for the restoration of discipline and order in the army and in the rear was shelved. The State Duma was formally dissolved on October 6. Prominent right-wing politicians, among them Guchkov, were arrested; organizations in sympathy with the Kornilov movement, such as the Officers' Union, were disbanded; and the higher army personnel, including the Mogilev headquarters, was drastically purged. In spite of Kerensky's orders for the strict observance of discipline, there were numerous arrests and lynching of officers, especially at the naval bases of Abo, Viborg, and Helsingfors.

The extreme revolutionary elements derived no mean benefit from the confusion created by the Kornilov affair. On August 27 Kerensky appealed for assistance to the Bolshevik Party; and the Soviets and other "democratic" agencies proceeded with the arming of workers (Red guards) and set up "committees for the salvation of the revolution" which showed no inclination to disband when directed to do so by Kerensky (September 4). Trotsky was freed on bail (September 4), as were other Bolshevik leaders arrested in connection with the July revolt, an act of clemency for which they showed no gratitude. The defeat, or rather the inevitable failure, of the counter-revolution from the right was a windfall to the inevitable upswing of the revolution from the left.

THE BOLSHEVIKS ON THE EVE OF OCTOBER

The July revolt marked the temporary retreat of Bolshevism. The closing of Bolshevik newspapers, exclusion of Bolshevik publications from the army, arrest or forced disappearances of Bolshevik leaders, and the intense campaign against Lenin and others accused of being German agents seemed, for a time, to have achieved their objective.

The ebbing of the Bolshevik tide, however, was brief, and within a few weeks the Bolshevik Party not only regained the ground lost but was expanding its influence. In August and September elections to municipal councils, Soviets, trade unions, and other agencies showed, as compared with the earlier period, a substantial increase in the Bolshevik vote at the expense of that of other socialist parties. The membership of the Bolshevik Party nevertheless remained small, though it rose from 24,000 at the beginning of 1917 to about 200,000 in August.

The anti-Bolshevik attitude of the Central Executive Committee during the July revolt led to the temporary abandonment of the slogan "All power to the Soviets." In the pamphlet *On Slogans* written early in July, Lenin argued that the slogan "All power to the Soviets" was appropriate for the opening phase of the revolution, when state power was shared by the "bourgeois" Provisional Government and the "democratic" Soviets, and when there was a strong probability that the Soviets would pass under Bolshevik control. It was the slogan of "peaceful transfer of power from the bourgeoisie to the workers and peasants." On July 4, however, according to Lenin's most questionable interpretation, state power was taken over by the counter-revolutionary bourgeoisie aided by the Mensheviks and the socialist revolutionaries. The "painless" assumption of power by the proletariat was no longer possible, and in the altered situation the slogan "All power to the Soviets" had become "a mockery." The Soviets, Lenin held, would reassert themselves in the future, but the *existing* Soviets, tainted by collaboration with the bourgeoisie, were not representative of the working class. The sixth congress of the Bolshevik Party (July 26 to August 3) endorsed Lenin's views, although not without misgivings: the discarded slogan was one of the pillars of Bolshevik propaganda. For a while factory committees and trade unions were singled out by the Bolsheviks as the true agencies of the revolutionary proletariat. Common opposition to the Kornilov movement, however, brought together the Bolsheviks and the Soviets and led Lenin, in the article *On Compromises* written on September 1, to revive the slogan "All power to the Soviets." Although the compromise he advocated (a cabinet of moderate socialists responsible to the Soviet) did not materialize, the Bolsheviks became the majority party in the Petrograd Soviet (August 31) and in the Moscow Soviet (September 6). The slogan "All power to the Soviets" was therefore retained but was given a sterner meaning: All power to the *Bolshevik* Soviets. It was no longer a question of the peaceful transfer of power to the proletariat. "The problem of the assumption of power by the Soviets," Lenin wrote early in October,[7] "is the problem of the successful insurrection." Armed insurrection was, indeed, the issue that dominated Bolshevik thought and the Russian scene in September and October.

Although, according to Lenin, the July revolt ended the regime of "dual power" and inaugurated that of the counter-revolutionary bourgeoisie which must be overthrown by force, he realized that Bolshevism had suffered a setback, and he did not advocate an armed uprising in the immediate future.[8] A resolution of the sixth congress of the Bolshevik Party, which Lenin directed from his hideout in Finland, urged the workers to wait and to avoid any action that might lead to an open clash. The events of the end of August and beginning of September brought a sharp reversal of Lenin's strategy. "Having obtained a majority in the Soviets of Workers' and Soldiers' Deputies in the two capital cities [Petrograd and Moscow] the Bolsheviks can and must take power," Lenin wrote to the central committee of the party in the middle of September. "The majority of the people is *for* us. . . . The Bolshevik government alone will satisfy the peasantry. . . . Why should power be taken by the Bolsheviks *now?* Because the impending surrender of Petrograd would reduce our chances a hundredfold. And we cannot prevent the surrender of Petrograd while the army is headed by Kerensky and Company. One cannot 'wait' for the Constituent Assembly. . . . Our party alone, by taking power, will assure the convocation of the Constituent Assembly. . . . Separate peace between the British and the German imperialists can and must be prevented only by rapid action. . . . The issue should be made clear to the party: to put on the order of the day *armed insurrection* in Petrograd and Moscow . . . conquest of power, overthrow of the government. . . . By taking power simultaneously in Moscow and Petrograd we shall win unconditionally and indubitably." The inter-

---

[7] *Theses for the Petrograd All-City Conference and Mandate for the Delegates to the Party Conference.*

[8] The doctrine of the counter-revolutionary character of the Provisional Government formed in July was endorsed by the sixth congress of the Bolshevik Party. Trotsky rightly observed that this formula was, "to say the least, inaccurate." If in July power had passed into the hands of the "military clique," why should the same "military clique" attempt a mutiny in August? Leon Trotsky, *The History of the Russian Revolution* (New York, 1934), II, 320.

national situation, especially disturbances in the German navy, made immediate action imperative, according to Lenin. "The world workers' revolution has begun . . ." he wrote on October 7. "Doubts are impossible. We stand on the threshold of the world proletarian revolution."

These views, like the *April Theses*, were at first strongly resisted in high party circles, where it was believed that an insurrection would be untimely and suicidal: even if it were successful the Bolsheviks would be speedily overthrown.[9] Lenin, however, refused to wait, and urged the Bolsheviks to arrest the Democratic Conference. "History will not forgive us if we do not take power now," he wrote to the central committee in the middle of September. He fought bitterly against the view that the insurrection should be postponed until the convocation of the second all-Russian congress of the Soviets, which was convened for October 20 but did not meet until the 25.[10] "To delay is a crime," Lenin wrote to the central committee early in October. "To

[9] Lenin, in *Letter to the Comrades* written on Oct. 16 and 17, dealt with the following arguments advanced by party members against the insurrection: "We have no majority among the people; without the fulfillment of this condition the insurrection is hopeless. . . . We are not strong enough to take power and the bourgeoisie is not strong enough to destroy the Constituent Assembly. . . . The Soviets must be the gun held at the forehead of the government to force it to convoke the Constituent Assembly and to give up 'Kornilov adventures.' . . . The bourgeoisie cannot surrender Petrograd to the Germans . . . because the fighting is done not by the bourgeoisie but by our heroic sailors. . . . We are getting stronger every day, we may form a powerful opposition in the Constituent Assembly: why should we risk everything? . . . If the Kornilov supporters start again, we will show them, but to begin ourselves—why take the chance? . . . There is nothing in the international situation to force us to intervene immediately; we shall rather harm the cause of the socialist revolution in the west if we let ourselves be shot down. . . . Everyone is against us [the Central Executive Committee and all non-Bolshevik left-wing groups], we are isolated. . . . We have no reliable ties with railway workers and postal employees . . . is it possible to win without the Post Office and the railways? . . . Petrograd has bread for two or three days: how shall we feed the insurgents? . . . The situation at the front is not really threatening; if the soldiers themselves conclude an armistice, what of it? . . . According to all reports the masses are not eager to dash into the streets. . . . A Marxist party . . . cannot reduce the question of insurrection to that of military conspiracy. . . ."

[10] The Central Executive Committee was still controlled by socialists of non-Bolshevik persuasion, and its leaders opposed the convocation of the congress of the Soviets on the ground that this would interfere with the elections to the Constituent Assembly. The decision to hold the congress was reached on Sept. 26, after Trotsky had threatened that in case of the inaction of the Central Executive Committee the initiative in summoning the congress would be taken by the Petrograd Soviet.

wait for the congress of the Soviets is a childish play with formalities, a disgraceful play with formalities, a betrayal of the revolution." On October 10 Lenin attended in disguise a meeting of the central committee of the Bolshevik Party held in Petrograd. Twelve of the twenty-one members were present. After a discussion lasting for nearly ten hours, the committee approved, by a vote of 10 to 2, Lenin's clumsily worded resolution declaring that "armed insurrection is inevitable and [the time for it] fully ripe." Party agencies were directed "to discuss and approach" all practical issues from that standpoint. The resolution gave the following reasons for the momentous decision: the international situation (mutiny in the German navy, manifest progress of "the world socialist revolution in the whole of Europe," threat of a peace between the imperialists in order to strangle the Russian revolution); the military situation ("the unquestionable determination of the Russian bourgeoisie and Kerensky" to surrender Petrograd to the Germans); the formation of the Bolshevik majorities in the Soviets; peasant uprisings and the shift of popular confidence towards the Bolsheviks; and, finally, "the indubitable preparation of a second 'Kornilov movement'" (withdrawal of revolutionary troops from Petrograd, sending of Cossacks to the capital). Of these reasons only three (not unimportant ones)—control of the leading Soviets by the Bolsheviks, intensification of the agrarian revolution, and the popularity of Bolshevik slogans with the masses—had any foundation in facts.

The two members who voted against the resolution were Zinovev and Kamenev, Lenin's political associates of long standing. The meeting of October 10 elected a political bureau of seven members, including Lenin, Trotsky, Zinovev, Kamenev, and Stalin. The political bureau, however, did not meet in October and had no part in organizing the insurrection. Kamenev, Zinovev, Lunacharsky, and several other prominent Bolsheviks continued openly to oppose the policy adopted by the central committee and had numerous adherents among the rank and file of the party. Party discipline and organization were still notoriously loose. Lenin, disgusted with the lukewarmness of the central committee towards the insurrection (prior to October 10), tendered his resignation from that body; Kamenev, too, offered his resignation, but because he disagreed with the decision of October 10. Although Kamenev's resignation was formally accepted, both he and Lenin, as well as Zinovev, remained members of the central committee.

OVERTHROW OF THE PROVISIONAL GOVERNMENT

The direction of the insurrection was in the hands of the military revolutionary committee set up by the Petrograd Soviet in order to prevent the removal of the Petrograd garrison and "to safeguard the revolutionary defense of Petrograd against the openly prepared attack by the military and civilian supporters of Kornilov." Accepted in principle on October 9 but not formally approved until a week later, the committee began to function on October 20. Trotsky, elected chairman of the Petrograd Soviet on September 23, was also chairman of the military revolutionary committee. On October 16 the central committee of the Bolshevik Party appointed a "party center" of five members, including Stalin, which was to be incorporated in the military revolutionary committee. Although held by Soviet historiography as the master-mind of the insurrection, the "party center" does not seem to have ever come into existence and no references to it are to be found in contemporary records. Lenin, still in hiding, did not appear at the Smolny, seat of the Petrograd Soviet and of the Bolshevik central committee, until the evening of October 24. The immediate responsibility for the planning of the insurrection rested with Trotsky, a revolutionary of fanatical devotion to the cause, resourcefulness, and imagination. The four or five days between the establishment of the military revolutionary committee and the overthrow of the Provisional Government were obviously too short a time for the adequate preparation of a major insurrection. Trotsky, in his history of the revolution, readily admits the clumsiness and crudities of the plans hastily devised by amateur strategists under his direction, and he suggests as the real explanation of the easy victory of the insurgents: "The weakness of the government exceeded all expectations."

The impending uprising was an open secret and was freely discussed in the Soviets, in the press, and elsewhere. The day of the actual outbreak, however, was not known and, indeed, was not decided upon by the Bolshevik leaders until the last moment, although it was understood that the insurrection should take place before the opening of the congress of the Soviets. Meanwhile the military revolutionary committee organized Red guards, distributed arms, appointed commissars to army units, and secured the allegiance of the Petrograd troops, whose pro-Bolshevik ardor was fanned by the refusal of the Soviet to countenance the government's decision to send to the front the regiments quartered in the capital. On October 21 the military revolutionary committee appointed commissars to supervise the activities of the commander of the Petrograd garrison, Colonel Polkovnikov: all his orders were to be counter-signed by a commissar. When Polkovnikov refused to submit to the dictation of the committee, the latter announced that it had assumed full control of the defense of the capital and that no one else had the power to issue military orders. The Provisional Government could not ignore this overt act, and in the night of October 23 decided to institute legal proceedings against the members of the military revolutionary committee, to rearrest the Bolshevik leaders free on bail, to close Bolshevik newspapers, and to bring to Petrograd from the near-by garrisons loyal troops, chiefly cadets of the military schools. In the morning hours of October 24, steps were taken to carry out these and kindred measures. The Bolshevik-controlled cruiser *Aurora*, which entered the Neva and came to anchor opposite the Winter Palace, was ordered to put out to sea. The editorial offices and plant of two Bolshevik papers (*Rabochii put* and *Soldat*) were seized by the cadets, who also occupied bridges and patrolled the main thoroughfares. The *Aurora* sailors, however, ignored the order and put themselves unreservedly at the disposal of the military revolutionary committee. By 11 A.M. the troops of the committee ejected the cadets from the offices of the Bolshevik papers, which were printed and distributed. Both the Provisional Government and the military revolutionary committee issued appeals charging each other with "provocation" and warning the population against unauthorized outbreaks by which counter-revolution alone was to profit.

At the afternoon session of the Council of the Republic, Kerensky, in a highly emotional speech, promised to crush the revolt of "the rabble" (*chern*) and called for the whole-hearted support of the assembly. The council, however, after hours of futile casuistry and wrangling, passed a resolution which partly blamed the Provisional Government for the existing situation and demanded the immediate transfer of all privately owned land to the land committees, an energetic peace policy including the publication of secret agreements, and the establishment of a committee of public salvation that would work "in contact with the Provisional Government." A. F. Dan, a Menshevik leader and chairman of the Central Executive Committee, who was a member of the delegation which communicated the resolution to Kerensky, asserted that Bolshevik influence was "rapidly declining," and stated shortly thereafter (at the night session of the Central Executive Committee) that never was the danger of counter-revolution from the right more imminent. Although the council had no authority and commanded no public support, Kerensky chose to regard the resolution as a vote of no confidence, and announced his intention to resign. Such were the insight and level of political maturity and statecraft of the men who nominally controlled Russia's destinies at a fateful turn of her history.

In the night of October 24 Lenin and Trotsky openly took the offensive. Armed detachments under the orders of the military revolutionary committee occupied railway terminals, bridges, the State Bank, the telephone exchange, the central post office, and other public buildings. Since all the troops (with the exception of a few "neutral" regiments, among them the Cossacks) were on the side of the insurgents, there was no opposition and no bloodshed. After a sleepless night spent in fruitless negotiations with the Cossacks and in desperate appeals to army headquarters for reinforcement, Kerensky decided to go to Gatchina in order to expedite the dispatch of loyal troops. Between 10 A.M. and 11 A.M. (October 25) he left the Winter Palace in an open touring car accompanied by another car flying the American flag.[11] No attempt was made to stop him as he drove through the streets crowded by Bolshevik soldiers. At 10 A.M. the military revolutionary committee announced that the Provisional Government was deposed. This announcement was premature.

Following the departure of Kerensky, the Provisional Government, now headed by Konovalov, remained in session at the Winter Palace under the protection of a women's battalion, detachments of cadets, a small number of Cossacks, and a few armored cars. The plans of the Bolshevik strategists calling for the seizure of the palace in the night of October 24–25 went astray, and the investment of the former im-

---

[11] According to Kerensky, the American car was sent on the initiative of the British and the United States embassies as a token of allied "solidarity" (Kerensky, *The Catastrophe*, pp. 336–337). According to the United States' version, the car was "commandeered" by Russian officers, but the ambassador raised no objection and tacitly approved the arrangement. (David Francis, *Russia from the American Embassy* [New York, 1921], pp. 179–180): Buchanan states that the American car was lent at Kerensky's own request (Buchanan, *My Mission to Russia*, II, 205–206).

perial residence was not completed until 6 P.M. Even then some of the palace telephones remained in service. At 6:30 P.M. the besiegers issued an ultimatum demanding the surrender of the Provisional Government under the threat of the bombardment of the palace by the *Aurora* and other ships which had entered the Neva, as well as by the guns of the fortress of Peter and Paul across the river. The time limit of twenty minutes stipulated in the ultimatum was extended by another ten minutes, but although no reply was received the guns remained silent: according to the fortress artillerymen they were not fit for use. At 9 P.M. the *Aurora* fired one blank shell followed by desultory rifle fire from both sides. There was much confusion among assailants and defenders alike. The Cossacks and some of the cadets withdrew from the palace, and at 10 P.M. the women's battalion surrendered. The Provisional Government, however, persisted in the belief that relief troops were about to arrive. The solitary attempt at comforting the besieged ministers came from the Petrograd municipal council. About midnight the councilors and representatives of other "democratic" non-Bolshevik organizations marched in a body towards the palace. At the head of the cortege was the minister of supplies and noted economist S. N. Prokopovich, who was carrying a lantern and an umbrella. The avowed purpose of the demonstrators (as stated in the resolution of the council) was to protest against Bolshevik violence and "to die together with our chosen representatives," but on meeting a Bolshevik patrol the marchers did not persevere in their heroic endeavor and meekly turned back. At 11 P.M. the attack on the palace was resumed, and the guns of the fortress of Peter and Paul finally went into action: thirty or thirty-five shells were fired, but only two of them hit the palace, causing minor damage to plastering. The closing stage of this strange struggle was infiltration, not direct assault. At 2:10 A.M., on October 26, all ministers, except Kerensky and Prokopovich, were arrested in the cabinet room of the Winter Palace and were marched to the fortress of Peter and Paul, where they joined their predecessors of the imperial regime.

Life in the capital was not seriously disturbed. Schools and government offices closed earlier than usual, but most of the shops, theaters, and moving-picture houses remained open. In the afternoon of October 25 Sir George Buchanan took a walk in the direction of the Winter Palace and noted that "the aspect of the quay was more or less normal."

CHAPTER XLVIII

THE MORROW OF THE OCTOBER REVOLUTION

PEACE, LAND, AND SOVIET POWER

The Bolsheviks, although men of action, shared their opponents' passion for public debate. In the afternoon of October 25, when the insurrection was at its height, Trotsky found time to preside at a session of the Petrograd Soviet, where Lenin made his first public appearance since July. There were long speeches in a self-congratulatory vein and a wordy resolution celebrating the still incomplete victory. The opening session of the second all-Russian congress of the Soviets was scheduled for the 25 but was postponed from hour to hour, partly because the Bolsheviks were waiting for the capture of the Winter Palace and partly because of factional strife among the delegates themselves. The congress finally met at 10:45 P.M., some three hours before the arrest of the Provisional Government. No information is available as to how the delegates were elected or as to their exact number and party affiliations. It is believed, nevertheless, that of the total of some 650 deputies, 390 were Bolsheviks, 80 were Mensheviks or representatives of groups close to the Mensheviks, and 150 or more were socialist revolutionaries. There was much dissension within both the Menshevik and the Socialist Revolutionary parties. The Menshevik "internationalists," led by L. Martov (J. O. Zederbaum), leaned on many issues towards the Bolsheviks, as did in an even greater degree the "left" socialist revolutionaries led by Marie Spiridonova, B. D. Kamkov, and M. A. Natanson. About three-fifths of the socialist revolutionary delegates to the congress belonged to the left faction, and their disagreement with party leadership precipitated a split and the establishment of the left socialist revolutionaries as an independent party.

The opening session of the congress was stormy. As a protest against the Bolshevik *coup d'état* the Mensheviks (both factions), the right socialist revolutionaries, and the delegates of some of the minor parties withdrew, leaving the Bolsheviks, the left socialist revolutionaries, and the groups affiliated with them in full control of the congress. The withdrawal of the opposition—always a foolish move—simplified the task of the second and the last session of the congress held in the evening of the 26. The assembly passed unanimously the decree on peace, nearly unanimously (one vote against and 8 abstentions) the decree on land, and confirmed the Council of People's Commissars, Russia's new chief executive agency. The peace and the land decrees were written and sponsored by Lenin. The former invited "all belligerent peoples and their governments to begin immediate negotiations for an honest democratic peace," that is, a peace "without annexations and indemnities." The Russian government, however, was prepared to consider peace proposals on any other terms provided they were made speedily, were unambiguous, and contained no secret clauses. Secret diplomacy was declared abolished; the Russian government was to publish at once all secret agreements "confirmed or concluded by the government of landlords and capitalists between February and October 25, 1917. All such agreements, in so far as they were directed . . . to the securing of advantages and privileges for the Russian landlords and capitalists, to the retention or expansion of Great Russian annexations" were annulled "unconditionally and immediately." Russia proposed the immediate conclusion of an armistice for a period of not less than three months. The decree closed with an appeal to "the conscious workers of the three most advanced nations of mankind . . . England, France, and Germany" to support Russia's peace move.

The decree on land, a hastily written document which Lenin was unable to read intelligibly at the congress from penciled notes, comprised two separate enactments: the decree, in the narrow meaning of the term, and the instruction on land organization. The decree abolished, without compensation, private ownership of large estates (*pomeshchichia sobstvennost na zemliu*). Pending the convocation of the Constituent Assembly all such land, as well as land belonging to appanages, monasteries, and the Church, was to be taken over by local land committees and peasant Soviets. The instruction (*nakaz*) reiterated that the land question could be settled only by the Constituent Assembly, but provided the following scheme of land organization which in the meantime was to be made effective as soon as possible.[1] Private ownership of land, including that of peasant farmers and village communes, was abolished forever; land could not be sold, bought, leased, mortgaged, or alienated in any way. There was to be no compensation, but the former owners were to receive temporary relief (maintenance) from public funds. All land removed from private ownership was to constitute the national land reserve. Every citizen willing to work on land was entitled to an allotment the size of which was to be determined either by the labor power (number of adult workers) or by the consumption needs (number of dependents) of the prospective farmer's family. The use of hired labor was prohibited. In order to safeguard the equalitarian principle the entire land reserve was to be subject to periodical reapportionments, and provisions were to be made for the mass resettlement of the population. This preposterous scheme, which extended to the cultivable portion of the national territory the principles of the antiquated Russian village commune (*obshchina*), was a characteristic product of the socialist revolutionary mythology, which the Bolsheviks had often and rightly derided. Lenin admitted that the land-organization scheme was borrowed from the arsenal of his opponents, but he excused it on the ground of expediency. "The root of the matter is that the peasantry should be given the assurance that there are no more large landed proprietors in the village," he said. "Let the peasants themselves decide all questions, let them build their own life." The latter admonition, which was hardly consonant with the Draconian terms of the decree, has been only too often disregarded by Lenin's successors.

The fifteen members of the Council of People's Commissars confirmed by the congress were drawn exclusively from the ranks of the Bolshevik Party. Lenin was chairman, Trotsky the commissar for foreign affairs, and Stalin the commissar for nationalities. After electing the All-Russian Central Executive Committee of 101 members (in-

[1] The instruction was the summary of 242 *nakaz* presented by the delegates to the peasant Soviet. The summary was prepared by the editors of the official organ of the All-Russian Soviet of Peasants' Deputies and was published in the press on Aug. 19.

cluding 62 Bolsheviks and 29 left socialist revolutionaries) [2] the congress adjourned at 5 A.M. on October 27.

RESISTANCE TO BOLSHEVISM

In spite of the ease with which the Bolsheviks overthrew the Provisional Government—the number of troops and Red guards participating in the seizure of the capital was probably smaller than the 25,000 to 30,000 estimated by Trotsky—the victory of the October revolution was far less complete than that of the revolution of February–March. Military revolutionary committees were set up in many cities and at the front, but this did not lead to the immediate and general recognition of the Bolshevik government. In Moscow, where, as Lenin wrote to the central committee of the party early in October, "victory is assured and there is no one to fight," civil war raged for a week (October 27 to November 2); the Kremlin was shelled, and there were heavy losses of life: 238 "victims of the October revolution" were solemnly buried in the Red Square, a figure which presumably did not include the enemies of the new regime. Fighting took place in many cities and towns (Voronezh, Kazan, Saratov, Smolensk, Tashkent, Kaluga, Kharkov, and others). In October 21 principal provincial cities (administrative centers of provinces) came under Bolshevik control, in November 15, in December 13, in January 15, in February 3, in March 5, and in April 2.

Resistance, however, did not crystallize, as was expected, around Kerensky and the Mogilev headquarters. Kerensky's final odyssey was brief and inglorious. On leaving the Winter Palace (October 25) he barely escaped arrest at Gatchina and drove to Pskov, where he secured the promise of support from General P. N. Krasnov, commander of a cavalry corps. On October 27 Kerensky and Krasnov, at the head of a small Cossack force, returned to Gatchina and the next day occupied Tsarskoe Selo. In an appeal to the troops, officials, and population of the capital Kerensky urged them not to comply with the orders of the Council of People's Commissars. "Bolshevism is breaking down," he wrote, "it is isolated and, as an organized force, has ceased to exist in Petrograd." On the 29, as the Krasnov detachments were approaching Pulkovo, twelve miles from the capital,

---

[2] The balance—ten members—was made up of six social democrats "internationalists," three Ukrainian social democrats, and one socialist revolutionary "maximalist."

the military cadets in Petrograd staged an uprising which, however, was suppressed within a few hours. The reinforcements eagerly awaited by Kerensky did not arrive, and the force at his disposal numbered barely 700 Cossacks and a regiment of infantry. The soldiers, demoralized and sulky, evinced no desire to fight for the hopeless cause of the Provisional Government. The "battle" of Pulkovo, therefore, was hardly more than a skirmish, and ended speedily in the rout of the government troops (October 30). Tsarskoe Selo was retaken by the Bolsheviks, Kerensky retreated to Gatchina and, when further appeals for reinforcements and attempts at negotiations proved equally futile, he escaped in disguise from the Gatchina Palace (November 1). This was none too soon: the Cossacks were about to hand him over to the Soviet emissary, the sailor P. E. Dybenko. The most spectacular career of the opening phase of the revolution was over. Krasnov was arrested, but escaped and took a prominent part in the organization of anti-Bolshevik armies in the south.

The much-dreaded resistance of army headquarters at Mogilev did not materialize. Some of the army committees passed resolutions condemning the Bolsheviks, and Dukhonin and other commanding officers went through the motions of making arrangements for the sending of troops to the assistance of the Provisional Government. The moods of the committees, however, were subject to rapid changes, and Kerensky was hated in army circles. Moreover, some of the generals believed that their primary duty was to hold the front as long as possible and that an intervention on their part in the civil strife would inevitably lead to the immediate and final breakdown of the army. These considerations were of small practical import. Any attempt at moving troops to Petrograd was foredoomed by the resistance of local Soviets, the hostility or "neutrality" of railway workers, and above all by the determination of the soldiers not to fight, especially against a government that had promised them immediate peace. Dukhonin, who after Kerensky's flight assumed the duties of commander in chief, was directed by the Council of People's Commissars to open peace negotiations with the enemy (November 8 and 9). This he declined to do, and he also refused to comply with the order of dismissal that followed. Irate and alarmed, the Council of People's Commissars appointed Ensign N. V. Krylenko his successor, branded Dukhonin "an enemy of the people," and made hasty preparations for a punitive military expedition to Mogilev. The latter measure was superfluous. Dukhonin, like Kornilov seven weeks earlier, offered no resistance, the officers and the few troops loyal to the Provisional Government left Mogilev, and the control of the city passed into the hands of the Bolshevik military revolutionary committee appointed by the local Soviet (November 19). The next day Krylenko took possession of the headquarters, most of the remaining officers (previously under arrest) were set free and returned to their work, but Dukhonin was dragged out of Krylenko's railway car and murdered by a drunken and infuriated soldiery. The much-talked-about counter-revolution of the generals was still a thing to come. At the end of October General Alekseev left Petrograd for Novocherkassk, in the Don region. On November 19 Kornilov, Denikin, and the other officers imprisoned at Bykhov were released by order of Dukhonin and fled to the Don, where, together with Alekseev, they proceeded to organize the anti-Bolshevik Volunteer Army. Russia was on the threshold of civil war.

In the opening weeks of the Bolshevik rule organized opposition to the new government came, not from the generals or the "bourgeoisie," but from the non-Bolshevik elements of Soviet "democracy," chiefly the socialist parties which withdrew from the second congress of the Soviets. The Petrograd municipal councilors and their supporters, having failed in the attempt to reach the Winter Palace in the night of October 25, returned to the City Hall and formed the Committee for the Salvation of the Country and the Revolution which comprised the presidium of the Council of the Republic, and representatives of the municipal council, of the Central Executive Committee of the Soviets of Workers' and Soldiers' Deputies (elected by the first congress in June), of the Central Executive Committee of the Soviets of Peasants' Deputies, of all the socialist parties opposing the Bolsheviks, and of a host of other "democratic" organizations. An appeal issued by the committee stigmatized the overthrow of the Provisional Government as an "unheard-of crime against the country" and closed with the battle call: "Do not recognize the power of the usurpers! Do not comply with their orders!" Appeals in a similar vein were issued by several left-wing groups. Committees for the Salvation were created in many cities and towns, for instance, in Moscow, and for a while became the rallying points of opposition to Bolshevism. The All-Russian Central Executive Committee of the Soviets of Workers' and Soldiers' Deputies elected in June refused to recognize the legality of the second congress of the Soviets and of the Central Executive

Committee it elected. The June Central Executive Committee continued to function for two months longer, held meetings, and published a newspaper.

There was much activity among the left-wing organizations. Trade unions, factory committees, socialist parties, institutions of local government—all held congresses at which political issues were hotly debated. Typical were the two congresses of peasants' deputies: the "extraordinary" congress (November 10 to 25) and the second "regular" congress (November 26 to December 11). Both were split by the conflict between the opponents and the supporters of Bolshevism, a division corresponding, roughly, to that between the right and the left socialist revolutionaries. The two warring factions met separately most of the time and passed diametrically opposed resolutions. Nevertheless the Bolsheviks and the left socialist revolutionaries, who were about to form an alliance, adopted a resolution merging the Central Executive Committee of the Soviets of Workers' and Soldiers' Deputies with the Central Executive Committee of the Soviets of Peasants' Deputies, a move designed to bring the peasant Soviets in line with the Bolshevik-controlled Soviets of Workers' and Soldiers' Deputies (November 15). Like the congresses of the peasant Soviets, other "democratic" organizations were divided and at odds among themselves. The interminable debate raging in the crowded halls was arid, confused, and replete with dogmatism and personal animosity; it revolved largely around the problems of peace, the Constituent Assembly, and the make-up of the government. Few of the socialist critics of Bolshevism believed in the possibility of continuing the war but no one seemed to know how to end it. There was general agreement that the salvation of Russia depended on the immediate convocation of the Constituent Assembly; opinions, however, were divided as to the political complexion of the government. Some favored a coalition with the non-socialists, others a coalition of all socialist parties, still others a coalition of all socialist parties except the Bolsheviks. The October revolution was not yet taken seriously.

The avowed objective of the Bolsheviks, often stated by Lenin, was to smash the machinery of the bourgeois government and to rebuild the administrative apparatus from the ground on a socialist basis. For obvious reasons, this could not be done at once; in the meantime anomalies developed. The socialist ministers of the Provisional Government were released from prison and reconstituted themselves as a cabinet which held regular meetings and for a time enjoyed a degree of authority. For instance, it increased the power of issue of the State Bank by 1,000 million rubles (November 2), made appropriations to the Petrograd municipality (November 7), and even discussed the use of treasury funds for anti-Bolshevik propaganda (November 11). In an appeal published on November 17 the Provisional Government proclaimed itself "the sole legitimate organ of power," restated its determination "to prevent the rebels from taking over the state administrative services," and urged the population to rally to the support of the Constituent Assembly. This pronouncement proved too much for the Bolsheviks. The nine papers which carried the appeal were closed and its signers—"to forestall excesses"—were ordered deported to Kronstadt. The Senate, the supreme court of imperial Russia, went on about its business unmolested until November 24, when it serenely adopted a decision denying the legality of the Council of People's Commissars. The printers, however, would not set it in type, and three days later the Senate was abolished. The Petrograd and the Moscow municipal councils were unwavering in their opposition to Bolshevism and were dissolved on November 16; they refused to recognize the validity of the dissolution decree and continued to meet for a while even after the new councils were elected. Civil servants (foreign office, the treasury, post and telegraph, and so on), as well as teachers and municipal employees, boycotted the Bolshevik government. The strike of the employees of the State Bank and the noncooperation of the employees of the joint-stock banks were the immediate cause of the nationalization of all banking institutions (December 14).

DISSENSIONS WITHIN THE BOLSHEVIK PARTY

The relative leniency displayed at first by the Bolsheviks towards their opponents—an attitude that might well appear surprising in the light of their subsequent record—may be explained by the insecurity of their position, the state of chaos inherited from the Provisional Government, the ignorance of the rudiments of the art of public administration, and the profound dissensions within the Bolshevik Party. On the morrow of the seizure of power, disagreement about principles, policies, and methods was as rife among the Bolshevik leaders as it was in April and in September and October. In spite of the formation of an all-Bolshevik Council of People's Commissars, negotiations (which began on October 26) concerning the inclusion in the government of representatives of other socialist parties continued but made little progress. On November 4 Kamenev, A. I. Rykov, V. Miliutin, Zinovev, and V. Nogin resigned from the central committee of the party as a protest against policies which blocked the establishment of a "socialist [coalition] Soviet government." Such a government, they held, was necessary "in order to prevent further bloodshed, impending famine, defeat of the revolution . . . and to ensure the convocation of the Constituent Assembly . . . and the enforcement of an effective peace program. . . ." Kamenev did not reject the possibility of a socialist government headed, not by Lenin, but by a right socialist revolutionary—Chernov or N. D. Avksentev, chairman of the peasant Soviet. Five people's commissars (including Rykov, Miliutin, and Nogin) and six other heads of departments resigned (November 4), but a severe admonition of the central committee and the threat of expulsion from the party made Zinovev recant his views (November 8).

A. Lozovsky, an old Bolshevik and later leader of Soviet trade unions, published in the press a bitter denunciation of the tactics of the central committee which "led to civil war . . . and to the defeat of the great revolution" (November 5). Every paragraph of his indictment began with the sentence, "I cannot keep silent for the sake of party discipline," and he cited, among other things, the "adulation of personalities" to which everything else was sacrificed—a reference to the insistence of the central committee on the inclusion of Lenin and Trotsky in the government. Dissensions within the party were the rule, not the exception. As with other socialist groups the most controversial issues were the freedom of the press, which was grievously curtailed by a decree of October 27, the Constituent Assembly, and peace policies. The inclusion in the government of several left socialist revolutionaries (A. L. Kolegaev, as commissar for agriculture, on November 17, and of six others on December 10) added a new element of discord. The left socialist revolutionaries were never fully converted to the Bolshevik doctrine, and in March, 1918, after the Treaty of Brest-Litovsk, withdrew from the Council of People's Commissars.

EARLY LEGISLATION

Doctrinaire, inexperienced, harassed, insecure, and divided, the Bolshevik government could hardly be expected to produce an integrated and carefully thought-out program of reform. Its early measures were, indeed, hasty improvisations which Trotsky has well described as the "enunciation of a party program in the language of power." Much of this legislation was eventually discarded or drastically amended, but some came to stay. A decree of October 29 introduced the eight-hour day in all enterprises irrespective of size. The decree on workers' control (November 14) conferred upon the workers' committees in each enterprise the right to supervise production, sales, purchases of raw materials, and financial transactions. Business secrecy was abolished. The committees were given access to books and business correspondence, and their directions were mandatory on the owners but could be appealed to the higher organs of workers' control. An instruction appended to the decree, however, prohibited the committee from interfering with the executive orders of the owners or "to take possession of the enterprise or direct it." The decree was little more than the recognition of the powers which the factory committees had exercised since the early days of the revolution. The uneasy dualism in the management of industry it sanctioned was not viable, and was swept away by the decree of June 28, 1918, which nationalized all industrial enterprises. On December 1 there was established the Supreme Economic Council which for over a decade was the central organ for the regulation of the economic life of the Soviet state. Banks, as already noted, were nationalized on December 14. Another decree of the same date ordered the search of safe-deposit boxes and the confiscation of the valuables they contained. On December 29 payments of interest and dividends, as well as dealings in securities, were prohibited.

A drastic program of democratization was instituted in the army. Commanders (no longer called officers), from platoon leaders to the commander in chief, were to be elected by the soldiers of the unit or by appropriate committees (decree of December 16), and all ranks, titles, decorations, and insignia were abolished (decree of December 23). These striking innovations served well the purpose of dealing the *coup de grâce* to the moribund old army, which was rapidly demobilized; they were not retained, however, when the Red Army was organized early in 1918. A decision of the Council of People's Commissars of December 24 did away with the institutions of local government, including the township (*volost*) zemstvos established by a law of May 21, 1917. Local affairs were to be administered by a network of Soviets arranged in a hierarchical order. Each Soviet was to be autonomous, but the lower Soviets were to conform with the directions of the Soviets on higher levels. The system of law courts which was inherited from the imperial regime and preserved under the Provisional Government was abolished by a decree of November 24 which introduced the electability of judges but provided that, as a temporary measure, judges could be appointed by local Soviets. Existing laws were to be applied "only in so far as they have not been annulled by the revolution and were not in conflict with revolutionary conscience and the revolutionary concept of right." Offenses against the new order were to be tried by special revolutionary tribunals (decree of December 19). On December 5 the Petrograd military revolutionary committee was dissolved, and its police powers were transferred to the Special Committee for the Struggle against Counter-Revolution, Sabotage, and Speculation, or the Cheka (decree of December 7). This sinister institution, headed by F. E. Dzerzhinsky, has since acquired world-wide notoriety and has evolved into the security police, endowed with extra-judicial powers, which became one of the pillars of the Soviet regime. The "separation of the Church from the state and from the schools" was promulgated on January 23, 1918.

THE CONSTITUENT ASSEMBLY

The approach of the date when the Constituent Assembly was expected to meet put the Soviet government in an awkward and, it was imagined, potentially dangerous position. The Bolsheviks, like all revolutionary and liberal parties, were pledged to support the Constituent Assembly, and Kerensky's alleged intention to "torpedo" it has been used as a justification for the overthrow of the Provisional Government. "Comrades," *Pravda* wrote on the morrow of the October revolution, "by shedding your blood you have assured the convocation . . . of the Constituent Assembly." Elections were held, as scheduled, in the middle of November, but in some districts there were delays and in others no voting took place. According to Lenin's analysis of the data available in 1918, the Bolsheviks received 25 per cent of the total vote; the socialist revolutionaries, 58 per cent; other socialist parties, 4 per cent; and the Constitutional Democratic Party and other "parties of the landowners and the bourgeoisie," 13 per cent. Of the 703 delegates accounted for in 1918, 168 were Bolsheviks, 39 left socialist revolutionaries, 380 right socialist revolutionaries, 18

Mensheviks, 17 constitutional democrats and "bourgeois," and 81 belonged to national groups, practically all of them strongly anti-Bolshevik.[3] The Bolsheviks and the left socialist revolutionaries thus controlled less than one-third of the total vote, and if the Constituent Assembly had been permitted to function freely the Bolshevik regime would have had little chance to survive.

Dissolution, therefore, appeared imminent and was generally expected, but Lenin would seem to have hesitated at first to violate openly a tenet of the Bolshevik program which many party members still regarded as sacred.[4] A subterfuge was tried. A decree written by Lenin gave the Soviets the power to recall the delegates to the Constituent Assembly (November 21). A justification for this decree was the peculiar position in which the Socialist Revolutionary Party found itself. The elections were held under the system of proportional representation, that is, ballots were cast, not for individual candidates, but for party lists. As lists were drawn prior to the October revolution, the socialist revolutionaries appeared in the election as one party, while they had actually split into two independent parties. It was claimed that because of this anomaly the small representation of the left socialist revolutionaries in the Constituent Assembly was out of proportion to their actual weight in the country. Proportional representation, however, presented baffling technical difficulties for the recall of delegates, and it would seem that the procedure proposed in the decree of November 21 was never used. Sterner measures were applied. The members of the commission on the elections to the Constituent Assembly were arrested (November 23), and although they were soon released the commission itself was disbanded (decree of November 30). On November 28 a decree of the Council of People's Commissars ordered the arrest of the leaders of the Constitu-

---

[3] The statute on the Constituent Assembly provided for 808 delegates, but the fate of about 100 is not known; probably they were never elected. No complete election returns are available. The total number of votes cast was given in 1918 as 36.3 million; additional returns found since by O. H. Radkey bring the total vote to 41.7 million. Pertinent figures are well and clearly summarized in O. H. Radkey, *The Elections to the Russian Constituent Assembly of 1917* (Cambridge, 1950).

[4] "Even in our ranks there are comrades who have not yet lived down the illusions about the Constituent Assembly," M. S. Uritsky, Bolshevik commissar for the Constituent Assembly, said on Dec. 12. The disagreement between the central committee of the party and the bureau of the Bolshevik faction of the Constituent Assembly was the immediate reason why Lenin wrote his *Theses on the Constituent Assembly* (about which more will be said below).

tional Democratic Party because of their alleged connection with the Kornilov anti-Bolshevik army. Four prominent constitutional democrats still in Petrograd—Prince P. D. Dolgorukov, F. E. Kokoshkin, A. I. Shingarev, and Countess Panin—were arrested, as were somewhat later Avksentev (December 19) and other leading right socialist revolutionaries.[5] These were ominous developments. Nevertheless, on December 6 Lenin officially denied the rumors that the Constituent Assembly would not be allowed to meet.

The attitude of the government was formulated in the *Theses on the Constituent Assembly* written by Lenin and published on December 13. The gist of Lenin's argument was that while in a bourgeois republic the demand for a Constituent Assembly was "fully legitimate," this was no longer true under the dictatorship of the proletariat. "The republic of the Soviets is in a higher form of democratic organization than the usual bourgeois republic with a Constituent Assembly." From these bold and questionable generalizations Lenin drew important practical conclusions. "The only painless solution of the crisis," he wrote, "is the unconditional declaration by the Constituent Assembly of acceptance of Soviet power, Soviet revolution, and its policies in questions of peace, land, and workers' control." If these conditions were ignored, "the crisis in connection with the Constituent Assembly could be solved only by revolutionary means." The warning could not be plainer.

Summoned by the Council of People's Commissars (decree of December 20) the Constituent Assembly held its first and only session on January 5, 1918, in the Taurida Palace packed with armed and hostile soldiers and sailors. Chernov was elected president and there was the customary flow of revolutionary oratory. After the rejection, 237 to 138, of the Bolshevik resolution framed along the lines of Lenin's *Theses*, the Bolsheviks and, later, the left socialist revolutionaries withdrew. The remaining delegates kept on talking until the sailor Zhelezniakov, acting on orders of the central committee of the Bolshevik Party, directed Chernov to close the proceedings because "the guards were tired." At 5 A.M. on January 6 the Constituent Assembly adjourned for twelve hours. It never met again: on the same day it was dissolved by the All-Russian Central Executive Committee.

---

[5] Kokoshkin and Shingarev, former ministers in the Provisional Government, were murdered by a band of soldiers and sailors in a prison hospital ward on Jan. 11, 1918.

Except for the small group of politically-minded intellectuals the event passed almost unnoticed. There was no ground for the extreme nervousness of Lenin and other Bolshevik leaders who spent most of the day and night of January 5 at the Taurida Palace. Ample evidence was available to show that the Constituent Assembly had never captured the imagination of the masses and that it was all but forgotten in the midst of the political, economic, and social chaos that overcame Russia in the winter of 1917–1918. Considerably less than half of the electorate—estimated at 90 million—went to the polls, and it is difficult to believe that the men and women who voted did so with conviction and understanding. Illiteracy, ignorance of democratic methods, absence of tradition of self-government, multiplicity of parties, and the system of proportional representation under which votes are cast for lists (identified by numbers)—all militate against the view that the Constituent Assembly reflected the feeling of the country. From the standpoint of western democracy the high-handed action of Lenin cannot be condoned, yet it would be idle to pretend that the Constituent Assembly had a real claim to speak for the nation. The indifference with which the dissolution was received is, perhaps, the most tragic and telling comment on what was to be a major landmark in Russian history but proved merely a passing and, by now, almost forgotten episode.

NATIONAL SELF-DETERMINATION: FINLAND AND UKRAINE

In the morass into which Russia had sunk by the end of 1917 the domestic policies of the Bolshevik government met with little resistance except for the helpless protestations of the socialist opposition. The peace policies proclaimed on October 26, however, raised problems of a different order and encountered serious difficulties. The attainment of peace involved three separate but closely interrelated issues: claims of the borderlands to independence; threat of the nascent anti-Bolshevik White armies; and, above all, the termination of war with the central Powers.

The question of the independence of the borderlands arose in the case of Finland and Ukraine and was dealt with in the light of the Bolshevik doctrine of national self-determination.[6] The "Declaration

---

[6] The right of Poland to independence was conceded and since the whole of that country was occupied by the enemy the issue, in a practical form, did not arise.

of the Rights of the Peoples of Russia" issued by the Council of People's Commissars under the signature of Stalin proclaimed the "equality and sovereignty of all the peoples of Russia" and their right to "free self-determination," including that of "secession and the formation of an independent state" (November 2, 1917). Stalin, however, qualified this seemingly liberal doctrine by explaining that the right of secession was determined "by the concrete factors of the international situation, by the interests of the revolution" (1920). Finland was the first country to experience what the right of self-determination, as understood by Lenin and Stalin, meant in practice. On December 19, N.S., the Finnish diet proclaimed the independence of Finland, which was duly recognized by the Russian Council of People's Commissars on December 31, N.S. On January 26, N.S., however, the non-socialist Finnish government of Svinhufud was overthrown by the extreme Finnish elements assisted by the Russian Bolsheviks. There followed a period of civil war. The north of Finland was in the hands of the Finnish White forces, which supported the Svinhufud government, while the Finnish Workers' Republic controlled the south. On March 1 the Soviets concluded a treaty of "friendship and brotherhood" with the Finnish Workers' Republic, but on March 7, four days after the signature of the Treaty of Brest-Litovsk, the Svinhufud government made a treaty of peace with Germany.[7] German troops were landed in Finland, the Red regime collapsed early in May, its leaders fled to Russia, and civil war in Finland was over.

Developments in Ukraine followed a somewhat similar pattern except that the situation was complicated by the fact that Ukraine, geographically, was situated between the Soviet state and the southern territories, where Kornilov, Alekseev, and Denikin were organizing the Volunteer Army in cooperation with the leader of the Don Cossacks, General A. M. Kaledin, and the leader of the Orenburg Cossacks,

---

The claims of Belorussia (White Russia) to independence were perfunctory and episodic. In August, 1917, a national Belorussian diet (Rada) of moderate political complexion was established in Minsk but was overthrown by the local Bolsheviks at the end of the year. This ephemeral regime was engulfed in the German advance in February, 1918, and the question of Belorussian independence was temporarily closed.

[7] On Feb. 1, 1918, the Soviet government introduced the western calendar; Feb. 1 became Feb. 14, and the difference between the Russian and the western calendar disappeared. Beginning with Feb. 14 all dates are given in accordance with the western calendar. For this reform the Soviets deserve the gratitude of all students of Russian affairs.

Colonel A. P. Dutov. At the end of 1917 and early in 1918 the Volunteer Army numbered merely a few thousand, its organization was rudimentary, and it was grievously short of supplies. Nevertheless it was a challenge and a threat to the Bolshevik rule, and its birth marked the beginning of the civil war.[8] The half-hearted cooperation between the Ukrainian Rada [9] and the White generals was a factor in shaping the course of affairs in Ukraine.

On November 7, 1917, the Rada proclaimed the establishment of the Ukrainian People's Republic but specified that the changed status did not imply secession from the Russian republic, which should be reorganized as "a federation of equal and free peoples." Pending the convocation of the Ukrainian Constituent Assembly, all powers were to be exercised by the Rada and by the general secretariat it elected. Although the program announced in the manifesto of November 7 was not lacking in radicalism,[10] Ukrainian nationalism proved incapable of checking the inroads of Bolshevism. The Bolsheviks were suppressed in Kiev but they won an easy victory in Kharkov, where, not without the connivance of the Russians, the All-Ukrainian Central Executive Committee of the Soviets formed a "people's secretariat" of Bolshevik complexion which proclaimed the deposition of the Rada (December 17). As in Finland, civil war followed, but in this instance the Russians made no pretense at non-intervention. The Council of People's Commissars accused the Rada of persecuting the Ukrainian Soviets, of supporting the counter-revolutionary forces of Kornilov and Kaledin, and of preventing the movement of Soviet troops through the Ukrainian territory (December 4). The general secretariat denied these allegations, questioned the validity of the Lenin-Stalin interpretation of self-determination, and observed rather pointedly that the Soviet form of government as applied in Russia had produced no "enviable" results. A resolution written by Lenin and adopted by the Council of People's Commissars on December 30

---

[8] The objectives of the Volunteer Army, as stated in a declaration of Dec. 27, 1917, were to repulse by armed force the German-Bolshevik invasion; to protect south and southwestern Russia from the intruders; to uphold civic liberties and to ensure the opportunity for the country to express its will through the Constituent Assembly.

[9] See p. 1424.

[10] Abolition of ownership of landed estates, introduction of the eight-hour day, immediate steps for the conclusion of a general peace, democratization of the judiciary and local government, freedom of the press, religion, assembly, unions, strikes, and so on.

branded the Ukrainian arguments as "mockery," and early in January, 1918, Soviet troops invaded Ukraine. On January 9 the Rada proclaimed Ukraine "a free and sovereign republic," but the achieving of this lofty status failed to bolster the flagging spirit of the Ukrainian troops. Although the Russians, too, made an exceedingly poor showing, the odds were overwhelmingly in their favor. After a siege lasting for several days Kiev was taken on January 27, Ukrainian resistance collapsed, and the Rada fled to Zhitomir and, later, to Sarny. Soviet detachments overran the entire country as well as the Cossack territories south of the uncertain Ukrainian border. There were mutinies and disaffection among the Cossacks, General Kaledin resigned and committed suicide (February, 1918), and the hard-pressed Volunteer Army retreated southeast in the Kuban Cossack territory, in the foothills of the Caucasian mountains. Bolshevism appeared triumphant. The Brest-Litovsk treaty temporarily reversed the situation.

BREST-LITOVSK

The Bolsheviks were eager to put into effect the peace program announced on October 26. On November 8 (November 21, N.S.) Trotsky in a circular note invited the ambassadors of the allied Powers to regard the peace decree "as a formal offer for an immediate armistice on all fronts and the immediate initiation of peace negotiations." Two days later a similar communication was sent to the ambassadors of neutral countries for transmission to the governments of the central Powers. No replies were forthcoming except for a protest by the allies to General Dukhonin against Russia's violation of the treaty of September 5, 1914, N.S., which bound the signatories not to conclude separate peace (November 10). On November 10 the first installment of the secret treaties was published in the Petrograd newspapers. In view of the attitude of the army, however, the most urgent question was that of an armistice. After Dukhonin's refusal to open peace negotiations with the enemy (November 9), Krylenko, the new commander in chief, directed the army units at the front to make their own armistice agreements, on a local basis, with the opposing forces. The first of these agreements were concluded in the Dvinsk sector on November 13 in connection with the acceptance by the German high command of Krylenko's offer for general armistice negotiations which were to be held at Brest-Litovsk. Other sectional cease-fire agreements followed but were superseded on November 24 (December 7, N.S.) by the comprehensive Brest-Litovsk armistice agreement. Concluded originally for ten days, the agreement was extended and remained in force until February 10, 1918, N.S., when it was denounced by the Germans. Commenting on the separate character of the armistice, Trotsky blamed for it the allies who had ignored his repeated invitations to take part in the negotiations (November 30).

The armistice negotiations at Brest-Litovsk, headquarters of the German eastern front, were but the preliminaries for the peace negotiations. The Bolsheviks approached the conference in an optimistic spirit. *Pravda* wrote triumphantly on November 15 that the acceptance by the central Powers of the armistice proposals was due "to the recognition of the strength of the Russian revolution, the recognition of the weakness of the invaders." "If Germany dares to send her troops against revolutionary Russia," Kamenev, a member of the Soviet peace delegation, declared on December 19, "this would unquestionably produce an explosion that would sweep away the stronghold of German imperialism"; and Trotsky expressed the belief that "our final negotiations will be with Karl Liebknecht," the future founder of the German Communist Party, who was imprisoned by the German authorities in 1916.

The Brest-Litovsk peace conference opened in the gloomy citadel of that war-torn city on December 9 (December 22, N.S.). The Soviet delegation was headed by Adolf Ioffe, an old Bolshevik who later held important diplomatic posts but eventually fell from grace and committed suicide in 1927. The genuine and picturesque worker, sailor, and peasant brought by Ioffe to the armistice negotiations were not present at the peace conference. On December 27 (January 9, N.S.) Trotsky succeeded Ioffe as head of the Soviet delegation. The principal representatives of the central Powers were the German foreign minister von Kühlmann and General Max von Hoffmann, of the German high command; the Austrian foreign minister Count Ottokar Czernin; the Turkish grand vizier Talaat Pasha; and V. Radoslavov, prime minister of Bulgaria. On ceremonial occasions Prince Leopold of Bavaria, commander of the German eastern front, presided.

It would be unreasonable to expect that a conference consisting of men of such divergent views and aspirations as the Russian revolutionaries and the old-school western diplomats and generals could have reached an agreement based on mutual concessions and understanding. Much of the discussion at Brest-Litovsk revolved around the question of national self-determination. The maneuvers of the German and Austrian diplomats led the Russians to believe that the central Powers were prepared to accept the principle of peace without annexations and indemnities. At the session of January 2 (January 15, N.S.) and 5 (18, N.S.), however, Hoffmann stated forcefully that self-determination, as understood by the Germans, justified the severance from Russia of the territories held by the enemy, that is, Russian Poland, most of the Baltic provinces, and parts of Belorussia (White Russia). If Petrograd was to have peace, it was to be purchased at the price of heavy territorial sacrifices.

The prospect of a separate peace with German "imperialists" threatened to split the Bolshevik Party. The Petrograd and the Moscow party organizations demanded the suspension of the negotiations while Trotsky advanced his celebrated formula "No war—no peace." On January 7 Lenin wrote *Theses on the Question of a Separate and Annexionist Peace*, which, however, were not published until February 24, that is, after the German terms were accepted. He argued that "the success of socialism in Russia" required a breathing space of at least a few months. "There is no doubt that the socialist revolution in Europe must and will come. All our hopes for the *final* victory of socialism are based on this conviction and this scientific foresight." But there was no assurance that the revolution would come "within the next half year (or a similar shorter period)." A defensive or "just" war against the German invasion would merely serve the objectives of the Anglo-French imperialists who were supporting the opponents of peace with Germany. The issue, however, was not the choice between two brands of imperialism, but how to protect the socialist revolution in one country until revolutions broke out in other countries. Moreover, the Russian army was incapable of fighting. It was certain that the peasants would support peace at any price, and if they were forced to wage war they would overthrow the Soviet government after the first defeat, within a month or, more likely, within a week. Immediate peace on any terms was the only way to save the revolution.

This pronouncement precipitated a new crisis. At a conference of Bolshevik leaders held in Petrograd on January 8 only 15 of the 63 participants voted for immediate peace; 32 voted for a "revolutionary" war, and 16 for Trotsky's formula. The "no war—no peace" policy was approved 9 to 7 by the central committee of the Bolshevik Party on January 11 and obtained a majority at a joint session of the central committees of the Bolshevik and the Left Socialist Revolutionary parties the next day. Lenin was defeated, and this explains why his *Theses* were not published until February 24.

Meanwhile the situation in Brest-Litovsk was complicated by the arrival of the delegation of the Ukrainian Rada, which was duly admitted, with the approval of Trotsky, to participate in the work of the conference (January 9, N.S.). On February 1, N.S., however, the central Powers recognized the Ukrainian People's Republic as a sovereign state, and on February 9, N.S., at the very time when the Bolsheviks were occupying Kiev, the central Powers concluded with the representatives of the Rada a peace treaty which put at their disposal the desperately needed Ukrainian grain and other agricultural products and paved the way for the Austro-German intervention in the south of Russia. The German high command was exasperated by Bolshevik procrastinations and the stream of vitriolic propaganda that poured across the Russian border: Lenin and Trotsky grossly exaggerated the revolutionary potentialities of Brest-Litovsk and were playing for time. A German ultimatum extending the areas of the proposed annexations was drafted but not delivered because of von Kühlmann's threat of resignation. The intolerable situation was brought to an end on February 10, N.S., when Trotsky dramatically announced that Russia refused to sign a peace of annexation but at the same time declared that the state of war with the central Powers was ended. Orders for the demobilization of the Russian army had already been issued. On the same day the Soviet delegation left Brest-Litovsk and was received with enthusiasm in Petrograd. On February 13, N.S., the Central Executive Committee approved the action of the Brest-Litovsk delegation, a motion in which Lenin concurred.

The German high command, however, meant business, and had no difficulty in overriding the hesitations of the civilians and the Austrians. The central Powers took the view that Trotsky's action had terminated the armistice, and on February 18 launched an offensive along the entire front, from the Baltic to the Black Sea.[11] The advancing armies met with no resistance.

In spite of the imminence of the danger the Bolshevik Party re-

[11] The armistice agreement provided for a seven-day notice prior to the resumption of the hostilities. The notice was actually served on the 16, but the breach of the armistice was reckoned from Feb. 10, N.S.

mained divided. On February 17 the central committee voted down, 5 to 6, Lenin's motion to accept the peace terms. Lenin was again defeated, 6 to 7, on February 18, with Trotsky voting against Lenin's resolution. Later in the day, however, Trotsky shifted his position, and the motion of Lenin for the immediate acceptance of the terms offered was carried by the central committee, 7 to 6. A radiogram to this effect was sent to Berlin, but the German reply was not forthcoming until the 23. The silence of Berlin and the relentless advance of the Austro-German armies unnerved the Bolshevik leaders and made even Lenin waver. On February 21 the Council of People's Commissars issued a hysterical appeal directing that "all forces and resources of the country shall be devoted wholly to the revolutionary defense," a policy that ran contrary to the cool analysis of Lenin's *Theses*. The German terms received in Petrograd on the 23 were considerably harsher than those stipulated heretofore. Lenin demanded their immediate acceptance; if this was not done he would resign. Of the 15 members of the central committee, 7 voted for his motion, 4 against, and 4—including Trotsky and Ioffe—abstained. On the night of the 23 the resolution of the central committee was approved by the Central Executive Committee, 116 to 85, with 26 abstentions. The peace treaty was signed at Brest-Litovsk on March 3, 1918. G. Sokolnikov headed the Russian delegation, Trotsky in the meantime having resigned as commissar for foreign affairs.

The treaty of Brest-Litovsk deprived Russia of her Polish, Baltic, and Belorussian (White Russian) provinces, as well as the districts of Kars, Batum, and Ardaghan in the Caucasus. Russia undertook to recognize the independence of Ukraine and Finland, to withdraw her troops from their territories, and to refrain from propaganda against the governments of Ukraine, Finland, and the central Powers. There were onerous provisions dealing with demobilization, disarmament, and trade relations, but no indemnities were imposed, although a supplementary treaty of August 27, 1918, provided that Russia should pay Germany, in installments, 6,000 million marks "for losses to Germans caused by Russian measures." The recognition of Ukrainian independence meant, in practice, the invasion of that country by the central Powers. The Austro-German troops entered Kiev on March 3, restored the Rada, and rapidly occupied the entire territory of the new republic. The Ukrainian Bolshevik government collapsed, as did, after the landing of German troops, the Bolshevik government of

RUSSIA
AFTER THE TREATY OF BREST-LITOVSK, MARCH 3, 1918

- ᗯᗯᗯ Russian frontier in 1914
- ▬▬ Russian frontier under the Treaty of Brest-Litovsk
- ▨ Territories severed from Russia, December 1917 to March 1918
- Dates in parentheses indicate when independency was proclaimed

Scale of Miles: 0 — 200 — 400

Finland. It is estimated that the Treaty of Brest-Litovsk removed from Russian sovereignty approximately 1.3 million square miles of territory with a population of 62 million. To these territorial losses must be added that of Bessarabia. The annexation by Rumania of that province, which was occupied by the Rumanians in December, 1917, was recognized by a treaty signed by the central Powers and Rumania on March 9, 1918.

Lenin's insistence on the acceptance of German terms in February, 1918, is usually regarded as one of his boldest strokes and as irrefutable proof of his power of foresight and capacity for clear thinking. There is little doubt that had the Soviets embarked on a "revolutionary" war or had they persisted in the "no war—no peace" extravaganza the Bolshevik regime would have been swept away. The masses accepted the "obscene" (*pokhabnyi*) peace with the same indifference with which they accepted the dissolution of the Constituent Assembly. Yet, as in so many other instances, the soundness of Lenin's practical conclusions is not necessarily decisive proof of the validity of the premises from which they were drawn. The international socialist revolution, that corner-stone of Lenin's theoretical structure, did not take place either in the defeated or in the victorious countries. The Treaty of Brest-Litovsk was not torn by the triumphant proletariat of Germany, France, and England, but was prosaically annulled by Article 15 of the armistice of November 11, 1918, written by "bourgeois" *entente* statesmen and soldiers.[12] Lenin had no preference among the "imperialists," but he certainly did nothing to facilitate the task of Lloyd George, Clemenceau, and Wilson. Nevertheless, since the international socialist revolution failed, the victory or defeat of the *entente* was not a matter of indifference from the Soviet point of view. Had the fortunes of war favored the central Powers, as they well might have, the fate of the Treaty of Brest-Litovsk would have been presumably very different from what it was and the urge to congratulate Lenin on his foresight less compelling.

A consequence of the Brest-Litovsk treaty was the transfer of the capital from Petrograd to Moscow (officially, March 10 and 11, 1918). The change was, perhaps, of more than passing interest. Petrograd, the Petrine "window on Europe," was Russia's geographical link with the western world, especially after the loss of the Baltic provinces.

[12] The abrogation of the Treaty of Brest-Litovsk was confirmed by Article 116 of the Treaty of Versailles.

It was also the most westernized of Russian cities. Moscow was different, and by tradition Russian to the core. From the graceful Italian and French palaces on the borders of the Neva the new rulers of Russia moved into the somber medieval splendor of the Kremlin, filled with the memories of the darkest age of Russian absolutism. It is not impossible—although, perhaps, not very plausible—that these gloomy semi-Asiatic surroundings had some effect upon the subsequent evolution of the doctrine and practice of Marxism-Leninism and have in some degree influenced the growth of that peculiar Byzantinism which may be regarded as a characteristic of the second Moscow period of Russian history.

THE "INEVITABILITY" OF BOLSHEVISM

A question that naturally arises in the mind of the student of the Russian revolution is whether the advent of Bolshevism could have been prevented. Like all broad historical generalizations, this question does not admit of a clear-cut, simple, and decisive answer. The intrinsic quality of the Bolshevik doctrine and the efficacy of party organization do not explain the triumph of Bolshevism. It is not open to doubt that the basic theories of Marxism-Leninism—the doom of capitalist society and the inevitability of the international socialist revolution—were not in agreement with the facts of the historical period about which Lenin was thinking. Nor is it obvious that these theories, even if they were true, would have won him a large following in an illiterate, backward, agricultural country such as Russia in 1917. The Bolshevik Party, like other Russian parties, was by no means of one mind. Contrary to the legend,[13] the authority of Lenin within the party was not supreme, and each major decision had to be fought out against a stubborn and unyielding opposition. To state these seemingly uncontroversial facts is not to minimize Lenin's preeminent part in the revolution. His devotion to the cause, singleness of purpose, ruthlessness, and above all his uncanny ability to draw—although by no means always—correct practical conclusions from often wrong or nebulous premises were essential elements in the victory of Bolshevism. A number of Lenin's grave and even ridiculous errors of judgment have been noted in these pages. His greatest contribution to the success of the Bolshevik revolution was the recognition of the

---

[13] "Lenin and the party, the man and the instrument, were now [after the October revolution] indissolubly one." E. H. Carr, *The Bolshevik Revolution*, I, 99.

importance of the peasantry as a revolutionary force and his wholehearted endorsement of the agrarian revolution and of soldiers' elemental longing for peace. The land-organization scheme provided by the decree of October 26 was, no doubt, scrapped, and the Brest-Litovsk treaty opened an era of German occupation, civil war, and foreign intervention. The fact nevertheless remains that the large landed proprietors disappeared and their estates were divided among the peasants; and while the civil war was cruel, ruinous, and savage it was on an entirely different plane from the struggle against the armed might of the central Powers. Moreover, the old army was demobilized, and the Red Army was much smaller than its predecessor. The Brest-Litovsk treaty was hardly a good specimen of a peace without annexations and indemnities, yet one may surmise that the Russian peasant soldier took a different view: he was at last allowed to go home and he got his share of the neighboring estate. The rest mattered little.

Bolshevism owed much of its success to the helplessness and blindness of its opponents. Miliukov's insufferable and complacent dogmatism and Prince Lvov's equally insufferable meekness did much to destroy whatever chance the frail Russian liberalism had to retain a foothold in the new revolutionary state. The theory espoused by the Provisional Government that the overthrow of the monarchy was an expression of the will of the nation to fight the war to a victorious end could lead nowhere but to disaster. The moderate socialists who through most of 1917 controlled the Soviets were as doctrinaire as the Bolsheviks and the liberals, but far less capable than Lenin of tackling practical situations. It was clear, not merely in retrospect, that the notions of legality, constitutionality, and democracy were alien to the Russian historical tradition, that the agrarian revolution could not be checked, and that the army was unwilling to fight. The facts of the situation were not in dispute. What was lacking was the capacity and courage to face them, to admit their irresistible logic, and act accordingly. The task was not a pleasant or an easy one, and success was not certain. Nevertheless if, instead of chasing the phantom of counter-revolution led by generals who had no soldiers to fight for them, Kerensky—for, distressingly, there was no one else—had made immediate peace and given all land to the peasants, it is possible that Lenin would never have come to the Kremlin. Such a program, of course, *was* Bolshevism in 1917, and would have been vehemently opposed by the allies and by liberal Russians. Yet it was the only practical policy that might have succeeded, and its rejection by the moderate elements assured the triumph of their opponents. It seems reasonably clear in retrospect that what in 1917 was treason to the allies and condonation of peasant lawlessness would have served, in the long run, the cause of democracy in Russia and throughout the world.

AUTHOR'S NOTE

※

I had originally intended to include in this discussion the Soviet phase of Russian history. After careful consideration, however, I have decided to abandon, at least temporarily, the writing of Part IV, which I proposed to call *The Second Moscow Period*. Two main reasons are responsible for this decision.

It is extremely difficult to fit into the framework of a study such as mine the relatively brief but vastly important span of the Soviet rule. The political, social, economic, and intellectual life of the U.S.S.R. is ordered by the communist doctrine. Even in the 1920's, when divergencies of views within the Communist Party were still tolerated, discussion centered on abstruse points of communist theory which are difficult to comprehend and even more difficult to make intelligible to a non-communist audience. Moreover, the distressing uniformity and one-sidedness of the information available confront the historian with problems which, to the best of my knowledge, still await solution. The rigidity of the dogma and the strict conformity in the modes of expression have all but obliterated the records of all manifestations of national life except those which the Kremlin desires to emphasize. The extent of this suppression by far exceeds the bounds of mere censorship, however rigorous, and imparts to the Russian scene an element of utter unreality. Soviet books, journals, and newspapers all say the same thing. Memoirs, diaries, letters, which are the meat of the historian, are rare and highly colored. Outside the narrow circle of the initiated the vast majority of Soviet leaders are mere names, lifeless and bloodless shadows about whom next to nothing is known. Lenin and Stalin, according to their official biographies, would seem to spend their lives reciting, to the applause of the worshipers, paragraphs from the writings of Marx or resolutions of the Communist Party. Surely, this cannot be the true picture.

I have quoted in its place the following characterization of the Russian Middle Ages given by Professor Solovev: "The actors perform silently, they make war and they make peace, but they will not say, nor will the chronicler explain, why they make war and why they make peace; in the city, at the court of the prince, all is quiet, all is still; every one keeps behind closed doors and thinks his thoughts all by himself; the door is open, the actors walk on the stage and do something, but they do it in silence." No one will accuse the Soviet leaders of keeping silent; yet, reversing the familiar saying *cum tacent clamant*, the torrents of Soviet propaganda are singularly unrevealing of what the Soviet leaders and people actually think and do. It is not suggested that the history of the Soviet Union cannot and should not be written, but merely that information for a broad and comprehensive picture such as I have attempted to trace for the earlier periods is not, and perhaps will never be, available. In spite of the unquestionable element of continuity of the Russian tradition, Soviet history, if it is to rise above the level of a mere catalogue of "facts" and repetition of communist propaganda, calls for a novel and fresh approach, the time for which is not perhaps ripe. There may be truth in Lenin's dictum that it is more pleasant to make a revolution than to write about it.[1]

The second compelling reason for not dealing with Soviet developments is the size of this study, which can be justified only by the vastness of the subject. The inclusion of an adequate discussion of the Soviet period either would make the length of this volume prohibitive or would necessitate the drastic pruning of the earlier portions of the book, which, I believe, would greatly impair its usefulness.

[1] Lenin, *The State and the Revolution* (1917), Preface.

GLOSSARY OF SELECTED RUSSIAN AND OTHER UNFAMILIAR TERMS

Some of the Russian terms have more than one meaning. The English interpretations given below are those used in this study.

Allotment land: land granted to the peasants at the emancipation of 1861.

Barshchina: compulsory labor performed by the serfs for their master; the French *corvée.*

Denshchik: orderly; under Peter I this office combined the duties of an orderly with those of an aide-de-camp.

Diaki (singular, *diak*): civil servants in medieval Russia, especially secretaries of central departments.

Druzhina: military retinue of the early Russian princes.

Duma: assembly or council.

Dvor: Household or homestead; basic unit of peasant organization.

Dvoriane (singular, *dvorianin*): noblemen, members of *dvorianstvo.*

Dvorianstvo: the nobility or upper class; in the Middle Ages its members held estates in service tenure but were relieved of the obligation of compulsory service in 1762.

Fiscaly (singular, *fiscal*): members of the secret service established in 1711.

Gosudarstvennye krestiane: peasants living on state-owned land.

Guberniia: province, an administrative territorial subdivision.

Kormlenie: "feeding"; administrative practice in ancient and medieval Russia which consisted of the appointment of governors who collected taxes, tributes, and judicial fines and retained, for their own use, the whole or a portion of the proceeds.

Namestnik: appointed governor in medieval Russia; later, viceroy.

Obrok: annual payments made by the serfs to their master for the use of land allotments which they farmed on their own account, or in commutation of compulsory services (*barshchina*); annual payments by state peasants to the treasury for the use of land allotments; also taxes consolidated into one payment.

Opolchenie: militia.

Oprichnik: a member of the group administering *oprichnina* under Ivan the Dread.

Oprichnina: an ancient term denoting an entailed domain; in Ivan the Dread's time, the tsar's personal domain exempt from the jurisdiction of the general administration.

Pomestie: estate held in service tenure in medieval Russia; later, any large estate, especially those held by the nobility.

Pop: colloquial for Orthodox priest.

Possadnik: governor, usually an elected one, in ancient and medieval Russia.

Possessionary peasants, possessionary works. See *Possessionnaia fabrika.*

Possessionnaia fabrika: industrial enterprises (chiefly in mining and metallurgy), first established in 1721, manned by servile labor, and subject to close government supervision; possessionary peasants—peasants attached to such enterprises.

Poteshnye: body of troops established by the future Emperor Peter I about 1683 and reorganized later as the regiments of the imperial guards.

Preobrazhenskii prikaz: security police under Peter I.

Prikazy (singular, *prikaz*): central government departments in medieval Russia.

Progymnasium: school offering the abridged course of a gymnasium (classical secondary school).

Soslove: social classes or "estates" (the French *état*), usually, but not always, hereditary.

State peasants. See *Gosudarstvennye krestiane.*

Tsarevich: son of the tsar, usually heir apparent.

Udel: appanage; small independent and semi-independent principalities in the X to XV centuries; later, domain of the imperial family.

Udelni order: a system under which the territory of Russia was divided

Glossary of Selected Russian and Other Unfamiliar Terms 1481

into small independent or quasi-independent principalities in the X to XV centuries.

Uezd: county or district, an administrative territorial subdivision.

Veche: popular assembly in ancient Russia.

Voevoda: appointed governor in medieval Russia.

Volost: township, an administrative territorial subdivision; after 1861, the basic unit of peasant self-government.

Votchina: hereditary estates originally unencumbered by obligations of service.

Yarlyk: decree of the khan usually confirming a Russian prince in office during the period of Tartar domination.

Zaporozhie or *Zaporozhskaia Sich:* Cossack settlement on an island near the Dnieper rapids in the XV to XVIII centuries.

Zemskii sobor: assembly of representatives of various social groups, XVI to XVII centuries.

Zemstvo: institutions of local self-government; their organization and functions varied greatly throughout history.

SOME RUSSIAN MEASURES AND THEIR EQUIVALENTS

One dessiatine = 2.7 acres
One pood = 36 lbs = 0.016 ton
One verst = 0.66 mile

PRINCIPAL SOURCES

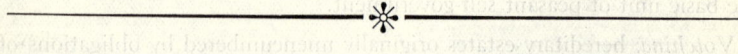

Adamov, E. A., ed., Konstantinopl i prolivy (Constantinople and the Straits), based on the secret documents of the former ministry of foreign affairs. 2 vols., Moscow, 1925–1926.

Akademiia Nauk SSSR, Institut Istorii, Protiv istoricheskoi kontseptsii M. N. Pokrovskago (Academy of Science of the USSR, Institute of History, Against the Historical Theories of M. N. Pokrovsky). Vol. I, Moscow-Leningrad, 1939.

Allen, W. E. D., The Ukraine: A History. Cambridge, 1941.

Antsiferov, A. N., Bilimovich, A. D., and others, Russian Agriculture During the War. New Haven, 1930.

Arkeograficheskaia Kommissiia, Pisma i doneseniia iezuitov o Rossii kontsa XVII i nachala XVIII veka (Archives Commission, Letters and Reports of the Jesuits About Russia at the End of the Seventeenth and the Beginning of the Eighteenth Centuries). St. Petersburg, 1904.

Arkhangelsky, A. S., Nil Sorskii i Vassian Patrikeev, ikh trudy i idei v drevnei Rusi (Nil Sorsky and Vassian Patrikeev, Their Literary Work and Ideas in Ancient Russia). Vol. I, St. Petersburg, 1882.

Arkhiv Russkoi Revoliutsii (Archives of the Russian Revolution). 22 vols., Berlin, 1921–1937.

Arkhiv Vorontsova (The Vorontsov Archives). 40 vols., Moscow, 1870–1895.

Arne, T. J., La Suède et l'Orient. Uppsala, 1914.

Arsenev, K. K., Zakonodatelstvo o pechati (Legislation on the Press). St. Petersburg, 1903.

Arsky, R., "Rabochii klas vo vremia voiny" (The Working Class During the War), Trud v Rosii (Labor in Russia), Vol. I, Leningrad, 1925.

Badayev, A., The Bolsheviks in the Tsarist Duma. New York, 1929.

Principal Sources

Baddeley, J. F., Russia, Mongolia, and China. 2 vols., London, 1919.

Bagalei, D. J., Russkaia istoriia, kniazheskaia Rus do Ioanna III (Russian History, Princely Russia Prior to Ivan III). Vol. I, Moscow, 1914.

Bain, R. N., The Pupils of Peter the Great. London, 1897.
———, The Daughter of Peter the Great. London, 1899.
———, Peter III, Emperor of Russia. London, 1902.

Bariatinsky, Prince V., Tsarstvennyi mistik, Imperator Aleksandr I—Fedor Kuzmich (The Mystic Tsar, Alexander I—Fedor Kuzmich). St. Petersburg, 1913; French version, Le Mystère d'Alexandre I-er, Paris, 1929.

Bartenev, P. I., ed., Osemnadtsatyi vek (The Eighteenth Century). Moscow, 1869.

Bell, H. C. F., Lord Palmerston. 2 vols., London–New York, 1936.

Benois, A., Istoriia russkoi zhivopisi v XIX veke (History of Russian Painting in the Nineteenth Century). St. Petersburg, 1902.

———, The Russian School of Painting, with an introduction by Christian Brinton. New York, 1916.

Beshkin, G., ed., Legalnaia sotsial-demokraticheskaia literatura v Rossii za 1906–1914 gody (Legal Social Democratic Literature in Russia in 1906–1914), a bibliography published by the Communist Academy. Moscow, 1924.

Beucler, A., La Vie de Ivan le Terrible. Paris, 1931.

Bogoliubov, V. P., Novikov i ego vremia (Novikov and His Time). Moscow, 1906.

Bogoslovsky, M. M., "Petr Velikii po ego pismam" (Peter the Great in His Letters), in Sbornik statei v chest M. K. Liubavskago (Symposium Dedicated to M. K. Liubavsky). Petrograd, 1917.

———, Petr I, materialy dlia biografii (Peter I, Materials for a Biography). 5 vols., Leningrad, 1940–1948.

Bolshaia Sovetskaia Entsiklopediia (Large Soviet Encyclopedia). 66 vols., Moscow, 1926–1948.

Bolshakov, A. M., and Rozhkov, N. A., Istoriia khoziaistva v Rossii v materialakh i dokumentakh (Economic History of Russia in Materials and Documents). Leningrad, 1926.

British Documents on the Origins of the War, 1894–1914, ed. G. P. Gooch, 11 vols. in 13. London, 1926–1938.

Brückner, A., Istoriia Ekateriny Vtoroi (History of Catherine II), 5 vols., St. Petersburg, 1885.

———, Smert Pavla I (The Death of Paul I). Moscow, 1909.

Bruun, G., Europe and the French Imperium, 1799–1814. New York–London, 1938.

Buchanan, Sir G., *My Mission to Russia, and Other Diplomatic Memories.* 2 vols., London, 1923.

Bukhovetsky, A. I., Materialy po denezhnoi reforme 1895–1897 gg. (Documents on the Monetary Reform of 1895–1897). Petrograd-Moscow, 1922.

Bukshpan, Ia. M., Voenno-khoziastvennaia politika: formy i organy regulirovaniia narodnago khoziaistva za vremia voiny 1914–1918 gg. (War Economic Policy: Methods of, and Institutions for, the Regulation of National Economy During the War of 1914–1918). Moscow-Leningrad, 1929.

Bunyan, J., and Fisher, H. H., The Bolshevik Revolution, 1917–1918, documents and materials. Stanford, 1934.

Byloe (The Past). 57 vols., St. Petersburg–Leningrad, 1906–1907, 1917–1926.

Cambridge History of British Foreign Policy, The, ed. Sir A. W. Ward and G. P. Gooch. 3 vols., Cambridge, 1922–1923.

Cambridge History of Poland, The, 1697–1935. Cambridge, 1941.

Cambridge Modern History, The. 13 vols., Cambridge, 1902–1911.

Catherine II, Empress, Sochineniia Imperatritsy Ekateriny II (Collected Works of Empress Catherine II), ed. A. N. Pypin. 12 vols., St. Petersburg, 1901–1907.

———, Correspondence of Catherine the Great when Grand Duchess with Sir Charles Hanbury-Williams, ed. the Earl of Ilchester and Mrs. Langford-Brooke. London, 1928.

Chamberlin, W. H., The Russian Revolution, 1917–1921. 2 vols., New York, 1935.

Chechulin, N. D., Russkoe provintsialnoe obshchestvo vo vtoroi polovine XVIII veka (Russian Provincial Society in the Second Half of the Nineteenth Century). St. Petersburg, 1889.

———, Ocherki po istorii russkikh finansov v tsarstvovanie Ekateriny II (Studies in the History of Rusian Finance in the Reign of Catherine II). St. Petersburg, 1906.

Principal Sources

Chechulin, N. D., Ekaterina II v borbe za prestol (Catherine II and the Struggle for the Throne). Leningrad, 1924.

Cheglokov, P., Ob organakh sudebnoi vlasti v Rossii ot osnovaniia gosudarstva do vstupleniia na prestol Alekseia Mikhailovicha (Organs of the Judiciary in Russia from the Founding of the State to the Accession of Alexis Mikhilovich). Kazan, 1885.

Chernov, V. M., Rozhdenie revoliutsionnoi Rossii: fevralskaia revoliutsiia (Birth of Revolutionary Russia: the February Revolution). Paris–Prague–New York, 1934.

Chicherin, B., Opyty po istorii russkago prava (Essays in the History of the Russian Law). Moscow, 1858.

Churchill, W. S., The World Crisis, 1915. London, 1923.

Cruttwell, C. R. M. F., A History of the Great War, 1914–1918. 2nd ed., Oxford, 1936.

Curtiss, J. S., Church and State in Russia: The Last Years of the Empire, 1900–1917. New York, 1940.

Czartoryski, Prince Adam, Mémoires du Prince Adam Czartoryski et sa correspondance avec l'Empereur Alexandre I-er. 2 vols., Paris, 1887.

Dan, F., Proiskhozhdenie Bolshevizma (The Origins of Bolshevism). New York, 1946.

Danilov, Yu. N., Rossiia v mirovoi voine, 1914–1915 (Russia in the World War, 1914–1915). Berlin, 1924.

———, Russkie otriady na frantsuzskom i makedonskom frontakh, 1916–1918 (Russian Troops on the French and the Macedonian Fronts, 1916–1918). Paris, 1933.

Dashkova, Princess E., Zapiski Kniagini Dashkovoi (Memoirs of Princess Dashkov). St. Petersburg, 1906.

Davydov, N. V., and Poliansky, N. N., Sudebnaia reforma (Reform of the Judiciary). 2 vols., Moscow, 1915.

Diakonov, M. A., Vlast moskovskikh gosudarei: ocherki po istorii politicheskikh idei drevenei Rusi do kontsa XVI veka (The Power of Muscovite Princes: Studies in the History of Political Ideas in Ancient Russia to the End of the Sixteenth Century). St. Petersburg, 1889.

———, Ocherki obshchestvennago i gosudarstvennago stroia dreveni Rusi (Studies in the Social and Constitutional Structure of Ancient Russia). 2nd ed., Moscow, 1908.

Dolgorukov, Prince L. D., and Tolstoi, Count S. L., eds., Kresianskii stroi (The Peasantry). Vol. I, St. Petersburg, 1905.

Dorn, W. L., Competition for Empire, 1740–1763. New York–London, 1940.

Dovnar-Zapolsky, M. V., Istoricheskii process russkago naroda (The Historical Process of the Russian People). Moscow, 1906.

———, Istoriia russkago narodnago khoziaistva (Economic History of Russia). Vol. I, Kiev, 1911.

———, Russkaia istoriia v ocherkakh i statiakh (Essays and Articles on Russian History). 3 vols., Moscow, 19(?)–1912.

Druzhinin, N., Iuridicheskoe polozhenie krestian (The Legal Status of the Peasants). St. Petersburg, 1897.

Dubnov, S. M., History of the Jews in Russia and Poland. 3 vols., Philadelphia, 1916–1920.

Dulles, F. R., The Road to Teheran. Princeton, 1944.

Dvesti let Kabinet Ego Imperatorskago Velichestva, 1704–1904 (Two Hundred Years of the Cabinet of His Imperial Majesty, 1704–1904). St. Petersburg, 1911.

Dzhanshiev, G. A., Epokha velikikh reform (The Era of Great Reforms). Moscow, 1900.

———, Sbornik statei (Essays). Moscow, 1914.

Eck, A., Le Moyen Âge russe. Paris, 1933.

Ekzempliarsky, A. V., Velikie i udelnye kniazia v severnoi Rossii s 1238 po 1505 g. (Grand Dukes and Appanage Princes in Northern Russia from 1238 to 1505). 2 vols., St. Petersburg, 1889–1891.

Entsiklopedicheskii slovar (Encyclopedia). St. Petersburg, F. A. Brockhaus and I. A. Efron, 43 vols. in 86, 1890–1907.

Falkenhayn, E. von, The German General Staff and Its Decisions, 1914–1916. New York, 1920.

Fay, S. B., The Origins of the World War. 2 vols., New York, 1928.

Ferrero, G., The Reconstruction of Europe: Talleyrand and the Congress of Vienna. New York, 1941.

Finn-Enotaevsky, A., Kapitalizm v Rossii, 1890–1917 (Capitalism in Russia, 1890–1917). 2nd ed., Moscow, 1925.

Firsov, N. N., "Aleksandr III: kharakteristika" (Alexander III: A Characterization), Byloe (The Past), Vol. XXIX, 1925.

Fisher, J. R., Finland and the Tsars, 1809–1899. London, 1899.

Fleer, M. G., ed., Rabochee dvizhenie v gody voiny (The Labor Movement During the War). Moscow, 1925.

Fletcher, Giles, O gosudarstve russkom (Of the Russe Common Wealth), ed. Prince N. V. Golitsin. St. Petersburg, 1911.

Florinsky, M. T., "The Russian Mobilization of 1914," Political Science Quarterly, Vol. XLII, 1927.

———, "Russia and Constantinople," Foreign Affairs, Vol. VIII, 1929.

———, The End of the Russian Empire. New Haven, 1931.

Florinsky, T. D., Slavianskoe plemia (The Slavs). Kiev, 1907.

———, Izbornik Kievskii posviashchennyi T. D. Florinskomu (Kiev Symposium Dedicated to T. D. Florinsky). Kiev, 1904.

Francis, D., Russia from the American Embassy. New York, 1921.

Friese, C., Russland und Preussen vom Krimkrieg bis zum polnischen Aufstand. Berlin, 1931.

Gankin, O. H., and Fisher, H. H., The Bolsheviks and the World War: The Origin of the Third International. Stanford, 1940.

Gershenzon, M. O., Istoriia molodoi Rossii (History of Young Russia). Moscow, 1908.

———, Epokha Nikolaia I (The Era of Nicholas I), Moscow, 1911.

Gimer, D., "9 ianvaria 1905 g. v SPB: vospominaniia" (January 9, 1905, in St. Petersburg: Reminiscences) Byloe (The Past), Vol. XXIX, 1925.

Glinsky, B. B., Revoliutsionnyi period russkoi istorii, 1861–1881 gg. (A Revolutionary Period of Russian History, 1861–1881). 2 vols., St. Petersburg, 1913.

Golovin, N. N., The Russian Army in the World War. New Haven, 1931.

Golubinsky, E., Istoriia russkoi tserkvi (History of the Russian Church). 2 vols. in 4, Moscow, 1900–1911.

Gooch, G. P., History of Modern Europe, 1878–1919. London, 1923.

———, Before the War: Studies in Diplomacy. 2 vols., London, 1936–1938.

Gorev, B. I., and Kozmin, B. P., eds., Revoliutsionnoe dvizhenie 1860-kh godov (The Revolutionary Movement of the 1860's). Moscow, 1932.

Goriainov, S., Bosfor i Dardanelly (The Bosphorus and the Dardanelles). St. Petersburg, 1907; French version, Le Bosphore et les Dardanelles, Paris, 1910.

———, "The End of the Alliance of the Three Emperors," The American Historical Review, Vol. XXIII, 1918.

Gosudarstvennyi kontrol, 1811–1911 (Department of State Control, 1811–1911). St. Petersburg, 1911.

Gosudarstvennyi soviet, 1801–1901 (The State Council, 1801–1901). St. Petersburg, 1901.

Grabar, I. E., Istoriia russkago iskustva (History of Russian Art). 6 vols., Moscow, 1909–1914.

Graham, S., Tsar of Freedom: The Life and Reign of Alexander II. New Haven, 1935.

Grekov, B. D., Feodalnyia otnosheniia v kievskom gosudarstve (Feudal Relationships in the Kievan State). Moscow-Leningrad, 1937.

———, Kievskaia Rus (Kievan Russia). 3rd ed., Moscow-Leningrad, 1939.

———, Krestiane na Rusi s drevneishikh vremen do XVII veka (Peasants in Russia from Ancient Times to the Seventeenth Century). Moscow, 1946.

———, and Iakubovsky, A., Zolotaia Orda (The Golden Horde). Leningrad, 1937.

Grey of Fallodon, Twenty-Five Years, 1892–1916. 2 vols., New York, 1925–1926.

Gronsky, P. P., and Astrov, N. J., The War and the Russian Government. New Haven, 1929.

Gudzy, N. K., History of Early Russian Literature. New York, 1948.

Gulishambarov, S. C., Vsemirnaia torgovlia v XIX v. i uchastie v nei Rossii (World Trade in the Nineteenth Century and Russia's Participation). St. Petersburg, 1898.

Gurev, A., Denezhnoe obrashchenie v Rossii v XIX stoletii (Money Circulation in Russia in the Nineteenth Century). St. Petersburg, 1903.

Gurko, V. I., Features and Figures of the Past: Government and Opinion in the Reign of Nicholas II. Stanford, 1939.

Gushchin, A. S., Pamiatniki khudozhestvennago remesla drevnei Rusi X–XII vv. (Monuments of Arts and Crafts of Ancient Russia in the Tenth–Twelfth Centuries). Moscow-Leningrad, 1936.

Hanbury-Williams, Sir J., The Emperor Nicholas II as I Knew Him. London, 1922.

Principal Sources

Handelsman, M., "Le Prince Adam Czartoryski: essai de caractéristique," Revue des travaux de l'Academie des Sciences Morales et Politiques, Paris, July–August, 1938.

Hildt, J. C., Early Diplomatic Negotiations of the United States with Russia. Baltimore, 1906.

Hoetzsch, O., Russland: Eine Einführung auf Grund seiner Geschichte vom japanischen bis zum Weltkrieg. Berlin, 1917.

How the War Began in 1914: Diary of the Russian Foreign Office. London, 1925.

Hrushevsky, M., A History of Ukraine. New Haven, 1941.

Iakhontov, A. N., Tiazhelye dni (Fateful Days), Arkhiv Russkoi Revoliutsii (Archives of the Russian Revolution). Vol. XVIII, 1926.

Iakovlev, A., Kholopstvo i kholopy v moskovskom gosudarstve XVII v. (Slavery and the Slaves in the Muscovite State of the Seventeenth Century). Moscow-Leningrad, 1943.

Iakushkin, B. E., Gosudarstvennaia vlast i proekty gosudarstvennoi reformy v Rossii (State Power and Projects of Constitutional Reform in Russia). St. Petersburg, 1906.

Ianson, Ia. E., Opyt statisticheskago izsledovaniia o krestianskikh nadelakh i platezhakh (Statistical Investigation of Peasant Allotments and Redemption Payments). St. Petersburg, 1877.

Ignatovich, I., Pomeshchii krestiane nakanune osvobozhdeniia (Serfs on the Eve of the Emancipation). 2nd ed., Moscow, 1910.

Ikonnikov, V. S., Opyt izsledovaniia o kulturnom znachenii Vizantii v russkoi istorii (Studies in the Cultural Influence of Byzantium in Russian History). Kiev, 1869.

———, Opyt russkoi istoriografii (Study in Russian Historiography). 2 vols. in 4, Kiev, 1891–1908.

International Cyclopedia of Music and Musicians. New York, 1946.

Istoricheskii Vestnik (Historical Messenger). 150 vols., St. Petersburg, 1880–1917.

Istoriia Pravitelstvuiushchago Senata za dvesti let, 1711–1911 (History of the Governing Senate for Two Hundred Years, 1711–1911). 5 vols., St. Petersburg, 1911.

Istoriia Rossii v XIX veke (History of Russia in the Nineteenth Century). St. Petersburg, A. I. Granat, 9 vols., 19(?).

Istoriia SSSR (History of the USSR), from ancient times to the end of the nineteenth century. Moscow, the Academy of Science of the USSR, 2 vols., 1939–1940.

Istoriia udelov za sto let ikh sushchestvovaniia, 1797–1897 (History of the Appanages for a Hundred Years of Their Existence, 1797–1897). St. Petersburg, 1902.

Izvolsky, A. P., The Memoirs of Alexander Izvolsky. London, 1920.

Kachorovsky, K. R., Russkaia obshchina (The Russian Land Commune). Moscow, 1900.

Kakurin, N. E., ed., Razlozhenie armii v 1917 godu (Breakdown of the Army in 1917). Moscow-Leningrad, 1925.

Kallash, V., ed., Tri veka: Rossiia ot smutnago vremeni do nashego (Three Centuries: Russia from the Time of Troubles to the Present). 6 vols., Moscow, 1912–1913.

Kareev, N. J., V kakom smysle mozhno govorit of sushchestvovanii feodalisma v Rossii? Po povodu teorii Pavlova-Silvanskago (What Is Meant by Russian Feudalism? Concerning the Theory of Pavlov-Silvansky). St. Petersburg, 1910.

Karnovich, E. P., Zamechatelnyia bogatstva chastnykh lits v Rossii (Remarkable Private Fortunes in Russia). St. Petersburg, 1885.

Kaufman, A. A., Agrarnyi vopros v Rossii (The Agrarian Problem in Russia). Moscow, 1919.

Kayden, E. M., and Antsiferov, A. N., The Cooperative Movement in Russia During the War. New Haven, 1929.

Kerensky, A. F., The Catastrophe. London, 1927.

Khodsky, L. V., Osnovy gosudarstvennago khoziaistva (Foundations of State Economy). 4th ed., St. Petersburg, 1913.

Khudekov, S. N., Istoriia tantsev (History of the Dance). Vol. IV, Petrograd, 1918.

Kizevetter, A. A., Istoricheskie ocherki (Historical Essays). Moscow, 1912.

———, Istoricheskie otkliki (Historical Notes). Moscow, 1915.

———, Na rubezhe dvukh stoletii: vospominaniia 1881–1914 (The Junction of Two Centuries: Reminiscences, 1881–1914). Prague, 1929.

———, Istoricheskie siluety: liudi i sobytiia (Historical Silhouettes: Men and Events). Berlin, 1931.

Kliuchevsky, V. O., Boyarskaia duma drevnei Rusi (The Boyar Council of Ancient Russia). 4th ed., Moscow, 1909.

Kliuchevsky, V. O., Opyty i izsledovaniia (Essays and Studies). Moscow, 191(?).

———, Istoriia soslovii v Rossii (History of the Social Classes in Russia). Moscow, 1913.

———, Otzyvy i otvety (Observations and Answers). Moscow, 1914.

———, Ocherki i rechi (Essays and Speeches). Petrograd, 1918.

———, Kurs russkoi istorii (Lectures in Russian History). 5 vols., Petrograd, 1918–1921.

Klochkov, M. V., Ocherki pravitelstvennoi deiatelnosti vremeni imperatora Pavla I (Essays in Public Administration of the Time of Emperor Paul I). Petrograd, 1916.

Kniga dlia chteniia po istorii novago vremeni (Readings in the History of Modern Times). Moscow, the Society for the Advancement of Technical Knowledge, Vol. II, 1911.

Knox, Sir A., With the Russian Army, 1914–1917. 2 vols., New York, 1921.

Kobiakov, R., "Gapon i okhrannoe otdelenie do 1905 g." (Gapon and the Security Police Before 1905), Byloe (The Past), Vol. XXIX, 1925.

Kohn, S., and Meyendorff, Baron A. F., The Cost of the War to Russia. New Haven, 1932.

Kokovtsov, Count V. N., Iz moego proshlago: vospominaniia 1903–1919 (Out of My Past: Reminiscences 1903–1919). 2 vols., Paris-Reval, 1933.

Kondakov, N. P., Russkie klady (Russian Treasure Troves). St. Petersburg, 1896.

———, The Russian Icon, Oxford, 1927.

Kondratev, N. D., Rynok khlebov i ego regulirovanie vo vremia voiny i revoliutsii (The Grain Market and Its Regulation During the War and the Revolution). Moscow, 1922.

"Konferentsiia soiuznikov v Petrograde v 1917 godu" (The Allied Conference in Petrograd in 1917), Krasnyi Arkhiv (Red Archives), Vol. XX, 1927.

Korf, Baron M. A., Zhizn Grafa Speranskogo (Life of Count Speransky). 2 vols., St. Petersburg, 1861.

Korkunov, N. M., Russkoe gosudarstvennoe pravo (Russian Constitutional Law). 2 vols., 7th ed., St. Petersburg, 1907.

Kornilov, A. A., Obshchestvennoe dvizhenie pri Aleksandre II (Social Movements under Alexander II). Moscow, 1909.

Kornilov, A. A., Kurs istorii Rossii v XIX veke (Lectures in the History of Russia in the Nineteenth Century). 3 vols., Moscow, 1912–1914.

———, Lappo-Danilevsky, A. S., Semevsky, V. I., and Strakhovsky, I. M., Krestianskii stroi (Conditions of the Peasantry). Vol. I, St. Petersburg, 1905.

Korsakov, D. A., Votsarenie Imperatritsy Anny Ioannovy (Accession of Empress Anna Ioannovna). Kazan, 1880.

———, Iz zhizni russkikh deiatelei vosemnadtsatago veka (Notes on Public Figures in Russia in the Eighteenth Century). Kazan, 1891.

Kostomarov, N. I., Sobranie sochinenii (Collected Works). 21 vols. in 8, St. Petersburg, 1903–1906.

———, Russkaia istoriia v zhizneopisaniiakh eia glavneishikh deiatelei (Russian History in Biographies of Its Principal Figures), the tenth–sixteenth centuries. Vol. I, St. Petersburg, 1880.

———, O znachenii Velikago Novgoroda (On the Significance of Novgorod the Great), Sobranie sochinenii (Collected Works). Vol. I, St. Petersburg, 1903.

———, Severnorusskiia narodopravstva (North Russian Democracies), Sobranie Sochinenii (Collected Works). Vol. III, St. Petersburg, 1904.

Krasnaia Letopis (Red Chronicle). 64 vols., Moscow, 1922–1936.

Krasnyi Arkhiv (Red Archives). 104 vols., Moscow, 1922–1941.

Krepostnaia Rossiia (Russia Under Serfdom), symposium published by the Petrograd section of the Communist Academy. Petrograd, 1922.

Kruglov, A. O., ed., Pisma Konstantina Nikolaevicha Bestuzheva-Riumina o smutnom vremeni (Letters of C. N. Bestuzhev-Riumin on the "Time of Troubles"). St. Petersburg, 1898.

Kulisher, I. M., Ocherk istorii russkoi promyshlennosti (Essay in the History of Russian Industry). Petrograd, 1922.

———, Ocherk po istorii russkoi torgovli (Essay in the History of Russian Commerce). St. Petersburg, 1923.

———, Istoriia russkago narodnago khoziaistva (Economic History of Russia). 2 vols., Moscow, 1925.

Labry, R., L'Industrie russe et la révolution. Paris, 1919.

Ladyzhensky, K. A., Istoriia russkago tamozhennago tarifa (History of the Russian Tariff). St. Petersburg, 1886.

Lamsdorf, Count V. N., Dnevnik, 1886–1890 (Diary, 1886–1890), ed. F. A. Rotshtein. Moscow-Leningrad, 1926.

Principal Sources 1493

Lamsdorf, Count V. N., Dnevnik, 1891–1892 (Diary, 1891–1892), Academia. Moscow-Leningrad, 1934.

Langer, W. L., European Alliances and Alignments, 1871–1890. New York, 1931.

———, The Diplomacy of Imperialism, 1890–1902. 2 vols., New York, 1935.

Lappo-Danilevsky, A. S., Russkiia promyshlennyia i torgovyia kompanii v pervoi polovine vosemnadtsatago stoletiia (Russian Industrial and Trading Companies in the First Half of the Eighteenth Century). St. Petersburg, 1899.

———, Ocherki istorii obrazovaniia glavneishikh razriadov krestianskago naseleniia v Rossii (Studies in the Formation of the Chief Groups of the Peasant Population in Russia). St. Petersburg, 1905.

———, Otzyv o sochinenii N. D. Chechulina: Ocherki po istorii russkikh finansov v tsarstvovanie Ekateriny II (A Critique of the Volume by N. D. Chechulin, Studies in the History of Russian Finance in the Reign of Catherine II). St. Petersburg, 1910.

———, Petr Velikii, osnovatel Imperatorskoi Akademii Nauk v S. Peterburge (Peter the Great, Founder of the Imperial Academy of Science in St. Petersburg). St. Petersburg, 1914.

Laugier, M. A., Histoire des négociations pour la paix conclue à Belgrade le 18 septembre 1739. 2 vols., Paris, 1768.

Lazarevsky, N. I., Lektsii po russkomu gosudarstvennomu pravu (Lectures on Russian Constitutional Law). 2 vols., 2nd ed., St. Petersburg, 1910.

———, Russkoe gosudarstvennoe pravo (Russian Constitutional Law). 3rd ed., Vol. I, St. Petersburg, 1913.

Lebedev, V. I., Reformy Petra I (The Reforms of Peter I), collection of documents. Moscow, 1937.

Lemke, M., Epokha tsenzurnykh reform, 1859–1865 (The Era of Censorship Reforms, 1859–1865). St. Petersburg, 1904.

———, Politicheskie protsesy (Political Trials). St. Petersburg, 1907.

———, Nikolaevskie zhandarmy i literatura, 1825–1855 (The Gendarmes of Nicholas and Literature, 1825–1856). St. Petersburg, 1908.

Lenin, V. I., Sochineniia (Works). 3rd ed. (reproduced without changes from the second), 30 vols., Moscow, 1928–1937.

Liashchenko, P. I., Istoriia russkago narodnago khoziaistva (Economic History of Russia). Moscow-Leningrad, 1927.

Likhachev, D. S., Russkiia letopisi i ikh kulturno-istoricheskoe znachenie (Russian Chronicles and Their Cultural and Historical Significance). Moscow-Leningrad, 1947.

Liubavsky, M. K., Ocherk istorii Litovsko-Russkago gosudarstva (A History of the Lithuanian-Russian State). Moscow, 1910.

———, Lektsii po drevnei russkoi istorii do kontsa shestnadtsatogo veka (Lectures on Ancient Russian History to the End of the Sixteenth Century). Moscow, 1915.

———, Obrazovanie osnovnoi gosudarstvennoi territorii velikorusskoi narodnosti (Formation of the Basic Territory of the Great-Russian State). Leningrad, 1929.

———, Sbornik statei v chest M. K. Liubavskago (Symposium Dedicated to M. K. Liubavsky). Petrograd, 1917.

Liubomirov, P. G., Torgovyia sviazi drevnei Rusi s vostokom v VIII–XI vv. (Commercial Relations Between Ancient Russia and the East in the Eighth–Eleventh Centuries), based chiefly on the treasure troves of eastern coins. Saratov, 1923.

———, Ocherki po istorii russkoi promyshlennosti XVII, XVIII i nachala XIX veka (Studies in the History of Russian Industry in the Seventeenth, Eighteenth, and the Beginning of the Nineteenth Centuries). Moscow, 1947.

Livanova, T., Istoriia russkoi muzyki (History of Russian Music). 2 vols., Moscow, 1940.

Lord, R. H., The Second Partition of Poland, a study in diplomatic history. Cambridge, 1915.

———, "The Third Partition of Poland," The Slavonic Review, Vol. III, London, 1925.

Lositsky, A., Vykupnaia operatsiia (Redemption Payments). St. Petersburg, 1906.

Lowe, C., Alexander III of Russia. London, 1895.

Macartney, C. A., The Magyars in the Ninth Century. Cambridge, 1930.

Maklakov, V. A., Vlast i obshchestvennost na zakate staroi Rossii: vospominaniia sovremennika (The Government and the Liberal Movement in the Closing Years of Old Russia: Reminiscences of a Contemporary). Paris, 1939(?).

———, Pervaia Gosudarstvennaia Duma: vospominaniia sovremennika (The First State Duma: Reminiscences of a Contemporary). Paris, 1939.

Principal Sources 1495

Maklakov, V. A., Vtoraia Gosudarstvennaia Duma: vospominaniia sovremennika (The Second State Duma: Reminiscences of a Contemporary). Paris, 1946.

"Mart-Mai 1917 goda" (March–May 1917), summary of reports on the political situation submitted to the State Duma, Krasnyi Arkhiv (Red Archives), Vol. XV, 1926.

Martens, F., ed., Recueil des traités et conventions conclus par la Russie avec les puissances étrangères. 15 vols., St. Petersburg, 1874–1909.

Martov, L., Maslov, P., and Potresov, A., eds., Obshchestvennoe dvizhenie v Rossii v nachale XX veka (The Social and Political Movement in Russia at the Beginning of the Twentieth Century). 4 vols., St. Petersburg, 1909–1910.

Materialy po istorii franko-russkikh otnoshenii za 1910–1914 gg. (Documents on the History of Franco-Russian Relations in 1910–1914). Moscow, 1922.

Medynsky, E. N., Istoriia russkoi pedagogiki do velikoi oktiabrskoi sotsialisticheskoi revoliutsii (History of Russian Pedagogy to the Great October Socialist Revolution). 2nd ed., Moscow, 1938.

Meller, V. L., and Pankratova, A. M., eds., Rabochee dvizhenie v 1917 godu (The Labor Movement in 1917). Moscow-Leningrad, 1926.

Mendeleev, D., K poznaniiu Rossii (Towards an Understanding of Russia). St. Petersburg, 1907.

Meyendorff, Baron A. F., Krestianski dvor (The Peasant Homestead). St. Petersburg, 1909.

Mezhdunarodnaia politika noveishago vremeni (International Policies in Modern Times). 2 vols., Moscow, 1925–1926.

Mezhdunarodnye otnosheniia v epokhu imperializma (International Relations in the Era of Imperialism), documents from the archives of the tsars and Provisional Government. 13 vols. in 15, Moscow, 1931–1939.

Michelson, A. M., Apostol, P. N., and Bernatzky, M. W., Russian Public Finance During the War. New Haven, 1928.

Migulin, P. P., Russkii gosudarstvennyi kredit (Russian State Loans). 3 vols., Kharkov, 1899–1904.

Miliukov, P. N., Spornye voprosy finansovoi istorii moskovskago gosudarstva (Unsolved Problems of the Financial History of the Muscovite State). St. Petersburg, 1892.

———, Iz istorii russkoi intelligentsii (Studies in the History of Russian Intellectual Movements). St. Petersburg, 1903.

Miliukov, P. N., Gosudarstvennoe khoziaistvo Rossii v pervoi chetverti XVIII stoletiia i reforma Petra Velikago (The Financial Administration of Russia in the First Quarter of the Eighteenth Century and the Reform of Peter the Great). 2nd ed., St. Petersburg, 1905.

———, Glavnyia techeniia russkoi istoricheskoi mysli (Chief Trends in Russian Historical Thought). 3rd ed., Moscow, 1913.

———, Istoriia vtoroi russkoi revoliutsii (History of the Second Russian Revolution). 3 vols., Sofia, 1921–1924.

———, Ocherki po istorii russkoi kultury (Essays in the History of Russian Culture). Rev. ed., 3 vols. in 4, Paris, 1930–1937.

———, Seignobos, C., and Eisenmann, L., Histoire de Russie. 3 vols., Paris, 1932–1933.

Miliutin, D., Istoriia voiny 1799 goda mezhdu Rossiei i Frantsiei v tsarstvovanie imperatora Pavla I (History of the War of 1799 Between Russia and France in the Reign of Emperor Paul I). 2nd ed., 5 vols., 1857.

Ministerstvo finansov, 1802–1902 (Ministry of Finance, 1802–1902). St. Petersburg, 1902.

Ministerstvo finansov, 1904–1913 (Ministry of Finance, 1904–1913). St. Petersburg, 1913.

Ministerstvo iustitsii za sto let, 1802–1902 (A Hundred Years of the Ministry of Justice, 1802–1902). St. Petersburg, 1902.

Ministerstvo vnutrennikh del (Ministry of the Interior). 3 vols., St. Petersburg, 1901.

Mirsky, Prince S. D., Contemporary Russian Literature, 1881–1925. New York, 1926.

———, A History of Russian Literature from the Earliest Times to the Death of Dostoyevsky (1881). New York, 1927.

———, Russia, A Social History. London, 1931.

Monarkhiia pered krusheniem (The Monarchy Before Its Downfall), papers of Nicholas II and other documents ed. V. P. Semennikov. Moscow-Leningrad, 1927.

Montagu-Nathan, M., A History of Russian Music. London, 1918.

Morokhovets, E. A., ed., Krestianskoe dvizhenie 1827–1869 gg. (The Peasant Movement in 1827–1869). Moscow, 1931.

Mosely, P. E., Russian Diplomacy and the Opening of the Eastern Question in 1838 and 1839. Cambridge, 1934.

———, "Russian Policy in 1911–1912," The Journal of Modern History, Vol. XII, 1940.

Nebolsin, G. P., Statisticheskoe obozrenie vneshnei torgovli Rossii (Statistical Survey of Russia's Foreign Trade). St. Petersburg, 1850.

Nevedensky, S., Katkov i ego vremia (Katkov and His Time). St. Petersburg, 1880.

Nicholas Mikhilovich, Grand Duke, Les Relations diplomatiques de la Russie et de la France d'après les rapports des ambassadeurs d'Alexandre et de Napoléon, 1808–1812. 7 vols., St. Petersburg, 1905–1914.

———, L'Impératrice Elisabeth, épouse d'Alexandre 1-er. 3 vols., St. Petersburg, 1908–1909.

———, Perepiska Imperatora Aleksandra I s sestroi Velikoi Kniaginei Ekaterinoi Pavlovnoi (Correspondence of Emperor Alexander I with His Sister the Grand Duchess Catherine Pavlovna). St. Petersburg, 1910.

———, Imperator Aleksandr I, opyt istoricheskago izsledovaniia (Emperor Alexander I, A Historical Study). 2 vols., St. Petersburg, 1912.

———, General-Adiutanty Imperatora Aleksandra I (Generals Aides-de-Camp of Emperor Alexander I). St. Petersburg, 1913.

Nicholas II, Emperor, Dnevnik Nikolaia II, 1890–1906 (Diary of Nicholas II, 1890–1906). Berlin, 1923.

———, The Letters of the Tsaritsa to the Tsar, 1914–1916, with an introduction by Sir B. Pares. London, 1923.

———, "Perepiska N. A. Romanova s P. A. Stolypinym" (Correspondence of N. A. Romanov with P. A. Stolypin), Krasnyi Arkhiv (Red Archives), Vol. V, 1924.

———, The Letters of the Tsar to the Tsaritsa, ed. C. E. Vulliamy. London, 1929.

———, The Secret Letters of the Last Tsar, ed. E. J. Bing. New York, 1938.

Nicolson, H., Sir Arthur Nicolson, Bart., First Lord Carnock. London, 1930.

Niederle, L., Manuel de l'antiquité slave. 2 vols., Paris, 1922–1926.

Nikitsky, A., Ocherk vnutrennei istorii Pskova (Outline of the Internal History of Pskov). St. Petersburg, 1873.

———, Istoriia ekonomicheskago byta Velikago Novgoroda (Economic History of Novgorod the Great). St. Petersburg, 1893.

Nolde, Baron B. E., Ocherki russkago gosudarstvennago prava (Studies in Russian Constitutional Law). St. Petersburg, 1911.

———, Vnehsniaia politika: istoricheskie ocherki (Foreign Policy: Historical Essays). Petrograd, 1915.

———, Yuri Samarin i ego vremia (Yuri Samarin and His Time). Paris, 1926.

Nolde, Baron B. E., L'Ancien Régime et la révolution russes. Paris, 1928.
——, Russia in the Economic War. New Haven, 1928.
——, Dalekoe i blizkoe (The Past, Distant and Recent), historical essays. Paris, 1930.
——, L'Alliance Franco-Russe. Paris, 1936.

Ocherk istorii ministerstva inostrannykh del, 1802–1902 (Survey of the History of the Ministry of Foreign Affairs, 1802–1902). St. Petersburg, 1902.

Odinetz, D. M., and Novgorotsev, P. J., Russian Schools and Universities During the War. New Haven, 1929.

Oganovsky, N. P., Selskoe khoziaistvo Rossii v dvadtsatom veke (Russian Agriculture in the Twentieth Century). Moscow, 1923.

Okun, S. B., Rossiisko-Amerikanskaia Kompaniia (The Russian-American Company). Moscow-Leningrad, 1939.

Oldenburg, S. S., Tsarstvovanie Imperatora Nikolaia II (The Reign of Emperor Nicholas II). 2 vols., Belgrade-Munich, 1939–1949.

Otechestvennaia voina i russkoe obshchestvo (The Patriotic War and Russian Opinion), ed. A. K. Dzhivelegov, S. P. Melgunov, and E. I. Pricheta. 7 vols., Moscow, 1912.

Ovsianikov-Kulikovsky, D. N., ed., Istoriia russkoi literatury XIX v. (History of Russian Literature in the Nineteenth Century). 5 vols., Moscow, 1908–1911.

Ozerov, I. Kh., Politika po rabochemu voprosu v Rossii za poslednie gody (Labor Policies in Russia in Recent Years). Moscow, 1906.

Padenie Tsarskago regima (Fall of the Tsarist Regime), verbatim reports of the Extraordinary Commission of Investigation appointed by the Provisional Government, ed. P. E. Shchegolev. 7 vols., Leningrad, 1925–1927.

Paléologue, M., La Russie des tsars pendant la guerre. 3 vols., Paris, 1921–1923.
——, Aleksandr II i Kniaginia Yurevskaia (Alexander II and Princess Yurevsky). Petrograd, 1924.
——, The Enigmatic Czar. New York, 1938.

Panchulidzev, S. A., Istoriia kavalergardov (History of the Horse Guards). 4 vols., St. Petersburg, 1899–1912.

Pares, Sir B., The Fall of the Russian Monarchy. New York, 1939.

Pasvolsky, L., and Moulton, H. G., Russian Debts and Russian Reconstruction. New York, 1924.

Principal Sources

Pavlov-Silvansky, N. P., Feodalizm v drevnei Rusi (Feudalism in Ancient Russia). St. Petersburg, 1907.

————, Sochineniia (Works). 3 vols., St. Petersburg, 1909–1910.

Pavlovich, P., ed., Avantiury ruskago tsarisma v Bolgarii (Adventures of Russian Tsarism in Bulgaria), collection of documents. Moscow, 1935.

Pazhitnov, K. A., Razvitie sotsialisticheskikh idei v Rossii (Development of Socialist Ideas in Russia). Kharkov, 1913.

Pchelin, N., Sila i pravo v deiatelnosti Petra Velikago (Right and Might in the Policies of Peter the Great). Yaroslavl, 1919.

Pekarsky, P. P., Nauka i literatura v Rossii pri Petre Velikom (Science and Literature in Russia Under Peter the Great). 2 vols., St. Petersburg, 1862.

Pervoe Maia v tsarskoi Rossii, 1890–1916 (May 1 in Tsarist Russia, 1890–1916), collection of documents. Moscow, 1939.

Petrushevsky, A., Generalissimus Kniaz Suvorov (Generalissimo Prince Suvorov). 2nd ed., St. Petersburg, 1900.

Phillipson, C., and Buxton, N., The Question of the Bosphorus and Dardanelles. London, 1917.

Platonov, S. F., K istorii poltavskoi bitvy (To the History of the Battle of Poltava). St. Petersburg, 1909.

————, Ocherki po istorii smuty v moskovskom gosudarstve XVI–XVII vv. (Studies in the History of the "Time of Troubles" in the Muscovite State in the Sixteenth–Seventeenth Centuries). 3rd ed., Moscow, 1910.

————, Stati po russkoi istorii, 1883–1912 (Essays in Russian History, 1883–1912). 2nd ed., St. Petersburg, 1912.

————, Drevnerusskiia skazaniia i povesti o smutnom vremeni kak istoricheskii istochnik (Ancient Russian Legends and Tales About the "Time of Troubles" as a Historical Source). 2nd ed., Moscow, 1913.

————, Lektsii po russkoi istorii (Lectures on Russian History). St. Petersburg, 1917.

————, Sbornik statei po russkoi istorii posviashchennykh S. F. Platonovu (Symposium of Articles on Russian History Dedicated to S. F. Platonov). St. Petersburg, 1922.

————, "Ivan Groznyi v russkoi istoriografii" (Ivan the Dread in Russian Historiography), Russkoe Proshloe (Russian Past), Vol. I, 1923.

————, Smutnoe vremia (The Time of Troubles). St. Petersburg, 1923.

————, Boris Godunov (Boris Godunov). Prague, 1924.

Platonov, S. F., Proshloe russkago severa (The Past of the Russian North). Berlin, 1924.

———, Sotsialnyi krizis smutnago vremeni (The Social Crisis of the "Time of Troubles"). Leningrad, 1924.

———, Moskva i zapad v XVI–XVII vekakh (Moscow and the West in the Sixteenth–Seventeenth Centuries). Leningrad, 1925.

———, Iz bytovoi istorii petrovskoi epokhi: liubimtsy Petra Velikago —Medved, Bitka, i drugie (From the Social History of the Petrine Era: The Favorites of Peter the Great—Medved, Bitka, and Others). Leningrad, 1926.

———, Petr Velikii, lichnost i deiatelnost (Peter the Great, the Man and His Work). Leningrad, 1926.

Plekhanov, G. V., Sochineniia (Works). 24 vols., Moscow, 1923–1927.

Pleshcheev, A., Nash balet, 1673–1896 (Our Ballet, 1763–1896). St. Petersburg, 1896.

K. P. Pobedonostsev i ego korrespondenty (C. P. Pobedonostsev and His Correspondents). 2 vols., Moscow, 1923.

———, Pisma Pobedonstseva k Aleksandru III s prilozheniem pisem k Velikomu Kniaziu Sergeiu Aleksandrovichu i Nikolaiu II (Letters of Pobedonostsev to Alexander III, the Grand Duke Serge Alexandrovich, and Nicholas II). 2 vols., Moscow, 1925–1926.

———, L'Autocracie russe: Constantin Pobédonostsev, mémoires politiques, correspondance officielle et documents inédits relatives à l'histoire du règne de l'empereur Alexandre III de Russie. Paris, 1927.

Pokrovsky, M. N., Russkaia istoriia s drevneishikh vremen (Russian history from the Earliest Time). 5 vols., Moscow, 1913.

———, Diplomatiia i voiny tsarskoi Rossii v XIX stoletii (Diplomacy and Wars of Tsarist Russia in the Nineteenth Century). Moscow, 1923.

———, ed., Russkaia istoricheskaia literatura v klassovom osveshchenii (Russian Historical Literature from the Class Point of View). 2 vols., Moscow, 1927–1930.

———, Istoricheskaia nauka i borba klassov (The Science of History and the Class Struggle). 2 vols., Moscow-Leningrad, 1933.

Pokrovsky, V. I., ed., Sbornik svedenii po istorii i statistike vneshnei torgovli Rossii (Collection of Materials Bearing on the History and Statistics of Russia's Foreign Trade). Vol. I, St. Petersburg, 1902.

Polievktov, M., Nikolai I (Nicholas I). St. Petersburg, 1914.

"Politicheskoe polozhenie Rossii nakanune fevralskoi revoiutsii v zhandarmskom osviashenii" (The Political Situation in Russia on the Eve of

Principal Sources   1501

the February Revolution as Viewed by the Security Police), Krasnyi Arkhiv (Red Archives), Vol. XVII, 1926.

Polner, T. I., Zhiznennyi put Kniazia Georgiia Evgenievicha Lvova (The Life Path of Prince G. E. Lvov). Paris, 1932.

———, and others, Russian Local Government During the War and the Union of Zemstvos. New Haven, 1930.

Polnoe Sobranie Zakonov Rossiiskoi Imperii, 1649–1916 (Full Collection of Laws of the Russian Empire, 1649–1916). 240 vols., St. Petersburg, 1830–1916.

Polovtzoff, A., Les Favoris de Catherine la Grande. Paris, 1939.

Popov, A., Istoriia vozmushcheniia Stenki Razina (History of the Rebellion of Stenka Razin). Moscow, 1857.

Porfirev, I. A., Istoriia russkoi slovesnosti (History of Russian Literature). 2 vols., Kazan, 1910–1913.

Potemkin, V. P., ed., Istoriia diplomatii (History of Diplomacy). 3 vols., Moscow, 1941–1945.

Presniakov, A. E., Kniazhoe pravo v drevnei Rusi, ocherky po istorii X–XII stoletiia (The Princely Law in Ancient Russia: Studies in the History of the Tenth-Twelfth Centuries). St. Petersburg, 1909.

———, Moskovskoe tsarstvo (The Moscow Tsardom). Petrograd, 1918.

———, Obrazovanie velikorusskago gosudarstva, ocherki po istorii XII–XV stoletii (Formation of the Great-Russian State, Studies in the History of the Twelfth–Fifteenth Centuries). Petrograd, 1918.

———, "Samoderzhavie Nikolaia I" (Autocracy under Nicholas I), Russkoe Proshloe (Russian Past), Vol. II, Petrograd, 1923.

———, "Samoderzhavie Aleksandra II" (Autocracy under Alexander II), Russkoe Proshloe (Russian Past), Vol. IV, Petrograd, 1923.

———, Apogei samoderzhaviia: Nikolai I (Apogee of Absolutism: Nicholas I). Leningrad, 1925.

———, 14 dekabria 1825 goda (December 14, 1825). Moscow-Leningrad, 1926.

———, Lekstsii po russkoi istorii: kievskaia Rus (Lectures in Russian History: Kievan Russia). Vol. I, Moscow, 1938.

Pribram, A. F., England and the International Policy of the European Powers, 1871–1914. Oxford, 1931.

Priselkov, M. D., Ocherki po tserkovno-politicheskoi istorii kievskoi Rusi X–XII vv. (Studies in the History of the Church and Politics in Kievan Russia of the Tenth–Twelfth Centuries). St. Petersburg, 1913.

Priselkov, M. D., Nestor Letopisets (Nestor the Chronicler). St. Petersburg, 1923.

Prokopovich, S. N., Krestianskoe khoziastvo (Peasant Economy). Berlin, 1924.

Pypin, A. N., Kharakteristika literaturnykh mnenii ot 20-kh do 50-kh godov (Characterization of Literary Opinions from the 1820's to the 1850's). St. Petersburg, 1890.

———, Istoriia russkoi etnografii (History of Russian Ethnography). 4 vols., St. Petersburg, 1890–1892.

———, Obshchestvennoe dvizenie v Rossii pri Aleksandre I (The Social Movement in Russia Under Alexander I). St. Petersburg, 1900.

———, Istoriia russkoi literatury (History of Russian Literature), 4 vols., St. Petersburg, 1911.

———, Panslavizm v proshlom i nastoiashchem (Panslavism, Its Past and Present). St. Petersburg, 1913.

———, Religioznyia dvizeniia pri Aleksandre I (Religious Movements Under Alexander I). Petrograd, 1916.

———, Ocherki literatury i obshchestvennosti pri Aleksandre I (Essays in Literature and Social Conditions under Alexander I). Petrograd, 1917.

Radkey, O. H., The Elections to the Russian Constituent Assembly of 1917. Cambridge, 1950.

Rashin, A. G., Formirovanie promyshlennago proletariata v Rossii (The Formation of the Industrial Proletariat in Russia). Moscow, 1940.

Reading, D. K., The Anglo-Russian Commercial Treaty of 1734. New Haven, 1938.

"Reforma 1861 goda i krestianskoe dvizhenie" (The Reform of 1861 and the Peasant Movement), Krasnyi Arkhiv (Red Archives), Vol. LXXV, 1936.

Revoliutsiia 1917 goda: khronika sobytii (The Revolution of 1917: A Chronicle of Events), A. Avdeev, V. Vladimirova, K. Riabinsky, and I. N. Liubimov, eds. 6 vols., Moscow-Leningrad, 1923–1930.

Riker, T. W., The Making of Roumania, 1856–1866. Oxford, 1931.

Robinson, G. T., Rural Russia Under the Old Regime. New York, 1932.

Rodzianko, M. V., "Gosudarstvennaia Duma i fevralskaia 1917 goda revoliutsiia" (The State Duma and the Revolution of February 1917), Arkhiv Russkoi Revoliutsii (Archives of the Russian Revolution), Vol. VI, 1922.

———, The Reign of Rasputin: An Empire's Collapse. London, 1927.

Principal Sources

Romanov, B. A., "Kontsessiia na Ialu" (The Yalu Concession), Russ-koe Proshloe (Russian Past), Vol. I, Petrograd, 1923.

———, Rossiia i Manzhuria, 1892–1906 (Russia and Manchuria, 1892–1906). Leningrad, 1928.

Romanovich-Slavatinsky, A., Dvorianstvo v Rossii ot nachala XVIII veka do otmeny krepostnogo prava (Russian Nobility from the Beginning of the Eighteenth Century to the Emancipation). Kiev, 1912.

Rosen, Baron R., Fifty Years of Diplomacy. 2 vols., New York, 1922.

Rossiia v mirovoi voine (Russia in the World War), official statistical summary. Moscow, 1925.

Rostowtzeff, M., Iranians and Greeks in South Russia. Oxford, 1922.

Rouire, A. M., La Rivalité anglo-russe au XIX-e siècle en Asie. Paris, 1908.

Roux, C., Alexandre II, Gorchakoff et Napoléon III. Paris, 1913.

Rozhdestvensky, S. V., Sluzhiloe zemlevladenie v moskovskom gosu-darstve XVI veka (Service Land Tenure in the Muscovite State of the Sixteenth Century). St. Petersburg, 1897.

———, Istoricheskii obzor deiatelnosti ministerstva narodnago pros-veshcheniia, 1802–1902 (Historical Survey of the Work of the Ministry of Education, 1802–1902). St. Petersburg, 1902.

———, Epokha preobrazovanii Petra Velikago i russkaia shkola novago vremeni (The Reforms of Peter the Great and the Russian Schools in Modern Times). St. Petersburg, 1903.

Rozhkov, N. A., Russkaia istoriia (History of Russia). 12 vols., Petrograd, 1919–1926.

———, Gorod i derevnia v russkoi istorii (Town and Village in Russian History). Petrograd, 1923.

Russkaia Starina (Russia That Was). 168 vols., St. Petersburg, 1870–1918.

Russkii Arkhiv (Russian Archives). 123 vols., Moscow, 1863–1917.

Russkii biograficheskii slovar (Russian Dictionary of Biographies). 25 vols., St. Petersburg, 1896–1913.

"Russko-Germanskii dogovor 1905 goda zakliuchennyi v Biorkakh" (The Russo-German Treaty of 1905 Concluded in Björkö), Krasnyi Arkhiv (Red Archives), Vol. V, 1924.

"Russko-Germanskiia otnosheniia" (Russo-German Relations), Krasnyi Arkhiv (Red Archives), Vol. I, 1922.

Savickij, N., "P. A. Stolypin," Le Monde slave, Paris, November-December, 1933; December, 1934; March, 1936.

Sazonov, S. D., Fateful Years, 1909–1916. London, 1928.

Sbornik Imperatorskago Russkago Istoricheskago Obshechestva (Symposium of the Imperial Russian Historical Society). 148 vols., St. Petersburg, 1867–1917.

Schiemann, T., Geschichte Russlands unter Kaiser Nikolaus I. 4 vols., Berlin, 1904–1919.

―――, and Brückner, A., Smert Pavla I (The Death of Paul I). Moscow, 1909.

Schmitt, B. E., The Coming of the War of 1914. 2 vols., New York, 1930.

Semevsky, M. I., Tsaritsa Praskovia, 1664–1723 (Tsarina Praskovie, 1664–1723). 2nd ed., St. Petersburg, 1883.

―――, Tsaritsa Ekaterina Alekseevna, Anna i Villim Mons, 1692–1724 (Tsarina Catherine Alekseevna, Anne and William Mons, 1692–1724). 2nd ed., St. Petersburg, 1884.

―――, Slovo i Delo! 1700–1725 (The Word and the Deed! 1700–1725). 3rd ed., St. Petersburg, 1885.

Semevsky, V. I., Krestianskii vopros v Rossii v XVIII i pervoi polovine XIX veka (The Peasant Question in Russia in the Eighteenth and in the First Half of the Nineteenth Century). 2 vols., St. Petersburg, 1888.

―――, Krestiane v tsarstvovanie imperatritsy Ekateriny II (Peasants in the Reign of Empress Catherine II). 2 vols., St. Petersburg, 1901–1903.

―――, Iz istorii obshchestvennikh idei v Rossii v kontse 40-kh godov (From the History of Social Ideas in Russia at the End of the 1840's). St. Petersburg, 1906.

―――, Politicheskiia i obshchestvennyia idei dekabristov (The Political and Social Ideas of the Decembrists). St. Petersburg, 1909.

Seredonin, S. M., ed. Istoricheskii obzor deiatelnosti komiteta ministrov (Historical Survey of the Work of the Committee of Ministers). 5 vols., St. Petersburg, 1902–1903.

―――, Otzyv of sochinenii A. M. Zaionchkovskago: Vostochnaia voina 1853–1856 gg. v sviazi s sovremennoi ei politicheskoi obstanovkoi (A Critique of the Volume by A. M. Zaionchkovsky: The War of 1853–1856 in the Light of the Contemporary Political Situation). St. Petersburg, 1911.

Principal Sources

Sergeevich, V. I., Veche i kniaz (The Veche and the Prince). Moscow, 1867.

———, Russkiia iuridicheskiia drevnosti (Russian Legal Antiquities). 3 vols., St. Petersburg, 1900–1903.

———, Russkaia Pravda v chetyrekh redaktiiakh (Russian Truth in Four Versions). St. Petersburg, 1904.

———, Lektsii i izsledovaniia po dreveni istorii russkago prava (Lectures and Essays in the History of Ancient Russian Law). 4th ed., St. Petersburg, 1910.

Seton-Watson, R. W., A History of the Roumanians. Cambridge, 1934.

Shakhmatov, A. A., Razyskaniia o drevneishikh russkikh letopisnykh svodakh (Studies in the Earliest Russian Chronicles). St. Petersburg, 1908.

———, Drevneishiia sudby russkago plemeni (The Earliest Destinies of the Russian People). Petrograd, 1919.

Shakhmatov, M. V., Kompetentsiia ispolnitelnoi vlasti moskovskoi Rusi (Competence of the Executive Power in Muscovite Russia). Prague, 1937.

Shchegolev, P. E., Nikolai I i dekabristy (Nicholas I and the Decembrists). Petrograd, 1919.

———, Dekabristy (The Decembrists). Moscow-Leningrad, 1926.

Shestakov, A. V., Ocherki po selskomu khoziaistvu i kresianskomu dvizeniiu v gody voiny i pered oktiabrem 1917 goda (Studies in Rural Economy and Peasant Movement in War Years and Prior to October 1917). Leningrad, 1927.

Shilder, N. K., Imperator Pavel I (Emperor Paul I). St. Petersburg, 1901.

———, Nikolai I (Nicholas I). 2 vols., St. Petersburg, 1903.

———, Imperator Aleksandr I, ego zhizn i tsarstvovanie (Emperor Alexander I, His Life and Reign). 4 vols., St. Petersburg, 1904–1905.

Shmelev, G. N., ed., Akty tsarstvovaniia Ekateriny II: uchrezhdenie dlia upravleniia gubernii i zhalovannyia gramoty dvorianstvu i gorodam (Statutes of the Reign of Catherine II: Law on the Organization of Provincial Government and the Charters of the Nobility and of the Towns). St. Petersburg, 1907.

Shmurlo, E., Istoriia Rossii, 862–1917 (History of Russia, 862–1917). Munich, 1922.

———, Kurs russkoi istorii (Lectures on Russian History). 3 vols., Prague, 1931–1935.

Shotwell, J. T., and Deák, F., Turkey at the Straits: A Short History. New York, 1940.

Shulgin, V., Dni (Days). Leningrad (?).

Shumigorsky, E. S., Imperator Pavel I: zhizn i tsarstvovanie (Emperor Paul I: Life and Reign). St. Petersburg, 1907.

Skazkin, S., Konets avstro-russkogo-germanskago soiuza (End of the Austro-Russian-German Alliance). Vol. I, Moscow, 1928.

Skobelev, M. D., "Posmertnyia bumagi M. D. Skobeleva" (Posthumous Papers of M. D. Skobelev), Istoricheskii Vestnik (Historical Messenger), Vol. X, 1882.

———, "Proekt M. D. Skobeleva o pokhode v Indiiu (M. D. Skobelev's Plan for a Campaign in India), Istoricheskii Vestnik (Historical Messenger), Vol. XIV, 1883.

Sliosberg, G. B., Dorevoliutsionnyi stroi Rossii (The Prerevolutionary Order in Russia). Paris, 1933.

Sobolev, M. N., Tamozhennaia politika Rossii vo vtoroi polovine XIX veka (The Tariff Policy of Russia in the Second Half of the Nineteenth Century). Tomsk, 1911.

Soiuz Russkogo Naroda (The Union of the Russian People), based on the materials of the Extraordinary Commission of Investigation appointed by the Provisional Government. Moscow-Leningrad, 1929.

Solovev, S. M., Imperator Aleksandr I (Emperor Alexander I). St. Petersburg, 1877.

———, Istoriia Rossii s drevneishikh vremen (History of Russia from the Earliest Time). 29 vols. in 6, St. Petersburg, 1894–1895(?).

———, Nachala russkoi zemli (Beginnings of Russia). St. Petersburg, 1895(?).

———, Drevniaia Rus (Ancient Russia), Sobranie sochinenii (Collected Works). St. Petersburg, 1895(?).

———, Istoriia padeniia Polshy (History of the Fall of Poland), Sobranie sochinenii (Collected Works). St. Petersburg, 1895(?).

Sorel, A., L'Europe et la révolution française. 8 vols., Paris, 1895–1910.

———, Napoléon et Alexandre, lectures historiques. Paris, 1923.

Speransky, M. N., Istoriia drevnei russkoi literatury (History of Early Russian Literature). 3rd ed., 2 vols., Moscow, 1920.

Spiridovich, A. I., Partiia sotsialistov-revoliutsionerov i eia predshestvenniki, 1886–1916 (The Socialist Revolutionary Party and Its Predecessors, 1886–1916). Petrograd, 1918.

Principal Sources 1507

Staal, Baron de, Correspondance diplomatique du Baron de Staal, 1884–1900, publiée par Alexander Meyendorff. 2 vols., Paris, 1929.

Stakelberg, N. S., "Zagadka smerti Nikolaia I" (The Puzzle of the Death of Nicholas I), Russkoe Proshloe (Russian Past), Vol. I, Petrograd, 1923.

Stankevich, V., Vospominaniia 1914–1919 (Reminiscences 1914–1919). Berlin, 1920.

Strumilin, S. G., Zarabotnaia plata Russkoi promyshlennosti za 1913–1922 gg. (Wages in Russian Industry in 1913–1922). Moscow, 1923.

Struve, P. B., Krepostnoe khoziaistvo (Economics of Serfdom). Moscow, 1913.

———, and others, Food Supply in Russia During the World War. New Haven, 1930.

———, Sushchestvoval li v drevnei Rusi feodalnyi pravoporiadok? (Did Feudal Order Exist in Ancient Russia?), in Sbornik Russkago Instituta v Prage (Symposium of the Russian Institute in Prague). Prague, 1929. Reprinted in Struve, P. B., Sotsialnaia i ekonomicheskaia istoriia Rossii (Social and Economic History of Russia). Paris, 1952.

Sukhanov, N. N., Zapiski o revoliutsii (Notes on the Revolution). 7 vols., Berlin, 1922–1923.

Sukhomlinov, V. A., "Perepiska V. A. Sukhomlinova" (Correspondence of V. A. Sukhomlinov), Krasnyi Arkhiv (Red Archives), Vols. I–III, 1922–1923.

Sumner, B. H., Russia and the Balkans, 1870–1880. Oxford, 1937.

Sviatoslavsky, V. V., Istoriia professionalnago dvizheniia v Rossii ot vozniknoveniia rabochago klassa do kontsa 1917 goda (History of the Trade Union Movement in Russia from the Appearance of the Working Class to the End of 1917). Leningrad, 1925.

Tarle, E., Nashestvie Napoleona na Rossiiu, 1812 god (Napoleon's Invasion of Russia, 1812). Moscow, 1938.

Tarnovsky, V., Otzyv o sochinenii V. I. Sergeevicha: Drevnosti Russkago Prava (A Critique of the Volume by V. I. Sergeevich: Russian Legal Antiquities). Yurev (Dorpat), 1911.

Tate, M., The Disarmament Illusion: The Movement for a Limitation of Armaments to 1907. New York, 1942.

Tatishchev, S. S., Vneshniaia politika Imperatora Nikolaia Pervago (Foreign Policy of Emperor Nicholas I). St. Petersburg, 1887.

Tatishchev, S. S., Imperator Nikolai i inostrannye dvory (Emperor Nicholas and the Foreign Courts). St. Petersburg, 1889.

———, Iz proshlago russkoi diplomatii (From the Past of Russian Diplomacy). St. Petersburg, 1890.

———, Alexandre I-er et Napoléon d'après leur correspondance inédite, 1801–1812. Paris, 1891.

———, Imperator Aleksandr II, ego zhizn i tsarstvovanie (Emperor Alexander II, His Life and Reign). 2 vols., St. Petersburg, 1903.

Taube, Baron M. de, La Politique russe d'avant guerre et la fin de l'empire des tsars, 1904–1917. Paris, 1927.

Temperley, H., England and the Near East: The Crimea. London, 1936.

Tikhonravov, N. S., Sochineniia (Works). 3 vols. in 4, Moscow, 1898.

Trotsky, L., 1905. Moscow, 1922.

———, Moia zhizn (My Life). 2 vols., Berlin, 1930.

———, Istoriia russkoi revoliutsii (History of the Russian Revolution). 3 vols., Berlin, 1931–1933.

———, Stalin, An Appraisal of the Man and His Work. New York, 1946.

Tsarskaia Rossiia v mirovoi voine (Tsarist Russia in the World War), introduction by M. N. Pokrovsky, Vol. I, Leningrad, 1926.

Tugan-Baranovsky, M. I., Russkaia fabrika v proshlom i nastoiashchem (The Russian Factory, Its Past and Present). Rev. ed., St. Petersburg, 1907.

Uchebnyia zavedeniia vedomstva ministerstva narodnago prosveshcheniia (Schools Under the Ministry of Education). St. Petersburg, 1895.

Valdenberg, V., Drevnerusskiia ucheniia o predelakh tsarskoi vlasti (Theories on the Limits of the Power of the Tsar in Ancient Russia). Petrograd, 1916.

Valuev, Count P. A., Dnevnik, 1877–1884 (Diary, 1877–1884), ed. V. Ia. Iakovlev-Bogucharsky and P. E. Shchegolev. Petrograd, 1919.

Vandal, A., Napoléon et Alexandre I-er: l'alliance russe sous le premier empire. 3 vols., Paris, 1893–1896.

Velikaia reforma: russkoe obshchestvo i krestianskii vopros v proshlom i nastoiashchem (The Great Reform: Russian Public Opinion and the Peasant Question in the Past and in the Present), A. K. Dzhivelegov, S. P. Melgunov, and V. I. Picheta, eds. 6 vols., Moscow, 1911.

Principal Sources

Vengerov, S. A., Ocherki po istorii russkoi literatury (Studies in the History of Russian Literature). St. Petersburg, 1907.

Vernadsky, G., and Karpovich, M., A History of Russia. Vols. I, II, New Haven, 1943–1948.

Veselovsky, A., Zapadnoe vliianie v novoi russkoi literature (Western Influence in the New Russian Literature). 4th ed., Moscow, 1910.

Veselovsky, V. B., Istoriia zemstva za sorok let (Forty Years of the History of the Zemstvo). 4 vols., St. Petersburg, 1909–1911.

———, and Frenkel, Z. G., eds., Iubileinyi zemskii sbornik, 1864–1914 (Jubilee Zemstvo Symposium, 1864–1914). St. Petersburg, 1914.

Vishniak, M. V., Vserossiiskoe uchreditelnoe sobranie (The All-Russian Constituent Assembly). Paris, 1932.

Vladimirovsky-Budanov, M. F., Gosudarstvo i narodnoe obrazovanie v Rossii s XVII veka do uchrezhdeniia ministerstv (The State and the Schools in Russia from the Seventeenth Century to the Formation of the Ministries). St. Petersburg, 1874.

———, Gosudarstvo i narodnoe obrazovanie v Rossii XVIII veka (The State and the Schools in Eighteenth Century Russia). Yaroslavl, 1874.

———, Obzor istorii russkago prava (Survey of the History of Russian Law). 5th ed., Kiev, 1907.

Voeikov, V. N., S Tsarem i bez tsaria (With and Without the Tsar). Helsingfors, 1936.

Volfson, I. V., ed., Gazetnyi mir (The Newspaper World). St. Petersburg, 1912.

"Vremennoe pravitelstvo posle oktiabria" (The Provisional Government after October), Krasnyi Arkhiv (Red Archives), Vol. VI, 1924.

Vsevolodsky, V., Istoriia russkago teatra (History of the Russian Theatre). 2 vols., Leningrad-Moscow, 1929.

Waliszewski, K., Ivan the Terrible. Philadelphia, 1904.

———, La Crise révolutionnaire, 1584–1614. 2 vols., Paris, 1906.

———, Le Berceau d'une dynastie: les premiers Romanovs, 1613–1682. Paris, 1909.

———, Pierre le Grand. Paris, 1907.

———, L'Héritage de Pierre le Grand: règne des femmes, gouvernement des favoris, 1725–1741. Paris, 1900.

———, La dernière des Romanovs: Elisabeth I-re, impératrice de Russie, 1741–1762. Paris, 1902.

———, La Russie du temps d'Elisabeth I-re, dernière des Romanovs. Paris, 1933.

Waliszewski, K., Autour d'un thrône: Catherine II de Russie. Paris, 1897.

———, Le Roman d'une impératrice: Catherine II de Russie. Paris, 1902.

———, Syn velikoi Ekateriny: imperator Pavel I (The Son of the Great Catherine: Emperor Paul I). St. Petersburg, 1914.

———, Le Règne d'Alexandre I-er. 3 vols., Paris, 1923–1925.

Weber, M., Zur Lage der bürgerlichen Demokratie in Russland, Archiv für Sozialwissenschaft und Sozialpolitik. Vol. XXII, Tübingen, 1906.

Webster, C. K., The Congress of Vienna. London, 1919.

———, The European Alliance, 1815–1925. Calcutta, 1929.

Wheeler-Bennett, J. W., The Forgotten Peace: Brest-Litovsk, March 1918. New York, 1939.

William II, Emperor, The Kaiser's Letters to the Tsar, ed. N. F. Grant. London, 1920.

———, Perepiska Vilgelma II s Nikolaem II (Correspondence of William II with Nicholas II), introduction by M. N. Pokrovsky. Moscow, 1923.

Witte, S. J., Samoderzhavie i zemstvo (Autocracy and the Zemstvo). Stuttgart, 1901.

———, Vospominaniia (Reminiscences). 3 vols., Berlin, 1922–1923.

Wolff, T., The Eve of 1914. New York, 1936.

Zabolotsky-Desiatovsky, A. P., Graf P. D. Kiselev i ego vremia (Count P. D. Kiselev and His Time). 4 vols., St. Petersburg, 1882.

Zabriskie, E. H., American Russian Rivalry in the Far East, 1895–1914. Philadelphia, 1946.

Zagorsky, S. O., State Control of Industry in Russia During the War. New Haven, 1928.

Zaionchkovsky, A. M., Vostochnaia voina 1853–1856 gg. v sviazi s sovremennoi ei politicheskoi obstanovkoi (The Eastern War of 1853–1856 in the Light of the Contemporary Political Situation). 2 vols. in 4, St. Petersburg, 1908–1912.

———, Podgotovka Rossii k mirovoi voine v diplomaticheskom otnoshenii (The Diplomatic Preparation of Russia for the World War). Leningrad, 1926.

Zaozersky, A. J., Tsar Aleksei Mikhailovich o svoem khoziastve (The Tsar Alexis Mikhailovich on His Business Establishment). Petrograd, 1917.

Principal Sources

Zaslavsky, D. O., and Kantorovich, V. A., Khronika fevralskoi revoliutsii (Chronicle of the February Revolution). Vol. I, Petrograd, 1924.

Zertsalov, A. N., K istorii miatezha 1648 goda v Moskve i drugikh gorodakh (A History of the Rebellion of 1648 in Moscow and Other Cities). Moscow, 1896.

Ziv, V. S., Inostrannyi kapital v russkikh aktsionernykh predpriiatiiakh (Foreign Capital in Russian Joint Stock Companies). Moscow, 1917.

Zweig, E., Die russische Handelspolitik seit 1877. Leipzig, 1906.

INDEX

Abaza, A. A., minister of finance, 936, 1090-1091
Abaza, A. M., Admiral, 1269
Abd ul-Aziz, Sultan, 993
Abd ul-Hamid, Sultan, 993, 1009
Abd ul-Mejid, Sultan, 846
Aberdeen, George Hamilton, Earl of, 827, 833, 848-850, 859, 863, 875; and 1853 crisis, 865, 867-868, 869 n.
Abrosimov, V. M., police agent, 1376
Absolutism, detested by Alexander I, 632; proposed limitations of, 634; maintained (1803), 695; unimpaired by State Council, 698; limited in Finland, 702-704, 881, 919-920; limited in Poland (1815), 705-706, 911; Karamzin on, 731; attempted limitation of (1730), 739; Nicholas I's conception of, 754; extolled by Uvarov, 777; slavophilism and, 809, 1068; eulogized by Gogol, 818; retained under Alexander II, 881, 920, 1066-1067; Witte on, 900, 1167, 1171 n., 1185; Alexander III and, 1087, 1090-1091, 1111; Pobedonostsev on, 1089-1091; and the judiciary, 1100; strengthened under Alexander III, 1139; Nicholas II attached to, 1142-1143, 1147; Empress Alexandra and, 1144; alliance against (1904), 1170; and 1905 revolution, 1177-1178, 1183; Goremykin on, 1190, 1363-1364; Kremlin, symbol of, 1474
Academy of Arts, 735, 822-823; revolt against, 1052-1053, 1245-1246
Academy of Science, 729 n., 1048, 1242; represented in State Council, 1187

Adams, John Quincy, 691
Addington, Henry, Viscount Sidmouth, 653-654
Administration of Empress Marie, 1041, 1042 n., 1046
Adrianople, Armistice of (1878), 1005, 1012-1013
Adrianople, Treaty of (1829), 832-833, 835, 842, 848, 866
von Aehrenthal, L. A., Count, foreign minister, 1293, 1303; and Izvolsky, 1293-1298; and annexation of Bosnia and Herzegovina, 1293-1298
Afghanistan, Anglo-Russian rivalries in, 843, 981, 984-986, 1288; crisis over (1885), 1029, 1127-1129
Africa, 982
Agadir crisis, 1289-1290, 1309
Agricultural Society, Polish, 910-912
Aigun, Treaty of (1858), 978
Aix-la-Chapelle, Congress of (1818), 687, 690
Akkerman, Convention of (1826), 828-830, 833, 848
Aksakov, Constantine, slavophile, 809, 893 n.
Aksakov, Ivan, slavophile, 809-810, 987-988, 995-996, 1000, 1028, 1068, 1087, 1092, 1139; decries Treaty of Berlin, 1024; anti-Semitism of, 1120; denounces *rapprochement* with Germanic Powers, 1127; and Bulgarian unification, 1130
Aksakov, Serge, author, 1060
Akselrod, P. B., Menshevik, 1150
Aland Islands, annexed, 665; occupied by England, 873; demilitarized, 950; Izvolsky and, 1291-1292

xxv

Alaska, annexed, 691; sold, 974-977
Albania, 997, 1020, 1022, 1304, 1339-1340
Aleko Pasha, 1023
Alekseev, E. I., Admiral, viceroy, 1270, 1272, 1274
Alekseev, M. V., General, 1321, 1323, 1332-1333, 1344, 1381, 1396, 1408, 1411 n., 1456, 1465; favors peace with Turkey, 1351; and army committees, 1394; and Kornilov "mutiny," 1439-1441
Alexander I, Emperor, 729 n., 738, 745, 754, 765, 771 n., 798 n., 832; characterization, 629; education, 630; approves removal of Paul I, 630-631; liberalism of, 630-631, 633-634, 636, 693, 695, 701, 706, 722; and Marie Naryshkin, 632; mysticism of, 632, 638-646; and Grand Duchess Catherine, 632-633; and direction of foreign policy, 635-636; statesmanship of, 636-637; expects defeat of Napoleon, 637-638; and Holy Alliance, 643-645, 685-686, 951; and Arakcheev, 647-650, 756 n.; and Fedor Kuzmich, 650; peace program of, 651; and defense of interests of Prussia, 653, 662; plans for aggrandizement and peace (1803–1804), 654-656; and 1805–1807 campaign, 657-661; offers alliance to France, 661-662; at Tilsit, 663-664; and execution of Tilsit agreement, 664; and Napoleon's proposal for partition of the world, 666-667; at Erfurt, 667-668; and Austrian war (1809), 668-669; rejects French dynastic alliance, 670; and 1812 war, 671-678, 692; and annexation of Georgia, 673 n.; and annexation of Poland, 679; messianic zeal of, 679, 685; and "war of liberation," 679-681; and Quadruple Alliance, 681, 686-687; and Congress of Vienna, 682-684; and Greek revolution (1821), 689, 828; and South American colonies, 690; and the United States, 690-692; early domestic policies of, 693; and reforms of Speransky, 696-700; and Finland, 702-704, 1157; and Poland, 705-707, 757, 956; public finance under, 708-709; and the serfs, 716-718; and military colonies, 719-720; and the nobility, 721; and schools, 722-725; reform movement encouraged by, 736; and the clergy, 737 n.; and secret societies, 742, 771; death of, and dynastic crisis, 745-749

Alexander II, Emperor, 745, 751, 756 n., 819, 845, 849, 941, 945, 952, 959 n., 961, 968, 1030, 1045, 1062, 1064, 1092-1093, 1106, 1113, 1118, 1139, 1162; and the emancipation, 778, 780-781, 883-885, 888; accepts allied terms (1856), 871, 947-948; education, 879-880; attitude towards reforms, 879-881, 921; and conduct of Turkish war, 881, 1003; and Bulgarian constitution, 881, 1023, 1131-1132; and Finland, 881, 909, 919-920, 1157; and Holy Alliance, 881-882, 951; marriage to Princess Yurevsky, 882, 1086; conciliatory policies of, in Poland, 909-911; anti-Catholic policies of in western provinces, 917; on finality of the emancipation, 922; expects revolution in France (1855), 948; and Napoleon's plea for Poland, 953; pro-Prussian and anti-French sentiments of, 953; and fear of international revolution, 955-956; and unification of Germany, 964-965; and Franco-Prussian War, 966-967, 970, 998, 1026; and three emperors' league, 970-972, 1005; Karakozov's attempt on life of, 974, 1075; and expansion in Central Asia, 984; and panslavism, 990, 995-996, 999-1000; and revolt in Bosnia and Herzegovina (1875), 991-992; and Balkan war (1876), 993, 995; and Reichstadt agreement (1876), 997; and Livadia conference, 999; and conversations with Loftus, 1000; declares war on Turkey (1877), 1001; and recovery of Bessarabian territories, 1002; and Russian peace terms, 1007, 1014; demands occupation of Constantinople, 1009-1010, 1016, 1025; and Bulgarian independence, 1013 n.; and Salisbury-Shuvalov agreement, 1017, 1025; and peace treaty with Turkey, 1022-1023; and Treaty of Berlin, 1024-

Index

1025; and William I, 1026-1027; murder of, 1027, 1033, 1072, 1081-1084, 1120, 1122; appraisal of foreign policy of, 1028-1029; and schools, 1035-1036, 1043; and censorship, 1054-1055; and Katkov, 1065-1066; rejects address of Moscow nobility, 1066-1067; Herzen and, 1069; Chigirin conspiracy and, 1079; approves Loris-Melikov's constitutional proposals, 1083, 1090; and the theatre, 1251

Alexander III, Emperor, 999, 1003, 1034, 1099, 1114, 1116 n., 1118, 1123, 1125, 1129, 1141-1144, 1147, 1185; and panslavism, 990, 996, 1025, 1087-1088, 1212; anti-Semitism of, 1047-1048 n., 1119, 1175, 1203; proposes dictatorship, 1083; nationalism of, 1086-1087; characterization of, 1086-1089; attempted murder of, 1087, 1122; and Pobedonostsev, 1088-1092; and Katkov, 1089-1090, 1134-1135; on representative government, 1090; and proposed *zemskii sobor*, 1092; and "counter-reforms," 1093, 1098; and university charter (1884), 1113; and "estate" (class) principle in schools, 1114; and direction of foreign relations, 1124; and Holy Alliance, 1126; on eventual occupation of Straits, 1126; and three emperors's league, 1126, 1135; anti-Austrian sentiments of, 1126, 1135; and Bulgaria, 1131-1134; and Alexander Battenberg, 1132-1133; proposes alliance with Turkey, 1135; and William II, 1136-1137; and termination of German alliance, 1137; and Franco-Russian Alliance, 1138-1139; appraisal of reign of, 1139-1140; and Finland, 1157-1158

Alexander III Museum, 1246

Alexander of Battenberg, Prince of Bulgaria, 1023, 1130-1133, 1136

Alexander Karageorgevich, Prince of Serbia, 954

Alexander Obrenovich, King of Serbia, 1293

Alexandra, Queen of England, 959 n., 1086

Alexandra Fedorovna, Empress, wife of Nicholas I, 753, 756 n., 880

Alexandra Fedorovna, Empress, wife of Nicholas II, 1144-1147, 1284, 1381, 1385; and Rasputin, 1145-1147, 1361-1366, 1373-1374; aversion of, for representative government, 1185; and temperance, 1211; ascendancy of, 1361; and tsar's assumption of high command, 1362; council of ministers and, 1362, 1364; correspondence of, with Nicholas II, 1362, 1365; in control of government, 1362-1365; urges prosecution of liberal leaders, 1372; removal of, deemed essential, 1373; reasons for unpopularity of, 1374; murdered, 1436 n.

Alexis, Grand Duke, son of Nicholas II, 1145, 1381-1382, 1436 n.

Alfred, Prince, Duke of Edinburgh, 959

Algeria, 836

Alice, Princess of England, 1144

Alice, Princess of Hesse-Darmstadt. *See* Alexandra Fedorovna, Empress, wife of Nicholas II

"All Power to the Soviets," slogan, origin of, 1391; meaning of, in April, 1405; abandoned and revived, 1443-1444; Lenin on, 1443-1444

All-Russian Central Executive Committee of Soviets of Peasants' Deputies, 1414-1415, 1427, 1433, 1453 n., 1456-1457

All-Russian Central Executive Committee of Soviets of Workers' and Soldiers' Deputies, formed, 1390; and July uprising, 1430-1431, 1443; and Democratic Conference, 1435; controlled by non-Bolsheviks, 1445 n., 1456; and October insurrection, 1448-1449

All-Russian Central Executive Committee of Soviets of Workers', Soldiers' and Peasants' Deputies, 1457; dissolves Constituent Assembly, 1463; approves Trotsky's peace policy, 1470; accepts German terms, 1471

All-Russian Conference of Soviets of Workers' and Soldiers' Deputies, 1402

All-Russian Conference of Trade Unions, 1418

All-Russian Congress of Soviets of Peasants' Deputies, *first*, 1414-1415, 1427-1429, 1456; "extraordinary" and "regular," 1457
All-Russian Congress of Soviets of Workers' and Soldiers' Deputies, *first*, 1390; and anarchists, 1429, 1456; *second*, 1445; complexion of, 1451; proceedings and decisions of, 1452-1454, 1456
All-Russian Congress of Trade Unions, 1418
All-Russian Union of Towns, 1367, 1369-1370; dissolution of, urged by Empress, 1372
All-Russian Union of Zemstvos, 1366-1367, 1369-1370; dissolution of, urged by Empress, 1372
All-Ukrainian Central Executive Committee of the Soviets, 1466
Allen, William, Quaker, 641-642
Alliance of the three emperors. See Three emperors' league
Amalia, Queen of Greece, 958
America, Russian colonies in, 690-692; sold, 973-977
Amiens, Treaty of (1802), 653-654
Amnesty (1905), 1080, 1180; (1917), 1392
Amur region, expansion in, 973, 977-979
Anarchism, 1071
Anarchists, 1429, 1431-1432
Anastasia, Grand Duchess, 1146
Andrássy, Julius, Count, foreign minister, and three emperors' league, 970-971, 973; and revolt in Bosnia and Herzegovina, 991-992; and Reichstadt agreement, 997; and Balkan war (1876), 997-999; and Austro-Russian agreement (1877), 998; and negotiations with England, 1006-1007, 1016; and Russian peace terms, 1008, 1015, 1017; and agreement with England, 1018; and Congress of Berlin, 1019
Andreev, Leonid, author, 1245
Anglo-French Alliance (1854), 869
Anglo-German Treaty (1890), 1138
Anglo-Russian Convention (1907), 1287-1288, 1292, 1309-1310

Anglo-Turkish Convention (1878), 1018, 1026
Anne, Empress, 730, 770
Anne, Grand Duchess, sister of Alexander I, 670
Antokolsky, M. M., sculptor, 1054
Appanage peasants, 896
Arakcheev, A. A., Count, 630, 636-637, 647, 679, 700, 728, 737, 739, 756 n.; and cult of memory of Emperor Paul, 631; career and influence with Alexander I, 647-649; prepares project of emancipation, 650, 716; and military colonies, 650, 720
Archeological and Numismatic Society, 805 n.
Architecture, 824, 1054; and "Russo-Byzantine" style, 824
Arensky, A. S., composer, 1250
Argentina, 1276
Armed Neutrality League, 652
Armenia, 1425
Armenians, 1170, 1283, 1385 n., 1408; and San Stefano, 1011; and Treaty of Berlin, 1021
Army, pre-reform, conditions in, 738, 906-908; in Russian Poland, 746; Jews and service in, 806-807 n., 1047-1048 n.; peasants and recruitment for, 895, 907; reform of (1860–1873), 907-908; and conscription law (1874), 908-909, 1003, 1119; and extension of Russian conscription to Finland, 1158; expelled students drafted in, 1166; mutinies in (1905–1906), 1180, 1182, 1195; poor leadership of, 1321; morale of, during World War I, 1326, 1330, 1377-1378, 1406-1408, 1411; size of, 1353; effects of demand of, 1355; Order No. 1 and, 1393-1394; and committee system, 1393-1395, 1407, 1409, 1411, 1427; and civilian commissars, 1407-1408; and shock battalions, 1408; national formations in, 1408; and women's battalions, 1408; and June offensive, 1409-1410; and revolutionary military tribunals, 1410-1411, 1433; disintegration of, 1411; democratization of, 1460
Artsybashev, M. P., author, 1244
Asquith, H. H., prime minister, 1316

Index

Assembly of Russian Workingmen, 1171
Association of Free Artists, 1052
Association of Industrialists of Southern Russia, 1421
Auckland, George Eden, Earl of, 843
Auer, Leopold, violinist, 1250
Austerlitz, battle of (1805), 657-658
Australia, and Japanese expansion, 1337
Austria, 655, 841, 858-860, 881, 966, 1110, 1226, 1260, 1268, 1340; joins anti-French coalition (1805), 656, 657; and Tilsit, 663; and Erfurt, 667-668; and war with France and Russia (1809), 668-669; and French alliance (1812), 673; and alliance with Russia (1813), 679-680; and Quadruple Alliance (1814), 681, 686-687; and Congress of Vienna, 682-684; and anti-Russian alliance (1815), 683; and Holy Alliance, 685, 689, 834-835, 840-841; and European Alliance, 687-690; and Polish insurrection (1830), 761-762; and Greek independence, 829, 834; favors Turkey (1828–1829), 832; and Turkish crisis (1832–1833), 836-837; and Münchengrätz Convention, 840-841, 845-846, 849; and near eastern crisis (1839), 846; and 1848 revolution, 851-855, 858; opposes German "union," 856-858; and dispute over Holy Places, 861-863; and 1853 crisis, 865-869; anti-Russian policy of, 870-872; ultimatum to Russia (1855), 871, 874, 947-948, 951, 997; Russian estrangement from, 953; and unification of Rumania, 954; and war with France (1859), 954-955; and Polish insurrection (1863), 956-957; and Schleswig-Holstein, 962-965; and war with Prussia (1866), 964-965; and Franco-Prussian War, 967; and abrogation of Black Sea clause, 969; and three emperors' league (1873), 970-973; and revolt in Bosnia and Herzegovina (1875), 991-992; and Balkan war (1876), 993-994, 997-999; and Constantinople Conference (1876–1877), 1001; and Russian peace terms, 1007-1008, 1015-1016; and San Stefano, 1012-1014; and Congress of Berlin, 1018-1019; war on, demanded by Aksakov, 1024; attacked in Russian press, 1025, 1134; and alliance with Germany (1879), 1027; and renewal of three emperors' league (1881, 1884), 1027, 1125-1127; Alexander III's dislike for, 1087-1088; and Afghan crisis (1885), 1129; and Bulgarian unification, 1132; and Triple Alliance, 1137; and Franco-Russian Alliance, 1139; and agreement with Russia (1897, 1903), 1284, 1292; annexes Bosnia and Herzegovina, 1288, 1293-1298; and Serbia, 1293; and Balkan wars (1911–1913), 1302-1304; and outbreak of World War I, 1312-1319; and World War I, 1322, 1324-1327, 1329, 1332-1333, 1347, 1410; and Brest-Litovsk, 1468-1470; occupies Ukraine, 1471
Austria-Hungary, panslavism and dissolution of, 988; dismemberment of, demanded by Kuropatkin, 1261. *See also* Austria
Austro-German Alliance (1879), 1027, 1135
Austro-German-Russian Alliance (1881), 1027
Austro-Prussian War (1866), 964-965
Austro-Russian agreement (1877), 998; (1878), 1126, 1296 n.; (1897, 1903), 1284, 1292
Autocracy. *See* Absolutism
Avksentev, N. D., socialist revolutionary, 1459, 1463
Azef, Evno, socialist revolutionary and police agent, 1154, 1166, 1170, 1172, 1196
Azerbaidzhan, 1425

Bagdad railway, 1290-1291
Bagot, Sir Charles, ambassador, 688
Bagration, P. I., Prince, General, 674-676
Bakst, L. S., painter, 1248
Bakunin, Michael, revolutionary, 915, 1070-1073, 1077-1078
Balakirev, M. A., composer, 1051-1052, 1249, 1254
Balaklava, battle of (1854), 875-876
Balashov, A. D., General, 637, 674
Baliev, Nikita, producer, 1252

Balkan League, 1300, 1340-1341, 1344
Balkan Slavs, 827, 1028; indifference of slavophiles towards, 810; panslavism and, 987-990; interests of, sacrificed to Italy (1915), 1340. *See also* Bulgaria, Montenegro, Serbia
Balkan wars (1911–1913), 1299-1305, 1340
Ballet, 1252-1255
Ballin, Albert, 1289
Balmashev, S. V., revolutionary, 1166
Balmont, Constantine, poet, 1245
Balta-Liman, agreement of (1849), 852
Baltic Declaration (1907), 1292
Baltic provinces, 813, 976, 1469, 1473; emancipation of serfs in, 718-719; Russification of, 1116-1117; prosecution of Protestant Churches in, 1117; agrarian disturbances in (1905), 1181; national movement in, 1425
Balugiansky, M. A., professor, 753
Banks, state-owned, crisis of (1857–1858), 789, 941-942; private, 941-944, 1225-1227, 1232; and promotion of industry, 1225; nationalization of, demanded, 1403; nationalized, 1458, 1460
Bar, The, established, 906; non-discriminatory admission of Jews to, 1047-1048 n.; restrictions on admission of Jews to, 1100, 1121
Barclay de Tolly, M. B., Prince, General, and Swedish campaign, 665; and Napoleonic invasion, 674-675, 704
Bark, P. I., minister of finance, 1211, 1230-1231, 1359, 1361, 1365
Barshchina (*corvée*), 886, 889; survivals of, after emancipation, 926
Batiushkov, Constantine, poet, 731-733
Bazaine, F. A., Marshal, 967
Bazili, N. A., diplomat, 1327, 1396
Beaconsfield, Benjamin Disraeli, Earl of, 985, 999, 1005 n., 1029, 1127; and revolt in Bosnia and Herzegovina, 992; and Constantinople Conference, 1000-1001; offers alliance to Austria, 1006-1007, 1016; orders fleet to Constantinople, 1008-1009; and Russian peace terms, 1015; and occupation of Cyprus, 1018; and Congress of Berlin, 1019; criticized, 1024

Beilis, Mendel, 1203
Beletsky, S. P., police official, 1146
Belgium, 652, 758, 834, 957, 1110, 1210, 1261, 1268; Russian investments of, 1226; and World War I, 1318-1319, 1322, 1347, 1400
Beliaev, N. D., historian, 893 n.
Belinsky, Vissarion, literary critic, 809-810, 820, 825, 1062
Bell (*Kolokol*), *The*, 811, 1068-1070, 1074
Belorussia (White Russia), 914, 1425, 1465 n.
Bely, Andrei (B. N. Bugaev), poet, 1245
Bem, Joseph, General, 853-855
Benckendorff, A. C., ambassador, 1335, 1340, 1342, 1349
Benckendorff, Alexander, Count, General, 742, 745, 771, 799, 813, 816
Bennigsen, Leon, Count, General, 631, 660-661, 677
Benois, A., painter and art critic, 1053 n., 1246, 1248
Bentham, Jeremy, 727, 731
Bentham, Samuel, 727 n.
von Berchtold, Leopold, Count, foreign minister, 1295, 1303-1304; and outbreak of World War I, 1313-1314, 1316
Berezowski, Anthony, Polish revolutionary, 1075
Berg, Theodore, Count, viceroy, 917
Bering, Vitus, 690
Berlin, Congress of (1878), 947, 1015, 1017-1019, 1024, 1026, 1028, 1125-1126
Berlin, Treaty of (1878), 1019-1021, 1026, 1125; execution of, 1022-1024, 1294-1295; criticized, 1024-1025
Berlioz, Louis Hector, composer, 1051
Bernstorff, Albrecht, Count, ambassador, 969
Berry, Duke of, 634
Bessarabia, 851, 871, 1000, 1343-1344; annexed, 673, 692; local institutions of, 707 n.; proposed severance of, 872; portion of, ceded to Moldavia (1856), 949-950, 952; Austria agrees to Russia's recovery of (1876), 997-

Index

998; and San Stefano, 1011, 1013; and Treaty of Berlin, 1019-1020; annexed by Rumania (1918), 1473
Bestuzhev, Michael, Captain, 750
von Bethmann Hollweg, Theobald, chancellor, 1289, 1291, 1304; and outbreak of World War I, 1313, 1315-1316
von Beust, Ferdinand Frederick, Count, chancellor, 966-967, 970
Bezak, A. P., governor general, 917
Bezobrazov, A. M., 1268-1270, 1272
Bezpopovtsy (priestless), 798 n.
Bibesco, Dimitry, Prince, 851
Bibikov, D. G., governor general, 779-780, 882
Bilibin, A., illustrator, 1248
von Bismarck-Schönhausen, Otto E. L., Prince, chancellor, 955-956, 1124; and Franco-Russian Alliance, 961; and Schleswig-Holstein, 961-964; and war with Austria (1866), 964-965; and unification of Germany, 961-966; and abrogation of Black Sea clause, 968-969; and three emperors' league (1873), 970-973; and revolt in Bosnia and Herzegovina, 992; and Balkan war (1876), 998-999; refuses to bring pressure on Austria, 1014; and Congress of Berlin, 1015, 1017-1019; attacked in Russian press, 1025-1026; and alliance with Austria (1879), 1027; and revival of three emperors' league, 1027; on representative government, 1090; and Afghan crisis, 1129; and Russo-German Alliance, 1135-1137; near eastern policy of, 1136
Björkö, Treaty of (1905), 1285-1286
Black Sea, neutralized (1856), 949-951; neutralization abrogated, 967-969; access to, and British security, 1129-1130; as *mare clausum*, 1292
Blanc, Louis, socialist, 808
Blanqui, Auguste, revolutionary, 1072
Blockade, 1319, 1358
Blok, Alexander, poet, 1245
"Bloody Sunday" (1905), 1171-1172
Bludov, D. N., Count, jurist, 903
Blue Rose, art society, 1247
Bobrikov, A. I., governor general, 1158, 1167

Bobrinsky, A. P., Count, minister of communications, 934, 936
Bobrinsky, G. A., Count, governor general, 1326
Bobrowsky, Stefan, 913
Bochkareva, woman army leader, 1408
Bogdanovich, N. M., governor, 1166
Bogolepov, N. P., minister of education, 1166
Bogoliubov, Alexis, revolutionary, 1080
Bogrov, Dimitry, revolutionary and police agent, 1204
Bokhara, khanate, 842, 980, 1131; Russian protectorate over, 981-982
Bolshevik Party (Bolshevik Faction of Russian Social Democratic Labor Party), 1242-1243, 1360, 1388, 1392, 1408-1409; beginning of, 1124, 1150-1151; ridicules socialist revolutionary agrarian program, 1153 n.; following of (1905), 1155; rejects alliance with liberals (1904), 1170; and elections to first Duma, 1189; and the press, 1239; deputies of, arrested, 1368, 1379; attitude towards the war, 1368, 1400-1401; and war industries committees, 1370, 1379; central committee of, revived in Petrograd, 1379; and cooperation with liberals, 1390-1391; early attitude of, towards Provisional Government, 1391; and war aims, 1397; part of, in February revolution, 1401; Petrograd organization of, 1401-1402; proposed change of name of, 1403; Petrograd committee of, rejects *April Theses*, 1403; conference of, endorses Lenin's program, 1405; and peasant Soviets, 1414, 1417; controls factory committees, 1421; takes over trade unions, 1421; progress of, 1428; and first congress of Soviets, 1428; and threat of insurrection, 1428-1429, 1434; and June demonstration, 1429-1430; and July uprising, 1430-1433, 1442; excluded from State Conference, 1435; withdraws from Council of the Republic, 1435-1436; setback of, 1436-1437, 1442-1443; controls Petrograd and Moscow Soviets, 1439 n., 1443, 1446; and Kornilov "mutiny," 1442; position of, strength-

Bolshevik Party (*continued*)
ened, 1443; membership of, 1443; sixth congress of, 1443-1444; central committee of, and insurrection, 1446; appoints "party center," 1447; and military revolutionary committees, 1447-1449, 1461; and second congress of Soviets, 1451; and decree on peace, 1452; and decree on land, 1452-1453; and Council of People's Commissars, 1452-1453; dissension within, 1458-1459; and Constituent Assembly, 1461-1463; divided on Brest-Litovsk, 1469-1471; reasons for success of, 1474-1475
Bookmaking, 824
Boris, Grand Duke, 1336
Borisov, Peter, Lieutenant, 744
Börgo, Finnish diet at (1809), 665, 703-704
Borodin, A. P., composer, 1051, 1254
Borodino, battle of (1812), 676
Borovikov, V. L., painter, 735
Borovkov, A. D., official, 754, 766
Bosnia and Herzegovina, 970, 1312, 1340, 1347; revolt in (1875), 987, 991-992; Russia agrees to annexation of, by Austria, 997-998, 1014, 1126, 1293-1295, 1296 n.; and San Stefano, 1011, 1012; occupied by Austria under Treaty of Berlin, 1020, 1022, 1127; annexed by Austria, 1283, 1291, 1293-1298
Bosphorus. *See* Dardanelles
Bouche, Madame, 641
Boulanger, Georges, General, 1137
Bourbon, Duke of, 654
Boxer Rebellion, 1267, 1269
Brandenburg, Frederick William, Count, prime minister, 857
Bratenstein, Convention of (1807), 660
Bratiano, Ion, prime minister, 1343-1344
Breshko-Breshkovsky, Catherine, socialist revolutionary, 1152, 1154
Breslau, 1334
Brest-Litovsk, negotiations of, 1467-1470
Brest-Litovsk, Treaty of (1918), 1459, 1465, 1467, 1475; terms of, 1471, 1473

Bright, John, 877
British Committee of Imperial Defense, 1349 n.
British and Foreign Bible Society, 641
Briusov, Valery, poet, 1245
Brok, P. F., minister of finance, 786
Brotherhood of Cyril and Methodius, 811
Brüllow, K. P., painter, 811 n., 822-823
Bruni, F. A., painter, 822-823
Brunnow, Ernest, Baron, ambassador, 845, 847, 849-850, 859, 863, 879, 962, 965, 967-969, 971; and Congress of Paris (1856), 948
Brusilov, A. A., General, 1323, 1406-1407 n., 1408, 1410; and 1916 offensive, 1332-1333, 1344
Buchanan, Sir George, ambassador, 1299, 1310, 1335-1336, 1347, 1352, 1373, 1404 n., 1440, 1450
Bucharest, Treaty of (1812), 673, 828; (1913), 1302, 1340
Buchlau, Aehrenthal and Izvolsky at, 1295-1296
Budberg, A. Ia., Baron, foreign minister, 658, 662
Budberg, Andrew, Baron, ambassador, 956
Budget, 708, 787, 943, 1106, 1209-1210; unification of, 941-942; partly exempt from legislative control, 1187; in wartime, 1367-1368
Bulatov, Alexander, Colonel, 750
Bulgaria, 860, 881, 1299, 1350; panslavism and, 990, 995; revolt in (1876), 993, 996; Austro-Russian agreements (1876–1877) and, 997-998; Turkish atrocities in, 999, 1005; Russian governor appointed for, 1000; Constantinople Conference and, 1001; San Stefano and, 1010-1014; Treaty of Berlin and, 1019-1022; constitution of, 1023, 1088; Russian troops withdrawn from, 1023-1024, 1130; promotion of railways in, 1028; Russian policies in (1881–1887), 1124-1125, 1130-1134, 1139; unification of, approved by Austria, Germany, and Russia (1881), 1126, 1130; unification of, 1132-1133; recognition of Ferdinand withheld, 1134; Russo-German Alli-

Index xxxiii

ance and, 1136; independence of, 1295; and Balkan wars (1911–1913), 1299-1305; joins central Powers, 1331, 1351; negotiates with both sides, 1335, 1340-1343, 1345-1346; invades Serbia, 1343
von Bülow, Bernhard, Prince, chancellor, 1124, 1138, 1285, 1287, 1289, 1297
Bulygin, A. G., minister of interior, 1172
Bunge, N. C., minister of finance, 1106-1107, 1109, 1158, 1206
Bunin, Ivan, author, 1240, 1243
von Buol-Schauenstein, Karl Ferdinand, Count, foreign minister, 866-867, 871; and Congress of Paris, 948-949
Bureaucracy, 699, 756, 1256; under Nicholas I, 765, 769; and great reforms, 880, 897, 901; and emancipation, 884; and local government, 896-897, 927; hostility of, to zemstvos, 899-900; and reform of judiciary, 904; alleged bankruptcy of, 1066; slavophilism and, 1068; Alexander III and, 1087-1088; denounced by Pobedonostsev, 1088; decadence of, 1365-1366; disappearance of, under socialism, envisaged, 1403
Burghers, granted right to own agricultural land, 717; lowly status of, 720 n.; and "honorary citizens," 786; and former "possessionary" peasants, 794; and army service, 907; land purchases by, 929; and handicrafts, 1232 n. *See also* Government, municipal; Merchants
Burns, Alexander, Captain, 843
Burns, John, cabinet minister, 1318
Burtsev, V. L., journalist, 1154
Butashevich-Petrashevsky, M. V., and his group, 811-812, 1059, 1062, 1065
Butenev, A. P., ambassador, 836-837, 845
Buturlin, D. P., Count, 813, 1055

Cabet, Étienne, 808
Cadets. *See* Constitutional Democratic Party
Calendar, Gregorian adopted, 1465 n.
Cambon, Paul, ambassador, 1340
Canada, detains political *émigrés*, 1399

Canning, George, foreign minister, 660, 664, 688-690, 828-830
Canning, Sir Stratford, 852, 854, 877, 949, 954 n., 992; anti-Russian feeling of, 827, 841, 863-867, 869 n., 1349; pro-Turkish feeling of, 836
Capital, foreign, 1111, 1226; and railway construction, 935-936; Russian, and railway construction, 936
Capital punishment, abolished, 1392; restored in army, 1410, 1433, 1438, 1440
Capitalism, Russian, 715, 945-946; weakness of, 1153
Capo d'Istria, John, Count, 679, 683, 687, 689, 737, 832, 834
Caprivi, Leo, Count, chancellor, 1137
Carol, Prince of Rumania, 1311
Carr, E. H., historian, upholds Lenin legend, 1401 n.
Castlereagh, Viscount, foreign secretary, 681, 683-684, 686-688, 690, 692
Catherine, Grand Duchess, sister of Alexander I, 632, 638, 640 n., 664, 668, 671-672, 676-677, 682, 700
Catherine II, Empress, 633, 693-695, 708, 716, 729, 731, 736, 769-770, 896, 1093, 1191, 1252; and education of Alexander I, 630; expansionist policies of, 651, 653, 689, 845
Cattaro, annexation of, demanded (1804), 655, 663
Caucasus, 754-755 n., 761, 831, 873, 904, 924, 988; annexation of, 673-674 n., 692, 743, 830, 833, 841-843; conquest of, completed, 980
de Caulaincourt, A. A. L., Marquis, Duke de Vicence, ambassador, 664-666, 669-670, 696
Cavaignac, Louis Eugène, General, 858
Cavos, Caterino, composer, 821
di Cavour, Camillo, Count, 948
Censorship, 695, 1121; in Russian Poland, 707, 764; in the eighteenth century, 727; preliminary, under Alexander I, 727-728; Golitsin and, 728; security police and, 728, 813; under Nicholas I, 804, 812-813, 815, 819, 1054-1055; and slavophiles, 810, 1056, 1068; Buturlin committee on, 813, 1055; of textbooks, 1044; under 1865 law, 1055-1056; and radical

Censorship (*continued*)
  authors, 1063-1064, 1074; Loris-Melikov and, 1083; Pobedonostsev on, 1111-1112; under 1882 law, 1112; dormant (1905), 1179; by printers' union, 1179; under 1905-1906 provisional rules, 1186, 1238-1239; suppresses parliamentary debates, 1373
Central Asia, 841, 1016, 1125; expansion in, 941, 951, 973, 979-986, 1027, 1124; nature of expansion in, 982-984; provinces of, disfranchised, 1200
Chaadaev, Peter, 799, 814-815
Chaikovsky, N. V., populist, 1076, 1078, 1084
Chaliapin, Fedor, singer, 1250-1251
de Champigny, Duke de Cadore, foreign minister, 670, 696
Chantilly, allied conference at (1915), 1332, 1406
Charles, Prince of Hohenzollern-Sigmaringen, Prince and King of Rumania, 960-961, 1002-1004, 1013, 1343
Charles XIII, King of Sweden, 665
Charles Albert, King of Sardinia, 852
Charlotte, Princess of Prussia. *See* Alexandra Fedorovna, wife of Nicholas I
Charter of the Cities (1785), 901
Charter of the Nobility (1785), 694, 1093; amended, 774-775; rights granted under, infringed, 776-777
Charykov, M., ambassador, 1306
Chaumont, Treaty of (1814), 681, 686
Chauve Souris, 1252
Cheka, 1461
Chekhov, Anton, author, 1239, 1243; life and work, 1241-1242
Cherkassky, V. A., Prince, 810, 887, 917, 990, 1000
Cherniaev, M. G., General, in central Asia, 980-984; in the Balkans (1876), 994-995, 1012
Chernov, Victor, socialist revolutionary, 1156, 1164, 1166, 1426, 1428, 1431, 1433-1434, 1441, 1459; and peasant Soviets, 1414-1415; and agrarian revolution, 1415-1416; president of Constituent Assembly, 1463
Chernyshevsky, Nicholas, literary critic, 893 n., 1063, 1065, 1072, 1074-1075

Chertkov, V. G., 1240
Chichagov, Paul, Admiral, 678
Chicherin, B. N., historian, 893 n., 1069
"*Chiffon de Carlsbad*," 834
Chile, 1276
China, 1261, 1337; trade with, 711; opening of, and Russia's American colonies, 975; and expansion in Far East, 977-979, 1266-1268; and war with England and France (1857-1858), 978; and Korea, 1263-1264; and Boxer Rebellion, 1267; revolution in, 1279
Chinese Eastern Railway, 1265, 1268, 1278-1279, 1283
Chkheidze, N. S., Menshevik leader, 1381, 1387-1388, 1390
Chlopicki, Joseph, General, 759-760
Christian, Prince of Schleswig-Holstein-Glücksburg. *See* Christian IX, King of Denmark
Christian VIII, King of Denmark, 856
Christian IX, King of Denmark, 959 n., 962-963
Christian population of Ottoman Empire, protection of, 655-656, 862, 871, 951 n.; expected uprising of, 658, 872-873; Treaty of Paris (1856) and, 949-950, 955; Gorchakov admits Austria's interest in, 971; San Stefano and, 1013-1014; Treaty of Berlin and, 1019
Church, Russian Orthodox, 698; opposes Bible Society, 641; decadence of, 737; as a government agency, 798; controlled by lay authorities, 798 n.; slavophilism and, 798, 809-810, 987-988; and dissenters, 798-799 n.; and schools, 806, 1043, 1047, 1115-1116, 1235-1237; and dispute over Holy Places, 861, 863-864; landholding of (1877), 923; and panslavism, 987-988, 996; and Balkan war (1876), 994, 996; and county school boards, 1043; and art, 1053; attacked by Leo Tolstoy, 1058, 1240; upheld by Dostoevsky, 1059; religious intolerance of, 1117; and proselytizing of dissenters, 1118; Empress Alexandra and, 1144-1145; represented in State Council, 1187; clergy, number of, in State Dumas, 1200 n.; and Rasputin,

Index

1205; failure of, to exercise unifying influence, 1257; and persecution of Uniats in Galicia, 1326-1327; and annexation of Constantinople, 1348 n.; land decree and, 1452; "separation" of from state and schools, 1461
Churchill, Winston Spencer, 1336, 1345-1346, 1350
Civil war, 1456, 1475
Clanricarde, Marquis, ambassador, 848
Clarendon, George W. F. Villiers, Earl of, foreign minister, 865-867, 868 n., 869, 985; and Congress of Paris, 948-950
von Clausewits, Karl, General, 676
Clodt, P. K., Baron, sculptor, 824
Cobden, Richard, 842, 1349-1350 n.
Code of 1649, 770; of 1833, 770, 784; of 1845 (criminal), 763, 771
Codification, 694, 770-771
Codrington, Sir Edward, Admiral, 830, 832
Colonization, internal. *See* Siberia
Commercial treaties, with Prussia (1818), 712; Russo-German, 1110
Committee for the Advancement of Literacy, 1157
Committee of ministers, and Arakcheev, 649
Committee of Public Safety (1807), 695 n.
Committees for the Salvation of the Country and of the Revolution, 1456
Committees for the Salvation of the Revolution, 1442
Communal tenure. *See* Village commune
Communist Party of the U.S.S.R., 1124
Complete Collection of Laws of the Russian Empire, 770
Concordat, abrogated, 958
Confederation of the Rhine, 659, 680
Conference on the needs of agricultural industry, 1213
Conrad von Hötzendorf, Baron, chief of staff, 1298, 1303, 1313
Conservatism, 1065, 1102, 1174-1176, 1189; slavophilism and, 1068; and the peasantry, 1176, 1190, 1199; not represented in first Duma, 1191; in second Duma, 1198; in third and fourth Duma, 1200; triumph of, 1200-1201; and village commune, 1213; and land expropriation, 1214; and the press, 1239; and annexation of Constantinople, 1348, 1352; and proposed palace revolution, 1373
Constantine, Grand Duke, brother of Alexander II, 884-885, 911, 976, 1090-1091; viceroy of Poland, 912-913, 917
Constantine, Grand Duke, brother of Nicholas I, 661, 675-676, 679, 706, 738, 778; and dynastic crisis (1825), 745-748; and December insurrection, 750; and Polish insurrection (1830), 757-760
Constantine I, King of Greece, 1345-1347
Constantinople, proposed annexation of (1804), 655; and Tilsit treaty, 663; annexation of, discussed, 667; proposed occupation of, 1006-1007; Russian occupation of, regarded inevitable, 1009; seizure of, vetoed by Totleben, 1016-1017. *See also* Dardanelles
Constantinople, Conference of (1876-1877), 1000-1001, 1010, 1011
Constituent Assembly, 1391, 1407, 1434 n., 1444, 1445 n., 1452, 1457-1459, 1466 n.; and People's Will, 1082; demand for, 1170-1171, 1173, 1177; dropped by Constitutional Democratic Party, 1188; convocation of, announced, 1382, 1392-1393; land reform and, 1413-1414, 1416; Polish independence and, 1422; statute on elections to, 1435; complexion of, 1461-1462; meets and is dissolved, 1463; indifference to fate of, 1464, 1473
Constitutional Democratic Party, 1186, 1384-1386, 1399; program of, 1188; and elections to first Duma, 1189; dominates first Duma, 1190-1191; expects to form cabinet, 1192; and Viborg appeal, 1192, 1195, 1197, 1383 n.; and elections to second Duma, 1197; in second Duma, 1198; in third and fourth Duma, 1200; and Progressive Bloc, 1371; members of, resign from government, 1430; repre-

Constitutional Dem. Party (*cont.*) sentation of, in Constituent Assembly, 1461-1462
Continental system, 659, 664, 666, 672, 696, 714
Cooperative societies, 943-944, 1222, 1227, 1435
Corfu, annexation of, demanded (1804), 655, 663 n.
Corporal punishment, "honorary citizens" exempt from, 786; and the peasants, 895, 906, 1214, 1221; application of, restricted, 906; in armed forces, 908
Corti, Luigi, Count, 1019
Cossacks, 651, 719; zemstvos and, 898 n.; represented in second Duma, 1198; and congress of national minorities, 1425; and Kornilov "mutiny," 1440; and October insurrection, 1446, 1449-1450; and resistance to Bolshevism, 1454-1455, 1465, 1467
Cottage industry, 933, 1213, 1232 n.
Council of ministers, 1173, 1185, 1191, 1203, 1330, 1377-1378; status of (1905), 1187; in wartime, 1320, 1363; complexion of (1915), 1362-1363; and tsar's assumption of high command, 1363-1364
Council of People's Commissars, 1452-1454; orders peace negotiations, 1455; legality of, denied by Senate, 1458; and Constituent Assembly, 1462-1463; and Finland, 1465; and Ukraine, 1466-1467; calls for defensive war, 1471
Council of the United Nobility, 1201, 1373
Counter-revolution, fear of, 1429, 1433-1434, 1439 n., 1441, 1448-1449, 1475
Courts. *See* Judiciary
Cracow, established as free city, 684; annexed by Austria, 850
Crete, Island of, 860, 1011-1012; Russia and revolt of, 960
Crimea, annexed, 845 n.; proposed secession of, 872; rumored sale of, 977
Crimean War, 756, 786, 788-789, 825, 861, 881-883, 906, 908, 947, 952, 969, 971, 975, 979, 985, 997, 1002, 1028, 1031, 1052, 1057, 1287, 1291; general causes of, 826-827; events leading to, 858-868; and allied peace program (1854), 870-871, 947-948; and Danubian campaign, 873-874; and campaign in Crimea, 874-876; and Caucasian campaign, 876; cost of, 876, 941, 944; interpretations of, 877, 1001; and Greek national aspirations, 958
Croats, panslavism and, 988, 989 n.
Crowe, Sir Eyre, 1319
Cubism, 1248, 1252
Cui, C. A., composer, 1051-1052, 1249
Currency, depreciation of, 671, 708-709, 787-788, 795, 944-945, 1106-1107; Speransky's proposals on, 699, 709; attempted reform of, under Alexander I, 709; attempted stabilization of (1839–1843), 786-788; depreciation of, and tariff policy, 940; attempted stabilization of, under Alexander II, 942, 944-945; and introduction of gold standard, 1206-1207; criticism of, 1207-1208; strain on, 1208; convertibility suspended, 1359-1360; increase in circulation of, 1360, 1420
Curzon of Kedleston, George Nathaniel, Marquis, 831
Cuza, Alexander, Prince, 960-961
Cyprus, 1015; occupied by England, 1019
Czartoryski, Adam, Prince, 632, 656 n., 661, 683, 694, 722, 737, 909; foreign minister, 655; supports France (1806), 658; resigns, 658; and Russian annexation of Poland, 673, 679, 705-706; and Polish insurrection, 759-762
Czechs, 810 n., 852, 1347; panslavism and, 988, 989 n., 990
Czernin, Ottokar, Count, foreign minister, 1468

Dan, A. F., Menshevik leader, 1448-1449
Dana, Francis, envoy, 690 n.
Danilevsky, N. Ya., author, 988-989
Danilov, G. A., General, 1322-1323, 1350

Index

Danube, internationalization of, 671, 945, 1021
Danubian Principalities, 663, 666, 828-829, 845, 851, 864, 868, 870, 873. *See also* Moldavia, Rumania, Wallachia
Dardanelles, open to Russian merchantmen, 829-830, 833; and Treaty of Unkiar-Skelesi, 838-839; and 1840 and 1841 Straits conventions, 847-848, 855, 867, 871, 1021; Nicholas I's proposal for control of, 860; French and British squadrons sent to, 865, 867; and Treaty of Paris, 949, 1292; and Treaty of London (1871), 969, 1292; status of, recognized as of "general concern," 1006, 1008, 1011; British fleet sent to, 1008-1009, 1017; seizure of, vetoed by Totleben, 1016-1017; Salisbury's statement on (1878), 1021; and Treaty of Berlin (1878), 1021, 1292; British squadron withdrawn from, 1023; *status quo* guaranteed (1881), 1027, 1125-1126; and Russo-German alliance, 1136; occupation of, demanded by Kuropatkin, 1261; "European character" of, recognized (1897), 1284; Izvolsky and revision of status of, 1288, 1291, 1293-1299; annexation of, demanded by Rodzianko (1913), 1305; negotiations for opening of (1911–1912), 1305-1306; Russian conference on (Jan., 1914), 1308; allied expedition to, 1328, 1331, 1334, 1337, 1342, 1345; closure of (1914), 1338-1339, 1357-1358; wartime agreements on, 1347-1352; annexation of, demanded by Miliukov, 1396, 1398
Dargomyzhsky, Alexander, composer, 822, 1051
Dashkov, Andrew, diplomat, 690
D'Aumale, Duke, 959
Davout, Louis Nicholas, Duke d'Auerstaedt, Marshal, 659
Debt, public, 708-709, 787-789, 945, 1106-1107, 1207-1209, 1359
December insurrection (Dec. 25, 1825), 736, 887; plans for, 748-749; course and failure of, 749-751; and Southern Army, 751; trial and fate of participants in, 751-752, 1065; "inevitability" of failure of, 752; influence of, 752, 754-755, 757, 766, 807-808; Alexander II and, 881. *See also* Northern Society, Southern Society
Declaration of Rights of the Peoples of Russia, 1464-1465
Declaration of the Rights of Soldiers, 1394
Delcassé, Théophile, foreign minister, 1339-1341, 1344, 1346
Delianov, I. D., Count, minister of education, 1034, 1092, 1113-1114, 1164, 1234
Dembinski, Henry, General, 854
Democratic Conference, 1411, 1435, 1445
D'Enghien, Antoine Henri de Bourbon, Duke, 654, 664
Denikin, A. I., General, 1383, 1465
Denmark, 727, 810 n., 869, 957, 1226, 1292, 1347; and Treaty of Tilsit, 663; and Schleswig-Holstein, 856-857, 961-965
Derby, Edward G. G. Stanley, fourteenth Earl of, prime minister, 859
Derby, Edward H. Stanley, fifteenth Earl of, foreign secretary, 985, 1000, 1015; and revolt in Bosnia and Herzegovina, 992; and Russo-Turkish War, 1006
Déroulède, Paul, poet, 1137
Derzhavin Gabriel, author, 729
D'Hédouville, G. T. J., Count, ambassador, 854
Diaghilev, Serge, 1244, 1248, 1254
Dibich, Ivan, Baron, Field Marshal, 747, 761, 831
Didlo, Charles Louis, choreographer, 1253
Dimitriev, Radko, General, 1133, 1323, 1328
Dimitry Pavlovich, Grand Duke, 1373-1374
Dissenters, persecution of, 798 n., 1117-1119; increase in number of, 798-799 n., 1119; status of, under 1883 law, 1118; disabilities of, removed, 1119, 1173
Dmowski, Roman, Polish leader, 762 n., 918

Dobroliubov, Nicholas, literary critic, 1063-1064, 1072
Dogger Bank incident, 1276, 1284-1286
Dolgorukov, P. D., Prince, cadet leader, 1463
Dolgoruky, Catherine, Princess. See Yurevsky, Princess
Dolgushin, A., populist, 1076-1077
Dondukov-Korsakov, A. M., Prince, 1023
Donets (Don) region, industrial development of, 931, 1111, 1225-1226, 1231
Dorpat, university of, 723, 804, 1032, 1046 n.
Dostoevsky, Fedor, novelist, 812, 819, 1056-1057, 1072; life and work, 1058-1060
Doumergue, Paul, 1411 n.
Draga, Queen of Serbia, 1293
Drenteln, A. R., General, 1081
Dreyfus affair, 1241
Drouyn de Lhuys, Edouard, foreign minister, 864, 868-869 n.
Drunkenness, and spirits monopoly, 1210-1211
"Dual power," 1391-1400, 1426
Dubrovin, A. I., reactionary leader, 1174-1175, 1201
Dufferin and Ava, F. T. H., Marquis of, viceroy, 1128
Dukhobory, 798 n., 1118-1119
Dukhonin, N. N., General, 1441, 1455-1456, 1467
Dulebov, E., revolutionary, 1166
Duncan, Isadora, dancer, 1254
Durnovo, I. N., minister of interior (1889–1895), 1093, 1098, 1104
Durnovo, P. N., minister of interior (1905), 1186, 1204
Duroc, G. C. M., Duke de Frioul, ambassador, 652
Dutov, A. P., Colonel, 1466
Dvoriane (singular *dvorianin*). See *Dvorianstvo*
Dvorianstvo, privileges restored, 694; and tax on landed estates, 699; and industrial labor, 714; and restriction on right of "personal" nobles to own serfs, 717; restlessness among, 721; and absolutism, 731; corporate institutions of remodeled, 775-776; and entailed estates, 776, 1212; access to dignity of, restricted, 776, 1222 n.; and "inventories" in western provinces, 779-780; and depression in agriculture, 782-783; economic status of, 784; separate schools for members of, 801-802, 805-806 n.; and school population, 802, 1234-1235; and reforms of Alexander II, 880; and the emancipation, 883-885, 1066; and provincial committees, 886-887; and local government, 896-897; and zemstvos, 897-900; judicial powers of, under serfdom, 902; landholding of (1877), 923; and decay of large-scale farming, 928; indebtedness of, 928; decline of landholding of, 929, 1218, 1223-1224; loses control over industrial enterprises, 930; and girls' schools, 1041; demands social and constitutional reforms, 1066; Katkov spokesman of, 1066; and counter-reforms, 1093; and office of land captain, 1094-1095; and 1890 zemstvo act, 1096-1097; decline of, 1098, 1212, 1223-1224; indifference of, to free trade, 1108; and State Nobility Bank, 1111; and movement for constitutional reform, 1170; represented in State Council, 1187; and Council of the United Nobility, 1201, 1373; opposes monetary reform, 1207; committee on needs of, 1212
Dybenko, P. E., Bolshevik, 1455
Dzerzhinsky, F. E., Bolshevik, 1461

Eastern question, defined, 826. See also Ottoman Empire, dissolution of
Eastern Rumelia, 1020, 1022-1023, 1126, 1132-1133. See also Bulgaria
Edward VII, King of England, 1134, 1287, 1289
Egypt, 667, 844, 860, 988, 1006, 1141, 1349
Ehrnroth, Johan Casimir, General, 1131
Elizabeth, Empress, wife of Alexander I, 632-633, 650
Elliot, Sir Henry, ambassador, 992, 1001
Elman, Misha, violinist, 1250
Emancipation of serfs, Arakcheev's

Index xxxix

project for, 650; Napoleon's reasons for not proclaiming, 678; Speransky on, 697; and Novosiltsev's constitutional proposal, 701; discussion of, 715-716; in Baltic provinces, 718-719; expected by peasants (1812), 720; and liberal opinion, 737; Freemasonry and, 740; secret societies and, 742; Nikita Muravev and Pestel and, 743; Constantine's rumored support of, 745; Nicholas I on, 754, 778; rejected by 1826 committee, 777; Alexander II and, 778, 780, 881, 883-885, 888; and rationalization of farming, 782-783; upheld by slavophiles, 810, 990; expected by peasants after Crimean War, 882; framing of legislation on, 884-888; public discussion of permitted, 886; and provincial committees, 886-888, 891, 896; and editorial commissions, 887-888; and State Council, 888, 891; statutes on, promulgated, 888; stages of, 888-890; complexity of, 888, 921-922; and redemption payments, 889-892, 896, 1159, 1212-1214; and legal status of former serfs, 890; and communal tenure, 890, 892-893, 896, 1159, 1212; and peasant government, 890, 893-894, 896; and peasant allotments, 890-891, 896; and former household serfs, 896; and local government, 896; in western provinces, 896, 916-917, 1101; and reform of judiciary, 902; and army reform, 907; and Russia's alleged leadership in eastern Europe, 915; slow progress of, 922-923; effects of, on industry, 929-930; and American view of Karakozov's attempted regicide, 974; Dimitry Tolstoy opposed to, 1033; criticized by Chernyshevsky; acclaimed by slavophiles and liberal westerners, 1065; criticized by radicals, 1074-1075; statutes on, believed a forgery, 1079; and program of Social Democratic Party, 1150

Enemy aliens, policy towards, 1360-1361
Engelhard, Colonel, 1321
Engels, Frederick, 760, 850, 914, 1123; on Russian expansion in Asia, 986

England, 645, 694, 786, 858, 982, 1210, 1258, 1260, 1473; *rapprochement* with (1801), 651-652; alliance with, against France (1805), 655; blockade of, proclaimed (1806), 659; and anti-French coalition (1806–1807), 660-661; Napoleon bent on defeat of, 662; and Tilsit, 663; Russia forced into conflict with, 664; and Erfurt, 667-668; and Franco-Austrian War (1809), 669; Russian trade of, and Continental System, 671; and Russo-Persian negotiations (1813), 673 n.; military agreement with Russia (1812), 674; and Quadruple Alliance, 681, 686-687; and Congress of Vienna, 682-684; and anti-Russian alliance (1815), 683-684; and second Peace of Paris, 684-685; and Holy Alliance, 685; and European Alliance, 687-689; subsidizes Russia during Napoleonic wars, 709; and Russian trade, 711, 790, 792, 938, 1231, 1358; and Polish insurrection (1830), 760-761; repeal of Corn Laws and Russian grain exports, 781; Nicholas I's inability to understand government of, 827; and Greek independence, 828-829, 832, 834; and Russian expansion in Near East, 830-831; and Turkish crisis (1832–1833), 836-841; pro-Turkish sentiment in, 841; rivalry with Russia in Persia, 843; and near eastern crisis (1839), 846; and Rumanian independence, 852; and Hungarian revolution, 854-855; and Schleswig-Holstein, 856, 961-963; Nicholas I offers cooperation to (1853), 860-861, 863, 865; and dispute over Holy Places, 861-864; sends squadron to Dardanelles, 865; and 1853 crisis, 865-869; eagerness for war in, 868, 951 n., 1001; sends fleet to Black Sea, 868, 877; ultimatum to Russia (1854), 868-869; diplomacy of, during Crimean War, 869-872; and Crimean campaign, 873-876; and interpretations of Crimean War, 877, 951 n.; and Polish insurrection, 914, 951; finances Russian railway construction, 935-936; builds merchant ships for Russia, 937; and Congress

England (*continued*)
of Paris (1856), 948-950; Russia's estrangement from, 953; diplomatic intervention of, on behalf of Poland, 956-958; and accession of George I of Greece, 958-960; and Franco-Prussian War, 967; and abrogation of Black Sea clause, 967-969; and Russian colonies in America, 973-976; and China (1840's–1860's), 977-978; and Russian expansion in Central Asia, 984-986, 1125; and revolt in Bosnia and Herzegovina (1875), 992; and Balkan war (1876), 993, 999; and Constantinople Conference, 1000-1001; and Russo-Turkish War (1877–1878), 1005-1007; and Russian peace terms, 1007-1008, 1014-1015, 1017-1018; orders fleet to Constantinople, 1008; and San Stefano, 1014-1016; and Congress of Berlin, 1017-1019, 1024; fleet of, withdrawn from Dardanelles, 1023; war on, demanded by Aksakov, 1024; Russian hostility towards, 1026-1027; Alexander III's dislike for, 1087-1088; and persecution of Russian Jews, 1121, 1287; and Afghanistan crisis (1885), 1127-1129; approves Bulgarian unification, 1132; Balkan policy of, attacked, 1134; Russian investments of, 1226; and Russian expansion in Far East, 1262-1264, 1266, 1268; and Japanese alliance, 1269-1270; and Dogger Bank incident, 1276, 1285; and Russo-Japanese *rapprochement*, 1282; and *rapprochement* with Russia, 1283, 1286-1287; and German big-navy program, 1287, 1289-1290; and Russian convention (1907), 1287-1288, 1309-1310; and Bagdad railway, 1290-1291; and opening of Straits to warships, 1292, 1294, 1306; and annexation of Bosnia and Herzegovina, 1296; and Balkan war (1911–1913), 1302-1304, 1309; and outbreak of World War I, 1313, 1315-1316, 1318-1319; and World War I, 1322, 1328, 1332, 1334, 1400; and Triple Entente treaty, 1335, 1467; decline of pro-Russian sentiment in, 1336; animosity towards, 1336-1337; and Japanese expansion, 1337; and negotiations with Turkey, Italy, Bulgaria, Serbia, Rumania, and Greece, 1338-1347; and Russian war aims, 1347-1352; and Russian trade *via* Sweden, 1358; portion of Russian gold reserve transferred to, 1359; recognizes Provisional Government, 1359; detains political *émigrés*, 1399; asylum for Nicholas II, 1436 n.

Entente Cordiale (Anglo-French), 1282, 1287

Enver Pasha, 1334, 1338

Erfurt, conference and convention of (1808), 667-668, 670, 696

Ermolov, A. P., General, 831

Ernest II, Duke of Saxe-Coburg-Gotha, 957

"Estates" (classes), bill on, 767; and admission to schools, 776; and "honorary citizens," 786; and school system, 800-802; and peasant government, 893-895; and legal status of peasantry, 895; and zemstvos, 897, 898 n., 899; and local and municipal government reform (1864, 1870), 902; and pre-reform army, 907; and army reform (1874), 908-909; school system based on, advocated, 1036; and admission to girls' schools, 1040-1041; abolition of, demanded, 1066; allegedly weakened by great reforms, 1093; proposed limitation of influence of, in local government, 1094; and 1890 zemstvo act, 1096; and school policies under Alexander III, 1113-1115; survivals of, 1222; abolished, 1392

Estonia, 718-719, 1425

Eugene, Metropolitan, 641

Eugénie, Empress of France, 953

European Alliance, 687-690

Evlogius, Bishop, 1326

Executive Committee of the Petrograd Soviet, 1382, 1387, 1392-1393; established, 1389-1390; and Kerensky's participation in Provisional Government, 1391; and Army Order No. 1, 1393-1394; approves "coalition" government, 1399-1400

Expressionism, 1247, 1252

Index

Factory committees, 1417-1420, 1457, 1560
Factory legislation, 796-797, 933; and employer-employee relations, 1105; and factory inspectors, 1105; and factory boards, 1105; and employment of women, 1105-1106; and juvenile labor, 1105-1106; and 11½-hour day, 1149, 1160-1161; and employers' accident liability, 1160, 1228-1229; and factory elders, 1160-1161; and trade unions, 1186, 1228; and sick benefit funds, 1228; and factory committees, 1419; and 8-hour day, 1419, 1460
Fadeev, R. A., author, 988
von Falkenhayn, Erich, General, 1328
Famine, 1139, 1148, 1152, 1159, 1167, 1212
Far East, expansion in, 951, 1108
Faure, Félix, President, 1283
Fedotov, Paul, painter, 823
Ferdinand, Prince of Saxe-Coburg-Gotha, King Consort of Portugal, 959
Ferdinand, Prince of Saxe-Coburg-Gotha, King of Bulgaria, 1134, 1295, 1340, 1346 n.
Ferdinand, King of Rumania, 1343
Ferdinand I, Emperor of Austria, 852-853
Ferdinand VII, King of Spain, 688, 736
Ferdinand Maximilian Joseph, Archduke, 959
Fet, Athanasius, poet, 819, 1061
Fichte, Johann Gottlieb, philosopher, 808
Fighting Union for the Liberation of the Working Class, 1148, 1160
Filonenko, M., army commissar, 1410, 1437, 1439
Finland, 634, 718, 736, 873, 902, 964, 1172 n., 1182 n., 1192, 1238, 1358, 1444, 1466; annexation of, 665, 667, 671, 692; constitutional arrangements in (1809), 702-704; abrogation of autonomy of, demanded, 743; proposed severance of, 869, 872; 1863 diet and constitution of, 881, 919-920; under Nicholas I, 919; pro-Swedish sympathies in, 947; and Fundamental Statutes (1899), 1158; defends her liberties, 1158; and murder of Bibikov, 1167; and revolutionary movement (1904-1905), 1169-1170, 1179; restrictive legislation on, abrogated, 1180, 1202; represented in Russian State Council, 1187; and 1910 legislation, 1202-1203; Progressive Bloc and, 1371; independence movement in 1422-1423; independence of, 1423, 1465; and Brest-Litovsk, 1471
Finnish Party of Active Resistance, 1169
Finnish Workers' Republic, 1465
First World War, 1144, 1146, 1206, 1208-1209, 1216, 1222, 1229, 1232, 1237-1238, 1243, 1245, 1255, 1258, 1261, 1291, 1303, 1309, 1383; causes of, 1312-1313, 1318-1319; outbreak of, 1312-1319; and "Russian steam roller," 1320, 1411, 1411-1412 n.; and east Prussian campaign, 1322-1324, 1326, 1336; and Galician campaign, 1323-1327; and German offensive on eastern front, 1328-1330; and shortage of supplies, 1329; size of armies in, 1329; casualties in, 1329, 1333, 1377; and "scorched earth" policy, 1330-1331, 1363; and Brusilov offensive, 1332-1333, 1344; on Caucasian front, 1333-1334; and Russian navy, 1334; and Russian war aims, 1347-1352; cost of, 1359; patriotism and breakdown of national morale in, 1375-1379; and June (1917) offensive, 1408-1409, 1422, 1430, 1437; and Russian armistice agreements, 1467-1468; and Brest-Litovsk, 1467-1473
"Five, The," composers, 1051-1052, 1249
Fokine, Michael, choreographer, 1254
Fontainbleau, Treaty of (1814), 681
Formosa, 1263-1264
Fourier, François Marie Charles, 808, 811-812
Fox, Charles James, prime minister, 658
Fox, Gustavus V., American politician, 974
France, 645, 736, 789, 844, 860, 982, 1178, 1210, 1258, 1473; estrangement from (1801), 652, 654; treaty of friendship with (1801), 653-654;

France (continued)
 war with (1805–1807), 657-661; and Russian alliance (1807–1812), 661-671; and 1812 war, 671-678; and "War of Liberation," 679-681; and Congress of Vienna, 682-684; and anti-Russian alliance (1815), 683; and European Alliance, 687-690; and Polish insurrection (1830), 760-761; and Russian trade, 790, 938, 1358; Nicholas I's hostility towards, 827; and Greek independence, 829, 832; and Turkish crisis (1832–1833), 836-837, 840-841; and near eastern crisis, 846-847; Russian ambassador to, recalled (1842), 849 n.; and 1848 revolution, 850-852; and Hungarian revolution, 854; and Schleswig-Holstein, 856-857, 962; and dispute over Holy Places, 861-862, 864; and 1853 crisis, 865-869; and Crimean War, 869-870, 873-877; and Polish insurrection (1863), 914, 951, 953; finances Russian railway construction, 935; and Congress of Paris (1856), 948-950; *rapprochement* with Russia, 953; and diplomatic intervention on behalf of Poland, 956-958, 961; and accession of George I of Greece, 958-960; and Crete uprising, 960; and war with Prussia, 966-967; and abrogation of Black Sea clause, 969; and revolt in Bosnia and Herzegovina (1875), 992; and Constantinople Conference, 1001; and Congress of Berlin, 1019; and Afghanistan crisis (1885), 1129; and loan to Russia, 1209; Russian investments of, 1226; and China, 1266, 1268; and Russo-Japanese War, 1277; and Russo-Japanese *rapprochement*, 1282; and Bagdad railway, 1290-1291; and Aland Islands, 1292; and annexation of Bosnia and Herzegovina, 1296, 1306; and opening of Straits, 1296, 1306; and Balkan wars (1911–1913), 1301-1303; and von Sanders' appointment, 1307; and outbreak of World War I, 1313, 1315, 1318-1319; and World War I, 1322, 1328, 1332-1334, 1400; and Triple Entente treaty, 1335, 1467; anti-Russian feeling in, 1336; and Turkey, 1338; and negotiations with Italy, Bulgaria, Rumania and Greece, 1339-1341, 1344, 1346-1347; and Russian war aims, 1347, 1349-1352; recognizes Provisional Government, 1395; detains political *émigrés*, 1399; Russian brigades in, 1411-1412 n.

Francis, D. F., ambassador, 1404

Francis I, Emperor of Austria, 657, 659, 668, 670, 674, 681, 685, 834

Francis II, Holy Roman Emperor. *See* Francis I, Emperor of Austria

Francis Ferdinand, Archduke, 1311-1312

Francis Joseph, Emperor of Austria, 853-854, 856, 858, 866, 870, 872, 954-955, 1284, 1296; and three emperors' league (1873), 971-972; and revolt in Bosnia and Herzegovina (1875), 991; and Reichstadt agreement (1876), 997; and Russian peace terms, 1014; and outbreak of World War I, 1313

Franco-Austrian Alliance (1812), 673, 685

Franco-Austrian War (1859), 954-955

Franco-Prussian Alliance (1812), 673

Franco-Prussian Treaty (1807), 663

Franco-Prussian War (1870), 966-967

Franco-Russian Alliance (1895), 953, 955, 961, 1109, 1125, 1141, 1260, 1271, 1283, 1287; advocated by Katkov, 1134, 1137; terms of, 1138-1139; consequences of, 1140; and proposed Anglo-German alliance, 1285; unaffected by Björko Treaty, 1286

Frederick, Prince of Augustenburg, 963

Frederick III, Emperor of Germany, 961, 1136

Frederick VII, King of Denmark, 962-963

Frederick William III, King of Prussia, 636, 653, 657-658, 660, 674, 680-683, 754, 845; and Alexander I at Memel, 660; at Tilsit, 662

Frederick William IV, King of Prussia, 856-858, 866, 870-871

Frederikshamn, Peace of (1809), 665, 703

Free Economic Society, 715-716

"Free farmers," 717, 778

Index

Free School of Music, 1051
Freemasonry, 639, 641; and Decembrist movement, 740, 740-741 n.; dissolved, 742
Friedland, battle of (1807), 661
Fuad Pasha, 855, 863
Fundamental Laws (1906), 1187-1189, 1194, 1199, 1215, 1259, 1421
Futurism, 1245, 1247-1248, 1252

de Gabriac, P. J. A. M. E. de Cadoine, Marquis, diplomat, 639, 641
Gagarin, P. P., Prince, president council of ministers, 1035
Galicia, 672, 852, 955, 957, 1334, 1347, 1400, 1423; occupied, 1326-1327; retreat from, 1328, 1330, 1342; Brusilov offensive in, 1332-1333; 1917 offensive in, 1409-1410, 1430
Galicia, eastern, annexed by Russia (1809), 669; by Austria (1815), 684
Gamble, Sir Douglas, Admiral, 1307
Gapon, George, priest, 1171, 1172 n.
Garibaldi, Giuseppe, 914, 955
Gastein, Convention of (1865), 963
Geltser, Catherine, ballerina, 1253
Gendarmery, 771-772, 906
General Company of Russian Railways, 935
George, Prince of Greece, 1142
George I, King of Greece, 959-960
George III, King of England, 659
George IV, King of England, 682
George V, King of England, 1436 n.
Georgia, 1170, 1425; annexed, 845, 872
German Confederation, 855-858, 960, 962, 965
German settlers, policy towards, 1360
Germany, 674, 789, 810 n., 1178, 1210, 1248, 1258, 1260; federation of proposed (1804), 655; and Russian trade, 790, 938, 1231, 1358; national movement in, 855-856; finances Russian railway construction, 936; unification of, 961-967; and abrogation of Black Sea clause, 969; and three emperors' league (1873), 970-973; panslavism and, 988-989; and revolt in Bosnia and Herzegovina, 991-992; **and** Balkan war (1876), 997-998; **and** Constantinople Conference, 1001; and Russian peace negotiations (1878), 1014-1015; and Treaty of Berlin, 1017-1019; tariff measures and estrangement from Russia, 1025-1026; and revival of three emperors' league, 1027; and alliance with Austria (1879), 1027, 1135; and tariff war with Russia, 1109-1110; and Bulgarian unification, 1132; Balkan policy of, attacked, 1134; and Russian alliance (1887), 1135-1139; and Triple Alliance, 1137; and Franco-Russian Alliance, 1138-1139; Russian investments of, 1226; and colonial expansion, 1258, 1287; and Korea, 1263-1264; and Kiaochow, 1266, 1284; and Boxer Rebellion, 1267; and Russo-Japanese War, 1271-1276, 1277; and Anglo-Russian *entente*, 1287; and big navy program, 1287, 1289; and annexation of Bosnia and Herzegovina, 1288, 1297-1298; and Bagdad railway, 1290-1291; and Aland Islands, 1292; and Balkan wars (1911–1913), 1302-1304; and von Sanders' appointment, 1307; and outbreak of World War I, 1313, 1315-1316, 1318-1319; and World War I, 1322, 1324, 1327, 1332-1333, 1340, 1349-1350, 1397, 1410; and offensive on eastern front, 1328-1329; and Turkey, 1337-1338; colonies of, partitioned, 1340, 1346-1347; and Bulgaria, 1342; urged to overthrow bourgeois government, 1397; Lenin travels through, 1401; proletariat of, extolled by Lenin, 1402 n.; Lenin allegedly agent of, 1432; occupies Riga, 1438; mutiny in navy of, 1446; and Finland, 1465; and Brest-Litovsk, 1467-1470, 1473; advances in Russia, 1470; recognizes Ukrainian People's Republic, 1470; occupies Ukraine, 1471

Gershuni, G. A., terrorist, 1152, 1154, 1166
von Gerstner, professor, 789
Giers, M. N., ambassador, 1306
Giers, N. K., foreign minister, 1007, 1024, 1090, 1110, 1259, 1296 n.; and *rapprochement* with Germany, 1026-1027; characterization, 1124-

Giers, N. K. (*continued*) 1125; and three emperors' league (1881–1887), 1126-1127, 1135; and Afghan crisis, 1129; and Bulgaria, 1130-1132, 1134-1135; and Katkov, 1134-1135; and Russo-German Alliance, 1135-1138; and Franco-Russian Alliance, 1137-1139

Giesl von Gieslingen, Waldimir, Freiherr, ambassador, 1315

Gladstone, William Ewart, 951 n., 967, 969, 985, 999, 1005, 1127, 1129

Glazunov, A. K., composer and conductor, 1250, 1254

Glinka, Michael, composer, 821-822, 1254

Gnedich, Nicholas, poet, 731

Göben, 1334

Goderich, Viscount. *See* Ripon, F. J. Robinson

Godnev, I. V., politician, 1435

von Goethe, Johann Wolfgang, 686

Goetz, Michael (A.R.), socialist revolutionary, 1152

Gogol, Nicholas, novelist, 715, 815, 820-821, 1055-1057; life and work, 817-819

Golenishchev-Kutuzov-Smolensky, M. I., Prince. *See* Kutuzov, M. I.

Golitsin, Alexander, Prince, chief procurator, 634, 641-649, 737 n., 739, 746; religious doctrines of, 638-640, minister of education, 724-725; and censorship, 728

Golitsin, N. D., Prince, president council of ministers, 1365

Golovnin, A. V., minister of education, 1032-1034, 1043, 1065, 1075

von der Goltz, Kolmar, Baron, General, 1307

Goncharov, Alexander, novelist, 819, 1061

Goncharova, N., painter, 1248

Gorchakov, Alexander, Prince, chancellor, 871, 961, 1124; characterization, 952; and *rapprochement* with France, 953-954, 956; and Anglo-French intervention in Poland, 957, 961; and Crete uprising, 960; and unification of Germany, 964-965; and revision of Treaty of Paris, 966-969, 1292; and Franco-Prussian War, 967; and three emperors' league, 970-973, 1005, 1014, 1025, 1027; and American Civil War, 973-974; and sale of Alaska, 975; and expansion in Far East, 979; and expansion in central Asia, 982, 984-985; and panslavism, 990, 995-996, 1017; and revolt in Bosnia and Herzegovina (1875), 991-992; and Balkan war (1876), 993, 999; and Reichstadt agreement (1876), 997; and Austro-Russian agreement (1877), 998; and peaceful solution of Balkan conflict, 1000-1001; and Rumania, 1002, 1004, 1013; and war with Turkey, 1006; and Russian peace program, 1007-1008, 1012; and San Stefano, 1011-1012; and Congress of Berlin, 1015, 1018-1019, 1025; and negotiations with England, 1016; and Treaty of Berlin, 1025; retires, 1026

Gorchakov, Michael, Prince, General, 865, 870-871, 873, 875-876; viceroy of Poland, 910-912, 948

Goremykin, I. L., 1156, 1158, 1167, 1175, 1214; president, council of ministers (1906), 1190-1193; dismissed, 1192; president, council of ministers (1914–1916), 1205, 1363, 1368-1370; dismissed, 1364, 1372; and Progressive Bloc, 1371

Gorky, Maxim (Alexis Peshkov), author, 817, 1149, 1240; life and work, 1242-1243

Gossner, priest, 643

Government, central, and establishment of ministries (1802), 692; advisory council (1769) abolished, 694; and "permanent council," 694; and "nonofficial committee," 694, 716, 722; administrative colleges abolished, 695; and status of the Senate, 695; and reform of ministries (1811), 697-698; and State Council, 697-698; and modernization of civil service, 699, 724; and administrative practice, 701-702; and Finland, 702-704; in Poland (1815), 705-706; and abolition of Polish autonomous institutions, 762-764; and "committee of December 6, 1826," 765, 767, 776, 786; and secret committees, 765-767,

Index

"land and freedom," 1069, 1413; and movement "to the people," 1069, 1076; founder of populism, 1072
Hesse-Cassel, electorate of, 857-858
Highways, 789
von Hindenburg, Paul, Field Marshal, 1322, 1325, 1328
Hippius, Zinaida, poet, 1245
His Majesty's Own Chancery, 695 n., 768, 770-772, 785, 813, 1040, 1083
Historiography, Russian, 730-731, 799, 803, 805, 1050
Hobart Pasha, Admiral, 960
von Hoffmann, Max, General, 1468-1469
Hofmann, Joseph Casimir, pianist, 1250
Hohenberg, Duchess of, 1312
Holland, 672, 674, 683, 861, 957, 982, 1226, 1258; finances Russian railway construction, 935
Holstein, Duchy of, 856-858, 961-965, 1347
Holy Alliance, 636, 724, 727 n., 739, 869, 947, 956, 1126; and Baroness Krüdner, 642; religious basis of, 643-645; establishment and status of, 685-687, 689, 692; in abeyance, 827-829, 834, 844-845, 848; revived (1830, 1833) 834, 840; weakened, 858; restored (1873), 971-972
Holy Host, 1121-1122
Holy Places, dispute over, 859, 861-864, 868
Holy See, 957, 1327 n.
Holy Synod, 737 n., 764, 806, 1088, 1112, 1205, 1363 n.; opposes Bible Society, 641, 764 n.; and dynastic crisis (1825), 746, 751; dependence of, on chief procurator, 798 n.; and schools, 806, 1042, 1046 n., 1047, 1116; excommunicates Tolstoy, 1240
Horowitz, Vladimir, pianist, 1250
Hrushevsky, Michael, Ukrainian leader, 1327, 1424
Hudson's Bay Company, 975
Hughes, John, industrialist, 932
Hungary, 689, 955, 966; revolution and Russian intervention in, 788, 804, 853-855, 872

Iakubovich, Alexander, Decembrist, 737, 748, 750
Ianson, Ia. E., economist, 1100-1101
Ianushkevich, N. N., General, 1317-1318, 1321, 1332, 1344; and demoralization of the army, 1378
Ibrahim Pasha, 828, 832, 836, 846
Ignatev, N. P., Count, General, 967, 971; and panslavism, 990, 996, 1028, 1091; and war with Turkey, 999, 1001; and peace negotiations, 1007, 1010, 1015-1016; and San Stefano, 1010-1013, 1125, 1130; dismissed, 1017; minister of interior, 1091-1092, 1112
Ignatev, P. N., Count, minister of education, 1238
Illiteracy, prevalence of, 903, 1048, 1184, 1235; decline of, 1256-1257
Imperial Archeological Society, 805 n.
Imperial Odessa Society of History and Antiquities, 805 n.
Impressionism, 1247, 1252
Income tax, 1359
India, 982, 1141, 1288; expedition for conquest of, recalled, 651-652; Franco-Russian plan for conquest of, 666-667; England and Russian threat to, 841, 844, 877, 984, 986, 1006; Skobelev and conquest of, 986; Alexander II denies threat to, 1000
Industry, growth of, 713, 791-792, 931, 1224-1225, 1232; uncertainties of statistics of, 713, 930; servile and hired labor in, 713-714, 792-794, 929-930; mechanization of, 795; and cyclical recessions, 929, 1224; effects of emancipation on, 929-930; cotton, and American Civil War, 930; concentration of production in, 930-931, 1225, 1232; conditions of workers in, 932-934; investments in, 944, 1226; represented in State Council, 1187; and national income, 1232 n.; and war industries committees, 1370; seizure of, by workers, 1420; financial burdens of, 1421; closing of enterprises and decline of production of, 1421; nationalization of, 1460. *See also* Factory committees; Factory legislation; Labor, industrial; "Possessionary" enterprises
Institut Pasteur, 1050

International, First, 1064, 1071, 1073, 1077; Second, 1400
Ioffe, Adolf, Bolshevik, 1468
Iollos, G. B., cadet deputy, 1201
Ionin, A. S., diplomat, 1132
Ishutin, Nicholas, revolutionary, 1075
Istomin, V. I., Admiral, 875-876
Italo-Turkish War (1911–1912), 1299
Italy, 652, 674, 739, 872, 958, 960, 964, 1071, 1110, 1226, 1268; federation of, proposed (1804), 655; and Black Sea trade, 790; and Franco-Prussian War, 967; and abrogation of Black Sea clause, 969; and revolt in Bosnia and Herzegovina (1875), 992; and Constantinople Conference, 1001; and Congress of Berlin, 1019; and Afghan crisis, 1129; and Triple Alliance, 1137; and annexation of Bosnia and Herzegovina, 1296; and opening of Straits, 1299, 1306; and Balkan wars (1911–1913), 1302-1304; and outbreak of World War I, 1315, 1318; and World War I, 1328, 1332-1334, 1344; wartime negotiations with, 1335, 1339-1341; and war aims, 1347, 1350; recognizes Provisional Government, 1395
Ito, Hirobumi, Marquis, Japanese statesman, 1270
Iurovsky, Z., revolutionary, 1166
Ivan IV, Tsar, 772
Ivanov, Alexander, painter, 823
Ivanov, Ivan, revolutionary, 1071-1072
Ivanov, N. J., General, 1323, 1327, 1383
Ivanov, Viacheslav, author, 1245
Izvestiia, first issue of, 1177
Izvolsky, A. P., foreign minister, 1192, 1259, 1285-1287, 1335-1336, 1344; and opening of Straits to warships, 1288, 1291, 1293-1299, 1306; and Aland Islands, 1291-1292; and annexation of Bosnia and Herzegovina, 1293-1298

Japan, 1141, 1258, 1261; exchanges Sakhalin for Kurile Islands (1875), 979; expansion of, in Korea and Manchuria, 1263-1264, 1268; and alliance with England, 1270; and war with Russia (1904–1905), 1270-1277; British and American support of, 1271; and *rapprochement* with Russia (1905–1914), 1279, 1282, 1286; and World War I, 1335, 1337; and Russian war aims, 1347; and Russian trade, 1358
Jefferson, Thomas, President, 692
Jena, battle of (1806), 659
Jews, non-discrimination against in schools, 726-727, 806 n., 1047 n.; legal disabilities of (1804–1825), 726-727 n.; Pestel on, 743 n.; policy of assimilation of, 806-807 n., 1047-1048 n.; disabilities of, in Poland removed, 912; legal disabilities of, eased (1860–1880), 1047-1048 n.; and pogroms (1871), 1047-1048 n.; and alleged ritual murders, 1047-1048 n., 1175, 1203; denied zemstvo franchise, 1096, 1202; representation of, in city government, 1098; *de facto* exclusion of from the bar, 1100; quotas for, in higher and secondary schools, 1115; Alexander III on, 1119; and growth of anti-Semitism, 1119-1120; and pogroms (1881), 1120; repeal of discriminatory legislation recommended, 1120; discriminatory legislation on (1882–1893), summarized, 1120-1121; consequences of persecution of, 1121; union for the emancipation of, 1173 n.; and pogroms (1903–1906), 1175-1176, 1179, 1191, 1196, 1198, 1287; and Polish municipal government bill, 1202; eligible to serve in Duma, 1203; Nicholas II and, 1203; and the judiciary, 1203; and government service, 1221; and the press, 1239; eviction of, 1330; Progressive Bloc and, 1371; emancipation of, 1392
Jomini, A. H., Baron, General, 879
Joseph Bonaparte, King of Spain, 667
Joseph Semashko, Bishop, 764
Josephine, Empress of France, 670
Joyce, James, 1059
Judiciary, and mitigation of penal procedure, 693; reform of, postponed, 698; reform of (1809), in Russian Poland, 705 n.; conditions of, prior to 1864, 902-903; statutes (1864)

Index xlix

of, 902-905, 1094; and administrative practice, 905-906; and the press, 1055-1056; reform of, favored by Katkov, 1065, 1099; reform of, favored by Pobedonostsev, 1088, 1099; and "state of emergency" legislation, 1091; justices of the peace abolished, 1094; curtailment of jurisdiction and independence of, 1099-1100; and factory boards, 1105; and 1906 military courts, 1196; justices of the peace restored, 1203; and the Jews, 1203; and abolition of the Senate, 1458; under the Soviets, 1461

Jung-Stilling, Johann Heinrich, mystic, 642

Kabul, Anglo-Russian rivalries in, 843
Kachura, F., revolutionary, 1166
Kahanov, M. S., committee of, 1092-1094, 1098
Kakhovsky, Peter, Decembrist, 750
Kaledin, A. M., General, 1465-1467
Kaliaev, I. P., terrorist, 1172
Kalish, Treaty of (1813), 680, 682
Kamenev, L. B. (Rosenfeld), Bolshevik, 1402, 1432, 1446, 1459, 1468
Kamensky, S. M., Count, Field Marshal, 660
Kamkov, B. D., socialist revolutionary, 1451
Kankrin, Egor, Count, minister of finance, 709, 767, 786, 789, 791, 879, 934; and currency reform, 787
Kant, Immanuel, 808
Karakozov, D. V., revolutionary, 974, 1033, 1035, 1065, 1075
Karamzin, Nicholas, historian, 700, 729-733
Karpovich, P., revolutionary, 1166
Karsavina, Tamara, ballerina, 1253-1254
Kartsov, A. N., consul general, 994
Kasso, L. A., minister of education, 1233
Katkov, M. N., journalist, 915, 1058, 1066; and panslavism, 989, 996, 1000, 1025, 1139; on Balkan "crusade," 1028; on class principle in school organization, 1035-1036, 1114; evolution and influence of, 1065; and the judiciary, 1065, 1099 1100; opposes Loris-Melikov's constitutional proposals, 1083; and Alexander III, 1089-1090, 1098; and counter-reforms, 1093, 1098; on independence of Russian press, 1112-1113 n.; advocates French alliance, 1134-1135, 1137

Katsura, Taro, Prince, Japanese statesman, 1270
von Kaufman, C. P., General, 917; and expansion in central Asia, 981-984
Kaulbars, Alexander, Baron, General, 1131
Kaulbars, Nicholas, Baron, General, 1133-1134
Kavelin, K. D., jurist, 885, 1032
Kazan, university of, 724-726, 1031-1032, 1049, 1057
Kazantsev, A. E., police agent, 1201
Kerensky, A. F., 1368, 1381, 1383, 1396, 1428-1429, 1461, 1475; characterization, 1386-1388; vice-chairman of Soviet, 1388, 1390; minister of justice, 1388, 1391; and Army Order No. 1, 1394; repudiates Miliukov's program, 1398; favors peace without annexations and indemnities, 1399; upholds fiction of Russia's determination to fight, 1405, 1413; and army morale, 1408-1410; and June (1917) offensive, 1409-1410; president of Provisional Government, 1410, 1433; and capital punishment, 1410-1411; peasant Soviets and, 1414-1415; minister of war and navy, 1426; escapes arrest, 1431; accuses Lenin of being German agent, 1432; and second coalition government, 1433-1434; and substitutes for parliament, 1435-1436; and Kornilov, 1435-1442; on exile of tsar to England, 1436 n.; commander in chief, 1440; and third coalition, 1441-1442; alleged intention of, to surrender Petrograd, 1444, 1446; and October insurrection, 1448-1449; leaves Petrograd, 1449-1450; and resistance to Bolshevism, 1454-1455; escapes, 1455
Khabalov, S. S., General, 1380
Kharkov, university of, 724, 726, 1031-1032

Khiva, khanate, 842, 980; attempted invasion of (1839), 843; Russian protectorate over, 981-982, 984-985
Khlysty (flagellants), 798 n.
Khodynka, disaster of, 1147, 1165
Khomiakov, Alexis, slavophile, 809, 893 n.
Khrulev, S. A., General, 875
Khrustalev-Nosar, G. S., Menshevik, 1176, 1181
Khvostov, A. A., minister of justice, 1364
Kiahkta, agreement of (1915), 1282 n.
Kiaochow, leased to Germany, 1266; taken over by Japan, 1337
Kienthal Conference (1916), 1400-1401
Kiev, university of, 764, 1031-1032
Kiprensky, O. A., painter, 822
Kireevsky, Ivan, slavophile, 809
Kireevsky, Peter, slavophile, 809
Kiselev, Nicholas, diplomat, 858
Kiselev, P. D., Count, administrator, 778-779, 838; and administration of state peasants, 785-786, 925; establishes protectorate in Danubian principalities, 835; urges acceptance of allied terms (1855), 947; and *rapprochement* with France, 953-956
Kitchener, Horatio Herbert, Earl of, 1350 n.
Kiutayeh, Peace of (1833), 837, 844
Kizevetter, A. A., historian, 1189, 1233
Kleigels, General, 1166
Kleinmichel, P. A., Count, 756 n., 789
Kliuchevsky, V. O., historian, 1050, 1233
Knave of Diamonds, art society, 1247
Knipper, Olga, actress, 1241
Knox, Sir Alfred, General, 1321, 1336
Knox, Philander, secretary of state, 1279
Kochubey, V. P., Prince, foreign minister, 653, 694, 696, 765
Kokand, khanate, annexed, 980-981, 984
Kokoshkin, F. E., cadet leader, 1463
Kokovtsov, V. N., Count, minister of finance and president of council of ministers, 1143-1144, 1178, 1191-1192, 1198, 1205, 1208-1209, 1213, 1231-1232, 1283, 1308, 1308-1309 n., 1372; and the Duma, 1204-1205; on budget and economic advancement, 1209-1210
Kolegaev, A. L., left socialist revolutionary, 1459
Kolmakov, N. M., writer, 771
Koltsov, Alexis, poet, 815, 817, 820, 825
Komissarzhevsky, Vera, actress, 1252
Komura, Juichiro, Baron, Japanese statesman, 1278
Koni, A. F., jurist, 903
Königsberg, Convention of (1807), 663-664
Konovalov, A. I., industrialist, 1429, 1449
Korea, 978, 1271, 1277; Russian expansion in, 1262-1263, 1265-1266, 1268, 1270; and Treaty of Portsmouth, 1278
Korf, M. A., Count, 897
Kornilov, L. G., 1410, 1433; career and outlook, 1436-1438, 1440; program of, 1438-1439; dismissed, 1439; arrested, 1439; released, 1456; organizes Volunteer Army, 1456, 1463, 1465-1466. See also Kornilov "mutiny"
Kornilov, V. K., Admiral, 875-876
Kornilov "mutiny," 1411, 1435-1441, 1443, 1445 n., 1446-1447; significance of, 1442
Kornilovich, Alexander, Decembrist, 754-755 n.
Korolenko, V. G., author, 1242, 1244
Korovin, K. A., painter, 1247-1248
Korvin-Krukovsky, Sophie, mathematician, 1050
Kosciuszko, Thaddeus, 706, 912
Koshelev, A. I., slavophile, 780, 809, 893 n., 921
Koshelev, Rodion, and Alexander I, 634-635, 641-644, 648, 706; religious doctrines of, 638-639
Kossuth, Louis, 853-855
Kostomarov, N. I., historian, 811
von Kotzebue, Augustus, 740, 819
Koussevitzky, Serge, conductor, 1250
Kovalevsky, E. P., minister of education, 1031, 1041
Kramskoy, I. N., painter, 1053
Krasinski, Sigmunt, 910
Krasnov, P. N., General, 1454-1455

Index

Krause, N. E., zemstvo leader, 1067
Krivoshein, A. V., minister of agriculture, 1330-1331, 1378
Kropotkin, D. N., Prince, governor general, 1081
Kropotkin, Peter, Prince, anarchist, 1076-1077, 1084
von Krüdner, Barbara Juliane, Baroness, 642-643, 646, 649
Krukoviecki, John, General, 761
Krushevan, P. A., reactionary leader, 1175, 1198
Krylenko, N. N., Ensign, Bolshevik, 1455-1456; orders armistice negotiations, 1467
Krylov, Ivan, author, 732, 734, 824
Krymov, A. M., General, 1440
Kryzanowski, Severin, Colonel, 757
Kryzhanovsky, S. E., official, 1199
Kshesinsky, Mathilda, ballerian, 1144, 1253; palace of, occupied by Lenin, 1404
Kuchuk-Kainardzhi, Peace of (1774), 845, 848, 861, 863, 866-867
Kudair Khan, 981
Kudashev, N. P., Prince, ambassador, 1348-1349 n., 1350
von Kühlmann, Richard, foreign minister, 1468, 1470
Kukolnik, N. V., playwright, 819
Kukolnik, V. G., professor, 753
Kulisher, P. A., historian, 811
Kuprin, A. I., author, 1244
Kurakin, Alexander, Prince, 662, 672, 692
Kurakin, Alexis, Prince, 696
Kurile Islands, 979
Kuropatkin, A. N., General, 1158, 1261, 1384; and the Japanese war, 1272-1274
Kustodiev, V. M., painter, 1247-1248
Kutler, N. N., cadet leader, 1186, 1214
Kutuzov, M. I., Prince, Field Marshal, 637, 675-676; and 1805 campaign, 657; and Turkish war, 673; and Napoleonic invasion, 675-680

Labor, industrial, sources of, under serfdom, 713-715, 792-794; female, 793, 932, 1354; juvenile, 793, 796, 932, 1354; wages of, prior to emancipation, 794-795; number of (1860-1900), 930; conditions of, after emancipation, 931-933; and strikes, 932, 1105, 1149, 1159-1160, 1162, 1171, 1174, 1229, 1314, 1375-1376; wages of, after emancipation, 932-933, 1105-1106, 1161, 1229, 1375; and "link with land," 933, 1230; indifference of, to populism, 1077; and police-sponsored labor organizations, 1161-1163, 1171, 1172 n.; representation of, in State Duma, 1176, 1187; and general strike (1905), 1176-1177, 1179-1180, 1182; and 1907 election law, 1199; number of (1900–1913), 1224; and trade unions, 1186, 1228-1229, 1417-1419, 1421; and sick benefit funds, 1228; living standards of, 1229-1230, 1257, 1420; sources of, in wartime, 1353-1354; productivity of, declines, 1354, 1420-1421; and arrest of Bolshevik deputies, 1368, 1379; and war industries committees, 1370, 1376, 1389; economic status of, in wartime, 1375-1376; economic status of, after the revolution, 1417-1421; and "workers' control," 1420-1421, 1460
Labor Group (Party), 1190-1191, 1386; in first Duma, 1190-1191; in second Duma, 1198; in third and fourth Dumas, 1200; attitude of, towards the war, 1368; and provisional committee of the Duma, 1381
de La Ferronays, P. L. A. F., Count, ambassador, 629, 631-632, 634-635, 640, 645
Lagovsky, revolutionary, 1166
La Harpe, César, 630-631, 633, 645, 683, 722, 737
Lambert, Charles, Count, viceroy, 912
Lamsdorf, V. N., Count, foreign minister, 1259-1260, 1267-1268, 1270, 1279, 1294; and Björko Treaty, 1286
Land and Freedom, revolutionary society, 915, 1064, 1074, 1078, 1080, 1083; and regicide, 1081-1082, 1084
Land captains, 1093-1095, 1099, 1102, 1104, 1221; status of, revised, 1215
Land committees (1917), 1393, 1414 1416, 1448
Landholding, of the nobility (1859), 784; distribution of, according to

Landholding (*continued*)
class of owners (1877), 923; peasant, purchases and leases, 925-927, 929 n., 1217-1218; of the nobility, decline of, 929, 1218, 1223-1224; and restrictions attached to allotment land, 1103-1104, 1221-1222; social democracy and, 1150; and socialization of land, 1153; expropriation of large estates demanded by cadets, 1188; first Duma and, 1191; and Stolypin land reform, 1193, 1198, 1203, 1215-1217, 1220-1221, 1224; peasant, expansion of (1905–1914), 1218; and peasant Soviets, 1414; and decree on land, 1452-1453

Langiewicz, Marian, General, 914

Language, Russian, evolution of, 729-730, 732, 809

Lanskoï, S. S., Count, minister of interior, 883-886, 897

Larionov, M., painter, 1248

Latvia, 1170, 1425, 1428

Lauenburg, Duchy of, 962-963

Lauriston, J. A. B. L., General, 677

Lausanne, Treaty of (1912), 1299

Lavrov, Peter, revolutionary, 1063-1064, 1072-1073, 1080

Law Society, 1157

Layard, Sir Henry, ambassador, 1001, 1005, 1008, 1023

Laybach, Congress of (1821), 688

Learned societies, 1049

Lebzeltern, Ludwig, Count, ambassador, 643-644

Left Socialist Revolutionaries (Party), 1451-1454, 1470; participate in Council of People's Commissars, 1459; representation of, in Constituent Assembly, 1461-1462

Legion of Pulawy, 1422

Lelewel, Joachim, Polish leader, 758-760, 762, 764

Lenin, V. I. (Ulianov), 1070, 1072, 1085, 1152, 1392, 1412, 1428, 1457, 1459, 1465, 1477-1478; on Herzen, 809, 1069; on zemstvos, 900; on Polish insurrection, 915; on survivals of serfdom, 926; on industry and concentration of production, 930-931; on colonial expansion, 982-983; on populism, 1073; and Fighting Union for the Liberation of the Working Class, 1148; not present at founding of party, 1149; editor of *Iskra*, 1149-1150; and party split, 1150-1151; and 1905 Soviet, 1177; and boycott of elections to first Duma, 1189, 1195; and elections to second Duma, 1197; emigrates, 1201, 1379; and imminence of international revolution, 1396, 1401, 1445, 1469, 1473-1474; wartime theories and writings, 1400-1401; returns to Petrograd, 1400-1401, 1404; and the legend, 1400-1401, 1475; and *April Theses*, 1402-1403, 1445; repudiated by Petrograd committee, 1403-1404; and efficacy of slogan "peace and land," 1404-1405; endorsed by party conference, 1405; and agrarian revolution, 1413-1414, 1417; peasant Soviets and, 1414; and "workers' control," 1420; and July uprising, 1430, 1432; allegedly German agent, 1431-1432, 1442; goes into hiding, 1432; on Constituent Assembly, 1444, 1445 n., 1461, 1463-1464; on insurrection, 1444-1446; and October insurrection, 1447, 1449, 1451; and decree on peace, 1452; and decree on land, 1452-1453; chairman Council of People's Commissars, 1453; and resistance to Bolshevism in Moscow, 1454; and Ukraine, 1466-1467; on separate and annexionist peace, 1469; peace program of, defeated, 1469-1470; approves Trotsky's policy, 1470; secures acceptance of German terms, 1471; policy of, appraised, 1473-1475

Leontev, Tatiana, revolutionary, 1154

Leopold, Prince of Bavaria, Field Marshal, 1468

Leopold, Prince of Coburg, 834

Lermontov, Michael, author, 815, 820, 1056, 1064; life and work, 816-817

Leroux, Pierre, 808

Leroy-Beaulieu, Anatole, historian, 1137-1138

Lesser, Paul, explorer, 1128

Leuchtenberg, Duke of, 959

Levitan, J. I., painter, 1247

Levitsky, D. G., painter, 735

Index

Li Hung-chang, Chinese statesman, 1265
Liaotung peninsula, 1264; annexed by Russia, 982 n., 1266, 1269; ceded to Japan, 1278-1279
Liberal movement, zemstvos and, 900-901; and Polish insurrection, 915; prominence of Jews in, 1047-1048 n.; estrangement of, from government, 1065; demands of, 1066; policies of, fail, 1068; Loris-Melikov's concessions to, 1083; ebbing of, 1121-1122; definition of, 1155; revival of, 1155-1157; and violations of Finnish constitution, 1159; and university students, 1164-1165; intensification of, 1167-1168; alliance of, with revolutionaries (1904), 1169-1170; and campaign for constitutional reforms, 1169-1170, 1173; opposes consultative Duma, 1176; and October manifesto, 1178; lack of parliamentary experience in, 1184; leaders of, decline participation in Witte's cabinet, 1186; decline of, 1201; and the press, 1238; popularity of, 1255; and annexation of Constantinople, 1348, 1352; and *union sacrée*, 1366; wartime demands of, 1369
Liberation of Labor, revolutionary society, 1123, 1148, 1150
Lichnowsky, K. M., Prince, ambassador, 1316
Liders, A. N., Count, viceroy, 912-913
von Liebig, Justus, Baron, chemist, 1049
Liebknecht, Karl, 1468
Lilienthal, Marx, Jewish leader, 806-807 n.
Limpus, Sir Arthur Henry, Admiral, 1307
Lindel, priest, 643
Linevich, N. P., General, 1267, 1275
Liquor, taxation of, 788, 943, 1107; state monopoly of, 788, 1107, 1210-1211; monopoly abolished, 1211, 1359
Liszt, Franz, composer, 1051
Literature, 728-734, 815-819, 1030, 1239-1245; and pseudo-classicism, 729-730, 732, 734; and sentimentalism, 729-730, 732, 734, 819; and romanticism, 729, 732, 734, 816, 819, 1243; and realism, 729, 734, 816, 819, 1056, 1239, 1243-1245; and translations, 731-732; national character of, 734; contemporary, and Napoleonic wards, 734 n.; golden age of, 815; and literary criticism, 820, 1062-1064; and age of the Russian novel, 1056-1061; and decline of poetry, 1061-1062; and symbolism, 1244-1245; and futurism, 1245
Lithuania, 1425, 1428
Lithuanian provinces, 718; incorporation of, with Poland rumored, 737; Poland's claim to, 757-760, 913, 915; and official Russian historiography, 803; repercussions in, of Polish insurrection, 914; Russification of, 916
Lithuanian Statute, 771
Livadia, Treaty of (1879), 978
Liven, C. A., Prince, ambassador, 644
Liven, K. A., Prince, minister of education, 802 n., 812
Livonia, 718-719
Lizogub, Dimitry, revolutionary, 1084
Lloyd George, David, 1473
Lobachevsky, N. I., mathematician, 805
Lobanov-Rostovsky, A. B., Prince, foreign minister, 1023-1024, 1026, 1259-1260, 1296 n.
Lobanov-Rostovsky, Dimitry, Prince, diplomat, 662
Loftus, Lord Augustus, ambassador, 1000, 1005, 1008
Lomonosov, Michael, author, 729
London, agreement of (1878), 1017
London, Treaty of (1827), 829; (1852), 962-965; (1863), 959, (1864), 960; (1871), 969, 1008, 1012, 1021; (1913), 1302; (1915), 1339-1340
Loris-Melikov, M. T., Count, 1083, 1090-1092, 1111
Louis, Georges, ambassador, 1309
Louis I, King of Bavaria, 834
Louis XVIII, King of France, 681, 683-684, 687
Louis Napoleon, Prince, President. *See* Napoleon III, Emperor
Louis Philippe, King of France, 834-835, 850-851
Louise, Princess of Baden. *See* Elizabeth, Empress, wife of Alexander I

Louise, Queen of Prussia, 636, 653, 659, 662
Lowicz, Princess (Countess Jeanette Gruzinska), 745-746
Lozovsky, A., Bolshevik, 1459
Lubecki, Ksavery, Prince, 759-760
von Ludendorff, Erich, General, 1322
Lukomsky, A. S., General, 1406
Lunacharsky, A. V., Bolshevik, 1433, 1446
Lunéville, Treaty of (1801), 652
Luxemburg, 652
Lvov, G. E., Prince, president Provisional Government, 1201, 1366, 1388, 1413, 1426, 1428, 1436; characterization, 1383-1385, 1475; favors peace without annexations and indemnities, 1399; and agrarian revolution, 1416; resigns, 1433
Lvov, V. N., politician, part of in Kornilov "mutiny," 1439, 1441

Mack von Lieberich, Karl, Baron, General, 657
Mackensen, Augustus, General, 1325, 1328
McNeil, John, publicist and diplomat, 841
Madison, James, President, 690
Magnitsky, Michael, school official, 724-725
Magyars, panslavism and, 988-989
Mahmud II, Sultan, 828, 832, 836-838, 844
Maiakovsky, Vladimir, poet, 1245
Maikov, Apollon, poet, 819, 1062
Makarov, Senator, 695 n.
Makarov, S. A., Admiral, 1275
Makary, Bishop, 1119 n.
Maklakov, N. A., minister of interior, 1142-1143, 1363 n., 1369
Maklakov, V. A., cadet deputy, 1164
Makovsky, Vladimir, painter, 1246
Malachowski, Casimir, General, 761
Malinovsky, R. V., Bolshevik deputy and police agent, 1205
Malta, 653, 655-656
Maltese Order of the Knights of St. John of Jerusalem, 654
Manchuria, 1169, 1173, 1263-1265; occupied by Russia, 1268, 1270; and Portsmouth Treaty, 1278; partition of, 1282
Manifesto of October 17 (1905), 1177, 1184, 1186, 1188, 1190; public response to, 1178-1179, 1203
Manteuffel, Edwin Hans Karl, Count, Field Marshal, 857, 966
Maria Aleksandrovna, Empress, wife of Alexander II, 882, 996
Maria Fedorovna, Empress, widow of Paul I, 658, 671, 745, 748 n.
Maria Fedorovna, Empress, wife of Alexander III, 959 n., 1086, 1197
Marie Louise, Empress of France, 670, 674
Martos, I. P., sculptor, 735
Martov, L. (J. O. Zederbaum), Menshevik, 1148, 1451
Marx, Karl, 850, 1071-1073, 1123
Marxism, Russian, 808, 1064, 1073, 1152-1153; beginnings of, 1123-1124, 1148-1151. *See also* Bolshevik Party, Lenin, Mensheviks, Plekhanov, Russian Social Democratic Labor Party
Masséna, André, Duke de Rivoli, Marshal, 652
Mechnikov, I. I., biologist, 1049-1050
Mehemet Ali, Pasha of Egypt, 828, 832, 836-837, 844, 846-847
Melbourne, Viscount, 842
Melnikov, P. L., General, 934
Melnikov, Pavel (Andrew Pechersky), author, 1061
Mendeleev, D. I., chemist, 1049
Mensheviks (Menshevik Faction of Russian Social Democratic Labor Party), 1428, 1443; origins of, 1150-1151; reject alliance with liberals (1904), 1170; dominate 1905 Soviet, 1177; and elections to first Duma, 1189; and the press, 1239; attitude of, towards the war, 1368; and war industries committees, 1370; and cooperation with liberals, 1390-1391; and peace manifesto, 1396; control trade unions, 1421; and second congress of Soviets, 1451-1452; "internationalists," 1451-1452; representation of, in Constituent Assembly, 1462
Menshikov, A. S., Prince, General, 777,

Index

874-875; mission to Constantinople (1853), 863-865
Merchant marine, 711, 791, 937; predominance of foreigners in, 711, 937
Merchants, granted right to own populated estates, 717; social status of, 790-791; exempt from recruitment, 907; land purchases by, 929; and control of industry, 930
Merder, Charles, Captain, 880
Merezhkovsky, D. S., author, 1244-1245, 1397-1398
Merv, annexed, 982, 984, 986, 1128
Meshchersky, V. P., Prince, journalist, 1120, 1143-1144, 1167
von Metternich, C. W. L., Prince, 635-637, 643, 668, 683-684, 686-689, 829, 834, 836, 840-841, 846, 850, 852
von Metternich, Paul Wolff, Count, ambassador, 1289
Meyendorf, P. K., Baron, ambassador, 858
Meyendorff, F. K., Baron, diplomat, 958
Meyerhold, V. E., producer, 1252
Mezentsev, N. V., General, 1081
Miasoedov, S. N., Colonel, 1331-1332 n.
Michael, Grand Duke, brother of Alexander I, 738, 748, 750, 778, 885
Michael, Grand Duke, brother of Alexander II, 983; and war with Turkey, 999-1000, 1002-1003
Michael Alexandrovich, Grand Duke, brother of Nicholas II, 1381-1382, 1386
Mickiewicz, Adam, author, 609-610
Middleton, John, American diplomat, 685
Mieroslawski, Ludwik, General, 909, 914
Mikhailov, M. I., novelist, 1074
Mikhailovsky, Nicholas, literary critic, 1064, 1072
Milan Obrenovich, Prince and King of Serbia, 1293; and war with Turkey (1876), 993, 995; and war with Bulgaria (1885), 1133
Military colonies, 636, 646, 648-649, 700-701 n., 719-720, 728

Military League, 1433
Military Medical Academy, 1042
Militsa, Grand Duchess, 1146
Miliukov, P. N., 1164, 1168, 1170, 1173, 1256, 1372, 1382, 1432 n., 1434, 1436, 1441, 1475; leader of Constitutional Democratic Party, 1188-1189; and proposed cadet cabinet, 1192-1193; and Viborg appeal, 1192-1193 n.; demands annexation of Constantinople, 1348, 1351, 1396, 1398; denounces Empress and Stürmer, 1364, 1373; foreign minister, 1385-1386; on war to victory, 1395-1399, 1413; outlines program of annexations, 1396, 1398; and peace manifesto, 1397; policies of, attacked, 1399, 1400, 1405, 1426; on Lenin's impending arrest, 1404 n.
Miliutin, Dimitry, Count, war minister, 880, 994, 999, 1026, 1036, 1040, 1090-1091; and army reforms, 907-908
Miliutin, Nicholas, official, 887-888, 897, 900, 907, 917
Miliutin, V. P., Bolshevik, 1459
Miloradovich, Nicholas, Count, General, 747, 750
Milosh Obrenovich, Prince of Serbia, 954
Minkin, Anastasia, 649
Mir Iskustva, art society and journal, 1244, 1246-1248
Mishchenko, A. V., General, 1274
Mobilization, Russian (1914), 1211, 1353, 1375
"Mobilization of industry," 1356, 1367, 1369
Mohommad, Shah of Persia, 843
Mohrenheim, Arthur, Baron, ambassador, 1138
Moldavia, 707 n., 743, 785, 827, 831, 860, 862, 870-871, 873; annexation of, demanded and abandoned (1804-1811), 655, 673; Tilsit agreement and, 667; Russian protectorate over (1829), 833, 835; constitution of, amended, 852; Treaty of Paris (1856) and, 950; and founding of Rumania, 954, 960
Molodetsky, I., revolutionary, 1083
Molokhane, 798 n.

Molotov, V. M. (Scriabin), Bolshevik, 1401
Mongolia, 978-979, 1282
Monroe, James, President, 692
Monroe Doctrine, 691, 974
Montenegro, 863, 870, 954, 991, 997, 1339; and war with Turkey (1876), 993-996, 1001; San Stefano and, 1011, 1013; Treaty of Berlin and, 1019-1020, 1022; and Balkan wars (1911–1913), 1300-1304; conquered, 1331
de Montmorency, Duke, diplomat, 688
Morgan, J. P., banker, 1279
Morkov, A. I., Count, ambassador, 654
Morley of Blackburn, John Morley, Viscount, 1287, 1318
Moroccan crisis (1905), 1289-1290
Morozov, Savva, industrialist and art collector, 1247
Moscow, the French in (1812), 676-677; insurrection in (1905), 1182, 1195; capital transferred to (1918), 1473-1474
Moscow, university of, 723, 726, 803, 805, 1032, 1034, 1046, 1050, 1056, 1157, 1162, 1233, 1241, 1348
Moscow Agricultural Society, 1356
Moscow Art Theatre, 1251-1252
Moscow People's Bank, 1227
Moscow Slavonic Benevolent Committee, 990
Moscow Soviet of Workers' and Soldiers' Deputies, 1443-1444
Mukden, battle of (1905), 1174, 1274-1275, 1385 n.
Münchengrätz, Convention of (1833), 840-841, 845-846, 849
Murad V, Sultan, 993
Murat, Joachim, Prince, Marshal, 678
Muravev, Alexander, Decembrist, 740, 916
Muravev, M. N., 722
Muravev, M. N., Count, foreign minister, 1259-1261, 1266-1267, 1284
Muravev, Michael, Count, 740, 916, 1075; and Russification of western provinces, 916-917
Muravev, N. N., General, 836, 876
Muravev, Nikita, Decembrist, 740, 742-744
Muravev-Amursky, Nicholas, Count, General, and expansion in Far East, 977-979, 983
Muravev-Apostol, Mathew, Decembrist, 740
Muravev-Apostol, Serge, Colonel, Decembrist, 740, 751
Muromtsev, S. A., cadet leader, 1157, 1191-1193
Mürtzsteg, agreement of (1903), 1284, 1292
Music, 821-822, 1030, 1048, 1050-1052, 1248-1251, 1254; neo-Russian school of, 1051-1052, 1250
Mussorgsky, M. P., composer, 1051-1052, 1249

Nakhimov, P. S., Admiral, 867, 875-876
Nanking, Treaty of (1842), 977
Napier, Sir Charles, Admiral, 847, 873
Napier, Francis, Baron Napier and Baron Ettrick, ambassador, 957
Naples, Kingdom of, 634, 645, 658, 688, 740
Napoleon I, Emperor, 637-638, 642, 645, 652-654, 656, 659, 695, 700, 706, 736, 841 n., 845, 853; at Tilsit, 661-664; encourages Russia to annex Finland, 665; and Sweden, 665-666; plans for Franco-Russian conquests (1808), 666-667; at Erfurt, 667-668; indifference of, to fate of Poland, 669-670, 673; and dynastic alliance with Russia, 670; and Franco-Russian convention on Poland, 670-671; and 1812 war, 671-678, 720, 1330; and "war of liberation," 680; and first Peace of Paris, 681; escapes from Elba and second Peace of Paris, 684-686
Napoleon III, Emperor, 827, 854, 858-859, 964; and dispute over Holy Places, 861-862; and 1853 crisis, 865-868; and Crimean War, 872, 875, 877; offers "peace with honor," 948; and Congress of Paris, 948-950; and *rapprochement* with Russia, 953-956; and Rumanian unification, 954; and diplomatic intervention on behalf of Poland, 956-958; overthrown, 966
Napoleonic wars, 651-685, 708-709,

Index

719-720, 724, 734 n., 738, 759, 1360
Napravnik, E. F., conductor, 1250
Naryshkin, Dimitry, 632
Naryshkin, Maria, 632
Naryshkin, Sophie, 640
National minorities, alliance for defense of, 1170; in first Duma, 1191; in second Duma, 1198; representation of, reduced, 1200; persecution of, 1202, 1257; and the press, 1239; military formations of, 1408, 1422; national movement among, 1421-1425; congress of (1917), 1425; and right of secession, 1427-1428; and State Conference, 1435. *See also* Finland, Jews, Poland, Ukraine
Nationalism, Russian, 1258; Gogol on, 818; panslavism and, 987; Dostoevsky and, 1059-1060; Katkov and, 1065; resurgence of, 1074; Alexander III and, 1086-1088; and school policies, 1115-1116; and persecution of national minorities, 1116-1117; and religious intolerance, 1117; and Bulgarian crisis, 1134-1135; and Finland, 1157-1158, 1202-1203; Stolypin and, 1193, 1202-1204; and 1907 election law, 1200; and annexation of Bosnia and Herzegovina, 1295-1296; and Balkan wars (1911–1913), 1304-1305; and occupation of Galicia, 1326-1327, 1330. *See also* "Official patriotism," "Orthodoxy, autocracy, and nationality," doctrine of
Nationalists (Party), in third and fourth Dumas, 1200
Navarino, battle of (1827), 830, 867
Navy, Russian, in Turkish war (1877–1878), 970, 1009; visits the United States, 974; mutinies in (1905–1906), 1174, 1180, 1182, 1195; in Japanese war, 1271-1273, 1275-1277, 1334; visits Portsmouth, 1287; in World War I, 1334; Black Sea, hoists Ukrainian flag, 1424
Nazimov, V. I., governor general, 884-885
Nebogatov, N. I., Admiral, 1276
Nechaev, Serge, revolutionary, 1070-1073, 1079-1080
Nekludov, A., diplomat, 1300, 1304, 1306

Nekrasov, N. A., poet and editor, 817, 819, 1062
Nekrasov, N. V., cadet deputy, 1383-1384, 1399, 1428, 1434
Nelidov, A. I., ambassador, 1007, 1283
Nelidov, Barbara, 756
Nelson, Horatio, Viscount, Admiral, 652
Nemirovich-Danchenko, V. I., author, 1252
Neratov, A. A., diplomat, 1300, 1305-1306
Nesselrode, Charles, Count, foreign minister, 647, 683, 687, 689, 836, 845, 851-852, 859, 861, 863, 948, 956; on future of Ottoman Empire, 826, 833; on Dardanelles and intervention in Turkey, 839; and Straits convention (1841), 847; and London conversations (1844), 849-850; and ultimatum to Turkey (1853), 864-865; and expected uprising of Balkan Christians, 872-873; hostility of, towards Danubian principalities, 950; and expansion in Far East, 979
Nesterov, M. V., painter, 1247-1248
New Zealand, and Japanese expansion, 1337
Ney, Michael, Marshal, 879
Nicholas, Grand Duke, brother of Alexander II, and Turkish war, 999-1000, 1002-1005, 1007-1009, 1016
Nicholas, Grand Duke, brother of Alexander III, 1086
Nicholas, Prince and King of Montenegro, 993, 995, 1301, 1304
Nicholas I, Emperor, 629, 689, 701 n., 704, 714, 717, 720, 738, 745, 791, 795, 797, 798 n., 800, 803-804, 845, 879-881, 1030, 1041, 1047-1048 n., 1048, 1117; and dynastic crisis (1825), 745-748; and December insurrection, 748-752, 754-755; characterization of, 773-776; views of, on monarchical government, 754; and Holy Alliance, 755, 828-829, 840, 844-845, 951; and reforms, 755, 765-769, 903; and Poland, 756; and Barbara Nelidov, 756; death of, 756, 871, 882, 910; crowned king of Poland, 757; and Polish insurrection, 758-760, 762-765, 909, 912; and codifica-

Nicholas I (*continued*)
tion, 770; and security police, 771-772; quasi-dictatorship of, 773; and the nobility, 774-775; and the peasants, 777-779; and the state peasants, 785-786; and currency reform, 787; and taxation of spirits, 788; and road and railway construction, 789; and "official nationalism," 797; and the Jews, 806 n.; and censorship, 812-814; and Pushkin, 816; and art, 823-824; and dissolution of Ottoman Empire, 826-827; and British constitutional government, 827; hostility of, towards France, 827, 845, 848, 850; and Seymour conversations, 827 n., 860-861, 865; indifference to fate of Balkan Christians, 827-828, 864; ultimatum to Turkey (1826), 828; and Greek independence, 828-829, 832-834; and Turkish war, 830-833; proposes intervention in France (1830), 835; and intervention in Turkey (1833), 836-837; and the Russo-Turkish alliance, 838-839; Brunnow on foreign policy of, 845; and near eastern crisis (1839), 846-847; and London conversations (1844), 849-850; and 1848 revolution, 851, 858; and intervention in Danubian principalities, 851-852; and intervention in Hungary, 853-855, 870; and German unification under Prussia (1850), 855-858; and Schleswig-Holstein, 856-857, 961; and Napoleon's imperial title, 859, 862; and dispute over Holy Places, 861-863; proposes alliance with Turkey (1853), 863; accepts "Vienna note," 866; and outbreak of Crimean War, 868-869; and wartime diplomatic negotiations, 870-871, 875; expects uprising of Balkan Christians, 872; and defeat in Crimean War, 877-878; and Finland, 919

Nicholas II, Emperor, 633, 1087-1088, 1212, 1222 n., 1284, 1339, 1342, 1385; characterization of, 1141-1147; aversion of, for representative government, 1142-1143, 1185, 1190; address to zemstvo delegates, 1147, 1156; hostility to Finland, 1158; rejects Sviatopolk-Mirsky's constitutional proposals, 1171; receives labor delegates (1905), 1172; and Union of the Russian People, 1175, 1201; and October manifesto, 1177-1178; and Witte, 1177-1178, 1185, 1190; and first Duma, 1190; and proposed liberal cabinet, 1192; and the Jews, 1203; and Stolypin, 1204; on drunkenness and state monopoly of spirits, 1211; and land expropriation, 1214; and direction of foreign policy, 1259; and universal peace, 1260-1261; and expansion in Far East, 1262-1264; and Kiaochow, 1266, 1284; and Yalu concession, 1269; and recall of Alekseev, 1272; and dispatch of Baltic fleet to Far East, 1275-1276; approves occupation of Bosphorus (1896), 1283-1284; and proposed German alliance, 1284-1285; and Björkö Treaty, 1285-1286; and annexation of Bosnia and Herzegovina, 1295, 1296 n.; allegedly offered Constantinople by Bulgarians (1913), 1305; and von Sanders' appointment, 1307; and outbreak of World War I, 1316-1319; commander in chief, 1321, 1361-1362; and conquest of Galicia, 1327-1328; and Sukhomlinov, 1331-1332 n.; bars Greek participation in Dardanelles campaign, 1346; surrenders to Empress and Rasputin, 1362, 1364-1366; on ministerial changes, 1365; and Union of Zemstvos, 1366-1367; visits Duma, 1372; ignores appeals and warnings, 1373; and outbreak of the revolution, 1380; abdicates, 1381-1382; on Kerensky, 1436 n.; murdered, 1436 n.

Nicholas Nikolaevich, Grand Duke, 1178, 1201, 1320-1321, 1323, 1327-1328, 1334, 1344-1345, 1350, 1362, 1381

Nicholson, Sir Arthur, Lord Carnock, ambassador, 1287-1288, 1297, 1299, 1318

Nicodimus, Bishop, 798 n.

Nihilism, 1063, 1065

Nijinsky, Waslav, dancer, 1254

Nikolai, Alexander, Baron, minister of education, 1092

Index

Nikolsburg, preliminary peace of (1866), 964-965
de Noailles, Antoine C. J., Duke de Poix, ambassador, 736-737
Nobility, The. *See Dvorianstvo*
Nogin, V. P., Bolshevik, 1459
Norov, A. S., minister of education, 1031, 1034, 1041
North German Confederation, 964, 966
Northern Society, 742-745, 749
Norway, 673, 810 n., 1226, 1291
Novibazar, sanjak, 1011, 1020, 1126, 1284, 1294-1295, 1301
Novikov, E. P., ambassador, 1007, 1025
Novikov, N. I., 740
Novosiltsev, Nicholas, 661, 671, 694, 706, 722; prepares draft constitution, 635, 701, 736; mission to London (1804), 655-656, 656 n.

Obolensky, Eugene, Prince, Decembrist, 742, 745, 749-750
Obolensky, I. M., Prince, 1166
Obrok (annual payment to state or landowner), of serfs, raised, 718, 783; and emancipation, 885-886, 889, 926
Obruchev, N. N., General, 999, 1009
Octobrists. *See* Union of October 17
Odessa, university of, 1046, 1050
Officers' Union, 1433, 1442
"Official patriotism," 799-800, 809, 814, 819, 824
Ogarev, N. P., radical journalist, 1068
Old-believers, 798 n., 1061, 1119 n. *See also* Dissenters
Oldenburg, Duchy of, 672
Oldenburg, George, Prince of, 632, 640 n., 672
Oldenburg, Peter, Grand Duke of, 965
Olga, Queen of Greece, 959 n.
Olmütz "punctation" (1850), 858
Omar Pasha, 874
Open Door in China, Russia and, 1267, 1270, 1279, 1282
Opium War, 977
Oprichnina, 772
Orloff, Nicholas, pianist, 1250
Orlov, A. F., Prince, 772, 838-839, 870; at Congress of Paris (1856), 948-950
Orlov, Anne, Countess, 646
Orlov, Michael, General, 742
Orlov, Vasili, 652

"Orthodoxy, autocracy, and nationality," doctrine of, 754, 797-800, 803, 1087
Osman Pasha, 1004
Ostrovsky, Alexander, playwright, 735, 819-820
Otto I, King of Greece, 834, 958-959
Ottoman Empire, dissolution of, Russian view on, 826-827, 833, 849, 859-860; America's alleged interest in, 974; panslavism and, 988, 989 n.; and the Austro-German-Russian treaty (1881), 1125-1126; and allied wartime agreements, 1347-1352. *See also* Turkey
Oubril, Peter, diplomat, 658-659, 661, 854
Oyama, Marquis, Marshal, 1274
Ozerov, M., diplomat, 863 n.
Ozerov, Vladislav, playwright, 735
Ozol, I. P., deputy, 1198

Padlewski, Zygmunt, 913
Pahlen, C. I., Count, minister of justice, 905, 1078, 1120
Pahlen, Peter, Count, 631
Painting, 735, 822-823, 1052-1054, 1245-1248, 1254
Paléologue, Maurice, ambassador, 882, 1335-1336, 1347, 1350-1351 n., 1352, 1396
Palmerston, Henry John Temple, Viscount, 835-836, 842-844, 846-852, 854-855, 857, 859, 865, 868, 877; anti-Russian sentiment of, 827, 840, 952-953, 1349; and threat to India, 831, 841, 844; and the Unkiar-Skelesi Treaty, 840-841, 846; and peace with victory, 871-872, 948; and Crimean campaign, 874-875; and Congress of Paris, 948-949; opposes unification of Rumania, 954; and diplomatic intervention on behalf of Poland, 956-957; and abrogation of Black Sea clause, 967
Pamir, annexations in region of (1895), 982 n.
Panin, N. P., Count, 631, 652
Panin, Sophie, Countess, 1463
Panin, V. N., Count, minister of justice, 887, 903, 906
Panslavism, Russian, 809-810, 827, doc-

Panslavism (*continued*)
trine of, 987-990, 1014; Alexander III and, 990, 996, 1025, 1087-1088; and revolt of Herzegovina (1875), 991; and Balkan war (1876), 994-998; social complexion of, 995-996; the government and, 995-996; opposed by foreign office, 1007; anti-British campaign of, 1009; program of, abandoned by government, 1027, 1125-1126; collapse of, 1029; Bulgarian nationalism and, 1130; and Balkan wars (1911–1913), 1300, 1304-1305

Paris, Congress of (1856), 871, 947-951

Paris, Treaty of (1806), 957; (1814), 681, 684; (1815), 684; (1856), 883, 947, 949-952, 954, 1008, 1012, 1014-1015, 1021, 1291-1292; revision of, demanded, 966; amended, 967, 969, 1027

Parker, Sir Hyde, Admiral, 652

Parker, Sir William, Admiral, 855

Pashitch, N., prime minister, 1315, 1342

Paskevich, F. I., Prince, 887

Paskevich, I. F., Prince of Warsaw, 761-762, 831, 853-854, 874, 910; and integration of Poland with Russia, 763-765, 912, 917

Passports, 895, 925, 1101-1102, 1104, 1215, 1221

Patriotic Society, Polish, 707, 757, 759

Paul I, Emperor, 630-631, 639, 647, 651-652, 654, 693-695, 705 n., 708, 716, 723, 745, 771 n., 774, 784, 815; annexes Georgia, 673 n.

Pavlov, I. P., physiologist, 1049

Pavlova, Anna, ballerina, 1253-1254

Pazukhin, A. D., and local government reform, 1093-1095, 1098

Peasant War, 774

Peasants, uprisings of, 720, 922, 1159, 1221; "obligated" (1842), 778; not represented in provincial committees, 886; emancipation of, 888-890; "temporary obligated," 889, 1101; and redemption payments, 890-892, 1101, 1159, 1212; government of, 890, 893-896, 1221; status of, under emancipation acts, 890-896, 906; in western and Polish provinces, 916-917, 1101; disappointed with emancipation, 922-923; landholding of (1877), 923; and size of allotments, 923-924, 1100-1101; obstacles to progressive farming of, 924; yield of land of, 924, 1222; and resettlement, 924-925, 1101-1102, 1104, 1218-1219; land purchases by, 925, 929 n., 1101, 1217-1218; land leasing by, 925-927, 1101; and survivals of serfdom, 926-927; poverty of, 927, 1159, 1212, 1223; long for more land, 927-928, 1224, 1412-1413; disproportionate tax burden of, 943; alleged revolutionary proclivities of, 1073; and movement "to the people," 1076-1079, 1100; and Chigirin conspiracy, 1079-1080; representation of, in proposed *zemskii sobor* (1881), 1091; land captains and, 1093-1095, 1099, 1215, 1221; 1890 zemstvo act and, 1096-1097; and breaking up of households, 1102; and restrictions on allotment land, 1103, 1221-1222; submissiveness of, 1139; importance of, in populist and socialist revolutionary doctrine, 1153; and 1905 agrarian revolution, 1174, 1180; favored by 1905 election law, 1176; in first Duma, 1190; and 1907 election law, 1199; redemption debt of, written off, 1214; corporal punishment for, abolished, 1214, 1221; passport disabilities of, removed, 1215, 1221; and the Stolypin land reform, 1215-1217, 1220-1221, 1224; increase their landholding, (1905–1914), 1218; legal status of, after the reform, 1221-1222; living standards of, 1222-1223, 1257; and handicrafts, 1232 n.; social isolation of, 1256; farmed area of, expanded, 1354; effects of prohibition on, 1359; Progressive Bloc and, 1371; economic status of, in wartime, 1376-1377; and draft evasion, 1377; and longing for peace, 1377; meaning of revolution to, 1412-1413; Soviets and committees of, 1414-1415; and agrarian revolution (1917), 1415-1417, 1446, 1475; Bolshevik propaganda and, 1417

Index

Peasants' Union, 1173, 1181, 1182 n.
Peking, Treaty of (1860), 978
People's Socialists (Party), 1197-1198
People's Will, revolutionary society, 1082-1084, 1120, 1122, 1152-1153
Pereverzev, P. N., minister of justice, 1431-1432
Perov, V. G., painter, 1053
Perovsky, Sophie, revolutionary, 1076, 1082, 1084
Perovsky, V. A., Count, General, 844, 980
Persia, 754-755 n., 841, 981, 1261; war with Russia (1804-1813), 674 n.; (1826–1828), 787, 830-831; Anglo-Russian rivalries in, 842-843, 984, 986; Treaty of Berlin and, 1019; Anglo-Russian Convention (1907) and, 1287-1288, 1309-1310
Pestel, Paul, Decembrist, 737, 740-741, 743-745, 751
Pétain, Henri Philippe, Marshal, 1412
Peter I, Emperor, 694, 715, 809
Peter III, Emperor, 770
Peter Karageorgevich, King of Serbia, 1293
Petipas, Marius, choreographer, 1253-1254
Petlyura, S., Ukrainian leader, 1424
Petrashevsky. *See* Butashevich-Petrashevsky
Petrograd, renamed St. Petersburg, 1320; allied conference in (1917), 1334-1335, 1351, 1381, 1406
Petrograd Association of Manufacturers, 1419
Petrograd Soviet of Workers' and Soldiers' Deputies, 1381, 1386, 1388-1397, 1399, 1409, 1414, 1419, 1422, 1429, 1434-1435, 1443-1444
Petrova, Valentina, 1408 n.
Petrunkevich, I. P., zemstvo leader, 1067
Philaret, Archbishop, 746-747
Philaret, Metropolitan, 888, 906
Philippe, M., impostor, 1145-1146
Photius, Archimandrite, 641, 646
Phull, K. L. A., General, 675
Pichon, Stephen, foreign minister, 1296
Picot (Georges–Picot), C. F., 1351
Pilsudski, Joseph, Marshal, 1324
Pirogov, N. I., educator, 805

Pisarev, Dimitry, literary critic, 1063, 1074-1075
Pisemsky, Alexis, author, 1061
Pitt, William, prime minister, 653-654, 656-658
Pius IX, Pope, 858, 861, 957-958
von Plehve, V. K., minister of interior, 1075-1076, 1119, 1166, 1168-1169, 1175, 1269-1270, 1277
Plekhanov, George, social democrat, 1081-1082, 1123, 1148-1150, 1396, 1403
Pleshcheev, A. N., poet, 812, 1062
Pobedonostsev, K. P., chief procurator, and panslavism, 996, 1025; and Alexander III, 1088-1089, 1098; and representative government, 1089-1090, 1192; anti-Semitism of, 1096, 1119-1120, 1175; and counter-reforms, 1102; on censorship, 1111-1112; on "estate" (class) principle in schools, 1114; on Church schools, 1115-1116, 1237; intolerance of, 1117; and Nicholas II, 1142, 1147, 1157-1158, 1171-1172; attempts on life of, 1166; Witte on, 1185
Pogodin, M. P., historian, 799, 990
Poincaré, Raymond, President, 1229, 1289, 1301, 1335, 1339; visits Russia, 1309, 1314; and outbreak of World War I, 1316, 1318
Pokrovsky, N. N., foreign minister, 1336, 1351, 1364, 1396
Poland, 634, 702, 718, 736, 756, 810 n., 845, 902, 904, 948, 953, 955-956, 966, 1422, 1425; annexation of, demanded (1804), 655; Russian fear of restoration of, 658; and Napoleonic invasion, 674-675, 705; Congress of Vienna and, 682-684, 692, 705; constitution of (1815), 705-706, 911; abrogated, 707; trade relations of, 712; the Decembrists and, 743-74; insurrection (1830–1831) in, 757-762, 767, 787, 834-835, 853, 1117; and Organic Statute (1832), 762-763, 911, 918; Russification of, 764-765, 810, 1000, 1116; slavophilism hostile to, 810; and 1848 revolution, 850, 852, 856; proposed severance of, from Russia, 872; national movement in, 909-912; and 1863 insur-

Poland (*continued*)
rection, 913-915, 941, 944, 1117; and Russian liberal and revolutionary movement, 914-915, 1065, 1070, 1074; administrative assimilation of, 917-918, 1075; anti-Russian sentiment in (1855), 947; and Anglo-French diplomatic intervention, 956-958, 973-974; panslavism and, 988, 989 n., 990; and revolutionary movement (1904–1905), 1170, 1179; representation of, in first, second, and third Dumas, 1191, 1198, 1200; and World War I, 1322, 1324-1325, 1329-1330, 1332, 1334, 1342, 1469; Russian plans for (1914), 1323-1324, 1347; Progressive Bloc and, 1371; independence of, conceded, 1422, 1427, 1464 n. See also Warsaw, Duchy of

Polevoy, N. A., playwright, 819

Poliakov, financier, 1028

Police, ministry of, 728

Polish Democratic Society, 909

Polish Military Academy, 758

Polish National Party, 1170 n.

Polish Rifle Brigade, 1422

Polish Socialist Party, 1170 n., 1182 n.

Political parties, 1112 n., 1184, 1188-1191, 1197

Polivanov, A. A., General, 1320, 1331, 1363 n., 1364 n., 1372, 1378, 1394

Polkovniko, Colonel, 1448

Poll tax, 786, 895, 907, 943, 1041; abolished, 1101-1102, 1104, 1107

Polner, T. I., zemstvo leader, 1384

Polonsky, Jacob, poet, 819, 1062

Poniatowski, Joseph, Prince, General, 680

Ponsonby, John, Viscount, ambassador, 838, 841-842, 844-845

Population, urban, 714 n., 720, 781, 1235 n.; servile, 784; total, 784 n., 1046, 1119, 1235 n.; Slavic, 988 n., and school attendance, 1046-1047, 1234-1238; dissenters in, 1119; pressure of, and migration to Siberia, 1219; and literacy, 1235, 1256; of Galicia, 1327 n.; and army drafts, 1353

Populism, 1072-1074, 1076, 1100; and movement "to the people," 1077-1079, 1100; and terrorism, 1079, 1081; social complexion of, 1084; decline of, 1122-1123; revival of, 1148, 1152

Port Arthur, 1270, 1272, 1275; annexed by Russia, 982 n., 1266; capitulates, 1273; ceded to Japan, 1278-1279

Portsmouth, Treaty of (1905), 1176, 1178, 1277-1279, 1282

Portugal, 634, 645, 663, 674, 688, 740, 957

Posen, Grand Duchy of, 684

"Possessionary" enterprises, 714 n., 715; difficulties of, 793-794; effects of emancipation on, 930

"Possessionary" peasants, 714 n., 715, 792-794, 930

Postal service, 937

Potemkin, battleship, mutiny of, 1174

Potemkin, Gregory, Prince of Taurida, 1191

Pourtalès, Friedrich, Count, ambassador, 1297-1298

Pozzo di Borgo, Charles, Count, 679, 683, 690, 737

de Pradt, Abbé, 686

Prague, Peace of (1866), 964

Preobrazhenskaya, Olga, ballerina, 1253

Press, The, educational, 1235; on eve of World War I, 1238-1239, 1255-1256. See also Censorship

Pressburg, Peace of (1805), 657, 663 n.

Princip, G., Bosnian revolutionary, 1312

Pritchett, V. S., author, 1070

Prodamet, 1225

Professional unions, 1156, 1170, 1173, 1177

Progressists (Party), 1200

Progressive Bloc, 1365, 1371-1372, 1374, 1381

Prokofiev, Serge, composer, 1250

Prokopovich, S. N., economist, 1450

Protasov, N. A., chief procurator, 798 n.

Protectionism, and Tariff Act of 1810, 672, 711; of 1816, 711-712; of 1819, 712; of 1822, 791; of 1850, 791; of 1857, 791, 940; of 1868, 940, 1109; of 1891, 1108-1109; and Russo-German tariff war, 1109-1110; monetary reform and, 1207; and Tariff Act of 1903, 1231-1232

Index

Protestantism, panslavism and, 988; persecution of, 1117, 1257
Protopopov, A. D., minister of interior, 1365-1366, 1376, 1387, 1389
Proudhon, Pierre-Joseph, 808, 1071
Proust, Marcel, 1059-1060
Provisional committee of the Duma, 1380-1382, 1386, 1392-1393, 1435
Provisional Council of the Republic (pre-parliament), 1427, 1435-1436, 1448, 1456
Provisional Government, 1351, 1357, 1360, 1379, 1434, 1455; formed, 1382, 1390-1391; complexion of, 1383-1388; and Petrograd Soviet, 1391; program of, 1392; and local administration, 1392-1393; and Army Order No. 1, 1393-1394; and peace through victory, 1395-1396; and fiction of Russia's will to win the war, 1395-1396, 1405, 1475; and declaration on war aims, 1398-1399; reorganized on "coalition" basis, 1400; branded as capitalist by Lenin, 1402, 1443; and June offensive, 1409-1410; and land reform, 1413, 1416; and peasant Soviets, 1415; and factory committees, 1419-1420; and Poland, 1422; and Finland, 1422-1423; and Ukraine, 1424-1425; and congress of national minorities, 1425; and first coalition, 1426-1429; cleavage in, 1428-1430; and June demonstration, 1429; repudiated by Kronstadt Soviet, 1429; and anarchists, 1429; and July uprising, 1430-1433, 1442; and second coalition, 1433-1434; and Kornilov "mutiny," 1439; and third coalition, 1441-1442; and October insurrection, 1447-1450, 1454; arrested, 1450-1451; functions after October, 1457-1458
Prussia, 645, 841, 859, 881; and French alliance (1812), 673; Alexander I's support of, 636; and treaty with France (1802), 653; and proposed German federation, 655; and French alliance (1806), 657; and convention with Russia (1805), 657, 660; and war with France (1806), 659-660; and Tilsit, 662-664, 666; and Russian alliance (1813), 680; and Quadruple Alliance, 681, 686-687; and Congress of Vienna, 682-684; and Holy Alliance, 685, 689, 834, 840; and European Alliance, 687-690; trade convention with (1818), 712; and Polish insurrection (1830), 761-762; and Greek independence, 829; and Turkish crisis (1832–1833), 837; assumes no obligations in Levant (1833), 844-845; and near eastern crisis (1839), 846; and 1848 revolution, 850-851, 855-858; and war with Denmarks (1848), 856-857; and 1853 crisis, 865-869; and Crimean War, 869-872; and Congress of Paris (1856), 948; *rapprochement* with Russia, 955; and Polish insurrection (1863), 956, 961; and Schleswig-Holstein, 961-965; and war with France (1870), 966-967. *See also* Germany
Prutkov, Kosma, humorist, 1062
Public finance, 708-709, 786-789, 941-945, 1106-1107, 1206-1211, 1358-1359
Pugachev, Emilian, peasant leader, 815, 1079
Purishkevich, V. M., conservative deputy, 1198, 1201, 1365; denounces Rasputin, 1205, 1373; participates in Rasputin's murder, 1373
Pushkin, A. S., 730, 732, 739-740, 813, 817, 820, 1056, 1059, 1061, 1063, 1157, 1240; life and work, 733-734, 815-816
Putiatin, E. V., Count, Admiral, and Chinese treaty, 978; minister of education, 1031-1032

Quadruple Alliance (1814), 681, 686-687, 845
Quadruple Alliance (1834), 841

Rachau, K. K., architect, 1054
Radetsky, F. F., General, 1004
Radetzky, Joseph, Count, Field Marshal, 852
Radishchev, Alexander, 727, 729
Radoslavov, V., prime minister, 1340, 1468
Raevsky, Nicholas, General, 675
Raevsky, Vladimir, Major, 742

Railways, 787, 873; construction of, 789, 934, 942, 1224; and industrial recovery, 929; financing of, 935-936, 944-945, 1106-1108, 1208; Nikolaevsky, rumored sale of, 976; state management of, 1107-1108; breakdown of, 1355-1356, 1406, 1420

Rakhmaninoff, Serge, composer, 1250

Rasputin, Gregory, doctrine and influence, 1145-1147; ascendancy of, 1205, 1361-1366, 1372-1373, 1385; and temperance, 1211, 1359; and tsar's visit to the Duma, 1372; murdered, 1373-1374, 1381; and the revolution, 1374

Rawlinson, Sir Henry, publicist, 984, 986

Red Army, 1460, 1475

Red guards, 1432, 1442, 1447, 1454

Refugees, 1330, 1354-1355, 1359; special council on, 1370

Reichenbach, Treaty of (1813), 680, 689

Reichstadt, agreement of (1876), 997-998, 1012, 1014

Rennenkampf, E. K., General, 1322-1323

Repin, I. E., painter, 1053, 1246

Repnin, Nicholas, Prince, 683

Resanov, A. I., architect, 1054

Reutern, Michael, Count, minister of finance, 934, 942-943; and currency stabilization, 935, 944-945, 1106; opposes Turkish war, 945, 999-1000; and sale of Alaska, 976

Revolution, of 1830, 758, 767, 812, 834; of 1848, 804, 813, 850-858, 909; of 1905, 1142, 1148, 1171-1183, 1267, 1293

Revolutionary movement, zemstvos and, 752, 900-901; and Polish insurrection, 914-916; beginnings of, 1030, 1063-1065; and the Jews, 1047-1048 n.; and terrorism, 1067, 1078-1079; Herzen and, 1068-1070; Bakunin and, 1070-1072; Nechaev and, 1070-1072; Tkachev and, 1072; populism and, 1072-1073; centers of, in Russia, 1074; and crusade "to the people," 1076-1079; trial of leaders of, 1077-1078; and Chigirin conspiracy, 1079-1080; nature of, 1084-1085; decline of, 1122-1123, 1139-1140; revival of, 1147-1148; weakness and strength of, 1154-1155; and university students, 1163-1164; opposition of, to consultative Duma, 1176; decline of, after 1905, 1200-1201, 1204; reasons for appeal of, 1374; rise of, free from organized leadership, 1379. *See also* Bolshevik Party, December insurrection, Land and Freedom, Mensheviks, People's Will, Populism, Russian Social Democratic Labor Party, Socialist Revolutionary Party, Terrorism

de Richelieu, A. E. du Plessis, Duke, 687

Rieger, Francis Ladislav, Czech leader, 990

Rimsky-Korsakov, N. A., composer, 1051-1052, 1249, 1254

Ripon, F. J. Robinson, Viscount Goderich, Earl of, 830

Ripon, G. F. S. Robinson, Marquis of, 949, 1128

River shipping, 789

Rodzianko, M. V., president of State Duma, 1035, 1268, 1372, 1381

Roerich, N. K., painter, 1247-1248

Roman Catholic Church, 1257; properties of, secularized in Poland, 674; prosecution of, in Poland, 918, 1117; criticized by slavophiles, 987-988

Romme, Gilbert, mathematician, 694

Roosevelt, Theodore, President, 1174, 1260-1261 n., 1271, 1279; and the Peace of Portsmouth, 1277-1278

Ropet-Petroff, I. P., architect, 1054

Rose, H. H., diplomat, 865

Rostopchin, F. V., administrator, 671, 675 n., 679

Rostovtsev, J. I., General, 747-749, 752, 887; and the emancipation, 887-888, 893-894 n.

Roussin, Admiral, ambassador, 837

Rozhdestvensky, Z. P., Admiral, 1275-1276, 1284

Rubinstein, Anton, pianist and composer, 1050-1051

Rubinstein, Nicholas, pianist, 1051

Rukhlov, S. V., minister of transportation, 1355-1366

Index lxv

Rumania, 851-852, 997; Russia and unification of, 954; recognition of Prince Charles withheld, 961; panslavism and, 989; independence of, proclaimed, 1002; and the Turkish war (1877–1878), 1002-1004; San Stefano and, 1011, 1013, 1016; Treaty of Berlin and, 1019-1021; and Balkan wars (1911–1913), 1300-1303; and Triple Entente, 1310-1311; joins allies, 1333, 1336; wartime negotiations with, 1335, 1340-1341, 1343-1344

Rumelia, Tilsit Treaty and, 663

Rumiantsev, Nicholas, Count, chancellor, 635, 662, 668, 670, 672, 679, 683

Rumiantsev, S. P., Count, 717

Runich, Dimitry, school official, 725

Russell (Lord John), Earl, prime minister and foreign secretary, 855 n., 860, 865, 871, 956, 961, 985

Russell, Lord Odo, 968

Russian Academy, 729 n.

Russian American Company, 691-692, 977; liquidated, 975-976

Russian Assembly, 1174

Russian Bible Society, 641, 643-644, 646, 648-649, 724, 729 n.

Russian brigades in France and Macedonia, 1411-1412 n.

Russian Music Society, 1050-1051, 1248-1249

Russian Social Democratic Labor Party, 1124, 1182 n., 1188, 1205, 1242, 1387, 1390; founding of, 1149-1150; program of, 1150, 1152; splits into Bolsheviks and Mensheviks, 1150-1151; in first Duma, 1191; in second Duma, 1197-1198; in third and fourth Duma, 1200; decline of, 1201; and the press, 1239; attitude of, towards the war, 1368; and war industries committees, 1370; and provisional committee of the Duma, 1381. *See also* Bolshevik Party, Mensheviks

Russian Steamship Company, 937

Russo-American Treaty (1824), 691, 975

Russo-Chinese Bank, 1265, 1269

Russo-German Alliance (1887), 1090, 1125, 1135-1136, 1138

Russo-Japanese agreement (1896), 1266

Russo-Japanese War (1904–1905), 1108, 1110, 1142, 1148, 1158, 1168-1169, 1208, 1260, 1286, 1292, 1334, 1360, 1385 n.; cost of, 1209, 1278; forces engaged in, 1271; and naval warfare, 1272, 1275-1277; and siege of Port Arthur, 1272-1274; and Manchurian campaign, 1272-1275, 1277; economic factors and, 1282-1283

Russo-Montenegrin Convention (1910), 1301 n.

Russo-Rumanian agreement (1914), 1343

Russo-Rumanian Conventions (1877), 1002

Russo-Turkish peace treaty (1879), 1023

Russo-Turkish War (1877–1878), 880-881, 900, 945, 1001-1005, 1067, 1087, 1125, 1360; cost of, 941, 944, 1106; the navy and, 970, 1009; size of armies and military campaign, 1002-1005; and Russian peace program, 1007-1008; as a war of liberation, 1013 n., 1029, 1130; economic factors and, 1028

Rutenber, P., revolutionary, 1172 n.

Ruzsky, N. V., General, 1323, 1381

Rykov, A. I., Bolshevik, 1459

Ryleev, Konrad, Decembrist, 742, 745, 749-752

Rysakov, Nicholas, revolutionary, 1084

Ryss, Solomon, revolutionary, 1196

Sabler, V. K., chief procurator, 1205, 1361, 1363 n., 1369

Saburov, A. A., minister of education, 1034

Saburov, P. A., ambassador, 1026-1027, 1088, 1090, 1126-1127

Safonov, V. I., conductor, 1250

Saint Helens, Alleyne Fitzherbert, Baron, 652

Saint Julien, Count, ambassador, 635-637, 639

Saint-Léon, Charles Victor, choreographer, 1253

St. Petersburg, Conference of (1825), 689
St. Petersburg, Convention of (1801), 652
St. Petersburg, Treaty of (1875), 979; Treaty of (1881), 979
St. Petersburg, university of, 724-726, 805, 817, 1031-1032, 1046, 1049, 1056, 1071, 1165
St. Petersburg Historico-Philological Institute, 1038
St. Petersburg Soviet of Workers' Deputies (1905), 1176-1177, 1180-1182
de Saint Simon, Claude H. de Rouvroy, Count, 808, 811
Sakhalin Island, 977, 1277; annexed, 979; half of, ceded to Japan, 1278-1279
Salandra, Antonio, prime minister, 1339
Salisbury, Robert A. T. G. Cecil, Marquis of, 985, 1001, 1010 n.; on San Stefano, 1015-1016; negotiates with Shuvalov, 1017-1018; and agreement with Austria, 1018; and Congress of Berlin, 1019, 1021; on status of Straits, 1021, 1026
Salonika, 1333, 1345-1346
Saltykov-Shchedrin, Michael, author, 1061
Samarin, A. D., chief procurator, 1363 n.
Samarin, Yuri, slavophile, 780, 810, 813, 885, 887, 893 n., 915-917; on representative government, 1068
Samsonov, A. V., General, 1322
San Stefano, Treaty of (1878), 1008, 1010-1015, 1017-1021, 1024, 1028, 1125, 1130
Sand, Karl, German student, 740
von Sanders, Liman, General, 1306-1308, 1310
Sarajevo assassination, 1312
Sardinia, Kingdom of, 869, 948, 954
Savary, René, General, ambassador, 664
Savinkov, Boris, revolutionary, 1154, 1166, 1172, 1195, 1410, 1436, 1441; and Kornilov, 1437-1440
Savinsky, A. A., ambassador, 1341
Saxony, and the Grand Duchy of Warsaw, 663; and the Congress of Vienna, 683
Sazonov, E. S., revolutionary, 1167

Sazonov, S. D., foreign minister, 1259-1260, 1309, 1324, 1327; and the Bagdad railway, 1290-1291; and panslavism, 1300, 1304, 1308-1309 n.; and Balkan wars (1911-1913), 1300-1305; and opening of Straits (1911-1912), 1305-1306; and von Sanders' incident, 1306-1308; and the Straits conference (Jan., 1914), 1308; and Rumania, 1310-1311; and outbreak of World War I, 1314-1319; dismissed, 1335; and Dardanelles expedition, 1336 n., 1350; and concessions to Turkey, 1338-1339; and annexation of Constantinople, 1339, 1342, 1345-1352; and wartime negotiations with Italy, Bulgaria, Serbia, Rumania, and Greece, 1339-1346; and war aims, 1347-1352
von Schelling, Friedrich Wilhelm Joseph, philosopher, 807
Schiff, Jacob, banker, 1279
Schilling, Maurice, Baron, diplomat, 1315
Schleswig, Duchy of, 856-857, 961-965, 1447
Schmidt, N. P., Lieutenant, 1182
von Schön, Wilhelm Edward, Freiherr, foreign minister, 1296
Schönbrunn, Convention of (1873), 971-973
Schönbrunn, Treaty of (1809), 669-670
Schools, 695, law on organization of (1803), 722-723, 800; universities under Alexander I, 724-725; shortage of teachers in, 725; beginnings of classicism in, 725; statistics of (1824), 726; private, 726, 802; non-discrimination against Jews in, 726, 806 n., 1047 n.; liberal tendencies in, 739; under ministry of state domains, 785, 806, 1043; dissenters excluded from, 798 n.; "estate" (class) principle in, under 1828 law, 800-802; and classical studies, 801; universities under 1835 charter, 803, 1032; oppressive control of (1848-1850), 804; higher, cultural tradition of, 805; statistics of (1825-1854), 805-806; Church, 806, 1043, 1047, 1115-1116, 1235-1237; number of Jewish students in,

806 n., 1047 n.; Jewish, 806-807 n., 1047 n.; zemstvo, expenditure on, 899, 1236; military, under Miliutin, 907, 909, 1040; Russification of, in Poland, 918; budget appropriations for, 943, 1236; more liberal attitude towards, 1031; universities under 1863 charter, 1032-1033; higher, women barred from, 1032-1033, 1042, 1076; D. Tolstoy's reactionary policies in, 1033-1034; universities, under 1884 charter, 1034, 1113, 1163, 1232; gymnasiums, under 1864 law, 1034-1035, 1114; strengthening of classicism in, 1035-1037; "estate" (class) principle in, 1036, 1113-1115; gymnasiums, under 1871 law, 1036-1038, 1114; regimentation of teachers and students in, 1037-1038; and foreign teachers, 1038; failure of classicism in, 1038-1039; *Realschulen*, under 1872 law, 1039-1040; boarding and day, for girls, 1040-1042; universities for women, 1042, 1113, 1233; Sunday, 1042; primary, under 1864 law, 1043; compulsory attendance at, 1044, 1235-1236; county, under 1872 law, 1044-1045; and training of teachers, 1045; statistics of (1881), 1045-1047; number of Catholic and Protestant students in universities, 1046 n.; and circular on "cook's children," 1114-1115; and discrimination against Jewish students, 1115, 1121; policy of Russification in, 1116-1117; zemstvo, rumored taking over of, by government, 1167; higher, closed (1905), 1172; universities, autonomy granted to (1905), 1176, 1232-1233; universities, represented in State Council, 1187; higher (1905–1914), 1232-1233; secondary, mitigation of classicism in, 1233-1234; secondary (1895–1915), 1234-1235; primary (1890–1915), 1235-1238. *See also* University students

Schumann, Robert, composer, 1254
Schwarts, A. N., minister of education, 1233
Schwarzenberg, Felix, Prince, prime minister, 852-853, 857

Schwarzenberg, K. P., Prince, Field Marshal, 669, 678, 680-681
von Schweinitz, Hans Lothar, General, ambassador, 965, 1137
Science, 805, 1030, 1048-1050
Scriabin, A. N., composer, 1249-1250
Sculpture, 735, 824, 1054
Sébastiani, H. F. B., Count, General, 659
Second World War, 1360, 1425
Secret treaties (World War I), concluded, 1348-1352; publication of, demanded, 1399; annulled, 1452; published, 1467
Security police, abolished, 693; restored, 695; and censorship, 728, 813; and secret societies, 739; under Nicholas I, 771-772, 1083; under Alexander II, 906; and department of police, 1083; agents of, in terrorist organizations, 1154; and police-sponsored labor organizations, 1161-1163; Gapon agent of, 1171, 1172 n.; and Stolypin's assassination, 1196, 1204; under Stolypin, 1196-1197; and dissolution of second Duma, 1198; agent of elected Bolshevik deputy, 1205; agent of, on central war industries committee, 1376; report of, on national morale (1916), 1377-1378; foretold outbreak of revolution, 1401
Selivachev, V. J., General, 1378
Senate, 694-695, 757 n., 763, 766, 903, 906, 921, 1080, 1095; and dynastic crisis (1825), 746-747; and December insurrection, 749-751; status of, under Nicholas I, 767-768; remains supreme court under 1864 reform, 904; abolished, 1458
Seraphim, Metropolitan, 641, 646
Serbia, 828-829, 833, 860, 870, 954, 991, 1347; Treaty of Paris (1856) and, 950; panslavism and, 990, 995; and war with Turkey (1876), 993-996, 998-999; and Russian volunteers, 994-995, 998, 1012; Austro-Russian agreements (1876–1877) and, 997-998; San Stefano and, 1011-1012; Treaty of Berlin and, 1020; and war with Bulgaria (1885–1886), 1133, 1135; and "greater Serbia"

Serbia (*continued*)
movement, 1293; and annexation of Bosnia and Herzegovina, 1295, 1297-1299; and Balkan wars (1911–1913), 1299-1304; and outbreak of World War I, 1312-1317; and World War I, 1324, 1339-1341, 1343; conquered, 1331

Serfs, and ownership of industrial enterprises, 714-715; and industrial employment, 714-715; status of (1800–1825), 716-718; burden of, lightened in Poland, 760; status of, under Nicholas I, unchanged, 778-779; and "inventories" in western provinces, 779-780; economic status of, on eve of emancipation, 783; number of, 784; expect emancipation, 882. *See* Appanage peasants, Emancipation, Peasants, "Possessionary" peasants

Serge Alexandrovich, Grand Duke, 1172
Serov, Alexander, music critic, 822
Serov, V. A., painter, 1247
Servan de Gerbey, General, 719
Sevastopol, 825, 868, 1057; siege and fall of, 871, 874-876, 947, 999
Seward, William Henry, 976
Seymour, Sir George Hamilton, ambassador, 827 n., 860-861, 863, 865
Shakhovskoy, Alexander, Prince, playwright, 732, 735
Shakhovskoy, D. I., Prince, 1356
Shakhovskoy, V. N., Prince, minister of commerce, 1228, 1365
Shamil, Caucasian leader, 842, 980
Shauman, Eugene, Finnish nationalist, 1167
Shchapov, A. P., professor, 1031
Shcheglovitov, I. G., minister of justice, 1203-1204, 1363 n., 1369
Shchepin-Rostovsky, Dimitry, Prince, Captain, 750, 752
Shchepkin, M. S., actor, 735, 811 n.
Shcherbatov, Michael, Prince, 730
Shcherbatov, N. B., Prince, minister of interior, 1228, 1363, 1377
Shchukin, S. J. and D. J., art collectors, 1247
Sheremetev, Count, 718
Shevchenko, Taras, poet, 811, 825
Shimonoseki, Treaty of (1895), 1264, 1269-1270
Shingarev, A. I., cadet leader, 1463

Shipov, D. N., zemstvo leader, 1156, 1169-1170, 1192
Shirinsky-Shikhmatov, P. A., Prince, minister of education, 804, 1030
Shishkov, A. S., minister of education, 637, 729-730, 809, 812, 1114
Shornikov, Catherine, police agent, 1198
Shulgin, V. V., conservative deputy, 1371, 1381-1382, 1387
Shuvalov, P. A., Count, St. Petersburg marshal of nobility, 887
Shuvalov, P. P., Count, military governor, 1174
Shuvalov, Paul, Count, ambassador, 1135, 1137
Shuvalov, Peter, Count, ambassador, 984, 1006-1007, 1009-1010; negotiates with Salisbury, 1017-1018; at Congress of Berlin, 1018-1019; dismissed, 1025
Siberia, 880, 1222, 1225, 1357, 1368, 1372; colonization of, 924-925, 1104, 1213, 1217-1219
Siberia Railway Committee, 1104, 1142
Simonich, J. S., Count, diplomat, 843
Sino-Japanese Treaty (1885), 1263
Sino-Japanese War (1894–1895), 1264
Sino-Russian Alliance (1896), 1262, 1265, 1267-1268 n.
Sinope, battle of (1853), 867-868
Sipiagin, D. S., minister of interior, 1118, 1166-1168
Sistova, Bulgarian national assembly at, 1131
Skobelev, M. D., General, and expansion in central Asia, 981-983, 1128; and Turkish war, 1003; on conflict with Teutons, 1127
Skobelev, M. I., Menshevik, 1390, 1427-1428
Skoptsy (castrates), 798 n., 1118
Slavonic Benevolent Committees, 990, 994
Slavophilism, doctrine of, 798, 809-810, 987-988, 1068, 1091; government opposed to, 810; censorship and, 810, 1056, 1068; and the village commune, 893-894 n., 1102; and Polish insurrection, 915-916; Bakunin and, 1071; Sazonov and, 1300, 1304; Prince Lvov and, 1384
Slovaks, panslavism and, 988, 989 n.
Slowacki, Julius, author, 910

Index

Sobinov, Leonid, tenor, 1250
Sobolev, L. N., General, 1131
Social conditions (1800–1825), 716-721; prior to emancipation, 774-786, 824-825; in post-emancipation era, 921-929; under Alexander II, 1064-1085; in late nineteenth century, 1100-1106; on eve of World War I, 1255-1257; and lack of social unity, 1256, 1374; and fall of the monarchy, 1374-1379
Socialist Revolutionary Party, 1073, 1172 n., 1182 n., 1188, 1197-1198, 1387, 1390, 1428; founded, 1152; doctrine of, 1152-1153; terroristic organization of, 1153-1154, 1166; and political terror, 1166-1167, 1172, 1174, 1195; boycotts first Duma, 1189; in second Duma, 1197; boycotts third and fourth Dumas, 1200; decline of, 1201; and cooperation with liberals, 1390-1391; and peace manifesto, 1396; and peasant Soviets, 1414-1415; controls trade unions, 1421; and second congress of Soviets, 1451-1452; controls Constituent Assembly, 1461. *See also* Left Socialist Revolutionaries
Society for the Advancement of Literacy, 1157
Society of Circulating Exhibitions, 1053, 1246
Society for the Encouragement of Artists, 822
Society of the United Slavs, revolutionary organization, 743-744
Sokolnikov, G., Bolshevik, 1471
Sologub, Fedor (F. K. Terenikov), author, 1245
Solovev, Alexander, revolutionary, 1081
Solovev, S. M., historian, 805, 878, 1034, 1086, 1478
Solovev, Vladimir, philosopher, 816
Somov, K. A., painter, 1247
Sophie Frederica Dagmara, Princess of Denmark. *See* Maria Fedorovna, Empress, wife of Alexander III
Soult, N. J., Duke of Dalmatia, Marshal, 847
South America, 645, 740
Southern Society, revolutionary organization, 742, 743 n., 744-745, 757
Soviets (1905), 1180, 1389
Soviets (1917), provincial and local, 1390, 1433, 1443, 1455. *See also* All-Russian Central Executive Committee of Soviets, Petrograd Soviet
Spain, 634, 645, 674, 677, 688, 691, 739-740, 869
Special councils (1915), 1369-1370
Speransky, Michael, Count, influence of, with Alexander I, 634, 647, 703; fall of, 634, 648, 700, 731; on the Treaty of Tilsit, 664; rise of, and plans for reform, 696-697, 706, 716; and reform of civil service, 699; financial program of, 699, 717; and Finland, 704; on lack of freedom, 721; and December insurrection, 749, 751-752; and reforms under Nicholas I, 766; and codification, 770-771
Spiridonova, Marie, socialist revolutionary, 1451
Sports, organized, lack of, 1163, 1257
Sprengtporten, J. M., Finnish leader, 704
Stackelberg, Count, ambassador, 635
de Staël-Holstein, Anne L. G. Necker, Baroness, 734
Stalin, J. V. (Dzhugashvili), 1085, 1477; deported, 1201, 1379; returns to Petrograd, 1402; and October insurrection, 1446-1447; commissar for nationalities, 1453; and right of secession, 1465
Stambulov, Stephen, Bulgarian leader, 1132-1133
Stanislavsky, K. S., producer, 1251-1252
Stasov, V. V., music and art critic, 1051
Stasov, Vasili, architect, 735
State Bank, 1111, 1207-1208, 1227, 1449; founded, 941-942; taken over by Soviets, 1458
State Conference (1917), 1435, 1437
State Council, 646, 700 n., 716, 754, 763, 766-767, 778, 880, 897, 1034, 1036, 1043, 1090, 1102, 1112, 1196 n., 1210-1211, 1324; established, 697, 700; and dynastic crisis (1825), 746-747; and December insurrection, 749-751; statue on, amended (1842), 767; and emancipation acts, 888, 891; and anti-Jewish legislation, 1047-1048 n.; and

State Council (*continued*)
Loris-Melikov's constitutional proposals, 1083; opposition in, to counter-reforms, 1098, 1100; and peasant passport regulations, 1101; and restrictions on allotment land, 1103; and protectionism, 1109; rejects university charter, 1113; jurisdiction of, extended to Finland (1899), 1158; proposed reform of, 1171; as upper house of legislature (1906), 1187; rejects western zemstvos bill, 1194; rejects Polish-provinces municipal government bill, 1202; rejects primary schools bill, 1236; and Progressive Bloc, 1371-1372; urges change of policies, 1373; dissolution of, demanded, 1420

State Duma, 1142, 1146, 1206, 1211, 1230, 1255, 1287, 1305, 1321; Speransky's proposal for, 697; consultative (1904), 1172, 1176; and 1906 election law, 1176, 1187; established, 1178, 1187-1188; and the budget, 1187, 1210; powers for, to frame constitution demanded, 1188; and legislation under Article 87, 1194-1195, 1197, 1368; and 1907 election law, 1199-1200; number of ecclesiastics in, 1200 n.; and labor legislation, 1228; joint session of, 1384, 1435

first, 1186, 1197, 1200 n., 1201; elections to, 1189; convocation of, 1190; complexion of, 1190-1191; and land reform, 1191, 1224; dissolved, 1191-1192, 1214, 1383, 1383 n.

second, 1186, 1196 n., 1200 n., 1235; elections to, 1197; complexion of, 1197-1198; and alleged conspiracy to murder the tsar, 1198; dissolved, 1198, 1214; and land reform, 1198, 1224

third, 1202, 1205, 1365, 1377; elections to, 1199-1200; complexion of, 1200; and land reform, 1215-1216; and schools, 1235-1236, 1238

fourth, 1202, 1205, 1359, 1361, 1365, 1386, 1389; elections to, 1199-1200; complexion of, 1200; and annexation of Constantinople, 1348, 1352; and ascendancy of the Empress, 1361; restlessness of, 1364; and cooperation with the government, 1368; appoints provisional committee (1914), 1368-1369; status of, in wartime, 1368-1369; estrangement of, from officialdom, 1369, 1371-1372; and wartime agencies, 1369-1370; and Progressive Bloc, 1371-1372; as spokesman of the middle class, 1373, 1375; unrepresentative character of, 1374; convoked and prorogued, 1380; elects provisional committee (1917), 1380-1381; crests the revolution, 1381; dissolved, 1420, 1435, 1442

"State of emergency" legislation, 1091, 1099, 1170, 1177, 1181, 1196

State monopoly of grain trade, 1357

State Nobility Bank, 1111

State Peasant Bank, 1101, 1217-1218

State peasants, granted right to own agricultural land, 717; and Kiselev's reforms, 784-786, 924-925; and former "possessionary" peasants, 794; land allotments and financial burdens of (1866–1886), 896, 923-925, 1102

von Stein, Henry, Freiherr, 679, 683, 737

Stepniak-Kravchinsky, S. M., revolutionary, 1078

Stessel, A. M., General, 1273

Stiglitz, Alexander, Baron, banker, 935

Stoeckl, Edward, diplomat, 973-976

Stolypin, P. A., 1190, 1259; president of council of ministers, 1192; forms bureaucratic cabinet, 1193; and land reform, 1193, 1198, 1202, 1204, 1215-1217, 1220-1221, 1224; seeks support of liberals, 1193, 1998-1199, 1383; and nationalism, 1193, 1200, 1202-1204, 1385 n.; and the Duma, 1193-1194; and legislation under Article 87, 1194-1195, 1198, 1215; prorogues legislative chambers (1911), 1194-1195, 1204, 1385; residence of, blown up, 1195-1196; and "state of emergency" regime, 1196; assassination of, 1196, 1204, 1300; and security police, 1196-1197; and elections, 1197, 1199-1200; and 1907 election law, 1199-1200; and trade unions, 1228; and opening of Straits, 1294

Storch, A. K., professor, 753

Index

Stratford de Redcliffe, Viscount. *See* Canning, Sir Stratford
Stratheden and Campbell, W. F. Campbell, Baron, 1129 n.
Stravinsky, Igor, composer, 1249-1250, 1254
Stroganov, Paul, Count, 661, 671, 694
Stroganov, S. G., Count, 1032
Struve, Peter, economist, 1149, 1164, 1168, 1170
Struve, V. J., astronomer, 805
Stundists, 1118, 1119 n.
Sturmer, B. V., president of council of ministers, 1335-1336, 1352, 1364, 1366, 1372; accused of treason, 1373; dismissed, 1373
Sukhanov, N. N., revolutionary, 1387
Sukhomlinov, V. A., General, minister of war, 1317, 1320, 1378, 1387; dismissed and tried, 1331, 1363 n., 1369, 1385
Sukhozanet, N. O., General, 912
Suleiman Pasha, 1004
Supreme Economic Council, 1460
Surikov, V. I., painter, 1053
Suvorin, A. S., publisher, 1241
Sviatopolk-Mirsky, P. D., Prince, minister of interior, 1169-1172
Svinhufud, P. E., Finnish leader, 1423, 1465
Sweden, 663, 703, 811 n., 964, 1226, 1401; and war with Russia (1808-1809), 665, 671-672; and Aland Islands, 665, 1291-1292; and treaty with Russia (1812), 673; joins anti-French coalition (1813), 680; neutral during Crimean War, 869; transit trade by way of, 1357-1358. *See also* Finland
Switzerland, 674, 957, 1110, 1226, 1400-1401
Sykes, Sir Mark, diplomat, 1351
Sykes-Pico agreement (1916), 1351
Symbolism, 1244-1245, 1252
Syria, 844, 847, 955
Szápáry, Count, ambassador, 1314
Szepticki, Andrew, Count, Uniat Metropolitan, 1327

Table of Ranks, 699, 776
Taiping Rebellion, 978
Talaat Pasha, 1338, 1468
de Talleyrand-Périgord, C. M., 668, 681, 683
Tariffs. *See* Protectionism
Tatarinov, Catherine, mystic, 642-643, 646
Tatarinov, V. A., economist, 942
Tatishchev, Dimitry, Count, ambassador, 690
de Taube, M., Baron, jurist, 1259, 1276 n., 1291
Taxation, of income from landed estates (1812), 699; direct and indirect, 943, 1107, 1210; yield of declines, 1359
Tchaikovsky, P. I., composer, 822, 1052, 1253-1254
Telegraph, 937
Teplitz, Treaty of (1813), 682
Tereshchenko, M. I., foreign minister, 1383, 1386, 1399, 1426-1427, 1434, 1439
Terrorism, beginnings of, 1071, 1075; populism and, 1078-1084, 1122; rejected by social democrats, 1153; upheld by socialist revolutionaries, 1153-1154; rising tide of, 1166-1167, 1172, 1174, 1195; collapse of, 1200-1201
Theatre, 734-735, 819-820, 1248, 1251-1252
Thiers, Louis Adolphe, President, 847
de Thomon, Thomas, architect, 735
Three emperors' league (1873), 952, 970-973, 997, 1005, 1014; renewed (1881, 1884), 1027, 1029, 1125-1127; and the Bulgarian crisis, 1130; existence of, disclosed by Katkov, 1134-1135; terminated, 1135
Tibet, 1287
Tientsin, Treaty of (1858), 978; Russian concession in, 1268
Tilsit, negotiations at, 661; treaty of (1807), 662-664, 672
Timashev, A. E., minister of interior, 1000, 1067
von Tirpitz, Alfred, Admiral, 1289
Tisza, Stephen, Count, 1314
Tittoni, Tommaso, foreign minister, 1296, 1299
Tiutchev, Fedor, poet, 819, 1061
Tkachev, Peter, revolutionary, 1070, 1072-1073, 1079-1080

Togo, Heihachiro, Admiral, 1275, 1277
Tolstoy, Alexandra, 1241
Tolstoy, Alexis, Count, author, 1062
Tolstoy, D. A., Count, chief procurator and minister of education, 880, 918, 1035, 1040, 1083, 1113, 1119, 1164, 1234; and classicism, 1036-1039, 1234; and curricula of girls' schools, 1041; and control of primary schools, 1044; and student disturbances, 1075; minister of interior, 1092; and local government reform, 1093-1096, 1098; and peasant institutions, 1102-1103; and factory legislation, 1105-1106; and censorship, 1112
Tolstoy, Fedor, Count, sculptor, 735, 824
Tolstoy, Leo, Count, author, 692, 819, 876, 1056, 1059-1060, 1100, 1239, 1242-1243; life and work, 1057-1058, 1240-1241
Tolstoy, P. A., Count, ambassador, 666
Tomsk, university of, 1046 n.
Ton, A. K., architect, 824
Tormasov, Alexander, General, 674
"Total Land Reapportionment" (*Cernyi peredel*), revolutionary society, 1082
Totleben, E. I., General, and defense of Sevastopol, 875-876; and the Turkish war, 999, 1003-1005, 1016-1017, 1022-1023
Trade
domestic, statistics of, 940-941; and fairs, 941; represented in State Council, 1187
foreign, and the Continental System, 671; and the Russian American Company, 691; liberalization of, under Alexander I, 693; in 1800–1860, 708, 710-711, 789-791; currency instability and, 767; predominance of foreigners in, 790-791; and opening of Dardanelles to merchantmen (1826), 829, 833; in 1861–1913, 938-940, 1230-1231; during World War I, 1358. *See also* Commercial treaties, Grain exports, Protectionism
Trade Unions, 1180, 1433, 1435, 1443; under 1906 "provisional rules," 1186, 1228-1229; Progressive Bloc and, 1371; after the revolution, 1417-1419, 1421, 1457

Trans-Siberian Railway, 1104, 1108, 1182, 1218, 1224, 1262, 1270-1271, 1279
Traugutt, Romuald, 914
Trepov, A. F., president of council of ministers, 1364-1365
Trepov, D. F., General, 1172, 1178-1179, 1192
Trepov, F. F., General, 1080
Trepov, V. F., 1204
Tretiakov, P. M., art collector, 1246-1247
Tretiakov, S. M., art collector, 1247
Trianon Tariff (1810), 672
Triple Alliance, 1137-1139, 1288, 1297, 1299, 1303, 1310, 1313, 1343
Triple Entente, 1260, 1287-1291, 1303, 1309-1310; strain on, 1298-1299; treaty of (1914), 1335, 1467
Troppau, Congress of (1820), 645, 688, 716
Trotsky, Leon (Bronstein), 1151, 1417, 1426, 1431, 1444 n., 1445 n., 1446; and 1905 Soviet, 1177, 1181; on October manifesto, 1178-1179; trial, sentence, and escape, 1182 n.; on 1905 revolution, 1183; emigrates, 1201, 1379; on Kerensky, 1386-1387; on Petrograd (1917) Soviet, 1389; on Army Order No. 1, 1393; arrested in Halifax, 1399; arrives in Petrograd, 1428; joins Bolshevik Party, 1428; arrested, 1433; released, 1442; directs October insurrection, 1447, 1449, 1451, 1454; commissar for foreign affairs, 1453, 1459; on early Soviet legislation, 1460; peace proposals of, 1467; and Brest-Litovsk, 1467-1470, 1473
Trubetskoy, E. N., Prince, professor, 1348
Trubetskoy, Paolo, Prince, sculptor, 1054
Trubetskoy, Serge, Prince, Decembrist, 737, 740, 742, 744-745, 748-750, 752
Tsarskoe Selo, lycée of, 726 n., 733, 739, 1046 n.
Tsereteli, I. G., Menshevik, 1429
Tsushima, battle of (1905), 1174, 1276-1277
Tugan-Baranovsky, M. I., economist, 1149

Index

Tugenbund, 741
Turgenev, I. S., novelist, 817, 819-820, 1060, 1070; life and work, 1056-1057
Turgenev, Nicholas, 742, 744
Turkestan, 978-979; annexed, 981
Turkey, 644, 653, 707 n., 739, 1027; partition of, proposed (1804), 655; integrity of, guaranteed by France and Prussia (1806), 657; war with Russia (1806–1812), 660, 673; Tilsit Treaty and, 663-664, 666; proposed partition of (1808), 666; and Greek revolution (1821), 689; and Greek independence, 828-829, 834; and war with Russia (1828–1829), 830-833; and Russian protectorate over Danubian principalities, 835; and 1832–1833 crisis, 836-840; and war with Egypt (1839), 844, 846-847; and 1848 revolution, 851-852; and Hungarian and Polish refugees, 854-855; Nicholas I's proposal for partition of, 860; and dispute over Holy Places, 861-863; Russian ultimatum to, 864-865; and Russian invasion of Danubian principalities, 865; rejects Vienna note, 866; declares war on Russia, 867; alliance with England and France, 868-869; and Crimean War, 870, 872-874, 876-877; and the Treaty of Paris (1856), 948-950; protest British fleet in Black Sea, 952-953; and intervention on behalf of Poland, 957; and abrogation of Black Sea clause, 969; and revolt in Bosnia and Herzegovina, 991-992; and Balkan war (1876), 993-995, 997-999; rejects proposals of European Powers, 1001; and war with Russia (1877–1879), 1001-1005; and Russian peace terms, 1008, 1015; cedes Cyprus to England, 1018; Treaty of Berlin and, 1019-1021; Russian troops withdrawn from, 1022-1023; three emperors' league and, 1125; and Afghan crisis (1885), 1129; and Bulgarian unification, 1133; and Russia's proposed occupation of Bosphorus (1896), 1283-1284; and Bagdad railway, 1290; Young Turk revolution in, 1294; and annexation of Bosnia and Herzegovina, 1295, 1298; and Balkan wars (1911–1913), 1299-1304; and von Sanders' appointment, 1306-1308; and World War I, 1328, 1333-1334, 1340, 1342, 1345, 1348; and wartime negotiations, 1335, 1337-1338; Alekseev favors peace with, 1351. *See also* Dardanelles, Ottoman Empire
Turkmanchay, Treaty of (1828), 831, 842
Tyrnowo, Bulgarian constitution of, 1023, 1131-1132

Ukhtomsky, E. E., Prince, orientalist, 1262, 1265
Ukraine, national movement in, and the slavophiles, 810-811; and the Polish insurrection (1863), 914, 916; panslavism and, 990; hostility towards, 1202; Progressive Bloc and, 1371; Austrian, proposed annexation of, 1398; independence movement in, after the revolution, 1423-1425, 1464-1467; and Brest-Litovsk, 1470-1471. *See also* Galicia
Ukrainian Central Rada, 1424, 1466-1467, 1470
Ukrainian Constituent Assembly, 1466
Ukrainian People's Republic, 1466, 1470
Ulianov, Alexander, revolutionary, 1122
Uniats, forcible return of, to Orthodoxy, 764, 918; persecution of, in Galicia, 1326-1327
Union of Liberation, revolutionary society, 1168, 1170, 1173
Union of Michael the Archangel, 1201
Union of October 17 (Party), 1188-1189, 1365, 1385; in first Duma, 1191; in second Duma, 1198; in third and fourth Dumas, 1200
Union of the Public Good, revolutionary society, 741-742
Union of the Russian People, 1174-1175, 1189; and elections to second Duma, 1197; terrorism of, 1201
Union of Salvation, revolutionary society, 740-741
Union of Socialist-Revolutionary Maximalists, 1195 n.
Union of the True and Faithful Sons of Russia. *See* Union of Salvation

Union of Unions, 1170, 1173, 1177, 1188-1189
United States, 806 n., 930, 982, 1078, 1110, 1258, 1261, 1359, 1388 n.; and Russian trade, 672, 938, 1231, 1358; and Holy Alliance, 685, 690; and Russian expansion in North America, 690-692; constitution of, and Russian censorship, 728; and intervention on behalf of Poland, 957, 973-974; Russia and Civil War in, 973-974; and visit of Russian fleet, 974; and mission to Russia (1866), 974; and purchase of Alaska, 974-976; and opening of China, 978; and proposed fitting of Russian privateers in (1878), 1016; migration of Russian Jewry to, 1121; and persecution of Russian Jews, 1121; Russian investments of, 1226; Gorky in, 1242-1243; and Russian expansion in Far East, 1263-1264, 1266, 1268; and *rapprochement* with Japan, 1269; and Russo-Japanese War, 1271, 1277-1278; and economic expansion in China, 1279, 1282; and World War I, 1320, 1337; recognizes Provisional Government, 1395
Universal Postal Union, 937
University students, unrest among, 1031, 1034, 1074-1075, 1113, 1165, 1179, 1233; denial of corporate rights to, 1113, 1163; Marxist groups among, 1123; contempt of, for sports, 1163; political-mindedness of, 1163; strength of revolutionary organizations among, 1163-1164; financial insecurity of, 1164; and mutual-aid associations, 1164-1165; first national strike of, 1165-1166; and murder of Bogolepov, 1166; and academic unions, 1174
Unkiar-Skelessi, Treaty of (1833), 838-839, 844-846, 848, 870
Unkovsky, A. M., zemstvo leader, 896-897, 1066
Uritsky, M. S., Bolshevik, 1462 n.
Urquart, David, publicist, 841, 843
Ustrialov, N. G., historian, 803
Uvarov, S. S., Count, minister of education, 725, 754, 797-800, 802, 804, 806 n., 810, 812-813, 815, 1087, 1114

Valuev, P. A., Count, minister of interior, 897, 898 n., 911, 1000, 1065-1067, 1083 n.
Vannovsky, P. S., General, minister of war, 1040, 1165
Vasnetsov, V. M., painter, 1248
V*eche*, 739
Venetsianov, A. G., painter, 811 n., 823
Venizelos, E., 1345-1347
Vereshchagin, V. V., painter, 1053
Vernadsky, I. V., historian, 893 n.
Verona, Congress of (1822), 636, 688, 690
Versailles, Treaty of (1919), 1473 n.
Verstovsky, Alexis, composer, 821
Viardot (Pauline Garcia), singer, 1056-1057
Viazemsky, P. A., Prince, 731, 995
Victor Emmanuel II, King of Italy, 955
Victor Emmanuel III, King of Italy, 1299
Victoria, Queen of England, 834, 849, 855 n., 860, 868, 954, 956, 959, 985, 1128; Russophobia of, 1005; demands war on Russia, 1009
Vienna, Congress of (1814–1815), 681-685, 687, 705, 857, 962, 965
Vienna, Treaty of (1815), 684, 687, 705, 833, 850, 954; (1864), 963
"Vienna note" (1853), 865-867, 947-948
Village commune, 1082 n., 1224; slavophilism and, 809, 893-894 n., westerns and, 809, 893-894 n., 1069; emancipation and, 885, 893, 895; origins of, 893-894 n.; reasons for retention of, 893-894 n.; and zemstvos, 897, 898 n.; land purchases by, 925, 929 n.; restrictions on withdrawal from, 925, 1103-1104; and primary schools, 1043-1044; populism and, 1073; powers of land captains over, 1095, 1104, 1215, 1221; land leasing by, 1101; and dissolution of peasant households, 1102-1103; powers of, over land, restricted, 1103; and "socialization" of land, 1153; and reassessment of redemption debt, 1212; bolstering of, 1212-1214; merits of, debated, 1213-1214; and abolition of joint responsibility, 1214, 1221; dissolution of, 1215-1216, 1220; State peasant Bank and, 1218; status of,

Index

after Stolypin reform, 1221; and agrarian revolution, 1415-1416; and decree on land, 1453
Vilna, university of, 723, 726, 758, 764
von Vincent, Karl, Baron, diplomat, 668
Vinnichenko, M., Ukrainian leader, 1424
Vinogradoff, Sir Paul, historian, 1233
Virigin, Peter, Dukhobor leader, 1119
Vitheft, V. K., Admiral, 1275
Vitkevich, Captain, 843
Vixen, The, 842-843
Vladivostok, founded, 978-979
Volkonsky, Peter, Prince, General, 647-648
Volkonsky, S. G., Prince, Decembrist, 771 n.
Volunteer Army, 1456, 1465-1467
Vonliarliarsky, V. M., 1267
Voronikhin, Andrew, architect, 735
Vorontsov, Simon, Count, ambassador, 651, 675 n.
Vorontsov-Dashkov, I. I., Count, 1122
Vorparlament, 856
Vronchenko, F. P., minister of finance, 786
Vrubel, M. V., painter, 1247-1248
Vyrubov, Anne, 1146, 1364, 1366
Vyshnegradsky, I. A., minister of finance, 1106-1107, 1110, 1114, 1206, 1208

Waddington, W. H., foreign minister, 1019
Wagner, Richard, composer, 1051, 1254
Wagram, battle of (1809), 669
Waldemar, Prince of Denmark, 1134
Waldersee, Alfred, Count, Field Marshal, 1267
Walewski, Alexander, Count, foreign minister, 948-950, 954
Wallachia, 667, 673, 785, 827, 831, 851, 853, 860, 862, 870-871, 873, 1057; Russian protectorate over (1829), 833, 835; constitution of, amended, 852; under Treaty of Paris, 950; and founding of Rumania, 954, 960
War industries committees, 1369-1370, 1372, 1385; dissolution of, urged by Empress, 1372; labor representatives on, arrested, 1375, 1389

"War of Liberation" (1813-1815), 677, 679-681
War profit tax, 1359
Warsaw, Duchy of, 663-664, 666, 668-669, 672-673, 682, 679, 705-706
Warsaw, university of, 764, 918, 1046 n.
Washington, George, President, 690 n.
Waterloo, battle of (1815), 642, 684, 951 n., 1275
von Weber, Karl M. F. E., Baron, composer, 1254
Wellington, Arthur Wellesley, Duke of, 684, 687-688, 828, 830-833, 836, 864
Westerners, 808-809, 892 n., 915
Wielopolski, Alexander, Marquis, 762 n., 911-913, 917-918
Wielopolski, S. I., Count, 1324
William, Archduke, 971
William I, King of Prussia, Emperor of Germany, 953, 955, 961, 965, 991, 1136; and abrogation of Black Sea clause, 966-968; and three emperors' league (1873), 970-972; and Russian peace terms, 1014; meets Alexander II (1879), 1026; and the Austro-German alliance (1879), 1027
William II, Emperor of Germany, 1136, 1138, 1290, 1345; and the Russian alliance, 1137; encourages Russian ambitions in Far East, 1262, 1266-1267, 1284; and Kiaochow, 1266, 1284; and Peace of Portsmouth, 1277-1278, 1284; and the Björkö Treaty, 1284-1286; and big navy program, 1289; and annexation of Bosnia and Herzegovina, 1297; and von Sanders' appointment, 1307; and outbreak of World War I, 1313, 1315-1316, 1318
Wilson, Sir Robert, 665, 677, 679
Wilson, Woodrow, 1398, 1473
Windischgrätz, Alfred, Prince, Field Marshal, 852-853
Witte, S. J., Count, 1086, 1124, 1147, 1157, 1179, 1197, 1201, 1208, 1276 n., 1283, 1286, 1308-1309 n., 1352; on autocracy and self-government, 900, 1167, 1171 n., 1185; and colonization of Siberia, 1104; and commercial treaty with Germany, 1110, 1231; and foreign investments, 1110-1111, 1226; on state interven-

Witte, S. J. (*continued*)
tion, 1110-1111; and the Holy Host, 1122 n.; and labor unrest, 1160, 1162; and Nicholas II, 1142, 1177-1178, 1185; and the October manifesto, 1177-1178; and Finland, 1180; and Poland, 1180; government of, 1180, 1185-1186, 1197; and the Soviet, 1180-1182; and Alexander III, 1185, 1262; seeks support of liberal opposition, 1185-1186; and the constitutional framework, 1187-1188; resigns, 1190; and the monetary reform, 1206-1207; on budget and economic advancement, 1209-1210; and the peasant question, 1213-1214; and far eastern policy, 1260, 1262, 1264-1266, 1267-1268 n., 1268-1270; and the Treaty of Portsmouth, 1277-1279
Wittgenstein, L. A. P., Prince, Field Marshal, 680
Wittgenstein, Peter, Prince, 678
Women's battalions, 1408, 1450
Wysocki, Peter, Lieutenant, 758

Yalu concession, 1268-1269, 1282
Yarmouth, F. C. Seymour-Conway, Earl of, 658-659
York von Wartenberg, Hans D. L., Count, Field Marshal, 679
Ypsilanti, Alexander, Prince, 689
Yurevsky, Princess, 882, 1086
Yusupov, Felix, Prince, 1373-1374

Zagoskin, Michael, playwright, 735
Zaionczek, Joseph, General, 706
Zakharov, Adrien, architect, 753
Zamiatin, D. N., minister of justice, 903, 905-906
Zamoyski, Andrew, Count, 910, 913
Zarudny, M. I., jurist, 902-903
Zasulich, M. I., General, 1273
Zasulich, Vera, revolutionary, 1080-1081, 1084, 1150
Zavadovsky, Peter, Count, minister of education, 722
Zemgor, 1367, 1369-1370
Zemskii sobor, 739, 809, 1091-1092
Zemstvos, Statutes (1864) on, 897, 1075, 1093-1096; structure of, 897-898; functions and powers of, 898-899, 1167; Witte on, 900, 1167, 1171 n., 1185; social complexion of, 900-901; and schools, 1042-1045, 1047, 1116, 1167, 1235-1238; Katkov favors introduction of, 1065; informal union of, 1067; government hostile towards, 1067, 1167; and the reform movement, 1067-1068, 1099, 1155-1156, 1170, 1172, 1372; Loris-Melikov's constitutional proposal and, 1083; consulted on local government reform, 1091-1092; under 1890 act, 1093, 1095-1097, 1121, 1155, 1194; and factory boards, 1105; indifference of, to free trade, 1108; and 1891 famine, 1148; national organization of, 1156; and Union of Liberation, 1168; conferences of, 1168, 1170, 1173, 1189; organize union for relief of war sufferers (1904), 1169, 1366; draft imperial constitution, 1173; leaders of, decline participation in Witte's cabinet, 1186; represented in State Council, 1187; influence of, declines, 1189; revolutionary tendencies in, 1201; and committee on impoverishment of central provinces, 1212-1213; and small credit funds, 1227; and wartime organizations, 1331, 1361, 1366-1367; Progressive Bloc and, 1371; reorganized after the revolution, 1392-1393; abolished, 1460
Zenger, G. E., minister of education, 1234
Zhelezniakov, sailor, 1463
Zheliabov, Andrew, revolutionary, 1072, 1082, 1084
Zhemchuzhnikov, A. M., and V. M., humorists, 1062
Zhinin, N. N., chemist, 805
Zhukovsky, Alexander, poet, 730-733, 811 n., 879-880
Ziloti, Alexander, conductor, 1250
Zimbalist, Efrem, violinist, 1250
Zimmerwald conference (1915), 1400-1401, 1426
Zinovev, G. E. (E. A. Radomyslovsky), Bolshevik, 1432, 1446, 1459
Zionist movement, 1121
Zubatov, S. V., police official, 1161-1163